Register Your Book

at ibmpressbooks.com/ibmregister

Upon registration, we will send you electronic sample chapters from two of our popular IBM Press books. In addition, you will be automatically entered into a monthly drawing for a free IBM Press book.

Registration also entitles you to:

- Notices and reminders about author appearances, conferences, and online chats with special guests
- Access to supplemental material that may be available
- Advance notice of forthcoming editions
- Related book recommendations
- Information about special contests and promotions throughout the year
- Chapter excerpts and supplements of forthcoming books

Contact us

If you are interested in writing a book or reviewing manuscripts prior to publication, please write to us at:

Editorial Director, IBM Press
c/o Pearson Education
800 East 96th Street
Indianapolis, IN 46240

e-mail: IBMPress@pearsoned.com

Visit us on the Web: ibmpressbooks.com

DB2® 9 for Linux®, UNIX®, and Windows®

Sixth Edition

DB2® 9 for Linux®, UNIX®, and Windows®

DBA Guide, Reference, and Exam Prep

Sixth Edition

George Baklarz and Paul C. Zikopoulos

IBM Press
Pearson plc

Upper Saddle River, NJ • Boston • Indianapolis • San Francisco
New York • Toronto • Montreal • London • Munich • Paris • Madrid
Capetown • Sydney • Tokyo • Singapore • Mexico City

ibmpressbooks.com

IBM Press Program Managers: Tara Woodman, Ellice Uffer
Cover design: IBM Corporation
Associate Publisher: Greg Wiegand
Marketing Manager: Kourtnaye Sturgeon
Publicist: Heather Fox
Acquisitions Editor: Bernard Goodwin
Managing Editor: John Fuller
Cover Designer: Alan Clements
Project Editor: Elizabeth Ryan
Proofreader: Diane Freed
Manufacturing Buyer: Anna Popick

Published by Pearson plc
Publishing as IBM Press

IBM Press offers excellent discounts on this book when ordered in quantity for bulk purchases or special sales, which may include electronic versions and/or custom covers and content particular to your business, training goals, marketing focus, and branding interests. For more information, please contact: U.S. Corporate and Government Sales, 1-800-382-3419, corpsales@pearsontechgroup.com.

For sales outside the United States, please contact: International Sales, international@pearsoned.com.

This Book Is Safari Enabled

The Safari® Enabled icon on the cover of your favorite technology book means the book is available through Safari Bookshelf. When you buy this book, you get free access to the online edition for 45 days. Safari Bookshelf is an electronic reference library that lets you easily search thousands of technical books, find code samples, download chapters, and access technical information whenever and wherever you need it.

To gain 45-day Safari Enabled access to this book:

- Go to http://www.awprofessional.com/safarienabled
- Complete the brief registration form
- Enter the coupon code E1GG-GU3I-KMAT-BZI5-KSEP

If you have difficulty registering on Safari Bookshelf or accessing the online edition, please e-mail customer-service@safaribooksonline.com.

Library of Congress Cataloging-in-Publication Data

Baklarz, George.
DB2 9 for Linux, Unix, and Windows : DBA guide, reference and exam prep / George Baklarz, Paul C. Zikopoulos. — 6th ed.
p. cm.
Revised ed. of: DB2 Universal Database v8.1 for Linux, UNIX, and Windows database administration certification guide. 5th ed. c2003.
Includes index.
ISBN 0-13-185514-X (hbk. : alk. paper)
1. IBM Database 2. 2. Relational databases. I. Zikopoulos, Paul. II. Baklarz, George. DB2 Universal Database v8.1 for Linux, UNIX, and Windows database administration certification guide. III. Title.
QA76.9.D3C6723 2007
005.75'65—dc22 2007039601

Pearson Education, Inc
Rights and Contracts Department
501 Boylston Street, Suite 900
Boston, MA 02116
Fax (617) 671-3447

ISBN-13: 978- 0-13-185514-4
ISBN-10: 0-13-185514-X

Text printed in the United States on recycled paper at Courier Westford in Westford, Massachusetts.
First printing, November 2007

Contents

Foreword

Today's business leaders agree that effectively managing and leveraging information to make decisions has never been more important. More than 60 percent of CEOs feel their organizations need to do better at leveraging their information (IBM® Attributes and Capabilities Study, 2005). CFOs feel that if they leverage their information effectively, they can create five times more value for their organization (IBM Global CFO Study, 2006). Meanwhile, the information challenges become more complicated by the hour as the amount of digital information will double every 11 hours by 2010! It is therefore no surprise that now, more than ever, database skills are in demand and commanding increasing salaries. Our value as technology professionals is further increased as we learn and develop new skills on industry leading products. One of the most technologically advanced products in the industry is IBM DB2® 9 for Linux®, UNIX®, and Windows® (LUW).

More than 20 years ago, relational database technology was invented in IBM Research delivering the first commercially available database in the early 1980s. Today, tens of thousands of businesses all over the world rely on DB2 databases to store key corporate data assets and run their business both traditionally and over the Web. IBM DB2 9 for Linux, UNIX, and Windows builds on this industry-leading success by providing cost effective management of both relational data and pure XML data in a single data server — to provide you with all of the business information you need to solve challenging new problems.

The demand for DB2 skills continues to grow. Certifications were awarded in over 60 countries around the world, and more than 1,000 institutions worldwide are teaching DB2-related courses. In 2006 alone more than 35,000 download requests were made from DBAs and Developers who have wanted to extend their skills from Microsoft®, Sybase®, and Oracle® to DB2. Meanwhile, the value of a DB2 certification has never been greater. In November 2006, *Certification Magazine* rated DB2 (UDB) one of the "Top Ten" IT specialty certifications, the only database that made the list (*Certification Magazine*, "Certification Top 10 Lists Revisited," Ed Tittel, Nov. 2006, pg. 25). Further, 2006 salary reports indicate that certified DB2 professionals' salaries are growing at a rate that exceeds those of rival database certifications. (*Certification Magazine*, "CerMag's 2006 Salary Survey," Tegan Jones, Daniel Margolis, Brian Summerfield, Kellye Whitney & Sarah Stone Wunder, Dec. 2006).

An ongoing challenge for today's computer professionals is reserving the time to develop new skills to keep up with changes in technology. *DB2® 9 for Linux®, UNIX®, and Windows® DBA Guide, Reference, and Exam Prep, Sixth Edition*, is an excellent way to learn about DB2, to develop new skills, prepare for the DB2 certification exams, and to provide new opportunities for yourself in the computer industry. I hope you use this book to advance your skills, enjoy the benefits of being a DB2 professional, and seize the opportunities ahead!

Michael Agostino
Business Unit Executive
Data Servers Education & Certification
IBM Software Group

Preface

This book is a complete guide to the IBM's relational database servers, known as DB2. DB2 is available on many operating systems, and the book has been written to cover the version available on Linux, UNIX, and Windows. Any significant differences in the implementation of DB2 on various operating systems are highlighted. If you are planning to become certified, or you would simply like to understand the powerful new DB2 database servers from IBM, then read on. Those interested in becoming an IBM Certified Professional will want to review the information found in Appendix A at the end of this book.

The book is divided into four parts:

- Part 1 — Introduction to DB2 (Chapters 1–4).
  Installing and configuring DB2 servers and clients are covered in Chapters 2–4.
- Part 2 — Using SQL (Chapters 5–10).
  The Structured Query Language (SQL) is discussed in Chapter 5, 6, and 7. Chapter 8 covers the new pureXML capabilities, while Chapter 9 discusses the SQL PL programming language. Database concurrency is discussed in Chapter 10.
- Part 3 — DB2 Database Administration (Chapters 11–14).
  Creating a DB2 database and its related table spaces is covered in Chapter 11. The common administration tasks are discussed in Chapters 12 and 13. Database monitoring and performance considerations are discussed in Chapter 14.
- Part 4 — Developing Applications with DB2 (Chapters 15–16).
  An introduction to application development for DBAs is given in Chapter 15. Chapter 16 deals with some of the DBA activities that are related to application development. Not all of the material in these chapters is necessary for you to pass your certification test, but it will definitely help you when applications go into production.

This book can be used as a self-study guide to help you prepare for the DB2 certification exams, or as a guide to DB2 on the Linux, UNIX, and Windows platforms. Experience with DB2 is the best way to prepare for any of the DB2 certification exams!

DB2 *Note*

More information about DB2 certification can be found at www.ibm.com/certify.

Conventions

Many examples of SQL statements, DB2 commands, and operating system commands are included throughout the book. SQL statements are usually displayed within a set of thin lines, and any of the mandatory sections of the statements are shown in uppercase letters. An example of an SQL statement is shown:

```
SELECT LNAME, FNAME FROM CANDIDATE
  WHERE LNAME = 'ZIKOPOULOS' OR
        LNAME = 'BAKLARZ'
```

SQL is not a case-sensitive language, so the above query would provide the same result regardless of the case of the SQL keywords or the database object (table names or column names). Of course, the data in the database is stored *exactly* as it was entered (including case). Therefore, the above query would only find the candidates with the last name of `'ZIKOPOULOS'` or `'BAKLARZ'`. If the data were stored as `'Zikopoulos'`, it would not be part of the result table.

If SQL keywords are referred to in the text portion of the book, they will be shown as a `monospaced` font. For example, the `SELECT` statement is used to retrieve data from a DB2 database.

DB2 commands will be shown using the same method as SQL keywords. For example, the `CREATE DATABASE` command lets you create a database. DB2 commands are issued from the Command Line Processor (CLP) utility. This utility will accept commands in upper- and lowercase letters. The CLP program itself is an executable called `db2`. In some operating systems, such as AIX®, the program names are case sensitive. Therefore, be careful to enter the program name using the proper case.

There are a few operating-system-specific commands in this book. If the commands must be in lowercase they will be shown as such. For example, the UNIX command to create a user is `mkuser`.

There are a few syntax diagrams shown in the book. We recommend that the Command Line Processor or the *DB2 Command Reference* be used to verify the syntax of DB2 commands. The *DB2 SQL Reference* should be used to verify the syntax of SQL statements. To emphasize a term or concept, the term is shown in **bold** type or emphasized with *italics*.

Contributions

The *DB2® 9 for Linux®, UNIX®, and Windows® DBA Guide, Reference, and Exam Prep* was updated for Version 9, making this the sixth edition. We would like to thank the many customers, colleagues, and technical support personnel we have worked with for their ongoing efforts to improve DB2 and their feedback on this book. In particular, we would like to thank:

- Bill Wong for his support of the two earlier versions.
- Susan Visser, for her continued encouragement and support in updating this book.
- Our publisher, Bernard Goodwin, for his guidance and infinite patience with us.
- Michelle Housley for working with our reviewers and making sure the feedback got back to us in a timely fashion.
- Elizabeth Ryan and her team of proofreaders, for finding and eliminating all spilling and gremmir mistakes in the text.

We appreciate the time and effort that our reviewers took in reading the material (as dull as some of it may be!) and providing their feedback. Their input and comments have made a considerable impact on the quality of the book. We'd like to thank:

- Rick Swagerman for his incredible insight into the SQL language, including features that we didn't think actually existed!
- Chris Eaton for his excellent transaction flow diagrams that formed a basis for our section on High Availability Disaster Recovery (HADR).
- Dale McInnis for reviewing our section on recovery and recommending some changes on how certain parameters were explained.
- Howard Fosdick for reviewing the entire book and suggesting some organizational changes that helped the flow of the material.
- Terry Mason for pointing out some jargon that needed better clarification for readers not familiar with them. We have also attempted to remove all noise words that would prevent him from buying this book!
- Nick Tchervenski for his unique ability at finding subtle errors in the examples. Some of these errors have been in prior editions and weren't found until now.
- Angela Yang for examining the many syntax diagrams and pointing out missing parameters as well as correcting the case on a number of the UNIX commands.
- The DB2 development team for their continued support of this book.
- Finally, a special thanks to Denis Vasconcelos who managed to find more formatting glitches than we thought were possible. He also tested many of the examples and made valuable suggestions throughout the book.

Acknowledgments

I'm always thankful that I have an understanding family (and dog and cat!) that could deal with the late nights and busy weekends when I was updating this book. You know that things are taking too long to get done when the cat eventually gives up on you and goes to bed.

Katrina had infinite patience during the creation of this book. Even though I would say (countless times!) it's almost done, she would nod her head in that understanding manner which really meant she didn't believe me. But, she supported my efforts and made sure I had the time to get things done.

Of course, my children were less sympathetic to my book writing, especially if it interfered with their social lives. However, the entire family chipped in and I couldn't have done this without their help and patience! Thanks Katrina, Geoff, Andrew, Tristan (cat), Ellie (dog), and Basil (dog-in-law)!

I'd also like to thank my in-laws, Jean and Pete, for their support. While they don't have a computer science background, they are interested in these books and even sometimes read them!

I have to also give additional credit to my mom. She had a tough life, growing up in Germany and being a prisoner of war during WW II. She had to deal with many challenges and never had the opportunity to further her education. Moving to Canada, Mom envisioned a better life for her children and she encouraged me to go to University and do the best I could. While Mom never learned about computers, she still reads my books and points out things in them to me. Thanks for all your encouragement Mom, and for reading the book.

George

I guess I should be thanking George for giving me the opportunity to join him on this book (if you knew the amount of work that went into this book, you'd understand why I'm saying "guess"). I also have to thank my wife, Kelly, and my angel, Chloë, for their understanding of the time commitment that goes into such a project, as well as ignoring (and not learning) the unpleasantries that echoed throughout the house when I suffered a blue screen after about six hours of unsaved work. Professionally, it's the usual list of suspects that help me to learn DB2 so I can help you learn it too; these folks know who they are at this point, so I'll just leave it at that.

I would like to dedicate this book to a number of people. Professionally, Jim Stittle. Jim has been a colleague of George and myself for a good many years. The guy is "off-the-hook" smart, but never really lets people know it — very humble. He's a great guy, big-time role model (in and outside of IBM), and, quite honestly, I'm not sure if I'd be where I am today without him. So three cheers for Jim Stittle!

Of course, my parents: they should be the source of any dedication for any book I've written (I think I'm at 10 now). They've always encouraged higher learning (even funded it — if you guys have spare change, pass it along by the way) and are just great parents with lots of love for my budding family. So thanks Mom and Dad: there's a feeling you get when you know your parents do their best for you, and not everyone gets parents like that, so I'm lucky. Really lucky. Really, really lucky.

Finally, to a former high school teacher of mine at Moira Secondary School in Belleville, Ontario: Ken Smith. Ken was my basketball coach during those years. I was always a good athlete growing up, used to lots of athletic success across the board. Basketball was a different story. I was good, but didn't excel. To make things worse, the top six guys on my team could have all had scholarships. The point is that I was just average on a well-above-average team (for a town of 35,000 at the time, we were ranked as high as seventh provincially).

Ken gave up his weekends for years to take us to tournaments all around the province to let our team play the best and achieve. He gave up his morning or afternoons to coach us. Gave up his spare time to help a kid if he had some issues in math or anything else. The guy loved our team as if he was getting paid for it or if we were his own kids. This is the nature of person that really shapes you when you're in high school. Of course, during those years you're too cool to realize it at the time, but when you get older and have a kid and reflect, it hits you. But Ken was more than all of this. Ken always knew when he could do something special to really make your day.

I recall practicing hours and hours extra because my parents were coming to a game. Their attendance really weighed heavy on me because they had always seen great successes when it came to athletics, but they hadn't been to a basketball game where I was just average. Well, Ken knew how I felt and played me when I likely shouldn't have gotten played. It was just for a short time, I think I missed two free throws and got 2 fouls in 5 minutes (I can still see his smile now when I peered at him off the court). The point was he knew I felt uneasy about my stature as a basketball player and played me because my parents were there. I never really thanked him for that; so thanks. However, the thing he taught me the most, and I have to admit it sounds so cliché but it's true: work hard and good things will come. He just taught me that even when you're not the best, work at it like you are and good things will come. Leave your life's court with everything you've got, and good things will come.

When I look at my successes as IBM, this is one of the core pillars that have helped me to achieve at this great company. The best part is that I just saw Ken earlier this year while golfing one of the best rounds of my life. After talking to him in the middle of a hole (which I subsequently doubled — thanks for nothing, Ken), I realized that Ken is alive and well. Past dedications have been to folks that aren't with me anymore — it's an amazing feeling to tell someone how they impacted your life while they are still around. Thanks, Ken. I wonder if today's students have it this good.

Paul

About the Authors

George Baklarz, B. Math, M.Sc., Ph.D., has spent 22 years at IBM working on various aspects of database technology. From 1987 to 1991 he worked on SQL/DS as part of the product planning department, system test team, performance team, and application development group. In 1991, Baklarz was part of the team that helped moved the OS/2 ES database to Toronto to become part of the DB2 family of products. Since that time he has worked on vendor enablement, competitive analysis, product marketing, product planning, and technical sales support. Today, Baklarz is the Program Director responsible for Dynamic Warehousing Pre-Sales Support, and he works with customers to help them understand DB2 technology directions and uses their feedback to improve the product. When not traveling the world, Baklarz lectures at the University of Guelph, teaching relational database concepts to students. You can reach him at gbaklarz@uoguelph.ca.

Paul C. Zikopoulos, B.A., M.B.A., is an award-winning writer and speaker with the IBM Database Competitive Technology team. He has more than thirteen years of experience with DB2 and has written more than 150 magazine articles and is currently working on book number twelve. Zikopoulos has authored the books *Information on Demand: Introduction to DB2 9.5 New Features*; *DB2 9 Database Administration Certification Guide and Reference (6th Edition)*; *DB2 9: New Features*; *Information on Demand: Introduction to DB2 9 New Features*; *Off to the Races with Apache Derby*; *DB2 Version 8: The Official Guide*; *DB2: The Complete Reference*; *DB2 Fundamentals Certification for Dummies*; *DB2 for Dummies*; and *A DBA's Guide to Databases on Linux*. Zikopoulos is a DB2 Certified Advanced Technical Expert (DRDA and Cluster/EEE) and a DB2 Certified Solutions Expert (Business Intelligence and Database Administration). In his spare time, he enjoys all sorts of sporting activities, including running with his dog Chachi, avoiding punches in his MMA class, and trying to figure out the world according to Chloë, his daughter. You can reach him at paulz_ibm@msn.com.

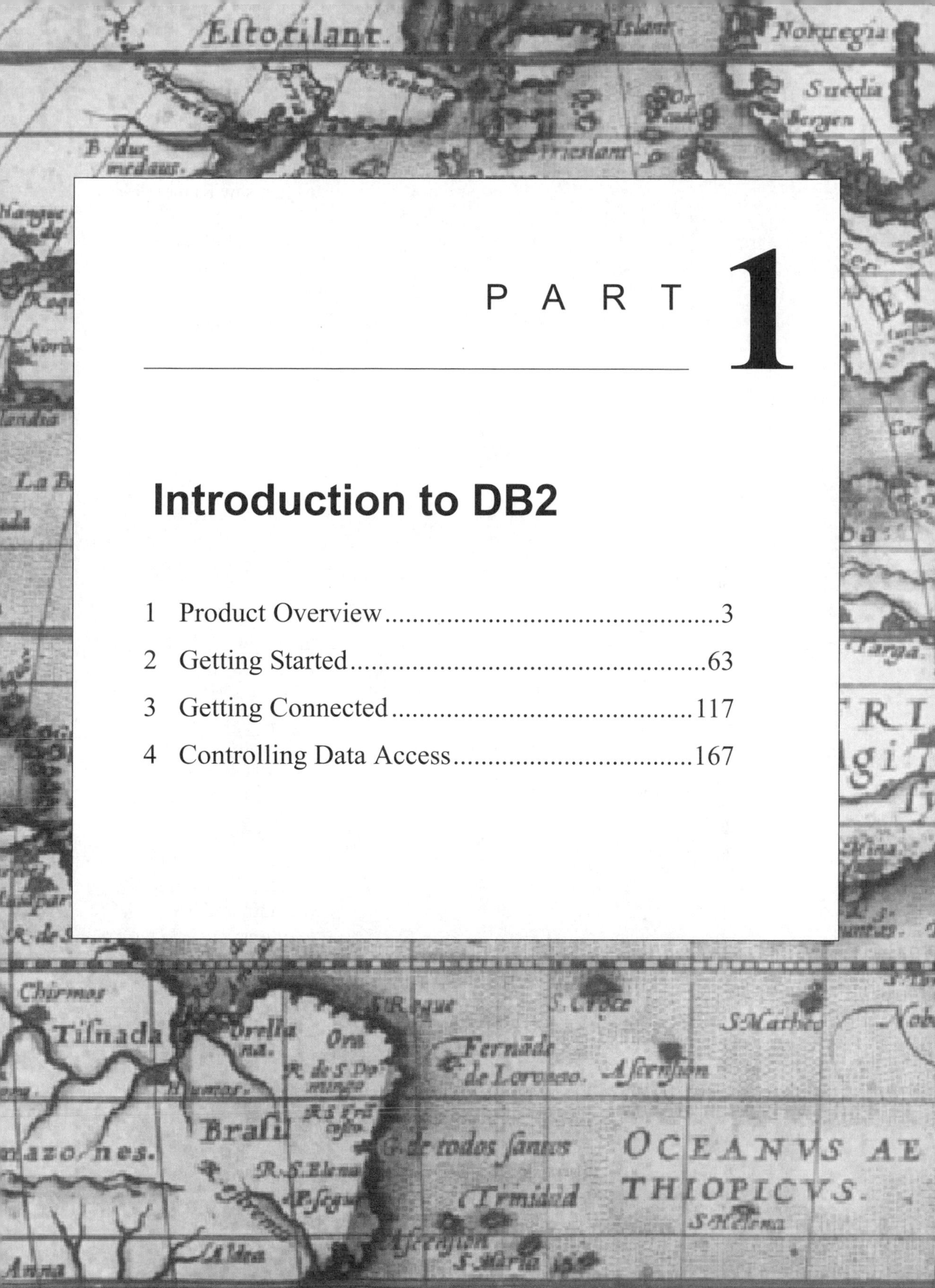

PART 1

Introduction to DB2

C H A P T E R 1

Product Overview

- DB2 PRODUCTS and PACKAGING
- DB2 CONNECTIVITY
- DB2 TOOLS
- DB2 ADMINISTRATION

*I*n this chapter you will be introduced to the DB2 family of products that run on the Linux, UNIX, and Windows operating systems. This version of DB2 is often referred to as the *distributed* version to differentiate it from the DB2 for z/OS® version that runs on an IBM mainframe.

DB2 has the ability to store all kinds of electronic information. This includes traditional relational data, data encoded within XML as well as structured and unstructured binary information, documents and text in many languages, graphics, images, multimedia (audio and video), information specific to operations like engineering drawings, maps, insurance claims forms, numerical control streams, or any type of electronic information. This chapter illustrates some of the ways to access data in a DB2 database using some of the interfaces provided within the DB2 family. A description of each of the DB2 products are provided to illustrate some of DB2's features and functions.

Information as a Service

The DB2 Data Server is an important part of IBM's Information as a Service software portfolio that serves as the atomic level for the broader IBM On Demand architecture.

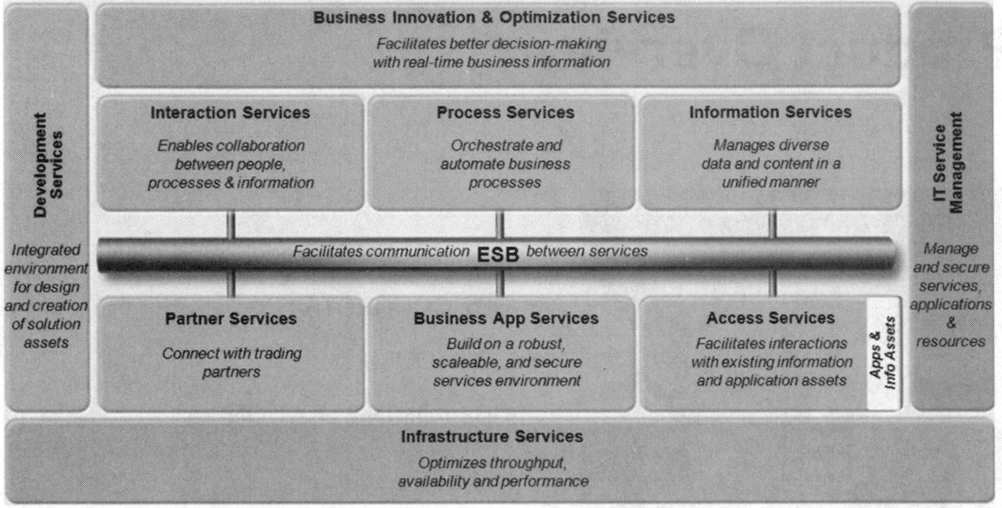

Figure 1–1 *IBM Service Framework for an On Demand business*

In Figure 1–1 you can see that the IBM software portfolio has really evolved into a collection of high value services provided by various IBM software portfolio offerings. The backbone fabric of this IBM reference architecture is the Enterprise Service Bus (ESB) that is used to facilitate communications across this rich set of services.

IT Service Management is mostly provided by various Tivoli® products. The Tivoli portfolio is built around four key disciplines or pillars:

- Security Management
- Storage Management
- Performance and Availability
- Configuration and Operations

Services from these pillars can be used to collectively manage your entire IT framework. For example, Tivoli Storage Resource Manager services can be used enterprise-wide to monitor and report on heterogeneous storage resources to increase storage utilization, identify and resolve potential problems, and ensure application availability through policy-based automation.

Development Services are the culmination of various Rational-based products that are built on the open source Eclipse platform. For example, Rational® ClearCase® provides source control services, and Rational Application Development empowers application developers with a rich set of services that can be used to develop applications, Web pages, and extended custom services for implementation in a Services Oriented Architecture (SOA) or loosely coupled application framework.

Services that enable interaction are typically part of the Lotus® suite of products that enhance collaboration and idea sharing across the enterprise and beyond. Products like Lotus Sametime® Connect can be used for messaging and more.

A number of services in the framework illustrated in Figure 1-1 are provided by the WebSphere® portfolio. For example, a product like WebSphere Integration Developer helps you define business process flows in the standard Business Process Execution Language (BPEL), which are used to implement process services that in turn help you define, orchestrate, and automate business policies. The Enterprise Service Bus (ESB) is provided by the WebSphere ESB product that provides your enterprise services with transformation, transport switching, and routing remediation among other services. Perhaps the most famous product of the WebSphere brand is the WebSphere Application Server that provides a runtime framework for J2EE®-based operations that are part of the Infrastructure Services component.

Finally there's the Information Services which represent the superset of the capabilities you'll learn about in this book. The specific set of services that are typically found in this part of the IBM reference architecture are shown in Figure 1–2.

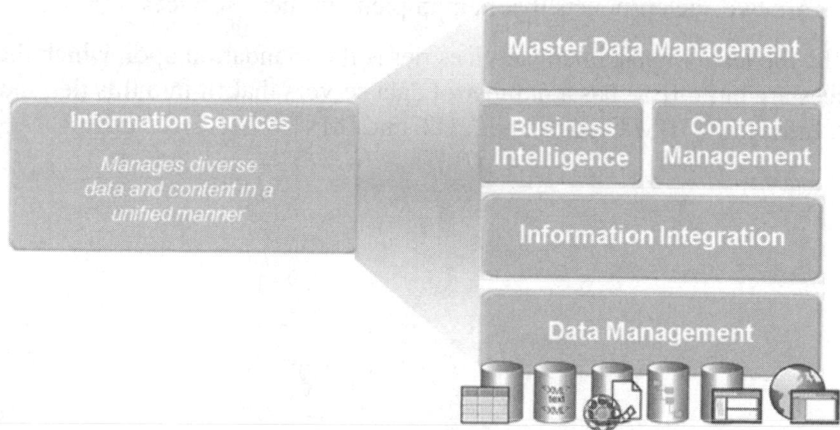

Figure 1–2 *IBM Information Services defined*

The services shown to the right in Figure 1–2 are hierarchical in nature. In other words, as you work from bottom to top, the services provided become richer and more business oriented.

For example, Master Data Management services are provided by the WebSphere Product Center and WebSphere Customer Center products. Master data are facts that describe your core business entities: customers, suppliers, partners, products, bill of materials, employees, and so on. The discipline of Master Data Management seeks to decouple master information from individual applications spread across the enterprise and create a central, application independent, resource. The end result is a simplification of ongoing integration tasks and new application development. This discipline addresses key issues such as data quality and consistency proactively rather than "after the fact"; for example, in a data warehouse (a lower service in this taxonomy). There is also a set of entity resolution services that fit within the Master Data Management service tier.

Business Intelligence services are provided by the DB2 Data Warehouse editions that you'll learn more about later in this chapter. Content Manager services are provided by the set of Content Management products and are used for document management, archiving, regulatory retention, and are a basis by which unstructured information (such as FAXes, video, voicemail, and so on) can be searched and folded into the information asset.

Information Integration services seek to provide enterprises with ways to share, place, publish, cleanse, and enrich data found in the lower-level data management services. WebSphere Federation Server and its parent WebSphere Information Server are two such products that help implement these services.

Finally, the Data Management services tier is the foundation upon which the other services are built. IBM has a number of data servers that fit into this tier, including DB2, Informix®, IBM Cloudscape™, U2, and IMS™.

This book is specifically about DB2 in this service tier. Specifically, you'll learn how DB2 can provide any number of the high-value data-centric services shown in Figure 1–3.

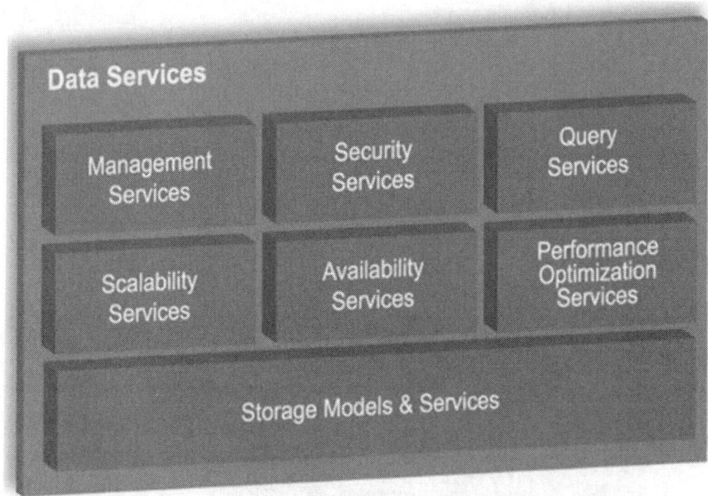

Figure 1–3 *The data services provided by DB2, the focus of this book*

For more information on the entire IBM software portfolio and how they are mapped to the illustrated services shown Figures 1–1 and 1–2, refer to the IBM Web site at www.ibm.com for more details.

The DB2 family of data servers executes on Windows, Linux (which can be run on the entire spectrum of IBM's hardware: System i™, System z™, System x™, and System p™), Solaris™ (both SPARC®-based and Intel®/AMD™-based installations), HP-UX™ (both PA-RISC™-based and Itanium-based installations), i5/OS®, VSE/VM, z/OS, and on pervasive platforms (like Windows Mobile Edition, Blue-Cat® Linux, Symbian®, Palm OS®, J2ME® platforms like the RIM® Blackberry®, and more).

The DB2 code base is optimized for each platform to ensure maximum performance and integration. DB2 for Linux, UNIX, and Windows shares about a 98 percent common code base with platform-specific optimizations at the operating system interface (OSI) level (Figure 1–4).

This means that once you've learned how to administer a DB2 for AIX system, for the most part you'll know how to manage DB2 for Linux or DB2 for Windows; this is the reason why there is a single DB2 certification for all the distributed platforms.

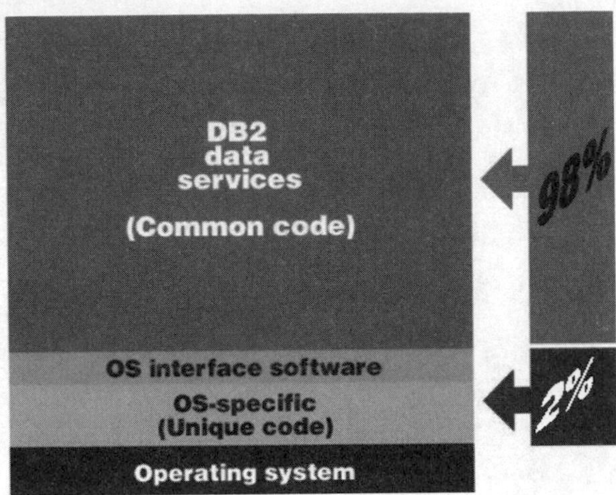

Figure 1–4 *The DB2 code for Linux, UNIX, and Windows is virtually the same*

DB2 for i5/OS and DB2 for z/OS are optimized for their respective environments. For example, DB2 for z/OS is based on a shared-everything disk architecture where the hardware-assisted Coupling Facility is used to serialize access to the shared disk. No such hardware exists for Linux, UNIX, and Windows, and therefore DB2 on these platforms uses a shared-nothing architecture. For this reason, administration tends to vary between these platforms (though many concepts and features are similar). However, the SQL API is 98% common to all the platforms where DB2 runs, allowing applications written on one platform to be easily ported to another. This means that you can build an application on DB2 for Windows and port it effortlessly to DB2 for z/OS. If you build your application according to the *SQL Reference for Cross-Platform Development* handbook, your application will be 100% portable across the DB2 family.

There are other synergies among DB2 running on Linux, UNIX, and Windows, as well as the other DB2 family members. For example, the JDBC driver used for DB2 for z/OS is exactly the same code as is used for DB2 for Linux, UNIX, and Windows. So while there may be variations in specific data definition language (DDL)-based tasks, the data manipulation language (DML) and client APIs are similar.

The DB2 for Linux, UNIX, and Windows Data Server

In the distributed environment, DB2 is available in a number of different packaging options, called *editions*. Furthermore, DB2 is also available as part of other packages that contain additional features and tooling rather than just the base data services provided by DB2.

The mainstream DB2 editions are shown in Figure 1–5:

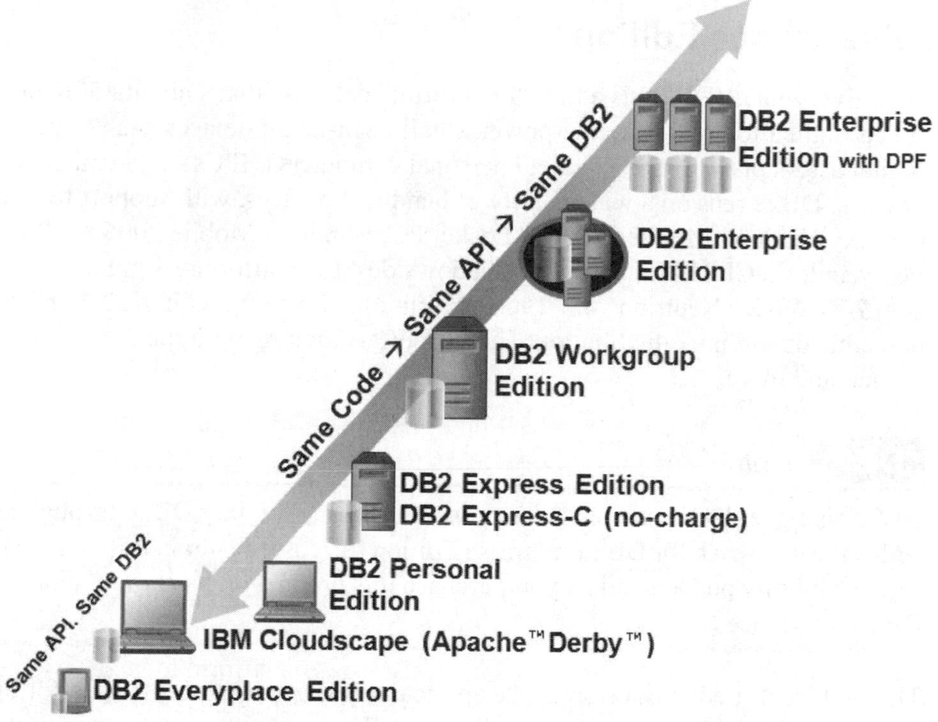

Figure 1–5 *The distributed DB2 family*

For the most part, each edition builds on its child in this hierarchy. For example, if a feature or functionality is available in DB2 Workgroup Edition, it's likely that it's also a part of a higher-level edition, like DB2 Enterprise Edition.

DB2 Note

The packaging and licensing of the DB2 product is very dynamic in nature. This chapter details how DB2 is licensed and packaged as of the time this book was written and is consistent with the focus area of the certification exam. Subsequent point releases could conflict with the information in this chapter, but the exam questions only change with versions.

DB2 Everyplace Edition

DB2 Everyplace (DB2e) is a tiny "fingerprint" database that's about 350K in size. It is designed for low-cost, low-power, small form-factor devices such as personal digital assistants (PDAs), handheld personal computers (HPCs), and embedded devices. DB2e runs on a wide variety of handheld devices, with support for Palm OS 5.x, Windows Mobile 2003 for Pocket PC, Windows Mobile 2005 for Pocket PC, Windows CE.NET, traditional Windows desktop platforms, Symbian OS Version 7/7s, QNX® Neutrino® 6.2, Linux distributions running with the 2.4 or 2.6 kernel, embedded Linux distributions (like BlueCat) running with the 2.4 or 2.6 kernel, and more.

DB2 Note

DB2e also goes by the name *Mobility on Demand;* if you buy DB2e through an add-on feature pack for DB2 Enterprise Edition (discussed later in this chapter), it's called Mobility on Demand. If you purchase this product on its own, it's known as DB2 Everyplace.

The SQL API used to develop DB2e applications is a subset of that used for building full-fledged DB2 data server applications. This means that enterprise applications, for the most part, can be easily extended to include mobile devices. More importantly, it means that if you have DB2 skills, you have DB2e skills. In addition, DB2e is extremely flexible for developers, with support for Open Database Connectivity (ODBC), Java Database Connectivity (JDBC), .NET (including the ADO.NET 2.0 API), and the DB2 Call Level Interface (CLI) APIs.

DB2e is a very simple-to-use data server that requires virtually no maintenance. Typical database administrator (DBA) operations like reorganizations and statistics collection are all performed automatically. Another nice thing about developing DB2e applications is that the database engine is platform independent, so it provides flexibility: You can seamlessly move DB2e databases between devices. For example, you could move a DB2e database populated on a Pocket PC device to a

Symbian smartphone, or whatever other supported device you have, without the need to do anything. This feature, coupled with the rich support for application development, enables developers to quickly build, deploy, and support mobile applications on all platforms.

DB2e is available in two editions: DB2 Everyplace Database Edition (DB2e DE) and DB2 Everyplace Enterprise Edition (DB2e EE). The database component of DB2e DE is the same as DB2e EE; however, DB2e DE has no synchronization middleware to extend or synchronize data to back-end enterprise data servers (although it does come with command line-based import and export utilities). DB2e DE is primarily used for applications that require an embedded database or a local relational storage facility that is exposed to endusers through some sort of application (they never really see the database) yet have stringent footprint requirements because of the device.

DB2e EE distinguishes itself from DB2e DE in that it comes with a data synchronization component called the DB2e Synchronization Server (DB2e Sync Server). The DB2e Sync Server allows you to manage subscriptions and security controls for data that is distributed wirelessly to your hand-held devices and manage data changes on the client devices back into the data center. The DB2e Sync Server also comes with facilities for conflict resolution, application deployment, device identification controls, management policies, and more.

The DB2e Sync Server can synchronize DB2e and Apache Derby/IBM Cloudscape data servers with back-end JDBC-enabled compliant data servers (for example, DB2, Oracle, Informix, SQL Server™, and so on). In addition, there is a special DB2 family synchronization adapter that uses the Data Propagator™ (DPROPR) SQL-based replication technology (which is included in the distributed version of DB2).

The number of concurrent synchronizations that the DB2e Sync Server can support is dependent on the hardware configuration of that server, the associated workload, and data change rates. If you need to scale to handle very large concurrent synchronizations, you can install any Java application server (like IBM WebSphere Application Server). DB2e also supports enhanced scalability and high-availability through its support for DB2e Sync Server farm configurations that allow you to cluster a number of DB2e Sync Servers to provide load balancing and high-availability services.

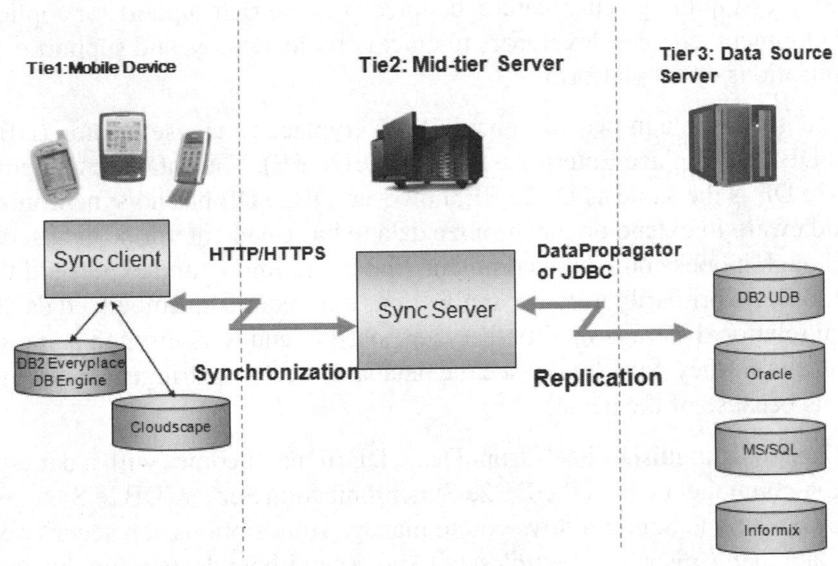

Figure 1–6 *A DB2e Enterprise Edition environment*

In Figure 1–6 you can see the flow of data in a DB2e EE environment. For example, data is pulled from a database in Tier 3 (the far right of the figure) and placed on a mobile device in Tier 1 (the far left). Tier 1 is typically composed of occasionally connected clients that operate on data and then use the services provided by Tier 2 (the middle of the figure where the DB2e Sync Server resides) to push those changes back to Tier 3. Tier 2 handles issues like conflict remediation and subscription management to ensure that the data quality is maintained throughout its lifecycle until it's at rest.

Apache Derby/IBM Cloudscape

In 2005, IBM donated $85 million worth of relational database management system (RDBMS) code to the open source community, and the Apache Derby database was born. Apache Derby and IBM Cloudscape are the same databases; the difference is that IBM Cloudscape is sold by IBM with IBM's award-winning 24*7 support and has some add-on features as well.

If you hadn't heard of IBM Cloudscape before the donation news, you'll probably be surprised to learn how many partners, customers, and software packages use this data server. In fact, more than 80 different IBM products use the IBM Cloudscape data server for its portability, easy deployment, open standards-based Java engine, small footprint, and more. IBM Cloudscape is a component that is transparent to products such as WebSphere Application Server, DB2 Content Manager, WebSphere Portal Server, IBM Director, Lotus Workplace, and many others.

IBM Cloudscape is a Java-based RDBMS that has a 2MB footprint. It's compatible with DB2, supports advanced functions (such as triggers and stored procedures), is easy to deploy, and requires no DBA effort. These same characteristics hold true for the open source Apache Derby as well.

We chose to include the Apache Derby/IBM Cloudscape data servers in this discussion because their SQL API is 100% compatible with the DB2 data server editions in Figure 1–5. This means that you can take any Apache Derby/IBM Cloudscape database and application and move it to a full-fledged DB2 data server if you need more scalability, or you need to take advantage of features that aren't found in these data servers. In fact, a component of DB2 9, called the DB2 Developer Workbench, provides a built-in facility to migrate Apache Derby/IBM Cloudscape schemas and data to a DB2 data server.

DB2 Personal Edition

DB2 Personal Edition (DB2 PE) is a full-function database that enables single users to create databases on their workstations. Since it's limited to single users (it doesn't support inbound client request for code), it's generally not referred to as a data server (although the DB2 engine behind DB2 PE is that same DB2 engine for all editions in Figure 1–5). This product is only available on Linux and Windows. DB2 PE can also be used as a remote client to a DB2 data server. Applications written to execute on DB2 PE are fully portable to the higher-level editions of the DB2 family in Figure 1–5.

DB2 PE is often used by end users requiring access to local and remote DB2 databases, or developers prototyping applications that will be accessing other DB2 databases. In addition, since it includes the pureXML™ technology free of charge, DB2 PE is also a good choice for those looking to acquire DB2 9 pureXML skills. In many cases, because it includes replication features, DB2 PE is used for occasionally connected applications (like field research, sales force automation, and so on) where a richer feature set is required than what's offered by DB2e or Apache Derby/IBM Cloudscape.

The DB2 Express and DB2 Workgroup Editions

Both DB2 Express Edition (DB2 Express) and DB2 Workgroup Edition (DB2 Workgroup) offer the same functions, features, and benefits; they are differentiated only with regard to licensing restrictions, which have a direct affect on the amount of scalability and performance that can be derived from each.

This section will detail these editions, point out differences where they exist, and describe the set of add-on feature packs that you can purchase to extend the scalability, capability, and availability of these data servers.

DB2 Express Edition

DB2 Express is a full-function, Web-enabled client/server RDBMS. DB2 Express is only available for Windows- and Linux-based workstations (unlike DB2 Workgroup). DB2 Express provides a low-cost, entry-level server that is intended primarily for small business and departmental computing. As previously mentioned, it shares the same functions and features as DB2 Workgroup, but is mainly differentiated from DB2 Workgroup by the amount of memory available on the server and the server's Value Unit (VU) rating (which equates to the power of a server's processor cores) on which it can be installed.

DB2 Express can be licensed using the VU methodology, which applies a per-VU charge for the VU rating of a server, or by an Authorized User metric. A DB2 Express server cannot use more than 4 GB of RAM on the server where it is installed. Authorized Users represent individual users that are registered to access the services and data of a single DB2 data server in the environment. For example, if you had a user that needed to access two different DB2 Express 9 data servers and wanted to license this environment with Authorized Users, that single user would require two DB2 Express Authorized User licenses (one for each server).

You can also license DB2 Express using the VU model. No matter what licensing methodology you choose, you cannot install DB2 Express on a server with more than 200 VUs.

DB2 Note

In September 2006, IBM Software Group (IBM SWG) announced a new licensing mechanism called Value Units (VUs) — for those seeking to deploy software for Internet use, or across environments where it isn't possible or feasible to identify users. Previous to this announcement, IBM SWG used to license its software products via a processor license. With the advent of dual core processors, each with different attributes, IBM converted the aggregated processor licensing metric to the more granular VU model. In this model, a core is converted to a number of VUs (referred to as the *VU rating of the server*) for which you are required to purchase the corresponding amount of VUs for the software you want to license. For example, an Intel dual core processor coverts to 50 VUs per core. If you had a two-way Intel dual core server, you'd have to buy 200 VUs of DB2. You can learn more about VU licensing at www.ibm.com/software/sw-lotus/services/cwepassport.nsf/wdocs/pvu_table_for_customers.

DB2 Express can play many roles in a business. It is a good fit for small businesses that need a full-fledged relational data server. A small business may not have the scalability requirements of some more mature or important applications, but they like knowing they have an enterprise quality data server backing their application that can easily scale (without a change to the application) if they need it to. As noted, an application written for any edition of DB2 is transparently portable to another edition on any distributed platform

DB2 Express-C: The Little Data Server that Could

DB2 Express-C isn't considered a "real" edition of DB2; however, we chose to include it here because it's very likely the case that this is the copy of DB2 that you're using to learn DB2.

DB2 Express-C is a free data server offering from IBM that you can download from www.ibm.com/software/data/db2/udb/db2express/ or order for free as part of the DB2 9 Discovery Kit. At the heart of the DB2 Express-C is the same scalable and robust data engine that you'll find in the other editions covered throughout this chapter. DB2 Express-C is optimized for two-way dual core servers with no more than 4 GB of memory. Because of the specific optimization in the code base for this architecture, many consider these the "license limitations" for this product.

DB2 Express-C was designed for the partner and development communities, but as you get to know this version, you'll realize it has applicability almost anywhere: as a student trying to learn or get certified in DB2, a hobbyist, and even large enterprises will find this product useful in their environments.

A defining characteristic of DB2 Express-C is that it's generally considered to be a *no limits* data server. DB2 Express-C doesn't have the limits that are typically associated with other competitor's free offerings (ironically, they also carry the Express moniker). For example, there is no database size limit with DB2 Express-C, you can address a 64-bit memory architecture, there are no limits on concurrency or on built-in self-managing features, and more. Where limits do exist, they are more than generous for the workloads for which DB2 Express-C has been optimized to run.

The main features that are *not* included in DB2 Express-C when compared to DB2 Express are:

- Support for high-availability clustering
- The ability to enhance the capabilities of the core data server using add-on feature packs (more on these later).
- Replication Data Capture
- 24x7 IBM Passport Advantage® support model (a special packaging of DB2 Express-C, called DB2 Express-C Fixed Term License, offers this support for

DB2 Express-C servers, but details on this option are outside the scope of this book).

If you want to use any of these features in your environment, you need to, at a minimum, purchase DB2 Express.

For the most part, all of the features found in DB2 Express-C are also available in any of the higher editions found in Figure 1–5. The exception for this product is the pureXML component. To help proliferate and grow XML skills across the database community, IBM generously decided to make this feature available for free with the DB2 Express-C data server. You'll note as you read this chapter that this feature is a chargeable add-on feature pack for all other DB2 data servers.

DB2 Workgroup Edition

DB2 Workgroup is also a full-function, Web-enabled client/server database. Unlike its DB2 Express-C and DB2 Express counterparts, it is available on all supported flavors of UNIX (AIX, HP-UX, and Solaris), Linux, and Windows — this is the main non-resource differentiator between DB2 Workgroup and DB2 Express.

DB2 Workgroup provides a low-cost, entry-level server that is intended primarily for small business and departmental computing. DB2 Workgroup supports all the same features as DB2 Express. Additional features and capabilities can also be added, via feature packs, without having to purchase DB2 Enterprise.

DB2 Workgroup can be licensed using the same options as DB2 Express — it only differs with respect to the architecture limits, which in turn optimize it for specific workloads. For example, the RAM limit for DB2 Workgroup is 16 GB, which is four times the amount you are entitled to use with a DB2 Express data server (which generally translates into better performance, or more supported users). The VU restriction is also more generous. DB2 Workgroup cannot be installed on a server that has a rating of more than 400 VUs, whereas the limit for DB2 Express is 200 VUs. DB2 Workgroup can also be licensed via the Authorized User model and shares the same minimum (five Authorized User licenses) as DB2 Express.

DB2 *Note*

In DB2 8 there were two types of Workgroup Editions in the DB2 lineup: DB2 Workgroup Server Edition (DB2 WSE) and DB2 Workgroup Unlimited Edition (DB2 WSUE). DB2 WSE was licensed by a concurrent or named user license, in addition to a base server license. DB2 WSUE was licensed by a processor metric. In DB2 9, these editions merged into one edition: DB2 Workgroup. The named user and server licenses have been replaced by the simplified Authorized User model and the processor license using the VU metric.

DB2 Workgroup can play many roles in a business. It's a good fit for small- or medium-sized businesses (SMBs) that need a full-fledged relational data server that is scalable and available over a wide area network (WAN) or local area network (LAN). DB2 Workgroup is also useful for enterprise environments that need silo servers for lines of business, or for departments that need the ability to scale in the future. As previously noted, an application written for any edition of DB2 is transparently portable to another edition on any distributed platform.

Add-on Feature Packs for DB2 Express and DB2 Workgroup Editions

DB2 Express and DB2 Workgroup come with the unique flexibility to add enterprise-like services (generally found in DB2 Enterprise) without having to buy a more expensive edition of DB2. Generally the price of these feature packs is such that if you only need one or two specific features, you can save money by purchasing the appropriate feature packs instead of purchasing DB2 Enterprise (as long as you remain within the architectural limitations of the DB2 edition you are implementing). This isn't the case with other competitive data server offerings.

Features Packs for DB2 Express and DB2 Workgroup are licensed in the same manner as the underlying data server. In other words, if you licensed your DB2 Express data server using the VU metric, you have to license any add-on feature packs using the VU metric as well.

The following feature packs are available for DB2 Express and DB2 Workgroup data servers:

- Workload Management Feature Pack

  Allows you to use the Connection Concentrator and the DB2 Governor, as well as install DB2 Query Patroller on a DB2 Express or DB2 Workgroup data server.

  The Connection Concentrator is useful for applications where multiple transient connections perform a limited amount of work in intervals. For example, think about a Web-based application where you browse around and selectively choose items to buy. You may be logged onto the system for a longer period of time while you browse potential items you wish to buy, but you're not making the data server work all the time because you're likely reading the page rather than continually clicking buttons. Concentrating a data server connection improves performance by allowing many more client connections to be processed efficiently, and it also reduces the memory used for each connection. This capability is part of a base DB2 Enterprise installation.

  The DB2 Governor, also included by default with DB2 Enterprise, is used to reactively monitor the behavior of applications that run against a DB2 data server. Using the DB2 Governor, you can alter the behavior of applications or the data server by taking corrective actions in response to thresholds that you define in a configuration file. For example, if an application is using too much CPU, you can set a rule that when this threshold is breached, the application is terminated or given less CPU priority.

DB2 Query Patroller (DB2 QP) is used to proactively manage the workload of a data server, the opposite of the reactive DB2 Governor. With DB2 QP, you can define a set of user and group business policies that are proactively monitored. For example, if a user submitted a query that the optimizer estimated would cost 1,000,000 timerons, and you set a business rule stating that no queries can be larger than 100,000 timerons, DB2 QP would stop this query from being processed on the data server. You can also use DB2 QP to perform charge-back accounting because it tracks valuable usage information (this information can also be used for performance tuning and more). DB2 QP is detailed in the "DB2 Query Patroller" section later in this chapter.

- Performance Optimization Feature Pack

  Makes available the use of materialized query tables (MQTs), multi-dimensional clustering (MDC) tables, and query parallelism for DB2 Express and DB2 Workgroup servers. All of these features are used to provide exceptional performance and are part of a base DB2 Enterprise installation.

  DB2 comes with a number of high-performance objects and capabilities that allow it to scale to hundreds of thousands of users and into the millions of transactions per minute or queries per hour. This feature pack provides the ability to create MDC tables and MQTs in your DB2 Express and DB2 Workgroup data servers. These objects provide immense benefits for applications running on DB2. In fact, we'd say that some of the most important components for any high-performing application are part of this feature pack. (If you're running a data warehouse be sure that you know what MDCs and MQTs are.) If you're looking to really boost the performance of an application running on the smaller servers for which DB2 Express and DB2 Workgroup were made, this feature pack has components that could prove very valuable to your business.

- High-Availability Feature Pack

  Gives DBAs a free two-node license of Tivoli System Automation (TSA) for high-availability failover clustering, the ability to run online table reorganizations, and the High-Availability Disaster Recovery (HADR) feature. All of the features in this feature pack are part of a base DB2 Enterprise installation.

  HADR is a high-availability feature that provides a database availability protection plan that is very simple to set up and use. The best part about HADR is that you set it up with mere clicks of a button. The online table reorganization capability, as its name implies, allows you to reorganize tables online. Finally, this feature pack includes a two-node cluster license for Tivoli System Automation (TSA) for AIX and Linux — you can use it to cluster together your servers for high-availability or to automate the failover of an HADR environment.

- pureXML Feature Pack

  Provides the ability to create pureXML columns in a DB2 Express or DB2 Workgroup data server and use an associated set of XML services when working with this data.

  You might be confused about the DB2 XML Extender (covered later in the "DB2 Extenders" section) and the pureXML add-on feature pack that's available in DB2 9. The DB2 XML Extender provides the XML capabilities that were part of the DB2 8 release. In contrast, the pureXML feature enables DB2 servers to exploit the new hybrid storage engine that stores XML naturally in DB2 9. The performance, usability, flexibility, and overall XML experience of pureXML can't even be compared to the older DB2 XML Extender technology; however, the DB2 XML Extender is still shipped in DB2 9 free-of-charge. If you are planning to use XML in your data environment we strongly recommended you use the pureXML feature.

  The pureXML feature lets you store XML in a parsed tree representation on disk, without having to store the XML in a large object or shred it to relational columns as you are forced to with the DB2 XML Extender. This can be very beneficial for applications that need to persist XML data. Access to XML data via the pureXML feature pack is a very natural experience; for example, you can use SQL or XQuery to get to relational or XML data.

  The pureXML feature also has facilities to store XML Schema Definition (XSD) documents in a native XML Schema Repository (XSR) service. It also supports schema annotations for document shredding, validation services, and more.

DB2 *Note*

DB2 9 supports the shredding of XML data to relational in the same manner as the DB2 XML Extender, but it uses a different and far superior technology to do it. You may want to shred your XML to relational for any number of reasons, such as when the XML data is naturally tabular. To shred XML to relational using the DB2 XML Extender, you have to hand-generate Document Access Definition documents that map nodes to columns, and so on. With DB2 9, even without the pureXML feature, you can use the DB2 Developer Workbench (covered later in this chapter) to shred your data and automate the discovery of these mappings. The new mechanism in DB2 9 is also significantly faster than the DB2 XML Extender method.

- Homogeneous Federation Feature Pack

  Provides the ability to create nicknames across the DB2 family of data servers. This feature allows developers to build applications that access DB2 tables that reside on different platforms without regard to their location. For example, you could use this feature to easily create an application that performs a join of data that resides on a DB2 for i5/OS data server with one that's running on DB2 for Windows. Even if you were working within an integrated development environment (IDE) such as IBM Rational Application Developer or Microsoft Visual Studio 2005, you still wouldn't be able to tell where each table actually resides — which is the whole point. The capability of this feature pack is a subset of the WebSphere Federated Server product covered later in this chapter.

DB2 Enterprise Edition

DB2 Enterprise Edition (DB2 Enterprise) is the premier data server offering from IBM that is the foundation of many mission-critical systems and the primary focus of this book. It is fully Web-enabled, scalable from single core servers to symmetric multicore servers and to massively parallel systems.

This edition of DB2 is considered to be the full-function offering from IBM (for example, it's the only DB2 edition that includes table partitioning). It is available on the same supported flavors of Linux, UNIX, and Windows as DB2 Workgroup. Applications built for DB2 Enterprise can scale upward and execute on massively parallel systems or downward to smaller servers.

DB2 Enterprise is meant for large and mid-sized departmental servers. DB2 Enterprise includes all the functions of the DB2 Express and DB2 Workgroup editions, and more. Additionally, there is a set of feature packs that are exclusive to this edition, such as the new DB2 9 Storage Optimization feature that provides deep row compression, and more.

DB2 *Note*

Some feature packs, such as the Database Partitioning and the Storage Optimization features, are not available using the authorized user metric.

DB2 Enterprise can be licensed using the same VU metric as DB2 Express and DB2 Workgroup; however, in the case of DB2 Enterprise, there is no RAM or VU server rating limits for the server on which this product is installed. DB2 Enterprise can also be licensed via the Authorized User metric. In contrast to DB2 Express and DB2 Workgroup, when licensing DB2 Enterprise using the Authorized User metric, the minimum number of Authorized Users for which it must be licensed is 25 Authorized Users for every 100 VUs on the server where it is installed. For example, if you installed DB2 Enterprise on an 8-core System p server (rated at 800 VUs), you would have to buy 200 Authorized User licenses at a minimum to use this licensing option, even if you intended for this data server to support fewer than 200 users.

Add-on Feature Packs for DB2 Enterprise Edition

DB2 Enterprise also comes with a set of add-on feature packs just like DB2 Express and DB2 Workgroup. For the most part (the exception being the pureXML feature pack), the extensibility features that can be purchased for DB2 Enterprise are unique to this edition of the DB2 family and provide even richer enterprise-capabilities to the data run-time environment.

The way you license DB2 Enterprise feature packs must be identical to how the DB2 Enterprise data server was licensed. This is one area where DBAs must pay particular attention when deciding how to license their DB2 Enterprise data servers because some feature packs aren't available with the DB2 Enterprise Authorized User license.

The feature packs that are available in DB2 Enterprise via Authorized User or Value Unit licensing are:

- Performance Optimization Feature Pack

  DBAs get licenses to install DB2 Query Patroller and the DB2 Performance Expert tool with this feature pack. The DB2 Query Patroller component of this feature pack is the same one that's part of the Workload Management feature pack available for DB2 Express and DB2 Workgroup.

  The DB2 Performance Expert is a separately purchasable tool that's used to simplify performance management and tuning. It offers DBAs a consistent view into their instances, subsystems, databases, and applications across the DB2 family. It has a set of pre-canned reports to identify resource shortage and exception conditions in DB2 including locking conflicts, deadlocks, and application and SQL statements causing high workload. The DB2 Performance Expert also includes a set of detailed reports about SQL, database, and buffer pool activity with trend analysis and what-if hypothesis testing for performance evaluation.

DB2 *Note*

The version of the DB2 Performance Expert that's part of this feature pack can only be used for DB2 data servers running on Linux, UNIX, and Windows. The DB2 Performance Expert tool when purchased outside of this feature pack can be used across the DB2 family.

- pureXML Feature Pack

  This feature pack provides the same capabilities as the one offered for DB2 Express and DB2 workgroup detailed earlier in this section.

- Advanced Access Control Feature Pack

  Provides label-based access control (LBAC) protection services to data stored in a DB2 Enterprise data server. Using this feature, data stewards can control the read and write access of a user at the table column and row level. LBAC implements data access controls by creating an affinity between columns and generated protection security labels. If users attempt to get data from a table, they must have matching label credentials (or a parent label) granted to them. When there's a match, access is permitted; without a match, access is denied.

  You can use this feature pack to create a security framework whose architecture is built on a hierarchal representation that matches the data access hierarchy, an array of that business entity, or a mix of the two. LBAC can also be used to restrict access to XML documents in columns (though as of the time of this writing, you cannot attach labels to fragments within the document itself).

- Geodetic Data Management Feature Pack

  This feature pack includes the DB2 Geodetic Data Management Extender that can be used to provide advanced spatial analysis capabilities. What separates this feature from the free DB2 Spatial Extender that comes with all DB2 data servers is that the Geodetic Data Management feature pack contains a built-in set of algorithms that take into consideration the curvature of objects, such as the earth's surface and so on. For example, maps generally are associated with some sort of applied projection in consideration of the map's purpose. The Mercator projection is very popular for navigational maps. When you look at a map generated using this projection, you'll notice that the top and bottom of the map seem much bigger than they really are. The fact that Greenland is one fourteenth the size of Africa often comes as a surprise when people think back to their public school atlas — this feature pack compensates for these distortions.

  While distortions caused by projections may not be of significance to applications that attempt to locate an address or division of a city, for weather pattern analysis or defense programs it could be very significant. If you can't afford to lose accuracy because of a projection, the Geodetic Data Management feature pack may be appropriate for your applications.

- Real-Time Insight Feature Pack

  Useful for managing large volumes of incoming data streams. Existing infrastructures can be easily overwhelmed when trying to manage large volumes of incoming data. Incoming data with message rates of tens to hundreds of thousands of messages per second can make it difficult to analyze this high volume of data.

The DB2 Real-Time Insight feature pack is powered by the DB2 Data Stream Engine (not discussed in this chapter since it's beyond the scope of this book) that enables organizations to store and forward high volumes of data from multiple data streams. The data messages from the feed can be aggregated, filtered, and enriched in real time before being stored or forwarded.

DB2 Data Stream Engine can load high volumes of data into the DB2 data server and make that data available to queries in real time through SQL. One example is a financial market data stream that provides information about financial transactions, such as stock trades and quotes.

The benefits of the Real-Time Insight Feature include:

- Scalable solution loads large volumes of data with high throughput and low latency
- Simultaneous storing and publishing of data from multiple feeds
- Insight into the data with filtering and aggregation from feeds before storing and publishing
- Maintenance of metadata, such as current state, for entities that are processed from the feeds
- Simultaneous persistence of data to multiple database servers on multiple hosts
- Real-time access by use of shared memory storage
- Easy access to both real-time and historical data through standard SQL, C-API, and Java API interfaces.

- Mobility on Demand Feature Pack

  This feature pack provides the components of DB2 Everyplace Enterprise Edition detailed earlier in this chapter. When using DB2e via the feature pack, you need to be aware that the DB2 SyncServer must be collocated with the DB2 Enterprise data server (this is the reason for its reduced cost when compared to a full licensed version of DB2 Everyplace Enterprise Edition).

- Homogeneous Federation Feature Pack

  This feature pack provides the same capabilities as the one offered for DB2 Express and DB2 Workgroup detailed earlier in this section.

Two feature packs available in DB2 Enterprise only through Value Unit licensing (in other words, you can't buy these feature packs with DB2 Enterprise servers that are licensed with authorized users) are:

1. Database Partitioning Feature (DPF)

   DB2 Enterprise provides the capability to enable DB2 to partition data across clusters or massively parallel servers. To the end user or application developer, a partitioned database appears to be on a single system, yet SQL statements are processed in parallel across all servers, thus increasing the execution speed for any given query.

   The DPF delivers the true principals of scalability to a DB2 Enterprise environment, namely:

   - **Double the resources, double the data**: Each partition processes the same amount of data as before, and response times and throughput remain constant.
   - **Double the resources, keep data constant**: Each partition processes half the amount of data as before, and response times will be cut in half, and throughput will double.
   - **Keep resources constant, double the data**: Each partition processes double the amount of data as before, response times should double, and throughput will be cut in half.

   You can partition data using the DPF across logical (within a larger SMP) and physical servers. An example of a partitioned database across multiple physical servers (though each server typically is small SMP server) is shown in Figure 1–7.

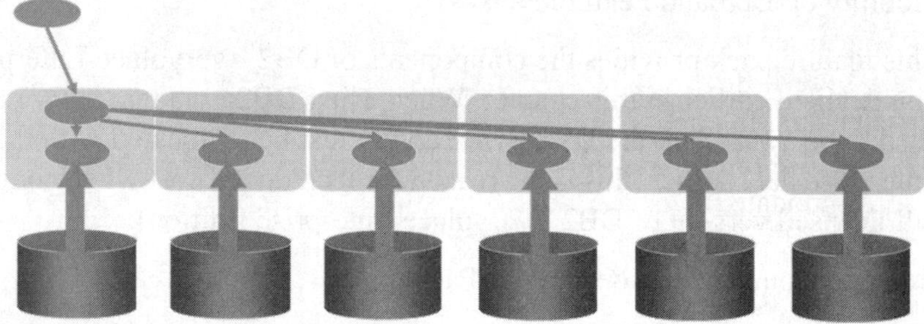

Figure 1–7 *DB2 partitioned across multiple servers using DPF*

In Figure 1–7 you can see that there are actually six copies of DB2. However, they all appear as a single copy to applications and administrators. Imagine the performance difference between a single copy of DB2 scanning 600,000 rows versus each copy of DB2 owning its own data and resources scanning just 100,000 rows. This is the power of the DPF.

Parallelism in DB2 is automatic and extended to the hash partitioning algorithm used in the DPF. If you are selecting just a few records (where partitioning key value = X), then DB2 will send that query directly to the node that contains that data. However, if you are scanning large amounts of data (as shown in Figure 1-7, typical in data warehousing), then DB2 will send the query to all partitions in the cluster and automatically parallelize the data access operations, driving more resources (RAM, CPU, and I/O) to get the job done faster.

It's not just query performance and faster maintenance operations that are delivered by the DPF. There is a significant resource savings per server because each server owns 1/nth of that data and generally requires fewer resources. Compare the partitioned database (shown on the left side in Figure 1–8) and the non-partitioned database on the right.

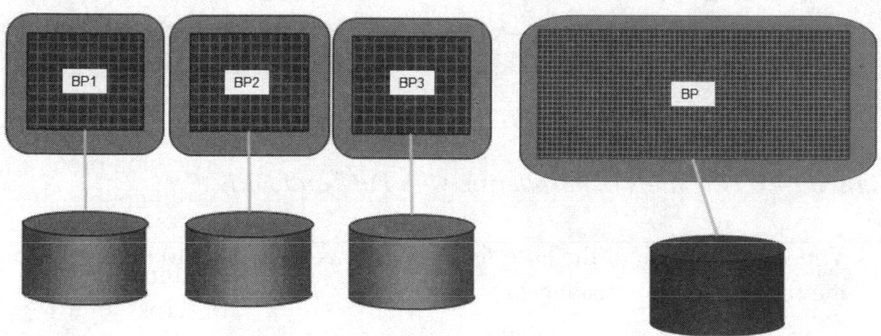

Figure 1–8 *Saving resources with the Database Partitioning Feature*

You can see that the servers comprising the partitioned database on the left side of Figure 1–8 require less memory, as each server is only responsible for 1/nth of the data. In contrast, the non-partitioned database on the right side of Figure 1–8 requires that much more memory be allocated to the buffer pool to accommodate the data.

Finally, DB2 can mix its intra-partition parallelism capabilities (where it runs components of an SQL statement in parallel on a single server) with its inter-partition parallelism (the DPF feature) as shown in Figure 1–9.

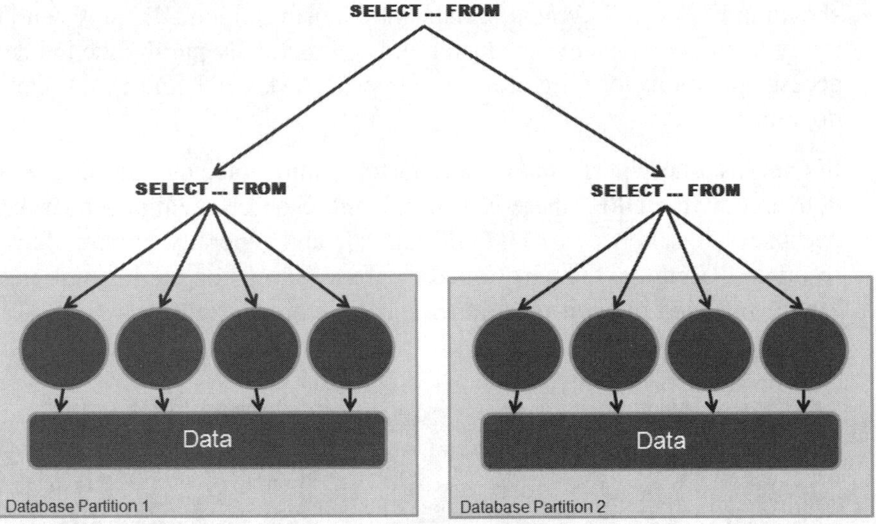

Figure 1–9 *Two kinds of parallelism with DB2 and DPF*

You should consider the DPF feature pack as an add-on to DB2 Enterprise in the following circumstances:

- The speed of database utility operations is key to your business operations. Operations like reorganizations, backups, and so on are parallelized with DPF so they can be performed much quicker. For example, if the six servers in Figure 1-7 all run the backup utility, they each only need to back-up one-sixth of the total data, and this operation should complete in one-sixth of the time when compared to a non-partitioned database.
- You need to shrink your batch window because of long extract, transform, and load processes (ETL). For example, data server load jobs are also parallelized. For example, if you had to load 600 GB of data, only 100 GB of data would need to be loaded into each server.
- Rolling window data update requirements for the warehouse make parallel SQL processing and additional log space essential. Not only does DPF give you more power to process the SQL, it gives you more resources (log space, memory, and so on).
- DPF should be considered if the database contains more than 400 GB of RAW data. Other indicators for using DPF are the total number of rows in the table and whether scan performance is critical to workload performance.

Large databases can be supported with DB2 Enterprise Edition, but large databases typically benefit from the DPF.

- Your environment is characterized by complex queries that involve large aggregations, multi-table joins, and so on. Having multiple servers working on the same SQL problem can generally return results faster than a single server.
- Your servers have plenty of available memory. Even though DB2 has 64-bit memory support for non-partitioned databases, multiple partitions have proven to provide more linear scalability and more efficient usage of memory than SMP parallelism alone.

2. DB2 Storage Optimization Feature

This feature provides deep row compression for you DB2 tables, as well as a backup compression utility that can significantly reduce the on disk size of your database backups. Tests have shown that more than 70 percent of table compression (data only) can be achieved when using this feature pack. Note that indexes remain uncompressed for performance reasons.

A number of other benefits, in addition to disk savings from having smaller tables, arise from row compression. Backups will be smaller (even without backup compression); maintenance operations (like backup) should run faster since there are fewer data pages to backup up; Q/A and test environments will be smaller; heating, ventilation, and air conditioning (HVAC) charges will be decreased since you need fewer disks; and query performance likely will increase because each I/O to disk brings back more rows into memory.

Row compression will drive up the CPU utilization of a data server. However, most systems (especially data warehouse systems) are I/O bound and, since compression will allow more rows on a data page and therefore more rows in the resident memory buffers, you'll likely see improved overall performance of your application.

Backup compression is also a part of this feature pack. The database backup architecture in DB2 is based on an open pluggable interface that allows you to use either the default compression algorithm that's shipped with DB2 or one of your own. The compression algorithm you use is embedded within the backup image so that it can be restored on a different server. Quite simply, if disaster happens and you lose the server where the compression algorithm is located, you can still get your data back because the compression algorithm is part of the backup image.

DB2 Connectivity

DB2 provides a variety of options for connecting to other DB2 and non-DB2 data servers:

- **DB2 Clients** — DB2 client code is required on workstations for remote users to access a DB2 database.
- **DB2 Drivers** — Some APIs that are part of a DB2 client are packaged on their own, outside of a client installation. DB2 drivers offer a more lightweight deployment option for specific API connectivity.
- **DB2 Connect™** — This add-on product provides support for applications executing on Linux, UNIX, and Windows to transparently access DB2 data servers on i5/OS, VM/VSE, and z/OS environments. DB2 Connect provides much more than just connectivity; more details of its capabilities are provided later in this chapter.

DB2 *Note*

DB2 Connect is not required to access DB2 for any of the LUW platforms.

- **DB2 Replication** — This feature provides replication capabilities for DB2 data servers. There are two kinds of replication, SQL-based replication and Queue-based replication (also know as Q-replication). Both are sometimes referred to as Data Propagator (DPROPR).

  SQL-based replication is included in all of the DB2 mainstream editions that run on Linux, UNIX, and Windows. It's made up of two components, CAPTURE and APPLY. It uses SQL to replay data on target servers.

  Q-Replication is built on the IBM WebSphere MQSeries® technology and is generally thought to be a more available and powerful replication technology. You can add this capability to a DB2 environment through one of the WebSphere Information Integrator products.
- **WebSphere Information Server** or **WebSphere Federation Server** — The WebSphere brand has a suite of products that help you publish, place, cleanse, transform, enrich, and access data across heterogeneous data sources.
- **WebSphere Application Server** — A part of this application server is shipped with DB2. It allows developers to use Java as a platform in a transaction processing environment.

DB2 Clients

Once a DB2 application has been developed, you need to install connectivity software on each client workstation in a two-tier environment. If you are deploying a Web-based application in a three-tier environment, you need to, at a minimum, install the DB2 client connectivity software on the application server. In DB2 9 there are basically two types of clients, the *DB2 Runtime Client* and the *DB2 Client*.

A DB2 Runtime Client provides the minimum *client* footprint (about 20–30 MB) to support connectivity to DB2 9 data servers (the exception to this is if you choose to support communication via specific API drivers, covered later in this section). When you install a DB2 Runtime Client, you install a driver to support all the common programming methodologies, including ADO.NET, ADO, OLE DB, ODBC, JDBC, SQLJ, static SQL, and more.

DB2 Note

In this chapter, the use of the term *client* with a lowercase c refers the DB2 client software in general, while an uppercase *C* refers to a specific DB2 client package.

Using a DB2 Runtime Client you can perform basic functions, such as running any DB2 commands or SQL statements from a DB2 CLP or CLP session; however, for the most part, this client comes with no other capabilities than supporting data connectivity. For example, there are no graphical-based management tools, documentation, and so on. You can download a DB2 Runtime Client at www14.software.ibm.com/webapp/iwm/web/preLogin.do?lang=en_US&source=swg-dm-db2rtcl.

DB2 Note

The DB2 8 Runtime Client is very different from the DB2 9 Runtime Client. In DB2 8, there was a special client only available on Windows called the *DB2 Runtime Client Lite*. This client had a reduced footprint compared to the DB2 9 Runtime Client and didn't include tooling, documentation, and so on. The DB2 9 Runtime Client is analogous to the DB2 8 Runtime Client Lite, only is now available on all supported platforms.

A special DB2 Runtime Client is made available as Windows Merge Modules (.msi files), which makes the installation of this software within Windows applications more natural. You can download these files at http://www-304.ibm.com/jct03002c/software/data/db2/runtime.html.

In contrast, the DB2 Client includes all the functions found in the DB2 Runtime Client plus functions for client-server configuration, tools for database administration and application development, samples, and more. For example, this client includes the Configuration Assistant that provides graphically administration and connectivity tools, as well as a host of programming samples, and so on. The DB2 9 Client replaces the functions found in both the DB2 8 Application Development and DB2 8 Administration clients.

A DB2 Client's footprint is directly correlated to the components you select to install and can take between 200 MB and 800 MB depending on the options you select. The process to install a DB2 Client is very similar to a DB2 data server. You can download a DB2 Client at http://www-304.ibm.com/jct03002c/software/data/db2/runtime.html.

The choice of which DB2 client to install should be based on the requirements of the application on the client machine. For example, if you have a database application developed for Linux, UNIX, or Windows and you do not require the DB2 administration or application development tools from a Windows workstation, yet want to support applications written in multiple programming languages like .NET and Java, you should install the DB2 Runtime Client on that workstation.

Some enterprises prefer to deploy the DB2 Runtime Client code remotely on a dedicated server. In these environments, remote workstations need to access the DB2 Runtime Client code remotely from a code server before accessing to DB2. This type of configuration is known as a thin client. A thin-client configuration can provide many benefits, such as a central catalog directory of all database connections and a single footprint of code to manage. The trade-off is that clients must load the client *.dlls* from the code server before accessing the remote data server. It should be noted however that this performance hit is only "noticed" on the initial connection. Once the client code is loaded on the client workstation, subsequent calls to the code server are not needed.

When you want to deploy your DB2 application, you only need to ensure that a DB2 Runtime Client is installed on each workstation executing the application. Figure 1-10 shows the relationship between an application, a DB2 Runtime Client, and the DB2 data server. If the application and database are installed on the same server, connectivity is considered to come from a local client. If the application is installed on a system other than the DB2 data server, its connectivity is considered to come from a *remote client*.

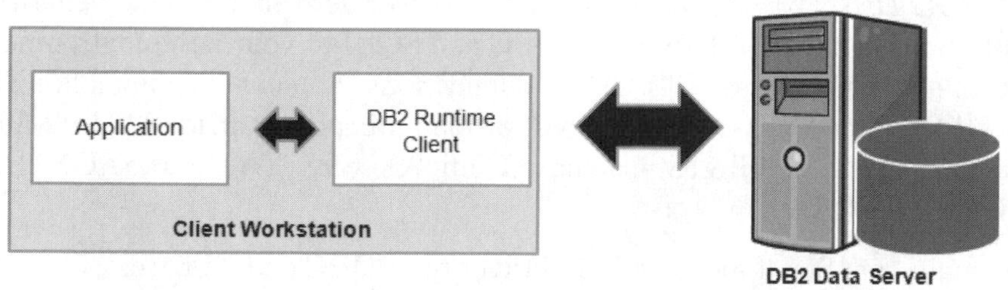

Figure 1–10 *Accessing a DB2 data server using the DB2 Runtime Client*

DB2 client connectivity can be configured using various supported communication protocols. The supported protocols vary according to operating system:

- TCP/IP — used in all environments
- Named Pipe — used in Windows environments

DB2 Drivers

Some larger enterprises and independent software vendors (ISVs) want to deploy their applications written in single language without the overheard of installing and maintaining a DB2 client on each client workstation. Despite the much smaller footprint of the DB2 Runtime Client in DB2 9, IBM makes available two drivers that can be deployed for connectivity on their own, outside of a DB2 Runtime Client or DB2 Client installation.

The *IBM Driver for JDBC and SQLJ* can be deployed to support Java-based connectivity to a DB2 data server. This driver is about 2 MB in size and can easily be embedded within your application. In fact, it comes with a royalty-free distribution license for this very purpose.

You should note however that although this driver can connect to the entire DB2 family, if you're connecting to a DB2 for i5/OS, DB2 for VM/VSE, or DB2 for z/OS data server, you need to additionally license this connectivity with DB2 Connect (covered in the next section) to ensure you are compliant with respect to licensing.

It's important to note that the IBM Driver for JDBC and SQLJ solely supports Java applications. Aside from not including tooling and documentation, this driver doesn't support data server connectivity using other APIs. For example, you can't support a .NET application using this driver. You can download this driver at www14.software.ibm.com/webapp/download/preconfig.jsp?id=2004-09-20+10%3A09%3A21.003415R&cat=database&fam=&s=c&S_TACT=105AGX11&S_CMP=DB2.

DB2 9 includes a new standalone driver for CLI and ODBC applications called the *IBM DB2 Driver for ODBC and CLI*. This driver delivers the same benefits and restrictions as the IBM Driver for JDBC and SQLJ to your DB2 environment, except it solely supports CLI/ODBC connections. You can download this driver at www14.software.ibm.com/webapp/download/preconfig.jsp?id=2004-09-20+13%3A44%3A48.813589R&cat=database&fam=&s=c&S_TACT=105AGX11&S_CMP=SPLT.

The main benefits of the IBM DB2 Driver for ODBC and CLI are:

- Light-weight deployment solution for ODBC/CLI applications
- Much smaller footprint (25M installed) than DB2 RTCL and DB2 Client
- No need to have DB2 RTCL or DB2 Client installed on the client machines
- Same concept as the JDBC/SQLJ driver but for ODBC/CLI applications

DB2 Connect

DB2 Connect is a separate product family that licenses client connectivity from distributed platforms to the DB2 family running on i5/OS, VM/VSE, and z/OS operating systems (hereafter referred to as *mainframe*). Although communications between any members of the DB2 family use the Distributed Relational Database Architecture (DRDA), you have to explicitly license access from DB2 for Linux, UNIX, and Windows clients to these data servers.

A client accessing DB2 running on the mainframe is generally referred to as a *DRDA Application Requester (DRDA AR)* and the DB2 server that manages the client connection as a *DRDA Application Server* (*DRDA AS*). DB2 Connect only uses TCP/IP as the transport protocol between a DRDA AR and DRDA AS.

DB2 Note

If you are connecting to DB2 for Linux, UNIX, and Windows from a client running on a mainframe, you don't need DB2 Connect. DRDA AS functionality is built into DB2 data servers running on distributed platforms.

Some of the major capabilities provided by DB2 Connect include:

- Support for programming APIs such as ADO, ODBC, OLE DB, CLI, JDBC, SQLJ, ADO.NET (and more) to DB2 running on the mainframe.
- Federation across the DB2 and Informix data servers. You can extend the reach of this federation capability to heterogeneous sources by adding either WebSphere Federation Server or WebSphere Information Server.
- Connection pooling and the more powerful connection concentration services

that provide minimal resource consumption on the mainframe.

- System z Sysplex exploitation for failover and load balancing. For example, DB2 Connect includes high-availability features such as z/OS Workload Manager Integration (WLM) and automatic re-direct to a data-sharing group.
- Integration into mainstream development environments for mainframe data access. For example, DB2 Connect makes data artifacts on the mainframe (including nonrelational-related services like CICS and VSAM) transparent to the world's most popular IDEs; for example, a .NET developer can use Microsoft Visual Studio 2005 and build stored procedures without knowing where the data actually resides.

DB2 Connect is often used to enable mainframe resources for Web access, better integrate legacy and heritage systems with new deployments on distributed platforms, modernize the application development experience for mainframe development (for example, moving from COBOL to Java), and off-loading development cycles to lower-cost operational environments.

Depending on the DB2 Connect edition you purchase, you can create a connectivity architecture for single- or multi-tier environments.

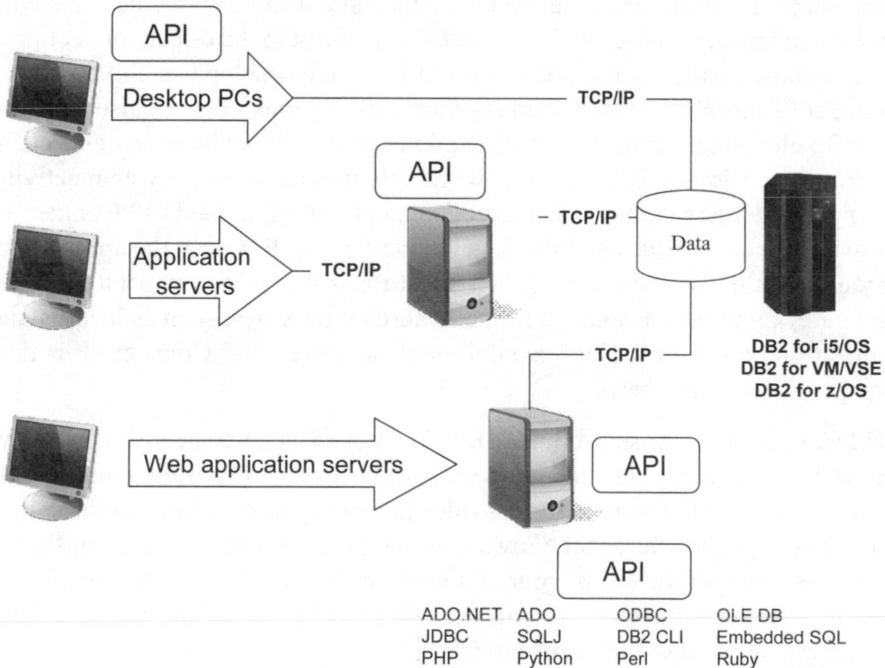

Figure 1–11 *Using DB2 Connect is a single-tier or multi-tier environment*

You can see in Figure 1–11 that there are many ways to implement a DB2 Connect product. In a multi-tier environment, you use DB2 client software to connect to the DB2 Connect gateway (in a client/server model) passing the connection context to to the mainframe resource. In a Web-based deployment, you may have DB2 Connect on its own or collocated with the application server. Depending on your configuration, you may or may not need to install a DB2 client.

DB2 Connect products can be added on to an existing DB2 data server installation, or act as a standalone gateway. Either way, it's purchased separately from DB2. If you are using one of drivers discussed earlier in this chapter, technically you can make the connection to a mainframe DB2 resource, but you still need to purchase a valid DB2 Connect license. There are a number of DB2 Connect editions available and each is suited for a particular implementation of the DB2 Connect software. With the exception of DB2 Connect PE, all of the DB2 Connect editions offer the same function and features; they are merely differentiated by capability. All editions of DB2 Connect PE are considered *gateways* since they provide client/server access to workstations. To connect to a DB2 Connect gateway, you simply use a DB2 client.

DB2 Connect Personal Edition (DB2 Connect PE) is similar to DB2 Personal Edition in that it is used for single workstations and doesn't provide its users with any server capabilities. Using DB2 Connect PE, you can make direct connections to DB2 running on the mainframe. In Figure 1–11, the desktop users likely have DB2 Connect PE installed in their workstations. DB2 Connect PE can also act as a regular DB2 client and connect to distributed versions of the data server as well. Some environments deploy DB2 Connect with both direct and gateway connectivity. For example, a developer may make direct connections using the DB2 Connect PE software for certain stages of the development cycle. But once the application is in production, they may use the DB2 Connect PE software to connect to a DB2 Connect gateway to take advantage of the features it provides, such as load balancing, connection optimization, high-availability, and more. DB2 Connect PE is licensed on a per-workstation basis.

DB2 Connect Enterprise Edition (DB2 Connect EE) can be licensed using two different user-based options: the number of Authorized Users or the number of Concurrent Users. DB2 Connect EE provides the ability to implement a three-tier connectivity architecture that allows you to isolate connectivity to mainframe resources to a specific tier in your architecture. Again, DB2 clients (or drivers) are used to connect to the gateways, and then the DB2 Connect software manages the connection context to the mainframe.

DB2 Connect Application Server Edition (DB2 Connect ASE) is licensed by the total VU rating of all the applications servers that connect to the mainframe. The VUs that you purchase have nothing to do with how many DB2 Connect servers you set up, or what their rating is. For example, if your Web server farm was rated at 1,000 VUs and you set up a DB2 Connect gateway farm rated at 5,000 VUs, you would have to buy 1,000 VUs of DB2 Connect ASE. DB2 Connect ASE is well suited for environments where you expect to see more growth of mainframe resource than your Web tier because its costs are directly linked to the VU rating of the Web serving tier.

DB2 Connect Unlimited Edition (DB2 Connect UE) is available for i5/OS and z/OS. DB2 Connect UE for i5/OS is licensed by the number of managed processors attached to the i5/OS partition while DB2 Connect UE for z/OS is licensed with a base server license plus a per-unit charge for the MSU rating of the System z server you are connecting to. DB2 Connect UE is well suited for environments that have flat mainframe cycle growth and heavy Web tier growth as the costs of DB2 Connect UE are directly correlated with the capacity of the mainframe resource. DB2 Connect UE comes with a free copy of Mobility on Demand to move mainframe data to occasionally connected devices, as well as DB2 Connect PE. Essentially, this edition of DB2 Connect, as its name would imply, allows for unlimited deployments.

There's so much more to the DB2 Connect product than what's detailed in this section. In fact, the name DB2 Connect is misleading because connectivity is just a small part of what this product can do; however, these details are outside the scope of this book.

DB2 Replication

DB2 Replication allows for data to be propagated from one location to another. SQL-based replication, also know as Data Propagator (DPROPR) replication, is a free component of the DB2 for Linux, UNIX, and Windows data servers (it's a paid feature on the mainframe). You can also extend this replication capability to support a wide variety of data servers, including DB2, Oracle, Microsoft, Sybase, Informix, IMS, Lotus Notes, and flat files with WebSphere Replication Server.

DB2 *Note*

SQL replication is also the core technology behind the DB2e SyncServer that enables mobile users to keep their data synchronized with corporate data.

An example of SQL-based replication is shown in Figure 1–12. SQL-based replication has been around for over a decade and has proven itself to be extremely flexible, resilient, easy to set up, and scalable.

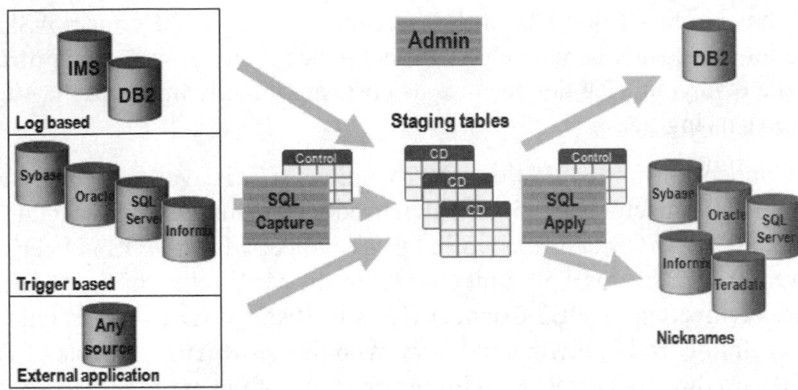

Figure 1–12 *SQL-based replication extended with WebSphere Replication Server*

In Figure 1–12 you can see the broad reach of the SQL-based replication technology when it is extended with the WebSphere Replication Server product. As you may recall, distributed versions of DB2 come with the DPROPR technology built in and can support replication subscriptions across the DB2 family. The core capabilities of a distributed data server with respect to replication are shown in the top-left and top-right portions of Figure 1–12.

When you buy WebSphere Replication Server, you also get Q-based replication (Figure 1–13). In Q-based replication, each message represents a transaction that is placed on a WebSphere MQ Series message queue. This replication is known for its highly parallel apply process and rich conflict detection and resolution services.

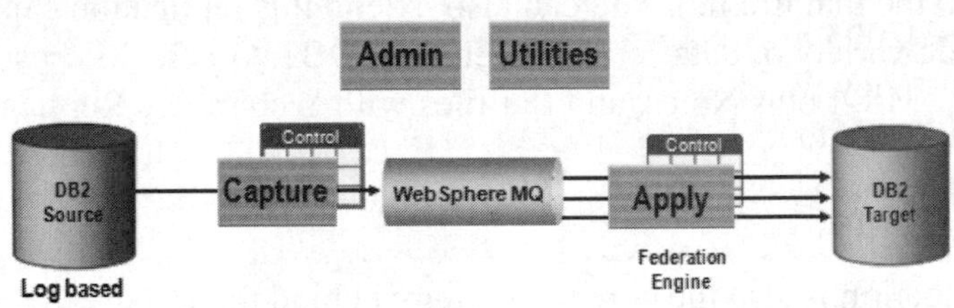

Figure 1–13 *The power of Q-based replication*

WebSphere Federation Server and WebSphere Information Server

WebSphere Information Server provides features and functions to place, publish, integrate, find, cleanse, and access data. The *federation* capabilities are worth mentioning as they relate to data access. WebSphere Federation Server contains a subset of the functionality found in WebSphere Information Server, namely the federation capabilities (and hence will be the focus of this section). You can learn more about WebSphere Federation Server and WebSphere Information Server at www.ibm.com/software/data/integration/.

A federated system is a distributed database environment that appears as a single virtual database to end users and applications. The WebSphere Federation Server technology (some of which is built into DB2) allows SQL statements to transparently access, join, or update data located across heterogeneous data sources. Federated support enables the DB2 data server to evaluate global statistics on all data sources in order to optimize requests for the remote data. For example, the global optimizer can use knowledge of source statistics, source indexes, source functions, server and network speeds, and so on.

The SQL support in a DB2 federated environment supports the same SQL as a non-federated environment, including advanced object-relational SQL operations across the federated data sources, such as recursive SQL, common table expressions (CTEs), and more. If the remote data source doesn't have this capability, DB2 will compensate for the missing functions.

Perhaps the greatest benefit to a federated system is that developers only have to learn a single dialect of SQL; namely, the DB2 ANSI-compliant SQL API. If an external data source has different data types or non-standard SQL, DB2 will transparently compensate for missing functions and convert data types. For example, SQL Server 2005 has a `MONEY` data type whereas DB2 uses a `DECIMAL` data type to support currency. Without the WebSphere Federation Server technology, a developer would have to know the differences between these data servers, or cast them to like data types using OLE DB. With WebSphere Federation Server, developers just code as if they were always accessing DB2 data, and the rest is taken care of.

An example of federated access is shown in Figure 1–14.

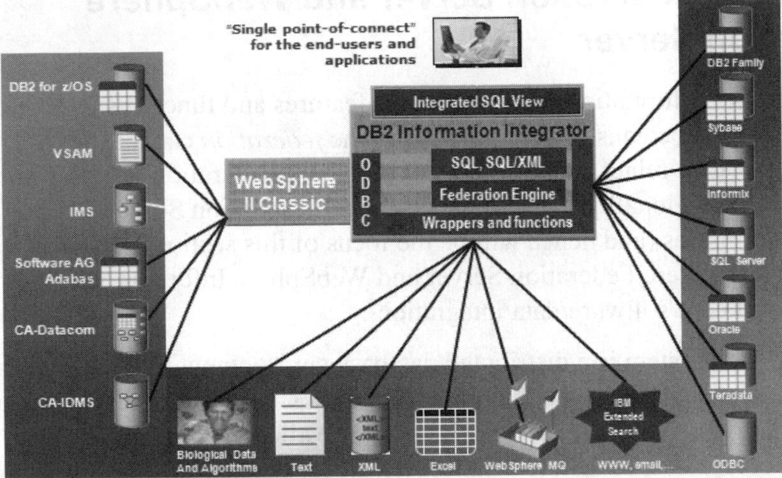

Figure 1–14 *The power of federation — any data, one API*

In Figure 1–15 you can see the technology components that make up a federated database. *Nicknames* are used to implement a low form of granularity with respect to the data sources you want to make available. Nicknames essentially are local aliases on remote tables, although they can be mapped to specific rows and columns. A collection of nicknames is located within a *server* that represents that actual data source. For example, in Figure 1–15 Oracle is one such data source, so the server component would represent a specific Oracle database. All the SQL eventually flows through a *wrapper*, which is a library of code that allows access to a particular class of data servers. Connections made to these servers use their native protocol; for example, the Oracle connection will use the Net8 client.

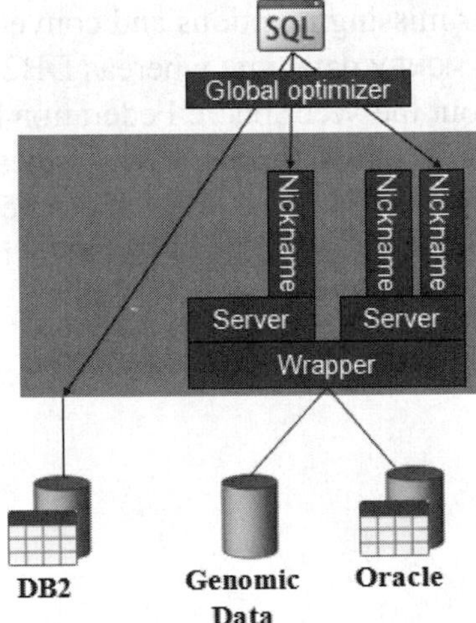

Figure 1–15 *How federation works*

You can see in Figure 1–14 that with WebSphere Federation Server you can pretty much extend the reach of DB2 to *any* data source in your environment. For example, in the life sciences industry, scientists need access to specialized data to support their research related to drug discovery. IBM offers a set of Life Sciences wrappers that can be used to build a federated system that can access data useful to scientists, including Excel spreadsheets, image data, flat files, and BLAST (Basic Local Alignment Search Tool).

If a wrapper is not available for purchase, there is a software developer's kit (SDK) that you can use to build your own.

Database Enterprise Developer's Edition

IBM offers a special discounted suite of Information Management products that you can purchase at a discount for development, evaluation, demonstration, and testing of your application programs; this edition is called Data Enterprise Developer Edition (DEDE).

Some of the products included in this comprehensive developer offering are:

- DB2 Express 9
- DB2 Workgroup 9
- DB2 Enterprise 9
- DB2 Runtime Client (including .msi merge modules on Windows)
- DB2 Client
- IBM Driver for ODBC and CLI
- IBM Driver for JDBC and SQLJ
- DB2 Developer Workbench
- DB2 Embedded Application Server (components of WebSphere Application Server)
- DB2 Information Center
- DB2 Documentation CD
- DB2e Enterprise Edition
- WebSphere MQ (this is a restricted copy that can only be used in conjunction with the DB2 software)
- Rational Web Developer (this is a restricted copy that can only be used in conjunction with the DB2 software)
- Tivoli System Automation (TSA) for Linux and AIX
- Informix IDS Enterprise Edition
- IBM Cloudscape/Apache Derby
- DB2 Connect Unlimited Edition for i5/OS and z/OS

- All the DB2 Extenders™, namely DB2 Spatial Extender, DB2 Geodetic Extender, DB2 Net Search Extender, and the DB2 XML Extender
- All of the DB2 add-on feature packs outlined earlier in this chapter

Most of the products within DEDE are available for all the platforms that DB2 Enterprise supports (unless of course a product doesn't exist on a specific platform). The data server where you install DEDE can be on a platform that is different from the one on which the application will eventually be deployed or tested because of the common code base used in the distributed DB2 environment. In fact, almost any applications developed using DEDE can be executed on any system that has DB2 client software (or specific drivers for which the application is written) installed.

The application development environment provided with DEDE allows application developers to write programs using today's most popular methodologies, including:

- Embedded SQL
- Call Level Interface (CLI)/Open Database Connectivity (ODBC)
- .NET Framework 2.0
- DB2 Application Programming Interfaces (APIs)
- Web Services
- Java Database Connectivity (JDBC) and SQLJ
- Python™
- PHP
- Perl™
- Ruby on Rails™

DEDE also includes the necessary programming libraries, header files, code samples, and pre-compilers for all of the supported programming languages.

DB2 Developer Workbench

The DB2 9 Developer Workbench (DB2 DWB) replaces the DB2 8 Development Center. The DB2 DWB is an Eclipse-based graphical environment that supports the rapid development of DB2 SQL and Java stored procedures, SQL scalar and table user defined functions (UDFs), SQL statements, XQuery statements, and Web Services. However, there's so much more to this list. For example, the DB2 DWB includes an SQL editor that's enriched with syntax colorization and code assistants, as well as teaming support, compare utilities, and more.

The DB2 DWB is a separate tool and is maintained separate from a DB2 data server. You can download it from www-304.ibm.com/jct03001c/software/data/db2/ad/dwb.html.

The DB2 DWB is really meant for power DBAs that aren't coding experts but require rapid development assistance for building business logic for their data servers. Depending on your environment, you may elect to use another tool like Toad for DB2 or Visual Studio. Pure developers will likely choose to use the plug-ins provided with DB2 9 into their respective IDEs, although they are free to use the DB2 DWB. For the most part, you can perform the same tasks in any of the tools that IBM ships or the integration points in specific IDEs.

A snapshot of the Developer Workbench screen is shown in Figure 1–16.

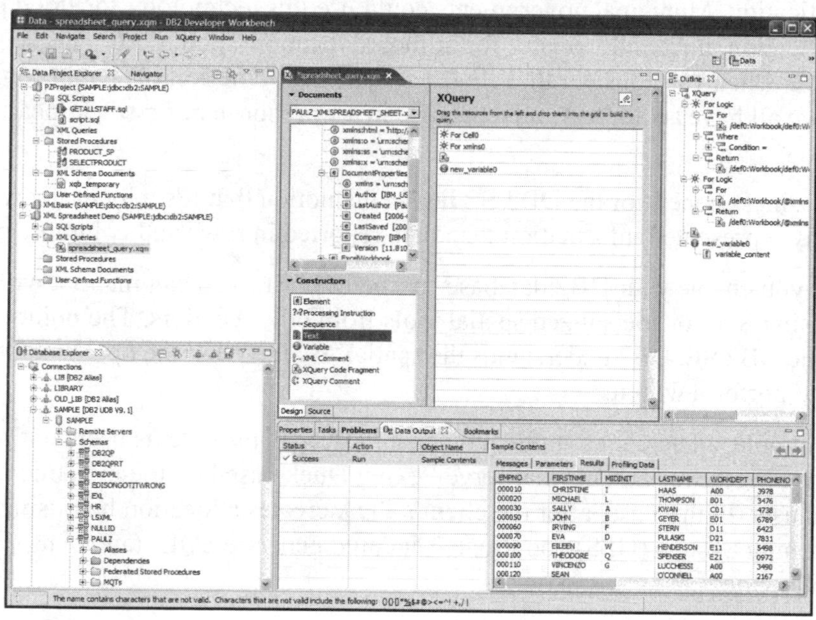

Figure 1–16 *The DB2 Developer Workbench*

DB2 Extenders

DB2 Extenders offer the ability to manipulate data outside of conventional rows and columns to include the manipulation of special data types (for example, spatial types that have associated LAT/LONG coordinates and SQL-based functions to operate on them), searching services, and more. The purpose of the DB2 Extenders is to provide for the management of this data through the familiar DB2 SQL API.

The DB2 Extenders encapsulate the attributes, structure, and behavior of these unstructured data types and stores this information in DB2. From the developer's perspective, the DB2 Extenders appear as seamless extensions to the database and enable the development of multimedia-based applications. In other words, a spatial data type is no different than a built-in data type that they may be accustomed to. This section briefly details the DB2 Extenders that are provided by IBM.

DB2 Spatial Extender

The DB2 Spatial Extender (DB2 SE) provides the ability to create spatially aware data objects and store them within your DB2 database, along with other spatially related objects like (LAT/LONG) coordinates and more. Almost all industries could benefit from this free technology in DB2. For example, the banking and finance industry could visually envelope customer segments for brand location identification. Municipal governments could use this technology for flood plain identification, the retail industry for billboard locations, and more. This seems apparent when you consider that almost all data has some sort of spatial component to it: we all have an address, merchandise in a warehouse has a stock location, and so on.

The business benefit of the DB2 SE lies in the notion that it's a lot easier to spot visually represented information than data reported in rows and columns.

When you enable your DB2 database for the DB2 SE, you can interact with your data using SQL or specialized spatial tools from other vendors. The point is that with the DB2 SE, DB2 understands the spatial "dialect" and the operations that you want to perform with it.

For example, a telematics application on a PDA may provide its users with a list of nearby Chinese restaurants that serve Peking Duck based on the dynamic request of this user. In this case, after the client's PDA creates a location box using Global Positioning System (GPS) coordinates, it could generate SQL statements similar to the following:

```
SELECT NAME, DESCRIPTION, ADDRESS FROM RESTAURANTS
  WHERE
    OVERLAPS (LOCATION, BOX(GETGPS(),2000,2000))
    AND CATEGORY = 'CHINESE'
    AND DOC CONTAINS(MENU,'PEKING DUCK');
```

`OVERLAPS` is a spatial function that shows interested data in a binding box defined by the `OVERLAPS` boundary specification; there are many other spatial functions, including `INTERSECTS`, `WITHIN`, `BUFFERS`, and so on.

DB2 Geodetic Extender

The DB2 Geodetic Extender builds upon capabilities available in the DB2 Spatial Extender and adds compensation for real-world objects like the curvature of the earth's surface. The algorithms in this extender seek to remove the inaccuracies introduced by projections and so on. This extender is available only for DB2 Enterprise as part of the Data Geodetic Management feature.

DB2 Net Search Extender

The DB2 Net Search Extender (DB2 NSE) combines in-memory database technology with text search semantics for high-speed text search in DB2 databases. Searching with it can be particularly advantageous in Internet applications where performance is an important factor. The DB2 NSE can add the power of fast full-text retrieval to your DB2 applications. Its features let you store unstructured text documents of up to 2 GB in databases. It offers application developers a fast, versatile, and intelligent method of searching through such documents.

Additionally, the DB2 NSE provides a rich set of XML searching capabilities with advanced search features like sounds-like, stemming, and so on. It is shipped free in DB2 9 (it was a chargeable extender in DB2 8) to facilitate non-XML index searching of XML data stored in pureXML columns.

DB2 XML Extender

The DB2 XML Extender is provided with DB2 and allows you to store XML documents in DB2; it also gives you the ability to shred and store XML in its component parts as columns in multiple tables. In either case, indexes can be defined over the elements or attributes of an XML document for fast retrieval. Furthermore, text and fragment search can be enabled on the XML column or its decomposed parts via the DB2 Net Search Extender. The DB2 XML Extender can also help you formulate an XML document from existing DB2 tables for data interchange in business-to-business environments.

You may recall that the pureXML add-on feature pack is available for all DB2 9 data servers. Indeed, this can cause confusion since the DB2 XML Extender is shipped for free in DB2 9. You should consider the DB2 XML Extender as stabilized technology. In other words, it is no longer being enhanced and shouldn't be considered for most XML applications. The DB2 XML Extender's approach to storing XML is to shred the XML to relational tables or stuff it into a large object. When you use this technology to persist XML data, you have to make serious trade-offs with respect to performance, flexibility, and so on. In addition, you have to use specialized functions to implement Spathe searches, and data types are abstracted from base DB2 data types. Quite simply, the way you interact with the DB2 XML Extender isn't natural for XML programmers and DBAs alike.

In contrast, the pureXML feature in DB2 9 provides services such that no compromises between flexibility (what XML was designed for) and performance (one of the reasons why you want the data server to store your XML) need to be made when storing your XML data. For example, to generate XML documents from relational tables, you simple use the SQL/XML API instead of the cumbersome DB2 XML Extender functions. You can validate XML documents against Sods instead of only document type definitions (Ds) as is the case with the DB2 XML Extender, and more. We strongly recommend this feature for most of your XML-based applications.

DB2 Administration

DB2 DBAs have a number of graphical-based tools they can use to manage and administer DB2 data servers. Alternatively, a DBA can also use a script-based approach to administer the data environment using the DB2 tools to create and schedule the scripts. This section briefly details the main graphical tools available with DB2.

Control Center

The Control Center is the central point of administration for DB2. The Control Center provides DBAs with the tools necessary to perform typical database administration tasks. It allows easy access to other server administration tools, gives a clear overview of the entire system, enables remote database management, and provides step-by-step assistance for complex tasks.

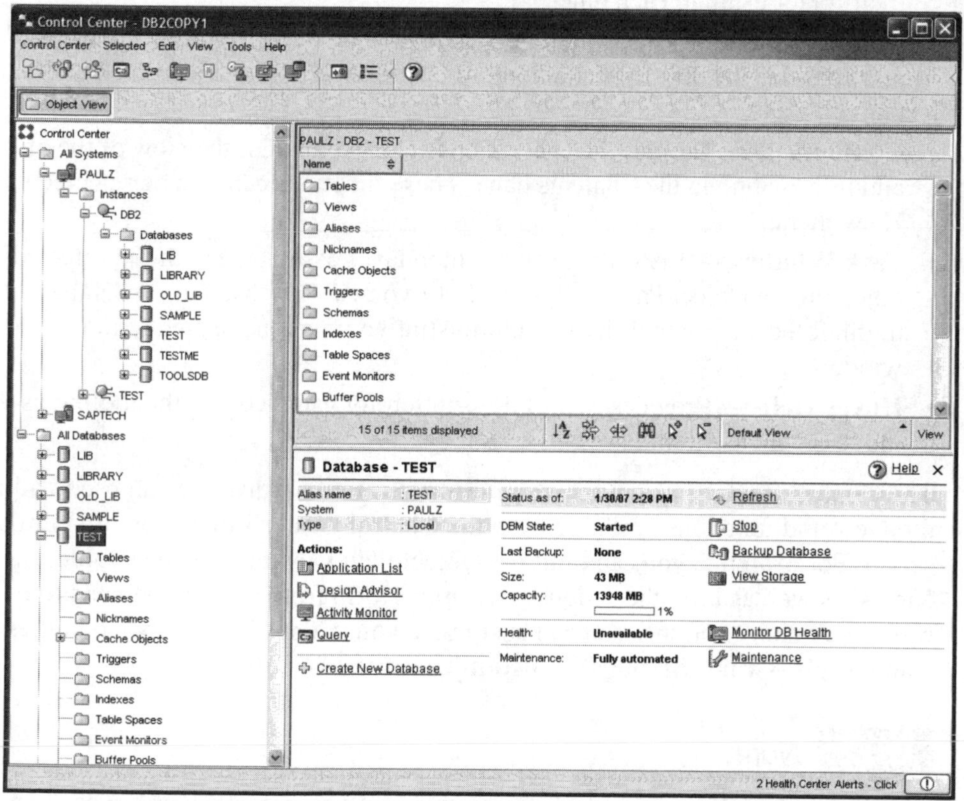

Figure 1–17 *The DB2 Control Center*

The **All Systems** object represents both local and remote data servers. To display all the DB2 systems that your system knows about, expand the object tree by clicking on the plus sign (+) next to **All Systems**. In Figure 1–17, you can see a DB2 data server called PAULZ contains a DB2 instance called DB2, in which the database TEST is located.

When you highlight an object, details about that object are shown in the Contents Pane.

The main components of the Control Center are:

- **Menu Bar** — Used to access Control Center functions and online help.
- **Tool Bar** — Used to access other DB2 administration tools, such as the Command Editor, Task Center, and more.
- **Objects Pane** — This is shown on the left side of the Control Center window. It contains all the objects that can be managed from the Control Center as well as their relationship to each other.
- **Contents Pane** — This is found on the right side of the Control Center window and contains the objects that belong or correspond to the object selected in the Objects Pane.
- **Contents Pane Toolbar** — These icons are used to tailor the view of the objects and information in the Contents pane. These functions can also be selected in the View menu.
- **Task Window** — Lists the most common tasks associated with the selected object in the Object Pane. In Figure 1–17 you can see that since a database is highlighted, common tasks and administrative functions related to it are in this window.
- **Hover Help** — Provides a short description for each icon on the toolbar as you move the mouse pointer over the icon.

The Control Center also comes with *personality control* that you can use to adjust the view and functions available from the Control Center's tree view of your data server. For example, you can limit the Object Pain view to show just Tables or Views, as well as limit the actions you can perform from the context-sensitive right-click menu options. You can customize your Control Center personalities using **Tools → Tools Settings → Customize Control Center**.

DB2 *Note*

The facility to define a Control Center personality by defaults pops up each and every time you start the Control Center. You can turn off this option by deselecting the **Show this window at startup time** checkbox.

DB2 Replication Center

The DB2 Replication Center is a graphical tool that allows DBAs to quickly set up and administer all forms of data replication, including the options offered by WebSphere Replication Server. The main functions in setting up a replication environment can be performed with this tool, including:

- Registering replication sources
- Monitoring the replication process
- Operating the CAPTURE and APPLY programs
- Defining alerts

You can use the Replication Center to set up all kinds of DB2 replications, as shown in Figure 1–18.

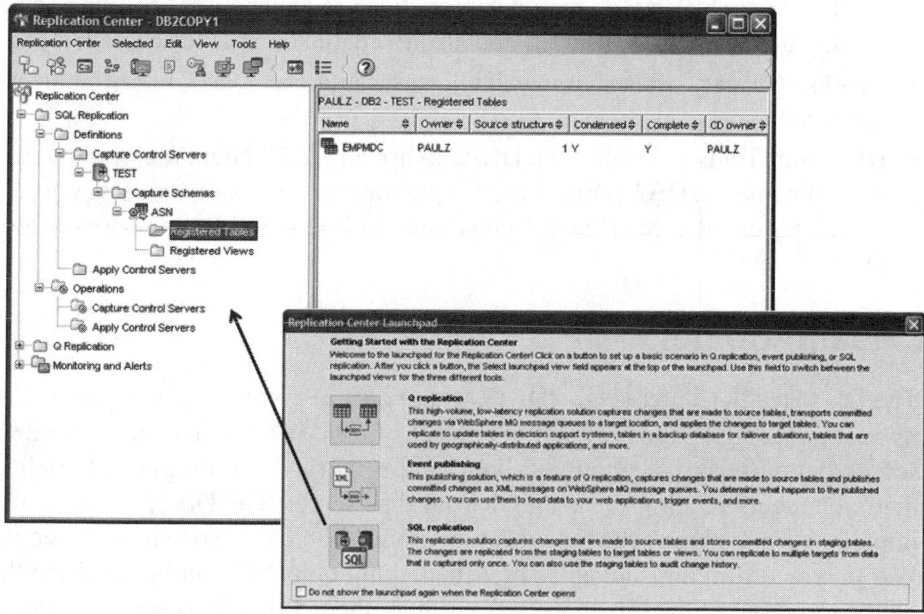

Figure 1–18 *The DB2 Replication Center*

Other Tools Available from the Control Center

By using the Control Center tool bar, you can access a host of other graphical administration tools to help you manage and administer databases in your environment:

- **Satellite Administration Center** — Used to manage groups of DB2 data servers through push/pull management scripts and more.
- **Command Editor** — Provides an interactive window that facilitates the building of SQL statements or DB2 commands, the viewing of execution results, and explain information. This graphical command utility is often the preferred method for text commands as it provides enormous flexibility and functionality.
- **Task Center** — Used to create, schedule, and manage scripts that can contain SQL statements, DB2 commands, or operating systems commands.
- **Journal** — Keeps a record of all script invocations, all DB2 messages, and the DB2 recovery history file for a database. It is used to show the results of a job, to display the contents of a script, and also to enable or disable scheduled jobs.
- **License Center** — Used to manage licenses and check how many connections are used.
- **DB2 Web Tools** — Allows the DBAs to use an HTTP client to remotely execute SQL statements, DB2 commands, or operating system commands against a DB2 server. Essentially, the Health Center and the Command Editor are exposed in this tool set.

DB2 Health Center

The DB2 Health Center (Figure 1–19) is the central point of information with respect to managing the health of your DB2 system. When you install a DB2 9 data server, out of the box it automatically monitors 27 (and counting) health indicators that proactively monitor the health of your data server. The DB2 Health Center implements a management-by-exception model whereby alerts are surfaced when Warning or Alarm thresholds are breached. Although DB2 configures these thresholds for you out of the box, you can configure them yourself as well as specify scripted actions to occur in the event of an alert.

You don't have to use the DB2 Health Center to work with DB2's health information or set triggered actions to occur on threshold breaches. You can use a number of SQL-based user defined functions to work with the DB2 health facilities from the command line.

The DB2 Health Center can monitor indicators across the following health categories:

- Application concurrency (e.g., Deadlock rate)

- DBMS (e.g., Instance operational state)
- Database (e.g., Database operational state)
- Logging (e.g., Log utilization)
- Memory (e.g., Monitor heap utilization)
- Sorting (e.g., Percentage of sorts that overflowed)
- Table space storage (e.g., Table space utilization)
- Database maintenance (e.g., Reorganization required)
- High-Availability Disaster Recovery (e.g., HADR log delay)
- Federated (e.g., Nickname status)
- Package and catalog caches (e.g., Package cache hit ratio)

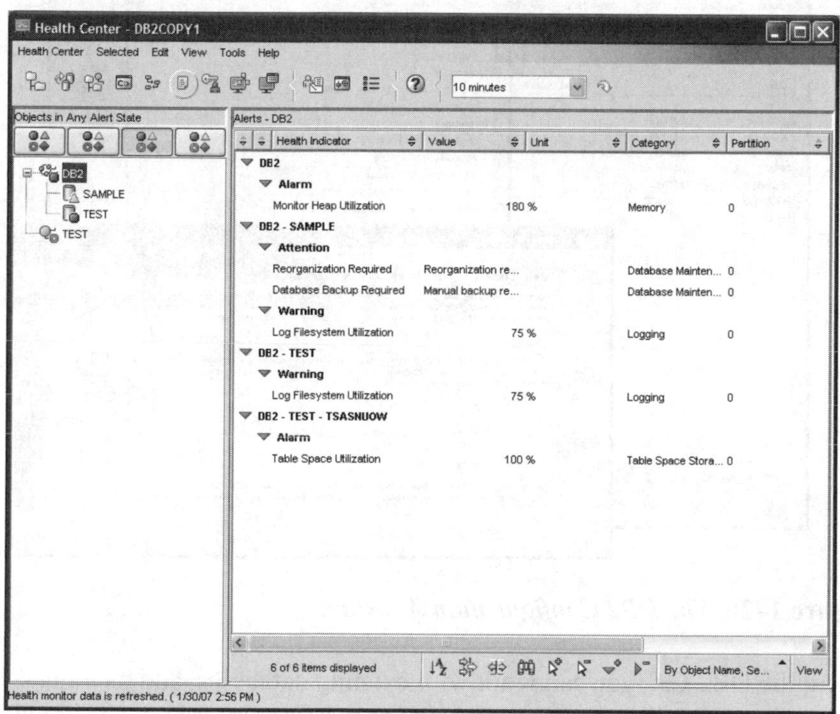

Figure 1–19 *The DB2 Health Center*

The DB2 Health Center's graphical user interface allows DBAs to select database objects and drill down on its details, current alerts, and the recommended actions. The DB2 Health Center also includes the DB2 Recommendation Advisor that can be used to walk through potential fixes to alerts and alarms raised in this facility.

DB2 Configuration Assistant

The DB2 Configuration Assistant (DB2 CA) lets you maintain a list of databases to which your applications can connect, as well as manage and administer those connections. It is mostly used for client connectivity configuration. You can start the DB2 CA by entering the `db2ca` command from your operating system's command-line shell or from the DB2 folder in the **Start** menu. Some of the functions available in the DB2 CA are shown in Figure 1–20.

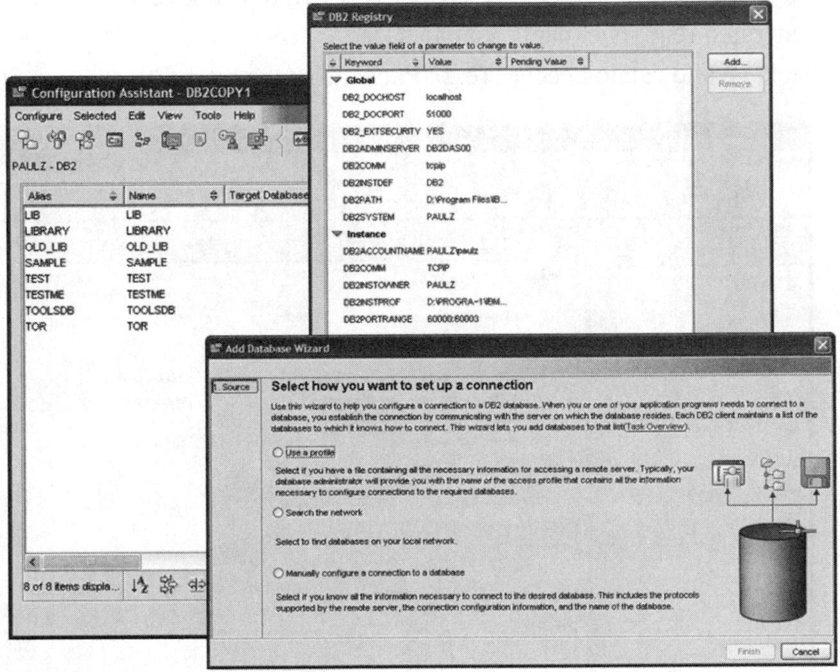

Figure 1–20 *The DB2 Configuration Assistant*

Using the DB2 CA, you can work with existing databases, add new ones, bind applications, set client configuration and registry parameters (also shown in Figure 1–20), test connectivity, and import and export configuration profiles.

The DB2 CA's graphical interface makes these complex tasks easier by means of the following:

- Wizards that help you perform certain tasks
- Dynamic fields that are activated based on your input choices
- Hints that help you make configuration decisions
- The Discovery feature, which can retrieve information that is known about databases that reside on your network

The DB2 CA's Discovery feature is very useful because it allows you to add a database connection without having to know the syntax of DB2 CATALOG NODE and DB2 CATALOG DATABASE commands, or even the location information of the remote data server.

As you can see in Figure 1–20, the DB2 CA displays a list of the databases to which your applications can connect from the workstation where it was started. Each database is identified first by its database alias, then by its name. You can use the Change Database Wizard to alter the information associated with databases in this list. The CA also has an Advanced view, which uses a notebook to organize connection information by the following objects:

- Systems
- Instance nodes
- Databases
- Database Connection Services (DCS) for System i and System z databases
- Data sources

Advisors and Wizards

DB2 comes with a set of Wizards and Advisors to help you with day-to-day tasks. Wizards can be very useful to both novice and expert DB2 users. Wizards help you complete specific tasks by taking you through each task one step at a time and recommending settings where applicable. Wizards are available through both the Control Center and the Configuration Assistant.

There are wizards for adding a database to your system, creating a database, backing up and restoring a database, creating tables, creating table spaces, configuring two-phase commit environments, configuring database logging, updating your documentation, setting up a High-Availability Disaster Recovery (HADR) pair, tuning your performance, and more.

Figure 1–21 shows a portion of the Create Database wizard in DB2 9.

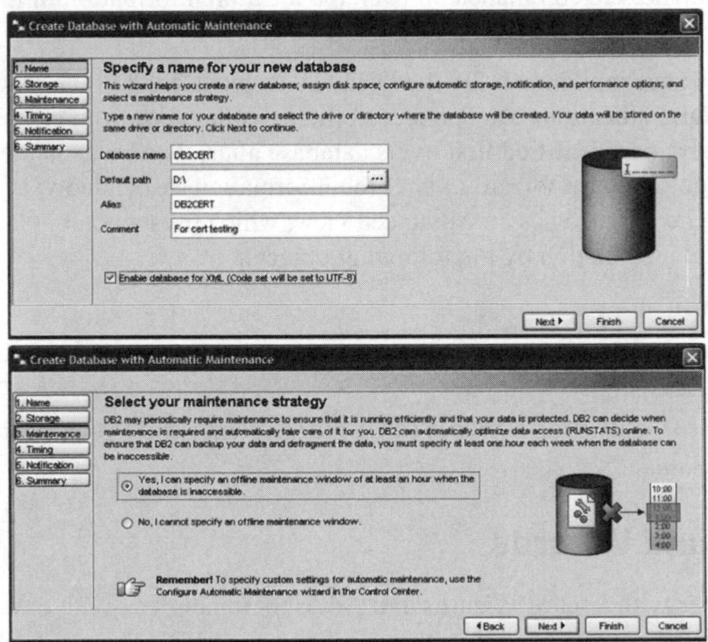

Figure 1–21 *The Create Database wizard*

Advisors are special types of wizards that do more than provide assistance in completing a task. Traditional wizards take you step-by-step through a task, simplifying the experience by asking important questions or generating the complex command syntax for the action you want to perform. When a wizard has more intelligence than just task completion and can offer advisory-type functions, DB2 calls them *advisors*. They operate just like wizards but are intelligent enough (having some pretty complex algorithms) to generate advice based on input factors such as workload or statistics. Advisors help you with more complex activities, such as tuning tasks, by gathering information and recommending options that you may not have considered. You can then accept or reject the advisor's advice. You can call advisors from context menus in the DB2 administration tools, from APIs, and the command-line interface.

Advisors are part of the IBM autonomic computing effort, which aims to make software and hardware more SMART (self-managing and resource tuning). There are three main advisors in DB2 9: the DB2 Configuration Advisor, the DB2 Recommendation Advisor, and the DB2 Design Advisor.

The DB2 Configuration Advisor is automatically run for you whenever you create a new database in DB2 9. It can configure up to 35 instance-level and database-level parameters for you based on responses to high-level questions that describe the data server environment and type of application you plan to support.

The DB2 Recommendation Advisor, as previously mentioned, is closely associated with the DB2 Health Center and is used to offer solutions to raised alerts and alarm breeches in this facility.

The DB2 Design Advisor is used to identify objects such as materialized query tables (MQTs), multidimensional clustering tables (MDCs), indexes, and partitioning keys that could optimize a given SQL workload. The DB2 Design Advisor can also identify indexes that aren't needed as well (shown in Figure 1–22).

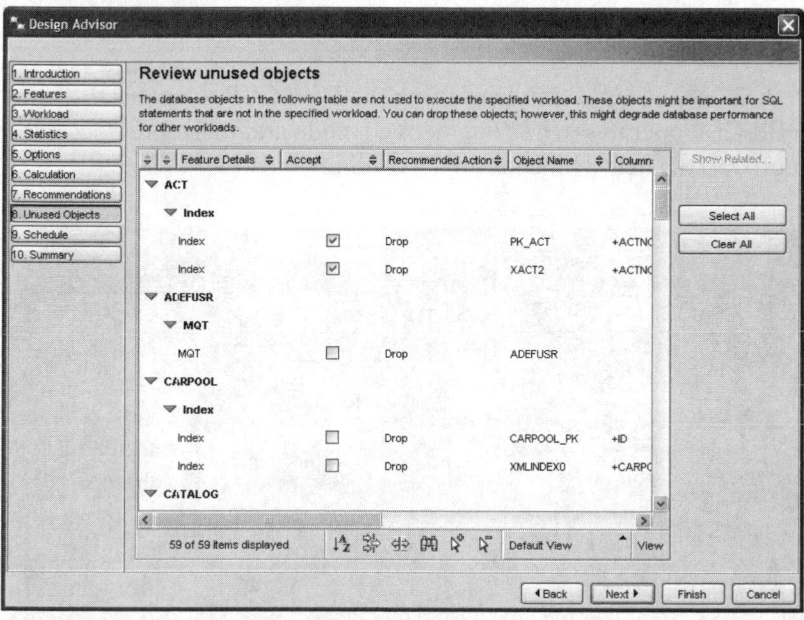

Figure 1–22 *The DB2 Design Advisor*

When using this advisor it's important to note that the suggestions it provides are based on a submitted workload. If you've left out significant portions of a workload, the answer will not reflect the impact of the missing workload. In addition, the DB2 Design Advisor gives you the ability to heavily weight SQL statements in a submitted workload over others, giving you more control with respect to how the DB2 Design Advisor will recommend the creation of performance objects with respect to your real workload characteristics.

The DB2 Command Line Processor

The DB2 Command Line Processor (DB2 CLP) is a component common to all DB2 products. It is a text-based application that can be used to issue interactive SQL statements or DB2 commands. For example, you can create a database, catalog a database, and issue dynamic SQL statements all from the DB2 CLP. Your DB2 statements and commands can also be placed in a file and executed in a batch environment, or they can be entered in interactive mode.

DB2 Note

Commands issued from the DB2 CLP can also be issued from the DB2 Command Editor or from most operating system's command line processor (CLP) using the `db2` prefix.

Figure 1–23 shows an example of using the DB2 CLP to enter DB2 commands. The DB2 CLP operates in an "interactive" mode and therefore does not require the db2 prefix associated with entering DB2 commands.

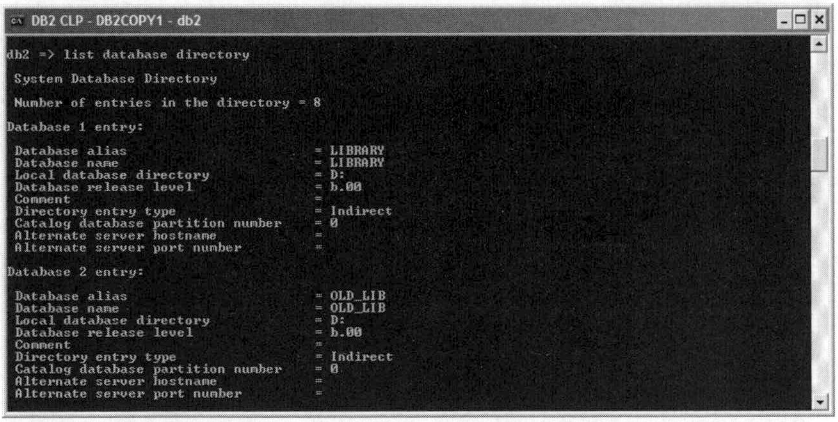

```
DB2 CLP - DB2COPY1 - db2

db2 => list database directory

 System Database Directory

 Number of entries in the directory = 8

Database 1 entry:

 Database alias                       = LIBRARY
 Database name                        = LIBRARY
 Local database directory             = D:
 Database release level               = b.00
 Comment                              =
 Directory entry type                 = Indirect
 Catalog database partition number    = 0
 Alternate server hostname            =
 Alternate server port number         =

Database 2 entry:

 Database alias                       = OLD_LIB
 Database name                        = OLD_LIB
 Local database directory             = D:
 Database release level               = b.00
 Comment                              =
 Directory entry type                 = Indirect
 Catalog database partition number    = 0
 Alternate server hostname            =
 Alternate server port number         =
```

Figure 1–23 *Using the DB2 CLP to enter commands*

The DB2 CLP is provided with all DB2 and DB2 Connect products. All SQL statements issued from the DB2 CLP are dynamically prepared and executed on the data server. The output, or result, of the SQL query is displayed on the screen by default. All of the DB2 commands that you can enter in the DB2 CLP are documented in the *DB2 Command Reference*. You learn more about the DB2 CLP and how to enter DB2 commands from an operating system's native CLP in Chapter 2.

Visual Explain

Other graphical tools can be used for tuning or monitoring performance. Visual Explain is a graphical utility that provides a visual representation of the access plan that DB2 uses to execute an SQL statement.

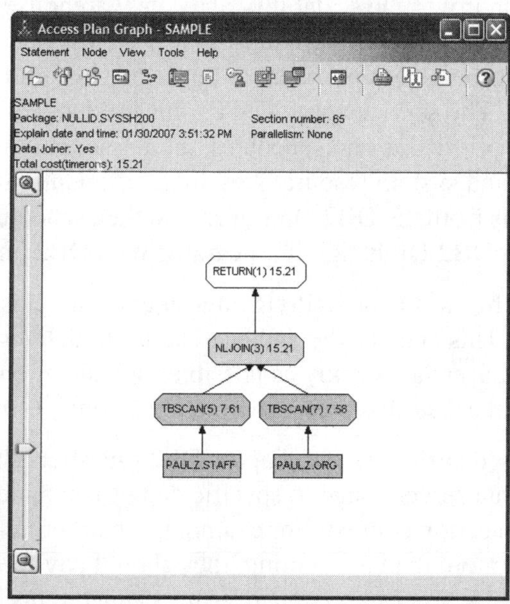

Figure 1–24 *Using Visual Explain to look at how your query is run by DB2*

Visual Explain can be invoked from the Control Center, the DB2 CLP (though the output in textual and not graphical), the DB2 DWB, or from the Command Editor.

Figure 1–24 shows the type of information that is displayed. You can see that the query is accessing two tables and an approximation of the cost of each step of this query is also provided in the Visual Explain output. The estimated query costs represent the complexity and resource usage expected for a given SQL query. There are many more details and features provided in Visual Explain under the **Statement** menu option.

DB2 Query Patroller

DB2 Query Patroller (DB2 QP) is an add-on product that can be used to control and monitor query execution, as well as work with queries to prioritize and schedule user queries based on user profiles and cost analysis performed on each query. Large queries can be put on hold and scheduled for a later time during off-peak hours. Queries with high priority (based on user profiles) are promoted to the top of the schedule.

In addition, DB2 QP monitors resource utilization statistics. DB2 QP can use this information to determine the load distribution of the system, which can allow it to balance the number of users allowed to submit queries at any given time.

DB2 QP greatly improves the scalability of a data warehouse by allowing hundreds of users to safely submit queries on multi-terabyte class data servers. Its components span the distributed environment to better manage and control all aspects of query submission. The services provided by this product act as an agent on behalf of the end user. It prioritizes and schedules queries so that query completion is more predictable and system resources are more efficiently utilized. DB2 QP obtains query costs from the DB2 Optimizer and then schedules them for execution — this means that DB2 QP is tightly integrated with DB2 engine.

DB2 QP can also be used to set individual user and user class priorities as well as user query limits. This enables the data warehouse to deliver the needed results to its most important users as quickly as possible. If desired, an end user can choose to receive notice of scheduled query completion through e-mail.

Finally, as discussed earlier in this chapter, DB2 QP offers the ability to perform charge back for data server usage to specific departments identified by accounting strings on the connection context. For example, if marketing is using the data warehouse three times more than accounting, they should pay three times the charge back. In Figure 1–25, you can see one of many canned reports that come with DB2 QP. This one shows the number of statements run by month. You can drill down into this view to the minute and second interval, as well as access a host of other reports such as average execution time, average wait time, average queue time, and more.

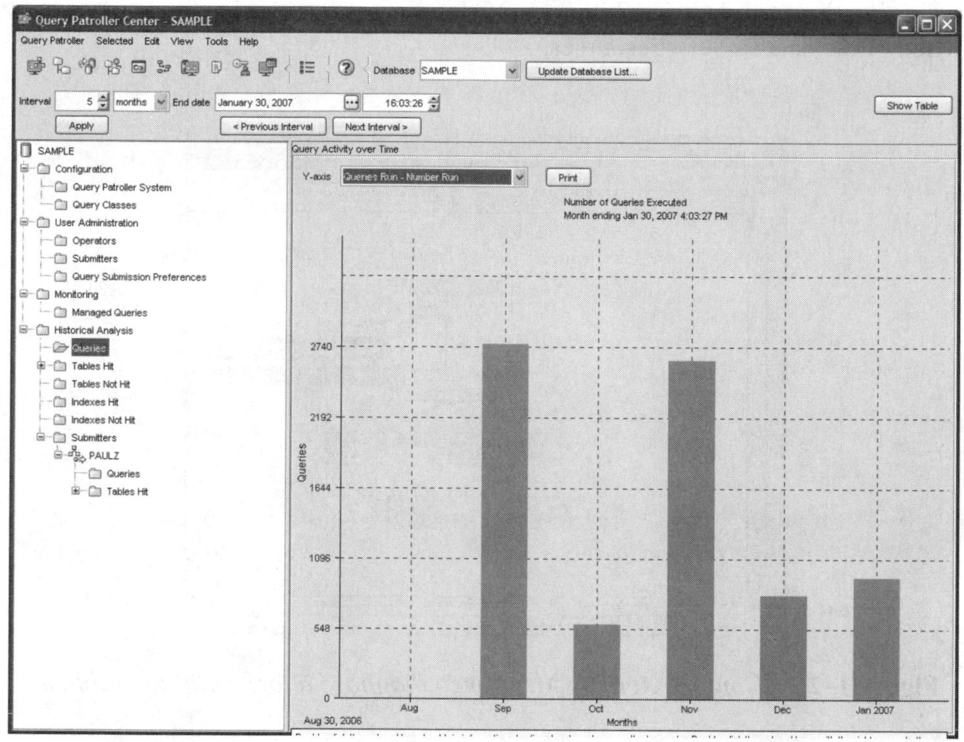

Figure 1–25 *Performing charge back with DB2 Query Patroller*

Database Monitoring Tools

The *Snapshot Monitor* captures database information at specific intervals. The interval time and data represented in the performance graph can be configured. The Snapshot Monitor can help analyze performance problems, tune SQL statements, and identify exception conditions based on limits or thresholds.

The *Event Monitor* captures database activity events as defined by the event monitor definition. Event Monitor records are usually stored on disk and then analyzed after the data has been captured. The *Event Analyzer* graphical tool provided with DB2 can be used to analyze the captured data.

The *Activity Monitor* help you improve the efficiency of database performance monitoring, problem determination, and resolution. By tracking a set of predefined monitor data, the Activity Monitor allows you to quickly locate the cause of a problem. You can then take direct action to resolve the problem or invoke another tool for further investigation. The Activity Monitor can help you monitor application performance, application concurrency, resource consumption, and SQL statement usage. It can also assist you in diagnosing performance problems such as lock waiting situations (as shown in Figure 1–26), and in tuning queries for optimal utilization of the data server's resources.

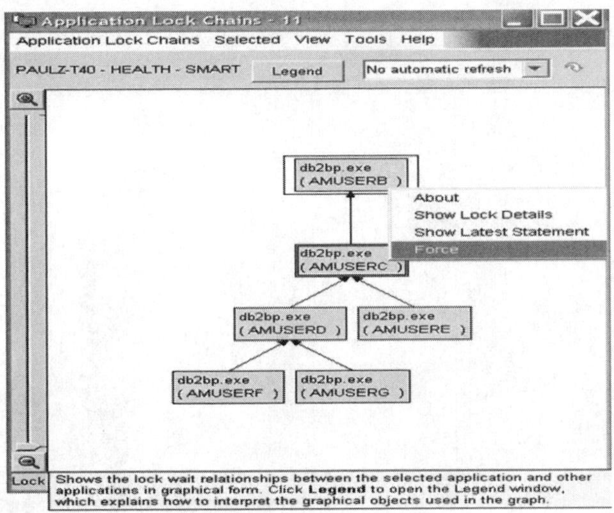

Figure 1–26 *Using the Activity Monitor to diagnose a lock waiting problem*

The DB2 Storage Management Tool

The DB2 Storage Management Tool can be used to monitor the storage state of a database. You can use this facility to take storage snapshots for a database or a table space. When a database or snapshot is taken, statistical information is collected for all the table spaces defined in the given database (you can also snapshot at the table space level).

The Storage Management Tool enables you to set thresholds for data skew, space usage, and index cluster ratio. If a target object exceeds a specified threshold, the icons beside the object and its parent object in the Storage Management view are marked with a warning flag or an alarm flag — similar to the DB2 Health Center.

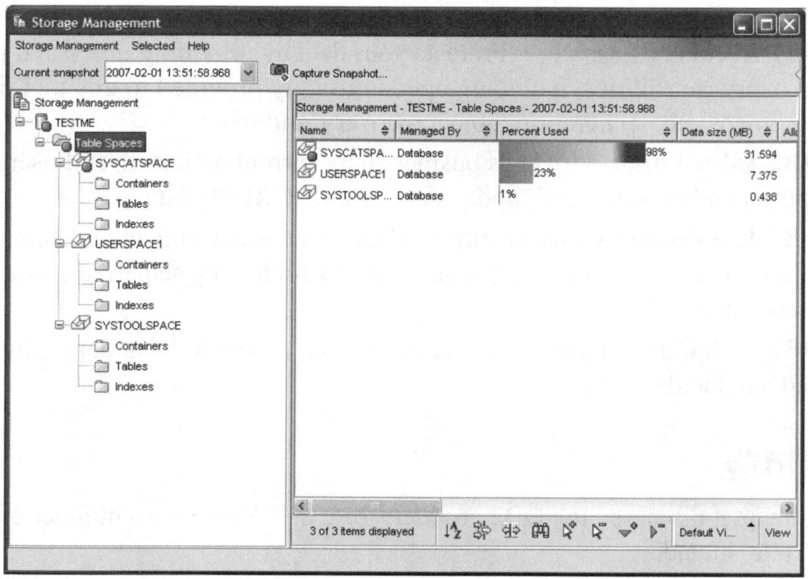

Figure 1–27 *Using the DB2 tools to manage storage activity*

You can see in Figure 1–27 that the SYSCATSPACE table space is running out of space as it's 98 percent used.

The DB2 Aftermarket Tools

There are two kinds of tools for DB2: those that are free and those that are add-ons that can be purchased separately. The free tools come as part of a DB2 installation and can be launched from the Control Center, the Configuration Assistant, or on their own. A separate set of purchasable tools are available to help ease a DBA's task of managing and recovering data, tuning performance, and more. The DB2 suite of these tools includes (www-306.ibm.com/software/data/tools/mptools.html):

- **DB2 Change Management Expert** — Improves DBA productivity and reduces human error by automating and managing complex DB2 structural changes.
- **Data Archive Expert** — Responds to legislative requirements like Sarbanes-Oxley by helping DBAs move seldom-used data to a less costly storage medium without additional programming.
- **DB2 High Performance Unload** —Maximizes DBA productivity by reducing maintenance windows for data unloading and repartitioning.
- **DB2 Performance Expert** — Makes DBAs more proactive in performance management to maximize database performance. (This tool was discussed in the

"Add-on Feature Packs for DB2 Enterprise Edition" section earlier in this chapter).

- **DB2 Recovery Expert** — Protects your data by providing quick and precise recovery capabilities, including operations only provided in this tool like SQL statement undo generation, object recovery, and more.
- **DB2 Table Editor** — Keeps business data current by letting end users easily and securely create, read, update, and delete (CRUD) data.
- **DB2 Test Database Generator** — Quickly creates test data and helps avoid liabilities associated with data privacy laws by protecting sensitive production data used in test.
- **DB2 Web Query Tool** — Broadens end user access to DB2 data using the Web and handheld devices.

Summary

This chapter discussed the DB2 products for LUW. There are a number of offerings available, including:

- DB2 Enterprise Edition
- DB2 Workgroup Edition
- DB2 Express Edition
- DB2 Express-C
- DB2 Personal Edition
- DB2 Everyplace Edition
- Various DB2 Connect Editions
- DB2 Query Patroller

These products provide the flexibility to execute database applications running on pervasive devices up to multi-node clusters. DB2 provides support for the commonly used communication protocols.

Each of the DB2 data server editions comes with a set of purchasable add-on feature packs that you can use to extend the capabilities of the core data server. There are also number of add-on tools and products that you can also buy for DB2, including DB2 Query Patroller and a myriad of DBA-focused tools such as High Performance Unload, the DB2 Recovery Expert, and more.

SQL-based replication is integrated into all DB2 for Linux, UNIX, and Windows servers. Replication can be used to move data between members of the DB2 family, or from and to members of the DB2 family and non-DB2 data servers (like Oracle, SQL Server, and more) if you're using WebSphere Replication Edition. DB2 Connect is used to access DB2 data that resides on DB2 for i5/OS, VM/VSE, and z/OS operating systems, and it comes with federated capabilities that can also be added to a DB2 data server installation.

DB2 9 includes a number of application development enhancements, including the DB2 Developer Workbench and integration into the world's most popular IDEs such as Rational Application Developer, Zend Core, and Microsoft Visual Studio 2005.

Significant new features have been added to make DB2 easier to manage. SMART technology (Self-managing and Resource Tuning) has been integrated into a number of DB2 components, including installation, configuration, utilities, problem determination and resolution, and availability. This is part of IBM's autonomic computing initiative and new features will continue to be added to make DBAs more productive.

This chapter also introduced some of the graphical and command line tools available in DB2. The Command Line Processor (CLP) is a text-based application that allows you to enter DB2 commands and SQL statements and is found in all DB2 products. From the desktop, an administrator can configure remote and local systems, administer instances and databases, and create database objects graphically using the Control Center or the Configuration Assistant. Tools like the DB2 Health Center and DB2 Activity Monitor also help manage DB2 environments while export support is provided in the form of Wizards and Advisors. In the remaining chapters, additional DB2 functions and tools will be examined for how they assist the end user, application developer, and administrator.

CHAPTER 2

Getting Started

- INSTALLING DB2 SOFTWARE
- USING THE DB2 COMMAND LINE PROCESSOR
- CREATING INSTANCES
- SETTING UP THE DB2 ENVIRONMENT
- INSTANCE ADMINISTRATION

This chapter provides an overview of the first steps in getting started with your DB2 data server. First, this chapter covers the overall installation process for a DB2 for Linux, UNIX, and Windows (DB2) data server with specific details for the Windows operating system.

A mass deployment installation will also be reviewed. If you are planning to install DB2 products across your network, a response file-based installation can provide you with numerous benefits such as speed of deployment, simplification of the deployment, and more. Rolling out multiple identical copies and configurations of a DB2 product is also possible using the installation response file architecture.

Once you have successfully installed a DB2 data server, the environment that is created by the installation process will be examined. This requires an understanding of the different levels of managing the DB2 environment from a global, instance, and user perspective. DB2 databases are created within an instance on a DB2 data server. The management of multiple instances including administration commands and tooling will also be reviewed.

Product Installation

This section discusses the installation of DB2 on Linux, UNIX, and Windows. While the installation has differences among the supported platforms (although the concepts are the same), once the DB2 data server is installed, the administration skill set is pretty much the same.

The DB2 installation process will check to see if TCP/IP or Named Pipes is running on your system and automatically configure the default DB2 instance it creates as part of the DB2 installation.

Windows Installation

This section illustrates installing DB2 on a Windows XP workstation.

Before beginning the installation on a Windows machine, make sure that the user account performing the installation is:

- Defined on the local machine
- A member of the `LOCAL ADMINISTRATORS` group
- Given the `ACT AS PART OF THE OPERATING SYSTEM` advanced user right
- Ensure that you system meets the installation, memory, and disk requirements for a DB2 9 installation. The most up to date operating system requirements for DB2 9 data server installations is available on the Web at www-306.ibm.com/software/data/db2/udb/sysreqs.html.
- Although not mandatory, it is recommended that you close all programs so that the installation program can update any files on the computer without requiring a reboot.

In general, the installation of a DB2 data server, as well as the application of DB2 Fix Packs (maintenance), requires access to the Windows system registry and windows services — hence the requirement for user accounts to belong to the `ADMINISTRATORS` group to complete the installation. In DB2 9, the restriction on requiring a user account that belongs to the Administrators group was lifted. Users belonging to the `POWER USERS` or `USERS` groups can use the Windows elevated privileges features to perform an installation. To use this feature, a user with administrative rights needs to setup his computer and grant the special authorities to the user accounts before the elevated feature can be used. You use the Windows Group Policy Editor (`GPEDIT.MSC`) to elevate user account privileges. Refer to your DB2 9 documentation for more information on this process.

DB2 *Note*

Support for non-Administrators group installations have been supported for DB2 clients and DB2 Connect Personal Edition since the Version 8 release. There is no need to use the elevated privileges method for these products.

To install DB2 on Windows XP, insert the DB2 media into the CD-ROM drive. The auto-run feature automatically starts the setup program (Figure 2–1) for the underlying language installed on your server (you can override this feature and launch the DB2 installation program with a different language as well).

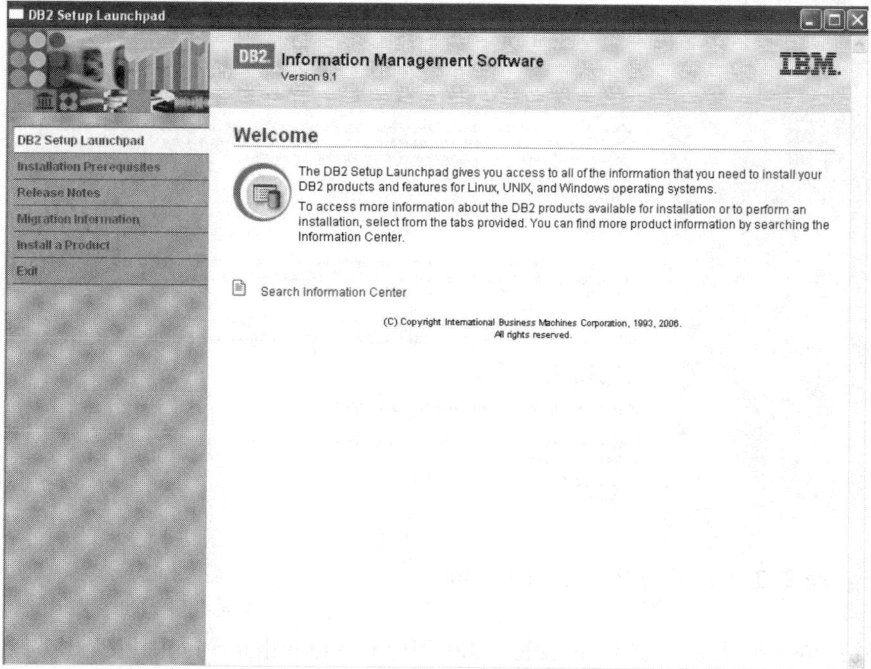

Figure 2–1 *The DB2 Launchpad*

If the DB2 installation program failed to auto-start (or you want to launch it from an image of the software deployed on your network), locate and execute the following command from an operating system window: `X:SETUP` (where x: is the location of the CD-ROW or DVD drive).

You can use the launchpad to find installation prerequisites, migration information, view the release notes, and install a product. To install DB2, click **Install a Product**. The Install a DB2 Product window opens (Figure 2–2).

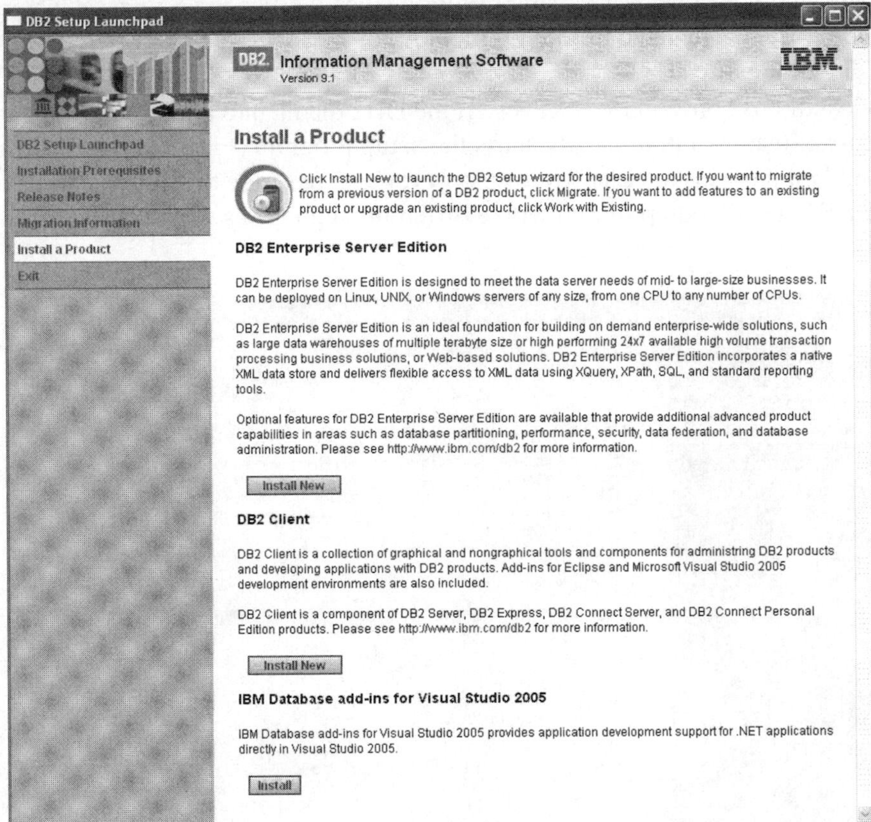

Figure 2–2 *Install a Product window*

You can use this window to select the DB2 product that's available on the media. This CD-ROM happens to have the DB2 Enterprise Server Edition (DB2 Enterprise) code on it, along with DB2 Client code, and the IBM Database add-ins for Visual Studio 2005.

To install a product click the corresponding **Install New** button and its corresponding Welcome window will open as shown in Figure 2–3. Click **Next**.

The IBM Database add-ins for Visual Studio 2005 installs a number of DB2 features into a local copy of Visual Studio 2005 that allows for rapid application development in a .NET environment.

DB2 Note

If the DB2 Enterprise Server Edition installation process detects a copy of Visual Studio 2005 on your server, it will give you the opportunity to install this plug-in; however, if you want to add support for .NET to an existing server or client installation, you can select the **Install** button that corresponds to this option.

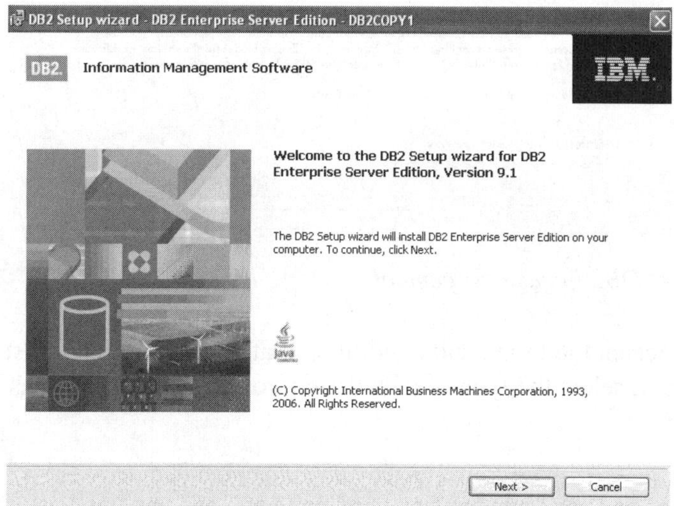

Figure 2–3 *The DB2 Enterprise Server Edition Welcome window*

Accept the licensing terms for the DB2 data server product you are installing and click **Next** to continue (Figure 2–4).

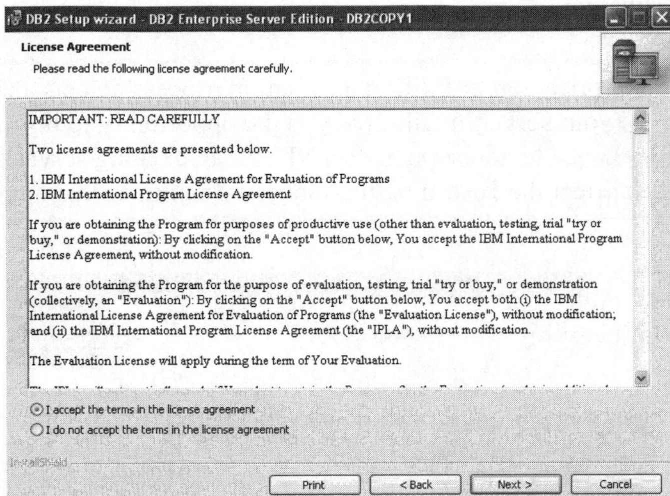

Figure 2–4 *DB2 license agreement*

After you accept the terms and conditions that are bound to the installation of any DB2 product, select the type of installation you want to perform as shown in Figure 2–5.

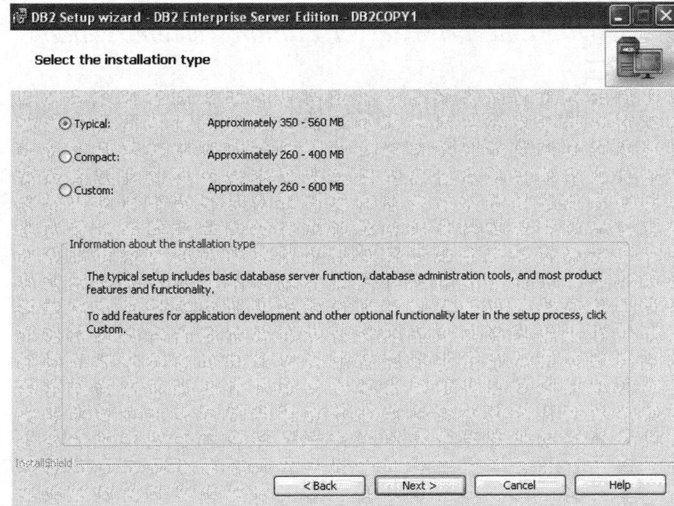

Figure 2–5 *Select the installation type*

DB2 Enterprise 9 comes with three installation types that allow you to control the components that will be installed as part of the installation process:

- **Typical** includes basic data server functions, database administration tools, and most of the product features and functionality. A Typical installation also creates and configures a default DB2 instance (named DB2). This type of installation will require between 350 to 560 MB of disk space.
- **Compact** will install basic data server functionality and limited tooling. This installation type will perform a minimum amount of configuration during the installation process. If you are new to DB2, we don't recommend this option. Depending on the platform, this installation type could require between 260 to 400 MB of disk space.
- **Custom** gives you the ability to selectivity choose the components that you want included as part of your DB2 data server installation. By default, a Custom installation is identical to a Typical installation unless you further customize it by adding or removing components that are not part of the default Typical installation. For this reason, the amount of disk space you could require will vary depending on the selections you make. A Custom installation can take as little as approximately 260 MB to as much as 600 MB of disk space.

The components and features that you have control over with a Custom installation are shown in Figure 2–6.

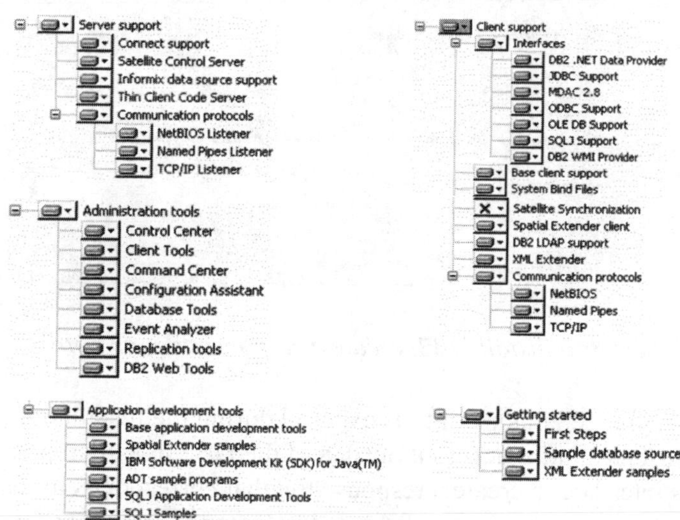

Figure 2–6 *Installation components and features*

Figure 2–6 shows all of the default components and features that are part of a Typical installation. These defaults serve as the starting point for a Custom installation from which you can add or remove components. For example, you can see that the Satellite Synchronization capability of DB2 Enterprise is not part of a Typical or a Custom installation since it has an x beside it.

DB2 Note

The ability to select the components of a DB2 installation will only appear during the installation if you perform a Custom install. In fact, the option to customize your installation won't appear until after Figure 2-7 during the installation process; however, we chose to include it here so you can also see the components that are installed by default as part of a Typical installation.

Once you select an installation type — we recommend you select **Typical** — click **Next**. The remainder of this chapter assumes you are performing a Typical installation (Figure 2–7).

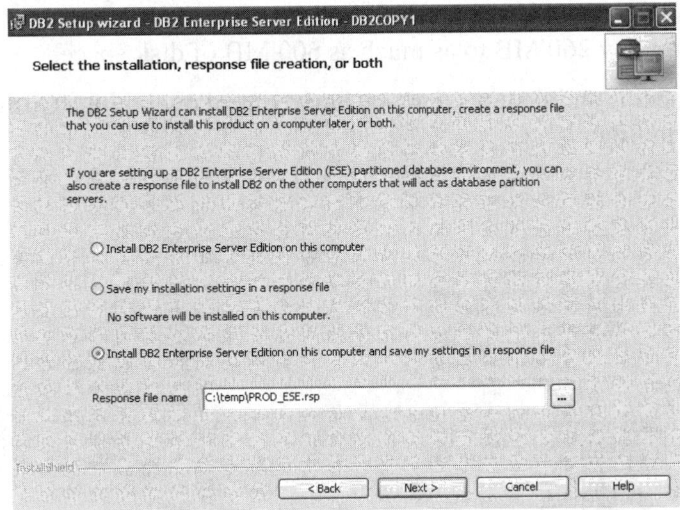

Figure 2–7 *Select to install DB2, create a response file, or both*

The response file generator utility is exposed during the installation, as shown in Figure 2–7 (you can also access it outside of the DB2 installation program). You can use this interface to create a response file that corresponds to the options you select from the installation process (including components that you include or exclude in a Custom installation), or both. Behind this installation window, DB2 uses the `DB2RSPGN` (DB2 response file generator) utility to create the response file. If you were to run the `DB2RSPGN` utility on an existing DB2 data server, it could generate a response file that not only installs the same DB2 data server (its components and so on), but also mimics the DB2 registry, database manager configuration settings, database settings, database connections, and more.

The DB2RSPGN utility (whether used on an existing installation or as part of a new server installation as described in this section) is a great way to create an installation script for all your DB2 data server and client installations. It's part of any experienced database administrator's (DBA's) toolkit.

To work through examples in the remainder of this chapter, select the **Install DB2 Enterprise Server Edition on this computer and save my settings in a response file radio button**, enter a path for the response file in the **Response file name** field, and click **Next**. The Installation Folder (Figure 2–8) opens.

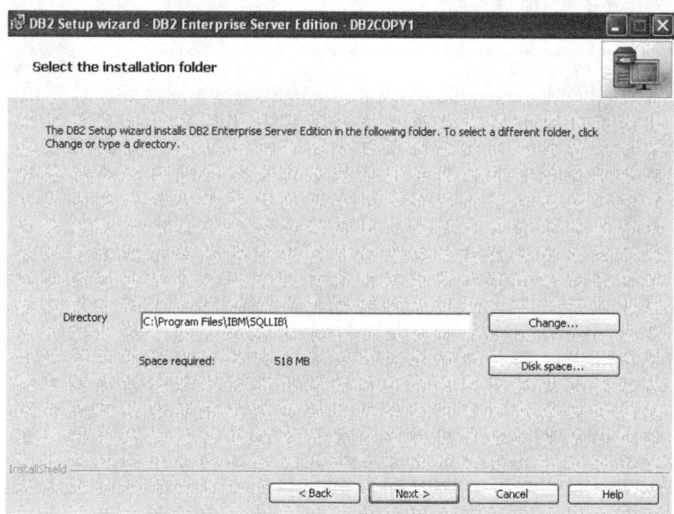

Figure 2–8 *Installation directory where to install the DB2 data server*

Enter the directory where you want to install DB2 in the **Directory** field and click **Next**. Click **Change** to change the default installation directory (*C:\Program Files\IBM\SQLLIB*) and **Disk Space** to check the amount of available space on the destination drive.

After you select the target installation directory, you should configure the DB2 Administration Server (DAS) (Figure 2–9). The DAS is an administration control point used only to assist with administrative tasks for your DB2 data server. You must have a running DAS if you want to use available tools like the Configuration Assistant, the Control Center, or some other management features in DB2 9. Basically, the DAS assists the Control Center and Configuration Assistant when working on the following administration tasks:

- Enabling remote administration of DB2 database instances.
- Providing a facility for job management, including the ability to schedule the

running of both DB2 database manager and operating system command scripts.

- Defining the scheduling of jobs, viewing the results of completed jobs, and performing other administrative tasks against jobs located either remotely or locally to the DAS using the Task Center.
- Providing a means for discovering information about the configuration of DB2 instances, databases, and other DB2 data servers in conjunction with the built-in DB2 data server discovery feature. This information is used by the Configuration Assistant and the Control Center to simplify and automate the configuration of client connections to DB2 databases.

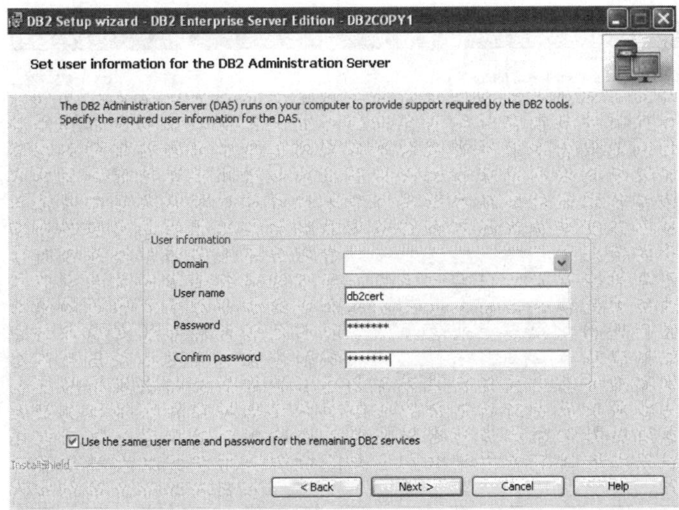

Figure 2–9 *Set user information for the DB2 Administration Server*

The DB2 installation program lets you associate an existing user account with the DAS service or create a new one. To create a new user account for the DAS you must be logged on to your domain as a user with authority to administer groups and users.

Typically we recommend that you select a user account that belongs to the `ADMINISTRATORS` group on the local machine (the account you use for the installation is one option). There are a number of other services that DB2 will configure and as a best practice you should associate those services with this user account as well by selecting the **Use the same user name and password for the remaining DB2 services** check box and click **Next** (Figure 2–10).

DB2 *Note*

If you choose not to configure the DAS during the installation process, or performed a Compact installation, you could create the DAS at a future time using the `DASCRT -u <das_user_account>` command. However, it's much easier for the DB2 installation program to do this for you.

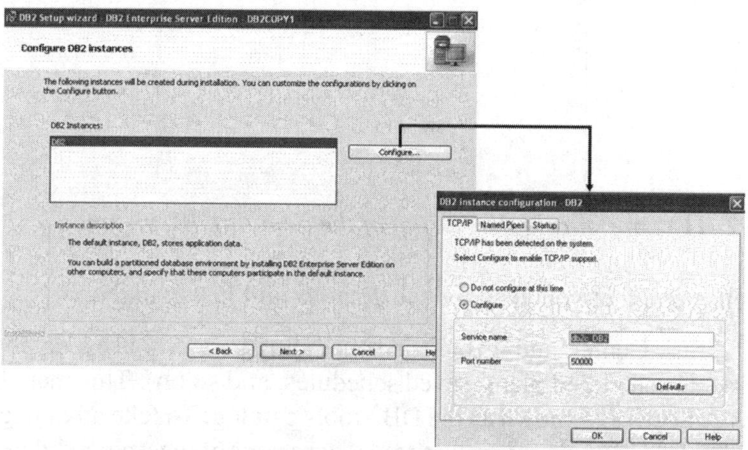

Figure 2–10 *Configure the default instance called DB2*

During a Typical installation, the DB2 installation program will create a default instance called DB2. While the instance is being created, the DB2 installation program automatically detects any supported communication protocols configured on the server, selects them for use, and generates default values for the DB2 instance to use for each detected protocol. You can override the selections and generated values by selecting **Configure**.

As mentioned, the DB2 installation program examines your system to see what communication protocols are installed and configured to use with the DB2 instance. If the DB2 installation program does not detect a protocol, the **Do not configure at this time** radio button is highlighted (Figure 2–11).

The DB2 installation program generates default values for the TCP/IP Service name and Port number parameters. Both must be entered and unique on the computer. The Port number designates the particular TCP/IP port on which the server listens for requests from DB2 clients. It is recommended to use the default values unless they will conflict with other services you plan to support on your server.

You can also specify the startup characteristics of the default `DB2` instance such that it's started when the server is started, or it must be manually started using the db2start command (or the Quick Launch icon that's created in the Windows taskbar).

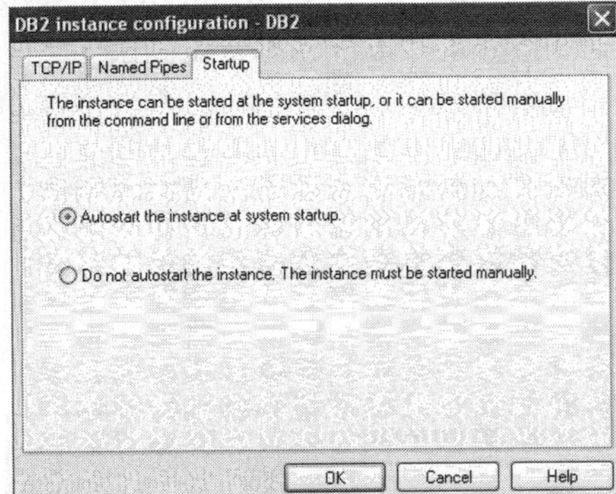

Figure 2–11 *Configuring the startup of the default DB2 instance*

We recommend that you examine the defaults and just click **Next**.

The DB2 Task Center, and its built-in scheduling services, use a database to store metadata (its scheduled plans, saved schedules, and so on). This metadata is stored in tables collectively known as the DB2 tools catalog. To take advantage of the rich features of the DB2 administration tools, we strongly recommend that scheduling be enabled by creating the DB2 tools catalog (Figure 2–12).

There can be multiple DB2 tools catalogs on the same system, but only one DB2 tools catalog can be actively used by a DB2 scheduler at any given time.

DB2 Setup wizard - DB2 Enterprise Server Edition - DB2COPY1
Prepare the DB2 tools catalog
Certain DB2 tools such as the Task Center and scheduler require a DB2 tools catalog on one of the DB2 servers in your environment. The DB2 tools catalog must be stored in a DB2 database.
Prepare the DB2 tools catalog
Instance DB2
Database
New TOOLSDB
Existing
Schema
New SYSTOOLS
Existing
InstallShield
< Back
Next >
Cancel
Help

Figure 2–12 *Prepare the DB2 tools catalog*

Select **Prepare the DB2 tools catalog** to create the DB2 tools catalog during the installation process and click **Next**. You can select an existing database to house the DB2 tools catalog or specify a new database that will be created for you by the DB2 installation program (you can also specify the schema where you want this database to be created).

The DAS can store a contact list that is used to notify database administrators (DBAs) by email or pager when certain conditions occur — for example, breach of a default health threshold. This contact list can be stored locally on each server, or a global contact list can be maintained by the DAS on designated server.

You use the Set Up Notifications window to configure this contact list as shown in Figure 2–13.

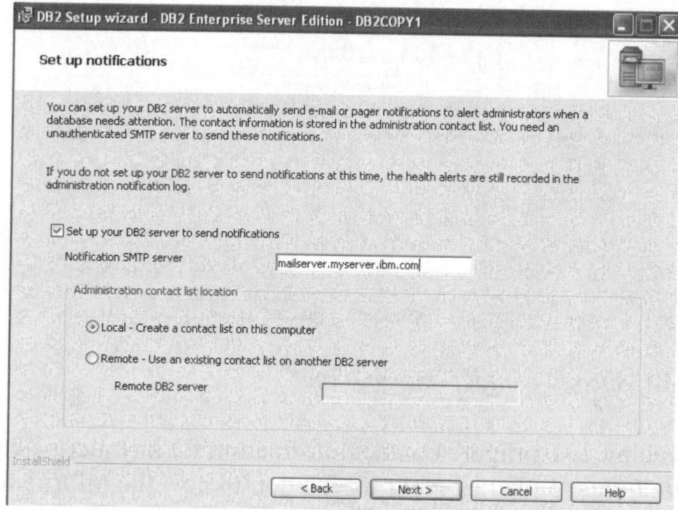

Figure 2–13 *Setting up notifications for your DB2 server*

Select **Set up your DB2 server to send notifications** to specify that you want an SMTP server to send email and pager notifications to your administration contacts (which you'll define in a moment). Type the TCP/IP host name of the SMTP server to use in the **Notification SMTP server** field.

For the purposes of this book, we recommend you select **Local — Create a contact list on this computer** and store the administration contact list on the local system. This list will be used by all instances. As previously mentioned, this list can be used by other servers. To configure remote notification lists, select **Remote — Use an existing contact list on another DB2 server** and enter the hostname of the remote server in the **Remote DB2 server** field, and click **Next**.

The Specify a Contact for Health Monitor Notification window opens (Figure 2–14). If you don't know the information required in this window, just skip this configuration step for now by de-selecting the **Set up your DB2 server to send notifications checkbox**. For information about enabling notification after installing DB2, refer to the `UPDATE ADMIN CONFIG` command in the *DB2 Command Reference*.

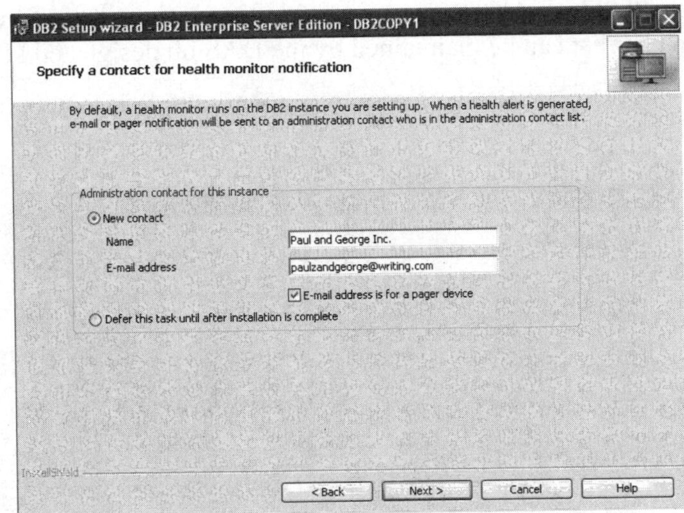

Figure 2–14 *Specify contact information*

Use this window to configure contact information for any alerts generated by the DB2 Health Center and click **Next**. If you don't know the information required in this window, just skip this configuration step for now by selecting the **Defer this task until after the installation is complete**. For information about enabling notification after installing DB2, refer to the `UPDATE ADMIN CONFIG` command in the *DB2 Command Reference* or use the Health Center's Contact List feature (located in the **Tools** menu).

Click **Next**. The Enable Operating System Security for DB2 Objects window opens as shown in Figure 2–15.

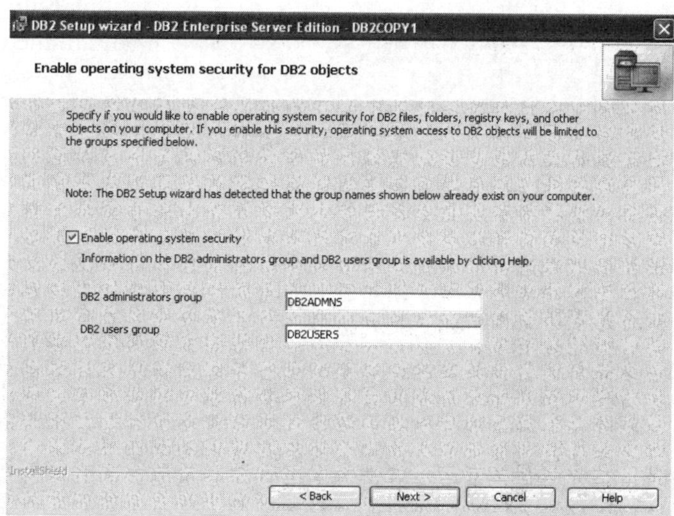

Figure 2–15 *Controlling access to the folders where DB2 is installed*

To make your DB2 environment as secure as possible, specify the particular user groups that should have access to DB2 objects (files, folders, registry keys, and other objects) at the file system level on this computer. Enabling this operating system security feature protects your DB2 objects from unwanted file-level access by unauthorized user groups.

You can also specify whether you want access to these DB2 objects to be limited to either the DB2 administrators group or the DB2 users group. The DB2 administrators group will have complete access to all DB2 objects on this computer, but the DB2 users group will have only read and execute access to all DB2 objects through your Windows operating system.

To enable this security, select **Enable operating system security**. Accept the default values for the DB2 administrators group and DB2 users group. You can specify your own values, if necessary. To ensure greater security, the values in the **DB2 administrators group** and **DB2 users group** fields should be different. Now click **Next**.

The Start Copying Files and Create Response File window opens (Figure 2–16); this window contains a summary for what the DB2 installation program is about to do.

Getting Started

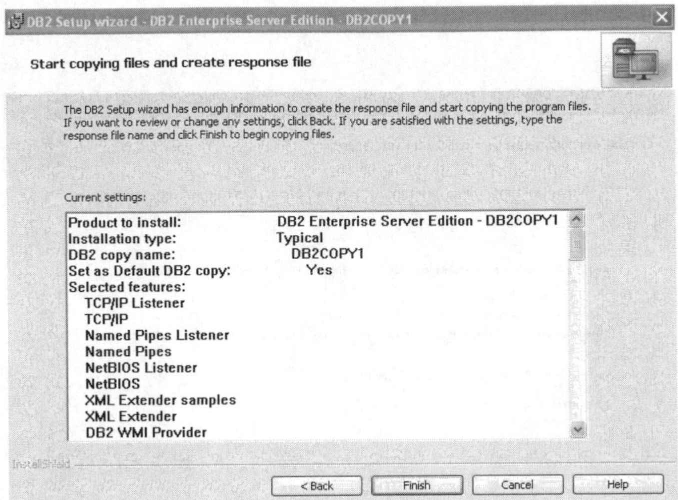

Figure 2–16 *A summary of installation options*

DB2 Enterprise 9 will be installed on your server after you click the **Finish** button. If you're installing DB2 Enterprise 9 on a Windows server, you are presented with an additional option to install the IBM Add-ins for Visual Studio 2005. By selecting the corresponding check box at the bottom of Figure 2–17, a new installation program will be invoked to install the IBM Add-ins for Visual Studio 2005, once you click **Finish**.

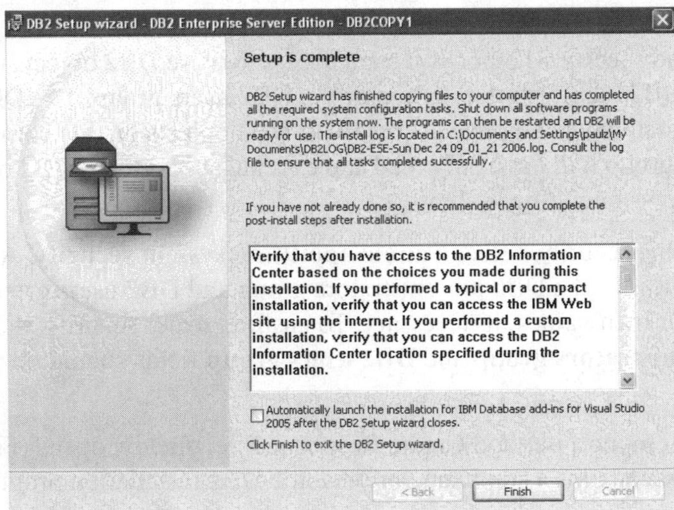

Figure 2–17 *DB2 installation is complete*

First Steps is a tool that is automatically started after you complete an installation of a DB2 data server (Figure 2–18), although you can generally access it at any time from the **Set-up Tools** folder for DB2 9 from the Start menu.

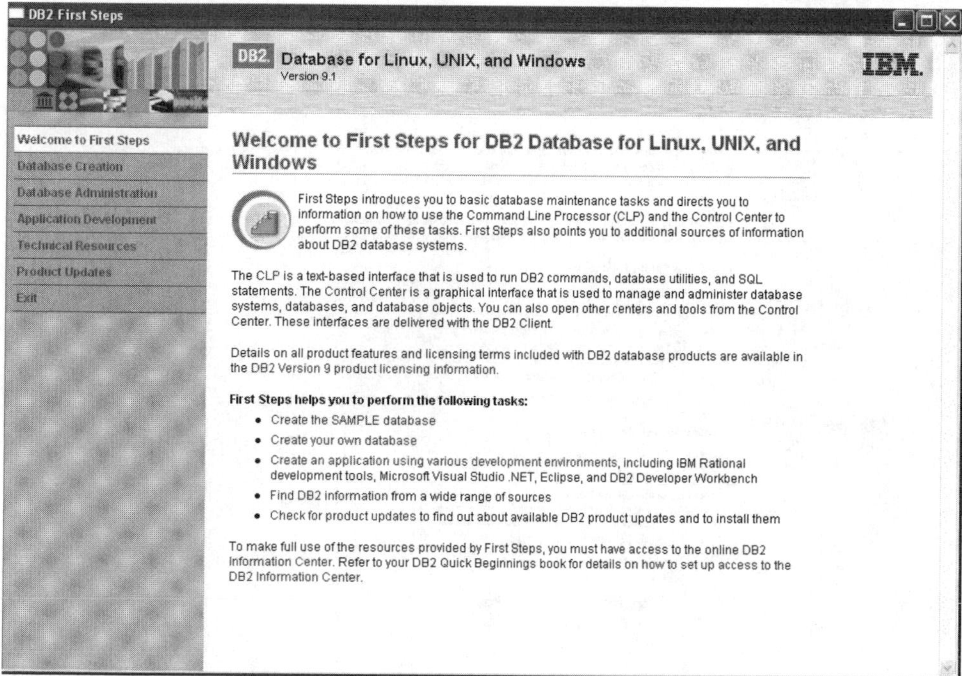

Figure 2–18 *If you're new to DB2, First Steps helps you get going*

Using First Steps you can:

- Create the SAMPLE database
- Create your own database
- Configure access to remote databases
- Connect to a database on a remote server
- Get help for creating applications using various development environments, including IBM Rational development tools, Microsoft Visual Studio .NET, Eclipse, and DB2 Developer Workbench
- Perform basic database administration tasks
- Find DB2 information from a wide range of sources
- Check for product updates and optionally install them

We recommend you explore the different First Steps options. For the purposes of this book, you should also create the SAMPLE database by selecting **Database Cre-**

ation from the left margin of the main First Steps window and clicking **Create SAMPLE Database** (Figure 2–19).

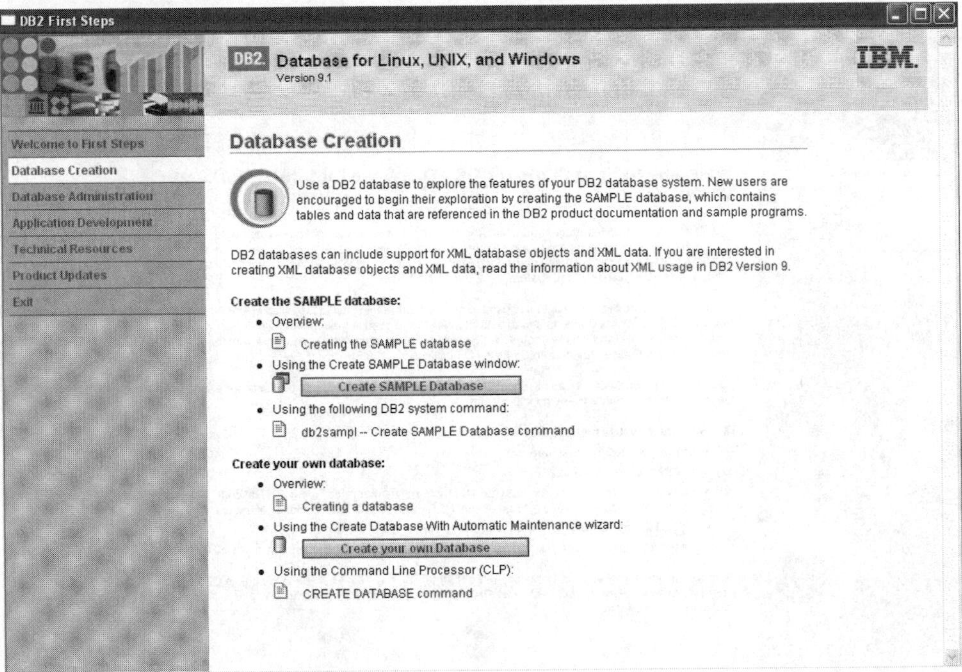

Figure 2–19 *Using First Steps to create the SAMPLE database*

In DB2 9, you can create the SAMPLE database with or without XML data. If you want to follow along with some of the examples in this book, you should ensure you create the SAMPLE database with the XML data (Figure 2–20).

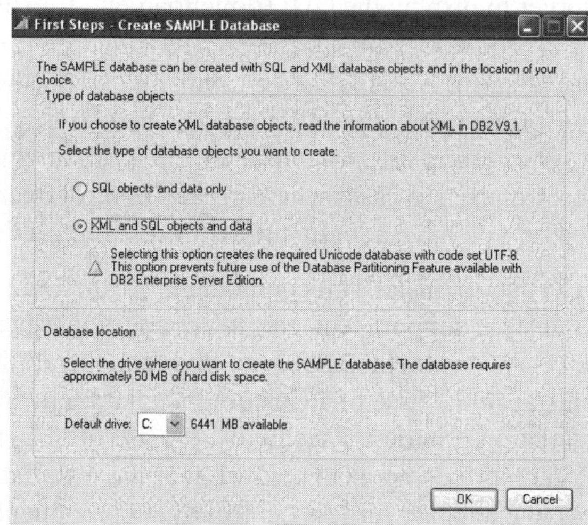

Figure 2–20 *Creating the SAMPLE database with XML data using First Steps*

By default, the `SAMPLE` database is created with a Unicode (UTF-8) codepage and meets all of the pureXML requirements.

Linux and UNIX Installation

A graphically driven DB2 installation program is also available in DB2 9 on the Linux and UNIX platforms. Linux and UNIX platforms can also use response files (covered later in this chapter) to enable distributed installations. Response files store the same values and parameters that were selected during the initial installation of DB2 on the local system as discussed in the "Windows Installation" section earlier in this chapter.

As of DB2 9, data server installations are no longer shipped as native operating system packages, and as a result, you can no longer use operating system commands to install a DB2 9 data server. For example, on AIX, the `installp` command can no longer be used to install a DB2 product.

For Linux and UNIX-based DB2 installations, an administrator can select from the following installation methods:

- The `db2setup` utility — this program is supplied with the DB2 product and is the recommended installation method. It is similar to the DB2 installation program for Windows in that it detects and configures communication protocols to use with the DB2 instances and is graphically driven; other methods require you to manually configure your system. To use `db2setup` on Linux and UNIX you require an Xserver to display the GUI (download one for free at: www.freedesktop.org/wiki/Software/Xserver among other places on the Web).

- The `db2_install` script is available for Linux and UNIX-based administrators that want to perform a manual installation. The `db2_install` script does not perform any user or group creation, instance creation, or configuration. This method may be preferred in cases where greater control over the installation process is required or, you have a lot of skill with respect to DB2 installations.

  The `db2_install` script installs all components for the DB2 product you specify with English interface support. You can select additional languages with the `-L` parameter; however, this method does not give you the ability to select or deselect components as in the case of a Custom installation available through the `db2setup` installation program. Essentially, the use of `db2_install` results is a trade-off: you get more component control over the installation and auto-configuration process in exchange for less control over components that are installed as `db2_install` installs everything in the language(s) you specify. In contrast, the `db2setup` installation program allows you more control over the installation process by choosing exactly what gets installed using the Custom installation option.

- Response file installation — a response file is an ASCII file that contains setup and configuration values. The file is passed to the `db2setup` program and the installation is performed according to the values that have been specified. This type of installation is covered later in this chapter.
- There may be an installation utility available in your operating system environment that allows you to perform manual installations. You can perform a manual installation by installing corresponding payload files. A payload file is a compressed tarball that contains all of the files and metadata for an installable component. A manual installation provides no automation and configuration and is generally not a recommended method for installing a DB2 data server.

DB2 *Note*

Before installing DB2 9 on a Linux-based server, you should ensure that your distribution meets the Linux validation criteria for DB2 data servers. You can get the most up to date Linux support information at: www-306.ibm.com/software/data/db2/linux/validate/.

So far, this chapter has detailed the installation of a DB2 9 data server on Windows. For completeness, we'll cover the installation process on a Linux or UNIX server, however, not in the same depth as a Windows installation.

Before you start a DB2 installation on Linux or UNIX, you should ensure that you have the following:

- Ensure that your system meets installation memory and disk requirements outlined in the DB2 documentation or the accompanying *README* file.
- You must have `root` authority to perform the installation as of DB2 9.1.
- You must have X windows software capable of rendering a graphical user interface for the `db2setup` utility to run on your machine. Ensure that the X windows server is running and that you've properly exported your display; for example, `export DISPLAY=9.26.163.144:0`.

To install DB2 9 using the `db2setup` utility, perform the following steps:

3. Log in as a user with `root` authority.
4. Mount the CD-ROM file system and change to the `disk1` directory where the CD-ROM is mounted by entering the `cd /cdrom/disk1` (where `cdrom` is the mount point of your product CD-ROM).

   If you have an image of DB2 on the mount point, you may need to decompress and untar the product file before you can proceed. You can decompress a product file using `GZIP`. For example:

```
gzip -d <product_name>.tar.gz
```

   Then you must untar the file using the `TAR` command. For example:

```
tar -xvf <product_name>.tar
```

5. Enter the `./db2setup` command to start the DB2 installation program and follow steps similar to those covered in the "Windows Installation" section.

When the installation is complete, by default the DB2 code will be installed in the */opt/IBM/db2/V9.1* directory for AIX, HP-UX, and Solaris installations, and the */opt/ibm/db2/V9.1* directory for Linux; of course, you can choose any installation path you want (so long as you can write to it and it's initially empty).

Multi-Copy Installations

DB2 9 gives you the ability to install and run multiple DB2 copies on the same server. While this feature was always available in UNIX and Linux in one form or another (both could support multiple versions of a DB2 data server, as well as maintenance via Alternate FixPacks), it wasn't available in a DB2 for Windows installation. Furthermore, the use of Alternate FixPacks wasn't always meant for production purposes. In DB2 9, this all changes and you can install multiple versions and release levels of the code, and have them coexist, side-by-side on any platform.

The ability to support various versions and maintenance levels of a DB2 data server provides administrators with a lot of advantages, including:

- The ability to run independent copies of DB2 products for different lines of business functions. For example, one line of business may need to use new features right away, while others may not have a need for a new feature and don't want to go through a lengthy quality assurance process to roll in new code or risk production downtime.
- The ability to test applications and the DB2 code on the same server before moving the production database to a newer version of the DB2 product.
- The ability to support various application packages like enterprise resource planning (ERP), supply chain management (SCM), planning and logistics management (PLM), and more. For example, you could have an SAP™ running on one level of DB2, and a Siebel™ application running on another.

You can even have a copy of DB2 8 running side-by-side with a copy of DB2 9; however, there are some considerations that you should be aware of. For example, they cannot share .NET providers, each copy must contain a unique instance name, and some more. Refer to the DB2 documentation for more information.

The term *DB2 Copy* is used in DB2 9 to refer to one or more installations of a DB2 product in a particular location on the same server. When you have more than a single copy of DB2 on your server, you have to specifically work with each copy when applying maintenance, or when going about your day-to-day routines of connectivity, administration, and so on.

For example, if you were to rerun the DB2 installation program on a server where a copy of DB2 9 was already installed, the DB2 Launchpad would look like that shown in Figure 2–21.

Figure 2–21 *Multiple DB2 installations on a single server in DB2 9*

You can see in Figure 2–21 that you could either work with the existing DB2 installation on this server or install a separate code path for another DB2 copy.

After you have installed a second copy of DB2 on your server, you will see that it has its own DB2 copy name, as well as its own links (for example, in the Start menu). Each of these links will launch tools and utilities that are bound by default to the copy of DB2 from which they are launched.

For example, if you started a CLP session from the DB2COPY2 folder, the corresponding window would work with that copy. You can see in Figure 2–22 that DB2COPY1 (the copy installed at the start of this chapter) already has a sample database installed, but DB2COPY2 does not.

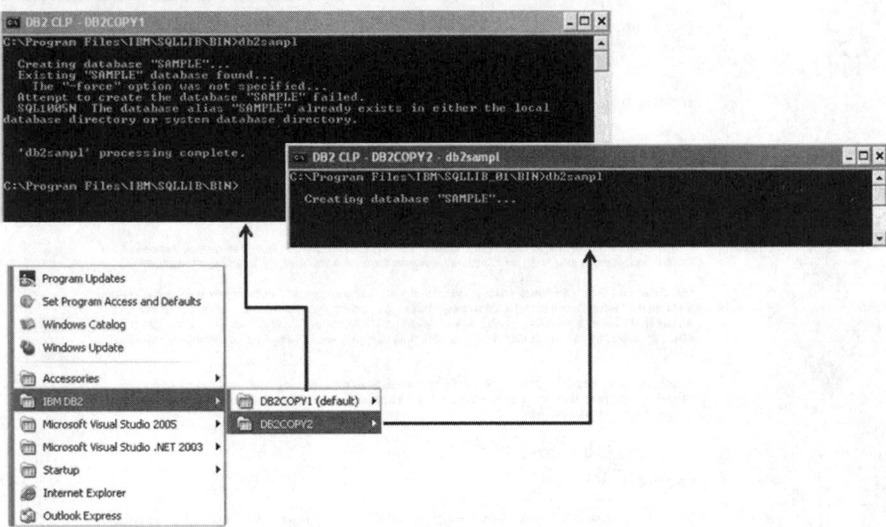

Figure 2–22 *Use the appropriate Start menu to work with a DB2 copy*

Notice in Figure 2–22 that every server where one or more copies of DB2 is installed has to have a default DB2 copy. On Windows, you can use the DB2SWTCH command to switch the default DB2 copy for your server. When you issue this command, it launches the DB2 Copy Select Wizard (this wizard is also available from the **IBM DB2** folder in the Start menu (Figure 2–23).

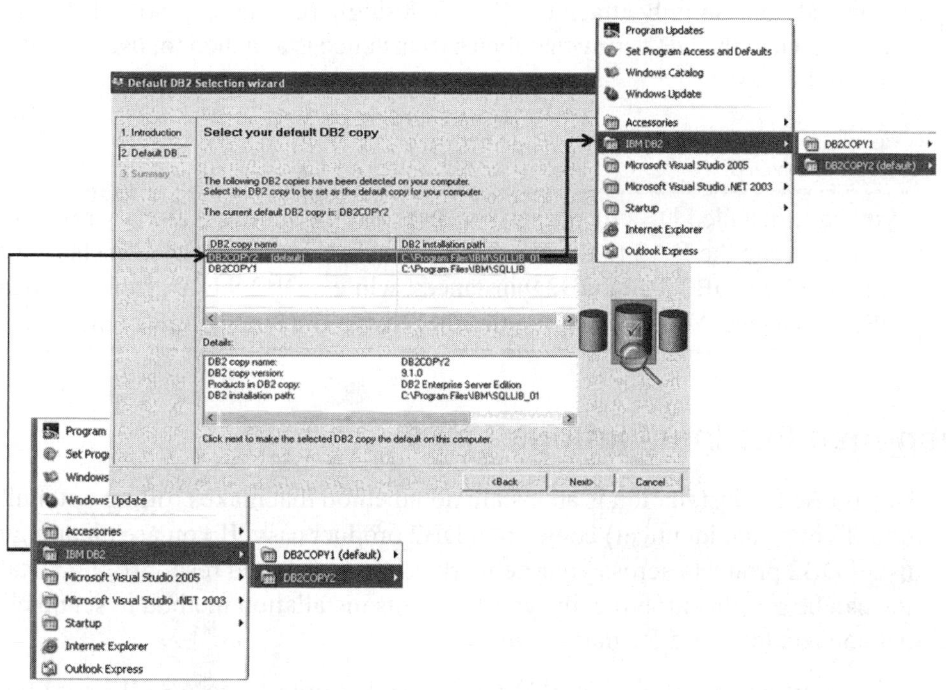

Figure 2–23 *Changing the default DB2 copy*

The DB2SWTCH command also has two optional flags that can be used as an alternative to launching this wizard. You can use the -l flag to list all the DB2 copies on your server and the -d flag to set the default copy. The following shows how you could switch the default DB2 copy on a Windows machine:

```
DB2SWTCH -l
DB2COPY2 C:\Program Files\IBM\SQLLIB_01 (default)
DB2COPY1 C:\Program Files\IBM\SQLLIB

DB2SWTCH -d DB2COPY1

DB2SWTCH -l

DB2COPY2 C:\Program Files\IBM\SQLLIB_01
DB2COPY1 C:\Program Files\IBM\SQLLIB (default)
```

On UNIX- and Linux-based systems, you use the db2ls command to list DB2 installations on your server.

When you have multiple DB2 copies running on the same computer, you may need pay some consideration to how the DB2 Administration Server (DAS) operates. The DAS is a unique component within DB2 that is limited to having only one version active, despite how many DB2 copies are installed on the same computer. This means that you can only attach the DAS to a single running copy of DB2 at any time. To switch the DB2 copy that the DAS instance is attached to, use the DASUPDT command.

DB2 Note

If you have installed DB2 9 on a server where a copy of DB2 8 already resides, you need to migrate the DAS to the Version 9 format. A Version 9 DAS instance can administer both DB2 8 and DB2 9 instances, while a DB2 8 DAS can only manage a DB2 8 instance. You can migrate the DAS using the DASMIGR command.

Response File Installations

A response file installation is an installation method that makes rolling out multiple (and if you want, identical) copies of a DB2 product easy. If you are planning to install DB2 products across your network, a network-based response file installation can be significant; typically, you'll use this installation method to set up clients that connect to your DB2 data server.

Before starting an installation of DB2 you need to prepare an ASCII-based file called a *response file* that can be customized with setup and configuration data that will automate an installation. This setup and configuration data would have to be entered during an interactive install; however, with a response file, the installation can proceed without any intervention.

A response file specifies such configuration and setup parameters as the destination directory and the products and components to install. It can also be used to set up the following settings:

- Global DB2 registry variables
- Instance variables
- Instance database manager configuration settings

You can use a response file to install an identical configuration across every system on your network or to install multiple configurations of a DB2 product. For example, you can customize a response file that will install a DB2 client that has the database connections already defined. You can then distribute this file to every system where you want the client to be installed.

You can create a response file by:

- Modifying a provided sample response file.
- Using the response file generator command (DB2RSPGN) available on Windows.
- Using the DB2 installation program previously detailed in this chapter

Sample Response Files

The DB2 CD-ROM includes a ready-to-use sample response file with default entries. The sample response files are located in the *db2/platform/samples* directory. Remember to select the directory that corresponds to the operating system and the processor architecture of your system.

You can copy any of these sample response files onto a hard disk drive, and then modify each parameter and save it for your own personal use. Refer to the *Installation and Configuration Supplement* manual for more information about available parameters for a response file installation.

For example, the following sample response files are shipped on the DB2 Enterprise 9 for Windows CD-ROM (each product and platform will vary):

- *db2ese.rsp* — DB2 Enterprise Server Edition
- *db2vsai.rsp* — IBM add-ins for Visual Studio 2005
- *db2client.rsp* — DB2 Client
- *db2un.rsp* — Used to uninstall a DB2 product on a machine
- *db2fixpk.rsp* — Used for Fix Pack installations

DB2 Note

DB2 Enterprise 9 comes with two additional response file for use with the Database Partitioning Feature (DPF). The *db2eseio.rsp* file is used for the instance-owning node in a DPF environment, while the *db2esenn.rsp* file is used for new nodes. Since these response files are only used when deploying DB2 in a partitioned database environment, they are outside the scope of this book.

If you recall from Figure 2–7, the option to generate the a response file called *DB2ESESampleResponseFile*, based on the options selected during the installation process, was selected. Part of the response file created from the Windows installation example (called) in this chapter is shown in Figure 2–24.

```
PROD=ENTERPRISE_SERVER_EDITION
LIC_AGREEMENT=ACCEPT
FILE=C:\Program Files\IBM\SQLLIB\
INSTALL_TYPE=TYPICAL

LANG=EN
DAS_CONTACT_LIST=LOCAL

CONTACT=CONTACT
DATABASE=TOOLS_DB
TOOLS_CATALOG_DATABASE=TOOLS_DB
TOOLS_CATALOG_SCHEMA=SYSTOOLS
TOOLS_DB.DATABASE_NAME=TOOLSDB

INSTANCE=DB2

CONTACT.INSTANCE=DB2
TOOLS_DB.INSTANCE=DB2
TOOLS_DB.LOCATION=LOCAL
DB2.NAME=DB2
CONTACT.CONTACT_NAME=Paul and George Inc.
CONTACT.NEW_CONTACT=YES
CONTACT.EMAIL=paulzandgeorge@writing.com
CONTACT.PAGER=0

DEFAULT_INSTANCE=DB2
DB2.SVCENAME=db2c_DB2
DB2.DB2COMM=TCPIP
DB2.PORT_NUMBER=60098
DB2.AUTOSTART=YES
DB2.USERNAME=db2admin
DB2.PASSWORD=644014635329164416901202265101758104061 4...
ENCRYPTED=DB2.PASSWORD
DAS_USERNAME=db2admin
DAS_PASSWORD=6440146353291644169012022651017581040614...
ENCRYPTED=DAS_PASSWORD
DAS_SMTP_SERVER=d25ml01.torolab.ibm.com
DB2_EXTSECURITY=YES
DB2_USERSGROUP_NAME=DB2USERS
DB2_ADMINGROUP_NAME=DB2ADMNS
RSP_FILE_NAME=c:\temp\DB2ESESampleResponseFile.rsp
DB2_COPY_NAME=DB2COPY1
DEFAULT_COPY=YES
```

Figure 2–24 *Windows response file*

DB2 Note

You may be concerned about using a password as part of a response file installation. The best part about generating a response file using the DB2 installation program is that it will encrypt the password field for you. In the sample response file in Figure 2–24, you can see the `DB2.PASSWORD` keyword has been encrypted.

Response File Generator (Windows only)

The response file generator utility creates a response file and instance profiles from an existing installed and configured DB2 product. You can use the generated response file to recreate the exact setup on other machines. This is by far the best method to redistribute DB2 code that has been set up and configured to your specifications.

For example, you could install and configure a DB2 client to connect to various databases across your network. Once this client is installed and configured to access all the database that your users must have access to, you can run the response file generator to create a response file as well as a configuration profile for each instance.

To generate a response file, execute the following command:

```
db2rspgn -d x:\path
```

A response file is generated in the path you specify with the `-d` option. The file name is fixed depending on which product has been installed. For example, a DB2 Enterprise 9 installation will always call this response file `DB2ESE.RSP`.

In addition to a generated response file, instance profiles are also generated in the same path for all instances on the profiled server (you can instruct the response file generator to only create profiles for a specific instances using the `-i` option). Each instance profile contains all the settings of a DB2 registry, database manager configuration parameters, node directory, database directory, and so on. The name of an instance profile is for the form *<name>.ins*. A sample of an instance profile is shown in Figure 2–25.

```
[FILE_DESCRIPTION]
APPLICATION=DB2/NT 9.1.0
FILE_CONTENT=DB2 CCA Exported Data Sources
FILE_TYPE=CommonServer
FILE_FORMAT_VERSION=2.0
Platform=5
DB2SYSTEM=DB28PAULZ
Instance=DB2

[REGISTRY_LOCAL]
DB2ACCOUNTNAME=DB28PAULZ\db2cert
DB2INSTOWNER=DB28PAULZ

...

[DBM_CONFIG]
NODETYPE=4
RELEASE=0xb00
DIAGLEVEL=3
RQRIOBLK=32767

...

[DB>!LOCAL:SAMPLE]
Dir_entry_type=INDIRECT
Drive=C:
DBName=SAMPLE
Comment=A sample database
```

Figure 2–25 *Instance Profile*

Although several DB2 copies could already be installed on your system, the response file generator only generates the response file for the current copy (that is, where you run the DB2RSPGN utility from.)

If you are planning to set up and configure multiple identical DB2 products (typically a client), you only need to specify the installation response file when you perform the DB2 installation. The installation response file created by the response file generator will automatically call each instance profile. You only need to ensure that the instance profiles are located in the same drive and directory as the installation response file.

Although this utility is not available on Linux- and UNIX-based servers, you can still create instance profiles using the Configuration Assistant, Control Center, or the client profile import (DB2CFIMP) and export commands (DB2CFEXP); both of these methods are available on Windows as well.

On Linux and UNIX, you can still have a response file installation automatically call your instance profiles as part of the installation process using the CLIENT_IMPORT_PROFILE keyword. The difference between this method and the db2rspgn method is that the response file generator will automatically fill in the

CLIENT_IMPORT_PROFILE keyword for you for the generated profiles. On Linux and UNIX, you'll have to do this yourself if you want to call the instance profiles during the installation.

Distributed Installation with a Response File

With a response file, the installation can proceed without any intervention. You can configure a CD-ROM drive or a hard disk drive to be shared and make the DB2 install files and response files accessible to the machines where the DB2 product will be installed. To use a response file, you use the same installation program as a normal installation, only you pass the option to specify a response file to the command to start the DB2 installation program. For example, you could start a response file installation by running the following command on Windows:

```
<DB2_image_path>:\SETUP /U <response_file_name> /M
```

The /U option specifies that the installation configuration information will come from a response file and the /M option instructs the DB2 installation program to show a progress bar (great for an application that embeds a DB2 data server installation, like SAP). A list of additional options are shown in Table 2–1.

Table 2–1 *Setup Flags*

Flag	Purpose
/U	Specifies the fully qualified response file name. This is a required parameter.
/N	Specifies the installation name. This installation name overrides the value in the response file.
/L	Specifies the fully qualified log file name, where setup information and any errors occurring during setup are logged. Optional.
/F	Forces any DB2 processes to stop before installation. Optional.
/T	Creates a file with installation trace information. Optional.
/C	Ensures that the setup.exe exits immediately after starting the installation. Optional.
/P	Changes the installation path of the product. Specifying this option overrides the installation path that is specified in the response file. Optional.
/M	Used with -u option to show the progress dialog during the installation. Optional.

Refer to the DB2 documentation for more information on these flags.

Using the DB2 Command Line Processor

The DB2 Command Line Processor (DB2 CLP) was introduced in Chapter 1. This section discusses how the DB2 CLP and your operating system's command line processor (CLP) — which requires you to manually add the db2 prefix to each command — work with DB2. You should also be aware that most commands can also be issued from the DB2 Command Editor, which as you'll recall from Chapter 1, is just a graphical front-end to the DB2 CLP.

If you plan to work with your operating system's CLP to interact with DB2 (also known as the DB2 Command Window in an Windows installation), you need to be careful that the operating system does not parse your SQL statements and incorrectly interpret part of the SQL statement as an operating system command. If you enclose any SQL statements or DB2 commands within *double* quotation marks ("..."), it will ensure that they are not parsed by the operating system.

For example, the following commands will not return the same results. The first would return all the rows in the STAFF table and store them in a file called 20, while the other would return all of the rows in the STAFF table where DEPT=20 to the standard output of your machine.

```
db2 SELECT * FROM STAFF WHERE DEPT > 20
db2 "SELECT * FROM STAFF WHERE DEPT > 20"
```

Within the DB2 CLP you can issue operating system commands by prefacing them with an exclamation mark (!). For example, the following command would return the contents of the c:\ directory on a Windows-based server:

```
db2 => !dir c:\
```

If a command ever exceeds the limit allowed by the operating system, use a backslash (\) as a line continuation character. In the DB2 CLP, the command you are entering will simply continue to the next line:

```
db2 => SELECT * FROM \
db2 (cont.) => STAFF WHERE DEPT > 20
```

The continuation character is also supported when entering DB2 commands from the operating system's CLP; however, you still must prefix the start of the command with the db2 prefix. The complete syntax and explanation for almost every command is documented in the *DB2 Command Reference*.

DB2 *Note*

You can download the DB2 library in PDF format at: www.ibm.com/software/data/db2/udb/support/manualsv9.html, or simply access this information via the online Information Center at publib.boulder.ibm.com/infocenter/db2luw/v9/index.jsp.

You can obtain syntax and information for all of the DB2 commands from the Command Line Processor using the `DB2 ?` command as follows:

- `DB2 ? command` displays information about a specific command
- `DB2 ? SQLnnnn` displays information about a specific SQLCODE
- `DB2 ? DB2nnnn` displays information about a DB2 error

To examine the current settings for entering DB2 command (they apply to both the DB2 CLP and the CLP), issue the following command:

```
db2 => LIST COMMAND OPTIONS
```

The results are shown in Figure 2–26.

```
DB2 CLP - DB2COPY1 - db2
db2 => list command options

   Command Line Processor Option Settings

 Backend process wait time (seconds)        (DB2BQTIME) = 1
 No. of retries to connect to backend        (DB2BQTRY) = 60
 Request queue wait time (seconds)          (DB2RQTIME) = 5
 Input queue wait time (seconds)            (DB2IQTIME) = 5
 Command options                           (DB2OPTIONS) =

 Option  Description                                Current Setting
 ------  ----------------------------------------   ---------------
   -a    Display SQLCA                              OFF
   -c    Auto-Commit                                ON
   -d    Retrieve and display XML declarations      OFF
   -e    Display SQLCODE/SQLSTATE                   OFF
   -f    Read from input file                       OFF
   -i    Display XML data with indentation          OFF
   -l    Log commands in history file               OFF
   -m    Display the number of rows affected        OFF
   -n    Remove new line character                  OFF
   -o    Display output                             ON
   -p    Display interactive input prompt           ON
   -q    Preserve whitespaces & linefeeds           OFF
   -r    Save output to report file                 OFF
   -s    Stop execution on command error            OFF
   -t    Set statement termination character        OFF
   -v    Echo current command                       OFF
   -w    Display FETCH/SELECT warning messages      ON
   -x    Suppress printing of column headings       OFF
   -z    Save all output to output file             OFF

db2 =>
```

Figure 2–26 *Command Line Processor option settings*

You can update these settings permanently or for each session.

Use the `DB2OPTIONS` environment variable to customize defaults. A minus sign (-) immediately following an option letter turns the option off. You can use the ? flag to get more help; for example, `DB2 ? OPTIONS` gives you all of the options.

To update the options permanently for any CLP, or when using the file input method to run commands, use the following syntax:

```
db2 UPDATE COMMAND OPTIONS USING OPTIONS ...
```

The DB2 CLP has two parts: a front-end process and a back-end process. The front-end process is called `db2` and the back-end is `db2bp`. The back-end process will maintain a connection to the database. To release this connection, use the `TERMINATE` command. To end an interactive DB2 CLP session, issue the `QUIT` command (this does not release the database connection).

DB2 for Windows CLP Considerations

The Windows platform does not allow you to enter commands directly from its CLP (also known as the Windows Command Prompt). Other operating systems, AIX for example, allow you to enter DB2 commands from their native operating system's CLP using the `db2` prefix. To enter DB2 commands from the CLP on Windows, you have to initiate the CLP to accept DB2 commands by starting the DB2 Command Window process. The DB2 Command Window functions exactly like the Windows Command Prompt, only it can process DB2 commands.

You can start the DB2 Command Windows (DB2 CW) from the **Command Line Tools** folder for your DB2 installation or by running the db2cmd command from the a Windows CLP.

DB2 *Note*

For simplicity, the remainder of this chapter will refer to the DB2 Command Window and the Windows Command Prompt simply as the CLP, or the *native operating system's CLP.*

The biggest difference between the DB2 CLP and an operating system's CLP is that the DB2 CLP alleviates the need to prefix all of your DB2 commands with `db2`.

As indicated earlier, the DB2 Command Editor can also be used to enter DB2 commands. This is often the most productive method as it allows entry of multiple commands/statements; saving commands to a script; recalling commands; basic copy, paste, and edit operations; viewing the `EXPLAIN` output of a statement; and much more.

You can start the Command Editor by entering the `db2ce` command from any operating system's CLP, from the **Command Line Tools** folder for your DB2 installation, or from the Control Center (started by entering db2cc in any CLP session for any operating system). The Command Editor is shown below in Figure 2–27.

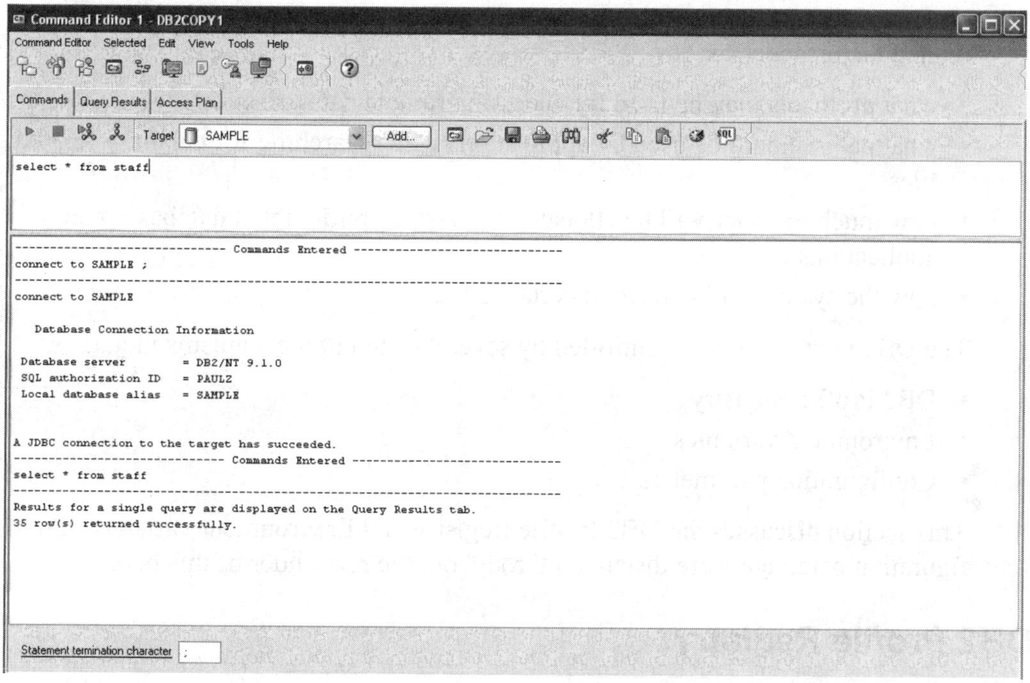

Figure 2–27 *DB2 Command Editor*

The Command Editor is an intuitive tool, just add the database connection you want to work with (using the **Add** button) and the rest is fairly self-explanatory. We recommend you experiment with entering commands with this tool, as well as learning some of the other valuable features it offers.

The DB2 Environment

Before creating and working with DB2 databases, you need to understand the DB2 environment. The DB2 environment controls many data server and database-related factors, such as:

- what protocols may be used for accessing remote databases
- what paths should be used by applications when searching for database-related files
- how much memory will be allocated for various buffers that databases and applications use
- how the system will behave in certain situations

The DB2 environment is controlled by several different mechanisms including:

- DB2 Profile Registry
- Environment variables
- Configuration parameters

This section discusses the DB2 Profile Registry and Environment variables. Configuration parameters are discussed throughout the remainder of this book.

DB2 Profile Registry

Much of the DB2 environment is controlled by entries stored in the DB2 Profile Registry. The objective of the Profile Registry is to consolidate the DB2 environment, thereby creating a central repository for key controlling factors that affect a DB2 server outside of the instance and database configuration settings. Many of these registry values control DB2 interfaces, communication parameters, and so on, so the variables that are set in this registry may vary by platform.

The DB2 Profile Registry can be used to alter the operations of your DB2 data server. For example, you can affect the locking mechanism to address concurrency issues or specifically define the communication protocols that can be used for client/server communications. The best thing about altering a data server's environment by changing the profile registry is that you don't need to reboot your server for the changes to take effect. This is the compelling reason why this feature was implemented in DB2. Before, a change to a data server at an environment variable level would require a system reboot. Note, however, that depending on the variable you change, you may need to recycle the database or database instance for the change to take effect.

The DB2 Profile Registry is divided into four regions, namely:

- **DB2 Instance Level Profile Registry** — The majority of DB2 environment variables are placed within this registry. The environment variable settings for a particular instance are also kept in this registry. Values defined in this level override their settings at the global level.
- **DB2 Global Level Profile Registry** — If a variable is not set for a particular instance, this registry is used. This registry contains machine-wide variable settings.
- **DB2 Instance Node Level Profile Registry** — This registry level contains variable settings that are specific to a partition in a partitioned-database environment (if you're using the Database Partitioning Feature, then you need to concern yourself with this registry). Values defined in this level override their settings at the instance and global levels.
- **DB2 Instance Profile Registry** — This registry contains a list of all instance names recognized by the system. You can see the complete list of all the instances available on the system by running `DB2ILIST`. You don't use this registry to alter that behavior of a system, it's more for information purposes.

There are literally dozens of registry values that you can set in the DB2 Profile Registry and it isn't necessary to memorize all of them for day-to-day operations (or to get certified). However, it is important to fundamentally understand how the behavior of DB2 can be altered using this infrastructure.

The following list gives some example of parameters that may be set in the DB2 Registry:

- `DB2_SKIPINSERTED` — Controls whether uncommitted insertions can be ignored for cursors using the Cursor Stability (CS) or Read Stability (RS) isolation levels.
- `DB2_MDC_ROLLOUT` — Instructs DB2 to use a special delete algorithm for MDC tables such that they are minimally logged thereby making them very quick. When DB2 uses this algorithm, logging and processing associated with the deletion of rows in an MDC table and its corresponding block indexes are drastically reduced.
- `DB2COMM` — Specifies the communication protocol listeners that are enabled for the current DB2 instance. If this registry variable is undefined or set to NULL, no protocol connection listeners are started when the database manager is started.

Some DB2 Registry Profile variables are platform specific. For example, the following registry variables are examples of those that can only be set on the Windows platform:

- DB2NTNOCACHE —Specifies whether the DB2 database systems opens database files with the NOCACHE option to avoid double-caching effects when both the data server software and the file system are involved in caching.
- DB2NTPRICLASS — Specifies the priority class for a DB2 instance (normal, the default, realtime, and high). You use this registry variable with individual thread priorities (set using the DB2PRIORITIES registry variable) to determine the priority of a DB2 thread relative to other threads on the operating system.

The following is an example of a registry variable that is only available on AIX:

- DB2_EXTENDED_IO_FEATURES — Enables features that can enhance I/O performance by raising the hit rate of the memory caches as well as reducing the latency associated with high-priority I/O operations.

The following registry variables are available for Windows and AIX, but not for Linux, Solaris, or HP-UX:

- DB2_LARGE_PAGE_MEM — Denotes that all applicable memory regions should use large page memory. You can also select individual memory regions that will use large page memory. Large page memory is primarily intended to provide performance improvements to high-performance computing applications.

Environment Variables

There are some environment variables that you can choose to specify, or not to specify, in the DB2 Profile Registry (depending on the operating system). They are also some system environment variables used by DB2 that must be stored in a location where the operating system stores its own system variables. The following are examples of some DB2 system environment variables:

- DB2INSTANCE — Specifies the active DB2 instance
- DB2PATH — Specifies the path for the DB2 executables

On Windows, DB2 Environment Variables are defined with the Windows' Environment Variables (press the **Environment Variables** button in the **Advanced** tab of the System Properties view). On UNIX and Linux, you define them within a called db2profile (Bourne or Korn shell) or db2cshrc (C shell) depending on the platform. It's often a best practice to incorporate this with the user's initialization file (.profile or .login). For further details on environment variables and on which operating system platforms you may see them or need them, please refer to the *DB2 Administration Guide*.

Declaring Registry and Environment Variables

Registry information is stored in files containing variable names and their set values. However, these files should not be edited or manipulated directly. To update registry and environment values, use the `db2set` command. Any changes made to the values in a registry are applied dynamically, and you do not need to reboot your system for the changes to take effect.

Using the `db2set` command with the `-all` option, you can see the list of all of the profiles variables set for your environment (Figure 2–28).

```
DB2 CLP - DB2COPY1
C:\temp\ESE\image>db2set -all
[e] DB2PATH=C:\Program Files\IBM\SQLLIB
[i] DB2ACCOUNTNAME=DB28PAULZ\db2cert
[i] DB2INSTOWNER=DB28PAULZ
[i] DB2PORTRANGE=60280:60283
[i] DB2INSTPROF=C:\PROGRA~1\IBM\SQLLIB
[i] DB2COMM=TCPIP
[g] DB2_EXTSECURITY=YES
[g] DB2SYSTEM=DB28PAULZ
[g] DB2PATH=C:\Program Files\IBM\SQLLIB
[g] DB2INSTDEF=DB2
[g] DB2ADMINSERVER=DB2DAS00

C:\temp\ESE\image>
```

Figure 2–28 *The db2set -all command*

The output of the `db2set` command with the `-all` option is shown Figure 2–28. Notice that instance-level settings are preceded with an `[i]`, global settings are preceded with a `[g]`, and the overall environment itself with an `[e]`.

DB2 *Note*

In a partitioned database environment, specific node settings are preceded with an `[n]`.

If you enter the `db2set` command on its own, it returns a list of all the instance-level registry settings. The following are some examples of usage of the `db2set` command.

- To set a parameter for the current instance:

```
db2set parameter=value
```

- To set a parameter's value for a specific instance:

```
db2set parameter=value -I instance_name
```

- To set a parameter at the global level:

```
db2set parameter=value -g
```

- To view a list of all variables that can be set in the profile registry:

```
db2set -lr
```

- To delete a registry variable setting, omit any values to the right of the = (equal) sign:

```
db2set parameter=
```

- To set a registry variable to NULL (different than deleting it), list the variable name with the -null option following it:

```
db2set parameter -null
```

Hierarchy of the DB2 Environment

Since there are multiple places where a variable can be set, DB2 uses a hierarchy to determine where it will look to determine a variable's value. It uses the following search order:

1. Environment variables set with the db2set command (or the EXPORT command on UNIX and Linux platforms)
2. Registry values set at the instance node level profile when using DB2 in a partitioned database environment (using the db2set -n <INSTANCE NAME><NODE-NUM> command)
3. Registry values set with the instance level profile (using the db2set -i command)
4. Registry values set with the global level profile (using the db2set -g command)

Although most DB2 environment settings can be set either in the DB2 Profile Registry or in the operating system's facility for environment settings, it's strongly recommended that the DB2 Profile Registry be used whenever possible. If DB2 variables are set outside of the DB2 Registry, remote administration of those variables is not possible and any changes made usually mean that the system must be rebooted for any changes to take effect.

The DB2 Instance

A DB2 instance is defined as a logical data server environment. DB2 databases are created within DB2 instances on a data server. The creation of multiple instances on the same physical server provides a unique database server environment for each instance. For example, you can maintain a test environment and a production environment on the same machine using the same code path (of course in DB2 9, you can separate these environments with different code levels using DB2 copies as well).

Each instance has an administrative group associated with it. This administrative group must be defined in the instance configuration file known as the *database manager configuration file*. Creating user IDs and user groups is different for each operating environment; by default, DB2 uses the operating system's underlying security controls to instantiate authentication levels. You can use almost any authentication mechanism you want in DB2 via security plug-ins, but that is out of the scope of this chapter.

Unless you specify otherwise, the installation process creates a default DB2 instance. This is the recommended method for creating instances. However, instances may be created (or dropped) after installation.

The instance directory stores all information that pertains to a database instance. The location of the instance directory cannot be changed once it is created. The directory contains information such as:

- The database manager configuration file
- The system database directory
- The node directory
- The node configuration file (*db2nodes.cfg*)
- Other files that contain debugging information, such as the exception or register dump, or the call stack for the DB2 processes

DB2 Instances on Windows

The default instance created during the installation of DB2 for Windows is called DB2. Some DB2 environment variables are set during install. If you want to create another instance, you can using the `DB2ICRT <name_of_instance>` command. For example, to create an instance in addition to the default DB2 instance created during the installation, enter this command as follows:

```
db2icrt db2cert
```

Getting Started

The instance name is specified at creation time and does not have to directly correspond to a user ID as it does in UNIX environments.

DB2 Instance Considerations on Windows

When installing DB2 on Windows, the DB2 instance is defined as a Windows service. Therefore, the DB2 instance name must adhere to any naming rules for Windows services. The DB2 Administration Server (DAS) is defined as a Windows service as well (more on that later in this chapter). You can configure these services to start automatically either during the installation process or through the Services control interface in the Windows operating system.

You can use the **Services** icon (located in the Windows Control Panel) to see the various services that DB2 uses on Windows (Figure 2–29).

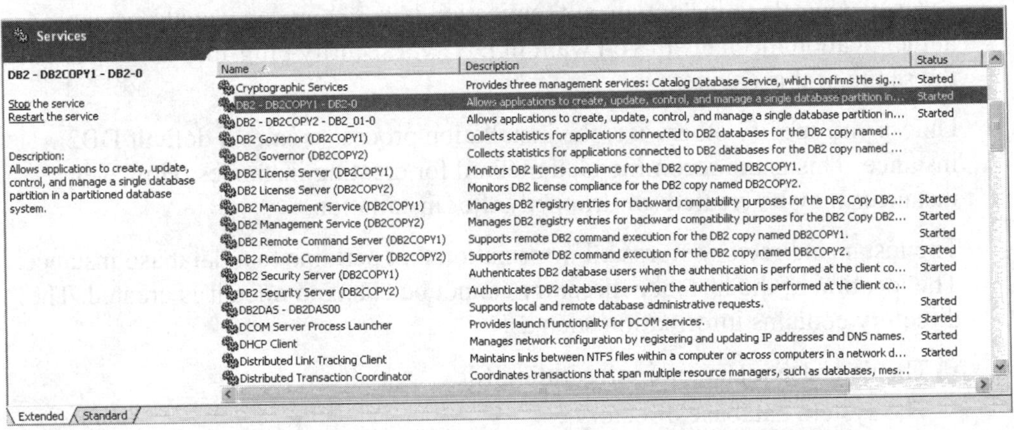

Figure 2–29 *DB2 uses services on the Windows platform*

You can see in Figure 2–29 that there are multiple services for each instance and copy of DB2. A single instance will use a number of services to perform various support functions for the instance.

For example, `DB2 - DB2COPY1 - DB2-0` in Figure 2–29 is the actual database instance, whereas a `DB2 SECURITY SERVER` service is used to perform security services for a specific DB2 copy. Note that there is a single `DB2DAS - DB2DAS00` instance and that this administrative instance is not associated with any copy of DB2; as you may recall, there can only be a single DAS instance on any machine.

A DB2 instance can be started from the Windows Control Panel or from any Windows CLP using the `NET START <service_name>` command (and stopped using `NET STOP <service_name>` command). DB2 has its own set of commands (covered later in this chapter) that can be used to more natively start instances from a DB2 perspective.

DB2 Instances on Linux and UNIX

Instances operate a little differently on UNIX and Linux workstations because the name of the instance owner dictates the name of the instance; however, the concepts and purpose of an instance are identical.

If a DB2 installation was done manually, or you specifically chose for the installation program to not create an instance, the following tasks must be completed before an instance can be created on the server:

1. Create the support groups and user IDs for a DB2 instance.

   Three users and groups are required to operate DB2 (Table 2–2).

Table 2–2 *Required Users and Groups*

Required User	Example User Name	Example Group Name
Instance owner	db2inst1	db2iadm1
Fenced user	db2fenc1	db2fadm1
DB2 administration server	db2as	db2asgrp

   - The `instance owner` home directory is where the DB2 instance will be created.
   - The `fenced user` is used to run user defined functions (UDFs) and stored procedures outside of the address space used by the DB2 database.
   - The `user ID` for the DB2 administration server is used to run the DAS service on your system.

   The commands to create the required groups and user IDs for DB2 will depend on the operating system. The following illustrates an example of performing these tasks on AIX:

```
mkgroup id=999 db2iadm1
mkgroup id=998 db2adm1
mkgroup id=997 db2asgrp
```

To create users for each group:

```
mkuser id=1004 pgrp=db2iadm1 groups=db2iadm1 home=/home/db2inst1
db2inst1 passwd mypasswrd
mkuser id=1003 pgrp=db2fadm1 groups=db2fadm1 home=/home/db2fenc1
db2fenc1 passwd mypasswrd
mkuser id=1002 pgrp=db2asgrp groups=db2asgrp home=/home/db2as
db2as passwd mypasswrd
```

DB2 Note

You must have root authority to create users and groups on most operating systems. Additionally, the names and passwords you specify must adhere to not only the operating system naming rules, but DB2 naming rules as well. You can find more information in the *DB2 Quick Beginnings* manual

2. Create the DAS using the `DASCRT -u <DAS_user_name>` command as follows:

```
/usr/opt/db2_08001/instance/dascrt -u DASuser
```

3. Create an instance using `DB2ICRT`.

```
DB2DIR/instance/db2icrt -a AuthType -u FencedID InstName
```

- `DB2DIR` is the DB2 installation directory; for example, on AIX it is */usr/opt/db2_09_01*.
- `-a AuthType` is the authentication type for the instance; values such as `SERVER`, (the default), `CLIENT`, `SERVER_ENCRYPT`, and more are supported. This parameter is optional.
- `-u FencedID` represents the name of the user under which fenced user-defined functions (UDFs) and fenced stored procedures will run.
- `InstName` is the name of the DB2 instance. The name of the instance is the same as the name of the instance-owning user. The instance will be created in the instance-owning user's home directory.

4. Set up communications for the instance.

   The `DB2COMM` registry variable allows you to set communication protocols for the DB2 instance. This variable can be set to any combination of the following keywords, separated by commas (though some settings have no effect on platforms where the communication protocol isn't supported by the operating system):

   - `NETBIOS` starts `NETBIOS` support
   - `NPIPE` starts `NAMED PIPE` support
   - `TCPIP` starts `TCP/IP` support

   For example, to set the database manager and DAS service to start connection managers for TCP/IP, enter the commands on the next page.

```
db2set DB2COMM=tcpip
db2set DB2DAS00 DB2COMM=tcpip
db2stop
db2start DBM CFG USING svcename db2c_DB2
```

The database manager configuration file has a parameter SVCENAME that is assigned as the main connection port name for the instance and defined in the \etc\services file. For example, if the name defined in the services file is db2c_DB2, the command to update the database manager configuration file is:

```
UPDATE DBM CFG USING svcename db2c_DB2
```

The corresponding entries in the /etc/services file would be:

```
db2c_DB2      5000/tcp
db2i_DB2      5001/tcp
```

5. Update the product license key.

   Refer to the db2licm command in the *DB2 Command Reference.*

Starting the DB2 Instance

Now that a DB2 instance has been created, it must be initialized or started. The process of starting an instance is similar to starting a network file server; until the instance is started, DB2 clients will not be able to access the databases on the server.

The DB2 specific command to start a DB2 instance is called DB2START. This command will allocate all of the required DB2 resources on the server. These resources include memory and communications support.

```
DB2START
SQL1063N DB2START processing was successful.
```

As previously mentioned, on Windows you may also start an instance using native Windows operating system commands. For example:

```
NET START <instance_name>
```

Stopping the DB2 Instance

The command to stop the current database manager instance is DB2STOP. Messages are sent to standard output indicating the success or failure of the DB2STOP command.

```
DB2STOP
SQL1064N DB2STOP processing was successful.
```

On Windows, you may also stop an instance with this command:

```
NET STOP <instance_name>
```

DB2 Note

Sometimes you want to stop and restart the database instance, for example, after you change a registry variable. This operation is referred to as recycling the instance. If you want to stop and restart a DB2 instance in a single command, you can enter the required commands as follows:

```
DB2STOP & DB2START
```

Instance Administration

This section discusses how to administer DB2 instances, both locally and remotely. Certain tasks in DB2 can only be performed at the instance level, such as creating a database or updating the database manager configuration. Other tasks require a database connection, such as issuing SQL Data Manipulation Language (DML) statements, using the LOAD utility, or using the BIND command.

Both remote and local administration of instances via the ATTACH command can be done using the DB2 CLP, CLP, or the Control Center. For example, you may use the ATTACH command when you have multiple instances on a single machine and want to work with each of them regardless of the current setting of DB2INSTANCE (the environment variable that dictates the instance to which a default DB2 CLP or CLP is attached). Use the ATTACH command as follows:

```
ATTACH [TO nodename] [USER username [USING password]]
```

If the ATTACH command is executed without arguments, the node name you are currently attached to is returned. If you attempt to attach to an instance while attached to another instance, the current instance will be detached and the new attachment is attempted. In other words, you can only be attached to one instance at a time.

DB2 Note

The currently active instance can be identified using the GET INSTANCE command, which returns the current setting of the DB2INSTANCE environment variable.

Database connections are independent of instance attachments. A single application can maintain several database connections at the same time, but it can only maintain a single instance attachment at any one time.

A database connection can be implicit or explicit. An implicit database connection will connect to the database specified by the DB2DBDFT registry variable. An explicit database connection can be made using the CONNECT TO <database_name> statement.

The local instance is determined by the value contained in the DB2INSTANCE variable. When attached to a second instance, you are using the directory services of the local instance. You cannot make catalog changes, list, update, or reset catalogs for database, node, or DCS directories (used only if DB2 Connect is installed) in the second instance. If you want to update catalog entries and so on, you need to change the focus of the session by setting the DB2INSTANCE environment variable (discussed in the "Working with Multiple Instances — A Shortcut" section later in this chapter).

Local Instance Administration

After DB2 has been installed on a server and an instance created, a user can access this instance in one of two ways:

- By setting the DB2INSTANCE environment variable to the name of the instance. The DB2PATH environment variable must be set to the location of the DB2 executables. This is known as an *implicit attachment*.
- By cataloging a local instance and issuing the ATTACH command. This is known as an *explicit attachment*.

Instance Attach Scenario

This scenario examines a situation in which a local user wants to access two instances on the same database server without changing the environment when the user logs into the system.

The two local instances are called DB2CERT and DB2. They are located on an AIX database server. The user, Tasha, is a local user on the database server. Tasha has set the DB2INSTANCE and DB2PATH variables to allow access to the DB2CERT instance. In AIX, Tasha would edit her profile to include the following entry:

```
. /home/db2test/sqllib/db2profile
```

Tasha also wants to access the DB2 instance on the same server. To do this, she catalogs the DB2 instance as a local node by using the following command:

```
CATALOG LOCAL NODE MYDB2 INSTANCE DB2
```

In this example:

- LOCAL identifies that this is a local instance.
- MYDB2 is the local alias for the node to be cataloged. This can be whatever name you want to represent this connection
- DB2 is the name of the local instance to be accessed.

The contents of the node directory can be examined using the LIST NODE DIRECTORY command shown in Figure 2–30.

```
 Node Directory

 Number of entries in the directory = 2

Node 1 entry:

 Node name                          = MYDB2
 Comment                            =
 Protocol                           = LOCAL
 Instance name                      = db2
```

Figure 2–30 *List Node Directory output*

To access a database in the instance named db2, Tasha must catalog the local database using the following command:

```
CATALOG DB DB2CERT AS MYCERT AT NODE MYDB2
```

In this example:

- DB2CERT is the name of the database as it exists in the instance on the database server.
- MYCERT is the alias name for the database that user Tasha will use when connecting to it.
- MYDB2 is the local alias given for the instance by Tasha in the CATALOG NODE command.

If Tasha issues the `LIST DATABASE DIRECTORY` command, the output is similar to that shown in Figure 2–31.

```
System Database Directory

Number of entries in the directory = 1

Database 1 entry:

 Database alias                          = MYCERT
 Database name                           = DB2CERT
 Node name                               = MYDB2
 Database release level                  = b.00
 Comment                                 =
 Directory entry type                    = Remote
 Catalog database partition number       = -1
 Alternate server hostname               =
 Alternate server port number            =
```

Figure 2–31 *List Database Directory output*

You can see from Figure 2–31 that the `DB2CERT` database has been cataloged at the `MYDB2` node. Also not that to connect to this database, you would actually connect to its alias name, `MYCERT`.

The `Alternate server hostname` and `Alternative server port number` entries are used by the Automatic Client Reroute (ACR) facility. ACR can be used to provide transparent failover of a failed DB2 server to its failover partner. When a client with this directory structure successfully connects to the `MYCERT` (the alias for `DB2CERT`) database, and this server is set up in a failover partner pair (for example, via High Availability Disaster Recovery — HADR), a successful connection would automatically populate these two entries. If a failure were to occur, the ACR facility would automatically retry the failed server to ensure it didn't accidentally determine the primary database to be down when it wasn't. If the primary database still wasn't responding, HADR would initiate the ownership transfer of the database (it would do more, such as ensure it's consistent) to the secondary server and the client (through ACR) would automatically try to connect to the database on the secondary sever through using this information.

Working with Multiple Instances — A Shortcut

As previously mentioned, you can work with different instances using the `DB2INSTANCE` environment variable. Since this variable can be set at a session level, it provides you with the ability to quickly move between instances from a CLP session.

Figure 2–32 shows the use of the `SET DB2INSTANCE` and `GET INSTANCE` commands to illustrate switching between different instances on the same server.

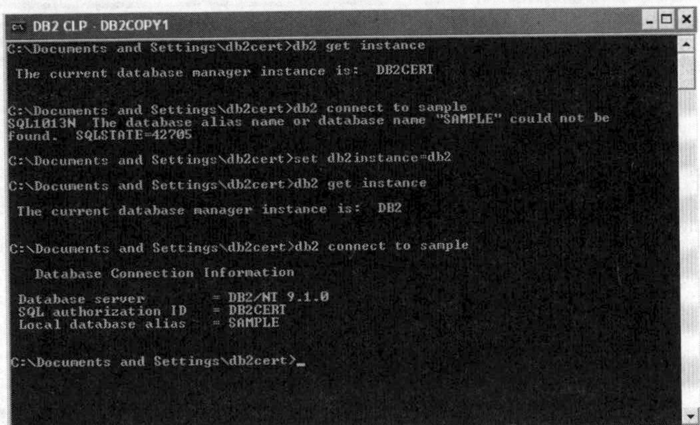

Figure 2–32 *Using DB2INSTANCE to work with multiple instances*

You can see in Figure 2–32 that the default instance is `DB2CERT`. Assuming this instance is started, a connection is made to the `SAMPLE` database. Since this database doesn't exist in this instance, an error is returned. Using the `SET DB2INSTANCE` command, the default attach for this session is changed from the `DB2CERT` instance to the DB2 instance (where the `SAMPLE` database resides). At this point the connection to the `SAMPLE` database is successful and the default instance attachment for the remainder of this session is DB2. Note that once you close the CLP session where you made this change, the operating system's setting for `DB2INSTANCE` (in this case `DB2INSTANCE=DB2CERT`) will revert back to the default instance attachment. By setting `DB2INSTANCE=DB2` at the session level, we temporarily overrode the default instance used in this example.

Attaching to an Instance Using the Control Center

So far, DB2 commands have been used to attach to an instance. This can also be done using the Control Center. To do this, right-click on the required instance and select Attach from the menu as shown in Figure 2–33.

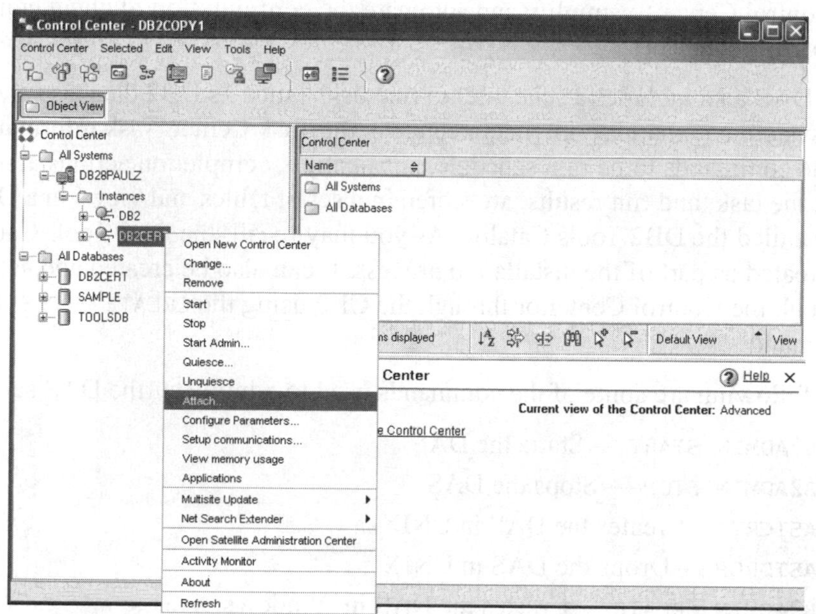

Figure 2–33 *Attaching to an instance using the Control Center*

DB2 Administration Server (DAS)

The DB2 Administration Server (DAS) is a control point used only to assist with tasks on DB2 instances. You must have a running DAS if you want to use available tools like the Control Center or Configuration Assistant's auto-catalog database discovery feature, the scheduling facilities of the Task Center, and so on. When the DAS is created, the DB2 global-level profile registry variable `DB2ADMINSERVER` is set to the name of the DAS.

Specifically, the DAS assists the DB2 tools when working on the following administration tasks:

- Enabling remote administration of DB2 database instances.
- Providing a facility for job management, including the ability to schedule the running of both DB2 database manager and operating system command scripts. These command scripts can be user defined.
- Defining the scheduling of jobs, viewing the results of completed jobs, and performing other administrative tasks against jobs located either remotely or locally to the DAS using the Task Center.
- Providing a means for discovering information about the configuration of DB2 instances, databases, and other DB2 servers in conjunction with the DB2 discovery function. This information is used by the Configuration Assistant and the

Control Center to simplify and automate the configuration of client connections to DB2 databases.

The DAS also includes a scheduler to run tasks (such as DB2 database and operating system command scripts) defined using the Task Center. Task information such as the commands to be run, schedule, notification, completion actions associated with the task, and run results, are stored in a set of tables and views in a DB2 database called the DB2 Tools Catalog. As you may recall, the DB2 Tools Catalog can be created as part of the installation process. It can also be created and activated through the Control Center or through the CLP using the `CREATE TOOLS CATALOG` command.

The following are some of the commands used to administer the DAS service:

- `DB2ADMIN START` — Starts the DAS
- `DB2ADMIN STOP` — Stops the DAS
- `DASICRT` — Creates the DAS in UNIX
- `DASIDROP` — Drops the DAS in UNIX
- `DB2ADMIN CREATE` — Creates the DAS in Windows
- `DB2ADMIN DROP` — Drops the DAS instance in Windows
- `DB2 GET ADMIN CFG` — Displays the database manager configuration for the DAS
- `DB2 UPDATE ADMIN CFG` — This command allows you to update individual entries in the database manager configuration file for the DAS. (The changes become effective only after the `DB2ADMIN STOP` and `DB2ADMIN START` commands are executed.)
- `DB2 RESET ADMIN CFG` — Resets the DAS configuration to the recommended defaults. (The changes become effective only after the `DB2ADMIN STOP` and db2admin start commands are executed.)

Summary

In this chapter, the process of installing DB2 on the Windows platform was detailed, along with considerations for UNIX and Linux. The creation of a DB2 instance and the role of the DB2 Administration Server (DAS) in a DB2 system were also described.

The DB2 installation program is a graphical installation utility available on Linux, UNIX, and Windows environments. The DB2 installation program provides an easy-to-use interface for installing DB2 and performing initial setup and configuration tasks.

The DB2 installation program can also be used to create instances and response files. The selections you make as you proceed through the DB2 installation program are recorded in a response file that you can save to a location on your system. For your convenience, the DB2 installation program allows you to create a response file without performing an installation. This feature may be useful in an environment where a DBA does not have the authority required to perform an installation. The DBA can create a response file for the installation and provide it to the system administrator who will install the product on the DBA's behalf.

A DB2 instance can be defined as a logical database server environment. For each environment, the instance creation process (including any special user ID and group setup required for Linux and UNIX) was reviewed.

The DB2 environment variables, including `DB2INSTANCE` and `DB2PATH`, were discussed, as they are defined on every DB2 system. The location of the DB2 environment variables differs by platform. Also discussed were the DB2 profile variables and the DB2 Profile Registry, how the various levels of the registry can contain different levels of information, and how settings variables at different levels can affect your system.

Throughout this chapter, DB2 commands were demonstrated through the DB2 Command Window or an operating system's native CLP. The DB2 CLP has settings that can be modified for each session or changed globally using the `DB2OPTIONS` profile variable.

Instance management, including starting and stopping a DB2 instance, was reviewed. DB2 for Windows is integrated with the Windows services environment, and each DB2 instance is a Windows service. The general commands used to start and stop a DB2 instance are `DB2START` and `DB2STOP`.

CHAPTER 3

Getting Connected

- DB2 CLIENT OVERVIEW
- INSTALLING A DB2 CLIENT
- AUTOMATING CONFIGURATIONS
- MANUAL CONFIGURATIONS
- BINDING DATABASE UTILITIES

DB2 databases can be accessed by applications that run on the same machine as the database or from remote clients using a distributed connection. In addition to providing client access to a centralized database running on a server, distributed connections can also be used by database administrators (DBAs) to perform remote administrative tasks via the Control Center or the DB2 Command Line Processor (DB2 CLP).

DB2 Client Overview

In Chapter 2 we introduced you to the installation of a DB2 data server. Specifically, we detailed the process of how to install DB2 Enterprise 9 for Windows with some auxiliary coverage on UNIX and Linux.

In contrast, a DB2 client provides the runtime environment that's required for DB2 applications to access a data server's resources. For example, a DB2 client contains the communications infrastructure to communicate with remote data servers. You can also execute SQL, bind packages, use data manipulation utilities (`IMPORT`, `LOAD`, `EXPORT`, and so on), catalog remote nodes and databases, and more using a DB2 client. In fact, most of the database administration tasks DBAs perform are typically done from a DB2 client workstation.

DB2 *Note*

In this chapter, the use of the term *client* with a lowercase **c** refers the DB2 client software in general, while an uppercase **C** refers to a specific DB2 client package.

- **DB2 Runtime Client** — Provides the minimum *client* footprint (about 20-30 MB) to support connectivity to DB2 9 data servers (the exception to this is if you choose to support communication via specific API drivers, covered later in this section). When you install a DB2 Runtime Client, you install a set of drivers that support all the programming languages supported in DB2 9, some of which include ADO.NET, ADO, OLE DB, ODBC, JDBC, SQLJ, static SQL, and more.
- **DB2 Client** — Includes all the functions found in the DB2 Runtime Client *plus* tools for client-server configuration, and database administration, as well as application development files that accelerate application development such as header files, samples, and more. For example, this client includes the Configuration Assistant that provides graphical tools for client administration and connectivity. A DB2 Client's footprint is directly correlated to the components you select to install and can take between 200 MB and 800 MB depending on the options you select. The process of installing a DB2 Client is similar to that of a DB2 data server.

For independent software vendors (ISVs) and enterprises that want to set up connectivity between client workstations and DB2 data servers with minimal disk footprint, they can alternatively use a standalone *driver*. A driver can be used to set up connectivity using a specific API; for example, there's a driver for JDBC/SQLJ connections and one for ODBC/CLI connections.

Drivers are sometimes preferred over DB2 clients since they have a small footprint (for example, the IBM Driver for JDBC and SQLJ is about 2 MB) and therefore are easily embedded within an application. They also come with royalty-free distribution licenses for this very purpose.

The main difference between a DB2 Runtime Client and a driver is that a DB2 Runtime Client supports all the connectivity APIs supported by DB2 9, whereas a driver only supports the API for which it was created.

For example, as of when this book was written, there was no specific driver for .NET applications. Therefore, to connect an application written using the ADO.NET API to a DB2 data server, you need to install one of the DB2 clients.

The drivers available in DB2 9 are:

- **IBM Driver for JDBC and SQLJ** — Used to support Java-based connectivity to a DB2 data server. This driver is about 2 MB in size and can easily be embedded within your application. This driver is common between the version of DB2 that runs on the distributed platforms and DB2 for z/OS; in other words, it's the same code. A DB2 Connect license enables this driver to connect to DB2 for i5/OS and DB2 for z/OS data sources.
- **IBM Driver for ODBC and CLI** — Used to support open database connectivity (ODBC) or call-level interface (CLI) connectivity to a DB2 9 data server (essentially the same concept as the IBM Driver for JDBC and SQLJ for Java, only this driver is for ODBC and CLI connections). This driver is about 2 MB in size and can easily be embedded within your application. If you want to use this driver to connect to a DB2 for z/OS or DB2 i5/OS data server, you need to license the DB2 Connect software as well.

DB2 *Note*

A DB2 9 application written for ODBC uses the same programming skill as one written for CLI. In other words, if you know ODBC, you know CLI. Some people choose to develop to the CLI layer because they can avoid the extra code path length required by calling the Windows ODBC Driver Manager (so theoretically the application should perform faster), and there are some additional binding options that offer advantages as they relate to the efficiency of your application.

You can use a DB2 client to connect to a DB2 9 or DB2 8 data server — prior versions of DB2 are not supported. If you are connecting to a DB2 8 data server, you must be aware of some of the functions and SQL that you try to execute on this server. If it was introduced in DB2 9, it won't obviously work on a DB2 8 server. For the most part, we strongly recommend running your DB2 data servers and DB2 clients at the same version level, and ideally at the same maintenance level.

Installing a DB2 Client

The process you follow to install a DB2 client is similar to the process of installing a DB2 data server covered in Chapter 2. The common method for installing a DB2 client is to run the DB2 installation program provided on one of your product's media. DB2 client install images are included on both DB2 data server install images and on client-only media.

The DB2 installation program allows you to perform a graphical assisted installation of the DB2 client software. For mass deployments, the same response file options available for a DB2 data server are also supported; you can also use manual options like the `db2_install` script on UNIX and Linux.

You can install a DB2 client (and data server for that matter) using deployment tools or methods such as Windows Active Directory, Windows Systems Management Server (SMS), an array of Tivoli products, and so on. Finally, in the same manner that a DB2 data server supports the coexistence of multiple versions and maintenance levels of the same product, so does a DB2 client.

You can install a DB2 for Windows client without a user account that belongs to the `ADMINISTRATORS` group, and instead with a user account that belongs to the Windows `POWER USERS` group or `USERS` group. This method is suitable when the user account used to perform the installation does not have administrator privileges. It's important to note that unlike the ability to install a DB2 data server without a user account belonging to the `ADMINISTRATORS` group (that method uses the Windows elevated privileges mechanism, which is also available for a DB2 client install), setting up elevated privileges is not required for this type of installation for a DB2 client.

Since the installation of a DB2 client so closely resembles that of a DB2 data server, we won't detail its process in this chapter. You should, however, make yourself aware of the different components of a DB2 Client to give you insight into whether a DB2 Runtime Client installation may be more suitable, whether you should customize a DB2 Client install, or whether you should perhaps use a driver.

Figure 3–1 shows the components selected by default during a DB2 Client installation.

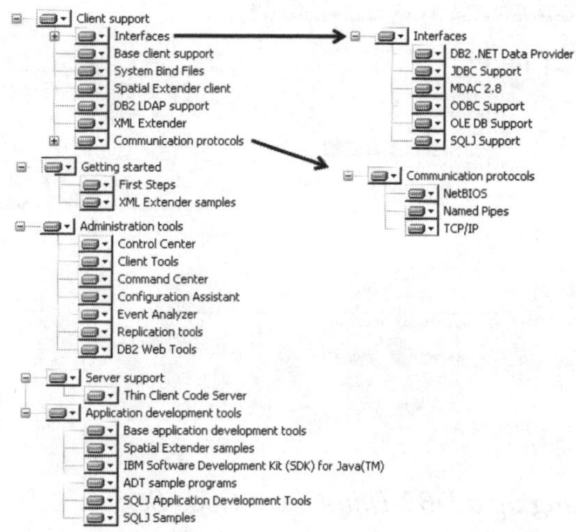

Figure 3–1 *The default components of a DB2 Client installation*

The DB2 Thin Client for Windows

There's a special way to implement the DB2 client code (and DB2 Connect Personal Edition for that matter) on Windows such that one machine acts as a code server to multiple client machines that download a set of required dynamic-link libraries (*DLLs*) to provide themselves with connectivity functionality. In this environment, DB2 client software (or driver) needs to be installed.

You set up a DB2 Thin-Client architecture by first customizing a DB2 Client installation such that the **Thin Client Code Server** component (a subcomponent within the **Server support** component group) is installed (Figure 3–2). Once this component is installed on a target workstation, it becomes known as a *DB2 Thin-Client Code Server* and the target machine that loads the code is known as the *DB2 Thin-Client*.

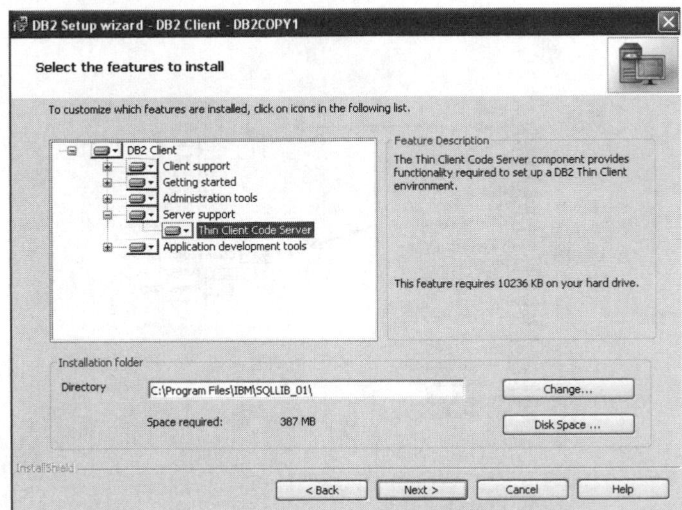

Figure 3–2 *Setting up a DB2 Thin-Client Code Server*

DB2 Note

In a DB2 Connect Personal Edition (DB2 Connect PE) environment, the code server known as the *DB2 Thin-Connect Code Server* and the client that loads its code is known as the *DB2 Connect Thin-Client.*

Once the DB2 Thin-Client Code Server is installed and configured, other workstations are configured to load the DB2 client code across a network connection from the DB2 Thin-Client Code Server. A DB2 Thin-Client functions like any other DB2 client workstation; the architecture is transparent to the end user or application.

When operating within a DB2 Thin-Client environment, no processing is done at the DB2 Thin-Client Code Server; the code is simply loaded from it. In sharp contrast to a locally installed DB2 client, each target DB2 Thin-Client workstation needs only a minimal amount of code and configuration to establish links to the DB2 Thin-Client Code Server.

Figure 3–3 shows a typical DB2 Thin-Client environment. The lighting bolts represent the code that is being pulled and loaded to the DB2 Thin-Client workstation from the DB2 Thin-Client Code Server. The arrows represent connections to a remote DB2 data server. Once the code is loaded, all processing and activity is handled at the DB2 Thin-Client workstations.

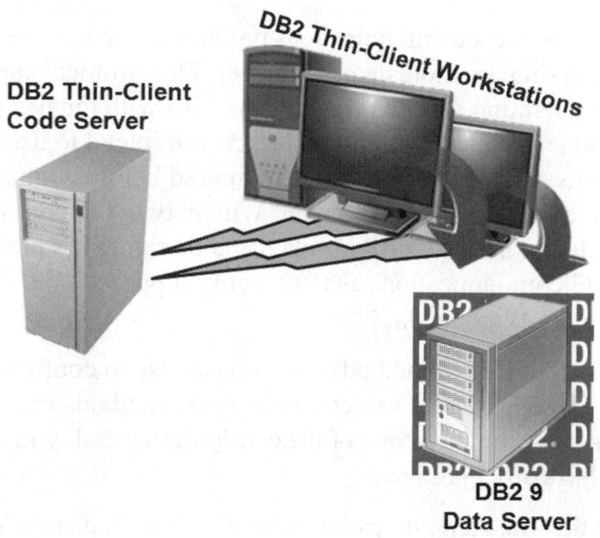

Figure 3–3 *How a DB2 Thin Client connects to a DB2 9 data server*

Because DB2 Thin-Client workstations access the DB2 Thin-Client Code Server and dynamically load the DB2 client code when needed, there is a performance hit while the code is retrieved and loaded locally into memory. After the initial loading of required DLLs, the DB2 Thin Client no longer needs to communicate with its associated DB2 Thin-Client Code Server, so there shouldn't be any measurable performance penalty after the first connection is established to the target database.

Database connection for DB2 Thin Client is configured using database configuration information from the DB2 Thin-Client Code Server which acts like a central repository (kind of like an LDAP or Active Directory environment). Remember, the DB2 code is actually run on the DB2 Thin Client: there is no DB2 code installed on the these workstations.

The major advantage of a DB2 Thin-Client solution is that the code is installed (and maintained) at only one location: the DB2 Thin Client Code Server. This gives the benefit of a touch-one, touch-all maintenance plan.

The major drawback of this solution is that it is not suitable for DBAs that want to use graphical tools like the Control Center, and generally it won't yield good results unless the target DB2 Thin-Client workstations are on a local area network (LAN). With the advent of packaged DB2 drivers, this installation is being used less and less; however, it still offers the aforementioned advantages.

Roadmap to Distributed Communications

All remote clients use a communications product to support the protocol the client uses when accessing a remote database server. This protocol support is either part of the client's operating system (typically the case with today's systems) or available as a separate product. The protocol stack you intend to use to support client communications must be installed and configured before a remote client can communicate with a remote DB2 data server. With networked computers today, existing machines likely have TCP/IP installed and therefore it's pretty much your only choice for DB2 communications as DB2 9 only supports TCP/IP and Named Pipes (only available on Windows).

DB2 provides a number of methods that you can use to configure remote clients that want to access DB2 data servers. Though the methods may differ, and the one you choose is based on the scope of the configuration task you are trying to solve, the steps are basically the same:

- Make sure that the communication product is installed and configured on the client workstation. For example, can the client and server workstations on your network ping each other?
- Perform the communication-specific steps. For example, when you configure DB2 communications for TCP/IP, you need to update the services file on the data server with the port number that the data server is listening on (if you are using the Database Partitioning Facility, you will likely need to define a port range). If you installed a DB2 data server using the DB2 Installation program, this is likely already done for you.
- Catalog the remote data server node. This is the data server to which you want to establish the connection represented in the communication infrastructure.
- Catalog the remote database. This is the database that resides on the data server node server (previous bullet) to which you want to establish the connection. A DB2 data sever can support both local and remote clients concurrently.

There are several methods that you can use to set up communications between a DB2 client and a DB2 data server. These methods are discussed in this chapter to enable you to decide which is best suited for your requirements. For example, the easiest way to configure a single remote client for communication with a DB2 data server is to use the DB2 Discovery feature and the Configuration Assistant; however, this isn't the most optimal approach for a large-scale deployment of connected clients.

There are four basic methods you can use to connect a DB2 client to a DB2 data server:

- Automated Configuration using DB2 Discovery
- Automated Configuration using Access Profiles
- Manual Configuration using the Configuration Assistant
- Manual Configuration using the Command Line Processor

Automated Configuration Using DB2 Discovery

DB2 Discovery is a helpful concept and feature to understand before attempting to set up any DB2 client connections. The DB2 Discovery feature allows you to automate the configuration of remote clients connecting to DB2 databases. Specifically, it allows you to easily catalog a remote database from a client workstation without having to know any detailed communication information or typing a command on a command line processor (CLP). Because of its interactive nature, this method is well suited for configuring a limited number of clients for communications. For larger-scale solutions, you should consider using Access Profiles or the CATALOG CLP commands in a batch script of some sort.

The way DB2 Discovery works is pretty simple. A DB2 client with the Configuration Assistant installed uses the DB2 Discovery feature to broadcast requests for DB2 data server connection information. DB2 data servers that are configured to respond to these requests subsequently return required connection information to the Configuration Assistant issuing the discovery request.

The returned data includes:

- The instances on the DB2 data server that have discovery enabled and information about the protocols that each instance supports for client connections
- The databases defined within these instances that have discovery enabled, including the name and description for each available database

DB2 Discovery offers granular controls that allow DBAs to selectively ask specific DB2 data servers, their instances, or their databases not to respond to these broadcasts. Details on these settings are covered in the "Configuring DB2 Discovery" section later in this chapter.

DB2 Discovery can operation in one of two modes as shown in Figure 3–4.

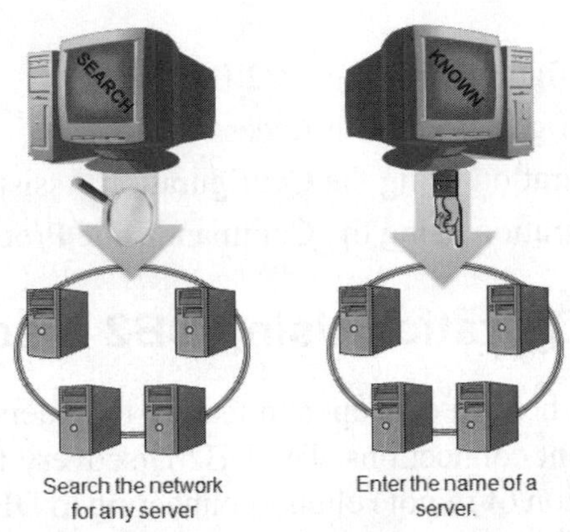
SEARCH
KNOWN
Search the network
for any server
Enter the name of a
server.

Figure 3–4 *DB2 Discovery SEARCH and KNOWN methods*

As Figure 3–4 illustrates, the SEARCH discovery method searches the network for valid DB2 database servers that a client workstation can access. You do not need to provide any configuration details. The remote client, using the Configuration Assistant, searches the network to obtain a list of valid servers. In the KNOWN discovery method, you must provide information about the server that you want to access, specifically the server name.

DB2 Note

You can also use the Control Center to exploit the DB2 Discovery feature and add servers to this tool for remote management or profile creation.

Configuring DB2 Discovery

As previously mentioned, DB2 Discovery offers granular controls that allow DBAs to selectively ask specific DB2 data servers, their instances, or their databases not to respond to these broadcasts.

The discover configuration parameter is the most important parameter as it controls the way DB2 Discovery feature works. This parameter is set in the DB2 Administration Server (DAS) configuration file and it instructs DB2 how to make DB2 Discovery requests. If DISCOVER=SEARCH (the default setting), a client can issue search discovery requests to find DB2 data server systems on the network. If DISCOVER=KNOWN, only known discovery requests can be issued from the client. When DISCOVER=DISABLE, discovery is disabled at the client. SEARCH discovery provides a superset of the functionality provided by KNOWN discovery. If DISCOVER=SEARCH, both search and known discovery requests can be issued by the client.

DB2 *Note*

In addition to having an installed and configured TCP/IP or Named Pipes communication infrastructure running, various parameters need to be correctly configured for DB2 Discovery to work. As mentioned previously, as long as DB2 is installed after the communications protocols have been installed and configured on your operating system, DB2 communications (as well as DB2 Discovery-related parameters) should be set automatically. However, if you add a new communications protocol after DB2 is installed, or if DB2 Discovery is not working, you may need to check these parameter settings.

The next level of DB2 Discovery configuration controls the instances that can be discovered. By setting the DISCOVER_INST database manager configuration parameter, you can configure an instance to not respond to these requests, thereby restricting discovery of its databases as well.

Finally, a level of security control is provided at the database level. You use the DISCOVER_DB database configuration parameter to restrict discovery responses at the database level. For example, you could have only a specific database in an instance that has four databases respond to DB2 Discovery requests.

DB2 Discovery is not supported for databases that reside on DB2 for z/OS or DB2 for i5/OS data servers. However, if you have a DB2 Connect server already configured with connections to either of these data servers, DB2 Discovery will discover the associated DB2 Connect servers. You can then choose to connect through the DB2 Connect server or use its information to configure a direct connection to the remote database (assuming you have the appropriate DB2 Connect software installed on your local client machine.

Figure 3–5 illustrates the hierarchal manner in which you configure DB2 data servers to respond to DB2 Discovery requests.

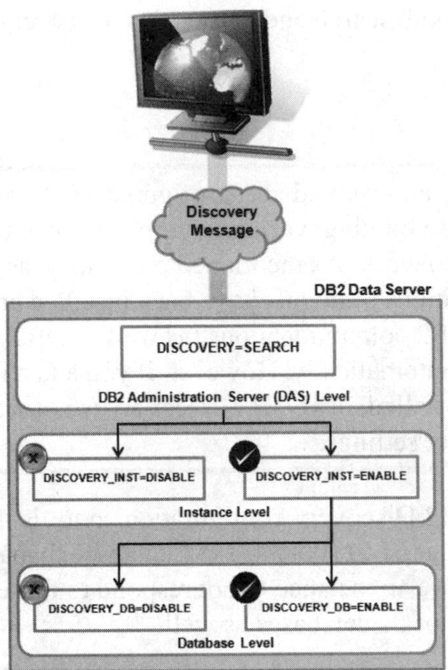

Figure 3–5 *DB2 Discovery hierarchy*

An Example of Configuring DB2 Discovery

The way that DB2 Discovery operates is specified in the *administration configuration* file. This file is similar to the *database manager configuration* file you use to configure a DB2 instance, but it's specifically designed for DAS administration.

The DAS's configuration can only be maintained through a CLP session. This can be a source of confusion because there are DB2 Discovery-related settings that occur at the database manager configuration (instance) and database configuration levels in addition to configuring the DAS.

For example, to set `DISCOVER=SEARCH` and `DISCOVER_COMM=TCP/IP` from a CLP session, enter the following commands:

```
UPDATE ADMIN CFG USING DISCOVER SEARCH
UPDATE ADMIN CFG USING DISCOVER_COMM TCPIP
```

To view the parameter values currently set for the DAS service, enter the following command:

```
GET ADMIN CFG
```

DB2 *Note*

In the previous commands, the `cfg` key word was used: this is short for `CONFIGURATION`. You can use either when entering a DB2 command that requires this keyword.

To configure the discovery of an instance or database, you could use the CLP to interact with the *database manager configuration* and *database configuration files*, or one of the graphical tools.

For example, Figure 3–6 shows how you would configure the `SAMPLE` database, located in the `TEST` instance, for discovery. This figure shows that currently the `TEST` instance will respond to discovery requests, and it will also surface the `SAMPLE` database that's located within it.

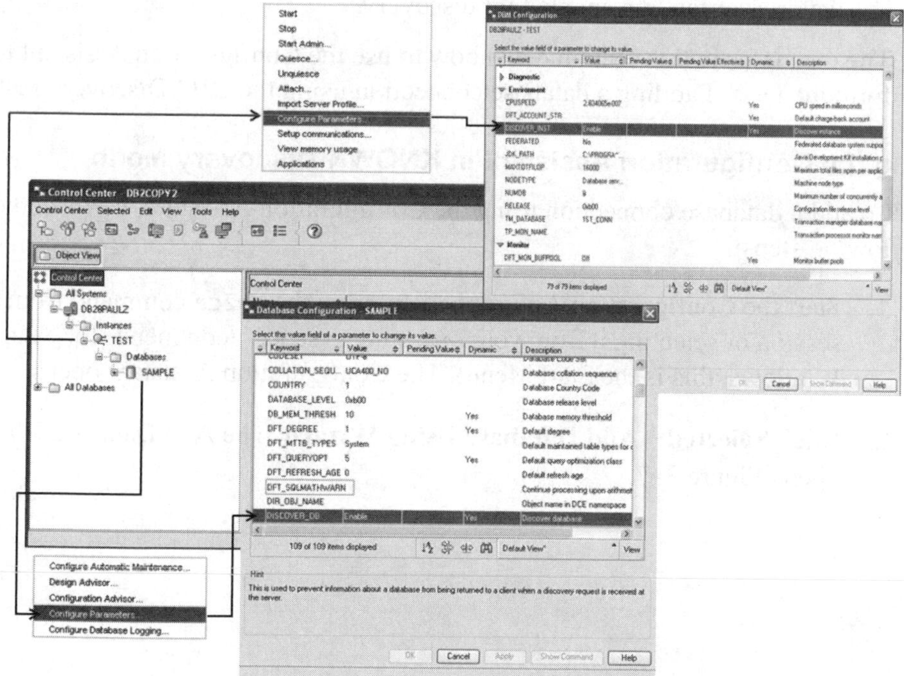

Figure 3–6 *Configuring instances and databases to respond to DB2 Discovery*

DB2 Note

The DAS service must be configured and running on each DB2 data server you wish to locate in this manner. If you installed a DB2 data server using the DB2 installation program, this should be the default. You can start a DAS by entering the `DB2ADMIN START` command from a CLP session.

Using the Automated Configuration Method

You can use the DB2 Discovery function through the Configuration Assistant or the Control Center to automate the addition of remote DB2 databases. This can be done in one of two ways:

1. Using the *Known discovery* method by entering the target data server's hostname, at which point DB2 will automatically return the instances and databases on that machine that are enabled for discovery.
2. Using the *Search discovery* method to search the network for data servers, at which point DB2 will automatically return the instances and databases for each data server that are enabled for discovery.

The examples in this section detail how to use the Configuration Assistant to perform the task of adding a database connection using the DB2 Discovery feature.

Using the Configuration Assistant in KNOWN Discovery Mode

To add a database connection using the Configuration Assistant, perform the following steps:

1. Start the Configuration Assistant by entering the `db2ca` command from a CLP session or selecting it from your operating system's icon menu (for example, in Windows, this is the Start Menu). The Configuration Assistant opens.
2. Click **Selected→Add Database Using Wizard**. The Add Database Wizard opens Figure 3–7.

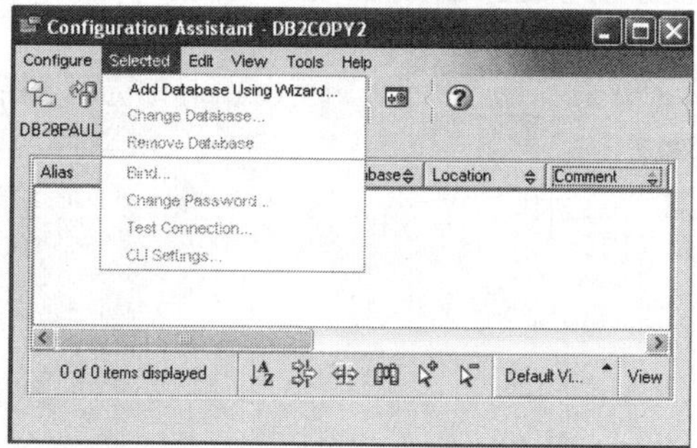

Figure 3–7 *Adding a database using the Configuration Assistant*

If no databases are cataloged on the client, the Welcome window is displayed; otherwise, the databases that are cataloged on the client workstation are shown.

DB2 *Note*

If you start this utility on a server, and you created the SAMPLE database, you will see an entry for that database automatically since it is local and you don't have to add local databases to the Configuration Assistance.

3. Select **Search the network** to use the DB2 Discovery feature to add a database connection to your client workstation and click **Next** (Figure 3–8).

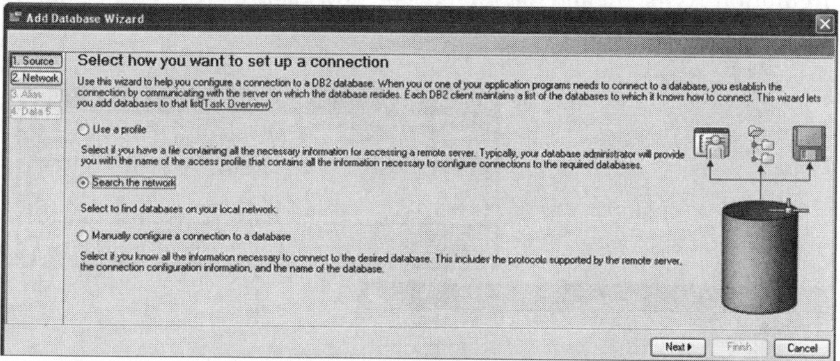

Figure 3–8 *Selecting how you want to find or specify a database connection*

4. Double-click **Known systems** and expand the list of data servers already known to your client (Figure 3–9).

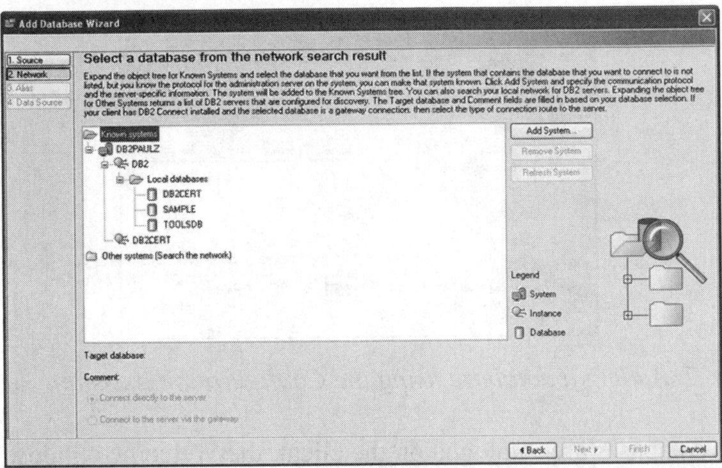

Figure 3–9 *Using Known discovery to find a DB2 database*

DB2 Note

In Figure 3-9, the Configuration Assistant was started on a workstation where we installed a DB2 data server. This is why you see the data server, instances, and databases under the **Known systems** folder.

5. Click **Add System** to add a data server to the **Known systems** folder. The Add system window opens (Figure 3–10).

6. Enter the required information for the data server you want known to the Configuration Assistant and click **OK**. The new data server is now added to the **Known systems** folder.

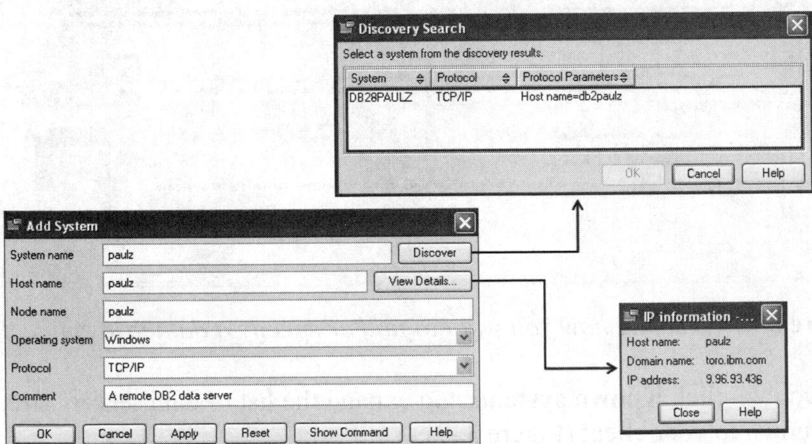

Figure 3–10 *Adding a data server to the KNOWN discovery list*

You can also use the **Discover** and **View Details** buttons in Figure 3-10 to find information about data servers on your network.

7. Select the database that you want to add a connection to and click **Next** (Figure 3–11).

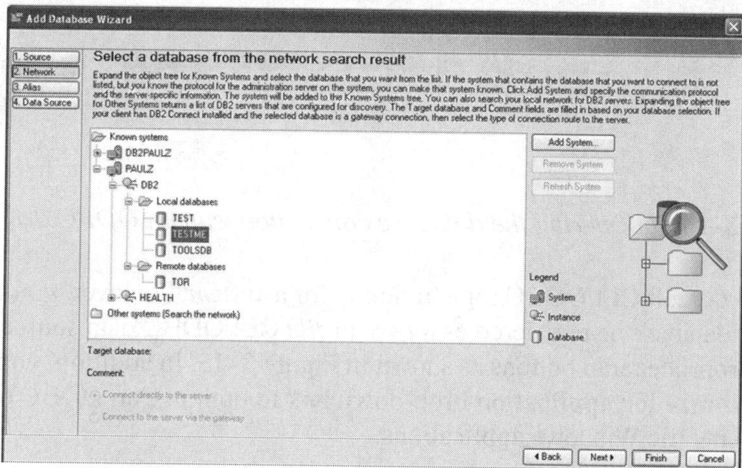

Figure 3–11 *Adding a new database connection using Known discovery*

8. Enter a database alias name for the database connection you want to add in the **Database alias** field and an optional accompanying comment in the **Comment** field, and then click **Next** (Figure 3–12).

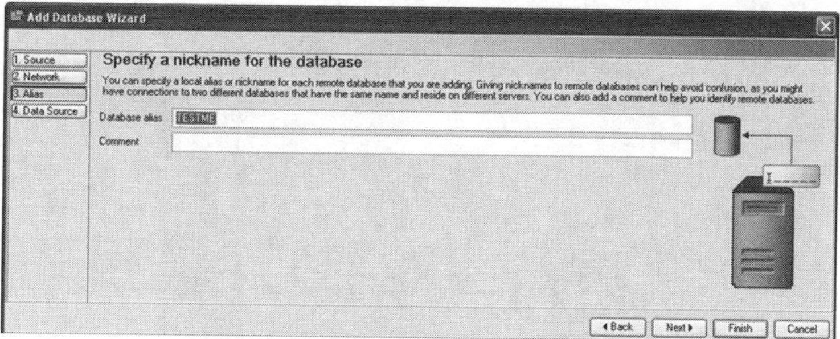

Figure 3–12 *Specifying the database alias for a new database connection*

9. Optionally select the **Register this database for CLI/ODBC** to register the data server with the local ODBC Driver Manager, and click **Finish** (Figure 3–13). The Add Database Confirmation window opens.

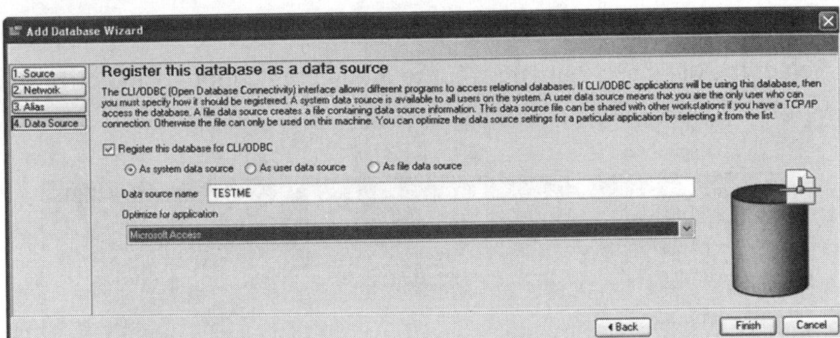

Figure 3–13 *Registering the database connection with an ODBC driver manager*

The default CLI/ODBC registration is for a *system*; however, you can specify this database be registered as a *user* or *file* CLI/ODBC data source using the appropriate radio buttons as shown in Figure 3–13. In addition, you can use the **Optimize for application** drop-down box to optimize an ODBC connection for specific Windows applications.

When the registration process is complete, the ODBC Driver manager will show the cataloged database. Figure 3–14 shows the Windows ODBC Data Source Administrator showing the TESTME database was successfully registered.

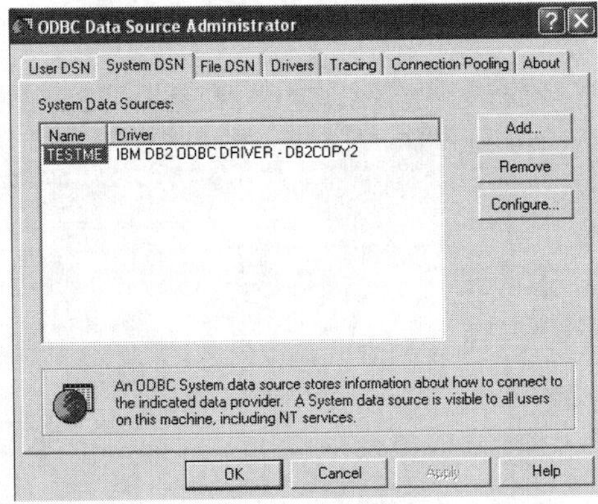

Figure 3–14 *The database automatically registered as an ODBC data source*

10. Click **Test Connection**, select the connection type you want to test, and click **Test Connection** again (Figure 3–15).

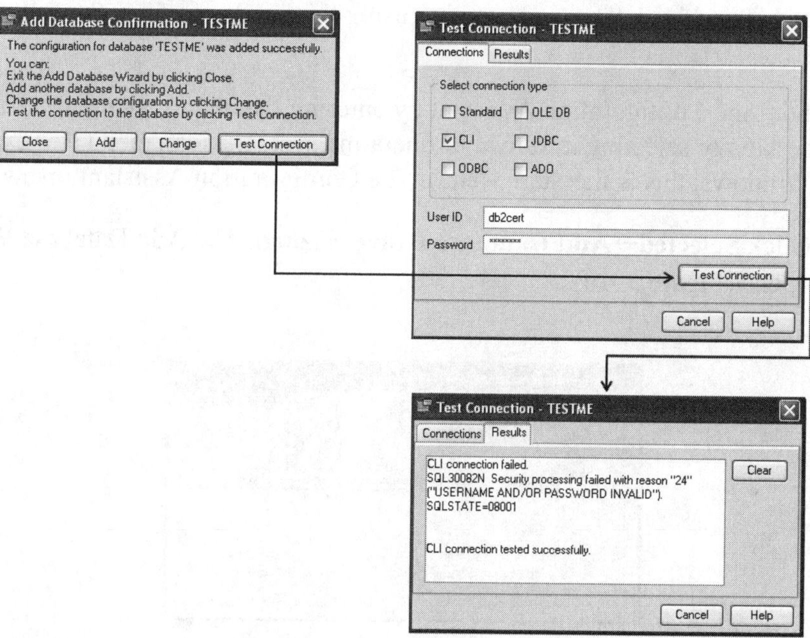

Figure 3–15 *Testing the new database connection*

If the connection is successful, you will receive a message indicating this in the **Results** tab. In Figure 3–15 you can see that we purposely made an initial connection that failed by not providing the correct user account and password. Depending on the authorization setting for the DB2 data server, you have to ensure that the user accounts defined on it support database connections. Since the default authentication type of a DB2 data server is SERVER, the user account specified must exist on the server, not the DB2 client. You learn more about security in Chapter 4.

11. Click **Cancel** then **Close**. If you want to add another database connection, select **Add**. You can change any of the settings you specified by clicking **Change**.

Using the Configuration Assistant in SEARCH Discovery Mode

Adding a database connection using the Search discovery method is very similar to the steps performed to add a database connection using the Known discovery method. To add a database connection using this mode, perform the following steps:

1. Start the Configuration Assistant by entering the `db2ca` command from a CLP session or selecting it from your operating system's icon menu (for example, in Windows, this is the Start Menu). The Configuration Assistant opens.

2. Click **Selected→Add Database Using Wizard**. The Add Database Wizard opens (Figure 3–16).

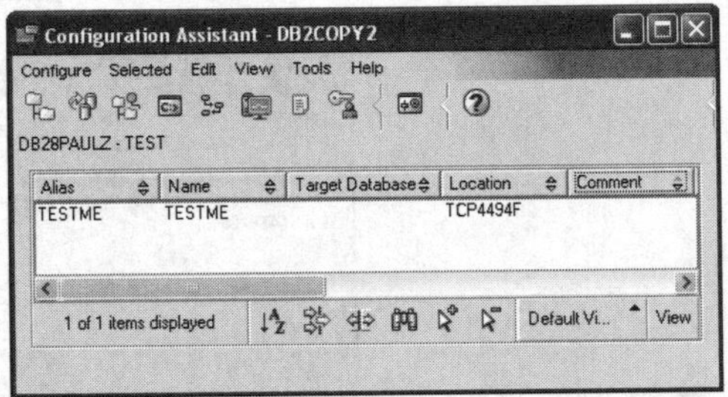

Figure 3–16 *The Configuration Assistant with an existing database connection*

In Figure 3–16 you can see that the `TESTME` database connection added in the previous section is shown.

3. Select **Search the network** to use the DB2 Discovery feature to add a database connection to your client workstation, and click **Next** as you did in the previous section (refer to Figure 3–8 for details).

4. Double-click **Other systems (Search the network)**, which causes the DB2 client to launch a DB2 Discovery request to locate any remote data servers on the network along with their respective instances and databases (Figure 3–17).

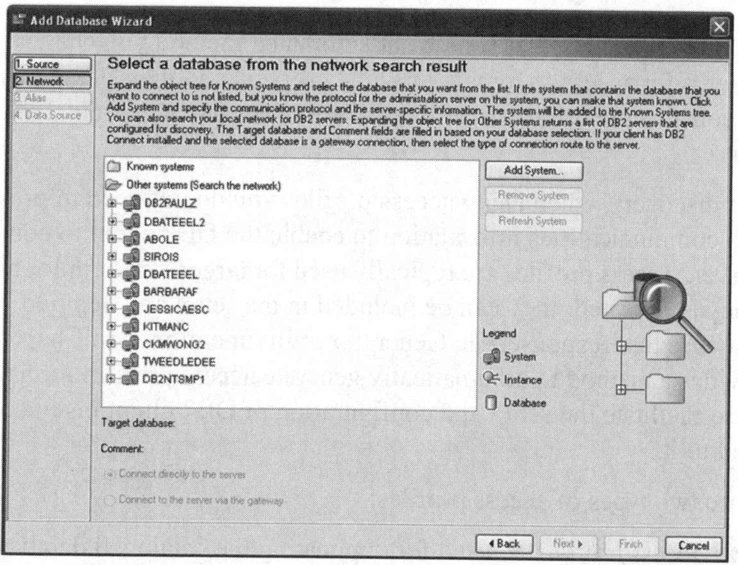

Figure 3–17 *Adding a new database connection using Search discovery*

DB2 *Note*

To avoid network overhead, we recommend that you first check the **Known Systems** folder to ensure that the data server that contains the database you are trying to add is not already known to the client.

In Figure 3–17 you can see that the DB2PAULZ data server (and a number of others) was automatically discovered by the DB2 Discovery process, as opposed to the previous section where configuration details were provided so that the Configuration Assistant could locate it.

Using the Search discovery method may appear to be simpler than Known discovery. However, in larger networks, routers and bridges can filter the messages Search discovery uses to find DB2 data servers on the network. This may result in incomplete or even empty lists. In these cases, use Known discovery. In addition, depending on your network, you may have to wait awhile for this list to populate. Finally, routers and switches can directly impact what data servers are returned to this list. Work with your network administrator if you encounter any difficulties using this option.

5. Complete the same steps you did for adding a database connection using the Known discovery method in the previous section.

Getting Connected

Automated Configuration Using Access Profiles

Access profiles are another somewhat automated method you can use to configure DB2 clients for access to remote DB2 data servers and their databases. An access profile contains the information that a client needs to catalog databases on a DB2 data server.

As with discovery, when using access profiles you do not need to provide any detailed communications information to enable the DB2 client to contact the DB2 data server. Access profiles are typically used for larger-scale deployments because once they are created, they can be included in the setup and deployment process. You may use the Response File Generator utility mentioned in Chapter 2. This utility provides a method to automatically generate access profiles for a target workstation to facilitate the setup and configuration of DB2 client installations that are identical to it.

There are two types of access profiles:

- *Client access profiles* — used for duplicating the cataloged databases and, optionally, the configuration settings for a client (for example, CLI/ODBC settings or local configuration settings)
- *Server access profiles* — used to copy DB2 data server configurations and database connection information for all the instances and databases that the data server has cataloged

Both types of profiles can be exported and then imported to another DB2 system using the Configuration Assistant, Control Center, or CLP command.

DB2 Note

If you have a large number of clients to configure, you should also consider making use of Lightweight Directory Access Protocol (LDAP). This allows you to store catalog information in one centralized location. Each client only needs to know this centralized location to be able to connect to any database that has been made available in the network. DB2 9 comes with a pre-built LDAP plug-in that also supports authentication as well as catalog directory lookup operations. As this is out of the scope of this book, refer to the *DB2 Administration Guide* for more information on this topic.

The generation of an access profile requires that the `DISCOVER` configuration parameter of the DAS service be set to either `SEARCH` or `KNOWN`. When an access profile is generated, it includes all the instances that have `ENABLE` in the `DISCOVER_INST` database manager configuration parameter and all the databases that have the `DISCOVER_DB` database configuration parameter set to `ENABLE`. You can create a profile using the Control Center, the Configuration Assistant, or the DB2CFEXP command.

An access profile is a text-based file, and although you can view it, we recommend not changing it directly. Rather, you should use the response file generator and recreate it with the different options you want.

After you create an access profile, you need to import it to your target workstations. To do this, the profile file must be made available to the DB2 client machine and imported using the Configuration Assistant, or using the DB2CFIMP command from a deployment script or CLP session.

Using the Configuration Assistant to Export a Client Profile

You can create a client profile using the Configuration Assistant, the Control Center (if you are profiling a server that you want to act as a client), or the DB2CFEXP command. During the profile creation process, the information necessary to create a connection between the client and server is created along with additional optional information such as the DB2 registry and configuration settings. The information in the client profile can subsequently be imported to configure other clients.

To create a client profile using the Configuration Assistant, perform the following steps:

1. Start the Configuration Assistant by entering the db2ca command from a CLP session or selecting it from your operating system's icon menu (for example, in Windows, this is the Start Menu). The Configuration Assistant opens.

2. Click **Configure→Export Profile** and select either **All**, **Database Connection**, or **Customize**. For this example, select Customize. The Customize Export Profile window opens (Figure 3–18).

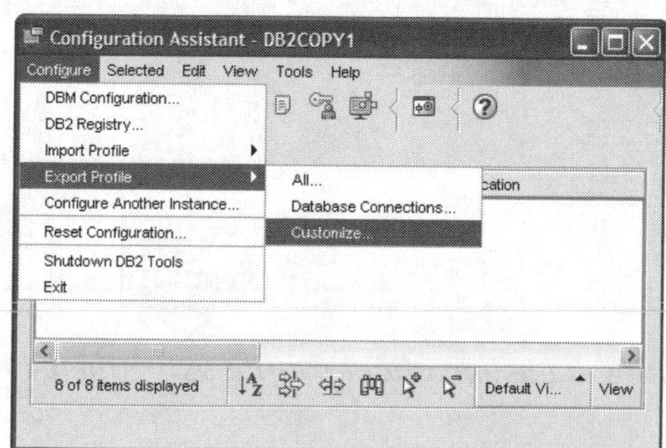

Figure 3–18 *Creating a custom client profile using the Configuration Assistant*

You can see in Figure 3–18 that you can select from one of three options when creating a client profile:

- **All** — creates a profile that contains all the databases cataloged on the workstation including all configuration information for the client
- **Database connection information** — creates a profile that contains all of the databases cataloged on the workstation without any client configuration information
- **Customize** — allows you to create a profile that contains specific databases and/or configuration information for the workstation

3. Enter a path and name for the client profile in the **File name** field, select the components you want the profile to contain, and then click **Export**. Focus will shift to the **Results** tab, which indicates whether or not the operation completed successfully.

You can see in Figure 3–19 that you have a lot of options to include or exclude from your client profile. To include database connection information, you must select **Database connections** and move the databases that you want included in the profile to the **Selected database aliases** box; notice that a single client profile can include multiple databases.

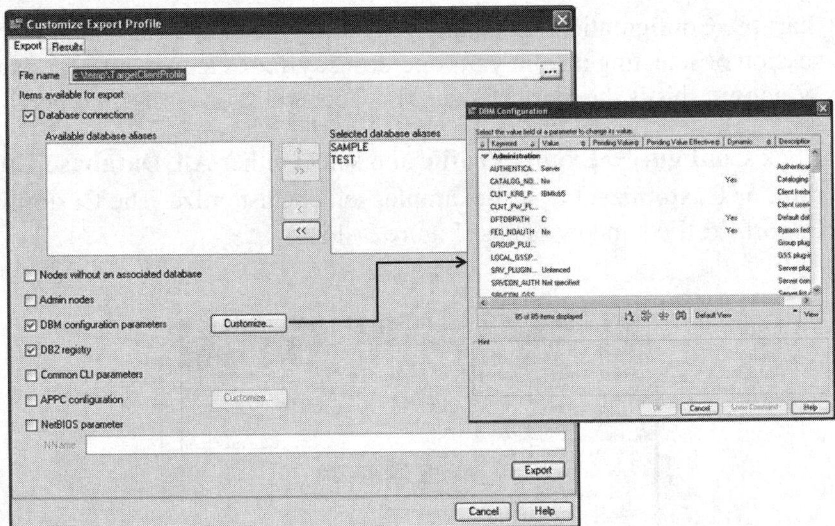

Figure 3–19 *Creating a custom client profile using the Configuration Assistant*

In addition, you can optionally include configuration information such as DB2 registry and configuration parameters. In fact, you can even override the configuration settings on the profiled client by clicking **Customize** beside **DBM configuration**

parameters. Any changes to these configuration parameters take effect only for clients deployed with this profile; the configuration for the client being profiled remains unchanged.

Figure 3–20 show parts of a client profile.

```
;Use BINARY file transfer

[FILE_DESCRIPTION]
APPLICATION=DB2/NT 9.1.2
FILE_CONTENT=DB2 CA Exported Data Sources
FILE_TYPE=CommonServer
FILE_FORMAT_VERSION=2.0
Platform=5
DB2SYSTEM=DB2PAULZ
Instance=DB2_011

[REGISTRY_GLOBAL]
DB2_EXTSECURITY=YES
DB2INSTDEF=DB2

[REGISTRY_LOCAL]
DB2ACCOUNTNAME=DB2PAULZ\db2cert
DB2INSTOWNER=DB2CERT
DB2PORTRANGE=62304:62307
DB2COMM=TCPIP

[DBM_CONFIG]
NODETYPE=4
RELEASE=0xb00
DIAGLEVEL=3
RQRIOBLK=32767
DOS_RQRIOBLK=4096
AUTHENTICATION=0
DIR_CACHE=1
.
.
.
```

Figure 3–20 *Client profile*

DB2 *Note*

As indicated at the top of any generated profile, remember to use `BINARY` file transfer settings if you are FTPing a generated profile to a target workstation.

Using the Configuration Assistant to Import a Client Profile

You can use a client profile to configure a client's database connection information and configuration by importing it using the Configuration Assistant, the Control

Center (if you profiled a server that you want to act as a client), or the `DB2CFIMP` command.

To create a client profile using the Configuration Assistant, perform the following steps:

1. Start the Configuration Assistant by entering the `db2ca` command from a CLP session or selecting it from your operating system's icon menu (for example, in Windows, this is the Start Menu). The Configuration Assistant opens.

2. Click **Configure→Import Profile** and select either the **All** or **Customize** options. For this example, select **Customize**. The Customize Import Profile window opens (Figure 3–21).

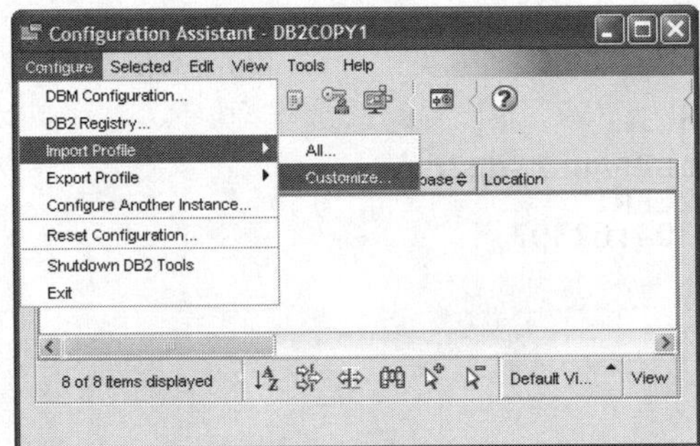

Figure 3–21 *Customizing the import process of a client profile*

In the same way that you can customize the creation of a client profile, when you import one you can choose to import all of the profile's information (both database connection and configuration) or a subset of it.

3. Select the client profile using the Ellipsis (…) or directly enter the name of the client profile in the **File name** field and click **Load**. The **Items available for import** fields are populated with information from the client profile (Figure 3–22).

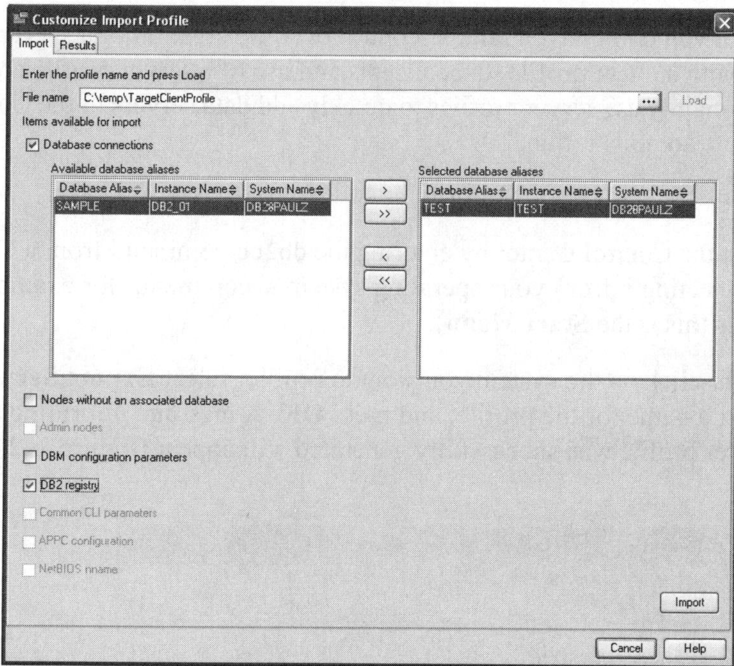

Figure 3–22 *Selecting the information you want to import from a client profile*

Notice in Figure 3–21 that we chose to only import a single database connection from the client profile despite the fact that it contained connection information for two separate databases. In addition, this particular client profile happens to contains DB2 registry and configuration information (you can see these options enabled for selection in Figure 3–20), yet we chose to only import the DB2 registry settings.

4. Select the components you want to import from this client profile and click **Import**. If successful, you will receive the following message. Now click **Cancel** (Figure 3–23).

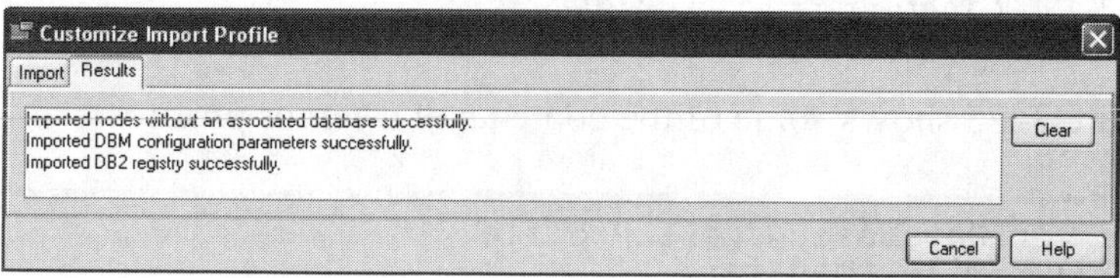

Figure 3–23 *Success! An imported client profile*

Using the Control Center to Export and Import a Server Profile

Although you don't have granular control over the creation of a server profile like you do with a client profile, the concepts and use of a server profile are very similar. You mainly use server profiles to quickly add data servers to the Control Center for remote administration.

To create a server profile, perform the following steps:

1. Start the Control Center by entering the `db2cc` command from a CLP session or selecting it from your operating system's icon menu (for example, in Windows this is the **Start Menu**).
2. Right-click on the system you want to profile, select **Export Server Profile**, enter a name for the profile, and press **OK**. A message informing you that the server profile was successfully generated will appear (Figure 3–24).

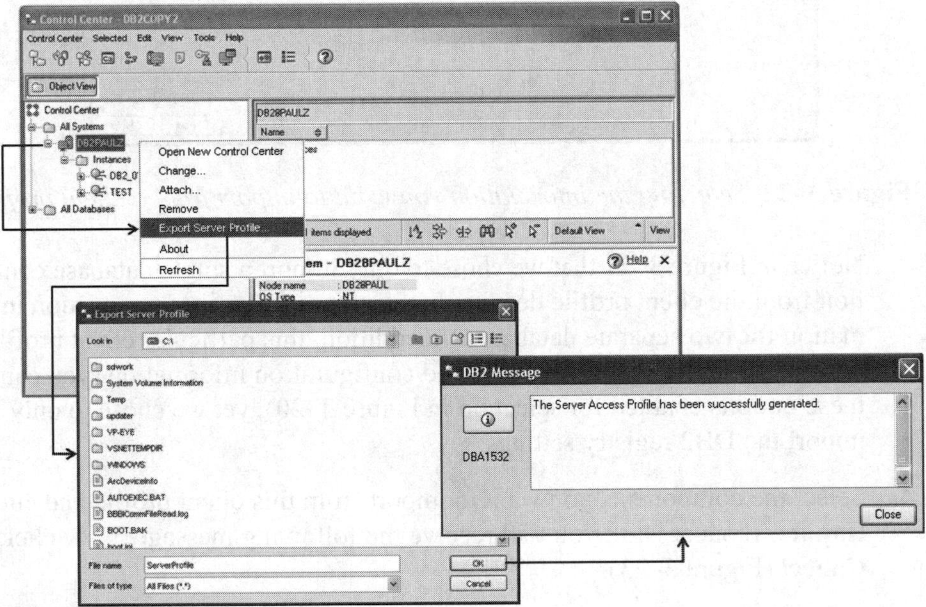

Figure 3–24 *Creating a server profile*

Figure 3–25 shows some of the contents of a server profile:

```
;DB2 Server Database Access Profile
;Use BINARY file transfer
;Comment lines start with a ";"
```

Figure 3–35 *Sample server profile*

```
;Other lines must be one of the following two types:
;   Type A: [section_name] or Type B: keyword=value

[File_Description]
Application=DB2/NT 9.1.2
Platform=5
File_Content=DB2 Server Definitions
File_Type=CommonServer
File_Format_Version=1.0
DB2System=DB2PAULZ
ServerType=DB2NT

[adminst>DB2DAS00]
NodeType=1
DB2Comm=TCPIP
Authentication=SERVER
HostName=db2paulz.torontolab.ibm.com
PortNumber=523
IpAddress=192.123.121.191

[inst>DB2]
NodeType=4
NodeNumber=0
DB2Comm=TCPIP
Authentication=SERVER
HostName=db2paulz.torolab.ibm.com
ServiceName=db2c_DB2
PortNumber=80000
IpAddress=192.123.121.191
QuietMode=No
SPMName=DB28PAUL
TMDatabase=1ST_CONN

[db>DB2:DB2CERT]
DBAlias=DB2CERT
DBName=DB2CERT
Drive=C:
Dir_entry_type=INDIRECT
Authentication=NOTSPEC

[db>DB2:SAMPLE]
DBAlias= SAMPLE
DBName= SAMPLE
Drive=C:
Dir_entry_type=INDIRECT
Authentication=NOTSPEC
```

Figure 3–25 *Sample server profile (continued)*

You can see that this server profile has as single instance called DB2 (also note the DAS instance included in the profile). In this instance are two databases: DB2CERT and SAMPLE.

3. Import the server profile by right-clicking on the first instance in the **Instance** folder, select **Import Server Profile**, select the server profile, and click **OK**, as shown in Figure 3–26.

Getting Connected

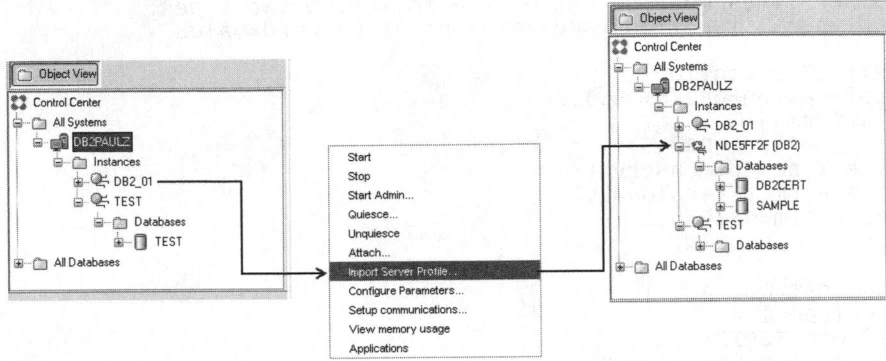

Figure 3–26 *Importing a server profile*

You can see in Figure 3–26 that DB2 automatically generated a node name for the remote system and references the instance it connects to within parentheses. This data server now has access to the DB2CERT and SAMPLE databases that exist on another DB2 data server and can now remotely administer them.

DB2 Note

Although not shown in Figure 3–26, the name of the remote server is also added to the **All systems** folder. Figure 3–26 shows the attached instance within the existing data server.

Using the Configuration Assistant to Import a Server Profile

You can also use the Configuration Assistant to import a server profile so that you can extract database connection information from it. The steps to import a server profile are the same as importing a client profile (see Figure 3–19); however, with a server profile you don't have the ability to import the configuration information as with a client profile.

In addition, you can use the **Add Database wizard** to also add database connections from a server profile by selecting the **Use a profile** radio button in Figure 3–8 by selecting the appropriate database connections you want to import and assigning database alias names to them. The details of this process aren't covered in this chapter because they are a combination of the search and profile options previously discussed and are relatively self-explanatory at this point.

Manual Configuration Using the Configuration Assistant

If you know the connectivity information required to configure communications between DB2 clients and servers, you can still simplify this process by using the Configuration Assistant to add connections without having to memorize command syntax (as in the case with the "Manual Configuration using the Command Line Processor" method covered in the next section).

To manually configure a connection, you must know the following:

- The protocol connection information required to configure the connection to the server instance
- The server name
- The name of the database on the remote data server

You may want to use the Configuration Assistant's manual configuration method for a relatively small number of connections (for example, on a development machine) where the connectivity information is well known to you and you don't want the overhead associated with DB2 Discovery, the target database cannot be discovered because it sits behind a firewall or wasn't configured to respond to DB2 Discovery requests, or you want to exploit some advanced options that are not available using either of the automated methods (for example, you want to alter the default behavior with respect to where authentication should take place).

To manually configure a connection using the Configuration Assistant, perform the following steps:

1. Start the Configuration Assistant by entering the db2ca command from a CLP session or selecting it from your operating system's icon menu (for example, in Windows, this is the **Start Menu**).
2. Click **Selected→Add Database Using Wizard**. The Add Database wizard opens. (This window is the same window shown in Figure 3–7.)
3. Select **Manually configure a connection to a database** and click **Next**. (This window is the same window shown in Figure 3–8.)
4. Select the protocol you want to use to connect to the remote data server (in most cases this will be **TCP/IP**) and click **Next** (Figure 3–27).

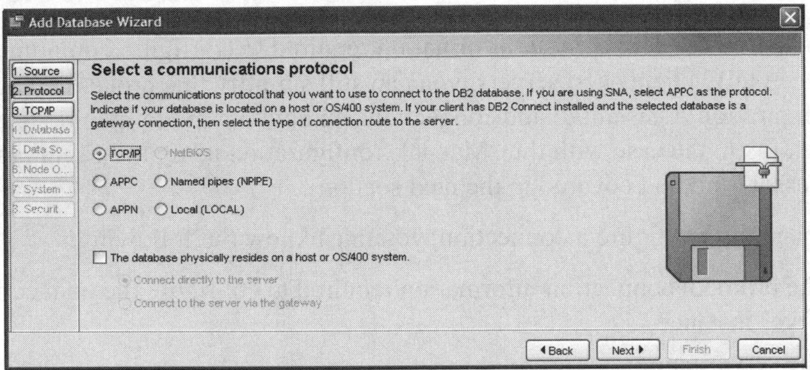

Figure 3–27 *Using the Configuration Assistant to manually add a TCP/IP-based connection to a remote database*

If you want to connect to a DB2 for i5/OS (formerly known as OS/400®) or DB2 for z/OS (formerly known as S/390®) data server, select **The database physically resides on a host or OS/400 system**. If you select this option, you must either choose the **Connect directly to the server** option that makes a direct connection from the client to the remote host or mainframe data server, or the **Connect to the server via the gateway** option. The gateway option makes a connection to a DB2 Connect server, which then handles the communications between the client and the host or mainframe data server. If you select either of these options, you must have a valid DB2 Connect license. If you don't have a valid DB2 Connect license and you choose to make a direct connection to the remote host or mainframe data server, the Configuration Assistant will fail.

DB2 Note

In Figure 3–27 you can see that protocols other than the supported TPC/IP and Named Pipes protocols are shown. This is for backwards compatibility.

5. Enter the required protocol parameters and click **Next** (Figure 3–28).

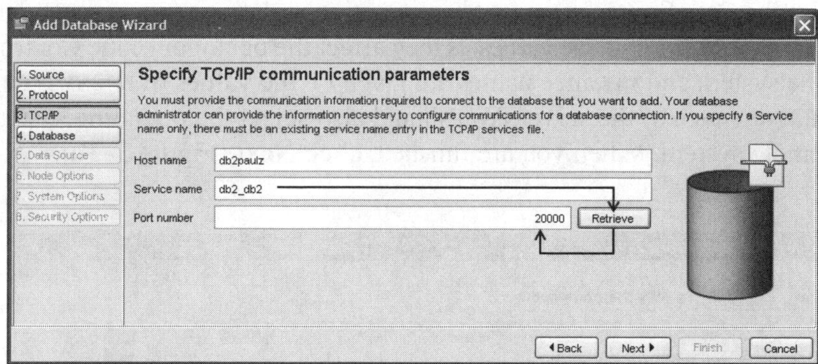

Figure 3–28 *Entering specific protocol information for the database connection*

You don't have to fill in all the fields in Figure 3–28. For example, if you know the port number, you don't need to specify the service name. In addition, if you know the service name, you can resolve the port number using the **Retrieve** button as shown in Figure 3–28. Configuration details of TCP/IP are out of the scope of this book; we're merely trying to illustrate the capabilities and options you have in this section. If you want more details on these related parameters or this process, refer to the *DB2 Installation and Configuration Supplement*.

6. Specify the database name you want to connect to, its alias, and, optionally, a comment describing the connection and click **Next** (Figure 3–29).

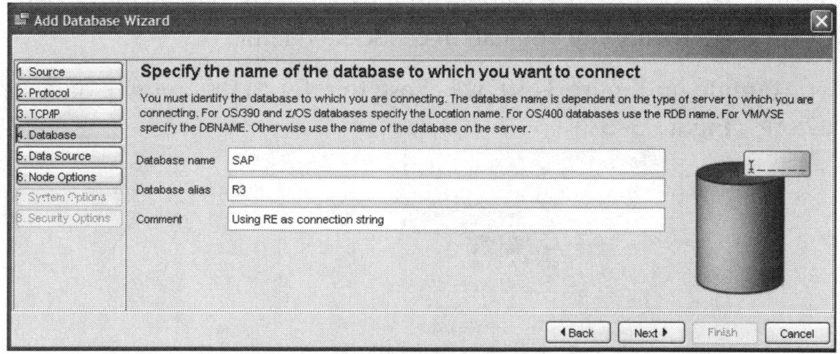

Figure 3–29 *Specifying the target database, alias, and an optional comment*

In Figure 3–29 you can see that although the database we are connecting to is called `SAP`, its alias name, `R3`, will be used for all connections.

7. Optionally register this database connection as an ODBC data source and click **Next**. (Refer to Figure 3–13 for more information.)

8. Use the Data Source window to enter options relating to the remote data server. You should fill in these values as they affect the behavior of the Control Center. The system and instance names are given by the values of `DB2SYSTEM` and `DB2INSTANCE` at the server. You should also select the operating system of the remote system. When you are finished, click **Next** (Figure 3–30).

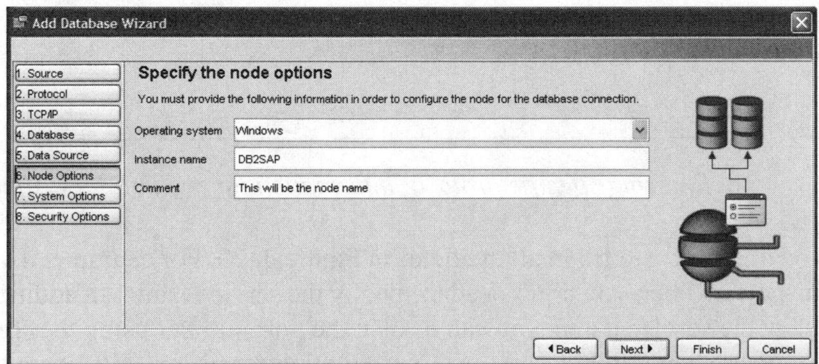

Figure 3–30 *Specifying the type and name of the target data server where the database you want to connect to resides*

Figure 3–30 is a good example of an option you don't get to configure when using any of the previous methods covered in this chapter. If you recall from Figure 3–24, DB2 generated a rather cryptic name of the remote data server and attached the instance name within parenthesis. The manual method gives you a method whereby you can override this name.

For example, in Figure 3–30, we chose to refer to this remote data server as `DB2SAP` (Figure 3–31).

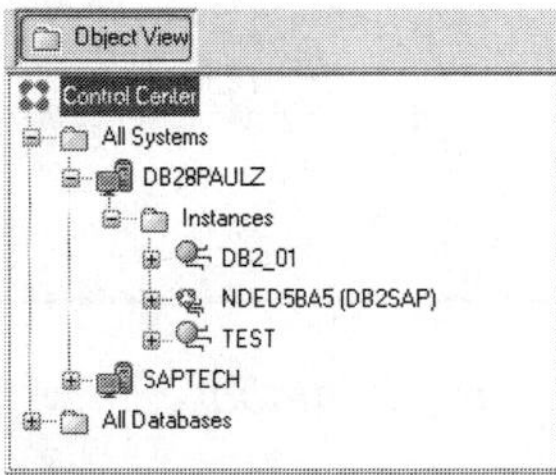

Figure 3–31 *A customized node name*

9. The Systems Options window (not shown) should be pre-filled for you based

on earlier information you supplied. Click **Next**.

10. Specify a security option for this connection and click **Finish** (Figure 3–32).

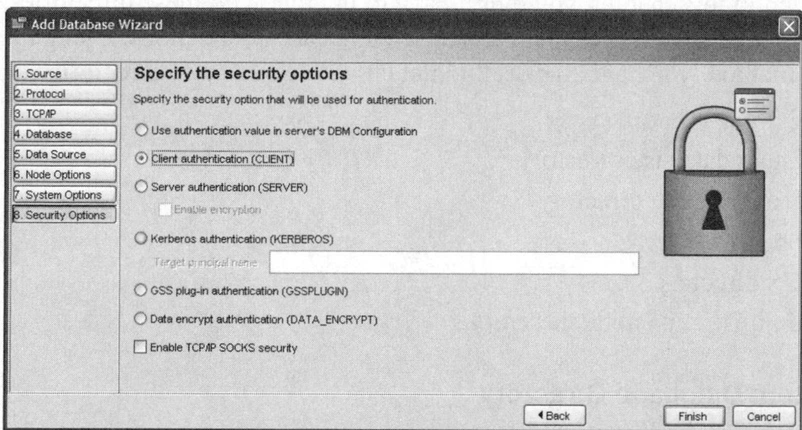

Figure 3–32 *Choosing a security model for the database connection*

You can see in Figure 3–32 that we chose the **Client authentication (CLIENT)** option. If you recall, the first connection in Figure 3–15 received an error that had to do with an incorrect user account and password defined on the server. If that connection had been made with this authentication setting (and the server was configured to allow client connections), it would have worked the first time since authentication would occur on the client.

Generally, client side authentication isn't the best choice for an enterprise; we simply put it here to illustrate the difference. Figure 3–32 shows that you have many options when it comes to authentication for client communications. More details on this topic are out of the scope of this chapter; however, security is covered in Chapter 4.

11. Optionally test the database connection as shown in Figure 3–15.

Manual Configuration Using the Command Line Processor

You can use the `CATALOG NODE` and `CATALOG DATABASE` commands to configure client server connections. This method requires more work and is more prone to errors; however, it gives you the ability to generate rich scripts that can be used in a roll-your-own framework you may have built for this purpose. Generally, this approach is reserved for advanced users, and therefore we only cover the details of this method at a high level.

Access to both local and remote databases uses entries in the DB2 directories. The directories hide the requirement that users or applications know where a database actually resides. Using directories, users are able to connect to local and remote databases by simply specifying the database name. In the previous methods detailed in this chapter, you didn't have to interact with these directories, but each method added entries to them to support database connections. Using the manual CLP method, you have to directly interact with connection directories that include the:

- System database directory
- Local database directory
- Node directory
- DCS directory
- Administration node directory

System Database Directory

The *system database directory* resides in the *SQLDBDIR* subdirectory in the instance directory. This directory is used to catalog both local and remote databases. The directory contains the database name, alias, type, and node where the database resides. If the database is local, a pointer to the local database directory is located in the system database directory. If the database is remote, there is a pointer to the node directory.

Local Database Directory

The *local database directory* resides in every drive/path that contains a database. It's used to access local databases in that subdirectory as each entry contains the database name, alias, type, and location information about the database.

Node Directory

Each database client maintains a *node directory*. The node directory contains entries for all instances that the client will access. The node directory contains communication information about the network connection to the instance. If multiple instances exist on a remote machine, then each instance must be cataloged as a separate node before you are able to access any information contained within the instance.

DCS Directory

The connection information for DB2 for z/OS and DB2 for i5/OS databases is different from the information for DB2 databases running on Linux, UNIX, and Windows. A separate directory maintains this host information. This directory is the *DCS directory*. It only exists if the DB2 Connect product is installed on your system. The DCS directory stores information used by the database manager to access databases on a DRDA Application Server.

Administration Node Directory

The *administration node directory* contains one definition for each remote system that is known to a DB2 client. Most of the entries for this directory are made during product installation, by the Control Center, or by the CA.

Examining DB2 Directories

Consider a scenario with two systems, a data server and a remote client. From the data server, issue the `LIST DATABASE DIRECTORY` command to see the contents of the system database directory as shown in Figure 3–33.

```
 System Database Directory

 Number of entries in the directory = 3

Database 1 entry:
 Database alias                       = DB2CERT
 Database name                        = DB2CERT
 Local database directory             = C:
 Database release level               = b.00
 Comment                              =
 Directory entry type                 = Indirect
 Catalog database partition number    = 0
 Alternate server hostname            =
 Alternate server port number         =
Database 2 entry:

 Database alias                       = TOOLSDB
 Database name                        = TOOLSDB
 Local database directory             = C:
 Database release level               = b.00
 Comment                              =
 Directory entry type                 = Indirect
 Catalog database partition number    = 0
 Alternate server hostname            =
 Alternate server port number         =
Database 3 entry:

 Database alias                       = SAMPLE
 Database name                        = SAMPLE
 Local database directory             = C:
 Database release level               = b.00
 Comment                              = A sample database
 Directory entry type                 = Indirect
 Catalog database partition number    = 0
 Alternate server hostname            =
 Alternate server port number         =
```

Figure 3–33 *Listing the databases cataloged on a workstation*

DB2 Note

You can use the short form db to represent the database keyword when entering DB2 commands from a CLP.

Figure 3–33 shows that there are three databases cataloged on this server. The first database is the DB2CERT database. When a database is created, an entry is automatically placed in the system database directory and the local database directory on the sever. Note the Alternative server hostname and Alternate server port number entries, as these are used to configure automated client reroute to a standby server and are automatically populated at database connection time (assuming the data server is configured for failover).

If you wanted more details, you can issue the LIST DB DIRECTORY ON <PATH> command as shown in Figure 3–34.

```
 Local Database Directory on C:\

 Number of entries in the directory = 3

Database 1 entry:
 Database alias                         = DB2CERT
 Database name                          = DB2CERT
 Local database directory               = SQL00003
 Database release level                 = b.00
 Comment                                =
 Directory entry type                   = Home
 Catalog database partition number      = 0
 Database partition number              = 0

Database 2 entry:

 Database alias                         = TOOLSDB
 Database name                          = TOOLSDB
 Local database directory               = SQL00001
 Database release level                 = b.00
 Comment                                =
 Directory entry type                   = Home
 Catalog database partition number      = 0
 Database partition number              = 0

Database 3 entry:

 Database alias                         = SAMPLE
 Database name                          = SAMPLE
 Local database directory               = SQL00002
 Database release level                 = b.00
 Comment                                = A sample database
 Directory entry type                   = Home
 Catalog database partition number      = 0
 Database partition number              = 0
```

Figure 3–34 *Getting even more details about the database directory*

If you were to run these commands from a client workstation (such that it had no local databases) you would not see the fields that relate to a database in Figure 3–34; rather, you would see the node name that's used to represent the remote data server where the database you are trying to connect to is located, as shown in Figure 3–35.

```
Database 6 entry:

 Database alias                          = TOR
 Database name                           = TOR
 Node name                               = TPCE379
 Database release level                  = b.00
 Comment                                 = SAP database TOR
 Directory entry type                    = Remote
 Catalog database partition number       = -1
 Alternate server hostname               =
 Alternate server port number            =
```

Figure 3–35 *The LIST DB DIRECTORY command from a client*

Figure 3–35 shows part of the output from the `LIST DB DIRECTORY ON` command on a machine where only a DB2 client is installed. You can see that the TOR database resides on a server known to this client as `TCPE379`, and an optional comment describing what that server does is there as well (since it isn't evident by the database name or database alias name). Also note that the `DIRECTORY ENTRY TYPE` is `REMOTE` for a remote connection and `INDIRECT` for a local connection on a server.

When cataloging a remote database on a client, the database name on that client must match the database alias on the server. The database alias specified on the client workstation is used in the `CONNECT TO` statement. Therefore, if the name used to connect to the `TOR` database in Figure 3–35 is `TOR`, you would have to use the `CONNECT TO R3` for the database connection defined in Figure 3–29.

There is always an associated node name with a client system database directory entry. The node name (in this example `TCPE379`) defines the location of the remote DB2 data server on the network.

To discover more information about the location of the database server, you can examine that node's directory information using the `LIST NODE DIRECTORY` command as shown in Figure 3–36.

```
 Node Directory

 Number of entries in the directory = 2

Node 1 entry:
 Node name                                  = TPCE379
 Comment                                    =
 Directory entry type                       = LOCAL
 Protocol                                   = TCPIP
 Hostname                                   = saptech
 Service name                               = 5912

Node 2 entry:

 Node name                                  = Test
 Comment                                    =
 Directory entry type                       = LOCAL
 Protocol                                   = LOCAL
 Instance name                              = TEST
```

Figure 3–36 *Viewing the node directory*

The first entry in the node directory shown in Figure 3–36 is for the workstation that corresponds to a TCP/IP connection. The TCP/IP host name for the DB2 server is SAPTECH and the service name is 5912. The TCP/IP information in the client's node directory must match the information in the server's database manager configuration file.

In this example, the port number was used in place of the service name. You can use this shortcut if you know the details of the remote data server. There are other options available when cataloging a database and node, such as where authentication takes place. These options are explained in Chapter 4. Again, since this method of configuration is for more advanced users, it's outside the scope of this chapter to go into details of this approach other than to introduce you to the high-level concepts associated with it.

Using the CATALOG Commands

You use the CATALOG NODE and CATALOG DATABASE commands from a DB2 CLP, a script file, or the DB2 Command Center to manually add a remote database connection. Before cataloging a remote database, you should check that the client machine can communicate with the remote DB2 server. The client must then catalog the remote node and the remote database.

DB2 Note

The CATALOG commands support advanced options such as retrieving connection information from an LDAP server and the ability to use IPv6 addresses. For details on these cataloging options, please refer to the *DB2 Command Reference*.

Cataloging a TCP/IP Node

When cataloging a client to use TCP/IP to communicate with a DB2 data server, you must catalog the node as type TCPIP as well as a unique name within the client node directory using the CATALOG DATABASE command.

To catalog the TCP/IP node used in Figure 3–36, you would enter a command similar to the following:

```
CATALOG TCPIP NODE TCPE379 REMOTE PAULZ SERVER 20000
```

In the previous example, TCPE379 is the name you assign to the node. REMOTE is a keyword that provides the catalog entry with the hostname, though you could directly use the IP address of the remote DB2 data server (you may need to fully qualify it, for example, *paul.torontolab.com*). The SERVER keyword in this example denotes the port number that the data server is listening on for incoming data requests (though it could have been the *service name* that would use the services file to map this port number). Once the node has been cataloged, you can then catalog the remote database.

Cataloging a Named Pipe Node

Named Pipes is a communication protocol whose support in DB2 is only available on Windows. When cataloging a Named Pipe node to communicate with a DB2 data server, you must specify parameters such that DB2 can locate the computer name of the data server and the instance where the target database resides. You register this information in the node directory in a similar fashion to TCP/IP connections, except you use the CATALOG NPIPE NODE command. This node name will also be used in the CATALOG DATABASE command and must be unique in the client node directory.

For example, to catalog a Named Pipes node, you would enter a command similar to the following:

```
CATALOG NPIPE NODE MYNODE REMOTE LITTLECHLOE INSTANCE DB2
```

In the previous example, MYNODE is the name you assign to the node. REMOTE is a keyword that provides the catalog entry with the Windows Computer Name (specified in the **Computer Name** tab in the **My Computer** properties in Windows XP) of the DB2 data server, and INSTANCE denotes the instance where the database you want to connect to resides. Once the node has been cataloged, you can then catalog the remote database.

Cataloging a Database

Once you've cataloged a node entry for a remote data server, you've essentially told the DB2 client software how to find the remote data server on the network. To make a connection to a database, you need to tell DB2 what database you want to connect to, by what name it will be known to your local applications, and where the database is located on the network (the node name).

You catalog a database using the CATALOG DATABASE command as follows:

```
CATALOG DATABASE DATABASENAME AS DATABASE_ALIAS AT NODE_NAME
```

For example, to catalog the TOR database in Figure 3–35 whose location is identified at node TCPE379 you would enter the following command:

```
CATALOG DATABASE TOR AS TOR AT TCPE379
```

DB2 *Note*

If you plan to use the same database alias name as the database name, you can omit the AS clause since the default database alias name is the database name. For example, in the previous example, you could enter: CATALOG DATABASE TOR AT TCPE379.

Once the database is cataloged, you can connect to it using the database alias name with the following command:

```
CONNECT TO DATABASE_ALIAS USER USER_NAME USING PASSWORD
```

If you don't use the database alias name to connect to the database, you will receive an error as shown in the scenario illustrated in Figure 3–37.

```
list db directory;

System Database Directory

 Number of entries in the directory = 1

Database 1 entry:
 Database alias                        = SAMPOTHR
 Database name                         = SAMPLE
 Local database directory              = C:
 Database release level                = b.00
 Comment                               =
 Directory entry type                  = Indirect
 Catalog database partition number     = 0
 Alternate server hostname             =
 Alternate server port number          =

connect to sample;

SQL1013N The database alias name or database name "SAMPLE"
could not be found. SQLSTATE=42705

connect to sampothr;

   Database Connection Information

 Database server        = DB2/NT 9.1.2
 SQL authorization ID   = DB2CERT
 Local database alias   = SAMPOTHR
```

Figure 3–37 *Connecting with the proper database alias name*

Summary of Configuring Connections

Choosing a client configuration method will depend on the number of database clients, the number of different configurations needed, and network complexity. Table 3–1 gives general recommendations on when to use each configuration method.

Table 3–1 *Connection Considerations*

Environment Considerations	Configuration Method
Large number of clients to configure. Clients may have access to different databases.	Server Access Profile
Large number of clients to configure. Clients will have access to the same databases.	Client Access Profile
Large network with many routers and bridges.	Known discovery
Simple network. Many clients. Dynamic environment, new servers added frequently.	Search discovery
Experienced DBA. Know the connectivity information from memory. Development environment.	Manually from Configuration Assistant
Need to be able to redo the setup using scripts.	Manual using CLP

Binding Utilities

When a remote client wants access to a data server, the database utilities must be bound on the server for the client to use. The most important database utilities that a remote client must bind to a DB2 server include:

- CLI/ODBC support
- DB2 Command Line Processor
- Data import/export utilities

If you create a new database on a server, packages for the database utilities must also be created in the system catalog tables. All of the client utility packages are contained in a file called DB2UBIND.LST. Call Level Interface and ODBC packages are grouped together in the DB2CLI.LST file. These packages can be created by executing the BIND command from the client workstation after a connection has been made to the data server.

The BIND command must be run separately for each database that you wish to access. Once a package has been successfully bound to the database, all DB2 clients can access it. If you have different types or versions of clients on your network, you must bind the utilities from each type and version of the client.

DB2 Note

Bind files can be different for each client platform and each version of DB2. You have to bind these files for each platform you want to use. Every time you install an update to a DB2 product that comes with new bind files, you have to bind these new files as well. With recent versions of DB2 (and planned point releases), the amount of manual binding you have to do is less and less. However, we recommend you bind packages just in case. For the most up-to-date information on the packages that need to be bound to the DB2 software, refer to the product *README* file.

Figure 3–38 shows an example of binding a Windows client to the SAMPLE database that resides on a Windows-based data server.

```
bind @db2ubind.lst blocking all grant public

LINE    MESSAGES FOR db2ubind.lst
------  --------------------------------------------------------
        SQL0061W  The binder is in progress.

LINE    MESSAGES FOR db2clpnc.bnd
------  --------------------------------------------------------
        SQL0595W  Isolation level "NC" has been escalated to "UR".
                  SQLSTATE=01526

LINE    MESSAGES FOR db2arxnc.bnd
------  --------------------------------------------------------
        SQL0595W  Isolation level "NC" has been escalated to "UR".
                  SQLSTATE=01526

LINE    MESSAGES FOR db2ubind.lst
------  --------------------------------------------------------
        SQL0091N  Binding was ended with "0" errors and "2" warnings.
```

Figure 3–38 *Binding client utilities to a remote database*

As you can see, the output of the BIND command defaults to your display terminal; however, you can direct the contents to a file using the MESSAGES parameter. In addition, the file you want to bind must be in the same directory where the BIND command is run (or explicitly pointed to in the command). For example, if you wanted to run the same command in Figure 3–38 but were in the *D:\Program Files\IBM\SQLLIB* directory, you would have to enter this command as follows:

```
DB2 BIND BND\@DB2UBIND.LST BLOCKING ALL GRANT PUBLIC
```

You can see in Figure 3–38 that the `GRANT PUBLIC` option of the `BIND` command was used. This option provides `EXECUTE` and `BIND` privileges to all users that can access the database. (You should also be aware that there are different `BIND` command options for DB2 for z/OS and DB2 for i5/OS data servers; refer to the *DB2 Command Reference* for more information).

The @ symbol in Figure 3–38 is used to specify that `DB2UBIND.LST` is a list of bind files and not a bind file itself. You can verify this by looking at the contents of this file shown in Figure 3–39.

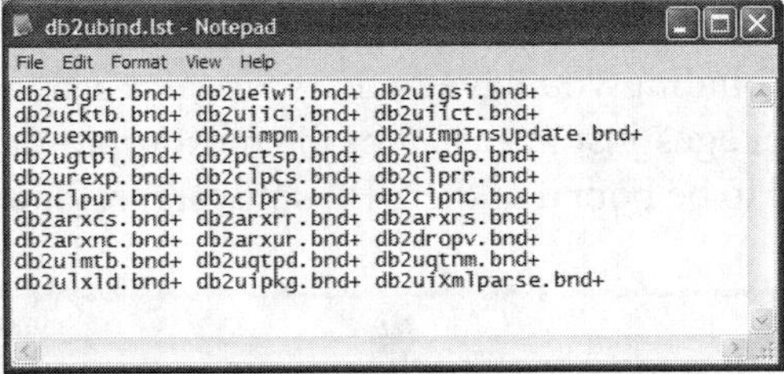

Figure 3–39 *Binding client utilities to a remote database*

The utilities that are bound with this bind file list, shown in Figure 3–39, include `IMPORT`, `EXPORT`, `LOAD`, `CLP`, `BACKUP`, `RESTORE`, and `REORG`, and more. In essence, the `DB2UBIND.LST` file contains the list of bind (`.BND`) files that are required to create the packages for these utilities.

DB2 *Note*

You must have `BINDADD` authority to create new packages in a database. If the package already exists, then you only need the `BIND` privilege for the package to update it. If you don't have these authorities, you can still use this command if you have `SYSCTRL` or `SYSADM` authority on the instance.

Binding Utilities Using the Configuration Assistant

You can also bind utilities using the Configuration Assistant. We chose to briefly cover this method after the manual method because typically binding is done via the CLP or a script file. In addition, while the Configuration Assistant offers a GUI-friendly, convenient way to bind utilities against a database, it only supports a subset of the BIND options available from the CLP.

To bind utilities using the Configuration Assistant, perform the following steps:

1. Start the Configuration Assistant by entering the db2ca command from a CLP session or selecting it from your operating system's icon menu (for example, in Windows, this is the **Start Menu**). The Configuration Assistant opens.
2. Select the database you want to bind the utilities again and click **Selected→Bind**. The Bind dialog-box opens (Figure 3–40).

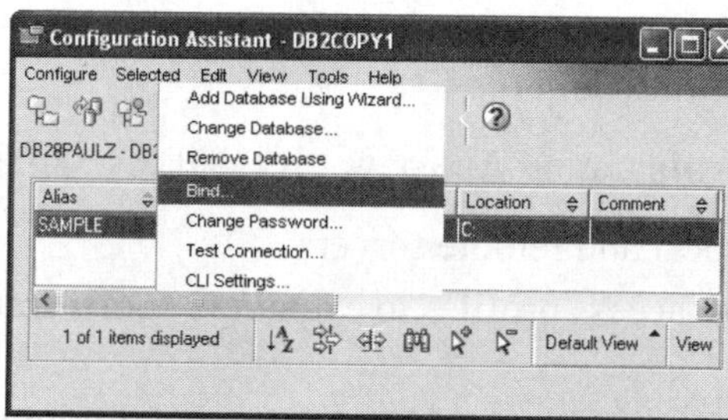

Figure 3–40 *Binding client utilities using the Configuration Assistant*

Select the utilities or files to bind and any bind options, enter the proper credentials in the **Enter connection information field**, and click **Bind** (Figure 3–41).

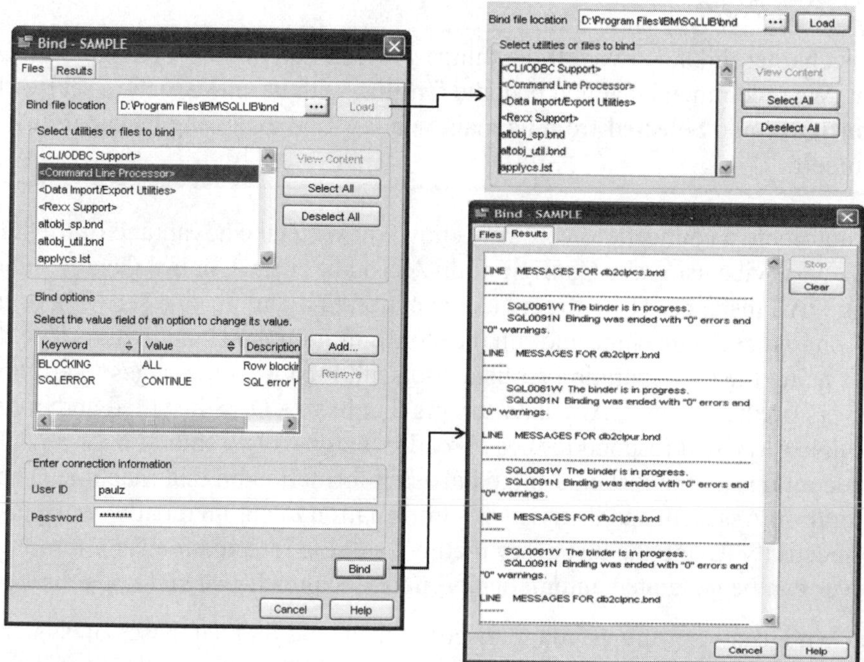

Figure 3–41 *Binding client utilities using the Configuration Assistant*

You can see in Figure 3–41 that you have a lot of options. You must select a utility before you can bind anything to the database. Note that you can use the **Load** button to load more bind files (or bind file lists) from the local workstation. In addition, you can use the **Add** button to add bind options to the bind process you are about to perform (this is not shown in Figure 3–41).

Summary

This chapter presented an overview of manual and automated configuration methods that can be used to set up a remote database connection using the Configuration Assistant, access profiles, and the CLP.

Specifically, the Configuration Assistant gives DBAs with the ability to:

- Configure both local and remote servers
- Import and export access profiles to exchange configuration information with other systems
- View and update applicable database manager configuration parameters and DB2 registry variables
- Bind utilities and packages to the database
- And more

DB2 *Note*

This chapter did not cover all the things you can do with the Configuration Assistant. We recommend that you become familiar with its entire feature set by clicking **Configure** and **Selected** from its main window and exploring its capabilities for yourself.

To automate a connection, you were shown how to take advantage of the DB2 Discovery service using the Configuration Assistant or the Control Center and a running DAS instance. To configure a connection to a remote data server, a user could log on to a client machine and run the Configuration Assistant to automate this process using the Configuration Assistant to send broadcast messages to all the data servers on the network. Any data servers that have a DAS installed and configured for discovery will respond to these broadcast signals by sending back a package that contains all the instance and database information on that machine. The Configuration Assistant can then use this information to automatically configure client connectivity. Using the discovery method, catalog information for a remote data server can be generated automatically in the local database and node directory.

Known Discovery allows you to discover instances and databases on systems that are known to a client workstation, and to add new systems so that their instances and databases can be discovered. Search Discovery provides all of the facilities of Known Discovery and adds the option to allow your local network to be searched for other DB2 servers. For environments with a large number of clients, an alternative is to use a directory service such as LDAP. DB2 also supports IPv6 addresses.

Server and client profiles were introduced and detailed such as their usefulness for larger scale deployments. For more experienced DBAs, or those that prefer scripting commands, the ability to manually configure connections using the Configuration Assistant and the CLP was covered.

Finally, how to bind the utilities to the server database when the client and server are on different systems was reviewed.

CHAPTER 4

Controlling Data Access

- AUTHENTICATING USERS
- BUILT-IN AUTHORITY ROLES
- ASSIGNING AUTHORITIES
- ASSIGNING PRIVILEGES
- USERS AND GROUPS
- AUDIT FACILITY

Security is an important consideration whenever data is stored in a relational database management system. In this chapter, we discuss controlling data access using many different methods. Access to data within DB2 is controlled at many levels, including instance, database, database object, application package, rows, columns, and more. This chapter includes an overview of how authentication and authorization are managed in DB2 — two key components to building a secure data server. In addition, assigning group rights and privileges for groups of typical database users, such as database administrators (DBAs), transactional processing personnel, and decision support users, is also discussed. Each of these database user types may require different access privileges. Finally, we briefly cover a very important security concept in today's marketplace: auditing that allows you to monitor security-related events.

Overview of Security

An important aspect of making a data server secure is controlling access to it. One of the responsibilities of a database administrator (DBA) is to secure the data server. It's recommended that DBAs implement the principle of least privilege, in which users aren't given capabilities or rights beyond the scope of their current roles or requirements. For example, if user Chloë is given access to a table to facilitate the reporting of absenteeism for a specific line of business, she shouldn't be able to view sick day records for another line of business, or be allowed to alter sick day data that's automatically entered into the database via a timekeeping system.

When implementing security controls for your data server, DBAs should start by considering these factors:

- Who will access the instance or its databases? For example, which users should be allowed to access the data server irrespective of the data?
- Where will authentication of the user identified for access in the previous point take place? For example, is the user authorized by the operating system on the server? The client? Or is a central authorization scheme used, such as the Lightweight Directory Access Protocol (LDAP)?
- Once a user is identified and connected to the database, what authority level should that person have over it? For example, a DBA should have further reaching authority than a business analyst that needs to look at data, but the DBA may not be allowed to access certain sensitive data details such as credit card numbers and so on.

  Authority levels can also include the types of commands a user is allowed to run. For example, an extract, transform, and load (ETL) programmer may only be allowed to run the LOAD command to populate the atomic layer of a data warehouse, whereas an individual charged with system maintenance may not be allowed to load a table but has authority to run maintenance activities against it, such as a backup or statistics collection job.
- What will be accessed? Quite simply, you should develop a security plan that identifies users, or groups of users, and what data (and objects) they are allowed to access or create. For example, many users may be allowed to read production line defect data, but only certified control engineers have the authority to populate it through their front-end application.
- What data objects are users allowed to create or modify? It's not just data that you have to consider with respect to your data server's access patterns. Various objects can be accessed, altered, created, or deleted by users and administrators, such as instances, configurations, tables, views, federated wrappers, and so on. For example, a certain group of users may be allowed to change the data table to

reflect the business model it represents while others can only read the data within it.

Figure 4–1 illustrates the three main categories of a framework that you should consider when applying a security plan to your environment.

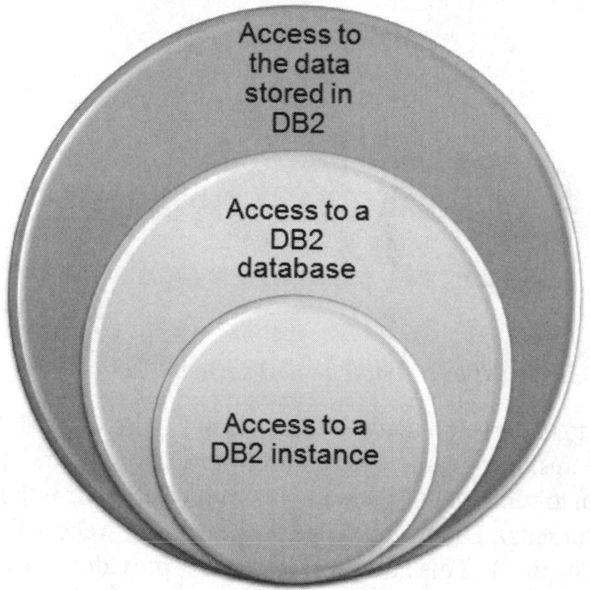

Figure 4–1 *A security control framework for a DB2 data server*

First, controls should be in place to define and manage access to the instances on a DB2 data server. All access to a DB2 instance is managed by a security facility external to DB2. This security facility can be the host operating system (which is typically the case) or a another facility via a customized plug-in. This facility allows the system to make sure that the user really is who he or she claims to be and may also control access to other objects such as files and programs. Users and groups they may belong to are normally used by these security facilities.

Within each instance resides one or more databases, and this represents the second level of control within a DB2 data server. Access to a database and its objects is controlled at the database level by the database manager. Here, administrative authorities and user privileges are used to control access to objects that reside within a database.

Finally, the last level of data server and database controls relates to the access of data or data-associated objects within a database. As previously stated, a DBA needs to ensure that sensitive information is not accessed by those without a need-to-know mandate. A security plan for DB2 should be developed by defining your objectives and implementing them using the appropriate privileges and authorities that you'll learn about in this chapter.

Once a security framework has been identified it needs to be physically implemented on the data server. DB2 provides three main mechanisms to implement the framework derived from Figure 4–1 on the data server as shown in Figure 4–2.

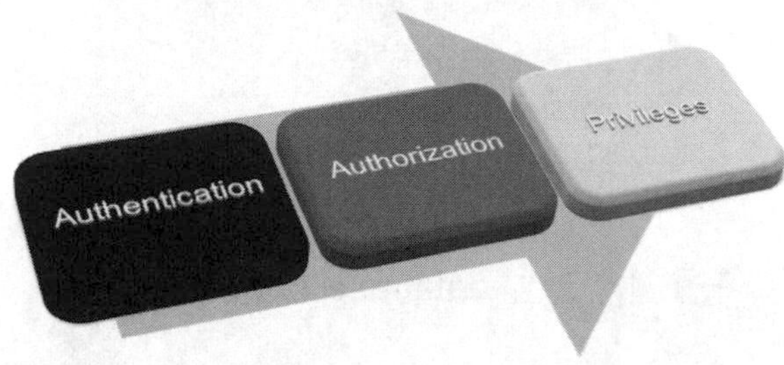

Figure 4–2 *DB2 facilities to implement a security framework*

It's important to understand that the facilities in Figure 4–2 can be made up of multiple DB2 features. For example, to control the ability to view data DBAs can assign the right to run a `SELECT` statement. To further control the ability to view the data that is returned, a DBA would use the Advanced Access Control feature pack discussed in Chapter 1. This add-on feature pack provides label-based access control such that specific data can be viewed by some users and not others within the same table; it even controls what a system administrator can see (more on this topic later in this chapter).

Authentication

The first step in managing security is to verify a user's identity. This is called *authentication*. Authentication is the operation of verifying whether a user or an application is who they claim to be. This is typically accomplished by forcing the user or application to provide a valid user ID and password.

DB2 Note

The Windows operating system uses the term *username* to identify an individual assigned to a specific user account. Most other operating systems, and DB2, use the term *user ID*. This chapter uses the more common *user ID* terminology; however, if you're a Windows DBA you can use *username* as a synonym for this term and concept unless otherwise noted.

Every time a user tries to connect to a local or remote database, he or she is authenticated. DB2 works closely with the hosting operating system's security facilities to handle its authentication requirements, but can also work with standard security protocols such as Kerberos™, Active Directory, and even custom-built authentication mechanisms developed with the GSS-API standard security model. When a user attempts to connect to a data server, DB2 passes the user ID and password to the operating system or the external security facility for verification.

A DBAs configuration of DB2 authentication addresses two of the security considerations mentioned earlier in this chapter whenever a CONNECT or ATTACH statement is issued against a target data server:

- Who is allowed to access the data server or its databases?
- Where should the authentication of a user trying to access the data server or database take place, and how should verification proceed?

Supplying a User ID and a Password for Authentication

A user can establish a connection between a client and an instance or between a client and a database. DB2 has two commands that can be used to establish these connections. For an instance connection, the ATTACH command is used. For a database connection, the CONNECT statement is used.

With either method, a user may or may not supply a user ID and password. If a user ID is not supplied and the authentication type is CLIENT (details on all authentication types in DB2 are discussed later in this chapter), DB2 uses the user ID and password with which the user logged on. Depending on the operating system and configuration, DB2 could prompt the user to supply a user ID and password.

If a user ID and password is supplied with either the ATTACH or CONNECT statement, DB2 will use them to authenticate the user. The user ID and password specified may differ from those used to log on to the client.

When using either of these statements, a user or application can request a password change by supplying the user ID, password, new password, and confirmation of the new password in the ATTACH or CONNECT statement. In this case, DB2 would first authenticate the user before requesting the password change from the security facility.

DB2 *Note*

Connecting to a database in an embedded SQL program does not require a user to supply confirmation of the new password.

The following examples use the CONNECT statement by specifying a specific user as part of the connection.

Example 1

A user wants to connect to a database called SAMPLE using his user ID MKELLY and his password BOGGARTS. The statement he would use would look like this:

```
CONNECT TO SAMPLE USER MKELLY USING BOGGARTS
```

Example 2

The same user in Example 1 wants to connect to the same database; however, this time he wants to change his password from BOGGARTS to BIRDIES. In this case, he would use the following statement:

```
CONNECT TO SAMPLE USER MKELLY USING BOGGARTS
           NEW BIRDIES CONFIRM BIRDIES
```

If you were to reissue the CONNECT statement in this example with the password BOGGARTS after running this example statement, the attempted connection would fail. Also note that if you change your user ID's password with this approach, you must use this password when subsequently logging on to the operating system irrespective of DB2.

Example 3

An application written using embedded SQL modules needs to connect to a database called SAMPLE. The application could assign the user ID used for the connection to the USERID host variable. If the application gave end users the capability to change their passwords at login time, it would present them with a dialog box to perform this action as well. The code behind this dialog box would further assign a host variable for the old password (OLDPWD), new password (NEWPWD), and new password confirmation (CONFIRMNEWPWD). For example, the embedded SQL statement could look like:

```
EXEC SQL CONNECT TO SAMPLE USER:USERID USING:OLDPWD
     NEW:NEWPWD CONFIRM:CONFIRMNEWPWD
```

Example 4

The user MKELLY wants to attach to the DB2CERT instance using his user account and the new password defined in Example 3, as shown.

```
DB2 ATTACH TO DB2CERT USER MKELLY USING BIRDIES
```

Controlling Where Authentication Takes Place

The authentication type defines where and how authentication will take place. The location where authentication takes place on a data server is determined by the value of the AUTHENTICATION parameter in an instance's database manager configuration file on the DB2 data server.

You may recall from Chapter 3 that when cataloging a remote client to connect to a DB2 data server you can optionally specify the AUTHENTICATION parameter with the CATALOG DATABASE command to specify the type of authentication the client will attempt to follow. In most cases, this setting must match the authentication setting of the instance that uses the same parameter name within the database manager configuration to define how connect requests to it are authenticated.

DB2 also gives you the ability to designate whether each client's own facilities can also handle the authentication process on behalf of the data server. If you configure your data server to use client authentication (which in many cases isn't recommended), you must depend on each client's integrated security facilities, which can vary in robustness and richness from platform to platform.

By default, an instance is set up to use the same authentication mechanism for all the instance-level (ATTACH) and connection-level (CONNECT) requests. DB2 9 introduced a new authentication setting for database connections called SRVCON_AUTH. By default, this parameter is not set, meaning that authentication behaves as discussed thus far in this chapter. When you set this parameter, it has the effect of instructing DB2 how to handle local authorizations versus external ATTACH or CONNECT requests.

This new parameter will typically be used for environments that use a GSS-API or Kerberos-defined authentication scheme because it allows local administrators to avoid the need to allocate a ticket to these users when they locally log on to the data server to perform maintenance activity, such as a TRACE and so on.

The remainder of this chapter assumes that only the AUTHENTICATION parameter is used to determine how authentication will occur, and therefore examples are based on the same authorization paradigm for both local and remote ATTACH or CONNECT requests.

DB2 Data Server Authentication Types

The authentication types available in DB2 9 are:

- SERVER

  This forces all authentications to take place at the server; therefore, a user ID and a password must be supplied when attaching to an instance or connecting to a database. With this setting, neither the data nor the user ID's password are encrypted when they flow across the connection between the DB2 client and the data server. This is the default authorization type for a newly created instance.

- SERVER_ENCRYPT

  This operates in the same manner as authentication SERVER in the sense that all authentications will take place at the server. However, all passwords are encrypted by DB2 at the client before they are sent to the remote data server. At the data server, these passwords are decrypted and the user ID is subsequently authenticated. If a data server is using this authentication scheme, as of DB2 9, it will not accept clients using SERVER authentication.

DB2 Note

If you request a password change at connect or attach time, and the target data server uses the SERVER_ENCRYPT authentication type, the new password will not be encrypted before it is sent to the server on the initial connection that requests the password change. Subsequent connection flows, however, will encrypt the password.

- CLIENT

  This assigns authentication responsibility to the client's operating system to perform user authentication on behalf of the data server. You should pay special consideration to this authentication model because this setting doesn't guarantee that authentication will take place at the client because of the concept of untrusted clients (discussed later in this chapter). For the most part, we generally don't recommend this authentication method because of the differentiation in password strength, protection, and facilities from a wide array of client operating systems; however, it all depends on your environment.

- KERBEROS

  This setting specifies that authentication is to be handled by Kerberos-based security software. It can only be used when both the DB2 client and data server are on operating systems that support the Kerberos security protocol. The Kerberos security protocol performs authentication as a third-party authentication service by using conventional cryptography to create a shared secret key that subsequently becomes a user's credential for verifying the identity of users during all occasions when local or network services are requested. A Kerberos key eliminates the need to pass user ID and password credentials across the network and helps to enable the concept of single sign-on to a remote DB2 data server.

DB2 *Note*

DB2 9 does not support any Kerberos authentication schemes on HP-UX.

- KRB_SERVER_ENCRYPT

  This specifies that the remote data server is enabled for Kerberos connections if the connecting client's authentication setting in its catalog directory is also set to use Kerberos. This setting, however, compensates clients that don't support Kerberos in that it will also accept client connections with the SERVER_ENCRYPT authentication setting. Quite simply, if the client authentication is KERBEROS, the client is authenticated using the Kerberos security system. If the client authentication is not KERBEROS, then the system authentication must be SERVER_ENCRYPT.

  This authentication setting does not support the encryption of data flows at the time DB2 9 was made generally available. In the case of Kerberos connected clients, passwords aren't passed around, since this setting also supports clients with SERVER_ENCRYPT authentication (where passwords are protected). If you want to use this authentication setting and encrypt data, you need to turn to alternative technologies such as IPSec encryption on a network card, SSL tunneling, and so on.

DB2 *Note*

Technologies that off-load encryption from the data server are generally considered to be ideal choices for high performing databases. For example, IPSec is an excellent data flow encryption option for any data server for any authentication scheme.

- DATA_ENCRYPT

  Authentication takes place on the data server. When DATA_ENCRYPT is used for authentication, the behavior for authentication is similar to SERVER_ENCRYPT; in addition to encrypting the password that flows across the wire, all data flows are encrypted as well.

With this setting, the following data flows are encrypted:

- SQL and XQuery statements
- SQL program variable data
- Output data from the server processing of an SQL or XQuery statement (including a description of the data)
- Some or all of the answer set data resulting from a query
- Large object (LOB) data streaming
- SQLDA descriptors

When using this authentication method, you should be aware that older clients that don't support encryption (any DB2 client before DB2 V8.2 or DB2 V8.1 with FixPack 7 applied) will not be able to connect to the remote data server. If you have a mix of older DB2 clients connecting to a DB2 9 data server, in addition to DB2 9 clients, and you want to support the encryption of the data, you should use the DATA_ENCRYPT_CMP authentication type.

- DATA_ENCRYPT_CMP

  This authentication setting behaves in the same manner as DATA_ENCRYPT. The difference is that this setting compensates back-level clients that don't support the encryption of data flows to authenticate using the SERVER_ENCRYPT option. Examples of clients that don't support the DB2 encryption of the data flows include older versions of the Java Common Client (JCC) and pre-V8.2 DB2 client code.

- GSSPLUG-IN

  This specifies that the data server's authentication is controlled by an external facility (not the operating system) that was developed using the GSS-API plug-in.

  If a client's authentication is not specified, the remote data server returns a list of server-supported plug-ins, including any Kerberos plug-ins that are listed in the srvcon_gssplug-in_list database manager configuration parameter. The client then selects the first plug-in found in the client plug-in directory from this list. If the client does not support any plug-ins in the list, the client is authenticated using the KERBEROS authentication scheme.

- GSS_SERVER_ENCRYPT

  This specifies that the data server's authentication is controlled by an external facility (not the operating system) that was developed using the GSS-API plug-in. If client authentication occurs through a plug-in, the client is authenticated using the first client-supported plug-in in the list of server-supported plug-ins.

If the connecting client doesn't support one of the server's GSS-API plug-ins, the SERVER_ENCRYPT authentication type is used. If the client isn't using the GSS-API, then the data server will accept its requests if it is using the KERBEROS (a subset of the GSS-API) or SERVER_ENCRYPT authentication schemes; it will reject all other authorization settings, including DATA_ENCRYPT and DATA_ENCRYPT_CMP.

The open security plug-in infrastructure in DB2 allows for the use of custom-built GSS-API compliant plug-ins to take over the job of authenticating the user ID to an external security program. For more information on GSS-API security mechanisms, or Kerberos, refer to the DB2 documentation.

DB2 *Note*

Understanding the implementation of the authentication mechanisms in DB2 can be somewhat confusing since they are all based on a plug-in architecture. In DB2 V8.2, the traditional data server authentication schemes were migrated to the plug-in architecture. Despite this technical fact, references in this book to DB2's security plug-in architecture refers to the KERBEROS, KRB_SERVER_ENCRYPT, GSSPLUG-IN, and GSS_SERVER_ENCRYPT authentication settings only. Since the GSS-API plug-in authentication (which includes Kerberos authentication) is an advanced topic, it is not covered in this book. A number of security samples are provided in the samples\security\plug-in directory on your data server.

Setting the Authentication Type on a Data Server

The authentication type for a database is specified in the database manager configuration file so that it is shared among all the databases contained in an instance; that is, authentication is controlled at the instance level and therefore all the databases in an instance will have the same authentication type. You can check the authentication type associated with the current instance using the following command:

```
GET DATABASE MANAGER CONFIGURATION
```

The current authentication type will be seen next to the AUTHENTICATION parameter in the database manager configuration file. The default setting for AUTHENTICATION is SERVER. You can change it by issuing a command similar to the following:

```
UPDATE DBM CFG USING AUTHENTICATION DATA_ENCRYPT_CMP
```

DB2 Note

You can see in the previous command we used the shorthand method for some of this command's parameters within the DB2 CLP; `DATABASE MANAGER` can be abbreviated with the short-form `DBM`, and `CONFIGURATION` can be abbreviated using the short-form `CFG`.

You can also use the Control Center to change this parameter as show in Figure 4–3.

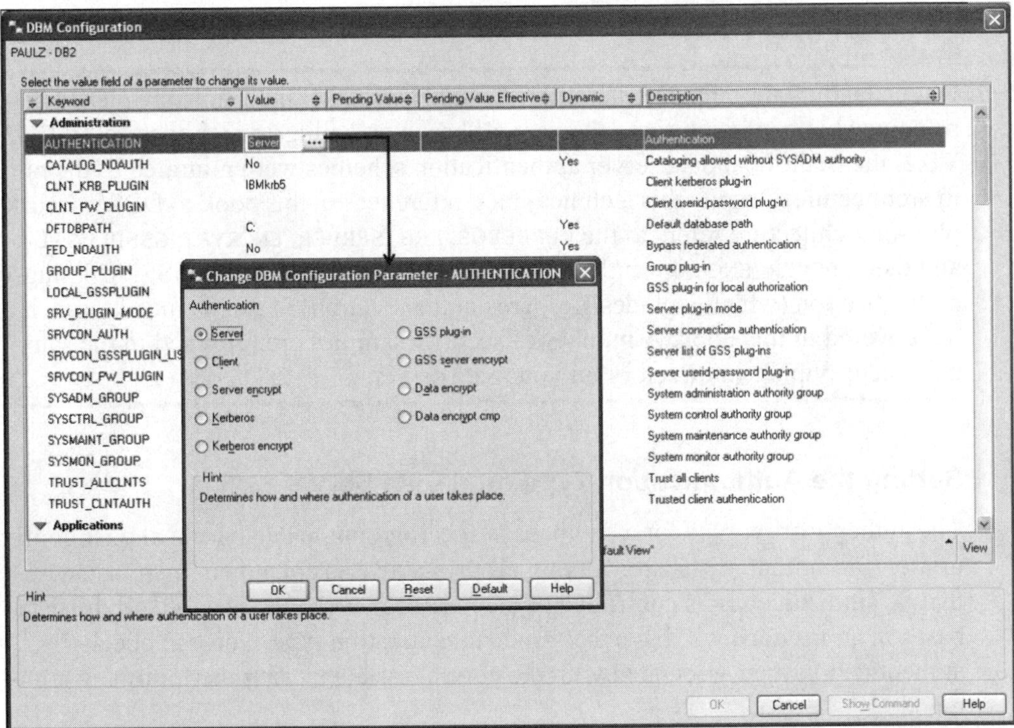

Figure 4–3 *Setting the AUTHENTICATION security setting*

In Figure 4–3 you can see all of the different database manager configuration settings that relate to security. Some of the parameters in Figure 4–3 have already been discussed in this chapter, others will be, and some are beyond the scope of this book. For example, the `CLNT_PW_PLUG-IN` parameter is used to specify the name of the client plug-in used for client and local authentication, whereas the `GROUP_PLUG-IN` parameter is used to specify the name of a user-defined plug-in that will be invoked for all group enumeration instead of relying on the operating system group lookup function. Both of these parameters (and some others) are beyond the scope of this chapter.

The remainder of this chapter assumes you understand that the DB2 CLP commands illustrated in this chapter can also be performed using the DB2 graphical tools, namely, the Control Center. The examples in this chapter are mainly shown using the DB2 CLP syntax.

Certain authentication types, such as CLIENT, GSSPLUG-IN, and KERBEROS, require that other database manager configuration settings be made. For example, if you change the authentication of a data server to CLIENT, you need to additionally set the TRUST_ALLCLNTS (and possibly TRUST_CLNTAUTH) parameters.

You can see in Figure 4–3 that the AUTHENTICATION parameter is not dynamic (see the **Dynamic** column in the figure). This means that if you change this parameter (using the Control Center or the DB2 CLP), you must recycle the instance using the db2stop and db2start commands before the new change will take effect. For the most part, security changes require a recycling of the instance, although there are some security parameters that are dynamic. You must be a member of the SYSADM group to make changes to security-related configuration parameters for an instance.

DB2 Client Authentication Types

Authentication at the client is specified in the client's database directory using the CATALOG DATABASE command; however, you can omit specifying an authentication type when configuring a client connection. If you specify an authentication type at the client, it must match (or be compatible with) the value specified at the remote DB2 data server. If they don't match (or aren't compatible), the requested connection will fail.

If CLIENT authentication is being used on the remote data server, this implies that it's up to the client to authenticate users on behalf of the remote data server. CLIENT authentication introduces the concept of trusted clients because some clients may not have native security functions available to them; examples are Windows ME and Windows 98. While DB2 9 doesn't support these client platforms, you may be administering an environment that has down-level clients that run on such platforms, so you should be aware how to handle them.

When using client-driven authentication, two other database manager configuration parameters need to be considered: TRUST_ALLCLNTS and TRUST_CLNTAUTH. (Another factor you need to consider when configuring an environment for client-side authentication is whether a user's credentials are explicitly provided — more on this in a bit.) Using these parameters, DB2 allows DBAs to specify whether they want their data server to trust all clients despite the fact that they could have a heterogeneous mix of authentication capabilities and security levels. In other words, a DBA can specify whether all clients can authenticate users.

It's pretty obvious that if there are clients without a reliable security facility, you probably do not want them to authenticate users. You can configure this by changing the TRUST_ALLCLNTS parameter in the database manager configuration file on your data server. The TRUST_ALLCLNTS parameter is used to determine what type of clients are allowed to connect without having password validation occur on the data server.

The TRUST_ALLCLNTS parameter can be set to:

- YES

  Setting this parameter to YES forces all clients, whether they are trusted or not, to authenticate at the client. This is the default.

- NO

  This specifies that all untrusted clients be authenticated at the data server meaning that a user ID and a password must be provided from the client. If the client is trusted, it will be locally authenticated. If it is not trusted, it must be authenticated at the server. If you are using CLIENT authentication, we strongly recommend setting TRUST_ALLCLNTS=NO to protect against insecure clients from connecting without providing a valid password. Since TRUST_ALLCLNTS is an instance-level parameter, all databases in the instance will use this setting (just like the AUTHENTICATION parameter).

The TRUST_CLNTAUTH parameter allows you to specify where the authentication will take place when a user ID and a password are supplied with the CONNECT or ATTACH statements. It's used in conjunction with the TRUST_ALLCLNTS parameter. This parameter is only used if the authentication type is CLIENT and if it affects clients that can authenticate users on behalf of a server; in other words, it affects all clients if TRUST_ALLCLNTS is set to YES.

Valid values for this parameter are:

- CLIENT (default)

  Authentication is performed by the client. A user ID and a password are not required. If a user ID and password are not supplied, authentication will take place on the client with the user ID and password that the user used to log on to the client.

- SERVER

  If SERVER is specified, authentication is done at the data server.

Table 4–1 summarizes where authentication will occur when a database connection or instance attachment is performed by each type of client to a data server using client-based authentication.

Table 4–1 *Setting the authentication type on a client*

User ID/Password Supplied?	TRUST_ALLCLNTS	TRUST_CLNTAUTH	UNTRUSTED CLIENT	TRUSTED CLIENT
No	Yes	CLIENT	CLIENT	CLIENT
No	Yes	SERVER	CLIENT	CLIENT
No	No	CLIENT	SERVER	CLIENT
No	No	SERVER	SERVER	CLIENT
Yes	Yes	CLIENT	CLIENT	CLIENT
Yes	Yes	SERVER	SERVER	SERVER
Yes	No	CLIENT	SERVER	CLIENT
Yes	No	SERVER	SERVER	SERVER

Setting the Authentication Type on a Client

As you learned in Chapter 3, DB2 has multiple directories that are used to direct an application to the location of a database. These directories allow DB2 to find data servers and their databases whether they are on a local or remote instance. The system database directory contains a list and pointers to where all known databases can be found. The node directory contains information relating to how and where remote systems or instances can be found. To put an entry into any of these directories, the CATALOG command is used. To remove an entry, the UNCATALOG command is used.

When setting up the data server, you can choose who should be able to CATALOG and UNCATALOG databases. This can be done in the database manager configuration file by setting the CATALOG_NOAUTH parameter. The two available values are YES and NO. NO is the default value for a DB2 data server and has the effect of preventing users without SYSADM or SYSCTRL authority from using the CATALOG or UNCATALOG commands. Setting it to YES allows all users to use these commands. YES is the default value for a DB2 client and a DB2 data server with local clients.

The client authentication type for a connection is stored in the system database directory. This is a list of all the databases known to the system.

To see the list of databases known to the system, use the following command:

```
LIST DATABASE DIRECTORY
```

All remotely cataloged databases will show the authentication type with which the client will attempt to connect to the data server. To change the authentication type for a connection, the database needs to be recataloged from the database directory with the new authentication type.

When you set the authentication type on a client, you must ensure that it matches (or is compatible with) the setting of the AUTHENTICATION parameter for the remote instance. The exceptions to this rule of thumb are the KRB_SERVER_ENCRYPT, DATA_ENCRYPT_CMP, and GSS_SERVER_ENCRYPT authentication settings since they offer multiple compatibilities, as discussed in the previous section.

The following gives an example of a command that catalogs a database connection using server-based authentication:

```
CATALOG DATABASE SAMPLE AT NODE MYNODE AUTHENTICATION SERVER
```

If an authentication type is not defined for a specific database connection, the connection manager will use the default SERVER_ENCRYPT.

A Server-based Authentication Example

In this example, a decision was made to have authentication take place at the data server and for all data and password flows to be encrypted for security reasons. With that noted, this environment has a mix of older and newer client code, and therefore some clients connecting to the data server don't have the ability to natively encrypt the data flow using the DB2 client code. For this reason, the data server uses the DATA_ENCRYPT_CMP authentication type.

The DB2 9 client that supports data encryption uses DATA_ENCRYPT while the back-level DB2 8 client that doesn't support encryption (data flow encryption was added in DB2 8.2 or DB2 8.1+Fix Pack 7) uses the SERVER_ENCRYPT authentication setting. This authentication setting would be accepted by the data server since its authentication setting is DATA_ENCRYPT_CMP. This environment is configured such that all user IDs and passwords are sent to the data server for authentication. Because AUTHENTICATION=DATA_ENCRYPT_CMP was used, all passwords that flow across the network are encrypted as well (Figure 4–4).

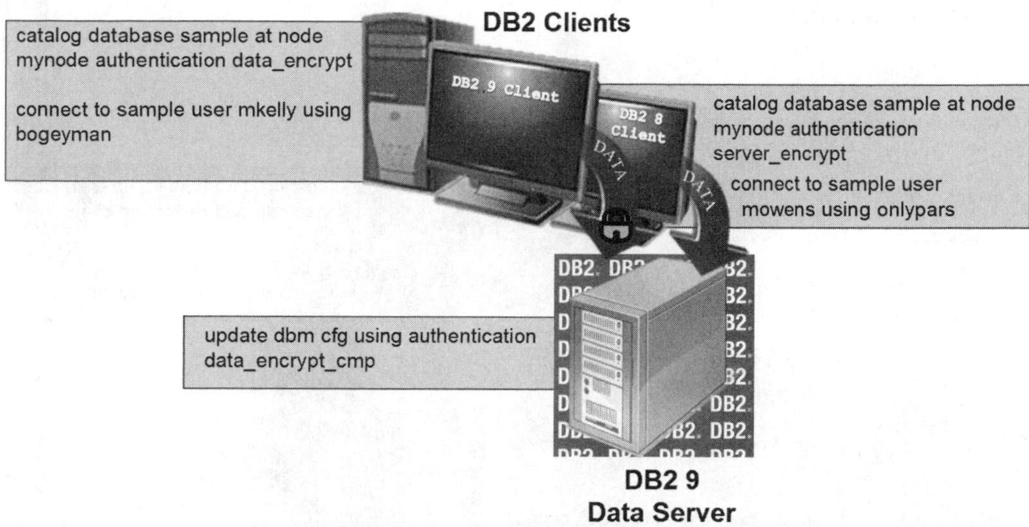

Figure 4–4 *Connecting using* DATA_ENCRYPT_CMP

Figure 4–4 shows the authentication type setting in the database manager configuration file on the data server and the authentication type settings in each client's system database directory (specified when each remote database connection was cataloged at the client).

When the DB2 9 client connects to the DB2 9 data server, both the password and the data is encrypted (as shown by the lock on the data stream). The DATA_ENCRYPT setting on the client is compatible with a server configured for DATA_ENCRYPT or DATA_ENCRYPT_CMP authentication. The DB2 8 client can connect to the DB2 9 data server even though it doesn't support data flow encryption because it was cataloged using SERVER_ENCRYPT authentication, which the DB2 9 data server will accept because its authentication is set to DATA_ENCRYPT_CMP. The data that flows from the DB2 8 client is not encrypted (although it could be if a technology like IPSec was used); however, the password is still encrypted as it flows to the DB2 9 data server.

A Client-based Authentication Example

In this example, a decision was made to have authentication take place on the client where it's deemed secure, as shown in Figure 4-5. You can see in this figure that the data server was configured with AUTHENTICATION=CLIENT and, additionally, client specific authentication settings (TRUST_ALLCLNTS=YES and TRUST_CLNTAUTH=SERVER) were specified such that if a user ID and password were not specified, authentication would occur at the client (if possible). If these credentials were explicitly specified, authentication would take place at the server as shown in Figure 4–5.

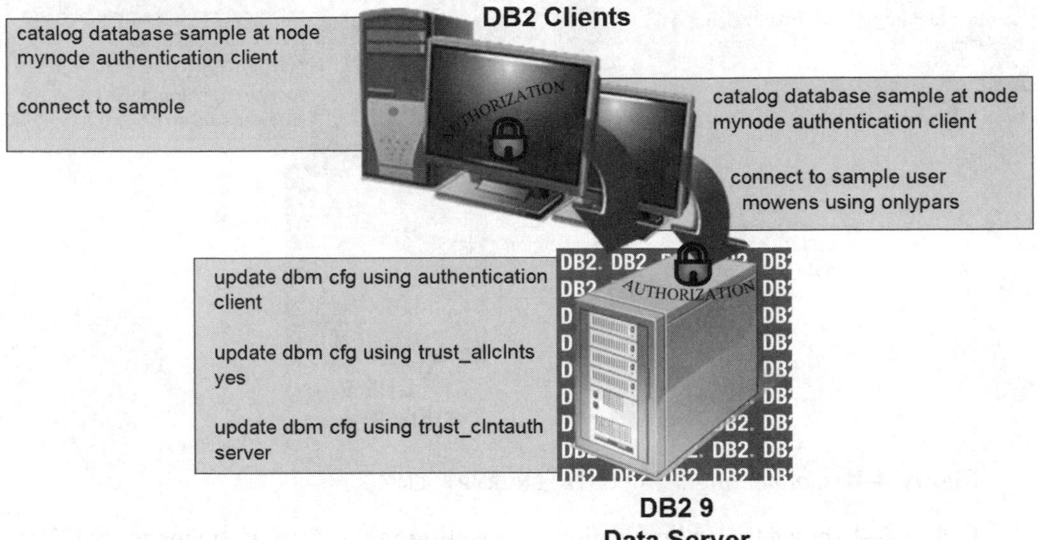

Figure 4–5 *Connecting using* `AUTHENTICATION=CLIENT`

Authorization

After successful authentication, access to database objects is controlled by DB2 through process authorization. Some access control is also controlled by associating users and groups with specific privileges, depending on what type of access the user or group is trying to perform. This type of access control is covered in the next section. If a certain authority is given to a group, each member of that group has the same DB2 authority unless they have had that authority explicitly revoked.

DB2 *Note*

Remember that users and groups are defined on the operating system level, and therefore references to group membership in this section imply that the group has already been defined on the operating system.

DB2 9 authorities can be used to control:

- The authority level that is granted to a user or group
- The commands that a user or group is allowed to run
- The "CRUDability" of the data; in other words, create, read (select), update, and

delete (CRUD)
- The database objects that a user or group is allowed to create, alter, or drop

Authorities can be used to answer such security questions as:

- Who is allowed to administer the data server or perform maintenance operations on it?
- How can I quickly assign privileges to users that need to perform common higher-level administrative functions?
- What authority levels should certain high-level users and groups be allotted?

Authorities are normally required for maintaining databases and instances, and therefore DB2 comes with a number of built-in authorization levels that determine the operations that can be performed within a database or instance. Quite simply, a user's or group's ability to perform high-level database and instance management operations is determined by the built-in DB2 authorities that they have been assigned to. DB2 provides six built-in authority levels:

- `SYSADM` — System Administration Authority
- `SYSCTRL` — System Control Authority
- `SYSMAINT` — System Maintenance Authority
- `SECADM` — Security Administration Authority
- `DBADM` — Database Administration Authority
- `LOAD` — Load Table Authority

Authorities in DB2 provide a hierarchy for data server administration capabilities as shown in Figure 4–6.

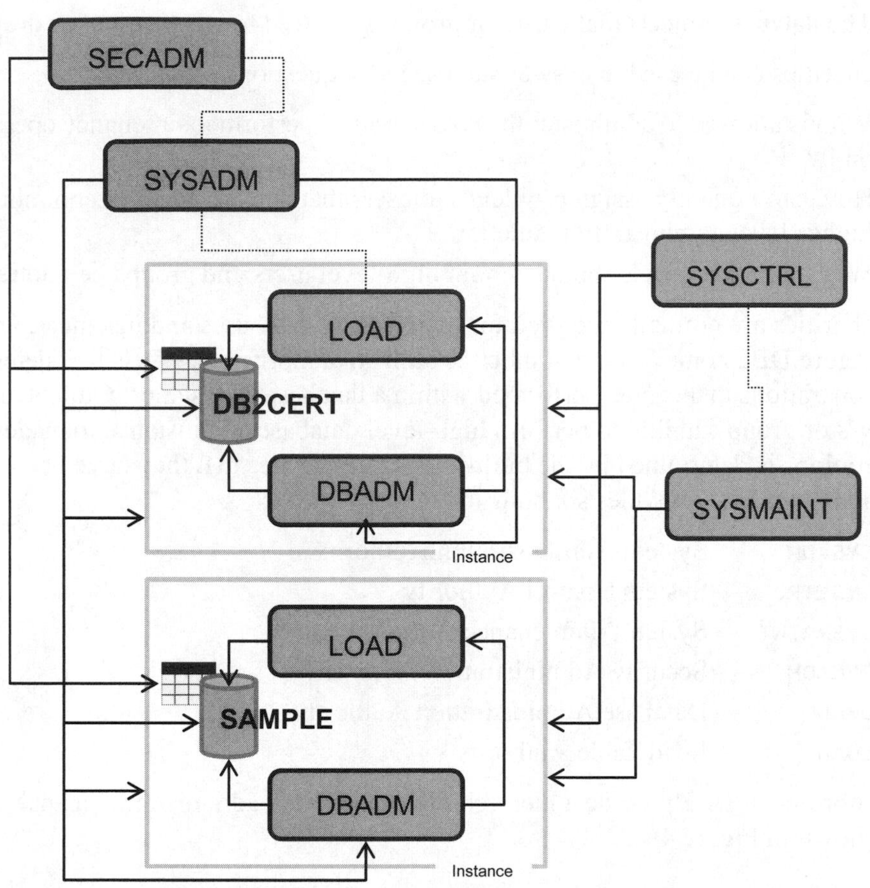

Figure 4–6 *Built-in DB2 authorities*

For the most part, the built-in authorities in DB2 can be thought of as pre-determined roles that contain a set of privileges and higher-level database manager, database maintenance, and utility operations so that users can administer and control their data servers and databases.

Some authority levels (SYSADM, SYSCTRL, and SYSMAINT) are instance-level authorities in that their inherent privileges include commands and operations that can run against an instance or databases that reside within them. These authorities, as you will see, are granted through the database manager configuration (at the instance level) and can only be assigned at the group level. This means that you must create a group even if you want to just grant any of these authorities to a single user.

In contrast, authorities such as LOAD, DBADM, and SECADM are considered database-level authorities and can be granted to users and groups using the GRANT statement.

SYSADM Authority

At the top of the DB2 security hierarchy is the DB2 System Administrator or SYSADM authority. Figure 4–6 shows the SECADM authority above the SYSADM authority because this authority level can access data that SYSADM cannot, yet it cannot perform the same actions as SYSADM. Any member of the SYSADM group is able to perform any of the DB2 administration operations as well as access all database objects – except for data specifically restricted through LBAC controls as implemented by the SECADM user. SYSADM group members are the only users allowed to configure the DB2 instance.

By default, on UNIX systems, the SYSADM group is set to the primary group of the instance owner, and therefore any users that belong to this group have SYSADM authority on the data server. On Windows, members of the local Administrators group are all granted SYSADM authority.

To change the default group to which SYSADM authority is assigned, you need to change the SYSADM_GROUP database manager configuration parameter using a command similar to the following:

```
UPDATE DBM CFG USING SYSADM_GROUP TOPADMINGROUP
```

The SYSADM_GROUP parameter isn't dynamic, so if you change it you have to recycle the database instance for the change to take effect.

DB2 Note

DB2 does not verify that the operating system group exists during the modification of a database manager configuration parameter that is set to an operating system group. Therefore, you must ensure that these groups exist on the operating system before assigning authorities to them within DB2.

Since group authorities are also related to the security mechanisms of the operating system, users granted a DB2 authority could end up inheriting special access to unrelated DB2 resources and vice versa. For example, by default, Windows operating system administrators have SYSADM control over a data server. For this reason, the creation of users and group assignments should be strictly controlled on any DB2 data server.

SYSCTRL Authority

System control (SYSCTRL) authority provides the ability to perform most administration tasks; in fact, SYSCTRL offers almost complete control of database objects defined in a DB2 instance. This authority allows members to perform pretty much all administrative and maintenance commands within the database instance. In contrast to the SYSADM authority, SYSCTRL users cannot access any data within the database unless specifically given the privilege by a user with the authority to do so.

Some of the tasks a user or group with SYSCTRL authority can perform include:

- Creating or dropping databases
- Forcing applications off the database
- Restoring an image to a new database
- Creating, dropping, or altering a table space
- Performing any actions that the SYSMAINT authority provides

Only a user with SYSADM authority can grant SYSCTRL authority. You grant SYSCTRL authority in the same manner that SYSADM authority is granted only you update the SYSCTRL_GROUP parameter. For example:

```
UPDATE DBM CFG USING SYSCTRL_GROUP MIDADMINGROUP
```

The SYSCTRL_GROUP parameter isn't dynamic, so if you change it you have to recycle the database instance for the change to take effect.

SYSMAINT Authority

System Maintenance authority (SYSMAINT) gives its users the ability to perform a subset of the actions that a user with SYSCTRL authority can perform. Much like the SYSCTRL authority, this authority's privileges center on maintenance operations. This authority doesn't allow access to user data.

The SYSMAINT authority provides privileges to perform the following tasks:

- Update database configuration files
- Backup databases and table spaces
- Restore to an existing database
- Perform roll forward recovery
- Restore table spaces
- Start and stop the DB2 instance
- Run the database monitor
- Start and stop traces
- Query the state of a table space

- Update log history files
- Quiesce a table space
- Reorganize a table
- Execute the RUNSTATS utility

Also note that users with SYSADM or SYSCTRL authorities can perform any of the previously listed actions since they sit above the SYSMAINT authority in the DB2 authority hierarchy.

Only users with SYSADM or SYSCTRL authorities can grant the SYSMAINT authority. You grant SYSMAINT authority in the same manner that the SYSADM authority is granted, only in this case you update the SYSMAINT_GROUP parameter. For example:

```
UPDATE DBM CFG USING SYSMAINT_GROUP TIREKICKERS
```

The SYSMAINT_GROUP parameter isn't dynamic, so if you change it you have to recycle the database instance for the change to take effect.

SECADM Authority

The security administrator (SECADM) authority collects several security-related privileges under one authority. The abilities given to SECADM are not given to any other authority, not even SYSADM.

In the DB2 9.1 release, SECADM authority is used for the administration of label-based security controls through the label-based access control (LBAC) facility available for DB2 Enterprise. Future releases of DB2 will build on this security authority to provide more security controls on that data within the data server, for example, the use of a customizable role-based security mechanism as opposed to the built-in static roles that exist in DB2 9.

Having SECADM authority allows you to perform the following actions:

- Create, drop, or grant permission to access or revoke the various objects that are part of label-based access control (LBAC)
- Use of the TRANSFER OWNERSHIP statement on objects that you do not own
- Grant or revoke the SETSESSIONUSER privilege

SECADM authority can only be granted by a user with SYSADM authority to a specific user. Unlike other authorities in DB2, SECADM can only be assigned to a single user, not a group. In addition, a SYSADM user cannot grant SECADM privileges to themselves.

The only way to get around this restriction is to change the session authorization to that of a user without the SECADM authority. To do this, a SYSADM user must have

SETSESSIONUSER privileges; however, SYSADM users can't grant this privilege to themselves either!

If users attempt to grant rights to themselves, they would get the following error message:

```
SQL0554N  An authorization ID cannot grant a privilege to itself.
SQLSTATE=42502
```

In order to give a SYSADM user the ability to perform actions associated with the SECADM authority, the following steps need to be taken:

1. Create a SECADM user using the operating system. Any user ID could be used, but we recommend creating a user account with the name SECADM because it's a convenient user ID to remember.

2. SYSADM grants SECADM privileges to new users since they cannot use the privilege themselves by entering the following command after making a connection to the target database:

```
GRANT SECADM ON DATABASE TO USER SECADM
```

3. Connect as SECADM and issue the following commands (assuming PAULZ is a user with SYSADM authority):

```
GRANT SETSESSIONUSER ON PUBLIC TO USER PAULZ
```

This command gives the SYSADM the ability to take on the identity of any user:

```
GRANT SECADM ON DATABASE TO USER PAULZ
```

The SECADM user then needs to grant back the SECADM privilege to the SYSADM user PAULZ.

DB2 *Note*

Depending on your operating system, you may need to login separately as these users to perform the steps in this example.

While these steps appear to be cumbersome, they have been created explicitly to delineate the role of the System Administrator versus the Security Administrator.

In many installations, the security administrator is a separate role, and this user should not have any administrative privileges. In smaller shops, the roles could be combined, or kept as separate users but managed by the same individual.

DBADM Authority

DBADM is a database-level authority as opposed to an instance-level authority. A user with DBADM authority can perform just about any administrative task on the database. For example, this authority gives users the ability to load data, create objects within a database, monitor database activity, and so on. A user with DBADM authority basically has complete control over a specific database; the users can query, drop, or create any table; grant or revoke privileges to users within the database; collect statistics via the RUNSTATS command; and more. It's possible for a single user or group to have DBADM authority for multiple databases.

Users with this authority cannot, however, perform maintenance and administrative tasks such as dropping a database, dropping or creating a table space, backing up or restoring a database, and so on.

Any user that creates the database is automatically granted the DBADM authority for the newly created database. DBADM authority can then be subsequently granted to other users by a user with SYSADM authority using the GRANT statement.

For example, consider the following statement:

```
CREATE DATABASE DB2CERT
```

This statement implicitly grants DBADM authority on a database called DB2CERT to the user who issued the command (of course, we assume the user account used to log on to the system has the authority to create a database).

Now consider the following statement:

```
GRANT DBADM ON DATABASE TO USER MOWENS
```

This statement gives DBADM authority to the user MOWENS on the DB2CERT database. This statement can only be issued once a connection is made to the DB2CERT database and can only be issued by a user with SYSADM authority.

Finally, consider this statement:

```
GRANT DBADM on DATABASE TO GROUP DBAS
```

This statement grants DBADM authority to all users that belong to the DBAS group. This statement can only be issued once a connection is made to the DB2CERT database and by a user with the correct authority to do so.

LOAD Authority

Users granted LOAD authority can run the LOAD utility without the need for SYSADM or DBADM authority. The LOAD command is typically used as a faster alternative to INSERT or IMPORT commands when populating a table with large amounts of data.

The LOAD authority was introduced in a previous version of DB2 to address the requirement to give an excessive number of privileges (breaking the principal of least privileges outlined earlier in this chapter) for users whose job it is to simply load a database, a role that's especially common in data warehousing environments. For example, the SYSADM authority provides the ability to stop and start an instance. An employee whose sole responsibility is to load data shouldn't have access to this elevated privilege.

Users granted the LOAD authority can perform the following tasks:

- If they have INSERT privilege on a table, they can use the LOAD INSERT command to load data into a table.
- If they have INSERT privilege on a table, they can LOAD RESTART or LOAD TERMINATE commands if the previous load operation was a load to insert data.
- If the previous load operation was a LOAD REPLACE, the DELETE privilege must also have been granted to that user before performing a LOAD RESTART or LOAD TERMINATE.
- Use exception tables (the user must have INSERT privilege on the exception tables to do this).
- Run the QUIESCE TABLESPACES FOR TABLE, RUNSTATS, and LIST TABLESPACES commands.

Depending on the type of LOAD you wish to perform, having LOAD authority alone may not be sufficient. Specific privileges on the table may also be required.

Since the LOAD authority is considered a database-level authority, it can be granted to users or groups. Only users with SYSADM or DBADM authority can grant the LOAD authority to a user or a group.

For example, to enable the user MKELLY to perform a LOAD INSERT, LOAD RESTART, or terminate a load after a LOAD INSERT, you would need to issue commands similar to the following after connecting to the database:

```
GRANT LOAD ON DATABASE TO USER MKELLY
GRANT INSERT ON TABLE ATOMICLAYER to USER MKELLY
```

DB2 *Note*

Since the LOAD authority can be granted to users or groups, simply substitute the USER parameter with GROUP to assign these same privileges to a group.

Table 4–2 illustrates some of the tasks that can be performed by the built-in authority levels in DB2.

Table 4–2 *Common database tasks and their required authority levels*

Function	SYSADM	SYSCTRL	SYSMAINT	DBADM	LOAD
UPDATE DBM CFG	YES				
GRANT/REVOKE DBADM	YES				
ESTABLISH/ CHANGE SYSCTRL	YES				
ESTABLISH/ CHANGE SYSMAINT	YES				
FORCE USERS	YES	YES			
CREATE/DROP DATABASE	YES	YES			
RESTORE TO NEW DATABASE	YES	YES			
UPDATE DB CFG	YES	YES	YES		
BACKUP DATABASE/ TABLE SPACE	YES	YES	YES		
RESTORE TO EXISTING DATABASE	YES	YES	YES		
PERFORM ROLL FORWARD RECOVERY	YES	YES	YES		
START/STOP INSTANCE	YES	YES	YES		
RESTORE TABLE SPACE	YES	YES	YES		
RUN TRACE	YES	YES	YES		

Table 4–2 *Common database tasks and their required authority levels*

Function	SYSADM	SYSCTRL	SYSMAINT	DBADM	LOAD
OBTAIN MONITOR SNAPSHOTS	YES	YES	YES		
QUERY TABLE SPACE STATE	YES	YES	YES	YES	YES
PRUNE LOG HISTORY FILES	YES	YES	YES	YES	
QUIESCE TABLE SPACE	YES	YES	YES	YES	YES*
LOAD TABLES	YES			YES	YES*
SET/UNSET CHECK PENDING STATUS	YES			YES	
CREATE/DROP EVENT MONITORS	YES			YES	

Privileges

Privileges are more granular than authorities. In fact, a number of privileges serve as the building blocks for the built-in DB2 authorities. A privilege is the right to create or access a database object. Privileges can be assigned to users and/or groups, and their assignments are stored in the DB2 catalog.

DBAs use privileges to help define the objects that a user or group can create, alter, or drop, and the types of commands they can use to access objects like tables, views, indexes, packages, and so on. If a certain privilege is given to a group, all members of that group have the same DB2 privilege unless they have had that authority explicitly revoked.

Privileges can be used to answer such security questions as:

- What users or groups can access what objects?
- What users and groups can create, alter, or drop what objects?
- Should certain users be allowed to give privileges to other users or groups?
- Who will have administrative authority on the database?
- What data will be accessed? Do we need a security plan that places security labels on the data?

There are basically two categories of privileges in DB2: database-scoped privileges and database object-scoped privileges. These categories can contain up to three types of privileges: ownership, individual, and implicit.

1. **Ownership privileges (referred to as CONTROL privileges in the DB2 command syntax)**

   For most objects, the user who creates an object has full access to that object, and therefore the CONTROL privilege is automatically granted to the creator of an object. There are some database objects, such as views, that are exceptions to this rule.

   When you have the CONTROL privilege on an object, you have ownership of that object. This means you have the right to access the object, give access to this object to others, and give others permission to grant privileges on the object to other users or groups. Privileges are controlled by users with ownership or administrative authority. These users can grant or revoke privileges using GRANT or REVOKE SQL statements.

2. **Individual privileges**

   These are privileges that allow you to perform a specific function, sometimes on a specific object. These privileges include SELECT, DELETE, INSERT, and UPDATE.

3. **Implicit privileges**

   An implicit privilege is one that is granted to a user automatically when that user is explicitly granted certain higher-level privileges. These privileges are not revoked when the higher-level privileges are explicitly revoked.

   In addition, an implicit privilege can also be associated with a package. For example, when a user executes a package that involves other privileges, the user executing the package obtains those privileges while executing the package. These users do not necessarily require explicit privileges on the data objects accessed within the package. These privileges are sometimes referred to as indirect privileges.

Figure 4–7 illustrates the hierarchy of authorizations and privileges. At the top of this figure are the built-in authorization groups in DB2. Note that the SECADM authorization is missing from this picture. We purposely excluded it because it controls security labels and is only used with LBAC (an advanced add-on security feature) in the generally available version of DB2 9.

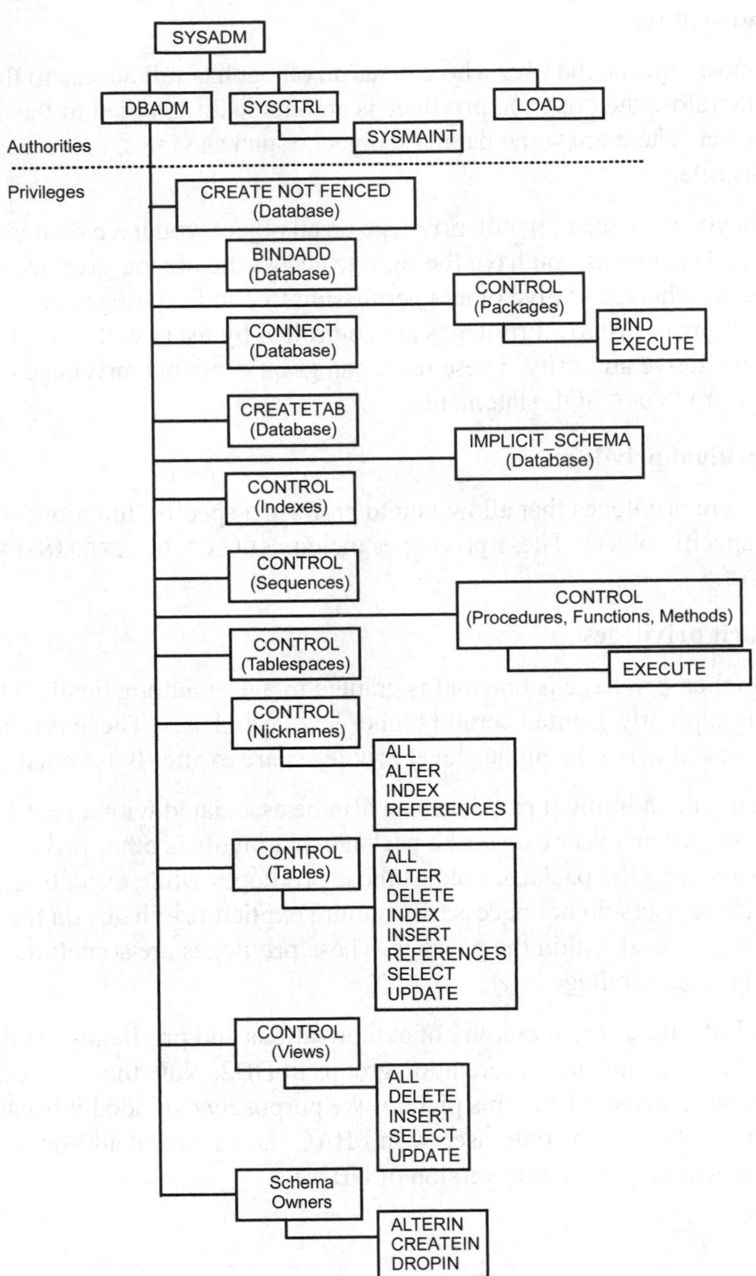

Figure 4–7 *Hierarchy of authorizations and privileges*

Database Privileges

Database privileges involve actions on a database as a whole, and only users with SYSADM or DBADM authority can grant and revoke these privileges. The database list of privileges in DB2 include:

- `CONNECT` allows a user to connect to a database.
- `BINDADD` allows a user to create new packages in a database using the `BIND` command
- `CREATETAB` allows a user to create new tables in a database.
- `CREATE_NOT_FENCED` allows a user to create a user-defined function (UDF) or stored procedure (collectively referred to as routines) that isn't fenced. Routines that aren't fenced must be extremely well tested because the database manager does not protect its storage or control blocks from them; as a result, a poorly written and tested routine that is allowed to run in an unfenced address space has the potential to cause serious problems for your system! We generally recommend not allowing users to create unfenced routines because the performance gains they can achieve versus fenced routines aren't worth the risk if the code used to implement the routine contains bad code.
- `IMPLICIT_SCHEMA` allows any user to create a schema implicitly by creating an object using a `CREATE` statement with a schema name that does not already exist. `SYSIBM` becomes the owner of any implicitly created schema, and `PUBLIC` is given the privilege to create objects in such a schema. For example, if user `MOWENS` creates a table called `MYGOLFSCORES` without specifying a schema name (and the schema name doesn't already exist), DB2 will create the table as `MOWENS.MYGOLFSCORES`.
- `LOAD` allows a user to load data into a table.
- `QUIESCE_CONNECT` allows a user to access the database while it is quiesced. A database may be placed into a quiesced state to allow for standalone maintenance or to allow an individual user or group of users to have exclusive use of the database.
- `CREATE_EXTERNAL_ROUTINE` allows a user to create an external routine for use by applications and other users of the database. Creating routines that run in this mode can result in much faster performance due to reduced calling overhead between the database manager and the routine. However, care must be taken in developing these types of routines since any incorrect memory allocations could affect the operation of the data server.

Controlling Data Access

Database Object Privileges

For each DB2 object, a specific authority or privilege is required to create it, and a specific authority or privilege is needed to have control over it.

The following list describes the privileges on various objects within the database:

- **Database authorities** — These include the ability to create and access a database. Any creator of a database automatically receives DBADM authority. The DBADM can issue any SQL statement against the database. A user with DBADM authority can grant the CONNECT privilege, the ability to create tables or new packages in the database, the ability to create a schema implicitly, and the ability to create unfenced routines.

  When a database is created, certain privileges are automatically granted to the group `PUBLIC`. If you want to control who can do what on the database, a `DBADM` or `SYSADM` user must revoke these privileges from `PUBLIC` (these include the `CREATETAB` and `BINDADD` privileges).
- **Schema privileges** — These include permissions to create, alter, or drop objects within schemas. The owner of the schema has all these permissions and the ability to grant them to others. The objects that belong to a schema include tables, views, indexes, packages, user-defined data types, user-defined functions, triggers, stored procedures, federated objects, XML Schema Documents, and aliases.
- **Table privileges** — `CONTROL` privilege on a table or view can only be granted by a user who has one of the `SYSADM` or `DBADM` authorities. (However, the creator of the table implicitly gets `CONTROL` privilege on that table.) Having `CONTROL` privilege on a table allows you to add columns; create a primary key; delete, retrieve, update, or insert rows; create indexes; create referential constraints; grant any of these privileges to others; use the `EXPORT` utility; and perform maintenance such as reorganizing tables or updating statistics on the table.

  The `UPDATE ON COLUMN` privilege allows users to modify only the specified columns of the table or view. In a similar way, the `REFERENCE ON COLUMN` privilege only allows for the creation of foreign keys on the stated columns.
- **View privileges** — To create a view, you must be able to issue an SQL `SELECT` statement or have `CONTROL` privilege on every table or view referenced in the statement used to instantiate the view. In order to grant delete, insert, select, and update privileges on a view, you need to have `CONTROL` privilege on that view unless the view is defined as a read-only view. The privileges required must be explicitly held by the user or be granted to PUBLIC (alternately, holding the `WITH GRANT OPTION` for each additional privilege would work as well).
- **Index privileges** — The user that creates the index receives `CONTROL` privileges on that index. This means that the user can drop the index. The table-level index privilege allows a user to create a new index on the table.
- **Procedures, Functions, and Methods privileges** — `EXECUTE` privileges involve actions on all types of routines such as functions, procedures, and meth-

ods within a database. Once a user has EXECUTE privileges on a routine, that user can invoke the routine, create a function that is sourced from that routine (applies to functions only), and reference the routine in any DDL statement such as CREATE VIEW, CREATE TRIGGER, or in the definition of a constraint. A user who creates an externally stored procedure, function, or method receives the EXECUTE WITH GRANT privilege.

- **Sequence privileges** — The creator of a sequence automatically receives the USAGE privilege. The USAGE privilege is needed to use the NEXTVAL and PREVVAL expressions for the sequence. To allow other users to use the NEXTVAL and PREVVAL expressions, sequence privileges must be granted to PUBLIC that would allow all users to use the expression for a specified sequence.
- **Nickname privileges** — Nicknames refer to tables in a federate DB2 system. A DB2 federated system is a special type of distributed database management system. The power of a DB2 federated system lies in its ability to:
  - Join data from local tables and remote data sources, as if all the data is local
  - Take advantage of a data source's processing strengths by sending distributed requests to federated data sources for processing
  - Compensate for SQL limitations at the data source by processing parts of a distributed request at the federated server.

  With a federated system you can send distributed requests to multiple data sources from a single SQL statement. For example, you can join data that is located in a DB2 table, an Oracle table, and a Sybase view in a single SQL statement.

  To define the data sources available to a federated application, the tables must first be defined using Nicknames. For more information on Federated Databases, see the *DB2 Administration Guide*.

- **Package privileges** — The creator of a package automatically receives CONTROL privilege on the package. That user can grant other users the ability to REBIND or EXECUTE the package. However, the person that rebinds a package must have the necessary privileges to access the objects referenced in the embedded static SQL statements. The required privileges must be obtained before doing the rebind.

  CONTROL privilege on a package also allows you to drop the package. Any user who has EXECUTE privilege on the package can execute the package without possessing the required privileges. To bind a new package to a database, you must have BINDADD database authority, be a user with DBADM authority, or belong to the SYSADM group.

Most of the database object privileges (tables, views, indexes, schemas, packages, and so on) are self-explanatory. Use Table 4–3 as a quick reference guide to the aforementioned privileges.

Table 4–3 *Privileges Reference Guide*

Privilege Name	Objects It Pertains To	Details
CONTROL	Table, View, Index, Package, Alias, Distinct Type, User, Defined Function, and Sequences	Provides full authority on the object. Users with this privilege can also GRANT or REVOKE privileges on an object to other users.
DELETE	Table or View	Allows users to delete records from an object using the DELETE statement.
INSERT	Table or View	Allows users to insert records into an object via the INSERT or the IMPORT commands.
SELECT	Table or View	Provides the ability to view the contents of an object using the SELECT statement.
UPDATE	Table or View	Allows users to modify records within an object using the UPDATE statement.
ALTER	Table	Allows users to alter an object definition using the ALTER statement.
INDEX	Table	Allows users to create indexes on an table using the CREATE INDEX statement.
REFERENCES	Table	Provides the ability to create or drop foreign key constraints on an object.
BIND	Package	Allows users to bind and rebind existing packages.
EXECUTE	Routines (package, procedure, functions, and methods)	Allows users to execute packages and routines.
ALTERIN	Schema	Allows users to modify the definition of an object within the schema.
CREATEIN	Schema	Allows users to create objects within a defined schema.
DROPIN	Schema	Allows users to drop objects within a defined schema.

DB2 stores the information of privileges that are granted to objects within the database in its system catalog views. Specifically, you can find such information in the following tables:

- SYSCAT.TABAUTH (for table and view privileges)
- SYSCAT.COLAUTH (for column privileges)
- SYSCAT.INDEXAUTH (for index privileges)
- SYSCAT.SCHEMAUTH (for schema privileges)
- SYSCAT.ROUTINEAUTH (for routine privileges)
- SYSCAT.PACKAGEAUTH (for package privileges)

To examine the groups specified for SYSADM, SYSCTRL, and SYSMAINT, view the database manager (DBM) configuration file. For all other authorities and privileges, examine the catalog views listed in this section to determine the users and groups that have access rights (or graphically using the Control Center).

Assigning Privileges

Two SQL statements are used to administer privileges:

- The GRANT statement grants privileges.
- The REVOKE statement revokes privileges.

For example, suppose you want user ANDREW to be able to drop the CANDIDATE table in the DB2CERT database. A DBA could issue a statement like the following to enable this action:

```
GRANT CONTROL ON TABLE CANDIDATE TO ANDREW
```

Unless Andrew is a SYSADM or DBADM, he cannot grant another user the CONTROL privilege on the CANDIDATE table.

To grant privileges on a database object, a user must have SYSADM authority, DBADM authority, CONTROL privilege, or a privilege WITH GRANT OPTION on that object. A user can grant privileges only on existing database objects. A user must have SYSADM or DBADM authority to grant CONTROL privilege. To grant DBADM authority, a user must have SYSADM authority.

As previously mentioned, you can also use the DB2 Control Center to easily view and change the privileges and authorities granted to users and groups as shown in Figure 4–8.

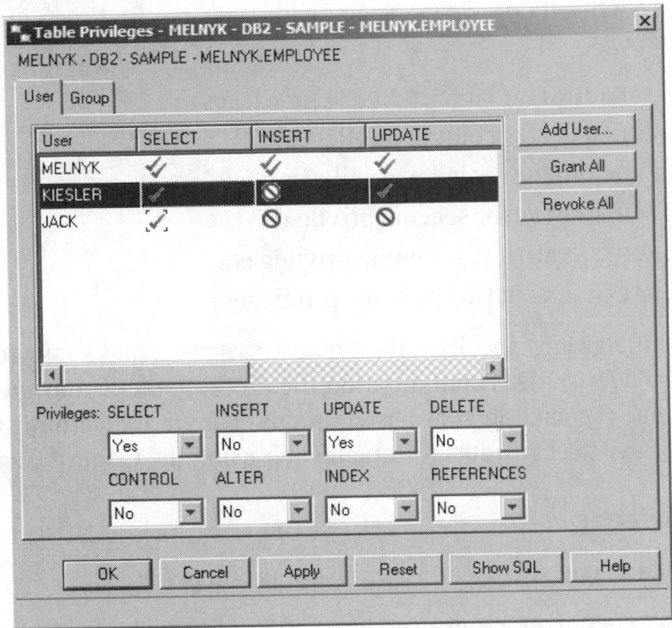

Figure 4–8 *Using the Control Center to administer privileges*

Table 4–4 summarizes some of the privileges required for database objects within DB2 to create a resource (database, schema, table, view, index, or package) or control the object.

Table 4–4 *Privileges and Authorities Related to Database Objects*

Object	Authority/Privilege Needed to Create	Authority/Privilege Needed to Control	Other Privileges on Object
DATABASE	SYSADM	DBADM	CONNECT BINDADD CREATETAB CREATE_NOT_FENCED IMPLICIT_SCHEMA CONNECT
SCHEMA	DBADM or IMPLICIT_SCHEMA	Ownership or IMPLICIT_SCHEMA	CREATEIN ALTERIN DROPIN
PACKAGE	BINDADD	CONTROL	BIND EXECUTE

Table 4–4 *Privileges and Authorities Related to Database Objects*

Object	Authority/Privilege Needed to Create	Authority/Privilege Needed to Control	Other Privileges on Object
TABLE or VIEW	CREATETAB (Table) CONTROL or SELECT (View)	CONTROL	SELECT (Table/ View) INSERT (Table/ View) DELETE (Table/ View) UPDATE (Table/ View) ALTER (Table) INDEX (Table) REFERENCES (Table)
INDEX	INDEX	CONTROL	NONE
ALIAS	If the schema differs from current authid, requires DBADM or IMPLICIT_SCHEMA. If schema is the same as an existing schema, may need CREATEIN privilege.	CONTROL	NONE
DISTINCT TYPE (UDT)	If the schema differs from current authid, requires DBADM or IMPLICIT_SCHEMA. If the schema is the same as an existing schema, may need CREATEIN privilege.	CONTROL	NONE
USER DEFINED FUNCTION (UDF)	If the schema differs from current authid, requires DBADM or IMPLICIT_SCHEMA. If the schema is the same as an existing schema, may require CREATIN privilege.	CONTROL	NONE
SEQUENCE	DBADM, SYSADM or CREATEIN privilege for the implicitly or explicitly specified schema.	DBADM, SYSADM, Ownership or IMPLICIT_SCHEMA	NONE

Application Development Privileges

There are certain privileges that you only need to concern yourself with if you are dealing with application developers. Each step of the development process requires certain privileges on database objects for which their code intends to operate. To better understand these requirements, it's useful to understand the typical steps that surround application development for database logic.

This methodology, and required privileges, is summarized in Table 4–5.

Table 4–5 *Privileges Required for Application Development*

Action	Privileges Required
Precompile to bindfile	CONNECT on database
Create a new package	CONNECT on database BINDADD on database Privileges needed to execute each static SQL statement explicitly or to PUBLIC
Modify an existing package	CONNECT on database BIND on package Privileges needed to execute each static SQL statement explicitly or to PUBLIC
Re-create an existing package	CONNECT on database BIND on package
Execute a package	CONNECT on database EXECUTE on package
Drop a package	CONNECT on database CONTROL on package or creator of package

An embedded SQL program must have its SQL statements prepared and bound as a package in a DB2 database before it can be successfully run by an application. The preparation step for a program with embedded static SQL does not require any privileges for the database objects by the user executing the application. If you attempt to compile your embedded SQL when required privileges on objects are not held, or the objects do not exist, warning messages are generated (the objects must exist during the bind phase as the existence and privileges of the objects are verified). In contrast, if a program contains dynamic embedded SQL statements, the statements are prepared and executed at run time.

To create a new package for any embedded SQL application you need to have both the CONNECT and BINDADD privileges on a database. You will also need the BIND privilege on the package to update its contents. To execute a package, you need EXECUTE privilege on that package.

Consider a simple scenario where all the privileges granted to the group PUBLIC, except CONNECT, were removed. In this scenario, let's determine the necessary database object authorities and privileges required according to the function that a user will be performing. In our scenario, we have a database where an application, called APP1, is used to manipulate names and addresses.

User GEORGE wants to execute a program called APP1. He also wants to be able to have his own table called GEORGE.PERSONAL to store other data. Therefore, we grant George EXECUTE privilege for the APP1 package. We also grant George the

CONTROL privilege for the PERSONAL table that resides in the GEORGE schema. We could have given him CREATETAB authority for the database and let him create the GEORGE.PERSONAL table himself; however, this would allow him to create many tables and we don't really trust him enough to do that. Remember, the APP1 package must exist in the database before we can grant George the EXECUTE privilege on it.

Katrina is an application developer who is writing the APP1 program. She needs to have SELECT, INSERT, UPDATE, and DELETE access to the various tables in the database. We need to GRANT these required privileges to Katrina in order for her to build the application logic. She also needs to be able to add new packages to the database and execute the application to test it; therefore, she needs to be granted the BINDADD authority.

Paul needs to be able to load data using the LOAD utility into various tables, but he will never execute the application. He needs DBADM authority. Another option for Paul is to grant him LOAD authority on the database, rather than DBADM authority. In DB2, we can use the LOAD authority to allow him to run the LOAD utility against this table and circumvent assigning him too many rights on the database – but we trust Paul, so we grant him DBADM authority. As far as the LOAD utility goes, SYSADM and DBADM also have this authority by default. However, if a user only has LOAD authority (not SYSADM or DBADM), the user is also required to have table-level privileges.

Chloë needs to be able to create a database to store personal information. Chloë is granted SYSADM authority for the DB2 instance. Therefore, Chloë can create the database and modify the database manager configuration file for the instance. As you may recall, SYSADM, SYSCTRL, and SYSMAINT authorities are not granted in the same way as the DBADM authority: they must be specified in the database manager configuration file.

Figure 4–9 depicts the authorities and privileges for the scenario we have just discussed.

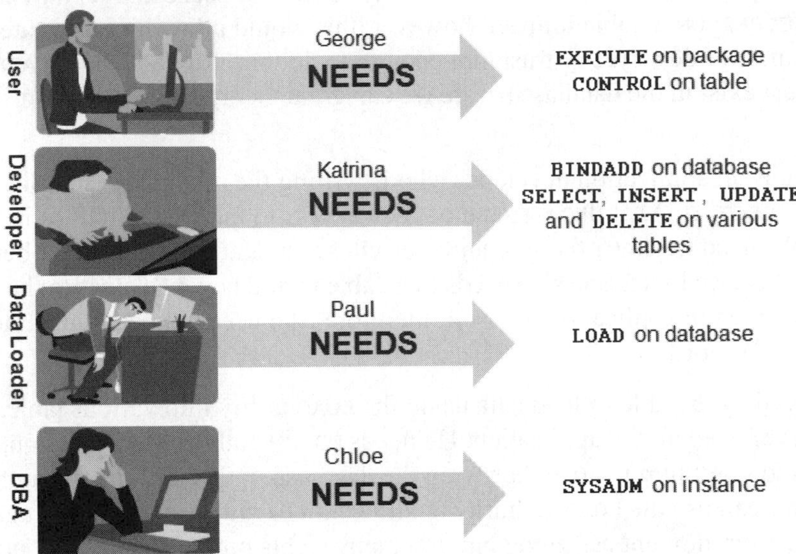

Figure 4–9 *Authority and privilege scenario*

Privileges of Groups

In addition to granting privileges to users of the database, one could grant privileges to groups. These group definitions are not handled in DB2 but in the operating system. A group consists of one or more users as defined in the security system. Every member of the group will have the same access privileges and authorities as granted to the group they belong to unless they have been granted higher-level privileges individually or have had privileges individually revoked.

Explicit, Implicit, and Indirect Privileges and Authorities

Privileges and authorities within DB2 can be obtained either explicitly, implicitly, or indirectly to users or groups. As a database administrator, you should be aware of the ways that users can obtain access to objects in your databases. This section examines the various ways that privileges and authorities can be obtained or revoked.

If a user who has SYSADM or SYSCTRL authority creates a database, the user is implicitly granted DBADM authority on that database. If that user has SYSADM or SYSCTRL authority removed, the user maintains DBADM authority on each database created. Removing DBADM authority must be done explicitly for each database using the REVOKE statement.

DB2 Note

A rule of thumb to differentiate between privileges that are granted implicitly or explicitly is to know whether a GRANT or REVOKE statement was used to assign the privilege in the first place. If this is the case, the privileges are explicit; otherwise they are implicit (or indirect).

When a user is granted DBADM authority on a database, the user is also implicitly granted CONNECT, CREATETAB, BINDADD, IMPLICIT_SCHEMA, and CREATE_NOT_FENCED privileges. If DBADM authority is later revoked, the implicitly granted privileges remain unless they are explicitly revoked.

When a user is granted CONTROL privilege on a table, that user is implicitly granted all of the other table privileges with the capability of allowing others access to it. If the CONTROL privilege is removed, the implicitly granted privileges remain unless they are explicitly revoked as well.

DB2 Note

You can quickly remove all remaining privileges for such a scenario using the REVOKE ALL statement. For example:

```
REVOKE ALL ON <tablename> FROM <username/groupname>
```

SYSADM or DBADM authority or CONTROL privilege on the table or view is required to revoke a privilege that was granted through the use of the WITH GRANT option. You should be aware, however, that in our example if Paul was granted privileges and the WITH GRANT option was specified, Paul can subsequently grant privileges to other users as well. Both Paul and the users he grants new privileges to under this authority are considered explicitly granted privileges.

If Paul were to have his privileges revoked, the privileges that Paul may have granted to others are unaffected. In other words, there is no cascade effect when using the WITH GRANT option.

When users attempt to perform an action that they do not have the necessary privileges for, DB2 will return an error. For example, in our scenario, George has CONTROL privilege on the GEORGE.PERSONAL table. This means that George can do about anything to this table.

However, suppose a table by the same name exists in the PAULZ schema. If George went to access this data, DB2 would return an error similar to the following since George doesn't have any privileges on the PAULZ.PERSONAL table:

```
SQL0551N "GEORGE" does not have the privilege to perform operations
"SELECT" on object "PAULZ.PERSONAL".
```

How could you solve this problem if you wanted George to be able to only select data from the PAULZ.PERSONAL table as well as his own? You could issue the following statement:

```
GRANT SELECT ON TABLE PAULZ.PERSONAL TO USER GEORGE
```

However, a need has arisen for George to insert data into the PAULZ.PERSONAL table as well. Indeed, a DBA could grant him this privilege; however, there are a number of other users that need to perform this same task on the PAULZ.PERSONAL table as well. In this case, it may be a good idea to just grant the INSERT privilege to a group. For example, the following statement grants the INSERT privilege to the INSERTERS group:

```
GRANT INSERT ON TABLE PAULZ.PERSONAL TO GROUP INSERTERS
```

The benefit of this approach is less administrative overhead with respect to granting and revoking privileges. While you could handle the granting of privileges to multiple users programmatically, controlling privileges via groups is a convenient and logical way to handle some administration tasks for your database.

If you wanted to remove all the privileges you just granted, you would enter the following commands:

```
REVOKE SELECT ON TABLE PAULZ.PERSONAL FROM USER GEORGE
REVOKE INSERT ON TABLE PAULZ.PERSONAL FROM GROUP INSERTERS
```

If you were concerned that over the course of time other privileges had been granted to the INSERTERS group, you could revoke privileges (except the CONTROL privilege if it had been granted) in a single statement as follows:

```
REVOKE ALL ON TABLE PAULZ.PERSONAL FROM GROUP INSERTERS
```

As previously mentioned, DB2 can grant privileges implicitly as well. As a DBA you'll want to ensure you understand this so that certain users or groups don't have privileges that you're not aware of as a result of performing (or allowing them to perform) some action on the database. Unlike the explicit privileges detailed earlier in this section, implicit privileges don't require the use of the GRANT statement to allocate them.

If an object that was created assigned implicit privileges, but was subsequently dropped, the implicitly granted privileges are also dropped. However, if higher-level privileges were granted and then revoked, the implicit privileges are not.

You should also be aware that DB2 also has a special group definition: the PUBLIC group. This group consists of all users, and CONNECT privilege is granted automatically to this group. Granting a privilege to PUBLIC provides all users with that privilege. There are certain privileges granted to PUBLIC by default. For example, PUBLIC also has SELECT privileges on the catalog tables. To follow the principle of least privileges approach to securing your data server, we recommend removing the SELECT privilege using the REVOKE statement after creating a database.

Table 4–6 summarizes the implicit privileges in DB2.

Table 4–6 *Implicit privileges*

Command Issued	Privilege Granted	To Whom It Is Granted
CREATE TABLE <table>	CONTROL on <table>	User issuing the command
CREATE TABLE <schema>	CREATEIN, ALTERNIN CREATEIN on <schema>, as well GRANT authority	User issuing the command
CREATE VIEW <view>	CONTROL on <view> if CONTROL is held on all tables and views referenced in the definition of the view	User issuing the command
CREATE VIEW <database>	SELECT on <database>'s system catalog tables and IMPLICIT_SCHEMA on <database>	PUBLIC

You may have noticed that in our working application development scenario a *package* was being created, and we had to assign the correct privileges to not only facilitate its execution but the creation of the package as well.

Privileges can be obtained indirectly when packages are executed by the database manager. A package contains one or more SQL statements that have been converted into a format that DB2 uses internally to execute them. In other words, a package contains multiple SQL statements in an executable format.

For example, let's assume that the package that Katrina created in our working scenario issued the following static SQL statements:

```
SELECT * FROM ORG
INSERT INTO TEST VALUES (1,2,3)
```

Katrina would need the `SELECT` privilege on the `ORG` table and the `INSERT` privilege on `TEST` table to build and bind the package. George would indirectly have the `SELECT` privileges on the `ORG` table and `INSERT` privileges on the `TEST` table because he was granted `EXECUTE` privilege on the package. However, if George were to directly try to select data from the `ORG` table, he would receive the SQL0551N error mentioned earlier in this section.

When Users and Group Have the Same Name

Some operating systems allow users and groups to have the same names, which can cause confusion for authorization and privilege checking within DB2. This is a concern you should be aware of when administering DB2 on UNIX operating systems (AIX, HP-UX, Solaris, and Linux). The Windows operating system doesn't permit a group and a user to have the same name.

Again, to better understand how DB2 would handle such a situation, it's best to work through a scenario. Suppose we have a user and group named `CHLOE` and we want to allow her to perform a `SELECT` on the `CANDIDATE` table. We could do this using either of the following two commands:

```
GRANT SELECT ON CANDIDATE TO CHLOE
GRANT SELECT ON CANDIDATE TO USER CHLOE
```

What happens if the operating system also has a group named `CHLOE`? The first command in the previous example is ambiguous. If the operating system had a user and group named Chloe, you may not be sure to which entity the privilege would be granted. In fact, if the user `CHLOE` didn't exist in the previous example, DB2 would grant the `SELECT` privilege on the `CANDIDATE` table to all the users in the group called `CHLOE` (assuming it exists). For this reason, we strongly recommend specifying the type of target entity your `GRANT` or `REVOKE` statements are intended for using either the `GROUP` or `USER` keywords. For example, you would use one of the following commands:

```
GRANT SELECT ON CANDIDATE TO USER CHLOE
GRANT SELECT ON CANDIDATE TO GROUP CHLOE
```

Set Session

This new privilege in DB2 9 provides more control over who has authority to switch session user identities. In DB2 8, users with DBADM or SYSADM authority could assume another user's identity by using the SET SESSION AUTHORIZATION statement. In DB2 9, the new SETSESSIONUSER privilege, can only be granted by the security administrator (SECADM) authority.

For backward compatibility, upon migration to DB2 9, any ID that holds DBADM authority is automatically granted the SETSESSIONUSER privilege on PUBLIC. A user who acquires DBADM authority after migration to DB2 9 will not be able to change the session authorization ID unless explicitly granted the SETSESSIONUSER privilege.

You can grant the new SETSESSIONUSER privilege to a user or to a group. This privilege allows the holder to switch identities to any of the authorization IDs to which you granted the privilege. The identity switch is made using the SET SESSION AUTHORIZATION SQL statement. For example:

```
SET SESSION AUTHORIZATION NAME ALLOW ADMINISTRATION
```

This statement can only be issued as the first statement in a new unit of work and only without any open WITH HOLD cursors. If the ALLOW ADMINISTRATION clause is specified, the following types of statements or operations can precede the SET SESSION AUTHORIZATION statement:

- Data definition language (DDL), including the definition of savepoints and the declaration of global temporary tables, but not including SET INTEGRITY
- GRANT and REVOKE statements
- LOCK TABLE statement
- COMMIT and ROLLBACK statements
- SET of special registers

Transfer Ownership

The TRANSFER OWNERSHIP SQL statement is new in DB2 9 and provides the security administrator or database object owner with the ability to change the ownership of a database object. For example, a test system may have been created with a particular developer being the owner of these objects. In DB2 9, all of the objects that make up the test system can now be transferred to a different user. A similar situation would arise if an employee changed jobs or left the company and their database objects needed to be assigned to someone else.

The `TRANSFER OWNERSHIP` SQL statement automatically grants the new owner the same privileges that the previous owner had that were obtained when the object was created. The syntax of this statement is:

```
TRANSFER OWNERSHIP OF <objects> TO <new owner>
   PRESERVE PRIVILEGES
```

The new owner can be one of the following:

- `USER`

  This specifies that the value of the USER special register is to be used as the authorization ID to which ownership of the object is being transferred.

- `SESSION_USER`

  This specifies that the value of the `SESSION_USER` special register is to be used as the authorization ID to which ownership of the object is being transferred.

- `SYSTEM_USER`

  This specifies that the value of the `SYSTEM_USER` special register is to be used as the authorization ID to which ownership of the object is being transferred.

The `PRESERVE PRIVILEGES` option in this command specifies that the current owner of an object that is to have its ownership transferred will continue to hold any existing privileges on the object after the transfer. If this clause is not specified, the creator (or original owner) of the objects will no longer have any privileges associated with those objects.

The objects can be any one of the following:

- ALIAS
- CONSTRAINT
- DATABASE PARTITION GROUP
- EVENT MONITOR
- FUNCTION, SPECIFIC FUNCTION, FUNCTION MAPPING
- INDEX, INDEX EXTENSION
- METHOD, SPECIFIC METHOD
- NICKNAME
- PACKAGE
- PROCEDURE, SPECIFIC PROCEDURE
- SCHEMA
- SEQUENCE
- TABLE, TABLE HIERARCHY

- TABLESPACE
- TRIGGER
- TYPE, TYPE MAPPING
- VIEW, VIEW HIERARCHY
- XSROBJECT

Note that all objects that need to be transferred must be specified in the command. Although the command can be specified multiple times, there is no equivalent of transferring "ALL" objects to another user. For instance, the following command will transfer the table BAKLARZ.EMPLOYEE to the user PAULZ:

```
TRANSFER OWNERSHIP OF TABLE BAKLARZ.EMPLOYEE
  TO PAULZ PRESERVE PRIVILEGES
```

Label-Based Access Control

Users attempting to access information from within a database needed at least three levels of authentication before retrieving any data:

- Valid credentials

  The user must be verified as a valid user in the system.

- Access to Database

  The user must be identified as someone who can "connect" to the database.

- SELECT Privilege

  Access to the underlying tables is required to be granted to the user.

While these three levels of authentication were normally sufficient for most applications, sensitive data required an extra level of security.

DB2 9 introduces an optional add-on security layer called Label-Based Access Control (LBAC). You can add LBAC capabilities to your data server by purchasing the Advanced Access Control feature pack. LBAC provides the ability to restrict read and write privileges at the row and column levels of a table. Before (or without) this feature, the only way to introduce these restrictions was to create a view on a table, authorize that view's use by the user in question, and remove access to the base table. Now imagine doing this for hundreds or thousands of users and you will see that this model doesn't scale well.

LBAC controls access to table objects by attaching security labels to rows and columns so that users attempting to access an object must have its security label granted to them. The LBAC capability is very configurable and can be tailored to match any specific security environment.

LBAC requires careful planning in the design of the labels, components, and security policies, but the end result will be a system that maintains the security and integrity of the records within the database.

LBAC Overview

Label-Based Access Control (LBAC) is commonly referred to as the ability to control access to data rows based on security labels. The DB2 LBAC solution is extremely flexible in that it allows you to implement access control at:

- Row level
- Column level
- Table level (simulated using column level labeling)

Row-level and column-level protection can be used either separately or combined. LBAC complements the traditional DB2 access control, which is implemented via the GRANT command.

In addition to the three levels of authentication discussed previously, DB2 will enforce a number of additional rules when LBAC is associated with a table:

- Access control at the table level

  Does the user hold the required privilege to perform the requested operation on the table?

- Label-based access control

  LBAC controls access to table objects by attaching security labels to rows and columns. Labels can be at either the row level, column level, or both.

Users attempting to access an object must have its security label granted to them. Assuming that the user has access to the table, a SELECT statement with LBAC will only return rows they are allowed to see. No indication is given that they did not retrieve any rows because of insufficient security clearance.

The steps that are required to implement an LBAC solution are:

1. Define the security policies and labels.
   - Define the security label component.
   - Define the security policy.
   - Define the security labels.
2. Create the protected table by including a column that holds the security label and attaching the security policy to the table.
3. Create the appropriate security labels to users.

Figure 4–10 shows how these different security components are related.

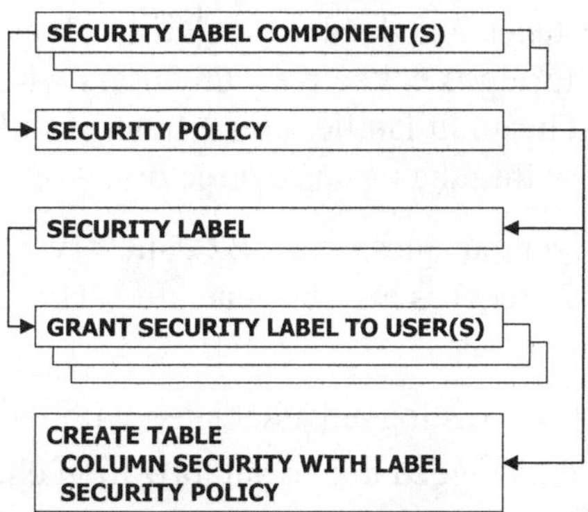

Figure 4–10 *Relationship between security components*

All of the LBAC definitions and granting of security labels to users are under the control of the security administrator (SECADM). The new security administrator authority collects several security-related privileges under one authority. The primary reason for this new security administrator is to separate the management of the data from the security controls on it. In many customer installations, the administrators of the data should not be able to view or manipulate the data. By implementing the SECADM authority, and using LBAC, a DBA can be prevented from manipulating the data they manage.

What LBAC Does Not Prevent

There are a number of things that LBAC cannot do:

- LBAC will never allow access to data that the user does not have permission to read (SELECT) from in the first place.
- A user's LBAC credentials only limit access to protected data. Any data in the table that has not been protected can be accessed regardless of LBAC settings.
- LBAC credentials are not checked when a table or database is dropped, even if the table or database contains protected data.
- LBAC credentials are not checked when data is backed up. The rows that are backed up are not limited in any way by the LBAC protection on the data. Also, data on the backup media is not protected by LBAC. Only data in the database is protected.
- LBAC cannot be used to protect materialized query tables (MQT), staging tables, or typed tables.

For more detailed information on LBAC and how to implement it, please refer to the *DB2 Administration Guide*.

Auditing

The DB2 audit facility is associated with an instance. It records auditable events associated with the instance and databases within it. It can be active even though the instance it is monitoring is not active. Only users with SYSADM authority can use the audit facility. The audit facility uses a binary configuration file located in the security directory within the instance directory.

For each operation a user executes on a DB2 data server, such as a SELECT statement, one or more audit records may be generated. These audit records are categorized into the following groups:

- `AUDIT` All records logged associated with the audit facility.
- `CHECKING` Events logged due to authorization checking when accessing DB2 objects.
- `OBJMAINT` Records logged caused by dropping or creating objects.
- `SECMAINT` Records logged due to changing `SYSADM_GROUP`, `SYSCTRL_GROUP`, `SYSMAINT_GROUP`, grant/revoke `DBADM`, or any privileges on any database objects.
- `SYSADMIN` Records logged for operations that required `SYSADM`, `SYSCTRL`, and `SYSMAINT` authority.
- `VALIDATE` Records are generated when authenticating users or retrieving system security information.
- `CONTEXT` This type of audit record shows detailed information about an operation. This operation may have caused multiple records to be logged in the audit log. Such records can be associated with the `CONTEXT` record using the event correlator field.

The audit facility may generate multiple audit records for a single operation, each of which may belong to a different record category.

Buffering Audit Log Writes

When configuring the audit facility, a `SYSADM` user can specify whether the audit facility should write audit records directly to disk in a synchronous mode or buffer the records in an audit buffer for asynchronous writing. This buffer size can be specified using the `AUDIT_BUFF_SZ` parameter located in the database manager configuration file. If the `AUDIT_BUFF_SZ` is set to 0, all audit record writing will be done synchronously; any number larger than zero indicates the buffer size as a multiple of 4KB.

If a buffer size is specified, the buffer will be written out to disk at regular intervals, or if the buffer becomes full. A `SYSADM` user can also force the audit buffer to be flushed to disk.

Configuring the Audit Facility

Before starting the audit facility, you need to configure it for use with the DB2AUDIT CONFIGURE command. The syntax for the command is:

```
db2audit CONFIGURE SCOPE scope STATUS status ERRORTYPE errortype
```

- SCOPE refers to which set of audit record categories should be logged. If ALL is specified as the category, it includes all the categories except the CONTEXT category.
- STATUS refers to whether an event should be logged if it returned successfully, failed, or both. The available values are SUCCESS, FAILURE, or BOTH.
- ERRORTYPE is either AUDIT or NORMAL. By setting ERRORTYPE to AUDIT, any error occurring in the audit facility will return the SQLCODE of the error to the application for which the audit record was logged during the failure. It will also cause the operation attempted by the application to fail. If ERRORTYPE is set to NORMAL, none of the applications executing will be affected if an attempt to generate an audit record fails.

For example, the following command will configure auditing to capture all events that are failures and not to affect the transaction that was running in the event of an audit error.

```
db2audit CONFIGURE SCOPE ALL STATUS FAILURE ERRORTYPE NORMAL
```

Looking at the Current Configuration

To see the current audit configuration, use the DESCRIBE option of the db2audit command as shown next.

```
db2audit DESCRIBE

DB2 AUDIT SETTINGS:
Audit active: "FALSE "
Log errors: "TRUE "
Log success: "FALSE "
Log audit events: "TRUE "
Log checking events: "TRUE "
Log object maintenance events: "TRUE "
Log security maintenance events: "TRUE "
Log system administrator events: "TRUE "
Log validate events: "TRUE "
Log context events: "FALSE "
Return SQLCA on audit error: "FALSE "

AUD0000I  Operation succeeded.
```

Starting the Audit Facility

Once the audit facility is configured, it can be started regardless of whether the instance is started. Use the following command to start the audit facility:

```
db2audit START
```

Flushing the Audit Buffer

Before extracting an audit log, SYSADM may want to make sure the audit buffer is flushed to disk using the following command:

```
db2audit FLUSH
```

Extracting the Audit Log

When the audit facility is started, it starts generating a binary audit log. This binary audit log writes information about each audit record category monitored. The audit log can be extracted by a SYSADM user to one of two formats: a text-based file containing the audit records or an ASCII-delimited file (DELASC).

The audit log's file names correspond to the names of the categories being audited When choosing an audit log output type, users can also override the default delimiter 0xFF by specifying the delimiter to use. These files can then be used to populate tables in a database by using the LOAD or IMPORT utilities.

For example, if a SYSADM user wanted to extract all the records in the validate and checking categories for the database SAMPLE to ASCII-delimited files using the "!" character as the delimiter, you would use the following command:

```
db2audit EXTRACT delasc DELIMITER ! CATEGORY validate, checking
        DATABASE sample
```

The output of this command will be two files named VALIDATE.DEL and CHECKING.DEL. The default delimiter 0xFF was overridden by the DELIMITER option. If a SYSADM user wanted to extract all the validation records to a text file, the command would look like this:

```
db2audit EXTRACT file myfile.txt CATEGORY validate
        DATABASE sample
```

In this case, the output will be in a file named MYFILE.TXT. If the file existed prior to executing the command, the command would fail. The following shows a sample of an audit log file:

```
timestamp=2007-04-17-15.03.17.131001;category=VALIDATE;audit event=AUTHENTICATION;
  event correlator=2;event status=-30082;
  database=SAMPLE;userid=BAKLARZ;execution id=BAKLARZ;
  origin node=0;coordinator node=0;
  application id=*LOCAL.DB2.070417190319;application name=db2demo.exe;
  auth type=SERVER;plugin name=IBMOSauthserver;
```

You can see in the previous example that a user named BAKLARZ connected to the SAMPLE database using the DB2DEMO.EXE program.

Pruning the Audit Log

To delete all the audit records from the audit log, use the following command:

```
db2audit PRUNE all
```

If the audit facility is set up to record events categorized as AUDIT events, an entry will be made in the audit log after the log has been cleared. Another way to prune is to specify the date/time before which all entries should be cleared out of the audit log. For example:

```
db2audit PRUNE DATE <yyyymmddhh> PATHNAME <pathname>
```

Adding the optional pathname parameter allows a user with SYSADM authority to prune the audit log if the drive or file system on which it is logged becomes full.

Stopping the Audit Facility

To stop the audit facility, use the following command:

```
db2audit STOP
```

Figure 4–11 shows a potential auditing scenario.

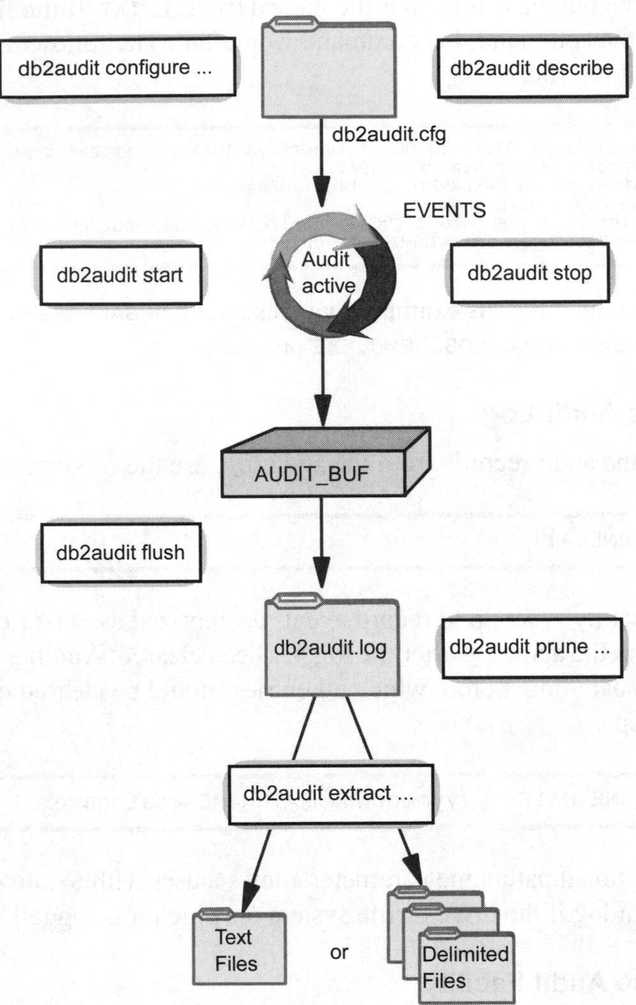

Figure 4–11 *The audit facility*

You can see in Figure 4–11 that the audit facility is first configured and checked before it's started. If the SYSADM user wants to look at the audit log, the audit buffer can then be flushed and the audit log extracted either as a text file or as delimited file. Using this output file, the administrator populates the audit tables. At some point, the user can stop the audit facility and, if desired, clear the audit log of all or some of the records.

Summary

This chapter discussed a number of topics relating to controlling access to a data server, its databases, and the data contained within. We started this chapter by talking about the component of a security framework and then highlighted the DB2 facilities to implement it: authentication, encryption of passwords and data, authorities, privileges, and more.

A server's authentication method is defined within the database manager configuration file of an instance. Clients that connect to these servers must have a compatible authentication setting in their client directory in order to connect to the remote data server. All databases within an instance share the same authentication type.

This chapter also talked about several of the authorization levels that are built into DB2: SYSADM, SYSCTRL, SYSMAINT, LOAD, DBADM, and SECADM. SYSADM has system administrative authority over an instance and is able to perform any administration operations as well as access any information from any database that exists within that instance (there are exceptions, for example, if an LBAC security control is being used).

SYSCTRL does not have the authority to access the database (unless explicitly granted), nor can SYSCTRL modify the database manager configuration; however, SYSCTRL can perform a lot of administration functions.

SYSMAINT also cannot access user data but allows you to perform a subset of the maintenance functions that SYSCTRL can perform, such as backup or restore databases and table spaces, and so on.

At the database level, DBADM has complete authority over the database objects. This authority includes creating or dropping tables, running a query, and setting privileges for other users of the database. Other database-level authorities include LOAD (self-explanatory) and SECADM for administration of an LBAC environment.

This chapter also examined the granting and revoking of authorities and privileges using the GRANT and REVOKE statements, and it provided working examples to illustrate their use. It also covered the different types of privileges and what they allow a user to do. Examples are CONTROL, INSERT, DELETE, CREATEIN, DROPIN, REFERENCES, and SELECT. Differentiation among implicit, explicit, and indirect (for packages only) privileges was done too.

Finally, we talked about the DB2 audit facility. It allows you to monitor security-related events and possible system abuse.

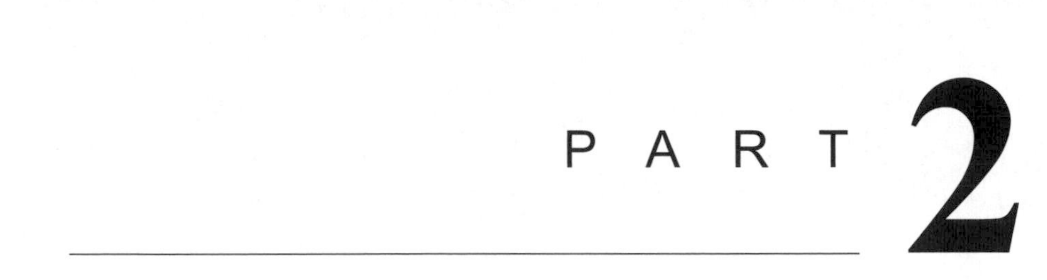

PART 2

Using SQL

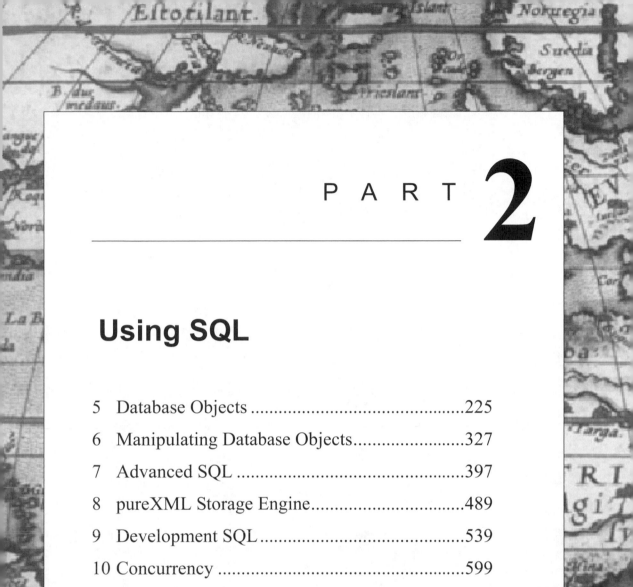

C H A P T E R 5

Database Objects

- CREATING DATABASE OBJECTS
- DATA TYPES
- TABLES
- CONSTRAINTS
- VIEWS
- INDEXES

The standard language of relational database access is SQL (Structured Query Language). SQL is not a conventional programming language. It was designed for the purpose of accessing tabular data. Every Relational Database Management System (RDBMS) implements a slightly different version of SQL.

In this chapter we examine the DB2 implementation of the SQL language. If you are familiar with other RDBMS products, you will already understand many aspects of the DB2 implementation of SQL thanks to the industry acceptance of the ISO®/ANSI® SQL standard.

We first examine the DB2 database objects that can be referenced in an SQL statement; then, we examine the SQL language elements. A database object, for the purpose of this book, is any component of a DB2 database, such as table spaces, tables, views, indexes, packages, logs, and locks. It is important to note that some of these database objects cannot be directly referenced using the SQL language.

SQL is divided into three major categories:

- DDL (Data Definition Language) — Used to create, modify, or drop database objects
- DML (Data Manipulation Language) — Used to select, insert, update, or delete database data (records)
- DCL (Data Control Language) — Used to provide data object access control

As SQL has evolved, many new statements have been added to provide a more complete set of data management methods. We explore some of these features, including constraints, triggers, outer joins, large object data access, and common table expressions.

Later in this chapter, the use of DDL (Data Definition Language) to create database objects is discussed.

DCL is discussed in Chapter 4.

Understanding Database Objects

A database is an organized collection of objects. Each database has its own system catalog, log files, security, and tuning parameters.

SQL is used throughout the database industry as a common method of issuing database queries. SQL is a language, composed of statements, functions, and data types. Before we examine the SQL language, we need to understand some DB2 terminology. We will be referring to the basic components or objects that are defined for each DB2 database. These objects include:

- Tables
- Schemas
- Table spaces
- Views
- Indexes
- Packages
- Buffer pools
- Locks
- Triggers
- Stored procedures
- Log files

Data Types

Each column in a DB2 table must be associated with a *data type*. The data type indicates the kind of data that is valid for the column. There are two major categories of data types in DB2.

- Built-in data types
- User-defined data types

Built-in data types are defined by DB2. DB2 supports a number of built-in data types that are described later in this chapter. DB2 also provides support for *user-defined data types*. User-defined types are classified into the following three types:

- User-defined distinct type
- User-defined structured type
- User-defined reference type

User-defined distinct types (UDT) enable you to create a new data type that has its own semantics based on existing built-in data types. *User-defined structured types* enable you to create a structure that contains a sequence of named attributes each of which has a data type. This is one of the extensions of DB2 Object Relational functions. A *user-defined reference type* is a companion type to a user-defined structured type. Similar to a user-defined distinct type, a user-defined reference type is a scalar type that shares a common representation with one of the built-in data types. A user-defined reference type may be used to reference rows in another table that uses a user-defined structured type. User-defined distinct types (UDTs) will be discussed in this chapter; user-defined structured types and user-defined reference types will be discussed in Chapter 7.

DB2 Note

User-defined structured types allow a user to create structures in DB2 and use them as columns within a table. This is one way that DB2 extends the relational model to be more object-oriented.

Tables

A *table* is an unordered set of rows. Rows consist of columns. Each column is based on a data type. Tables, once created and populated with data, are referenced in the `FROM` and `INTO` clauses of the DML statements. There are three types of tables:

- Permanent (base) tables
- Temporary (declared) tables
- Temporary (derived) tables

We only discuss permanent tables in this chapter. These tables are created using the `CREATE TABLE` statement and each is a logical representation of the way the data is physically stored on disk. We discuss the temporary tables in Chapter 7.

DB2 Note

Temporary declared tables allow an application developer or user to create tables that exist only for the duration of the program.

Schemas

Schemas are database objects used in DB2 to logically group other database objects. Most database objects are named using a two-part naming convention (`SCHEMA_NAME.OBJECT_NAME`). The first part of the name is referred to as the schema (otherwise known as a qualifier for the database object). The second part is the *object name*.

When you create an object and do not specify a schema, the object will be associated with an *implicit schema* using your *authorization ID*. When an object is referenced in an SQL statement, it is also implicitly qualified with the authorization ID of the issuer (dynamic SQL) if no schema name is specified in the SQL statement.

The CURRENT SCHEMA special register contains the default qualifier to be used for unqualified objects referenced for dynamic SQL statements issued from within a specific DB2 connection. This value can be modified by the user with the SET CURRENT SCHEMA statement. Static SQL statements are qualified with the authorization ID of the person binding the application (by default). For example, if user KATRINA connected to the database and created a table called TASKS, the complete name of the table as stored in the database would be: KATRINA.TASKS. You can use the QUALIFIER option of the BIND command to define the default qualifier at bind time.

One additional schema qualifier is the SESSION keyword. This keyword is used for temporary tables that are created and used during a connection. The SESSION qualifier is discussed later in the section "The DECLARE Statement" on page 236.

DB2 *Note*

When a program or user declares a temporary table, the only way to reference it in the SQL is through the use of the SESSION qualifier. If the SESSION qualifier is not used, DB2 will attempt to find the table using the current schema.

Table Spaces

Table spaces are the logical layers between the database and the tables stored in that database. Table spaces are created within a database, and tables are created within table spaces. DB2 supports two kinds of table spaces:

- System Managed Space (SMS) — The operating system's file system manager allocates and manages the space where the table space is to be stored. SMS is the default table space type.
- Database Managed Space (DMS) — The database manager controls the storage space. This is, essentially, an implementation of a special-purpose file system designed to best meet the needs of the database manager.

When a table is defined using the CREATE TABLE statement, you can explicitly state in which table space the table will reside. By default, all tables will be created in the USERSPACE1 table space. Table spaces provide the database administrator with the ability to control the location of tables, indexes, and large objects. You can define any number of table spaces within a single database and any number of tables within a table space.

Views

Views are virtual tables that are derived from one or more tables or views and can be used interchangeably with tables when retrieving data. When changes are made to the data through a view, the data is changed in the underlying table itself. Views do not contain real data. Only the definition exists in the database. Views can be created to limit access to sensitive data while allowing more general access to other data. Views can be deletable, updatable, insertable, and read-only. The classification indicates the kind of SQL operations allowed against the view.

Indexes

Indexes are physical objects that are associated with individual tables. Any permanent table or declared temporary table can have indexes defined on it. You cannot define an index on a view. You can define multiple indexes for a single table. Indexes are used for two primary reasons:

- Ensure uniqueness of data values
- Improve SQL query performance

Indexes can be used to access data in a sorted order more quickly and avoid the time-consuming task of sorting the data using temporary storage. Indexes can also be created on computed columns so that the optimizer can save computation time by using the index instead of doing the calculations. Indexes are maintained automatically by DB2 as data is inserted, updated, and deleted.

DB2 *Note*

Another important feature in index creation is the ability to add additional values to the index, which can be used by the optimizer to get non-key data. This can also result in much faster performance for queries, which can get their answer sets from the index rather than from the data pages.

The maintenance overhead of indexes can negatively impact the performance of `INSERT`, `UPDATE`, and `DELETE` statements.

Indexes can be defined in ascending or descending order. They can be defined as unique or nonunique, and they can be defined on a single column or multiple columns. They can also be defined to support both forward and reverse scans. In DB2 9, all indexes are automatically created with forward and reverse scans. For prior releases, the index direction must be explicitly stated. The Visual Explain utility provides index usage information for every explainable SQL statement (if the explain data is gathered).

DB2 Note

DB2 8 introduced a new index structure in the database. These new indexes are referred to as "Type-2" indexes and help to eliminate a phenomena called "next-key locking." Transactions in prior releases could lock an adjacent record during processing. This could result in unnecessary delays in completing transactions that depended on this record. Any new indexes created in Version 8 or 9 will use this new index structure, while existing indexes will be replaced only when the user drops and recreates them, or reorganizes the indexes and specifies that they should be converted.

In addition, DB2 8 also allows indexes to be created on temporary tables. Prior to this, any query against a temporary table object would result in a complete scan of the table.

Packages

Packages are database objects that contain executable forms of SQL statements. These packages contain statements that are referenced from a DB2 application. A package corresponds to a program source module.

DB2 Note

Only the corresponding program source module can invoke the contents of a package.

Packages are stored in the catalog. Packages contain access plans selected by DB2 during the `BIND` or `PREP` process. This type of `BIND` is known as static binding since it is performed prior to the execution of the SQL statement. Packages cannot be directly referenced in DML statements.

Most applications that access a DB2 database will have a package or group of packages in the catalog.

DB2 Note

Packages can now exist with different version numbers. This option allows multiple versions of the same package name (package name and creator name) to coexist. This allows you to make changes to an existing application and not invalidate the existing package that users are running.

Buffer Pools

Buffer pools are database objects used to cache data pages in memory. Once a data page is placed in a buffer pool, physical I/O access to disk can be avoided. Buffer pools can be assigned to cache only a particular table space.

Every DB2 database must have a buffer pool. For each new database, DB2 defines the IBMDEFAULTBP default buffer pool for the database.

The CREATE BUFFERPOOL statement is used to define buffer pools other than the default IBMDEFAULTBP buffer pool. Once a buffer pool is created, table spaces can be assigned to it using the CREATE TABLESPACE statement or the ALTER TABLESPACE statements.

The SYSCAT.BUFFERPOOLS catalog view accesses the information for the buffer pools defined in the database.

Transactions

A *transaction* is a sequence of SQL statements that execute as a single operation. The term *unit of work* is synonymous with the term *transaction*.

A transaction either succeeds or fails. A transaction starts implicitly with the first executable SQL statement in a program. The transaction ends when either an explicit or implicit COMMIT or ROLLBACK statement is encountered. An implicit COMMIT or ROLLBACK can occur when a DB2 application terminates.

DB2 also allows supports SAVEPOINTs within a transaction. This allows a selective rollback without undoing work prior to the savepoint. More details on COMMIT, ROLLBACK, and SAVEPOINTS can be found in Chapter 9.

DB2 Note

Application savepoints provide control over the work performed by a subset of SQL statements in a transaction or unit of work. Within your application you can set a savepoint, and later either release the savepoint or roll back the work performed since you set the savepoint.

It is best to explicitly COMMIT or ROLLBACK outstanding SQL transactions prior to terminating a DB2 application. Whether DB2 implicitly performs a COMMIT or ROLLBACK depends on the operating environment.

Locks

DB2 is a multiuser database product. As users request data, the DB2 locking mechanism attempts to avoid resource conflicts yet still provide full data integrity. As SQL statements are processed, the transactions may obtain locks. The locks are released when the resource is no longer required at the end of the transaction. The locks are stored in memory on the database server (in a structure known as the *locklist*). DB2 supports two types of locks, table locks and row locks.

The locking strategy used by DB2 during transaction processing is specified using an *isolation level* as defined when binding the application.

DB2 *Note*

Locking levels can be dynamically set in DB2. As part of the SQL statement, developers can assign the type of locking level they wish to have during the duration of that statement. This allows the developer more flexibility in the types of locks that are held at the statement level, rather than using one type of locking for the entire application.

Log Files

A number of *log files* are associated with each DB2 database. As transactions are processed, they are tracked within the log files. DB2 will track all of the SQL statements that are issued for a database within its database log files.

DB2 uses *write-ahead logging* for database recovery. The changes are first written to the log files and, at a later time, applied to the physical database tables.

DB2 *Note*

There are physical limits to the size that an individual log file can grow to, so DB2 will "chain" log files together so that a user should never run out of log space. This should allow long-running transactions to finish without filling up one log file. However, applications should commit their work at regular intervals so that this type of log chaining does not occur!

Creating a DB2 Database

A DB2 database must exist before any of the database objects can be created in it. The database must be given a name. (There is no schema associated with the database.) Once the database has been created, the next logical step is to create the table spaces that will be used to store the user tables.

DB2 Note

The CREATE DATABASE command is not an SQL statement but is a DB2 CLP command. The database name can be 1 – 8 characters long.

When you create a database without any table space options, three table spaces are created by default:

- SYSCATSPACE — Contains the system catalog tables
- TEMPSPACE1 — Contains temporary tables used by DB2
- USERSPACE1 — Contains the user tables unless other user table spaces are created

These table spaces can be specified as either SMS or DMS table spaces in the CREATE DATABASE command. Prior to DB2 9, the default table space format was SMS. Starting with DB2 9, the new default uses automatic DMS storage. If applications require temporary table storage, an addition table space type, USER temporary table space, needs to be defined.

Please refer to Chapter 11 for more information about databases and table spaces.

DB2 Note

Temporary tables that are DECLARED in a transaction require the use of a USER temporary table space. This needs to be created and access granted to users before temporary tables are used.

Managing Database Objects

To create, modify, or delete objects in a database, SQL Data Definition Language (DDL) is used.

Using SQL Data Definition Language (DDL)

DDL has four basic SQL statements:

- CREATE
- ALTER
- DROP
- DECLARE

DB2 Note

The DECLARE statement is used for temporary tables in an application. This can only be used for temporary tables and requires the use of USER temporary table spaces.

The CREATE Statement

```
CREATE <database object>....
```

The CREATE statement is used to create database objects. The list of database objects that can be created are:

- Table
- Index
- Schema
- View
- User-defined function
- User-defined data type
- Buffer pool
- Table space
- Stored procedures
- Trigger
- Alias
- Method
- Transform

- Nickname
- Sequence
- Server
- Wrapper

The creation of any database object updates the catalog tables. Specific authorities and privileges are required to create database objects.

The DECLARE Statement

```
DECLARE <database object>....
```

The DECLARE statement is very similar to the CREATE statement, except that it is used to create temporary tables that are used only during a session. The only object that can be DECLARED is a table, and it must be placed into an existing USER temporary table space.

The creation of a temporary table does not update the catalog, so locking, logging, and other forms of contention are avoided with this object.

DECLARED tables can be DROPPED and ALTERED, but no other database objects (other than indexes) can be created to act against them. Temporary tables do allow for the specification of a partitioning key and the creation of indexes for improved performance.

Once a table is declared, it can be referenced like any other table. The following example shows a temporary table being declared and then used in a subsequent SQL statement.

```
DECLARE GLOBAL TEMPORARY TABLE T1
   LIKE TRANSACTIONS
   ON COMMIT PRESERVE ROWS NOT LOGGED IN SESSIONTEMP;

INSERT INTO SESSION.T1
  SELECT * FROM TRANSACTIONS WHERE SALES < 3000;

SELECT * FROM SESSION.T1;
```

Example 5–1 *Using a temporary table*

DB2 Note

The DECLARE statement is used to create temporary tables that are used only during the duration of session. The table does not cause any logging or contention against the catalog and is very useful for working with intermediate results. Users can also create indexes on temporary tables. This can dramatically improve the performance of queries against these objects. In addition, transactions against temporary tables can now be logged so that the user has the ability to undo transactions against these tables.

The DROP Statement

```
DROP <database object>....
```

The DROP statement is used to delete objects from the database. Since database objects can be dependent on other database objects, the act of dropping an object can result in a related object being rendered invalid. You can drop any object created with the CREATE <database object> and the DECLARE <table> statements.

The ALTER Statement

```
ALTER <database object>....
```

The ALTER statement allows you to change some characteristics of existing database objects. The types of database objects that can be altered are:

- Table
- Table space
- Database partition
- Server
- Procedure
- Function
- Nickname
- Sequence
- Type
- Wrapper
- View
- Method
- User mapping
- Buffer pool

DB2 Note

You cannot alter an index. You must drop and create a new index.

Every time you issue a DDL statement (except for the `DECLARE` statement), the catalog is updated. The update includes a creation or modification timestamp and the authorization ID of the user issuing the statement.

Let's look in detail at some of the objects that can be created in a database. We will cover data types, tables, views, and indexes.

DB2 Note

It is useful to store all of the DDL statements for the database in a script file to allow for easier creation of the database objects. This script can either be used from the DB2 CLP or the DB2 Command Center. It is possible to extract the DDL for objects using the `DB2LOOK` utility if you haven't kept a copy of the database creation commands.

Data Types

Every column in a table must be assigned a data type. Before discussing tables, we have to understand the various data types supplied by DB2 or defined by users.

First let us look at the built-in data types supplied by DB2.

DB2 Built-in Data Types

Every DB2-supplied data type belongs to one of these three major categories (`DATALINK` is not included in this categorization list but is represented in Figure 5–1):

- Numeric
- String (Binary, Single Byte, Double Byte)
- Datetime

The built-in DB2 data types are shown in Figure 5–1.

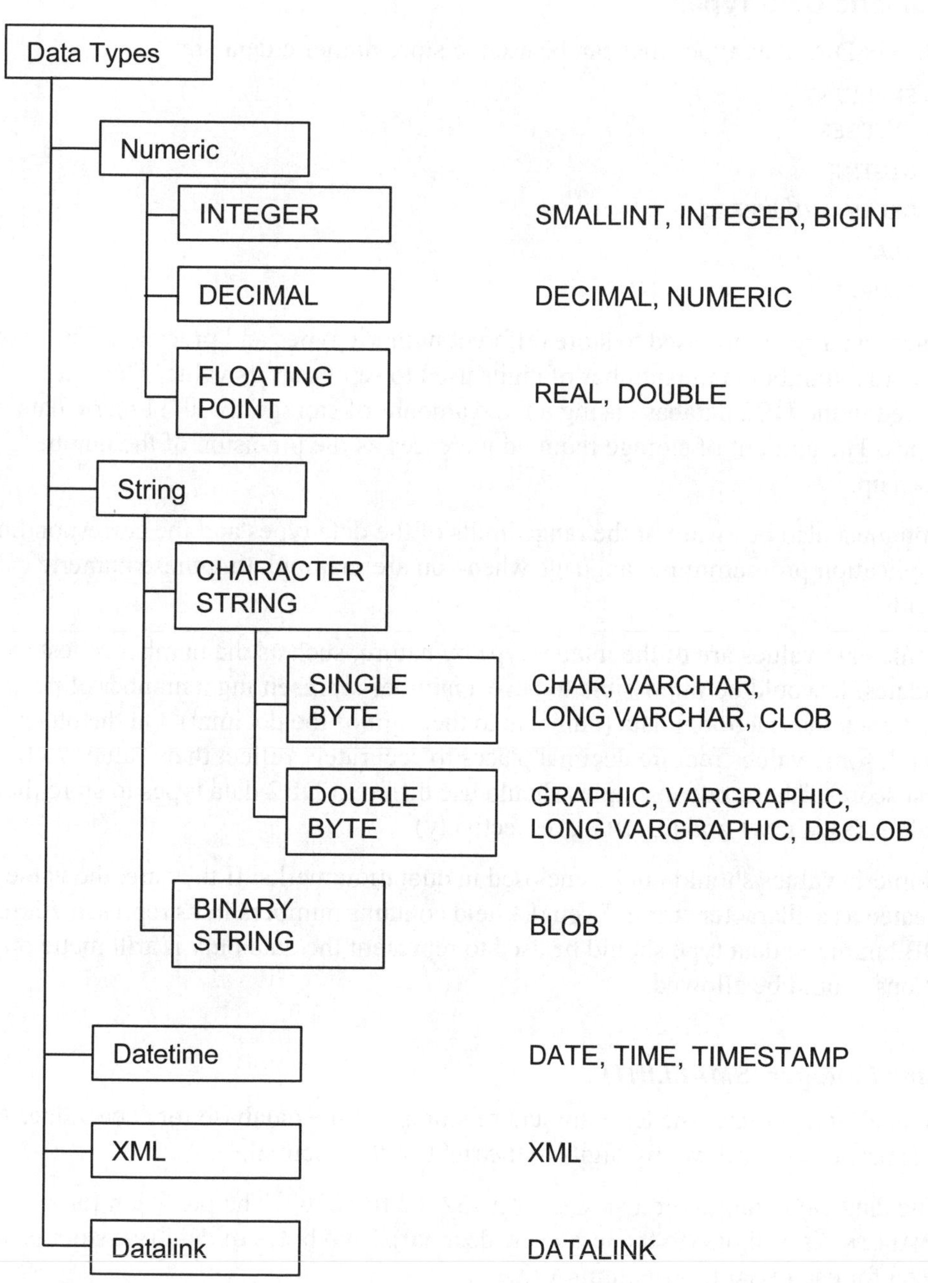

Figure 5–1 *DB2 built-in data types*

Numeric Data Types

The six DB2 data types that can be used to store numeric data are:

- `SMALLINT`
- `INTEGER`
- `BIGINT`
- `DECIMAL/NUMERIC`
- `REAL`
- `DOUBLE`

These data types are used to store different numeric types and precision. The precision of a number is the number of digits used to represent its value. The data is stored in the DB2 database using a fixed amount of storage for all numeric data types. The amount of storage required increases as the precision of the number goes up.

You must also be aware of the range limits of the data types and the corresponding application programming language when you are manipulating these numeric fields.

Some data values are of the integer type by nature, such as the number of test candidates. It would be impossible to have a number representing a number of people that contains fractional data (numbers to the right of the decimal). On the other hand, some values require decimal places to accurately reflect their value, such as test scores. These two examples should use different DB2 data types to store their values (`SMALLINT` and `DECIMAL`, respectively).

Numeric values should not be enclosed in quotation marks. If they are, the value is treated as a character string. Even if a field contains numbers in its representation, a DB2 numeric data type should be used to represent the data only if arithmetic operations should be allowed.

Small integer (SMALLINT)

A small integer uses the least amount of storage in the database for each value. An integer does not allow any digits to the right of the decimal.

The data value range for a `SMALLINT` is -32768 to 32767. The precision for a `SMALLINT` is 5 digits (to the left of the decimal). Two bytes of database storage are used for each `SMALLINT` column value.

Example: `AGE SMALLINT`

Integer (INTEGER)

An INTEGER takes twice as much storage as a SMALLINT but has a greater range of possible values.

The range value for an INTEGER data type is -2,147,483,648 to 2,147,483,647. The precision for an INTEGER is 10 digits to the left of the decimal. Four bytes of database storage are used for each INTEGER column value.

Example: STREET_NO INT

Big integer (BIGINT)

The BIGINT data type is available for supporting 64-bit integers. The range for BIGINT is -9,223,372,036,854,775,808 to +9,223,372,036,854,775,807. As platforms include native support for 64 bit integers, the processing of large numbers with BIGINT is more efficient than processing with DECIMAL and more precise than DOUBLE or REAL. Eight bytes of database storage are used for each BIGINT column value.

Example: TRANSACTION_NO BIGINT

Decimal (DECIMAL/NUMERIC)

A DECIMAL or NUMERIC data type is used for numbers with fractional and whole parts. The DECIMAL data is stored in a packed format.

The precision and scale must be provided when a decimal data type is used. The precision is the total number of digits (range from 1 to 31), and the scale is the number of digits in the fractional part of the number. For example, a decimal data type to store currency values of up to $1 million would require a definition of DECIMAL(9,2). The terms NUMERIC, NUM, DECIMAL, and DEC can all be used to declare a decimal/numeric column. If a decimal data type is to be used in a C program, the host variable must be declared as a double. A DECIMAL number takes up p/2 + 1 bytes of storage, where p is the precision used. For example, DEC(8,2) would take up 5 bytes of storage (8/2 + 1), whereas DEC(7,2) would take up only 4 bytes (truncate the division of p/2).

Example: SALARY DEC(13,2)

DB2 *Note*

If the precision and scale values are not supplied for a DECIMAL column definition, a default value (5,0) is used. This column would take up 3 bytes of space in the row.

Single-precision floating-point (REAL/FLOAT)

A REAL data type is an approximation of a number. The approximation requires 32 bits or 4 bytes of storage. To specify a single-precision number using the REAL data type, its length must be defined between 1 and 24 (especially if the FLOAT data type is used, as it can represent both single- and double-precision and is determined by the integer value specified).

Example: `LATITUDE REAL` or `LATITUDE FLOAT(20)`

Double-precision floating-point (DOUBLE/FLOAT)

A DOUBLE or FLOAT data type is an approximation of a number. The approximation requires 64 bits or 8 bytes of storage. To specify a double-precision number using the FLOAT data type, its length must be defined between 25 and 53.

Example: `DISTANCE DOUBLE` or `DISTANCE FLOAT(50)`

DB2 *Note*

Exponential notation is used to represent REAL, DOUBLE, and FLOAT data values.

String Data Types

This section discusses the string data types that include CHAR, VARCHAR, and LONG VARCHAR.

Fixed-length character string (CHAR)

Fixed-length character strings are stored in the database using the entire defined amount of storage. If the data being stored always has the same length, a CHAR data type should be used.

Using fixed-length character fields can potentially waste disk space within the database if the data is not using the defined amount of storage. However, there is overhead involved in storing varying-length character strings. The term CHARACTER can be used as a synonym for CHAR.

The length of a fixed-length string must be between 1 and 254 characters. If you do not supply a value for the length, a value of 1 is assumed.

Example: `LASTNAME CHAR(20)`

DB2 Note

Character strings are stored in the database without a termination character. Depending on the development environment, a null-terminator may or may not be appended to the end of a character string when the data is stored or retrieved.

Varying-length character string (VARCHAR)

Varying-length character strings are stored in the database using only the amount of space required to store the data. For example, a name would be stored as varying-length strings (VARCHAR) because each person's name has a different length. The term CHAR VARYING or CHARACTER VARYING can be used as a synonym for VARCHAR.

If a varying-length character string is updated and the resulting value is larger than the original, the record will be moved to another page in the table. These rows are known as *tombstone* records or pointer records. Too many of these records can cause significant performance degradation since multiple pages are required to return a single row. The maximum length of a VARCHAR column is 32,672 bytes.

Example: `ADDRESS VARCHAR(128)`

Varying-length long character strings (LONG VARCHAR)

This data type is used to store character data with a varying length. In the past it was used when the VARCHAR was not large enough; however, with the increase of the VARCHAR column to 32,672, the LONG VARCHAR data type may not be used as often.

A VARCHAR column has the restriction that it must fit on one database page. This means that a 4K page would allow a VARCHAR of approximately 4000 characters long, an 8K page would be 8000, and so on up to a 32K page. This means that you must create a table space for this table that can accommodate the larger page size, and you must have sufficient space in the row to accommodate this string. A LONG VARCHAR only takes up 24 bytes of space in the row, no matter what the length is. The LONG VARCHAR format will result in the strings being stored in a separate database page, and this will result in longer processing time for these strings since the database will always need to make an extra hop to get to this data.

The maximum length of a LONG VARCHAR column is 32,700.

Example: `RESUME LONG VARCHAR`

DB2 Note

LONG VARCHAR data types are similar to CLOB data types. (Both types have usage restrictions.)

The FOR BIT DATA clause can be used following a character string column definition. During data exchange, code page conversions are not performed. Rather, data is treated and compared as binary (bit) data.

Character large object (CLOB)

Character large objects are varying-length SBCS (single-byte character set) or MBCS (multibyte character set) character strings that are stored in the database. There is a code page associated with each CLOB. For more details regarding a DB2 code page, please see "Code Page Considerations" on page 259. CLOB columns are used to store greater than 32KB of text. The maximum size for each CLOB column is 2GB (gigabytes). Since this data type is of varying length, the amount of disk space allocated is determined by the amount of data in each record. Therefore, you should create the column specifying the length of the longest string.

Example: `COURSE_ABSTRACT CLOB (50 K)`

Double-byte character strings (GRAPHIC)

The GRAPHIC data types represent a single character using 2 bytes of storage. The GRAPHIC data types include:

- GRAPHIC (fixed length — maximum 127 characters)
- VARGRAPHIC (varying length — maximum 16336 characters)
- LONG VARGRAPHIC (varying length — maximum 16350 characters)

Double-byte character large objects (DBCLOB)

Double-byte character large objects are varying-length character strings that are stored in the database using 2 bytes to represent each character. There is a code page associated with each column. DBCLOB columns are used for large amounts (>32KB) of double-byte text data such as Japanese text.

The maximum length should be specified during the column definition because each row will be variable in length.

Example: `MENU_ITEMS DBCLOB (1 M)`

Binary large object (BLOB)

Binary large objects are variable-length binary strings. The data is stored in a binary format in the database. There are restrictions when using this data type including the inability to sort using this type of column. The BLOB data type is useful for storing nontraditional relational database information such as images, audio, and large documents.

The maximum size of each BLOB column is 2GB (gigabytes). Since this data type is of varying length, the amount of disk space allocated is determined by the amount of data in each record, not by the defined maximum size of the column in the table definition.

Example: `LOCATION_MAP BLOB (2 M)`

Large Object Considerations

Traditionally, large unstructured data was stored somewhere outside the database. Therefore, the data could not be accessed using SQL. Besides the traditional database data types, DB2 implements data types that will store large amounts of unstructured data. These data types are known as Large Objects (LOBs). Multiple LOB columns can be defined for a single table.

DB2 provides special considerations for handling these large objects. You can choose not to log the LOB values to avoid exhausting the transaction log files. There is a NOT LOGGED option that can be specified during the CREATE TABLE statement for each LOB column that you want to avoid logging any modifications. If you would like to define a LOB column greater than 1GB, you must specify the NOT LOGGED option.

There is also a COMPACT option that can be specified during the CREATE TABLE statement. This option is used to avoid allocating extra disk space when storing these large data objects, not for the compression of these objects!

In a database, you may choose to use BLOBs for the storage of pictures, images, or audio or video objects, along with large documents. BLOB columns will accept any binary string without regard to the contents.

If you would like to manipulate textual data that is greater than 32 KB in length, you would use CLOB or a character large object data type. For example, potential employees could submit their resumes to a company and have that information stored in the database as a CLOB column along with the rest of their information. There are many SQL functions that can be used to manipulate large character data columns.

Date and Time Data Types

There are three DB2 data types specifically used to represent dates and times:

- `DATE` — This data type is stored internally as a (packed) string of 4 bytes. Externally, the string has a length of 10 bytes (`MM-DD-YYYY` — this representation can vary and is dependent on the country code).
- `TIME` — This data type is stored internally as a (packed) string of 3 bytes. Externally, the string has a length of 8 bytes (`HH-MM-SS` — this representation may vary).
- `TIMESTAMP` — This data type is stored internally as a (packed) string of 10 bytes. Externally, the string has a length of 26 bytes (`YYYY-MM-DD-HH-MM-SS-NNNNNN`).

From the user perspective, these data types can be treated as character or string data types. Every time you need to use a datetime attribute, you will need to enclose it in quotation marks. However, datetime data types are not stored in the database as fixed-length character strings.

DB2 provides special functions that allow you to manipulate these data types. These functions allow you to extract the month, hour, or year of a date–time column.

The date and time formats correspond to the country code of the database or a specified format (since the representation of dates and times varies in different countries). Therefore, the string that represents a date value will change depending on the country code (or format specified). In some countries, the date format is `DD/MM/YYYY`, whereas in other countries, it is `YYYY-MM-DD`. You should be aware of the country code/format used by your application to use the correct date string format. If an incorrect date format is used, an SQL error will be reported.

As a general recommendation, if you are interested in a single element of a date string, say month or year, always use the SQL functions provided by DB2 to interpret the column value. By using the SQL functions, your application will be more portable.

DB2 *Note*

`TIMESTAMP` fields use the most storage, but they contain the most accurate time since they include microseconds.

We stated that all datetime data types have an internal and external format. The external format is always a character string. Let us examine the various datetime data type formats available in DB2.

Date string (DATE)

There are a number of valid methods of representing a DATE as a string.

Table 5–1 *Valid Date Formats*

Format Name	Abbreviation	Date Format
International Organization for Standardization	ISO	YYYY-MM-DD
IBM USA Standard	USA	MM/DD/YYYY
IBM European Standard	EUR	DD.MM.YYYY
Japanese Industrial Standard	JIS	YYYY-MM-DD
Site Defined	LOC	Depends on database country code

Any of the string formats shown in Table 5–1 can be used to store dates in a DB2 database. When the data is retrieved (using a SELECT statement), the output string will be in one of these formats. There is an option of the BIND command called DATETIME, which allows you to define the external format of the date and time values. The abbreviation column in Table 5–1 contains some possible values for the DATETIME option of the BIND command.

Example: `HIRE_DATE DATE`

Time string (TIME)

There are a number of valid methods for representing a TIME as a string. Any of the string formats in Table 5–2 can be used to store times in a DB2 database. When data is retrieved, the external format of the time will be one of the formats shown in Table 5–2.

Table 5–2 *Valid Time Formats*

Format Name	Abbreviation	Date Format
International Organization for Standardization	ISO	HH.MM.SS
IBM USA Standard	USA	HH:MM AM or PM
IBM European Standard	EUR	HH.MM.SS
Japanese Industrial Standard	JIS	HH:MM:SS

Table 5–2 *Valid Time Formats*

Format Name	Abbreviation	Date Format
Site Defined	LOC	Depends on the database country code

There is a BIND option, called DATETIME, which allows you to define the external format of the date and time values. The abbreviation column in Table 5–2 contains some possible values for the DATETIME BIND option.

DB2 Note

Regardless of the date and time format of the applications, TIME data types have the same internal representation. Their external representation can be changed with the BIND option.

Timestamp string (TIMESTAMP)

The timestamp data type has a single external format. Therefore, the DATETIME BIND option does not affect the external format of timestamps. Timestamps have an external representation as YYYY-MM-DD-HH.MM.SS.NNNNNN (Year-Month-Day-Hour-Minute-Seconds-Microseconds).

Example: TRANSACTION_RECORD TIMESTAMP

External File Data Types (DATALINK)

A DATALINK value is an encapsulated value that contains a logical reference from the database to a file stored in a Data Links Manager Server, which is outside the database. The attributes of this encapsulated value are as follows:

- Link type — The currently supported type of link is a URL (Uniform Resource Locator).
- Scheme — For URLs, this is a value like HTTP or FILE. The value, no matter what case it is entered in, is stored in the database in uppercase characters. If a value is not specified, FILE is included in the DATALINK value.
- File server name — The complete address of the file server. The value, no matter what case it is entered in, is stored in the database in uppercase characters. If a value is not specified, the file server name of the database server is selected and included in the DATALINK value.
- File path — The identity of the file within the server. The value is case-sensitive

and, therefore, it is not converted to uppercase characters when stored in the database.

- Access control token — When appropriate, the access token is embedded within the file path. It is generated dynamically when a DATALINK value is extracted, and it is not necessary to provide it when a DATALINK value is inserted. In other words, it is not a permanent part of the DATALINK value that is stored in the database.
- Comment — Up to 254 bytes of descriptive information. This is intended for application-specific uses such as further or alternative identification of the location of the data.

Insert and extract DATALINK values

When you are inserting rows into a table that has DATALINK columns, you should use a built-in scalar function, DLVALUE, to provide each attribute of the DATALINK value.

To extract encapsulated attributes of the DATALINK value, DB2 provides several built-in scalar functions, such as DLLINKTYPE, DLURLSCHEME, DLURLSERVER, DLURLCOMPLETE, DLURLPATH, DLURLPATHONLY, and DLCOMMENT.

Refer to the *DB2 SQL Reference* for more detailed information about these built-in scalar functions.

DB2 *Note*

The DATALINK type is included in this book for historical purposes. This data type is not longer supported in DB2 9, although it is still available in prior releases. Applications being written on versions prior to DB2 9 should not use this feature if the application will be run against future versions of DB2.

XML (Extensible Markup Language)

XML stands for Extensible Markup Language and is a new data type introduced in DB2 9. XML is a general-purpose markup language that can be used to share information between different information systems.

XML is sometimes described as a “self-describing data structure” since the XML tags describe each element and their attributes. Some of the benefits of XML are:

- Extensible
- No fixed format or syntax

- Structures can be easily changed
- Platform independent
- Not tied to any platform, operating system, language, or software vendor
- XML can be easily exchanged
- Fully Unicode™ compliant

The XML data type introduces a number of new concepts and language extensions to SQL (including a brand-new language called XQuery). More details on XML are found in Chapter 8.

User-Defined Data Types

User-defined types (UDTs) allow a user to extend the data types that DB2 understands. There are three kinds of UDTs:

- User-defined distinct type — User-defined data types (UDTs) can be created on an existing data type. UDTs are used to define further types of data being represented in the database. If columns are defined using different UDTs based on the same base data type, these UDTs cannot be directly compared. This is known as *strong typing*. DB2 provides this strong data typing to avoid end-user mistakes during the assignment or comparison of different types of real-world data.
- User-defined reference type — A UDT can also be a user-defined reference type used to reference rows in another table that uses a user-defined structured type. A structured type can be a subtype of another structured type (called supertype) defining a type hierarchy. User-defined structured types (for type hierarchy) are discussed in Chapter 7.
- User-defined structured data type — Structured type support has been extended to provide the ability to create tables with structured type columns. Additionally, structured types can be nested within a structured type. This means that the attributes of structured type are no longer restricted to the base SQL types, they can now be of another structured type. User-defined structured types are discussed in Chapter 7.

DB2 Note

The user-defined structured data type allows the DBA or developer to create columns that are actually made up of a structure. This is part of the object-relational support found within DB2.

The `SYSCAT.DATATYPES` catalog view allows you to see the UDTs that have been defined in your database.

Creating User-Defined Distinct Types (UDTs)

Let us say we have a table that will be used to store different measures of weight such as pounds and kilograms. We should use a numeric data type for these columns since arithmetic operations are appropriate. We will use the INTEGER data type as the base DB2 data type for the UDTs, KILOGRAM and POUND. The values represent different units and, therefore, should not be directly compared.

DB2 Note

User-defined data types (UDTs) can only be based on existing DB2 data types.

Here we define two new data types: KILOGRAM and POUND. These data types will be based on the integer (INTEGER) data type. Once the KILOGRAM and POUND UDTs have been defined, they can be referenced in the CREATE TABLE statement.

When the UDTs are defined, system-generated SQL functions are created. These functions are known as *casting functions*. The casting functions allow comparison between the UDT and its base type. In the real world, you cannot directly compare pounds and kilograms without converting one of the values. In DB2, a user-defined function is required.

The following SQL creates the user-defined data types for POUND and KILOGRAM.

```
CREATE DISTINCT TYPE POUND
      AS INTEGER WITH COMPARISONS;
CREATE DISTINCT TYPE KILOGRAM
      AS INTEGER WITH COMPARISONS;
```

Example 5–2 *Creating DISTINCT types*

In the example above, we are creating the new data types known as POUND and KILOGRAM.

The keyword DISTINCT is mandatory for all user-defined data types. The WITH COMPARISONS clause is also a mandatory clause (except for LOB, LONG, and DATALINK data types). The following table uses the pound and kilogram data types (Example 5–3).

```
CREATE TABLE HEALTH
  (
  F_NAME             VARCHAR(30),
  WEIGHT_P           POUND,
  WEIGHT_K           KILOGRAM
  );
```

Example 5–3 *Creating a table with user-defined types*

The new data types are used in the table definition just like the DB2 built-in data types. DB2 will not allow you to compare or perform arithmetic operations on the POUND and KILOGRAM typed columns directly. A casting function would need to be used to perform arithmetic operations using the columns defined with these types. In other words, you could not use built-in functions, such as the average function (AVG), for a column defined as POUND or KILOGRAM, unless you use the appropriate casting functions or create a new user-defined function that can use those UDTs as an input parameter.

The following SQL will result in an error (Example 5–4). The data type for the constant value of 30 is of type INTEGER, and the INTEGER data type cannot be directly compared with the POUND data type.

```
SELECT F_NAME, WEIGHT_P FROM HEALTH
  WHERE WEIGHT_P > 30;

SQL0401N  The data types of the operands for the operation ">"
 are not compatible.  SQLSTATE=42818
```

Example 5–4 *Invalid comparison of a user-defined type*

To resolve the error, a cast of the constant value of 30 is required. By casting, the value of 30 is treated as an POUND data type. In Example 5–5, the POUND(INTEGER) casting function is being used to convert the value of 30 to the POUND data type.

```
SELECT F_NAME, WEIGHT_P FROM HEALTH
  WHERE WEIGHT_P > POUND(30);
```

Example 5–5 *Using casting functions for comparisons*

Let us look at a simple example of a UDT involving telephone numbers. This example is here for the purpose of describing the use of user-defined types. Be aware that this example would not restrict the phone number to be numeric. You always compare phone numbers with other phone numbers; you do not compare them with street numbers or department numbers. This means that a column representing telephone numbers would be an ideal candidate to be defined using a distinct type or UDT.

Should telephone numbers be stored as numeric or string data? Does it make sense to perform arithmetic operations on a telephone number? No, a telephone number has no significant mathematical properties (e.g., adding one to your telephone number is not a useful operation). Therefore, we should base the new data type on a CHARACTER or CHAR type. A varying-length character string or VARCHAR is not required because the length of a telephone number is consistent.

We start by creating a user-defined data type for the telephone numbers. This will ensure that all the columns containing telephone numbers share the same data type.

DB2 *Note*

The valid data values for a user-defined data type cannot be specified. Therefore, any valid value for the base data type is allowed. Additional constraints can be placed on the column within the table.

The SQL statement to create the distinct type PHONENO is shown (Example 5–6).

```
CREATE DISTINCT TYPE PHONENO
  AS CHAR(10) WITH COMPARISONS;
```

Example 5–6 *Creating a user-defined type with comparisons*

The creation of this user-defined data type will result in the creation of the following casting functions:

- CHAR(PHONENO), which translates data values from the PHONENO data type to the base data type CHAR
- PHONENO(CHAR), which translates data values from the base data type CHAR to the PHONENO data type

In fact, DB2 will create two PHONENO casting functions: one that converts fixed CHAR strings and another that works with VARCHAR columns. The number of casting functions created will vary according to the base data type being used. In addition, a casting function VARCHAR(PHONENO) is also created.

Let us say that we have two columns that represent phone numbers: HPHONE (home phone number) and WPHONE (work phone number). Both of these columns should be defined using the same data type PHONENO.

Here are some examples of using these columns in expressions:

- An expression involving the same data type (PHONENO) —
  `PHONENO = HPHONE` or `HPHONE <> WPHONE`
- An expression using the casting function PHONENO(CHAR) —
  `HPHONE = PHONENO('5555551234')`
- A similar expression using the casting function CHAR(PHONENO) —
  `CHAR(hphone) = '5555551234'`

Removing a User-Defined Distinct Type

User-defined distinct types (UDTs) are defined at the database level. They can only be created and dropped from a database by someone with database administrator (or higher) authority. If tables have been defined using a UDT, you will not be allowed to drop the UDT. The table would need to be dropped before the UDT could be dropped.

Assuming there is no table defined using the pound data type, you could remove the definition of the POUND data type using the following statement (Example 5–7).

```
DROP DISTINCT TYPE POUND;
```

Example 5–7 *Dropping a distinct type*

The DROP DISTINCT TYPE statement will drop the POUND data type and all of its related casting functions.

DB2 Note

Remember that if you do not qualify a DB2 object, the current authorization ID will be used as the schema name. For example, if you are connected to the database as user GEOFFREY, the DROP statement in the previous example would attempt to drop the data type GEOFFREY.POUND.

Null Considerations

A null represents an unknown state. Therefore, when columns containing null values are used in calculations, the result is unknown. All of the data types discussed in the previous section support the presence of nulls. During table definition, you can specify that a value must be provided. This is accomplished by adding a phrase to the column definition. The CREATE TABLE statement can contain the phrase NOT NULL as part of the definition of each column. This will ensure that the column contains a value, i.e., is not null.

Special considerations are required to properly handle nulls when coding a DB2 application. DB2 treats nulls differently than it treats values.

DB2 Note

Relational databases allow nulls. It is important to remember that they can be appropriate for your database design.

To define a column not to accept nulls, add the phrase NOT NULL to the end of the column definition, for example:

```
CREATE TABLE T1 (C1 CHAR(3) NOT NULL);
```

Example 5–8 *NOT NULL specification on a column*

From the example above, DB2 will not allow any nulls to be stored in the C1 column. In general, avoid using nullable columns unless they are required to implement the database design. There is also overhead storage you must consider. An extra byte per nullable column is necessary if nulls are allowed.

Null with Default

When you insert a row into a table and omit the value of one or more columns, these columns may either be null (if the column is defined as nullable) or given a default value. If the column is defined as not nullable, the insert will fail unless a value has been provided for the column. DB2 has a defined default value for each of the DB2 data types, but you can explicitly provide a default value for any column. The default value is specified in the CREATE TABLE statement. By defining your own default value, you can ensure that the column has been populated with a desired value.

DB2 Note

The DB2 default values may not be what you want! Explicitly define the default values in your CREATE TABLE statement.

Example 5–9 demonstrates how the default values can be specified in a CREATE TABLE statement.

```
CREATE TABLE STAFF (
  ID     SMALLINT NOT NULL,
  NAME   VARCHAR(9),
  DEPT   SMALLINT NOT NULL WITH DEFAULT 10,
  JOB    CHAR(5),
  YEARS  SMALLINT,
  SALARY DECIMAL(7,2),
  COMM   DECIMAL(7,2) WITH DEFAULT 15);
```

Example 5–9 *Default Values*

Now, all the INSERT statements that omit the DEPT column will populate the column with the default value of 10. The COMM column is defined as WITH DEFAULT, but allows NULLs. In this case, you can choose at insert time between NULL or the default value of 15.

To ensure that the default value is being used during an INSERT operation, the keyword DEFAULT should be specified in the VALUES portion of the INSERT statement. Example 5–10 shows two examples of inserting a record with user-defined default values. In this case, both cause the same result.

```
INSERT INTO STAFF
 VALUES(360,'Baklarz',DEFAULT,'SE',8,20000,DEFAULT);

INSERT INTO STAFF (ID,NAME,JOB,YEARS,SALARY)
 VALUES(360,'Baklarz','SE',8,20000);

ID     NAME      DEPT   JOB   YEARS  SALARY      COMM
------ --------- ------ ----- ------ ----------- ---------
   360 Baklarz       10 SE         8  20000.00       15.00
   360 Baklarz       10 SE         8  20000.00       15.00

1 record(s) selected.
```

Example 5–10 *Inserting a row with a default value*

DB2 *Note*

Columns can also contain generated values, including a new sequence number value.

Identity Column

The previous section discussed how columns can be populated with values if no value was supplied by the user. It is also possible to have DB2 generate sequence numbers or other values during record insertion.

Often, a single column within a table represents a unique identifier for that row. This identifier is usually a number that gets sequentially updated as new records are added.

DB2 can automatically generate sequential values. Example 5–11 shows a table definition with the EMP_NO column automatically being generated.

```
CREATE TABLE EMPLOYEE (
  EMPNO  INT GENERATED ALWAYS AS IDENTITY,
  NAME CHAR(10));

INSERT INTO EMPLOYEE(NAME) VALUES 'George','Paul';

SELECT * FROM EMPLOYEE;

EMPNO       NAME
----------- ----------
          1 George
          2 Paul
```

Example 5–11 *Inserting rows with generated values*

If the column is defined with GENERATED ALWAYS, then the INSERT statement cannot specify a value for the EMPNO field. By default, the numbering will start at 1 and increment by 1. The range and increment can be specified as part of the column definition (Example 5–12):

```
CREATE TABLE EMPLOYEE (
  EMPNO  INT GENERATED ALWAYS AS
     IDENTITY(START WITH 100, INCREMENT BY 10)),
  NAME CHAR(10));

INSERT INTO EMPLOYEE(NAME) VALUES 'George','Paul';

SELECT * FROM EMPLOYEE;

EMPNO       NAME
----------- ----------
        100 George
        110 Paul
```

Example 5–12 *Inserting records with generated values*

DB2 *Note*

Sequences do not guarantee unique values in the column. The user must specify either a unique index, or a primary key on this column to insure that values are not duplicated.

In addition, the default value can be GENERATED BY DEFAULT, which means that the user has the option of supplying a value for the field. If no value is supplied (indicated by the DEFAULT keyword), DB2 will generate the next number in sequence.

One additional keyword is available as part of IDENTITY columns. As a DBA, you can decide how many numbers should be “pregenerated” by DB2. This can help reduce catalog contention since DB2 will cache that many numbers in memory rather than go back to the catalog tables to determine which number to generate next.

Identity columns are restricted to numeric values (integer or decimal) and can only be used in one column in the table. The GENERATE keyword can be used for other columns, but they cannot be IDENTITY columns.

The GENERATE keyword can be applied to other columns to generate values automatically. For instance, the EMPLOYEE table could include two columns that are components of the individuals' pay.

```
CREATE TABLE EMPLOYEE (
   EMPNO  INT GENERATED ALWAYS AS IDENTITY,
   NAME   CHAR(10),
   SALARY INT,
   BONUS  INT,
   PAY    INT GENERATED ALWAYS AS (SALARY+BONUS)
   );

INSERT INTO EMPLOYEE(NAME, SALARY, BONUS) VALUES
  ('George',20000,2000),
  ('Paul',30000,5000);

SELECT * FROM EMPLOYEE;

EMPNO       NAME       SALARY      BONUS       PAY
----------- ---------- ----------- ----------- ----------
          1 George           20000        2000      22000
          2 Paul             30000        5000      35000
```

Example 5–13 *Inserting records with a generated column*

EMPNO is generated as an IDENTITY column, and PAY is calculated automatically by DB2. If SALARY or BONUS are modified at a later time, DB2 will recalculate the PAY. A GENERATED column has the same options as an IDENTITY column. The value can be either calculated ALWAYS or generated by DEFAULT.

For more information on this powerful feature, please refer to the *DB2 SQL Reference*.

DB2 Note

DB2 also has a SEQUENCE object that can be used in place of a generated column. See Chapter 7 for more information.

Code Page Considerations

A character *code page* is associated with all DB2 character data types (CHAR, VARCHAR, CLOB, DBCLOB). This code page is set at the database level during the CREATE DATABASE command.

A code page is a mapping between an alphanumeric "code" and its binary "encoding" (representation) in the database. A DB2 database can only use a single code page. The code page is established during the CREATE DATABASE command using the options CODESET and TERRITORY. The code page can use a single byte to represent an alphanumeric (a single byte can represent 256 unique elements) or multiple bytes.

Languages such as English contain relatively few unique characters; therefore, a single-byte code page is sufficient to store data. Languages like Japanese require more than 256 elements to represent all unique characters; therefore, a multi-byte code page (usually a double-byte code page) is required.

A code point is the location of a character within the code page. DB2 will attempt to perform *code page conversion* if the application and the database have not been defined using the same code page.

	0	1	2	3	4	5	6	7	8	9	A	B	C	D	E	F
0				0	@	P	`	p								
1			!	1	A	Q	a	q								
2			"	2	B	R	b	r								
3			#	3	C	S	c	s								
4			$	4	D	T	d	t								
5			%	5	E	U	e	u								
6			&	6	F	V	f	v								
7			"	7	G	W	g	w								
8			(	8	H	X	h	x								
9			)	9	I	Y	i	y								
A			*	:	J	Z	j	z								
B			+	;	K	[	k	{								
C			,	<	L	\	l	|								
D			-	=	M	]	m	}								
E			.	>	N	^	n	~								
F			/	?	O	_	o									

Figure 5–2 *Code page*

In Figure 5–2, an example code page is shown. This example represents a portion of the ASCII character set (e.g., hexadecimal code point 41 represents the character A).

DB2 Note

Binary data, such as columns specified with `FOR BIT DATA` and `BLOB` columns, do not require alphanumeric translation and are not associated with the database code page.

When a DB2 application is bound to a DB2 database, the application and database code page are compared. If the code pages are not the same, code page conversion will be attempted for each SQL statement. If you are using a code page other than that of the database you are accessing, it is important to ensure that the code pages are compatible and conversion can be accomplished.

By default, the collating sequence of a database is defined according to the code set used in the `CREATE DATABASE` command. If you specify the option `COLLATE USING SYSTEM`, the data values are compared based on the `TERRITORY` specified for the database. If the option `COLLATE USING IDENTITY` is used, all values are compared using their binary representation in a byte-to-byte manner.

When you need to store data in its native (binary) format, avoid using data types associated with code pages. It is generally advantageous to have the application and the database code page the same to avoid the code page conversion process.

Unicode Support in DB2

The *Unicode* character encoding standard is a fixed-length, character-encoding scheme that includes characters from almost all the living languages of the world. Unicode characters are usually shown as U+xxxx, where xxxx is the hexadecimal code of the character. Each character is 16 bits (2 bytes) wide regardless of the language. While the resulting 65,536 code elements are sufficient for encoding most of the characters of the major languages of the world, the Unicode standard also provides an extension mechanism that allows for encoding as many as a million more characters. This extension reserves a range of code values (U+D800 to U+D8FF, known as *surrogates*) for encoding some 32-bit characters as two successive code elements.

DB2 supports ISO/IEC 10646 standard UCS-2, that is, Unicode without surrogates. UCS-2 is implemented with UTF-8 (UCS Transformation Format 8) algorithmic transformation.

DB2 supported code page/CCSIDs are shown in Table 5–3.

Table 5–3 *Supported Code Pages/CCSIDs*

CP/CCSID	Single-Byte (SBCS) Space	Double-Byte (DBCS) Space
1200	N/A	U+0020
13488	N/A	U+0030

These are handled the same way except for the value of their DBCS space. Regarding the conversion table, since code page 1200 is a super set of CCSID 13488, the exact same tables are used for both.

UTF-8 has been registered as CCSID 1208, which is used as the multibyte (MBCS) code page number for the UCS-2/UTF-8 support of DB2. This is the database code page number and the code page of character string data within the database.The double-byte code page number (for UCS-2) is 1200, which is the code page of graphic string data within the database.

When a database is created in UCS-2/UTF-8, `CHAR`, `VARCHAR`, `LONG VARCHAR`, and `CLOB` data are stored in UTF-8, and `GRAPHIC`, `VARGRAPHIC`, `LONG VARGRAPHIC`, and `DBCLOB` data are stored in UCS-2. We will simply refer to this as a UCS-2 database.

If you are working with character string data in UTF-8, you should be aware that ASCII characters are encoded into 1-byte lengths; however, non-ASCII characters are encoded into 2- or 3-byte lengths in a multiple-byte character code set (MBCS). Therefore, if you define an n-byte length character column, you can store strings anywhere from n/3 to n characters depending on the ratio of ASCII to non-ASCII characters.

Following is the example to create a UCS-2 database named `UCS2DB` with the territory code for United States (Example 5–14).

```
CREATE DATABASE UCS2DB USING CODESET UTF-8 TERRITORY US
```

Example 5–14 *Creating a UNICODE database*

DB2 Note

Code set should be specified in uppercase characters.

For further DB2-supported code set or territory information, please refer to the National Language Support (NLS) section in the *DB2 Administration Guide: Planning.*

Selecting the Correct Data Type

Knowledge of the possible data values and their usage is required to be able to select the correct data type. Specifying an inappropriate data type when defining the tables can result in:

- Wasted disk space
- Improper expression evaluation
- Performance considerations

A small checklist for data type selection is shown in Table 5–4.

Table 5–4 *Data Type Checklist*

Question	Data Type
Is the data variable in length?	VARCHAR
If the data is variable in length, what is the maximum length?	VARCHAR
Do you need to sort (order) the data?	CHAR, VARCHAR, NUMERIC
Is the data going to be used in arithmetic operations?	DECIMAL, NUMERIC, REAL, DOUBLE, BIGINT, INTEGER, SMALLINT
Does the data element contain decimals?	DECIMAL, NUMERIC, REAL, DOUBLE
Is the data fixed in length?	CHAR
Does the data contain XML?	XML or CLOB, BLOB
Does the data have a specific meaning (beyond DB2 base data types)?	USER DEFINED TYPE
Is the data larger than what a character string can store, or do you need to store nontraditional data?	CLOB, BLOB, DBCLOB

When using character data types, the choice between CHAR and VARCHAR is determined by the range of lengths of the columns. For example, if the range of column length is relatively small, use a fixed char with the maximum length. This will reduce the storage requirements and could improve performance.

DB2 Note

Remember that you need to create page sizes that are large enough to contain the length of a row in a table. This is particularly important for tables with large character columns. See "User Tables" on page 274.

Tables

Tables are composed of rows; rows are composed of columns. Tables can have constraints to guarantee the uniqueness of rows maintaining relationships between tables. A constraint is a rule that the database manager enforces. There are three types of constraints:

- Unique constraint — Ensures the unique values of a key in a table. Any changes to the columns that comprise the unique key are checked for uniqueness.
- Referential integrity — Enforces referential constraints on insert, update, and delete operations. It is the state of a database in which all values of all foreign keys are valid.
- Table check constraint — Verifies that changed data does not violate conditions specified when a table was created or altered.

Unique Constraints

A *unique constraint* is the rule that the values of a key are valid only if they are unique within the table. Each column making up the key in a unique constraint must be defined as `NOT NULL`. Unique constraints are defined in the `CREATE TABLE` statement or the `ALTER TABLE` statement using the `PRIMARY KEY` clause or the `UNIQUE` clause.

A table can have any number of unique constraints; however, a table cannot have more than one unique constraint on the same set of columns.

DB2 Note

The `UNIQUERULE` column of the `SYSCAT.INDEXES` view indicates the characteristic of the index. If the value of this column is `P`, the index is a primary key, and if it is `U`, the index is an unique index (but not a primary key).

When a unique constraint is defined, the database manager creates (if needed) a unique index and designates it as either a primary or unique system-required index. The enforcement of the constraint is through the unique index. Once a unique constraint has been established on a column, the check for uniqueness during multiple row updates is deferred until the end of the update (deferred unique constraint).

A unique constraint can also be used as the parent key in a referential constraint.

Referential Integrity

Referential integrity allows you to define required relationships between and within tables. The database manager maintains these relationships, which are expressed as referential constraints and requires that all values of a given attribute or table column also exist in some other table column. Figure 5–3 shows an example of the referential integrity between two tables. This constraint requires that every employee in the EMPLOYEE table must be in a department that exists in the DEPARTMENT table. No employee can be in a department that does not exist.

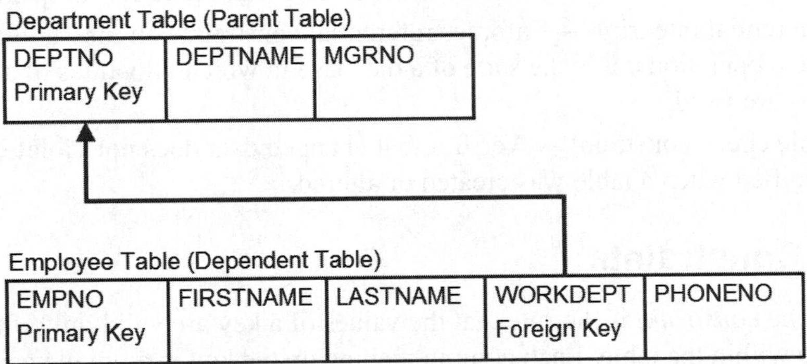

Figure 5–3 *Referential integrity between two tables*

A *unique key* is a set of columns in which no two values are duplicated in any other row. Only one unique key can be defined as a primary key for each table. The unique key may also be known as the *parent key* when referenced by a foreign key.

A *primary key* is a special case of a unique key. Each table can only have one primary key. In this example, DEPTNO and EMPNO are the primary keys of the DEPARTMENT and EMPLOYEE tables.

A *foreign key* is a column or set of columns in a table that refer to a unique key or primary key of the same or another table. A foreign key is used to establish a relationship with a unique key or primary key and enforces referential integrity among tables. The column WORKDEPT in the EMPLOYEE table is a foreign key because it refers to the primary key, column DEPTNO, in the DEPARTMENT table.

A parent key is a primary key or unique key of a referential constraint.

A *parent table* is a table containing a parent key that is related to at least one foreign key in the same or another table. A table can be a parent in an arbitrary number of relationships. In this example, the DEPARTMENT table, which has a primary key of DEPTNO, is a parent of the EMPLOYEE table, which contains the foreign key WORKDEPT.

A dependent table is a table containing one or more foreign keys. A dependent table can also be a parent table. A table can be a dependent in an arbitrary number of relationships. For example, the EMPLOYEE table contains the foreign key WORKDEPT, which is dependent on the DEPARTMENT table that has a primary key.

A referential constraint is an assertion that non-null values of a designated foreign key are valid only if they also appear as values of a unique key of a designated parent table. The purpose of referential constraints is to guarantee that database relationships are maintained and data entry rules are followed.

Enforcement of referential constraints has special implications for some SQL operations that depend on whether the table is a parent or a dependent. The database manager enforces referential constraints across systems based on the referential integrity rules. The rules are

- INSERT rule
- DELETE rule
- UPDATE rule

INSERT Rules

The INSERT rule is implicit when a foreign key is specified.

You can insert a row at any time into a parent table without any action being taken in the dependent table.

You cannot insert a row into a dependent table unless there is a row in the parent table with a parent key value equal to the foreign key value of the row that is being inserted unless the foreign key value is null.

If an INSERT operation fails for one row during an attempt to insert more than one row, all rows inserted by the statement are removed from the database.

DELETE Rules

When you delete a row from a parent table, the database manager checks if there are any dependent rows in the dependent table with matching foreign key values. If any dependent rows are found, several actions can be taken. You determine which action will be taken by specifying a delete rule when you create the dependent table.

- `RESTRICT` — This rule prevents any row in the parent table from being deleted if any dependent rows are found. If you need to remove both parent and dependent rows, delete dependent rows first.
- `NO ACTION` — This rule enforces the presence of a parent row for every child after all the referential constraints are applied. This is the default. The difference between `NO ACTION` and `RESTRICT` is based on when the constraint is enforced. See the *DB2 SQL Reference* for further details.
- `CASCADE DELETE` — This rule implies that deleting a row in the parent table automatically deletes any related rows in the dependent table.
- `SET NULL` — This rule ensures that deletion of a row in the parent table sets the values of the foreign key in any dependent row to null (if nullable). Other parts of the row are unchanged.

UPDATE Rules

The database manager prevents the update of a unique key of a parent row. When you update a foreign key in a dependent table and the foreign key is defined with `NOT NULL` option, it must match some value of the parent key of the parent table. Two options exist:

- `RESTRICT` — The update for the parent key will be rejected if a row in the dependent table matches the original values of the key.
- `NO ACTION` — The update operation for the parent key will be rejected if any row in the dependent table does not have a corresponding parent key when the update statement is completed (excluding after triggers). This is the default.

Check Constraints

Table-check constraints will enforce data integrity at the table level. Once a table-check constraint has been defined for a table, every `UPDATE` and `INSERT` statement will involve checking the restriction or constraint. If the constraint is violated, the row will not be inserted or updated, and an SQL error will be returned.

A table-check constraint can be defined at table creation time or later using the `ALTER TABLE` statement.

The table-check constraints can help implement specific rules for the data values contained in the table by specifying the values allowed in one or more columns in every row of a table. This can save time for the application developer since the validation of each data value can be performed by the database and not by each of the applications accessing the database.

The check constraint's definition is stored in the system catalog tables, specifically the `SYSIBM.SYSCHECKS` table. In addition you can use the `SYSCAT.CHECKS` system catalog view to view the check constraint definitions.

Adding Check Constraints

When you add a check constraint to a table that contains data, one of two things can happen:

- All the rows meet the check constraint.
- Some or all the rows do not meet the check constraint.

In the first case, when all the rows meet the check constraint, the check constraint will be created successfully. Future attempts to insert or update data that does not meet the constraint business rule will be rejected.

When there are some rows that do not meet the check constraint, the check constraint will not be created (i.e., the ALTER TABLE statement will fail). The ALTER TABLE statement, which adds a new constraint to the EMPLOYEE table, is shown below. The check constraint is named CHECK_JOB. DB2 will use this name to inform us which constraint was violated if an INSERT or UPDATE statement fails. The CHECK clause is used to define a table-check constraint (Example 5–15).

```
ALTER TABLE EMPLOYEE
 ADD CONSTRAINT check_job
 CHECK (JOB IN ('ENGINEER','SALES','MANAGER'));
```

Example 5–15 *Adding a check constraint*

An ALTER TABLE statement was used because the table had already been defined. If there are values in the EMPLOYEE table that conflict with the constraint being defined, the ALTER TABLE statement will not be completed successfully.

It is possible to turn off constraint checking to let you add a new constraint. The SET INTEGRITY statement enables you to turn off check constraint and referential constraint checking for one or more tables. When you turn off the constraint checking for a table, it will be put in a CHECK PENDING state, and only limited access to the table will be allowed. For example, once a table is in a check-pending state, use of SELECT, INSERT, UPDATE, and DELETE is disallowed on a table. See the *DB2 SQL Reference* for the complete syntax of the SET INTEGRITY statement.

DB2 *Note*

It is a good idea to label every constraint (triggers, table-check, or referential integrity). This is particularly important for diagnosing errors that might occur.

Modifying Check Constraints

As check constraints are used to implement business rules, you may need to change them from time to time. This could happen when the business rules change in your organization.

There is no special command used to change a check constraint. Whenever a check constraint needs to be changed, you must drop it and create a new one. Check constraints can be dropped at any time, and this action will not affect your table or the data within it.

When you drop a check constraint, you must be aware that data validation performed by the constraint will no longer be in effect. The statement used to drop a constraint is the `ALTER TABLE` statement.

The following example shows how to modify the existing constraint. After dropping the constraint, you have to create it with the new definition.

```
ALTER TABLE STAFF DROP CONSTRAINT CHECK_JOB;

ALTER TABLE STAFF
  ADD CONSTRAINT CHECK_JOB
  CHECK (JOB IN ('Mgr','Sales','Clerk','Admin'));
```

Example 5–16 *Dropping and recreating a check constraint*

The two `ALTER` statements can be combined into one (Example 5–17):

```
ALTER TABLE STAFF
  DROP CONSTRAINT CHECK_JOB
  ADD CONSTRAINT CHECK_JOB
    CHECK (JOB IN ('Mgr','Sales','Clerk','Admin'));
```

Example 5–17 *Combining check constraint changes*

Informational Constraints

All of the constraints that have been defined up to this point in time are enforced by DB2 when records are inserted or updated. This can lead to high amounts of system overhead, especially when loading large quantities of records that have referential integrity constraints.

If an application has already verified information before inserting a record into DB2, it may be more efficient to use informational constraints, rather than normal constraints. These constraints tell DB2 what format the data should be in, but are not enforced during insert or update processing. However, this information can be used by the DB2 optimizer and may result in better performance of SQL queries.

The following table will illustrate the use of information constraints and how they work. This simple table contains information on some employee salaries and gender (Example 5–18):

```
CREATE TABLE EMPDATA
  (
  EMPNO    INT NOT NULL,
  SEX      CHAR(1) NOT NULL
           CONSTRAINT SEXOK
               CHECK (SEX IN ('M','F'))
               NOT ENFORCED
               ENABLE QUERY OPTIMIZATION,
  SALARY INT NOT NULL,
           CONSTRAINT SALARYOK
               CHECK (SALARY BETWEEN 0 AND 100000)
               NOT ENFORCED
               ENABLE QUERY OPTIMIZATION
  );
```

Example 5–18 *Employee table with informational constraints*

This example contains two statements that change the behavior of the column constraints. The first option is NOT ENFORCED, which instructs DB2 not to enforce the checking of this column when data is inserted or updated.

The second option is ENABLE QUERY OPTIMIZATION, which is used by DB2 when SELECT statements are run against this table. When this value is specified, DB2 will use the information in the constraint when optimizing the SQL.

If the table contains the NOT ENFORCED option, the behavior of insert statements may appear odd. The following SQL will not result in any errors when run against the EMPDATA table (Example 5–19):

```
INSERT INTO EMPDATA VALUES
   (1, 'M', 54200),
   (2, 'F', 28000),
   (3, 'M', 21240),
   (4, 'F', 89222),
   (5, 'Q', 34444),
   (6, 'K',132333);
```

Example 5–19 *Inserting into the Empdata table*

Employee number five has a questionable gender (Q) and employee number six has both an unusual gender and a salary that exceeds the limits of the salary column. In both cases DB2 will allow the insert to occur since the constraints are NOT ENFORCED.

What probably will cause more confusion is the result of a select statement against this table (Example 5–20):

```
SELECT * FROM EMPDATA
  WHERE SEX = 'Q';

EMPNO       SEX SALARY
----------- --- -----------

  0 record(s) selected.
```

Example 5–20 *Selecting from the Empdata table*

So DB2 instantly returned the incorrect answer to our query! We know that the value `'Q'` is found within the table, but the constraint on this column tells DB2 that the only valid values are either `'M'` or `'F'`. The `ENABLE QUERY OPTIMIZATION` keyword also allowed DB2 to use this constraint information when optimizing the SQL statement. If this is not the behavior that the user wants, then the constraint needs to be changed through the use of the `ALTER` command (Example 5–21):

```
ALTER TABLE EMPDATA
  ALTER CHECK SEXOK DISABLE QUERY OPTIMIZATION
```

Example 5–21 *Alter query optimization*

If the query is reissued, DB2 will return the following results (Example 5–22):

```
SELECT * FROM EMPDATA
  WHERE SEX = 'Q';

EMPNO       SEX SALARY
----------- --- -----------
          5 Q         34444

  1 record(s) selected.
```

Example 5–22 *Selecting from the Empdata table without optimization*

This result takes longer to retrieve than the last one, but at least it is correct! So when should informational constraints be used in DB2? The best scenario for using informational constraints occurs when the user can guarantee that the application program is the only application inserting and updating the data. If the application already checks all of the information beforehand (like sex), then using informational constraints can result in faster performance and no duplication of effort.

The other possible use of information constraints is in the design of data warehouses. Many customers use a star schema (see "STAR Schemas" on page 414) in the design of their data warehouse. The following points are characteristic of a STAR schema design:

- There is a large *fact* table that contains data relating to *dimension* tables.
- The fact table contains the raw data or transactions that have been generated by an application.
- There are a number of small dimension tables that hold descriptive information about entities found in the fact table.
- The primary keys of the dimension tables involved in the STAR schema supply foreign key entries in the fact table. The concatenation of foreign keys from the dimension tables usually forms a small subset of the fact table.

The primary/foreign key constraints within the fact and dimension tables will cause significant amounts of overhead during load times (using `INSERT` commands) or during a validation step after loading the data. This validation can take more time than the load step itself due to the large number of checks that must take place.

If the application has already generated correct foreign/primary key values in the tables, then it may appropriate to define the referential integrity constraints as information constraints and avoid the large overhead of checking these values. These referential integrity constraints should not be removed from the table definition since DB2 can use them to optimize access to the fact table through the known relationships with the dimension tables. For this reason, the referential constraints should be kept as informational, and query optimization enabled so that DB2 can use this during `SELECT` optimization.

As with any optimization techniques, DBAs should prototype the changes on a smaller scale to ensure that the changes have the desired effects!

DB2 Note

Informational constraints allow DB2 to continue to optimize `SELECT` statements based on these constraints, but not have the overhead associated with enforcing these rules. For more information see "Informational Constraints" on page 268.

Physical DB2 Tables

In DB2, there are two types of permanent tables. One type is the system catalog tables and the other is the user tables.

System Catalog Tables

There are special tables used by DB2 that contain information about all objects within the database and are created for you when the database is created (for instance, using the CREATE DATABASE command). These tables are called system catalog tables and they are examined by DB2 during query processing. Some of the information contained in the system catalog tables includes:

- Table/Index definitions
- Column data types
- Defined constraints
- Object dependencies
- Object privileges

When SQL Data Definition Language (DDL) statements are issued, the system catalog tables may in fact be updated for you. There are a number of base system tables and views in a DB2 database, and they always reside in a special table space called SYSCATSPACE.

DB2 *Note*

To display the names of the system catalog tables and views along with their creation time, enter the command LIST TABLES FOR SYSTEM or LIST TABLES FOR SCHEMA schemaname (SYSIBM, SYSCAT, or SYSSTAT).

The system catalog table data cannot be modified using an INSERT or DELETE SQL statement. However, some of the table data can be modified. For example, the COMMENT ON statement and ALTER statement will update information stored in the system catalog tables. For more details on the use of the ALTER statement, please refer to “The ALTER Statement” on page 237 and the *DB2 SQL Reference*.

The system tables also contain statistical information about the tables in the database. For example, the number of physical pages allocated for each table is stored in the system catalog tables. The statistical information is calculated and updated by the RUNSTATS command.

Database object privileges, such as INSERT, SELECT, and CONTROL, are also maintained within the system catalog tables. The privileges are established using special SQL statements known as Data Control Language (DCL) statements. The primary DCL statements are GRANT and REVOKE. These statements were discussed in Chapter 4.

The system catalog tables are primarily for read-only purposes since they are maintained by DB2. However, there is a special set of system catalog views that are updatable. This is a special set of views defined on the system catalog tables that are used to update database statistics. These views are defined in the SYSSTAT schema. For example, these views can be used to force the DB2 optimizer to change the access path when executing a query relating to a certain table.

DB2 *Note*

Use the RUNSTATS command to update the database statistics. Update the SYSSTAT schema views to perform *what if* analysis of performance statistics.

There is also a set of read-only views defined for the system catalog base tables. To determine information about a DB2 database, the most common method is to issue SELECT statements against the system catalog tables. There are views defined for this purpose and they have the schema name SYSCAT.

The system catalog base tables are defined under the SYSIBM schema. However, you should query the SYSCAT views instead.

In general, there is at least one system catalog table for each of the database object types. Table 5–5 lists some of the system catalog views.

Table 5–5 *System Catalog Tables and Views*

Database Object	SYSCAT System Catalog Views	SYSSTAT Updatable Views
Table space	TABLESPACES	-
Table	TABLES	TABLES
Schema	SCHEMATA	
View	VIEWS	-
Column	COLUMNS	COLUMNS
Index	INDEXES	INDEXES
Package	PACKAGES	-
Trigger	TRIGGERS	-
Data Type	DATA TYPES	-
Stored Procedures	PROCEDURES	-
Constraint	CHECKS	-
Referential Integrity	REFERENCES	-
Function	FUNCTIONS	FUNCTIONS

Table 5–5 *System Catalog Tables and Views*

Database Object	SYSCAT System Catalog Views	SYSSTAT Updatable Views
Buffer Pool	BUFFERPOOLS	

The number of views defined within the SYSCAT schema or defined within the SYSSTAT schema can differ based on the version of DB2. Remember, the SYSSTAT schema views are used for updating statistical information for the database. An attempt to update any nonstatistical value is rejected by DB2.

User Tables

The CREATE TABLE statement allows users to define tables. The definition must include its name and the attributes of its columns. The definition may include other attributes of the table such as its primary key or check constraints.

Once the table is defined, column names cannot be changed. However, some data types can be modified. For instance, the length of a varchar column or modifying a reference type column to add a scope are allowed. Columns can also be dropped or added to the table (be careful when adding new columns since default data values will be used for existing records). In addition, after a table is created you can change table options such as PCTFREE, the DATA CAPTURE option, LOCK SIZE, LOGGING, or APPEND MODE.

The RENAME TABLE statement can change the name of an existing table.

DB2 Note

The longest unqualified table name is 128 bytes and the longest unqualified column name is 30 bytes.

The maximum number of columns that a table can have is 1012. This will vary depending on the data page size. DB2 supports 4K, 8K, 16K, and 32K data page sizes. Table 5–6 shows the maximum number of columns in a table and maximum length of a row by page size.

Table 5–6 *Table Limits*

	4k Page	8k Page	16k Page	32k Page
Maximum columns	500	1012	1012	1012

Table 5–6 *Table Limits*

	4k Page	8k Page	16k Page	32k Page
Maximum row length (bytes)	4005	8101	16293	32677
Maximum table size GB (SMS/DMS)	64/2048	128/4096	256/8192	512/16384

DB2 *Note*

DB2 9 introduced a larger table space size. For DMS table spaces, the size of a 4K table space can grow from 64GB to 2TB, while a 32K table space can go up to 16TB in size. This increased capacity is only available for DMS table spaces.

By default, user tables are stored in the USERSPACE1 table space. Users can specify the table space name in which the table will be stored. Tables and indexes can be placed separately into different table spaces (using DMS table spaces). LOB columns can also be placed into another table space in which the table is created (using DMS table spaces). If the table space name is not specified explicitly when creating a table, a table space for the table is determined as follows (Figure 5–4):

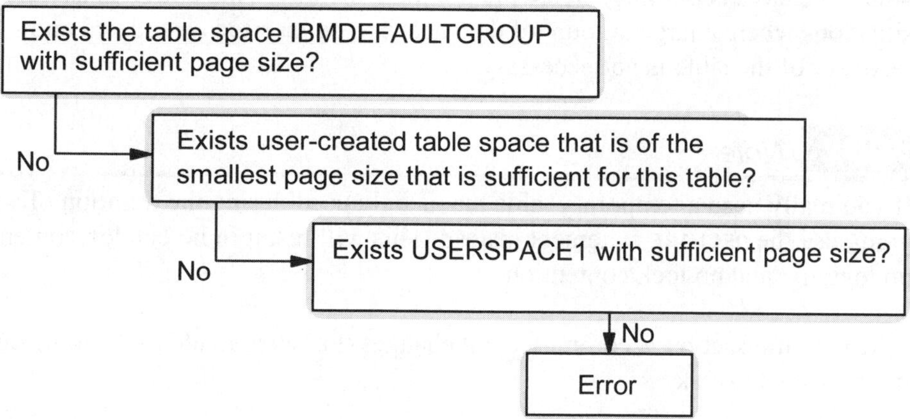

Figure 5–4 *How DB2 chooses a table space for a table*

For detailed information about table spaces, please refer to Chapter 11.

After creating a table, data can be stored in the table using one of these methods:

- INSERT statement
- IMPORT command
- LOAD command

DB2 *Note*

The terms *utility* and *command* are used interchangeably throughout the book. All of the DB2 utilities are documented in the *DB2 Command Reference*, but they can also be issued from an application using an API defined in the *DB2 API Reference.*

Not logged table

The NOT LOGGED INITIALLY option of the CREATE TABLE statement avoids the overhead of logging data. Any changes made to the table by an INSERT, DELETE, UPDATE, CREATE INDEX, DROP INDEX, or ALTER TABLE operation in the same transaction in which the table is created are not logged.

For a table created with the NOT LOGGED INITIALLY option, you can reactivate the not logged mode using the ALTER TABLE statement with the ACTIVATE NOT LOGGED INITIALLY option. Any changes made to the table by an INSERT, DELETE, UPDATE, CREATE INDEX, DROP INDEX, or ALTER TABLE operation in the same transaction in which the table is initially altered are not logged either. This option is useful for situations where a large amount of data needs to be inserted or updated and recovery of the table is not necessary.

DB2 *Note*

If you really need a temporary table that is only used during the duration of a program, use the DECLARE statement instead. This will result in no catalog contention, no logging, and no lock contention.

When the transaction is committed, all changes that were made to the table during it are flushed to disk.

When you run the ROLLFORWARD utility and it encounters a log record that indicates that a table in the database was created with the NOT LOGGED INITIALLY option, the table will be marked as unavailable. After the database is recovered, an error will be issued if any attempt is made to access the table (SQL1477N Table "" cannot be accessed. SQLSTATE=55019). The only operation permitted is to drop the table.

Sample Table Create Statements

Example 5–23 shows sample CREATE TABLE statements. This sample creates two tables. The definitions include unique constraints, check constraints, referential integrity, and NOT LOGGED INITIALLY attributes. In this example,

- The DEPARTMENT table has a primary key that consists of column DEPTNUMB.
- The EMPLOYEE table has a check constraint that says JOB should be Sales, Mgr, or Clerk.
- The default value is defined for the column HIREDATE in the EMPLOYEE table.
- EMPLOYEE table has a primary key that consists of column ID.
- A Referential constraint is defined between the DEPARTMENT table and the EMPLOYEE table.
- The EMPLOYEE table is created in the table space HUMRES, and its index is created in the table space HUMRES_IDX.
- Any changes made to the table by an INSERT, DELETE, UPDATE, CREATE INDEX, DROP INDEX, or ALTER TABLE operation in the same transaction in which the EMPLOYEE table is created are not logged for the EMPLOYEE table.

```
CREATE TABLE DEPARTMENT
(DEPTNUMB  SMALLINT NOT NULL,
 DEPTNAME  VARCHAR(20),
 MGRNO     SMALLINT,
 PRIMARY KEY(DEPTNUMB)
);
CREATE TABLE EMPLOYEE
(ID         SMALLINT      NOT NULL,
 NAME       VARCHAR(9)    NOT NULL,
 DEPT       SMALLINT,
 JOB        CHAR(5) CHECK (JOB IN ('SALES','MGR','CLERK')),
 HIREDATE   DATE WITH DEFAULT CURRENT DATE,
 SALARY     DECIMAL(7,2),
 COMM       DECIMAL(7,2),
 CONSTRAINT UNIQUEID PRIMARY KEY(ID),
 FOREIGN KEY(DEPT) REFERENCES DEPARTMENT(DEPTNUMB)
                             ON DELETE RESTRICT)
IN HUMRES
INDEX IN HUMRES_IDX
NOT LOGGED INITIALLY;
```

Example 5–23 *Create Table statement examples*

Compressed Tables

When creating a table the user has the option of using two forms of data compression. The first form, value compression, can be useful in environments where much of the data in a table consists of null or zero values. The second form, row compression, compresses data in the row regardless of the default values. Each type of compression can be used alone, or in combination. The decision of which form to use depends on many factors, including the types of workloads. The sections below elaborate on each form of compression in DB2.

Value Compression

DB2 allows two additional clauses on the CREATE TABLE statement to specify value compression:

```
CREATE TABLE PRODUCTS
(PRODNO       INT            NOT NULL,
 DESCRIPTION  VARCHAR(40),
 QUANTITY     NUMERIC(31,0)  NOT NULL COMPRESS SYSTEM DEFAULT,
 LOCATION     CHAR(10)
)
VALUE COMPRESSION;
```

Example 5–24 *Value compression example*

In order to take advantage of compression at the table level, the VALUE COMPRESSION clause must be used as part of the CREATE TABLE command. This parameter indicates to DB2 that it can use a different row format to store the default information in the row.

The normal row format in DB2 contains information on each column value, including whether or not it can contain a null value. For fixed-length fields, like numbers, the entire object is still stored in the row whether or not the field contains null or zero. This can result in a large amount of wasted space, especially in data warehousing applications where much of the data may not contain a value.

The DB2 row format will add an extra two bytes of storage to each variable length data type (i.e., BLOB, CLOB, DBCLOB, LONG VARCHAR, and LONG VARGRAPHIC) in the table when the VALUE COMPRESSION clause is used. This can result in a new row being longer than the original one if all of the fields are filled. However, if only a few of the fields have default or null values then the space savings can be significant.

In addition, other data types like SMALLINT, INTEGER, BIGINT, NUMERIC, FLOAT, DOUBLE, and REAL can be compressed if the COMPRESS SYSTEM DEFAULT clause is added to the column definition. These values will only be compressed out if the field is NULL or contains the system default value of zero. If the field contains anything other than the system default value, it cannot be compressed, even if it contains a user-defined default value.

All of these data types, regardless of length or precision, will be compressed to three bytes per column. The savings in space are dependent on the data type. SMALLINT fields only occupy two bytes, so compressing them to three bytes is not really any savings! However, large numeric columns like NUMERIC(31,0) can be compressed from 16 bytes of storage to only three.

The TIME, TIMESTAMP, and DATE data types are not supported for value compression. The system default value for these fields are continually changing, so there is no way for the system to know what the default value should be.

The space saving achieved from using compression comes at the cost of higher maintenance time in the database. Although retrieval of values will be extremely efficient, updating a value from a default of zero to something else will require that the row be expanded to accommodate the new column size. This additional work will impact total response time. In systems where update transactions are minimal, compressing the table may result in considerable space savings.

Row Compression

Row compression in DB2 is different from value compression in that it examines all of the data in a table to determine what repeated patterns can be compressed out. Value compression only looks at null and default values within a column, so the opportunity for compressing values is limited to the amount of data that has not yet been assigned a value.

Compressing data within a table requires three steps:

1. Creating or altering the table to be eligible for compression
2. Generating the compression dictionary
3. Reorganizing existing data

Enabling a Table for Compression

The first step involves either creating the table with the compression clause or altering the table to include this characteristic. The previous PRODUCTS table is made eligible for row compression by adding the additional COMPRESS YES option to the table definition (Example 5–25).

```
CREATE TABLE PRODUCTS
(PRODNO        INT            NOT NULL,
 DESCRIPTION   VARCHAR(40),
 QUANTITY      NUMERIC(31,0)  NOT NULL,
 LOCATION      CHAR(10)
)
COMPRESS YES;
```

Example 5–25 *Turning on row compression*

The COMPRESS option can also be combined with the VALUE COMPRESSION clause, although the benefit of doing this will likely be minimal.

An existing table can be made eligible for compression by using the ALTER TABLE command (Example 5–26):

```
ALTER TABLE PRODUCTS
  COMPRESS YES;
```

Example 5–26 *Altering a table to enable compression*

Either of these commands will update the SYSCAT.TABLES catalog table. To determine if a table has compression enabled, the COMPRESSION column can retrieved to determine the type of compression in effect.

In DB2 9, the COMPRESSION column will have one of the four values shown in Table 5–7.

Table 5–7 *Compression Settings in SYSCAT.TABLES*

Value	Definition
N	No compression of any kind is being deployed within the table
V	Value compression is specified for this table
R	Row compression is enabled for this table
B	Both row compression and value compression are specified for this table

It is possible to use both value compression (which can remove nulls and system defaults) and row compression together. However, it is not recommended to use value compression in this case. Row compression will be able to find the repeating system-defined default values and null values and replace those values.

In releases prior to DB2 9, the COMPRESSION column had a value of Y if value compression was turned on and N if there was no value compression for the table. When migrating to DB2 9, this value will be changed from Y to V.

Once the table has been made eligible for compression, DB2 needs to generate a compression dictionary for the table. The row compression feature examines rows looking for patterns across the entire row, rather than at a column level like value compression. For instance, Figure 5–5 shows some sample data from an employee table.

Name	Dept	Salary	City	State	ZipCode
Fred	500	35324	Plano	TX	24355
John	500	35422	Plano	TX	24355

Figure 5–5 *Sample data to be compressed*

When DB2 uses row compression, it looks for patterns in the entire row of data, not just at the column level. Figure 5–6 shows the potential patterns that DB2 will extract from the two rows.

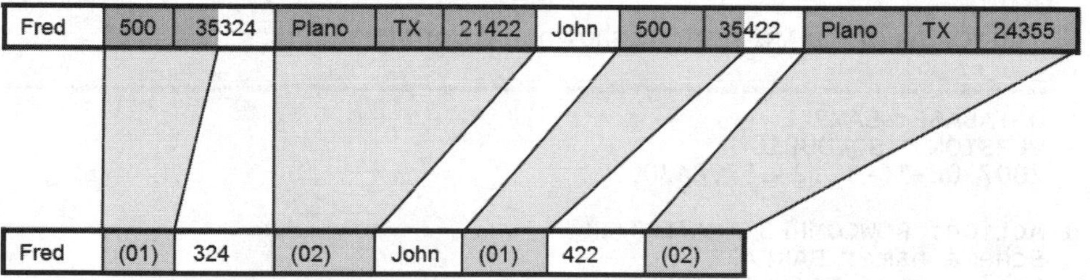

Figure 5–6 *Row level compression*

Note that compression can span multiple columns, as is the case with the CITY, STATE, and ZIPCODE fields. In addition to recognizing patterns within columns, DB2 row compression can also find patterns within columns as well. The DEPARTMENT column has a pattern that can be combined with a portion of the SALARY column. The ability to find patterns across columns and within columns increases the effectiveness of the compression algorithm.

Generating the Compression Dictionary Using INSPECT

DB2 must generate a compression dictionary before it can compress individual rows. There are two approaches to creating a compression dictionary. The first approach is to use the INSPECT command to determine the amount of compression that can be achieved on a table (Example 5–27).

```
INSPECT ROWCOMPESTIMATE
  TABLE NAME TRANSACTIONS
  SCHEMA BAKLARZ
  RESULTS KEEP TRANSACTIONS_OUTPUT;
```

Example 5–27 *Using INSPECT to return a compression estimate*

The `INSPECT` command must be run from a DB2 command line or the Control Center. The `INSPECT` command samples all of the data within the existing table and builds a compression dictionary from this information. The file called `TRANSACTIONS_OUTPUT` will be written out to the diagnostic data directory path. The DB2 Inspect Format command (`DB2INSPF`) can then be used to view the results (Example 5–28):

```
DB2INSPF C:\PROGRAM FILES\IBM\SQLLIB\DB2\TRANSACTIONS_OUTPUT
         C:\PROGRAM FILES\IBM\SQLLIB\DB2\TRANSACTIONS.TXT
NOTEPAD C:\PROGRAM FILES\IBM\SQLLIB\DB2\TRANSACTIONS.TXT
```

Example 5–28 *Using the INSPECT format command to view the results*

The results of the `INSPECT` are shown in Example 5–29.

```
DATABASE: SAMPLE
VERSION : SQL09010
2007-02-15-12.24.57.843001

Action: ROWCOMPESTIMATE TABLE
Schema name: BAKLARZ
Table name: TRANSACTIONS
Tablespace ID: 2  Object ID: 16
Result file name: transactions_output

 Table phase start (ID Signed: 16, Unsigned: 16;
      Tablespace ID: 2) : BAKLARZ.TRANSACTIONS

      Data phase start. Object: 16 Tablespace: 2
      Row compression estimate results:
      Percentage of pages saved from compression: 60
      Percentage of bytes saved from compression: 60
     Percentage of rows ineligible for compression due to small
          row size: 0
      Compression dictionary size: 43264 bytes.
      Expansion dictionary size: 32768 bytes.
      Data phase end.
    Table phase end.
Processing has completed. 2007-02-15-12.24.58.015000
```

Example 5–29 *Results of formatting the INSPECT data*

The key information contained within this report is the percentage of compression that DB2 can achieve on this table. There are two numbers that are of interest:

- Percentage of pages saved from compression
- Percentage of bytes saved from compression

These fields tell us how well the table will be compressed. If this number is too small, or if the `INSPECT` indicates that some rows are ineligible for compression, then you may want to reconsider whether or not compression should be used.

DB2 may decide not to compress the row if it becomes too small. If SMS table spaces are used, the maximum number of rows per page is approximately 255 (for any page size). If 255 rows can be placed on a page *without* compression, then compressing them will not reduce the amount of storage. The remainder of a page will simply be wasted space. However, if DMS table spaces are used, there is an option to use large row identifiers (RIDs) that will allow in excess of 2,000 rows on a page. In this case, many more rows could be contained on the page, in which case DB2 will decide to compress them.

There are two additional rows in the output that indicate the size of the compression and expansion dictionary. The dictionary is stored as part of the table being compressed. This dictionary is loaded into memory the first time the table is referenced and remains in memory until either the database is deactivated or shut down.

When DB2 needs to expand a row or compress it, it will refer to this dictionary.

The following workloads are all eligible for compression:

- `INSERT`
- `IMPORT`
- `UPDATE`
- `LOAD`

DB2 continues to compress rows as new data is loaded into the table. This makes DB2 compression much more effective at compression than other competing technologies in the marketplace. From a table compression perspective, there are a few table types that cannot be compressed:

- System Catalog Tables
- Temporary Tables
- Range Clustered Tables (Range Partitioned Tables are eligible)

In addition to these table types, DB2 cannot compress columns that contain:

- `CLOB`, `BLOB`, `DBCLOB`
- `DATALINK` (not supported in DB2 9)
- `XML`

- LONG VARCHAR

The other data types in the row will be compressed.

Reorganizing Data and Creating the Compression Dictionary

Another technique for compressing a table is through the use of the REORG command. The REORG command will be the only way to compress existing tables in the database. The INSPECT command will generate a compression dictionary for a table, but it will not compress existing rows. Any new data that is inserted or updated in the table will become compressed, but rows that are not updated will always remain in an uncompressed format.

The REORG command has two additional parameters that tell DB2 how to create or update the compression dictionary. These parameters are KEEPDICTIONARY and RESETDICTIONARY.

The effects of the KEEPDICTIONARY option are summarized in Table 5–8 and those of RESETDICTIONARY in Table 5–9.

Table 5–8 *KEEPDICTIONARY Behavior*

Compression Value	Dictionary Exists	Result of Reorg
R, B	Yes	Dictionary is preserved and rows are compressed based on that dictionary.
R, B	No	A new dictionary is created and rows are compressed.
N	Yes	Dictionary is preserved but all rows are uncompressed by the reorg.
N	No	No effect. Normal reorg is performed.

Table 5–9 *RESETDICTIONARY Behavior*

Compression Value	Dictionary Exists	Result of Reorg
R, B	Yes	The current dictionary is discarded, a new one is created and the rows are compressed.
R, B	No	A new dictionary is created and the rows are compressed.
N	Yes	The current dictionary is discarded and rows are uncompressed.
N	No	No effect. Normal reorg is performed.

The first time that a table is reorganized for compression, the KEEPDICTIONARY or RESETDICTIONARY option can be used. Once the dictionary has been created, which option to use is dependent on whether or not the existing dictionary needs to be updated:

- Compress existing data in a table

  ALTER the table to turn on compression and then use either RESETDICTIONARY or RESETDICTIONARY with the REORG command.

- Uncompress all of the data

  ALTER the table to turn off compression and then use the RESETDICTIONARY in the reorg command. You need to make sure you have enough space for the uncompressed table.

- Reorg existing rows without changing the compression dictionary

  Use KEEPDICTIONARY with the REORG command.

- Reorg existing rows but update the compression dictionary

  Use RESETDICTIONARY with the REORG command. Note that the REORG will need to expand existing rows before recompressing them with a new dictionary.

A few special notes about using REORG to compress data. The REORG must be offline, not online. These means that you must schedule some time for the table to be properly reorganized. Secondly, the compressed format is not compatible with replication. If you have a requirement to replicate tables between different DB2 servers, you currently cannot compress the tables that are being replicated.

On the other hand, compressing a table in DB2 has some significant benefits:

- Storage for tables can be reduced in excess of 50%.
- I/O can be reduced along with a corresponding reduction in CPU usage.
- Logging is reduced since rows are written out in compressed format.
- More efficient use of bufferpools can be achieved since more data is now held in pages.

Using compression will generate more CPU usage in an application. However, the corresponding drop in I/O rates and the increased amount of data in memory more than makes up for this cost. DBAs should examine the potential space savings against the increased processing time when doing updates against the data. Data warehousing applications are good candidates for compression and should be considered first.

Table Modification

After creating a table, the ALTER TABLE statement enables you to modify existing tables. The ALTER TABLE statement modifies existing tables by:

- Adding or dropping one or more columns to a table
- Adding or dropping a primary key
- Adding or dropping one or more unique or referential constraints
- Adding or dropping one or more check constraint definitions
- Altering the length of a VARCHAR column
- Altering a reference type column to add a scope
- Altering or dropping a partitioning key
- Changing table attributes such as the DATA CAPTURE, PCTFREE, LOCKSIZE, or APPEND mode option
- Activating the not logged initially attribute of the table

In this chapter, not all of these operations are discussed. Refer to the *DB2 SQL Reference* for each option of the ALTER TABLE statement.

Some of the attributes of a table can be changed only after the table is created. For example, if users want to change the default lock level or enable insert by append mode for a table, the ALTER TABLE statement should be issued for a table. Example 5–30 shows us the ALTER TABLE statement with these options used.

```
ALTER TABLE EMPLOYEE
 ACTIVATE NOT LOGGED INITIALLY
 LOCKSIZE TABLE
 APPEND ON
 VOLATILE;
```

Example 5–30 *Alter Table statement*

The LOCKSIZE option indicates the granularity of locks used when the table is accessed; in this case, the use of a table lock. By default, row-level locks are used when tables are accessed. This option of the ALTER TABLE statement allows locking to be pushed up to the table level. Using table-level locks may improve the performance of queries by reducing the number of locks that need to be obtained and released. However, concurrency may be reduced since all locks are held over the complete table.

The APPEND ON option indicates whether data is appended to the end of a table or inserted where free space is available. Specifying APPEND ON can improve performance by allowing for faster inserts and eliminating the maintenance of free space information. Note that the table must not have a clustered index when specifying this option.

If you want to activate the NOT LOGGED attribute of the table for the current transaction, the ACTIVATE NOT LOGGED INITIALLY option enables you to do this. However, notice that if you want to specify this option, the table must have been originally created with the NOT LOGGED INITIALLY attribute, and the create table transaction committed.

The VOLATILE parameter indicates to the optimizer that the cardinality of the table can vary significantly at run time, from empty to quite large. To access the table, the optimizer will use an index scan rather than a table scan, regardless of the statistics, if that access is index only (all columns referenced are in the index) or that access is able to apply a predicate in the index scan. An optional key word, CARDINALITY, is used to indicate that it is the number of rows in the table that is volatile and not the table itself.

Dropping Columns in a Table

Prior to DB2 9, the ALTER TABLE command would not allow you to drop a column. In order to remove a column from a table, a DBA needed to perform the following steps:

- Unload all table data
- Drop the table
- Recreate it along with all its previous authorities, indexes, and related objects
- Reload the table data

This task ends up being one of the highest administrative costs involved in maintaining a table. Dropping columns in a production table is a relatively rare event (considering the impact it would have on a system) but it is quite common in a development environment. In order to make it simpler to drop columns, change a column type, or change the nullability of a column, the ALTER command has been modified to allow these changes.

The ALTER command will now allow:

- ALTER TABLE DROP COLUMN
- ALTER TABLE ALTER COLUMN TYPE
- ALTER TABLE ALTER COLUMN NULLABILITY

When an alter of any of these types is performed, the table is updated to the new design, but only SELECT scans will be allowed (no inserts or updates) until a REORG is completed. DB2 will keep track of the schema changes that have been made and will materialize these changes when a SELECT command is issued against the table. However, the physical structure of the row will not change (i.e., the column will not be removed) until a reorganization is performed.

The table in Example 5–31 will be used to illustrate how the new ALTER command behaves with SQL statements.

```
CREATE TABLE EMPLOYEE_DET
  (
  EMPID SMALLINT NOT NULL,
  EMPNAME VARCHAR (20) NOT NULL,
  EMP_POSITION VARCHAR (10) NOT NULL,
  SALARY DECIMAL (5, 2),
  BONUS  DECIMAL (7, 2),
  PROMOTION_DATE DATE NOT NULL
  );

INSERT INTO EMPLOYEE_DET VALUES
  (1,'MARK WRIGHT','ENGINEER',745.40,35.00,'2006-02-02');
```

Example 5–31 *Table for ALTER examples*

The first modification to the table involves dropping the EMP_POSITION column (Example 5–32):

```
ALTER TABLE EMPLOYEE_DET
  DROP COLUMN EMP_POSITION;

SELECT * FROM EMPLOYEE_DET;

EMPID  EMPNAME                   SALARY  BONUS     PROMOTION_DATE
------ ------------------------- ------- --------- --------------
     1 MARK WRIGHT                745.40     35.00 02/02/2006

  1 record(s) selected.
```

Example 5–32 *Dropping EMP_POSITION column*

While SELECTs will work against the modified table, any INSERT or UPDATE statements will fail (Example 5–33):

```
INSERT INTO EMPLOYEE_DET VALUES
  (2,'PAUL RIVOT',500.00,45.00,'2006-07-31');

SQL0668N  Operation not allowed for reason code "7" on table
"BAKLARZ.EMPLOYEE_DET".  SQLSTATE=57016
```

Example 5–33 *INSERT failure*

Reason code "7" indicates that the table is in a reorg pending state. Additional ALTER commands can be issued against the table up to a total of three. After three ALTER commands, DB2 will require a full reorg of the table. An ALTER command can contain more than one change to the table and still be considered as one ALTER command invocation (Example 5–34).

```
ALTER TABLE EMPLOYEE_DET
  ALTER COLUMN SALARY SET DATA TYPE DECIMAL (6, 2)
  ALTER COLUMN PROMOTION_DATE DROP NOT NULL;
```

Example 5–34 *ALTER with multiple changes*

From a development perspective, this will make changing of table designs very simple. From a production perspective, it will eliminate many of the steps involved in changing the table, but a full reorganization will be required before the table can be used for anything other than SELECT statements.

Removing a Table

When you want to remove a table, issue this statement:

```
DROP TABLE EMPLOYEE;
```

Note that any objects that are directly or indirectly dependent on this table are deleted or made inoperative, for example, indexes, triggers, and views. Whenever a table is deleted, its description is deleted from the catalog and any packages that reference the object are invalidated.

DB2 *Note*

To delete all of the rows from a table, without actually dropping it, you can use the ALTER TABLE statement:

```
ALTER TABLE NAME ACTIVATE NOT LOGGED INITIALLY WITH EMPTY TABLE
```

The advantage of using this format over a DROP table is that all of the security definitions, indexes, and other database objects are preserved.

Multidimensional Clustering

Multidimensional clustering (MDC) provides an elegant method for flexible, continuous, and automatic clustering of data along multiple dimensions. This results in significant improvement in the performance of queries, as well as a reduction in the overhead of data maintenance operations, such as reorganization, and index maintenance operations during insert, update, and delete operations. Multidimensional clustering is primarily intended for data warehousing and large database environments, but it can also be used in online transaction processing (OLTP) environments.

MDC enables a table to be physically clustered on more than one dimension simultaneously, rather than only one with a clustering index. In particular, an MDC table ensures that rows are organized on disk in blocks of consecutive pages, such that all rows within any block have the same dimension values. All blocks contain the same number of pages and multiple blocks can have the same dimension values.

DB2 Note

Multidimensional Clustering (MDC) tables store rows into extents based on dimension values, resulting in faster performance for range queries as well as eliminating the need for table reorganization.

When a clustering index is defined for a table, DB2 attempts to organize the rows on pages according to these index values (Figure 5–7).

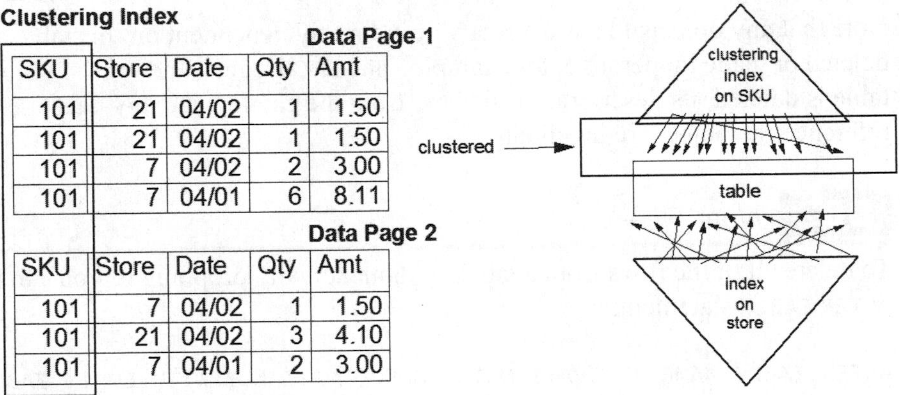

Figure 5–7 *Clustering index*

In this example, the DBA has chosen the SKU column (product number) as the clustering index, so DB2 will attempt to place product records with the same SKU close to one another on the pages. From a query perspective, any range queries like `SKU BETWEEN 101 AND 102` will result in very efficient retrieval of the records since they will all be close to one another on disk.

Any other indexes that might be created on this table will not be clustered. For instance, an index on the store number will not have the data on the pages ordered by store number. DB2 can still use this index for optimizing retrieval from the disk, but the record retrieval will be in a much more random fashion rather than sequentially if it was a clustering index.

With an MDC table, the data is clustered according to the dimensions you have defined for the table. The following diagram illustrates how DB2 would manage a table of two dimensions that have been specified for the table (Figure 5–8):

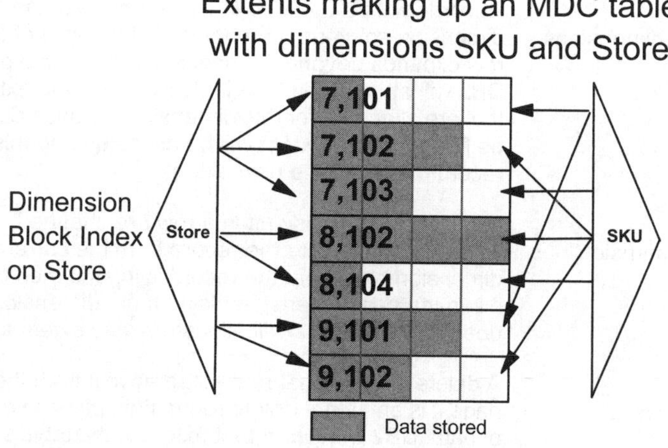

Figure 5–8 *MDC table*

Each block in an MDC table corresponds to an extent in a DB2 table space. This can be as little as two physical pages (which can be 4, 8, 16, or 32K in size) up to whatever amount the DBA thinks is reasonable. Each one of these blocks will only contain records that have the same dimension values. The intersection of unique dimension values is called a cell, and a cell is placed into its own extent. An MDC table can have up to 16 dimensions, but most tables will only have a small number of significant dimensions. In the previous diagram, one cell contains only records for store 7 and product number 101.

As records are added to the system, MDC will maintain these blocks automatically. The following table describes the actions that DB2 would take when inserts, deletes, and updates take place against an MDC table (Table 5–10).

Table 5–10 *MDC SQL Processing*

SQL statement	MDC Processing
INSERT - new dimensions	When a record with new dimension values (dimensions that are not already represented in the table) is inserted into an MDC table, DB2 will allocate a new extent for this record and place that record into this extent.

Table 5–10 *MDC SQL Processing*

SQL statement	MDC Processing
INSERT — existing dimension	If the record being inserted already has dimensions that exist in the table, DB2 will place the record into the same set of extents that contain records with the same dimensions. If the extent is full, DB2 will allocate another extent and place this record into it.
UPDATE — maintaining dimensions	Records will be updated in place if none of the dimension columns are changed. If the size of the row expands beyond the space available on a page, DB2 will attempt to place it elsewhere in the extents that are allocated for this dimension. If space cannot be found, a new extent will be allocated and this record moved to the new extent.
UPDATE — changing dimension	If any of the dimensions in a row are changed, DB2 will physically delete the record from the current dimension block that the record is in, and then place it into the new dimension block. If the dimension does not exist, DB2 will allocate a new extent for it.
DELETE — individual rows	A delete of individual row will remove it from the page it is on. If that delete request empties an extent of data, DB2 will return that extent to the table space for use in future inserts or updates.
DELETE — entire dimension	A delete of all values in a dimension will result in the extents being returned to the table space for future use in inserts and updates.

Block Indexes

In order to track the blocks that comprise a slice, or which blocks contain all records having a particular dimension key value, a dimension block index is automatically created for each dimension when an MDC table is created. The following SQL illustrates how a table is created with two dimensions (Example 5–35):

```
CREATE TABLE SALES
   (
   STORE    INT  NOT NULL,
   SKU      INT  NOT NULL,
   DIVISION INT  NOT NULL,
   QUANTITY INT  NOT NULL,
   TXDATE   DATE NOT NULL,
   )
ORGANIZE BY DIMENSIONS(STORE,SKU);
```

Example 5–35 *MDC table creation*

The `ORGANIZE BY` option tells DB2 that you want to create an MDC table with two dimensions. In this case, the STORE and SKU columns will be the dimensions that DB2 will keep track of. With two dimensions, DB2 will create three block indexes:

- One block index for the unique STORE values
- One block index for the unique SKU values
- One composite block index for STORE/SKU pairs

The composite index is used by DB2 to find a block to insert a new record into as well as find the blocks for select processing. This index will contain all STORE/SKU pairs that have been inserted into the table (as opposed to all possible combinations). This is sometimes referred to as a sparse index since not every possible value in the cartesian join of department and division values is represented in the index.

The individual dimension blocks are used for quickly locating blocks of records in that particular dimension. The block indexes for the store example are illustrated in the following diagram (Figure 5–9):

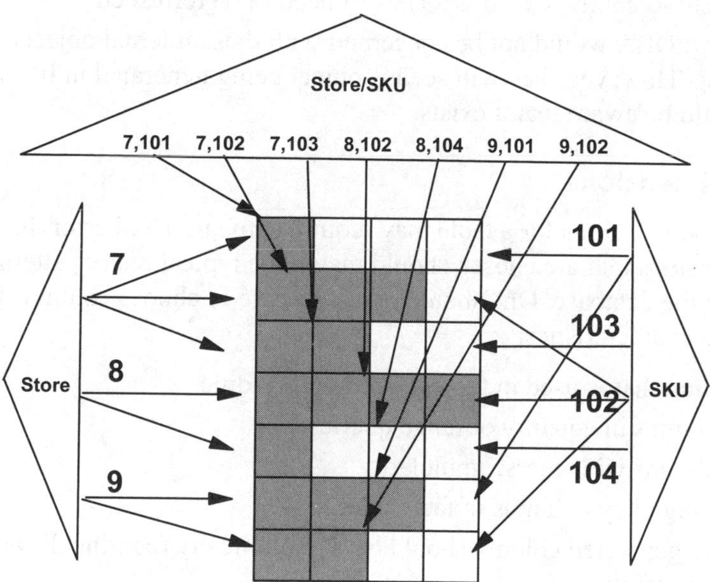

Figure 5–9 *Block indexes*

These block indexes are typically very small since they only contain entries for the dimensions values and not for every possible record. Since these indexes are relatively small, they can be quickly traversed to find which block a record needs to be placed into, rather than using complicated clustering logic. This short search time can help OLTP workloads, especially if most dimension values have already been inserted into the table. In the event that a particular dimension does not exist, DB2 will need to acquire another extent to insert this record into, and that will increase the transaction for this particular case. However, this can also occur with tables that are not defined as MDC.

Block Map

In addition to the new block indexes that are created for an MDC table, DB2 will also create a new structure which stores the status of each block of the table. This block map is stored as a separate `BMP` file in an SMS table space and as a new object in the object table in a DMS table space.

This file comprises an array containing an entry for each block of the table, where each entry is a set of status bits for a block. These status bits indicate:

- In-use: Currently contains data and block is assigned to a cell
- Load: Recently loaded; not yet visible by scans
- Constraint: Recently loaded; constraint checking still to be done
- Refresh: Recently loaded; MQTs still need to be refreshed

Normally a DBA would not be concerned with these internal objects that DB2 is generating. However, they will see his object being generated in file systems so they should be aware that it exists.

Candidate Dimensions

Choosing dimensions for a table may require some trial and error. In many cases the dimensions that are chosen should match the typical query patterns that users submit to the database. One should also take care to choose columns that have the following characteristics:

- A column that is used in typical queries including:
  - columns in equality or range queries
  - columns with coarse granularity
  - foreign key columns in fact tables
  - any generated column should be monotonically (continually) increasing or decreasing
- A column that has a low cardinality, or unique number of values

Choosing a column with a high cardinality may result in a lot of wasted space. For instance, a salary field is probably not a suitable candidate for a dimension since there is very low probability that any two salaries will be the same.

If the skew of the data is such that some cells will be sparsely populated while others will be full, you may wish to have a smaller block size, so that the sparse cells will not take up as much wasted space. For this reason, a DBA may want to create the table with a smaller extent size (2) to avoid wasting space in each extent. It is important to remember that each unique cell (combination of all dimensions) will occupy a minimum of one extent as opposed to a page.

If some of the dimensions do not have sufficient values, then it is possible to combine them with another column to create a composite dimension. In the sales table, the DBA may determine that store and division are always used together in a query. Since there may only be a handful of divisions, creating a dimension just on division may not be useful. The table creation command would be changed to that in Example 5–36:

```
CREATE TABLE SALES
   (
   STORE    INT  NOT NULL,
   SKU      INT  NOT NULL,
   DIVISION INT  NOT NULL,
   QUANTITY INT  NOT NULL,
   TXDATE   DATE NOT NULL,
   )
ORGANIZE BY DIMENSIONS((STORE,DIVISION),SKU);
```

Example 5–36 *MDC table with composite dimensions*

Note how STORE and DIVISION are combined as one dimension. This design still gives the user access to store and division ranges, but can also be used for store lookups as well.

Dimensions that have too many values can be modified through functions to lower their cardinality. A typical example would be salaries where it would not be practical to use this column as one of the dimensions, but the integer portion of SALARY/1000 might result in a reasonable number of values. To implement this type of dimension, the user must create a column in the table that contains this value. The easiest way to implement this is through the use of a generated column. If the use of the sales table indicates that the quantity field is used in many queries, a generated column on this field may be useful (Example 5–37).

```
CREATE TABLE SALES
   (
   STORE    INT  NOT NULL,
   SKU      INT  NOT NULL,
   DIVISION INT  NOT NULL,
   QUANTITY INT  NOT NULL,
   QTY_1K   INT  NOT NULL
     GENERATED ALWAYS AS (QUANTITY/1000),
   TXDATE   DATE NOT NULL,
   )
ORGANIZE BY DIMENSIONS(SKU, QTY_1K);
```

Example 5–37 *MDC table with a generated column*

One important caveat of using generated columns concerns the monotonicity of the function that is used. Generally, the value generated by the function should be going up if the base value goes up and it should go down when the base value goes down. In algebraic terms where A and B are values and f(A) and f(B) are functions against A and B:

$$A \geq B \rightarrow f(A) \geq f(B)$$
$$A \leq B \rightarrow f(A) \leq f(B)$$

If the values in the generated column holds to these rules, DB2 will be able to do range queries across the dimensions. SQL statements which include `BETWEEN` predicates are ideal candidates for this. The `QTY_1K` field in the `SALES` table follows this rule since the calculation for this field will increase as the quantity of sales increases.

A calculation that would not be a good candidate for generated column is the `MONTH` function. Over the course of a year, the function `MONTH(DATE)` would increase in value. As we go into the next year, the `MONTH` function will return a value of one for January, which would be less than December. However, from a date perspective, it should be greater than December. This function fails the monotonicity test and should not be used as one of the dimensions. While there is nothing that restricts you from using this type of generated column, DB2 will only be able to use the dimensions that are generated to search for exact matches and will not be able to do efficient range searching.

As an alternative to using the `MONTH` function, the `INTEGER` function has been extended to work with date fields. When the `INTEGER` function is used against a date, it returns a numeric representation of that date. For instance, `INTEGER('2007-09-14')` will return an integer value of `20070914`. To generate an equivalent `MONTH` function using this new `INTEGER` function, the result can be divided by 100 to create a year and month value. This will always increase in value, and so any dimension that is generated with this function will be eligible for range queries.

Alternative Index Considerations

An MDC table creates additional indexes that are used to track blocks within the table. These indexes are not under user control and are created automatically when you create the table.

Even though these indexes exist, there is no limitation on the type of indexes you can create on this table. A primary key, partitioning key, or any other type of key can work in conjunction with the MDC indexes.

MDC indexes can also be used to AND/OR with other indexes if they exist. This means that MDC indexes can be used to reduce the answer set before needing to use one of the other indexes. Using an MDC table may also reduce the need for many of the additional indexes that are in place.

Loading and Delete Pocessing

An MDC table can be loaded using the high-speed LOAD command that is shipped with DB2. The loader is aware of the structure of an MDC table and so will generate the appropriate blocks of information. It will also take advantage of free extents that may be created during delete activity.

One important aspect of MDC tables is the reclamation of existing space after a delete. When an extent is cleared of records due to a delete operation, DB2 will release this extent back to the table space for future use. With standard SQL tables, space will not be reclaimed until a reorganization command is issued. In the case of MDC, the free space is instantly available to the user, thus eliminating the need for reorganizing the table. It may still be possible that pages within the extent become fragmented over a long period of time (row overflows), so the DBA may want to run a reorganization command against an MDC table. In most cases this will be a very infrequent activity.

MDC Performance

Tests have shown that MDC can speed up certain queries by over 50%. Much of this improvement comes from shortening the search and access time to blocks of records. Selecting individual records will still need traditional indexes to ensure good performance, but MDC will significantly improve access to groups of records. This benefit can be gained for both transactional (OLTP) and business intelligence (BI) workloads.

For OLTP workloads, MDC tables should improve insert time since the records are placed into existing extents based on dimensions, so the overhead of free space checking is reduced. For block deletes or updates, DB2 can go directly to the cell containing the appropriate records and modify all of the values in that extent. Contrast this to having to traverse an index and looking for individual rows that meet the update or delete criteria.

When creating a database for BI workloads, MDC tables will offer superior performance for any queries that access ranges of data. In these situations, DB2 can go directly to the cells that contain the required dimensions and read the values in the extent. This is much faster than using a traditional index to find the records. In addition, block indexes can be used with traditional indexes by using index ANDing or ORing to reduce the scope of searches within the table.

MDC tables offer an alternative to traditional clustering indexes for maintaining data order in tables. DBAs should access their table designs to see whether or not they can take advantage of this key technology that is found in DB2. In many cases a significant benefit in performance and a reduction of maintenance can be achieved.

Range Clustered Tables

Range Clustered Tables (RCT) are a specialized type of table that behave similar to an index. In a RCT table, the records are laid out in key-ordered sequence.

1	George	Rockwood	156
2	Paul	Oshawa	264
3	Kelly	Oshawa	143
4	Katrina	Rockwood	644
...			
100	Chloe	Oshawa	913

Figure 5–10 *RCT Table*

When a RCT is defined, the maximum number of rows allowed within the table must be known. The table is created with exactly that number of slots available for inserting records. Consequently, records are inserted into exactly the “nth slot of the table based on the key that is being used to define the table. For instance, in Figure 5–10, the table has exactly 100 slots.

There are a couple of reasons why a RCT may be desirable:

- Accessing a RCT is fast
- An index is not required when using a RCT since it provides direct record access
- There is no logging for secondary structures (indexes) on insert, update, delete
- No key locking
- No traversal through the B-Tree levels
- Uses less buffer pool space
- No reorganizations required

However, while the RCT has lots of advantages, there are some drawbacks to using them:

- No vertical partitioning

  You cannot use table partitioning against a table that is defined with RCT.

- Reserves space for unused records

  If you required a million rows in the table, it will take up the entire space for the million rows immediately. RCT tables must preallocate all of the storage for the table, regardless if the rows will actually exist. In addition, the size of the row will be based on the maximum possible size of the columns in the row. In the case of VARCHAR columns, the row size will assume that the column will be at its maximum size.

- Overflow causes performance degradation

  RCT can allow for overflow records. These are records that are not contained in the original definition of the table. These records are appended to the end of the existing table and are not ordered. In other words, any query that needs to search for records beyond the original limit of the RCT will end up scanning all records at the end of the table. This can slow down performance, especially if there are a high number of overflow records.

- Cannot ALTER the RCT definition

  Once a decision has been made on the size of the RCT, it cannot be altered. In order to change the number of slots, the table will need to be unloaded and recreated.

The best application for RCTs involves lookup tables, or tables that are frequently used in applications but do not grow in size.

Example 5–38 shows a RCT table being created using the STUDENT_ID column as the sequence value.

```
CREATE TABLE STUDENTS
  (
  STUDENT_ID      INT NOT NULL,
  FIRST_NAME      CHAR(10) NOT NULL,
  LAST_NAME       CHAR(10) NOT NULL,
  GPA             DECIMAL(3,2) NOT NULL
  )
  ORGANIZE BY KEY SEQUENCE
     (STUDENT_ID STARTING FROM 1 ENDING AT 100)
  DISALLOW OVERFLOW;
```

Example 5–38 *Sample Range Clustered table*

The ORGANIZE BY KEY SEQUENCE clause indicates to DB2 that this table will be a RCT type and that the STUDENT_ID will be used as the direct key into the table. The STARTING FROM option tells DB2 how many slots to allocate for this particular table. In this case, 100 slots are defined and no additional records can be added at the end of the table (DISALLOW OVERFLOW).

If an insert was attempted beyond the end of the table definition, DB2 would issue an error message and the insert would be unsuccessful (Example 5–39).

```
INSERT INTO STUDENTS VALUES
    (1, 1, 1, 1001, 'THIS','NOWORK', 4.0);

SQL1870N A row could not be inserted into a range-clustered
         table because a key sequence column is out of range.
```

Example 5–39 *Error on inserting beyond the RCT range*

If the ALLOW OVERFLOW keyword were used instead, the insert would work, but the row would be placed at the end of the table. Note that 900 empty slots would not be generated after the end of the table to accommodate student 1001! Records inserted after the initial range are simply placed at the end of the table, regardless of the key value.

Multiple ranges can also be specified in a RCT definition. Example 5–40 shows a RCT table being generated that uses three dimensions: SCHOOL_ID, CLASS_ID, and STUDENT_NUM. The total number of rows in this table is equal to the cardinality (values) for each of these keys multiplied together. In this case, it will be 5×10×20 or 1000 rows.

```
CREATE TABLE STUDENTS
  (SCHOOL_ID       INT NOT NULL,
   CLASS_ID        INT NOT NULL,
   STUDENT_NUM     INT NOT NULL,
   STUDENT_ID      INT NOT NULL,
   FIRST_NAME      CHAR(10) NOT NULL,
   LAST_NAME       CHAR(10) NOT NULL,
   GPA             DECIMAL(3,2) NOT NULL)
   ORGANIZE BY KEY SEQUENCE
      (SCHOOL_ID       STARTING FROM 1 ENDING AT 5,
       CLASS_ID        STARTING FROM 1 ENDING AT 10,
       STUDENT_NUM     STARTING FROM 1 ENDING AT 20)
       ALLOW OVERFLOW;
```

Example 5–40 *RCT with multiple dimensions*

Views

Views are virtual tables that are created using the CREATE VIEW statement. Once a view is defined, it may be accessed using DML statements, such as SELECT, INSERT, UPDATE, and DELETE, as if it were a table. A view is a temporary result and available only during query processing. We will talk about the *typed view* in Chapter 7.

With a view, you can make a subset of table data available to an application program and validate data that is to be inserted or updated. A view can have column names that are different from the names of corresponding columns in the original tables. The use of views provides flexibility in the way the application programs and end-user queries look at the table data.

A sample CREATE VIEW statement is shown below (Example 5–41). The underlying table, EMPLOYEE, has columns named SALARY and COMM. For security reasons, this view is created from the ID, NAME, DEPT, JOB, and HIREDATE columns. In addition, we are restricting access on the column DEPT. This definition will only show the information of employees who belong to the department whose DEPTNO is 10.

```
CREATE VIEW EMP_VIEW1
(EMPID,EMPNAME,DEPTNO,JOBTITLE,HIREDATE)
AS SELECT ID,NAME,DEPT,JOB,HIREDATE FROM EMPLOYEE
   WHERE DEPT=10;
```

Example 5–41 *View Creation*

After the view has been defined, the access privileges can be specified. This provides data security since a restricted view of the base table is accessible. As we have seen above, a view can contain a WHERE clause to restrict access to certain rows or can contain a subset of the columns to restrict access to certain columns of data. The column names in the view do not have to match the column names of the base table. The table name has an associated schema as does the view name.

Once the view has been defined, it can be used in DML statements such as SELECT, INSERT, UPDATE, and DELETE (with restrictions). The database administrator can decide to provide a group of users with a higher level privilege on the view than the base table.

Views with Check Option

If the view definition includes conditions (such as a WHERE clause) and the intent is to ensure that any INSERT or UPDATE statement referencing the view will have the WHERE clause applied, the view must be defined using WITH CHECK OPTION. This option can ensure the integrity of the data being modified in the database. An SQL error will be returned if the condition is violated during an INSERT or UPDATE operation. Example 5–42 is an example of a view definition using the WITH CHECK OPTION. The WITH CHECK OPTION is required to ensure that the condition is always checked. You want to ensure that the DEPT is always 10. This will restrict the input values for the DEPT column. When a view is used to insert a new value, the WITH CHECK OPTION is always enforced.

```
CREATE VIEW EMP_VIEW2
   (EMPNO,EMPNAME,DEPTNO,JOBTITLE,HIREDATE)
AS SELECT ID,NAME,DEPT,JOB,HIREDATE FROM EMPLOYEE
   WHERE DEPT=10
WITH CHECK OPTION;
```

Example 5–42 *View definition using* WITH CHECK OPTION

If the view in Example 5–42 is used in an INSERT statement, the row will be rejected if the DEPTNO column is not the value 10. It is important to remember that there is no data validation during modification if the WITH CHECK OPTION is not specified.

If the view in Example 5–42 is used in a SELECT statement, the conditional (WHERE clause) would be invoked and the resulting table would only contain the matching rows of data. In other words, the WITH CHECK OPTION does not affect the result of a SELECT statement.

The WITH CHECK OPTION must not be specified for the following views:

- Views defined with the READ ONLY option (a read-only view)
- Views that reference the NODENUMBER or PARTITION function, a nondeterministic function (e.g., RAND), or a function with external action
- Typed views (refer to Chapter 7 for detailed information about typed views)

Nested View Definitions

If a view is based on another view, the number of predicates that must be evaluated is based on the WITH CHECK OPTION specification.

If a view is defined without WITH CHECK OPTION, the definition of the view is not used in the data validity checking of any insert or update operations. However, if the view directly or indirectly depends on another view defined with the WITH CHECK OPTION, the definition of that super view is used in the checking of any insert or update operation.

If a view is defined with the WITH CASCADED CHECK OPTION or just the WITH CHECK OPTION (CASCADED is the default value of the WITH CHECK OPTION), the definition of the view is used in the checking of any insert or update operations. In addition, the view inherits the search conditions from any updatable views on which the view depends. These conditions are inherited even if those views do not include the WITH CHECK OPTION. Then, the inherited conditions are multiplied together to conform to a constraint that is applied for any insert or update operations for the view or any views depending on the view.

As an example, if a view V2 is based on a view V1, and the check option for V2 is defined with the WITH CASCADED CHECK OPTION, the predicates for both views are evaluated when INSERT and UPDATE statements are performed against the view V2. Fig. 5–43 shows a CREATE VIEW statement using the WITH CASCADED CHECK OPTION. The view EMP_VIEW3 is created based on a view EMP_VIEW2, which has been created with the WITH CHECK OPTION (Example 5–42). If you want to insert or update a record to EMP_VIEW3, the record should have the values DEPTNO=10 and EMPNO>20.

DB2 *Note*

Notice that the condition DEPTNO=10 is enforced for inserting or updating operations to EMP_VIEW3 even if EMP_VIEW2 does not include the WITH CHECK OPTION.

```
CREATE VIEW EMP_VIEW3 AS
 SELECT EMPNO,EMPNAME,DEPTNO FROM EMP_VIEW2
    WHERE EMPNO >20
WITH CASCADED CHECK OPTION;
```

Example 5–43 *View definition using the* WITH CASCADED CHECK OPTION

We can also specify the WITH LOCAL CHECK OPTION when creating a view. If a view is defined with the WITH LOCAL CHECK OPTION, the definition of the view is used in the checking of any insert or update operations. However, the view does not inherit the search conditions from any updatable views on which it depends.

As an example, refer to the nested view example shown in Example 5–44.

```
CREATE TABLE T1
  (C1 INT, C2 INT, C3 INT, C4 INT, C5 INT);
CREATE VIEW V1 AS
     SELECT * FROM T1 WHERE C1=1;
CREATE VIEW V2 AS
     SELECT * FROM V1 WHERE C2=1 WITH LOCAL CHECK OPTION;
CREATE VIEW V3 AS
     SELECT * FROM V2 WHERE C3=1;
CREATE VIEW V4 AS
     SELECT * FROM V3 WHERE C4=1 WITH CASCADED CHECK OPTION;
CREATE VIEW V5 AS
     SELECT * FROM V4 WHERE C5=1;
```

Example 5–44 *Nested view table and view creation statements*

We created one table and five views. V2 depends on V1, V3 on V2, V4 on V3, and V5 on V4. V2 includes WITH LOCAL CHECK OPTION and V4 includes WITH CASCADED CHECK OPTION.

Let us test some insert statements against these views.

1. This insert statement succeeds because the view V1 does not include the WITH CHECK OPTION.

```
INSERT INTO V1 VALUES (2,1,1,1,1);
```

2. The next insert statement will cause an error because V2 includes the WITH LOCAL CHECK OPTION, and the value does not conform to the definition of V2.

```
INSERT INTO V2 VALUES (1,2,1,1,1);
```

3. The following insert statement succeeds because V2 includes the WITH LOCAL CHECK OPTION, which means the definition of V2 is used for the checking but the one of V1 is not. Therefore, it succeeds regardless of the value of the column C1.

```
INSERT INTO V2 VALUES (2,1,1,1,1);
```

4. The next insert returns an error even though V3 does not include the WITH CHECK OPTION, because V3 inherits search conditions from the views on which V3 depends directly or indirectly if those views have the WITH CHECK OPTION. Therefore, the search condition of V2, which is C2=1, is inherited and used for the checking of this insert.

```
INSERT INTO V3 VALUES (1,2,1,1,1);
```

5. The next insert succeeds because V3 does not inherit the definition of V1.

```
INSERT INTO V3 VALUES (2,1,1,1,1);
```

6. The next insert should return an error because V4 includes the WITH CASCADED CHECK OPTION, but the value does not conform to the definition of V4.

```
INSERT INTO V4 VALUES (1,1,1,2,1);
```

7. These insert statements return errors because V4 inherits all search conditions

of V4, V3, V2, and V1. Each of these statements does not conform to the definition of V3 or V1.

```
INSERT INTO V4 VALUES (1,1,2,1,1);
INSERT INTO V4 VALUES (2,1,1,1,1);
```

8. This one succeeds because V5 does not include WITH CHECK OPTION, which means the condition C5=1 is not used.

```
INSERT INTO V5 VALUES (1,1,1,1,2);
```

9. This insert statement returns an error for the same reason as does the fourth example: V5 inherits the definition of V4, that is, C4=4. This insert does not conform to this condition.

```
INSERT INTO V5 VALUES (1,1,1,2,1);
```

10. This last example returns an error because the inserting row is checked using V4 and V4 inherits the definition of V3.

```
INSERT INTO V5 VALUES (1,1,2,1,1);
```

The inserting of rows into V5 must conform to the search conditions of V1, V2, V3, and V4. If the WITH LOCAL CHECK OPTION is specified for V4, the search conditions of V2 and V4 must be met. If the WITH CHECK OPTION is not specified for V4, the search condition of V2 must be met.

Modifying a View

Views are virtual table definitions. The view definition is stored in the catalog. Therefore, if a backup of the database is performed, the view definition is contained in the backup image. The data contained in the view is only available when the view is being referenced in an SQL statement.

Unlike some other DB2 objects, a view definition cannot be altered using the ALTER statement. If a view definition needs to be changed in any way, the original view must be dropped and re-created with the desired configuration. (Note that in DB2 there is the option to use the ALTER VIEW statement to alter a reference type column to alter the scope; however, this is the only action on a view definition that can be done.)

A view can become inoperative if any of the referenced database objects are dropped from the database. These view dependencies are stored in the system catalog view called SYSCAT.VIEWDEP.

The system catalog view SYSCAT.VIEWS and the system catalog table SYSIBM.SYSVIEWS contain a column called VALID that contains the character X if the view has become inoperative. If the base table EMPLOYEE is dropped, the views EMP_VIEW1 and EMP_VIEW2 would become inoperative as shown in Example 5–45.

```
SELECT VIEWNAME,VIEWCHECK,READONLY,VALID
  FROM SYSCAT.VIEWS
  WHERE VIEWSCHEMA ='DB2ADMIN'

VIEWNAME           VIEWCHECK READONLY VALID
------------------ --------- -------- -----
EMP_VIEW1          N         N        X
EMP_VIEW2          C         N        X

 2 record(s) selected.
```

Example 5–45 *Inoperative views*

Two inoperative views are shown in Example 5–45 since the valid column contains the value X (a value of Y means that the view is valid). The query in Example 5–45 does not show the contents of the TEXT column. This column contains the original CREATE VIEW statement text. The column VIEWCHECK corresponds to the WITH CHECK OPTION in the CREATE VIEW statement. A value of N means that no check option was specified, L means that the WITH LOCAL CHECK OPTION was specified, and C means that the WITH CASCADED CHECK OPTION was specified.

DB2 *Note*

A view will always enforce the base table constraints. These constraints could include a primary key, foreign key, table-check, or not-null constraint.

Removing a View

When you want to remove a view, issue the statement in Example 5–46:

```
DROP VIEW EMP_VIEW1;
```

Example 5–46 *Dropping a view*

Note that when the specified view is deleted, the definition of any view or trigger that is directly or indirectly dependent on that view is marked inoperative, and any packages dependent on a view that is dropped or marked inoperative will be invalidated.

View Classifications

Views can be classified by the operations they allow. Views can be deletable, updatable, insertable, and read only. Essentially a view type is established according to its update capabilities, and the classification of the view indicates the kind of SQL operation that can be performed using the view.

Referential and check constraints are not taken into account when determining the classification of the view.

The rules determining the classification of a view are numerous and are not listed here. For details on DB2 classification of views, please refer to the `CREATE VIEW` statement description in the *DB2 SQL Reference*.

DB2 *Note*

DB2 allows views with `UNION ALL` statements to be used in `INSERT`, `UPDATE`, `DELETE`, and `SELECT` commands. The only requirement is that an appropriate `CHECK CONSTRAINT` has been applied to each underlying table so that DB2 can determine which table is affected by the SQL statement. If the view is too complex for DB2 to determine which table gets modified, an `INSTEAD OF TRIGGER` can be used to allow for user-defined handling of view operations.

Nicknames

A DB2 federated system is a special type of distributed database management system (DBMS). With a federated system you can send distributed requests to multiple data sources within a single SQL statement. For example, you can join data that is located in a DB2 Universal Database table, an Oracle table, and a Sybase view in a single SQL statement.

The base DB2 product contains support for federating SQL requests between all DB2 family members and Informix. Support for other database platforms is also available but requires an optional product.

The basic steps to set up the federated server are:

1. Install and configure the client configuration software.
2. Install the DB2 server software on the server that will act as the federated server. This includes:
    - Creating a DB2 instance on the federated server.
    - Specifying the user authorities information for the instance.
3. Install and configure any additional required software on the federated server.

4. Check the server setup. This includes:
   - Confirming the link between the client libraries and DB2.
   - Ensuring the proper permissions are on the wrapper library files.
   - Checking the data source environment variables.
   - Verifying the FEDERATED parameter is set to YES.
5. Create a DB2 database on the federated server instance that will act as the federated database.

Once a federated server and nicknames have been established, these tables can be used in an SQL statement along with other tables. From a user perspective, these tables are no different from tables that are found in a local database. Most of the DML that is described in this book can be used against federated objects.

The first step in setting up a federated system is to enable federated support in the database engine. This can be done either through the control center, or via a CLP command (Example 5–47):

```
UPDATE DATABASE MANAGER CONFIGURATION USING FEDERATED YES
```

Example 5–47 *Enable federated support*

For each data source that you intend to select from you will need an appropriate wrapper. For DB2 sources this will be the DRDA wrapper, and it needs to be created before you can catalog any remote data sources.

```
CREATE WRAPPER DRDA;
```

Example 5–48 *Create DB2 wrapper*

Once the wrapper is defined, the servers for the remote databases must be defined. These server definitions will then be used for the nickname definitions. For instance, the following server definition redefines the SAMPLE database as a remote server (Example 5–49):

```
CREATE SERVER V9SAMPLE
  TYPE DB2/UDB VERSION 9.1
  WRAPPER DRDA
  AUTHID "BAKLARZ"
  PASSWORD "********"
  OPTIONS ( DBNAME 'SAMPLE' );
```

Example 5–49 *Create server definition*

The CREATE SERVER command must specify a userid and password that can connect to the remote source with SYSADM or DBADM privileges. This statement tells DB2 that the local server name V9SAMPLE maps to the real database called SAMPLE. For all subsequent commands, V9SAMPLE will be the name of the database we refer to.

Now that the server definition is complete, a user mapping needs to be created (Example 5–50) so that the user issuing the SQL can be authenticated on the remote site.

```
CREATE USER MAPPING FOR USER
  SERVER V9SAMPLE
  OPTIONS( REMOTE_AUTHID 'BAKLARZ',
           REMOTE_PASSWORD '********');
```

Example 5–50 *Create user mapping*

Now all of the pieces are in place so that a nickname can be created for the remote tables that a user wants to access. The nickname command is used to create a local definition of a table that is found on a remote site. The following example illustrates how a remote table is defined (Example 5–51):

```
CREATE NICKNAME R_DEPT FOR V9SAMPLE.BAKLARZ.DEPARTMENT;
```

Example 5–51 *Table nickname*

This simple example creates a nickname on the DEPARTMENT table that is found in the V9SAMPLE database (which is really the SAMPLE database). This means that the R_DEPT table is exactly the same as the DEPARTMENT table, but DB2 still considers them to be two different objects. Now that the nickname has been created, this table can be used in the same way as another local table. For instance, the following select statement would access this remote table, but this fact is hidden from the user (Example 5–52):

```
SELECT * FROM R_DEPT;

DEPTNO DEPTNAME                      MGRNO  ADMRDEPT LOCATION
------ ----------------------------- ------ -------- --------
A00    SPIFFY COMPUTER SERVICE DIV.  000010 A00      -
B01    PLANNING                      000020 A00      -
C01    INFORMATION CENTER            000030 A00      -
D01    DEVELOPMENT CENTER            -      A00      -
D11    MANUFACTURING SYSTEMS         000060 D01      -
D21    ADMINISTRATION SYSTEMS        000070 D01      -
E01    SUPPORT SERVICES              000050 A00      -
E11    OPERATIONS                    000090 E01      -
E21    SOFTWARE SUPPORT              000100 E01      -
```

Example 5–52 *Select against federated table*

```
F22     BRANCH OFFICE F2                  -      E01     -
G22     BRANCH OFFICE G2                  -      E01     -
H22     BRANCH OFFICE H2                  -      E01     -
I22     BRANCH OFFICE I2                  -      E01     -
J22     BRANCH OFFICE J2                  -      E01     -

  14 record(s) selected.
```

Example 5–52 *Select against federated table (continued)*

Much more sophisticated SQL can be issued against a federated table. For instance, joins between local and federated tables are allowed (Example 5–53), along with the creation of summary tables based on nicknames.

```
SELECT R.MGRNO, E.LASTNAME, R.DEPTNAME FROM
  R_DEPT R, EMPLOYEE E
WHERE R.MGRNO = E.EMPNO ;

MGRNO  LASTNAME        DEPTNAME
------ --------------- ------------------------------------
000010 HAAS            SPIFFY COMPUTER SERVICE DIV.
000020 THOMPSON        PLANNING
000030 KWAN            INFORMATION CENTER
000050 GEYER           SUPPORT SERVICES
000060 STERN           MANUFACTURING SYSTEMS
000070 PULASKI         ADMINISTRATION SYSTEMS
000090 HENDERSON       OPERATIONS
000100 SPENSER         SOFTWARE SUPPORT

  8 record(s) selected.
```

Example 5–53 *Joining local and federated tables*

The `EXPLAIN` facility included with DB2 will also describe access to remote objects as shown in the following diagram (Figure 5–11):

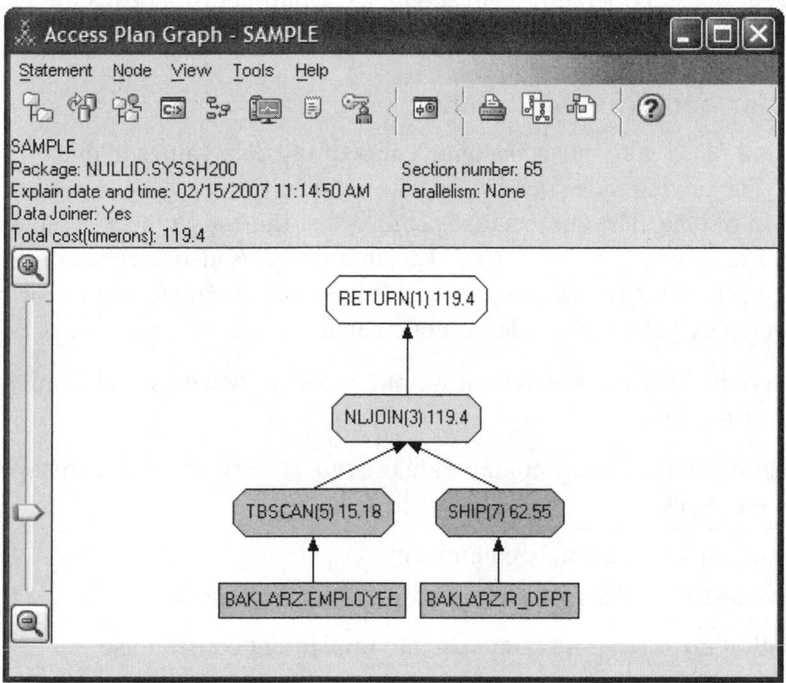

Figure 5–11 *Visual Explain of a federated join*

For more information on federated databases and tables, refer to the *DB2 SQL Reference*.

Indexes

An *index* is a list of the locations of rows sorted by the contents of one or more specified columns. Indexes are typically used to improve query performance. However, they can also serve a logical data design purpose. For example, a primary key does not allow the entry of duplicate values in columns, thereby guaranteeing that no rows of a table are the same. Indexes can be created to specify ascending or descending order by the values in a column. The indexes contain a pointer, known as a *record id (RID)*, to the physical location of the rows in the table.

These are two main purposes for creating indexes:

- To ensure uniqueness of values
- To improve query performance

More than one index can be defined on a particular table, which can have a beneficial effect on the performance of queries. However, the more indexes there are, the more the database manager must work to keep the indexes current during update, delete, and insert operations. Creating a large number of indexes for a table that receives many updates can slow down processing.

Unique Index and Non-unique Index

A *unique index* guarantees the uniqueness of the data values in one or more columns. The unique index can be used during query processing to perform faster retrieval of data. The uniqueness is enforced at the end of the SQL statement that updates rows or inserts new rows. The uniqueness is also checked during the execution of the `CREATE INDEX` statement. If the table already contains rows with duplicate key values, the index is not created.

A *nonunique index* can also improve query performance by maintaining a sorted order for the data.

Depending on how many columns are used to define a key, you can have one of the following types:

- An *scalar key* is a single column key.
- A *composite key* is composed of two or more columns.

The following are types of keys used to implement constraints:

- A *unique key* is used to implement unique constraints. A unique constraint does not allow two different rows to have the same values on the key columns.
- A *primary key* is used to implement entity integrity constraints. A primary key is a special type of unique key. There can be only one primary key per table. The primary key column must be defined with the `NOT NULL` attribute.
- A *foreign key* is used to implement referential integrity constraints. Referential constraints can only reference a primary key or unique constraint. The values of a foreign key can only have values defined in the primary key or unique constraint they are referencing or `NULL` values. (A foreign key is not an index.)

Referential Integrity and Indexes

We have discussed how defining a primary key will ensure the uniqueness of rows and that the primary key is maintained using an index. The index supporting a primary key is known as the primary index of the table. If a constraint name is not provided, DB2-generated indexes are given the name `SYSIBM.SQL<timestamp>`.

Indexes supporting primary or unique key constraints cannot be dropped explicitly. To remove primary or unique key constraints indexes, you need to use the `ALTER TABLE` statement. Primary key indexes are dropped with the `DROP PRIMARY KEY` option. Unique key indexes are dropped using the `DROP UNIQUE (CONSTRAINT NAME)` option.

DB2 *Note*

DB2 uses unique indexes and the `NOT NULL` option to maintain primary and unique key constraints.

Null Values and Indexes

It is important to understand the difference between a primary or unique key constraint and a unique index. DB2 uses two elements to implement the relational database concept of primary and unique keys: unique indexes and the `NOT NULL` constraint. Therefore, unique indexes do not enforce the primary key constraint by themselves since they can allow nulls. Nulls, when it comes to indexing, are treated as equal to all other nulls. You cannot insert a null twice if the column is a key of a unique index because it violates the uniqueness rule for the index.

General Indexing Guidelines

Indexes consume disk space. The amount of disk space will vary depending on the length of the key columns and the number of rows being indexed. The size of the index will increase as more data is inserted into the table. Therefore, consider the disk space required for indexes when planning the size of the database. Some of the indexing considerations include:

- Primary and unique key constraints will always create a system-generated unique index.
- It is usually beneficial to create indexes on foreign key constraint columns.

You can estimate the disk space consumed by an index using the Control Center. If you are creating an index using the Control Center, you can see the **Estimate Size** button. Clicking this button brings up the Estimate Size panel. You can supply the total number of rows and so forth from this panel and get the estimated size.

DB2 *Note*

The maximum columns for an index key is 64 and the maximum indexes allowed on a table is 32,767. The longest index key (including all overhead) is 8096 bytes. Note that the maximum index size is 1/4 the page size in use. For a 4K page, the maximum index size would be 1024 bytes.

Index Only Access (Unique Index Include)

The INCLUDE clause specifies additional columns to be appended to the set of index key columns. Any columns included with this clause are not used to enforce uniqueness. These included columns may improve the performance of some queries through index only access. This option may:

- Eliminate the need to access data pages for more queries
- Eliminate redundant indexes
- Maintain the uniqueness of an index

See the following example. If SELECT EMPNO,FIRSTNME,JOB FROM EMPNO is issued to the table on which this index resides, all of the required data can be retrieved from the index without reading data pages. It may improve performance.

```
CREATE UNIQUE INDEX EMP_IX
 ON EMPLOYEE(EMPNO)
 INCLUDE(FIRSTNME,JOB);
```

Example 5–54 *Creating a unique index*

Bi-Directional Index

The ALLOW REVERSE SCANS clause enables both forward and reverse index scans, that is, in the order defined at index creation time and in the opposite (or reverse) order. This option allows you to:

- Facilitate MIN and MAX functions
- Fetch previous keys
- Eliminate the need for DB2 to create a temporary table for the reverse scan
- Eliminate redundant reverse order indexes

If the index is ordered in ascending order from left to right across its leaf pages, a bidirectional index contains leaf pointers pointing in both directions, that is, to left and right neighboring leaf pages. Therefore, a bidirectional index can be scanned or leaf-traversed from left to right (ascending) or right to left (descending). For example:

```
CREATE UNIQUE INDEX EMP_IX
 ON EMPLOYEE(EMPNO)
 INCLUDE(FIRSTNME,JOB)
 ALLOW REVERSE SCANS;
```

Example 5–55 *Bidirectional indexes*

If a user issued the following select statement:

```
SELECT * FROM EMPLOYEE
ORDER BY EMPNO DESC;
```

Example 5–56 *A sort that takes advantage of the bidirectional index*

DB2 would not need to sort the results since the index already has the data in the proper sequence.

DB2 *Note*

DB2 9 creates bi-directional indexes by default. Prior releases of DB2 require that the reverse scans be explicitly defined as part of the index creation.

Modifying an Index

Index attributes cannot be changed without recreating the index definition. For example, you cannot add a column to the list of key columns without dropping the previous definition and creating a new index. You can add a comment to describe the purpose of the index using the `COMMENT ON` statement.

If you want to modify your index, you have to drop the index first and then create the index again. There is no `ALTER INDEX` statement.

Removing an Index

When you want to remove an index, issue the following statement (Example 5–57):

```
DROP INDEX EMP_IX;
```

Example 5–57 *Dropping a view*

Note that packages having a dependency on a dropped index are invalidated.

Index Advisor

The DB2 Design Advisor is a utility for automatically recommending indexes for the user to create. The Design Advisor helps you to:

- Find the best indexes for a problem query
- Find the best indexes for a set of queries (a workload), subject to resource limits that are optionally applied
- Test an index on a workload without having to create the index

The Design Advisor can be invoked using either:

- The Control Center
- The command `db2advis`

For more information on the Index Advisor, refer to the *DB2 Administration Guide: Performance.*

Database Design and Implementation

The best way to understand data type selection is to design an application and implement the design using DB2. We will create a number of tables in the `SAMPLE` database that can be used to schedule and track the results of a certification program. These tables will be used to illustrate many aspects of the SQL language and features of DB2.

DB2 *Note*

The `SAMPLE` database is normally created as part of the installation process. If you do not have access to the `SAMPLE` database, run the First Steps program and select "Create Sample Database." Alternatively you can run the `DB2SAMPL` program to generate the database.

This set of tables will be used to schedule test candidates' exams, and following the completion of the test, it will contain the candidates' test scores.

The tables and the application will need to support the following tasks:

1. Insert/update/delete testing center information
2. Insert/update/delete test information
3. Insert/update/delete test candidate information
4. Guarantee a uniquely identified test name, regardless of the test number
5. Schedule a candidate to take a test
6. Update candidate test scores once exams have been completed
7. Determine which candidates qualify for certification
8. Generate various reports on the candidates and tests

Usually an application would be designed to access its own database. In the case of this application, the `SAMPLE` database will be used since it is assumed that is available to the majority of readers of this book. If this application were placed into its own database, then a CREATE DATABASE command would need to be issued and then all of the subsequent examples in this book could be used with this database.

The data to be stored for the DB2CERT application can easily be grouped into three reference tables and a fourth table used to relate the other tables. The primary relationship can be defined as *a test candidate takes a specific test at a test center.*

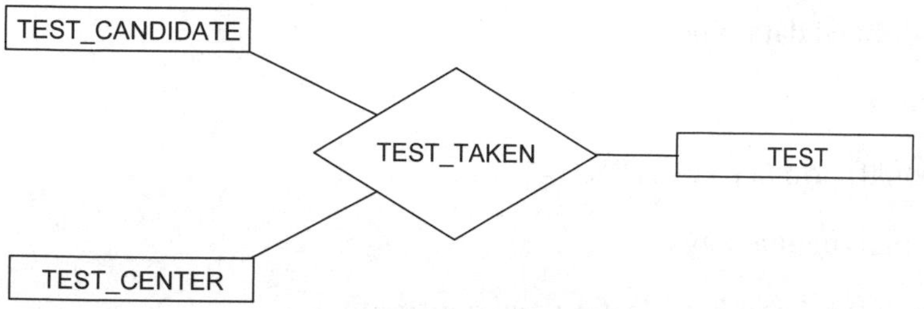

Figure 5–12 *Tables for the Certification Test Management application*

Figure 5–12 shows the relationships within the problem domain. The rectangles represent the tables: TEST_CANDIDATE, TEST_CENTER, and TEST. The fourth table is a relationship table called TEST_TAKEN.

Certification Test Table Descriptions

The following is the list of tables in the Certification Test Management application:

- The TEST_CANDIDATE table stores information about each test candidate for the DB2 Certification Program. Data such as candidate name, address, ID, and phone number will be stored in this table. A row represents a single test candidate (person).
- The TEST_CENTER table stores information about the test centers where a candidate can take a DB2 Certification exam. Data such as the test-center name, address, number of seats, ID, and phone number will be stored in this table. A row represents a single test-center location.
- The TEST table stores information about each of the DB2 Certification exams. Data such as the test name, type, test ID, cut score (passing percentage), and length will be stored in this table. A row represents a single test. For our example, there are three tests in the DB2 Certification Program; therefore, there are only three rows in this table.
- The TEST_TAKEN table associates the rows from the other three tables. It serves the dual purpose of scheduling tests and tracking each test result. Data such as

the candidates' test scores, date taken, start time, and seat numbers will be stored in this table. This will be the most active of the four tables since multiple exams must be taken by each candidate to become certified, and each test taken will have a corresponding row in this table.

Once you have defined the tables and their relationships, the following should be defined:

1. User-defined data types
2. Columns
3. (Optional) primary keys (PK)
4. (Optional) unique keys
5. (Optional) foreign keys (referential constraints)
6. (Optional) table check constraints
7. (Optional) triggers

In Figure 5–13, the DBACERT design is shown. The rectangles represent entities (tables). The ellipses represent attributes (columns). Note that some of the columns are derived (virtual) columns. A derived column is a column that represents a concept and not a physical attribute of an object. The derived columns are included in the model since their values will be populated by the database using a constraint mechanism.

We must map the attributes shown in Figure 5–13 to DB2 built-in or user-defined data types. To demonstrate some of the powerful features of DB2, we have decided to create distinct types for many of the attributes.

It is beneficial to have a primary key defined for each of the tables since this will ensure uniqueness of the rows. The attributes that are underlined will be used as primary keys. We will also create unique keys to illustrate their use. Unique key attributes are double underlined.

In the previous section, we mentioned that there are four tables used in the DB2CERT application. However, the design shown in Figure 5–13 has only three tables defined. There is an implied table defined in the relationship *candidate takes a test*. A table is required to store each occurrence of a candidate taking a certification test.

We will impose a restriction on the candidates: They can take the test only once on any given day. A candidate can take different tests on the same day, but not the same test. With this restriction in place, we will define a primary key for the *test_taken* table as a composite key including NUMBER (test ID), CID (candidate ID), and DATE_TAKEN (the date of the test). Defining the primary key as a combination of these three values facilitates enforcing this constraint.

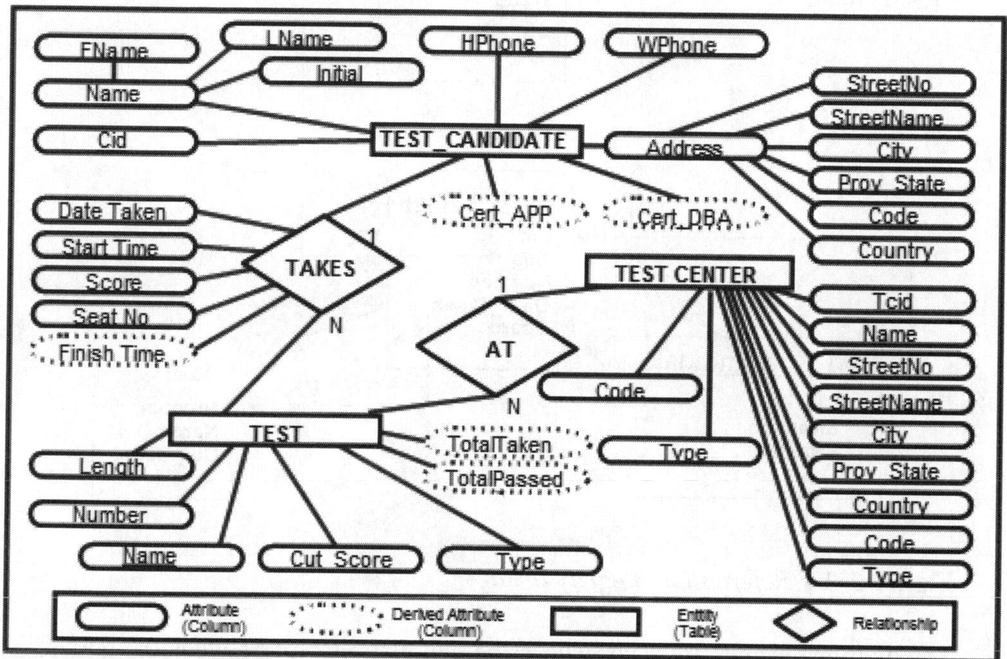

Figure 5–13 *Certification Test Application Entity - Relationship diagram*

Figure 5–14 shows the referential relationship between the four main tables.

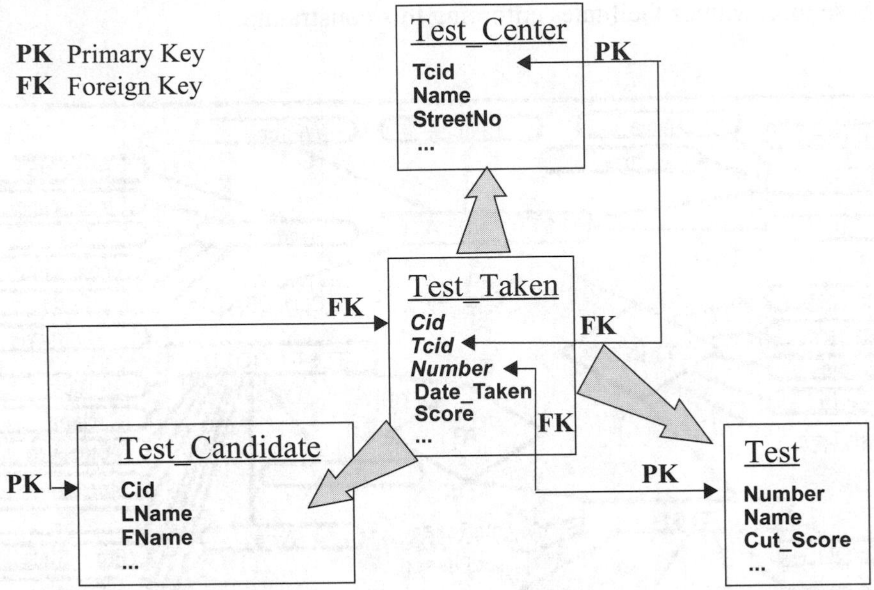

Figure 5–14 *Referential integrity linkage*

The diamond shapes are used to describe the relationships between the tables, including parent-child relationships. For example, there is a one-to-many relationship between the CANDIDATE and the TEST_TAKEN table because a single candidate can take many tests. This relationship is shown by denoting the values of 1 and N (many) on the appropriate side of the diamond.

The database design shown in Figure 5–13 is just one type of diagramming technique. A logical database design can be represented in a number of ways, but it should not dictate the physical implementation of the database. We have included it here because it will be used in many of the SQL statements throughout the rest of the book.

Defining User-Defined Data Types

If you wish to utilize user-defined data types, they must defined before they can be referenced in a CREATE TABLE statement.

We have decided to create a number of user-defined data types as shown in Example 5–58. The CANDIDATE_ID, TEST_ID, CENTER_ID, and PHONE data types are all fixed-length strings based on the CHAR data type. These attributes were chosen to be user defined because they have meaning in their structure, and they should not be used in expressions with other character data types. For example, a telephone number data type could be defined and then a user-defined function could be created to extract the area code. The function would only be used for phone data types.

```
CREATE DISTINCT TYPE CANDIDATE_ID AS CHAR(8)
   WITH COMPARISONS;
CREATE DISTINCT TYPE TEST_ID AS CHAR(6)
   WITH COMPARISONS;
CREATE DISTINCT TYPE CENTER_ID AS CHAR(4)
   WITH COMPARISONS;
CREATE DISTINCT TYPE PHONE AS CHAR(10)
   WITH COMPARISONS;
CREATE DISTINCT TYPE SCORE AS DECIMAL(6,2)
   WITH COMPARISONS;
CREATE DISTINCT TYPE MINUTES AS SMALLINT
   WITH COMPARISONS;
```

Example 5–58 *Defining the user-defined data types*

We also decided to create some numeric user-defined data types, including SCORE and MINUTES.

Defining Columns

Designing a database involves many considerations. We will only examine some of these considerations in this book. If we use the database design in Figure 5–13 as a starting point, we can start defining database objects.

The first step in creating a database is to issue the CREATE DATABASE command. This command is not an SQL statement since each database product has a different syntax for the creation of a database. In the case of the Certification Test Management system (DBACERT), the SAMPLE database will be used instead in order to simplify the SQL.

Once the database has been created, we can start defining objects. Let us start creating tables. The E-R diagram had a number of attributes shown. Each of these attributes will be a column in a table.

Every DB2 table contains one or more columns. Tables and their columns are given names. In previous sections, we discussed all of the data types that can be used for column definitions.

Data is stored in a DB2 table using the SQL statement INSERT or UPDATE. (The LOAD and IMPORT utilities are other options.) Usually, it is desirable for each column to have a value. Sometimes, no value is provided for a column in an INSERT statement. If the column is defined as NOT NULL, the INSERT statement will fail. If a default value is defined, it will be used.

The table in Example 5–59 is called TEST_CANDIDATE and contains 14 columns.

Each column must have a name and a data type. There are two user-defined data types used in the TEST_CANDIDATE table. These data types are CANDIDATE_ID and PHONE. There are also constraints defined for some of the columns. For example, the NOT NULL constraint is specified for all of the columns except HPHONE, WPHONE, INITIAL, and PHOTO.

```
CREATE TABLE TEST_CANDIDATE (
   CID         CANDIDATE_ID NOT NULL,
   LNAME       VARCHAR(30)  NOT NULL,
   FNAME       VARCHAR(30)  NOT NULL,
   INITIAL     CHAR(1),
   HPHONE      PHONE,
   WPHONE      PHONE,
   STREETNO    VARCHAR(8)   NOT NULL,
   STREETNAME  VARCHAR(20)  NOT NULL,
   CITY        VARCHAR(30)  NOT NULL,
   PROV_STATE  VARCHAR(30)  NOT NULL,
   CODE        CHAR(6)      NOT NULL,
   COUNTRY     VARCHAR(20)  NOT NULL,
   CERT_DBA    CHAR(1)      NOT NULL WITH DEFAULT 'N',
   CERT_APP    CHAR(1)      NOT NULL WITH DEFAULT 'N',
   CONSTRAINT UNIQUE_CANDIDATE PRIMARY KEY (CID));
```

Example 5–59 *Creating the CANDIDATE table*

Keys

Keys are sets of columns. They can be used to uniquely identify a row. Keys can be classified either by the columns they are composed of or by the database constraint they support.

Defining Primary Keys

It is usually beneficial to define a primary key for each table since this guarantees the uniqueness of the rows. In Example 5–59, the primary key for the table CANDIDATE is defined as the column CID (candidate ID). By specifying this column as a primary key, DB2 will create a system-unique index if one does not already exist.

Let us look at the other tables representing the tests and the test centers. In Example 5–60, the TEST and TEST_CENTER tables are shown. These tables each have a primary key defined.

In our example, the primary key constraint was given a name (unique_test and unique_center) for referencing purposes. If a name is not provided, DB2 will assign a system-generated name to the constraint.

```
CREATE TABLE TEST (
  NUMBER        TEST_ID          NOT NULL,
  NAME          VARCHAR(50)      NOT NULL,
  TYPE          CHAR(1)          NOT NULL,
  CUT_SCORE     SCORE            NOT NULL,
  LENGTH        MINUTES          NOT NULL,
  TOTALTAKEN    SMALLINT         NOT NULL,
  TOTALPASSED   SMALLINT         NOT NULL,
  CONSTRAINT    UNIQUE_TEST      PRIMARY KEY(NUMBER),
  CONSTRAINT    UNIQUE_TEST_NAME UNIQUE (NAME),
  CONSTRAINT    TEST_TYPE CHECK (TYPE IN ('P','B')));

CREATE TABLE TEST_CENTER (
  TCID          CENTER_ID        NOT NULL,
  NAME          VARCHAR(40)      NOT NULL,
  STREETNO      VARCHAR(8)       NOT NULL,
  STREETNAME    VARCHAR(20)      NOT NULL,
  CITY          VARCHAR(30)      NOT NULL,
  PROV_STATE    VARCHAR(30)      NOT NULL,
  COUNTRY       VARCHAR(20)      NOT NULL,
  CODE          CHAR(6)          NOT NULL,
  TYPE          CHAR(1)          NOT NULL,
  PHONE         PHONE            NOT NULL,
  NO_SEATS      SMALLINT         NOT NULL,
  CONSTRAINT    UNIQUE_CENTER PRIMARY KEY (TCID));
```

Example 5–60 *Defining the test and test_center tables*

Defining Unique Keys

Unique keys can be used to enforce uniqueness on a set of columns. A table can have more than one unique key defined. The TEST table definition in Figure 5–60 uses a unique constraint (UNIQUE_TEST_NAME) on column NAME to ensure that a test name is not used twice. There is also a primary key constraint on the column NUMBER to avoid duplicate test numbers.

Having unique constraints on more than one set of columns of a table is different than defining a composite unique key that includes the whole set of columns. For example, if we define a composite primary key on the columns NUMBER and NAME, there is still a chance that a test name will be duplicated using a different test number.

DB2 *Note*

A unique index is always created for primary (if one does not already exist) or unique key constraints. If you define a constraint name, it will be used to name the index; otherwise, a system-generated name will be used for the index.

Defining Foreign Keys

A foreign key is a reference to the data values in another table. There are different types of foreign key constraints. Let us look at the remaining tables in the application and, in particular, its foreign key constraints. In Example 5–61, there is one composite primary key defined and three foreign key constraints.

The primary key is defined as the columns CID, TCID, and NUMBER. The foreign key constraints will perform the following:

- If a record in the candidate table is deleted, all matching records in the test_taken table will be deleted (DELETE CASCADE).
- If a test center in the test_center table is deleted, all of the matching records in the test_taken table will be deleted (DELETE CASCADE).
- If a test in the test table is deleted and there are matching records in the test_taken table, the DELETE statement will result in an error (DELETE RESTRICT).
- If a test in the test table is updated and there are matching records in the test_taken table, the UPDATE statement will result in an error (UPDATE RESTRICT).

DB2 Note

A foreign key constraint always relates to the primary or unique constraint of the table in the references clause.

```
CREATE TABLE TEST_TAKEN (
   CID CANDIDATE_ID NOT NULL,
   TCID CENTER_ID NOT NULL,
   NUMBER TEST_ID NOT NULL,
   DATE_TAKEN DATE NOT NULL WITH DEFAULT,
   START_TIME TIME NOT NULL,
   FINISH_TIME TIME NOT NULL,
   SCORE SCORE,
   SEAT_NO CHAR(2) NOT NULL,
   CONSTRAINT NUMBER_CONST
PRIMARY KEY (CID,TCID,NUMBER),
FOREIGN KEY (CID)
   REFERENCES TEST_CANDIDATE ON DELETE CASCADE,
FOREIGN KEY (TCID)
   REFERENCES TEST_CENTER ON DELETE CASCADE,
   FOREIGN KEY (NUMBER)
   REFERENCES TEST ON DELETE RESTRICT
                         ON UPDATE RESTRICT);
```

Example 5–61 *Defining the TEST_TAKEN table*

Defining parent-child relationships between tables is known as declarative referential integrity because the child table refers to the parent table. These constraints are defined during table creation or by using the ALTER TABLE statement. DB2 will enforce referential constraints for all INSERT, UPDATE, and DELETE activity.

The relationship between all of these tables was previously illustrated in Figure 5–14.

Summary

In this chapter, we concentrated on the SQL Data Definition Language (DDL). DDL is used to create, modify, and remove database objects. There are three main statements in DDL: CREATE, ALTER, and DROP. If you want to use a DB2 database, you may learn DDL first to create some database objects. There are many kinds of objects in a DB2 database. Some of them are created by a DB2 command, but most of them are created by DDL statements.

Here we focused on data types, tables, views, and indexes among the database objects created by DDL. A data type must be specified for every column in a table. DB2 has two kinds of data types: built-in data types and user-defined data types. The built-in type is a DB2-supplied data type and falls into four main categories: Numeric, String (including large object [LOB]), Datetime, and DATALINK. Character data types (part of the String category) are associated with a character code page. We also discussed that DB2 supports Unicode. The user-defined data type enables you to create your application-oriented data type based on the built-in data type.

Tables are composed of rows; rows are composed of columns. Each column has a data type. A table itself can have some rules called CONSTRAINTS to guarantee the uniqueness of records or maintain the relationship between tables. A view may also reduce some application development workload. A logical table is created and is based on tables or other views. An index is one of the most important objects for performance. It can also be used to guarantee the uniqueness of each record. We also introduced some new options in the CREATE and ALTER statements.

CHAPTER 6

Manipulating Database Objects

- DATA MANIPULATION LANGUAGE
- RETRIEVING DATA
- INSERTING DATA
- UPDATING DATA
- DELETING DATA
- MERGING DATA
- VIEW CLASSIFICATION

In the previous chapter, we discussed the definition of various database objects using the Data Definition Language (DDL). In this chapter, we start manipulating database objects using the part of SQL known as Data Manipulation Language (DML). We will be populating (inserting) data into the database and retrieving the data using many powerful methods. The majority of the SQL statements within a DB2 application involve DML statements. Therefore, application developers must understand the various methods of inserting, updating, and retrieving data from the database. We will start with simple retrieval statements and gradually introduce more complex methods of data manipulation. The DB2 Certification database will be used for most of the examples. There are five main DML SQL statements we consider: `SELECT`, `INSERT`, `UPDATE`, `DELETE`, and `MERGE`.

Data Retrieval

SQL is a set-oriented language and many of its language elements are directly related to relational algebraic terms, such as *PROJECTION, RESTRICTION, JOIN,* and *UNION*.

Data is represented in a DB2 database as tables and is stored in tables without regard to order. To retrieve data in a particular order, an ORDER BY clause must be added to a SELECT. Similarly, if the data is to be grouped, then a GROUP BY clause must be added to the statement.

Now, let's review the DB2 certification test tables that were defined in the previous chapter. There are three main tables: TEST_CANDIDATE, TEST, and TEST_CENTER. Each of these tables is a set of rows that correspond to test candidates (persons), tests, and test centers (locations). There is an associative table, known as the TEST_TAKEN table, that is used to reflect the relationships among the three main tables. The TEST_TAKEN table is used to schedule the test candidates and also to maintain their test scores.

DB2 *Note*

An SQL statement can be up to 2M bytes long. Normally this wouldn't be a problem for most queries that developers or users may generate, but it does become a concern with large SQL PL statements or procedures. Customers who are converting from other database products will occasionally come across this problem.

Remember that to execute any SQL operation, one must have the necessary privileges.

Retrieving the Entire Table

The most basic of all retrieval commands involves the SELECT statement, with no clauses other than FROM, that specifies the name of the table. The following SELECT retrieves all of the candidates who have taken a DB2 Certification exam. The information requested is contained in the table TEST_TAKEN.

```
SELECT * FROM TEST_TAKEN;
```

SQL is a data access language that consists of language statements. There are many optional clauses that can be used to modify the statement. The SELECT is referred to as a *query* and the results are known as a *result set* or *result table*. The results from the previous SELECT are shown in Example 6–1.

```
CID TCID NUMBER DATE_TAKEN START_TIME FINISH_TIME SCORE       PASS_FAIL SEAT_NO
--- ---- ------ ---------- ---------- ----------- ----------- --------- -------
111 TX01 500    01/01/2007 11:30:00   12:30:00             65 P         1
111 TX01 501    02/02/2007 10:30:00   11:45:00             73 P         1
111 TX01 502    03/03/2007 12:30:00   13:30:00             67 P         1
222 TR01 500    01/01/2007 14:00:00   15:30:00             55 F         2
222 TR01 502    01/02/2007 09:00:00   10:15:00             53 F         2
222 TR01 502    02/18/2007 10:00:00   11:30:00             75 P         2
333 TX01 500    03/01/2007 11:30:00   13:00:00             82 P         2
333 TX01 501    12/29/2007 14:00:00   -                     - -         1
333 TX01 502    03/02/2007 14:00:00   14:30:00             92 P         1

  9 record(s) selected.
```

Example 6–1 *Result from a simple SELECT*

In SQL, the asterisk **(*)** is used to indicate that all columns of a table are being referenced. In this example, the SELECT refers to all of the columns in the TEST_TAKEN table.

If the table is altered and a new column is added, the result set would contain the new column.

DB2 *Note*

Adding a new column to an existing table (with NOT NULL specified) will result in default values being populated for the existing rows. If default values are not specified, the alter will fail.

Since the results of a SELECT using the asterisk (*) varies according to the table definition, it is recommended that you explicitly specify all of the column names you want to see in any SELECT. By explicitly stating all of the columns, the results will be guaranteed to have the same columns returned. If an asterisk were used, the columns that are returned could be different due to changes in the table structure. In addition, retrieving all of the columns from a the table requires more processing by the database. Eliminating columns that are not required will result in faster processing and less chance of retrieving incorrect results.

We could have obtained the same result as in Example 6–1 with the following SQL (Example 6–2).

```
SELECT CID, TCID, NUMBER,DATE_TAKEN,START_TIME,
       FINISH_TIME,SCORE,SEAT_NO
FROM TEST_TAKEN;
```

Example 6–2 *Result from a simple SELECT*

This SQL will provide the same result table even if new columns are added to the table.

DB2 Note

The asterisk (*) is used to refer to all of the columns in a table. In this case, the order of the columns in the result table is the same order as specified in the CREATE TABLE or CREATE VIEW statement.

The FROM clause is required in every SELECT since it describes the source of the data. Our example references a single table called TEST_TAKEN. The list of columns following the SELECT keyword is referred to as the *select list.*

Projecting Columns from a Table

Projection is a relational operation that allows you to retrieve a subset of the columns from a table. The next example limits the output from the SELECT so that only the candidate ID, test center, and test number columns from the TEST_TAKEN table are shown (Example 6–3).

```
SELECT CID,TCID,NUMBER FROM TEST_TAKEN;

CID TCID NUMBER
--- ---- ------
111 TX01 500
111 TX01 501
111 TX01 502
222 TR01 500
222 TR01 502
222 TR01 502
333 TX01 500
333 TX01 501
333 TX01 502
 9 record(s) selected.
```

Example 6–3 *Result table of a projection*

The order of the columns in the result table will always match the order in the select list. The order of the columns as they were defined in the CREATE TABLE or CREATE VIEW statement is ignored when a select list is provided.

Changing the Order of the Columns

Permutation is the relational operation that allows you to change the order of the columns in your result table. Permutation is used every time you select columns in an order different than their order in the CREATE TABLE statement.

For example, to display the test center ID prior to the candidate IDs and the test number you could execute the following (Example 6–4):

```
SELECT TCID,CID,NUMBER FROM TEST_TAKEN;

TCID CID NUMBER
---- --- ------
TX01 111 500
TX01 111 501
TX01 111 502
TR01 222 500
TR01 222 502
TR01 222 502
TX01 333 500
TX01 333 501
TX01 333 502

 9 record(s) selected.
```

Example 6–4 *Result table of a permutation*

This SELECT retrieves the columns in a different order than defined in the table is shown in Example 6–3.

DB2 *Note*

We refer to the result of a SELECT as a *result table* because the results of all SELECTs are tables, but are not stored permanently in the database.

Restricting Rows from a Table

Restriction is a relational operation that filters the resulting rows of a table. Restriction is accomplished through the use of *predicates* specified in an SQL WHERE clause.

DB2 *Note*

A predicate is a condition placed on the data. The value of condition can be TRUE, FALSE, or UNKNOWN.

To restrict the result set, we need to add a WHERE. The WHERE clause specifies conditions (predicates) that must be evaluated by DB2 before the result table is returned. There are many types of predicates. In the following example, the equality (=) predicate is used to restrict the rows to only those candidates who have taken a DB2 Certification test at the test center TR01 (Example 6–5).

```
SELECT TCID,CID FROM TEST_TAKEN
  WHERE TCID ='TR01';
```

Example 6–5 *Restricting rows*

Other comparison operators, such as greater than (>), less than (<), greater than or equal to (>=), less than or equal to (<=), and not equal to (<>, !=) can be used in a WHERE clause. This statement is an example of a *basic predicate*. A basic predicate compares two values.

DB2 *Note*

Trying to execute this sample SELECT will result in a data type compatibility error, because the column TCID is defined with a user-defined distinct data type (UDT).

Limiting Result Table Size

DB2 does not limit the amount of rows returned from a SELECT. Occasionally a user may only require the first 100 rows instead of the entire list. To indicate that the SELECT is to return only a subset of rows, the FETCH FIRST ... ROWS must be appended to the end of the SQL (Example 6–6):

```
SELECT * FROM TEST_TAKEN
  FETCH FIRST 5 ROWS ONLY;

CID TCID NUMBER DATE_TAKEN START_TIME FINISH_TIME SCORE PASS_FAIL SEAT_NO
--- ---- ------ ---------- ---------- ----------- ----- --------- -------
111 TX01 500    01/01/2007 11:30:00   12:30:00       65 Y               1
111 TX01 501    02/02/2007 10:30:00   11:45:00       73 Y               1
111 TX01 502    03/03/2007 12:30:00   13:30:00       67 Y               1
222 TR01 500    01/01/2007 14:00:00   15:30:00       55 N               2
222 TR01 502    01/02/2007 09:00:00   10:15:00       53 N               2

  5 record(s) selected.
```

Example 6–6 *Result table from a SELECT limited to 5 rows*

Predicate Evaluation for UDTs

The column TCID was defined as a *user-defined distinct data type* (UDT). To make the comparison in the WHERE clause valid, a casting function needs to be used. This technique is shown in Example 6–7.

```
SELECT TCID, CID FROM TEST_TAKEN
  WHERE TCID=CAST('TR01' AS CENTER_ID);
```

Example 6–7 *Casting function*

Predicate evaluation requires that the data types be compatible (same data type or a convertible data type).

We can accomplish the data type conversion (cast) using one of two methods:

- Use the CAST expression
- Use a casting function

In the example above, we used the CAST expression to perform a comparison using compatible data types.

The CAST expression requires that you specify the input data value and the output data type. In our example, the input data value is TR01 and the output data type is CENTER_ID (the full two-part name of the UDT).

The other method of converting UDTs involves the use of a system-generated SQL function known as a *casting function*. When we created the user-defined data type called CENTER_ID, functions to cast between the distinct type (CENTER_ID) and its source type (CHAR) and six comparison operators (=, <>, <, <=, >, and >=) were also generated.

The following example uses the casting function (Example 6–8):

```
SELECT TCID,CID FROM TEST_TAKEN
  WHERE TCID=CENTER_ID('TR01');
```

Example 6–8 *Additional casting function*

The casting function used in this example is called CENTER_ID. It is easy to remember the name of the casting function, since it is the same as the UDT itself. It is also possible to cast the left-side argument using the CHAR casting function as follows (Example 6–9):

```
SELECT TCID,CID FROM TEST_TAKEN
    WHERE CHAR(TCID)='TR01';
```

Example 6–9 *CHAR casting function*

Restricting Rows Using Multiple Conditions

It is possible to combine multiple conditions (predicates) in a single WHERE clause. The predicates can be combined using boolean operators, such as the AND operator. These operators allow you to combine conditions. The order in which the predicates are specified does not affect the result table. The DB2 optimizer decides the order in which the conditions are applied to maximize query performance based on statistical information and other factors.

The next example retrieves the rows for the test candidates who took a test at test center TR01 and achieved a score greater than 65. The rows that satisfy the predicates are known as the *qualifying rows.* The following example is an SQL statement using multiple predicates (Example 6–10):

```
SELECT TCID,CID,SCORE FROM TEST_TAKEN
    WHERE TCID=CENTER_ID('TR01')
         AND SCORE > TEST_SCORE(65);
```

Example 6–10 *Multiple conditions*

DB2 *Note*

In addition to user-defined data types, structured types can also be used within table definitions. User-defined types and structured types allow for greater control of data comparisons within a database as well as giving the relational model a more object-oriented feel. However, UDTs require the use of casting functions that require more knowledge by end users and developers.

Selecting Columns from Multiple Tables

There are basically two operations that retrieve columns from multiple tables in a single SELECT. These operations are:

- Cartesian product
- Join

Cartesian Product

A *cartesian product* is a relational operation that will merge all the rows from one table with all the rows from another table. This operation is primarily of theoretical interest. In theory, any multitable access can be performed by constructing the Cartesian product and then removing extraneous rows and columns. In practice, this is almost always the most expensive way to do things.

The number of rows in the result table is always equal to the product of the number of rows in the qualifying rows for each of the tables being accessed.

The following example retrieves all test numbers and test names from the TEST table (Example 6–11).

```
SELECT NUMBER,NAME FROM TEST;

NUMBER NAME
------ ----------------------------------------------------------
500    DB2 Fundamentals
501    DB2 Administration
502    DB2 Application Development

 3 record(s) selected.
```

Example 6–11 *Simple query (1)*

The following example retrieves all candidate and test center IDs from the TEST_TAKEN table (Example 6–12).

```
SELECT CID,TCID FROM TEST_TAKEN;

CID TCID
--- ----
222 TR01
222 TR01
222 TR01
111 TX01
111 TX01
111 TX01
333 TX01
333 TX01
333 TX01

 9 record(s) selected.
```

Example 6–12 *Simple query (2)*

An example of a cartesian product is shown in Example 6–13.

```
SELECT TEST_TAKEN.NUMBER,CID,TCID
   FROM TEST_TAKEN,TEST;

NUMBER CID TCID
------ --- ----
500    111 TX01
501    111 TX01
502    111 TX01
500    222 TR01
502    222 TR01
502    222 TR01
500    333 TX01
501    333 TX01
502    333 TX01
500    111 TX01
501    111 TX01
```

```
502     111 TX01
500     222 TR01
502     222 TR01
502     222 TR01
500     333 TX01
501     333 TX01
502     333 TX01
500     111 TX01
501     111 TX01
502     111 TX01
500     222 TR01
502     222 TR01
502     222 TR01
500     333 TX01
501     333 TX01
502     333 TX01

 27 record(s) selected.
```

Example 6–13 *Cartesian product query (continued)*

There are two tables referenced in the FROM clause in this SELECT. The tables are separated by commas. There is no predicate limiting the rows to be retrieved. This type of SELECT results in a cartesian product.

The result table is a representation of all possible combinations of the input tables. The TEST table has three rows and the TEST_TAKEN table has nine rows. Therefore, the SELECT shown in Example 6–13 returns 27 rows. Note the first column name in Example 6–13. It is necessary to fully qualify the column name with the schema and table name because the column exists in both the TEST and TEST_TAKEN tables. In this case, we needed to specify that the NUMBER column is to be retrieved from the TEST_TAKEN table and not the TEST table.

By adding a predicate to a the original statement, the result table can represent a more useful representation of the data. In Example 6–14, the query represents all of the tests that were taken by the candidate whose ID is 111.

```
SELECT TEST_TAKEN.NUMBER,CID,TCID
   FROM TEST_TAKEN,TEST
      WHERE CID=CANDIDATE_ID('111');

NUMBER CID TCID
------ --- ----
500     111 TX01
500     111 TX01
500     111 TX01
501     111 TX01
501     111 TX01
501     111 TX01
502     111 TX01
502     111 TX01
502     111 TX01

 9 record(s) selected.
```

Example 6–14 *Adding additional predicates to the SELECT*

Adding a WHERE clause to your query does not always provide the desired result. In the example shown in Example 6–14, you want to know all of the tests that were taken by the candidate whose ID is 111 and the query returns nine rows. However, as the result in Example 6–15 shows, the candidate took only three tests. The query in Example 6–14 uses a WHERE clause to filter out the candidates whose ID is 111 from the TEST_TAKEN table, but there was no filter on the TEST_CENTER table. Therefore, the result of the query would always be a multiple of the number of testing centers. Usually, when multiple tables are referenced, you should include a cross-table relationship using a table join as shown in Example 6–15. We will examine table join methods in the next section.

```
SELECT TEST_TAKEN.NUMBER,CID,TCID
   FROM TEST_TAKEN,TEST
      WHERE CID=CANDIDATE_ID('111')
            AND TEST_TAKEN.NUMBER=TEST.NUMBER;

NUMBER CID TCID
------ --- ----
500    111 TX01
501    111 TX01
502    111 TX01

  3 record(s) selected.
```

Example 6–15 *Join tables example*

Join

To avoid data redundancy it is recommended that the database tables be *normalized.* Following a normalization process, a number of related tables will exist. To satisfy some of the required queries, the tables must be reconstructed. The tables are reconstructed temporarily using a table join strategy to produce a single-result table.

The result tables in the previous examples usually provided candidate ID numbers and not the complete name of the test candidates. The candidate IDs are stored in the TEST_TAKEN table, and the full names are stored in the TEST_CANDIDATE table. To obtain the name of a candidate, the data must be retrieved from the TEST_CANDIDATE table using a relationship or join strategy.

Consider an example that will list the name and phone numbers of candidates who were registered to take a DB2 Certification test in 2007. To accomplish this, we need to select data from two different tables:

- TEST_CANDIDATE
- TEST_TAKEN

Let's retrieve a list of candidate names, phone numbers, and IDs from the TEST_CANDIDATE table. The candidate names were stored in multiple columns to allow for easy retrieval by last name (Example 6–16).

```
SELECT FNAME,INITIAL,LNAME,HPHONE,CID
  FROM TEST_CANDIDATE;

FNAME    INITIAL LNAME      HPHONE     CID
-------- ------- ---------- ---------- ---
Bill     W       Wong       1115551234 111
George           Baklarz    2226543455 222
Susan    M       Visser     4442314244 333
Glen     R       Sheffield  5552143244 444
Jim      G       Stittle    6662341234 555
Kevin    W       Street     7773142134 666
Bert     F       Nicol      8886534534 777
Paul     C       Zikopoulos 9992112212 888

  8 record(s) selected.
```

Example 6–16 *A sample query result*

Pay special attention to the values in the CID column. It will be used as the *join column* in the next example.

Now, let's retrieve the ID numbers of those candidates who were registered to take the test in 2007.

```
SELECT DISTINCT CID FROM TEST_TAKEN
  WHERE YEAR(DATE_TAKEN) = 2007;

CID
---
222
111
333

  3 record(s) selected.
```

Example 6–17 *Retrieving the candidate IDs*

The candidate IDs in the TEST_TAKEN table must correspond to a candidate ID in the TEST_CANDIDATE table because of the declarative referential integrity constraints. The parent table in the relationship is the TEST_CANDIDATE table and the child table (dependent table) is the TEST_TAKEN table.

The result table from the second query in Example 6–17 does not include the test candidate 444 since that candidate did not have a test scheduled for 2007. We need to join the two result tables based on the candidate ID values. This column is known as the *join column*.

DB2 Note

Query performance can significantly improve if the join columns are appropriately indexed.

The following single query will satisfy the end-user requirement (Example 6–18).

```
SELECT DISTINCT FNAME, INITIAL, LNAME, HPHONE
    FROM TEST_TAKEN, TEST_CANDIDATE
    WHERE YEAR(DATE_TAKEN) = 2007
         AND TEST_TAKEN.CID = TEST_CANDIDATE.CID;
```

Example 6–18 *Selecting candidates taking tests in 2007*

A table join requires a predicate that includes an expression based on columns from the tables referenced in the `FROM` clause. This is known as a *join predicate*. The `FROM` clause has not changed from the cartesian product examples. The only difference is in the join predicate (`TEST_TAKEN.CID = TEST_CANDIDATE.CID`).

DB2 Note

This kind of join operation is also known as `INNER JOIN`. An inner join displays only the rows that are present in both of the joined tables.

The table names needed to be explicitly stated because there is a column named `CID` in both of the referenced tables. When multiple tables are being accessed in a single query, you have to qualify the column names with the table name.

DB2 Note

An error will occur if the columns being referenced are ambiguous (not properly qualified).

There is no defined limit, except in storage, to the number of tables that can be referenced in a single SQL statement. However, there is a 1012 column limit in the `SELECT` list of a query. (If the page size is 4K, the maximum number of columns in a select list is 500.)

Using Correlation Names

If each of the columns needed to be fully qualified with the table name, such as tableschema.tablename.columnname, queries would very large and cumbersome to work with. Fortunately, there is an easier way to disambiguate columns in multi-table SELECTs.

Columns can be qualified using *correlation names*. A correlation name is an alias for a table in an SQL statement. We can rewrite the previous query using correlation names as follows (Example 6–19):

```
SELECT DISTINCT FNAME, INITIAL, LNAME, HPHONE
  FROM TEST_TAKEN TT, TEST_CANDIDATE AS C
  WHERE YEAR(DATE_TAKEN) = 2007
        AND TT.CID = C.CID;
```

Example 6–19 *Correlation name*

The correlation name immediately follows the name of the table in the FROM clause. In this example, the correlation name for the TEST_TAKEN table is TT and the correlation name for the TEST_CANDIDATE table is C. The AS keyword can also be used to clarify that a correlation name is being used.

Correlation names are accessible within the SQL statement only. Following the execution of the SQL statement, the correlation name is no longer defined. Once a correlation name has been defined, it can be referenced in the rest of the query in place of the table name.

DB2 Note

Use simple, easy-to-remember correlation names. Table initials are good candidates for correlation names.

Sorting Your Output

The order of the rows in the result table has not been specified in any of the SQL so far. Data is retrieved in an undetermined order if there is no ORDER BY clause in the SQL.

The following example produces a list of the test candidates in alphabetical order by last name for the candidates who have taken a DB2 Certification test at the TR01 test center (Example 6–20).

```
SELECT LNAME, INITIAL, FNAME
  FROM TEST_CANDIDATE C, TEST_TAKEN TT
  WHERE C.CID = TT.CID AND
        TCID = CENTER_ID('TR01')
  ORDER BY LNAME;
```

Example 6–20 *Sorting the results*

This example contains a new clause, ORDER BY. After the ORDER BY clause, you list the columns that specify the sort order and the direction of the of sort.

The SQL above can be modified to descending order by last name and first name in ascending order (Example 6–21).

```
SELECT LNAME,FNAME,HPHONE
  FROM TEST_CANDIDATE C, TEST_TAKEN TT
  WHERE C.CID=TT.CID
        AND TCID=CENTER_ID('TR01')
  ORDER BY LNAME DESC, FNAME ASC;
```

Example 6–21 *Multiple sort columns*

In this example, the DESC keyword that follows the LNAME column indicates that the result table should be in descending order based on the last name. More than one record can have the same last name. This situation is quite common. There is a second column specified in the ORDER BY clause, FNAME ASC. The ASC keyword specifies that the values should be sorted in ascending sequence. The ASC keyword can be omitted from a column specification since that is the default way of sorting a column.

The next example contains three columns: LNAME, FNAME, and HPHONE. You can reference the column that should be used to sort the data using the column name or by specifying its position in the select list. Using the column position is very useful when the column in the select list is made up of derived columns (calculated columns) that have no explicit name.

```
SELECT LNAME,FNAME,HPHONE
  FROM TEST_CANDIDATE C, TEST_TAKEN TT
  WHERE C.CID = TT.CID
        AND TCID=CENTER_ID('TR01')
  ORDER BY 1 DESC, 2;
```

Example 6–22 *Sorting by column position*

In this example, the sort order is specified using the column position. Yet, the query result is exactly the same as the previous example.

You can also rename a column using an *alias*. The alias can then be referenced in the ORDER BY clause.

DB2 *Note*

The ORDER BY clause, if used, must be the last clause in your SQL statement.

Limiting Sort Results

The result set from a SELECT can be limited through the use of the FETCH FIRST ... ROWS clause. This same clause can be applied to an ORDER BY clause to reduce the size of the sorted result table. Example 6–23 returns the highest marks across all candidates and restricts the sorted results to 5 rows:

```
SELECT CID, TCID, NUMBER, SCORE FROM TEST_TAKEN
  WHERE SCORE IS NOT NULL
ORDER BY SCORE DESC FETCH FIRST 5 ROWS ONLY;

CID TCID NUMBER SCORE
--- ---- ------ -----------
333 TX01 502             92
333 TX01 500             82
222 TR01 502             75
111 TX01 501             73
111 TX01 502             67
  5 record(s) selected.
```

Example 6–23 *Result table from an ORDER BY limited to 5 rows*

Sorting by Subselect

The ORDER BY ORDER OF clause specifies that the ordering used in a prior table-designator should be applied to the result table of the subselect. The following select statement illustrates how this is used (Example 6–24):

```
SELECT E.EMPNO, E.LASTNAME, PAY FROM EMPLOYEE E,
   (SELECT EMPNO, SALARY+BONUS AS PAY FROM EMPLOYEE
    WHERE (SALARY+BONUS)>40000
   ORDER BY PAY DESC) AS TOTAL_PAY
WHERE
   E.EMPNO = TOTAL_PAY.EMPNO
ORDER BY ORDER OF TOTAL_PAY;
```

Example 6–24 *ORDER BY ORDER OF*

The SELECT statement specifies four columns that are to be returned in the answer set: employee number, last name, pay, and the total_pay column as a combination of pay and bonus columns. This subselect within the select list further restricts the records to only those employees who make more than 40,000 in total pay.

The WHERE clause restricts the employee records to those that meet the minimum total pay as defined in the subselect.

Finally, the ORDER BY ORDER OF statement tells DB2 to sort the result set in the same order as that returned in the subselect. The results from this statement are found in (Example 6–25):

```
EMPNO  LASTNAME        PAY
------ --------------- ------------
000010 HAAS                53750.00
000110 LUCCHESSI           47400.00
000020 THOMPSON            42050.00
000050 GEYER               40975.00
  4 record(s) selected.
```

Example 6–25 *ORDER BY ORDER OF results*

Changing the sort order of the subselect to ORDER BY PAY ASC results in the following answer (Example 6–26):

```
EMPNO  LASTNAME        PAY
------ --------------- ------------
000050 GEYER               40975.00
000020 THOMPSON            42050.00
000110 LUCCHESSI           47400.00
000010 HAAS                53750.00
  4 record(s) selected.
```

Example 6–26 *Change in sort order*

Derived Columns

There are some cases when you will need to perform calculations on the data. The SQL language has some basic mathematical and string functions built in. Mathematical operations include standard addition, subtraction, multiplication, and division.

The calculation can be defined in the WHERE clause of the SQL statement or in the select list. Suppose that you need to calculate a passing rate for a DB2 test. The passing rate is defined as the percentage of candidates that pass the test (totalpassed*100/totaltaken).

Manipulating DB Objects

The following SQL (Example 6–27) will accomplish this for us for test number 500:

```
SELECT NUMBER, TOTALPASSED*100/TOTALTAKEN
  FROM TEST
  WHERE NUMBER=TEST_ID('500');
```

Example 6–27 *Derived columns*

In this example, the second column of the results is a calculated column. Remember that you must use the column position if you want to use this calculated column in an ORDER BY clause unless you name it (as we now discuss).

DB2 *Note*

Occasionally, the values of a derived column may not display as expected. The example using TOTALPASSED*100/TOTALTAKEN will result in a value of 66 being retrieved. Since both the TOTALPASSED and TOTALTAKEN columns are integers, the final result is also an integer and the fractional part is discarded. If this is not your desired result, you should use other functions (like DECIMAL) to change the way the calculation is done or displayed.

Naming Derived Columns

You can specify a column name for any calculation. By providing the derived (calculated) column with a name, the ORDER BY clause can reference the name to allow for more readable SQL.

The following SQL calculates the percentage of people that have passed the DB2 Certification exams and orders the result in descending order by the passing rate (Example 6–28).

```
SELECT NUMBER,TOTALPASSED*100/TOTALTAKEN AS PASSEDRATE
  FROM TEST
  ORDER BY PASSEDRATE DESC;
```

Example 6–28 *Naming a derived column*

The AS clause is used to override the default name of a column in the select list. In this example, we are giving the name PASSEDRATE to the result of the division of columns TOTALPASSED by TOTALTAKEN. The named column is used in the query to specify the column that should be used for the sorting of the output. The AS keyword is optional, but it is good practice to include it to differentiate the meaning of the field. Without the AS clause, someone reading the SQL may mistake it for a column name.

A calculation could also be in the sort column and it does not need to be found in the select list. Example 6–29 accomplishes the same results as in the previous example, but uses the calculation instead of the column name.

```
SELECT NUMBER,TOTALPASSED*100/TOTALTAKEN AS PASSEDRATE
  FROM TEST
  ORDER BY TOTALPASSED*100/TOTALTAKEN DESC;
```

Example 6–29 *Using a calculation to sort the results*

DB2 Functions

In DB2, there are four different types of functions provided. For example, two types of functions provided by DB2 are scalar and column functions (there are two additional functions called *table* and *row functions* — for details on these functions please refer to "Development SQL" on page 539):

- *Scalar functions* (also known as row functions) provide a result for each row of the result table. A scalar function can be used any place an expression is allowed.
- *Column functions* (also known as vector functions). They work on a group of rows to provide a result. The group is specified using a fullselect and optionally grouped using the GROUP BY clause.

In this section, we introduce you to some of the SQL functions provided with DB2. SQL functions are categorized by their implementation type. Either the functions are built-in or they are extensions of DB2 and are known as user-defined functions (UDFs).

- *Built-in functions* are provided by DB2. These can be either scalar, column or table functions.
- *User-defined functions (UDFs)* are extensions of the current SQL language. These functions can be developed by a DB2 administrator or application developer. Once the UDFs have been created, they can be invoked by any user with the proper privileges. Some of the new functions provided in DB2 are scalar UDFs. The functions with the schema name of SYSFUN are provided by DB2.

DB2 *Note*

For detailed information about UDFs, refer to "Advanced SQL" on page 397.

Scalar Functions

Scalar functions are applied to each row of data, and there is a per-row result provided. If we wanted to retrieve only the first three digits of telephone numbers for each candidate, we could use a scalar function. The function that will be used is called SUBSTR. The arguments for this function include a string data type column, a beginning offset, and length. The output data type are dependent on the definition of the function.

The following example extracts the telephone area code from the column WPHONE (Example 6–30).

```
SELECT LNAME, SUBSTR(CHAR(WPHONE),1,3)
  FROM TEST_CANDIDATE;
```

Example 6–30 *Using a scalar function*

The SUBSTR function is a scalar function. In this example, SUBSTR returns a character string of three characters.

The result string corresponds to the first three characters of the WPHONE column. This function is known as a string function because it works with any string data type. If we wanted to provide the output column with a meaningful name, we could provide an alias, as was done for calculated columns.

In the example above, the substring starts from the beginning of the string because we indicate one (1) as the second parameter of the function. The length of the result string is indicated by the third argument. In our example, the length is three. Note that the data type of the WPHONE column is PHONE, so a casting function is used to convert the PHONE data type to the CHAR data type.

The following query will provide the month when the exam was taken. The input for this function is a DATE and the output is a character string (Example 6–31).

```
SELECT FNAME, MONTHNAME(DATE_TAKEN)
  FROM TEST_CANDIDATE C, TEST_TAKEN TT
  WHERE C.CID=TT.CID;
```

Example 6–31 *Date functions*

Column Functions

Column functions provide a single result for a group of qualifying rows for a specified table or view. Many common queries can be satisfied using column functions, such as finding the smallest value, the largest value, or the average value for a group of rows.

Let's obtain the maximum length of time of any of the DB2 Certification exams (Example 6–32):

```
SELECT MAX(SMALLINT(LENGTH)) FROM TEST;
```

Example 6–32 *Column function*

Because the column LENGTH is specified as the MINUTES data type, a casting function is required to convert the MINUTES data type to the SMALLINT data type in this example.

If we added a WHERE clause to this example, the maximum would represent the maximum length for the qualifying rows.

This next example calculates the average of the number of seats for all of the test centers. Notice the column function AVG is used in this example (Example 6–33):

```
SELECT AVG(NOSEATS) FROM TEST_CENTER;
```

Example 6–33 *Average column function*

DB2 does provide many more built-in functions. If you are interested in calculating statistical information, you can use Business Intelligence-related functions, such as CORRELATION, COVARIANCE, and some regression functions. See the *DB2 SQL Reference* for more detailed information.

Grouping Values

Many queries require some level of aggregated data. This is accomplished in SQL through the use of the GROUP BY clause.

The following SQL obtains the average number of seats for each country (Example 6–34):

```
SELECT COUNTRY, AVG(NOSEATS) FROM TEST_CENTER
  GROUP BY COUNTRY;
```

Example 6–34 *Average by Country*

This SELECT obtains the average number of seats per country. The GROUP BY clause tells DB2 to group together the rows that have the same values in the columns indicated in the group by list. In our example, we are grouping countries into subsets. As the subsets are created, DB2 calculates the average of each of those groups or subsets, in this case, by each country.

When you combine vector functions and other elements, such as column names, scalar functions, or calculated columns, you must use the GROUP BY clause. In this case, you must include every element that is not a column function in the group by list. The only elements that can be omitted in the GROUP BY list are constant values.

The next SELECT retrieves data that includes the average cut score and minimum test length for the DB2 Certification exams. We group this list data by the type of exam as follows (Example 6–35):

```
SELECT TYPE, AVG(INTEGER(CUT_SCORE)), MIN(SMALLINT(LENGTH))
  FROM TEST
  GROUP BY TYPE;
```

Example 6–35 *Multiple column functions*

It is possible to sort the output of the previous example using an ORDER BY clause. Note that the ORDER BY clause should always be the last clause in an SQL statement.

On-line analytical processing (OLAP) applications use different levels of grouping within the same data. DB2 supports OLAP requirements implementing *super group* or aggregation features. OLAP-oriented grouping functions will be discussed in "Advanced SQL" on page 397.

Restricting the Use of Sets of Data

Up to now, we have discussed how to restrict rows based on row conditions. With SQL, it is also possible to restrict rows using vector functions and the GROUP BY clause.

Suppose you want a list of all the test centers that have administered more than five DB2 Certification exams.

To make it easier to understand, let's first get the number of tests that have been taken in each test center (Example 6–36).

```
SELECT TCID, COUNT(*) FROM TEST_TAKEN GROUP BY TCID;
```

Example 6–36 *Count of tests taken*

We use the COUNT vector function to get the total number of tests that have been taken in each test center. When you use an asterisk (*) with the COUNT function, you are indicating that you want the number of rows in a table that meet the selection or aggregation criteria in the WHERE or GROUP BY clauses. In this example, we are grouping by TCID because we have a number of occurrences for all the test centers in the TEST_TAKEN table. The TEST_TAKEN table has an entry for every DB2 Certification exam that has been taken.

If you include a column name as part of the COUNT function, it will only count NOT NULL values. This behavior means that you could get different results on the between COUNT(*) and COUNT(COLUMN).

Finally, the result is restricted to only those test centers that have administered more than four exams (Example 6–37).

```
SELECT TCID FROM TEST_TAKEN
  GROUP BY TCID HAVING COUNT(*) > 4;
```

Example 6–37 *Having clause*

This example introduces the HAVING clause. The HAVING clause for groups, is analogous to the WHERE clause for tables. The HAVING clause will restrict the result to only the groups of rows that meet the condition specified in it.

In our example, only the test centers that have administered more than four DB2 Certification exams will be displayed.

DB2 Note

If you have an extremely large table (>2 147 483 647 rows), it is possible that the COUNT function cannot return the proper result. In this case you should use the COUNT_BIG function which will return a DECIMAL(31,0) result instead of an integer value.

Eliminating Duplicates

When you execute a query, you might get duplicate rows in the results. The SQL language provides a special keyword to remove the duplicate rows from your output.

The following SQL generates a list of names and phone numbers for all the candidates who have taken a test. In the following example, we eliminate the duplicate rows from our output list using the DISTINCT keyword (Example 6–38).

```
SELECT DISTINCT FNAME,WPHONE,HPHONE
  FROM TEST_CANDIDATE C,TEST_TAKEN TT
  WHERE C.CID=TT.CID;
```

Example 6–38 *DISTINCT keyword*

The DISTINCT keyword can also be used with the COUNT function. When you use DISTINCT inside a COUNT function, it will not count the duplicate entries for a particular column.

Let's say that you want to count how many different test centers have candidates registered (Example 6–39).

```
SELECT COUNT(DISTINCT CHAR(TCID)) FROM TEST_TAKEN;
```

Example 6–39 *Count of distinct candidates*

This example provides the number of test centers that are registered in the test taken table. Remember that all the candidates who have registered for DB2 Certification exams are stored in this table.

Make sure that you understand the difference between COUNT(*) and COUNT(DISTINCT colname). They are very similar in syntax but differ in function.

Searching for String Patterns

SQL has a powerful predicate that allows you to search for patterns in character strings columns. This is the LIKE predicate.

Suppose you want to generate a list of the candidates whose first name starts with the letter G (Example 6–40).

```
SELECT FNAME,LNAME,WPHONE,HPHONE FROM TEST_CANDIDATE
  WHERE FNAME LIKE 'G%' ORDER BY LNAME, FNAME;
```

Example 6–40 *String searching*

In this query, we are using a *wildcard character* with the LIKE predicate.

In SQL, the percent character (%) represents zero or more characters. The search string (G%) can be matched with names like George, Geoffrey, Ginger, and so on (since the percent character can match zero or more characters, the search string can also match a single letter G).

The percent character can be used any place in the search string. It also can be used as many times as you need it. The percent sign is not case sensitive, so it can take the place of uppercase or lowercase letters. However, the constant characters included in your search string are case sensitive.

Another wildcard character used with the LIKE predicate is the underline character (_). This character represents one and only one character. The underline character can take the place of any character. However, the underline character does not represent and cannot match an empty character.

The previous SQL can be modified to include all candidates' names and the telephone numbers for those candidates whose name has a lowercase letter "a" as its second letter (Example 6–41).

```
SELECT FNAME,LNAME,WPHONE,HPHONE FROM TEST_CANDIDATE
  WHERE FNAME LIKE '_A%' ORDER BY LNAME,FNAME;
```

Example 6–41 *Like function*

This example uses two wildcard characters that work with the LIKE predicate. The search string, in this example, can include names, such as Paul, Gabriel, or Natalie. (The first character may be any character, the lowercase letter "a" is the second character in the string, and the string ends with any number of characters.)

Searching for Data in Ranges

SQL also offers us a range operator. This operator is used to restrict rows that are in a particular range of values.

Consider the requirement to list those candidates whose scores in the DB2 Certification exam are between 60 and 75 (Example 6–42).

```
SELECT DISTINCT FNAME,LNAME,WPHONE,HPHONE
  FROM TEST_CANDIDATE C, TEST_TAKEN TT
  WHERE C.CID=TT.CID
        AND INTEGER (SCORE) BETWEEN 60 AND 75;
```

Example 6–42 *Range searching*

The BETWEEN predicate includes the values that you specify for searching your data. An important fact about the BETWEEN predicate is that it can work with character ranges as well.

In addition to the score requirement, this example modifies the SQL to include only those candidates whose last name begins with a letter between B and G (Example 6–43).

```
SELECT DISTINCT FNAME,LNAME,WPHONE,HPHONE
  FROM TEST_CANDIDATE C, TEST_TAKEN TT
  WHERE C.CID=TT.CID
        AND INTEGER(SCORE) BETWEEN 60 AND 75
        AND LNAME BETWEEN 'B' AND 'GZ';
```

Example 6–43 *Multiple ranges*

In Example 6–43, the second `BETWEEN` predicate contains character values. We need to specify the `GZ` value to include all the possible names that start with the letter `G`. This was done assuming that the letter `Z` is the last possible value in the alphabet.

Searching for Null Values

`NULL` values represent an unknown value for a particular occurrence of an entity. We can use a `NULL` value in the cases where we don't know a particular value of a column.

Let's say that we want a list of all those candidates whose score is not yet input. This condition is represented with a `NULL` value (Example 6–44).

```
SELECT FNAME,LNAME,WPHONE,HPHONE
  FROM TEST_CANDIDATE C, TEST_TAKEN TT
  WHERE C.CID=TT.CID AND SCORE IS NULL;
```

Example 6–44 *Handling NULL values*

The `IS` predicate is used to search for the `NULL` value in this example. Remember that the `NULL` value means "unknown." Because it has no particular value, it can't be compared with other values. You can't use relational operators, such as equal (=), with null values.

Searching for Negative Conditions

The `BETWEEN`, `IS`, and `LIKE` predicates always look for the values that meet a particular condition. These predicates can also be used to look for values that don't meet a particular criterion. The `NOT` predicate can be used to look for the opposite condition, combined with the `LIKE`, `BETWEEN`, and `IS` predicate, to accomplish negative searches. The following example has a `LIKE` predicate combined with the `NOT` predicate. We want a list of those candidates whose last names do not start with the letter S (Example 6–45).

```
SELECT DISTINCT FNAME,LNAME,WPHONE,HPHONE FROM TEST_CANDIDATE
      WHERE LNAME NOT LIKE 'S%'
ORDER BY LNAME,FNAME;
```

Example 6–45 *Candidates that begin with S*

Example 6–46 has a BETWEEN predicate combined with the NOT predicate. We want the list of those candidates whose score, in any test, is not in the range 60 to 75.

```
SELECT DISTINCT FNAME,LNAME,WPHONE,HPHONE
   FROM TEST_CANDIDATE C, TEST_TAKEN TT
   WHERE C.CID=TT.CID
      AND INTEGER(SCORE) NOT BETWEEN 60 AND 75;
```

Example 6–46 *NOT predicate*

In this example, the NOT predicate will exclude all the values that are in the range 60 to 75.

Negation can also be applied to the NULL value. This SQL produces a report that searches for those candidates that have a seat number assigned. This is expressed with a NOT NULL value (Example 6–47).

```
SELECT DISTINCT FNAME,LNAME,WPHONE,HPHONE
  FROM TEST_CANDIDATE C, TEST_TAKEN TT
  WHERE C.CID=TT.CID AND SEAT_NO IS NOT NULL;
```

Example 6–47 *NOT NULL*

Searching for a Set of Values

In SQL, it is possible to select rows based on a set of values. Suppose that you need the test centers that have candidates registered for the DB2 Fundamentals test and for the DB2 Application Development test. This can be queried with the following statement (Example 6–48):

```
SELECT DISTINCT NAME,PHONE
   FROM TEST_CENTER TC, TEST_TAKEN TT
   WHERE TC.TCID=TT.TCID
  AND CHAR(NUMBER) IN ('500','502');
```

Example 6–48 *IN list*

The IN clause is used to denote a set of values. In this example, we are using a constant set of values. In this particular case, the SQL statement could also be written using the OR operator to restrict the test numbers.

You can also use the NOT predicate with the IN clause. In this case, the condition will be true when a value is not present in the set of values provided to the IN clause.

You can use as many values as you wish in the IN clause. However, there will be cases when the list of values is very long, and it would be better to retrieve them using another SQL statement.

The IN predicate can also be used to define a set based on conditions. In this case, the IN predicate also accepts an SQL statement that defines the set of values. When you define the set of values using an SQL statement, the SQL statement that defines that set is called a subquery.

Subqueries

Subqueries can be used in the IN clause to specify the search arguments for an SQL statement.

Consider the difficulty of producing a report on the number of DB2 Certification exams if the name and number of the exams is unknown. The following SQL produces a report that includes all the test centers that have candidates registered for the DB2 Certification exams.

In the example, we'll use the word DB2 as the search string to find the numbers of the DB2 Certification program exams (Example 6–49):

```
SELECT DISTINCT NAME,PHONE
  FROM TEST_CENTER TC, TEST_TAKEN TT
  WHERE TC.TCID=TT.TCID
        AND NUMBER IN
          (SELECT NUMBER FROM TEST
             WHERE NAME LIKE 'DB2%');
```

Example 6–49 *Using a subquery*

In this example, the subquery appears as part of the IN clause. In the subquery, we are retrieving all the numbers for those tests that have the word DB2 in their name.

As you can see in the last example, the subquery looks like a standard SQL statement. The only difference here is that the subquery is used as a selection criterion. You will never see its results. We are only using the subquery to create a list of values that will be used later by the outer SELECT.

The subquery used in this example is known as an uncorrelated subquery. An uncorrelated subquery is one where the values retrieved by the subquery are not directly related to the rows processed by the outer SELECT. A correlated subquery is a query in which the subquery references values of the outer SELECT.

In the next example, you want to count how many candidates are registered in each test center. This time you want to display the name of the center near the number of candidates. We use a correlated subquery to accomplish this (Example 6–50).

```
SELECT TC.NAME, COUNT(*)
  FROM TEST_CENTER TC,TEST T
  WHERE TC.TCID IN
        (SELECT TCID FROM TEST_TAKEN TT
            WHERE TT.NUMBER=T.NUMBER)
  GROUP BY TC.NAME;
```

Example 6–50 *Correlated subquery*

Observe the WHERE clause in the subquery in this example. It references a table in the outer FROM clause.

If you write this query as a uncorrelated subquery, you will have different results. In this example, you need to use a correlated subquery to be sure that all the rows of the TEST_TAKEN table are counted. When you use an uncorrelated subquery, you will only count one occurrence of the test number for each test center.

DB2 *Note*

You should understand the difference between subselects and subqueries. Subselects are queries that do not include an ORDER BY clause, an UPDATE clause, or UNION operators. Subqueries are to be used with the IN clause to specify the search arguments for an SQL statement as already described.

Quantified Predicates

A quantified predicate is used to compare a value or values with a collection of values. In Figure 6–1, the partial syntax diagram for a quantified predicate is shown (please refer to the *DB2 SQL Reference* for the complete discussion). The right side of the expression is a fullselect.

A *fullselect* is a subselect, a VALUES clause, or a number of both that are combined by set operators.

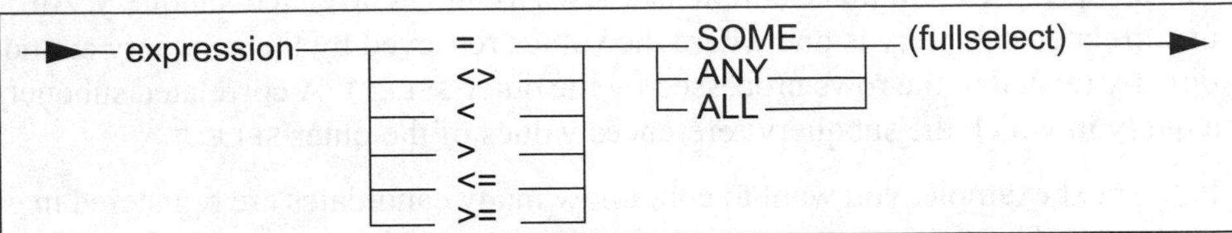

Figure 6–1 *Quantified predicates*

Let's examine the use of a quantified predicate in a SELECT. First we look at the original queries (Example 6–51):

```
SELECT CID, LNAME, FNAME FROM TEST_CANDIDATE;

CID LNAME      FNAME
--- ---------- --------
111 Wong       Bill
222 Baklarz    George
333 Visser     Susan
444 Sheffield  Glen
555 Stittle    Jim
666 Street     Kevin
777 Nicol      Bert
888 Zikopoulos Paul

  8 record(s) selected.
```

Example 6–51 *A simple query (1)*

```
SELECT CID FROM TEST_TAKEN;

CID
---
222
222
222
111
111
111
333
333
333

  9 RECORD(S) SELECTED.
```

Example 6–52 *A simple query (2)*

```
SELECT C.CID, LNAME, FNAME FROM TEST_CANDIDATE C
  WHERE CID = SOME
        (SELECT TT.CID FROM TEST_TAKEN TT
           WHERE C.CID = TT.CID);

CID LNAME      FNAME
--- ---------- --------
111 Wong       Bill
222 Baklarz    George
333 Visser     Susan

 3 record(s) selected.
```

Example 6–53 *Using a quantified predicate in a SELECT*

A *quantified predicate* is used in Example 6–53 to find the test candidates who have taken or are scheduled to take a test. When SOME or ANY is specified for the fullselect statement, the predicate is true if the relationship is true for at least one value returned by the fullselect. The clause ALL would result in all of the test candidate names being returned because the specified relationship is true for every value returned by the fullselect. The relationship CID = fullselect is true for all values returned by the fullselect because of the referential integrity constraints between our defined tables. It is impossible to have a cid value in the TEST_TAKEN table that does not have a corresponding value in the TEST_CANDIDATE table.

Note that if you use an equality predicate in with a subselect, the subselect must only return one row, or else an error message will be returned. If the previous example was rewritten without the SOME operator, an error would occur (Example 6–54):

```
SQL0811N  The result of a scalar fullselect, SELECT INTO
statement, or VALUES INTO statement is more than one row.
SQLSTATE=21000
```

Example 6–54 *Error when returning more than one row*

This is due to the SQL restriction that only one value can be compared with the equal sign. To avoid this problem, you can use the FETCH FIRST ROW ONLY clause to force only one row to be returned (Example 6–55):

```
SELECT C.CID, LNAME, FNAME FROM TEST_CANDIDATE C
  WHERE CID =
     (SELECT TT.CID FROM TEST_TAKEN TT
          WHERE C.CID = TT.CID FETCH FIRST ROW ONLY);
```

Example 6–55 *Fetch first clause*

Case Expressions

You can add some logic to your SQL using CASE expressions. Consider the generation of a list of those candidates who have passed the DB2 Fundamentals exam.

In the report, you want to print the score of the tests, but instead of printing the numeric score, you want to print a message. If the score is below the cut_score, you want to print Not Passed. If it is between the cut_score and 90, you want to print Passed, and if the score is above 90, you want to print "Excellent".

The following SQL statement using a CASE expression accomplishes this (Example 6–56):

```
SELECT FNAME,LNAME,
       CASE
         WHEN  INTEGER(SCORE) < 65 THEN 'Not Passed'
         WHEN  INTEGER(SCORE) <=90 THEN 'Passed'
         ELSE 'EXCELLENT'
       END
  FROM TEST_CANDIDATE C, TEST_TAKEN TT
  WHERE C.CID=TT.CID
        AND CHAR(NUMBER)='500';
```

Example 6–56 *CASE expressions*

The SQL presented in Fig. 6–56 provides string messages based on the conditions of the CASE expression. In this example, the SCORE column features a numeric value, but we are using it to produce a character string.

The order of the conditions for the CASE expression is very important (similar to the BETWEEN operator). DB2 will process the first condition first, then the second, and so on. If you do not pay attention to the order in which the conditions are processed, you might retrieve the same result for every row in your table. For example, if you coded the "<=90" option before the "<65", all the data that is lower than 91, even 64 or 30, will display the message "Passed".

DB2 *Note*

You must use the END keyword to finish a CASE expression.

CASE expressions can also be used in places other than select lists. CASE expressions can be used inside functions and in a group list. Samples of these features will be presented in "Advanced SQL" on page 397.

Nested Table Expressions

A nested table expression is a special kind of subquery. This subquery is used in the FROM clause to create local temporary tables that are only known in the SQL that defines them.

Consider the problem of obtaining the maximum average score for the DB2 Certification program exams. To gather this result, you must first obtain the averages and then you must select the maximum value from that list.

Let's use a nested table expression to accomplish this request (Example 6–57):

```
SELECT MAX(AVG_SCORE)
 FROM (
    SELECT NUMBER,
    AVG(INTEGER(SCORE)) AS AVG_SCORE
    FROM TEST_TAKEN
    GROUP BY NUMBER
) AS AVERAGES;
```

Example 6–57 *Using table expressions*

In this example, the nested sub-select will create a temporary table that will be used by the outer SELECT to obtain the maximum average score. This temporary table is called AVERAGES.

The NUMBER column is included in the subquery to be able to gather the average for each one of the exams. After the subquery is completed, the outer SELECT will be able to obtain the maximum value of the averages calculated in the nested table expression.

An advantage of using nested table expressions over views is that nested table expressions exist only during the execution of the query, so you don't have to worry about their maintenance. They reduce contention over the system catalog tables, and since they are created at execution time, they can be defined using host variables.

DB2 *Note*

The TABLE clause can also be used to denote that the subquery following it will create a temporary table. This keyword is also used to denote TABLE user-defined functions. Refer to "Advanced SQL" on page 397 for information about UDFs.

Scalar Fullselect

A scalar fullselect is a SELECT that returns only one value. This type of SELECT can be used in different parts of an SQL statement. It can be used in the select list or in the WHERE clause. Scalar fullselects can be used to combine grouped information, such as averages or sums, with detailed information in a single query.

Occasionally, you may need to include row data in the report that includes information based on the entire table. For instance, you may want a report that shows the candidate's ID, score, the average score, and the maximum score for the DB2 Certification exams. This information cannot be gathered without the help of temporary tables or views. Let's see how the scalar fullselect can be used to assist in the retrieval of this data (Example 6–58):

```
SELECT CID,NUMBER,SCORE,
     (SELECT AVG(INTEGER(SCORE))
       FROM TEST_TAKEN) AS AVG_SCORE,
     (SELECT MAX(INTEGER(SCORE))
       FROM TEST_TAKEN) AS MAX_SCORE
  FROM TEST_TAKEN;
```

Example 6–58 *Combining detailed and aggregated information*

In Example 6–58, we are using two scalar fullselects to retrieve the information about the aggregated data. The first scalar fullselect calculates the average SCORE and the second one calculates the maximum SCORE for the DB2 Certification exams. Observe how the SQL statements that produce the average and the maximum values are scalar fullselects. Now, let's extend this SQL to calculate the average and maximum scores for each one of the DB2 Certification exams.

To accomplish this request you need to use a correlated sub-select. This is because you must ensure that the SELECT returns only one value at a time. The correlated sub-select will let you generate the average and maximum scores for each one of the DB2 Certification exams (Example 6–59):

```
SELECT CID,NUMBER,SCORE,
     (SELECT AVG(INTEGER(SCORE))
       FROM TEST_TAKEN TT1
       WHERE TT1.NUMBER=TT.NUMBER
  ) AS AVG_SCORE,
     (SELECT MAX(INTEGER(SCORE))
       FROM TEST_TAKEN TT2
       WHERE TT2.NUMBER=TT.NUMBER
  ) AS MAX_SCORE
 FROM TEST_TAKEN TT;
```

Example 6–59 *Using a correlated scalar fullselect*

Examine the WHERE clauses in Example 6–59. They both make reference to the table of the outer SELECT. The WHERE clauses are used to obtain a separate average and maximum value for each one of the test numbers in the TEST_TAKEN table.

Now, let's use a scalar fullselect to create a list of those candidates who have a higher SCORE than the average for the DB2 Fundamentals exam (Example 6–60).

```
SELECT FNAME,LNAME,SCORE
  FROM TEST_CANDIDATE C, TEST_TAKEN TT
  WHERE C.CID=TT.CID AND NUMBER=TEST_ID('500')
  AND INTEGER(TT.SCORE) > (SELECT AVG(INTEGER(SCORE))
                             FROM TEST_TAKEN
                             WHERE NUMBER=TEST_ID('500'));
```

Example 6–60 *Using a scalar fullselect in the WHERE clause*

In Example 6–60, the scalar fullselect is used in the WHERE clause. This scalar fullselect calculates the average score for the DB2 Fundamentals exam.

The value returned from the scalar fullselect is compared with the score of the candidate. In this way we retrieve those candidates whose SCORE is higher than the average.

Common Table Expressions

A common table is a local temporary table that can be referenced many times in an SQL statement. However, this temporary table only exists for the duration of the SQL statement in which it is used. A common table expression defines a common table and provides many of the advantages of nested table expressions discussed earlier.

Every time that you reference a common table expression, the result will be the same. This means that the SELECT statement that generates it will not be re-executed each time the common table expression is referenced.

Consider a report that lists the candidates who have earned the highest score for each of the DB2 Certification program exams.

This can be accomplished using three common table expressions. Each of them corresponds to one of the DB2 Certification program exams. The common table expressions will be called MAX500, MAX501, and MAX502. They will contain the maximum score value for each one of the DB2 Certification program exams.

After calculating the maximum score for each one of the tests, we use those values to search for the candidates whose score is equal to the maximum score for a particular test. This will be accomplished by joining the score of each candidate with the maximum score of each one of the exams.

After specifying a common table expression, you can refer to the common table like any other table. An example is shown in Example 6–61.

```
WITH
  MAX500 AS
    (SELECT MAX(INTEGER(SCORE)) AS M500 FROM TEST_TAKEN
       WHERE NUMBER=TEST_ID('500')),
  MAX501 AS
   (SELECT MAX(INTEGER(SCORE)) AS M501 FROM TEST_TAKEN
       WHERE NUMBER=TEST_ID('501')),
  MAX502 AS
   (SELECT MAX(INTEGER(SCORE)) AS M502 FROM TEST_TAKEN
       WHERE NUMBER=TEST_ID('502'))

SELECT FNAME, LNAME, WPHONE
   FROM MAX500, MAX501, MAX502, TEST_CANDIDATE C, TEST_TAKEN TT
   WHERE C.CID=TT.CID
   AND ((INTEGER(SCORE)=M500 AND NUMBER=TEST_ID('500'))
   OR (INTEGER(SCORE)=M501 AND NUMBER=TEST_ID('501'))
   OR (INTEGER(SCORE)=M502 AND NUMBER=TEST_ID('502')));
```

Example 6–61 *Using common table expressions*

The `WITH` clause is used to specify a common table expression. Example 6–61 specifies three different common table expressions: `MAX500`, `MAX501`, and `MAX502`. Observe the commas that are used to separate each one of the common table expressions.

You can refer to a common as many times as you wish. You can specify a common table expression based on a previously defined common table. However, you can only use common tables in the SQL statement that defines them.

Set Operators

SQL offers a group of operators that are used to implement the relational algebra operations union (`UNION` operator), intersection (`INTERSECT` operator), and difference (`EXCEPT` operator).

Union

The `UNION` operator lets you combine the results of two or more different `SELECT`s into one result table. You can combine up to 16 different result tables using the `UNION` operator; the only restriction is that every table or SQL statement must be *`UNION` compatible*, i.e., have the same type, number, and order of columns.

Suppose you wanted to combine the minimum and maximum score for each of the DB2 Certification program exams and add a string constant that indicates which values are the maximum and minimum (Example 6–62).

```
SELECT NUMBER,'MINIMUM:', MIN(INTEGER(SCORE))
  FROM TEST_TAKEN
  GROUP BY NUMBER
UNION
SELECT NUMBER,'MAXIMUM:', MAX(INTEGER(SCORE))
  FROM TEST_TAKEN
  GROUP BY NUMBER
ORDER BY NUMBER,2;
```

Example 6–62 *UNION operator*

The UNION operator combines the results of two or more separate queries into a single result. In our example, the first query calculates the minimum score of the TEST_TAKEN table. The the second query calculates the maximum score value. Both select lists have the same type, order, and number of columns.

In Example 6–62, the two queries are very similar. However, you can combine very different queries using the UNION operator. Just remember the results must be UNION compatible.

The UNION operator removes duplicate rows from the result table. However, there will be times when you'll need to list all the rows processed by your SQL statements.

SQL provides you with a way keep all the rows involved in a UNION operation. This is the ALL keyword. Let's create a list of all the first names and last names in our TEST_CANDIDATE table. In this example, shown in Example 6–63, we want all the first names that start with a letter G and all the last names for the candidates who have taken the DB2 Administration exam.

```
SELECT FNAME FROM TEST_CANDIDATE
  WHERE FNAME LIKE'G%'
UNION ALL
SELECT LNAME FROM TEST_CANDIDATE C,TEST_TAKEN TT
  WHERE C.CID=TT.CID
        AND   CHAR(NUMBER) = '501';
```

Example 6–63 *An example of UNION ALL*

DB2 *Note*

Only code a UNION when duplicates are not desired. The UNION ALL offers better performance since it avoids sorting to eliminate duplicates. However, you can't always substitute a UNION for a UNION ALL.

The UNION ALL operator provides us with a powerful mechanism, but unions are usually no longer needed, superseded by the far more powerful outer join operators. However as we will see when we discuss advanced SQL, it is required when writing recursive SQL.

Intersection (Intersect Operator)

The intersection operation is implemented in DB2 using the INTERSECT operator. Using INTERSECT, we can find the rows that belong to two different result tables.

For example, we want a list of all the candidate IDs that are present in the TEST_TAKEN table and in the TEST_CANDIDATE table. This requirement can be seen as the intersection of the set *candidate IDs* and the set *candidates IDs* present in TEST_TAKEN (Example 6–64).

```
SELECT CID FROM TEST_CANDIDATE
 INTERSECT
SELECT CID FROM TEST_TAKEN;
```

Example 6–64 *INTERSECT operator*

Like the UNION operator, there is an INTERSECT ALL operator. If you use the INTERSECT ALL operator, the result table can contain duplicate rows, which is sometimes desirable.

Difference (Except Operator)

The difference operation is the complement of the intersection operation. It is implemented in DB2 using the EXCEPT operator. Using EXCEPT, we can find out which rows of one result table are not present in another result table.

This time, we want to know which candidate IDs are not present in the TEST_TAKEN table. This is effectively saying, "Show me all the candidate IDs except those candidate IDs present in the TEST_TAKEN table."

The query using the EXCEPT operator is shown in the following example (Example 6–65):

```
SELECT CID FROM TEST_CANDIDATE
 EXCEPT
SELECT CID FROM TEST_TAKEN;
```

Example 6–65 *EXCEPT operator*

The first part of the example retrieves all the candidate IDs. The second section of the query retrieves the candidate IDs present in the TEST_TAKEN table. Finally, the

EXCEPT operator performs the difference operation that selects only those candidate IDs not present in the TEST_TAKEN table. Without the EXCEPT operator, the query would have been more complicated. As with the other relational algebra operators, there is also an EXCEPT ALL operator that does not eliminate duplicates from the result.

DB2 *Note*

The select lists of the operands of UNION, INTERSECT, and EXCEPT, must be "compatible."

Data Modification

Up to now, we have discussed retrieval queries. The SELECT statement allows you to retrieve data from your database and assumes the data has been previously loaded into tables. Now we will concentrate on getting data into the database using SQL. There are three main statements that can be used to add and change data stored in a DB2 database table. They are the INSERT, DELETE, and UPDATE statements.

To perform these operations, you must have the required privileges on the tables being accessed. These privileges must be granted with caution since they can allow the end user to modify rows.

Inserting Rows

To initially populate a DB2 table with data, the INSERT statement can be used to store one row or many data records at a time. The statement can be targeted to insert data directly into a table; or a view, if updatable, can be used instead. If a view is being used as the target, remember that it is a table where the data actually is stored.

Every row that is populated using the INSERT statement must adhere to table-check constraints, data type validation, dynamic (trigger) constraints, and referential integrity constraints. An SQL error will occur if any of these conditions are violated during the processing of the INSERT statement.

DB2 *Note*

Remember that you must have the necessary privileges to perform an INSERT statement.

The first example is a simple INSERT statement. This statement will insert the data for the DB2 Data Propagation (#508) exam into the test table (Example 6–66).

```
INSERT INTO TEST
  (NUMBER,NAME,TYPE,CUT_SCORE,LENGTH,TOTALTAKEN,TOTALPASSED)
  VALUES
  ('508','DB2 Data Propagation','P',NULL,90,0,0);
```

Example 6–66 *Inserting into the TEST table*

In this example, we specify all the column names and their corresponding values for this row. Following the VALUES clause, we include values for each column.

In the VALUES clause, the number and order of the inserted elements must match the number and order of the column names specified in the INSERT column list. However, the order of the columns doesn't have to match the order in which they are defined in the table. For those columns that don't require a value, you can indicate null or default values. In this example, we are using the NULL value for the CUT_SCORE column.

DB2 *Note*

The number of values in the VALUES clause must match the number of names in the insert column list.

Depending on your column definition, the DEFAULT value can cause a system-defined default, a user-defined default, or NULL to be inserted. Be aware that if the column doesn't accept nulls (NOT NULL) and wasn't defined as WITH DEFAULT, you will receive an error message when using the DEFAULT value. This error is because the default value for those columns not using the WITH DEFAULT option is the NULL value.

When you want to insert values into all the columns of a table, you do not have to provide a column list in the INSERT statement. This example is shown next (Example 6–67).

```
INSERT INTO TEST VALUES
('508','DB2 Data Propagation','P',DEFAULT,90,79,11);
```

Example 6–67 *Insert without column names*

This method will only work if you specify a value for all the columns in a table and that they are in the same order as defined in the table. If you miss one of the columns of the table, DB2 will not allow you to insert the row into the table. The

DEFAULT keyword used in this example will insert the default value for the CUT_SCORE column.

DB2 Note

Remember, depending on the column definition, the default value could be a user-defined default value, a system-defined default value, or NULL.

Inserting Data into Specific Columns

There are times when you need to insert data only for specific columns. Every column that is not included in the INSERT statement will receive its default value.

This operation can be accomplished only if the omitted columns accept nulls or have a default value definition. This means that you must specify a value for the columns defined as NOT NULL. This restriction excludes columns defined as NOT NULL WITH DEFAULT.

Let's insert a row into the TEST_TAKEN table. In the following example, we will only insert data for the columns CID, TCID, NUMBER, and SEAT_NO (Example 6–68).

```
INSERT INTO TEST_TAKEN
 (CID,TCID,NUMBER,SEAT_NO)
   VALUES('888','TR01','508','1');
```

Example 6–68 *Insert with specific columns*

Remember that columns defined using WITH DEFAULT that are not listed in the INSERT statement will receive the NULL value or a default value.

DB2 Note

The TEST_TAKEN table has referential constraints with three other tables. If you want to insert a record into the TEST_TAKEN table, the appropriate values should be inserted into the other three tables in advance.

Inserting Multiple Rows

You can insert multiple rows into a table using a single INSERT statement. For instance, you may want to schedule a candidate for the DB2 Certification exams. This candidate will take all the exams on three different days (Example 6–69).

```
INSERT INTO TEST_TAKEN
 (CID,TCID,NUMBER,DATE_TAKEN,SEAT_NO)
VALUES
 ('888','TR01','500','2007-06-04','1'),
 ('888','TR01','501','2007-07-11','2'),
 ('888','TR01','502','2007-11-08','1');
```

Example 6–69 *Multiple row INSERT statement*

In Example 6–69, we enclose the values for each row in parentheses and separate each value list with a comma. When inserting multiple rows with a single statement, you have to consider that all the rows must have the same number, type, and order of columns. This means, for example, that you cannot insert values into one column in the first row and into five columns in the last row.

Inserting a Set of Values

Using INSERT, you can insert the result of a subselect into the same or a different table. The subselect must follow these rules:

- The number of columns must equal the number of columns in the INSERT list.
- The data type of each of the columns must match the data type of the corresponding columns in the INSERT list.
- The INSERT column list can be omitted only if values are inserted into all the columns in the table.
- Only columns defined to allow NULL or defined as NOT NULL WITH DEFAULT can be omitted from the INSERT column list.

In some situations, it might be useful to create tables that are duplicates of others so that you can do multiple calculations against them. The next example uses a table called TEST_PASSED, which is a copy of the TEST_TAKEN table. This new table will be used to extract the information about those candidates who have passed any of the DB2 Certification exams (Example 6–70).

```
CREATE TABLE TEST_PASSED LIKE TEST_TAKEN;

INSERT INTO TEST_PASSED
 (CID,TCID,NUMBER,
 DATE_TAKEN,START_TIME,FINISH_TIME,
 PASS_FAIL,SCORE,SEAT_NO)
(SELECT CID,TCID,NUMBER,
        DATE_TAKEN,START_TIME,FINISH_TIME,
        PASS_FAIL,SCORE,SEAT_NO
 FROM TEST_TAKEN
   WHERE PASS_FAIL='P');
```

Example 6–70 *Using a subselect to insert values*

The select list used in the subselect in Example 6–70 can also be replaced by an asterisk (*). This is possible because the TEST_PASSED table has the same column structure as does the TEST_TAKEN table. However, to keep this query independent of future table modifications, it is recommended that you use the explicit select list instead of an asterisk.

When you use a subselect to insert data into a table, you must enclose it in parentheses. You can also use a common table expression to insert values into a table or view using the INSERT clause.

Inserting Large Amounts of Data

It is recommended that you do not load large amounts of data into a table using the INSERT statement as the transaction logging overhead can be unmanageable.

DB2 provides you with two utilities that are designed to load large amounts of data into a table. These utilities are IMPORT and LOAD and are described in "Maintaining Data" on page 701.

DB2 *Note*

The NOT LOGGED INITIALLY option on table creation can improve your performance on high-volume inserts. This option tells DB2 not to log changes to the table during the current unit of work. Subsequent changes to the table will be logged. If future loads require that logging be turned off, the table can be placed back into a no-logging status with the command: ALTER TABLE ... ACTIVATE NOT LOGGED INITIALLY.

DB2 *Note*

Before taking advantage of this feature, make sure you understand the recovery implications of logging being turned off during loads.

Updating Rows

So far we have looked at the INSERT statement as a method of loading data into your DB2 table. You may wish to update only a column with values for a group of rows. There is an SQL UPDATE statement that can be used to specify the column and its new values. A table or a view can be referenced as the target for the UPDATE statement.

DB2 Note

Remember that you must have the correct privileges in order to execute the UPDATE statement.

The UPDATE statement can be used in two forms:

- *Searched update.* This type of UPDATE statement is used to update one or more rows in a table. It requires a WHERE clause to select which rows are to be updated.
- *Positioned update.* This kind of UPDATE statement is always embedded in a program. It uses *cursors* to update rows where the cursor is positioned. As the cursor is repositioned using the FETCH statement, the target row for the UPDATE statement changes.

We focus on searched updates in this chapter.

Similar to INSERT, all relevant constraints are enforced during an UPDATE. Update constraints can be different from insert constraints.

For example, the following is a transaction that updates candidate ID 888's exam date for the DB2 Fundamentals certification exam (Example 6–71).

```
UPDATE TEST_TAKEN
 SET DATE_TAKEN=DATE_TAKEN + 3 DAYS
 WHERE CHAR(CID) ='888'
       AND NUMBER=TEST_ID('500');
```

Example 6–71 *Updating values*

In this example, we are using an operation known as a *labeled duration* to add three days to the original date. DB2 labeled durations for data types include: YEARS, MONTHS, DAYS, HOURS, MINUTES, SECONDS, and MICROSECONDS.

It is very important that you provide the proper WHERE clause to avoid updating unintended rows. In this example, we needed to specify the predicate number=test_id('500') to avoid changing the date for any of the other tests that the candidate can be scheduled for.

The UPDATE statement can also be used with scalar fullselects. In this case, the fullselect must return a row with exactly the same number of columns and column data types of the row that will be updated. Observe that this scalar fullselect must return only one row.

Let's update a row using a scalar fullselect to set the new value. Candidate ID 888 decides to take the DB2 Fundamentals test today in the test center located in Markham, Canada (Example 6–72).

```
UPDATE TEST_TAKEN
 SET (DATE_TAKEN,TCID)=
     (SELECT CURRENT DATE,TCID FROM TEST_CENTER
        WHERE CITY='MARKHAM'
        AND COUNTRY='CANADA')
 WHERE CID = CANDIDATE_ID('111') AND NUMBER=TEST_ID('500');
```

Example 6–72 *Using a scalar fullselect to update data*

In Example 6–72, we are updating two different columns. These columns are listed in the parentheses following the SET clause.

After indicating which columns are going to be updated, we use a scalar fullselect to retrieve the current date (today) and the test center ID for the test center located in Markham, Canada. Notice the last WHERE clause in the statement will restrict the rows that will be updated.

DB2 *Note*

If you forget the WHERE clause in an UPDATE, all of the rows in your table will be updated.

The SQL statement that will update the DATE_TAKEN and TCID columns is known as a scalar fullselect. This name is given because it returns only one row. Observe that the scalar fullselect can be considered a special case of a row fullselect.

DB2 *Note*

CURRENT DATE is a DB2 special register that gives the system date. Others include CURRENT TIME, CURRENT TIMESTAMP, and USER (the authid).

Updating Large Amounts of Data

There are times when you need to update a large number of rows of a particular table. This can be accomplished by issuing a searched update. However, this also could allocate a large amount of transactional log space. You can accomplish updates using positioned updates, where you can easily control the commit frequency. The other option is to create tables with the NOT LOGGED INITIALLY attribute and turn logging off during large update operations.

Removing Data

There are many methods available to remove data from a DB2 database. To remove all of the data within a database, perform the DROP DATABASE command. This may remove more data than you intended because the entire database, including its configuration, will be physically removed.

It is also possible to remove data using the DROP TABLESPACE or DROP TABLE statements. These statements are usually only issued by the SYSADM or DBADM, since they will remove large amounts of data. If you wish to remove all of the rows from a table, it is easier and quicker to perform the DROP TABLE statement. If the table is dropped, it must be re-created before any data can be populated again in the table.

The DELETE statement removes rows from tables. The syntax of the DELETE statement is different from the SELECT or INSERT statements because columns cannot be selected, only rows can be deleted.

The DELETE statement can also be used with views. However, there are restrictions on the type of views that can be used within a DELETE statement. Views must be considered deletable in order to allow deletes to be performed against them.

DB2 Note

Remember that you must have the necessary privileges over a table to execute the DELETE statement.

In general, there are two kinds of DELETE statements:

- *Searched delete* — This DELETE statement is used to delete one or multiple rows from a table. It uses a WHERE clause to select the rows to be deleted.
- *Positioned delete* — This kind of DELETE operation is always embedded into a program. It uses *cursors* to delete the row where the cursor is positioned.

In this section we will focus on the searched delete.

The following DELETE statement deletes candidates who don't have telephone numbers. We use a searched delete to accomplish this (Example 6–73).

```
DELETE FROM TEST_CANDIDATE
  WHERE HPHONE IS NULL
        AND WPHONE IS NULL;
```

Example 6–73 *Deleting rows in the TEST_CANDIDATE table*

This example uses a WHERE clause to delete the data that meets a specific criterion.

To verify the result of the DELETE statement, you can issue a SELECT with the same WHERE clause. If the DELETE was successful, the SELECT will return an empty result table.

A delete can also become more sophisticated by using subselects. The next SQL statement deletes all the candidates who took the DB2 Certification exams in February of any given year (Example 6–74).

```
DELETE FROM TEST_CANDIDATE
 WHERE CID IN (SELECT CID FROM TEST_TAKEN
                WHERE MONTH(DATE_TAKEN)=2);
```

Example 6–74 *Searched delete*

In this example, we are using a subselect to retrieve the CID values of the candidates who took a DB2 Certification exam in the month of February. This list will be used to search for the candidates we want to delete.

Deleting All the Rows in a Table

You will delete all the rows in a table if you don't specify a search condition in your DELETE statement. You must be aware of the implications of this type of statement. However, this is not the only way to delete all the rows in a table. You will also delete all the rows in a table if all the rows meet the search condition.

Deleting all the rows in a table by using a DELETE statement may not be the most efficient method. This kind of statement can consume a lot of log space when your tables are big.

DB2 *Note*

If a table has been created with the NOT LOGGED INITIALLY option, there is a way to delete all of the contents of the table without physically dropping it. Use the following command to tell DB2 to drop the contents of the rows (without logging): ALTER TABLE ... ACTIVATE NOT LOGGED INITIALLY WITH EMPTY TABLE. The advantage of deleting rows with this technique is that definitions relying on this table do not get dropped.

Searched INSERT, UPDATE, and DELETE

One additional technique that can be applied to INSERT, UPDATE, and DELETE statements is the use of fullselects as the argument to the statement. This feature enables you to reduce work that might otherwise require two statements (a fullselect and an

INSERT, UPDATE, or DELETE on the results of the fullselect) to a single statement. By combining this work into a single statement, you can reduce the potential for deadlocks and possibly eliminate the need for view and cursor definitions. Any query that can be used to produce an insertable, updatable, or deletable view can be the target of searched INSERT, UPDATE, or DELETE statements.

The following example shows how only one employee record will be deleted from a table even if multiple employees match the WHERE clause (Example 6–75).

```
DELETE FROM (
  SELECT * FROM EMP_PROFILE
    WHERE EMP_NAME LIKE '%A%'
    FETCH FIRST ROW ONLY);
```

Example 6–75 *Searched delete with fullselect*

SELECT from Updates, Inserts, and Deletes

In prior INSERT, UPDATE, and DELETE examples, there was no easy way for determining which rows were affected by the command. Unless an application did a SELECT statement prior to issuing the UPDATE, there would be no record of what was done to the rows.

DB2 allows the use of a SELECT statement to be processed along with an INSERT/UPDATE/DELETE statement. This allows the developer to run one SQL statement that updates the corresponding data and at the same time returns the values of the rows that were changed. This eliminates the need to run a SELECT statement separate from the INSERT/UPDATE/DELETE. In addition, it may be difficult to determine which rows are affected by the corresponding action, so this form of SQL guarantees that the actual rows affected will be returned.

The EMP_PROFILE table will be used to illustrate the use of this feature in Example 6–76.

```
CREATE TABLE EMP_PROFILE
  (
  EMP_NAME VARCHAR(20),
  EMP_SALARY INT,
  EMP_BONUS INT GENERATED ALWAYS AS (EMP_SALARY / 10)
  );
```

Example 6–76 *EMP_PROFILE table*

Example 6–77 show the results obtained when issuing an INSERT statement against the EMP_PROFILE table.

```
SELECT * FROM FINAL TABLE
  (INSERT INTO EMP_PROFILE(EMP_NAME, EMP_SALARY)
    VALUES
      ('JACQUES',30000),
      ('KEVIN',20000),
      ('JIM',40000),
      ('PAUL',50000),
      ('GEORGE',10000)
  );

EMP_NAME             EMP_SALARY  EMP_BONUS
-------------------- ----------- -----------
Jacques                    30000        3000
Kevin                      20000        2000
Jim                        40000        4000
Paul                       50000        5000
George                     10000        1000

  5 record(s) selected.
```

Example 6–77 *SELECT with INSERT*

The SELECT statement retrieves the results of the INSERTs that were performed against the EMP_PROFILE table. Note that the INSERT statement did not include the EMP_BONUS field because it is a generated column. However, the SELECT statement will return all values from the table. This technique is very useful for returning values that are automatically generated by DB2 such as sequence numbers and generated columns.

A SELECT can also be applied against UPDATE and DELETE statements as shown in Example 6–78.

```
SELECT * FROM OLD TABLE
  (UPDATE EMP_PROFILE
   SET EMP_SALARY = EMP_SALARY * 1.2
   WHERE EMP_SALARY <= 20000
  );

EMP_NAME             EMP_SALARY  EMP_BONUS
-------------------- ----------- -----------
Kevin                      20000        2000
George                     10000        1000

  2 record(s) selected.
```

Example 6–78 *SELECT with UPDATE*

The contents of the intermediate result table are dependant on the qualifier specified in the FROM clause. You must include one of the following FROM clause qualifiers in SELECT statements that retrieve result sets as intermediate result tables.

- `OLD TABLE`

  The rows in the intermediate result table will contain values of the target table rows at the point immediately preceding the execution of before triggers and the SQL data-change operation. The `OLD TABLE` qualifier applies to `UPDATE` and `DELETE` operations.

- `NEW TABLE`

  The rows in the intermediate result table will contain values of the target table rows at the point immediately after the SQL data-change statement has been executed, but before referential integrity evaluation and the firing of any after triggers. The `NEW TABLE` qualifier applies to `UPDATE` and `INSERT` operations.

- `FINAL TABLE`

  This qualifier returns the same intermediate result table as `NEW TABLE`. In addition, the use of `FINAL TABLE` guarantees that no after trigger or referential integrity constraint will further modify the target of the `UPDATE` or `INSERT` operation. The `FINAL TABLE` qualifier applies to `UPDATE` and `INSERT` operations.

Merging Data

One of the most common types of data maintenance applications written today involves the merging of data from a set of new transactions into an existing table. Logic used within these applications follow a set of logic similar to the following (Example 6–79):

```
For each record in the transaction table
    Find the corresponding record in the base table
    If the record does not exist in the base table
        Insert this record into the base table (new record)
       Or Issue an error message that the record does not exist
    Else
        Update the existing record with the information from
          the transaction
    End if
End For
```

Example 6–79 *Logic for updating a master table with transactions*

Some applications also include logic that would delete records from the existing table that are not found in the transaction table. Rather than write an application in a conventional programming language, the SQL language includes the MERGE (or UPSERT) statement that mimics this functionality in a single SQL statement.

A simple example will illustrate the power of the MERGE statement. Consider a retail store where a list of products, their description, and quantity are kept in a single table. The definition of this table is found in Example 6–80.

```
CREATE TABLE PRODUCTS
  (
  PROD_NO     INT            NOT NULL,
  DESCRIPTION VARCHAR(20),
  QUANTITY    INT            NOT NULL
  );
```

Example 6–80 *PRODUCT table definition*

Every morning, stock is delivered to the store and a transaction table is created that includes all of the new merchandise that has been delivered to the store. This transaction table is identical to the PRODUCTS table defined in Example 6–80. The SQL language has a simple way of creating a table based on an existing table definition Example 6–81:

```
CREATE TABLE PRODUCT_TXS LIKE PRODUCTS;
```

Example 6–81 *PRODUCT_TXS table definition*

The following MERGE command will take the contents of the transaction table and update the existing product table (Example 6–82):

```
MERGE INTO PRODUCTS PR
   USING (SELECT PROD_NO, DESCRIPTION, QUANTITY
          FROM PRODUCT_TXS) TX
          ON (PR.PROD_NO = TX.PROD_NO)
   WHEN MATCHED THEN
        UPDATE SET
               PR.QUANTITY = PR.QUANTITY + TX.QUANTITY
   WHEN NOT MATCHED THEN
        INSERT (PROD_NO, DESCRIPTION, QUANTITY)
               VALUES (TX.PROD_NO, TX.DESCRIPTION,
                                   TX.QUANTITY);
```

Example 6–82 *MERGE command*

The original table contains the following rows (Example 6–83):

```
PROD_NO DESCRIPTION QUANTITY
------- ----------- --------
      1 Pants             10
      2 Shorts             5
      3 Shirts            20
      4 Socks             12
      5 Ties               5
```

Example 6–83 *PRODUCT table contents*

In addition, the PRODUCT_TXS (transaction) table contains the following data (Example 6–84):

```
PROD_NO DESCRIPTION QUANTITY
------- ----------- --------
      1 Pants             15
      3 Shirts            30
      6 Shoes              5
      7 Belts             10
```

Example 6–84 *PRODUCT_TXS (Transaction) table contents*

After the MERGE command has run, the PRODUCT table will contain the following rows (Example 6–85):

```
PROD_NO DESCRIPTION QUANTITY
------- ----------- --------
      1 Pants             25
      2 Shorts             5
      3 Shirts            50
      4 Socks             12
      5 Ties               5
      6 Shoes              5
      7 Belts             10
```

Example 6–85 *Final PRODUCT table results*

The number of pants and shirts available has increased by the quantity found in the transaction table, while two new entries have been added for shoes and belts.

MERGE Syntax

A closer inspection of the MERGE command illustrates how the command operates against the PRODUCT table. The original MERGE command in Example 6–82 contains 9 statements that are described in detail below.

1. `MERGE INTO PRODUCT PR`

   The MERGE INTO command indicates to DB2 that this is a MERGE command and it will be modifying the PRODUCT table. The PR after the table name is a label that can be used to refer to this table, rather than using the full name. The MERGE can update either a table or a view, but the view must not identify a catalog table, a system-maintained materialized query table, a view of a catalog table, or a read-only view.

2. `USING (SELECT PROD_NO,DESCRIPTION,QUANTITY FROM PRODUCT_TXS) TX`

   The USING clause indicates which table will be used to modify the original table. In this case, the three columns from the PRODUCT_TXS table are going to retrieved and used in the MERGE logic. Note that a label is required after this SELECT logic to identify the rows being returned. The portion within the SELECT statement can contain addition logic to restrict the rows being returned from the PRODUCT_TXS table. For instance, the SELECT could contain the following logic to restrict rows only containing products that have an "S" in their first letter (Example 6–86).

```
USING (SELECT PROD_NO, DESCRIPTION, QUANTITY FROM PRODUCT_TXS
          WHERE DESCRIPTION LIKE 'S%') TX
```

Example 6–86 *Selecting descriptions starting with S*

3. `ON (PR.PROD_NO = TX.PROD_NO)`

   The `ON` clause determines how the base table (`PRODUCT`) and the transaction table (`PRODUCT_TXS`) are going to be combined. In the majority of cases, this column should be the primary key of both tables. Trying to run a `MERGE` command against a table without an index would result in poor performance since the tables would need to be completely scanned to determine the answer set.

4. `WHEN MATCHED THEN`

   The `WHEN MATCHED` clause tells DB2 what to do when a row in the transaction table matches a corresponding record in the base table. The `WHEN` clause can also contain additional logic to determine what happens to the base records. In this example, all transaction records that match base records will execute this logic.

5. `UPDATE SET`

   The `UPDATE` command is part of the `WHEN MATCHED THEN` clause. When a transaction record matches a base record, the record can either be updated, deleted, or an error condition raised. In this case, the `UPDATE` command will change the base record contents.

6. `PR.QUANTITY = PR.QUANTITY + TX.QUANTITY`

   The value of the `QUANTITY` field in the `PRODUCT` table is updated to reflect the addition of new stock (`TX.QUANTITY`).

7. `WHEN NOT MATCHED THEN`

   The `WHEN NOT MATCHED THEN` clause is executed when the transaction record is not found in the base table. In this situation, only an `INSERT` or raising an error condition is allowed.

8. `INSERT (PROD_NO, DESCRIPTION, QUANTITY)`

   The `INSERT` statement is part of the `WHEN NOT MATCHED THEN` clause. These fields are inserted into the base (`PRODUCT`) table.

9. `VALUES (TX.PROD_NO, TX.DESCRIPTION, TX.QUANTITY)`

   The values that are being inserted are taken from the transaction (`PRODUCT_TXS`) table. This can include calculations and values from either the base table or the transaction table.

Additional WHEN MATCHED logic

Example 6–82 can insert new records and update existing ones, but it has no ability to delete records from the base table. In order to allow for this capability in the transaction table, the developer must create an additional column in the transaction table and add some logic that will identify which records to delete. A slight modification to the transaction table makes this possible (Example 6–87):

```
CREATE TABLE PRODUCT_TXS
 (
 TX_TYPE      CHAR(1)        NOT NULL,
 PROD_NO      INT            NOT NULL,
 DESCRIPTION VARCHAR(20),
 QUANTITY     INT
 );
```

Example 6–87 *Modified product transactions table*

This table includes an additional column that determines the transaction type. For simplicity, these codes are "I" for insert, "D" for delete, and "U" for update. A sample set of transactions are found in Example 6–88:

```
TX_TYPE PROD_NO     DESCRIPTION          QUANTITY
------- ----------- -------------------- -----------
U                 1 -                             15
D                 3 -                              -
I                 6 Shoes                          5
I                 7 Belts                         10
```

Example 6–88 *Sample transactions*

In this example, product 1 has 15 additional items, product 3 is deleted from inventory, and products 6 and 7 are added to the product line. The MERGE statement that implements the insert, update, and delete logic is found in Example 6–89:

```
MERGE INTO PRODUCTS PR
  USING (SELECT TX_TYPE, PROD_NO, DESCRIPTION, QUANTITY
      FROM PRODUCT_TXS) TX
           ON (PR.PROD_NO = TX.PROD_NO)
  WHEN MATCHED AND TX_TYPE = 'U' THEN
        UPDATE SET
               PR.QUANTITY = PR.QUANTITY + TX.QUANTITY
  WHEN MATCHED AND TX_TYPE = 'D' THEN
        DELETE
  WHEN NOT MATCHED AND TX_TYPE = 'I' THEN
        INSERT (PROD_NO, DESCRIPTION, QUANTITY)
               VALUES (TX.PROD_NO, TX.DESCRIPTION, TX.QUANTITY);
```

Example 6–89 *MERGE with insert, update, and delete logic*

The WHEN MATCHED clause now contains additional logic to determine when the transaction is applied. For instance, the WHEN MATCHED AND TX_TYPE='D' indicates to DB2 that any base record that matches a transaction record with a transaction type of "D" should be deleted from the table.

IGNORING records

What happens when a record does not match any of the criteria in the MERGE command? In all cases, DB2 will ignore the transaction record and continue onto the next one. You can explicitly code this behavior in the MERGE statement by adding the ELSE IGNORE clause. You cannot include any logic with the ELSE clause, so you must use a generic WHEN MATCHED or WHEN NOT MATCHED clause to deal with records that do not match any of the other criteria.

The MERGE command gets executed sequentially, which means that each WHEN clause of the MERGE statement is executed until one of the conditions is met. Once a condition is met, the logic associated with that statement is executed and processing continues on with the next transaction record. Only one of the WHEN clauses is matched, and the remainder are ignored. This prevents more than one action occurring against the same record.

Raising Error Conditions

There will be occasions where transaction records are not matched and you want to be able to stop the process of the MERGE command. In order to do this, the SIGNAL command can be used.

The following MERGE command expands upon the example in Example 6–89 and adds two additional error conditions (Example 6–90).

```
MERGE INTO PRODUCTS PR
  USING (SELECT TX_TYPE, PROD_NO, DESCRIPTION, QUANTITY FROM
    PRODUCT_TXS) TX
         ON (PR.PROD_NO = TX.PROD_NO)
  WHEN MATCHED AND TX_TYPE = 'U' THEN
       UPDATE SET PR.QUANTITY = PR.QUANTITY + TX.QUANTITY
  WHEN MATCHED AND TX_TYPE = 'D' THEN
       DELETE
  WHEN MATCHED AND TX_TYPE = 'I' THEN
       SIGNAL SQLSTATE '70001'
         SET MESSAGE_TEXT = 'Record already exists for an INSERT'
  WHEN NOT MATCHED AND TX_TYPE = 'I' THEN
       INSERT (PROD_NO, DESCRIPTION, QUANTITY)
              VALUES (TX.PROD_NO, TX.DESCRIPTION, TX.QUANTITY)
  WHEN NOT MATCHED THEN
       SIGNAL SQLSTATE '70002'
         SET MESSAGE_TEXT = 'Record not found for Update or Delete'
  ELSE IGNORE;
```

Example 6–90 *MERGE with SIGNAL statement*

The first error condition is raised when an insert is processed and a record already exists in the transaction table. The `SIGNAL` statement raises the error code `70001` with the associated error message that the record already exists. For instance, the following transaction record will cause the `MERGE` to fail (Example 6–91):

```
TX_TYPE PROD_NO     DESCRIPTION         QUANTITY
------- ----------- ------------------- -----------
D                10 -                             -

MERGE INTO PRODUCT ...

SQL0438N  Application raised error with diagnostic text:
 "Record already exists for an INSERT".  SQLSTATE=70001
```

Example 6–91 *Error in MERGE processing*

When the `SIGNAL` statement is executed, all processing that has been done up to this point in time will fail. In other words, the entire statement is rolled back.

Any valid `SQLSTATE` value can be used in the `SIGNAL` statement. However, it is recommended that programmers define new `SQLSTATEs` based on ranges reserved for applications. This prevents the unintentional use of an `SQLSTATE` value that might be defined by the database manager in a future release.

`SQLSTATES` should follow these rules:

- `SQLSTATE` classes that begin with the characters '7' through '9' or 'I' through 'Z' may be defined. Within these classes, any subclass may be defined.
- `SQLSTATE` classes that begin with the characters '0' through '6' or 'A' through 'H' are reserved for the database manager. Within these classes, subclasses that begin with the characters '0' through 'H' are reserved for the database manager. Subclasses that begin with the characters 'I' through 'Z' may be defined.

View Classification

Now that we have examined various SQL DML statements, let's take a closer look at views. We have already discussed creating views. Now we'll examine the different types of views.

Views are classified by the operations they allow. They can be:

- Deletable
- Updatable
- Insertable
- Read-only

The view type is established according to its update capabilities. The classification indicates the kind of SQL operation that is allowed against the view.

Referential and check constraints are treated independently. They do not affect the view classification.

For example, you may not be able to insert a value into a table because of a referential constraint. If you create a view using that table, you also can't insert that value using the view. However, if the view satisfies all the rules for an insertable view, it will still be considered an insertable view. This is because the insert restriction is on the base table, not on the view definition.

Deletable Views

Depending on how a view is defined, the view can be deletable. A deletable view is a view against which you can successfully issue a DELETE statement. There are a few rules that need to be followed for a view to be considered deletable:

- Each FROM clause of the outer fullselect identifies only one base table (with no OUTER clause), deletable view (with no OUTER clause), deletable nested table expression, or deletable common table expression.
- The outer fullselect doesn't use the VALUES clause.
- The outer fullselect doesn't use the GROUP BY or HAVING clauses.
- The outer fullselect doesn't include column functions in its select list.
- The outer fullselect doesn't use set operations (UNION, EXCEPT, or INTERSECT) with the exception of UNION ALL.
- The base tables in the operands of a UNION ALL must not be the same table, and each operand must be deletable.
- The select list of the outer fullselect does not include DISTINCT.

A view must meet all the rules listed above to be considered a deletable view.

```
CREATE VIEW DELETABLE_VIEW
 (TCID,CID,NUMBER,DATE_TAKEN,START_TIME,SEAT_NO,SCORE)
AS
 SELECT TCID,CID,NUMBER,DATE_TAKEN,
        START_TIME,SEAT_NO,SCORE
 FROM TEST_TAKEN
 WHERE TCID=CENTER_ID('TR01');
```

Example 6–92 *Example of a deletable view*

The view shown in Example 6–92 is deletable. It follows all the rules for a deletable view.

Updatable Views

An updatable view is a special case of a deletable view. A deletable view becomes an updatable view when at least one of its columns is updatable.

A column of a view is updatable when all of the following rules are true:

- The view is deletable.
- The column resolves to a column of a table (not using a dereference operation) and the READ ONLY option is not specified.
- All the corresponding columns of the operands of a UNION ALL have exactly matching data types (including length or precision and scale) and matching default values if the fullselect of the view includes a UNION ALL.

```
CREATE VIEW UPDATABLE_VIEW
  (TCID,CID,NUMBER,CURRENT_DATE,CURRENT_TIME,SEAT_NO,SCORE)
AS
 SELECT TCID,CID,NUMBER,CURRENT DATE,
                       CURRENT TIME,SEAT_NO,SCORE
 FROM TEST_TAKEN
 WHERE CHAR(TCID)='TX01';
```

Example 6–93 *Example of an updatable view*

The view definition in Example 6–93 uses constant values that cannot be updated. However, the view is a deletable view and at least you can update one of its columns. Therefore, it is an updatable view.

Insertable Views

Insertable views allow you to insert rows using the view definition. A view is insertable when all of its columns are updatable.

```
CREATE VIEW INSERTABLE_VIEW
  (TEST_NUMBER,TEST_NAME,TOTAL_TAKEN)
AS
  SELECT NUMBER,NAME,TOTALTAKEN FROM TEST;
```

Example 6–94 *Example of an insertable view*

The view shown in Example 6–94 is an insertable view. However, an attempt to insert the view will fail. This is because there are columns in the table that don't accept null values. Some of these columns are not present in the view definition. When you try to insert a value using the view, DB2 will try to insert a NULL into a NOT NULL column. This action is not permitted.

Manipulating DB Objects

DB2 *Note*

Remember, the constraints defined on the table are independent of the operations that can be performed using a view based on that table.

Read-Only Views

A read-only view is a nondeletable view. A view can be read-only if it is a view that doesn't comply with at least one of the rules for deletable views.

The `READONLY` column in the `SYSCAT.VIEWS` catalog view indicates a view is read-only (R).

Let's examine a read-only view:

```
CREATE VIEW READ_ONLY_VIEW
   (NAME,WORK_PHONE,HOME_PHONE)
AS
SELECT DISTINCT FNAME,WPHONE,HPHONE
    FROM TEST_CANDIDATE C, TEST_TAKEN TT
    WHERE C.CID=TT.CID;
```

Example 6–95 *Example of a read-only view*

The view shown in Example 6–95 is not a deletable view as it uses the `DISTINCT` clause and the SQL statement involves more than one table.

DB2 *Note*

Even if a view is considered Read-only, a DBA can create `INSTEAD OF` triggers to handle the `INSERT`, `UPDATE`, and `DELETE` processing against the view. For more information on triggers, see "Triggers" on page 398.

Views with UNION ALL

Views with tables connected through the use of `UNION ALL` have been supported for a number of releases. `SELECT`, `DELETE`, and `UPDATE` operators have been allowed as long as DB2 could determine which table the corresponding command was to be applied to.

In DB2, the INSERT operator can be used with views that contain the UNION ALL, as long as the following conditions hold:

1. The expressions have the same datatypes.
2. A constraint exists on at least one column that can be used to uniquely identify where a row should be inserted and the constraint ranges are non-overlapping.

Views defined in this fashion will also support UPDATE operations as long as the column being changed does not violate the constraint for that column. In this case, the user must first DELETE and then INSERT the record.

A few examples will clarify how this will work.

Consider four tables that have been created to represent the sales for each quarter of the year. The tables all have the same definition as shown in Example 6–96.

```
CREATE TABLE Q1SALES
  (
  STORE     INT      NOT NULL,
  TX_DATE   DATE     NOT NULL,
  ITEM      INT      NOT NULL,
  QUANTITY  INT      NOT NULL
  );
CREATE TABLE Q2SALES LIKE Q1SALES;
CREATE TABLE Q3SALES LIKE Q1SALES;
CREATE TABLE Q4SALES LIKE Q1SALES;
```

Example 6–96 *Multiple tables representing a year of sales*

These tables could be UNIONed together to create a single view of the entire year as shown in Example 6–97.

```
CREATE VIEW ALLQ AS
  (
  SELECT * FROM Q1SALES
  UNION ALL
  SELECT * FROM Q2SALES
  UNION ALL
  SELECT * FROM Q3SALES
  UNION ALL
  SELECT * FROM Q4SALES
  );
```

Example 6–97 *View of entire year's sales*

Although DB2 could use this view for a SELECT, it will not work for an UPDATE, INSERT, or DELETE since DB2 has no way of knowing which underlying table the record needs to be placed into. Attempting an INSERT statement against this view would fail (Example 6–98).

```
INSERT INTO ALLQ
  VALUES (1,'2006-05-01', 25, 100);

SQL20154N  The requested insert or update operation into view
"BAKLARZ.ALLQ" is not allowed because no target table can be
determined for a row. Reason code = "2".  SQLSTATE=23513
```

Example 6–98 *Invalid INSERT*

The original tables need to be altered to create constraints that identify what records are allowed to be stored in them. In addition, creating constraints gives DB2 more information on how to handle a `SELECT` statement against this view.

For instance, consider the `SELECT` in Example 6–99.

```
SELECT * FROM ALLQ WHERE
  ITEM = 142 AND
  TX_DATE BETWEEN '2006-05-14' AND '2006-07-21';
```

Example 6–99 *SELECT against view ALLQ*

When DB2 optimizes this statement, it has no information about where the data might reside in the four tables. A Visual Explain of this `SELECT` shows the work that DB2 must do in order to satisfy this request (Figure 6–2).

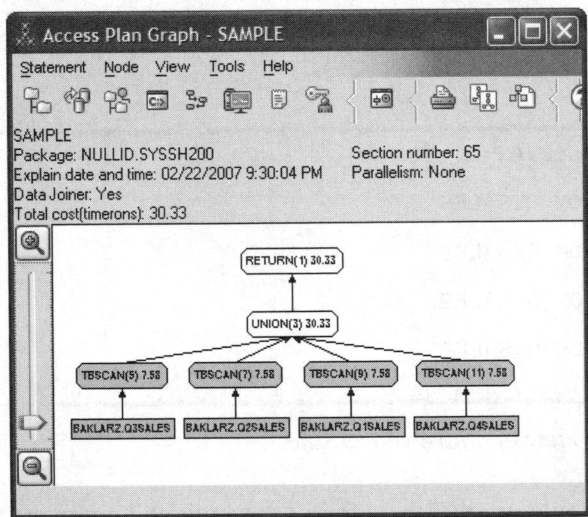

Figure 6–2 *EXPLAIN statement of SELECT across UNION ALL*

In order to give DB2 better information on how to handle these rows, a check constraint needs to be added to the original table definition. This can be accomplished at either table creation time or through the use of the ALTER TABLE command. For the existing tables defined above, the ALTER TABLE command would be similar to that found in Example 6–100.

```
ALTER TABLE Q1SALES
  ADD CONSTRAINT Q1_DATES
  CHECK (TX_DATE BETWEEN '2006-01-01' AND '2006-03-31');
```

Example 6–100 *Adding constraints to the table definitions*

Each table would have its own range of dates in the TX_DATE field. With this additional constraint added, the query will now be executed using the following explain plan (Figure 6–3):

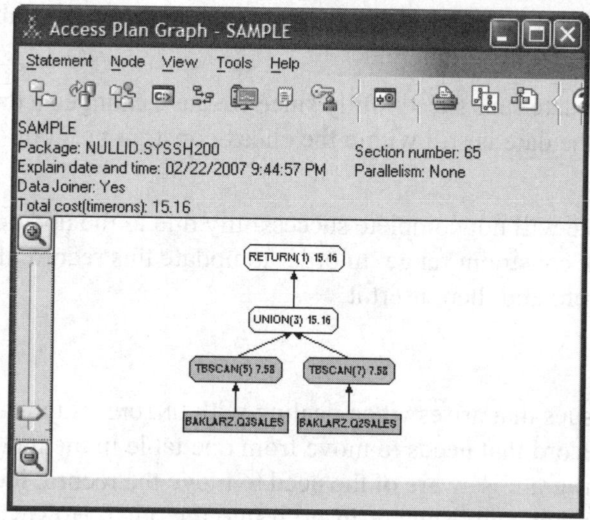

Figure 6–3 *Explain plan after addition of check constraints*

Note how DB2 is able to eliminate two tables (Q1SALES and Q4SALES) from the access logic since the constraints tell DB2 that only Q2SALES and Q3SALES have the ranges of dates that we are interested in.

When a user issues an INSERT, DELETE, UPDATE, or SELECT against the ALLQ view, DB2 can use this new constraint information to direct the transaction to the proper table. This is especially important in the case of queries where tables that are not appropriate to the query can be eliminated from the search. Note that for proper handling of this view, the check constraints (range) must not overlap. In addition, modification to the column defined in the check constraint must not be updated outside the range. For instance, consider the `UPDATE` statements found in Example 6–101.

```
UPDATE ALLQ
  SET    STORE = 4
  WHERE STORE = 1;

UPDATE ALLQ
  SET    TX_DATE = '2006-02-26'
  WHERE TX_DATE = '2006-02-27';

UPDATE ALLQ
  SET    TX_DATE = '2006-04-01'
  WHERE TX_DATE = '2006-03-30';
```

Example 6–101 *Update commands against a UNION ALL View*

The first update does not change any value in the check constraint so it will run successfully. Note that since we don't define a date range, all tables will have store number 4 changed to store number 1.

The second update runs successfully since we have changed a date from the 27th to the 26th and the date is still within the check constraint (`'2006-01-01'` to `'2006-03-31'`).

The last update will not complete successfully due to the updated value being outside the check constraint range. In order to update this record, the user must first delete the record and then insert it.

Row Migration

One of the issues that arises when dealing with `UNION`s of tables is handling the update of a record that needs to move from one table in the union to another. If the application program is aware of the need to move the record, it could simply delete the record from one table and re-insert it into the other. However, this approach is not satisfactory because the an application cannot control what may happen when multiple records are impacted by an update.

For instance, a number of records may need to have their transaction date changed because of a clerical error. This type of change could not be done using an `UPDATE` statement as shown in Example 6–102.

```
UPDATE ALLQ
  SET   TX_DATE = '2006-04-01'
  WHERE TX_DATE = '2006-03-30';

SQL0545N  The requested operation is not allowed because a row
does not satisfy the check constraint BAKLARZ.Q1SALES.Q1_DATES.
SQLSTATE=23513
```

Example 6–102 *Update command fails*

The problem with the update is that the new date of the record does not fit the range of values that are allowed for the underlying table it came from. This could be fixed by writing a `DELETE` and then an `INSERT` statement, but an additional option exists on view definitions that lets DB2 do it for you automatically (Example 6–103).

```
CREATE VIEW ALLQ AS
  (
  SELECT * FROM Q1SALES WHERE
     TX_DATE BETWEEN '2006-01-01' AND '2006-03-31'
  UNION ALL
  SELECT * FROM Q2SALES WHERE
     TX_DATE BETWEEN '2006-04-01' AND '2006-06-30'
  UNION ALL
  SELECT * FROM Q3SALES WHERE
     TX_DATE BETWEEN '2006-07-01' AND '2006-09-30'
  UNION ALL
  SELECT * FROM Q4SALES WHERE
     TX_DATE BETWEEN '2006-10-01' AND '2006-12-31'
  )
 WITH ROW MOVEMENT;
```

Example 6–103 *ROW MOVEMENT option*

The `WITH ROW MOVEMENT` clause will allow records to move between the underlying tables if their constraint value changes. This option avoids the need of having the application physically move the records between tables. Note that an error can still occur if the change to the constraint value does not fit within the ranges of the existing tables.

Using Tables Spaces with UNION ALL

A `UNION ALL` in a view can be used to circumvent some restrictions in DB2 and allow for more flexible maintenance in time-series data.

Tables in DB2 can only occupy 64GB of storage if a 4K data page is specified. Increasing the page size to 8K, 16K, or 32K can result in larger table sizes, but the restriction of 255 rows per page may still limit the amount of data that you can store.

DB2 Note

Depending on which release of DB2 you have, the size of a table space can be greater than 64GB with a 4K page. In DB2 9, a new row identifier (RID) was introduced that allows DMS table spaces to grow up to 2TB in size. In addition, pages using this new RID format can have in excess of 2,000 rows per page. However, if you are using System Management Storage (SMS), the limit of 64GB per table space and 256 rows per page remains.

A user could get around this space limitation by breaking up a table into smaller units and placing each one of these units into a separate table space. Consider the quarterly sales data tables found in Figure 6–96 where each table was placed into the default table space. This designed limited all tables to a limit of 64GB of data. Instead of using the default table space for these tables, the user could create a separate table space for each individual table (Example 6–105).

```
CREATE REGULAR TABLESPACE Q1_2006
  PAGESIZE 4 K MANAGED BY SYSTEM
  USING('Q1_2006') EXTENTSIZE 2;
CREATE REGULAR TABLESPACE Q2_2006
  PAGESIZE 4 K MANAGED BY SYSTEM
  USING('Q2_2006') EXTENTSIZE 2;
CREATE REGULAR TABLESPACE Q3_2006
  PAGESIZE 4 K MANAGED BY SYSTEM
  USING('Q3_2006') EXTENTSIZE 2;
CREATE REGULAR TABLESPACE Q4_2006
  PAGESIZE 4 K MANAGED BY SYSTEM
  USING('Q4_2006') EXTENTSIZE 2;
```

Example 6–104 *Creation of table spaces*

Once these table spaces have been created, each table can be placed into its own table space. Only one table definition is show in Example 6–105.

```
CREATE TABLE Q1SALES
  (
  STORE    INT      NOT NULL,
  TX_DATE  DATE     NOT NULL,
  ITEM     INT      NOT NULL,
  QUANTITY INT      NOT NULL
  ) IN Q1_2007;
```

Example 6–105 *Creation of Q1SALES table in a separate table space*

At this point, each quarterly sales table can take up to 64GB of space using a 4K page size. All transactions against this view, including `INSERTs`, will be directed to the appropriate table. Applications could still be written that directed their transactions to the appropriate quarterly sales table, but the view makes the handling of queries much easier. In addition, by designing the view as a `UNION ALL` of four separate tables, it is possible for the user to load new data into the system without impacting current workloads and then making the new data "live" with a minimum of administration.

If data is continually being refreshed on a monthly or quarterly basis, a user could create a separate table and table space and load the information into that table first. When the load is complete, then only a few commands need to be issued to make this data "live" to all users. In the case of the quarterly data, assume that a new set of data comes in for the first quarter of 2007 and you want to be able to make that part of the four quarters of information rather than the first quarter of 2006. A new table for the first quarter of 2007 has to be created that mimics the same table design as the prior four quarters of information (Example 6–106).


```
CREATE REGULAR TABLESPACE Q1_2007
  PAGESIZE 4 K MANAGED BY SYSTEM
  USING('Q1_2007') EXTENTSIZE 2;

CREATE TABLE Q1SALES_2007
  (
  STORE     INT     NOT NULL,
  TX_DATE   DATE    NOT NULL,
  ITEM      INT     NOT NULL,
  QUANTITY  INT     NOT NULL
  ) IN Q1_2007;
```

Example 6–106 *New quarter of sales information*

We need to change the name of the table since `Q1SALES` already exists in our database. Once the table is loaded with data from quarter 1, the existing `Q1SALES` table needs to be dropped and the view recreated to include the new `Q1SALES_2007` table (Example 6–107).

```
DROP TABLESPACE Q1_2006;
CREATE VIEW ALLQ AS
  (
  SELECT * FROM Q1SALES_2007
  UNION ALL
  SELECT * FROM Q2SALES
  UNION ALL
  SELECT * FROM Q3SALES
  UNION ALL
  SELECT * FROM Q4SALES
  );
```

Example 6–107 *New quarter of sales information*

When a DROP statement is issued against a table space, typically no logging occurs. This means that a user can eliminate these rows from the database without the overhead associated with logging row deletes. An added benefit of separating the tables is the ability to manage loads and other activities on this new quarterly information without affecting production data.

There are some maintenance aspects that a user must be aware of when separating tables into different table spaces. Although SELECT processing can be relatively efficient, INSERT statements running against these tables will require some additional overhead to determine which base table the transaction needs to be directed to. This may only amount to a few milliseconds of additional optimization time, but may make a difference on a heavily loaded system.

Finally, DB2 does not recognize the relationship between the tables that make up the view from a recovery perspective. Normal logging and transaction rollbacks are handled the same as any other SQL statement. However, the table spaces that make up the various tables need to be backed up at the same time (if doing individual table space backups) so that they are recovered as one complete unit. If the table spaces are not recovered based on the same unit, it may be possible that transactions across the tables are not synchronized.

DB2 Note

An alternative to UNION ALL views is to use Range Partitioning. Range Partitioning is described in detail in Chapter 11.

Inoperative Views

A inoperative view is a view that is no longer available for SQL statements. A view becomes inoperative if:

- A privilege on which the view definition is dependent is revoked.
- An object, such as a table, alias, or function, on which the view definition is dependent is dropped.
- A view on which the view definition is dependent becomes inoperative.
- A view that is the superview of the view definition (the subview) becomes inoperative.

Summary

In this chapter, we have discussed SQL's Data Manipulation Language (DML). DML has four primary statements: `SELECT`, `UPDATE`, `INSERT`, and `DELETE`. These statements enable all database object data manipulation.

The `SELECT` statement has a rich set of features that allow a user to specify what rows should be retrieved and how they should be formatted. The columns to be retrieved from a table are specified in the select list. These columns can also contain calculations and functions that aggregate rows over ranges of values. The rows that are retrieved from tables must match the criteria in the `WHERE` clause. Result sets are returned to the user, optionally sorted by column values.

Multiple tables can be joined together in `SELECT` statements. Result sets can be further manipulated using `UNION`, `INTERSECT`, and `EXCEPT` operators. These operators add additional flexibility to the `SELECT` statement. Temporary result sets can be created using the `WITH` operator and subsequently used in the `SELECT` statement it was defined in.

The `INSERT`, `UPDATE`, `DELETE`, and `MERGE` statements modify the contents of a table. These statements allow for the use of `SELECT` logic to limit the number of rows that are affected by the data modification.

Views are virtual tables. Views do not exist until a query is executed that requires the contents. Views can be classified deletable, updatable, insertable and read-only. The classification is important when designing applications or queries that need to access these views.

DB2 supports many more powerful SQL features, and these will be discussed in the next chapter.

CHAPTER 7

Advanced SQL

- TRIGGERS
- RECURSIVE SQL
- OUTER JOIN
- OLAP
- CASE EXPRESSIONS
- TYPED TABLES
- SUMMARY TABLES
- SEQUENCES
- ADVANCED FUNCTIONS

This chapter will cover some very powerful features found in DB2 SQL. Features, such as triggers, recursion, outer join, OLAP features, and uses of the case expression, will be discussed. In addition, we will discuss structured types, typed tables, user-defined functions, summary tables, sequences and some advanced functions.

Triggers

A *trigger* is a set of actions that will be executed when a defined event occurs. The triggering events can be the following SQL statements:

- `INSERT`
- `UPDATE`
- `DELETE`

Triggers are defined for a specific table and once defined, a trigger is automatically active. A table can have multiple triggers defined for it, and if multiple triggers are defined for a given table, the order of trigger activation is based on the trigger creation timestamp (the order in which the triggers were created). Trigger definitions are stored in the system catalog tables. You can see them through these catalog views:

- `SYSCAT.TRIGGERS` — contains the trigger definition information, one row for each trigger defined
- `SYSCAT.TRIGDEP` — contains one row for every dependency of a trigger on some other object

Triggers can also be defined on views. These types of triggers would be created when you need to manage how `INSERT`s, `DELETE`s, or `UPDATE`s need to be handled against the base tables. There are situations where DB2 cannot determine which table in a view needs to modified, so `INSTEAD OF` triggers can be used to direct the update to the proper tables.

Trigger Usage

Some of the uses of a trigger include:

- Data Validation — ensures that a new data value is within the proper range. This is similar to table-check constraints, but it is a more flexible data validation mechanism.
- Data Conditioning — implemented using triggers that fire before data record modification. This allows the new data value to be modified or conditioned to a predefined value.
- Data Integrity — can be used to ensure that cross-table dependencies are maintained. The triggered action could involve updating data records in related tables. This is similar to referential integrity, but it is a more flexible alternative.
- View Handling — DB2 cannot always determine how an update should be applied to a view. Instead-of triggers allow the user to control how modifications through a view should be handled.

Trigger Activation

A trigger can be defined to fire (be activated) in one of two ways:

- A *before trigger* will fire for each row in the set of affected rows before the triggering SQL statement executes. Therefore, the trigger body is seeing the new data values prior to their being inserted or updated into the table.
- An *after trigger* will fire for each row in the set of affected rows or after the statement has successfully completed (depending on the defined granularity). Therefore, the trigger body is seeing the table as being in a consistent state. (All transactions have been completed.)

Another important feature about triggers is that they can fire other triggers (or the same trigger) or other constraints. These are known as *cascading triggers*.

During the execution of a trigger, the new and old data values can be accessible to the trigger depending on the nature of the trigger (before or after). By using triggers you can:

- Reduce the amount of application development and make development faster. Since triggers are stored in DB2 itself and are processed by DB2, you do not need to code the triggers or their actions into your applications.
- Provide a global environment for your business rules. Since the triggers only have to be defined once and then are stored in the database, they are available to all applications executing against the database.
- Reduce the maintenance of your applications. Again, since the trigger is handled by DB2 and is stored in the database itself, any changes to the trigger due to changes in your environment only have to occur in one, not multiple, applications.

The best method of understanding the usage of triggers is to see some in action. The `DB2CERT` application contains many relationships that can be maintained using triggers.

Trigger Example (After Trigger)

In Example 7–1, a trigger is defined to set the value of the `PASS_FAIL` column for each of the tests taken by a candidate. (Note that we add this column for this scenario.) The trigger has been given the name `PASSFAIL` (no relationship with the column called `PASS_FAIL`). Once the trigger has been created, it is active.

The `PASSFAIL` trigger is an `AFTER`, `INSERT`, and `FOR EACH ROW` trigger. Every time there is a row inserted into the `TEST_TAKEN` table, this trigger will fire. The trigger body section will perform an `UPDATE` statement to set the value of the `PASS_FAIL` column for the newly inserted row. The column is populated with either the value `P` (representing a passing grade) or the value `F` (representing a failing grade).

DB2 *Note*

Remember that a trigger defined against one table can modify other tables in the trigger body.

```
CREATE TRIGGER PASSFAIL AFTER INSERT ON TEST_TAKEN
     REFERENCING NEW AS N
     FOR EACH ROW MODE DB2SQL
UPDATE TEST_TAKEN
SET PASS_FAIL =
          CASE
          WHEN N.SCORE >=
              (SELECT CUT_SCORE FROM TEST
                WHERE NUMBER = N.NUMBER)
               THEN 'P'
          WHEN N.SCORE <
              (SELECT CUT_SCORE FROM TEST
                WHERE NUMBER = N.NUMBER)
               THEN 'F'
          END
WHERE N.CID          = CID
 AND N.TCID          = TCID
 AND N.NUMBER        = NUMBER
 AND N.DATE_TAKEN    = DATE_TAKEN;
```

Example 7–1 *Creating an AFTER trigger*

Trigger Example (Before Trigger)

A before trigger will be activated before the trigger operation has completed. The triggering operation can be an INSERT, UPDATE, or DELETE statement. This type of trigger is very useful for three purposes: to condition data, to provide default values, or to enforce data value constraints dynamically.

There are three before trigger examples shown in Example 7–2 through Example 7–4 that are used in the DB2 Certification application.

All three of these triggers have been implemented to avoid seat conflicts for test candidates. The triggers will fire during an insert of each new candidate for a test.

```
CREATE TRIGGER PRE9 NO CASCADE BEFORE
   INSERT ON TEST_TAKEN
      REFERENCING NEW AS N
      FOR EACH ROW MODE DB2SQL
      WHEN (N.START_TIME <'09:00:00')
   SIGNAL SQLSTATE '70003'
   ('CANNOT ASSIGN SEAT BEFORE 09:00:00!');
```

Example 7–2 *Before trigger example (1)*

```
CREATE TRIGGER AFT5 NO CASCADE BEFORE
   INSERT ON TEST_TAKEN
      REFERENCING NEW AS N
      FOR EACH ROW MODE DB2SQL
      WHEN (N.START_TIME +
             (SELECT SMALLINT(LENGTH) FROM TEST
               WHERE NUMBER = N.NUMBER) MINUTES
                                        > '17:00:00')
   SIGNAL SQLSTATE '70004'
   ('CANNOT ASSIGN SEAT AFTER 17:00:00!');
```

Example 7–3 *Before trigger example (2)*

```
CREATE TRIGGER START NO CASCADE BEFORE
   INSERT ON TEST_TAKEN
      REFERENCING NEW AS N
      FOR EACH ROW MODE DB2SQL
      WHEN (
       EXISTS (SELECT CID FROM TEST_TAKEN
                WHERE SEAT_NO    = N.SEAT_NO    AND
                      TCID       = N.TCID       AND
                      DATE_TAKEN = N.DATE_TAKEN AND
                      N.START_TIME BETWEEN
                        START_TIME AND FINISH_TIME))
   SIGNAL SQLSTATE '70001'
   ('START TIME CONFLICT!');
```

Example 7–4 *Before trigger example (3)*

If the conditions are encountered, an SQL error will be flagged using the SQL function called SIGNAL. A different SQLSTATE value will be provided when the triggered conditions are encountered.

The PRE9 trigger, shown in Example 7–2, is used to ensure that a test candidate is not scheduled to take a test before 9:00 a.m. The AFT5 trigger is used to ensure that a test candidate is not scheduled to take a test after 5:00 p.m. The START trigger is used to avoid conflicts during a testing day.

Instead of Triggers

In many installations, views are used as a way of limiting access to base tables. With a view, a DBA can restrict both the columns and sets of rows that a user can access. However, the use of views causes some difficulties when data modification commands need to be applied to rows in the base table. For instance, a user may have created a customer reference table with the following definition (Example 7–5):

```
CREATE TABLE CUSTOMERS
  (
  CUSTNO      INT              NOT NULL,
  CUSTNAME    VARCHAR(20)      NOT NULL,
  PHONE       CHAR(12)         NOT NULL,
  CREDIT_CARD VARCHAR(20)      FOR BIT DATA NOT NULL,
  YTD_SALES   DECIMAL(15,2)    NOT NULL
  );
```

Example 7–5 *Customer reference table*

This table needs to be made available to a variety of people in the company including the sales people, order desk, customer service, and accounts receivable. However, some of this information is not relevant to all users, and from a security perspective you may not want all users to see everything in the table. A possible solution is to create a view for each group of users. The customer service staff may have the following view defined for them (Example 7–6):

```
CREATE VIEW CUSTOMER_SERVICE AS
  (
  SELECT CUSTNO, CUSTNAME, PHONE, CREDIT_CARD
    FROM CUSTOMERS
  );
```

Example 7–6 *Customer reference table*

Now the customer service staff can select from this table and get all of the contact information from the customer table without seeing the yearly sales numbers. Although this fixes the security problem, it raises new issues when the service staff have to add new records. Based on their knowledge of the view that they have access to (CUSTOMER_SERVICE), adding a new customer to their table would look like this (Example 7–7):

```
INSERT INTO CUSTOMER_SERVICE VALUES
  (1234, 'WONGS DONUTS','887-555-1212','3922 1111 2222');
```

Example 7–7 *Insert into the Customer_Service table*

Unfortunately, DB2 will issue an error message (Example 7–8) since this insert violates a constraint on the base table. In this case, the YTD_SALES column is not included as part of the INSERT statement and it must be supplied according to the original table definition (NOT NULL).

```
SQL0407N  Assignment of a NULL value to a NOT NULL column
"TBSPACEID=5, TABLEID=61, COLNO=4" is not allowed.
SQLSTATE=23502
```

Example 7–8 *Error on insert*

In order to get around this problem the DBA can do one of the following steps:

- Create a better database design to avoid this error
- Allow NULL values in the YTD_SALES field or set the DEFAULT to zero
- Create an INSTEAD OF trigger

One could argue that the system should be redesigned not have to this problem, but if we are stuck with the current table definitions an INSTEAD OF trigger will help solve the problem.

An INSTEAD OF trigger is used only on VIEWS, not base tables. It has similar characteristics to a normal trigger except for the following restrictions:

- Only allowed on views
- Always FOR EACH ROW
- DEFAULT values get passed as NULL
- Cannot use positioned UPDATE/DELETE on cursor over view with INSTEAD OF UPDATE/DELETE trigger

For the CUSTOMER_SERVICE view, we can create an INSTEAD OF trigger that will handle the missing field during an insert operation (Example 7–9):

```
CREATE TRIGGER I_CUSTOMER_SERVICE
  INSTEAD OF INSERT ON CUSTOMER_SERVICE
  REFERENCING NEW AS CUST
  FOR EACH ROW MODE DB2SQL
BEGIN ATOMIC
  INSERT INTO CUSTOMERS VALUES (
     CUST.CUSTNO,
     CUST.CUSTNAME,
     CUST.PHONE,
     CUST.CREDIT_CARD,
     0);
END
```

Example 7–9 *Instead of trigger on insert*

Advanced SQL

When an INSERT is executed against this view, DB2 will now invoke this INSTEAD OF trigger and the record will be successfully inserted into the table. Although this is a trivial example, the INSTEAD OF trigger can be used for variety of purposes, including encrypting and decrypting fields in the table. For instance, the CREDIT_CARD information in this table could be encrypted for security reasons. If we decide to use a fixed password for the encryption and decryption, we can create the following view to select the records with the values decrypted (Example 7–10):

```
CREATE VIEW CUSTOMER_SERVICE AS
  (
  SELECT CUSTNO, CUSTNAME, PHONE,
    DECRYPT_CHAR(CREDIT_CARD,'SECRET') AS CREDIT_CARD
    FROM CUSTOMERS
  );
```

Example 7–10 *View with decryption*

The INSTEAD OF trigger also needs to modified to encrypt the values as well as insert the zero sales for the year (Example 7–11):

```
CREATE TRIGGER I_CUSTOMER_SERVICE
  INSTEAD OF INSERT ON CUSTOMER_SERVICE
  REFERENCING NEW AS CUST
  DEFAULTS NULL
  FOR EACH ROW MODE DB2SQL
BEGIN ATOMIC
  INSERT INTO CUSTOMERS VALUES (
     CUST.CUSTNO,
     CUST.CUSTNAME,
     CUST.PHONE,
     ENCRYPT(CUST.CREDIT_CARD,'SECRET'),
     0);
END
```

Example 7–11 *Instead of trigger with encryption*

When a user does a select from the CUSTOMER_SERVICE view, they would see the following results (Example 7–12):

```
CUSTNO CUSTNAME        PHONE        CREDIT_CARD
------ --------------- ------------ --------------
  1234 WONGS DONUTS    887-555-1212 3922 1111 2222
```

Example 7–12 *Select from Customer_Service view*

Note what happens if another user selected from the base table instead (Example 7–13):

```
CUSTNO CUSTNAME       PHONE        CREDIT_CARD
------ -------------- ------------ --------------
  1234 WONGS DONUTS   887-555-1212 X'00B749FFE...
```

Example 7–13 *Select from Customers table*

Since the decryption is not occurring on the base table, any other user accessing this field will not see the results.

In summary, the `INSTEAD OF` trigger can give you greater flexibility in the use of views and allow you to handle situations with `INSERTs`, `UPDATEs`, and `DELETEs` that DB2 cannot figure out on its own.

Recursive SQL

A *recursive SQL* statement is one where an SQL statement repeatedly uses the resulting set to determine further results. This kind of SQL statement is built using a common table expression that make references to itself (i.e., it uses its own definition).

Such statements are useful to solve queries, such as hierarchical trees, routing airline flights, or bill-of-material types of queries.

Let's say that we have a table that indicates the distance between two cities. For this example, we are using the `FLIGHTS` table. It contains information about the origin, destination, and distance between cities.

The table is shown in Example 7–14.

```
ORIGIN     DESTINATION DISTANCE
---------- ----------- -----------
Germany    New York           8000
Germany    Chicago            8700
Chicago    Austin             1300
New York   Houston            2100
Houston    Austin              300
New York   Chicago             950
Italy      New York          10000
Italy      Chicago           11000
Ireland    Chicago           10700
Chicago    Toronto             400
New York   Toronto             350
Mexico     Houston             770
```

Example 7–14 *Recursive SQL: Content of the flights table*

Our goal is to obtain a list with the distance and number of stops of all the destinations you can reach departing from Germany. We will create a recursive SQL statement to retrieve this information.

Let's first explain why this kind of query is resolved using recursive SQL. The table contains information about destinations and origins. After reaching one specific destination, this destination can be treated as an origin. This is where the recursion appears: The destination becomes an origin, and the next destination can become a new origin, and so on.

The way to resolve this query is by writing an SQL statement that, given an origin, will retrieve its destinations, then treat them as origins, obtain the new destinations, and so on.

```
       WITH PATH (ORIGIN,DESTINATION,DISTANCE,STOPS) AS
          (
          SELECT F.ORIGIN, F.DESTINATION, F.DISTANCE,0
            FROM FLIGHTS F
[1]              WHERE ORIGIN='Germany'
          UNION ALL
          SELECT P.ORIGIN,F.DESTINATION,
[2]              P.DISTANCE+F.DISTANCE, P.STOPS+1
          FROM FLIGHTS F, PATH P
                WHERE P.DESTINATION=F.ORIGIN
          )
[3] SELECT ORIGIN, DESTINATION, DISTANCE, STOPS FROM PATH;
```

Example 7–15 *Recursive SQL: Obtaining all the destinations from Germany*

As we have said before, recursion is built on common table expressions. In the recursive SQL example shown in Example 7–15, the common table expression is called `PATH`.

In `[1]`, we are obtaining the destinations that can be reached directly from Germany. In this case, the stops column is set to `0`, because the flights are nonstop.

Then, in `[2]`, we are referencing the recently created common table expression path. In this part, we join the common table expression with the base table to create the recursion. This is where the destination becomes a new origin. We are also incrementing the distance and the number of stops. Observe that a `ALL` clause is needed in the definition of a recursive query.

Finally, in `[3]`, we are retrieving all the possible routes accessible from Germany, the distance, and the number of stops.

The output of the recursive SQL statement is show in Example 7–16.

```
ORIGIN   DESTINATION DISTANCE    STOPS
-------- ----------- ----------- -----------
SQL0347W  The recursive common table expression "BAKLARZ.PATH"
 may contain an infinite loop.  SQLSTATE=01605

Germany  New York           8000           0
Germany  Chicago            8700           0
Germany  Houston           10100           1
Germany  Chicago            8950           1
Germany  Markham            8350           1
Germany  Austin            10000           1
Germany  Markham            9100           1
Germany  Austin            10400           2
Germany  Austin            10250           2
Germany  Markham            9350           2

  10 record(s) selected with 1 warning messages printed.
```

Example 7–16 *Recursive SQL: Destinations reached from Germany*

The SQL statement shown in Example 7–15 can run forever if there is a loop found in the flights table. When you are coding this kind of SQL statement, you must be aware of the possibility of infinite loops. To avoid an infinite loop, you can restrict the query using the number of stops.

Let's say that you are only interested in the routes that make less than five stops. You need to add the following restriction to the last SQL statement (Figure 7–17):

```
WHERE STOPS < 5
```

Example 7–17 *Limiting recursion*

This condition can be used to avoid an infinite loop.

Now, let's create a more complex example based on the same idea. We want to obtain a list of the possible flights from Germany to Austin. This time, we want to obtain the flight route, the distance, and the number of stops.

As we can see from the output in Example 7–16, there are three different paths to reach Austin from Germany. Let's create the SQL statement that can tell us the complete path for each case (Example 7–18).

```
    WITH DETAIL_PATH (ORIGIN,DESTINATION,ROUTE,DISTANCE,STOPS) AS
      (
      SELECT F.ORIGIN, F.DESTINATION,
[1]          VARCHAR(SUBSTR(F.ORIGIN,1,2),35),F.DISTANCE,0
         FROM FLIGHTS F WHERE ORIGIN='Germany'
      UNION ALL
      SELECT P.ORIGIN,F.DESTINATION,
[2]          ROUTE ||'>' || SUBSTR(P.DESTINATION,1,2),
             P.DISTANCE+F.DISTANCE, P.STOPS+1
         FROM FLIGHTS F,DETAIL_PATH P
         WHERE P.DESTINATION=F.ORIGIN
      )
    SELECT ROUTE ||'>' || SUBSTR(DESTINATION,1,2),
[3]        DISTANCE, STOPS
       FROM DETAIL_PATH WHERE DESTINATION='Austin'
    ORDER BY DISTANCE;
```

Example 7–18 *Recursive SQL: Obtaining routes from Germany to Austin*

The basics of the SQL statement in Example 7–18 are the same as the previous example. The difference is that now we are creating the route column. This column is created by extracting the first two characters of each visited airport on the way from Germany to Austin. The || (concatenation) operator is used to link each one of the cities visited to another.

In [1], we are using the VARCHAR function to create a varchar column that will store all the cities visited in a specific path. This step will also add the origin city.

Then, in [2], we are linking the route with each one of the intermediary cities visited.

Finally, in [3], we link the final destination to the path. Also in this step, we specify the desired destination. The results are shown in Example 7–19.

```
1                                        DISTANCE    STOPS
---------------------------------------- ----------- -----------
SQL0347W  The recursive common table expression
 "BAKLARZ.DETAIL_PATH" may contain an infinite loop.
 SQLSTATE=01605

Ge>Ch>Au                                       10000           1
Ge>Ne>Ch>Au                                    10250           2
Ge>Ne>Ho>Au                                    10400           2

  3 record(s) selected with 1 warning messages printed.
```

Example 7–19 *Detailed path from Germany to Austin*

Outer Join

The join operation used most often is the one we have been using in the book exercises, which is known as an INNER JOIN. Now, we will talk about a different kind of join operation.

The result set of an inner join consists only of those matched rows that are present in both joined tables. What happens when we need to include those values that are present in one or another joined table, but not in both of them? This is the case when we need to use an OUTER JOIN operation. Outer joins are designed to generate an answer set that includes those values that are present in joined tables and those that are not. There are different kinds of outer joins as we will see.

Before getting into the details of the outer join, we will examine the explicit syntax used to code joins between tables. Let's start with an inner join coded with this syntax. The following join example produces an answer set containing the first name, the phone number, and the highest score for each candidate in the TEST_TAKEN table (Example 7–20).


```
SELECT FNAME, WPHONE, MAX(INTEGER(SCORE))
 FROM TEST_CANDIDATE C
    INNER JOIN TEST_TAKEN TT ON C.CID=TT.CID
GROUP BY FNAME, WPHONE;
```

Example 7–20 *Inner Join*

In this syntax, you indicate the tables that will be joined, along with the join operation, and the join columns that are required.

Observe the INNER JOIN operator in the example above. It belongs to the FROM clause of the statement. The INNER JOIN operator specifies that an inner join operation will be used for the statement. The keyword ON is used to specify the join conditions for the tables being joined. In our example, the join condition is based on the join columns, CID of the TEST_CANDIDATE table, and CID of the TEST_TAKEN table.

The explicit join syntax also allows you to specify an outer join as we will see in the next sections.

Left Outer Join

A LEFT OUTER JOIN operation, also known as left join, produces an answer set that includes the matching values of both joined tables and those values only present in the left joined table. The left joined table is the one used in the left part of the LEFT OUTER JOIN operator when coding the join operation.

DB2 Note

You can also use `LEFT JOIN` to indicate a left outer join operation.

We have been requested to generate a report that includes the first name, the phone number, and the highest score for all the candidates present in the `TEST_CANDIDATE` table. If an inner join is used, as is shown in the last example, the report will only include data of those candidates present in the `TEST_TAKEN` table.

The request could be solved using some SQL statements already discussed; however, the construction will be complex. We will use the left outer join to satisfy the request as the following example shows (Example 7–21).

```
SELECT FNAME, WPHONE, MAX(INTEGER(SCORE))
 FROM TEST_CANDIDATE C
    LEFT OUTER JOIN TEST_TAKEN TT ON C.CID=TT.CID
GROUP BY FNAME, WPHONE;
```

Example 7–21 *Left Outer Join*

Observe the syntax used to indicate a left outer join. The `LEFT OUTER JOIN` operator is used to indicate the left outer join operation. In this example, the answer set includes those candidates not present in the test_taken table. The `MAX(INTEGER(SCORE))` column will show nulls for those candidates.

Right Outer Join

A `RIGHT OUTER JOIN` operation, also known as right join, produces an answer set that includes the matching values of both joined tables and those values only present in the right joined table. The right joined table is the one used in the right part of the `RIGHT OUTER JOIN` operator when coding the join operation.

The example using a right outer join is shown below (Example 7–22):

```
SELECT NAME, COUNT(DISTINCT CHAR(TT.CID))
   FROM TEST_TAKEN TT
     RIGHT OUTER JOIN TEST T
     ON TT.NUMBER = T.NUMBER
   GROUP BY NAME;
```

Example 7–22 *Right Outer Join*

In this example, all test names present in the `TEST` table and the number of candidates who scheduled or took each test are requested. Notice there may be some tests for which no candidate was scheduled. You cannot report such tests using a inner join statement; however, you can do it using a right outer join.

Full Outer Join

The FULL OUTER JOIN operation produces an answer set that includes the matching values of both joined tables and those values not present in one or the other of the tables.

To show a full outer join operation, we will create two sample tables: city and country. They show the relationship between a city and a country (CITY table) and a country and a continent (COUNTRY table). The city table is designed to have countries that are not in the country table. The country table is also designed to have countries that are not in the city table. The contents of both tables are shown in Examples 7–23 and 7–24.

```
CITY_NAME        COUNTRY_NAME
---------------  ---------------
Sidney           Australia
London           England
Dublin           Ireland
Firenze          Italy
Milano           Italy
Mexico           Mexico
Lima             Peru
Toronto          Canada
Vienna           Austria
Hannover         Germany
```

Example 7–23 *City table used in outer join*

```
COUNTRY_NAME     CONTINENT
---------------  ---------------------------
Australia        Australian Continent
England          European Continent
Ireland          European Continent
Italy            European Continent
Mexico           American Continent
Austria          European Continent
South Africa     African Continent
Spain            European Continent
```

Example 7–24 *Country table used in outer join*

We want to show all the countries, cities, and the continents that are in the tables. Therefore, we are using a full outer join as the following example shows (Example 7–25):

```
SELECT CTRY.CONTINENT, CTRY.COUNTRY_NAME,
       CTY.COUNTRY_NAME, CTY.CITY_NAME
        FROM COUNTRY CTRY
             FULL OUTER JOIN
             CITY CTY
             ON CTY.COUNTRY_NAME=CTRY.COUNTRY_NAME
       ORDER BY CTRY.CONTINENT,
                CTY.COUNTRY_NAME,
                CTY.CITY_NAME;

CONTINENT              COUNTRY_NAME  COUNTRY_NAME  CITY_NAME
---------------------- ------------- ------------- ----------
African Continent      South Africa  -             -
American Continent     Mexico        Mexico        Mexico
Australian Continent   Australia     Australia     Sidney
European Continent     Austria       Austria       Vienna
European Continent     England       England       London
European Continent     Ireland       Ireland       Dublin
European Continent     Italy         Italy         Firenze
European Continent     Italy         Italy         Milano
European Continent     Spain         -             -
-                      -             Canada        Toronto
-                      -             Germany       Hannover
-                      -             Peru          Lima

 12 record(s) selected.
```

Example 7–25 *Full outer join*

As shown in Example 7–25, the rows that have a null value were added by the outer join operation. The COUNTRY_NAME column is shown twice to see those countries present in the country table that are not present in the city table and vice versa.

Combining Outer Joins

Up to now we have discussed each outer join operation separately. Now, we will show a more complex example combining two outer joins in one single query. Let's display all the candidates and all the tests with their respective scores.

To create this query, we need two outer joins. The first outer join will obtain all candidates and their scores including candidates who did not schedule or take any tests. The second outer join will retrieve all the tests present in the test table even if no candidate scheduled or took those tests (Example 7–26).

```
     SELECT C.CID, T.NAME, SCORE
[1]         FROM (TEST_CANDIDATE C
                 LEFT OUTER JOIN TEST_TAKEN TT
                     ON TT.CID=C.CID)
[2]                     FULL OUTER JOIN TEST T
                     ON TT.NUMBER = T.NUMBER
     ORDER BY C.CID;
```

Example 7–26 *Two outer joins in one SQL statement*

The first outer join [1] is enclosed in parentheses. The parentheses are used for readability and to denote that the left outer join will be resolved first. This left outer join gathers all the candidate IDs. We only need a left outer join here. Because of referential integrity constraints, table TEST_TAKEN can only have candidates present in the TEST_CANDIDATE table.

The second part is a full outer join [2]. With this outer join, we take all the tests taken by the candidates, the result of the left outer join, and join them with all the tests in the TEST table. We need a full outer join this time even though the TEST_TAKEN table can only have test numbers that are present in the TEST table, because the left table of this outer join, which is the result of the first join, may include NULL values as a test number. The TEST table does not have null values, so we need to use a full outer join.

The output of the SQL statement is shown in Example 7–27.

```
CID NAME                              SCORE
--- -------------------------------- -----------
111 DB2 Fundamentals                          65
111 DB2 Administration                        73
111 DB2 Application Development               67
222 DB2 Fundamentals                          55
222 DB2 Application Development               53
222 DB2 Application Development               75
333 DB2 Fundamentals                          82
333 DB2 Administration                         -
333 DB2 Application Development               92
444 -                                          -
555 -                                          -
666 -                                          -
777 -                                          -
888 -                                          -

 14 record(s) selected.
```

Example 7–27 *Result of two outer joins combined*

Advanced SQL

OLAP Features

Databases normally hold large amounts of data that can be updated, deleted, queried, and inserted on a daily basis. Databases in which data is constantly updated, deleted, and inserted are known as *Online Transaction Processing (OLTP)* systems. Databases that hold large amounts of data and do not have a heavy transaction work load but do have a large number of concurrent queries executing all the time, are known as *Decision Support Systems (DSS)*. Certain decision support systems have fewer queries, but each query can be very complex. These allow users to examine the data from different perspectives by performing *Online Analytical Processing (OLAP)*.

The functionality of the database is required to provide multidimensional views of relational data, without a significant performance effect. DB2 provides this capability, using a number of joining methods, SQL statements, and other database features. The next few sections explain the database technology found in DB2 that enhances the performance of OLAP queries.

STAR Schemas

The concept of a *STAR schema* is illustrated in Figure 7–1. A business view of a highly normalized database often requires a number of attributes associated with one primary object. Each of these attributes is contained in separate tables.

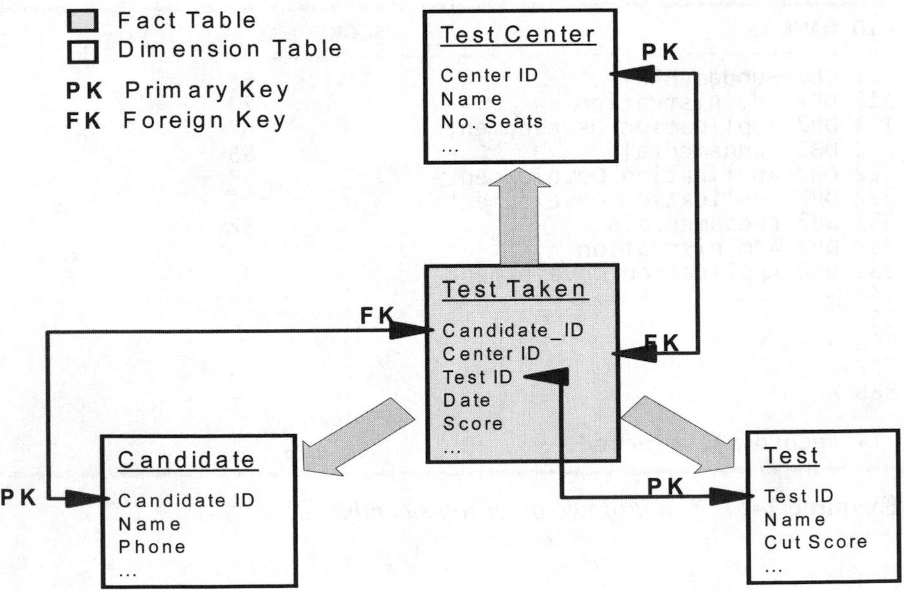

Figure 7–1 *STAR schema in the DB2CERT application*

The following points are characteristic of a STAR schema design:

- There is a large Fact table that contains data relating to the Dimension tables. In Figure 7–1, the Fact table is the test_taken table. It contains detailed information on each test taken, including exactly which test was taken, in which center the test was taken, and who took the test.
- There are a number of small Dimension tables that typically hold descriptive information about an entity that has a small number of rows. In Figure 7–1, the Dimension tables are test, candidate, and test_center.
- The primary keys of the Dimension tables involved in the STAR schema supply foreign key entries in the Fact table. The concatenation of foreign keys from the Dimension tables usually forms a small subset of the Fact table. In Figure 7–1, the foreign keys are Candidate ID, Center ID, and Test ID.

This approach allows as few attributes as possible to be stored in the Fact table. The benefit of this is that the Fact table is usually very large, and therefore any data duplication in this table would be very costly in terms of storage and access times. If the DB2CERT database were used to store information on a university's entrance examinations, for example, the test_taken table could grow enormously.

OLAP schemas, such as the STAR schemas, are frequently used for large databases. These schemas make it very important to access the data in these databases in the optimal manner. Otherwise, the joins involved in the schemas may result in poor performance.

OLAP Indexes

A typical STAR schema includes a large number of indexes. This is due to the adhoc nature of queries in an OLAP environment. Such an environment is typically not subjected to constant insert or update activity and, therefore, does not have to suffer from significant performance degradation as a result of index maintenance.

The prime consideration of indexes in an OLAP environment is to facilitate the joining of tables and the ordering of output. This is particularly important for the fact table where multiple indexes are defined, especially on foreign key columns relating to the dimension tables. The benefit of multiple indexes in this environment is improved query performance against the fact table. The indexes defined on the tables could either be single-column or multicolumn indexes.

There are also certain issues to be considered when using multiple indexes in the OLAP environment. The first is that multiple indexes will require a certain amount of space, depending on the number of columns in each index and the size of the tables. The second is that there will be a significant one-time cost when building indexes, perhaps during a bulk load.

STAR Joins

A typical query against databases designed with the STAR schema would consist of multiple local predicates referencing values in the dimension tables and contain join predicates connecting the dimension tables to the fact table as shown in Example 7–28. These types of queries are called *STAR joins*.

In this example, we wish to find the average score of DB2 tests taken by Canadian citizens in the small test centers year by year. A STAR join query is difficult to execute efficiently, because no single join predicate reduces the cardinality of the fact rows significantly, although the combination of join predicates results in a small answer set. The more dimension tables involved in the join result, the more potential there is to plan an inefficient access path. To execute STAR join queries efficiently, multiple index access can be performed by the optimizer.

```
SELECT T.NAME, YEAR(TT.DATE_TAKEN) AS YEAR,
       AVG(INTEGER(TT.SCORE)) AS AVGSC
FROM TEST T, TEST_TAKEN TT, TEST_CENTER TC,
     TEST_CANDIDATE C
WHERE C.CID = TT.CID          AND
      TC.TCID = TT.TCID        AND
      T.NUMBER = TT.NUMBER     AND
      T.NAME LIKE 'DB2%'       AND
      C.COUNTRY='CANADA'       AND
      TC.NOSEATS < 10
GROUP BY T.NAME, YEAR(TT.DATE_TAKEN);
```

Example 7–28 *STAR join*

Super Grouping

We will now discuss OLAP features known as *super grouping* functions. These functions are used to analyze data in multiple dimensions. The dimensions can be seen as different levels of aggregation over a set of tables. The term *super grouping* is used to describe OLAP features, because they allow the retrieval of multiple aggregation levels in one single pass of data.

Multiple Groups (Grouping Sets)

The `GROUPING SETS` specification in the `GROUP BY` clause is used to generate multiple aggregation groups in a single SQL statement. This feature is used to generate aggregated data based on different grouping criteria. Using `GROUPING SETS`, it is possible to calculate aggregations that would otherwise require a set operation, such as a UNION, to put together the different aggregated answer sets.

Let's suppose we want to know the following:

- How many tests have been taken at the test centers?
- How many tests of each type have been taken in each test center?

To gather this information, we first need to count the tests taken grouped by test center and then count the tests taken in each test center. This requirement needs two different grouping sets, one grouped by test center and another grouped by test name and test center. See the following example and the result (Example 7–29):

```
SELECT TT.TCID,T.NAME,COUNT(*)
   FROM TEST_TAKEN TT, TEST T
   WHERE TT.NUMBER=T.NUMBER
   GROUP BY
        GROUPING SETS (TT.TCID,(TT.TCID,T.NAME));

TCID NAME                                   3
---- -------------------------------------- -----------
TR01 -                                                3
TX01 -                                                6
TR01 DB2 Application Development                      2
TR01 DB2 Fundamentals                                 1
TX01 DB2 Administration                               2
TX01 DB2 Application Development                      2
TX01 DB2 Fundamentals                                 2

7 record(s) selected.
```

Example 7–29 *Grouping sets used in an SQL statement*

The `GROUPING SETS` specification calculates the first requirement, which is the number of tests taken at each test center, by listing the `TCID` column of the `TEST_TAKEN` table. Then the second requirement, which is the number of tests by test center and test name, is calculated by listing `TCID` column of the `TEST_TAKEN` table and `NAME` column of the `TEST` table. This second grouping is the same as if you coded a regular `GROUP BY` by using `GROUP BY TT.TCID,T.NAME`.

As seen in the result set shown in Example 7–29, the grouping sets can be formed by one or more columns.

Adding a Grand Total

Using the `GROUPING SETS` specification, you can add a grand total to your query. The example shown in Example 7–29 doesn't display the total of all tests taken at all test centers. This can be calculated by adding the grand total group to the grouping sets list.

As groups are created, null values are added to those columns that don't have a value in a particular group. In this way, the grand total row will show null values in all columns except for the grand total itself.

In this next example, we are including a grand total group and converting the null-generated values to character strings using the VALUE SQL function. This SQL is very similar to the example shown in Example 7–29. In Example 7–30, if the first argument of the VALUE function is null, the character string supplied as the second argument will be the result of the VALUE function.

```
SELECT VALUE(CHAR(TT.TCID),'ALL'),
       VALUE(T.NAME,'ALL TESTS'),
       COUNT(*)
 FROM TEST_TAKEN TT, TEST T
 WHERE TT.NUMBER=T.NUMBER
 GROUP BY
    GROUPING SETS
        (CHAR(TT.TCID),(CHAR(TT.TCID),T.NAME),());

1    2                                          3
---- ----------------------------------------- -----------
All  All Tests                                           9
TR01 All Tests                                           3
TX01 All Tests                                           6
TR01 DB2 Application Development                         2
TR01 DB2 Fundamentals                                    1
TX01 DB2 Administration                                  2
TX01 DB2 Application Development                         2
TX01 DB2 Fundamentals                                    2

8 record(s) selected.
```

Example 7–30 *Grouping sets with a grand total*

The grand total group is specified with a pair of empty parentheses () in the grouping set list.

Recognizing Group Added Null Values

There will be cases when the data used in a grouping function contains null values. In this case, is important to be able to distinguish between a null value and a group-generated null value.

DB2 provides the GROUPING function that identifies those null-generated values by giving them a value of 1.

DB2 Note

The GROUPING function returns only the values of 1 or 0. One (1) means that the null value was generated by DB2, and 0 means that the value was not generated by DB2.

Now, let's use the GROUPING function inside a CASE expression to differentiate between those groups with added null values and regular null values. To keep the query small, the example will only use the CASE expression for the TT.TCID column.

```
     SELECT
       CASE
[1]      WHEN GROUPING(TT.TCID)=1
             THEN 'All'
         WHEN GROUPING(TT.TCID)=0
             THEN CHAR(TT.TCID)
       END,
       VALUE(t.name,'All Tests'),
       GROUPING(TT.TCID) AS GROUPED_TCID,
       GROUPING(T.NAME) AS GROUPED_NAME,
       COUNT(*)
     FROM TEST_TAKEN TT, TEST T
       WHERE TT.NUMBER=T.NUMBER
[2]  GROUP BY
       GROUPING SETS (TT.TCID,(T.NAME,TT.TCID),());

1    2                              GROUPED_TCID GROUPED_NAME 5
---- ------------------------------ ------------ ------------ --
All  All Tests                                 1            1  9
TR01 All Tests                                 0            1  3
TX01 All Tests                                 0            1  6
TR01 DB2 Application Development               0            0  2
TR01 DB2 Fundamentals                          0            0  1
TX01 DB2 Administration                        0            0  2
TX01 DB2 Application Development               0            0  2
TX01 DB2 Fundamentals                          0            0  2

8 record(s) selected.
```

Example 7–31 *Using the grouping function to identify group added null*

The case expression [1] uses the GROUPING function over the TCID column. If a value of 1 is returned, then ALL will be printed. In our example, ALL indicates that the row contains a group-added null value. A null-generated value represents all the tests centers. If the GROUPING function returns a 0, it means that the value of the TCID column for that row was not generated by DB2.

The GROUPING functions shown in [2] will display a value of 1 or 0 depending on the value of the columns TT.TCID and T.NAME for a particular row. A value of 1 in GROUPING(TT.TCID) means that the row is a total grouped on the TCID column.

ROLLUP

The GROUPING SETS specification shown in the previous section allows you to create different levels of aggregation in one single pass of data. However, you need to specify each of the groups you want. There are cases when you need to create a report in which you require a total for each column you are grouping. Here is when a super group feature such as ROLLUP is required.

The ROLLUP grouping can generate various groups in one single pass. This will allow you to review different levels of aggregation as if you created a control break report.

Let's say that you need a report showing the following:

- How many tests have been taken by country?
- How many tests have been taken by country and test center?
- How many tests have been taken by country, test center, and test name?
- What is the total number of tests taken?

To solve this requirement, we will use the ROLLUP grouping, which will generate the aggregations requested. The SQL statement is shown in Example 7–32.

```
SELECT
  C.COUNTRY,
  TT.TCID,
  SUBSTR(T.NAME,1,27) AS TEST_NAME,
  COUNT(*) AS TESTS_TAKEN
FROM TEST_TAKEN TT, TEST T, TEST_CANDIDATE C
  WHERE TT.NUMBER=T.NUMBER AND TT.CID=C.CID
GROUP BY ROLLUP (C.COUNTRY,TT.TCID,T.NAME)
ORDER BY C.COUNTRY,TT.TCID,T.NAME;

COUNTRY     TCID TEST_NAME                   TESTS_TAKEN
----------- ---- --------------------------- -----------
CANADA      TR01 DB2 Application Development           2
CANADA      TR01 DB2 Fundamentals                      1
CANADA      TR01 -                                     3
CANADA      TX01 DB2 Administration                    2
CANADA      TX01 DB2 Application Development           2
CANADA      TX01 DB2 Fundamentals                      2
CANADA      TX01 -                                     6
CANADA      -    -                                     9
-           -    -                                     9

  9 record(s) selected.
```

Example 7–32 *Using the ROLLUP operator*

The report generated allows you to roll up your information and drill down into your information. You can analyze the report from a grand-total level down to the country, test center, and test name.

DB2 *Note*

The ROLLUP operation is not commutative; the order in which you specify your groups is important. The resulting set of ROLLUP(COUNTRY, TCID, NAME) is different from ROLLUP(TCID, COUNTRY, NAME).

Super-group operations such as ROLLUP are built over the GROUPING SETS operation. The ROLLUP shown in Example 7–32 is equivalent to GROUPING SETS ((COUNTRY,TCID,NAME),(COUNTRY,TCID),COUNTRY,()). This is why they are considered super-groups operations.

CUBE

From the answer set obtained by the ROLLUP operation shown in Example 7–32, there are some groups not present that can be useful. These groups include the number of tests taken only by test center or by test number.

The CUBE operation obtains all combinations of groups that can be formed in a grouping list. The groups, listed in the grouping list of a CUBE operation, will be permuted to calculate all the groups possible in that list. This creates all the aggregations needed to construct a cube of data.

The resulting cube can be sliced and diced in multiple dimensions to allow the users multidimensional analysis of data stored in DB2.

Now use the CUBE operation to generate the following groups:

- Tests taken by country
- Tests taken by test center
- Tests taken by test number
- All intermediate groups

You can write a statement as shown in Example 7–33.

```
SELECT C.COUNTRY,TT.TCID,
       SUBSTR(T.NAME,1,27) AS TEST_NAME,
       COUNT(*) AS TESTS_TAKEN
       FROM TEST_TAKEN TT,
            TEST T,
            TEST_CANDIDATE C
              WHERE TT.NUMBER=T.NUMBER
              AND    TT.CID=C.CID
               GROUP BY
                 CUBE (C.COUNTRY,TT.TCID,T.NAME)
              ORDER BY C.COUNTRY,TT.TCID,T.NAME;
```

Example 7–33 *Using the CUBE operator*

```
COUNTRY    TCID TEST_NAME                          TESTS_TAKEN
---------- ---- ---------------------------------- -----------
CANADA     TR01 DB2 Application Development                  2
CANADA     TR01 DB2 Fundamentals                             1
CANADA     TR01 -                                            3
CANADA     TX01 DB2 Administration                           2
CANADA     TX01 DB2 Application Development                  2
CANADA     TX01 DB2 Fundamentals                             2
CANADA     TX01 -                                            6
CANADA     -    DB2 Administration                           2
CANADA     -    DB2 Application Development                  4
CANADA     -    DB2 Fundamentals                             3
CANADA     -    -                                            9
-          TR01 DB2 Application Development                  2
-          TR01 DB2 Fundamentals                             1
-          TR01                                              3
-          TX01 DB2 Administration                           2
-          TX01 DB2 Application Development                  2
-          TX01 DB2 Fundamentals                             2
-          TX01 -                                            6
-          -    DB2 Administration                           2
-          -    DB2 Application Development                  4
-          -    DB2 Fundamentals                             3
-          -    -                                            9

  22 record(s) selected.
```

Example 7–34 *The result of the CUBE operator*

The CUBE operation shown in Example 7–33 generates eight different groups, including a grand total group (Example 7–34). The number of groups generated by a CUBE operation is the result of the number of permutations that can be generated by the number of different groups listed in the grouping list.

The number of rows that super-group operations generate depends on the number of groups generated and the number of distinct values in each group.

The SQL statement shown in Example 7–33 can be written using the following GROUPING SETS Example 7–35:

```
GROUPING SETS ((COUNTRY,TCID,NAME),
               (COUNTRY,TCID),
               (COUNTRY,NAME),
               (TCID,NAME),
               (COUNTRY),
               (TCID),
               (NAME),
               ()
);
```

Example 7–35 *Grouping Sets generated by CUBE (COUNTRY, TCID, NAME)*

Moving Functions

DB2 contains a number of built-in functions that can help in the analysis of data. One type of calculation that is difficult to do in the relational model is one that is based on a "window" of data. For instance, you may want to know what the average of three sales is over a point in time. Column functions within DB2 (along with CUBE and ROLLUP) deal only with complete sets, not partial values.

Moving functions help to overcome this limitation with column functions. Along with the definition of a column function, a user can now supply a "window" specification to DB2 that defines how much data should be included as part of the calculation. For instance, Example 7–36 shows a table with 10 values in it. These values could represent the sales of a store over 10 days. An AVG function applied to this data would give the average sales across all 10 days.

```
CREATE TABLE SALES (DAY INT, SALES INT);
INSERT INTO SALES VALUES (1,10),(2,14),(3,13),(4,15),
  (5,20),(6,14),(7,16),(8,17),(9,18),(10,9);

SELECT AVG(SALES) FROM SALES;

1
-----------
         14
```

Example 7–36 *Simple average calculation*

This AVG function could be modified to use a moving window. This is accomplished through the use of the OVER specification. Example 7–37 shows the use of this function to calculate the moving 3-day average sales (1 day before and 1 day after).

```
SELECT DAY, AVG(SALES) OVER
  (ORDER BY DAY ROWS BETWEEN 1 PRECEDING AND 1 FOLLOWING)
  AS SMOOTH_VALUE FROM SALES;

DAY         SMOOTH_VALUE
----------- ------------
          1           12
          2           12
          3           14
          4           16
          5           16
          6           16
          7           15
          8           17
          9           14
         10           13
```

Example 7–37 *Moving average calculation*

Advanced SQL

The moving average function gives a completely different picture from just doing an average against the column!

SQL Sampling

While a database is often used for transactional purposes, one of the major benefits of the relational model is the ability to do complex analysis of the data. DB2 has many features and techniques that improve the performance of complex queries including summary tables, dynamic bitmaps indexes, multidimensional clustering, and a variety of SQL optimizations.

DB2 has another type of SQL optimization in the form of sampling of data during the execution of the statement. Databases are growing so large that it is often impractical to access all of the data relevant to a query. For instance, a query requesting the average sales per month in a large department store may need to read millions of records. In this example, it may be just as valid to sample a portion of the table to come up with an average number. The corresponding savings in execution time may be worth the slight inaccuracy of the result. This is particularly true when someone is trying to analyze trends and exact amounts are not as important as the magnitude of the number.

DB2 implements this type of sampling through the TABLESAMPLE clause on the SELECT statement. This additional specification is added after the table name in a select statement (Example 7–38):

```
SELECT ... FROM <TABLE> TABLESAMPLE (BERNOULLI | SYSTEM)
   REPEATABLE
```

Example 7–38 *Moving average calculation*

The TABLESAMPLE clause has two components. The first is the type of sampling that is to occur with the data and the second is the "seed" or randomization number that is to be used to determine which rows get selected. The various parameters and their usage are described in the sections below.

BERNOULLI Sampling

The TABLESAMPLE clause is used to obtain a random subset or sample of the rows from the specified table. Of course, this is in addition to any predicates or conditions that are applied to the rows themselves.

Unless the optional REPEATABLE clause is specified, you will get a different result each time the query is executed. In cases where there is a very small table, the results may be the same since DB2 cannot get a large enough sample size to generate a random set of records.

The BERNOULLI keyword includes a numeric specification that indicates the approximately percentage of the table that is to be returned. For instance, the following statement will only consider 10% of the total number of rows in the table (Example 7–39):

```
SELECT COUNT(*) FROM TRANSACTIONS TABLESAMPLE BERNOULLI(10);
```

Example 7–39 *BERNOULLI sampling*

The number in parenthesis must be greater than zero and can be up to 100. Of course, a value of 100 would be equivalent to retrieving the entire table!

Sampling using the BERNOULLI algorithm will consider every row individually. The probability of the row being included in the set is P/100 (where P is the percentage used with the BERNOULLI keyword) or excluded with probability 1 – P/100. An SQL count statement executed 5 times with BERNOULLI(10) sampling retrieves the following values from a table with 10,000 rows (Example 7–40):

```
VALUES (1, (SELECT COUNT(*) FROM TRANSACTIONS
  TABLESAMPLE BERNOULLI(10)))
UNION ALL
VALUES (2, (SELECT COUNT(*) FROM TRANSACTIONS
  TABLESAMPLE BERNOULLI(10)))
UNION ALL
VALUES (3, (SELECT COUNT(*) FROM TRANSACTIONS
  TABLESAMPLE BERNOULLI(10)))
UNION ALL
VALUES (4, (SELECT COUNT(*) FROM TRANSACTIONS
  TABLESAMPLE BERNOULLI(10)))
UNION ALL
VALUES (5, (SELECT COUNT(*) FROM TRANSACTIONS
  TABLESAMPLE BERNOULLI(10)));

1           2
----------- -----------
          1         988
          2         988
          3         988
          4         988
          5         988

  5 record(s) selected.
```

Example 7–40 *10% Sampling*

The result of the SQL statement appears to be exactly the same for each row. One would expect that the results would be random given the definition of the BERNOULLI function. However, the BERNOULLI sampling is done at the beginning of the SQL statement, and so any subsequent reference to the same set of rows will have

Advanced SQL

the same answer set returned. Each statement in Example 7–40 are identical, so the results will be the same. Using the following SQL logic, the random nature of the BERNOULLI statement can be illustrated (Example 7–41). Note that for this example, the "$" is used as a delimiter since SQL PL statements use a semicolon as a delimiter:

```
-- SET DELIMITER $

CREATE TABLE SAMPLES
  (
  RUN     INT,
  CNT     INT
  )
$

BEGIN ATOMIC
  DECLARE I INT DEFAULT 0;
  DECLARE ROWS_CNT INT DEFAULT 0;

  SET I = I + 1;
  WHILE I <= 5 DO
    SET ROWS_CNT = (SELECT COUNT(*) FROM TRANSACTIONS
                      TABLESAMPLE BERNOULLI(10));
    INSERT INTO SAMPLES VALUES (I,ROWS_CNT);
    SET I = I + 1;
  END WHILE;
END
$

SELECT * FROM SAMPLES
$
RUN         CNT
----------- -----------
          1         951
          2        1007
          3        1005
          4        1000
          5        1015

  5 record(s) selected.
```

Example 7–41 *Different Bernoulli results*

SYSTEM Sampling

SYSTEM sampling permits the database manager to determine the most efficient manner in which to perform the sampling. In most cases, SYSTEM sampling applied to a table means that each page of the table is included in the sample with probability P/100, and excluded with probability 1 – P/100. All of the rows found on that page qualify for the sample.

SYSTEM sampling of a table executes much faster than BERNOULLI sampling because fewer data pages need to be retrieved. Using BERNOULLI sampling requires that all pages be read to determine which rows are part of the set. The following SQL query (Example 7–42) was run against a 100,000 row table using BERNOULLI sampling:

```
SELECT TX_ITEM, AVG(TX_QUANTITY) FROM STORE_TXS
  TABLESAMPLE BERNOULLI(10)
GROUP BY TX_ITEM;
```

Example 7–42 *Select average from table with BERNOULLI sampling*

The corresponding visual explain statement for this SQL is shown in Figure 7–2:

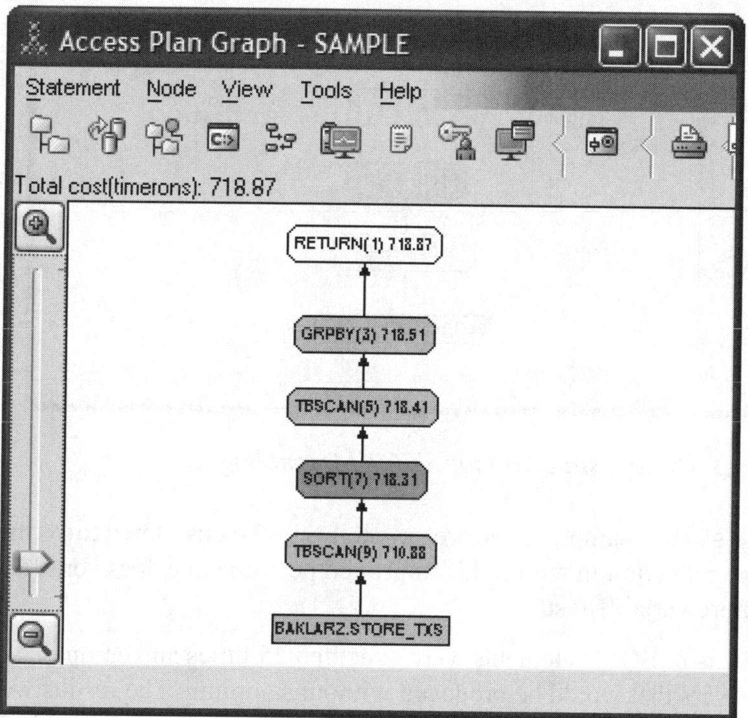

Figure 7–2 *Explain statement for BERNOULLI sampling*

The cost for this SQL statement is 718 units. Converting this statement to use SYSTEM sampling results in the following visual explain (Figure 7–3):

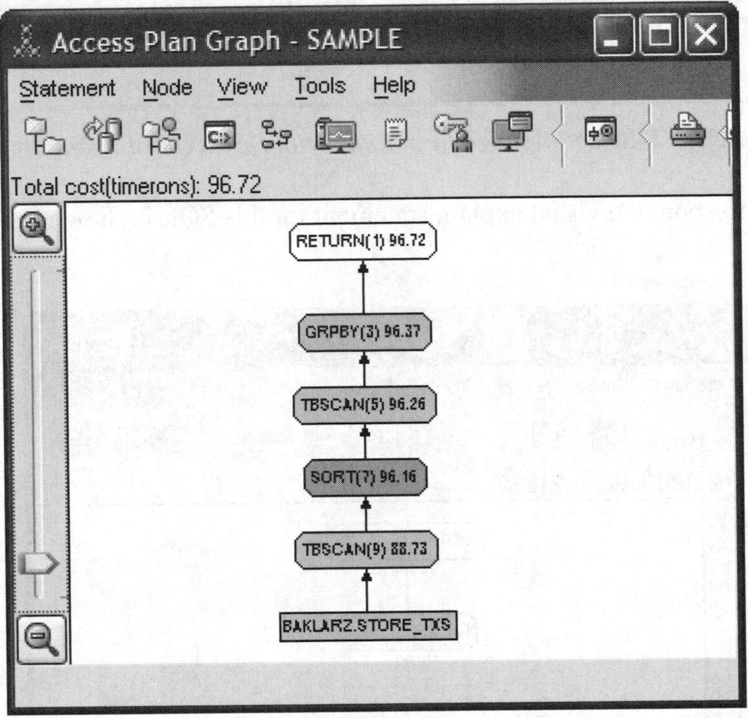

Figure 7–3 *Explain statement for SYSTEM sampling*

Using the SYSTEM sampling, we are able to bring the cost down to 96 units, or an eight-time reduction in work. This improved performance does come at the cost of having more variable results.

The two sets of SQL statements were executed 25 times and compared against the exact answers that would be produced without sampling. The results were plotted as a ratio against the correct result. For example, an exact result would score 100. Answers higher or lower than 100 would have slightly incorrect answers because of the sampling that was done.

The two SQL statements are compared in the following graph (Figure 7–4):

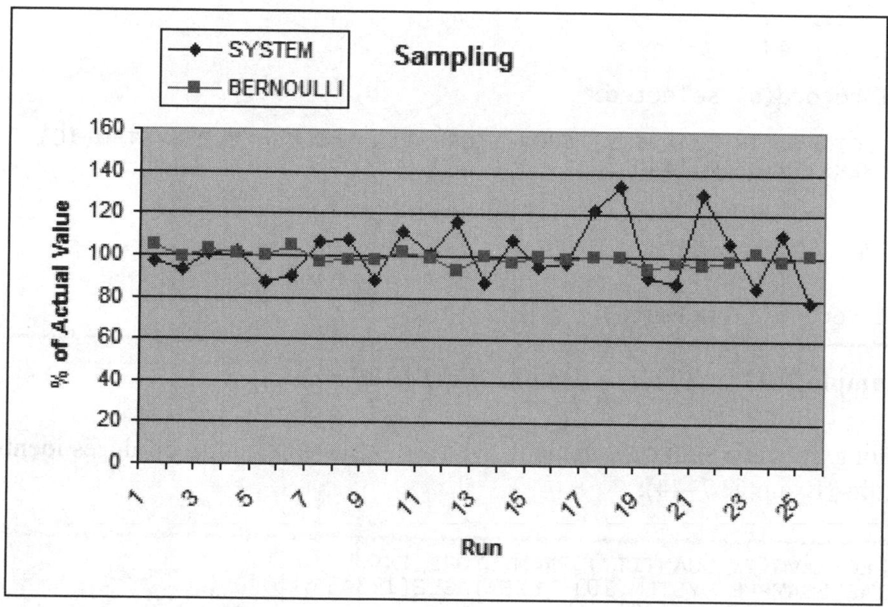

Figure 7–4 *Comparison of SYSTEM versus BERNOULLI accuracy*

With a 10% sampling of rows, the `BERNOULLI` sampling is less variable than the `SYSTEM` sampling. However, during the execution of this query, `SYSTEM` sampling took less time than `BERNOULLI` sampling. The user must choose between the trade-offs of fast execution speeds versus higher accuracy in the results.

REPEATABLE Sampling

During query testing or debugging, it may be useful to have exactly the same results returned during sampling. This can be accomplished by specifying the `REPEATABLE` clause after the sampling specification. Every time the query is executed, the same sample will be returned, unless the data has been changed or updated. The first example (Example 7–43) shows the results of two average calculations without the `REPEATABLE` clause.

```
SELECT AVG(TX_QUANTITY) FROM STORE_TXS TABLESAMPLE SYSTEM(10)
  WHERE TX_ITEM='A40';

1
-----------
         49

  1 record(s) selected.

SELECT AVG(TX_QUANTITY) FROM STORE_TXS TABLESAMPLE SYSTEM(10)
  WHERE TX_ITEM='A40';

1
-----------
         48

  1 record(s) selected.
```

Example 7–43 *SELECT without REPEATABLE clause*

Issuing the same SELECT statements with a REPEATABLE clause produces identical results (Example 7–44):

```
SELECT AVG(TX_QUANTITY) FROM STORE_TXS
  TABLESAMPLE SYSTEM(10) REPEATABLE(12345)
  WHERE TX_ITEM='A40';

1
-----------
         49

  1 record(s) selected.

SELECT AVG(TX_QUANTITY) FROM STORE_TXS
  TABLESAMPLE SYSTEM(10) REPEATABLE(12345)
  WHERE TX_ITEM='A40';

1
-----------
         49
  1 record(s) selected.
```

Example 7–44 *SELECT with REPEATABLE clause*

If the results are supposed to be consistent throughout a large set of SQL statements, a global temporary table should be used. Create the temporary table and populate it with a SELECT statement that uses the TABLESAMPLE clause to generate a subset to the data. Then the remainder of the SQL can refer to the temporary table. When the SQL goes into production, the TABLESAMPLE clause can be eliminated or the SQL modified to point to the original table.

Any numeric value can be used in the REPEATABLE clause. This value is used to seed the random number generator that is used to select the rows. In order to obtain the same sampling, the same number must be used in every TABLESAMPLE clause for that table. Otherwise, different results will be produced.

Additional Considerations

There are a few additional considerations when taking advantage of the TABLESAMPLE clause.

1. Sampling can only occur on base tables and materialized query tables.
2. Sampling occurs before any predicates are applied (the WHERE clause). Multiple tables can be sampled in the same SQL statement to test join conditions and other complex SQL without using entire tables.
3. Any calculations done in the SELECT list must account for the percentage of sampling done. For instance, the average calculation (AVG) should not be any different when working with 10% of the table or 50% of the table. However, a SUM or COUNT calculation must be scaled by multiplying the result by 100 and dividing by the sampling percentage to get the proper result. For instance, the following SQL scales SUM by 5 (100/20) to get the proper results since only 20% of the data was sampled (Example 7–45):

```
SELECT SUM(TX_QUANTITY) * 5 FROM STORE_TXS
  TABLESAMPLE SYSTEM(20)
  WHERE TX_ITEM='A40';
```

Example 7–45 *Scaling results with a TABLESAMPLE clause*

4. SYSTEM sampling is almost always faster than BERNOULLI sampling, but the results are often less accurate. This may be sufficient for testing and for quick reporting, but the results should be used with the appropriate caveats.

In general, the TABLESAMPLE clause can be extremely useful in prototyping SQL against large tables, and for getting quick answers to "what if" questions.

Advanced CASE Expressions

Up to now, we have been using the CASE expression in the select list of select statements. CASE expressions can also be used in other SQL statements, such as grouping lists, WHERE predicates, functions, and so on. We will review some of these uses in this section.

Using CASE Expressions to Group Values

As stated earlier, CASE expressions may be part of a grouping list. Being part of the grouping list can be used to rank data.

Suppose we want to know how many candidates have not passed the exams, how many have passed, and how many of them have an excellent score along with an average score for each classification. To solve this request, we will use a case expression in the select list and another one in the grouping list. The CASE expression used in the select list is used to rank the candidates. The CASE expression in the grouping list is used to create the groups based on the ranking defined in it (Example 7–46).

```
SELECT NUMBER,
  CASE
    WHEN INTEGER(SCORE) < 65 THEN 'Not Passed'
    WHEN integer(SCORE) < 90   THEN 'Passed'
    ELSE
      'Excellent'
  END AS GROUPBY_CASE,
  COUNT(*) AS COUNT,
  AVG(INTEGER(SCORE)) AS AVERAGE
FROM TEST_CANDIDATE C, TEST_TAKEN TT
  WHERE C.CID=TT.CID
GROUP BY
  NUMBER,
  CASE
    WHEN INTEGER(SCORE) < 65 THEN 'Not Passed'
    WHEN INTEGER(SCORE) < 90 THEN 'Passed'
    ELSE
      'Excellent'
  END;
```

Example 7–46 *Grouping with CASE expressions*

Whenever you group using a CASE expression, the CASE expression in the grouping list must be exactly the same as the one used in the select list. What can be different is the use of the AS clause, because it is not permitted in the grouping list.

Using CASE Expressions in Functions

CASE expressions can be embedded as functions parameters. This allows you to pass different parameters to the function in a single pass of the data. Suppose that the TEST_TAKEN table is very large and we have the following requirements:

- The number of tests taken with a score higher than 90
- The number of tests taken with a score of 90
- The number of tests taken with a score lower than 70
- The number of DB2 Fundamentals exams taken

Without the use of case expressions, this will require four different queries that will read the entire table. We want to do this in one single pass of the data, because the table is very large.

The query will use four count functions, each one evaluating different criteria using a CASE expression (Example 7–47).

```
SELECT COUNT (CASE WHEN INTEGER (SCORE) > 90 THEN 1
                   ELSE NULL
              END) AS MOREGB90,
       COUNT (CASE WHEN INTEGER (SCORE) = 90 THEN 1
                   ELSE NULL
              END) AS EQUALGB90,
       COUNT (CASE WHEN INTEGER (SCORE) < 70 THEN 1
                   ELSE NULL
             END) AS MINORGB70,
       COUNT (CASE WHEN NUMBER=TEST_ID('500') THEN 1
                   ELSE NULL
              END) AS EQUALGB500
FROM TEST_TAKEN;
```

Example 7–47 *Using CASE expressions in functions*

This type of query may be useful when performing data inspection analysis. Notice that the four different requirements are solved in a single pass of the data.

The query was created using a different column function for each one of the conditions presented as a requirement. The conditions are evaluated in the case expression inside each function. When the condition evaluates true, it will return a value of 1 and the row will be counted. When the condition evaluates false, the case expression will return a null value and the row will not be counted.

Structured Types and Typed Tables

As mentioned in Chapter 5, *user-defined structured types* are one of the data types in DB2 that allow you to create a structure that contains a sequence of named attributes, each of which has a data type. This structured type can be used as the type of a table or a view.

With typed tables, you can establish a hierarchical structure with a defined relationship between those tables called a table hierarchy. By using typed tables, a developer can avoid creating many separate tables that are essentially the same. For instance, an EMPLOYEE table is probably very similar to a MANAGER table. By basing the MANAGER table on the EMPLOYEE table, only one table has to be created and managed by DB2. The MANAGER table could contain attributes unique to a manager, but yet still be based on the underlying EMPLOYEE table. From an application perspective, MANAGER and EMPLOYEE would appear as two separate tables to the user.

A table defined using a structured type is called a *typed table*, whereas a view defined using a structured type is called a *typed view*. A structured type can be a *sub-type* of another structured type, called a *super-type*. A sub-type inherits all attributes from its super-type and can be added to other attributes. A sub-type can be a super-type for other structured types. Therefore, you can create a hierarchy of structured types using this relationship between sub-type and super-type. Also, a hierarchy of typed tables can be created based on the structured type hierarchy. Structured types and typed tables enable you to configure a better model of business entities and relationships in the real world.

A structured type can be created by using the CREATE TYPE SQL statement. As discussed in Chapter 5, a user-defined distinct type can also be created by a CREATE TYPE statement, and it represents a column type of a table. For a user-defined structured type, you can call it a row type of a table. See Figure 7–5 for an example.

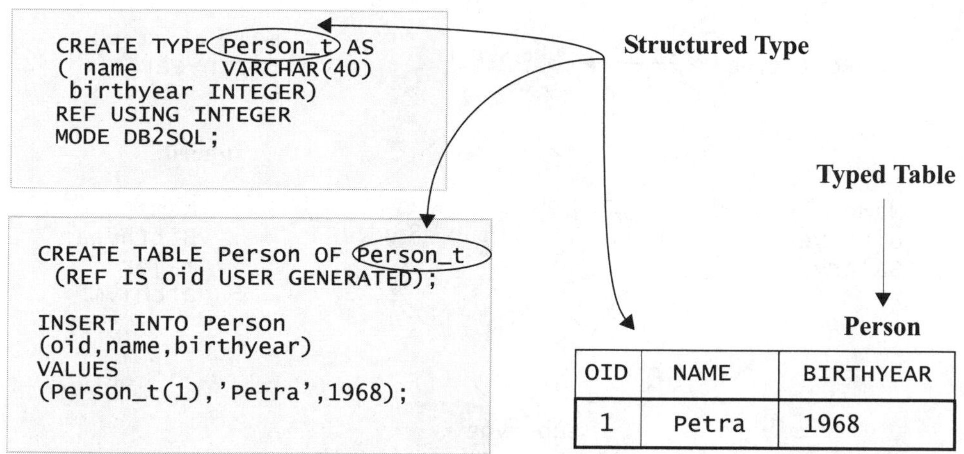

Figure 7–5 *User-defined structured type*

In this example, a structured type PERSON_T is defined with two attributes, NAME and BIRTHYEAR, and then a table PERSON is defined using the structured type. Notice the table PERSON has NAME and BIRTHYEAR columns that are defined by the PERSON_T type. The other column is called the *object identifier* (OID). Every typed table must have the OID column as its first column and the value of the OID column must be unique in the whole table hierarchy. The data type of the OID column is REFERENCE. Notice that the casting function PERSON_T is used to provide a value for the OID column in our example. The OID column will be talked about in greater detail later.

Creating Structured Types

A structured type supports a hierarchical structure. Therefore, a structured type can be created as a sub-type of another structured type (thereby inheriting the attributes of that type). Figure 7–6 shows a simple structured type hierarchy. PERSON_T is defined as a Root type (not depending on other types) with two attributes, NAME and BIRTHYEAR. EMP_T and STUDENT_T are defined as sub-types of PERSON_T. Thus, EMP_T and STUDENT_T inherit all attributes of PERSON_T. In addition, the structured types EMP_T and STUDENT_T have several additional attributes that are specific to their particular types.

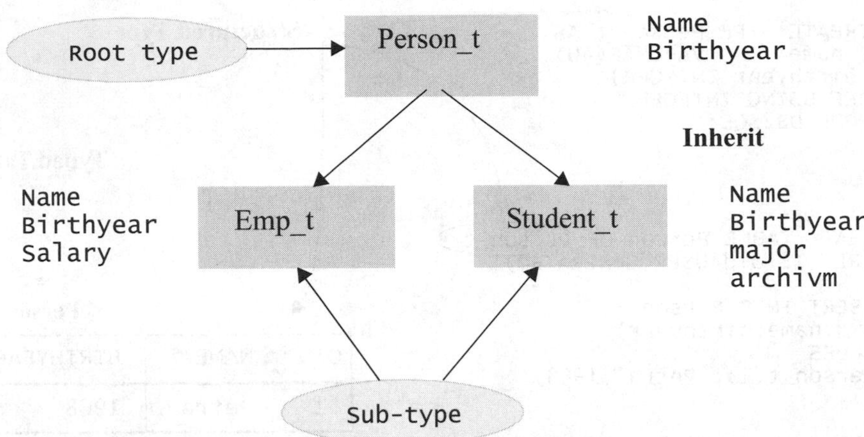

Figure 7–6 *Hierarchy of structured types*

Let's see how we can define this structured type hierarchy. Look at the example shown in Example 7–48.

```
CREATE TYPE PERSON_T AS
 (NAME VARCHAR(20),BIRTHYEAR SMALLINT)
   REF USING INTEGER
   MODE DB2SQL;

CREATE TYPE EMP_T UNDER PERSON_T
 AS (SALARY INT)
 MODE DB2SQL;

CREATE TYPE STUDENT_T UNDER PERSON_T
 AS (MAJOR VARCHAR(10),
     ARCHIVM DECIMAL(5,2))
 MODE DB2SQL;
```

Example 7–48 *Creating structured types and structured type hierarchies*

The `AS` clause provides the attribute definitions associated with the type. The `UNDER` clause specifies that the structured type is being defined as a sub-type of the specified super-type. In our example, the `EMP_T` type has `SALARY` as its attribute. The `STUDENT_T` type has `Major` and `Archivm` as its attributes. In addition, both have attributes `NAME` and `BIRTHYEAR`, which are inherited from the `PERSON_T` type.

The `REF USING` clause is used when defining a root-type and specifies the built-in data type used as the representation for the `REFERENCE` type of this structured type and all its sub-types. As seen in Example 7–48, a typed table must have the `OID` column, and a casting function is used when supplying a value for the `OID` column. This casting function casts the data type specified by the `REF USING` clause of the root type definition into the `REFERENCE` type. You can specify the following for the `REFERENCE` type: `INTEGER`, `SMALLINT`, `BIGINT`, `DECIMAL`, `CHAR`, `VARCHAR`, `GRAPHIC`, or `VARGRAPHIC`. The default type is `VARCHAR(16) FOR BIT DATA`.

DB2 *Note*

Note: Successful execution of the `CREATE TYPE` statement also generates functions to cast between the `REFERENCE` type and its representation type (the built-in type specified by `REF USING` clause) and generates support for the comparison operators (=, <>, !=, <, <=, >, and >=) for users with the `REFERENCE` type.

The `MODE` clause is used to specify the mode of the type. `DB2SQL` is the only value for `MODE` currently supported.

Altering Structured Types

The `ALTER TYPE` statement enables you to add or drop an attribute of an existing structured type. The following example shows the `ALTER TYPE` statements adding an attribute `TEL` to the `PERSON_T` type and dropping the attribute (Example 7–49).

```
ALTER TYPE PERSON_T ADD ATTRIBUTE TEL CHAR(12);
ALTER TYPE PERSON_T DROP ATTRIBUTE TEL;
```

Example 7–49 *Altering types*

DB2 *Note*

Note: The `ALTER TYPE` statement cannot be executed against a type if it, or one of its sub-types, is the type of an existing table.

Creating Typed Tables

A typed table is a table defined with a structured data type (refer to Figure 7–7). Typed tables can have a hierarchy of structured types. A sub-table inherits all attributes of its super-table. All tables in an inherit relationship form a table hierarchy. A table that does not have a super-table in a hierarchy is called a *root-table*. In other words, a root-table is a table defined with the root-type of a type hierarchy.

A simple hierarchy of a typed table is shown in Figure 7–7. You can see the two columns of the `PERSON` table are inherited by the `STUDENT` table and the `EMP` table.

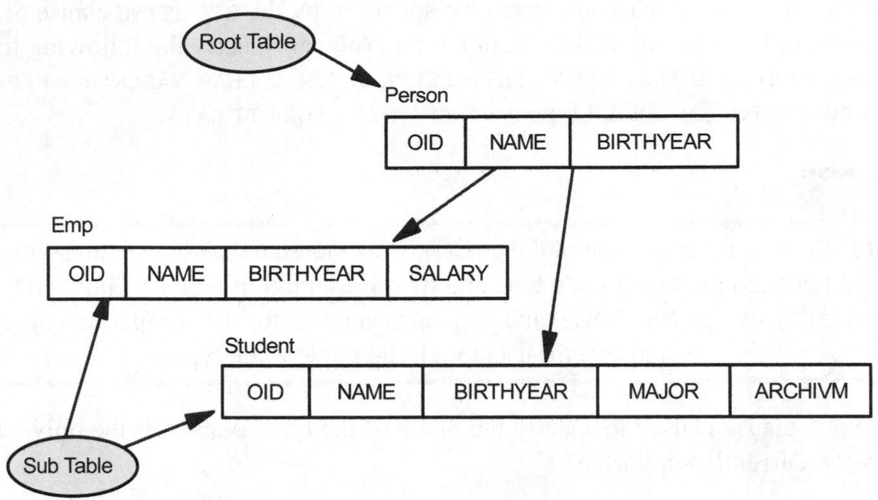

Figure 7–7 *Hierarchy of typed tables*

Example 7–50 shows sample statements to create these typed tables. Typed tables are created using the CREATE TABLE statement.

```
CREATE TABLE PERSON OF PERSON_T
      (REF IS OID USER GENERATED);

CREATE TABLE EMP OF EMP_T UNDER PERSON
      INHERIT SELECT PRIVILEGES;

CREATE TABLE STUDENT OF STUDENT_T UNDER PERSON
      INHERIT SELECT PRIVILEGES;
```

Example 7–50 *Create typed tables*

In our example, the PERSON table is the root-table, and the EMP table and the STUDENT table are sub-tables. The PERSON table is defined to be of the structured type PERSON_T. This means that it has a column corresponding to each attribute of the structured type PERSON_T. The EMP table and the STUDENT table inherit all attributes of the PERSON table.

As explained before, every typed table must have an OID column. The OID is defined at the root-table of a table hierarchy, and all sub-tables inherit the OID. The column name of the OID column is defined at the root-table of a table hierarchy using the REF IS clause. In our example, it is OID. Each row must have a unique value of OID in the whole hierarchy. The data type of the OID column is a system type REFERENCE.

The USER GENERATED clause indicates that the initial value for the OID column of each newly inserted row will be provided by the user when inserting a row. Once a row is inserted, the OID column cannot be updated.

The INHERIT SELECT PRIVILEGES clause means that any user or group holding SELECT privilege on the super table will be granted an equivalent privilege on the newly created sub-table. The definer of a sub-table is considered to be the grantor of this privilege.

DB2 *Note*

Note: Within a typed table hierarchy, only one sub-table may exist of a particular sub-type.

Dropping Typed Tables

You can use a DROP TABLE statement to drop a typed table as well as a regular table. When you drop a typed table, you must make sure it does not have any sub-tables. If the typed table being dropped has sub-tables, the DROP TABLE statement will return an error.

Dropping a sub-table has the effect of deleting all the rows of the sub-table from the super-tables. Therefore, this may result in the activation of triggers or referential integrity constraints defined on the super-tables.

If you want to drop a whole table hierarchy, you can use the DROP TABLE HIERARCHY statement. Unlike dropping a single sub-table, dropping the table hierarchy does not result in the activation of triggers nor in referential integrity constraints of any tables in the hierarchy. The following example shows dropping the whole table hierarchy (Example 7–51). You should specify the root table name of the table hierarchy.

```
DROP TABLE HIERARCHY PERSON;
```

Example 7–51 *Dropping a typed table*

DB2 *Note*

You can use the DROP VIEW HIERARCHY statement to drop a total view hierarchy. The view hierarchy is explained later.

Inserting Rows into a Typed Table

Rows can be inserted into a typed table using an INSERT SQL statement. Examples of this are shown in Figure 7–8.

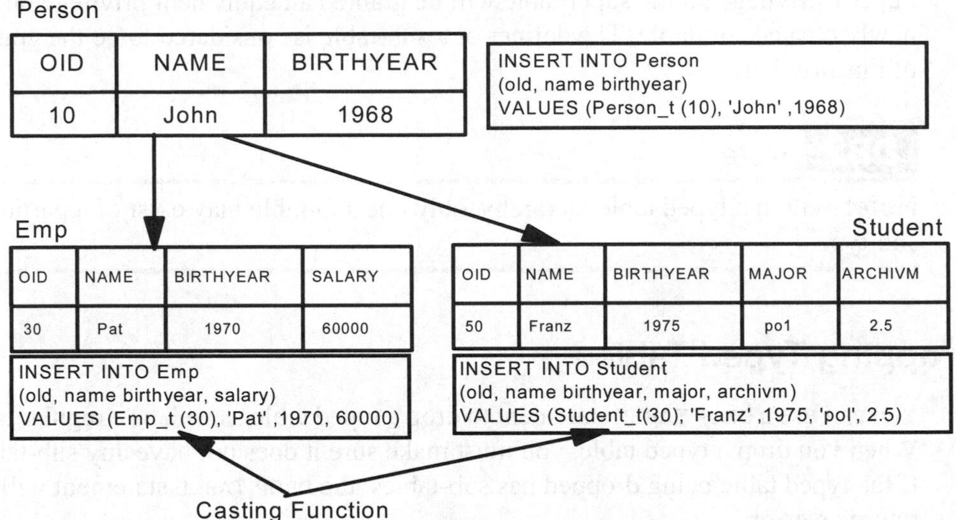

Figure 7–8 *Inserting into a hierarchy of typed tables*

Notice that each INSERT statement uses a casting function for the value of the OID column. All OID values (of type REFERENCE) must be cast into the REFERENCE type of the table to which the value is being inserted. When you create a structured type, the casting function is created implicitly. The argument of the casing function should be of the built-in data type specified with the REF USING clause of the root type definition. The name of the casting function is the same as the underlying structured type, but optionally, you can specify another casting function name in the CREATE TYPE statement. See the *DB2 SQL Reference* manual for further details.

Selecting a Row from a Typed Table

When you issue a select statement for a typed table, the rows are returned from the target table and all of its sub-tables in the table hierarchy. Example 7–52 shows the SELECT statements against some typed tables. Each SELECT statement retrieves all columns and all rows from each table. Notice the select statement for the PERSON table returns not only the rows of the PERSON table but also the rows of the EMP table and STUDENT table (Example 7–52).

```
SELECT * FROM PERSON;

OID  NAME   BIRTHYEAR
---- ------ -----------
  10 John          1968
  30 Pat           1970
  50 Franz         1975

SELECT * FROM EMP;

OID  NAME   BIRTHYEAR   SALARY
---- ------ ----------- ---------
  30 Pat           1970     60000

SELECT * FROM STUDENT;

OID  NAME   BIRTHYEAR  MAJOR  ARCHIVM
---- ------ ---------- ------ -------
  50 FRANZ        1975 POL        2.5
```

Example 7–52 *Issuing a SELECT statement against typed tables*

If you want to retrieve only rows of the PERSON table, you can use the ONLY clause for a select statement as follows (Example 7–53):

```
SELECT * FROM ONLY(PERSON);
```

Example 7–53 *ONLY qualifier*

If you want to retrieve columns from not only the specified table but also its sub-tables, you can use the OUTER clause for a select statement as follows (Example 7–54).

```
SELECT * FROM OUTER(PERSON);
OID  NAME  BIRTHYEAR  SALARY   MAJOR  ARCHIVM
---- ----- ---------- -------- ------ --------
  10 John        1968        - -             -
  30 Pat         1970    60000 -             -
  50 FRANZ       1975        - POL         2.5
```

Example 7–54 *Using the OUTER clause against a typed table*

Updating and Deleting Rows from Typed Tables

As in a regular table, you can use UPDATE and DELETE statements to update or delete rows of a typed table. Be aware that update and delete statements affect the target table and its sub-tables in a manner like a select statement. Let's take a look at some examples.

The first example changes the birthyear of a person whose OID is 10 to 1969. This statement will affect PERSON and its sub-tables (EMP and STUDENT). Notice that a casting function, EMP_T, is used to cast the type INTEGER into the REFERENCE type (Example 7–55).

```
UPDATE PERSON SET BIRTHYEAR=1969 WHERE OID=EMP_T(10);
```

Example 7–55 *Use OID for updates*

The next example deletes all rows from the PERSON table and its sub-tables (EMP and STUDENT) (Example 7–56).

```
DELETE FROM PERSON;
```

Example 7–56 *Deleting all entries including subtables*

If you want to update or delete rows of a particular typed table only (and not its sub-tables), you can use the ONLY clause for an update or a delete statement, as the following example shows (Example 7–57):

```
DELETE FROM ONLY(PERSON);
```

Example 7–57 *Deleting only the table and no sub-tables*

Physical Implementation of Typed Tables

The physical implementation of a typed table hierarchy is one table that holds all attributes of the tables in the table hierarchy. This table is called a *Hierarchy table* (H-Table). When a root-table is created, an H-Table is automatically created. Each time a sub-table having other columns different than its root table is created, the H-Table is altered and new columns are added. You can specify the name of the H-Table using the HIERARCHY option of the create table statement, but the default name is the root-table name followed by the suffix _HIERARCHY. This physical implementation has an advantage in performance and you can regard typed tables as if they are views defined for an H-Table. Figure 7–9 shows a logical view of the typed table hierarchy and H-Table.

DB2 *Note*

The H-Table cannot be manipulated with SQL statements.

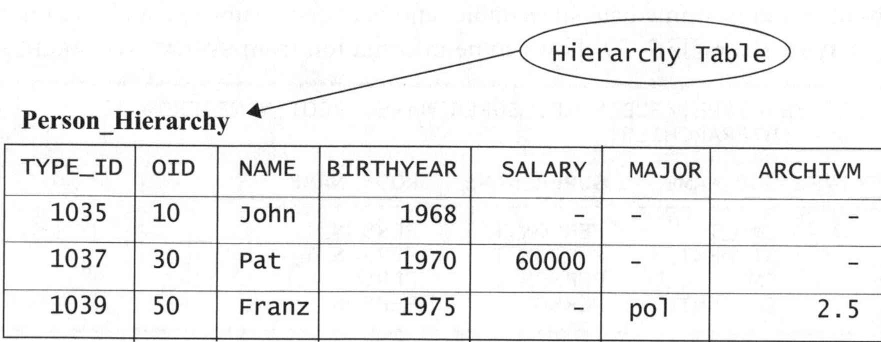

TYPE_ID	OID	NAME	BIRTHYEAR	SALARY	MAJOR	ARCHIVM
1035	10	John	1968	-	-	-
1037	30	Pat	1970	60000	-	-
1039	50	Franz	1975	-	pol	2.5

Figure 7–9 *Logical view of a Hierarchy table (H-Table)*

The first column of an H-Table is the TYPE_ID column. Each value of this column specifies the structured type of the typed table to which this row was inserted.

Once a structured type and a typed table are defined, the DB2 system catalog tables hold their information. Let's peek into the system catalog tables through some system catalog views.

You can see the ROWTYPESCHEMA and the ROWTYPENAME column from the SYSCAT.TABLES view. These columns have the information to maintain typed tables. You can see each structured type through the SYSCAT.DATATYPES view as shown in Figure 7–58. The values of the SOURCENAME column of the SYSCAT.DATATYPES catalog view is the name of the built-in type which was specified with the REF USING clause when creating the root type. You can see that EMP_T and STUDENT_T inherit the attributes from their root-type, PERSON_T.

```
SELECT TYPENAME,SOURCENAME,METATYPE FROM SYSCAT.DATATYPES;

TYPENAME           SOURCENAME         METATYPE
------------------ ------------------ --------
PERSON_T           INTEGER            R
EMP_T              INTEGER            R
STUDENT_T          INTEGER            R
```

Example 7–58 *System catalog view information for typed tables*

In this example, only rows for structured types are extracted. The SOURCENAME column would be NULL, and the METATYPE column would have an S for built-in data types. For user-defined distinct types, the METATYPE column would be T.

The SYSCAT.HIERARCHIES system catalog view contains the relationship between a sub-table and its immediate super-table, and between a sub-type and its immediate super-type. Example 7–59 shows some information from SYSCAT.HIERARCHIES.

```
SELECT METATYPE, SUB_NAME, SUPER_NAME, ROOT_NAME FROM
  SYSCAT.HIERARCHIES;

METATYPE SUB_NAME     SUPER_NAME    ROOT_NAME
-------- ------------ ------------- -----------
R        EMP_T        PERSON_T      PERSON_T
R        STUDENT_T    PERSON_T      PERSON_T
U        EMP          PERSON        PERSON
U        STUDENT      PERSON        PERSON
```

Example 7–59 *System catalog view information for hierarchy relationships*

The METATYPE column of the SYSCAT.HIERARCHIES catalog view encodes the relationship type of the object as follows:

- R — Between structured types
- U — Between typed tables
- W— Between typed views

Typed views are described later in this chapter.

Reference Columns

In a typed table definition, you can define columns as *reference columns* to another typed table. This referenced typed table is called a *target table*. A reference column holds values that correspond to OID values of the target table and clearly identify rows in the target tables. The data type of a reference column is REFERENCE, the same type as OID in the target table. The reference column is similar to a foreign key; however, the evaluation, like a foreign key, is not performed for operations such as insert, update, or delete.

Look at Figure 7–10. This shows you a typed table, EMP, which has a reference column referring another typed table DEPT. This relationship is defined when the CREATE TABLE statement is executed and is called a *scope*.

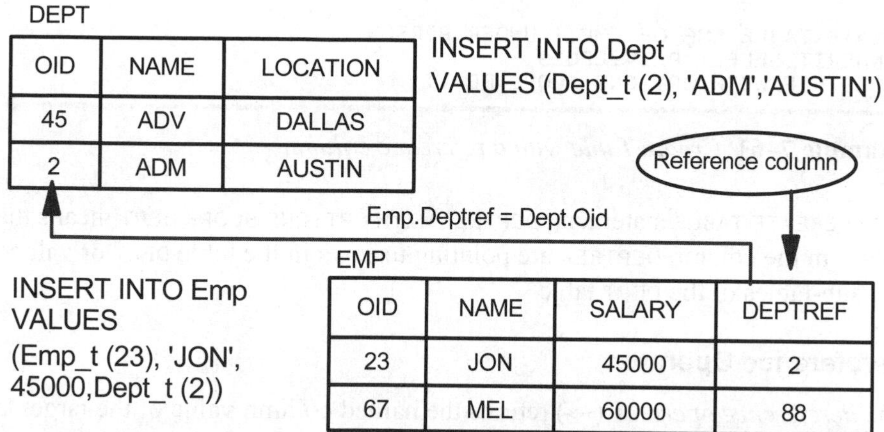

Figure 7–10 *Reference column relationship*

As shown in Figure 7–10, a reference column can have a value that the target table does not have. Notice the casting function DEPT_T is used to provide a value for the reference column.

The reference column is defined through the CREATE TYPE and CREATE TABLE statements. Example 7–60 shows CREATE TYPE statements to set up a reference column, assuming the root type PERSON_T is already defined, as shown in Example 7–48.

```
CREATE TYPE DEPT_T AS (NAME CHAR(40),LOCATION CHAR(20))
 REF USING INTEGER MODE DB2SQL;

CREATE TYPE EMP_T UNDER PERSON_T
 AS (SALARY INTEGER, DEPTREF REF(DEPT_T)) MODE DB2SQL;
```

Example 7–60 *Create Type statement to define a reference column*

In our example, DEPT_T is a root type of a different table hierarchy from the one to which EMP_T and PERSON_T belong. The definition of EMP_T supplies two attributes: one is SALARY, which is of the INTEGER type, and the other is DEPTREF, which is of the REFERENCE type. DEPTREF REF(DEPT_T) means that this attribute DEPTREF of EMP_T type is the reference type and the target of the reference is a row of the table whose row type is DEPT_T or its sub-type.

You then need to create typed tables based on the structured types defined in Example 7–60. Example 7–61 shows the sample CREATE TABLE statements to define a reference column (define a scope). The second CREATE TABLE statement in this example creates a table with a reference column.

```
CREATE TABLE DEPT OF DEPT_T (REF IS OID USER GENERATED);

CREATE TABLE EMP OF EMP_T UNDER PERSON
 INHERIT SELECT PRIVILEGES
 (DEPTREF WITH OPTIONS SCOPE DEPT);
```

Example 7–61 *Create Table with a reference column*

In the CREATE TABLE statement, DEPTREF WITH OPTIONS SCOPE DEPT means that the values in the column DEPTREF are pointing to rows in the table DEPT or values in any sub-tables of the DEPT table.

Dereference Operator

The *dereference operator* (->) returns the named column value of the target table or its sub-table from the row with the matching OID column. The following example shows a SELECT statement using the dereference operator.

```
SELECT E.NAME FROM EMP E
     WHERE E.DEPTREF->LOCATION ='AUSTIN';
```

Example 7–62 *Using dereference operator*

In this example, each DEPTREF column value is interrogated and checked. We check to see if the target table (DEPT table) or its sub-table has a row whose OID value is the same. If such a row is found, the value of the LOCATION column is taken from that row and returned. That is how DEPTREF->LOCATION works. This predicate is true if the returned value is AUSTIN.

The SELECT statement above using the dereference operator (->) can be rewritten using a JOIN operation. The next example shows the equivalent SQL statement using a JOIN operation (Example 7–63).

```
SELECT E.NAME FROM EMP E, DEPT D
     WHERE E.DEPTREF = D.OID
       AND D.LOCATION ='AUSTIN';
```

Example 7–63 *Using Joins instead of dereference operators*

View Hierarchies

Typed views are views whose definition is based on structured types. You can create a view hierarchy with typed views as you would create a table hierarchy with typed tables. Example 7–64 shows the CREATE VIEW statements to define typed views. In our example, two typed views PERSON_V and EMP_V are created using the

PERSON_T type and the EMP_T type. The PERSON_V view is defined as a root view of the view hierarchy and references all columns and rows of the PERSON table. The EMP_V view is defined as a sub-view of the PERSON_V view and references all columns and rows of the EMP table. Notice that the PERSON_V definition uses the ONLY clause so that rows are selected from only the PERSON table. This is necessary because the PERSON_V view has a sub-view (EMP_V), and the PERSON_V view should not have rows that are assigned to the EMP_V view. Remember, it is not allowed to have duplicated OID values in the same view hierarchy.

The first CREATE VIEW statement will succeed even if FROM PERSON is used instead of FROM ONLY(PERSON); however, you will get an error when creating the EMP_V view since all rows that conform to the full select of the EMP_V definition are referred to by the PERSON_V view (Example 7–64). You do not need to use the ONLY clause for the EMP_V view because the EMP_V view does not have any sub-views.

```
CREATE VIEW PERSON_V OF PERSON_T MODE DB2SQL
 (REF IS VOID USER GENERATED)
 AS SELECT PERSON_T(INTEGER(OID)),NAME,BIRTHYEAR
     FROM ONLY(PERSON);

CREATE VIEW EMP_V OF EMP_T MODE DB2SQL UNDER PERSON_V
 INHERIT SELECT PRIVILEGES
 AS SELECT EMP_T(INTEGER(OID)),NAME,BIRTHYEAR,SALARY
     FROM EMP;
```

Example 7–64 *Create typed views*

SQL Functions for Typed Tables and Typed Views

You can use the following SQL functions for typed tables or typed views:

- DEREF (function)
- TYPE_ID (expression)
- TYPE_NAME (expression)
- TYPE_SCHEMA (expression)

The DEREF function returns the structured type of the argument. The argument can be the OID column or a reference column. The value that the DEREF function returns is also called a *dynamic data type*. This function can only be used on the left side of the TYPE predicate (explained later) or in the argument of the TYPE_ID, TYPE_NAME, or TYPE_SCHEMA functions. Let's look at each of the functions.

The TYPE_ID function returns the internal type identifier of the dynamic data type. The argument must be a structured type. The data type of the result of this function is an INTEGER. The following example (Example 7–65) shows an SQL statement using the TYPE_ID function. It retrieves the type identifier of each row and the person's name from the PERSON table.

```
SELECT TYPE_ID(DEREF(OID)),NAME FROM PERSON;
1          NAME
---------- ----------------------------------------
      1065 JON

  1 record(s) selected.
```

Example 7–65 *TYPE_ID Function*

DB2 Note

Note: The values returned by the TYPE_ID function are not portable across databases. The type identifier may be different in each database even if the type schema and type name are the same.

The TYPE_NAME function returns the unqualified name of the dynamic data type. The argument must be a structured type. The data type of the result of the function is a VARCHAR(18). The next example shows an SQL statement using the TYPE_NAME function (Example 7–66). It retrieves the type name of each row (represented by OID values), NAME, BIRTHYEAR, and the SALARY from the table EMP.

```
SELECT TYPE_NAME(DEREF(OID)),NAME,BIRTHYEAR,SALARY
     FROM EMP;

1                  NAME          BIRTHYEAR   SALARY

------------------ ------------- ----------- -----------
EMP_T2             JON                  1980       45000

  1 record(s) selected.
```

Example 7–66 *TYPE_NAME function*

The TYPE_SCHEMA function returns the schema name of the dynamic data type. The argument must be a structured type. The data type of the result of the function is a VARCHAR(128). The next example shows an SQL statement using the TYPE_SCHEMA function (Example 7–67). It retrieves the schema name of the dynamic type of each row (represented by OID values) and the NAME from the table PERSON.

```
SELECT TYPE_SCHEMA(DEREF(OID)),NAME FROM PERSON;
1                            NAME
---------------------------- --------------------------------
BAKLARZ                      JON

  1 record(s) selected.
```

Example 7–67 *TYPE_SCHEMA function*

TYPE Predicate

The TYPE predicate compares the type of an expression with one or more user-defined structured types. The DEREF function should be used whenever a TYPE predicate has an expression involving a reference type value. It evaluates whether the value that the DEREF function returns matches one or more candidates in the list. If there is a match, the result of the predicate is true. The next example shows an SQL statement using the TYPE predicate (Example 7–68). It returns all attributes and rows whose OID type is PERSON_T and not a sub-type of PERSON_T.

```
SELECT * FROM EMP
     WHERE DEREF(OID) IS OF DYNAMIC TYPE (ONLY EMP_T);

OID         NAME        BIRTHYEAR   SALARY      DEPTREF
----------- ----------- ----------- ----------- -------
         23 JON                1980       45000       2

  1 record(s) selected.
```

Example 7–68 *TYPE predicate*

You can leave out the keywords DYNAMIC TYPE and rewrite this example as follows (Example 7–69):

```
SELECT * FROM EMP
     WHERE DEREF(OID) IS OF (ONLY EMP_T);
```

Example 7–69 *Equivalent TYPE function*

Considerations When Using Typed Tables and Views

Some considerations when using typed tables and views are:

- A primary key cannot be created on a sub-table (the primary key (OID) is inherited from the super table).

Advanced SQL

- An unique index cannot be created on a sub-table.
- A check constraint defined on a table automatically applies to all sub-tables of that table.
- The LOAD command is not supported.
- Replication is not supported.
- RUNSTATS, REORG, and REORGCHK can only be executed on a root-table.

Examples of a Typed Table Hierarchy

Now let's look at more examples of the user-defined structured type and typed table.

Assume you are building a data model of the people in a university. Each person has two base attributes, name and birth year. A person who works for the university is an employee. An employee belongs to a department and gets a salary. Therefore, salary and department are the attributes for an employee. A person who studies at the university is a student. A student majors in a subject and has an achievement record. Major and achievement are particular attributes for a student. A professor is working for the university, so he or she is an employee, but has a speciality. On the other hand, there are a lot of departments in a university. Each department has a manager, and the manager is working for the university as an employee.

The model of this example represents these relationships. Figure 7–11 shows these relationships using structured types and a typed table hierarchy. There is a hierarchy whose root-type is PERSON_T. EMP_T and STUDENT_T are the sub-types of PERSON_T, and PROF_T is a sub-type of EMP_T. There are two reference attributes, MGR in DEPT_T that points to EMP_T and DEPT in EMP_T that points to DEPT_T.

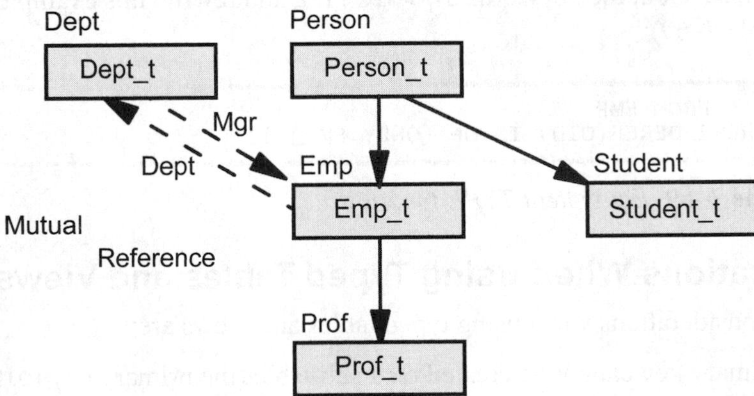

Figure 7–11 *Example: Hierarchy of structured types and typed tables*

DEPT_T and EMP_T reference each other. When you define two structured types referencing each other (mutual definition), you must create one of them first without the reference definition, and then add a reference attribute with the ALTER TYPE statement after the other type is created. This is because the referenced type should be defined in advance when a structured type is created with a reference.

In our example, the EMP_T type is created without a reference attribute first, and then the DEPT_T type is created with the reference attribute MGR, which refers the EMP_T type. Finally, the reference attribute DEPT is added to the EMP_T type using an ALTER TYPE statement. See the SQL statements shown in Example 7–70.

```
CREATE TYPE PERSON_T AS
 (NAME VARCHAR(20), BIRTHYEAR SMALLINT)
 REF USING INTEGER MODE DB2SQL;

CREATE TYPE EMP_T UNDER PERSON_T
 AS (SALARY INT) MODE DB2SQL;

CREATE TYPE STUDENT_T UNDER PERSON_T
 AS (MAJOR CHAR(20), ARCHIVM DECIMAL(5,2))
 MODE DB2SQL;

CREATE TYPE DEPT_T AS
 (NAME VARCHAR(20), BUDGET INT, MGR REF(EMP_T))
 REF USING INTEGER MODE DB2SQL;

ALTER TYPE EMP_T ADD ATTRIBUTE DEPT REF(DEPT_T);

CREATE TYPE PROF_T UNDER EMP_T
 AS (SPECIALITY VARCHAR(20)) MODE DB2SQL;
```

Example 7–70 *Example: Creating structured types*

Now let's create the table hierarchy. The table PERSON, which is created based on the PERSON_T type, is a root-table and has two sub-tables, EMP and STUDENT. PROF is a sub-table of EMP. The table DEPT has a scope of the reference column MGR, which points to rows in the table EMP. The table EMP has a scope of the reference column DEPT, which points to rows in the table DEPT. Therefore, you should create the EMP table without a reference column, and then add a reference column after the DEPT table is created. See the SQL statements shown Example 7–71.

```
CREATE TABLE PERSON OF PERSON_T (REF IS OID USER GENERATED);

CREATE TABLE EMP OF EMP_T UNDER PERSON
  INHERIT SELECT PRIVILEGES;

CREATE TABLE STUDENT OF STUDENT_T UNDER PERSON
  INHERIT SELECT PRIVILEGES;

CREATE TABLE DEPT OF DEPT_T
 (REF IS OID USER GENERATED, MGR WITH OPTIONS SCOPE EMP);
```

```
ALTER TABLE EMP ALTER COLUMN DEPT ADD SCOPE DEPT;

CREATE TABLE PROF OF PROF_T UNDER EMP
    INHERIT SELECT PRIVILEGES;
```

Example 7–71 *Example: Creating typed tables (continued)*

The content of all the tables are shown in Figure 7–12 (assuming these rows are previously inserted).

Person

OID	NAME	BIRTHYEAR
10	John	1968
20	Paul	1961

Dept

OID	NAME	BUDGET	MGR
10	math	300000	80
20	oec	500000	70
30	headq	5000000	90
40	itso	1000000	60

Emp

OID	NAME	BIRTHYEAR	SALARY	DEPT
30	Pat	1970	60000	10
40	Hitomi	1977	65000	20
90	Lou	-	-	-
50	Sam	1968	60000	40
60	Uta	1961	95000	30

Student

OID	NAME	BIRTHYEAR	MAJOR	ARCHIVM
100	Franzis	1975	pol	2.50
110	Herb	1980	math	1.70

Prof

OID	NAME	BIRTHYEAR	SALARY	DEPT	SPECIALITY
70	Rich	1941	90000	30	oec
80	Herb	1962	120000	30	math

Figure 7–12 *Example: Records that each typed table contains*

As already described, one hierarchy table (H-Table) is created for a table hierarchy. All columns and all rows of typed tables in a table hierarchy are stored in one hierarchy table. Let's look at the PERSON_HIERARCHY table, which is the hierarchy table of our example, and see how a SELECT statement against typed tables is processed. Note that a hierarchy table cannot be directly manipulated by an SQL statement. See the following three examples. Each of them is a simple query from a typed table (Example 7–72).

```
SELECT * FROM PERSON;
SELECT * FROM EMP;
SELECT * FROM OUTER(EMP);
```

Example 7–72 *Creating structured types and structured type hierarchies*

The answer set is shown in Figure 7–13. This figure shows the hierarchy table of our example and the answer set of the previous queries.

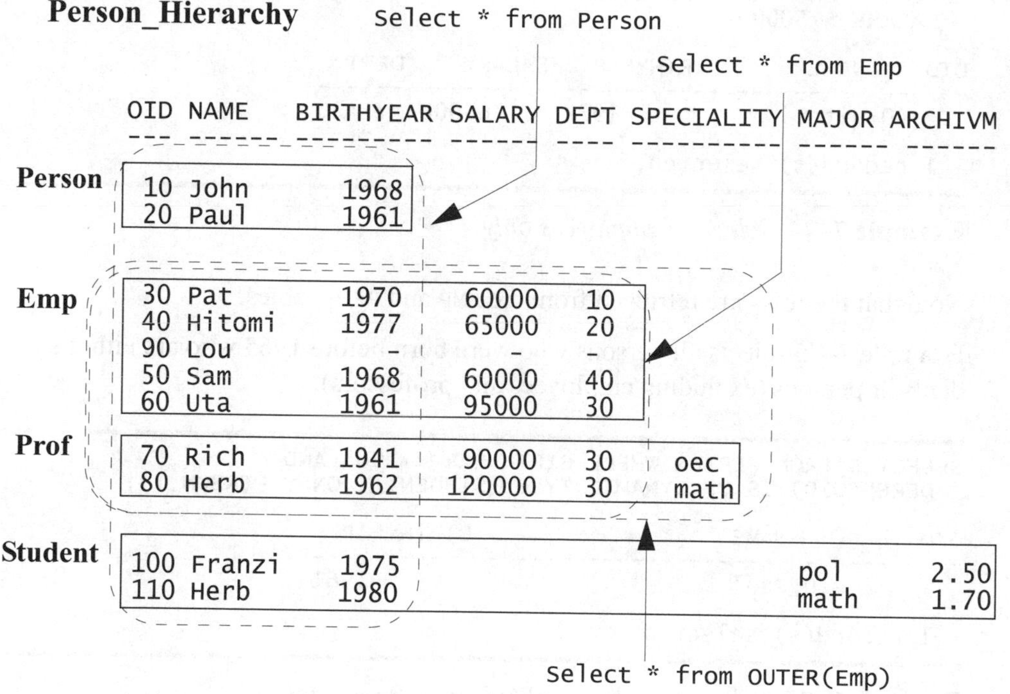

Figure 7–13 *Example: Logical view of hierarchy tables (H-table)*

DB2 *Note*

Note: Remember you cannot select rows directly from the hierarchy table.

Now let's look at other examples.

This example inserts an employee TETSU with the OID 200, born in 1968, earning a $65,000 salary, and working in the ITSO department (Example 7–73).

```
INSERT INTO EMP (OID, NAME, BIRTHYEAR, SALARY, DEPT)
 VALUES(EMP_T(200),'TETSU',1968,65000,
        (SELECT OID FROM DEPT WHERE NAME='ITSO'));
```

Example 7–73 *Inserting into a hierarchy*

The next example selects all attributes of all employees born after 1970 who earn more than $50,000 a year (Example 7–74).

```
SELECT * FROM EMP WHERE BIRTHYEAR > 1970 AND
  SALARY > 50000;

OID    NAME      BIRTHYEAR   SALARY    DEPT
------ --------- ----------- --------- ------
    40 Hitomi           1977     65000 20

  1 record(s) selected.
```

Example 7–74 *Selecting employees only*

Note that the rows are retrieved from the EMP and PROF tables.

Example 7–75 selects all persons who were born before 1965 who are either students or persons (excluding employees and professors).

```
SELECT * FROM PERSON WHERE BIRTHYEAR < 1965 AND
  DEREF(OID) IS OF DYNAMIC TYPE (STUDENT_T,ONLY PERSON_T);

OID         NAME                 BIRTHYEAR
----------- -------------------- -----------
         20 Paul                        1961

  1 record(s) selected.
```

Example 7–75 *Selecting only from Student or Person types*

This example uses the TYPE predicate, which compares a dynamic data type with a list of types. As already explained, the predicate is true if the dynamic type is specified in the list. In our example, STUDENT_T and PERSON_T (with the keyword ONLY) are specified. Therefore, only rows whose data type is STUDENT_T, its sub-types (although STUDENT_T does not have any sub-types), or PERSON_T type are returned.

Let's look at some reference column examples. Remember the DEPT table and EMP table have a mutual reference relationship as shown in Figure 7–14.

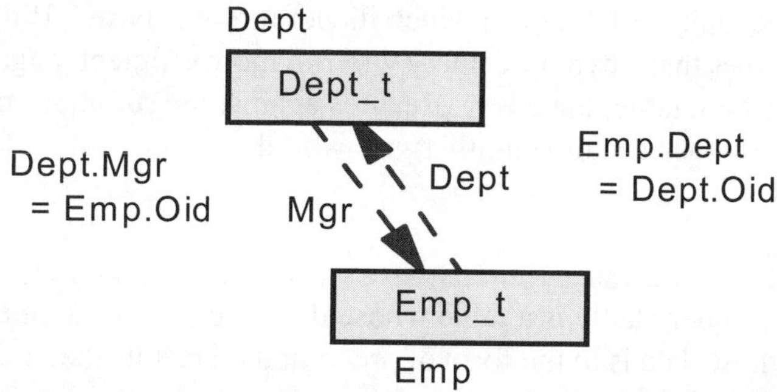

Figure 7–14 *Reference column*

The next example finds the employee's name, salary, department name, and budget (Example 7–76). It selects only the employees whose department's budget is greater than $500,000.

```
SELECT NAME, SALARY, DEPT->NAME, DEPT->BUDGET FROM EMP
                                WHERE DEPT->BUDGET > 500000;

NAME     SALARY     NAME       BUDGET
------- --------- ---------- -----------
Sam         60000 itso          1000000
Uta         95000 headq         5000000
Rich        90000 headq         5000000
Herb       120000 headq         5000000
Tetsu       65000 itso          5000000

  5 record(s) selected.
```

Example 7–76 *Creating structured types and structured type hierarchies*

Notice the department's name and the department's budget are retrieved from the DEPT table, which is referenced by the reference column DEPT of the EMP table and its sub-table, the PROF table.

Summary Tables

A *summary table* is a table whose definition is based on the result of a query. As such, the summary table typically contains precomputed results based on the data existing in the table, or tables, on which its definition is based. If the DB2 optimizer determines that a dynamic query will run more efficiently against a summary table than the base table, the query executes against the summary table, and you obtain the result faster than you otherwise would.

DB2 *Note*

A materialized query table is a table whose definition is based on the result of a query, and whose data is in the form of precomputed results that are taken from one or more tables on which the materialized query table definition is based. A materialized query table whose fullselect contains a GROUP BY clause is summarizing data from the tables that are referenced in the fullselect. Such a materialized query table is also known as a summary table. A summary table is a specialized type of materialized query table.

The query rewrite function of the optimizer will access a summary table if it determines that the query can be answered by using the data in the summary table instead of accessing the base tables (Figure 7–15).

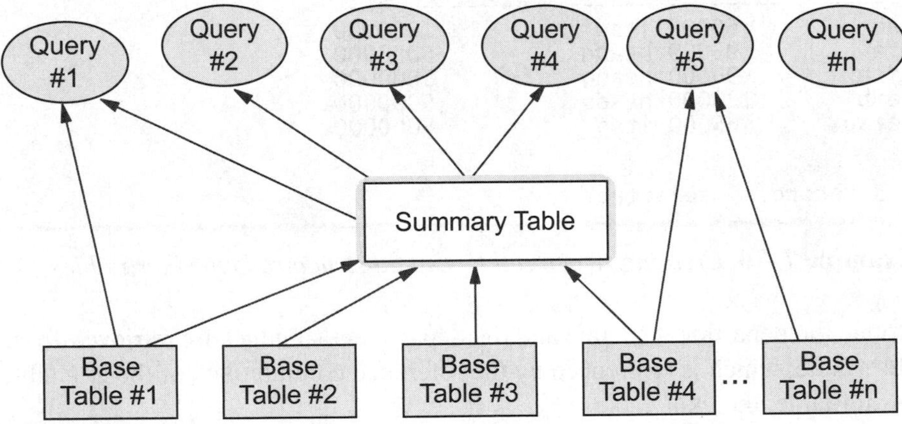

Figure 7–15 *Summary table concept*

DB2 *Note*

Note: Summary tables are only accessed for dynamic SQL.

Creating a Summary Table

A summary table can be created by a CREATE TABLE statement. Example 7–77 shows the CREATE TABLE statement to create a summary table.

```
CREATE SUMMARY TABLE DEPT_GROUP
 AS (SELECT WORKDEPT,
            SUM(SALARY) AS SALARY,
                SUM(BONUS) AS BONUS
        FROM EMPLOYEE GROUP BY WORKDEPT)
      DATA INITIALLY DEFERRED
      REFRESH DEFERRED;
```

Example 7–77 *Create a summary table*

In this example, the keyword SUMMARY is used to indicate that this is a summary table; however, you can omit this keyword if you so choose. The keyword AS followed by a fullselect means that this is a summary table. The column attributes of the summary table are defined by this fullselect.

There are two options to update the data in the summary table, deferred refresh and immediate refresh. This is specified in the CREATE TABLE statement using REFRESH DEFERRED or REFRESH IMMEDIATE. The last example uses REFRESH DEFERRED, which means that the data in the table is refreshed when a REFRESH TABLE statement is executed. The data in the summary table reflects the result of the query at the time the REFRESH TABLE statement is executed. REFRESH IMMEDIATE means that the changes made to the underlying tables as part of a DELETE, INSERT, or UPDATE statement are cascaded to the summary table immediately.

The DATA INITIALLY DEFERRED clause indicates that data is not inserted into the table as part of the CREATE TABLE statement, and the REFRESH TABLE statement is the only way to populate the table.

DB2 *Note*

After creating a summary table, the table is in check-pending state. The REFRESH TABLE statement or SET INTEGRITY statement with the IMMEDIATE CHECKED option enables you to get out of this check-pending state.

Example 7–78 shows a CREATE TABLE statement to create a summary table with the REFRESH IMMEDIATE option.

```
CREATE SUMMARY TABLE DEPT_GROUP2
 AS (SELECT WORKDEPT,
            COUNT(*) AS RECCOUNT,
                SUM(SALARY) AS SALARY,
                SUM(BONUS) AS BONUS
         FROM EMPLOYEE GROUP BY WORKDEPT)
      DATA INITIALLY DEFERRED
      REFRESH IMMEDIATE;
```

Example 7–78 *Create a Summary table with the REFRESH IMMEDIATE option*

DB2 *Note*

The summary table cannot be directly modified by the INSERT, UPDATE, or DELETE statements.

CURRENT REFRESH AGE Special Register

The CURRENT REFRESH AGE special register specifies a timestamp duration value with a data type of DECIMAL(20,6). This duration is the maximum duration, since a REFRESH TABLE statement has been processed on a deferred refresh summary table. It determines if a summary table can be used to optimize the processing of a query. The SET CURRENT REFRESH AGE statement enables you to change the value of the CURRENT REFRESH AGE special register. The value must be 0 or 99999999999999 (9999 years, 99 months, 99 days, 99 hours, 99 minutes, and 99 seconds).

- Zero (0) means that only summary tables defined with REFRESH IMMEDIATE may be used to optimize the processing of a query.
- 99999999999999 means that any summary tables defined with REFRESH DEFERRED or REFRESH IMMEDIATE may be used to optimize the processing of a query.

DB2 *Note*

Note: The keyword ANY is shorthand for 99999999999999.

The initial value of CURRENT REFRESH AGE is 0. If you want the DB2 optimizer to consider using the deferred refresh summary tables, you must set the CURRENT REFRESH AGE special register to ANY or 99999999999999 as follows in Example 7–79:

```
SET CURRENT REFRESH AGE ANY;
```

Example 7–79 *REFRESH AGE*

Considerations of Using Summary Tables

There are some considerations when you create a summary table. The fullselect of the summary table definition must not have following:

- References to a view (see *DB2 SQL Reference SQL Reference* for details), summary table, or typed table in any FROM clause
- Expressions that are a reference type or DATALINK type (or a distinct type based on these types)
- Functions that have an external action
- Functions that depend on physical characteristics (e.g., NODENUMBER, PARTITION)
- Table or view references to system objects (explain tables also should not be specified)

Other considerations you should be aware of include:

- The summary table does not support IMPORT or LOAD.
- A unique index cannot be created on a summary table.
- If the summary table is specified in the ALTER TABLE statement, the ALTER is limited to activating not logged initially, changing pctfree, locksize, append, or volatile.

Additionally, if you create a summary table with the REFRESH IMMEDIATE option, the following considerations exist:

- The fullselect in the summary table definition must be a sub-select and cannot include:
  - — Functions that are not deterministic
  - — Scalar full selects
  - — Predicates with full selects
  - — Special registers
- A GROUP BY clause must be included in the sub-select.
- The select list must have a COUNT(*) function (or COUNT_BIG(*)) and no DISTINCT.
- Only SUM (of not nullable columns), COUNT, or COUNT_BIG column functions are allowed in the select list (without DISTINCT), and other select list items must be included in the GROUP BY clause.
- All GROUP BY items must be included in the select list.
- No grouping sets are allowed (including CUBE and ROLLUP) or grouping on constants.
- A HAVING clause is not allowed.

System Catalog Information for Summary Tables

The system catalog tables maintain the information about summary tables as well as the usual tables. Here is the output of the `LIST TABLES` command (Example 7–80). The value `S` in the type column indicates that this table is a summary table.

```
TABLE/VIEW      SCHEMA      TYPE  CREATION TIME
--------------- ----------- ----- --------------------------
DEPT_GROUP      AUSRES33    S     1999-04-19-16.21.48.826001
DEPT_GROUP2     AUSRES33    S     1999-04-19-16.21.48.756001
```

Example 7–80 *Output of LIST TABLES command showing summary tables*

User-maintained Summary Tables

There may be circumstances where a user is already generating summarization data. For example, a nightly batch job may be run that calculates sales by store, region, and country before loading the raw data into the database tables. In this case, it might be to their advantage to take this summarization data and place it into a user-defined summary table.

A user-maintained summary table is no different than a system summary table other than the creation and loading of the summary table is under user control. Since the data is generated by the user, DB2 does not refresh this information, so the user must update the table on a periodic basis. In addition, DB2 will assume that information within the summary table is correct and may produce incorrect results if the user has not loaded valid information into the table.

To create a user-maintained summary table, the `CREATE SUMMARY TABLE` command must have the `MAINTAINED BY USER` option added to the end. The example found in Example 7–77 is changed to a user-maintained summary table in the following example (Example 7–81):

```
CREATE SUMMARY TABLE UMST_EMPLOYEE AS
  (
  SELECT
    WORKDEPT,
    COUNT(*) AS EMPCOUNT,
    SUM(SALARY) AS TOTSALARY,
    SUM(BONUS) AS TOTBONUS
  FROM EMPLOYEE GROUP BY WORKDEPT
  )
  DATA INITIALLY DEFERRED REFRESH DEFERRED
  MAINTAINED BY USER;
```

Example 7–81 *Create a Summary table that is user-defined*

Once the table is created, the user can load data into this table from their application and then have DB2 optimize queries based on this information. Before loading the data, the summary table must be taken out of the check pending state (Example 7–82):

```
SET INTEGRITY FOR UMST_EMPLOYEE ALL IMMEDIATE UNCHECKED;
```

Example 7–82 *Reset of check pending condition*

After the CHECK INTEGRITY command has been issued, the user can use insert statements to load this table. For instance, the following SQL can be used to load this summary table with current information from the EMPLOYEE table (Example 7–83):

```
INSERT INTO UMST_EMPLOYEE
  SELECT * FROM
    (
    SELECT WORKDEPT, COUNT(*), SUM(SALARY), SUM(BONUS)
      FROM EMPLOYEE
    GROUP BY WORKDEPT
    ) AS T;
```

Example 7–83 *Loading the summary table*

The user may also have to set the special optimization register to prevent other summary tables to be used when loading this table. Prior to running this insert statement, the user should issue the following command (Example 7–84):

```
SET CURRENT MAINTAINED TABLE TYPES FOR OPTIMIZATION = NONE;
```

Example 7–84 *Optimization setting*

Setting the register to NONE will prevent any summary tables from being used during SQL processing. However, this value should be set back on if you want to take advantage of the summary tables that have been created. This special register can contain one of four values:

- ALL — Specifies that all possible types of maintained tables controlled by this special register are to be considered when optimizing dynamic SQL queries.
- NONE — Specifies that none of the object types that are controlled by this special register are to be considered when optimizing the processing of dynamic SQL queries.
- SYSTEM — Specifies that system-maintained refresh-deferred materialized query tables can be considered to optimize the processing of dynamic SQL queries. (Immediate materialized query tables are always available.)

- USER — Specifies that user-maintained refresh-deferred materialized query tables can be considered to optimize the processing of dynamic SQL queries.

In addition to this optimization register, the user will also have to set the CURRENT REFERESH AGE register to ensure DB2 will use these user-maintained summary tables (Example 7–85). If this value is set to zero, DB2 will only consider summary tables that are automatically maintain by the system.

```
SET CURRENT REFRESH AGE ANY;
```

Example 7–85 *Current refresh age*

Materialized Query Tables

A materialized query table is a table whose definition is based on the result of a query, and whose data is in the form of precomputed results that are taken from one or more tables on which the materialized query table definition is based. The definition of a materialized query table contains joins, functions, and other SQL elements that are not allowed in automatic summary tables.

The following two SQL statements highlight the difference between an automatic summary table and a material query table. The first example (Example 7–86) is a typical summary table that contains summarization using a GROUP BY clause. The second example (Example 7–87) contains a join between two tables and does not have any summarization or grouping associated with it. Both tables need to be refreshed before they can be used in queries.

```
CREATE SUMMARY TABLE DEPT_GROUP
  AS (SELECT WORKDEPT,
             SUM(SALARY) AS SALARY,
                 SUM(BONUS) AS BONUS
         FROM EMPLOYEE GROUP BY WORKDEPT)
      DATA INITIALLY DEFERRED
      REFRESH DEFERRED;
```

Example 7–86 *Automatic summary table*

```
CREATE SUMMARY TABLE EPLUSD
  AS (SELECT EMPNO, LASTNAME, DEPT, DEPTNAME
      FROM EMPLOYEE E, DEPARTMENT D
      WHERE E.DEPT = D.DEPTNO)
      DATA INITIALLY DEFERRED
  REFRESH DEFERRED;
```

Example 7–87 *Materialized query table*

The materialized query table could be used to pre-join tables together. This allows the optimizer to bypass joining tables together if the materialized table contains the columns and rows that it needs.

MQT Design

To better support MQT design and query troubleshooting, the DB2 explain output indicates which MQTs were considered (but not chosen) by the optimizer for a query access plan. Previously, DB2 gives no indication if an MQT was even considered during the compilation process, which makes it extremely difficult for users to figure out if they have defined the proper MQT or if it is a configuration or costing issue. The explain output now provides information on which MQTs were considered, the one that was ultimately used, and the reason why the others were rejected.

As a query goes through the optimization process, wherever a particular MQT is skipped from usage, its name is logged and diagnostic messages will be logged into the explain tables. The mechanism for generating these high-level diagnostic messages are in the EXPLAIN tool. Two tables that were added in DB2 Version 8.2.2, EXPLAIN_DIAGNOSTICS and EXPLAIN_DIAGNOSTICS_DATA tables, are populated with these error messages, and the DB2 table function EXPLAIN_GET_MSGS can be issued to retrieve the diagnostic information from them.

The format of the EXPLAIN_GET_MSGS table function is shown in Example 7–88:

```
CREATE FUNCTION EXPLAIN_GET_MSGS
  (
  EXPLAIN_REQUESTER VARCHAR(128),
  EXPLAIN_TIME      TIMESTAMP,
  SOURCE_NAME       VARCHAR(128),
  SOURCE_SCHEMA     VARCHAR(128),
  SOURCE_VERSION    VARCHAR(64),
  EXPLAIN_LEVEL     CHAR(1),
  STMTNO            INTEGER,
  SECTNO            INTEGER,
  INLOCALE          VARCHAR(33)
  )
RETURNS
  (
  EXPLAIN_REQUESTER, EXPLAIN_TIME, SOURCE_NAME, SOURCE_SCHEMA,
  SOURCE_VERSION, EXPLAIN_LEVEL, STMTNO, SECTNO, DIAGNOSTIC_ID,
  LOCALE, MSG
  );
```

Example 7–88 *Explain_Get_Msgs definition*

The EXPLAIN_GET_MSGS table function takes as arguments the statement that you want diagnostic information on and returns all of the explain details as rows of data. If you keep explain information on multiple statements in the database then you will need to be very specific in the request to return information. However, if the explain is only done to diagnose information on a particular statement, it may be easier to delete all of the explain statements beforehand and just issue the function with NULL arguments (Example 7–89):

```
DELETE FROM EXPLAIN_INSTANCE;
EXPLAIN PLAN FOR
  SELECT C1, COUNT(*) FROM T1 WHERE C2 >= 10  GROUP BY C1;
SELECT * FROM
  TABLE(EXPLAIN_GET_MSGS(CAST (NULL AS VARCHAR(128),
                         CAST (NULL AS TIMESTAMP),
                         CAST (NULL AS VARCHAR(128)),
                         CAST (NULL AS VARCHAR(128)),...) AS T;
```

Example 7–89 *Retrieving messages*

Unfortunately, each argument to the EXPLAIN_GET_MSGS function must be cast to the proper data type in order for the function to perform properly. It may be more convenient to create a view on this function so that the implementation details are hidden from the user (Example 7–90).

```
CREATE VIEW MQT_MESSAGES AS
  (
  SELECT MSG FROM
    TABLE(
      EXPLAIN_GET_MSGS( CAST (NULL AS VARCHAR(128)),
                        CAST (NULL AS TIMESTAMP),
                        CAST (NULL AS VARCHAR(128)),
                        CAST (NULL AS VARCHAR(128)),
                        CAST (NULL AS VARCHAR(64)),
                        CAST (NULL AS CHAR(1)),
                        CAST (NULL AS INTEGER),
                        CAST (NULL AS INTEGER),
                        CAST (NULL AS VARCHAR(33))
                      )
      ) AS T
  );
```

Example 7–90 *Creating a view to hide complexity*

This view returns the diagnostic information associated with all of the statements in the explain tables. Since this function returns information on all statements, the explain information should be deleted before issuing the function.

```
DELETE FROM EXPLAIN_INSTANCE;
EXPLAIN PLAN FOR
  SELECT C1, COUNT(*) FROM T1 WHERE C2 >= 10  GROUP BY C1;
SELECT * FROM MQT_MESSAGES;
```

Example 7–91 *Diagnostic output*

The data that is returned from Example 7–91 includes information on:

- Status of statistics for the table (i.e., statistics may be out of date).

  EXP0021W Table column has no statistics. The column "C1" of table "BAKLARZ "."T1" has not had runstats run on it. This can lead to poor cardinality and predicate filtering estimates.

- Optimization settings that might affect MQT usage.

  EXP0054W The following REFRESH DEFERRED MQT was not considered for rewrite matching because the CURRENT REFRESH AGE register was not set to ANY: "BAKLARZ "."MQT1".

- MQTs that were considered for running the query.

  EXP0148W The following MQT or statistical view was considered in query matching: "BAKLARZ "."MQT3".

- MQTs that were eliminated from consideration, and the reasons why.

  EXP0073W The following MQT or statistical view was not eligible because one or more data filtering predicates from the query could not be matched with the MQT: "BAKLARZ "."MQT3".

- The final MQT that was used to satisfy the query.

  EXP0149W The following MQT was used (from those considered) in query matching: "BAKLARZ "."MQT1".

There are considerably more messages that can be generated based on the type of decision the optimizer made on using or excluding a particular MQT. The wealth of information that is returned as part of the explain statement can now be used to manage the MQTs that are built and used in the system. This will lead to a better understanding of the use of MQTs by the optimizer and help eliminate any MQTs that are not being used on a regular basis.

Functional Dependencies

Functional dependencies are used for improving query performance. Defining a functional dependency can allow DB2 to route a query to a particular summary table which may not have been considered previously.

Functional dependencies can be used for query rewrite but are not enforced by database manager. Functional dependencies can be defined in CREATE TABLE statement or ALTER TABLE statement through the check constraint syntax.

For instance, Example 7–92 demonstrates the use of a functional dependency that ties together the SMU_DESC and SMU_CODE columns.

```
CREATE TABLE PRODUCT
  (
  PROD_KEY CHAR(15) NOT NULL,
  SMU_CODE VARCHAR(6) NOT NULL,
  SMU_DESC VARCHAR(35),
  PROD_DESC VARCHAR(30),
  CONSTRAINT FD1 CHECK (SMU_DESC DETERMINED BY SMU_CODE)
    NOT ENFORCED ENABLE QUERY OPTIMIZATION
  );
```

Example 7–92 *Functional dependency*

DB2 will recognize that the two columns are related and may be able to improve the query rewrite or use a summary table that contains only one of the columns.

Statistical Views

DB2 system catalog tables contain critical statistical information about columns, tables, and indexes. Whenever a dynamic SQL statement is issued, the DB2 optimizer reads the system catalog tables to review the available indexes, the size of each table, the characteristics of a column, and other information to select the best access path for executing the query. This becomes more crucial as the complexity of the SQL statements increases. Choosing the correct access path can reduce the response time considerably.

Statistical views was introduced in DB2 to allow the optimizer to compute more accurate cardinality estimates for queries in which the view definition overlaps with the query definition. This feature provides the optimizer with accurate statistics for determining cardinality estimates for queries with complex sets of predicates involving one or more tables.

Examples of queries that would benefit from statistical views include:

- Correlated attributes

  These are columns within the same table that are correlated to one another. For instance, `CITY` and `ZIPCODE`.

- Expression Results

  Calculations in a query may benefit from additional statistics.

- Multiple Tables

  Statistics are usually based on individual tables. A statistical view can be used to generate statistics on tables that are joined together.

A statistical view does not need to be identical to a query in order to be used. In many cases, the view's statistics can be used if its definition overlaps the query.

Enabling Statistical Views

Statistical views are not enabled by default in DB2 9. The DBA must set the DB2 variable DB2_STATVIEW to YES in order for the RUNSTAT utility and the optimizer to allow the use of statistical views (Example 7–93).

```
db2set DB2_STATVIEW=YES
```

Example 7–93 *Turning on Statistical views*

If the DB2_STATVIEW setting has not been set to YES, DB2 will return a syntax error on the commands rather than a message suggesting that statistical views have not been turned on (Example 7–94). The message is misleading!

```
ALTER VIEW EMP_DEPT ENABLE QUERY OPTIMIZATION;

SQL0104N  An unexpected token "ENABLE" was found following
 "ALTER VIEW <view-name>".  Expected tokens may include:
 "ALTER SCOPE".  SQLSTATE=42601
```

Example 7–94 *Alter table error*

Advanced SQL

Statistical View Example

A classic case of using statistical views occurs when two tables are joined together and a number of columns are correlated. Statistics on any one of the tables will show that there are no columns related to one another. However, when the tables are combined, there are obvious correlations. In the SAMPLE database, there are two tables that are commonly joined together: the EMPLOYEE table and the DEPARTMENT table. The EMPLOYEE table includes a department number (WORKDEPT), while the DEPARTMENT table has a DEPTNO column. These two columns are joined together when a query is done that needs information on the employee along with the department that they work in. The following query retrieves a list of employees who work in the PLANNING department (Example 7–95):

```
SELECT EMPNO, DEPTNAME
  FROM DEPARTMENT, EMPLOYEE
WHERE
  DEPTNAME='PLANNING' AND WORKDEPT=DEPTNO;
```

Example 7–95 *Employees working in the Planning department*

The access plan in Figure 7–16 is created by DB2.

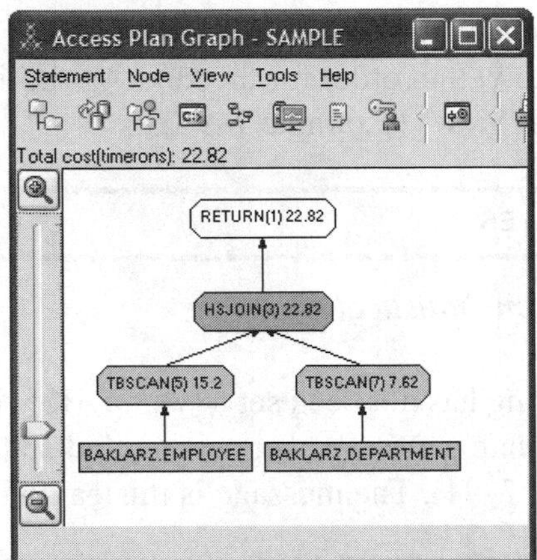

Figure 7–16 *Explain of two table join*

DB2 is scanning both tables and doing a hash-join to determine the final answer. The information that DB2 is missing from this query is that the name of the department (PLANNING) is directly correlated with the department number (DEPTNO). In order to give DB2 more information about this join, a view can be generated and statistics gathered for the join. The following view is created that closely mimics the query that was requested (Example 7–96):

```
CREATE VIEW EMP_DEPT AS
  (
  SELECT EMPNO, WORKDEPT, DEPTNAME, MGRNO
     FROM EMPLOYEE, DEPARTMENT
     WHERE WORKDEPT=DEPTNO
  );
```

Example 7–96 *Statistical view on the join*

Note that this view does not specifically state what department name is being searched for. In order to use statistical views, the DB2_STATVIEW variable must be set and the view altered to enable query optimization (Example 7–97):

```
ALTER VIEW EMP_DEPT ENABLE QUERY OPTIMIZATION;
```

Example 7–97 *Enabling query optimization*

Once the view has been altered to enable query optimization, the statistics for that view must be updated (Example 7–98).

```
RUNSTATS ON TABLE BAKLARZ.EMP_DEPT WITH DISTRIBUTION;
```

Example 7–98 *Updating statistics on the view*

Rerunning the identical query results in the access path found in Figure 7–17.

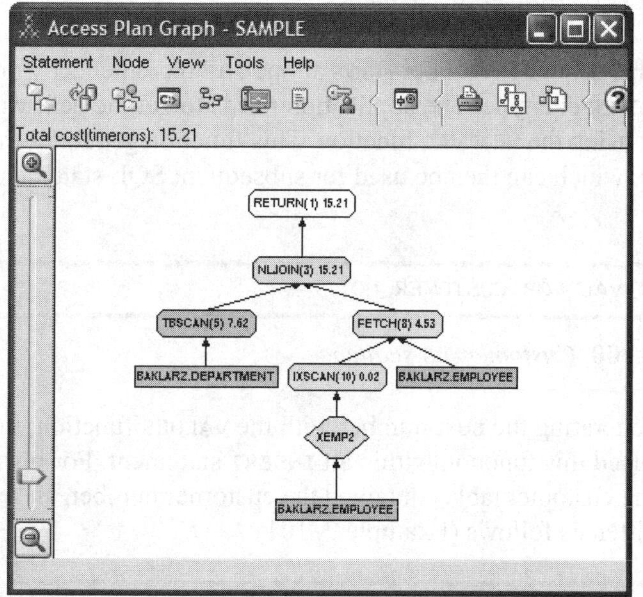

Figure 7–17 *Updated explain graph*

DB2 now takes advantage of an index that is available on the EMPLOYEE table to speed up the search for records. Even this simple example illustrates how DB2 can use additional statistics on a view to improve query performance.

Sequences

Many applications that are written require the use of sequence numbers to track invoice numbers, customer numbers, and other objects which get incremented by one whenever a new item is required. DB2 can autoincrement values in a table through the use of identity columns (See "Identity Column" on page 256.) Although this technique works well for individual tables, it may not be the most convenient way of generating unique values that need to be used across multiple tables.

The SEQUENCE object in DB2 lets the DBA or developer create a value that gets incremented under programmer control and can be used across many different tables. Example 7–99 shows a sample sequence number being created for customer numbers using a datatype of integer:

```
CREATE SEQUENCE CUSTOMER_NO AS INTEGER;
```

Example 7–99 *Customer_no sequence*

By default this sequence number starts at one and increments by one at a time and is of an INTEGER datatype. The application needs to get the next value in the sequence by using the NEXTVAL function. This function generates the next value for the sequence which can then be used for subsequent SQL statements (Example 7–100):

```
VALUES NEXTVAL FOR CUSTOMER_NO;
```

Example 7–100 *Customer_no sequence*

Instead of generating the next number with the VALUES function, the programmer could have used this function within an INSERT statement. For instance, if the first column of the customer table contained the customer number, an INSERT statement could be written as follows (Example 7–101):

```
INSERT INTO CUSTOMERS VALUE
  (NEXTVAL FOR CUSTOMER_NO, 'BERTS HOUSE OF MOVING', ...);
```

Example 7–101 *Insert with a sequence number*

If the sequence number needs to be used for inserts into other tables, the PREVVAL function can be used to retrieve the previously generated value. For instance, if the customer number we just created needs to be used for a subsequent invoice record, the SQL would include the PREVVAL function (Example 7–102):

```
INSERT INTO INVOICES
  (34,PREVVAL FOR CUSTOMER_NO, 234.44, ...);
```

Example 7–102 *Subsequent insert with PREVVAL*

The PREVVAL function can be used multiple times within the application and it will only return the last value generated by that application. It may be possible that subsequent transactions have already incremented the sequence to another value, but the user will always see the last number that they generated.

In addition to being simple to set up and create, the SEQUENCE object has a variety of additional options that allows the user more flexibility in generating the values:

- use a different datatype (SMALLINT, INTEGER, BIGINT, DECIMAL)
- change starting values (START WITH)
- change the sequence increment, including specifying increasing or decreasing values (INCREMENT BY)
- set minimum and maximum values where the sequence would stop (MAXVALUE/MINVALUE)
- allow wrapping of values so that sequences can start over again (CYCLE/NO CYCLE)
- allow caching of sequences to minimize catalog contention (CACHE/NO CACHE)

Even after the sequence has been generated, many of these values can be ALTERED by the user. For instance, the DBA may want to set a different starting value depending on the day of the week.

The one option that a DBA should be aware of is the caching value. This value tells DB2 how many sequence values should be generated by the system before going back to the DB2 catalog to generate another set of sequences. The CACHE value is set to a value of 20 if the user does not specify it at creation time. DB2 will automatically generate 20 sequential values in memory (1, 2,..., 20) when it first starts up the database. Whenever a new sequence number is required, this memory cache of values is used to return the next value to the user. Once this cache of values is used up, DB2 will generate the next twenty values (21, 21,..., 40).

By implementing caching of sequence numbers in this manner, DB2 does not have to continually go to the catalog tables to get the next value. This will reduce the overhead associated with retrieving sequence numbers, but it also leads to possible gaps in the sequences if a system failure occurs, or if the system is shut down at the end of the day. For instance, if the DBA decided to set the sequence cache to 100, DB2 will cache 100 values of these numbers and also set the system catalog to show that the next sequence of values should begin at 200. In the event that the database is shut down, the next set of sequence numbers will begin at 200. The numbers that were generated from 100 to 199 will be lost from the set of sequences if they were not used. If gaps in generated values cannot be tolerated in the application, the DBA will need to set the caching value to NO CACHE at the expense of higher system overhead.

Advanced Functions

DB2 contains a large number of built-in column and scalar functions that can add flexibility to the type of calculations the user can perform against the data. These functions can be broken down into the following categories:

- Trigonometric Functions (COS, SIN, TAN, COT, TANH, COSH, SINH, ATAH, ATAN2.)
- Math Functions (INTEGER, FLOOR, CEILING, TRUNC, SQRT, LN, EXP)
- String Functions (RTRIM, LTRIM, INSTR, TRANSLATE, REPEAT, REPLACE, CONCAT, SUBSTR, LENGTH, LOWER, UPPER)
- Statistical Functions (CORRELATION, STDDEV, VARIANCE)
- Date Functions (DATE, TIME, TO_CHAR, TO_DATE, DAYNAME, DAYOFWEEK)
- Logic Functions (COALESCE, NULLIF)
- Speciality Functions (MQPUBLISH, MQREAD, ENCRYPT, REC2XML)

There are many more functions available within DB2 that a user can take advantage of. For a complete listing of available functions, refer to the *DB2 SQL Reference*. Some specific functions that have been introduced over the last few releases of DB2 are described below.

ADMIN_CMD

DB2 contains a feature that allows administrators to run commands from an SQL interface. By using a new stored procedure named ADMIN_CMD you can run a set of administrative commands through SQL rather than using the DB2 CLP, or writing an application. This type of interface is also much more convenient for Java developers who no longer have to interface with C libraries in order to execute administrative commands against the database.

The list of administrative commands that are supported continues to grow from one DB2 release to another. The following list contains some of the functions that can be performed against a database.

- UPDATE DATABASE CONFIG
- RUNSTATS
- REORG TABLE/INDEX
- EXPORT/IMPORT/LOAD
- UPDATE DBM CFG
- UPDATE HISTORY
- QUIESCE TABLESPACES FOR TABLE
- FORCE APPLICATIONS
- DESCRIBE TABLE/INDEX/DATA PARTITION
- REDISTRIBUTE

- BACKUP/QUIESCE/UNQUIESCE DATABASE
- AUTOCONFIGURE
- PRUNE/UPDATE HISTORY

The general format of the ADMIN_CMD is shown in Example 7–103. This example shows a portion of the columns that the ADMIN_CMD returns when describing the columns in a select statement.

```
CALL ADMIN_CMD('DESCRIBE SELECT * FROM DEPT');

SQLTYPE_ID SQLTYPE   SQLLENGTH SQLSCALE SQLNAME_DATA SQLNAME_LENGTH
---------- --------- --------- -------- ------------ --------------
       452 CHARACTER         3        0 DEPTNO                    6
       448 VARCHAR          36        0 DEPTNAME                  8
       453 CHARACTER         6        0 MGRNO                     5
       452 CHARACTER         3        0 ADMRDEPT                  8
       453 CHARACTER        16        0 LOCATION                  8

  5 record(s) selected.
```

Example 7–103 *ADMIN_CMD results*

SQLERRM

SQLERRM is a scalar function that returns the message associated with a specific error code. Although considered an application development enhancement, this function is useful for DBAs to use to see the text associated with an error message.

The SQLERRM function has two forms:

- SQLERRM(SQLCODE)

  The short form takes the SQLCODE and returns the short message.

- SQLERRM(MESSAGEID, TOKENS, TOKEN_DELIMITER, LOCALE, SHORTMSG)

  The long form takes a locale input and returns the message in the specified locale if the locale is supported at the server. This form of the command can return either a short or long version of the message.

Example 7–104 shows the short error message for an SQL0526N (or -526) error.

```
VALUES SQLERRM(-526);

1
-------------------------------------------------------------
SQL0526N  The requested function does not apply to
  declared temporary tables.

  1 RECORD(S) SELECTED.
```

Example 7–104 *SQLERRM short message output*

The long form is where MESSAGEID is the SQL error message, TOKENS are those tokens that are passed to the error message, TOKEN_DELIMITER is the delimiter used in the token string, LOCALE is the language to use to print out the error message in, and SHORTMSG is 1 if you just want a short text description and 0 if you want the entire error message.

Example 7–105 shows the long format for the error message for an SQL0551N error.

```
VALUES
  SQLERRM('SQL551','AYYANG,UPDATE,SYSCAT.TABLES',',','EN_EN',1);

1
-------------------------------------------------------------
SQL0551N  "AYYANG" does not have the privilege to perform
  operation "UPDATE" on object "SYSCAT.TABLES".

  1 RECORD(S) SELECTED.
```

Example 7–105 *SQLERRM long message output*

MULTIPLY_ALT

The rules of decimal multiplication can cause problems when dealing with extremely large values. This is primarily due to the multiplication precision rules that have been developed over the years. The following SQL calculation highlights the problem with decimal math (Example 7–106):

```
VALUES 1234567890.0000000 * 1234567890.0000000;

SQL0802N  Arithmetic overflow or other arithmetic exception
 OCCURRED. SQLSTATE=22003
```

Example 7–106 *Large number multiplication*

If the decimal values had not been included in the calculation, DB2 would have returned a valid result (Example 7–107):

```
VALUES 1234567890.0 * 1234567890.0;

1
-------------------------
  1524157875019052100.00
```

Example 7–107 *Successful multiplication*

This bizarre behavior is due to the rules of decimal math. A calculation using decimal math uses the following rule to determine the number of significant digits and decimal places, where p is the precision of the number and s is the scale:

- Precision = min(31, p^1+p^2)
- Scale = min(31, s^1+s^2)

In our first example, the precision of both numbers was 17.7 (seventeen digits of precision with 7 decimal places). The rule would tell us that the final result should contain the minimum of (31, 17+17) = 31 digits of precision and at least (31, 7+7) = 14 digits in the scale (numbers after the decimal place). If we set aside 14 digits for the scale, this will only leave 17 digits for the significant part. The answer (Figure 7–107) contains 19 significant digits, so the number could not be placed into a normal numeric field. The only way to get around this limitation was to cast the values into floating point numbers, but this could result in a loss of precision.

The alternative way of doing decimal multiplication is also available in DB2. Instead of using the standard multiplication operator, the MULTIPLY_ALT function could be used instead to maintain the significant digit precision and limit the number of digits in the fractional portion. The original calculation in Example 7–106 can now be done using this new function (Example 7–108):

```
VALUES MULTIPLY_ALT(1234567890.0000000,1234567890.0000000);

1
---------------------------------
  1524157875019052100.00000000000
```

Example 7–108 *Successful multiplication using Multiply_Alt*

The decimal portion of the number is truncated, with the scale being reduced to accommodate the more significant digits. This function should be considered for any decimal multiplication where the scale may force arithmetic overflow situations.

SNAPSHOT Table Functions

DB2 has a number of table functions that return data on internal objects that are normally only accessible via an API call. The advantage of using SQL to retrieve this information is that scripts can be written to extract this information rather than writing C++ programs to do the same thing. In addition, Java developers can also take advantage of these SQL calls rather than having to link C routines into their applications.

These snapshot functions return information on a variety of objects within DB2 (Table 7–1):

Table 7–1 *Snapshot Functions*

Function	Purpose
SNAPSHOT_AGENT	The SNAPSHOT_AGENT function returns information about agents from an application snapshot.
SNAPSHOT_APPL	The SNAPSHOT_APPL function returns general information from an application snapshot.
SNAPSHOT_APPL_INFO	The SNAPSHOT_APPL_INFO function returns general information from an application snapshot.
SNAPSHOT_BP	The SNAPSHOT_BP function returns information from a buffer pool snapshot.
SNAPSHOT_CONTAINER	The SNAPSHOT_CONTAINER function returns container configuration information from a table space snapshot.
SNAPSHOT_DATABASE	The SNAPSHOT_DATABASE function returns information from a database snapshot.
SNAPSHOT_DBM	The SNAPSHOT_DBM function returns information from a snapshot of the DB2 database manager.
SNAPSHOT_DYN_SQL	The SNAPSHOT_DYN_SQL function returns information from a dynamic SQL snapshot. It replaces the SQLCACHE_SNAPSHOT function, which is still available for compatibility reasons.
SNAPSHOT_FCM	The SNAPSHOT_FCM function returns database manager level information regarding the fast communication manager (FCM).
SNAPSHOT_FCMPARTITION	The SNAPSHOT_FCMPARTITION function returns information from a snapshot of the fast communication manager in the database manager.
SNAPSHOT_LOCK	The SNAPSHOT_LOCK function returns information from a lock snapshot.
SNAPSHOT_LOCKWAIT	The SNAPSHOT_LOCKWAIT function returns lock waits information from an application snapshot.
SNAPSHOT_QUIESCERS	The SNAPSHOT_QUIESCERS function returns information about agents that are trying to quiesce the database.
SNAPSHOT_RANGES	The SNAPSHOT_RANGES function returns information from a range snapshot.

Table 7–1 *Snapshot Functions*

Function	Purpose
SNAPSHOT_STATEMENT	The SNAPSHOT_STATEMENT function returns information about statements from an application snapshot.
SNAPSHOT_SUBSECT	The SNAPSHOT_SUBSECT function returns information about subsections of access plans from an application snapshot.
SNAPSHOT_SWITCHES	The SNAPSHOT_SWITCHES function returns information about the database snapshot switch state.
SNAPSHOT_TABLE	The SNAPSHOT_TABLE function returns activity information from a table snapshot.
SNAPSHOT_TBS	The SNAPSHOT_TBS function returns activity information from a table space snapshot.
SNAPSHOT_TBS_CFG	The SNAPSHOT_TBS_CFG function returns configuration information from a table space snapshot.
SQLCACHE_SNAPSHOT	The SQLCACHE_SNAPSHOT function returns the results of a snapshot of the DB2 dynamic SQL statement cache.

The general form of a snapshot function is (Example 7–109):

```
SELECT *
  FROM TABLE(SNAPSHOT_FUNCTION(DATABASE, PARTITION)) AS S;
```

Example 7–109 *General Snapshot function*

The SNAPSHOT_FUNCTION is replaced with the appropriate snapshot command, and the DATABASE field contains the name of the database you want the snapshot to be taken against. The partition should be set to -1 to return information for the current partition and -2 for all partitions. If this field is not included or set to null, the command will only work against the current partition.

A DBA may want to use these commands to monitor the status of various objects within DB2 from within a script. For instance, the following SQL will retrieve information on all table spaces in the SAMPLE database (Example 7–110).

```
SELECT TABLESPACE_ID, TABLESPACE_NAME, TOTAL_PAGES
  FROM TABLE(SNAPSHOT_CONTAINER('SAMPLE',-2)) AS S;

TABLESPACE_ID TABLESPACE_NAME                TOTAL_PAGES
------------- ------------------------------ -----------
            0 SYSCATSPACE                           3644
            1 TEMPSPACE1                               1
            2 USERSPACE1                            4150
            3 DB2DEMO                                  1
            4 TEMPSESSION                              1
            5 MDC                                    458
            6 ORVRTS                                 108
            8 Q2_2001                                 22
            9 Q3_2001                                 23
           10 Q1_2002                                  2
           11 Q4_2001                                 22

  11 RECORD(S) SELECTED.
```

Example 7–110 *Output from snapshot function*

DB2 *Note*

The SNAPSHOT functions were introduced in DB2 Version 8.1. The SQL reference manuals lists these functions, but more details on the use of snapshots and monitoring can be found in the *DB2 System Monitor Guide and Reference*.

MQSeries Functions

DB2 provides a set of MQSeries functions and a MQ-Assist wizard. The MQ-Assist wizard helps you to create a table function that reads from an MQSeries queue using the MQSeries user-defined functions. The wizard treats each MQ message as a delimited string, parses the string according to user specifications, and returns the result as a row of the table function. It also allows you to create a view on top of the table function.

A set of MQSeries functions are provided with DB2 to allow SQL statements to include messaging operations. This means that this support is available to applications written in any supported language, for example, C, Java, or SQL, using any of the database interfaces. This SQL may be used from other programming languages in all the standard ways.

The MQSeries Functions can be used in a wide variety of scenarios, including basic messaging, application connectivity, and data publication. These functions are described in the following table (Table 7–2).

Table 7–2 *MQSeries Functions*

Function	Purpose
MQPUBLISH	The MQPUBLISH function publishes data to MQSeries. This function requires the installation of either MQSeries Publish/Subscribe or MQSeries Integrator.
MQREAD	The MQREAD function returns a message from the MQSeries service. The message does not get removed from the queue using this function. The maximum length of the message is 4000 bytes.
MQREADCLOB	The MQREADCLOB function returns a message from the MQSeries service. The message does not get removed from the queue using this function. The maximum length of the message is 1M bytes.
MQREADALL MQREADALLCLOB	The MQREADALL function returns a table of all messages returned from the MQSeries service.
MQRECEIVE	The MQRECEIVE function returns a message from the MQSeries service. The receive function does remove the message from the queue. The maximum length of the message is 4000 bytes.
MQRECEIVECLOB	The MQRECEIVECLOB function returns a message from the MQSeries service. The receive function does remove the message from the queue. The maximum length of the message is 1M bytes.
MQRECEIVEALL MQRECEIVEALLCLOB	The MQRECEIVEALL function returns a table of all messages returned from the MQSeries service and removes all of the messages from the queue.
MQSEND	The MQSEND function sends the data to an MQSeries service.
MQSUBSCRIBE	The MQSUBSCRIBE function is used to register interest in MQSeries messages.
MQUNSUBSCRIBE	The MQUNSUBSCRIBE function is used to unregister an existing message subscription.

Health Snapshot Functions

DB2 provided access to health snapshot data via DB2 C APIs and the DB2 CLP. While this is useful, some high-level programming languages cannot use these APIs directly. These languages can use SQL, so DB2 also provides an SQL interface into this data via a UDF that is callable from the SQL API.

This new feature is an extension of the `GET HEALTH SNAPSHOT` monitor data. DB2 introduces twelve new table functions that can be used to retrieve health snapshot information for the DBM, DB, table spaces, and containers.

The implemented table functions call the db2GetSnapshot() API. These functions can be used in a partitioned environment as well using the "partition" input parameter. The functions will convert the self-defining data stream returned from the API into a virtual table for SQL manipulation.

For each tracked group (DBM, DB, table spaces, and containers) there are three categories of functions: `INFO`, `HI` (Health Indicator) and `HI_HIS` (Health Indicator HIStory). As a general rule of thumb:

- `INFO` captures the global information for the specific logical group (for example, the server instance name for DBM)
- `HI` contains the latest health indicator information
- `HI_HIS` contains the health indicator history information

You can use these health functions as follows (Example 7–111):

```
SELECT * FROM
  TABLE( HEALTHFUNCTION( [<DATABASE>,] <PARTITION> ))
    AS <ALIASNAME>
```

Example 7–111 *Health snapshot syntax*

The <partition> field has the following values:

- 1..n — partition number
- –1 — means currently connected partition
- –2 — means all partitions

The current list of supported health snapshot calls are listed in Table 7–3.

Table 7–3 *Health Snapshot Functions*

Function	Purpose
HEALTH_DBM_INFO	Returns information from a health snapshot of the DB2 database manager
HEALTH_DBM_HI	Returns health indicator information from a health snapshot of the DB2 database manager
HEALTH_DBM_HI_HIS	Returns health indicator history information from a health snapshot of the DB2 database manager.
HEALTH_DB_INFO	Returns information from a health snapshot of a database.
HEALTH_DB_HI	Returns health indicator information from a health snapshot of a database.
HEALTH_DB_HI_HIS	Returns health indicator history information from a health snapshot of a database.
HEALTH_TBS_INFO	Returns table space information from a health snapshot of a database.
HEALTH_TBS_HI	Returns health indicator information for table spaces from a health snapshot of a database.
HEALTH_TBS_HI_HIS	Returns health indicator history information for table spaces from a health snapshot of a database.
HEALTH_CONT_INFO	Returns container information from a health snapshot of a database.
HEALTH_CONT_HI	Returns health indicator information for containers from a health snapshot of a database.
HEALTH_CONT_HI_HIS	Returns health indicator history information for containers from a health snapshot of a database.

The following SQL statement will retrieve health information about the status of the SAMPLE database (Example 7–112):

```
SELECT SNAPSHOT_TIMESTAMP,
       DB_NAME,
       ROLLED_UP_ALERT_STATE_DETAIL
FROM TABLE(HEALTH_DB_INFO('SAMPLE',-2)) AS S;

SNAPSHOT_TIMESTAMP         DB_NAME ROLLED_UP_ALERT_STATE_DETAIL
-------------------------- ------- ----------------------------
2007-02-26-17.17.39.092429 SAMPLE  Attention

  1 RECORD(S) SELECTED.
```

Example 7–112 *Snapshot function results*

Advanced SQL

A DBA can use these health center snapshots to write scripts that check on the status of databases and send appropriate alerts or invoke corrective actions. This type of functionality is also available in the Health Center, but the ability to get information through SQL gives the user more flexibility in retrieving the information.

Unicode Functions

The current SQL functions in DB2 that deal with text strings work on a byte or double-byte basis and ignore character boundaries. This means that a function applied to a character string treats the character string as an uninterpreted sequence of bytes. This mode of operation works fine and will not accidentally split characters when applied to single byte data. However, for multi-byte code pages, programmers currently need to know the width of each character before they can properly execute any string-based operation such as substringing, so as not to accidentally truncate a valid double-byte character or emit an invalid double-byte character.

A series of new functions were created in DB2 to deal with double-byte characters properly. In order to use these functions, three different length units need to be defined:

- CODEUNITS16

  Functions that use CODEUNITS16 calculates the length of a string based on 16-bit UTF-16 code units. This format is used by many C compilers and it is represented with the WCHAR_T datatype. This is the format that is also used by Java to represent the CHAR datatype.

- CODEUNITS32

  Functions that use CODEUNITS32 calculate the length of a string based on 32-bit UTF-32 code units. This is useful when an application wants to process data in a simple fixed length format, and needs the same answer regardless of whether the character is a Unicode supplementary character or not.

- OCTETS

  Functions that use OCTETS calculates the length of a string as a number of bytes. This is useful for applications that are interested in allocation buffer space, or operations where simple byte processing is needed.

The default string length unit used by DB2 is dependent on the context in which the string length unit is used:

- Character String — the default string length unit is a byte (or octet).
- Graphic String — the default string length unit is two bytes. For ASCII and EBCDIC this corresponds to a double byte character. For Unicode, this corre-

sponds to a UTF-16 code point.

- Binary String — the default string length unit is a byte (or octet).

From an output perspective, the Unicode functions return exactly the same data type as the arguments, i.e., a character string if the input is a character string.

The functions that are described below use the following table which contains a single-byte column (NAME) and a double-byte column (NAMEG) (Example 7–113).

The name "Jürgen" appears to be six characters long. In a UTF-8 Unicode format (single-byte variable length), this character string actually takes up seven bytes. The characters "Jrgen" all occupy one byte position, while "ü" takes up two. If this was using UCS-2 Unicode format (double-byte fixed length), each character would take up exactly two bytes.

```
CREATE TABLE UNICODE_TEST
  (
  TYPE  CHAR(10) NOT NULL,
  NAME  VARCHAR(32) NOT NULL,
  NAMEG VARGRAPHIC(32) NOT NULL
  ) ;

INSERT INTO UNICODE_TEST VALUES
  ('UTF-8','JÜRGEN','JÜRGEN');
```

Example 7–113 *Unicode table*

CHARACTER_LENGTH, CHAR_LENGTH, LENGTH

CHARACTER_LENGTH returns the length of a character (UNICODE) string. The length of character and graphic strings includes trailing blanks and the length of binary strings includes binary zeroes. The length of varying-length strings is the actual length and not the maximum length.

Example 7–114 demonstrates the use of this function.

```
SELECT 'NAME CODEUNITS16',
  CHARACTER_LENGTH(NAME USING CODEUNITS16) FROM UNICODE_TEST
UNION ALL
SELECT 'NAME OCTETS',
  CHAR_LENGTH(NAME,OCTETS) FROM UNICODE_TEST
UNION ALL
SELECT 'NAMEG CODEUNITS16',
  CHARACTER_LENGTH(NAMEG USING CODEUNITS16) FROM UNICODE_TEST
UNION ALL
SELECT 'NAMEG OCTETS',
  CHAR_LENGTH(NAMEG,OCTETS) FROM UNICODE_TEST
ORDER BY 1;
```

Example 7–114 *CHARACTER_LENGTH function*

The output from these function calls are found in Example 7–115.

```
1                 2
----------------- -----------
NAME CODEUNITS16            6
NAME OCTETS                 7
NAMEG CODEUNITS16           6
NAMEG OCTETS               12

  4 RECORD(S) SELECTED.
```

Example 7–115 *Output from CHAR_LENGTH function*

Whether the string is in single-byte Unicode format (UTF-8) or in double-byte format (UCS-2), the size of the string is exactly 6 characters. However, looking at the actual byte length, the string is 7 bytes long using UTF-8 and 12 bytes with UCS-2.

LOCATE POSITION

The LOCATE function (and POSITION) returns the starting position of the first occurrence of one string (called the search-string) within another string (called the source-string).

If the search-string is not found and neither argument is null, the result is zero. If the search-string is found, the result is a number from 1 to the actual length of the source-string. If the optional start is specified, it indicates the character position in the source-string at which the search is to begin. An optional string unit can be specified to indicate in what units the start and result of the function are expressed.

In Example 7–116 the letter “ü” is found in exactly the same character position in both string representations.

```
SELECT
  LOCATE('ü',NAME) AS NAME_LOCATION,
  LOCATE('ü',NAMEG) AS NAMEG_LOCATION
FROM UNICODE_TEST;

NAME_LOCATION NAMEG_LOCATION
------------- --------------
            2              2

  1 RECORD(S) SELECTED.
```

Example 7–116 *LOCATE function*

OCTET_LENGTH

The OCTET_LENGTH function returns the length of expression in octets (bytes). The results in Example 7–117 are identical to the CHAR_LENGTH function using OCTETS as the length measure.

```
SELECT
  OCTET_LENGTH(NAME) AS NAME_LENGTH,
  OCTET_LENGTH(NAMEG) AS NAMEG_LENGTH
FROM UNICODE_TEST;

NAME_LENGTH NAMEG_LENGTH
----------- ------------
          7           12

  1 RECORD(S) SELECTED.
```

Example 7–117 *OCTET_LENGTH function results*

SUBSTRING Function

The SUBSTRING function returns a substring of a string. This function is similar to, but is not a synonym of, the existing SUBSTR scalar function. The original SUBSTR function is not sensitive to Unicode characters.

The SUBSTRING function takes four arguments:

- Expression — The string being searched
- Start — Start specifies the position within expression to be the first string length unit of the result
- Length — Length is an expression that specifies the length of the resulting substring
- Unit of length — Which type of length unit to use — OCTET, CODEUNITS16, CONDEUNITS32

Example 7–118 demonstrates the use of the SUBSTRING function.

```
SELECT
  SUBSTRING(NAME FROM 1 FOR 3 USING CODEUNITS16) AS STRING1,
  SUBSTRING(NAMEG,1,3,CODEUNITS16) AS STRING2
FROM UNICODE_TEST;

STRING1            STRING2
------------------ ----------------
Jür                Jür

  1 RECORD(S) SELECTED.
```

Example 7–118 *SUBSTRING function results*

Advanced SQL

STRIP/TRIM

The `STRIP` function removes blanks or another specified character from the end, the beginning, or both ends of a string-expression. The `STRIP` and `TRIM` functions are the same except that they differ in syntax (Example 7–119).

```
VALUES
 STRIP('    123    '),
 STRIP('    123    ',BOTH,' '),
 STRIP('    123    ',TRAILING),
 STRIP('    123    ',LEADING),
 STRIP('****123****',BOTH,'*');

1
-----------
123
123
    123
123
123

  5 record(s) selected.
```

Example 7–119 *STRIP function results*

The `TRIM` function (Example 7–120) produces output identical to Example 7–119.

```
VALUES
  TRIM(' ' FROM '    123    '),
  TRIM(BOTH ' ' FROM '    123    '),
  TRIM(LEADING FROM '    123    '),
  TRIM(TRAILING FROM '    123    '),
  TRIM(BOTH '*' FROM '****123****');
```

Example 7–120 *TRIM function results*

Summary

In this chapter we have talked about very powerful SQL features, such as triggers, recursive SQL, outer joins, the OLAP functions, case expressions, and a number of advanced external functions. These SQL features that DB2 provides can reduce the amount of application development time and maintenance.

We have also discussed user-defined structured types. This is one of the capabilities that DB2 provides to manage the Object Relational Model. As explained in Chapter 5, DB2 has implemented some Object Relational functions, Large Object (LOB) support, user-defined distinct types, user-defined functions, and so on. The concept of structured types and tables is very similar to object-oriented programming.

We have also introduced the summary table. The summary table is a physical table that contains precomputed results based on the data existing in the table, or tables, on which its definition is based. Many customers execute complex SQL to summarize the operational data for reporting or analysis purposes. These types of SQL often take a long time to provide the result. The summary table can be helpful in improving query performance.

In addition to many of the advanced SQL features, DB2 also provides support for MQSERIES integration, health monitoring snapshots, and table functions for querying the operational status of DB2.

CHAPTER 8

pureXML Storage Engine

- XML OVERVIEW
- XML DATA TYPE AND STORAGE
- XPATH AND XQUERY
- SQL/XML FUNCTIONS
- ADDITIONAL CONSIDERATIONS

*T*he DB2 9 pureXML technology unlocks the latent potential of XML data by providing simple efficient access to it with the same levels of security, integrity, and resiliency taken for granted with relational data, thereby allowing you to seamlessly integrate XML and relational data. DB2 9 stores XML data in a hierarchical structure that naturally reflects the structure of XML. This structure along with innovative indexing techniques allows DB2 to efficiently manage this data and eliminate the complex and time-consuming parsing typically required for XML. This chapter details the pureXML feature available in DB2 9, as well as the advantages it has over a data server environment.

pureXML Feature Pack

DB2 9 includes an optional add-on feature pack, called pureXML. For all editions of DB2 9, except DB2 9 Express - C, you have to purchase pureXML services in addition to a base data server license. You can learn all about the DB2 9 editions, their corresponding feature packs, and guidance on which edition to choose for your business on the IBM DB2 9 Web site. For this reason, and more, it's important to not only understand the technology that pureXML provides, but the alternative solutions available to justify its use.

Before pureXML: How XML is Traditionally Stored

pureXML technology is truly unique in the marketplace. To best understand how it's so unique, it's best to understand the traditional options for storing XML. Before pureXML, XML could be stored in an XML-only database, shredded into a relational format, stored in a relational database intact within a large object (LOB), or stored on a file system (unfortunately the most common format). These options, and their respective trade-offs, are shown below (Figure 8–1):

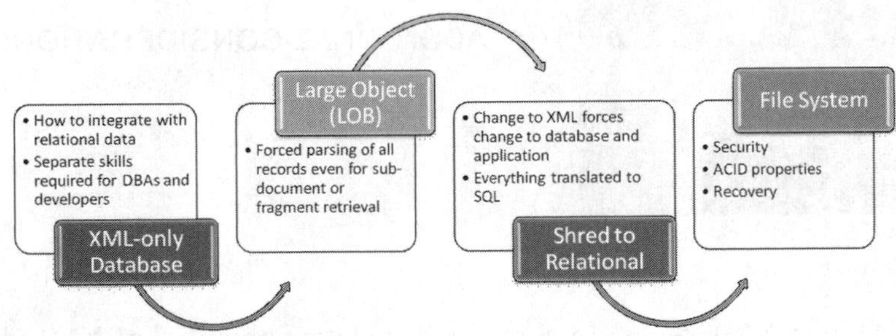

Figure 8–1 *XML Storage options*

The XML-only Database

For the longest time there have been a number of niche corporations that offer XML-only databases. While XML databases store XML as XML, their weakness is their only strength: they can only do that — store XML. In other words, they create a silo of information that ultimately requires more work and engineering to integrate with your relational systems. As more and more businesses move towards XML, challenges around integration with the relational data (which isn't going away; rather, it will be complimented by XML) arise. An XML-only database ultimately adds unforeseen costs to an environment because different programming models, administrative skills sets, servers, maintenance plans, and more are implicitly tagged to such a data storage solution. What's more, end users will experience different service levels since there is no capability to unify a service-level across separate servers. Database administrators (DBAs) live and breathe by their service-level agreements (SLAs), and the separation of data servers based on the semantic structure of the data is an obstacle to sustainable SLA adherence among other efficiencies.

Storing XML in a File System

Perhaps this most common way to store XML is on a file system, which is perhaps a risky practice considering today's regulatory compliance requirements.

The biggest problem associated with storing critical XML data on a file system is that file systems can't offer the Atomic, Consistent, Isolated, and Durable (ACID) properties of a database. Consider the following questions:

- How can file systems handle multiple changes that impact each other?
- What is the richness of the built-in recovery mechanism in case of a failure? (What about point-in-time recovery and recovery point objectives?)
- How do you handle complex relationships between your data artifacts in a heterogeneous environment?
- What type of facilities exist for access parallelism?
- Is there an abstracted data access language like XQuery or SQL?
- How is access to the same data handled?

Furthermore, storing your XML on a file system and then interacting with it from your application requires a lot of hand coding and is prone to errors. Quite simply, the decision to store critical XML data on a file system forces you to accept the same risks and issues associated with storing critical data in Excel spreadsheets, there is a serious issue associated with data integrity and quality.

How did all that XML get stored on a file system in the first place you may ask? Simple: application developers. If you're a DBA and you don't "sense" the need for XML, you need to talk to the application development team. You're bound to find many reasons why you need to take an active role in the decisions that affect the storage local of XML data in your enterprise.

XML Within a LOB in a Relational Database

One option provided by most of today's relational database vendors is to take the XML data, leave it as XML, and place it in a LOB column within a relational table. This solves a number of issues, yet it presents new ones too.

When the XML is placed in a LOB, you indeed unify XML and the relational data. And in most cases, you can take advantage of what XML was designed for — flexibility — because you are not tightly bound to a relational schema within the LOB container. The problem with storing XML data in a LOB is that you pay a massive performance price for this flexibility because you have to parse the XML when it is required for query.

It should be noted that this storage method may work well for large documents that are intended to be read as a whole (for example, a book chapter). However, by and large, XML is moving to facilitate transactional processing as evident by the growing number of standards that have emerged in support for this.

For example, the FiXML protocol is a standard XML-based markup language for financial transactions. Other vertically aligned XML-based markup languages include:

- Justice XML Data Dictionary (JXDD) and Justice XML Registry and Repository (JXRR) and their corresponding RapSheet.xsd, DriverHistory.xsd, and ArrestWarrent.xsd XML Schema Definition (XSD) documents
- Air Quality System Schema (Asbestos Demolition & Removal Schema)
- Health Level 7 (HL7®) for patient management, diagnosis, treatments, prescriptions, and so on
- Interactive Financial Exchange (IFX) standard for trades, banking, consumer transactions, and so on
- ACORD® standard for policy management such as underwriting, indemnity, claims, and so on
- IXRetail standard for inventory, customer transaction, and employee management
- and many, many more.

As companies store massive orders in XML and want to retrieve specific order details, they'll be forced to parse all of the orders with this storage mechanism. For example, assume a financial trading house is sent a block of stock trades on the hour for real-time input into a fraud detection system. To maintain the XML, the data is placed in a LOB. If a specific request came to take a closer look at trades by Mr. X, the database manager would have parsed all the trades in a block to find Mr. X's trades. Imagine this overhead if Mr. X made a single trade in the first hour and the block contained 100,000 trades. That's a lot of overheard to locate a single transaction.

It quickly becomes obvious that while LOB storage of XML unifies the data, it presents a new issue, namely performance. There are others, depending on a vendor's implementation of XML storage, but this is the main issue you should be aware of.

XML Shredded to a Table in a Relational Database

Another option provided by most of today's relational database vendors is to take XML data and shred it into a relational table. In this context, shred means that there is some mapping that takes the data from the XML format and places it into a relational table. Consider the following example (Figure 8–2):

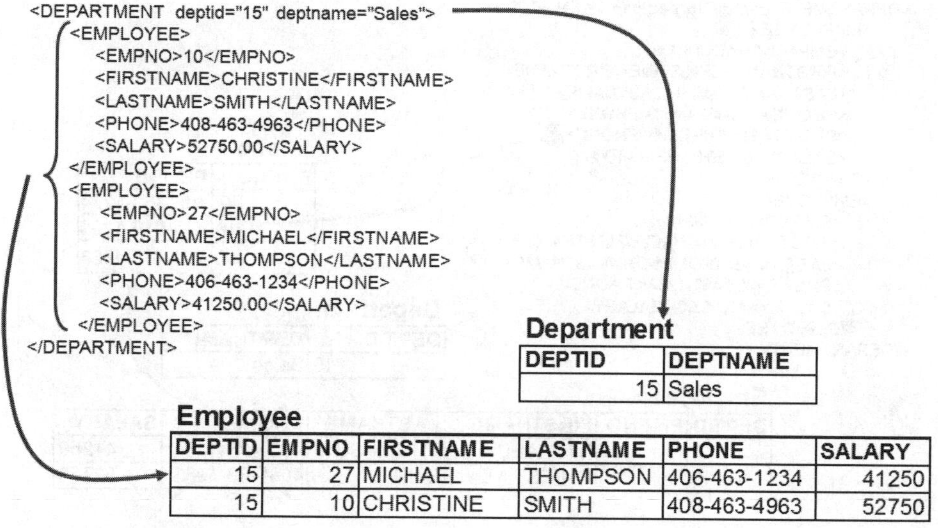

DEPTID	DEPTNAME
15	Sales

DEPTID	EMPNO	FIRSTNAME	LASTNAME	PHONE	SALARY
15	27	MICHAEL	THOMPSON	406-463-1234	41250
15	10	CHRISTINE	SMITH	408-463-4963	52750

Figure 8–2 *XML Shredding*

In the previous example you can see a single XML document has been shredded into two different relational tables: DEPARTMENT and EMPLOYEE. This example illustrates 3rd Normal Form (no repeating elements).

In this storage mechanism, XML data is unified with its relational counterpart since it's actually stored with the relational data. Additionally, there is no parsing overhead since data is retrieved as regular relational data via SQL requests.

From a performance perspective, shredding XML to relational data seems to solve the aforementioned issues; however, there are a number of disadvantages with this approach as well. XML is all about *flexibility*. It's the key benefit of this technology. Application developers (big proponents of XML) like the flexibility to alter a schema without the long process that's typically well understood by DBAs. Consider this example: If a new business rule established that the Human Resources department now required employee's cellular phone numbers for business emergencies, what ill effects would such a change present XML data whose storage mechanism was to shred it to a set of relational tables?

First, the mapping (not shown in Figure 8–2) between the XML data and the relational tables would have to be updated; this could cause application changes, testing requirements, and more. Of course, to maintain 3rd Normal Form you may actually be forced to create a new table for phone numbers and create referential integrity rules to link them together as shown below (Figure 8–3):

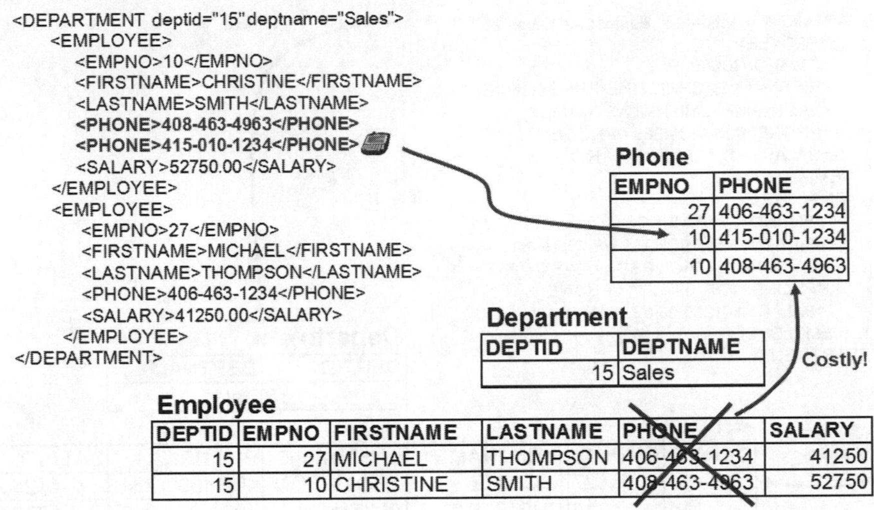

Figure 8–3 *XML schema changes*

You can see in this example that the flexibility promise associated with XML is quickly eroded when shredding is used for storage, because a change to the XML Schema requires a change to the underlying relational schema. In addition, a change to the XML Schema requires a change to the mapping tier between the XML document and the relational database.

Also consider that when shredded, access to the XML data is via SQL, meaning that the newly engineered language specific to querying XML data (XQuery) must be translated into SQL in this model. This can cause ineffectiveness, loss of function, and more.

Essentially, the shredding model solves the performance issue (although there is a performance penalty to rebuild the shredded data as XML), but it presents major flexibility issues that negate the most significant benefit of XML.

The Difference: pureXML

The LOB and shredded storage formats are used by every relational database vendor today, including DB2's XML Extender (which is available for free in DB2 9). The underlying architecture (the storage of the XML) is often overlooked because an XML data type is often presented at the top of the architecture, hence the term native XML. As a DBA, you should be sure to look beneath the veneer of a data type for true efficiencies when storing your XML data. This section introduces you to the pureXML feature and how to use it in DB2 9.

How DB2 Stores XML in a pureXML Column

pureXML introduces a new storage service that's completely transparent to applications and DBAs, yet it provides XML storage services that don't face any of the trade-offs associated with the XML storage methods discussed in the previous section.

DB2 *Note*

You can quickly get access to sample XML tables and data by creating the DB2 `SAMPLE` database with the XML extensions. When using UNIX-based platforms, at the operating system command prompt, issue

```
sqllib/bin/db2sampl -dbpath <path>
```

from the home directory of the database manager instance owner, where `path` is an optional parameter specifying the path where the `SAMPLE` database is to be created. If the path parameter is not specified, the sample database is created in the default path specified by the `DFTDBPATH` parameter in the database manager configuration file. The schema for `DB2SAMPL` is the value of the `CURRENT SCHEMA` special register.

When using a Windows platform, at the operating system command prompt, issue

```
db2sampl -dbpath e
```

where `e` is an optional parameter specifying the drive where the database is to be created. If the drive parameter is not specified, the sample database is created on the same drive as DB2.

The pureXML feature in DB2 stores XML data on-disk as XML in a query-rich DOM-like parsed tree format. This structure is similar to that of the XML-only databases and provides massive performance and flexibility benefits over the other approaches, and because it's within DB2, it's integrated with the relational data. At

pureXML

the same time, relational data is stored in regular rows and columns. In other words, DB2 has two storage services, one for XML and one for relational data. Both of these storage mechanisms are transparent to DBAs. An example is shown below (Figure 8–4):

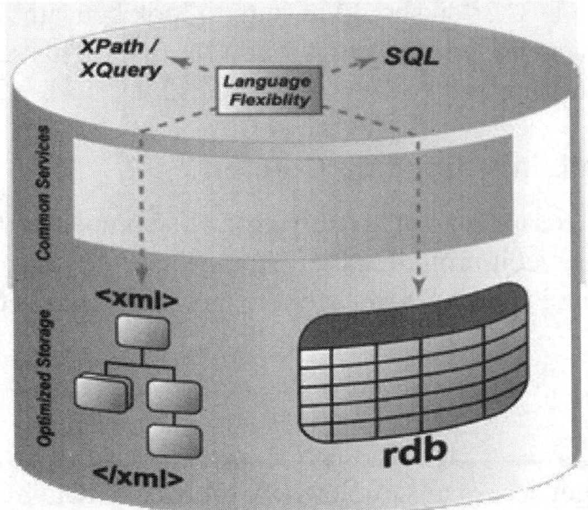

Figure 8–4 *XML schema changes*

In the previous figure you can see just how transparent these storage services are. If you are querying the database with SQL, you can access both XML and relational data (shown as **rdb** in the figure), or mix SQL and XQuery together. Likewise, you can use XQuery to get to both XML and relational data, or mix them together as well. DB2 is able to support this language flexibility because both access APIs are compiled down to an intermediate language-neutral representation called the Query Graph Model (QGM). The DB2 optimizer then takes the QGM and generates an optimized access plan for data access. The on-disk parsed representation of pureXML columns is done by the Xerces open source parser and is stored in the UTF-8 format regardless of the document encoding, the locale, or the codepage of the database.

The on-disk XML is often referred to as a *tree*. Branches of this tree represent elements, attributes, or text entities that contain name, namespace, namespace prefixes (stringIDs), type annotations (pathID), pointers to parent elements, pointers to child elements, and possible in-lined values.

The on-disk storage unit for DB2 is still a data page for XML, just like with relational data. This means that if an XML document or fragment can't fit on a single page (the maximum size is 32 KB), it has to be *chained* to other pages to create the document.

Since XML documents that don't fit on a single page must be split into multiple pages (referred to as regions in the XML tree), if your table space was using a 4 KB page size and your XML document was 12 KB in size after parsing, it would require 3 separate data pages to store it.

For example, consider the previously mentioned scenario with a single XML document of 12 KB. In this case, the XML document's on-disk representation may look like Figure 8–5:

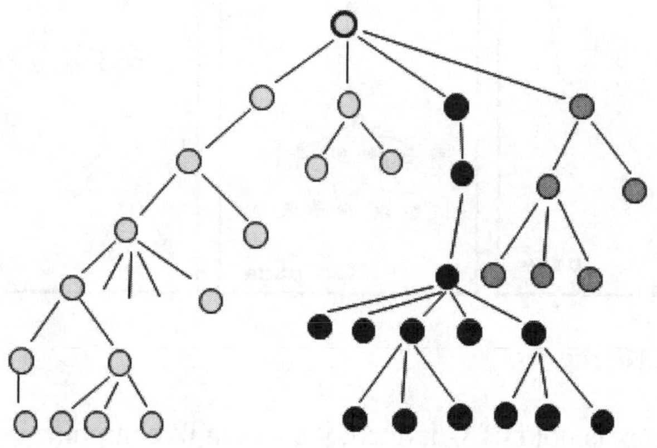

Figure 8–5 *XML spread across multiple disks*

If DB2 needs to find XML data that's stored on the same data page (for example, looking for data in the darker nodes), it can do so at pointer traversal speeds. However, what happens if data is requested from the XML document that resides on a different data page (region)? When the on-disk representation is created for your XML document, DB2 automatically creates (and maintains) a regions index such that portions of the same XML document that reside on different pages can be quickly located and returned to the database engine's query processing, as shown in Figure 8–6.

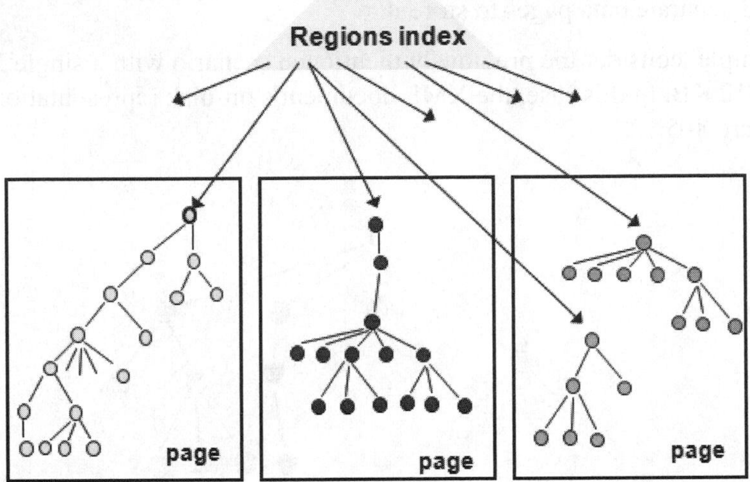

Figure 8–6 *XML regions*

Again, this index is not DBA-defined; it's a default component of the pureXML storage services. From the previous figure you can see that nodes are physically connected on the same data page, and regions (different pages) are logically connected and appropriately indexed.

Because an on-disk parsed representation of the XML data typically takes up more space than if the XML document were stored in an un-parsed format (plan for on-disk XML documents in pureXML to be at least twice as big as their serialized counterpart), pureXML columns automatically compress its data. (This compression shouldn't be confused with the Storage Optimization feature's Deep Compression capabilities; rather, it's an internal automatic compression algorithm.)

The reason that a pureXML column takes up extra space is because it's sitting on the disk in a parsed format such that query response times are incredibly fast, even for sub-document retrieval. In other words, it doesn't have to incur the overhead of parsing, which is associated with the LOB storage method, and it's never shredded (so all its flexibility is maintained), which was the issue with the shredding method.

With a pureXML column you can see that there's a trade-off as well; after all, nothing in the world is "free." pureXML columns offer you better performance, function, and flexibility than any other storage mechanism, but at the cost of more disk space. Considering that the per-MB cost of disk space has been decreasing at an incredible rate, these seem like a good trade-offs to make.

To see how DB2 handles XML data on its way to the on-disk format, start with an XML document like the one below (Figure 8–7):

```
<dept>
    <employee id=901>
          <name>John Doe</name>
          <phone>408 555 1212</phone>
          <office>344</office>
    </employee>
    <employee id=902>
          <name>Peter Pan</name>
          <phone>408 555 9918</phone>
          <office>216</office>
    </employee>
</dept>
```

Figure 8–7 *XML fragment*

The XML document in the previous form is considered *serialized.* When it's parsed, its representation turns into something that an application like DB2 can use.

There are two mainstream types of parsers in today's market: DOM and SAX. A DOM-parsed XML document takes up more disk space and is slower to get into its parsed format when compared to XML data that is SAX parsed. However, the DOM format is faster for queries because the on-disk format is optimized for query retrieval. A SAX parser is an event parser; it creates a stream of events that correlates to the XML document. A SAX-parsed XML document isn't as efficient for queries in that it typically takes some extra work to get it to perform; however, it parses faster than its DOM counterpart and takes up less space. DB2 9 attempts to combine the best of both worlds by SAX parsing the XML document and storing it in a DOM-like structure on disk. For example, the previous XML document after being parsed by DB2, but before DB2 compressed the data, would look like this (Figure 8–8):

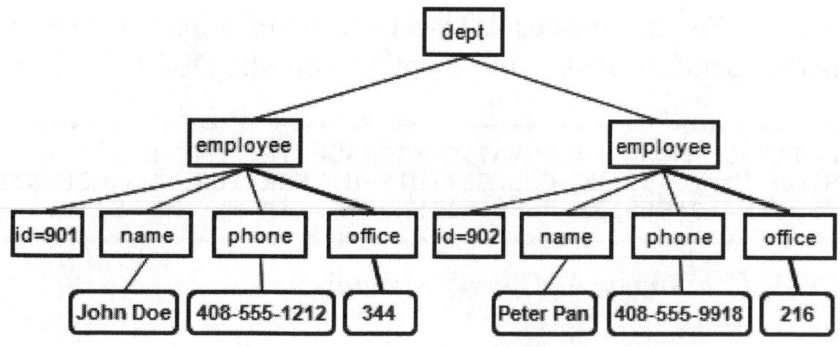

Figure 8–8 *Pre-compressed XML structure*

After DB2 9 compresses the XML document (its on-disk format), it would look like this (Figure 8–9):

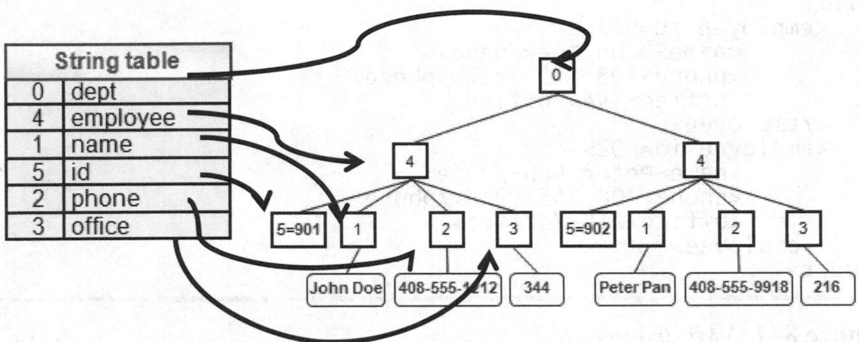

Figure 8–9 *Compressed XML structure*

You can see in the previous figure that a table is created to store the string values that are compressed. Essentially the compression algorithm converts tag names into integers, and the translation of this representation is held in an internal table called `SYSIBM.SYSXMLSTRINGS` (although you don't need to interact with this table). DB2's XML compression is efficient because not only does it reduce storage requirements (which should be obvious by the previous figure), it also creates an environment for faster string comparisons and navigation of the hierarchy because it can do so via integer math, which is generally faster than string comparisons.

Creating an XML-enabled Database

Before you can work with pureXML columns, you need to create a database that's capable of storing them. At the time DB2 9 became generally available, pureXML columns could only be stored in databases that were created to support the UTF-8 Unicode format. You can create a UTF-8 Unicode-enabled database in DB2 9 by specifying the `USING CODESET UTF-8` option from the DB2 CLP (Example 8–1):

```
CREATE DATABASE MYXML AUTOMATIC STORAGE YES ON 'D:\'
  DBPATH ON 'D:\' USING CODESET UTF-8 TERRITORY US COLLATE
  USING SYSTEM PAGESIZE 4096 WITH 'This is my XML Database'
```

Example 8–1 *Creating an XML enabled database*

There are some features in DB2 that do not support pureXML. For example, the Database Partitioning Feature (DPF) and the Storage Optimization Feature (for deep row compression) currently do not support pureXML columns.

The other option is to use the Create Database Wizard as shown below (Figure 8–10):

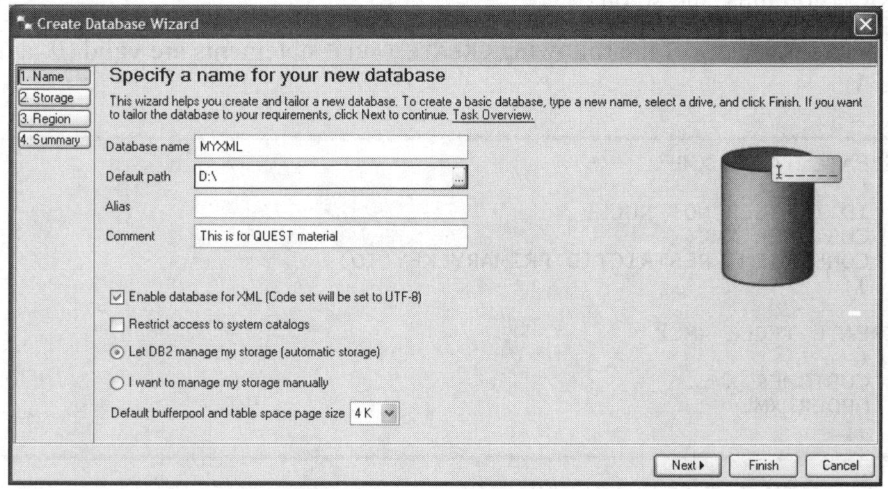

Figure 8–10 *Using the Create Database Wizard to create an XML-enabled database*

DB2 Note

Future versions of DB2 may alleviate this restriction of only supporting XML columns in Unicode databases (UTF-8). This information is current as of DB2 9 and Fix Pack 2.

The following database will be used in the examples throughout this help topic (Example 8–2):

```
CREATE DATABASE MYXML AUTOMATIC STORAGE YES
  USING CODESET UTF-8 TERRITORY US
```

Example 8–2 *Sample XML database*

Creating Tables with pureXML

Once a database has been enabled for pureXML, you create tables that store XML data in these columns in the same manner that you create tables with only relational data. One of the great flexibility benefits of pureXML is that it doesn't require supporting relational columns to store XML. You can choose to create a table that has single or multiple XML columns, that has a relational column with one or more XML columns, and so on.

For example, any of the following CREATE TABLE statements are valid (Example 8–3):

```
CREATE TABLE XML1
  (
  ID INTEGER NOT NULL,
  CUSTOMER XML,
  CONSTRAINT RESTRICTID PRIMARY KEY(ID)
  );

CREATE TABLE XML2
  (
  CUSTOMER XML,
  ORDER XML
  );
```

Example 8–3 *Tables with XML columns*

You can create tables with pureXML columns using either the DB2 CLP or the Control Center, as shown in Figure 8–11.

The XML data type integration extends beyond the DB2 tools and into popular integrated development environments (IDEs) like IBM Rational Application Developer, Microsoft Visual Studio 2005, Quest TOAD, and more. This means that you can work with pureXML columns from whatever tool or facility you feel most comfortable.

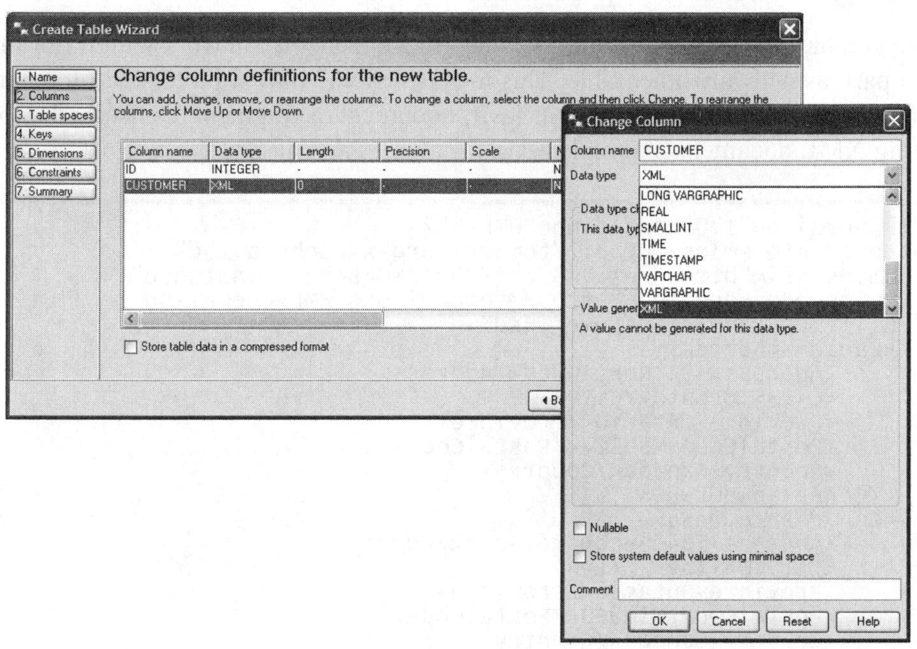

Figure 8–11 *Using the Create Table Wizard to create an XML column*

The examples in this chapter assume that the following table has been created in an XML-enabled database (Example 8–4):

```
CREATE TABLE COMMUTERS
  (
  ID        INTEGER NOT NULL,
  CUSTOMER XML,
  CONSTRAINT RESTRICTID PRIMARY KEY(ID)
  );
```

Example 8–4 *Table used to demonstrate XML capabilities*

This table will be used to store commuter information (based in XML) alongside an ID that represents the Web site's customer who is building the commuter community (the names of the commuters are purposely not entered into the database). Commuter information is retrieved from various customers who want to carpool to work, and their information is received via a Web form and passed to DB2 via XML — a typical Web application.

Inserting Data into pureXML Columns

Once you have a pureXML column defined in a table, you can work with it, for the most part, as with any other table. This means that you may want to start by populating the pureXML column with an XML document or fragment. Consider the following XML document (Example 8–5):

```
<?xml version="1.0" encoding="UTF-8"?>
<customerinfo xmlns="http://tempuri.org/XMLSchema.xsd"
    xmlns:xsi="http://www.w3.org/2001/XMLSchema-instance"
    xsi:schemaLocation="http://tempuri.org/XMLSchema.xsd
    C:\Temp\Example\Customer.xsd">
    <CanadianAddress>
        <Address>434 Rory Road</Address>
        <City>Toronto</City>
        <Province>Ontario</Province>
        <PostalCode>M5L1C7</PostalCode>
        <Country>Canada</Country>
    </CanadianAddress>
    <CanadianAddress>
        <Address>124 Seaboard Gate</Address>
        <City>Whitby</City>
        <Province>Ontario</Province>
        <PostalCode>L1N9C3</PostalCode>
        <Country>Canada</Country>
    </CanadianAddress>
</customerinfo>
```

Example 8–5 *Sample XML document*

Because this is a well-formed XML document, you will be able to see it in an XML-enabled browser, such as Internet Explorer (Figure 8–12).

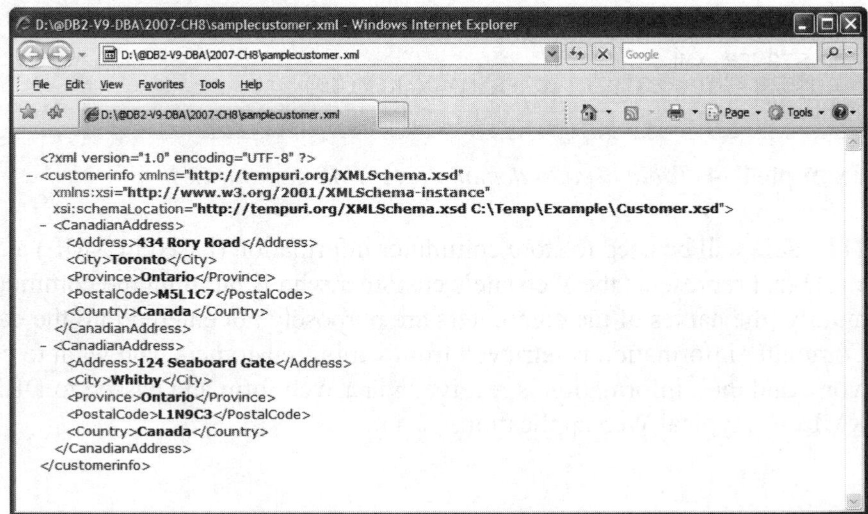

Figure 8–12 *XML document displayed in a browser*

You can use the SQL `INSERT` statement to add this data to the `COMMUTERS` table in the same manner that you would add it to a table with only relational data. The data inserted into the pureXML column must be a well-formed XML document (or fragment), as defined by the XML 1.0 specification.

For example, to insert the working example XML document using the CLP, issue the following command (Example 8–6):

```
INSERT INTO COMMUTERS VALUES (1,
 '<?xml version="1.0" encoding="UTF-8"?>
  <customerinfo xmlns...
  ...
  </customerinfo>')
```

Example 8–6 *Sample XML document*

The full XML document is placed between the two single quotes.

You can see this data is now in the pureXML column (Figure 8–13):

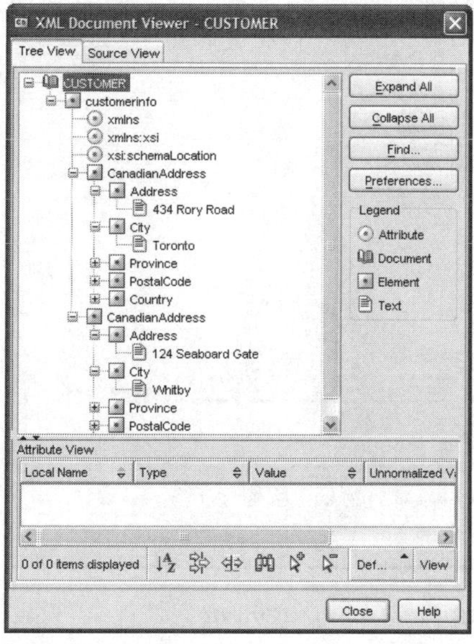

Figure 8–13 *Viewing XML data in the command center*

Since pureXML provides you with the utmost flexibility for storing XML, you don't have to just store full XML documents as in Example 8–6. You could store a fragment of that document in the same table.

For example, to add the XML document in the working example (one full `<CanadianAddress>` block), you could enter the following command (Example 8–7):

```
INSERT INTO COMMUTERS VALUES (2,
  '<CanadianAddress>
     <Address>434 Rory Road</Address><City>Toronto</City>
     <Province>Ontario</Province>
     <PostalCode>M5L1C7</PostalCode>
     <Country>Canada</Country>
  </CanadianAddress>')
```

Example 8–7 *Inserting an XML fragment*

Now the COMMUTERS table has two rows with XML data, one with a full XML document and the other with an XML fragment (Figure 8–14):

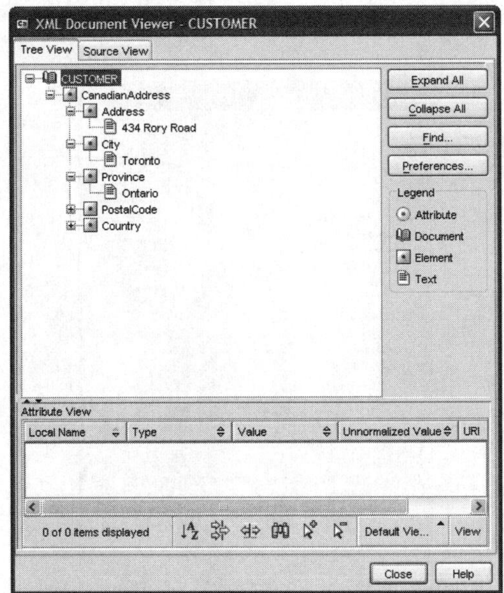

Figure 8–14 *Displaying the XML fragment*

The previous figure visualizes the XML data in the COMMUTERS table using the DB2 9 Command Editor, a tool that is included as part of the DB2 Control Center.

If you recall, DB2 must store well-formed XML documents and fragments, although you have the option of validating them against XML Schema Definition (XSD) documents.

If you tried to insert a non-well-formed XML document or fragment into a pureXML column you would receive an error as shown in Figure 8–15.

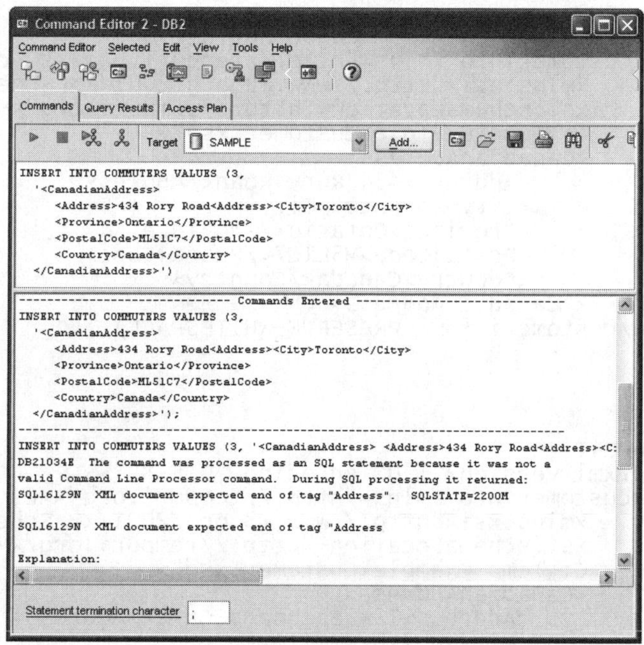

Figure 8–15 *Invalid XML fragment*

In the previous example you can see that the `<Address>` element isn't closed properly — it uses `<Address>` to close it instead of the proper `</Address>` element. Because this element isn't closed properly, as per the standard, this fragment isn't considered to be well-formed, and therefore the insert operation fails.

Finally, you should be aware that there are multiple options to use when using the `INSERT` command to insert XML data into a table.

```
INSERT INTO COMMUTERS VALUES
  (
  3,
  XMLPARSE
    (DOCUMENT
       '<?xml version="1.0" encoding="UTF-8"?>
        <customerinfo xmlns="http://tempuri.org/XMLSchema.xsd"
            xmlns:xsi="http://www.w3.org/2001/XMLSchema-instance"
            xsi:schemaLocation="http://tempuri.org/XMLSchema.xsd
            C:\Temp\Example\Customer.xsd">
            <CanadianAddress>
                <Address>434 Rory Road</Address>
                <City>Toronto</City>
                <Province>Ontario</Province>
                <PostalCode>M5L1C7</PostalCode>
                <Country>Canada</Country>
            </CanadianAddress>
        </customerinfo>' PRESERVE WHITESPACE)
  ),
  (
  4,
  XMLPARSE
    (DOCUMENT
       '<?xml version="1.0" encoding="UTF-8"?>
        <customerinfo xmlns="http://tempuri.org/XMLSchema.xsd"
            xmlns:xsi="http://www.w3.org/2001/XMLSchema-instance"
            xsi:schemaLocation="http://tempuri.org/XMLSchema.xsd
            C:\Temp\Example\Customer.xsd">
            <CanadianAddress>
                <Address>124 Seaboard Gate</Address>
                <City>Whitby</City>
                <Province>Ontario</Province>
                <PostalCode>L1N9C3</PostalCode>
                <Country>Canada</Country>
            </CanadianAddress>
        </customerinfo>')
  );
```

Example 8–8 *Inserting an XML fragment*

Looking at Example 8–8, the INSERT statement illustrates the flexibility you have when inserting XML data into pureXML columns. First, note that two separate XML documents were inserted in a single INSERT statement. Also note the use of various options that affect XML insert activity into pureXML columns, some of which include DOCUMENT, PRESERVE WHITESPACE, and so on. Others include the ability to validate the XML data against a registered XML schema definition document (the XMLVALIDATE option).

The first row in the INSERT statement (ID=3) specifically requests that whitespace be preserved in the on-disk format via the PRESERVE WHITESPACE option. In contrast, the second XML document doesn't make such a request, and therefore boundary whitespace will be stripped (the default) from this document.

White Space Preservation

The PRESERVE WHITESPACE option was specified in Example 8–8. This option, as its name indicates, instructs DB2 to preserve whitespace in the XML document when it parses out the on-disk format. This option specifies that all whitespace is to be preserved even when the nearest containing element has the attribute xml:space='default'.

Generally, this option is used when the highest level of fidelity is required for the XML document when it's stored in a pureXML column. For example, a typical trading order may be regulated to be returned to an application in the manner in which it was inserted into the data server.

In contrast, the STRIP WHITESPACE option specifies that any text nodes containing only whitespace characters up to 1,000 bytes in length be stripped, unless the nearest containing element has the attribute xml:space='preserve'. If any text node begins with more than 1,000 bytes of whitespace, an SQLSTATE 54059 error is returned. Whitespace characters in the CDATA section are also affected by this option.

When stripping whitespace you should be aware that, according to the XML standard, whitespace also includes space characters (U+0020), carriage returns (U+000D), line feeds (U+000A), or tabs (U+0009) that are in the document to improve readability. When any of these characters appear as part of a text string, they are not considered to be whitespace. When you use the STRIP WHITESPACE option, the whitespace characters that appear between elements are stripped.

For example, in the following XML fragment, the spaces between <a> and <b> and between </b> and </a> are considered to be boundary whitespace (Example 8–9).

```
<a>   <b><c>This and That</c></b>   </a>
```

Example 8–9 *Whitespace in XML*

If you want DB2 to preserve whitespace by default, you need to change the value of the special registers from STRIP WHITESPACE to PRESERVE WHITESPACE using the following command (Example 8–10):

```
SET CURRENT IMPLICIT XMLPARSE OPTION='PRESERVE WHITESPACE'
```

Example 8–10 *Preserving whitespace implicitly in all XML documents*

Depending on the business problem you're trying to solve, or the regulatory compliance issues that may govern your day-to-day operations, you need to carefully consider and interpret the term *fidelity* and how it applies to your business. For example, some financial compliance regulations state that a transaction action must look exactly as it did going into the database. The XML InfoSet standard actually breaks this rule, so depending on your application, the `PRESERVE WHITESPACE` option still won't guarantee the truest form of fidelity since DB2 follows the XML standard. In these circumstances, DBAs often store an XML transaction in a LOB (for audit purposes) and in a pureXML column (for speedy search, retrieval, and transaction processing).

Adding Data Through an Application

The pureXML support in DB2 9 has interfaces to support the most popular programming methodologies (CLI/ODBC, Java. ADO.NET, Ruby on Rails, PHP, and so on). Typically you're not going to manually insert XML data in your tables. If you insert XML data programmatically, it's recommended that the application insert the data from host variables rather than literals. This way, the DB2 data server can use the host variable data type to determine some of the encoding information.

For example, the code for a JDBC application that wants to read XML data in a binary format and insert it into a pureXML column may look like:

```
PreparedStatement insertStmt = null;
String sqls = null;
int cid = 1015;

sqls = "INSERT INTO MyCustomer (Cid, Info) VALUES (?, ?)";
insertStmt = conn.prepareStatement(sqls);
insertStmt.setInt(1, cid);
File file = new File("commuterdata.xml");
insertStmt.setBinaryStream(2, new FileInputStream(file),
                           (int)file.length());
insertStmt.executeUpdate();
```

Example 8–11 *Java application inserting XML into DB2*

Inserting Large Amounts of XML Data

If you're a DBA responsible for large data movement operations, you're already quite familiar with the IMPORT and LOAD utilities available in DB2. For pureXML columns, as of the time DB2 9 became generally available, large data population operations involving pureXML columns must be handled by the IMPORT utility.

DB2 Note

The population of large amounts of XML into pureXML columns is evolving throughout the DB2 9 release; you should monitor future DB2 9 releases for possible added support for pureXML columns and the LOAD utility.

If XML information is passed to you in an ASCII format (or you have the ability to easily put your XML documents into such a format), you can use the IMPORT utility to populate your pureXML columns in a more efficient manner than just running individual INSERT operations. What's nice about the IMPORT utility's support for pureXML columns is that you don't have to handle this process programmatically in an application; you simply need to have a delimited (DEL) ASCII file with the XML data. The XML data is placed into files that are separate from the delimited data.

IMPORT handles XML data bound for pureXML columns in a similar fashion to LOB data for LOB columns: a source file is used that contains the actual relational data and pointers are used to point the IMPORT utility to the location where the LOB data exists. In the case of pureXML columns, the pointer is called an XML Data Specifier (XDS) and it points to a file that contains the XML data.

For example, consider the IMPORT file for the COMMUTERS table in Figure 8–16. This file points to three separate XML fragments (not whole XML documents) that contain individual commuter information.

DB2 Note

If you had some rows that didn't have XML data associated with them, you could simply omit the "<XDS FIL='...'/>" pointer for that row.

pureXML

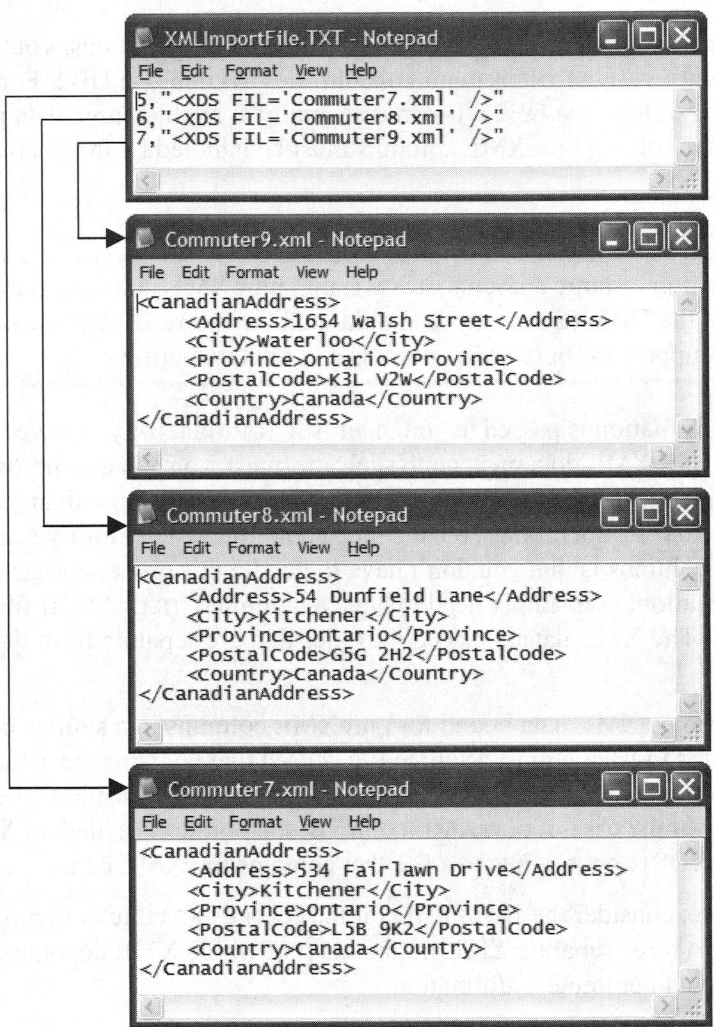

Figure 8–16 *IMPORT file specification of XML columns*

Once you've defined the import source file, simply call it from the `IMPORT` command as shown in Example 8–12.

```
IMPORT FROM 'C:\TEMP\XMLIMPORTFILE.TXT OF DEL'
   XML FROM 'C:\TEMP\'
    MODIFIED BY XMLCHAR
    MESSAGES 'C:\TEMP\IMPORTMESSAGES.TXT'
    INSERT INTO COMMUTERS
```

Example 8–12 *IMPORT command*

Selecting Data from pureXML Columns

You can use XQuery, SQL, SQL/XML, or any combination thereof, to retrieve data stored in pureXML columns as illustrated below (Figure 8–17):

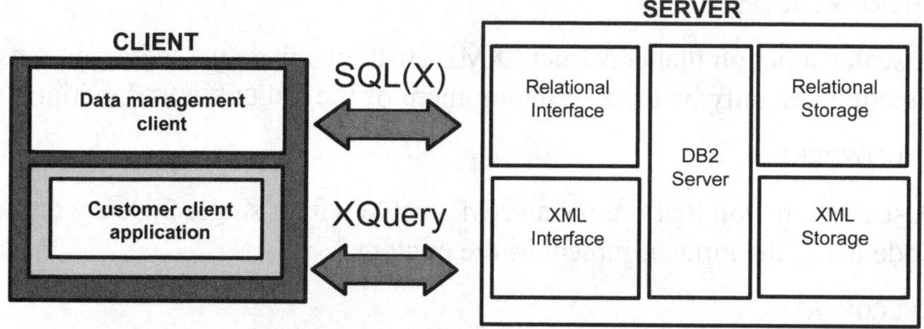

Figure 8–17 *XQuery and SQL relationship to DB2*

In practice, depending on the data you want to retrieve, you'll use different interfaces to solve different problems; however, this ultimately depends on your skill set. If your enterprise is well versed in all the XML data access methods, you'll be able to use varying approaches to data retrieval that will yield benefits that relate to development time, performance, efficiency, and more.

The easiest (yet perhaps most inefficient) method to retrieve data from a pureXML column is to use only SQL, as shown in some of the previous examples. However, generally more value can be delivered to an application that uses SELECT, SQL/XML, XQuery, or some combination thereof. The remainder of this section briefly discusses both SQL/XML and the XQuery approach for XML data retrieval.

An Introduction to SQL/XML

SQL/XML provides support for XML through the SQL syntax, an ANSI and ISO standard. It's somewhat popular because of the rich talent pool of SQL developers, and this standard syntax allows them to use their skill set to work with XML data in relational databases. DB2 supports SQL/XML.

There are at least a dozen SQL/XML functions in DB2 9, and the list keeps growing, adding more and more capability to the XML-ability of SQL.

Some of the SQL/XML functions include:

- `XMLAGG`

  An aggregate function that returns an XML sequence containing an item for each non-null value in a set of XML values.

- `XMLATTRIBUTES`

  A scalar function that constructs XML attributes from passed arguments. This function can only be used as an argument of the `XMLELEMENT` function.

- `XMLCOMMENT`

  A scalar function that returns an XML value with a single XQuery comment node using the input argument as the content.

- `XMLCONCAT`

  A scalar function that returns a sequence containing the concatenation of a variable number of XML input arguments.

- `XMLDOCUMENT`

  A scalar function that returns an XML value with a single XQuery document node with zero or more child nodes. This function creates a document node, which by definition, every XML document must have. A document node is not visible in the serialized representation of the XML; however, every document to be stored in a DB2 table must contain a document node. Note that the `XMLELEMENT` function does not create a document node, only an element node. When constructing XML documents that are to be inserted, it's not sufficient to create only an element node — the document must contain a document node.

- `XMLELEMENT`

  A scalar function that returns an XML value that is an XML element node.

- `XMLFOREST`

  A scalar function that returns an XML value that is a sequence of XML element nodes.

- `XMLNAMESPACES`

  Used to construct namespace declarations from passed arguments. This declaration can only be used as an argument of the `XMLELEMENT`, `XMLFOREST`, and `XMLTABLE` functions.

- `XMLPI`

  A scalar function that returns an XML value with a single XQuery processing instruction node.

- XMLTEXT

  A scalar function that returns an XML value with a single XQuery text node where the input argument is the actual content.

Example 8–13 creates a relational table and then populates it with `INSERT` statements.

```
CREATE TABLE CARPOOL
  (
  POOLER_ID          INT NOT NULL,
  POOLER_FIRSTNAME VARCHAR(20) NOT NULL,
  POOLER_LASTNAME  VARCHAR(20) NOT NULL,
  POOLER_EXTENSION INT NOT NULL
  );

INSERT INTO CARPOOL VALUES
  (1,'George','Martin',1234),
  (2,'Fred','Flintstone',2345),
  (3,'Barney','Rubble',3456),
  (4,'Wilma','Rockafeller',9876);
```

Example 8–13 *Sample tables for XML function examples*

An SQL/XML statement that would return relational data within XML tags is shown in Example 8–14:

```
SELECT XML2CLOB
  (XMLELEMENT(NAME "CarPoolers",
       XMLELEMENT(NAME "ID", C.POOLER_ID),
       XMLELEMENT(NAME "Firstname", C.POOLER_FIRSTNAME),
       XMLELEMENT(NAME "Lastname",  C.POOLER_LASTNAME),
       XMLELEMENT(NAME "Extension", C.POOLER_EXTENSION))
  )
AS "Result"
FROM CARPOOL C;
```

Example 8–14 *SQL/XML publishing example*

The results are returned as a character string to the application. You can see the use of SQL and SQL/XML on a relational table (note that this is not data stored in a pureXML column) in Figure 8–18.

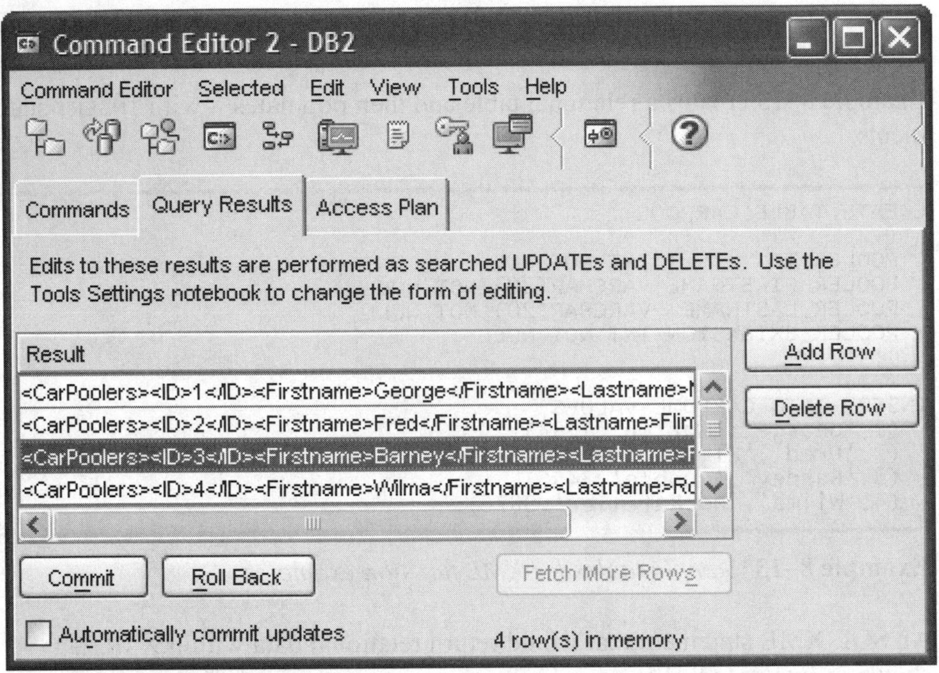

Figure 8–18 *SQL/XML results*

An Introduction to XQuery

XQuery is a programming language that was built from the ground up to query XML data. It's an open standard that has the full backing from the World Wide Web Consortium (W3C®). This language arose from the inefficiencies that were associated with using SQL to query XML hierarchies.

When you think about it, relational tables are sets of rows and columns. Operations on these relations are done with mathematics via abstracted algebraic expressions, namely SQL. SQL contains functions to work on relations, using a more natural language, with support for projections, restrictions, permutations, and more. However, XML data is hierarchal in nature, not flat like its relational counterpart. Therefore, a new language was built specifically to navigate hierarchical structures and the full flexibility of XML. The end result was the birth of XQuery.

For example, you might need to create XML queries that perform the following operations:

- Search XML data for objects that are at unknown levels of the hierarchy.
- Perform structural transformations on the data (for example, you might want to invert a hierarchy).

- Return results that have mixed types.

In XQuery, the FOR-LET-WHERE-ORDERBY-RETURN statement (commonly known as a FLWOR expression) is used to perform such operations. For example, the following XQuery statement would retrieve the first <PostalCode> element in the working example document (Example 8–15):

```
XQUERY FOR $y IN db2-fn:xmlcolumn
  ('COMMUTERS.CUSTOMER')/CanadianAddress/PostalCode
  RETURN $y
```

Example 8–15 *Retrieving the PostalCode from an XML document*

There are many operations and options available with XQuery. If you wanted to restrict the result set, you could enter something similar to the following (Example 8–16):

```
XQUERY FOR $y IN db2-fn:xmlcolumn
  ('COMMUTERS.CUSTOMER')/CanadianAddress/
  WHERE $y/PostalCode="ML51C7"
  RETURN $y
```

Example 8–16 *XQuery WHERE clause*

DB2 also has a rich XQuery builder available in the Developer Workbench that can make building these expressions easier (Figure 8–19).

DB2 *Note*

The purpose of this help topic wasn't to teach you about XQuery, but to introduce you to its existence. The DB2 Information Center and IBM Developers Domain Web sites have many tutorials and reference materials regarding this subject.

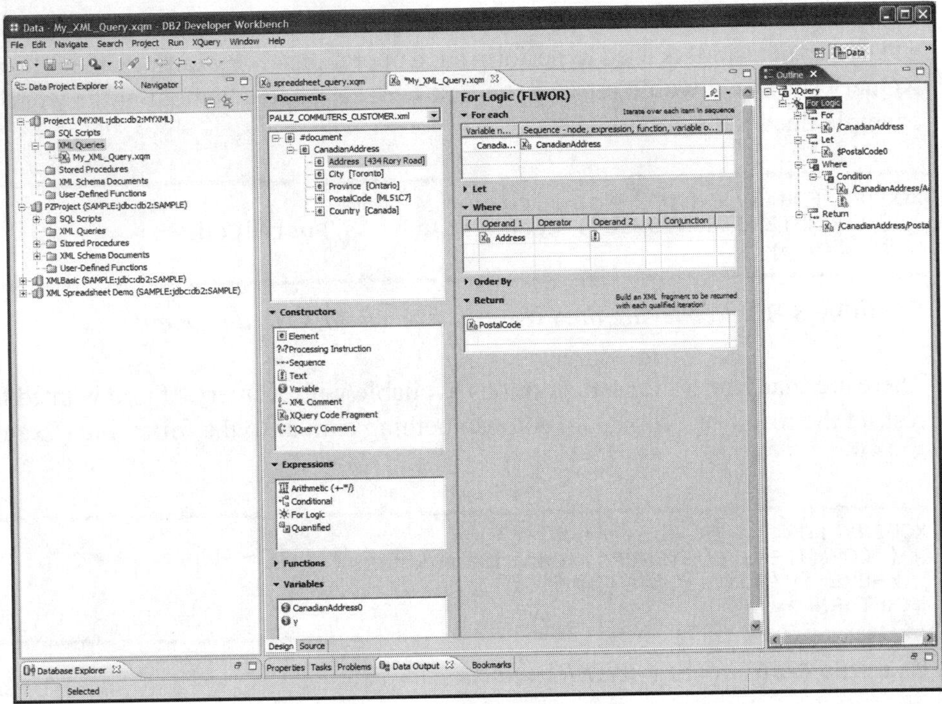

Figure 8–19 *DB2 Developer Workbench*

SQL/XML, SQL, or XQuery Best Practices

The following table summarizes which APIs are best suited to perform which kind of operations on XML data (Table 8–1):

Table 8–1 *XML API Summary*

Feature, Function, Benefit	SQL	SQL/XML	XQuery	XQuery & SQL/XML
XML Predicates	N/A	Best	Best	Best
Relational Predicates	Best	Best	N/A	Good
XML and Relational	N/A	Best	N/A	Best
Joining XML and Relational	N/A	Best	N/A	Best
Joining XML and XML	N/A	Good	Best	Best
Transforming XML Data	N/A	Awkward	Best	Best

Table 8–1 *XML API Summary*

Feature, Function, Benefit	SQL	SQL/XML	XQuery	XQuery & SQL/XML
INSERT, UPDATE, DELETE	Best	Best	N/A	N/A
Parameter Markers	Good	Best	N/A	N/A
Full Text Search	Good	Best	N/A	Best
XML Aggregation	N/A	Best	Awkward	Awkward
Function Calls	Best	Best	N/A	Best

Generally, the use of just SQL is only useful when retrieving a full document or fragment from a pureXML column (in which case you may want to have this information reside in a LOB depending on the data within it and your application's access patterns). The reason that solely using SQL is so limiting is that you can't select data based on the contents of the XML document or fragment, just the relational columns (if they exist) that surround it.

When SQL/XML is used as the top query language (and optionally mixed with XQuery) you get the richest functionality when it comes to querying the data with the least amount of restrictions. For example, with this method you can extract XML fragments from a pureXML column, use full-text searching, aggregate or group the data, and more. For the most part, this is the generally recommended method for pureXML data retrieval. Even if you don't need all of the capabilities this approach provides, it "leaves the door open" for future application flexibility.

As previously mentioned, XQuery is a language developed specifically for the querying of XML data. If you have an application that only works with XML data, this seems like an obvious choice.

Finally, you can embed SQL within an XQuery statement. This allows you to filter out some of the XML data using relational predicates on the columns that surround it in the schema. However, if you need to perform data analysis queries with grouping and aggregations, you may prefer SQL/XML.

Updating and Deleting pureXML Columns

To update or delete entire XML documents or fragment in a pureXML column, you can use traditional INSERT and UPDATE SQL statements. If you wanted to update an entire XML document in a pureXML column, you could enter an UPDATE statement similar to the following (Example 8–17):

```
UPDATE COMMUTERS SET CUSTOMER =
  XMLPARSE
    (
    DOCUMENT
        '<?xml version="1.0" encoding="UTF-8"?>
         <customerinfo xmlns="http://tempuri.org/XMLSchema.xsd"
              xmlns:xsi="http://www.w3.org/2001/XMLSchema-instance"
              xsi:schemaLocation="http://tempuri.org/XMLSchema.xsd
              C:\Temp\Example\Customer.xsd">
              <CanadianAddress>
                   <Address>434 Rory Road</Address>
                   <City>Toronto</City>
                   <Province>Ontario</Province>
                   <PostalCode>M5L1C7</PostalCode>
                   <Country>Canada</Country>
              </CanadianAddress>
         </customerinfo>'
    )
  WHERE ID=4;
```

Example 8–17 *Updating an XML column*

As you might expect, you delete rows with XML documents in the same manner as regular rows using the DELETE command (Example 8–18):

```
DELETE FROM COMMUTERS WHERE ID=4
```

Example 8–18 *Deleting a row with XML columns*

If you wanted to completely remove an XML document or fragment from a pureXML column you would use the UPDATE command and set the value to NULL (Example 8–19):

```
UPDATE COMMUTERS SET CUSTOMER=NULL WHERE ID=3
```

Example 8–19 *Setting an XML value to NULL*

At the time when DB2 9 generally became available, the XQuery standard really only defined what its name implies: query. There was no ANSI standard method for updating or deleting fragments of an XML document. As you've seen in the previous examples, you can manipulate data in existing pureXML columns, but only when you work on the entire document or fragment in a single operation. As XML proliferates into the mainstream, one should expect more and more operations to occur transactionally at child levels in the hierarchy.

For example, a commuter in the working example could move to a new location in the same city — this would likely require that the XML data be updated, but not all elements (you don't need to update `<Country>` or `<Province>`). If you considered these types of operations across a large number of documents (within a single column or spread across multiple pureXML columns), the overhead of having to work with the entire document for fragment could be quite high.

Because there was no defined standard for updating parts of an XML document or fragment when DB2 9 became generally available, a decision was made to provide the `DB2XMLFUNCTIONS.XMLUPDATE` stored procedure to offer the capability to update portions of an XML document or fragment in the interim.

Although the source for this routine is provided for you, you are required to build and install this stored procedure. (It's not considered part of the pureXML support, rather a work-around method until the XQuery standard evolves to support such activity.)

DB2 *Note*

This space should be watched closely. As the standard evolves, the reliance on this stored procedure may not be required.

Indexing pureXML Columns

Indexing support is available for data stored in XML columns. The use of indexes over XML data can improve the efficiency of queries issued against XML documents or fragments stored in a DB2 9 pureXML column.

As with a relational index, an index over XML data indexes the contents of the column. They differ, however, in that a relational index indexes an entire column, while an index over XML data indexes parts of the column. (It can also index the entire column.) You can define single or multiple XML indexes on a single pureXML column in the same manner as a relational index.

For DB2 XML indexes, you indicate which parts of the XML document stored in the column should be indexed. DBAs can specify parts of the XML document or fragment they want indexed using an XML Pattern expression (which is essentially a limited XPath expression).

Example 8–20 illustrates how an index is created on an XML column:

```
CREATE INDEX XMLINDEX ON DEPT(DEPTDOC)
  GENERATE KEY USING XMLPATTERN'/dept/name' AS VARCHAR(30);
```

Example 8–20 *XML index creation*

DB2 pureXML indexes are very powerful because they can index any element, attribute, or text within an XML document (or combination thereof) or the entire document itself (although you are not forced to do so). In addition, DB2 pureXML indexes can index repeating elements.

Figure 8–3 illustrated the complexities that arise when shredding XML data to relational format when the schema changes; the example was the addition of a new phone number to an employee's record. In that example, the XML document evolved such that it had multiple elements. DB2 9 could index these multiple elements. DB2 pureXML indexes are very powerful with respect to this capability when compared to other database offerings and their XML support.

The DDL used to create an XML index in DB2 9 is shown below (Figure 8–20):

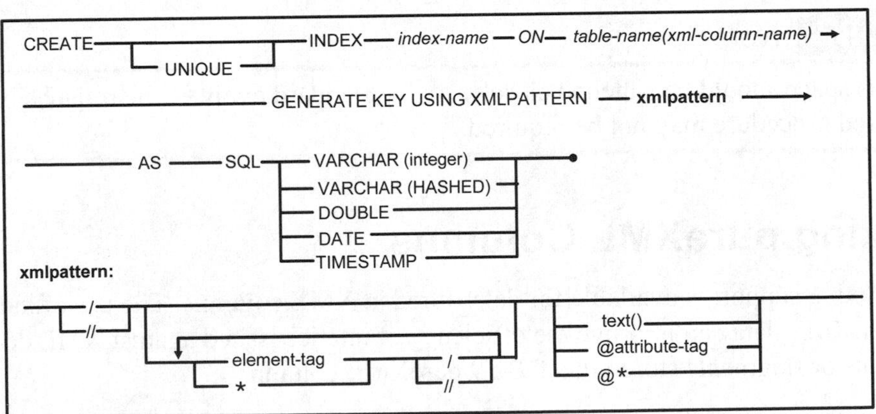

Figure 8–20 *XML Index creation syntax*

In the previous figure you can see that the actual search path differs from a traditional relational index. When you index a pureXML column you index an XMLPATTERN that points to the location of the information you want, and then optionally modify the pointer such that it returns text, attributes, elements, and so on.

DB2 Note

XMLPATTERN is a notation that's based on XPath, only it has no predicates. An XMLPATTERN expression is simply formulated with child axis (/) and descendent-or-self axis (//) operations.

You'll also note the AS clause in the previous DDL, which specifies the data type to which indexed values are converted before they are stored. Values are converted to the index XML data type that corresponds to the specified index SQL data type, which helps the index manager perform fast and efficient searches on the XML data.

More specifically, the AS clause is required because the DB2 9 engine was built for flexibility, and one of those flexible options is not to require an associated XML Schema Definition document to store your XML documents. Without an XML Schema Definition document there would be no way for DB2 9 to know the data type to use for the index for a specified XMLPATTERN expression. For example, you use AS SQL VARCHAR(X) for nodes to index values of a known maximum length, and AS SQL DATE and AS SQL TIMESTAMP for date-based nodes.

DB2 Note

The AS VARCHAR HASHED option is typically used when you don't know the length of the XML data, or for nodes whose lengths change frequently. This index will hash out the string values of your nodes. This may seem optimal, but these indexes won't support range predicate queries, just equality ones.

If you're indexing numeric data, use the AS SQL DOUBLE clause. For simplicity, the DB2 9 technology offers this single numeric data type for indexing XML numeric-based data. The reason for this is simple: Instead of weighing down DBAs with the complexity of choosing between multiple numeric-based data types, it was deemed a better option to cast all numeric-based data into a DOUBLE data type. The consequence is that the DBA could lose precision with this data type, which would create the side effect of the inclusion of some elements that wouldn't otherwise be in the index if it were able to accommodate a more precise numeric value.

The point here is that you'll always get the data you're looking for (and it'll be easier to define the structure to get it), though the index may contain more entries than needed. Your queries will filter out these results anyway and still get the data fast.

Consider the following XML fragment that describes books for an online retailer (Example 8–21):

```
<book>
  <authors>
    <author id="74">George Baklarz</author>
    <author id="85">Paul Zikopoulos</author>
    <author id="15">Roman Melnyk</author>
  </authors>
  <title>The Rise and Fall of White Knuckle Airlines</title>
  <price>35</price>
  <keywords>
    <keyword>business</keyword>
    <keyword>success</keyword>
    <keyword>failures</keyword>
  </keywords>
</book>
```

Example 8–21 *XML book descriptor*

The following table shows some examples of the information that would be indexed from different XMLPATTERNS (Figure 8–21):

XMLPATTERN	DATA INDEX
XMLPATTERN '//author' as sql varchar(35)	Indexes all <author> elements
XMLPATTERN '//@*' as sql double	Indexes all numeric attributes
XMLPATTERN '//text()' as sql varchar(hashed)	Indexes all text nodes and hashes them
XMLPATTERN '/keywords/keyword' as sqlvarchar(35)	Indexes all the <keyword>s under <keywords>
XMLPATTERN '/book//text()' as sql varchar(128);	Indexes all text nodes under <book>

Figure 8–21 *XMLPATTERN examples*

If you wanted to index the entire commuter pool based on their Postal Codes (Example 8–4), you would build an XMLPATTERN expression found in Example 8–22:

```
customerinfo/CanadianAddress[2]/PostalCode
```

Example 8–22 *Indexing an XML document based on PostalCode*

DB2 Note

The [2] notation in this `XMLPATTERN` expression actually indicates the second occurrence of the element. So this notation would actually index the Postal Code of the second Canadian address in this document.

While the previous `XMLPATTERN` expression indexes the `<PostalCode>` element's second occurrence, you could index the actual text of any `<PostalCode>` using the `text()` function as follows:

```
customerinfo/CanadianAddress/PostalCode/text()
```

Example 8–23 *Indexing all PostalCode occurrences*

As you might expect, it could become rather complex when trying to generate an XML index for a larger document. For this reason, it's often better to create XML indexes in DB2 9 using the Control Center or the Developer Workbench. These tools provide graphical tooling to inspect the hierarchical structure of an XML document (on the file system or within a DB2 pureXML column) and build the index using graphical tools.

For example, the following illustrates the process to build the `customerinfo/CanadianAddress[2]/PostalCode` index on the working example using the Control Center.

1. Start the Control Center by selecting it from the Start menu or entering **db2cc** from the CLP.

2. Select the **Indexes** folder, right-click, and select **Create→Index (**Figure 8–22). The Create Index wizard opens.

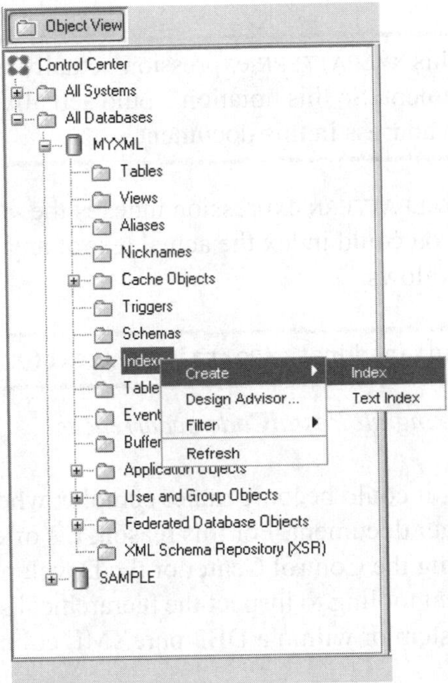

Figure 8–22 *Using the Control Center to create an index*

3. Select the table you want to index by specifying its schema and name, select **Yes** in the **XML columns options** box, and click **Next** (Figure 8–23).

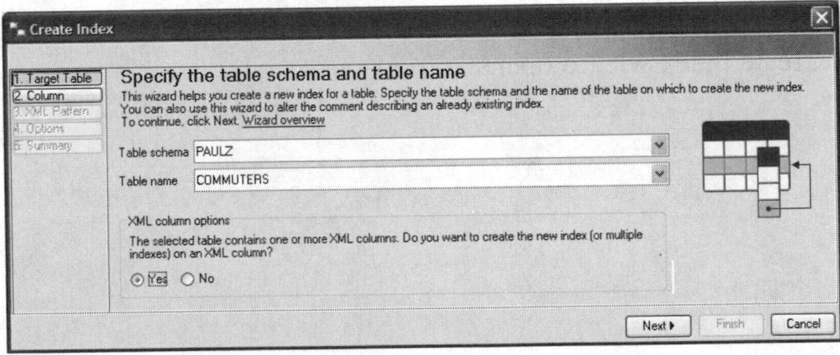

Figure 8–23 *Specifying table schema and name*

When you select a table to index that has an XML column, the **XML column options** box automatically appears. If you select the **Yes** radio button, it tells the Control Center that you want to build an XML-based index.

4. Select the column you want to create the XML index on (only columns of type XML are shown in the **Available XML columns** box), move it to the **Select XML column** box by clicking, then click **Next** (Figure 8–24).

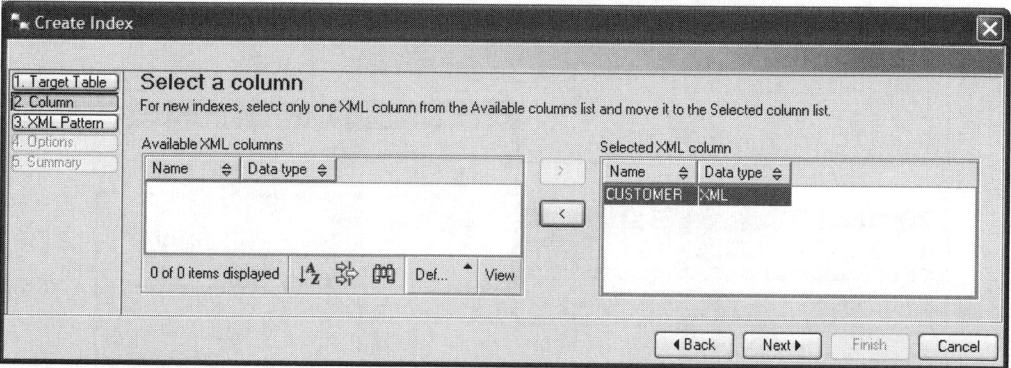

Figure 8–24 *XMLPATTERN examples*

5. Click **Open Document** and import the XML document you want indexed by selecting it from a column where it's already been inserted (the **Use an XML document from the column on which the index is to be built** radio button), or from the file system (the **Use the following local XML instance document** radio button), then click **OK**. The **Document from the select XML column** box is loaded with the selected XML document or fragment (Figure 8–25).

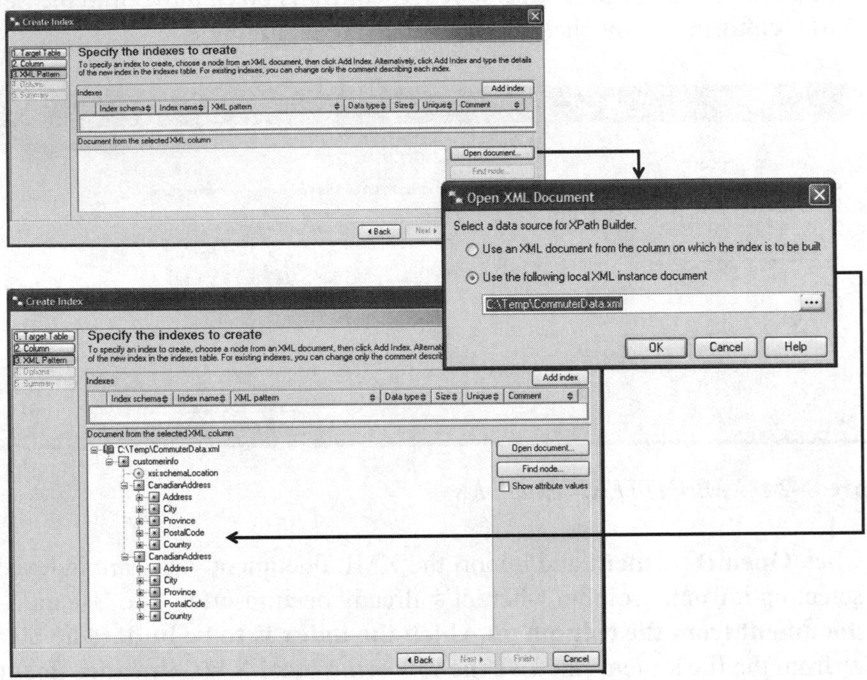

Figure 8–25 *Viewing document data to assist in index creation*

6. Select the `PostalCode` entry in the second `CanadianAddress` element, click **Add Index**, select **Selected element only**, and click **OK**. The **Indexes** field is populated with the `XMLPATTERN` for this new index (Figure 8–26).

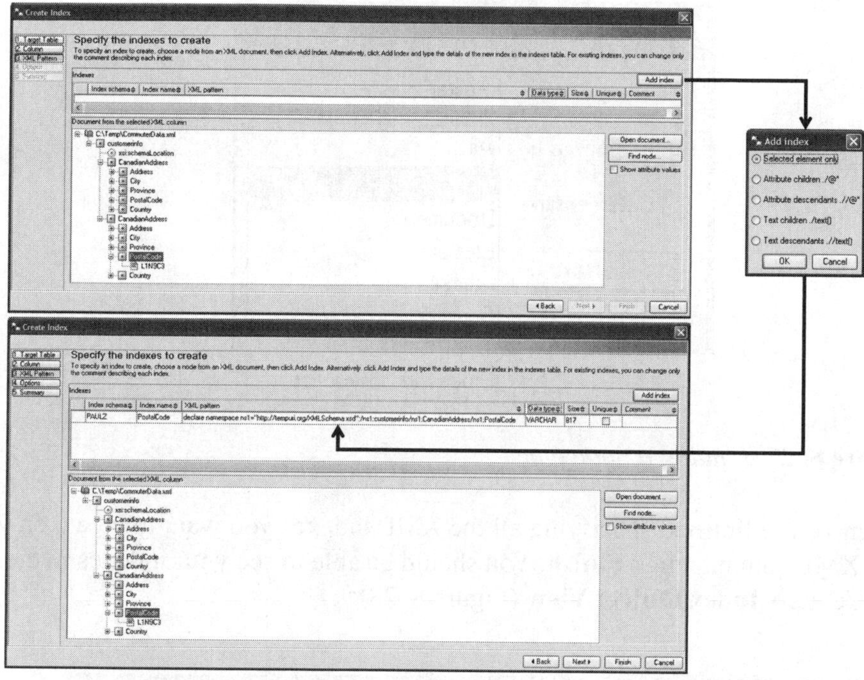

Figure 8–26 *Selecting the PostalCode element*

You can define more than one index at a time when specifying the XMLPATTERN for an XML index. For example, if you wanted to create a second XML index that used the `text()` function, you would click **Add index** and select the **Text children ./text()** option from the Add Index window.

DB2 automatically generates the names of the XML indexes based on the elements you select. You can override this by double clicking on the **Index name** field and entering your own name. Since you can't change the name of an XML index after it's created, you should ensure that you specify this option at index creation time if the default names generated by DB2 aren't suitable for your environment. XML indexes, for the most part, cannot be altered after they are created. In addition, if you are dealing with larger XML documents, you can search through them by clicking **Find node** (Figure 8–27).

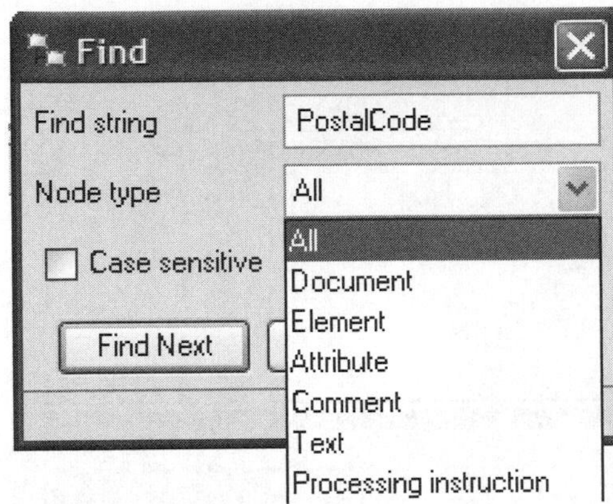

Figure 8–27 *Finding a node type*

When you're finished specifying all the XML indexes you want to create on your pureXML column, click **Finish**. You should be able to see your indexes in the Control Center's **Index Object View** (Figure 8–28).

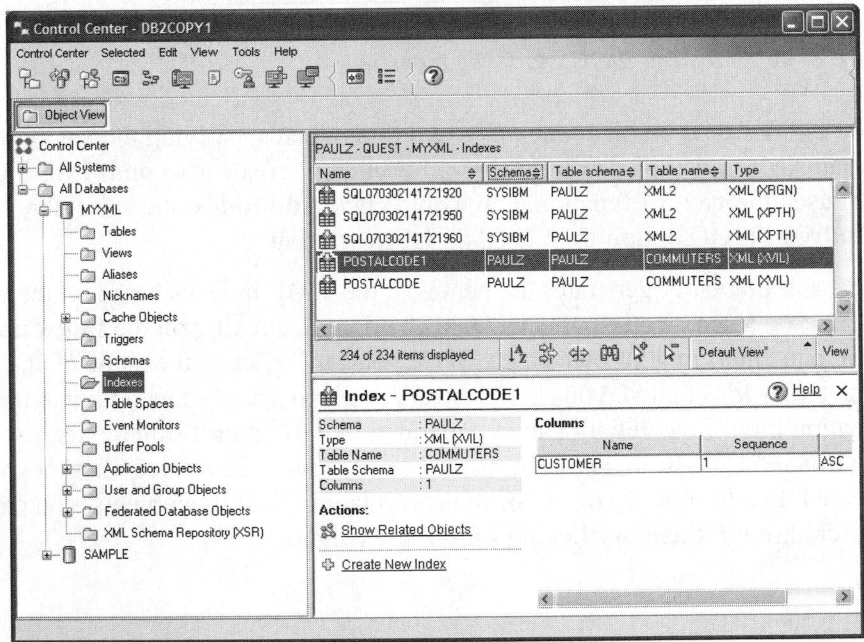

Figure 8–28 *Viewing indexes on the COMMUTERS table*

Creating XML indexes is much easier using the Control Center than manually using the CLP unless you're really familiar with the XML document or fragment you want to index. Even if you know the structure of the XML index, the Control Center's XML index creation facility gives you the opportunity to create multiple indexes very quickly.

The indexing features associated with pureXML are also tightly integrated into popular IDEs. Figure 8–28 shows the facility in Visual Studio 2005 that can be used to generate the exact same index without ever leaving the development environment:

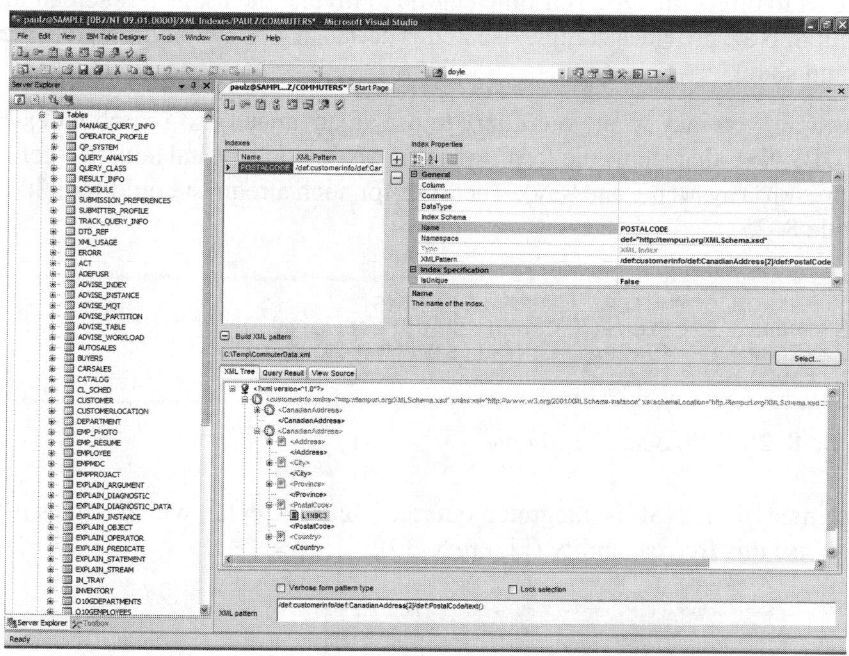

Figure 8–29 *Creating an index through Visual Studio 2005*

Full-text XML Indexing

The XMLPATTERN index is very useful to search subsets of an XML document or fragment (though as previously stated, it can be set to fully index the column's contents as well). In DB2 9, the DB2 Net Search Extender (DB2 NSE) is available free for all editions (it was a previously chargeable component in DB2 8). In DB2 9, the DB2 NSE has been enhanced for pureXML and offers the ability to create a fully XML-aware index for an entire XML document which aids free-form linguistic searching.

You can also use the DB2 NSE to index partial documents, but it's likely that you're indexing text within large fragments for free-form search; for example, a book chapter in an entire book delivered as an XML file.

For example, an NSE index on the COMMUTER table could look like (Example 8–24):

```
CREATE INDEX IDX_COMMUTERS FOR TEXT ON COMMUTERS(CUSTOMERS)
```

Example 8–24 *Text index on COMMUTERS table*

The DB2 NSE provides a set of easy-to-use functions that are simply added to SQL statements to direct the DB2 run-time engine to invoke the usage of such an index. In addition, NSE provides complex search criteria such as synonym match, stemming, and so on.

For example, you may want your query to use an advanced text search index built by the DB2 NSE that stems the forms of using Whitby in a postal address (common forms are: Whitby, Wtby, and Wby). The SQL for such a request could look like (Example 8–25):

```
SELECT * FROM COMMUTERS WHERE CONTAINS
  (CUSTOMERS,'SECTIONS("/CanadianAddress/City")
   FUZZY FORM OF 42 "PATTERN" | STEMMED FORM OF
   "Whitby"')=1
```

Example 8–25 *NSE Search example*

Management of the NSE is integrated into the Control Center, which makes it even easier to use this free capability (Figure 8–30):

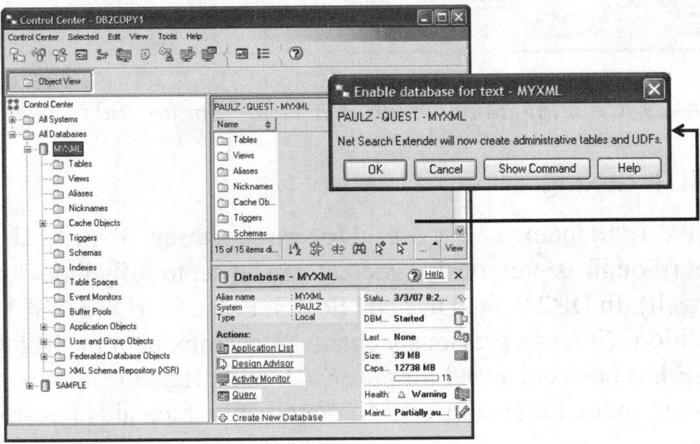

Figure 8–30 *Creating an NSE index through the Control Center*

XML Schema Repository (XSR)

DB2 9 doesn't just have industry leading support for XML, it also has a rich and flexible XML Schema repository (XSR) that can be used to store XML Schema Definition (XSD) documents for subsequent data validation on insertion into a DB2 9 database.

When storing data in DB2 9, all of the XML documents *must* be *well-formed.* This is much different from validation. Validation says that an XML document conforms to a strongly typed document (the XSD document), while an XML document that is well-formed may not be validated, but it confirms to the W3C standards for a well-formed document (matching opening and closing tags, single root node, and more).

Basically, you need to know that DB2 can only store well-formed XML documents (or fragments of XML for that matter) in a pureXML column; however, whether that XML data is valid according to a specific XML Schema is totally up to you. This provides immense flexibility to store *strongly typed* (validated), *typed* (not validated by an XML Schema), and *schema-less* documents — a key principal for any XML data server. What's more, the option to have a strongly typed, typed, or schema-less document stored in a pureXML column can be applied on a row by row basis within the same table (another mostly unique feature compared to other relational vendor's technology). Finally, the XSR in DB2 9 supports what is referred to as schema evolution.

The schema evolution concept considers that not all participants in an XML message may be at the same XML Schema version for your XML applications. For example, consider a brokerage clearing house that clears transactions for its clients. Perhaps the Canadian trading partner is at Version 1.1 of your XSD document while the U.S. trading house is at Version 1.2. DB2 gives you the ability to support *schema evolution* by allowing you to store XSD documents that are orthogonal and intersect. In other words, you can store multiple iterations of the same schema and apply them to each row. Again, this is unique in the industry — other relational vendors don't support this concept, which severely limits the flexibility (the whole point of XML) of an XML solution and creates a severe burden on the DBA to excessively manage tables and policies to support the XML application.

Before you can use an XML Schema Definition document to validate your XML data, you need to register it for use with DB2 in the XML Schema Repository (XSR). The ability to do this is part of the DB2 9 engine, and there are multiple interfaces to accomplish this task. For example, you can use the Control Center, the DB2 Developers Workbench, Visual Studio.NET, the DB2 command line processor (CLP), a stored procedure, and more, as shown in Figure 8–31.

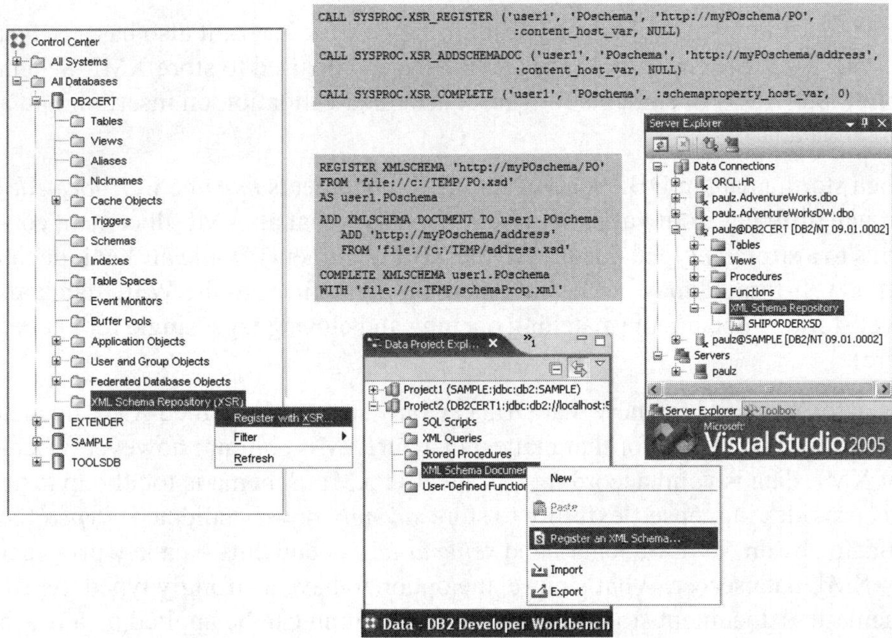

Figure 8–31 *Registering an XSD document in the DB2 9 XSR*

Obviously it stands to reason that you can't register an XSD document if you don't have one. In this chapter, we're trying to give you the basics of the pureXML support in DB2 9. Typically, a DBA isn't the person writing the XSD document. It's safe to say that there are literally hundreds of tools you can use to create an XSD document. Since an XSD document is merely an XML document, it doesn't matter how it was created — it can still be stored in DB2.

DB2 9 has some integration features that make some toolsets easier to work with than others. For example, from the DB2 Developers Workbench, Oxygen XML Editor, Visual Studio (and others), you can use the integrated XML Schema Definition document editors and register them right from the design template. An example of using the native XSD editor in Visual Studio (which has nothing to do with DB2 at all) and registering it in the DB2 9 XSR with a single click is shown in Figure 8–32.

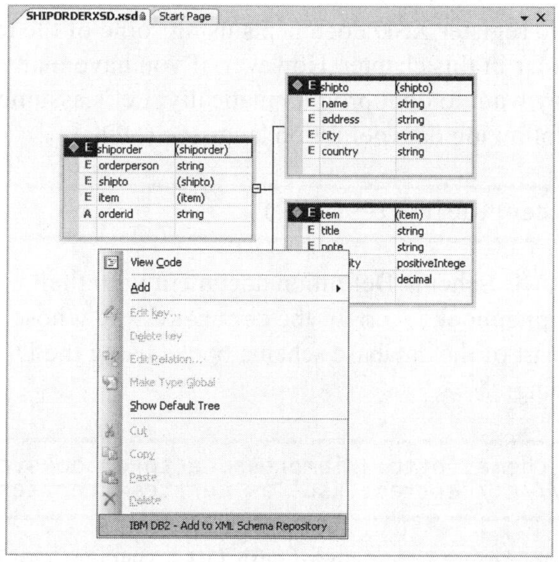

Figure 8–32 *Using native tooling to compose XML Schema Definition documents*

So why would you want to store your XSD documents in the DB2 9 XSR beyond the obvious benefits of a simplified topology? When you store your XSD documents in the XSR, performance of validation can be improved significantly. Generally, validation is a heavy process and can slow down application performance, so anything you can do to make your application go faster is generally a good thing. DB2 9 XSR services help to improve the performance of validation because you don't have to locate these validation documents across a network (or file system, and so on, or other storage configuration) to perform validation.

In addition, when you register an XSD document in the DB2 9 XSR, that document is stored in a parsed-out format with the catalog tables to assist in even faster validation. During the validation process of an XML document, DB2 9 annotates the nodes in the XML hierarchy with data rule information that resides in the XML Schema Definition document. In DB2 9, you can only validate XML documents against an XSD document. Support for document type definition (DTD) documents in DB2 9 is for entity resolution, not validation. Generally, today's XML application have evolved to solely use XSD documents for validation since they are much easier to work with (they are XML documents) and have gained industry and standards acceptance.

XML Schema Definition Document Registration Example

It's pretty easy to register XSD documents using some of the tooling that we've shown you thus far in this chapter. However, if you have many XSD documents to register, you may want to do it programmatically. Let's assume you have a table created by the following data definition language (DDL):

```
create table certtable (test xml)
```

To register an XML Schema Definition document with the URI `http://ibmpress.certprepbooks.com` for the `certtest.xsd` whose schema identifier `certtest` was part of the database schema books using the DB2 CLP, you would enter the following:

```
register xmlschema 'http://ibmpress.certprepbooks.com'
 from 'file:///c:/certtest.xsd' as certtest.certtest complete
```

After the XSD document is registered with DB2, you can validate your XML directly using the `XMLVALIDATE` function, as shown below:

```
insert into certtable(test) values xmlvalidate
  (? According to xmlschema uri
    'http://ibmpress.certprepbooks.com')
```

Of course, if you wanted to insert a document without validation, you could use a command similar to this:

```
insert into certtable(test) values (?,?)
```

DB2 *Note*

You can use any of the DB2 toolsets, or integration points, to do this example through a GUI. We're just trying to illustrate different methods throughout this section of working with your XML artifacts. In fact, you can also perform any of these functions from a Java or .NET application, and more.

DB2 can also try to deduce an XSD for validation based on the XML document without you explicitly specifying it with the `XMLVALIDATE` function by "guessing" at its contents.

To attempt to validate your XML document without specifically pointing to an XML Schema Definition, you could enter a command similar to the following:

```
insert into certtable(test) values (?,xmlvalidate(?))
```

As you can imagine, performing XML validation consumes CPU cycles on your data server. If you're managing a high-volume transactional data server, you shouldn't perform data validation unless it's really needed.

Since the XSR is really just a section of the DB2 storage engine, you can interact with it and view the registered XML Schema Definition documents in a natural way. For example, the following simple query would return a list of all registered XSD documents:

```
select * from syscat.xsrobjects
```

You could find out what XML Schema Definition document was used to validate a specific document using a query similar to the following:

```
select deptid, xsrobjects(test) from certtable where testid=704
```

Summary

In this chapter, we have examined the new XML capabilities within DB2, including the new XML data type, the pureXML implementation, and the SQL and XML features supporting this new data type.

DB2 has supported XML structures for a number of releases. These functions allowed a developer to store and retrieve XML information from a DB2 database. While the DB2 extender was acceptable for XML manipulation, it had a number of limitations that reduced its usability and performance.

The new pureXML support in DB2 adds significant new capability to the database and makes the manipulation of XML much more efficient and powerful.

CHAPTER 9

Development SQL

- USER-DEFINED FUNCTIONS
- USER-DEFINED STRUCTURED DATA TYPES
- SYNONYM AND ALIAS
- COMMIT AND ROLLBACK
- SQL PROCEDURAL LANGUAGE
- STORED PROCEDURES

This chapter will cover some of the additional SQL features that are included in DB2 that are primarily intended for developers. User-defined functions (UDFs) and user-defined structured data types can be used for enhancing the functions and data types available in DB2. SYNONYM, ALIAS, COMMIT, and ROLLBACK are used within programs for controlling the access to objects and determining changes in the database. Finally, the SQL Procedural Language (SQL PL) is introduced for its use in triggers, user-defined functions, stored procedures, and within SQL blocks.

User-Defined Functions

User-defined functions (UDF) form the basis of *Object-Relational* extensions to the SQL language along with user-defined types (UDT) and LOBs. Fundamentally, a database function is a relationship between a set of input data values and a result value. DB2 comes with many built-in functions; however, it is possible to create your own column, scalar, and table functions.

There are four types of functions:

- Column
- Scalar
- Row
- Table

Column functions take in a set of data values from a column and derive a single result. For example, to determine the average score of all tests taken (Example 9–1):

```
SELECT AVG(SCORE) FROM TEST_TAKEN;
```

Example 9–1 *Column function*

Scalar functions can have one or more arguments but return only one value. For example, to look at all tests taken since 1996 (Example 9–2):

```
SELECT * FROM TEST_TAKEN
  WHERE YEAR(DATE_TAKEN) > 1996;
```

Example 9–2 *Scalar function*

The third type of function, a row function, is used in combination with structured data types. The argument to a row function must consist of an abstract data type and it returns multiple values that are used as part of a transform function (Example 9–3).

```
CREATE FUNCTION PAY_COLUMNS (P COMPENSATION)
  RETURNS ROW(
              SALARY      INT,
              BONUS       INT,
              COMMISSION  INT
              )
  LANGUAGE SQL
  RETURN VALUES (P..SALARY, P..BONUS, P..COMMISSION);
```

Example 9–3 *Row function*

A row function is only used when passing a structured data type to an external routine. External routines are written in programming languages that need to have the components of a structured data type converted to data types the language understands. This function is never used in standard SQL so most users will not need to be aware of it.

The final type of function, a table function, can only be used in the FROM clause of an SQL statement. It returns columns of a table, resembling a regular created table. This type of function is used in the FROM clause of a SELECT statement and takes the place of a normal table name (Example 9–4).

```
SELECT * FROM TABLE(STORES(10,20)) AS STORE_NUMBERS;
```

Example 9–4 *Table function*

There are a large number of functions built-in to DB2 and they can be found in the *DB2 SQL Reference*.

In DB2, you can create your own functions (which can be scalar or table functions). A UDF can be written in a high-level programming language such as C, C++, Java, SQL PL, or you can use SQL statements.

You can also create a user-defined function based on another UDF or built-in function. This concept is similar to *overloading* classes in object-oriented programming. This is called a *sourced* function. A UDF that you write from scratch is called an *external* function.

DB2 *Note*

In a Windows environment, as part of the Microsoft Object Linking and Embedding (OLE) architecture, DB2 can act as an OLE Automation Controller. Through this mechanism, DB2 can invoke methods of OLE automation objects as external UDFs.

External UDFs, once written and generated as dynamically loadable libraries or classes, must be registered with the database.The CONGRAT function shown in Example 9–5 is registered using the CREATE FUNCTION statement.

```
CREATE FUNCTION CONGRAT(VARCHAR(30),VARCHAR(40))
       RETURNS CLOB(1K)
       EXTERNAL NAME 'CONGRAT.A!CONGRAT'
       LANGUAGE C
       PARAMETER STYLE DB2SQL
       DETERMINISTIC
       FENCED
       NO SQL
       NO EXTERNAL ACTION;
```

Example 9–5 *Registering a user-defined function*

Sourced UDFs are registered in the same way, simply by specifying the *parent* source function. Example 9–6 illustrates how an AVG function can be created for the SCORE data type:

```
CREATE FUNCTION AVG (SCORE)
       RETURNS SCORE
       SOURCE   SYSIBM.AVG(DECIMAL);
```

Example 9–6 *Registering a user-defined function based on another function*

These CREATE FUNCTION statements place an entry for each UDF in the view SYSCAT.FUNCTIONS. You can view the UDFs registered with the database in the Control Center.

User-defined functions are like any other database object in DB2, meaning that each UDF has a schema name associated with it. Ideally, each UDF is fully qualified when it is called. However, this can be quite difficult and can limit the flexibility of SQL queries. The alternative is to use the special register CURRENT FUNCTION PATH. DB2 uses this path to resolve unqualified function references. The path in this case is not a list of directories, but a list of schema names such as "SYSIBM", "SYSFUN", or "DB2CERT". SYSFUN is the schema used for built-in UDFs. Note that the authorities needed to create UDFs are the same as those required to create stored procedures.

For more information on the various types of UDFs and the parameters used in the CREATE FUNCTION statement, please refer to the *Developing SQL and External Routines Reference.*

SQL-Bodied Scalar Functions

The previous examples referred to user-defined functions and table functions that used a programming language such as C, C++, SQL PL, or Java to create the logic associated with the function. An alternative method of creating these functions is through the use of SQL statements as shown in Example 9–7.

```
CREATE FUNCTION BONUS(SALARY INT, BONUS_PERCENT INT)
  RETURNS INT
  LANGUAGE SQL CONTAINS SQL
  RETURN
    (
    SALARY * BONUS_PERCENT / 100
    );
```

Example 9–7 *User-defined function — BONUS*

The CREATE FUNCTION statement allows the use of one or more SQL statements to be used for the calculations. The BONUS function takes the salary value and calculates the bonus based on a percentage rate. This function could now be used in an SQL statement to calculate the bonus for an employee (Example 9–8).

```
VALUES BONUS(30000,10);

1
-----------
       3000
```

Example 9–8 *Using the BONUS function*

DB2 Note

The VALUES clause is a convenient short form when writing SQL that only needs to return a single value and isn't dependent on a table name.

This function could be used anywhere in an SQL statement where a normal function could be used. Example 9–9 illustrates how the BONUS function could be used as part of an UPDATE statement.

```
UPDATE STAFF
  SET BONUS_PAY = BONUS(STAFF.SALARY, 10);
```

Example 9–9 *Advanced use of the BONUS function*

The body of the function can only consist of one SQL statement. While this may seem like a big restriction, the SQL language includes the CASE statement which can allow for a limited form of logic. The BONUS function is modified in Example 9–10 to return different bonus values depending on the salary level.

```
CREATE FUNCTION BONUS(SALARY INT, BONUS_PERCENT INT)
  RETURNS INT
  LANGUAGE SQL CONTAINS SQL
  RETURN
    (
    CASE
      WHEN SALARY <= 20000 THEN SALARY / BONUS_PERCENT
      WHEN SALARY <= 30000 THEN SALARY / BONUS_PERCENT / 2
      WHEN SALARY <= 40000 THEN SALARY / BONUS_PERCENT / 4
      ELSE 0
    END
    );
```

Example 9–10 *BONUS function - Additional logic*

The following SQL shows the result from four different salary values (Example 9–11):

```
VALUES BONUS(20000,10), BONUS(30000,10), BONUS(40000,10),
       BONUS(50000,10);

1
-----------
       2000
       1500
       1000
          0
```

Example 9–11 *Using the BONUS function*

Note that the limitation of one SQL statement per function body only applies if the return statement is used. A developer can use SQL procedural statements (SQL PL) to add additional logic to a user-defined function. See the section on "SQL Procedural Language" on page 559.

SQL-Bodied Row Functions

A row function is similar to a scalar function, but it can only be used with user-defined structured types. Each set of one or more scalar parameters returns a single row instead of a single value. Row functions can only be used as a transform function mapping attributes of a structured type into built-in data type values in a row.

More information on transform functions can be found in the section "Structured Data Types" on page 549.

SQL-Bodied Table Functions

A table function is a UDF that returns a table to the SQL statement that calls it. This means that a table function can only be referenced in the `FROM` clause of a `SELECT` statement. The table function provides a means of including external data in SQL queries. Table functions can read non-DB2 data, for instance, a file on the operating system, tabularize it, and return the data to DB2 as a result set that can subsequently be treated like any other table.

For example, the `APPFORM` table function in Example 9–12 takes in a candidate application form, processes it, and returns the data in an appropriate format to be inserted in the `CANDIDATE` table (except for the candidate ID, which is generated):

```
CREATE FUNCTION APPFORM(VARCHAR(30))
RETURNS TABLE (LNAME VARCHAR(30),FNAME VARCHAR(30),
               INITIAL CHAR(1), HPHONE PHONE,
               WPHONE PHONE, STREETNO VARCHAR(8),
               STREETNAME VARCHAR(20),
               CITY VARCHAR(20),
               PROV_STATE VARCHAR(30),
               CODE CHAR(6), COUNTRY VARCHAR(20))
EXTERNAL NAME 'TBUDF!APPFORM'
LANGUAGE C PARAMETER STYLE DB2SQL
NO SQL DETERMINISTIC
NO EXTERNAL ACTION
FINAL CALL
CARDINALITY 20;
```

Example 9–12 *User-defined table function - APPFORM*

If we wanted to insert a new candidate into the `CANDIDATE` table based on his or her application form, we could use the following `SELECT` statement (Example 9–13):

```
INSERT INTO TEST_CANDIDATE
   SELECT SUBSTR(GENERATE_UNIQUE(),1,9) AS CID,
          LNAME, FNAME, INITIAL,
          HPHONE, WPHONE,
          STREETNO, STREETNAME, CITY,
          PROV_STATE, CODE, COUNTRY
   FROM TABLE(APPFORM('D:\DOCS\NEWFORM.TXT')) AS CANDIDATE;
```

Example 9–13 *Using a table function*

DB2 needs the additional `TABLE()` clause to identify the fact that the results will be returned from a table function rather than a traditional table.

DB2 *Note*

DB2 also provides table functions for accessing data from OLE DB providers. This allows you to incorporate data into your DB2 database or application from a wide variety of relational and non-relational data sources including Oracle, Microsoft SQL Server, and Microsoft Access.

User-defined table functions can also be written using one or more SQL statements. This gives the user the capability of creating a table UDF without the need to write a program in C, C++, or Java.

The table UDF can only access database tables as part of the definition, so it is not as flexible as an external UDF. The example in Example 9–14 creates a table UDF that returns records from the TEST_TAKEN table where the test scores are between two values.

```
CREATE FUNCTION GET_MARKS(
     BEGIN_RANGE INT,
     END_RANGE   INT)
  RETURNS TABLE(CID      CANDIDATE_ID,
                NUMBER TEST_ID,
                SCORE  TEST_SCORE)
  LANGUAGE SQL READS SQL DATA
  RETURN
    SELECT CID, NUMBER, SCORE FROM TEST_TAKEN
       WHERE
         INTEGER(SCORE) BETWEEN BEGIN_RANGE AND END_RANGE;
```

Example 9–14 *GET_MARKS table function*

Note the extensive use of user-defined types in this example. The function takes two SCORE arguments that represent the range of marks that we want to retrieve from the table. This table function can now be used as part of a select statement. The SQL in Example 9–15 retrieves the list of candidates who scored between 60 and 70 percent on their test.

```
SELECT * FROM TABLE(GET_MARKS(60,70)) AS MARKS;

CID NUMBER SCORE
--- ------ -----------
111 500             65
111 502             67
```

Example 9–15 *GET_MARKS table function usage*

In order to use the table function, the SQL statement must make use of the TABLE clause with the table function imbedded within it. In addition, the resulting table must be named with the AS clause.

The table that is returned via the table function can also have additional SQL predicates applied to it. For instance, the SQL could have been modified to only return those marks for test number 500 (Example 9–16):

```
SELECT * FROM TABLE(GET_MARKS(60,70)) AS MARKS
  WHERE NUMBER = TEST_ID('500');

CID NUMBER SCORE
--- ------ -----------
111 500             65
```

Example 9–16 *GET_MARKS table function usage with additional logic*

The table UDF can be used in situations where the developer wants to dynamically control the rows being returned to a user. A view definition could have been created to return information about the TEST_TAKEN table, but the definition would have been static. For instance, the following view definition would return exactly the same result (Example 9–17):

```
CREATE VIEW GET_MARKS AS (
   SELECT CID, NUMBER, SCORE FROM TEST_TAKEN
     WHERE
          INTEGER(SCORE) BETWEEN 60 AND 70;
```

Example 9–17 *GET_MARKS as a VIEW*

However, this view will only return the scores between 60 and 70. In contrast, the table UDF can use variables to change the rows that are returned.

Updating Data with Table Functions

User-defined table functions can also include SQL statements that modify other tables. This is sometimes useful when a system needs to track access to a table or update some statistics.

For instance, a table that tracks who used the GET_MARKS function could be easily incorporated into the function. Whenever someone attempts to access the table via the GET_MARKS function, their userid, time of access, and the parameters that were used are recorded in the AUDIT_MARKS table. The following table will track all access to the table (Example 9–18):

```
CREATE TABLE AUDIT_MARKS
  (
  TX_TIME TIMESTAMP,
  TX_USER VARCHAR(30),
  BEGIN_RANGE INT, END_RANGE INT
  );
```

Example 9–18 *Audit table*

The table function is changed to use BEGIN ATOMIC, MODIFIES SQL DATA, and an insert statement (Example 9–19):

```
DROP FUNCTION GET_MARKS;

CREATE FUNCTION GET_MARKS(
     BEGIN_RANGE INT,
     END_RANGE   INT)
  RETURNS TABLE(CID CANDIDATE_ID, NUMBER TEST_ID,
              SCORE TEST_SCORE)
  LANGUAGE SQL MODIFIES SQL DATA
  BEGIN ATOMIC
    INSERT INTO AUDIT_MARKS VALUES(CURRENT TIMESTAMP,
      CURRENT USER, BEGIN_RANGE, END_RANGE);
    RETURN
      SELECT CID, NUMBER, SCORE FROM TEST_TAKEN
        WHERE INTEGER(SCORE) BETWEEN
                 BEGIN_RANGE AND END_RANGE;
  END;
```

Example 9–19 *Audit access via table function*

The following two select statements are executed against this table, and the audit results displayed (Example 9–20):

```
SELECT * FROM TABLE(GET_MARKS(60,70)) AS MARKS
  WHERE NUMBER = TEST_ID('500');

SELECT * FROM TABLE(GET_MARKS(90,100)) AS MARKS;

SELECT * FROM AUDIT_MARKS;

TX_TIME                    TX_USER    BEGIN_RANGE END_RANGE
-------------------------- ---------- ----------- ----------
2007-02-26-10.31.54.721000 BAKLARZ             60         70
2007-02-26-10.31.54.721000 BAKLARZ             90        100

  2 record(s) selected.
```

Example 9–20 *Audit results*

More information on user-defined table definitions can be found in the *DB2 SQL*

Reference and how to develop these functions using a high-level language are found in the *Developing SQL and External Routines Reference*.

Structured Data Types

Structured data types (or sometimes referred to as abstract data types) is extended to table definitions. The structured data type is similar to the typed tables discussed in "Advanced SQL" on page 397. However, these data types are used within the definition of the table itself, rather than being used to define tables.

For instance, our DB2CERT database contained information about the candidates taking the test. The original definition for the table is shown in Example 9–21.

```
CREATE TABLE TEST_CANDIDATE
 (CID            CANDIDATE_ID      NOT NULL,
 LNAME           VARCHAR(10)       NOT NULL,
 FNAME           VARCHAR(8)        NOT NULL,
 INITIAL         CHAR(1),
 HPHONE          PHONE, WPHONE     PHONE,
 STREETNO        VARCHAR(8),
 STREETNAME      VARCHAR(15)       NOT NULL,
 CITY            VARCHAR(10)       NOT NULL,
 PROV_STATE      VARCHAR(10)       NOT NULL,
 CODE            CHAR(6)           NOT NULL,
 COUNTRY         VARCHAR(10)       NOT NULL,
 CERT_DBA        CHAR(1) NOT NULL WITH DEFAULT,
 CERT_APP        CHAR(1) NOT NULL WITH DEFAULT,
 PRIMARY KEY (CID));
```

Example 9–21 *Table definition for the CANDIDATE table*

A number of UDTs were used in the definition of this table. For instance, a UDT called CANDIDATE_ID was created to represent a unique identifier for this individual. Further down the table definition, a number of fields were created for storing the address information of the candidate in the table. These multiple fields could be combined into one structured data type definition as shown in Example 9–22.

```
CREATE TYPE ADDRESS_TYPE AS
 (
 STREETNO        VARCHAR(8),
 STREETNAME      VARCHAR(15),
 CITY            VARCHAR(10),
 PROV_STATE      VARCHAR(10),
 CODE            CHAR(6),
 COUNTRY         VARCHAR(10)
 )
MODE DB2SQL WITH FUNCTION ACCESS INSTANTIABLE;
```

Example 9–22 *Creating structured data type*

Now that the definition has been created, we can use it as part of the table creation (Example 9–23):

```
CREATE TABLE TEST_CANDIDATE
  (
  CID            CANDIDATE_ID      NOT NULL,
  LNAME          VARCHAR(10)       NOT NULL,
  FNAME          VARCHAR(8)        NOT NULL,
  INITIAL        CHAR(1),
  HPHONE         PHONE,
  WPHONE         PHONE,
  ADDRESS        ADDRESS_TYPE NOT NULL,
  CERT_DBA       CHAR(1) NOT NULL WITH DEFAULT,
  CERT_APP       CHAR(1) NOT NULL WITH DEFAULT,
  PRIMARY KEY    (CID)
  );
```

Example 9–23 *Creating TEST_CANDIDATE table with the address structure*

The use of structured data types can help simplify the definitions of tables that have many common elements. This will also make it much easier to develop applications that use object-oriented techniques. Your structured data types can contain other structured data types as well as UDTs within them.

There are a number of administrative changes that you need to be aware of when using these data types in the definition of the table. The first change is how elements are inserted into a table. The relational model always assumes that a column contains one value. Because of this restriction, a number of new operators were required to allow structures to be inserted into tables. For instance, the `INSERT` command needs to know how to insert a structure.

To illustrate the use of these new operators, we will create a new table with a structured data type of `COMPENSATION` (Example 9–24).

```
CREATE TYPE COMPENSATION AS
 (
 SALARY       INT,
 BONUS        INT,
 COMMISSION   INT
 )
MODE DB2SQL WITH FUNCTION ACCESS INSTANTIABLE;
```

Example 9–24 *Creating COMPENSATION data type*

The COMPENSATION structure contains three elements that make up a person's pay. This structure will be used in the creation of a EMPLOYEES table (Example 9–25).

```
CREATE TABLE EMPLOYEES
 (
 NAME   CHAR(10),
 PAY    COMPENSATION
 );
```

Example 9–25 *Creating a table with the COMPENSATION data type*

At this point we need to insert some information into the EMPLOYEES table. To insert values into the PAY column, we use the COMPENSATION constructor which is similar to a casting function (Example 9–26):

```
INSERT INTO EMPLOYEES VALUES
   (
   'KELLY',
   COMPENSATION()..SALARY(30000)..BONUS(1000)..COMMISSION(3000)
   );
```

Example 9–26 *Inserting a structure into the EMPLOYEES table*

The COMPENSATION constructor indicates to DB2 that the fields following it make up part of the structure and the double-dot ".." notation combines the elements. The values needed to be cast as a COMPENSATION type since the PAY column is defined as a COMPENSATION type. Fortunately for the developer, you can also generate a PAY SQL-bodied constructor that makes the syntax more readable (Example 9–27).

```
CREATE FUNCTION PAY(A INT, B INT, C INT)
  RETURNS COMPENSATION
  LANGUAGE SQL
  RETURN(
    COMPENSATION()..SALARY(A)..BONUS(B)..COMMISSION(C)
  );
```

Example 9–27 *Creating PAY constructor*

Now the SQL for inserting the structure can be simplified (Example 9–28):

```
INSERT INTO EMPLOYEES VALUES
   (
   'KATRINA',PAY(40000,2000,6000)
   );
```

Example 9–28 *Using PAY function to insert a structure*

After the data has been inserted into the table, you must use the ".." notation to extract the individual elements of the structure. When you define your structured data type, DB2 generates a number of functions that allow you to extract the values without using the double-dot notation. The two statements found in Example 9–29 generate identical results:

```
SELECT NAME, PAY..SALARY, PAY..BONUS, PAY..COMMISSION
  FROM EMPLOYEES;

SELECT NAME, SALARY(PAY), BONUS(PAY), COMMISSION(PAY)
  FROM EMPLOYEES;

NAME       2           3           4
---------- ----------- ----------- -----------
KELLY            30000        1000        3000
KATRINA          40000        2000        6000
```

Example 9–29 *Selecting information from the EMPLOYEES table*

When displaying structures, DB2 does not generate column names as in the case of regular column types. The user must supply column names through the use of the AS keyword in the SELECT list.

The structure elements can also be used in the where clause and in any part of the SQL that uses column information. For instance, the previous SQL could be modified to return only those employees who have a SALARY >= 30000 and a bonus and commission that do not exceed 5000 in value (Example 9–30).

```
SELECT NAME, PAY..SALARY, PAY..BONUS, PAY..COMMISSION
  FROM EMPLOYEES
WHERE
  SALARY(PAY) >= 30000 AND
  (BONUS(PAY) + PAY..COMMISSION <= 5000);

NAME       2           3           4
---------- ----------- ----------- -----------
KELLY            30000        1000        3000
```

Example 9–30 *Selecting information from the EMPLOYEES table with logic*

Example 9–30 illustrates the use of the double-dot notation and the casting functions against the same structure.

Finally, the developer or DBA needs to create some transform functions for DB2 so that it can handle SELECT commands that do not explicitly name the columns in the select list.

The following SQL statement will generate an error (Example 9–31):

```
SELECT * FROM EMPLOYEES;

SQL20015N  A transform group "DB2_PROGRAM" is not defined
  for data type "BAKLARZ.COMPENSATION".  SQLSTATE=42741
```

Example 9–31 *Error when selecting without column names*

DB2 does not know how to represent the PAY structure found within the EMPLOYEES table. In order to make a SELECT * work, two steps need to be taken. First, a UDF needs to be created that returns the contents of the structure as one value. This value must be a simple type, not a structure. For instance, we could create a function that returns the value of each field in the PAY structure as a string of values. The SQL in Example 9–32 returns the PAY structure as a character string.

```
CREATE FUNCTION SHOW_PAY (P COMPENSATION)
      RETURNS VARCHAR(25)
      LANGUAGE SQL
      RETURN '(' ||
               RTRIM(CHAR(P..SALARY)) || ',' ||
               RTRIM(CHAR(P..BONUS)) || ',' ||
               RTRIM(CHAR(P..COMMISSION)) ||')' ;

SELECT NAME, SHOW_PAY(PAY) FROM EMPLOYEES;

NAME       2
---------- -------------------------
KELLY      (30000,1000,3000)
KATRINA    (40000,2000,6000)
```

Example 9–32 *SHOW_PAY function for displaying PAY column*

After this function is defined, we need to create a transform for this column so that DB2 knows how to handle it in a select statement (Example 9–33).

```
CREATE TRANSFORM FOR COMPENSATION
      DB2_PROGRAM
      ( FROM SQL WITH FUNCTION SHOW_PAY(COMPENSATION));
```

Example 9–33 *Transform function for COMPENSATION type*

Once the transform is defined, the PAY column can be used in a select list without worrying about the structure underneath (Example 9–34).

```
SELECT * FROM EMPLOYEES;

NAME       PAY
---------- -------------------------
KELLY      (30000,1000,3000)
KATRINA    (40000,2000,6000)
```

Example 9–34 *Transform function for COMPENSATION type*

Since the PAY column can now be represented as a single value, DB2 places the column heading at the top of the results.

When creating transforms for columns, the developer or DBA should understand how a user would interpret the column. The transform function that was defined previously represents the PAY column as a character string. This may seem odd to a user who expects to see a single value being returned from the database. A more-intuitive definition would be to have the SHOW_PAY function calculate the actual employee PAY by summing the columns together. The SQL in Example 9–35 creates a function that returns the sum of the three PAY elements.

```
DROP FUNCTION SHOW_PAY;

CREATE FUNCTION SHOW_PAY (P COMPENSATION)
     RETURNS INT
     LANGUAGE SQL
     RETURN P..SALARY + P..BONUS + P..COMMISSION;

CREATE TRANSFORM FOR COMPENSATION
     DB2_PROGRAM
     ( FROM SQL WITH FUNCTION SHOW_PAY(COMPENSATION));

SELECT NAME, SHOW_PAY(PAY) FROM EMPLOYEES;

NAME       2
---------- -----------
SHIRLEY          34000
KATRINA          48000

SELECT * FROM EMPLOYEES;

NAME       PAY
---------- -----------
KELLY            34000
KATRINA          48000
```

Example 9–35 *Alternative function for displaying PAY column*

The advantage of creating a function like SHOW_PAY is that it can now be used in a regular SQL statement to select records based on the total pay of the individual. For instance, the following SQL statement will return only those employees who have a total pay greater than 45000.

```
SELECT * FROM EMPLOYEES
  WHERE SHOW_PAY(PAY) > 45000;

NAME       PAY
---------- -----------
KATRINA          48000
```

Example 9–36 *Alternative function for displaying PAY column*

User-defined structured data types and user-defined functions are powerful features within DB2. A development group can create common structures and routines to be used within the database. That can lead to better control of data definitions as well as to encourage more code reuse through the use of UDFs.

Schemas and Aliases

In this section, we will discuss two database objects, schemas and aliases, which have not been discussed in detail in the previous chapters.

Schema

A schema is a database entity that represents a collection of named objects within a DB2 database. The schema name is actually part of the fully qualified name of the object being accessed. When database objects are being defined using the SQL CREATE <DB OBJECT> statement, a qualifier or schema name should be provided in the name of the database object.

Schemas may be explicitly created using the CREATE SCHEMA statement with one user specified as the owner. If the user BERT wanted to create tables with a schema called DB2, the DBADM could use the Control Center to create the schema for BERT or use the following statement. Since BERT owns the schema, he can create objects within the schema (Example 9–37).

```
CREATE SCHEMA DB2 AUTHORIZATION BERT;
```

Example 9–37 *Creating a schema*

Schema names are associated with many database objects, including tables, views, indexes, and packages. For application development purposes, the table, view, and package objects are of primary interest because indexes cannot be directly referenced in SQL DML statements (INSERT, UPDATE, DELETE). If the creator of a database object does not include the schema name in the database object definition, then the object will be created using the creator's authorization ID (assuming IMPLICIT_SCHEMA has not been revoked for the creator).

For example, assume that a user called MARK created a table using the statement CREATE TABLE TABLE1 (C1 CHAR(3)). The complete name of the database object would be MARK.TABLE1, and the application would have to specify the entire name.

DB2 Note

Avoid using unqualified table or view names in SQL statements when creating a production application. This will avoid problems with applications referring to an incorrect table. For purposes of this book, we have tried to simplify the SQL by removing the schema name. In most instances this will be your own userid.

In Example 9–38, the schema for the table called TEST is DB2CERT. If you refer to this table in an embedded SQL application, you should reference the table using its fully qualified name, DB2CERT.TEST. Failure to include the schema name can result in unexpected behavior.

In an embedded SQL application, unqualified database objects are qualified with the authorization ID of the person who performed the BIND command to bind the application package to the database. In a dynamic SQL application, unqualified database objects are qualified with the authorization ID of the person who is executing the statement. This difference is a major consideration during application development because it affects the required data access privileges.

The fully qualified name of a database object must be unique within the database. Thus, from the previous example, another table can exist with the name TEST, if the schema name is something other than DB2CERT.

```
CREATE TABLE DB2CERT.TEST
  (
  NUMBER       TEST_ID      NOT NULL,
  NAME         VARCHAR(30)  NOT NULL,
  TYPE         CHAR(1)      NOT NULL,
  AVGSCORE     SCORE        NOT NULL,
  CUTSCORE     SCORE        NOT NULL,
  LENGTH       MINUTES      NOT NULL,
  TOTALTAKEN   INTEGER      NOT NULL,
  TOTALPASSED  INTEGER      NOT NULL,
  CONSTRAINT   PRIMARY KEY(NUMBER)
  );
```

Example 9–38 *Creating a table specifying a schema*

Alias

An alias can be used to refer to a table within the database. If an application contains SQL statements that access tables based on an alias, then the alias can be defined to represent different tables without modifying the application. An alias can be created for a table or another alias.

For example, assume a user named CHLOE created a table called PRICES, and a user named MAXINE created a table called PRICES. These tables reside in the same database and are named CHLOE.PRICES and MAXINE.PRICES. Suppose you are asked to develop an application that would access both of these tables and produce summary reports. Also assume that you are using an embedded SQL technique. Your application would require two sets of queries, one for each schema name: CHLOE and MAXINE. This is not a good programming technique and is prone to error. For instance, if you find a problem with one of the SQL statements, you may forget to make the corresponding change in the statement that accesses the other table. An alias can be used as the target table name for the SQL statements in your application. If the referenced object in your application is an alias, it can be defined to represent the table CHLOE.PRICES or MAXINE.PRICES.

Let's create the alias objects that could be used in the example scenario (Example 9–39).

```
CREATE ALIAS DB2CERT.PRICES FOR CHLOE.PRICES;
OR
CREATE ALIAS DB2CERT.PRICES FOR MAXINE.PRICES;
```

Example 9–39 *Creating Aliases*

The application could be developed referencing the table object as DB2CERT.PRICES. The application would then access whichever table has been defined as the source for the DB2CERT.PRICES alias. There can only be one definition for the DB2CERT.PRICES alias at any given time within the database. You could not create the DB2CERT.PRICES alias twice, for example. However, the same alias name could be used in different databases.

Another example of using aliases involves creating multiple aliases for the same source table or view. Assume that the database object was called DB2CERT.PRICES, and we wanted to allow the users ANDREW and GEOFF to issue the following SQL statement from the CLP (Example 9–40):

```
SELECT * FROM PRICES;
```

Example 9–40 *Unqualified SELECT*

The SELECT statement did not explicitly qualify the table name by using the table's schema name. Since the CLP interface is an embedded dynamic SQL interface, the table is implicitly qualified with the current authorization IDs. The target table for this query would be ANDREW.PRICES and GEOFF.PRICES. These are two different tables. However, the goal of the SELECT statement was to access the data in the DB2CERT.PRICES table. Create two aliases to provide the desired results (Example 9–41):

```
CREATE ALIAS ANDREW.PRICES FOR DB2CERT.PRICES;
CREATE ALIAS GEOFF.PRICES FOR DB2CERT.PRICES;
```

Example 9–41 *Qualified SELECT*

If you were not the user ANDREW, and you tried to create the alias ANDREW.PRICES, you would require CREATE_IN authority in the schema ANDREW, or DBADM or SYSADM authority to create the alias ANDREW.PRICES in the schema. Once you create the alias ANDREW.PRICES, the privileges on the referenced table or view (in this case, DB2CERT.PRICES) are used to determine if access is granted to users on ANDREW.PRICES.

COMMIT and ROLLBACK

A program must establish a connection to the target database server before it can run any executable SQL statements. This connection identifies both the authorization ID of the user who is running the program and the name of the database server against which the program is run. After the connection has been established, the program can issue SQL statements that manipulate data (SELECT, INSERT, UPDATE, or DELETE), define and maintain database objects (CREATE, ALTER, or DROP), and initiate control operations (GRANT, REVOKE, COMMIT, or ROLLBACK). These statements are considered parts of a transaction. A transaction is a sequence of SQL statements (possibly with intervening program logic) that the database manager treats as a whole. An alternative term that is often used for transaction is unit of work. To ensure the consistency of data at the transaction level, the system makes sure that either all operations within a transaction are completed or none are completed.

A transaction begins implicitly with the first executable SQL statement and ends with either a COMMIT or a ROLLBACK statement or when the program ends. In some DB2 programming interfaces, you do not issue the COMMIT or ROLLBACK SQL statements explicitly, but instead employ APIs or object methods to end transactions that result in a commit or a rollback. A commit makes the changes performed during the current transaction permanent, and a rollback restores the data to the state it was in prior to beginning the transaction.

A COMMIT statement normally releases any resources associated with the transaction. However, developers may want to save their work at a particular point in time (similar to saving a document while it is being edited) without losing their place in the table. This can be achieved by using the WITH HOLD option on any cursors that they open. This "hardens" the changes made to disk, but keep the cursor open for further processing.

To properly end a program, it must perform these steps:

- End the current transaction (if one is in progress) by explicitly issuing either a COMMIT statement or a ROLLBACK statement.
- Release the connection to the database server by using the CONNECT RESET statement or the appropriate function or method for your programming interface.
- Clean up resources used by the program. For example, free any temporary storage.

Developers can also create intermediate SAVEPOINTS within their SQL so that they can selectively ROLLBACK to a prior point in their code. This feature allows for greater flexibility when working with modular code and stored procedures.

SQL Procedural Language

The SQL procedural language (SQL PL) consists of SQL control statements that allow the structured query language to be used in a manner similar to writing a program in a programming language like C++ or Java. SQL control statements provide the capability to control the logic flow, declare and set variables, and handle warnings and exceptions. Some SQL control statements can also include other nested SQL statements.

While SQL PL was originally designed as a stored procedure language, it can also be used in the body of a routine, trigger, or a dynamic compound statement. The advantages of using SQL PL is that it does not require a compiler, can be created with any text editor, and can be run immediately. However, the drawbacks of SQL PL are that it does not have some of the sophisticated mathematical capabilities of other programming languages and it cannot perform any type of external input or output.

SQL PL blocks contain the following control statements, along with any SQL that might be required:

- DECLARE
- SET assignment statement
- FOR statement
- GET DIAGNOSTICS statement
- IF statement

- ITERATE statement
- LEAVE statement
- RETURN statement
- SIGNAL statement
- CALL statement
- WHILE statement

An SQL PL block can issue most SQL statements, except for the following:

- CREATE any object other than indexes, tables, or views
- DROP any object other than indexes, tables, or views
- FLUSH EVENT MONITOR
- REFRESH TABLE
- RENAME TABLE, RENAME TABLESPACE
- REVOKE
- SET INTEGRITY

A description of all of the SQL PL control statements follows.

BEGIN ATOMIC Statement

All SQL PL statement blocks must start with the BEGIN ATOMIC statement and end with a corresponding END statement. The SQL statements found between these keywords are interpreted as SQL PL control statements. Outside of this block, these keywords will cause an SQL error. To run a series of commands as a stand-alone block of SQL, make sure that you use a different SQL delimiter instead of the semi-colon. The semi-colon is used as a statement terminator in SQL PL, so you will need to use a different character to delimit multiple commands within your script or commands. The following example contains a set of SQL that will execute as part of an SQL PL block (Example 9–42):

```
CONNECT TO DB2CERT@
DROP TABLE TEST@
CREATE TABLE TEST (NUMBER INT)@

BEGIN ATOMIC
  DECLARE I INT DEFAULT 1;
  WHILE I <= 10 DO
    INSERT INTO TEST VALUES(I);
    SET I = I + 1;
  END WHILE;
END@

SELECT * FROM TEST@
QUIT@
```

Example 9–42 *SQL PL commands in a file*

Note how in the previous example that each command is terminated with a "@" sign. To execute this SQL as part of a script, the CLP command must be modified to allow the use of the at sign "@" as the delimiter.

Assuming the name of this file was called SQLBLOCK.DB2, the following command will execute this SQL (Example 9–43):

```
DB2 -td@ -v -f SQLBLOCK.DB2
```

Example 9–43 *Using an @ sign as a delimiter*

Rather than using a special delimiter throughout the script, the SET TERMINATOR statement can be used to change the delimiter in the script. The syntax of the statement is (Example 9–44):

```
--#SET TERMINATOR <char>
```

Example 9–44 *Setting the terminator character*

The --#SET command will be read as a comment in versions of DB2 prior to release V8.2.2. This allows scripts to be used with older releases of DB2, but the script will probably still fail if the delimiter was not used globally.

An example of a script that changes the delimiter is found in Example 9–45 below.

```
DROP TABLE TDEPT;
CREATE TABLE TDEPT (DEPTNO CHAR(4));

--#SET TERMINATOR @
BEGIN ATOMIC
  DECLARE COUNT INT DEFAULT 5;

  WHILE COUNT > 0 DO
    INSERT INTO TDEPT VALUES 'F'||
       RTRIM(CHAR(COUNT));
    SET COUNT = COUNT - 1;
  END WHILE;
END@

--#SET TERMINATOR ;

SELECT * FROM TDEPT;
```

Example 9–45 *Setting the terminator character*

The final option for allowing multiple statements to contain semicolons is the special ";--" sequence. When a statement includes the special sequence, the DB2 command line processor treats it as a continuation character and does not execute the statement until it finds a semicolon by itself (Example 9–46).

```
DROP TABLE TDEPT;
CREATE TABLE TDEPT (DEPTNO CHAR(4));

BEGIN ATOMIC
  DECLARE COUNT INT DEFAULT 5;--

  WHILE COUNT > 0 DO
    INSERT INTO TDEPT VALUES 'F'||
       RTRIM(CHAR(COUNT));--
    SET COUNT = COUNT - 1;--
  END WHILE;--
END;

SELECT * FROM TDEPT;
```

Example 9–46 *Using statement continuation characters*

While SQL PL can be used for a variety of SQL commands, a SELECT statement will not be returned to the calling program (either CLP or an application) as a open cursor that records can be fetched from. From a user perspective, issuing a SELECT statement within a BEGIN ATOMIC block will not return a result set, while outside of the block it will. For instance, if the SQL PL in Example 9–42 was modified to place the SELECT statement inside the control block, no result set would be returned when you issued the DB2 command (Example 9–47):

```
CONNECT TO DB2CERT@
DROP TABLE TEST@
CREATE TABLE TEST (NUMBER INT)@

BEGIN ATOMIC
  DECLARE I INT DEFAULT 1;
  WHILE I <= 10 DO
    INSERT INTO TEST VALUES(I);
    SET I = I + 1;
  END WHILE;
  SELECT * FROM TEST;
END@
QUIT@
```

Example 9–47 *SQL PL with no output*

Normally you would use SQL PL blocks to apply complex logic to INSERT, UPDATE, and DELETE statements. If you do need to see the results of these statements, you must issue the SELECT outside the scope of the SQL PL block. However, you can use a SELECT statement within an SQL PL block to calculate values, find values, or for any other purpose other than to display results.

For user-defined functions, the RETURN statement is replaced with the BEGIN ATOMIC block (Example 9–48).

```
CREATE FUNCTION TAX_PAYMENT(SALARY INT) RETURNS INT
  LANGUAGE SQL READS SQL DATA
  BEGIN ATOMIC
    ... SQL PL ...
  END
```

Example 9–48 *SQL PL for a user-defined function*

The same is true for a trigger definition where you can now replace a single SQL statement with a block of SQL PL (Figure 9–49):

```
CREATE TRIGGER CHECK_TAXES NO CASCADE BEFORE
  INSERT ON EMPLOYEE_WAGES REFERENCING NEW AS X
  FOR EACH ROW MODE DB2SQL
  BEGIN ATOMIC
    ... SQL PL ...
  END
```

Example 9–49 *SQL PL for a trigger*

SQL PL can extend the capabilities of triggers and user-defined functions within a DB2 database, as well as give the developer and DBA more flexibility in the types of SQL scripts that they can create. The following sections describe in more detail the syntax that is allowed in SQL PL command blocks. For a more detailed discussion of SQL PL in the use of stored procedures, please refer to the *Developing SQL and External Routines Reference.*

DECLARE Statement

The DECLARE statement is used to specify which variables will be used within the SQL PL block as well as error handling definitions. The basic structure of the DECLARE statement is (Example 9–50):

```
DECLARE SQL-VARIABLE-NAME DATA-TYPE DEFAULT NULL
                                    DEFAULT DEFAULT-VALUES
DECLARE CONDITION-NAME CONDITION FOR SQLSTATE VALUE ...
```

Example 9–50 *DECLARE statement*

The variable name can be any valid SQL identifier and contain any SQL data type, including user-defined data types and structured types. Along with the definition, the user can include a default value for the variables. Users should take care in not

Development SQL

creating variables that conflict with DB2 special register names or column names that may be returned as part of a FOR loop.

The following example lists some valid DECLARE statements (Example 9–51):

```
DECLARE PAY DECIMAL(15,2) DEFAULT 10000.00;
DECLARE SALARY COMPENSATION;
```

Example 9–51 *DECLARE examples*

Note that only one variable can be defined per DECLARE statement. In addition to defining the variables that will be used in the SQL PL block, the DECLARE statement can also be used to assign a symbolic name to a specific SQL error code. This declaration is only used for simplifying coding within the SQL PL block and does not give the block of code any error-handling capability. For more details on how these error codes are handled, see the section on the SIGNAL command.

CALL

The CALL statement is used to invoke a stored procedure (Example 9–52):

```
CALL PROCEDURE_NAME (PARM1, PARM2, …)
```

Example 9–52 *CALL statement*

The stored procedure cannot return a result set (cursor) since there is no facility available to the read the rows. Result sets can only be handled in a stored procedure.

SET Statement

The SET command is used to assign values to declared variables, or to columns in a table in a trigger definition. Many program languages drop the requirement of using a SET statement when assigning variables, but this is a mandatory clause in the SQL PL language.

A variable can be assigned any one of the following values:

- a constant

  `SET BONUS = 5000.00;`

- the contents of another variable or a parameter from the function arguments

  `SET PAY = EMPLOYEE_SALARY;`

- the result of a calculation

  `SET PAY = EMPLOYEE_SALARY + BONUS + COMMISSION * 1.53;`

- result of an SQL statement that returns only one value

  ```
  SET PAY = SELECT SALARY FROM EMPLOYEE WHERE EMPNO = 5;
  ```
- the NULL value

  ```
  SET PAY = NULL;
  ```
- the default value, based on the definition of the variable

  ```
  SET PAY = DEFAULT;
  ```
- the contents of a special register

  ```
  SET USERID = USERID;
  SET TODAY = CURRENT DATE;
  ```

The same rules that apply to SQL statements are used to determine the way that calculations are performed on variables, including operator precedence and casting to other data types.

Multiple assignments can be performed in one SET statement as illustrated in the following example (Example 9–53):

```
SET PAY = 10000.00; SET BONUS = 1500.00;

SET PAY = 10000.00, BONUS = 1500.00;

SET (PAY, BONUS) = (10000.00, 1500.00);

SET (PAY, BONUS) =
    SELECT (PAY, BONUS) FROM EMPLOYEE WHERE EMPNO = '000010';
```

Example 9–53 *SET statement*

The last form of the SET statement is very useful when retrieving column values via a SELECT statement.

IF/THEN/ELSE Statement

SQL PL contains a number of logical constructs that allow the user to modify processing based on the outcome of some test. There are three forms of the IF statement:

- IF THEN/END IF block

  The logic within the IF THEN/END IF block is executed when the condition found within the IF statement is TRUE. If the value is not TRUE, processing continues after the END IF statement.

- IF THEN/ELSE/END IF block

  The IF THEN/ELSE/END IF is similar to the IF statement, except that if the condition found within the IF statement is true, processing will continue until the

ELSE statement is found, and then skip down to the END IF statement. If the condition is FALSE, processing continues from the ELSE statement to the END IF statement.

- IF THEN/ELSEIF/ELSE/END IF block

  Although SQL PL control statements lack the CASE statement, this limitation can be overcome through the use of IF THEN/ELSEIF logic. The ELSEIF is a convenient short form of having multiple IF THEN/ELSE IF THEN blocks of code. When the IF statement is evaluated and the result is FALSE, the processing jumps down to the next ELSEIF block.

  If this ELSEIF is false, then processing will continue with the next ELSEIF block in the list and so on until one of the ELSEIF blocks is true. If none of the sections is true, processing will go to the final ELSE clause. This structure lets you handle multiple conditions and allow for a final section of logic that catches errors that were not handled in previous code.

The example shown in Example 9–54 shows all three types of IF statements. The logic within the IF statement can contain any valid SQL that will result in a TRUE or FALSE value. Boolean expressions that include the standard comparison operators are allowed (<,=,>,<>,<=,>=,NOT), along with SQL statements that result in a true or false value.

```
IF (COMMISSION > 30000) THEN
   BONUS = COMMISSION / 100;
END IF;

IF (PAY + BONUS + COMMISSION > 100000) THEN
   SALARY = 0.90 * (PAY + BONUS + COMMISSION);
ELSE
   SALARY = PAY + BONUS + COMMISSION;
END IF;

IF (SALARY > 100000) THEN
   TAX_RATE = 0.50;
ELSEIF (SALARY > 70000) THEN
   TAX_RATE = 0.40;
ELSEIF (SALARY > 50000) THEN
   TAX_RATE = 0.30;
ELSE
   TAX_RATE = 0.10;
END IF;
```

Example 9–54 *IF statement*

The previous example uses only boolean expression to determine whether or not a condition was TRUE or FALSE. In addition to regular expression operators, the user can also include SQL statements to determine how processing should continue.

A few simple examples illustrate the use of SQL in IF statements.

- Using SQL operators to check values

  Instead of using complex comparison statements, a user can take advantage of the SQL syntax available to them and use that instead.

```
IF (SALARY BETWEEN 10000 AND 90000) THEN ...
IF (DEPTNO IN ('A00','B01','D11')) THEN ...
```

- Check for NULL values

```
IF (SALARY IS NULL) THEN ...
```

- Check for the existence of values within a table

```
IF (EXISTS (SELECT * FROM EMPLOYEE)) THEN ...
IF ((SELECT COUNT(*) FROM EMPLOYEE) > 0) THEN ...
```

- Check for values based on a SELECT statement

```
IF (EMP.SALARY < (SELECT AVG(SALARY) FROM EMPLOYEE)) THEN ...
```

In summary, the IF statement gives the user a large degree of flexibility in modifying the behavior of their code. The additional power of SQL can also be used as a means of controlling the logic within the IF statement.

WHILE Statement

The WHILE statement gives the user the ability to loop within a section of code until the while condition is no longer met. A WHILE statement has the following format (Example 9–55):

```
LABEL:
  WHILE CONDITION DO
    ... SQL PL ...
  END WHILE LABEL;
```

Example 9–55 *WHILE statement*

The condition field within the WHILE clause is identical to the IF statement. You can use either boolean expressions or SQL operators to generate a TRUE or FALSE value. If the calculated value is FALSE, processing will skip all of the logic within the WHILE block and start execution of the first statement after the END WHILE keyword.

The LABEL field is optional for a WHILE statement and can be used to uniquely identify this block of code. The LABEL consists of a unique name that follows the same naming conventions as an SQL column. If LABEL is specified for a WHILE statement, it must be placed on the END WHILE statement as well.

A sample WHILE statement is shown below (Example 9–56):

```
BEGIN ATOMIC
  DECLARE COUNT INT DEFAULT 5;

  WHILE COUNT > 0 DO
    INSERT INTO DEPARTMENTS VALUES 'F'|| RTRIM(CHAR(COUNT));
    SET COUNT = COUNT - 1;
  END WHILE;
END
```

Example 9–56 *WHILE example*

FOR Statement

Users familiar with other programming languages may expect the FOR statement to work in a similar fashion. However, the FOR statement is not intended to be used for executing program logic "n" number of times depending on a loop counter, but rather for executing logic on the rows being returned as the result of a SELECT statement. The syntax of the FOR statement is found in Example 9–57.

```
LABEL:
  FOR ROW_LABEL AS SELECT STATEMENT DO
     ... SQL PL ...
  END FOR LABEL;
```

Example 9–57 *FOR statement*

The LABEL field is optional for a FOR statement and can be used to uniquely identify this block of code. The LABEL consists of a unique name that follows the same naming conventions as an SQL column. If LABEL is specified for a FOR statement, it must be placed on the END FOR statement as well.

The ROW_LABEL is similar to a FOR label but it is used to identify the row of data being returned by the SELECT statement. For example, the following block of code selects data from the EMPLOYEE table based on BONUS data (Example 9–58):

```
SET TOTAL_BONUS = 0;
FOR EMP AS SELECT * FROM EMPLOYEE WHERE BONUS > 1000 DO
  SET TOTAL_BONUS = TOTAL_BONUS + EMP.BONUS;
END FOR;
```

Example 9–58 *FOR statement example*

When using FOR loops, a user should not declare variables that may conflict with columns being returned in the SELECT statement. In the event that the column name is already defined as a variable, you will end up getting error messages referring to invalid use of a variable in assignment statements. This is caused by DB2 trying to assign values to a variable that is considered part of a row, rather than to the variable you DECLARED at the beginning. The result set names take precedence over DECLARED variables. This problem does not occur with multiple nested FOR statements that may have the same column names since each answer set will have a different row label.

When results are returned as part of the FOR statement, each column can be accessed either through the direct column name or through the row label. It is better to use the explicit row label and column name together to avoid ambiguity when trying to modify (or debug) the code at a later date.

ITERATE Statement

The ITERATE statement is used to cause processing to continue from the beginning of a FOR or WHILE loop. This is used in circumstances where the record does not match a certain criteria and the logic needs to get the next record and start processing over again.

The ITERATE statement must have a label supplied as an argument, so any FOR or WHILE statement that is being used with this function must have a corresponding label associated with it. Users should be cautious in the use of the ITERATE statement in a WHILE loop to ensure that any variable found in the loop logic is incremented or decremented before iterating! A sample use of an ITERATE statement is found below (Example 9–59):

```
SET TOTAL_BONUS = 0;
CHECK_BONUS:
FOR EMP AS SELECT * FROM EMPLOYEE DO
  IF (EMP.BONUS > 1000) THEN
     SET TOTAL_BONUS = TOTAL_BONUS + EMP.BONUS;
  ELSE
     ITERATE CHECK_BONUS;
  END IF;
END FOR CHECK_BONUS;
```

Example 9–59 *ITERATE statement*

LEAVE Statement

The LEAVE statement compliments the ITERATE statement in FOR and WHILE loops. In the event that the user needs to get out of a loop, the LEAVE statement can be used to transfer processing to the first statement after the END that terminates this loop.

LEAVE statement require that a label be supplied as an argument, so any FOR or WHILE statement that you want to exit from must have a label supplied. The following SQL PL will stop processing of records if the maximum bonus for all employees is exceeded (Example 9–60):

```
SET TOTAL_BONUS = 0;
ADD_BONUS:
FOR EMP AS SELECT * FROM EMPLOYEE DO
  SET TOTAL_BONUS = TOTAL_BONUS + EMP.BONUS;
  IF (TOTAL_BONUS > 10000) THEN
    LEAVE ADD_BONUS;
  END IF;
END FOR ADD_BONUS;
```

Example 9–60 *LEAVE statement*

RETURN Statement

The RETURN statement is used to exit out of a function and return a value. The RETURN statement is not supported in SQL PL command blocks or in triggers. If a return code is required then the SIGNAL command should be used instead.

The RETURN statement has a single argument which can be a constant, a variable, a SELECT statement that returns a single value, or the NULL value. Table functions can return multiple rows in the form of a SELECT statement.

The following function returns the cube of a input value (Example 9–61):

```
CREATE FUNCTION CUBEIT(CUBE INT) RETURNS INT
  LANGUAGE SQL READS SQL DATA
  BEGIN ATOMIC
    DECLARE CUBE_NUMBER INT DEFAULT 0;
    SET CUBE_NUMBER = CUBE * CUBE * CUBE ;
    RETURN CUBE_NUMBER;
  END
```

Example 9–61 *RETURN statement*

SIGNAL Statement

In the event that something abnormal happens during the processing of your SQL PL code, you may want to use the SIGNAL command to alert the application of the problem. The SIGNAL command has the following formats (Example 9–62):

```
SIGNAL SQLSTATE VALUE SET MESSAGE_TEXT='...';
SIGNAL CONDITION SET MESSAGE_TEXT='...'
```

Example 9–62 *SIGNAL statement*

The first form of the SIGNAL command requires that you know the SQLSTATE that you want to raise. For instance, SQLSTATE '02000' indicates that no records were found. The SET MESSAGE_TEXT keyword allows you to return diagnostic information back to the calling application so that additional error handling can be done.

There are a variety of ways that this function can be used. An initial SELECT statement may return may valid rows, but none may match the criteria required by the function. In this event, an SQLSTATE '02000' may be a valid error to send back to the calling application.

In other cases, the user may want to set up specific error codes that they want to use to signify errors that are generated by a function, and not the SQL code itself. For these types of error codes, users should consider using SQLSTATEs that start with 7, 8, 9, and I through Z. These ranges are not used by DB2 and are available for user-defined errors.

The original CUBEIT function is modified in the following example to raise an error when the number is too big to cube (Example 9–63):

```
CREATE FUNCTION CUBEIT(CUBE INT) RETURNS INT
  LANGUAGE SQL READS SQL DATA
  BEGIN ATOMIC
    DECLARE CUBE_NUMBER INT DEFAULT 0;
    IF (CUBE > 500) THEN
      SIGNAL SQLSTATE '98000'
        SET MESSAGE_TEXT = 'NUMBER TOO BIG TO CUBE!';
    END IF;
    SET CUBE_NUMBER = CUBE * CUBE * CUBE ;
   RETURN CUBE_NUMBER;
  END
```

Example 9–63 *SIGNAL example*

The results of an invalid cube value are show in Example 9–64:

```
VALUES CUBEIT(600);

1
-----------
SQL0438N  Application raised error with diagnostic text:
   "Number too big to cube!".  SQLSTATE=98000
```

Example 9–64 *SIGNAL results*

As an alternative to placing SQLSTATE codes throughout an application, the user can declare symbolic names for SQLSTATES. This is accomplished with the DECLARE statement. Example 9–65 declares the bad cube number SQLSTATE with the symbolic name of TOOBIG

```
CREATE FUNCTION CUBEIT(CUBE INT) RETURNS INT
  LANGUAGE SQL READS SQL DATA
  BEGIN ATOMIC
    DECLARE CUBE_NUMBER INT DEFAULT 0;
    DECLARE TOOBIG CONDITION FOR SQLSTATE '98000';
    IF (CUBE > 500) THEN
      SIGNAL TOOBIG
        SET MESSAGE_TEXT = 'NUMBER TOO BIG TO CUBE';
    END IF;
    SET CUBE_NUMBER = CUBE * CUBE * CUBE ;
   RETURN CUBE_NUMBER;
  END
```

Example 9–65 *SIGNAL with DECLARE statement*

Instead of signalling an error based on the exact SQLSTATE, the program can now just use the symbolic name (TOOBIG) to raise the error. Note that the message text must still be set where the error is raised, rather than in the declare section.

GET DIAGNOSTICS Statement

The GET DIAGNOSTICS statement is used within an SQL PL trigger or block to return the number of records that were affected by an UPDATE, INSERT, or DELETE statement. The GET DIAGNOSTICS command is found below (Example 9–66):

```
GET DIAGNOSTICS VARIABLE = ROW_COUNT;
```

Example 9–66 *GET DIAGNOSTICS statement*

The VARIABLE referenced in the statement is a declared variable that will contain the number of rows that were affected by the previous SQL statement. The following SQL will raise an SQLSTATE when no records are updated as part of an UPDATE command (Example 9–67):

```
BEGIN ATOMIC
  DECLARE REC_COUNT INT DEFAULT 0;
  UPDATE EMPLOYEE
     SET BONUS = 10000
     WHERE EMPNO = '000000';
  GET DIAGNOSTICS REC_COUNT = ROW_COUNT;
  IF (REC_COUNT = 0) THEN
    SIGNAL SQLSTATE '75000'
      SET MESSAGE_TEXT = 'NO EMPLOYEES FOUND';
  END IF;
END
```

Example 9–67 *GET DIAGNOSTICS example*

SQL PL Example

The following SQL shows SQL PL being used in stored procedures, triggers, and user-defined functions. The example will not only illustrate the level of procedural complexity that you can now have in all of these SQL features, but also how portable the language is across all of these environments.

The system that is being designed consists of two simple tables. The EMPLOYEE table contains information on all employees within a company, including their personal information and salary. Along with the salary is a tax field that indicates how much tax the individual needs to pay a year, based on their current salary.

The tax amount in the EMPLOYEE table is calculated from a TAX_RATE table that contains tax percentages based on incremental amounts of salary. This table contains the following data (Table 9–1):

Table 9–1 *Taxation table*

Salary Ranges	Tax Percentage
First 10000	10
Second 10000	15
Next 30000	20
Anything Left	30

Tax is calculated in increments, where the first 10000 is taxed at 10%, the next amount (to 20000) at 15% and so on until we have the final taxation amount. For example, someone earning 35000 a year would pay the following amount:

```
TAX = (10000)*.10 + (10000)*.15 + (15000)*.20 = 5500
```

The table definition for the TAX_RATE table is found in Example 9–68.

```
CREATE TABLE TAX_RATE
  (
  TAX_BRACKET    INT NOT NULL,
  INCOME_AMOUNT  INT NOT NULL,
  TAX_PCT        DECIMAL(5,2) NOT NULL
  );
INSERT INTO TAX_RATE VALUES
  (1,10000,0.10),
  (2,10000,0.15),
  (3,30000,0.20),
  (4,0,0.30);
```

Example 9–68 *TAX_RATE table definition*

Processing of the tax rate information is based on the following logic:

1. Set the tax payable to zero and the remaining salary to the current salary.
2. Set the current tax bracket to one.
3. Set the taxable amount equal to the lesser of the taxable income amount or the remaining salary. If the taxable income amount is zero then the taxable amount becomes the remaining salary.
4. Add the taxable amount times the tax percentage into the tax payable.
5. Subtract the taxable amount from the remaining salary.
6. If the remaining salary is not zero, go to the next tax bracket and repeat step 3.

In order to make sure the tax brackets are in the proper order, the TAX_RATE table must be sorted in ascending sequence. Otherwise, it may be possible to get the wrong tax bracket being selected first and generating incorrect results.

This TAX_PAYMENT calculation can be implemented in a number of ways. The first approach is to create a user-defined function that will calculate the tax and have it included as part of an INSERT statement (Example 9–69).

```
CREATE FUNCTION TAX_PAYMENT(SALARY INT) RETURNS INT
  LANGUAGE SQL READS SQL DATA
  BEGIN ATOMIC
    DECLARE REMAINDER INT DEFAULT 0;
    DECLARE TAX_INCR  INT DEFAULT 0;
    DECLARE TAX_PAID  INT DEFAULT 0;
    DECLARE TAX_RANGE INT DEFAULT 0;
    DECLARE TAXABLE   INT DEFAULT 0;

    IF (SALARY <= 0) THEN
       SIGNAL SQLSTATE '75000'
         SET MESSAGE_TEXT = 'BAD SALARY';
    END IF;

    SET TAX_PAID = 0;
    SET REMAINDER = SALARY;

L1: FOR TAX_RATES AS
      SELECT * FROM TAX_RATE ORDER BY TAX_BRACKET ASC DO
        SET TAX_RANGE = TAX_RATES.INCOME_AMOUNT;
        IF (TAX_RANGE = 0) THEN
            SET TAX_RANGE = REMAINDER;
        END IF;
        IF (TAX_RANGE >= REMAINDER) THEN
           SET TAX_INCR = REMAINDER * TAX_RATES.TAX_PCT;
           SET TAX_PAID = TAX_PAID + TAX_INCR;
           LEAVE L1;
        ELSE
           SET TAX_INCR = TAX_RANGE * TAX_RATES.TAX_PCT;
           SET TAX_PAID = TAX_PAID + TAX_INCR;
           SET REMAINDER = REMAINDER - TAX_RANGE;
```

```
      END IF;
    END FOR L1;
    RETURN TAX_PAID;
  END
```

Example 9–69 *TAX_PAYMENT function*

After this function is created, a user can reference this function in any SQL statement.

The VALUES clause can be very useful in testing the functionality of a new user-defined function (Example 9–70):

```
VALUES TAX_PAYMENT(35000);

1
-----------
       5500
```

Example 9–70 *Sample TAX_PAYMENT calculation*

This function can now be used as part of an INSERT statement to update the tax payable. Assume that the EMPL (employee) table has the following simple design:

```
CREATE TABLE EMPL
  (
  EMPNO    INT NOT NULL,
  SALARY   INT NOT NULL,
  TAX      INT NOT NULL
  );
```

Example 9–71 *EMPL table*

To insert records into this table (Example 9–71) with the proper tax value, the SQL would look similar to this (Example 9–72):

```
INSERT INTO EMPL VALUES
  (1, 50000, TAX_PAYMENT(50000)),
  (2, 30000, TAX_PAYMENT(30000)),
  (3, 64000, TAX_PAYMENT(64000));

SELECT * FROM EMP;

EMPNO       SALARY      TAX
----------- ----------- -----------
          1       50000        8500
          2       30000        4500
          3       64000       12700
```

Example 9–72 *Inserting records into the EMPL table*

Development SQL

Since we have placed the tax payment calculation into a function, every SQL INSERT or UPDATE statement will require that this function be used. This is probably not the best way to implement this logic since it is possible that a user may forget to use this function. Another approach would be to use this logic within a trigger statement. A trigger will get fired on every INSERT or UPDATE statement and we can guarantee that this logic is used. Example 9–73 shows the TAX_PAYMENT function moved into the body of an INSERT trigger.

```
CREATE TRIGGER CHECK_TAXES
  NO CASCADE BEFORE
  INSERT ON EMPL
  REFERENCING NEW AS X
  FOR EACH ROW MODE DB2SQL
  BEGIN ATOMIC
    DECLARE REMAINDER INT DEFAULT 0;
    DECLARE TAX_INCR  INT DEFAULT 0;
    DECLARE TAX_PAID  INT DEFAULT 0;
    DECLARE TAX_RANGE INT DEFAULT 0;
    DECLARE TAXABLE   INT DEFAULT 0;

    IF (SALARY <= 0) THEN
       SIGNAL SQLSTATE '75000'
         SET MESSAGE_TEXT = 'BAD SALARY';
    END IF;

    SET TAX_PAID = 0;
    SET REMAINDER = X.SALARY;

L1: FOR TAX_RATES AS
      SELECT * FROM TAX_RATE ORDER BY TAX_BRACKET ASC DO
        SET TAX_RANGE = TAX_RATES.INCOME_AMOUNT;
        IF (TAX_RANGE = 0) THEN
            SET TAX_RANGE = REMAINDER;
        END IF;
        IF (TAX_RANGE >= REMAINDER) THEN
           SET TAX_INCR = REMAINDER * TAX_RATES.TAX_PCT;
           SET TAX_PAID = TAX_PAID + TAX_INCR;
           LEAVE L1;
        ELSE
           SET TAX_INCR = TAX_RANGE * TAX_RATES.TAX_PCT;
           SET TAX_PAID = TAX_PAID + TAX_INCR;
           SET REMAINDER = REMAINDER - TAX_RANGE;
        END IF;
     END FOR L1;
     SET X.TAX = TAX_PAID;
  END
```

Example 9–73 *TAX_PAYMENT in a trigger body*

The only changes that had to made to the logic (other than defining a trigger instead of a function) was the substitution of REMAINDER = X.SALARY at the beginning of the logic and SET X.TAX = TAX_PAID instead of a RETURN statement at the end.

If the INSERT statements are run again (without the TAX_PAYMENT function) the following results would be returned (Example 9–74):

```
INSERT INTO EMPL VALUES
  (1, 50000, 0),
  (2, 30000, 0),
  (3, 64000, 0);

SELECT * FROM EMPL;

EMPNO       SALARY      TAX
----------- ----------- -----------
          1       50000        8500
          2       30000        4500
          3       64000       12700
          1       50000        8500
          2       30000        4500
          3       64000       12700
```

Example 9–74 *Inserting records into the EMPL table with triggers*

The good news is that the trigger had the same effect as the function! This trigger could have been simplified by making use of the existing TAX_PAYMENT function. The following trigger definition replaces all of the logic with a call to the TAX_PAYMENT function (Example 9–75):

```
CREATE TRIGGER CHECK_TAXES
  NO CASCADE BEFORE
  INSERT ON EMPL
  REFERENCING NEW AS X
  FOR EACH ROW MODE DB2SQL
  BEGIN ATOMIC
    SET X.TAX = TAX_PAYMENT(X.SALARY);
  END
```

Example 9–75 *TAX_PAYMENT function in a trigger*

Issuing the INSERT statements will result in exactly the same results as before.

Finally, the logic within the TAX_PAYMENT function can also be placed into a stored procedure. The stored procedure would look similar to the following code (Example 9–76):

```
CREATE PROCEDURE INSERT_WAGES
    (
    I_EMPNO INT,
    I_SALARY INT
    )
    LANGUAGE SQL MODIFIES SQL DATA
  BEGIN ATOMIC
    DECLARE REMAINDER INT DEFAULT 0;
```

```
    DECLARE TAX_INCR   INT DEFAULT 0;
    DECLARE TAX_PAID   INT DEFAULT 0;
    DECLARE TAX_RANGE  INT DEFAULT 0;
    DECLARE TAXABLE    INT DEFAULT 0;

    IF (I_SALARY <= 0) THEN
       SIGNAL SQLSTATE '75000'
         SET MESSAGE_TEXT = 'BAD SALARY';
    END IF;

    SET TAX_PAID = 0;
    SET REMAINDER = I_SALARY;

L1: FOR TAX_RATES AS
      SELECT * FROM TAX_RATE ORDER BY TAX_BRACKET ASC DO
        SET TAX_RANGE = TAX_RATES.INCOME_AMOUNT;
        IF (TAX_RANGE = 0) THEN
            SET TAX_RANGE = REMAINDER;
        END IF;
        IF (TAX_RANGE >= REMAINDER) THEN
           SET TAX_INCR = REMAINDER * TAX_RATES.TAX_PCT;
           SET TAX_PAID = TAX_PAID + TAX_INCR;
           LEAVE L1;
        ELSE
           SET TAX_INCR = TAX_RANGE * TAX_RATES.TAX_PCT;
           SET TAX_PAID = TAX_PAID + TAX_INCR;
           SET REMAINDER = REMAINDER - TAX_RANGE;
        END IF;
    END FOR L1;
    INSERT INTO EMPL VALUES (I_EMPNO, I_SALARY, TAX_PAID);
  END
```

Example 9–76 *TAX_PAYMENT in a stored procedure*

This stored procedure would be called from an application program and it would INSERT the record into the table, along with calculating the proper tax payment. Before implementing this stored procedure, it would probably be beneficial to drop the INSERT trigger since it will be repeating the same logic on the tax column as the stored procedure would!

In summary, SQL PL can be extremely powerful for a developer, user, or DBA to create sophisticated logic within a number of SQL objects.The code is extremely portable and can be easily moved between different objects without much effort.

Stored Procedures

A database stored procedure is a dynamically loadable library (DLL) or an internal SQL PL routine that can be invoked from a database application by using the CALL statement.

Stored procedures can help improve application performance and reduce database access traffic. All database access must go across the network since the application must initiate a separate communication with DB2 for each separate SQL statement.

To improve application performance, a stored procedure can be created to run on the database server. A client application then calls the stored procedures to obtain results of the SQL statements that are contained in the procedure. Because the stored procedure runs the SQL statement on the server, database performance is improved. Stored procedures can also help to centralize business logic. Changes that are made to a stored procedure are immediately available to all client applications that use it.

Stored procedures are programs that have the following characteristics:

- Contain procedural constructs in a high-level programming language like C, C++, Java, or SQL PL and include embedded SQL statements
- Are stored in databases and run on DB2 servers
- Can be called by name by an application that is using SQL (CALL statement)
- Allow an application program to run in two parts: the application on the client and the stored procedure on the server

To use a stored procedure, you need to write two programs: the stored procedure, which runs on a database server, and a client application, which runs on a client workstation or a middleware server. The client application calls the stored procedure by using one of the available API methods.

A stored procedure does not connect to the database, but relies on the database connection already established by the client. The call across the network includes parameters that are required by the stored procedure, and the stored procedure then uses the parameters to complete its logic and return a set of values, rows, or modified parameters back to the calling application.

Benefits of Using Stored Procedures

Stored procedures provide many benefits to a system:

- Reduced network usage between clients and servers

  A stored procedure can perform processing on the database server, without transmitting unnecessary data across the network. Only records that meet the proper criteria are returned back to the application. Applications that execute SQL statements one at a time typically cross the network twice for each SQL statement. A stored procedure can group SQL statements together, making it necessary to only cross the network twice for each group of SQL statements.

- Enhanced capabilities

  Stored procedures have access to increased memory and disk space on the server computer. Applications also have access to software that is installed only on the database server.

- Improved security

  A DBA can improve security by building a stored procedure that has the appropriate database privileges rather than the end users. The users of the application can call the stored procedure but do not require direct access to the contents of the database.

- Reduced development cost

  Stored procedures can be used to centralize logic for the database. These centralized procedures can be used by many routines, thus reducing the amount of application development required.

- Centralized security, administration, and maintenance for common routines

  By managing shared logic in one place at the server, you can simplify security, administration, and maintenance. Applications can call stored procedures that run SQL queries with little or no additional processing.

SQL PL in Stored Procedures

Stored procedures can be written in a variety of languages, including C, C++, Java, and SQL PL. SQL PL is a language specifically designed for DB2 and offers a rich set of features that can make it suitable for many purposes, including writing stored procedures. It has the added benefit of not requiring any external compiler and is similar to many other high-level languages, so it is easy to learn.

SQL PL code can used in the body of DB2 stored procedures, but the syntax differs from SQL PL control statements in a number of aspects. SQL PL stored procedures support the following extensions which are not permitted in triggers, UDFs, or SQL statements:

- `ALLOCATE CURSOR`, `ASSOCIATE LOCATORS`, `CALL`

  SQL PL control statements can call stored procedures, but they cannot process answer sets. This is the reason why the `ALLOCATE` and `ASSOCIATE` statements are not supported in control statements.

- `PREPARE`, `DESCRIBE`, `OPEN`, `FETCH`

  No cursor processing is allowed in the body of an SQL PL block. The `FOR` control statement can be used to loop through a answer set.

- `CONNECT`, `DISCONNECT`, `SET CONNECTION`

  The body of an SQL PL block cannot change the current connection.

- `SAVEPOINT`, `COMMIT`, `ROLLBACK`

  SQL PL blocks cannot set savepoints or rollback work, but they are able to

COMMIT work if this is the last statement of the block.

- CASE, GOTO, LOOP, REPEAT statements

  Most of these control statements can be simulated using a combination of IF and WHILE statements. Although this may make for more complex logic, it doesn't reduce the capability of SQL PL.

- procedure compound statement

  An SQL control statement is already part of a procedure compound statement, and nesting of these structures is not supported.

- RESIGNAL

  SQL PL blocks can signal errors, but the ability to resignal to a different error is not supported.

- INSERT, UPDATE, DELETE

  SQL PL used within a user-defined function (UDF) has the added restriction that it cannot issue any data modification commands. Triggers, user-defined table functions, and SQL PL statements run as SQL commands can modify data. External UDFs written in C, C++, or Java can update data within the scope of the program.

For more information on SQL PL as a stored procedure language refer to the *DB2 SQL Reference* or the *Developing SQL and External Routines Reference.*

CREATE PROCEDURE Statement

An SQL PL procedure is created through the use of the CREATE PROCEDURE statement as shown in Example 9–77:

```
CREATE PROCEDURE CREATE_T_EMP()
  LANGUAGE SQL
BEGIN
  DECLARE EOF INT DEFAULT 0;
  DECLARE STMT VARCHAR(200);
  DECLARE CONTINUE HANDLER FOR NOT FOUND
    SET EOF = 1;
  EXECUTE IMMEDIATE 'DROP TABLE T_EMP';
  SET STMT =
    'CREATE TABLE T_EMP(EMP CHAR(6), SALARY INT)';
  EXECUTE IMMEDIATE STMT;
END
```

Example 9–77 *CREATE PROCEDURE statement*

Development SQL

The CREATE PROCEDURE statement allows the use of SQL PL statements in the routine body. The CREATE_T_EMP stored procedure drops the T_EMP table and re-creates it for further processing.

The simplified structure of the CREATE PROCEDURE command is (Example 9–78):

```
[1] CREATE PROCEDURE NAME(IN | OUT | INOUT ARG1 TYPE1,
                          IN | OUT | INOUT ARG2 TYPE2, ...)
[2]   LANGUAGE SQL CONTAINS SQL
[3]   BEGIN ... STATEMENTS ... END
```

Example 9–78 *Sections of the CREATE PROCEDURE statement*

The sections of the CREATE PROCEDURE are discussed below.

1. CREATE PROCEDURE NAME(...)

   The initial section of the CREATE PROCEDURE statement names the stored procedures and defines what the names and data types of the arguments will be. Each argument to the stored procedure must be defined including whether it is an input variable (IN), output variable (OUT), or both (INOUT). There is no notion of optional arguments within a stored procedure. The CREATE PROCEDURE command does not allow user-defined types to be used as arguments to the stored procedures.

2. LANGUAGE SQL CONTAINS SQL

   A mandatory clause that is required as part of the stored procedures definition. The options can be READ SQL DATA, CONTAINS SQL, or MODIFIES SQL DATA. There are additional options regarding result sets that are covered in the DB2 documentation on the command.

3. BEGIN ... END block

   All of the logic for a stored procedure are found within the BEGIN/END block.

Stored procedures can be dropped using the Control Center or the DROP command (Example 9–79):

```
DROP PROCEDURE STORED-PROCEDURE-NAME <type1, type2,...>
```

Example 9–79 *DROP PROCEDURE statement*

If there is more that one copy of the stored procedure in the current SCHEMA, the data types for the particular version of the stored procedure need to be included so DB2 can figure out which one needs to be removed.

Updating is not possible with stored procedures. The routines need to be dropped and re-created. That's one very good reason to keep a copy of all of your CREATE statements in a separate file.

CALL, ALLOCATE, and ASSOCIATE

The CALL, ALLOCATE, and ASSOCIATE keywords are all used when retrieving results from another stored procedure. The CALL statement is used to invoke the stored procedure (Example 9–80):

```
CALL PROCEDURE_NAME (PARM1, PARM2, …)
```

Example 9–80 *CALL statement*

If the stored procedure returns a result set (cursor), the calling program must ALLOCATE a cursor to process the rows and ASSOCIATE the cursor to the result set that was returned.

For instance, the stored procedure EMPR is called by another stored procedure. The result set is opened through the use of a cursor that was associated with it (Example 9–81):

```
CALL EMPR;
ASSOCIATE RESULT SET LOCATOR (LOC1) WITH PROCEDURE EMPR;
ALLOCATE C1 CURSOR FOR RESULT SET LOC1;
```

Example 9–81 *Using result sets from a procedure*

An OPEN is not required when reading the contents of the cursor. The EMPR stored procedure has already returned an open cursor for processing.

More details on ALLOCATE, ASSOCIATE, and CALL can be found in the *DB2 SQL Reference* documentation.

The CALL statement can be used in triggers, functions, SQL, and stored procedures.

PREPARE, EXECUTE, and Parameter Markers

During execution, a stored procedure may need to build SQL statement dynamically and then submit it for processing. This dynamic SQL execution can be accomplished through the use of the PREPARE and EXECUTE statements.

The PREPARE statement is used to check the statement syntax and convert it to a form that can be submitted to DB2 for execution. The EXECUTE statement submits the statement for execution in the database. Example 9–82 illustrates this concept.

```
DECLARE STMT VARCHAR(200);
SET STMT = 'CREATE TABLE T_EMP(EMP CHAR(6), SALARY INT)';
PREPARE S1 FROM STMT;
EXECUTE S1;
```

Example 9–82 *PREPARE and EXECUTE statements*

The STMT variable can be changed and a new statement executed. The PREPARE step can be avoided with the use of the EXECUTE IMMEDIATE statement (Example 9–83):

```
DECLARE STMT VARCHAR(200);
SET STMT = 'CREATE TABLE T_EMP(EMP CHAR(6), SALARY INT)';
EXECUTE IMMEDIATE STMT;
```

Example 9–83 *EXECUTE IMMEDIATE statement*

The SQL PL code should include an exception handler in the event that the SQL that was submitted was incorrect.

If a statement is to be executed multiple times with slightly different values, it may be more efficient to use parameter markers. Parameter markers are question marks (?) inserted into portions of the SQL and act as placeholders. These are meant to be used for select, insert, update, and delete statements.

For instance, the following SQL statement will delete an employee with an employee number that has yet to be defined (Example 9–84):

```
DELETE FROM EMPLOYEE WHERE EMPNO = ?;
```

Example 9–84 *Parameter marker usage*

This statement can be prepared once, and then executed subsequent times with different values for the employee number (Example 9–85).

```
DECLARE EMPNO CHAR(6);
SET STMT = 'DELETE FROM EMPLOYEE WHERE EMPNO = ?';
PREPARE S1 FROM STMT;
EMPNO = '111111';
EXECUTE S1 USING EMPNO;
EMPNO = '222222';
EXECUTE S1 USING EMPNO;
```

Example 9–85 *Executing statements with different parameter markers*

This is a much more efficient process than continually preparing a new SQL statement.

CURSORS, OPEN, CLOSE, and FETCH

The DECLARE CURSOR statement defines a cursor that will be subsequently used to OPEN and FETCH records. The DECLARE statement includes the SQL statement that will be used to retrieve data (Example 9–86):

```
DECLARE CURSOR-NAME CURSOR [WITH HOLD]
  [WITH RETURN [TO CALLER | TO CLIENT]]
  FOR SELECT-STATEMENT
```

Example 9–86 *Declaring a cursor*

The WITH HOLD specifies what happens to the cursor when a COMMIT WORK occurs. Normally a cursor will be closed when a COMMIT occurs, but when WITH HOLD is specified, it will remain open for further processing. This is useful when large amounts of data need to processed and the stored procedure wants to "save" the work that was done to this point in time.

The WITH RETURN clause is optional and specifies that the cursor will be returned to the calling program (TO CALLER) or directly to the client (TO CLIENT).

Once a cursor has been defined, it can subsequently be opened for processing. The OPEN statement includes the name of the cursor and the parameter marker values if any exist (Example 9–87):

```
OPEN CURSOR-NAME
```

Example 9–87 *OPEN statement*

When the statement has been opened, the FETCH statement can be used to retrieve values from the rows that are returned (Example 9–88):

```
FETCH FROM CURSOR-NAME INTO VAR1, VAR2, …
```

Example 9–88 *FETCH statement*

Once processing is complete, the cursor can be closed (Example 9–89):

```
CLOSE CURSOR-NAME
```

Example 9–89 *CLOSE statement*

The following code illustrates the use of all of the elements described in this section (Example 9–90).

```
CREATE PROCEDURE FIND_SALARY()
  LANGUAGE SQL
BEGIN
   DECLARE EOF INT DEFAULT 0;
   DECLARE STMT VARCHAR(200);
   DECLARE R_EMPNO CHAR(6);
   DECLARE R_SALARY DEC(9,2);
   DECLARE C1 CURSOR FOR
     SELECT EMPNO, SALARY FROM EMPLOYEE
       WHERE SALARY <= 50000;

   DECLARE CONTINUE HANDLER FOR NOT FOUND
     SET EOF = 1;

   SET STMT = 'DELETE FROM T_RESULTS';
   EXECUTE IMMEDIATE STMT;
   SET STMT = 'INSERT INTO T_RESULTS VALUES (?,?)';
   PREPARE S1 FROM STMT;
   OPEN C1;
   WHILE EOF = 0 DO
     FETCH FROM C1 INTO R_EMPNO, R_SALARY;
     EXECUTE S1 USING R_EMPNO, R_SALARY;
   END WHILE;
   CLOSE C1;
END
```

Example 9–90 *Using a cursor to process records*

This code selects all of the records in the EMPLOYEE table (CURSOR C1) and places them into the T_RESULTS table. Before the records are inserted into this table, the T_RESULTS contents are deleted (first EXECUTE IMMEDIATE) and then an INSERT statement is prepared with two parameter markers. As each record is read from the answer set, the prepared insert statement is executed with the values returned from the EMPLOYEE table. Note how the CONTINUE HANDLER has been set up to return a value for EOF that indicates that the end of records has been reached.

COMMIT, ROLLBACK, and SAVEPOINTS

Before a stored procedure can access a database, a connection must be established by the client application. An SQL PL stored procedure cannot connect to a database itself; it relies on the application program to do this for it.

COMMITs and ROLLBACKs can be issued from within SQL PL. Normally a COMMIT or ROLLBACK would be left to the calling application, except in the situation where the stored procedure must undo updates that it generated.

Developers can also create intermediate SAVEPOINTs within their SQL so that they can selectively ROLLBACK to a prior point in their code. This feature allows for greater flexibility when working with modular code and stored procedures. SAVE-POINTs are useful within stored procedures where portions of work may need to be rolled back due to an error. A SAVEPOINT definition is similar to the following (Example 9–91):

```
SAVEPOINT SAVEPOINT-NAME ON ROLLBACK RETAIN CURSORS;
```

Example 9–91 *SAVEPPOINT statement*

The use of a SAVEPOINT is best illustrated with the following example (Example 9–92):

```
INSERT INTO EMP VALUES ('111111','FRED','A20');
SAVEPOINT SP1 ON ROLLBACK RETAIN CURSORS;
INSERT INTO EMP VALUES ('222222','PAUL','A31');
ROLLBACK TO SAVEPOINT SP1;
```

Example 9–92 *Rolling back to a SAVEPOINT*

This example inserts the first employee (Fred) into the EMP table, followed by 'Paul'. The ROLLBACK statement causes the second INSERT to be rolled back so that only the first record remains.

Savepoints can also be nested in applications so that the developer can control which portion of the SQL should be rolled back. For instance, if a stored procedure is called, that stored procedure can have nested savepoints independent from the main program. This allows the stored procedure to selectively ROLLBACK portions of work without affecting the original application.

CASE

The CASE statement selects a suitable execution path based on multiple conditions. There are two forms of the CASE statement available (Example 9–93):

```
CASE SEARCHED CASE STATEMENT
  WHEN VALUE THEN …
  ELSE
END CASE

CASE
  WHEN VAR = VALUE THEN
  ELSE
END CASE
```

Example 9–93 *Two forms of CASE statement*

For instance, applying logic to a record based on which department an employee works for can be easily accomplished with the CASE statement (Example 9–94).

```
CASE WORKDEPT                          CASE
  WHEN 'A00' THEN …                      WHEN WORKDEPT='A00' THEN
  WHEN 'B01' THEN …                      WHEN WORKDEPT='B01' THEN
  ELSE …                                 ELSE …
END CASE                               END CASE
```

Example 9–94 *Checking for department values using the CASE statement*

The ELSE clause is executed when none of the other WHEN clauses is selected. If none of the WHEN clauses is selected and the ELSE clause is missing, DB2 will raise an error condition.

The order of the conditions for the CASE expression is very important. DB2 will process the first condition first, then the second, and so on. If you do not pay attention to the order in which the conditions are processed, you might execute the same condition for every value entering the CASE statement. For example, if you coded a condition like "AGE<=65" before "AGE<45", all the data that is lower than 65, even 40 or 30, will branch into the first WHEN clause.

GOTO

The GOTO statement is used to branch to a label within an SQL procedure (Example 9–95).

```
GOTO LABEL_NAME
```

Example 9–95 *GOTO statement*

The label must exist or else an error will be generated at procedure creation time. The use of the GOTO generates a lot of debate in the programming community. There are good arguments for not using the GOTO because of the poor maintainability and debugging of code. However, the GOTO can be used effectively to skip over large quantities of code to enter an error processing section. Coding this with IF/THEN/ELSE blocks may be awkward or create very complex logic structures.

There are some restrictions on the use of the GOTO within some control structures:

- If the GOTO statement is defined in a FOR statement, label must be defined inside the same FOR statement, excluding a nested FOR statement or nested compound statement.
- If the GOTO statement is defined in a compound statement, label must be defined inside the same compound statement, excluding a nested FOR statement or

nested compound statement.

- If the GOTO statement is defined in a handler, label must be defined in the same handler, following the other scope rules.
- If the GOTO statement is defined outside of a handler, label must not be defined within a handler.
- If label is not defined within a scope that the GOTO statement can reach, an error is returned.

LOOP

LOOP is a very simple control structure that continues to execute the statements within the loop until a RETURN or LEAVE statement is encountered (Example 9–96).

```
FETCH_LOOP:
  LOOP
    FETCH C1 INTO V_SALARY;
    IF V_SALARY = 0 THEN
       LEAVE FETCH_LOOP;
    END IF;
    SET V_COUNTER = V_COUNTER + 1;
  END LOOP FETCH_LOOP;
```

Example 9–96 *LOOP statement*

The beginning of a loop can have a label associated with it. The label can be used in a LEAVE statement to guarantee which LOOP statement is exited. This is particularly important in nested LOOP structures where it may not be clear where processing will continue after the LEAVE statement. In addition to the LEAVE statement, the ITERATE statement can also be used to change the order of execution in the LOOP. The ITERATE will return execution to the first statement in the LOOP.

REPEAT

The REPEAT statement executes a statement or group of statements until a search condition is true. This is similar to a WHILE statement except that the test is done at the end of the loop rather than at the beginning. The REPEAT structure also supports the use of the ITERATE and LEAVE statements (Example 9–97).

```
FETCH_LOOP:
  REPEAT
    FETCH C1 INTO V_SALARY;
    SET V_COUNTER = V_COUNTER + 1;
    UNTIL V_SALARY = 0
  END REPEAT FETCH_LOOP;
```

Example 9–97 *REPEAT statement*

The label at the beginning of the loop is optional but can make it easier to follow ITERATE and LEAVE instructions in nested loops.

RESIGNAL

The SQL Procedural Language section described the use of the SIGNAL statement to raise error handlers in the procedure. The RESIGNAL statement is similar to the SIGNAL statement, but it is only used in the body of an error handler for a specific error condition. The role of the RESIGNAL statement is to return back to the calling program another error code, other than the one that caused the initial problem (Example 9–98):

```
DECLARE OVERFLOW CONDITION FOR SQLSTATE '22003';
DECLARE CONTINUE HANDLER FOR OVERFLOW
  RESIGNAL SQLSTATE '22375';
```

Example 9–98 *RESIGNAL statement*

When the overflow handler is invoked, the SQLSTATE 22375 is returned to the calling application, rather than the 22003 that cause the original error.

Condition Handling

Every program language has its own way of handling error conditions. The techniques range from "checking the error code" after a transaction or statement to developing error or condition handlers.

In SQL PL, the error processing is usually done through the use of condition handlers. This simplifies development since rarely used error handling code can be placed into separate blocks of code. However, this technique of encapsulating error code in a condition handler isn't always used by developers, especially those coming from environments where this technique is not available.

The generic error handler approach, where all error information is saved in local variables, is usually a result of porting a stored procedure from some other database platform. An example of this technique is shown in Example 9–99 below:

```
DECLARE SQLCODE INT;
DECLARE SQLSTATE CHAR(5);
DECLARE RC_SQLCODE INT DEFAULT 0;
DECLARE RC_SQLSATTE CHAR(5) DEFAULT '00000';
DECLARE CONTINUE HANDLER FOR
  SQLEXCEPTION,
  SQLWARNING,
  NOT FOUND
VALUES (SQLCODE, SQLSTATE) INTO
  MY_SQLCODE, MY_SQLSTATE;
UPDATE EMPLOYEE SET SALARY=50000 WHERE EMPNO=20;
```

```
IF (MY_SQLCODE <> 0) THEN
  SIGNAL SQLSTATE '78001'
     SET MESSAGE_TEXT='ERROR FINDING EMPLOYEE';
END IF;
```

Example 9–99 *Condition handling example*

This technique is expensive from an SQL PL perspective since the condition handler is being invoked for almost all of the SQL statements. In addition, the NOT FOUND condition is actually a warning, and can be checked explicitly rather than using a CONTINUE HANDLER.

Instead of using the MY_SQLCODE in the body of the procedure, it can be replaced with the native SQLCODE value (Example 9–100):

```
UPDATE EMPLOYEE SET SALARY=50000 WHERE EMPNO=20;
IF (SQLCODE = 100) THEN
  SIGNAL SQLSTATE '78001'
    SET MESSAGE_TEXT='EMPLOYEE NOT FOUND';
END IF;
```

Example 9–100 *Using native SQLCODEs for capturing errors*

Any unexpected errors should be placed into the exception handler rather than using local variables to test for the type of error. This will result in much more readable code and reduce the possibility of errors if you forget to zero out the temporary return code variables.

The exception handler would be modified in the previous example to eliminate the NOT FOUND exception and to return an error directly within the exception handler (Example 9–101):

```
DECLARE CONTINUE HANDLER FOR SQLEXCEPTION
  SIGNAL SQLSTATE '78001'
    SET MESSAGE_TEXT='ERROR UPDATING RECORD';
```

Example 9–101 *Setting error description within the error handler*

The two variables, SQLCODE and SQLSTATE, must be defined within the routine and are reserved for DB2's use. These are set after each SQL statement is executed. The routine would now be updated to include the new condition handler, along with a direct check against the SQLCODE to determine whether a record was updated (Example 9–102).

```
DECLARE SQLCODE INT;
DECLARE SQLSTATE CHAR(5);
DECLARE CONTINUE HANDLER FOR SQLEXCEPTION
SIGNAL SQLSTATE '78001'
  SET MESSAGE_TEXT='ERROR UPDATING RECORD';
UPDATE EMPLOYEE SET SALARY=50000 WHERE EMPNO=20;
IF (SQLCODE = 100) THEN
  SIGNAL SQLSTATE '78001'
     SET MESSAGE_TEXT='EMPLOYEE NOT FOUND';
END IF;
```

Example 9–102 *Inline error handling*

External Stored Procedures

There are two different types of stored procedures. It takes significantly more work to create an external stored procedure than one based on SQL PL. All external stored procedures need to written and compiled using one of the supported programming languages. Stored procedures, once written and generated as dynamically loadable libraries or classes, must be registered with the database. The object code is placed into a library that DB2 has access to, and then the CREATE PROCEDURE command is used to catalog the stored procedure into the database.

An example of a stored procedure being registered using the CREATE PROCEDURE statement is found in Example 9–103.

```
CREATE PROCEDURE ASSEMBLY_PARTS
 (IN ASSEMBLY_NUM INTEGER,
  OUT NUM_PARTS INTEGER,
  OUT COST DOUBLE)
 EXTERNAL NAME 'PARTS!ASSEMBLY'
 DYNAMIC RESULT SETS 1 NOT FENCED
 LANGUAGE C PARAMETER STYLE GENERAL
```

Example 9–103 *Registering an external stored procedure*

The stored procedure ASSEMBLY_PARTS would need to be compiled and placed into a library that is accessible by DB2 at run time. Once the stored procedure has been registered, it can be called from an application (Example 9–104):

```
CALL ASSEMBLY_PARTS(NO_IN, COUNT_PARTS, COST);
```

Example 9–104 *Calling an external stored procedure*

In addition to user-defined scalar stored procedures, DB2 also allows external routines to return result sets. These result sets are handled like cursors for a prepared statement. The only difference is that the result set has already been opened on your behalf by the stored procedure. More information on External Routines can be found in the *Developing SQL and External Routines Reference*.

External stored procedures versus SQL PL

The reasons for writing a stored procedure in a language other than SQL PL are very few:

- The stored procedure ability required to do either text or mathematical computations are not available in SQL PL.
- Speed of execution is critical and there are a high number of computations required in the stored procedure.
- Some SQL is not supported in SQL PL.

Under normal circumstances, a native SQL PL stored procedure will outperform a stored procedure built in C or Java. However, in very heavy, compute-intensive routines, using external programs may be faster.

A distinct disadvantage of an external stored procedure is the dependency on the compiler and lack of portability between platforms. A stored procedure written and compiled on a Windows platform must be moved and recompiled on a different (non-Windows) platform.

The major advantage of SQL PL-based stored procedures is the ability to quickly write, debug, and implement a stored procedure, along with the portability to any other DB2 platform. If a routine can be easily developed in SQL PL, the effort to write it in an external language may not be economical.

External Stored Procedures and SCHEMAs

Stored procedures are like any other database object in DB2, meaning that each stored procedure has a schema name associated with it. Ideally, each stored procedure is fully qualified when it is called. However, this can be difficult to remember and can limit the flexibility of SQL queries.

The alternative is to use the special register `CURRENT PATH`. DB2 uses this path to resolve unqualified stored procedure references. The path in this case is not a list of directories, but a list of schema names such as "`SYSIBM`", "`SYSFUN`" or "`SAMPLE`".

An application would set this special register at initialization to the point proper libraries, and then all stored procedure calls would go to the specified libraries. One use for this is to have a routine use the stored procedures in the "`TEST`" library during development, and then switch to the "`PRODUCTION`" library when testing is complete. This eliminates the need to change the high-level schema qualifier for the stored procedures.

Locking Levels

If a stored procedure requires cursors, it's best to check what level of locking the procedure really needs for the rows it selects. The higher the isolation level (like RR or repeatable read), the more locks DB2 must acquire, with the potential impact of slowing down other applications or causing deadlock situations.

DB2 provides different levels of protection to isolate the data from each of the database applications while it is being accessed. These levels of protection are known as isolation levels or locking strategies. The isolation levels supported by DB2 include:

- Uncommitted read (UR)
- Cursor stability (CS)
- Read stability (RS)
- Repeatable read (RR)

The isolation level is defined for embedded SQL statements during the binding of a package to a database using the `ISOLATION` option of the `PREP` or the `BIND` command. If no isolation level is specified, the default level of cursor stability is used.

If you are using the command line processor, you may change the isolation level using the `CHANGE ISOLATION LEVEL` command. For DB2 Call Level Interface (DB2 CLI), you may change the isolation level as part of the DB2 CLI configuration (DB2CLI.INI) file. Finally, for an SQL PL procedure, you can change the isolation with the `CALL SET_ROUTINE_OPTS` routine.

Uncommitted Read

The Uncommitted Read (`UR`) isolation level, also known as dirty read, is the lowest level of isolation supported by DB2. It can be used to access uncommitted data changes of other applications. For example, an application using the uncommitted read isolation level will return all of the matching rows for a query, even if that data is in the process of being modified, and may not be committed to the database. If you decide to use this isolation level, your application might access incorrect data. There will be very few locks held by uncommitted read transactions.

Cursor Stability

The Cursor Stability (`CS`) isolation level locks any row on which the cursor is positioned during a transaction. The lock on the row is held until the next row is fetched or the transaction is terminated. If a row has been updated, the lock is held until the transaction is terminated. A transaction is terminated when either a `COMMIT` or `ROLLBACK` statement is executed.

An application using cursor stability cannot read uncommitted data. In addition, the application locks the row that has been currently fetched, and no other application can modify the contents of the current row.

Read Stability

The Read Stability (RS) isolation level locks those rows that are part of a result table. If you have a table containing 10,000 rows and the query returns 10 rows, then only 10 rows are locked. An application using read stability cannot read uncommitted data. Instead of locking a single row, it locks all rows that are part of the result table. No other application can change or modify these rows.

Repeatable Read

The Repeatable Read (RR) isolation level is the highest isolation level available in DB2. It locks all rows an application references within a transaction so the application is guaranteed that if it reads the same row again, it will get the same result.

Locks are held on all rows processed to build the result set, no matter how large the result set. DB2 may acquire a table lock if a substantial portion of the table needs to be referenced. An application using repeatable read cannot read uncommitted data of a concurrent application.

Setting Isolation Level for a Procedure

The isolation level for a procedure can be dynamically set through the use of the SET_ROUTINE_OPTS procedure. This procedure takes as its arguments the options that will be used to generate the stored procedure. One of these options is the ISOLATION keyword which can be set to either:

- UR — Uncommitted Read
- CS — Cursor Stability
- RS — Read Stability
- RR — Repeatable Read

For instance, to set the isolation level of a stored procedure before creation, issue the command before the CREATE PROCEDURE command (Example 9–105):

```
CALL SET_ROUTINE_OPTS('ISOLATION CS')
CREATE PROCEDURE …
```

Example 9–105 *Setting an SQL PL routine locking level*

Make sure you don't use an isolation level higher than what you need. The default isolation level is CS or cursor stability and will be suitable for most applications.

Another option for giving DB2 some help in managing rows is to declare cursors with the `FOR READ ONLY` option on the SQL statement. `FOR READ ONLY` gets added to the end of the `SELECT` statement and tells DB2 that it the cursor will not be updated and that it can do record blocking to retrieve the rows (Example 9–106):

```
SELECT * FROM EMPLOYEE
    FOR READ ONLY;
```

Example 9–106 *Forcing read-only results in SQL*

If the `FOR READ ONLY` is not specified on a cursor, DB2 must determine whether or not the cursor can update the rows and this could make a difference on how rows are fetched into the application.

Isolation Level on SQL Statements

When a stored procedure is developed, the default locking behavior is usually defined for all of the SQL within that application. Usually the default value for SQL calls will have the default locking level set to cursor stability. This may not be the behavior that the developer wants, especially if some of the SQL statements are only for quick table lookups and shouldn't be holding any locks. In this case, the developer should be using the `WITH` clause that is available on the `SELECT` statement.

The `WITH` statement is placed at the end of any `SELECT` statement, followed by the locking level that you want for that statement:

- RR — Repeatable Read
- RS — Read Stability
- CS — Cursor Stability
- UR — Uncommitted Read

The following example shows how a `SELECT` statement can be changed to hold no locks during the duration of the request (Example 9–107):

```
SELECT * FROM EMPLOYEE
  WHERE SALARY BETWEEN 10000.00 AND 30000.00
WITH UR;
```

Example 9–107 *Changing locking level on an SQL statement*

In order to guarantee the locking behavior of DB2 during the execution of your stored procedure, you should either set the default locking with the `SET_ROUTINE_OPTS` command or explicitly state it as part of the SQL statement.

Summary

In this chapter, we have examined additional SQL features used in DB2 application development.

User-defined functions allow a developer to extend the types of functions used within DB2 and allow for the sharing of common routines between users and application developers.

User-defined structured data types can be used to create common structures in database tables and allow for tighter control of data types in table definitions.

Schemas and aliases can be used to simplify application development and to reduce confusion when accessing objects in a database.

The Commit and Rollback commands provide a way of ensuring transaction integrity within the database.

Finally, the SQL PL language has been introduced as a way of extending the capabilities of triggers, user-defined functions, stored procedures, and SQL commands.

CHAPTER 10

Concurrency

- CONCURRENCY
- ISOLATION LEVELS
- LOCKS
- LOCK CONVERSION
- LOCK ESCALATION
- LOCK WAIT

A database server acts as a central source of data access for users. The number of users can vary from one to thousands. When more than one user accesses the same data source at the same time, some rules must be established for the reading, inserting, deleting, and updating of the data to guarantee data integrity.

The rules for data access are set by each application connected to a DB2 database and are established using two methods:

- Explicit control — Locking resources using an SQL statement or using a DB2 command
- Implicit control — Locking resources by specifying an *isolation level*

Some of the DB2 database resources, databases, table spaces, and tables can be explicitly controlled (for concurrency purposes). DB2 implicitly locks database resources at the row level. This can provide good concurrency and avoid resource conflicts. Record locking behavior is specified by isolation levels. We will examine the supported isolation levels and their locking semantics.

We will also examine the locks in DB2 and their behavior in an application environment. DB2 must also handle concurrency conflicts, including deadlocks, lock timeout, and resource contention. Some of the database configuration parameters affect the amount and type of locks acquired and the maximum length of time they are held by DB2 applications.

We will also examine concurrency problems that can occur in a multiuser environment. The concurrency examples are based on the DB2CERT certification testing application.

Concurrency

Data integrity is the primary concern in any database environment. The data server must guarantee the integrity of the data as it is modified. Every executable SQL statement that is issued is considered to be part of a *transaction*.

A transaction will contain at least one SQL statement. Multiple SQL statements can be grouped together and executed as a single transaction. Any data that has been accessed or modified by SQL statements will be tracked by DB2 and either permanently changed (committed) or returned to its original state (rolled back). This all-or-nothing behavior is known as *atomicity*. A transaction does not only guarantee atomicity, it also guarantees *persistency*. Persistency is provided through transactional logging. The log files are used to ensure that all committed transactions are physically applied to the database.

A transaction is started implicitly during the processing of the first SQL statement. The transaction is completed when a COMMIT or ROLLBACK statement has been issued, either explicitly or implicitly.

When the data has been permanently changed using the COMMIT or ROLLBACK statement, a point of consistency is established. A point of consistency is important because it is used during database crash recovery and roll forward recovery.

DB2 Note

The term *unit of work* is the same as *transaction*.

In a previous chapter, we discussed data access control. The GRANT and REVOKE statements can be used by users to provide and take away the ability to access tables, views, and packages. Once access control has been established, resource control must be considered. Concurrency problems can occur if resource control is not properly managed.

DB2 provides mechanisms to manage resource control. We will discuss the control of data modification using transactions, examine some of the possible concurrency problems and the strategies that can be used to avoid them, and examine some concurrency issues that need to be addressed by an application.

Concurrency Considerations

Database resource control requires the use of data modification rules. There are concurrency anomalies that we will consider when using the DB2CERT database application. They include:

- Lost update
- Uncommitted read
- Nonrepeatable read
- Phantom read

Lost Update Problem

A *lost update* problem occurs when the same data is retrieved by two individuals, both of whom change and save the data. The last successful change to the data will be kept, and the first change will be overwritten.

Suppose Kelly works in the Markham testing center and receives a call from Paul. Paul wants to see what the availability of seats are for taking the DB2 Certification test in Markham. Kelly needs to examine a table called TEST_SEATS to see what the availability of seats are. The TEST_SEATS table contains the location name, seat number, test date, and the first name of the person taking the test (Example 10–1).

```
CREATE TABLE TEST_SEATS
  (
  LOCATION  VARCHAR(25) NOT NULL,
  SEAT      INT NOT NULL,
  TEST_DATE DATE NOT NULL,
  NAME      VARCHAR(8)
  );
```

Example 10–1 *TEST_SEATS table design*

This table has been populated with four records for the Markham location, including one null record indicating an available seat (Example 10–2):

```
INSERT INTO TEST_SEATS VALUES
  ('MARKHAM',1,'2007-02-01','GEORGE'),
  ('MARKHAM',2,'2007-02-01','KATRINA'),
  ('MARKHAM',3,'2007-02-01','BILL'),
  ('MARKHAM',4,'2007-02-01',NULL);
```

Example 10–2 *Inserting seat information for the Markham testing center*

Kelly queries the availability of seats at the Markham testing center for the date that Paul wants and finds that a seat is available (Example 10–3):

```
SELECT SEAT, NAME FROM TEST_SEATS WHERE LOCATION='MARKHAM'
  AND TEST_DATE = '2007-02-01';

SEAT        NAME
----------- --------
          1 GEORGE
          2 KATRINA
          3 PAUL
          4 -
```

Example 10–3 *Available seats at Markham testing center*

Kelly decides to go get a coffee while Paul figures out if the exam date is good for him.

Meanwhile, another call comes into the testing center. Andrew, another test coordinator, takes a call from Geoffrey. Geoffrey wants to take the same DB2 exam on the day that Paul has requested. Andrew checks the seat availability and obtains the same list as Kelly. Andrew's screen is same as Kelly's that is shown in Example 10–3.

Paul finally decides to take the test and Kelly updates the record in the table (Example 10–4):

```
UPDATE TEST_SEATS
   SET NAME='PAUL'
   WHERE SEAT=4 AND TEST_DATE='2007-02-01';
```

Example 10–4 *Updating the seat record for Paul*

The other test candidate, Geoffrey, decides to take the test and Andrew assigns seat 4 to Geoffrey as well (Example 10–5).

```
UPDATE TEST_SEATS
   SET NAME='GEOFFREY'
   WHERE SEAT=4 AND TEST_DATE='2007-02-01';
```

Example 10–5 *Updating the seat record for Geoffrey*

Andrew does not see that Kelly has assigned seat 4 to Paul, so he assigns the same seat to Geoffrey. Remember, Andrew sees seat 4 as unassigned. The commit operation was successful for Andrew because no resource conflict was encountered.

If the list of seats is refreshed (retrieved again), we see that seat 4 was assigned to Geoffrey and the update made by Kelly was overwritten. Example 10–6 shows the refreshed screen.

```
SELECT SEAT, NAME FROM TEST_SEATS WHERE LOCATION='MARKHAM'
  AND TEST_DATE = '2007-02-01';

SEAT        NAME
----------- ----------
          1 GEORGE
          2 KATRINA
          3 BILL
          4 GEOFFREY
```

Example 10–6 *Lists of assigned seats*

On the day of the test, Paul and Geoffrey arrive at the testing center, and the database shows that Geoffrey has a proper seat assignment. Paul walks away unhappy and has to reschedule to take the exam another day.

What was the problem? To maintain the accuracy of the data, control mechanisms needed to be enforced. The goal of the database manager (DB2) is to avoid lost updates and guarantee the integrity of the data.

If table-level locking was used, then Kelly's application would have restricted any update to the table. However, if Kelly's application had update control for the table, then other test centers would not be able to assign seats since all test centers access the same table. Should only one test center coordinator be allowed to update data records for a given day? For some applications, this can be appropriate, but this does not provide a sufficient degree of concurrency for others.

In order to guarantee the integrity of the database, an application has to lock the updated data to make it impossible for another application to overwrite the data.

Lost Update Solution

To avoid lost updates, control of each data record must be maintained by DB2. The control mechanism involves obtaining update control of all of the matching records or possible matching records for the query. This is known as *repeatable read.* See "Repeatable Read" on page 609 for more details on establishing a repeatable read concurrency strategy.

The only explicit SQL control mechanism provided by DB2 is the LOCK TABLE statement. According to the design of the DB2CERT application, there is a table that represents all of the tests taken at all of the tests centers, the TEST_TAKEN table. If the application explicitly locked the table for update (known as EXCLUSIVE mode), other test centers would not be allowed to update or even read any of the committed data in the table. If the application explicitly locked the table not for update, (SHARE mode) other test centers would be allowed to read but not update the data.

Kelly's application could have obtained a share lock on the TEST_TAKEN table. The share lock would have prevented Andrew from successfully performing an UPDATE of the table (assignment of seat four to Geoffrey). The table lock would remain in effect until Kelly's application released the lock using the COMMIT or ROLLBACK statement.

An alternative method involves record or row-level locking. If Kelly's application acquired record locks for seat 4, Andrew's update would have failed. You cannot explicitly acquire row-level locks using an SQL statement. See "Cursor Stability" on page 608 for more details on row-level locking.

Uncommitted Read

Kelly's application locks the rows of unassigned seats and makes a temporary update to assign seat 4 to Paul. Until Kelly has committed or rolled back this update, no one else can update the record for seat 4.

Example 10–7 shows the list retrieved by George. George has permission to read uncommitted changes, so he can see Kelly assigned seat 4 to Paul.

```
SELECT SEAT, NAME FROM TEST_SEATS WHERE LOCATION='MARKHAM'
  AND TEST_DATE = '2007-02-01';

SEAT        NAME
----------- ----------
          1 GEORGE
          2 KATRINA
          3 BILL
          4 PAUL
```

Example 10–7 *List of assigned seats (including uncommitted)*

If George were to reissue his query after Andrew assigned seat 4 to Geoffrey, he would obtain a different result. This is known as an *uncommitted read* (dirty read).

If the test center secretary runs a report to determine how many people will be tested on February 1st she would get an inconsistent result if she used uncommitted read (Example 10–8) and Kelly had not yet issued a COMMIT for the update transaction.

```
SELECT COUNT(*) FROM TEST_SEATS
  WHERE TEST_DATE = '2007-02-01';

1
-----------
          4
```

Example 10–8 *Count of currently scheduled test (incorrect)*

The result will include the temporary assigned seat. To avoid this behavior, the application should not be able to read uncommitted changes.

Nonrepeatable Read

A nonrepeatable read scenario can obtain a different result set within the same transaction. Uncommitted read applications do not guarantee a repeatable read.

Let's look at an example of a nonrepeatable read scenario. Suppose Katrina is going to take the certification exam. She asks Kelly to check where (Markham or Rockwood) she can take the exam. For this example, the TEST_SEATS table has been repopulated with the new records (Example 10–9).

```
DELETE FROM TEST_SEATS;

INSERT INTO TEST_SEATS VALUES
   ('MARKHAM',1,'2007-02-01','GEORGE'),
   ('MARKHAM',2,'2007-02-01','KATRINA'),
   ('MARKHAM',3,'2007-02-01',NULL),
   ('MARKHAM',4,'2007-02-01',NULL),
   ('ROCKWOOD',1,'2007-02-01','GEOFFREY'),
   ('ROCKWOOD',2,'2007-02-01','PAUL'),
   ('ROCKWOOD',3,'2007-02-01','BILL'),
   ('ROCKWOOD',4,'2007-02-01',NULL);
```

Example 10–9 *Repopulating the TEST_SEATS table*

Kelly sends a request to the database and retrieves the list of available seats in Markham and Rockwood, as shown in Example 10–10.

```
SELECT SEAT, LOCATION FROM TEST_SEATS WHERE
  TEST_DATE = '2007-02-01' AND NAME IS NULL;

SEAT        LOCATION
----------- ----------
          3 MARKHAM
          4 MARKHAM
          4 ROCKWOOD
```

Example 10–10 *Available seats in Markham and Rockwood*

In the meantime, Andrew has assigned and committed the last available seat in Rockwood to Mike. Katrina would like to take the test in Rockwood, so Kelly attempts to assign the seat. The update fails, and when Kelly reissues the SQL, the seat in Rockwood is no longer available. Linda's refreshed screen is shown in Example 10–11.

```
SELECT SEAT, LOCATION FROM TEST_SEATS WHERE
  TEST_DATE = '2007-02-01' AND NAME IS NULL;

SEAT        LOCATION
----------- ----------
          3 MARKHAM
          4 MARKHAM
```

Example 10–11 *Rockwood location no longer available*

The application was coded to only lock the rows of data being updated. In this case, an exclusive lock was obtained by Andrew when he assigned the seat to Mike. This did not conflict with the locks held by Kelly because she did not have that row locked. We are assuming that the row is only locked when it is chosen for update by the administrator.

To avoid this type of nonrepeatable read scenario, all of the retrieved data needs to be locked. If you want to guarantee that none of the selected data is modified, locking these rows is sufficient. This is known as read stability in DB2. If you would like to guarantee that the rows you have selected in getting this result will never change within the transaction, use repeatable read. This may require additional locking.

Phantom Read Problem

The *phantom read* phenomenon occurs if an application executes the same query twice; the second time the query is issued additional rows are returned. For many applications, this is an acceptable scenario. For example, if the query involved finding all of the available seats at a concert, then reissuing the query and obtaining a better seat selection is a desirable feature.

Let's take a look at our application again. Assume that the `TEST_SEATS` table contains the same information as before (Example 10–9). Katrina wants to take the exam in Markham or Rockwood. Kelly requests the list of available seats for these locations, as shown in Example 10–12.

```
SELECT SEAT, LOCATION FROM TEST_SEATS WHERE
  TEST_DATE = '2007-02-01' AND NAME IS NULL;

SEAT        LOCATION
----------- ----------
          3 MARKHAM
          4 MARKHAM
          4 ROCKWOOD
```

Example 10–12 *Available seats in Markham and Rockwood (first query)*

Another test coordinator adds an additional seat to the Rockwood testing site using an INSERT statement (Example 10–13):

```
INSERT INTO TEST_SEATS VALUES
  ('ROCKWOOD',5,'2007-02-01',NULL);
```

Example 10–13 *Inserting an additional seat in Rockwood*

Now it is possible to test five candidates in Rockwood at the same time. If the query is issued again, Kelly retrieves a different result set that includes four available seats. Although the application locked the previously retrieved rows, the application was able to see the new row as shown in Example 10–14.

```
SELECT SEAT, LOCATION FROM TEST_SEATS WHERE
  TEST_DATE = '2007-02-01' AND NAME IS NULL;

SEAT        LOCATION
----------- ----------
          3 MARKHAM
          4 MARKHAM
          4 ROCKWOOD
          5 ROCKWOOD
```

Example 10–14 *Available seats in Markham and Rockwood (second query)*

Phantom Read Solution

Depending on the situation, a phantom read may be desirable. If you wish to avoid this behavior, the application has to lock all of the possible qualifying rows. This ensures that no other application can update, delete, or insert a row that would affect the result table. This is an important concept to understand.

DB2 *Note*

If DB2 needs to acquire locks for every row in the table to provide the required level of isolation, a table-level lock may be obtained instead of multiple row-level locks.

Isolation Levels

In the previous examples, we have seen some of the possible concurrency problems. DB2 Universal Database provides different levels of protection to isolate the data from each of the database applications while it is being accessed.

These levels of protection are known as isolation levels or locking strategies. The isolation levels supported by DB2 include:

- Uncommitted read
- Cursor stability
- Read stability
- Repeatable read

The isolation level is defined for embedded SQL statements during the binding of a package to a database using the `ISOLATION` option of the `PREP` or the `BIND` command. If no isolation level is specified, the default level of cursor stability is used.

If you are using the command line processor, you may change the isolation level using the `CHANGE ISOLATION LEVEL` command.

For DB2 Call Level Interface (DB2 CLI), you may change the isolation level as part of the DB2 CLI configuration (`DB2CLI.INI`) file.

Uncommitted Read

The Uncommitted Read (UR) isolation level, also known as dirty read, is the lowest level of isolation supported by DB2. It can be used to access uncommitted data changes of other applications. For example, an application using the uncommitted read isolation level will return all of the matching rows for a query, even if that data is in the process of being modified, and may not be committed to the database. If you decide to use this isolation level, your application might access incorrect data. Nonrepeatable read and phantom read phenomena are possible when this isolation level is being used.

There will be very few locks held by uncommitted read transactions. If the application is updating any data using a cursor (`FOR UPDATE`), the locking mode will be upgraded to Cursor Stability (CS). In addition, if the `SELECT` statement takes advantage of data found in an index (data in key), an IS lock will be held and prevent another application from taking an exclusive lock on the table. This behavior prevents an index from being removed during select statement processing.

Cursor Stability

The Cursor Stability (CS) isolation level locks any row on which the cursor is positioned during a transaction. The lock on the row is held until the next row is fetched or the transaction is terminated. If a row has been updated, the lock is held until the transaction is terminated. A transaction is terminated when either a `COMMIT` or `ROLLBACK` statement is executed.

An application using cursor stability cannot read uncommitted data. In addition, the application locks the row that has been currently fetched, and no other application can modify the contents of the current row.

If you decide to use this isolation level, your application will always read consistent data, but nonrepeatable read or phantom read situations are still possible.

Read Stability

The Read Stability (RS) isolation level locks those rows that are part of a result table. If you have a table containing 10,000 rows and the query returns 10 rows, then only 10 rows are locked.

An application using read stability cannot read uncommitted data. Instead of locking a single row, it locks all rows that are part of the result table. No other application can change or modify these rows.

If you decide to use this isolation level, your application will always get the same result if the query is executed more than once in a transaction, though you may get additional phantom rows.

Repeatable Read

The Repeatable Read (RR) isolation level is the highest isolation level available in DB2. It locks all rows and application references within a transaction. Locks are held on all rows processed to build the result set, no matter how large the result set. A table lock may be obtained instead depending on a number of factors.

An application using repeatable read cannot read uncommitted data of a concurrent application. If you decide to use this isolation level, none of the previous discussed situations (lost update, phantom read, or unrepeatable read) can occur in your application.

Choosing an Isolation Level

Choosing the proper isolation level is very important, because the isolation level influences not only the concurrency, but also the performance of the application. The more protection you have, the less concurrency is available.

Decide which concurrency problems are unacceptable for your application and then choose the isolation level that prevents these problems:

- Use the Uncommitted Read isolation level only if you use queries on read-only tables, or if you are using only SELECT statements and do not care whether you get uncommitted data from concurrent applications.

- Use the Cursor Stability isolation level when you want the maximum concurrency while seeing only committed data from concurrent applications.
- Use the Read Stability isolation level when your application operates in a concurrent environment. This means that qualified rows have to remain stable for the duration of the transaction.
- Use the Repeatable Read isolation level if changes to your result set are unacceptable.

Locking

DB2 provides isolation levels to control concurrency. In most cases, you do not need to take direct action to establish locks. In general, locks are acquired implicitly by DB2 according to the semantics defined by the isolation level.

Lock Attributes

The resource being locked is called an object. The only objects you can explicitly lock are tables and table spaces. Implicit locks on other types of objects, such as rows, index keys, and sometimes tables, are acquired by DB2 according to the isolation level and processing situations. The object being locked represents the granularity of the lock.

DB2 Note

The database itself can be locked if the `CONNECT` statement contains the clause `IN EXCLUSIVE MODE`. This will acquire an exclusive lock on the database and prevent any other users applications from connecting.

The length of time a lock is held is called the duration and is affected by the isolation level.

The access and rules that pertain to a lock are defined by the lock mode. Some lock modes are only used for locking table objects, while other lock modes are used for row objects. DB2 uses the following hierarchy of lockable database objects:

- Table spaces
- Tables
- Rows

The different modes of *table locks* are listed below in order of increasing control:

- IN (Intent None) — The owner of the lock can read any data, committed or noncommitted, in the table. Other applications can read or update the table.
- IS (Intent Share) — The owner of the lock can read any data in the table and

obtains an S or NS lock on each row read. Other applications can read or update rows in the table.

- S (Share) — The owner of the lock can read any data in the table and will not obtain row locks. Other applications can read the table data.
- IX (Intent Exclusive) — The owner of the lock can read any data in the table if a U, S, NS, or X lock can be obtained on rows and also can change any data in the table if an X lock can be obtained on rows. Other applications can both read and update table rows.
- SIX (Share with Intent Exclusive) —The owner of the lock can read any data in the table and change rows if it can obtain an X lock on the target row(s). Other applications can only read the table data.
- U (Update) — The owner of the lock can read any data in the table and can change data if an X lock on the table can be obtained prior to the update. Other applications can only read the table data.
- X (Exclusive) — The owner of the lock can read or update any data in the table. No row locks are obtained.Only other applications using the Uncommitted Read isolation level can read rows of the table.
- Z (Super exclusive) — No other application can access the table.

The different modes of *row locking* are listed below in order of increasing control over resources:

- NS (Next Key Share) — The row is being read by one application and can be read by concurrent applications. This lock type is held by applications using RS or CS isolation levels. It is compatible with the NX lock.
- S (Share) — The row is being read by one application and is available for *read-only* by concurrent applications.
- U (Update) — The row is being read by one application, which intends to update the data in this row. It is available for read-only by concurrent applications. Only one application can possess a U lock on a row. The lock owner will acquire X locks on the rows prior to update.
- NX (Next Key Exclusive) — This lock is acquired on the next row when a row is deleted from an index or inserted into an index in a table. The lock owner can read but not change the locked row. For type 2 indexes, this occurs only if the next row is currently locked by an RR scan.
- NW (Next Key Weak Exclusive) — This lock is acquired on the next row when a row is inserted into the index of a noncatalog table. The lock owner can read, but not change, the locked row. Only individual rows can be locked in NW mode. This is similar to X and NX locks except that it is compatible with the W and NS locks. For type 2 indexes, this lock occurs only if the next row is cur-

rently locked by an RR scan.

- X (Exclusive) — The row is being changed by one application and is not available for concurrent applications, except for those with uncommitted read isolation level. The lock owner can read and change data in the locked object.
- W (Weak Exclusive) — This lock is acquired on the row when a row is inserted into a noncatalog table. The lock owner can change the locked row. This lock is similar to a X lock except that it is compatible with the NW lock. Only uncommitted read applications can access the locked row.

The following table illustrates how all the lock modes work together (called *lock compatibility*). The table demonstrates whether one lock is compatible with another; "no" means the requesting application must wait for the lock to be released and "yes" means the lock can be granted.

Table 10–1 *Lock Type Compatibility*

State being	State of Held Resource												
Requested	**none**	**IN**	**IS**	**NS**	**S**	**IX**	**SIX**	**U**	**NX**	**X**	**Z**	**NW**	**W**
none	yes	yes	yes	yes	yes	yes	yes	yes	yes	yes	yes	yes	yes
IN	yes	yes	yes	yes	yes	yes	yes	yes	yes	yes	no	yes	yes
IS	yes	yes	yes	yes	yes	yes	yes	yes	no	no	no	no	no
NS	yes	yes	yes	yes	yes	no	no	yes	yes	no	no	yes	no
S	yes	yes	yes	yes	yes	no	no	yes	no	no	no	no	no
IX	yes	yes	yes	no	no	yes	no	no	no	no	no	no	no
SIX	yes	yes	yes	no	no	no	no	no	no	no	no	no	no
U	yes	yes	yes	yes	yes	no	no	no	no	no	no	no	no
NX	yes	yes	no	yes	no	no	no	no	no	no	no	no	no
X	yes	yes	no	no	no	no	no	no	no	no	no	no	no
Z	yes	no	no	no	no	no	no	no	no	no	no	no	no
NW	yes	yes	no	yes	no	no	no	no	no	no	no	no	yes
W	yes	yes	no	no	no	no	no	no	no	no	no	yes	no

Lock Conversion

If an application holds a lock on a data object, and the mode of access requires a more restrictive lock, the lock is converted to the more-restrictive lock. This process is known as *lock conversion*. During the lock conversion process, the more-restrictive lock may or may not be granted.

Let's look at an example of lock conversion. Assume that the application fetches a row from the test_taken table with the intent to update this row. The intent to update tells DB2 to acquire an update lock on the currently positioned row during the query processing.

The database manager holds an IX lock on the table and a U lock on the specified row. The SQL statements shown in Example 10–15 assign all test candidates currently scheduled to take the test at seat_no 1 to take the test at seat_no 2.

When the update statement of our example is issued, the database manager holds an IX lock on the test_taken table and an X lock on the changed row.

```
SELECT * FROM TEST_TAKEN
  WHERE SEAT_NO = '1' AND DATE_TAKEN = CURRENT DATE
  FOR UPDATE OF SEAT_NO;

UPDATE TEST_TAKEN
  SET SEAT_NO = '2'
WHERE SEAT_NO = '1' AND DATE_TAKEN = CURRENT DATE;
```

Example 10–15 *Update a row - Lock conversion*

All the locks are released when your application terminates the transaction with either a `COMMIT` or `ROLLBACK`.

The cursor stability isolation level was used in this example.

DB2 *Note*

When rows are being modified, an X lock is always required.

Lock Escalation

If your application changes many rows in one table, it may be better to have one lock on the entire table rather than many locks on each of the rows. DB2 requires memory for each lock; therefore, if a number of row locks can be replaced with a single table lock, the locking storage area can be used by other applications.

When DB2 converts the row locks to a table lock on your behalf, this is called *lock escalation*. DB2 will perform lock escalation to avoid resource problems by too many resources being held for the individual locks.

DB2 Note

Each DB2 lock consumes the same amount of memory.

Two database configuration parameters have a direct effect on lock escalation. They are:

- `LOCKLIST` — Defines the amount of memory allocated for the locks.
- `MAXLOCKS` — Defines the percentage of the total locklist permitted to be allocated to a single application.

There are two different situations for lock escalation:

- One application exceeds the percentage of the locklist as defined by the `MAXLOCKS` configuration parameter. The database manager will attempt to free memory by obtaining a table lock and releasing row locks for this application.
- Many applications connected to the database fill the locklist by acquiring a large number of locks. DB2 will attempt to free memory by obtaining a table lock and releasing row locks.

Also note that the isolation level used by the application has an effect on lock escalation:

- Cursor stability will acquire row level locks initially. If required, table level locks can be obtained. Usually, a very small number of locks are acquired by each cursor stability application since they only have to guarantee the integrity of the data in the current row.
- Read stability locks all rows in the original result set.
- Repeatable read may or may not obtain row locks on all rows read to determine the result set. If it does not, then a table lock will be obtain instead.

Lock Wait Behavior

What happens if one application requests to update a row that is already locked with an exclusive (X) lock? The application requesting the update will simply wait until the exclusive lock is released by the other application.

To ensure that the waiting application can continue without needed to wait indefinitely, the `LOCKTIMEOUT` configuration parameter can be set to define the length of the timeout period. The value is specified in seconds. By default, the lock timeout is disabled (set to a value of –1). This means the waiting application will not receive a timeout and will wait indefinitely.

Deadlock Behavior

In DB2, contention for locks by processes using the database can result in a deadlock situation.

A deadlock may occur in the following manner:

- Jon locks record 1.
- Finn locks record 5.
- Jon attempts to lock record 5, but waits since Finn already holds a lock on this record.
- Finn then tries to lock record 1, but waits since Jon already holds a lock on this record.

In this situation, both Jon and Finn will wait indefinitely for each other's locks until an external event causes one or both of them to ROLLBACK.

DB2 uses a background process, called the deadlock detector, to check for deadlocks. The process is activated periodically as determined by the DLCHKTIME parameter in the database configuration file. When activated it checks the lock system for deadlocks.

When the deadlock detector finds a deadlock situation, one of the deadlocked applications will receive an error code and the current transaction for that application will be rolled back automatically by DB2. When the rollback is complete, the locks held by this chosen application are released, thereby allowing other applications to continue.

Lock Table Statement

You can use the LOCK TABLE statement to override the rules for acquiring initial lock modes. It locks the specified table until the transaction is committed or rolled back. A table can be locked either in SHARE MODE or in EXCLUSIVE MODE.

When using the LOCK TABLE statement in SHARE MODE, no other application can update, delete, or insert data in the locked table. If you need a snapshot of a table that is frequently changed by concurrent applications, you can use this statement to lock the table for changes without using the repeatable read isolation level for your application.

The EXCLUSIVE MODE is more restrictive than SHARE MODE. It prevents concurrent applications from accessing the table for read, update, delete, and insert. If you want to update a large part of the table, you can use the LOCK TABLE statement in EXCLUSIVE MODE rather than locking each row.

LOCKSIZE Parameter of ALTER TABLE Statement

The default locking method for tables in DB2 is row locking. DB2 now provides you with the ability to override this default for a table by using the ALTER TABLE statement and the LOCKSIZE parameter.

The LOCKSIZE parameter allows you to specify the granularity of locking you wish DB2 to do for a particular table, either row or table-level locking. For example, to change the default locking method for the TEST_TAKEN table from row locking to table locking you would issue the following SQL statement (Example 10–16):

```
ALTER TABLE TEST_TAKEN LOCKSIZE TABLE;
```

Example 10–16 *Forcing table-level locking*

Whenever an application requires a lock to access data in the table, an appropriate table-level lock will be issued. It is important to realize that since all locks on the table are on the table level and not on the row level, it reduces the concurrency of applications accessing this table.

Changing the Locking Level in SQL

When a new application is developed, the default locking behavior is usually defined for all of the SQL within that application. For instance, a program using call-level interface SQL calls may have the default locking level set to cursor stability. This may not be the behavior that the developer wants, especially if some of the SQL statements are only for quick table lookups and shouldn't be holding any locks. In this case, the developer should be using the WITH clause that is available on the SELECT, INSERT, DELETE, and UPDATE statements.

The WITH statement is placed at the end of any of the SELECT or data modification statements, followed by the locking level that you want for that statement:

- RR — Repeatable Read
- RS — Read Stability
- CS — Cursor Stability
- UR — Uncommitted Read

The following example shows how a SELECT statement can be changed to hold no locks during the duration of the request (Example 10–17):

```
SELECT * FROM DB2CERT.TEST_TAKEN
  WHERE SEAT_NO = '1' AND DATE_TAKEN = CURRENT DATE
  WITH UR;
```

Example 10–17 *Changing isolation level at the statement level*

SET ISOLATION LEVEL

Sometimes the SQL that is being executed is found within stored procedures or other code that cannot be easily modified to change the locking behavior. In this type of situation, the SET CURRENT ISOLATION statement can be used to change the value of the CURRENT ISOLATION special register. The specific isolation level is then used when any select statement is executed, except in cases where the statement has already specified the locking level. The syntax of the command is shown in Example 10–18.

```
SET CURRENT ISOLATION = US | CS | RR | RS | RESET
```

Example 10–18 *Changing isolation level outside the statement*

When this SQL is executed, the CURRENT ISOLATION special register is replaced by the specified value or set to blanks if RESET is specified. The locking levels are identical to those used in Example 10–17. In addition to the two character locking codes, there are some synonyms that can be used instead:

- DIRTY READ can be specified in place of UR
- READ UNCOMMITTED can be specified in place of UR
- READ COMMITTED is recognized and upgraded to CS
- CURSOR STABILITY can be specified in place of CS
- REPEATABLE READ can be specified in place of RR
- SERIALIZABLE can be specified in place of RR

Locking Modification

DB2 contains two special registry variables that can be used to modify the way certain records are handled during SELECT processing:

- DB2_SKIPINSERTED controls whether uncommitted insertions can be ignored for cursors using the Cursor Stability (CS) or Read Stability (RS) isolation levels.
- DB2_SKIPDELETED allows statements using either Cursor Stability or Read Stability isolation levels to unconditionally skip deleted keys during index access and deleted rows during table access.

Both of these registry variables must be set using the db2set command (Example 10–19).

```
db2set DB2_SKIPINSERTED=ON
```

Example 10–19 *Changing the DB2_SKIPINSERTED value*

The DB2_SKIPINSERTED and DB2_SKIPDELETED registry values apply to the entire database and can only be changed before the database is started.

DB2_SKIPINSERTED

Usually DB2 will wait until an INSERT transaction completes before allowing a SELECT statement to read the value. In other words, any insert activity will cause a SELECT statement to wait until the insert is either committed or the work rolled-back. This is the default behavior of DB2 and when DB2_SKIPINSERTED is set to OFF.

However. there will be many cases where a report is being created that does not need to wait for the uncommitted data. This means that the report should skip data which has been inserted, but not committed, in the table. By setting DB2_SKIPINSERTED=OFF, the concurrency to the table can be increased, with a reduction in applications needing to wait for locks to free up.

DB2_SKIPDELETED

DB2_SKIPDELETED is similar to DB2_SKIPINSERTED except that it deals with deleted records. When this parameter is set to ON, any statements using either Cursor Stability or Read Stability isolation levels will skip deleted keys during index access and deleted rows during table access. Note that an additional registry variable, DB2_EVALUNCOMMITTED, can also improve concurrency with certain forms of SQL.

With DB2_EVALUNCOMMITTED enabled, the predicate evaluation will occur on uncommitted data. This means that predicate evaluation will wait until a uncommited update has completed. If the check was done before the row was commited, it may not satisfy the query, whereas if the predicate evaluation waited until the updated transaction completed, the row may satisfy the query. Additionally, uncommitted deleted rows are skipped during table scans.

This registry variable does not impact the behavior of cursors on the DB2 catalog tables.

Modifying Deadlock Time-outs

Traditional locking that is used to implement transaction isolation level can result in applications blocking each other. When this happens, one application must wait for another application to release the lock on a particular table, row, or index key value. A database has a configuration parameter called *locktimeout* that limits the amount of time that an application will wait for a lock before timing out. However, this database-level parameter may not be appropriate for many applications. On the other hand, in some cases it may be better to tell a user that the update cannot be done at the present time and to try it again later.

The lock wait mode timeout for an application/session can be set not to wait, to wait indefinitely, to wait for a specified amount of time (up to 32767 seconds), or to reset back to the value of database configuration. The syntax for this command is shown in Example 10–20.

```
SET CURRENT LOCK TIMEOUT = WAIT | NOT WAIT | NULL | 1..32767
```

Example 10–20 *Lock timeout setting*

Example 10–21 illustrates how the lock wait time can be modified so that the UPDATE will fail if there are any locks currently held on the same record. In the case that the UPDATE could not be performed, the application could display a message to the user indicating that someone else is performing maintenance on this record. If the lock wait time was not modified, the user may have to wait for a long time before the transaction goes through. In some cases, the user may think that the system has failed and cancel the transaction.

```
SET CURRENT LOCK TIMEOUT = NOT WAIT;

UPDATE TEST_SEATS
   SET NAME='PAUL'
   WHERE SEAT=4 AND TEST_DATE='2007-02-01';
```

Example 10–21 *Modifying lock timeout before issuing an UPDATE*

Using Temporary Tables

Declared temporary tables offer an alternative method for reducing lock contention. The DECLARE statement is very similar to the CREATE statement, except that it is used to create temporary tables that are used only during a session. The creation of a temporary table does not update the catalog, so locking, logging, and other forms of contention are avoided with this object.

If an application needs to create multiple reports from the same set of data, it may be more efficient to create a copy of the data rather than reissuing SQL statements against the original data. This technique is particularly important if the data needs to remain consistent between reports.

Example 10–22 shows how a temporary table can be created based on the original table design.

```
DECLARE GLOBAL TEMPORARY TABLE T1
   LIKE TRANSACTIONS
   ON COMMIT PRESERVE ROWS NOT LOGGED IN SESSIONTEMP;

INSERT INTO SESSION.T1
  SELECT * FROM TRANSACTIONS WHERE SALES < 3000;

SELECT * FROM SESSION.T1;
```

Example 10–22 *Using temporary tables to avoid locks*

Note that once the temporary table has been created, indexes can be created against it to improve performance of any additional queries.

The initial `SELECT` statement will cause some locking on the system unless `WITH UR` was added to the SQL. Once the temporary table has been populated, subsequent queries can access this table without locking any other users.

`DECLARED` tables can be `DROPPED` and `ALTERED`, but no other database objects (other than indexes) can be created to act against them. Temporary tables do allow for the specification of a partitioning key and the creation of indexes for improved performance.

From an SQL perspective, the temporary tables must have the `SESSION` schema prefixed to the table name in order to access them. Once the transaction has been completed and the application disconnected, the temporary tables will be removed from the system.

Summary

In this chapter, we have discussed some of the possible concurrency problems that can occur in a multiuser database environment. To protect the data as it is being modified, rules are established and the changes are grouped together in transactions.

The data updated by a transaction is either made permanent by the `COMMIT` statement or removed using the `ROLLBACK` statement. Each transaction is made up of one or more SQL statements. The rules of concurrent data access are determined by the isolation level, which are set for static and dynamic SQL application modules.

DB2 will implement the isolation level semantics of data access by implicitly acquiring locks on behalf of the applications. Applications can decide to lock a resource for `EXCLUSIVE` or `SHARE` mode. The only resource that can be directly locked using an SQL statement is a table. All row-level locks are acquired, according to the isolation level, by DB2.

If a requested lock is more restrictive, and another application already has the resource locked, a wait on the release of the lock will occur. The amount of time an application will wait is determined by a database configuration parameter known as `LOCKTIMEOUT`. The default amount of lock wait time is indefinite.

If multiple applications require access to data that is held by other applications, a deadlock scenario can occur. DB2 will detect the occurrence of any deadlocks and force one of the transactions to `ROLLBACK`. Every lock requested requires memory on the DB2 server. The amount of lock storage is configurable using the `LOCKLIST` and `MAXLOCKS` parameters.

Locking levels can be modified within SQL statements and by changing the `CURRENT ISOLATION` register. In addition to changing the locking levels, other techniques, including using temporary tables, can be used to help reduce contention in a database.

PART 3

DB2 Administration

CHAPTER 11

Data Storage Management

- PROCESSOR, MEMORY, DISK CONSIDERATIONS
- DB2 STORAGE MODEL
- TABLE SPACE DESIGN
- IMPLEMENTATION EXAMPLES
- MAINTENANCE

*B*eing able to efficiently store and quickly retrieve large amounts of data is one of the main functions of any relational database management system. The physical placement of the data can directly affect the query performance. It is the responsibility of the database administrator to understand the concepts of data placement and to create an appropriate physical database design.

Processor, Memory, and Disk Resources

Before looking at specific DB2 objects, you should consider the hardware that will be used to implement your DB2 system. Besides the minimum amount of processor, disk, and memory required to install the various DB2 components, how much of each component do you need to support your databases? Like most questions of this nature, the answer is: *it depends*.

Without adequate hardware resources, you will need to limit your performance expectations. No amount of tuning inside DB2 and/or the operating system can compensate for a hardware configuration that is lacking in processing power, hard disk capacity, or the amount of real memory.

On the other hand, if not enough attention is paid to configuring DB2 when there is enough hardware resource, your system may underperform.

Processors

DB2 can operate in the following hardware environments:

- Single partition on a single processor (uniprocessor).
- Single partition with multiple processors.
- Multiple partition configurations. These configurations are supported on a single machine or across multiple servers.

Single Partition on a Single Processor

The database in this environment serves the needs of a department or small office. A single processor system is restricted by the amount of disk-related processing the processor can handle. As workload increases, a single processor may become insufficient in processing user requests any faster, regardless of other additional components such as disk and memory that you may add to the system.

Single Partition with Multiple Processors

This environment is typically made up of several equally powerful processors within the same machine and is called a symmetric multiprocessor (SMP) system. Resources such as disk space and memory are shared. More disks and memory are found in this machine compared to the single-partition database, single processor environment.

This environment is easier to manage than multiple machines are since all components are physically contained in one machine. With multiple processors available, different database operations can be completed more quickly than with database operations assigned to only a single processor. DB2 can also divide the work of a single query among available processors to improve processing speed. Other database operations such as the LOAD, BACKUP, and RESTORE utilities, and the CREATE INDEX statement can take advantage of the multiple processors.

Parallel I/O operations are much more likely to occur in this environment, especially if data is spread out over multiple containers over multiple disk drives.

Memory

As previously mentioned, buffer pools are a very important tuning area in DB2 performance tuning. The way that you configure the system's real and virtual memory, DB2's internal memory usage, and the DB2 buffer pools will greatly influence the performance of the system.

Generally speaking, the more real memory, the better the overall performance. Balance this against the number of processors in the system. Not enough real memory will cause excessive paging in the operating system, which affects all applications, including DB2. The situation can arise where even though a page of DB2 data is sitting in the buffer pool, because the operating system does not have enough memory to keep that page in its real memory, it has to write it out to disk temporarily. This situation can have a severe performance effect on DB2.

Try to make the data server a dedicated machine. If DB2 has to share the machine with other applications, be aware of their memory requirements and factor that into how much memory is acquired for the machine.

Memory requirements are influenced by the number of concurrent users you will have. For example, in a Windows environment, it is recommended that you start with a minimum of 256 MB of memory and additional memory may be required as the number of users are increased. Refer to the *DB2 Quick Beginnings* manual for the relevant operating system for further exact details for your release level.

Disk

The amount of disk required will ultimately depend on the amount of data that is required to be stored in your databases. Factors to be aware of in planning your hard disk configuration include:

- The capacity of the disks used. Sometimes it is better to use multiple disks of lower capacity so that greater degrees of parallel I/O operations can take place. The tradeoff to this approach is that additional hardware is required.
- The speed of disks used. Hard disk attributes such as latency and seek time affect the I/O performance. DB2's optimizer can make use of disk attributes in its calculation for the best access path.
- Compressed file systems can be used to hold DB2 table space containers when disk space is at a premium and/or when the performance requirements allow for

the extra overhead incurred. Another option would be to use row compression as discussed in "Database Objects" on page 225.

- If availability is a high priority issue you may want to mirror disks. If so, this will double your disk requirements.

Performance and availability can be influenced by the hard disk controllers you use and how many disks are attached to the controller. By placing disks on separate controllers you can reduce the traffic going through the controllers, thereby reducing the contention for the disks.

DB2 Storage Model

The following data objects will be discussed:

- Buffer pool — allocates memory to DB2.
- Table space — logical layer between physical tables with data and the database.
- Table — represented by rows and columns. Several tables can reside in one table space.
- Container — allocates storage to a table space.

The DB2 storage model illustrates the relationship between tables, table spaces, databases, and a DB2 instance (Figure 11–1).

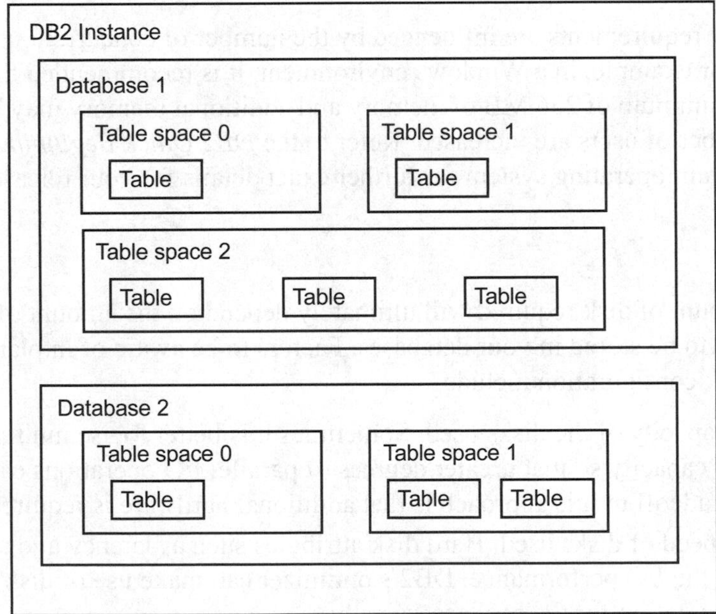

Figure 11–1 *DB2 storage model*

Normally an individual table would be placed into a single table space. However, table (or range) partitions allows the DBA to have portions of a table placed into separate table spaces. This feature allows the DBA to do more efficient maintenance of data that is frequently added and dropped from the table (like monthly or quarterly sales data). More information on this feature can be found in the section on "Table (Range) Partitioning" on page 674.

Buffer Pool

A *buffer pool* is an area of main memory allocated to the database manager to cache table and index data pages as they are read from disk or modified. The purpose of a buffer pool is to improve database system performance. The database manager decides when to bring data from disk into a buffer pool and when old data in a buffer pool is unlikely to be used in the short term and can be written back out to disk. Data can be accessed much faster from memory than from disk; therefore, the fewer times the database manager needs to read from or write to a disk, the better the performance. Multiple buffer pools can be created. The configuration of buffer pools is a very important tuning area, since you can reduce the delay caused by excessive physical I/O.

DB2 *Note*

On UNIX platforms, the creation of a DB2 database will create a default buffer pool called `IBMDEFAULTBP` of 1000 four-kilobyte pages. For other platforms, the buffer pool size is 250 four-kilobyte pages.

Table Spaces

One of the first tasks in setting up a relational database is mapping the logical database design to physical storage on your system. The object used to specify the physical location of data is known as a *table space*. A table space is used as a layer between the database and the container objects that hold the actual table data. A table space can contain more than one table.

As all DB2 tables reside in table spaces, this means you can control where table data is physically stored. This gives you the ability to create a physical database design to fit your particular environment. For example, you can choose slower disks to store less frequently accessed data.

Backup and recovery can be performed at the table space level. This will give you more granularity and control since you can back up or restore each table space individually.

There are three types of table spaces:

- System-Managed Space (SMS)

  The operating system's file system manager allocates and manages the space. Prior to DB2 9, creating a database or table space without any parameters will result in all table spaces being created as SMS objects.

- Database-Managed Space (DMS)

  The database manager controls the storage space. This table space is, essentially, an implementation of a special-purpose file system designed to best meet the needs of the database manager.

- Automatic Storage with DMS

  Automated storage is not really a separate type of table space, but a different way of handling DMS storage. DMS containers require more maintenance (see the section below) and Automatic Storage was introduced in DB2 V8.2.2 as a way of simplifying space management.

DB2 *Note*

The default storage mechanism for new databases created in DB2 9 is based on Automatic Storage. Prior to DB2 9, databases were created using System Managed Storage.

SMS Table Spaces

In a *System Managed Space* (SMS) table space, the operating system's file system manager allocates and manages the space where the table is to be stored. This storage model typically consists of many files representing table objects, stored in the file system space. The user decides on the location of the files, DB2 controls their names, and the file system is responsible for managing them. Each container is a directory in the file space of the operating system.

DMS Table Spaces

In a *Database Managed Space* (DMS) table space, the database manager controls the storage space. The storage model consists of a limited number of devices, whose space is managed by DB2. The Database Administrator decides which devices to use, and DB2 manages the space on the devices. This type of table space is essentially an implementation of a special-purpose file system designed to best meet the needs of the database manager. The table space definition includes a list of the devices or files belonging to the table space in which data can be stored. Each container is either a fixed size preallocated file or a physical device such as a disk.

Automatic Storage

Databases that are enabled for automatic storage have a set of one or more storage paths associated with them. A table space can be defined as "managed by automatic storage" and its containers assigned and allocated by DB2 based on those storage paths.

DMS versus SMS versus Automatic Storage

Although Table 11–1 is not exhaustive, it does contain some things for you to consider when deciding between DMS, automatic, and SMS table spaces.

Table 11–1 *SMS versus DMS versus Automatic Storage*

Feature	SMS	DMS	Automatic Storage
Striping?	Yes	Yes	Yes
Default type	Version 8	No	Version 9
Object management	Operating system	DB2	DB2
Space allocation	Grows//shrinks on demand.	Preallocated. Size can shrink and grow but requires DBA intervention.	Preallocated. Can grow automatically.
Ease of administration	Best. Little or no tuning required.	Good, but some tuning required (e.g. EXTENTSIZE PREFETCHSIZE)	Best. Little or no tuning required.
Performance	Very good	Best. Can achieve up to 5 to 10% additional performance with raw containers.	Best. Can't use raw containers however.
Maximum table space size	64GB (4K Page)	2TB (4K Page)	2TB (4K Page)

Aside from the simplified management using SMS table spaces, the most significant difference between the two storage models is the maximum size of a table space. Using SMS, the DBA is restricted to placing a maximum of 64GB in a table space. This amount can be increased by changing the page size to 32K (512GB), at the expense of possibly less useable space on a page. Moving to a DMS model will increase the table space limit to 2TB with a 4K page size. The amount of storage available can grow to as much as 16TB with a 32K page size. While there are other ways to increase the size of a table beyond the 64GB boundary, the simplest approach may be to use DMS table spaces initially.

DMS versus Automatic Storage

DB2 Version 8.2.2 introduced the notion of AUTOMATIC STORAGE. Automatic storage allows the DBA to set up the database with storage paths that can be used for all table space container creation. Rather than having the DBA explicitly code the location and size of the tablespaces, the system will automatically allocate them. In DB2 9, a database will be created with automatic storage unless the DBA explicitly overrides this setting.

A database can only be enabled for automatic storage when it is first created. You cannot enable automatic storage for a database that was not originally defined to use it. Similarly, you cannot disable automatic storage for a database that was originally designed to use it.

Table 11–2 summarizes some of the differences between managing non-automatic storage and automatic storage.

Table 11–2 *DMS storage versus automatic storage*

Feature	Non-automatic storage	Automatic storage
Container Creation	Containers must be explicitly provided when the table space is created.	Containers cannot be provided when the table space is created — they will be assigned and allocated automatically by DB2.
Container Resizing	Automatic resizing of table spaces is off (AUTORESIZE NO) by default.	Automatic resizing of table spaces is on (AUTORESIZE YES) by default.
Initial Size	The initial size for the table space cannot be specified using the INITIALSIZE clause.	The initial size for the table space can be specified using the INITIALSIZE clause.
Container Modification	Container operations can be performed using the ALTER TABLESPACE statement (ADD, DROP, BEGIN NEW STRIPE SET, and so on).	Container operations cannot be performed because DB2 is in control of space management.

Table 11–2 *DMS storage versus automatic storage*

Feature	Non-automatic storage	Automatic storage
Ease of administration	A redirected restore operation can be used to redefine the containers associated with the table space.	A redirected restore operation cannot be used to redefine the containers associated with the table space because DB2 is in control of space management.

The primary reason for the introduction of the automatic storage model was to simplify the management of DMS tablespaces while retaining the performance characteristics. There will situations where the DBA must define all of the characteristics of the tablespaces being used, but many applications will benefit from the reduced management required with automatic storage.

Regular versus Large Table Spaces

DB2 places rows on a data page, which can be either 4K, 8K, 16K, or 32K in size. Although the size of a page can vary, the maximum number of pages in a table space is limited to the size of the row identifier (RID). The RID is a reference to the location of a row in a table. The RID contains the page number in the table space and the slot number of the row on a page.

Prior to DB2 9, the row identifier was four bytes in length, with 3 bytes pointing to a page in a regular table space and 1 byte representing the row number within a page. Figure 11–2 illustrates the structure of the RID for DB2 8 and prior releases.

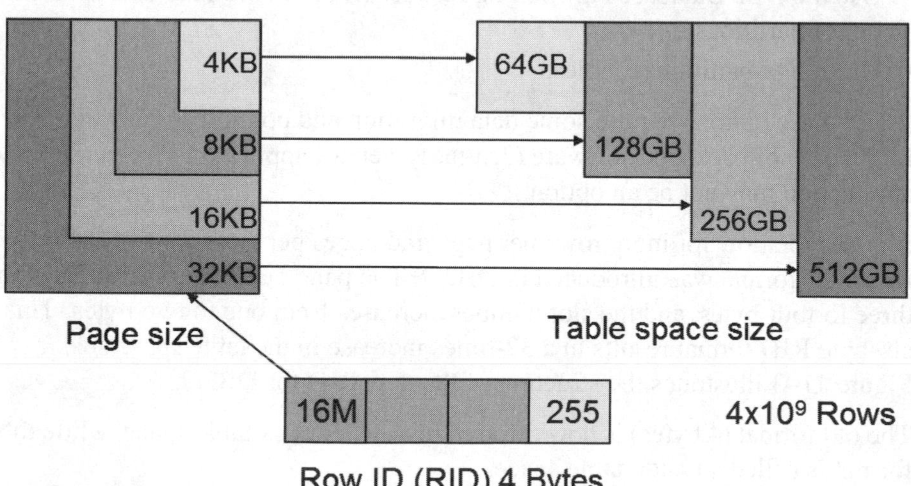

Figure 11–2 *Record Identifier (Regular Table Space)*

All regular, user, and temporary table spaces had a maximum of 224 (16 million) pages associated with it. This number is derived from the three-byte page number in the row identifier. Based on the size of page selected, a table space could contain anywhere from 64GB of data for a 4K page, up to 512GB for a 32K page.

With the four-byte RID, DB2 only reserves one byte for a row slot in a page. This one-byte value translates to a maximum of 255 rows being placed on one page. If the length of a row is relatively small, there may be a large amount of space wasted on a larger page size. Table 11–3 highlights the smallest row size before space will be wasted on the page.

Table 11–3 *Maximum row size by page size*

Page Size	Min Row Length	Max Records
4 KB	14	251
8 KB	30	253
16 KB	62	254
32 KB	127	253

Increasing the size of a page in DB2 would not necessarily guarantee more rows in a table since the maximum number of rows at any page size is still limited to 255.

Once the maximum page limit in a table space is met, there are three options available:

- Union a number of tables together in a view
- Use the DB2 Database Partitioning Feature (DPF) to hash the data across a number of partitions
- Use range-partitioned tables.

All of these options require some data migration and possible application changes. In the case of packaged software (3rd-party vendor applications), changing the application may not be an option.

In order to allow for more rows per page and pages per table space, a new row identifier format was introduced in DB2 9. The page number is increased from three to four bytes, and the slot number increases from one to two bytes. This new six-byte RID format results in a 32-times increase in the table space size. Figure 11–3 illustrates the structure of the new RID for DB2 9.

The old format (4 bytes) is now referred to as a REGULAR table space, while the new format is called a LARGE table space.

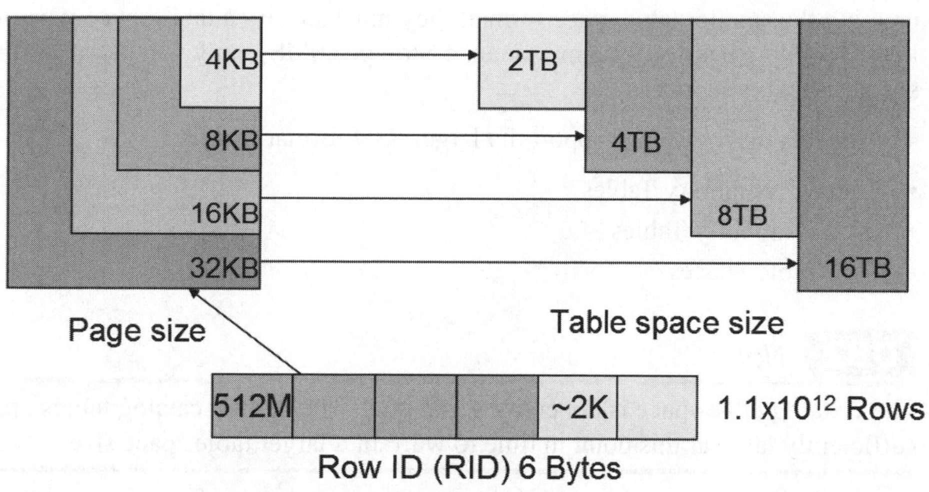

Figure 11–3 *Large Record Identifier (Large Table Space)*

In addition to the larger table space size, the number of rows on a page increases from 255 to over 2300 on a page. While the theoretical limit is 65,000 rows on a page, there is a minimum row size (approximately 12 bytes) that limits the total number of rows on a page. Table 11–4 summarizes the increased row capacity per various page sizes.

Table 11–4 *Maximum number of rows per page with Large RIDs*

Page Size (bytes)	Space for Data (bytes)	Number of Rows
4096	4028	366
8192	8124	738
16384	16316	1483
32768	32700	2972

While table spaces can now grow to 16TB in size, a table of this size will have challenges associated with it, including backup and recovery. When tables start to grow into terabyte sizes, it may more appropriate to use other techniques, like table partitioning or database partitioning, rather than placing all of the data in one table space. These options will allow for more granular backup and recovery, as well as options for tuning access to certain parts of a table.

Large table spaces are now the default type for any Database Managed Storage (DMS) table space in a DB2 9 database. This means that the CREATE TABLESPACE command does not have to explicitly state that a LARGE table space object is being created, although the syntax allows this to be specified. If a DBA wants to continue creating the smaller table space format, they must specify a table space type of REGULAR. Note that for System Managed Storage (SMS), only the REGULAR table space format is supported.

The objects that now can support the larger RID format include:

- System Temporary Tables
- User Temporary Tables
- User Table Spaces

DB2 Note

The Catalog table space is not created as LARGE. The current catalog tables are not sufficiently large at this point in time to warrant a larger table space size.

Migrating to Large Tablespaces

Migrating to DB2 9 from a prior release will not upgrade any of the table spaces to the new format. In order to change the table spaces to the LARGE format, the ALTER table space command must be used:

```
ALTER TABLESPACE tablespacename CONVERT TO LARGE
```

The ALTER command does not physically change the structure of the table space; it merely changes the catalog entry to indicate that the table space is eligible for the new RID format. All table spaces that are migrated from version 8 will be in the REGULAR format.

While the ALTER command does not take a great deal of time to execute, you must take care to COMMIT WORK immediately after the command completes. If the command is not committed, an exclusive lock will be held on the table space and no other work can be done against tables in the table space until the lock is released.

Once the table space has been altered, two additional steps need to be taken in order to gain the advantages associated with the larger RIDs:

- Reorganize the indexes
- Reorganize the data

Reorganizing the indexes will allow the table space to grow the amount of pages allocated to it. This step is required in order to grow tables beyond the 64GB boundary. Without reorganizing the indexes, the table space will continue to be limited to the original 64GB boundary.

Note that without having done the index reorganization, previously existing tables continue to be restricted to 255 rows per page and to three-byte page numbers until reorganization of the table or indexes occur. If the number of pages in a table space are exhausted, DB2 will issue an error message:

```
SQL1236N Table "<table-name>" cannot allocate a new page because
the index with identifier "<index-id>" does not yet support
large RIDs.
```

Reorganizing a table is not as critical as reorganizing the indexes. While the indexes control the growth of the number of pages in the table space, a reorganization of a table may result in more rows per page. The standard `REORG TABLE` command must be used to place more rows on a page. The online `REORG` command is not supported when converting to the new RID format.

Reorganizing the tables in `LARGE` table spaces is only necessary when the average row size is less than the minimum record length as shown in Table 11–3.

Containers

A container is a physical storage device. It can be identified by a directory name, a device name, or a file name (Figure 11–4).

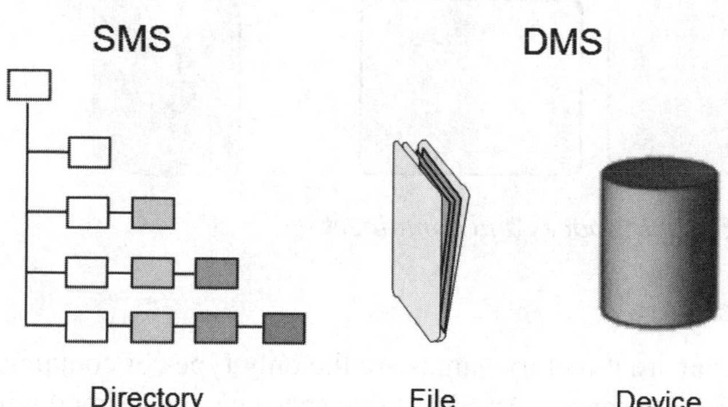

Figure 11–4 *Containers in DB2*

A container is assigned to a table space. All database and table data is assigned to table spaces. A table space's definitions and attributes are recorded in the database system catalog. Once a table space is created, you can then create tables within this table space. Details about containers can obtained by using the `LIST TABLESPACE CONTAINERS` command. A single table space can span many containers, but each container can belong to only one table space. Figure 11–5 shows an example of the relationship between tables and a table space within a database and the associated containers and disks.

Containers usually reside on disks that are local. Some LAN-redirected drives or NFS-mounted file systems can be used but care must be taken to ensure that the network latency does not impact performance of the system. In addition, only certain network file systems have been tested so it is wise to check on the DB2 support website to ensure that your particular configuration is supported:

```
www-306.ibm.com/software/data/db2/support/db2_9/
```

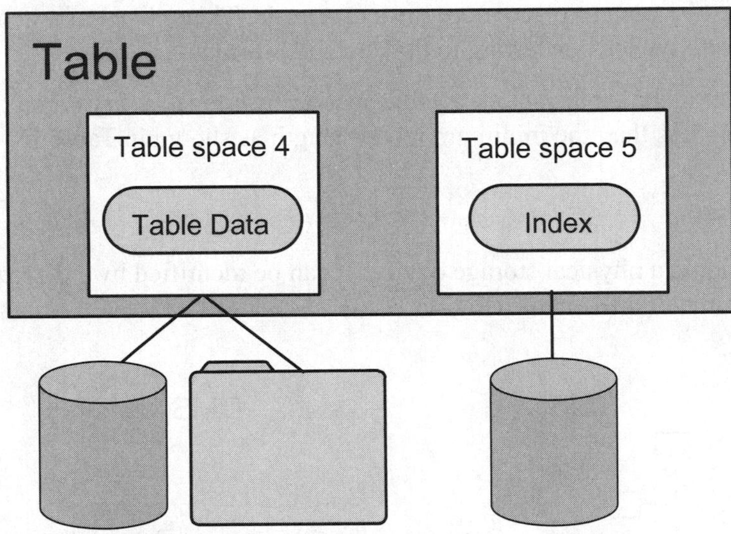

Figure 11–5 *Table spaces and containers*

Directory Containers

Containers that are directory names are the only types of containers that can be used in SMS table spaces. An SMS table space can be defined with more than one container, each one of which could be mapped to a different physical disk to balance the I/O workload. DB2 will balance the amount data written to the multiple containers. It is very important to identify all the containers you want to use, since you cannot add or delete containers to an SMS table space after it has been created using the `ALTER TABLESPACE` statement.

The name for a directory container identifies an absolute or relative directory name. The directory named must not contain any files or subdirectories. The relative directory name is relative to the database directory. Refer to the `CREATE TABLESPACE` statement in the *DB2 SQL Reference* for more details.

DB2 Note

A table space container layout can be redefined during a restore of the table space. This is known as a *redirected restore*.

Device Containers

The device that the container is created on cannot be used in another table space. So when specifying the size of the container, make sure that all the space on the device is used because any unused space will be wasted. The amount space required can be specified in pages, kilobytes, megabytes, or gigabytes.

File Containers

File containers are files of preallocated size used by DMS table spaces. No operational differences exist between a file and a device. When defining the container name, you can use an absolute or relative file name. If any component of the directory name does not exist, it will be created by DB2. Similarly, if the file does not exist, it will be created and initialized to the specific size by DB2. The amount of space specified must exist when the table space is created. The amount space required can be specified in pages, kilobytes, megabytes, or gigabytes.

DB2 Note

A container can only be added to a DMS table space. Containers cannot be added to an SMS table space with the ALTER TABLESPACE statement. You can add a container to an SMS table space during a *redirected restore* operation.

Table Space Design

In addition to defining whether a table space is SMS or DMS managed, there are several other parameters that may be specified during the `CREATE TABLESPACE` command.

Here is the syntax of the `CREATE TABLESPACE` statement (Figure 11–6):

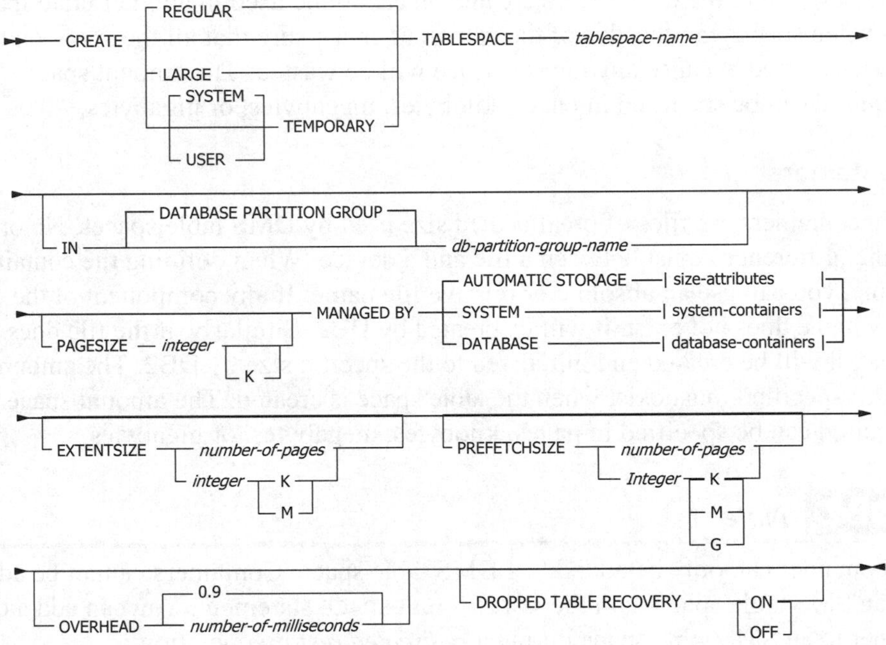

Figure 11–6 *Create Table space syntax*

Some of the key parameters to the `CREATE TABLESPACE` statement include (see the *DB2 SQL Reference* for further detail):

- `REGULAR | TEMPORARY | LARGE TABLESPACE` — specifies the type of table space to be created; `LARGE` will be selected if nothing is specified.
- `MANAGED BY SYSTEM | DATABASE USING | AUTOMATIC STORAGE` — specifies SMS (SYSTEM), DMS (DATABASE), or an `AUTOMATIC STORAGE` table space. For SMS or DMS table spaces the containers are defined with the `USING` clause. For SMS table spaces, the container is a directory name. For DMS table spaces, a `FILE` or `DEVICE` container is specified and its size in `PAGESIZE` pages. For

AUTOMATIC STORAGE table spaces, the size attributes are shown in Figure 11–7.

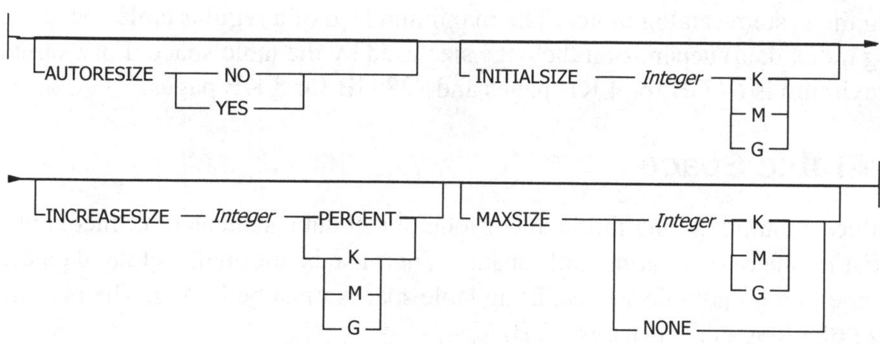

Figure 11–7 *Automatic Storage size attributes*

- PAGESIZE — allowable values for the page size of the table space: 4, 8, 16, or 32.
- EXTENTSIZE — number of PAGESIZE pages that are written to a container before moving to the next container.
- PREFETCHSIZE — number of PAGESIZE pages read if prefetch is performed.
- BUFFERPOOL — name of buffer pool to be used for tables in this table space.
- OVERHEAD — number of milliseconds for the I/O controller to read a page (disk seek and latency time, default = 24.1).
- TRANSFERRATE — number of milliseconds to read one page into memory; this value is used by the optimizer in calculating I/O costs (default = 0.9).
- DROPPED TABLE RECOVERY ON | OFF — specifies if dropped tables in the table space can be recovered using the RECOVER TABLE ON option of the ROLLFORWARD command.
- DATABASE PARTITION GROUP — used to specify which database partition group a table space will belong to in a clustered environment; the default assumes a non-clustered environment.

Some of the major table space parameters will now be reviewed in more detail.

Regular Table Space

Tables containing user data exist in one or many *regular* table spaces. By default, a table space called USERSPACE1 is created when the CREATE DATABASE command is executed. Indexes are also stored in regular table spaces. The system catalog tables exist in a regular table space as well. The default system catalog table space is called SYSCATSPACE. By default, both USERSPACE1 and SYSCATSPACE are created as SMSs, but can be defined as DMSs in the CREATE DATABASE command. While it is optional to use the USERSPACE1 table space (it is always created but may be dropped), it is mandatory to use SYSCATSPACE as the name of the table space holding the system catalog tables. The maximum size of a regular table space (including index data) depends on the page size used by the table space. For example, the maximum is 64 GB for 4 KB pages and 128 GB for 8 KB pages.

Large Table Space

Tables containing long field data or long object data, such as multimedia objects, exist in one or many *long* table spaces. Their use is optional, as long data can also reside in regular table spaces. Long table spaces must be DMSs. The maximum size of a long table space is 2 TB.

DB2 *Note*

Long table space have been renamed to large table spaces.

System Temporary Table Space

Temporary table spaces are used by the database manager during SQL operations for holding transient data such as immediate tables during sort operations, reorganizing tables, creating indexes, and joining tables. A database must have at least one temporary table space. By default, an SMS table space called TEMPSPACE1 is created when the database is created. It can be dropped after another temporary table space is created (one must always be in existence), and it can be called any legal table space name. The name TEMPSPACE1 does not have to be used. Temporary table spaces can be either SMSs or DMSs. The maximum size of a temporary table space is 2 TB.

DB2 *Note*

DB2 supports system temporary table spaces and user temporary table spaces. A system temporary table space must exist for DB2 to operate properly. User temporary table spaces are used for DECLARED TEMPORARY tables.

Extentsize

An *extent* is a unit of space within a container of a table space. Database objects are stored in pages within DB2 (except for LOBs and long varchars). These pages are grouped into allocation units called extents. The extent size is defined at the table space level. Once the extent size is established for the table space, it cannot be altered. A database configuration parameter DFT_EXTENT_SZ specifies the default extent size for all table spaces in the database. The range this value can take is from 2 to 256 pages; for example, 8 – 1024 KB for 4 KB pages or 16 – 2048 KB for 8 KB pages. This figure can be overridden by using the EXTENTSIZE parameter in the CREATE TABLESPACE statement. Although this parameter can be also specified in kilobytes or megabytes, DB2 ensures that the extent size is always a whole number of pages by taking the floor of the number of bytes divided by the page size.

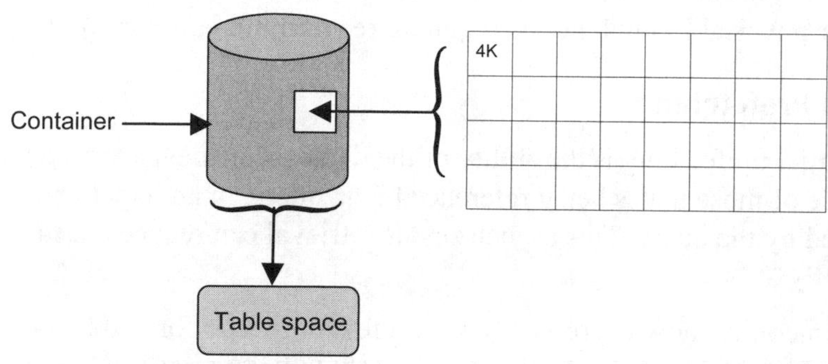

Figure 11–8 *Extents and containers*

DB2 *Note*

In addition to using extents for storing user data, extents are also used for space management within the table space.

Pagesize

Rows of DB2 table data are organized into blocks called *pages*. Pages can be four sizes: 4, 8, 16, and 32 KB. Table data pages do not contain the data for columns defined with LONG VARCHAR, LONG VARGRAPHIC, BLOB, CLOB, or DBCLOB data types.

In a page of table data, 68 bytes are reserved for DB2. The other 4028 bytes are available for user data, although no individual row can exceed 4005 bytes (8101 bytes for 8 KB pages) in length. The maximum number of columns in a table defined using a table space that uses 4 KB pages is 500; for 8, 16, and 32 KB pages, it is 1012 columns.

DB2 *Note*

LOB and long field data can reside in table spaces of any page size.

Performance Considerations

The type and design of your table space determines the efficiency of the I/O performed against that table space. The following concepts are important in understanding how DB2 performs I/O operations.

Big-Block Reads

If several pages (usually an extent) are retrieved in a single request, then *big-block reads* have occurred. If rows that are in pages within the extent retrieved are used, another physical I/O will not be required, resulting in optimum performance.

Sequential Prefetching

Sequential prefetching is the ability of the database manager to read pages in advance of those pages being referenced by a query, in anticipation of being required by the query. This asynchronous retrieval can reduce execution times significantly.

You can control how aggressively the prefetching is performed by changing the PREFETCHSIZE parameter on the CREATE TABLESPACE or ALTER TABLESPACE statement. By default, this value is set to the DFT_PREFETCH_SZ database configuration parameter. This value represents how many pages will be read at a time when a prefetch request is triggered by DB2. By setting this value to a multiple of the extent size, multiple extents can be read in parallel. This function is even more effective when the containers for the table space are on separate hard disks.

DB2 Note

On Linux and UNIX platforms, prefetching will create separate I/O processes. On Windows, prefetching is accomplished using threads.

To enable prefetching, DB2 starts separate threads of control, known as *I/O servers*, to perform page reading. These I/O servers wait for requests for pages from database agents that manage the processing of all SQL requests. The first available I/O server will read the prefetch request from a queue and read the data into the buffer pool. Depending on the number of prefetch requests in the queue and the number of I/O servers configured by the NUM_IOSERVERS database configuration parameter, multiple I/O servers can be fetching data at the same time.

DB2 can monitor I/O activity in the system. If sequential page reading is occurring, DB2 will initiate prefetching requests. The function is called *sequential detection* and is implemented via the SEQDETECT database configuration parameter. By default, this parameter is set to YES. If set to NO, DB2 will only initiate sequential prefetching in a predetermined manner during query optimization for activities such as table sorts and scans where sets of contiguous pages of data are required during query processing.

Another form of prefetching that can occur regardless of the SEQDETECT parameter is *list prefetching*. This is when DB2 builds up a list of internal row identifiers that are required, usually after scanning an index, then sorts them into physical address sequence and starts scanning the table for the rows. Because DB2 knows beforehand which pages are required, it can retrieve them ahead of when the application needs them; thus, the time to retrieve the data is shortened significantly due to the asynchronous processing.

Page Cleaning

As pages are read and modified, they accumulate in the buffer pool. Whenever a page is read in, there must be a buffer pool page to read it into. If the buffer pool is full of modified pages, one of these modified pages must be written out to the disk before the new page can be read in. To prevent the buffer pool from becoming full, *page cleaner* tasks write out modified pages to guarantee the availability of buffer pool pages for use by read requests. This feature is implemented via the NUM_IOCLEANERS database configuration parameter.

The CHNGPGS_THRESH database configuration parameter specifies the level (percentage) of changed pages at which the page cleaner tasks will start. When started, they will build a list of the pages to write to disk. Once they have completed writing the pages to disk, they will become inactive again and wait for the next trigger to start. The default value for this parameter is 60%.

In addition to I/O considerations, there are also considerations relating to the use of the table space containers. These are detailed as follows.

Number of Extents Required

Five is the minimum number of extents required in a DMS table space:

- Three extents for overhead and control information
- Two extents for each table object (always assume one object)

Number of Pages Required

In a DMS table space, one page in every container is reserved for overhead, and the remaining pages will be used one extent at a time. Only full extents are used in the container, so for optimum space management, you can use the following formula to help determine the appropriate size to use when allocating a container size:

```
(extent size in pages * n) + 1
```

In this formula, `extent size` is the size of each extent for the table space and `n` is the number of extents you want to store in the container. Recall above that you need a minimum of five extents for a DMS table space.

Recall that with SMS table spaces, space is allocated by the operating system file system as required.

Striping

Given that a table space can span multiple containers, DB2 writes to each container in a *round robin* fashion, where an extent as it is filled with data is written to each container in turn. This is known as striping.

In an SMS table space, if any container becomes full, then the entire table space is considered full, and no more data can be added.

In a DMS table space, if a container becomes full, DB2 will continue to use space available in other containers.

In both cases, it is preferable that containers be designed so that they are of equal size on different physical drives to optimize space usage and DB2 parallel operations.

Using RAID Devices

If you plan to use RAID devices, here are some guidelines. For further information and details, please refer to the *DB2 Administration Guide*.

- Define a single container for the table space (using the RAID device).
- Make the extent size equal to, or a multiple of the RAID stripe size.
- Ensure the prefetch size of the table space is the RAID stripe size multiplied by the number of RAID parallel devices (or a whole multiple of this product) and a multiple of the extent size.
- Use the DB2 registry variable `DB2_STRIPED_CONTAINERS` to align extents to the RAID stripe size.
- Use the DB2 registry variable `DB2_PARALLEL_IO` to enable parallel disk I/O.

Device Containers Versus File Containers

For DMS table spaces, files can be less efficient than devices due to the runtime overhead of the file system. Files are useful when:

- A device is not available.
- Maximum performance is not required. By bypassing the file system layer, DB2 manages device containers directly, improving performance, whereas for files,

DB2 interacts with the file system.

- You do not want the extra administrative overhead associated with setting up and maintaining devices.

Some operating systems allow you to have physical devices greater than 2 GB in size. You should consider partitioning the physical device into multiple logical devices so that no container is bigger than the size allowed by the operating system.

Here are some considerations specific to the different supported operating systems:

- In Windows, a DMS table space can use devices. If you want to use an entire physical drive as a container, specify `\\.\N`, where `N` is the physical drive number. If you want to use a logical drive as a container, specify `\\.\X:`, where `X` is the logical drive letter. The drive must not be formatted. Other applications must not use these container locations.
- In AIX, create a volume group over the physical disks you are going to use for DB2 containers.
- On UNIX platforms, the creator of the logical volume must have write access to the character portion of the device container being used.

Multipage File Allocation

In an SMS table space, the associated file is extended one page at a time as the object grows. When inserting a large number of rows, some delay may result from waiting for the system to allocate another page. If you need improved insert performance, you can enable *multipage file allocation*. This allows the system to allocate or extend the file by more than one extent at a time. It will allocate empty pages to fill up the last extent in all SMS table space containers (see the *DB2 Command Reference* for more information).

This facility is implemented by running the `DB2EMPFA` utility and is indicated by the `MULTIPAGE_ALLOC` database configuration parameter.

Comparison of SMS and DMS Table Spaces

The following table compares the key features of SMS and DMS table spaces.

Table 11–5 *Characteristics of SMS and DMS User Table Spaces*

Characteristics	SMS	DMS
Can dynamically increase number of containers in table spaces	No	Yes
Can store index data for a table in a separate table space	No	Yes
Can store long data for a table in a separate table space	No	Yes

Table 11–5 *Characteristics of SMS and DMS User Table Spaces*

Characteristics	SMS	DMS
One table can span several table spaces	No	Yes
Space allocated only when needed	Yes	No*
Table space can be placed on different disks	Yes	Yes
Can support large RID format (>64GB per table space)	No	Yes
Extent size can be changed after creation	No	No

* For automatic storage, the containers are extended when necessary.

DB2 Note

Administrators can drop a container from a table space and reduce the size of existing containers without the need to perform a redirected restore.

The Catalog Table Space

The DB2 system catalog is where DB2 keeps all its metadata about all the DB2 objects in the database. Previously we had mentioned that catalog table space is called SYSCATSPACE and that its definition occurs in the CREATE DATABASE command. The following are considerations when planning for the system catalog:

- The system catalog consists of many tables of varying sizes. In using a DMS table space, a minimum of two extents are allocated for each table object. Depending on the extent size chosen, a significant amount of allocated and unused space may result. If using a DMS table space, a small extent size (2 – 4 pages) should be chosen; otherwise, an SMS table space should be used.
- The catalog tables use large object data type columns. These columns are not kept in the buffer pool and are read from disk each time they are needed. By using an SMS table space or DMS table space with file containers, you can take advantage of the file system cache for LOB data types.
- As more DB2 objects are created, the size of the catalog will increase. If you use an SMS table space, you cannot add more containers. All you can do is use operating system functionality to increase the underlying file system size. If you use a DMS table space, you can add more containers.

Temporary Table Spaces

Temporary table spaces are important as they are DB2's work areas for placing intermediate tables as it determines the final result set of data in satisfying SQL queries. Therefore, a significant amount of activity takes place in temporary table spaces. Another important use is for intermediate storage during the REORG TABLE utility. Its use here is optional, as by default, DB2 will place the copy of the table in the same table space where the original table resides. Refer to the *DB2 Administration Guide* for more considerations about the REORG TABLE utility and temporary table spaces.

If a database has more than one temporary table space defined, temporary objects are allocated among the temporary table spaces in a round robin fashion. Each temporary table space must be large enough to accommodate the largest possible temporary table. An application may encounter a temporary table space full condition even though there is unused space in other temporary table spaces. It is recommended that just one temporary table space be defined for a database and that multiple containers on separate disks be used to improve performance.

Some guidelines for temporary table spaces are:

- Create one SMS temporary table space for every page size.
- Define the containers for these table spaces so that they share the same file system(s). This maximizes disk sharing and minimizes the total disk requirement. As each temporary table is created and deleted by DB2, the disk space used will be reclaimed.
- If you require the highest level of performance and can afford the dedicated disk space, consider using DMS for temporary table spaces. Although you will lose the benefits of flexibility that you have with SMS, you may benefit from the performance advantages of using DMS.

DB2 *Note*

There must be at least one temporary table space for use by the database at all times. In most cases, SMS is the preferred choice for TEMP table spaces.

Choosing an Extent Size

The extent size for a table space indicates the number of pages of table data that will be written to a container before data will be written to the next container. When selecting an extent size, you should consider the size and type of tables in the table space.

Space in DMS table spaces is allocated to a table an extent at a time. As the table is populated and an extent becomes full, a new extent is allocated. A table is made up of the following separate table objects:

- A DATA object — This is where the regular column data is stored.

- An INDEX object — All indexes defined on the table are stored here.
- A LONG FIELD object — If your table has one or more LONG columns, they are all stored here.
- Two LOB objects — If your table has one or more LOB columns, they are stored in these two table objects: one table object for the LOB data and a second table object for metadata describing the LOB data.

Each table object is stored separately, and each allocates new extents as needed. Each table object is also paired up with a metadata object called an *extent map*, which describes all the extents in the table space that belong to the table object. Space for extent maps is also allocated an extent at a time.

The initial allocation of space for a table is two extents for each table object. If you have many small tables in a table space, you may have a large amount of space allocated to store a relatively small amount of data. In such a case, you should specify a small extent size or use an SMS table space that allocates pages one at a time.

If, on the other hand, you have a very large table that has a high growth rate, and you are using a DMS table space with a small extent size, you could have unnecessary overhead related to the frequent allocation of additional extents.

In addition, the type of access to the tables should also be considered. Sequential scanning of tables, such as the type of SQL queries used in a data warehousing environment, will need to access a large percentage of rows in a table. In this type of workload, a larger extent size may be preferred to reduce the number of I/O operations DB2 has to perform. In addition, prefetching of data can also take place to reduce the time the application has to wait for DB2 to return data to it.

In contrast, an online transaction processing (OLTP) workload involves queries that access tables usually in a random manner, retrieving data by key values. In this case, a large extent would bring many data pages into the buffer pool that are not required by the application. In this case, a smaller extent size may be justified.

Long Field Data

For the data types of LONG VARCHAR and LONG VARGRAPHIC, 20 bytes are used for the descriptor that is kept in the table data row. For further information about how long field data is stored, see the *DB2 Administration Guide*.

Large Object Data

If a table has BLOB, CLOB, or DBCLOB data, in addition to the byte count (between 72 and 312 bytes) for the descriptor (in the table row), the data itself must be stored.

This data is stored in two separate table objects that are structured differently than other data types.

LOB Data Objects

Data is stored in 64 MB areas that are broken up into segments whose sizes are a power of two times 1 KB. Hence these segments can be 1024 bytes, 2048 bytes, 4096 bytes, and so on, up to 64 MB.

To reduce the amount of disk space used by the LOB data, you can use the COMPACT parameter in the lob-options-clause on the CREATE TABLE and ALTER TABLE statements. The COMPACT option minimizes the amount of disk space required by allowing the LOB data to be split into smaller segments so that it will use the smallest amount of space possible. This does not involve data compression but is simply using the minimum amount of space to the nearest 1 KB boundary. Without the COMPACT option, there is no attempt to reduce the space used to the nearest 1 KB boundary. Appending to LOB values stored using the COMPACT option may result in slower performance compared with appending LOB values for which the COMPACT option is not specified. The amount of free space contained in LOB data objects will be influenced by the amount of update and delete activity as well as the size of the LOB values being inserted.

LOB Allocation Objects

Allocation and free space information is stored in 4 KB allocation pages separated from the actual data. The number of these 4 KB pages is dependent on the amount of data, including unused space, allocated for the large object data.The overhead is calculated as follows: one 4 KB page for every 64 GB plus one 4 KB page for every 8 MB.

If character data is less than 4 KB in length, and it fits in the record with the rest of the data, the CHAR, GRAPHIC, VARCHAR, or VARGRAPHIC data types should be used instead of the large object data types.

Mapping Tables to Table Spaces

When determining how to map tables to table spaces in your design, consider the following:

- The *amount* of data. If your design involves tables with a small amount of data, consider using SMS table spaces for them. The effort in administering many small tables, each in their own DMS table space, would not be proportional to the benefit gained.

  It would be more prudent to concentrate on larger, more frequently accessed tables. Here you could justify placing each table in its own DMS table space.

- The *type* of data in the table. Historical data that is used infrequently and does not have a critical response time requirement can be placed on slower, less-expensive devices.

  Conversely, the tables with fastest response time requirements should be assigned to the fastest devices available. In extreme cases, these table spaces could be given their own buffer pool.

  Another approach is to group related tables together in table spaces. They may be related via referential integrity, triggers, or structured data types. Since the BACKUP and RESTORE utilities can work at the table space level, the related data between the tables can be relied on stay consistent and recoverable.

- Separating out index and long data components. By assigning the indexes for a table into a separate table space, the containers for this table space can be placed on different disks, thus reducing contention on the disks containing the actual table data. Indexes can then be given their own buffer pool to reduce index physical I/O.

  Similarly, contention is also reduced by separating the long data from the other components. In addition, if long data is included with the regular data, it will take longer because of the extra I/O required to sequentially scan the table.

Implementation Examples

Now that we understand the characteristics of the DB2 storage objects we can implement them via the commands and SQL statements that create and delete them. For a detailed description of all the options available on the following commands and SQL statements, see the *DB2 Administration Guide*, the *DB2 SQL Reference* and the *DB2 Command Reference*.

Creating a Database

This is the simplest form of the CREATE DATABASE command. Note that this is a command and not an SQL statement.

```
CREATE DATABASE DB2CERT
```

The LIST TABLESPACES SHOW DETAIL command output below shows us the result of the above CREATE DATABASE command. Note that for this example, these commands are being executed in a Windows environment (Figure 11–9).

```
CONNECT TO DB2CERT;
LIST TABLESPACES SHOW DETAIL;

           Tablespaces for Current Database
```

```
Tablespace ID                       = 0
Name                                = SYSCATSPACE
Type                                = Database managed space
Contents                            = All permanent data. Regular table space.
State                               = 0x0000
  Detailed explanation:
    Normal
Total pages                         = 8192
Useable pages                       = 8188
Used pages                          = 7924
Free pages                          = 264
High water mark (pages)             = 7924
Page size (bytes)                   = 4096
Extent size (pages)                 = 4
Prefetch size (pages)               = 4
Number of containers                = 1

Tablespace ID                       = 1
Name                                = TEMPSPACE1
Type                                = System managed space
Contents                            = System Temporary data
State                               = 0x0000
  Detailed explanation:
    Normal
Total pages                         = 1
Useable pages                       = 1
Used pages                          = 1
Free pages                          = Not applicable
High water mark (pages)             = Not applicable
Page size (bytes)                   = 4096
Extent size (pages)                 = 32
Prefetch size (pages)               = 32
Number of containers                = 1

Tablespace ID                       = 2
Name                                = USERSPACE1
Type                                = Database managed space
Contents                            = All permanent data. Large table space.
State                               = 0x0000
  Detailed explanation:
    Normal
Total pages                         = 8192
Useable pages                       = 8160
Used pages                          = 96
Free pages                          = 8064
High water mark (pages)             = 96
Page size (bytes)                   = 4096
Extent size (pages)                 = 32
Prefetch size (pages)               = 32
Number of containers                = 1
```

Figure 11–9 *Table space details*

Note how the default values have been applied. The default database organization in DB2 9 is AUTOMATIC STORAGE. Two of the three table spaces (SYSCATSPACE, USERSPACE1) are defined as Database Managed Space (DMS) with an extent size of 4 for the catalog, and 32 for the user data. The TEMPSPACE1 table space is defined as a System Managed Space (SMS) with an extent size of 32. The total page count for SYSCATSPACE is 7924 at a page size of 4 KB, which means the catalog by default occupies approximately 32 MB. This will grow as objects are created in the database. The user space contains 384K of data and the temp space has only 1 page allocated.

Here is a more complex example:

```
CREATE DATABASE DB2CERT
       DFT_EXTENT_SZ 4
       CATALOG TABLESPACE
               MANAGED BY DATABASE USING
                         (FILE 'C:\CAT\CATALOG.DAT' 6000
                         ,FILE 'D:\CAT\CATALOG.DAT' 6000)
               EXTENTSIZE 8
               PREFETCHSIZE 16
       TEMPORARY TABLESPACE
               MANAGED BY SYSTEM USING
                         ('C:\TEMPTS','D:\TEMPTS')
       USER TABLESPACE
               MANAGED BY DATABASE USING
                         (FILE 'C:\TS\USERTS.DAT' 8000)
               EXTENTSIZE 24
               PREFETCHSIZE 48
```

Here we are asking DB2 to create a database with:

- A default extent size of four pages
- The system catalog table space as a DMS table space with two file containers, each with 6000 pages, 8-page extents, and prefetch size of 16 pages
- The temporary table space `TEMPSPACE1` as an SMS table space with two containers
- The user table space `USERSPACE1` as a DMS table space of one container, with 8000 pages, 24-page extents, and prefetch size of 48 pages

The output from `LIST TABLESPACES SHOW DETAIL` in this case is as follows (Figure 11–10):

```
CONNECT TO DB2CERT;
LIST TABLESPACES SHOW DETAIL;

           Tablespaces for Current Database

 Tablespace ID                        = 0
 Name                                 = SYSCATSPACE
 Type                                 = Database managed space
 Contents                             = All permanent data. Regular table space.

 State                                = 0x0000
   Detailed explanation:
     Normal
 Total pages                          = 12000
 Useable pages                        = 11984
 Used pages                           = 9976
 Free pages                           = 2008
 High water mark (pages)              = 9976
 Page size (bytes)                    = 4096
 Extent size (pages)                  = 8
 Prefetch size (pages)                = 16
 Number of containers                 = 2

 Tablespace ID                        = 1
 Name                                 = TEMPSPACE1
 Type                                 = System managed space
 Contents                             = System Temporary data
 State                                = 0x0000
   Detailed explanation:
     Normal
 Total pages                          = 2
```

```
Useable pages                          = 2
Used pages                             = 2
Free pages                             = Not applicable
High water mark (pages)                = Not applicable
Page size (bytes)                      = 4096
Extent size (pages)                    = 4
Prefetch size (pages)                  = 8
Number of containers                   = 2

Tablespace ID                          = 2
Name                                   = USERSPACE1
Type                                   = Database managed space
Contents                               = All permanent data. Large table space.
State                                  = 0x0000
  Detailed explanation:
    Normal
Total pages                            = 8000
Useable pages                          = 7968
Used pages                             = 72
Free pages                             = 7896
High water mark (pages)                = 72
Page size (bytes)                      = 4096
Extent size (pages)                    = 24
Prefetch size (pages)                  = 48
Number of containers                   = 1
```

Figure 11–10 *Table space details from extended example*

Note how the number of usable pages in SYSCATSPACE is 11984. Because one page per container is required for overhead, this leaves 11984 pages available for use by extents.

Since the extent size is 8, this leaves a spare seven pages unable to be used for extents in each container because only full extents are used. Add to this the one mandatory page for overhead and you have a total of eight pages per container unusable. Therefore, 16 pages out of 4000 for the entire table space are unusable.

In the USERSPACE1 table space, note that the container size is 121. One page is used for overhead, leaving 120 pages usable. Three extents are also used for overhead, accounting for the used page count of 72. This leaves 48 pages (two extents) available free for user data. Given the extent size, this is minimum number of pages the container can be defined with.

The LIST TABLESPACE CONTAINERS FOR 2 SHOW DETAIL command produces the following output. Note that the table space ID that the command requires is for the table space USERSPACE1.

```
             Tablespace Containers for Tablespace 2

Container ID                       = 0
Name                               = C:\TS\USERTS.DAT
Type                               = File
Total pages                        = 121
Useable pages                      = 120
Accessible                         = Yes
```

Figure 11–11 *Table space containers*

Creating Buffer Pools

This statement creates a buffer pool of 2000 four-kilobyte pages (8 MB):

```
CREATE BUFFERPOOL BPCERT4K
       SIZE 2000
       PAGESIZE 4096
```

This statement creates a buffer pool of 1000 eight-kilobyte pages (8 MB):

```
CREATE BUFFERPOOL BPCERT8K
       SIZE 1000
       PAGESIZE 8192
```

A buffer pool with the same page size must exist before a table space with a non-4KB page size can be created.

Creating Table Spaces

This is an example of how to define a table space that has a raw device container under Windows. In this case, we are using an unformatted logical drive.

```
CREATE TABLESPACE RAWTS
       PAGESIZE 4096
       MANAGED BY DATABASE USING
            (DEVICE '\\.\E:' 8001)
       EXTENTSIZE 8
       PREFETCHSIZE 16
       BUFFERPOOL BPCERT4K
```

This example uses the buffer pool created previously. The reports on the table space and container are (Figure 11–12):

```
Tablespace ID                          = 3
Name                                   = RAWTS
Type                                   = Database managed space
Contents                               = Any data
State                                  = 0x0000
 Detailed explanation:
   Normal
Total pages                            = 8001
Useable pages                          = 8000
Used pages                             = 24
Free pages                             = 7976
High water mark (pages)                = 24
Page size (bytes)                      = 4096
Extent size (pages)                    = 8
Prefetch size (pages)                  = 16
Number of containers                   = 1

           Tablespace Containers for Tablespace 3

Container ID                           = 0
Name                                   = \\.\E:
```

```
Type                                         = Disk
Total pages                                  = 8001
Useable pages                                = 8000
Accessible                                   = Yes
```

Figure 11–12 *Table space and container information*

Creating Tables

This example shows how a table and its indexes can be separated into separate table spaces. Both table spaces must be defined as DMS.

```
CREATE TABLE CERTTAB
    (
    COL1     CHAR(7) NOT NULL,
    COL2     INTEGER NOT NULL
    )
    IN RAWTS
    INDEX IN USERSPACE1
```

Dropping Table Spaces

This example shows how to drop table spaces. More than one can be dropped at the same time. All objects defined in the table spaces will be implicitly dropped or invalidated. Containers that were created by DB2 are deleted.

```
DROP TABLESPACE RAWTS, USERSPACE1
```

Dropping Buffer Pools

This example shows how to drop buffer pools. Note that the default buffer pool `IBMDEFAULTBP` cannot be dropped. This command will fail if table spaces that use the buffer pool are still defined. Once dropped, the memory that the buffer pool used will not be released until the database is stopped.

```
DROP BUFFERPOOL BPCERT4K
```

Dropping a Database

A DB2 command (not an SQL statement) is used to drop a database. This completely deletes all objects in the database. All users must be disconnected from the database before this command can succeed.

```
DROP DATABASE DB2CERT
```

Creating Table Spaces Using the Control Center

Besides being able to execute the above statements via the command line processor or DB2 Command Center, you can also use the Control Center to create DB2 objects. Here is an example of creating the table space RAWTS, using the table space wizard. From the Control Center, right click on the Table Space icon to start the Create Table Space Wizard dialog (Figure 11–13).

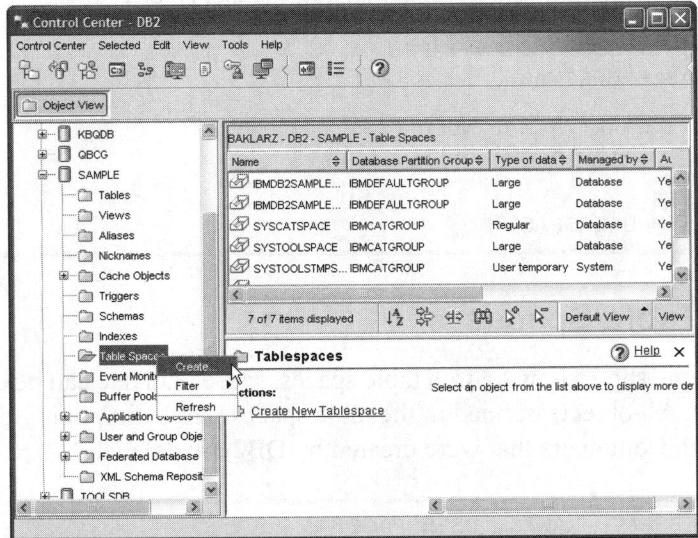

Figure 11–13 *Control Center — Create Table Space Wizard*

Enter the name of the table space and click **Next** (Figure 11–14).

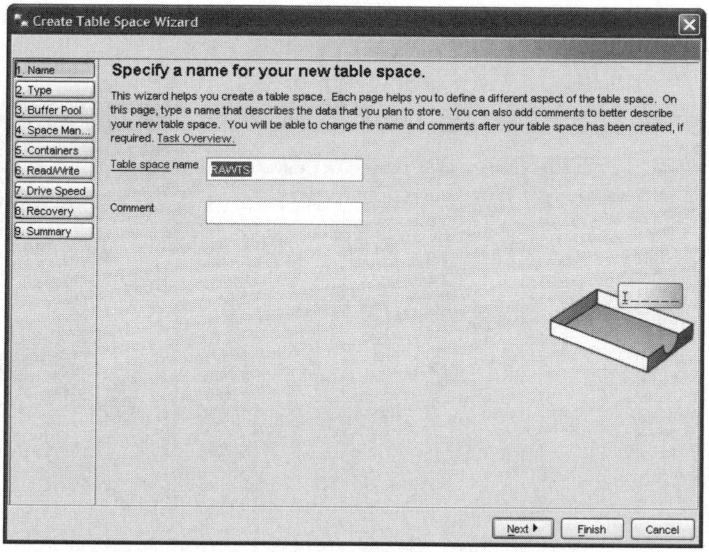

Figure 11–14 *Specify a name for your new table space*

Select whether the table space will be a regular, large, system temporary, or user temporary table space (Figure 11–15). Click **Next**.

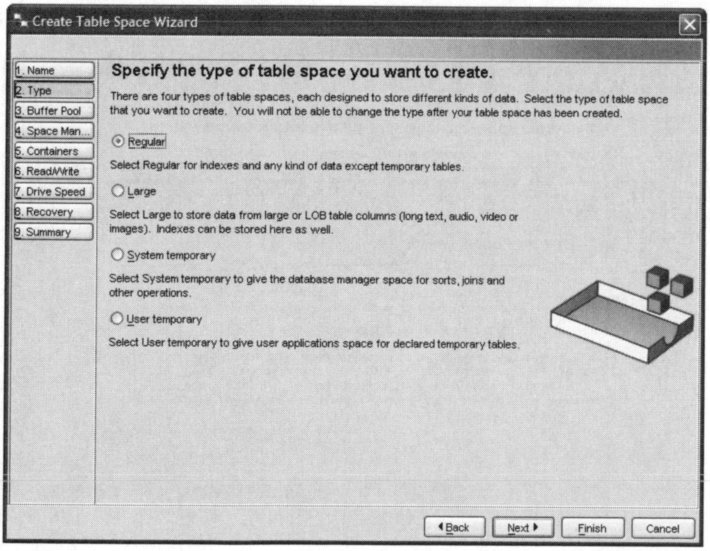

Figure 11–15 *Specify the type of table space you want to create*

Select which buffer pool you want the table space to be associated with. Note, that you have the option of creating a new buffer pool, rather than accepting the default buffer pool (Figure 11–16). Click **Next**.

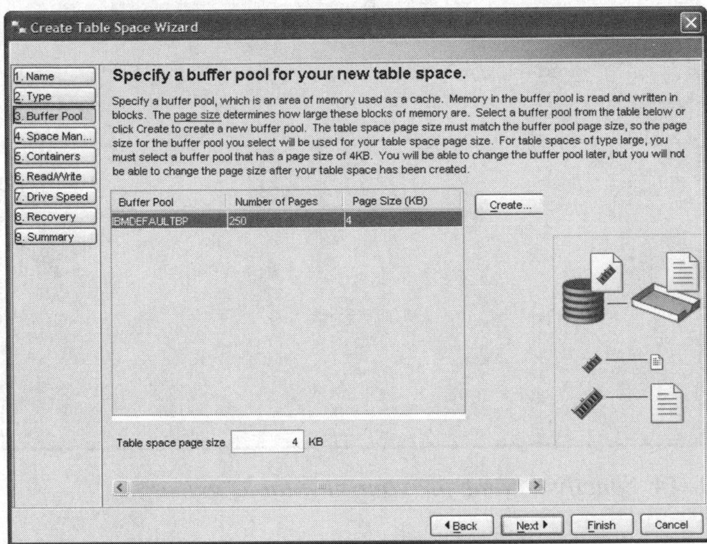

Figure 11–16 *Specify a buffer pool for you new table space*

Select whether the table space will be a SMS or DMS (Figure 11–17). Click **Next**.

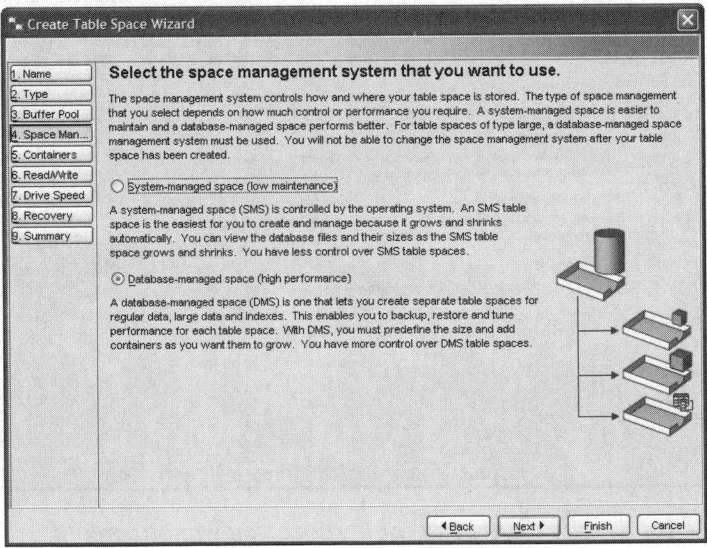

Figure 11–17 *Select the space management system that you want to use*

The next panel gives you the opportunity to add container for this table space (Figure 11–18).

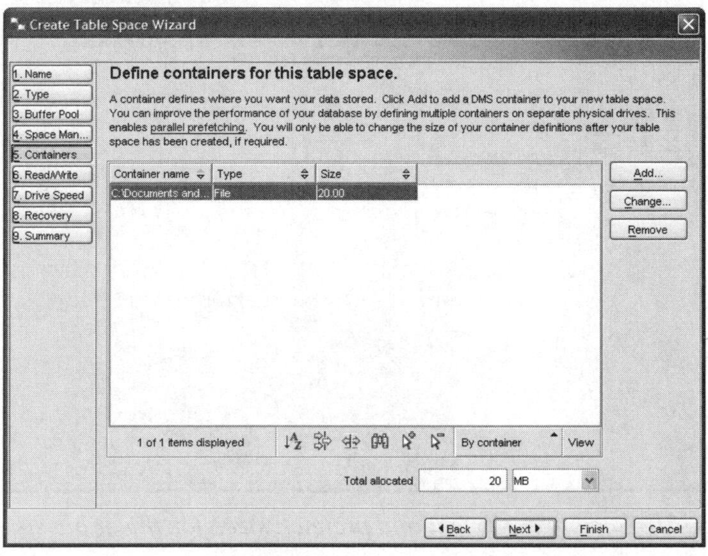

Figure 11–18 *Defining a container for this table space*

In this example, a file will be the container. Click the **Add** button to bring up the container definition dialog (Figure 11–19). Select or create a file name to be used and Click **OK**.

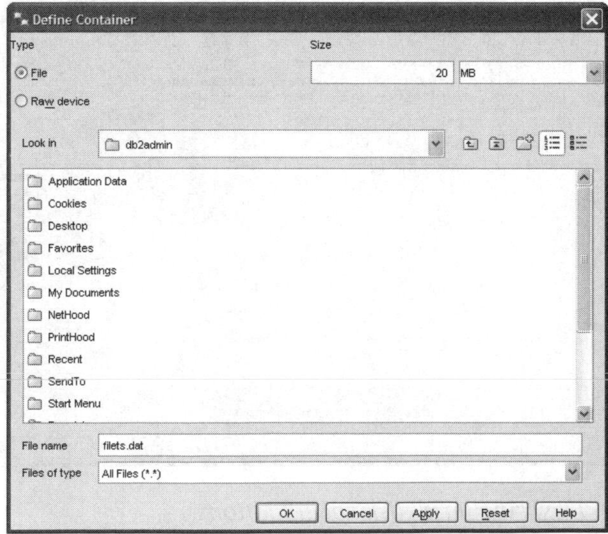

Figure 11–19 *Define Container*

Select extent and prefetch size. (Figure 11–20) Click **Next**.

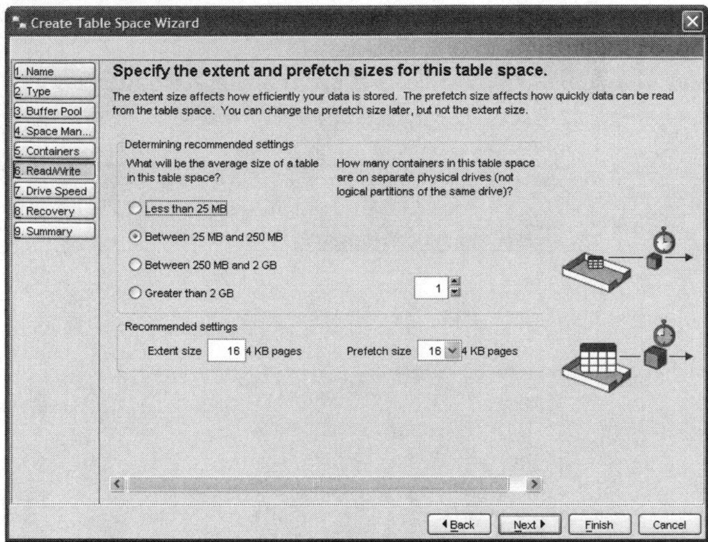

Figure 11–20 *Specify the extent and prefetch sizes for this table space*

Select disk specifications that the optimizer will consider for optimizing data access (Figure 11–21). Click **Next**.

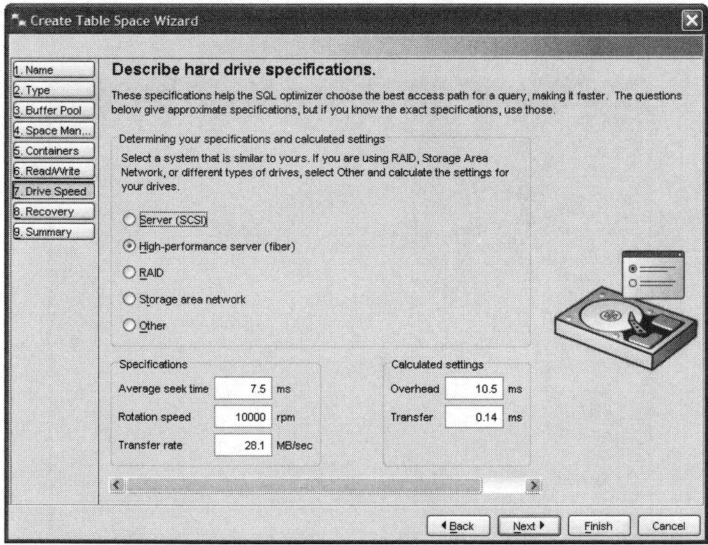

Figure 11–21 *Describe hard disk specifications*

This panel allows you the option of recovering a dropped table with a table space recovery (Regular table space only) (Figure 11–22). Click **Next**.

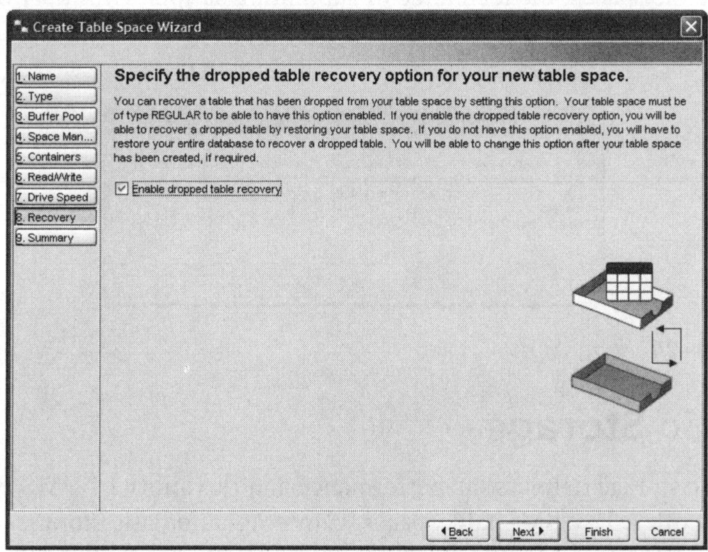

Figure 11–22 *Specify the dropped table recovery option for your new table space*

This final panel (Figure 11–23) summarizes the options specified for creating this table space.

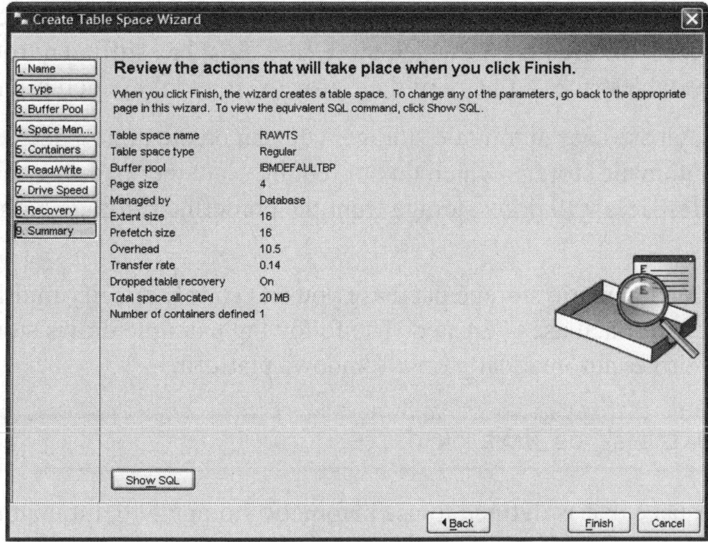

Figure 11–23 *Review the actions that will take place when you click Finish*

One additional option is to select Show SQL, which gives the further option of saving the results to a script (Figure 11–24). As a DBA becomes more familiar with creating table spaces, the technique of submitting scripts will likely be less time consuming.

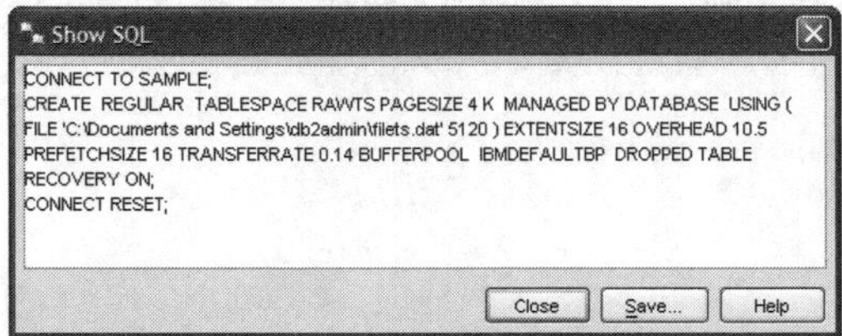

Figure 11–24 *Show SQL*

Automatic Storage

Automatic storage delivers the performance and flexibility of DMS with the ease of growth offered by SMS tablespaces. Choosing automatic storage (the default) allows the DBA to set up the database with storage paths that can be used for all table space container creations. Rather than having the DBA explicitly code the location and size of the tablespaces, the system will automatically allocate them.

The benefit of this new storage model is that you can have the flexibility and performance of DMS tablespaces without having to continuously monitor their capacity or the amount of free space within the tablespace. This new storage model only works with DMS file table spaces (not DMS raw) so there is still a need to ensure the file system or directory in which these files exist has sufficient room to accommodate the tablespaces and any of their growth should they increase in size.

When a database uses automatic storage, you can create tablespaces that are managed by automatic storage which do not require container paths to be specified. These tablespaces will draw storage from the predefined storage paths of the database.

To create an automatic storage database you can simply specify multiple storage paths when the database is created. The following example draws storage from the D: and E: drives automatically on a Windows platform:

```
CREATE DATABASE DB_NAME ON D:, E:
```

Any tablespace that is defined to use automatic storage will automatically have storage paths for its containers defined on both the D: and E: drives. The next example will set up automatic storage for all table spaces using three storage paths:

```
CREATE DATABASE TEST
  AUTOMATIC STORAGE ON
  /db2/storagepath001,
  /db2/storagepath002,
  /db2/storagepath003
  AUTORESIZE YES
  INITIALSIZE 300 M
  INCREASESIZE 75 M
  MAXSIZE NONE
```

After the AUTOMATED STORAGE ON option, three file directories (paths) are shown. These three paths are the locations where containers for a table space will reside. The remainder of the options are:

- AUTORESIZE YES

  In the event that a table space runs out of space, the system will automatically extend the size of the containers.

- INITIALSIZE 300 M (The INITIALSIZE integer [K | M | G])

  Any table space defined with no initial size will default to 300 MB in size. The containers will each be 100 MB in size (there are three storage paths).

- INCREASESIZE 75 M (or %) (INCREASESIZE integer [K | M | G])

  In the event that the table space runs out of space, the total space for the table space will be increased by 75 MB in size. A percentage can also be specified, in which case the table space will be increased in size as a percentage of its current size.

- MAXSIZE NONE (MAXSIZE integer [K | M | G])

  The maximum size of table space will be unlimited. If the DBA wants to place a limit on how much storage a table space can have, they can do so by specifying a maximum value.

Note that the values that are used in the CREATE DATABASE command are applied (by default) to all automatic tablespaces.

When a table space is defined using AUTOMATIC STORAGE, no additional parameters need to be supplied:

```
CREATE TABLESPACE TEST MANAGED BY AUTOMATIC STORAGE
```

There are no container definitions for tablespace TEST. Instead the storage for this tablespace is managed at the database level. Any of the parameters associated with a table space can be supplied in this command, including the AUTORESIZE,

INCREASESIZE, and MAXSIZE parameters. Note that these last three options can be used for standard table spaces as well.

When creating a table space in a database that is not enabled for automatic storage, the MANAGED BY SYSTEM or MANAGED BY DATABASE clause must be specified. Using these clauses results in the creation of a system managed space (SMS) table space or database managed space (DMS) table space respectively. An explicit list of containers must be provided in both cases.

Adding Additional Storage

If the database requires more space, more storage can be added by using the ALTER DATABASE command:

```
ALTER DATABASE DB_NAME ADD STORAGE ON F:
```

This command adds the F: drive to the storage pool and any automatic storage tablespaces will now automatically draw storage from the F: drive if they need additional space. Adding more space to the database in this manner will create a new stripe set. The containers that are created on the new storage paths will not be rebalanced with the existing containers. This avoids the overhead of container redistribution occurring.

Table Space Maintenance

We have covered the creation of the DB2 storage objects to hold the database data. There are some additional commands and concepts to be aware of for maintaining them and monitoring changes in their size.

Database Files

The physical files that DB2 creates to support the database need to be protected from any direct access from outside of DB2.

- Do not make any direct changes to these files. They can only be accessed indirectly using the documented application programming interfaces (APIs) and by tools that implement those APIs.
- Do not remove or move these files.
- Using the security functions of the operating system, make sure all DB2 files and directories are secured. No one other than DB2 itself requires direct access to DB2 files and directories.
- The only supported means of backing up a database or table space is through the BACKUP API, including implementations of that API, such as those provided by

the command line processor and Control Center.

Listing Table Spaces

To list basic or detailed information about table spaces, use the `LIST TABLESPACES` command. The syntax for this command is:

```
LIST TABLESPACES [SHOW DETAIL]
```

The basic information displayed by using this command is:

- Table space ID, the internal ID that DB2 uses for the table space
- Table space name
- Storage type (DMS or SMS)
- Table space type, which can be Regular (any data), Long, or Temporary
- State, a hexadecimal value indicating the current table space state

If the `SHOW DETAIL` option is used, the following additional details are normally shown:

- Total number of pages
- Number of usable pages
- Number of used pages
- Number of free pages
- High water mark (in pages)
- Page size (in bytes)
- Extent size (in bytes)
- Prefetch size (in pages)
- Extent size (in pages)
- Prefetch size (in pages)
- Number of containers

This information is important for informing you of how full the table spaces are and whether some action is required, such as adding new containers and running backups.

For examples of the output from this command, see the `CREATE DATABASE` command and the `CREATE TABLESPACE` statement in "Implementation Examples" on page 652.

Listing Table Space Containers

To list basic or detailed information about the table space containers for a specific table space, use the `LIST TABLESPACE CONTAINERS` command. The syntax for this command is:

```
LIST TABLESPACE CONTAINERS FOR tablespace_id [SHOW DETAIL]
```

The basic information displayed by using this command is:

- Container ID
- Container name
- Container type

When the `SHOW DETAIL` option is used the additional information shown is:

- Total number of pages
- Number of usable pages
- Accessible (yes or no)

Table Space States

DB2 maintains information about the states of table spaces and will not allow access using SQL (DML) statements if the table space is not in a *normal* state. Table space states are expressed in hexadecimal numbers. Sometimes, a table space can have more than one state associated with it. This will result in a combined hexadecimal number. There is a description of the state provided with the `LIST TABLESPACES SHOW DETAIL` command.

To view the table space state, issue the `LIST TABLESPACES` command and note the detailed explanation of the state. A table space is placed in a nonnormal state during load, backup, and recovery operations, or if placed in a quiesced condition via the `QUIESCE TABLESPACE` command. This command is not used very often by itself but is used by various DB2 utilities.

The `LOAD` command will place the table space in a `LOAD PENDING` state and leave the table space in this pending state until it has completed successfully. The `RESTORE` command will place the table space in `ROLLFORWARD PENDING` following a successful restore of the database. The table space will remain in this state until a successful `ROLLFORWARD DATABASE` command has been issued. The table space states are important to understand because if a table space is in any nonnormal state (not 0x0000) no `SELECT`, `INSERT`, `UPDATE`, or `DELETE` statements can be issued for any of the related table objects.

A list of some of the possible table space states follows:

- 0x0000 — Access to the table space is allowed (normal)
- 0x0001 — Quiesced share
- 0x0002 — Quiesced update
- 0x0004 — Quiesced exclusive
- 0x0008 — Load pending
- 0x0010 — Delete pending
- 0x0020 — Backup pending
- 0x0100 — Restore pending

For the further information about table space states, see the `LIST TABLESPACES` command in the *DB2 Command Reference*.

DB2 *Note*

If a container is not accessible, DB2 will place the associated table space in an `OFFLINE` state. Once the problem is resolved the `ALTER TABLESPACE` statement can be used with the `SWITCH ONLINE` option to make the table space available again.

System Catalog Information About Table Spaces

Table space information is kept in the `SYSCAT.TABLESPACES` catalog view. You are able to query this information using SQL. The layout of the view follows:

Table 11–6 *SYSCAT.TABLESPACES*

Column Name	Data Type	Nulls?	Description
TBSPACE	VARCHAR(18)		Name of table space
DEFINER	VARCHAR(128)		Authorization ID of table space definer
CREATE_TIME	TIMESTAMP		Creation time of table space
TBSPACEID	INTEGER		Internal table space identifier
TBSPACETYPE	CHAR(1)		The type of the table space: S = System managed space D = Database managed space
DATATYPE	CHAR(1)		Type of data that can be stored: A = All types of permanent data L = Long data only T = Temporary tables only

Table 11–6 *SYSCAT.TABLESPACES*

Column Name	Data Type	Nulls?	Description
EXTENTSIZE	INTEGER		Size of extent, in pages of size PAGESIZE
PREFETCHSIZE	INTEGER		Number of pages of size PAGESIZE to be read when prefetch is performed
OVERHEAD	DOUBLE		Controller overhead and disk seek and latency time in milliseconds
TRANSFERRATE	DOUBLE		Time to read one page of size PAGESIZE into the buffer
PAGESIZE	INTEGER		Size (in bytes) of pages in the table space
NGNAME	VARCHAR(18)		Name of the database partition group for the table space
BUFFERPOOLID	INTEGER		ID of buffer pool used by this table space (1 indicates default buffer pool)
DROP_RECOVERY	CHAR(1)		N = table is not recoverable after a DROP TABLE statement Y = table is recoverable after a DROP TABLE statement
REMARKS	VARCHAR(254)	Yes	User-provided comment

The following columns are of interest for table spaces from the SYSCAT.TABLES catalog view.

Table 11–7 *SYSCAT.TABLES*

Column Name	Data Type	Nulls?	Description
TBSPACEID	SMALLINT		Internal identifier of the primary table space of the table
TBSPACE	VARCHAR(18)	Yes	Name of primary table space for the table
INDEX_TBSPACE	VARCHAR(18)	Yes	Name of the table space that holds all indexes for the table
LONG_TBSPACE	VARCHAR(18)	Yes	Name of the table space that holds all long data for the table

Adding Containers to DMS Table Spaces

You can add a container to an existing table space to increase its storage capacity with the ALTER TABLESPACE statement. The contents of the table space are then rebalanced across all containers. Access to the table space is not restricted during the rebalancing. If you need to add more than one container, you should add them at the same time either in one ALTER TABLESPACE statement or within the same transaction to prevent DB2 from rebalancing the containers more than once.

You should check how full the containers are by using the LIST TABLESPACES and LIST TABLESPACE CONTAINERS commands. Adding new containers should be done before the existing containers are almost or completely full. The new space across all the containers is not available until the rebalance is complete.

Adding a container that is smaller than existing containers results in a uneven distribution of data. This can cause parallel I/O operations, such as prefetching data, to perform less efficiently than they otherwise could on containers of equal size.

Adding a New Container Using the CLP

This is an example of how to add another container, in this case, a file container to the table space that was created in an earlier example.

```
ALTER TABLESPACE RAWTS
      ADD (FILE 'C:\TS\FILECON1.DAT' 8001)
      PREFETCHSIZE 32
      BUFFERPOOL IBMDEFAULTBP
```

Note how the ALTER TABLESPACE statement can be used to change the prefetch quantity and the buffer pool for the table space.

DB2 *Note*

Prior to V8, when a new container was added, existing data would be automatically redistributed or rebalanced across all available devices. The new BEGIN STRIPE option of the ALTER command allows the addition of new containers to a table space such that a rebalance does not occur.

Adding a New Container Using the Control Center

Alternatively, you can also use the Control Center to add a container. In the list of table spaces, right-click on the table space you wish to alter (Figure 11–25).

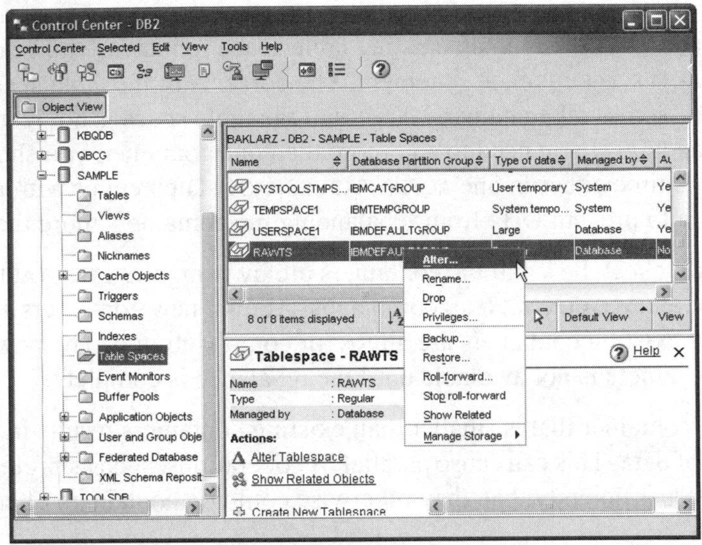

Figure 11–25 *Control Center — Choosing a table space to alter*

The Alter Table Space panel is displayed (Figure 11–26).

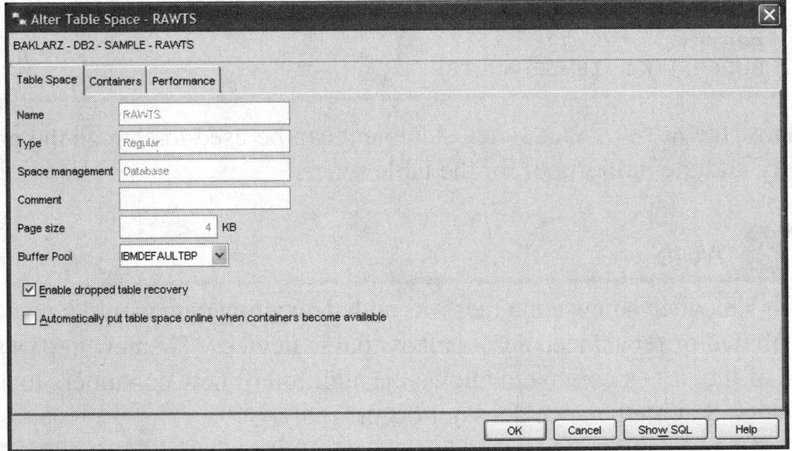

Figure 11–26 *Alter table space*

Click on the Containers tab and then **Add**. You can then enter the details of the new container (Figure 11–27). Options that cannot be changed have been grayed out.

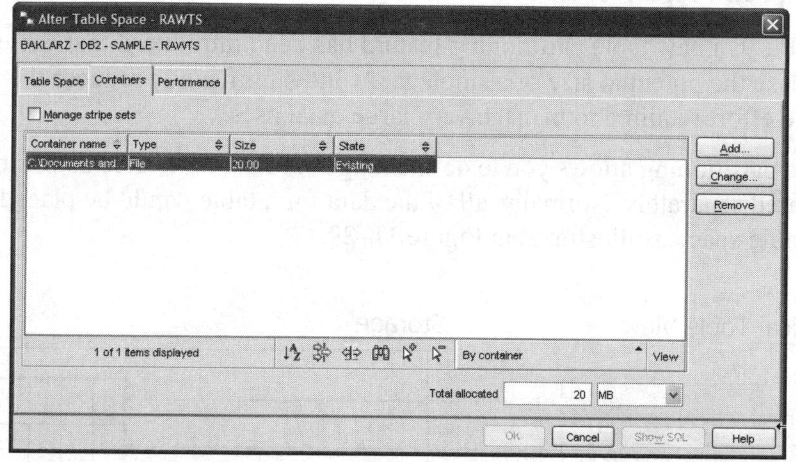

Figure 11–27 *Define Container*

After defining the additional containers, the Alter Table Space panel displays the following (Figure 11–28):

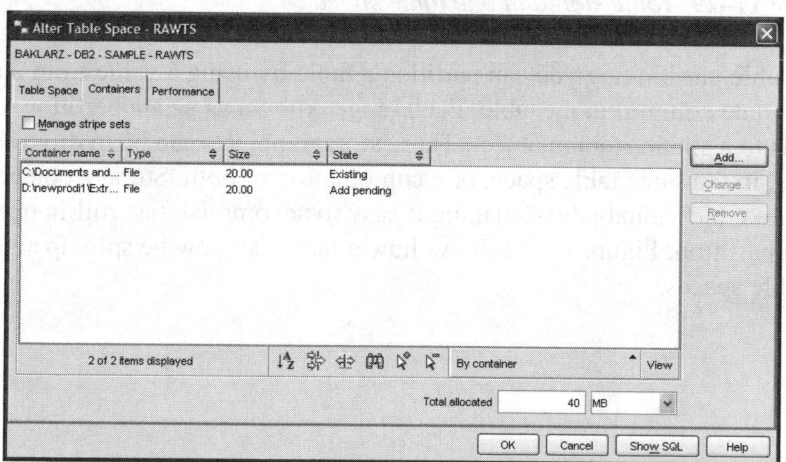

Figure 11–28 *Alter table space (2)*

Select **OK** to add the container and DB2 will automatically rebalance the data across the containers.

Table (Range) Partitioning

In DB2 9, a new table partitioning feature has been introduced that can effectively increase the potential size of a single table and significantly reduces the maintenance effort required to manage very large databases.

Table partitioning allows you to define ranges of data for a table so that each range is stored separately. Normally, all of the data for a table would be placed into a single table space as illustrated in Figure 11–29.

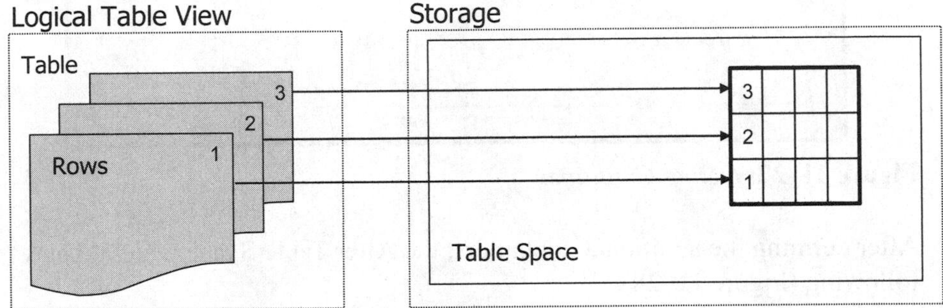

Figure 11–29 *Table stored in one table space*

With table partitioning you can partition a table by using a value from a column (like a date column) in the table. Each range, known as a data partition, corresponds to a single storage object. These storage objects can be in different table spaces, in the same table space, or a combination of both. Storage objects behave much like individual tables, making it easy to accomplish fast roll-in or roll-out of a data partition. Figure 11–30 shows how a table can now be split up among different table spaces.

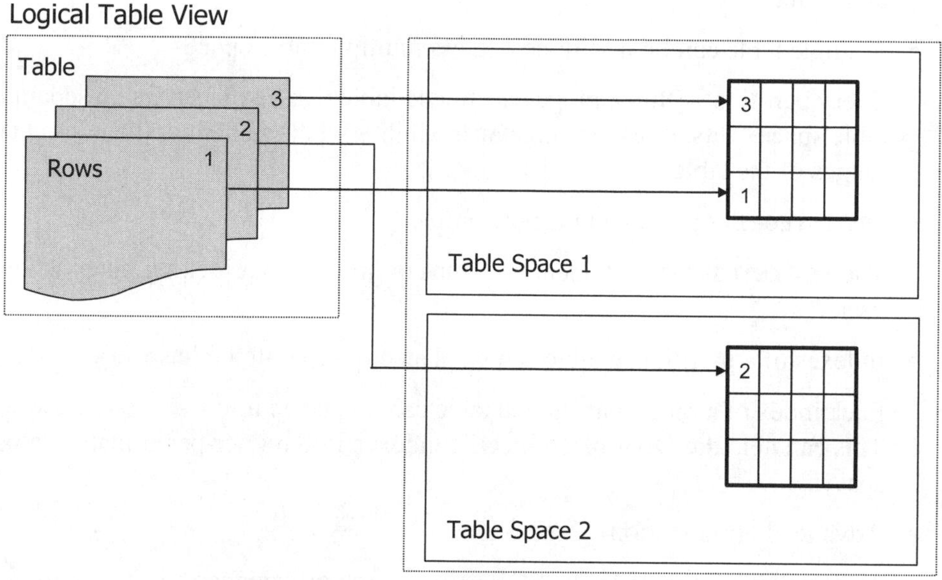

Figure 11–30 *Table split among multiple table space*

While the table may be split up into different table spaces, the table is still viewed as one logical entity by users, utilities, and applications.

The main benefits of table partitioning includes:

- Allows for optimized data roll-in and roll-out processing

  New data can be placed into a separate table without impacting the partitioned table. When the data is ready to be added, an `ALTER TABLE ATTACH` command followed by a `SET INTEGRITY` statement will make the data available as part of the partitioned table.

- Allows for the dividing of large tables into more manageable pieces

  Range partitioning allows for larger tables to be stored in DB2. Backing up data is simplified since individual portions of the partitioned table can be backed up and restored rather than managing one large object.

- Improved Hierarchical Storage Management (HSM) integration

  Selective ranges can be archived if they are not accessed on a regular basis, rather than having to archive the entire table.

- Eliminates the need for `UNION ALL` views

  `UNION ALL` views are not necessary since table partitioning does everything that a union all view provides, but also includes features for rolling in and rolling out table data.

- A single table can be partitioned across multiple table spaces

  Every partition within a range partitioned table can be placed into a separate table space. This allows for greater flexibility when managing the individual ranges of the table.

- `SET INTEGRITY` processing is now online

  The `SET INTEGRITY` statement now runs online without locking out existing users.

- Indexes of a partitioned table can be placed in separate table spaces

  Each index of a range-partitioned table can be placed into a separate table space. This can help the DBA place specific indexes into higher-performance table spaces.

- Advanced optimization

  Table partitioning allows the SQL compiler to performance partition elimination on the data. This technique refers to the ability to determine, based on the query predicates, that only a subset of the data partitions of a table need to be accessed to answer a query. Partition elimination can substantially increase the performance of certain queries.

With the introduction of table partitioning functionality, DB2 9 offers three levels of data organization. Each of these methods can be used by themselves, or in combination with the other ones. The following three clauses demonstrate the levels of data organization that can be used together in any combination:

- `DISTRIBUTE BY HASH`

  This clause is used to spread data evenly across database partitions. This concept is known as database partitioning and is enabled with the Database Partitioning Feature (DPF).

- `PARTITION BY RANGE`

  This clause group rows with similar values of a single dimension in the same data partition. This concept is known as table partitioning.

- `ORGANIZE BY DIMENSIONS`

  This clause group rows with similar values on multiple dimensions in the same table extent. This concept is known as multidimensional clustering (MDC).

These clauses can be combined in a single table to create more sophisticated partitioning schemes. Figure 11–31 illustrates how the three partitioning types can be combined when creating a table.

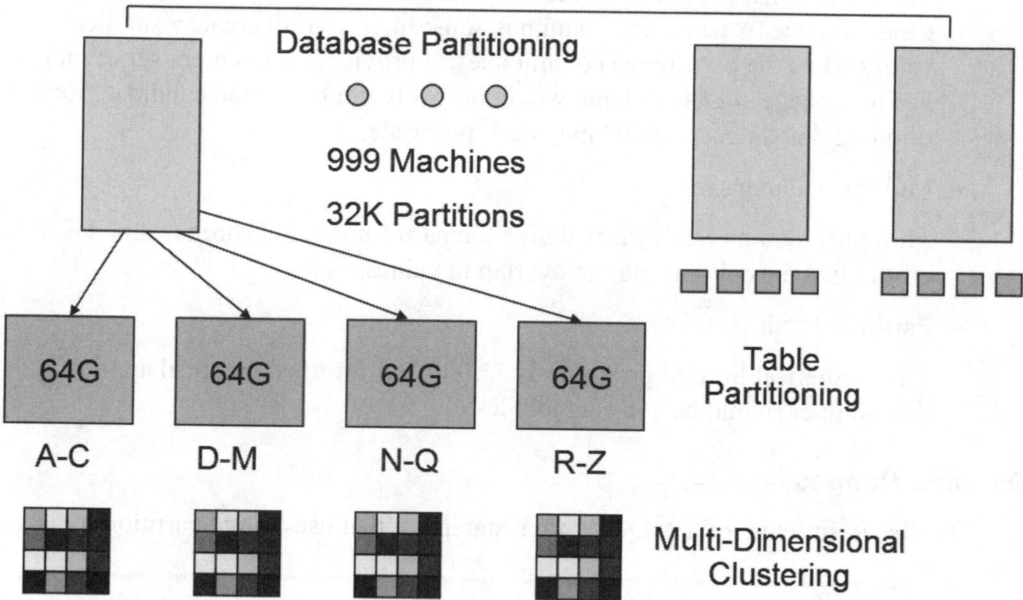

Figure 11–31 *Three forms of partitioning*

Creating a Range Partitioned Table

Range Partitioned Tables are created via the CREATE TABLE command. There is a long and short form of the command for creating partitions. The short form is convenient for developers and DBAs who want to prototype a partitioned table. The long form is the preferred method of creating the partitions for production system, especially if the partitions need to be managed with ATTACH and DETACH commands.

The partitioning column must be based on a regular data type — the following data types are not supported:

- XML data type
- LONG VARCHAR, LONG VARGRAPHIC
- BLOB, CLOB, DBCLOB
- User-defined distinct and structured data types
- DATALINK (also not supported as a data type in DB2 9)

All of the other standard data types are valid. Most typical usages of table partitioning would use DATE or TIMESTAMP columns. Some additional considerations when using table partitioning:

- Generated columns

  The column that is used to define the partitioning can be a regular column or a generated one. A generated column is sometimes used to create a smaller set of values when the partitioned column doesn't provide a convenient set of ranges. For instance, a SALARY column would probably not be a good candidate for partitioning, but SALARY/10000 may be appropriate.

- Multiple Columns

  Multiple columns can be used define the partitioning, but care must be taken to ensure that the columns do not overlap in values.

- Partition Limit

  The theoretical limit of partitions is 32,000, but for most practical applications this number should be considerably less.

Defining Ranges

The basic structure of a CREATE TABLE statement that uses range partitioning is:

```
CREATE TABLE NAME
  (
  COLUMN_NAME1 DATA TYPE ...,
  ...
  )
  IN TABLESPACE...
  PARTITION BY RANGE(COLUMN_NAME)
    (
    PARTITIONING STATEMENTS ...
    )
```

The PARTITION BY RANGE() specification includes the name of the column(s) that the table will be partitioned by. Within the brackets of the specification are statements which define what the individual partitions are and what ranges are associated with them. The IN clause specifies the table spaces where the partitions will be placed. For example, the following SQL statement creates four ranges:

```
CREATE TABLE SALES (SALE_DATE DATE, CUSTOMER INT)
PARTITION BY RANGE(SALE_DATE)
  (
  STARTING '2006-01-01' ENDING '2006-03-31',
  STARTING '2006-04-01' ENDING '2006-06-30',
  STARTING '2006-07-01' ENDING '2006-09-30',
  STARTING '2006-10-01' ENDING '2007-12-31'
  );
```

The STARTING clause indicates the starting value within a partition, while the ENDING indicates what the final value will be. Values that are specified with the START and ENDING clauses are considered to be part of the partition.

Ranges do not have to be contiguous, nor do they have to have the same range of values within them. However, anyone that inserts a row into a table that is missing a range would receive an error message if there was no partition available to handle the row they are trying to insert:

```
SQL0327N The row cannot be inserted into table "BAKLARZ.SALES"
because it is outside the bounds of the defined data partition
ranges.
```

In the previous table definition, partitions one through three covered a three-month period, while the last partition covered 15 months. The range of values within a partition is not relevant to the CREATE command. However, for tables that rely on quarterly data, the ranges would normally be based on three-month intervals.

Inserts and Updates

There are no changes required to applications that deal with range partitioned tables. Inserts and updates will continue to work as they have in the past, with two subtle differences. When an insert is done against a table where a value is not covered by one of the existing partitions, an error will be raised:

```
INSERT INTO SALES VALUES ('1999-12-31',5);
SQL0327N  The row cannot be inserted into table "BAKLARZ.SALES"
because it is outside the bounds of the defined data partition
ranges.  SQLSTATE=22525
```

A similar error would occur if a row was updated outside the existing ranges for the table.

When rows are updated to belong to a different partition, DB2 will automatically delete the row from one partition and re-insert it into another. This insert and delete processing is hidden from the application and is under full integrity control. In the event that the system were to fail during this row migration, DB2 would make sure that the update is rolled back.

Specifying Partition Ranges

There are a number of different ways to specify the range for a partition. This section describes how ranges are created and what some of the considerations are for using them.

Open Ended Ranges

One of the problems when defining ranges is how to represent the smallest or largest value for a column. A range starting with the smallest value may be used to capture transactions that are outside the normal range. The special values MINVALUE and MAXVALUE can be used to specify open ended ranges. For instance, the following example places everything before the year 2000 in the first range:

```
CREATE TABLE SALES (SALE_DATE DATE, CUSTOMER INT)
PARTITION BY RANGE(SALE_DATE)
  (
  STARTING MINVALUE     ENDING '1999-12-31',
  STARTING '2000-01-01' ENDING '2000-03-31',
  STARTING '2000-04-01' ENDING '2000-06-30',
  STARTING '2000-07-01' ENDING '2000-09-30',
  STARTING '2000-10-01' ENDING '2004-12-31'
  )
```

Any records that are inserted that contain dates less than or equal to '1999-12-31' will be placed into the first partition.

Note that MINVALUE and MAXVALUE are exclusive values, so they are never included as part of a range. The following create statement would fail because the first partition has effectively no range:

```
CREATE TABLE SALES (SALE_DATE DATE, CUSTOMER INT)
PARTITION BY RANGE(SALE_DATE)
  (
  STARTING MINVALUE ENDING MINVALUE,
  STARTING '2000-01-01' ENDING '2004-12-31'
  );

SQL0636N Range specified for data partition "PART0" is not valid.
Reason code = "1".
```

Generally the STARTING value for a partition must be less than the ENDING value. However, the starting value can be equal to the ending value if both bounds are inclusive. A bound which includes MINVALUE or MAXVALUE is considered exclusive.

Inclusive and Exclusive Bounds

There are two keywords which control how the values in the range specification are treated. The EXCLUSIVE keyword is used to indicate that range boundaries are exclusive, or not included in the range. The default value is INCLUSIVE which would include the values in the range.

Date ranges should always use exclusive date boundaries, especially when trying to deal with dates at the end of a month. Rather than having to guess what the last day of a range is, include the first day of the next range, but mark it as EXCLUSIVE. This will guarantee that everything up to but not including this date will be in the range.

This example avoid "holes" by making each ending bound the same as the next starting bound, and using EXCLUSIVE for the ending bound:

```
CREATE TABLE SALES (SALE_DATE DATE, CUSTOMER INT)
PARTITION BY RANGE(SALE_DATE)
  (
  STARTING MINVALUE     ENDING '2000-01-01' EXCLUSIVE,
  STARTING '2000-01-01' ENDING '2000-04-01' EXCLUSIVE,
  STARTING '2000-04-01' ENDING '2000-07-01' EXCLUSIVE,
  STARTING '2000-07-01' ENDING '2000-10-01' EXCLUSIVE,
  STARTING '2000-10-01' ENDING '2004-12-31'
  )
```

Implicit Bounds

DB2 will automatically generate the missing bounds if they are not included in the range specification. The starting and ending bounds can be left out as long as all the ranges are unambiguous. The following example creates five partitions:

```
CREATE TABLE SALES (SALE_DATE DATE, CUSTOMER INT)
PARTITION BY RANGE(SALE_DATE)
  (
  STARTING MINVALUE,
  STARTING '2000-01-01',
  STARTING '2000-04-01',
  STARTING '2000-07-01',
  STARTING '2000-10-01'
  ENDING   '2004-12-31'
  )
```

The first range will start from MINVALUE and end at '2000-01-01', exclusive. This means that the last effective date of the first range is '1999-12-31'. The second range starts at '2000-01-01' and ends at '2000-03-31' because it is '2000-04-01' exclusive. The final range starts at '2000-10-01' and ends at '2004-12-31'. There is no additional modifier on that line so '2004-12-31' is included as part of the last range.

Naming Partitions

When tables are placed into production, the DBA will need to be able to name individual partitions so that they can perform maintenance against them. If a partition is not explicitly named, DB2 will generate an SQL identifier that will be rather difficult to remember when doing any maintenance against the table.

A partition can be named with the PART or PARTITION keyword. This name will be used to specify a partition name during partition operations like ALTER TABLE DETACH.

An example of naming data partitions is found below.

```
CREATE TABLE SALES (SALE_DATE DATE, CUSTOMER INT)
PARTITION BY RANGE(SALE_DATE)
  (
  PART REST    STARTING MINVALUE,
  PARTITION Q1 STARTING '2000-01-01',
  PARTITION Q2 STARTING '2000-04-01',
  PARTITION Q3 STARTING '2000-07-01',
  PARTITION Q4 STARTING '2000-10-01' ENDING '2004-12-31'
  )
```

Handling NULL Values

If a table design requires that the partitioning column allows null values, you must tell DB2 where the null values should be placed during an INSERT statement. The NULLS FIRST/LAST keyword specifies what partition nulls are placed in:

- The default is NULLS LAST. Rows with null in the partitioning key column are placed in the range ending at MAXVALUE.
- Use NULLS FIRST to place nulls in the range starting with MINVALUE.

If a partition in the table does not contain the MINVALUE or MAXVALUE value, null values are considered to be out-of-range values.

```
CREATE TABLE SALES (SALE_DATE DATE, CUSTOMER INT )
PARTITION BY RANGE(SALE_DATE NULLS FIRST)
  (
  STARTING MINVALUE,
  STARTING '2000-01-01',
  STARTING '2000-04-01',
  STARTING '2000-07-01',
  STARTING '2000-10-01' ENDING '2004-12-31'
  )
```

If a table is continually updated with roll-in and roll-out operations, the location of the null values needs to be considered. Most applications that deal with date ranges will add a new partition at the end of the current table and drop the first one.

The problem with this approach is that the null values will be dropped with the first partition. This may not be the intended result since the null values may need to be kept for future processing.

In this case, it would be better to create a range using MINVALUE that goes up to, but does not include, the first valid date in the table. This partition would not be removed as part of maintenance as shown in Figure 11–32:

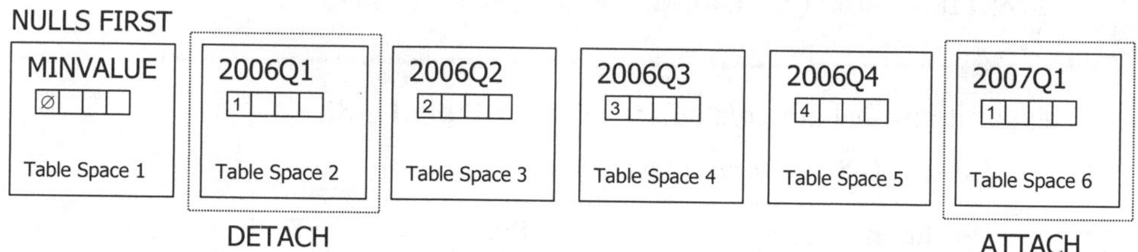

Figure 11–32 *Avoiding NULL detaches*

Computed Ranges

All of the examples up to this point use explicit starting and ending values for the partitions. DB2 includes a shortcut in the PARTITION command that will compute the ranges automatically, based on a starting value, an ending value, and an interval amount.

Short Syntax

The syntax within the PARTITION clause includes the STARTING ... ENDING ... EVERY keyword to quickly define ranges. This is a simple way of creating many partitions quickly and easily, and is appropriate for equal sized ranges based on dates or numbers. For example, this SQL creates 8 data partitions, one for each quarter:

```
CREATE TABLE SALES (SALE_DATE DATE, CUSTOMER INT)
PARTITION BY RANGE(SALE_DATE)
  (
  STARTING '2006-01-01' ENDING '2007-12-31' EVERY 3 MONTHS
  )
```

The first range starts at '2006-01-01' and ends at '2006-03-31'. The next one starts at '2006-04-01' and ends at '2006-06-30', and so on until '2007-12-31'. While this is a very efficient way of generating multiple ranges, it has the disadvantage that the ranges are not given any names, so issuing DETACH commands against them will require a lookup within the system catalog tables.

While all of the examples to this point have shown calculations on date ranges, regular numeric values can also be computed using the same syntax.

The following SQL generates four partitions:

```
CREATE TABLE T1 (C1 INT)
PARTITION BY RANGE(C1)
  (
  STARTING FROM (1) ENDING (400) EVERY (100)
  )
```

The partitions that are created are found in Table 11–8:

Table 11–8 *Computed partitions*

Partition	Start	End
1	1	100
2	101	200
3	201	300
4	301	400

Open Ended Ranges with Computed Ranges

The short form of calculating ranges can be mixed with the long syntax. This mixing of formats is particularly useful when an exception partition has to be created along with the normal partitions.

This example creates one catch-all partition with the long syntax, and then uses the short syntax to specify the remaining partitions:

```
CREATE TABLE SALES (SALE_DATE DATE, CUSTOMER INT)
PARTITION BY RANGE(SALE_DATE)
  (
  STARTING MINVALUE ENDING '2006-01-01' EXCLUSIVE,
  STARTING '2000-06-01' ENDING '20047-12-31' EVERY 3 MONTHS
  )
```

Partitioning on Multiple Columns

Multiple columns can be specified in the PARTITION BY clause. This is similar to defining multiple columns in an index key.

```
CREATE TABLE SALES (YEAR INT, MONTH INT)
PARTITION BY RANGE(YEAR, MONTH)
  (
  STARTING (2006,1)  ENDING (2006,3),
  STARTING (2006,4)  ENDING (2006,6),
  STARTING (2006,7)  ENDING (2006,9),
  STARTING (2006,10) ENDING (2006,12),
  STARTING (2007,1)  ENDING (2007,3)
  )
```

Note that multiple columns are not multiple dimensions. The ranges cannot overlap or else DB2 will raise an error condition:

```
CREATE TABLE NEIGHBORHOODS (STREET INT, AVENUE INT)
PARTITION BY RANGE(STREET, AVENUE)
  (
  STARTING (1,1)  ENDING (10,10),
  STARTING (1,11) ENDING (10,20)
  )

SQL0636N  Range specified for data partition "PART0" is not valid.
Reason code = "10".  SQLSTATE=56016
```

The reason for the error is due to the overlapping ranges between the two partition specifications. The first range goes from (1,1) to (10,20) while the second goes from (1,11) to (10,20). Ranges are linear so when the second range ends at (1,20), it starts back over at (2,1) instead of (2,11) as one might expect. If the data needs to be organized by grids or cubes the Multidimensional Clustering (MDC) feature should be used instead.

Partition Storage Mapping

One of the benefits of range table partitioning is the ability to place each table, index, and long field into their own table space. This section describes how these objects get mapped to different table spaces.

Automatically Mapping Ranges to Table Spaces

The `IN` clause on `CREATE TABLE` now accepts a list of table spaces that will be used for the various partitions:

```
CREATE TABLE SALES (SALE_DATE DATE, CUSTOMER INT)
  IN TBSP1, TBSP2, TBSP3
PARTITION BY RANGE(SALE_DATE)
  (
  STARTING '2006-01-01' ENDING '2007-12-31' EVERY 3 MONTHS
  )
```

Figure 11–33 illustrates how the partitions are placed into the table spaces.

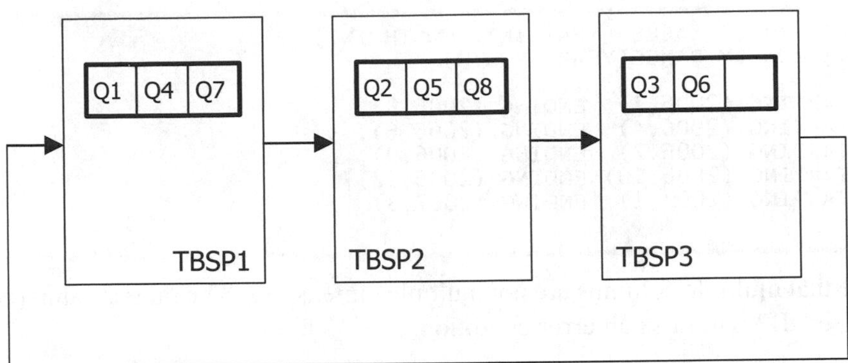

Figure 11–33 *Round-robin allocation of table spaces*

The ranges will cycle through the provided table spaces in round-robin fashion. Data for 1Q/2006 will be placed in TBSP1, 2Q/2006 in TBSP2, 3Q/2006 in TBSP3, 4Q/2006 in TBSP1, and so on until all of the partitions are allocated. The round-robin behavior can be disabled with the `NO CYCLE` option at the end of the table space list. If `NO CYCLE` is specified and not enough table spaces are available for the generated partitions, DB2 will generate an error message and the table will not be created.

```
CREATE TABLE SALES (SALE_DATE DATE, CUSTOMER INT)
  IN TBSP1, TBSP2, TBSP3  NO CYCLE
PARTITION BY RANGE(SALE_DATE)
  (
  STARTING '2006-01-01' ENDING '2007-12-31' EVERY 3 MONTHS
  );

SQL20250N  The number of data partitions exceeds the number of
table spaces for the table.  SQLSTATE=428G1
```

Manual Mapping of Ranges to Table Spaces

The previous example used the short syntax to assign partitions to table spaces. The long form uses the `IN` clause after each partition definition.

In this example, data before '2006-01-01' will be placed into the first partition, '2006-01-01' to '2006-06-01' (exclusive) in the second partition, and then '2006-06-01' to '2006-09-30' in the last partition.

```
CREATE TABLE SALES (SALE_DATE DATE, CUSTOMER INT)
PARTITION BY RANGE(SALE_DATE)
  (
  STARTING MINVALUE  IN TBSP1,
  STARTING '2006-01-01' IN TBSP2,
  STARTING '2006-06-01' ENDING '2006-09-30' IN TBSP3
  )
```

Mapping Indexes

The location of any indexes defined on a table are dependent on the type of storage being used.

- System Managed Storage (SMS)

  If the table is in an SMS table space, all index objects for that table are stored in the same table space.

- Database Managed Storage (DMS)

  If the table is in a DMS table space or using Automatic Storage, all indexes for that table can be stored in one different DMS table space via the `INDEX IN` keyword.

With range partitioning, each index for a partitioned table can now be placed into its own table space, regardless of the underlying table space type.

```
CREATE TABLE T1 (C1 INT, C2 INT)
  IN TBSP1, TBSP2, TBSP3
  INDEX IN TBSP4
PARTITION BY RANGE(c1)
  (
  STARTING FROM (1) ENDING (100) EVERY (25)
  );
CREATE INDEX I1 ON T1(C1);
CREATE INDEX I2 ON T1(C2) IN TBSP5;
```

The `INDEX IN` is used to specify the default location for indexes if no `IN` clause is specified in the `CREATE INDEX` command. In this example, index I1 does not have an `IN` specification, so it will be placed into `TBSP4`. If an index does contain the `IN` clause, the index will be placed into that particular table space.

From a table maintenance perspective, it is important to place indexes in a table space separate from that of the table. If no index location is given, it will default to the first table space defined for the table. If data is placed into the same table space, there will be disk contention between the different objects. In addition, the table space cannot be dropped without removing the index.

In addition to maintenance considerations, indexes may need to be separated from the main table because of their potential size. Indexes that are created on range partitioned tables are global. This means that one index structure contains the index entries for all partitions, rather than a separate index for each partition. While this may appear to be a limitation of range partitioned tables, a new feature called Asynchronous Index Cleanup ensures the highest availability of the index and table during any `DETACH` processing.

Mapping Large Objects

Large objects (LONG VARCHAR, BLOB, and XML) are similar to indexes as they are stored in different table spaces, as long as the LONG IN specification is included in the CREATE TABLE command. Normally large objects for a particular partition will be placed into the same table space as that partition. However, large objects can be placed into separate table spaces in a round robin fashion similar to data partitions:

```
CREATE TABLE SALES (SALE_DATE DATE, CUSTOMER INT)
  LONG IN TBSP6, TBSP7
PARTITION BY RANGE(SALE_DATE)
  (
  STARTING '2006-01-01' ENDING '2007-12-31' EVERY 3 MONTHS
  )
```

New Operations for Roll-Out and Roll-In

One of the most significant features of table partitioning is the ability to roll-in and roll-out table data. Two new commands are added to the ALTER TABLE command to roll data in and out: ATTACH PARTITION and DETACH PARTITION. Rolling in partitioned table data allows a new range to be easily incorporated into a partitioned table while rolling out partitioned table data allows you to separate ranges of data from a partitioned table for subsequent archiving.

Adding Partitions to an Existing Table

The ALTER TABLE ... ATTACH PARTITION command is used to incorporate an existing table as a new range. The simplest way to create a new partition is to use the CREATE TABLE LIKE command and then use this table to load in new data. Ultimately this table will be your new table partition. For instance, an existing partitioned table was created using the following SQL:

```
CREATE TABLE TXS
 (
 C1 INT NOT NULL,
 C2 INT NOT NULL
 )
PARTITION BY RANGE(c1)
 (
 PARTITION P1 STARTING 1 ENDING 1 IN TBSP1,
 PARTITION P2 STARTING 2 ENDING 2 IN TBSP2
 )
```

INSERT statements against a partitioned table continue to work similar to normal tables:

```
INSERT INTO TXS VALUES (1,1),(2,2),(1,1),(2,3),(1,1),(1,2)
```

Once the range partitioned table has been created, the LIKE option on the CREATE command can be used to generate a table that looks identical in structure to the TXS table:

```
CREATE TABLE NEWRANGE LIKE TXS IN TBSP3
```

This will create a table that has the same column names and data types as the base table. New data can now be loaded into this table, independent of the partitioned table.

```
INSERT INTO NEWRANGE VALUES (3,2),(3,3),(3,5)
```

Once the data has been successfully loaded into this NEWRANGE table, the ALTER command can be used to attach it to the existing range partitioned table:

```
ALTER TABLE TXS
  ATTACH PARTITION P3
  STARTING 3 ENDING 3
  FROM TABLE NEWRANGE
```

DB2 will issue a warning message regarding the status of the tables that are affected, but it is not an error condition and it will be fixed in a separate step.

```
SQL3601W  The statement caused one or more tables to automatically
be placed in the Set Integrity Pending state.  SQLSTATE=01586
```

The ALTER command only makes a catalog change and does not move any data. If the table had any dependent objects on it, like indexes, triggers, or views, they will be dropped. Once the ALTER command is committed, the existing table disappears from the catalogs and cannot be queried:

```
SELECT * FROM NEWRANGE;
SQL0204N  "BAKLARZ.NEWRANGE" is an undefined name.  SQLSTATE=42704
```

Trying to select the rows that were in the NEWRANGE table also fails:

```
SELECT * FROM TXS WHERE C1=3;

C1          C2
----------- -----------

  0 record(s) selected
```

The actual rows within the new partition are not available until a SET INTEGRITY command is used. This command is necessary to check that the data within the new partition matches the partition definition and any generated columns are properly created:

```
SET INTEGRITY FOR TXS ALLOW WRITE ACCESS
  IMMEDIATE CHECKED INCREMENTAL
```

Once this command completes, the data now becomes visible to an application:

```
SELECT * FROM TXS WHERE C1=3;

C1          C2
----------- -----------
          3           2
          3           3
          3           5

  3 record(s) selected.
```

Set Integrity Processing

The SET INTEGRITY command must be run before any ALTER TABLE ATTACH partition is brought online. The SET INTEGRITY command performs a number of functions:

- Checking the data in the new partition to make sure it matches the range defined for that partition
- Updating any generated columns and checking any constraints that may be on the table
- Updating any Materialized Query Tables (MQTs) that may be defined on the base table
- Updating the index with the new records

All of these activities are done as a background process that does not impact users of the existing partitioned table. Once the SET INTEGRITY command completes, the new data is made visible to applications.

The SET INTEGRITY command has a number of options, the most important shown below:

```
SET INTEGRITY FOR <table> ALLOW WRITE ACCESS
  IMMEDIATE CHECKED INCREMENTAL
  FOR EXCEPTION IN <table> USE <exception-table>
```

The ALLOW WRITE ACCESS provides for the most concurrency for existing users of the base table, but will take more processing time as the command needs to compete for resources on the table. The EXCEPTION statement is particularly important for tables that may not have been checked for data integrity. SET INTEGRITY is an atomic command, which means that the command must either complete successfully for all rows, or fail. If one row is incorrect in a million records, the entire command will fail. For instance, the following table is created that will be added as a partition to the base table:

```
CREATE TABLE NEWRANGE LIKE TXS IN TBSP4;
INSERT INTO NEWRANGE VALUES (4,4),(4,3),(4,5);
```

Attaching the table does not cause any error to occur, even though one of the values (5,3) is outside the defined range:

```
ALTER TABLE TXS
  ATTACH PARTITION P4
  STARTING 4 ENDING 4
  FROM TABLE NEWRANGE
```

The SET INTEGRITY command finds the error, but the correct records are not loaded into the table.

```
SET INTEGRITY FOR TXS ALLOW WRITE ACCESS
  IMMEDIATE CHECKED INCREMENTAL;

SQL3603N  Check data processing through the SET INTEGRITY statement
has found integrity violation involving a constraint or a unique
index with name "BAKLARZ.TXS.RANGE_CONSTRAINT".  SQLSTATE=23514
```

The way to handle rows that have constraint or integrity violations is to add the FOR EXCEPTION clause. This clause includes the name of the table or MQT that may have a violation occur against it.

In the previous example, the SET INTEGRITY can be run again with the FOR EXCEPTION clause to capture the bad record.

```
CREATE TABLE TXSBAD LIKE TXS IN USERSPACE1;
SET INTEGRITY FOR TXS ALLOW WRITE ACCESS
  IMMEDIATE CHECKED INCREMENTAL
  FOR EXCEPTION IN TXS USE TXSBAD;

SQL3602W  Check data processing found constraint violations and
moved them to exception tables.  SQLSTATE=01603

SELECT * FROM TXSBAD;
C1          C2
----------- -----------
          5           3

  1 record(s) selected.
```

The check constraint violations are placed into this error table and a warning message issued that indicates some rows had errors in them.

Data Availability During Attach and Set Integrity Processing

The ALTER TABLE ATTACH command takes a few milliseconds to process since it only needs to change a catalog entry to make an existing table part of a range partitioned table. The ALTER command does requires exclusive access to the table and the catalog to make a change, so there are some considerations when running this command:

- Table Locking

  The ALTER command needs to have an exclusive lock on the table. This means that any work that is currently running against the table must complete before the ALTER can operate.

- Catalog Locking

  The catalog must be briefly locked while the ALTER changes the catalog entries. If there are any other activities occurring against the catalog tables, the ALTER command must wait.

Since the ALTER requires exclusive locks, the DBA must insure that a COMMIT WORK or ROLLBACK be issued as soon as possible. An exclusive lock on the catalog may cause some work to pause waiting for the completion of the ALTER command.

The SET INTEGRITY has three options of how it should lock existing users:

- ALLOW NO ACCESS

  This will allow the SET INTEGRITY command to complete in the fastest amount of time, but will not allow any access to the table.

- ALLOW READ ACCESS

  SET INTEGRITY can also run with READ ACCESS which will allow users to query the table but not update any of its contents. All updates will queue up pending the completion of the SET INTEGRITY command.

- ALLOW WRITE ACCESS

  This mode of locking will result in the most availability to the users, but the slowest SET INTEGRITY performance.

When using the SET INTEGRITY command, the DBA must be sure to issue the COMMIT WORK as quickly as possible to avoid holding any locks.

Another consideration for running the SET INTEGRITY command is the setting of the lock time-outs. The following command may need to be issued — before issuing the SET INTEGRITY command is issued — to ask the database manager to not time-out while waiting on locks. This will prevent it from failing on lock conflicts at the end of its processing:

```
SET LOCK TIMEOUT WAIT
```

The system default may not allow enough time for the SET INTEGRITY command to start or complete successfully. By adjusting the SET LOCK value, the SET INTEGRITY command will wait until the appropriate locks are granted, and will not fail due to a lock time-out.

Deleting Partitions from an Existing Table

The ALTER TABLE ... DETACH command is used to remove a partition from an existing range partitioned table. A partition may be removed when the data needs to be rolled out for a new set of records. The format of the ALTER TABLE DETACH command is:

```
ALTER TABLE <table>
  DETACH PARTITION <partition-name> INTO TABLE <detached-table>
```

The partition-name is the name given to a partition when it is either attached to the table, or when it was created with the PART or PARTITION clause. The detached table name is the name of table that DB2 will create that will hold the detached partition. The DETACH only changes a catalog entry and makes the partition into a real table. There is no data movement as part of the ALTER TABLE DETACH command.

The following example illustrates the use of the command:

```
DROP TABLE OLDTABLE;
ALTER TABLE TXS
  DETACH PARTITION P1 INTO TABLE OLDTABLE;
```

The DROP statement is used to ensure that a table does not exist before the ALTER TABLE command is issued or else the command will fail since DB2 cannot create the table. Once the ALTER completes the range is removed from the existing table, and the new table is created. The DBA must make sure that a COMMIT WORK is issued immediately so that any locks held by the command are freed.

The detached partition is now available for use as a normal table. For instance, SELECT command can be issued against it:

```
SELECT * FROM OLDTABLE;

C1          C2
----------- -----------
          1           1
          1           1
          1           1
          1           2

  4 record(s) selected.
```

If there are any MQTs associated with this partition, the SET INTEGRITY command would need to be issued before the table can be dropped. MQTs on a partitioned table will be invalidated if they have any dependencies on the dropped range. For instance, the following MQT was defined on the base table:

```
CREATE SUMMARY TABLE TXSSUM AS
  (
  SELECT C1, SUM(C2) AS TOTAL, COUNT(*) AS QTY
  FROM TXS
  GROUP BY C1
  )
DATA INITIALLY DEFERRED REFRESH IMMEDIATE
```

Trying to drop the detached partition results in an error:

```
DROP TABLE OLDTABLE;
SQL20285N  The statement or command is not allowed while table
"VIPER.OLDTABLE" has detached dependents.  SQLSTATE=55057
```

If the detached partition is available, DB2 can do an incremental update of the MQT based on the contents of the partition. If the deleted partition was not available, DB2 would be required to do a refresh of the MQT from the entire table. The overhead of doing an entire refresh can be enormous, especially if the size of the partitioned table is significantly larger than an individual partition.

To complete the DETACH command, the SET INTEGRITY command can be used to update the MQTs:

```
SET INTEGRITY FOR T1SUM ALLOW WRITE ACCESS
  IMMEDIATE CHECKED INCREMENTAL;
DROP TABLE OLDTABLE;
```

Data Availability During Attach and Set Integrity Processing

The ALTER TABLE DETACH command only takes a few milliseconds to process. No data movement takes place during the DETACH and only catalog entries are changed. The DETACH command also requires exclusive access to the table and the catalog to make a change, so there are some considerations when running this command:

- Table Locking

  The ALTER command needs to have an exclusive lock on the table. Any work that is currently running against the table must complete before the ALTER can operate. Existing queries must be drained (completed) before the ALTER can start and any new queries that started after the ALTER command was issued will have to wait in queue.

- Catalog Locking

  The catalog must be briefly locked while the ALTER changes the catalog entries. If there are any other activities occurring against the catalog tables, the ALTER command must wait.

The DBA must insure that a COMMIT WORK or ROLLBACK be issued as soon as possible. In addition to detaching the partition from the table, DB2 will clean up the indexes associated with the detached partition using a new feature called Asynchronous Index Cleanup.

Asynchronous Index Cleanup after DETACH

Asynchronous Index Cleanup (AIC) is used to delete index entries after a partition has been detached from a table. When a DETACH is issued, any indexes entries associated with the partition are no longer considered and DB2 will begin removing these keys in a background process. The AIC has the following properties:

- It is a low-priority, throttled, background process
- Reclaims space in index (keys corresponding to data rolled-out)
- Automatically started when DETACH is committed (or after refresh of dependent MQTs)

- Pauses if would have caused a lock conflict with user activity
- Will not keep a database active
- Commits (hardens) its progress periodically
- Continues where it left off after a shutdown or recovery

The progress of the AIC can be monitored by using the LIST UTILITIES SHOW DETAIL command (Figure 11–34):

```
LIST UTILITIES SHOW DETAIL;

ID                              = 2
Type                            = ASYNCH INDEX CLEANUP
Database Name                   = SAMPLE
Partition Number                = 0
Description                     = Table: TXS, Index: I1
Start Time                      = 04/14/2007 11:15:01.978513
State                           = Executing
Invocation Type                 = Automatic
Throttling:
   Priority                     = 50
Progress Monitoring:
      Total Work                = 5 pages
      Completed Work            = 0 pages
      Start Time                = 04/14/2007 11:15:01.980518
```

Figure 11–34 *List Utilities details*

Additional Considerations for Range Partitioning

There are a number of other situations that warrant special consideration when using range partitioned tables. These situations are described in detail below.

Migration from a UNION ALL View

Many customers took advantage of the UNION ALL view capability in DB2 to create a form of range partitioning. A separate table would be created for each range and then all tables combined into a view.

Range Partitioning solves many of the problems associated with UNION ALL views and simplifies the roll-in and roll-out procedure. Only three steps are required in order to migrate existing UNION ALL views to a range partitioned table.

1. Create a partitioned table

   The first step would be to create a partitioned table with only one partition in it. The first partition will contain records with null values and for records that are below the normal ranges.

For instance, assume that the view SALES has a number of tables associated with it that have the following structure:

```
CREATE TABLE QTR1
  (
  TX_NUMBER   INT NOT NULL,
  TX_ITEM     CHAR(10) NOT NULL,
  TX_QUANTITY INT NOT NULL,
  TX_DATE     DATE NOT NULL,
     CHECK (TX_DATE BETWEEN '2006-01-01' AND '2006-03-31')
  )
```

Each quarter would have a table associated with it. A new partitioned table would be created that defines the range that catches null values and records that are less than the current ranges.

```
CREATE TABLE PARTITIONED_SALES BY (TX_DATE NULLS FIRST)
  (
  PARTITION EXCEPTION
         STARTING MINVALUE
         ENDING '2006-01-01' EXCLUSIVE
  )
```

2. Attach existing tables

   Each table in the existing view needs to be attached to the partitioned table.

```
ALTER TABLE PARTITIONED_SALES
  ATTACH PARTITION Q1
    STARTING '2006-01-01' ENDING '2006-03-31'
    FROM TABLE QTR1;
```

3. Run SET INTEGRITY

   The SET INTEGRITY statement needs to be issued to bring the data back online. After the SET INTEGRITY completes, the PARTITIONED_SALES table now contains the same contents as the original SALES view.

```
SET INTEGRITY FOR YEAR2005 ALLOW WRITE ACCESS
  IMMEDIATE CHECKED INCREMENTAL
```

Using MDC with Table Partitioning

Multidimensional clustering can be used with range partitioned tables, but the base table must have the ORGANIZE BY DIMENSIONS clause added to it to define the clustering that will be used.

```
CREATE TABLE SALES
  (
  TX_NUMBER   INT NOT NULL,
  TX_ITEM     CHAR(10) NOT NULL,
  TX_QUANTITY INT NOT NULL,
  TX_DATE     DATE NOT NULL
  )
PARTITION BY (TX_DATE)
 (PARTITION EXCEPTION
    STARTING MINVALUE ENDING '2005-01-01' EXCLUSIVE)
ORGANIZE BY (TX_ITEM)
```

Any table that now gets added to this range partition table must also have the same ORGANIZE BY DIMENSIONS clause:

```
CREATE TABLE SALESQ1 LIKE SALES
  ORGANIZE BY DIMENSIONS(TX_ITEM)
```

If the table being attached to the partitioned table does not have the same dimensions as the base table, DB2 will issue an error message. Unfortunately, the only way to correct this problem is to recreate the table, or create a copy of the table with the ORGANIZE clause included.

Compression and Table Partitioning

Row compression can also be used with range partitioning. In order to attach any partition that is compressed, the main table definition must include the COMPRESS YES option:

```
CREATE TABLE SALES
  (
  TX_NUMBER   INT NOT NULL,
  TX_ITEM     CHAR(10) NOT NULL,
  TX_QUANTITY INT NOT NULL,
  TX_DATE     DATE NOT NULL
  )
PARTITION BY (TX_DATE)
 (PARTITION EXCEPTION STARTING MINVALUE
                      ENDING '2005-01-01' EXCLUSIVE)
COMPRESS YES
```

If the table has been already defined, the ALTER TABLE command could be used to add the compression option to the table:

```
ALTER TABLE SALES COMPRESS YES
```

Once the range partitioned table is eligible for compression, any of the partitions can be compressed. There is no requirement that any one of the partitions be compressed in the table, even though it has been marked as eligible for compression. From a transactional perspective, it may be better to compress historical partitions and keep the current partitions uncompressed to reduce compression overhead.

Summary

This chapter discussed the physical placement of objects in DB2 databases. The types of objects discussed included:

- *Buffer pools* — Areas of main memory allocated to cache table and index data pages as they are being read or written to the hard disk.
- *Table spaces* — DB2 objects that isolate the logical definition of the table from the details of the physical storage. The storage types available are SMS (System Managed Space) and DMS (Database Managed Space). SMS is a storage model where space is acquired when needed. Its main benefit is its flexibility. DMS is preallocated storage space. Its main benefit is that it generally performs better than SMS. Regular table spaces can store any DB2 data. Optionally, indexes and long data can be placed in their own table spaces.
- *Containers* — Physical storage objects. They can be directories, files, or devices. Containers can be only assigned to one table space. Table spaces can consist of multiple containers.
- *Extents* — Units of space within a container. DB2 can use these units to transfer data between disk and buffer pools. Extents range in size from 2 to 256 pages. Once defined, the extent size for a table space cannot be changed.
- *Pages* — Blocks of storage that hold the rows of data. They can be either 4, 8, 16, or 32 KB in size. Buffer pool storage is divided into pages.
- *Large Object* (LOB) data is stored differently than other data types in DB2. LOB data objects are stored in 64 MB areas, broken up into segments. LOB allocation objects maintain allocation and free space information about large objects.

We discussed planning and design considerations for the DB2 physical environment:

- SMP systems have the capability of performing query and I/O operations in parallel.
- DB2 can operate in a single partition, single or multiple processor (SMP) environment. Multiple partition environments are also possible on SMP machines and across a cluster of SMP machines.
- The way DB2 is configured to use the available memory resources is critical to its performance characteristics.
- Placing containers on separate disks gives DB2 the opportunity to perform parallel I/O operations by using sequential prefetching of pages.

- When a database is created, the system catalog table space `SYSCATSPACE` is created along with the temporary table space `TEMPSPACE1` and user table space `USERSPACE1`.
- The choice of an extent size for a table space depends on factors such as the size and type of tables in the table space and the type of access to the tables.
- The mapping of tables to table spaces depends on factors such as the amount of data and the type of data in the table.

We then looked at how to implement, monitor, and change the objects via DB2 commands, SQL statements, and the Control Center.

Finally, we examined the new table partitioning feature that can help to significantly reduce the maintenance effort required to manage very large tables and increase the potential size of a single table.

Table partitioning is an important feature that should be considered by any installation that requires roll-in and roll-out capabilities, as well as the need to manage large tables.

CHAPTER 12

Maintaining Data

- EXPORTING DATA
- IMPORTING DATA
- LOADING DATA
- ANALYZING DATA PLACEMENT
- REORGANIZING DATA
- GATHERING STATISTICS

*I*n this chapter, the techniques of how to populate and extract DB2 data using the `LOAD`, `IMPORT`, and `EXPORT` utilities will be examined. The differences between these utilities will be examined along with the scenarios that would favor using one over another.

Additional maintenance topics will include examining the physical data placement and gathering statistics. Some of the utilities examined will include `REORGCHK`, `REORG`, `RUNSTATS`, and `REBIND`.

Moving Data

Whenever data is extracted or inserted into the database, particular care must be taken to check the format of the data. Sometimes a DBA may spend more time correcting the data format than actually inserting or extracting the data. To assist the DBA in this regard, DB2 supports various data formats for extraction and insertion. The formats include:

- DEL — Delimited ASCII files
- ASC — Fixed-length ASCII files
- IXF — Integrated Exchange Format files
- WSF — Worksheet Format files
- XML — XML documents
- LOB — Large objects (video, audio, text)

The following table summarizes the DB2 utilities and the file formats that they support.

Table 12–1 *Utilities by file format*

Utility	DEL	ASC	IXF	WSF	XML	LOB
IMPORT	Yes	Yes	Yes	Yes	Yes	Yes
EXPORT	Yes	No	Yes	Yes	Yes	Yes
LOAD	Yes	Yes	Yes	No	No	Yes

Delimited ASCII Files

This file type, used extensively in Relational Database Management Systems (RDBMS) and other software packages, makes use of delimiters. A delimiter is a character that is used to identify the beginning or end of a data element. Some of the most important delimiters used in delimited ASCII (DEL) files include:

- *Character* delimiter — As the name suggests, this is used to mark the beginning and end of a character field. By default, DB2 uses the double quote (") character as a character delimiter. The DBA can optionally override this default and cause DB2 to make use of another character as the character delimiter.
- *Column* delimiter — This delimiter is used to mark the end of a field. The default column delimiter used is the comma (,) character, but the DBA may choose another character to use.
- *Row* delimiter — Used to mark the end of a record or row. DB2 assumes the new line character X'0A' (commonly used on UNIX operating systems to mark a new line) to be the row delimiter. On Windows, the carriage return/linefeed

characters X'0D0A' are used by DB2 as the row delimiter.

In DEL files, the rows are streamed into the file one after the other. They are separated with the *row delimiter*. The fields in the row are separated from one another by a *column delimiter*.

Character fields are encapsulated by two character delimiters.

Numeric fields are represented by their ASCII equivalent. A period (.) character is used to indicate the decimal point, if required. Float values are represented with the E notation, negative values with a leading minus (-) character, and positive values with a plus (+) sign.

To illustrate, a table named NAMES contains the following data (Table 12–2):

Table 12–2 *Names Table*

EMP_NO	NAME	LASTNAME	DEPT_NO
10001	George	Baklarz	307
10002	Paul	Zikopoulos	204
10003	Beverly	Crusher	305

Assume the EMP_NO column is of type INTEGER and all the other columns are of a CHARACTER type. If the column delimiter is the comma (,), the row delimiter is the linefeed character and the character delimiter is the double quote (") character, a DEL file containing the data would consist of a datastream that looks like this:

```
10001,"George" ,"Baklarz",   "307"
10002,"Paul"   ,"Zikopoulos","204"
10003,"Beverly","Crusher",   "305"
```

When choosing the column delimiter and the row delimiter of a DEL file, be careful not to use characters that are used in the datastream.

Non-Delimited ASCII Files

Non-delimited ASCII (ASC) files are sometimes referred to as fixed-length ASCII files. This file consists of a stream of ASCII characters of data values organized by row and column. Rows in the data stream are separated by a carriage return/line feed or new line character, and all column values are of fixed length (if a record length is specified, there is no need for the row delimiter). All variable-length character types are padded with blanks and represented using their maximum length. There are no column or character delimiters. Using the same example as above, an ASC file representing the data in the NAMES table would look like this:

```
10001George Baklarz   307
10002Paul   Zikopoulos204
10003BeverlyCrusher   305
```

DB2 Note

The columns are aligned in non-delimited ASCII files.

IXF Files

Integrated Exchange Format (IXF) files are used to move data among DB2 databases. For example, you can export a data file from a host database and use it as input to populate a table in a database on a DB2 server. In general, an IXF file consists of an unbroken sequence of variable-length records. Numeric values are stored as packed decimal or binary values, depending on the data type. Character values are stored in their ASCII representation, and only the used part of variable-length character types are stored. An IXF file also has the table definition stored within it along with the data.

DB2 Note

If the host table contains packed fields, you will have to convert these fields before transferring the file to a DB2 database. To perform this conversion, create a view in the host database for all the columns that you require. A view automatically forms character fields out of the packed fields. From the view, you can export the required data as an IXF file.

IXF files cannot be edited by using a normal text editor.

An advantage of using this type of format is that the table definition is included in the file, so a table and its indexes can be recreated and populated with this file format.

Worksheet Format Files

Lotus 1-2-3 and Symphony products use this type of file format to extract or import data. Although different releases have new added functions in their release-specific file types, the Worksheet Format (WSF) only uses a subset of this functionality accepted by most versions of these products. This format is not used to move data from one DB2 table to another.

Data Movement Utilities

A set of utilities is provided with DB2 to populate tables or to extract data from tables. These utilities enable you to easily move large amounts of data into or out of DB2 databases. The speed of these operations is very important. When working with large databases and tables, extracting or inserting new data may take a long time.

In this section, three DB2 utilities will be examined. The various options for each utility will be reviewed to explore their function and performance benefit. These utilities are:

- `EXPORT`
- `IMPORT`
- `LOAD`

The Export Utility

The `EXPORT` utility is used to extract data from a table, view, or from any valid SQL statement into a file. Data can be extracted into several different file formats, which can be used by either the `IMPORT` or `LOAD` utilities to populate tables. These files can also be used by other software products such as spreadsheets, word processors, and other RDBMSs to populate tables or generate reports.

You must already be connected to the database from which data is to be exported, and you must have `SYSADM` or `DBADM` authority, or `CONTROL` or `SELECT` privilege on the tables or views you access during the export.

Here is an abbreviated syntax of the `EXPORT` utility (Figure 12–1):

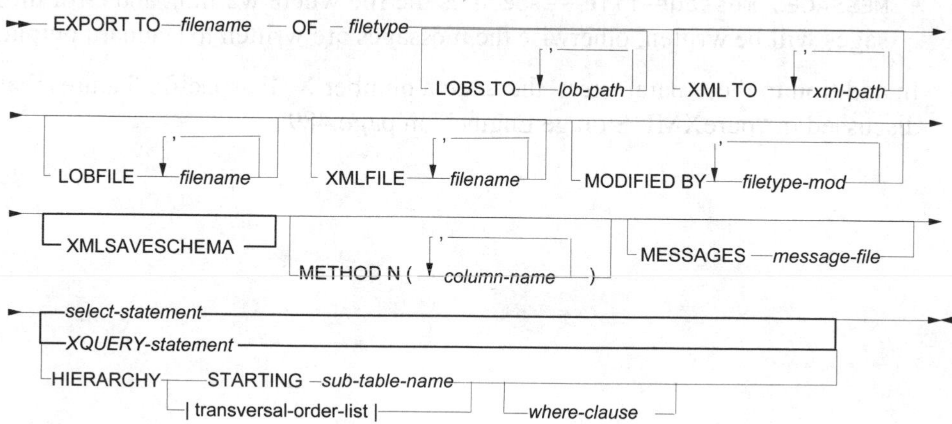

Figure 12–1 *Export command*

Using the EXPORT Command

To export all the data from a table `NAMES` into a file `NAMES.DEL` of type DEL using all the default options, one would use the command:

```
export to names.del of del select * from names
```

Figure 12–2 illustrates the results of running the `EXPORT` command.

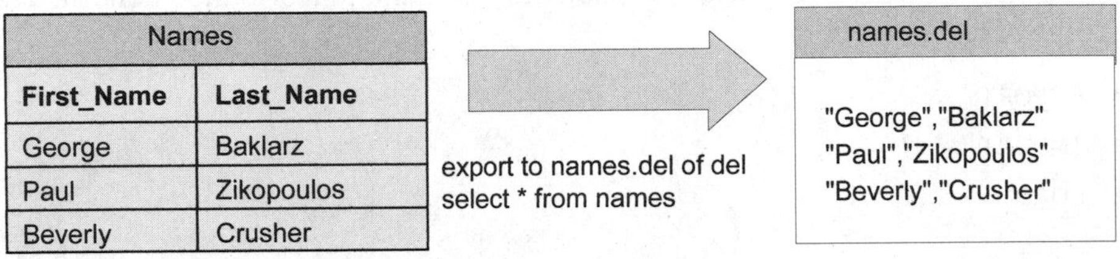

Names	
First_Name	**Last_Name**
George	Baklarz
Paul	Zikopoulos
Beverly	Crusher

export to names.del of del select * from names

names.del

"George","Baklarz"
"Paul","Zikopoulos"
"Beverly","Crusher"

Figure 12–2 *Simple export results*

Some of the key parameters to the `EXPORT` command include (see the *DB2 Command Reference* for further detail):

- `TO filename` — specifies the name of the file to which data is to be exported.
- `OF filetype` — specifies the format of the data in the output file: DEL, WSF, IXF.
- `METHOD N column-name` — specifies one or more column names to be used in the output file, valid only for WSF and IXF files.
- `select-statement` — specifies the `SELECT` statement that will return the data to be exported.
- `MESSAGES message-file` — specifies the file where warning and error messages will be written, otherwise the messages are written to standard output.

In addition to these parameters, there are a number XML-specific features that are discussed in "pureXML Storage Engine" on page 489.

Supported File Formats

The export utility allows the user to export data into one of three supported file types: IXF, DEL, or WSF.

To specify the file type, use the `OF FILETYPE` clause. For example, data from the `PRODUCT` table can be exported to a file `PRODUCT.IXF` of type IXF by using the command options (note that other options can also be specified):

```
export to product.ixf of ixf ... select ... from product ...
```

Although the ASC file type is not supported with the `EXPORT` command, the user can still generate a data file of type ASC by modifying the `SELECT` statement. For example, if two columns named `FIRST_NAME` defined as `CHAR(10)` and `EMP_NO` as `CHAR(5)` are to be exported to a file of type ASC, the user can specify the DEL file type and modify the select statement to:

```
export ... of del ... select first_name concat emp_no from ...
```

The output of the command is shown below:

```
"George     10001"
"Zikopoulos 10002"
"Beverly    10003"
```

When importing the data into a table, the column start position of the first column should be given as 2, thus ignoring the double quote (") character in the first position. Numeric values can be cast to a character type and then concatenated to the other columns.

Date Format Modification

For DEL and WSF files, the default format used for date values is *yyyymmdd*. The user has the option of changing the format to the ISO standard representation *yyyy-mm-dd* by specifying the `DATESISO` file type modifier with the `EXPORT` command:

```
export ... modified by datesiso ...
```

Delimiters Used with DEL Files

The default character delimiter is the double quote (") character. To override this, specify the CHARDEL file type modifier. For example, to use the asterisk (*) character as the character delimiter:

```
export ... modified by chardel*
```

DB2 Note

The same character cannot be used for more than one delimiter in the file.

Handling Decimal Columns

When exporting to DEL files, decimal data types are exported with a decimal point (.) character. Leading and trailing zeros and a plus (+) or minus (–) sign are inserted before (or after) the value. For example, a value of 22.5 in a column named AMOUNT defined as DECIMAL(8,2) will be exported as:

```
+000022.50
```

To change the decimal point delimiter, specify the DECPT file type modifier:

```
export ... modified by decpt^
```

The user can also change the way that positive decimal values are exported. By default, a plus (+) character is added in front of the value to identify it as a positive, value. By using the DECPLUSBLANK filetype modifier, no plus (+) will be added to positive values. Negative values are unaffected.

```
export ... modified by decplusblank
```

Derived Column Names When Exporting

In some cases, the user may want to export data derived from one or more columns into a single column in the output file. For example, the SELECT statement may include a derived column defined as "Salary minus Deductions." In this case, a number will be generated and used as the name of the derived column. There are two ways to force the column to be renamed. You can do this for IXF and WSF formats only.

First, you can use the AS clause in the SELECT statement. In our example, "Salary minus Deductions" can be written as SALARY - DEDUCTIONS AS PAY. The name of the derived column will now be PAY.

```
export ... select salary - deduction as pay ... from ...
```

Alternatively, you can specify the METHOD N option followed by the names to be used for the columns, in the order in which they are selected. In our example, if the first column is the "Salary minus Deductions" column, the first name specified after the METHOD N option would be PAY:

```
export ... method n ('PAY', ...) ...
  select salary - deduction, ... from ...
```

An IXF data file can be used to create a table in another database by using the table definition stored in the IXF file itself. By changing the names of the columns when exporting to the IXF file, the subsequent table can be created with the desired column names when the file is imported into the target database.

Capturing Error and Warning Messages

Use the MESSAGES option to specify a file that should be used to record all error and warning messages:

```
export ... messages x:\error_logs\exports\exp1.txt ...
```

Exporting Large Object Data

When exporting tables that contain LOB data types, the user has two options of how the LOB values can be exported. The first 32 KB of LOB data can be included in the target file with the regular table data, or the LOB can be stored separately, in a file. If the user decides on the first option, there are no extra parameters that need to be specified with the EXPORT command. However, only LOBs of 32 KB or less should be exported in this way. If a LOB value exceeds 32 KB in size, it will be truncated, and only the first 32 KB will be exported into the file.

For the export utility to export each LOB value to a separate file, the user must specify where the files are to be put and what names are to be used. This is done by specifying three parameters:

- LOBSINFILE — A file type modifier, which when specified, informs the EXPORT utility that all LOB values are to be exported into separate files (DB2 can concatenate multiple LOBs in a file). If it is not specified, the export utility will

Maintaining Data

ignore all other parameters related to exporting LOBs into separate files.

- LOBS TO lob-path specifies the path or paths where the LOB values will be exported as individual files. If the first path specified becomes full, the second will be used, and so on. When specifying the path name, make sure it ends with a "\" character for Windows or "/" for UNIX.
- LOBFILE filename tells the EXPORT utility what file name to use for the files. A three-digit number will be generated and added to the filename as an extension to ensure uniqueness.

In exporting LOB data from a table named EMP_PHOTO to a file named EMP_PHOTO.DEL and its LOB values to the directories D:\LOBDIR1 and D:\LOBDIR2 and the LOB file name to be used is EMP_PHOTO_LOB, the EXPORT command would be written as follows:

```
export to emp_photo.del of del lobs to
  d:\lobdir1\,d:\lobdir2\
  lobfile emp_photo_lob ... modified by lobsinfile
  select * from emp_photo
```

The first LOB files exported would be named as follows:

```
D:\LOBDIR1\EMP_PHOTO_LOB.001
D:\LOBDIR1\EMP_PHOTO_LOB.002
D:\LOBDIR1\EMP_PHOTO_LOB.003
.....and so on.......
```

If the D:\LOBDIR1 directory becomes full, the D:\LOBDIR2 directory will be used.

Exporting Typed Tables

There are two ways in which data can be exported from typed tables. The first way is to treat the typed table as a normal table by using a SELECT statement.

For example, if a user wants to export rows from the EMPLOYEE table and no records from any subtables defined under it, then the ONLY option in the SELECT statement should be used:

```
export ... select ... from only(db2cert.employee) ...
```

If all the records in the EMPLOYEE table should be returned, including records from subtables under it, do not specify the ONLY option in the SELECT statement:

```
export ... select ... from db2cert.employee ...
```

Another option is to export some or all tables in the hierarchy. The user needs to specify two things: which subtables to export and the order in which they are to be exported. This order is referred to as the *traversal order*. Figure 12–3 shows a table hierarchy.

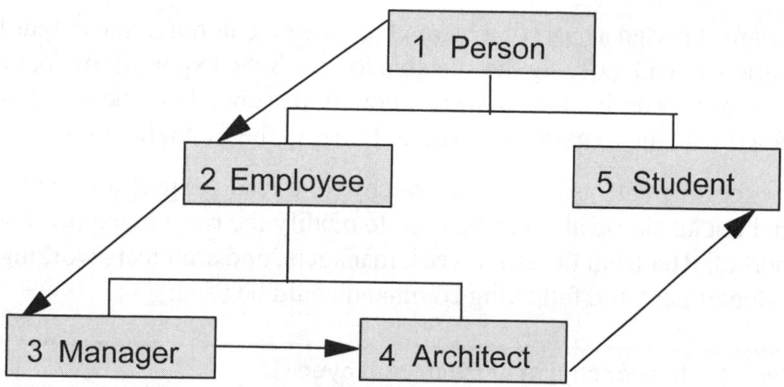

Figure 12–3 *Exporting a table hierarchy — Traversal order*

The default traversal order starts from the highest table in the hierarchy — in our example, the PERSON table. The next table in the list can be either STUDENT or EMPLOYEE, depending on which of the two was created first. Assume that the EMPLOYEE table was created first. The next table in the list could be MANAGER or ARCHITECT; this is also dependent on which was created earlier. Assume the MANAGER table was created before the ARCHITECT table. There are no tables defined under MANAGER, so the ARCHITECT table will be the next table in the traversal order. Because the ARCHITECT table has no tables defined under it, the next in the list will be the STUDENT table.

It is important to realize that databases with the same table hierarchies may have two distinctly different default traversal orders. Make a note of the traversal order in which the tables in the hierarchy are exported because the same order must be used to import the tables.

To use the default traversal order, specify the subtable to start the export from after the STARTING option, in our case, the root table of the hierarchy, DB2CERT.PERSON:

```
export ... hierarchy starting db2cert.person
```

To specify another traversal order to use for the export, list the order of the tables instead of the STARTING table_name option. All subtables must be listed.

```
export ... hierarchy (person,student,
  employee,architect,manager) ...
```

If rows are exported as part of a hierarchy, the first column in the output file will be a numeric value identifying the subtable to which the exported row belongs. The numeric value is derived from the position of the subtable in the traversal order list as defined with the EXPORT command, "1" being the first table in the list.

When exporting data as part of a hierarchy (or a result export for that matter), an optional WHERE clause also can be used to qualify the rows to export. For example, to export all data from the employees, managers, and architects working in the Sales Department, the following command could be used:

```
export ... hierarchy starting employee
  where dept = 'Sales'
```

Using the Control Center to Export a Table

The Control Center provides an easy interface to the EXPORT utility. To invoke it, select the table that needs to be exported and right-click on it. Select the **Export** option as shown in Figure 12–4.

Once invoked, the user may specify the different options as discussed above. The Control Center will also be used to demonstrate EXPORT by showing how a user can export a table named PRODUCT to a DEL file. The output file name and message file name are specified as: C:\EXTRACT\PROJECT.DEL and C:\EXTRACT\PROJECT.MSG.

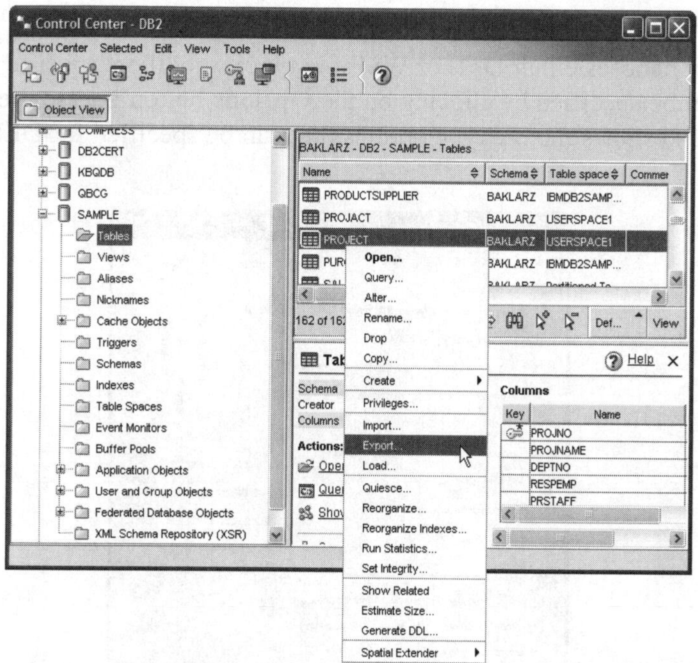

Figure 12–4 *Invoking the EXPORT utility from the Control Center*

The Export Table panel is displayed:

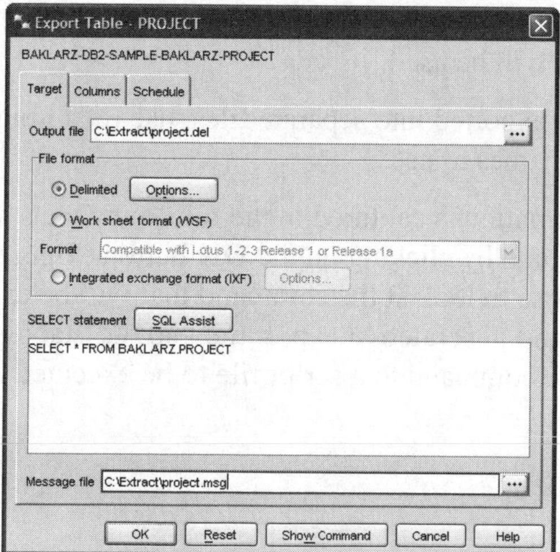

Figure 12–5 *The EXPORT utility*

As indicated by the SELECT statement in Figure 12–5, all rows and columns will be exported.

If the user chooses either DEL or WSF file types, modifiers specific to these file types may be specified by clicking on the **Options** button next to the file type. Figure 12–6 shows the file type options that can be specified for DEL files.

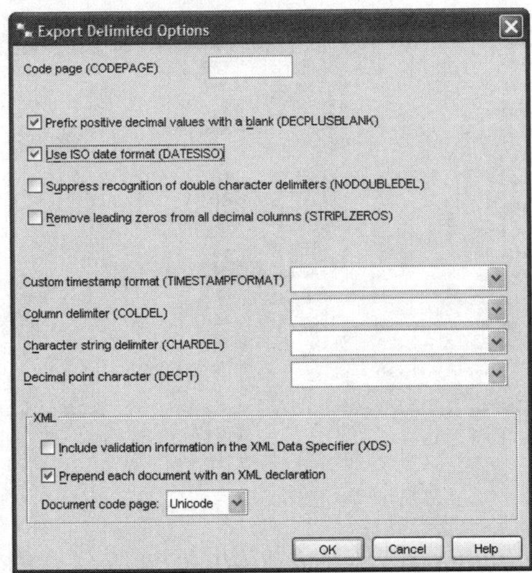

Figure 12–6 *Changing the DEL EXPORT options*

The Columns tab (see Figure 12–5) can be used to specify the column names to use in the exported file (IXF or WSF only). If not specified, the column names in the SELECT statement will be used.

If LOBs are to be exported into separate files, use the Large Objects tab to specify the paths and filenames to use.

Once all the information is captured in the relevant panels, the user may opt to run the EXPORT command by clicking on the **OK** button (Figure 12–7). Alternatively, the user may choose to look at the command that will be executed. Figure 12–8 shows the command generated to export the PROJECT table. The user may also choose to save the command to a script file to be executed at a later time.

Figure 12–7 *Schedule Tab*

If the tools catalog has been created, this panel will give you the option to schedule the this task, otherwise, you have the option to create the tools catalog from the panel that is displayed if the tools catalog has not been created. Type in a valid user id and password and click OK.

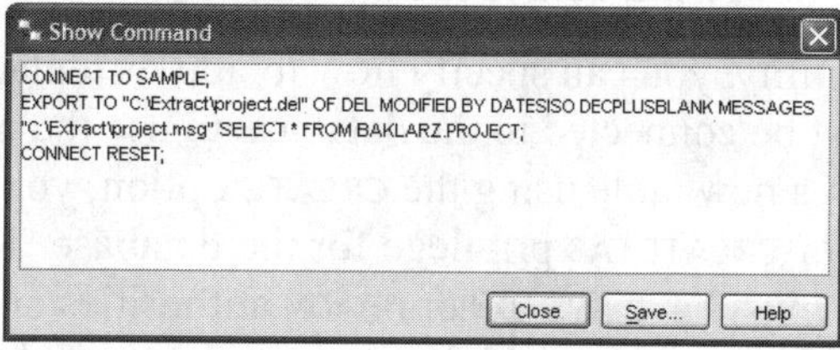

Show Command
CONNECT TO SAMPLE;
EXPORT TO "C:\Extract\project.del" OF DEL MODIFIED BY DATESISO DECPLUSBLANK MESSAGES "C:\Extract\project.msg" SELECT * FROM BAKLARZ.PROJECT;
CONNECT RESET;
Close
Save...
Help

Figure 12–8 *The EXPORT command generated*

EXPORT Considerations

The following information is required when exporting data:

- A SELECT statement (or hierarchy selection clause for typed tables) specifying the data to be exported
- The path and name of the file that will store the exported data
- The format the data will be written in (IXF, DEL, or WSF)

DB2 Note

An ASC format can be generated by translating and concatenating the columns in the SELECT statement.

The following information is optional when exporting data:

- A message file name
- New column names when exporting to IXF or WSF files
- A file type modifier to specify additional formatting when creating DEL and WSF files
- File names and paths for exported LOB columns

Performance of the EXPORT Utility

When using the EXPORT utility, a DBA should make sure that the utility extracts the data efficiently. The SELECT statement used with this utility has the greatest effect on performance. There are some tools (like Visual Explain) available in DB2 that can be used to evaluate the performance of a SELECT statement.

The IMPORT Utility

The IMPORT utility inserts data from an input file into a table or view. You can either replace data or append data to the table or view if it already contains data.

With the IMPORT utility, you can specify how to add or replace the data into the target table. You must be connected to the database to use the utility, and if you want to import data into a new table using the CREATE option, you must have SYSADM or DBADM authorities or CREATETAB privilege for the database. To replace data in a table or view, you must have SYSADM or DBADM authorities or CONTROL privilege for the table or view. If you want to add data to an existing table or view, you must have SELECT and INSERT privileges for the table or view.

DB2 Note

If the existing table contains a primary key or unique constraint that is referenced by a foreign key in another table, data cannot be replaced, only appended.

An abbreviated syntax of the IMPORT utility is shown in Figure 12–9. Note that there are additional XML options which are covered in "pureXML Storage Engine" on page 489.

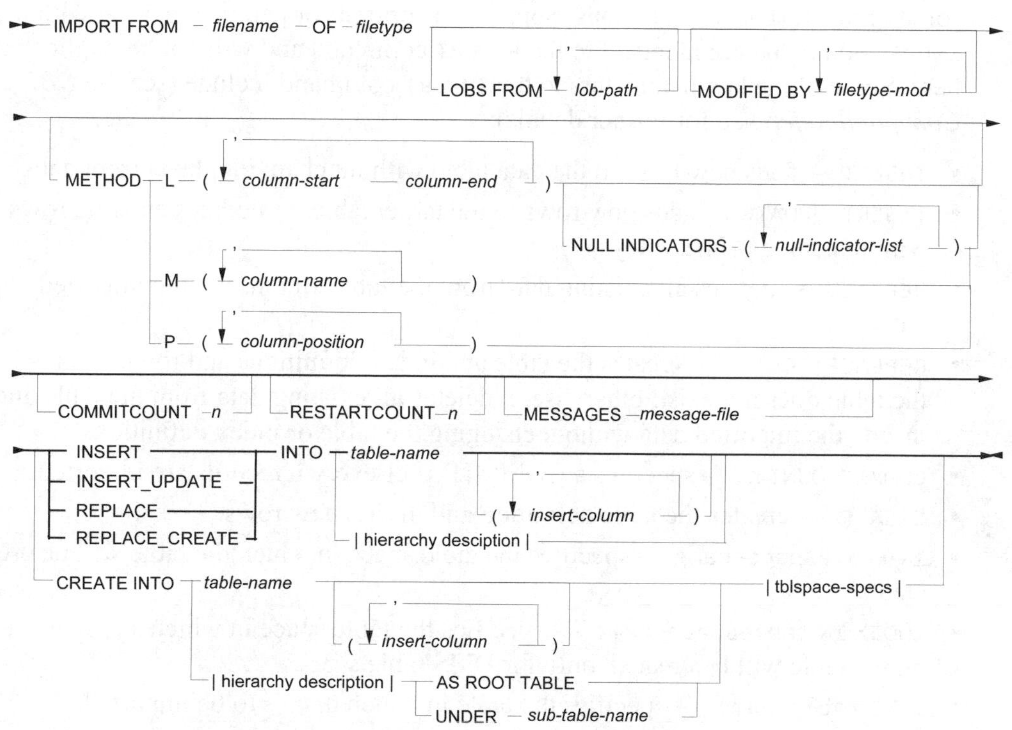

Figure 12–9 *IMPORT command syntax*

Using the IMPORT Command

To import data from a file named `NAMES.DEL` of type DEL into an empty table named `NAMES` using all the default options, use the following command (Figure 12–10):

```
import from names.del of del insert into names
```

Names.del

"George","Baklarz"
"Paul","Zikopoulos"
"Beverly","Crusher"

IMPORT FROM NAMES.DEL OF DEL
INSERT INTO NAMES

Names	
First_Name	**Last_Name**
George	Baklarz
Paul	Zikopoulos
Beverly	Crusher

Figure 12–10 *Simple import*

In this section, the use of the IMPORT command will be examined by looking at some of its most useful functions. Some of the options or parameters used with the IMPORT command are identical to the EXPORT command and will not be duplicated here. Some of the key parameters to the IMPORT command include (see the *DB2 Command Reference* for further details):

- INSERT — adds new rows to the data table without changing the current data.
- INSERT_UPDATE — adds new rows to the target table, or updates existing rows with matching primary keys.
- REPLACE — deletes all existing data from the table and inserts the imported data.
- REPLACE_CREATE — creates the table and index definitions and row contents if the table does not exist; otherwise, it deletes all existing data from the table and inserts the imported data without changing the table or index definitions.
- COMMITCOUNT n — specifies a COMMIT after every n records are imported.
- CREATE — creates the table definition and inserts new rows.
- IN tablespace-name — specifies the table space in which the table will be created.
- INDEX IN tablespace-name — specifies the table space in which any indexes on the table will be created, only for DMS table spaces.
- INTO table-name — specifies the table in which data is to be imported.
- METHOD L |N — L specifies the start and end column numbers from which to import data (numbering starts at 1, for ASC files only). N specifies the names of the columns being imported (IXF files only).

File Types Supported

The file types supported are IXF, DEL, WSF, and ASC. To specify the file type, use the OF FILE-TYPE clause. For example, a file named PRODUCT.IXF of type IXF can be imported by using the command:

```
import from product.ixf of ixf ...
```

Insert Mode

If the data in the source file is to be added to the data in the target table, the INSERT option should be used. For example, if the order of the columns in the exported file is the same as the order of the columns in the target table, the following command will insert the new rows into the existing table named PRODUCT:

```
import ... insert into product
```

If the order of the columns in the source file is not the same as the order in which columns in the target table, then the order of the columns must be specified after the table name. For example, if the Product table has three columns named PROD_NO, PRICE, and DESCRIPTION in that order, and the source file contains the three columns in the order PRICE, PROD_NO, DESCRIPTION, the following command needs to be specified:

```
import ... insert into product(price,prod_no,description)
```

Insert and Update Mode

Sometimes a DBA receives a file that contains updated data for a table. Some of the rows in the file do not exist in the target table, however, most do. Some of the existing data needs to be updated to reflect the new values. For example, the DBA receives a file named PRODUCT.DEL that contains the new prices for some of the existing products as well as for new products. He cannot *insert* all the new data because it contains values for some existing products nor can he *replace* all the data because some of the valid product values do not yet exist in the table. The only option is to use the INSERT_UPDATE option of the IMPORT command. This will *insert* all the new rows and *update* existing rows to reflect the new values.

The IMPORT utility uses the primary key and unique constraints defined on the table to determine if a row exists and whether it should be updated or inserted. In our example, the PRODUCT table has a primary key value defined as the product number (PROD_NO). In Figure 12–11, four rows in the input file and three rows in the table before the import are shown.

Product.del

```
00001,15.00,"Book"
00005,3.00,"Pen"
00003,35.00,"Lamp - Green"
00004,20.00,"Table"
```

Products table (before)

Prod_no	Price	Description
00001	10.00	Book
00002	20.00	Table
00003	30.00	Lamp

```
IMPORT FROM PRODUCT.DEL of DEL...
INSERT_UPDATE INTO PRODUCT
```

Products table (after)

Prod_no	Price	Description
00001	15.00	Book
00002	20.00	Table
00003	30.00	Lamp - Green
00004	20.00	Table
00005	3.00	Pen

Figure 12–11 *Using IMPORT with INSERT_UPDATE option*

The IMPORT command is invoked with the INSERT_UPDATE option. The first record in the input file will cause the first row in the table to be updated. The reason for this is that the PROD_NO value supplied in the file matches an existing row in the table. As shown in the PRODUCTS table after the import, the value associated with the PRICE column has been updated to show the new price.

The second record in the input file has a PROD_NO value that does not exist in the PRODUCT table before the import. It is therefore treated as a new row that needs to be inserted into the table.

The third record updates both the description and the price of an existing row.

The fourth record in the input file is inserted as a new row because the PROD_NO value does not match an existing row in the table, even though the PRICE and DESCRIPTION do match an existing row in the table.

Replace Mode

To replace existing data in the table, you can specify the REPLACE option. This option is not valid if the table for which data needs to be replaced has a primary key that is referenced by a foreign key in another table. This is to enforce referential integrity. Assume that the PRODUCT table did not have any referential dependencies and that it is desired to replace the existing data with data in a file named PRODUCT.IXF. The following would be specified with the IMPORT command:

```
IMPORT FROM PRODUCT.IXF OF IXF ... REPLACE INTO PRODUCT
```

Replace and Create Mode

When an IXF file is created using the EXPORT command, the table structure and definition is stored in it. The IMPORT utility can make use of the structure to recreate the table and its indexes. There are two ways to recreate the table. If the table already exists, it can be recreated by using the REPLACE_CREATE option. For example, if a table named Product exists and is to be recreated when importing new data, the IMPORT command can be invoked as follows. Note that this does not change the table definition — it only deletes all the data before doing the import. If the table does not exist and this option is used, the table will be created.

```
import from product.ixf of ixf ...
  replace_create into product ...
```

DB2 Note

If the PRODUCT table has a primary key defined that is referenced by another table's foreign key, the REPLACE_CREATE option can not be used.

If the PRODUCT table does not exist prior to the import, the CREATE option can be used to create it. For example:

```
import from product.ixf of ixf ...
  create into product ...
```

When creating a table in this way, a user can also specify the table space in which it should be created. Optionally, the index and long table spaces can also be specified. For example, assume the source table PRODUCT has two indexes and contains long data. This example has a new table named PRODUCT created in an existing table space named DMS1 of type DMS, its indexes in table space INDEXDMS1 of type DMS, and its long data in table space LONG1 of type DMS. To accomplish this, the following command would be issued on the command line:

```
import from product.ixf of ixf ...
  create into product in dms1
  index in indexdms1 long in long1
```

Forcing Intermediate Commits

By default, the IMPORT utility will only issue a commit at the end of a successful import. If the utility fails during its execution, all the changes to the table will be rolled back, so that it will seem as if the import never took place. The user may also direct the IMPORT utility to issue commit statements after a certain number of rows are successfully imported. If an error occurs during the import, only the changes since the last commit will be rolled back.

To specify the frequency of such intermediate commit statements, use the COMMITCOUNT option followed by the number of rows to be imported before a COMMIT is issued. (For more details on using IMPORT and committing records, please refer to the *DB2 Command Reference*.) For example, if a COMMIT is to be issued after every 50 records processed from the input file, the following command would be issued:

```
import ... commitcount 50 ...
```

Before and after the commit is executed, a message is written to the message file (if defined) or to the screen. The number of records read and committed are recorded in the message file. In the event of a failure, the DBA can find out how many records have been processed and which how many have not been imported by looking at the message file.

All changes to data are logged in the transaction log files, and they have to stay active for as long as they contain records of uncommitted transactions. The amount of available active log file space can be limited; therefore, an import of a large file may fail if the `COMMITCOUNT` option is not used. In the case of a failure, all the changes may be rolled back or an automatic commit done based on the type of `IMPORT` being done (see the *DB2 Command Reference* for details). It is highly recommended that this option be used when importing data.

Restarting a Failed Import

If an `IMPORT` operation that did not specify `COMMITCOUNT` fails, it can be restarted after fixing the problem that caused it to fail. The type of `IMPORT` being done will dictate the recovery needed.

If the `IMPORT` operation is invoked with the `COMMITCOUNT` option and subsequently fails, it can be restarted by using the `RESTARTCOUNT` option. This is used to tell the `IMPORT` utility to skip a certain number of records at the beginning of the file but to import the remainder.

For example, a file named `PRODUCT.DEL` was imported into a table named `Product` by making use of the `COMMITCOUNT 50` option. During the processing of the `IMPORT` command, the user accidently terminated the import session. This caused the import to fail half way through. The following extract is from the messages file (Figure 12–12):

```
SQL3109N The utility is beginning to load data from file
   "Product.del".
SQL3221W...Begin COMMIT WORK. Input Record Count = "50".
SQL3222W...COMMIT of any database changes was successful.
SQL3221W...Begin COMMIT WORK. Input Record Count = "100".
SQL3222W...COMMIT of any database changes was successful.
SQL3005N Processing was interrupted.
SQL3110N The utility has completed processing. "100" rows were
   read from the input file.
```

Figure 12–12 *IMPORT message file extract*

This shows that the first 100 records were committed. By restarting the `IMPORT` utility with the `RESTARTCOUNT 100` option, the first 100 records found in the input file are skipped.

Processing will continue starting with record 101 of the input file.

```
import from product.del of del ...
  commitcount 50 restartcount 100 ...
  into product ...
```

Importing ASC Files

When importing a file of type ASC, the IMPORT utility needs to be told where the column values start and end. The starting position and the ending position for all columns to be imported must be specified. This is done by making use of the METHOD L modifier. In Figure 12–13, an input file of type ASC is shown. It consists of three columns that match the type and length of the three columns of the PRODUCT table. The first is the PROD_NO column, which is of type CHAR(5); the second is the PRICE column of type DECIMAL(8,2); and the last is DESCRIPTION of type VARCHAR(10). All blanks will be represented with the character "~".

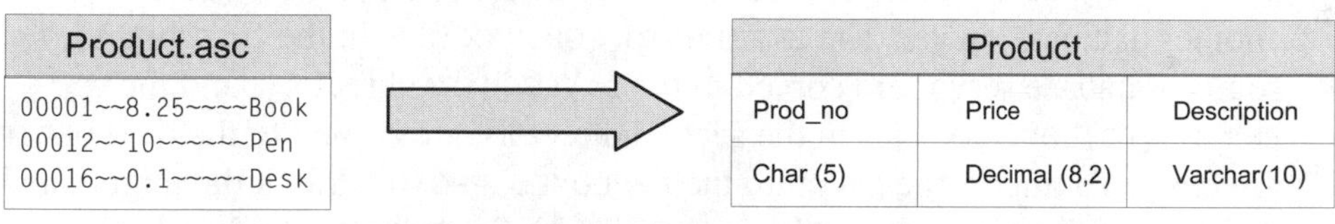

Figure 12–13 *Import using METHOD L*

Selecting Columns to Import

Sometimes a data file contains more columns than required by the target table. If the file is of type IXF or DEL, column numbers can be used to import it by specifying the METHOD P option. For example, a DEL file contains data in four columns, PROD_NO, PRICE, SUPPLIER, and DESCRIPTION. The target table PRODUCT only requires the columns PROD_NO, PRICE, and DESCRIPTION (columns 1, 2, and 4 of the input file). To import the data into the PRODUCT table, the following command can be used:

```
import from product.del of del ... method p (1,2,4) ...
  into product(prod_no,price,description) ...
```

Importing Large Objects

LOBs can be exported as part of the table data in the exported file or in separate files. If the LOB data is in the same file as the rest of the table data, it can be imported without any extra parameters being specified with the IMPORT utility.

If the LOB values are exported into separate files, the IMPORT utility needs two things: the directory or directories where the LOB files can be located and the file names of the LOB files.

Since the file names of the LOB files are stored in the exported file, the user does not need to specify them. To specify the source directory, use the LOBS FROM option followed by one or more directories that will serve as the source directories. Then specify the LOBSINFILE file-type modifier. If the LOBSINFILE modifier is not specified, the LOBS FROM option will be ignored.

For example, a table named EMP_PHOTO was exported to a file named EMP_PHOTO.DEL of type DEL, and its LOB files were exported with filenames EMP_PHOTO_LOB.XXX into two directories. The EMP_PHOTO.DEL file is copied to another database server. The EMP_PHOTO_LOB.XXX files in the first directory on the source database server are copied to the D:\LOBDIRA directory, and the EMP_PHOTO_LOB.XXX files in the second directory are copied to the D:\LOBDIRB directory. To import the data into the EMPLOYEE_PHOTO table in the target database, the following options should be specified with the IMPORT command.

```
import from emp_photo.del of del
  lobs from d:\lobdira\,d:\lobdirb\
  modified by lobsinfile ... into employee_photo ...
```

DB2 *Note*

When specifying the path, it must include the "\" character at the end for a Windows path or "/" when it is a UNIX path.

Importing Typed Tables

When importing data into a hierarchical structure, the user can specify the traversal order, which must match the order used when it was exported. It may be that the hierarchy structure at the destination differs from the one the data was exported from. For example, an extra table named TEMP_EMPLOYEES was created under the EMPLOYEE table as in our example. In this case, the default traversal order and the number and/or names of the tables are different than those in the original design. The user can compensate for these differences by specifying a list of subtables to import into.

For example, an exported file contains the data associated with the `Employee` and the `Manager` subtables only. The default traversal order can be used and imported with the command options:

```
import ... (employee,manager)
  in hierarchy starting employee ...
```

The traversal order could also be specified as:

```
import ... (employee,manager)
  in hierarchy (employee,manager)
```

If all the subtables named in the traversal order are to be imported, the `ALL TABLES` option could be used. In our example, this is only the `EMPLOYEE` and `MANAGER` tables:

```
import ... all tables in hierarchy (employee,manager) ...
```

To import all tables including the `EMPLOYEE` table using the default traversal order, issue the command as follows:

```
import ... all tables in hierarchy starting employee ...
```

DB2 *Note*

If one of the records in the compound group cannot be inserted, all will be rejected. Use this option only if you know the data to be correct.

Invoking Import Using the Control Center

The `IMPORT` utility can also be invoked from the Control Center. Select the target table and click the right mouse button, then select the **Import** option. Figure 12–14 shows the File tab of the Import Notebook. This next example will demonstrate the use of the Import Notebook.

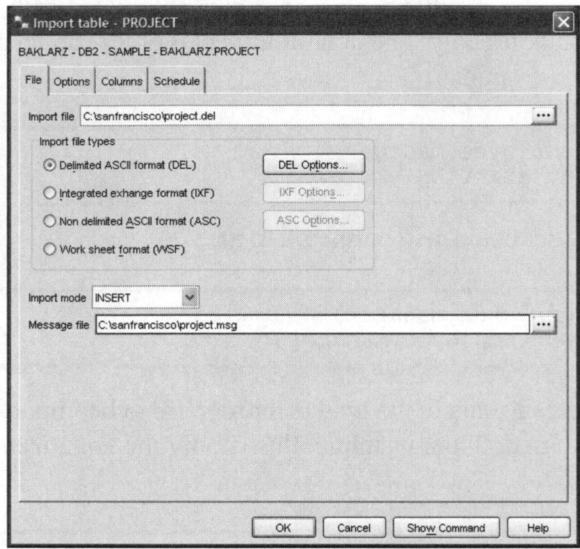

Figure 12–14 *Import GUI in the control center*

A file named `C:\SANFRANCISCO\PROJECT.DEL` will be inserted into an existing table named `PROJECT`. The table is empty, so all the data in the DEL file has to be inserted. The file `C:\SANFRANCISCO\PROJECT.MSG` is used as the import message file. Since a large number of records are to be imported, a `COMMITCOUNT` of 50 will be used to make sure the log files do not fill up. Finally, the `COMPOUND=5` file type modifier will cause five records to be grouped together when inserted to improve the performance of the import (Figure 12–15).

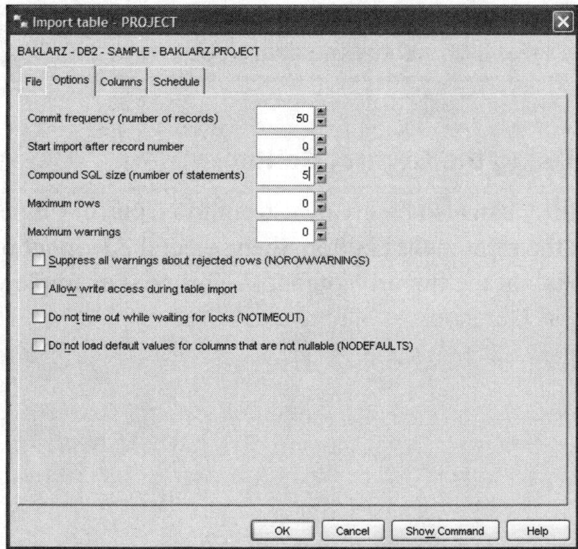

Figure 12–15 *Import Options*

Delimited Options

Specify delimiters for Delimited ASCII (DEL) file format.

Code page (CODEPAGE)

Delimiters

Column delimiter (COLDEL) <default>

Character string delimiter (CHARDEL) <default>

Decimal point character (DECPT) <default>

Insert an implied decimal point on decimal data (IMPLIEDDECIMAL)

Suppress recognition of character x'1A' as the end-of-file character (NOEOFCHAR)

Prioritize character string delimiter over record delimiter (DELPRIORITYCHAR)

Prefix positive decimal values with a blank (DECPLUSBLANK)

Preserve leading and trailing blanks in each field (KEEPBLANKS)

Suppress recognition of double character delimiters (NODOUBLEDEL)

Use ISO date format (DATESISO)

Use graphic code page for graphic or DBLOB data fields (USEGRAPHICCODEPAGE)

Custom date format (DATEFORMAT) <none>

Custom time format (TIMEFORMAT) <none>

Custom timestamp format (TIMESTAMPFORMAT) <none>

XML

Validate incoming documents Options

Whitespace handling: <default>

Code page: Unicode, or specified in document

OK Cancel Help

Figure 12–16 *Delimiter options*

Figure 12–16 shows the file-type-specific options for DEL files. The `DATESISO` option has been selected, since the file was produced with this option.

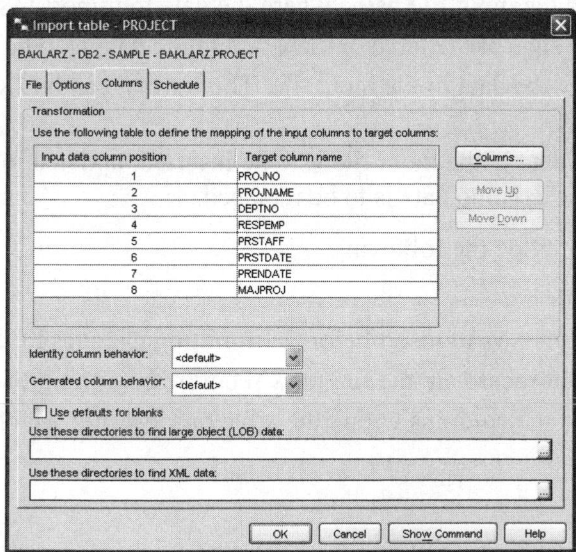

Figure 12–17 *Columns Tab*

The Columns tab (Figure 12–17) can be used to specify which columns are present in the source file. The user can also use it to specify the order of the columns and new names to use if the file is an IXF file and if the table is to be created with the `CREATE` or `REPLACE_CREATE` options.

If LOBs are to be imported from separate files, fill in the field at the bottom of this panel.

Once all the information is captured in the relevant panels, the user may opt to run the `IMPORT` command by clicking on the **OK** button. Alternatively, the user may choose to look at the command that is to be executed. Figure 12–18 shows the command generated to import the file into the `PROJECT` table. The user may also choose to save the command to a script file to be executed at a later time.

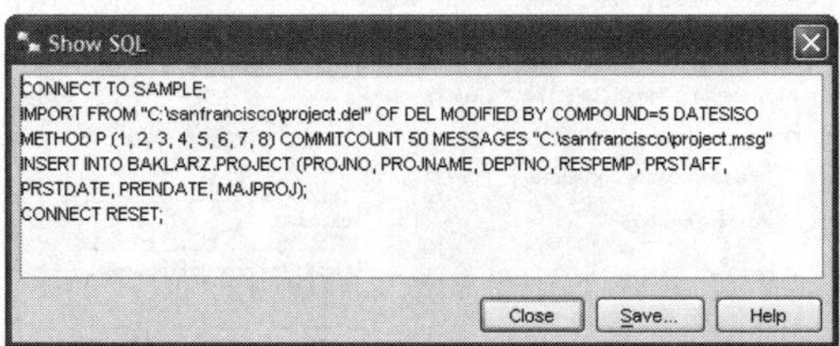

Figure 12–18 *The IMPORT command generated*

IMPORT Considerations

The following information is required when importing data into a table or view:

- The path and the input file name where the data to import is stored.
- The name or alias of the table or view where the data is to be imported.
- The format of the data in the input file. This format can be IXF, DEL, ASC, or WSF.
- Whether the data in the input file is to be inserted, updated into the table, or view, or if the existing data is to be replaced.

You may also provide the following:

- A message file
- The number of rows to insert before committing changes to the table
- The number of records in the file to skip before beginning the import
- The names of the columns within the table or view into which the data is inserted

DB2 Note

The `IMPORT` utility will issue a `COMMIT` or a `ROLLBACK`, depending on the success or failure of the import.

Examples of Using EXPORT and IMPORT

The first example shows how to export information from the `PRODUCT` table in the `SALES` database. Export to the file `product.ixf` with the output in IXF format:

```
export to product.ixf of ixf messages product.msg
  select * from products
```

You must be connected to the database before you issue the command. To import the data into another database and create a table named `PRODS` in an existing table space named `SMS1`, the following command can be used:

```
import from product.ixf of ixf
  commitcount 50 messages product.msg
  create into prods in sms1
```

Note the use of the `COMMITCOUNT` option. This may prevent the log files from filling up.

In this second example, export all the data in a table hierarchy defined in the `SALES` database. The table hierarchy is defined as shown in Figure 12–19:

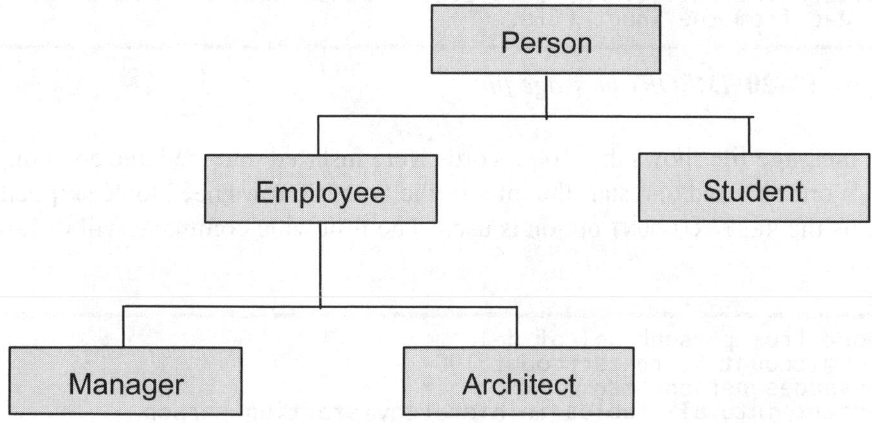

Figure 12–19 *Table hierarchy of the Sales database*

Export the data to a DEL file named PERSONH.DEL:

```
export to personh.del of del messages personh.msg
  hierarchy starting person
```

A portion of the output file looks like this:

```
2,"y","James         ","Kirk          ",35,"000054",90000,"b",,,,
2,"z","Leonard       ","McCoy         ",45,"000145",120000,"b",,,,
2,"A","Hikaru        ","Sulu          ",31,"000167",11000,"b",,,,
2,"B","Pavel         ","Chkalov       ",28,"000170",90000,"b",,,,
2,"C","Montgomery    ","Scott         ",42,"000301",100000,"b",,,,
```

Import the PERSONH.DEL file into the entire PERSON hierarchy. Assuming all the tables in the hierarchy are empty, use the INSERT command option. The command to issue is:

```
import from personh.del of del
  commitcount 50 messages personh.msg
  insert into all tables in hierarchy starting person
```

Assume the import failed. The message file shows the following entries (Figure 12–20):

```
SQL3109N The utility is beginning to load data from file
  "personh.del".
SQL3221W...Begin COMMIT WORK. Input Record Count = "50".
SQL3222W...COMMIT of any database changes was successful.
SQL3221W...Begin COMMIT WORK. Input Record Count = "100".
SQL3222W...COMMIT of any database changes was successful.
SQL3005N Processing was interrupted.
SQL3110N The utility has completed processing. "100" rows were
   read from the input file.
```

Figure 12–20 *IMPORT message file*

The message file shows that 100 records were inserted into the table and committed. If one selected to restart the import, the first 100 rows need to be skipped. To do this the RESTARTCOUNT option is used. The following command will restart the import:

```
import from personh.del of del
  commitcount 50 restartcount 100
  messages personh.msg
  insert into all tables in hierarchy starting person
```

The Load Utility

The LOAD utility, like the IMPORT utility, moves data supplied in an input file into a target table. Unlike the IMPORT utility, the target table *must* exist within the database prior to the start of the load process. The target table may be a new table that was created just before the load or an existing table in which data will be added to or replaced. Indexes on the table may or may not already exist. The load process does not create new indexes – it only maintains indexes that are already defined on the table.

To the DBA, the most important difference between the IMPORT and LOAD utilities relates to performance. The IMPORT utility inserts the data one row at a time. Each row inserted has to be checked for compliance with constraints (such as foreign key constraints or table check constraints). Changes are also logged in the log files.

The LOAD utility will insert data into a table much faster than will the IMPORT utility, because instead of inserting one row at a time, the LOAD utility will use the rows read from the input file to build pages which are then written directly into the database. Existing indexes (including primary keys or unique indexes) may be rebuilt after the data pages are inserted (rebuilt either totally or partially based on newly added data), and finally all the duplicate rows that do not comply with unique or primary key constraints are deleted from the table. During the load operation, individual records loaded are not logged in the log files.

Since the LOAD utility changes are not logged, it cannot be rolled forward by using the log files. However, the LOAD utility can use a copy of the source data (a load copy), so it can be reloaded if required.

Use of the LOAD utility requires either SYSADM, DBADM, or LOAD authority on the database with INSERT privilege on the table. The DELETE privilege on the table is also required when REPLACE mode is selected, TERMINATE mode (to terminate a previous load replace operation), or RESTART mode (to restart a previous load replace operation).

Before using the LOAD utility, the DBA must understand how it works to exploit its performance benefits and to avoid any problems that may occur if it is used incorrectly.

DB2 *Note*

Load operations now take place at the table level. This means that the load utility no longer requires exclusive access to the entire table space, and concurrent access to other table objects in the same table space is possible during a load operation.

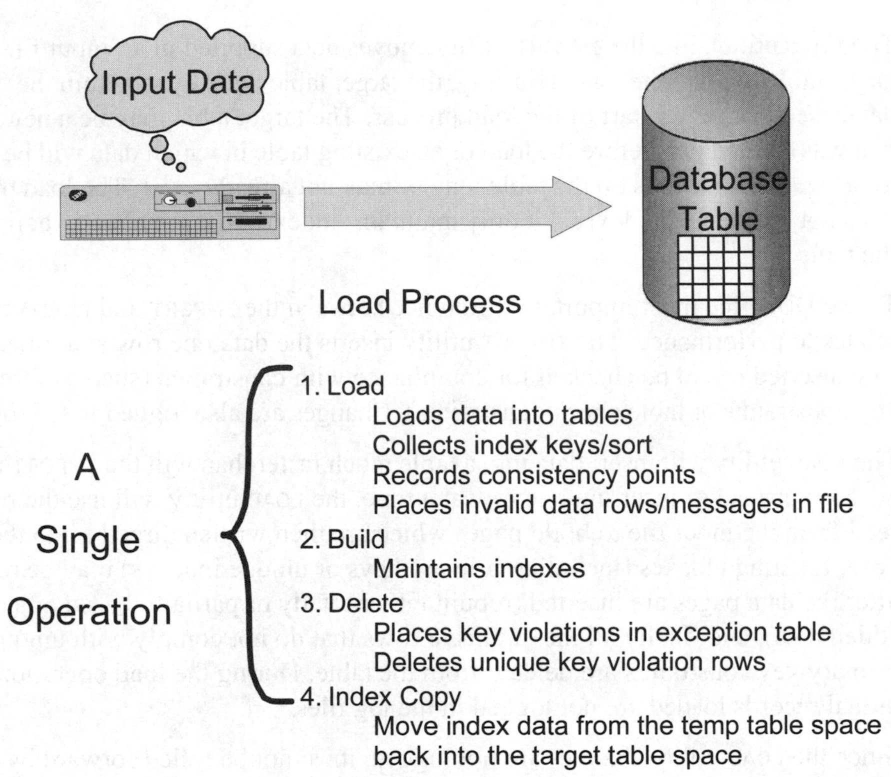

Figure 12–21 *Phases of LOAD*

The phases of the LOAD utility as shown in Figure 12–21 will now be examined.

1. *Load* phase — Two things happen during the load phase: Data is stored in the table, and index keys are collected and sorted.

   When running the LOAD utility the DBA can specify how often it should generate points of consistency. A consistency point serves as a checkpoint to the LOAD utility. If the LOAD is interrupted during its execution, it can be restarted and will continue from the last consistency point. As part of taking a consistency point, the LOAD utility will write a message to the message file stating how many records have been loaded. This can then be used by the DBA to monitor the progress of the LOAD utility.

2. *Build* phase — During the build phase, indexes are created based on the index keys collected in the load phase. If a failure occurs during the build phase and the LOAD utility is restarted (with the RESTART option), it will restart from the beginning of the build phase.

3. *Delete* Phase — During the delete phase, all rows that have violated a unique or primary key constraint are deleted and copied to an exception table (if it is specified when the LOAD utility is invoked). Only these two constraint types are checked. If a failure occurs during the delete phase and the LOAD utility is restarted, it will do so from the beginning of the delete phase; however, if an online LOAD was invoked or COPY YES was specified, then restart will occur from the BUILD phase if a failure occurs here.

   When input rows are rejected, messages are generated in the message file.

4. *Index Copy* Phase — If a system temporary table space was specified for index creation during a load operation and the READ ACCESS option selected, this index data will be copied from the system temporary table space to the original table space.

All phases of the load process are part of one operation that is complete only after all four phases complete successfully. The LOAD utility will generate messages during the progress of each phase. Should a failure occur during one of the phases, these messages can assist the DBA in problem analysis and resolution.

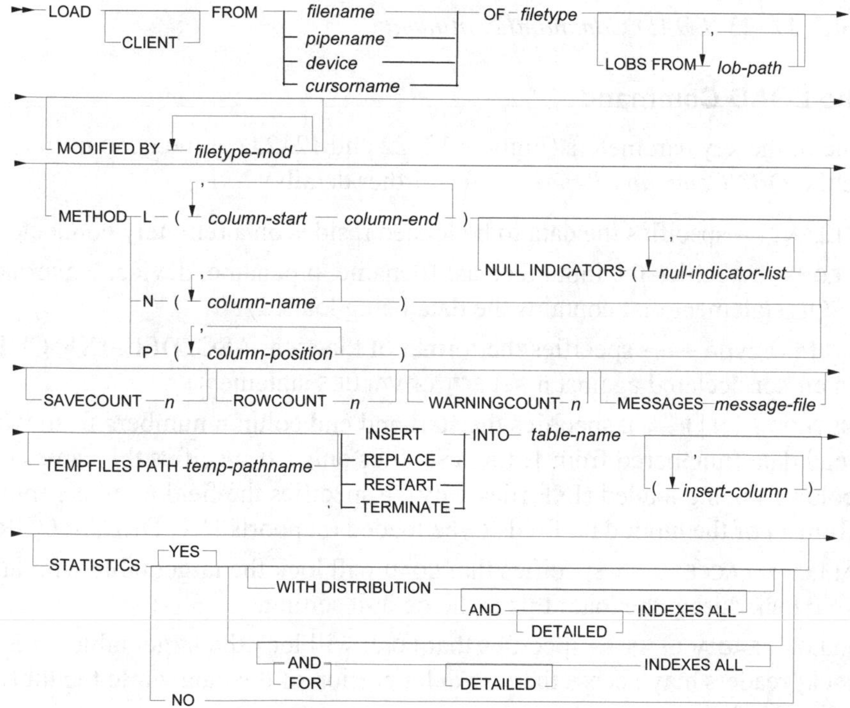

Figure 12–22 *LOAD Command*

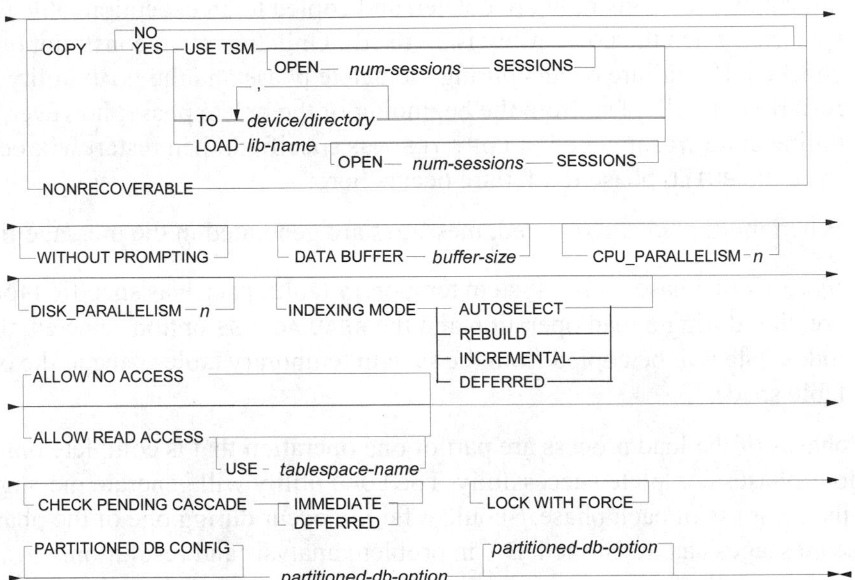

Figure 12–23 *LOAD Command continued*

Using the LOAD Command

Some of the key parameters (Figures 12–22 and 12–23) of the LOAD utility are here (see the *DB2 Command Reference* for further details):

- CLIENT — specifies the data to be loaded resides on a remotely connected client.
- FROM — specifies the input data as: filename, pipename, device, cursorname (SQL statement that contains the data being loaded).
- OF filetype —— specifies the format of the data: ASC, DEL, IXF, CURSOR (a cursor declared against a SELECT or VALUES statement).
- METHOD L | N | P — L specifies the start and end column numbers from which to load data (numbered from 1, for ASC files only). N specifies the names of the columns being loaded (IXF files only). P specifies the field numbers (numbered from 1) of the input data fields to be loaded (supports IXF, DEL, or CURSOR).
- ALLOW NO ACCESS — specifies that LOAD will lock the target table with an exclusive lock during the load; this is the default setting.
- ALLOW READ ACCESS — specifies that LOAD will lock the target table with a share lock; readers may access the non-delta portion of the data while the table is being loaded.

DB2 Note

The LOAD utility has the ability to query preexisting data in a table while new data is being loaded. You can do this by specifying the READ ACCESS option of the LOAD command.

Insert Mode

By using the INSERT option with the LOAD command, all data in the input file will be inserted as new data into an existing table. For example, to load the table named PRODUCT by inserting the data contained in PRODUCT.IXF, the user would specify the following command:

```
load from product.ixf of ixf ... insert into product ...
```

Replace Mode

By using the REPLACE option, the LOAD utility will delete all the data in an existing table before loading the new data. It will not recreate the table. For example, if a file named PRODUCT.IXF contains data that should replace the data in an existing table named PRODUCT, the user would use the following command:

```
load from product.ixf of ixf ... replace into product ...
```

Terminate Mode

Sometimes it is necessary to terminate a load process; for example, the user is loading the wrong file, or the LOAD utility was invoked with the wrong options. To terminate the interrupted load operation, the user has to invoke the LOAD utility again, using the exact options it was invoked with the first time, but replacing the INSERT or REPLACE option with the TERMINATE option. For example, if the LOAD utility was invoked with the following options and then interrupted:

```
load from product.del of del
  insert into product
```

The load operation can be terminated by replacing the INSERT option with TERMINATE:

```
load from product.del of del
  terminate into product
```

In the case of the original load being invoked with the INSERT option, all the new records loaded into the table will be deleted, and the state of the table will be the same as it was before the LOAD utility was invoked.

DB2 *Note*

The LOCK WITH FORCE option has been introduced in this release. It allows you to force applications to release the locks they have on a table, allowing the load operation to proceed and to acquire the locks it needs.

If the original load was invoked with the REPLACE command option, all the records in the table, old and new, will be deleted.

Restart Mode

If the load operation should fail, the DBA should look at the message file and error logs to determine the reason for the failure. Once the problem has been identified and fixed, the user can than reinvoke the LOAD utility with the RESTART command option. Care should be taken to reinvoke it with the same options as the first invocation, replacing the INSERT or REPLACE command option with the RESTART command option.

If the load failed during the load phase and consistency points were generated, it will restart the load phase from the last consistency point.

If the load failed in the build or delete phases, it will restart from the beginning of the phase in question (with the exception of an online load or if COPY YES was specified, restart will occur at the build phase even if failure occurs during the delete phase).

Cursor File Type

By specifying the CURSOR file type when using the LOAD command, you can load the results of an SQL query directly into a target table without creating an intermediate exported file. By referencing a nickname within the SQL query, the LOAD utility can also load data from another database in a single step.

To execute a load from cursor operation from the CLP, a cursor must first be declared against an SQL query. Once this is done, you can issue the LOAD command using the declared cursor's name as the cursorname and CURSOR as the file type.

```
declare mycurs cursor for select one,two,three from abc.table1
load from mycurs of cursor insert into abc.table2
```

In the above example, the column names of each table are the same, however, the source column types of the SQL query do not need to be identical to their target column types, although they do have to be compatible.

Generated Columns

The load utility can be used to load data into a table containing (non-identity) generated columns. The column values will be generated by this utility. This means that following a load operation, the target table will not be left in check pending state if the only constraints on the table are generated column constraints.

The GENERATEDMISSING modifier makes loading a table with generated columns more convenient if the input data file does not contain any values (not even nulls) for all generated columns present in the table.

```
load from load.del modified by generatedmissing
  replace into table1
```

The GENERATEDIGNORE modifier is in some ways the opposite of the GENERATED-MISSING modifier: it indicates to the load utility that even though the input data file contains data for all generated columns present in the target table, the data should be ignored, and the computed values should be loaded into each generated column.

Both modifiers simplify the syntax of the load operation especially if many columns are involved. The GENERATEDOVERRIDE modifier is used for loading user-supplied values into a table with generated columns. This can be quite useful when migrating data from another database system, or when loading a table from data that was recovered using the RECOVER DROPPED TABLE option of the ROLLFORWARD DATABASE command. When this modifier is used, any rows with no data (or null data) for non-nullable generated columns are rejected (SQL3116W).

Generating Consistency Points

The user may choose to generate consistency points during the load operation. During the generation of consistency points, all internal buffers are flushed to disk. A record is also written to the message file. These consistency points are used to monitor the progress of the LOAD utility and to restart a failed load.

DB2 Note

The generation of a consistency point has some performance overhead.

To specify the frequency with which the consistency points should be generated, use the SAVECOUNT command option followed by the number of rows to load between consistency points. For example, if roughly 500 rows should be loaded between consistency points, the following option should be used with the LOAD command:

```
load from ... savecount 500 ...
```

Although the user specifies the number of rows with this option, it is converted internally to the number of pages on which that number of rows will fit. It is then rounded up to the nearest extent.

Limiting the Number of Rows to Load

Sometimes the DBA may want to load only part of the data file, for example, to test the load options without loading all the data. When invoking the LOAD utility, the ROWCOUNT command option can be used to specify the number of records to load from the beginning of the file.

```
load from ... rowcount 10000 ...
```

Forcing the Load to Fail on Warnings

In some cases, all the rows in the input file *must* be loaded into the target table, for example, an account table at a bank. If even a single record is not loaded correctly, this could cause a problem. To specify that the load should fail if one or more warnings are generated, use the following option when invoking the LOAD utility:

```
load from ... warningcount 1 ...
```

If the load fails because of the WARNINGCOUNT option, it can be restarted by using the RESTART option.

Preventing Generation of Warning Messages

If the user is not interested in warning messages about rejected rows, he can suppress them by using the NOROWWARNINGS file type modifier to specify that they should not be recorded. This can enhance the performance of the LOAD utility if large amounts of row warning messages would otherwise be generated.

```
load from ... modified by norowwarnings ...
```

Specifying a File for Rejected Rows

Rows that are not formatted correctly may be rejected by the LOAD utility and not be loaded. For example, if a row has a character value where the load expects a numeric or date value, it will not be loaded. These rows can be placed separately, from the other records, in a file by specifying the DUMPFILE file type modifier. This option is only valid for DEL and ASC filetypes. For example:

```
load from ... of del ... modified by dumpfile=c:\dump.del ...
```


Using an Exception Table

A user-defined exception table can be used to store rows that do not comply with unique or primary key constraints. Using an exception table is an optional parameter of the LOAD command. However, if an exception table is not specified with the LOAD utility, any rows that violate unique constraints will be discarded without any chance of recovering or altering them.

The exception table definition is very similar to the target table definition. The first n columns match exactly the column names and data types of the target table. The $n + 1$ column is an optional column, which if defined must be of data type TIMESTAMP. The $n + 2$ column is also an optional column. It can only be created if the TIMESTAMP column $n + 1$ precedes it. It should be defined as type CLOB of 32 KB or larger. This is to be used as a message column. It stores information about the particular constraint that caused the rejection of the row (Figure 12–24).

DB2 *Note*

The LOAD exception table is defined without any constraints or triggers.

Target Table

Name CHAR(20)	Age INT	Serial_num CHAR(3)	Salary INT	Department CHAR(25)
George	26	105	30000	Toy
Paul	31	83	45000	Shoe
Kelly	28	214	39000	Shoe
Katrina	35	251	55000	Toy
Chloe	10	317	85000	Shoe

Valid exception table 1

Name CHAR(20)	Age INT	Serial_num CHAR(3)	Salary INT	Department CHAR(25)	Timestamp TIMESTAMP

Valid exception table 2

Name CHAR(20)	Age INT	Serial_num CHAR(3)	Salary INT	Department CHAR(25)	Timestamp TIMESTAMP	Description CLOB(32k)

Figure 12–24 *Exception table definition*

Indexing Modes

During the build phase, the indexes that existed prior to the load can be rebuilt. The user can define the method to be used for the rebuild. There are four options available:

- *Rebuild* — This option will force all indexes to be recreated independent of the type of load, INSERT or REPLACE.
- *Incremental* — This will allow the LOAD utility to use the data in the existing indexes and add the new data to them when the load is invoked with the INSERT option. This is useful if the amount of data loaded into the table is small compared with the existing data.
- *Deferred* — This option will prevent the LOAD utility from rebuilding indexes; instead, the indexes will be flagged as needing a refresh. They will subsequently be rebuilt upon the first access to the table or when the database is restarted. The value specified for the INDEXREC parameter in the database configuration file is used to determine when the indexes are recreated. This option is not supported for tables that have a primary key index or unique indexes defined, since they need to be used for checking for duplicates.
- *Autoselect* — Will allow the LOAD utility to choose between the REBUILD and INCREMENTAL options.

For example, if a table named Product has two indexes defined and no unique or primary key constraints, and the LOAD utility is used to replace all existing data, the following options specified with the LOAD command will allow the index build to be deferred:

```
load from ... indexing mode deferred ...
  replace into product ...
```

If the DBA needs to add some data to the PRODUCT table immediately after the load completes, the following options can be used to rebuild the indexes:

```
load from ... indexing mode rebuild ...
  insert into product ...
```

When performing consecutive load operations on the same table, the index build should be deferred until the last LOAD is performed on the table.

Leaving Free Space

The LOAD utility provides the functionality to leave some free space on the pages created during the load for both index and data pages. It can also format some additional pages and leave them empty. This space can then be used for subsequent inserts into the table or indexes. The file type modifiers used to do this are:

- PAGEFREESPACE — Indicates the percentage free space to leave at the end of each data page
- INDEXFREESPACE — Indicates the percentage free space to leave at the end of each index page
- TOTALFREESPACE — Indicates the number of empty pages to be added to the table as a percentage of the total number of used pages

For example, if you want to load a table named PERSON by replacing all the existing data, leaving 20% of each data page empty, 20% of each index page empty, and ensuring that 15% of the total number of used pages are to be empty pages at the end of the table, use the following options:

```
load from ... modified by pagefreespace 20
  indexfreespace 20 totalfreespace 15 ...
  into person ...
```

Generating Statistics

The LOAD utility can be used to generate statistics associated with the table and or indexes. These statistics are used by the optimizer to determine the most efficient way in which an SQL statement should be executed. The user can also specify how detailed the statistics should be for tables and/or indexes if they use the REPLACE load option. Table 12–3 shows the different combinations of statistics that can be generated for tables and indexes.

Table 12–3 *Load – Generating Statistics*

	Max Table Stats	Min Table Stats	No Table Stats
Max Index Stats	YES WITH DISTRIBUTION AND DETAILED INDEXES ALL	YES AND DETAILED INDEXES ALL	YES FOR DETAILED INDEXES ALL
Min Index Stats	YES WITH DISTRIBUTION AND INDEXES ALL	YES AND INDEXES ALL	YES FOR INDEXES ALL
No Index Stats	YES WITH DISTRIBUTION	YES	NO

For example, if you require the maximum statistics to be generated for both indexes and the associated table, use the following command:

```
load from ... statistics yes with distribution and
  detailed indexes all ...
```

If minimal statistics need to be generated for both indexes and the associated table, use the following options:

```
load from ... statistics yes and indexes all ...
```

For maximum statistics on the table only:

```
load from ... statistics yes with distribution ...
```

If no statistics should be generated, use the following option:

```
load from ... statistics no ...
```

Statistical Profiles

The LOAD command can include a RUNSTATS profile instead of specifying what statistics to use during the load command. The RUNSTATS utility provides an option to register and use a statistics profile, which is a set of options that specify which statistics are to be collected on a particular table. This feature simplifies statistics collection by allowing you to store the options that you specify when you issue the RUNSTATS or LOAD command so that you can collect the same statistics repeatedly on a table without having to re-type the command options.

A statistics profile can be created without actually collecting statistics. For example, the following command registers a profile against the TRANSACTIONS table:

```
runstats on table baklarz.transactions for indexes all
  tablesample system(10) set profile only
```

The SET PROFILE ONLY option is used to register the profile. To query the system to determine which profiles are available, the following SQL will return the RUNSTATS command used as part of the SET PROFILE ONLY option.

```
select statistics_profile from sysibm.systables
  where name = 'TRANSACTIONS'
```

To use this profile as part of a LOAD command, use STATISTICS USE PROFILE instead of explicitly stating the statistics to use.

Specifying a Temporary Directory

By default, the LOAD utility uses a subdirectory in the directory where the database is created to store temporary files. These files are deleted after successful completion of the LOAD utility. The user may specify a directory to use as the temporary directory. Specifying a directory on a separate device where the data is read from and written to may increase the performance of the LOAD utility.

```
load from ... tempfiles path e:\tempdir ...
```

DB2 *Note*

Do not modify or tamper with these temporary files! It could cause the load to fail and put the database in jeopardy.

Loading Large Object Files

The same considerations that apply to the IMPORT utility apply to the LOAD utility. See "Importing Large Objects" on page 724. The parameter names and specification are also the same.

Performance Considerations

The LOAD utility has a number of performance-related options. Some of these are:

- COPY YES/NO
- NONRECOVERABLE
- FASTPARSE
- ANYORDER
- DATA BUFFER
- CPU_PARALLELISM
- DISK_PARALLELISM

These options are now examined in more detail.

COPY Yes/No and NONRECOVERABLE

During the load process, no logging of changes is done. This means that a user cannot perform roll-forward recovery for the load operation using the RESTORE and ROLLFORWARD commands. The user can choose to make the table recoverable but at the expense of performance.

DB2 *Note*

When the COPY NO option is specified for a recoverable database, the table space will be placed in the backup pending table space state when the load operation begins.

The LOAD utility provides three ways in which the performance and recoverability can be balanced. The options are:

- *Nonrecoverable* — Specifies that the load operation is to be marked as nonrecoverable and that it will not be possible to recover it by a subsequent roll forward action. The rollforward utility will skip the transaction and will mark the table into which data was being loaded as "invalid." The utility will also ignore any subsequent transactions against that table. After the roll forward operation is completed, such a table can only be dropped or restored from a backup (full or table space) taken after a commit point following the completion of the nonrecoverable load operation. With this option, table spaces are not put in backup pending state following the load operation, and a copy of the loaded data does not have to be made during the load operation. A nonrecoverable load is useful when loading large read-only tables. You could also load multiple tables into a table space with the nonrecoverable option. Then, once the last table has been loaded, you can back up the database or the table spaces in which the table, its indexes, and long data reside.

- *Copy No* — (Default) If this option is specified and archival logging is enabled for the database, the table space in which the table resides will be placed in backup-pending state after the load. The table space will not be accessible for write operations until a database or table space backup is made. Since the LOAD utility's changes to the data are not logged, taking a backup of the table space or database is required to be able to recover it in the event of damage after the load operation has completed.
- *Copy Yes* — If YES is specified for the COPY option and archival logging is enabled for the database, a copy of the changes caused by the load process will be saved to tape, directory, or TSM server, and the table spaces will not be left in backup-pending state. This option does not apply to a database that uses circular logging and is thus nonrecoverable. If database damage occurs just after the load operation has completed, an existing backup can be restored and rolled forward (assuming archival logging is used).

```
load from ... copy yes to tsm ...
```

FASTPARSE

This is a file type modifier that can be used to reduce the amount of data checking. It should only be used if the data is known to be correct. Since IXF files can only contain the data in the correct format, this parameter may not improve the performance of the LOAD when IXF file types are used. If DEL or ASC files are used, the LOAD utility may perform faster.

```
load from ... modified by fastparse ...
```

ANYORDER

If the SAVECOUNT option is not used, this parameter will allow the LOAD utility to load the data into the table without having to respect the order in which the data appears in the input file. If the data in the input file is ordered according to a clustering index, then this option may not be a very good choice because it will affect the performance of a subsequent REORG operation. When used, this file type modifier may improve the performance of the LOAD utility, particularly in SMP systems (and the CPU_PARALLELISM option is > 1).

```
load from ... modified by anyorder ...
```

DATA BUFFER

Specifies the amount of memory in 4 KB pages allocated from the Utility Heap to be used as an internal load buffer. If not specified, a calculated default will be used that takes into consideration the size allocated in the Utility heap and the characteristics of the table being loaded. Specifying a large buffer size may improve the performance of the load.

```
load from ... modified by data buffer 5000 ...
```

CPU_PARALLELISM

This option should be used on SMP machines to indicate how many processes or threads should be used to parse, convert, or format the data. If no value is specified, a default is calculated based on the number of CPUs on the machine. The data is loaded using the order that it appears in the input file. Choosing the correct value may considerably improve the performance of the LOAD utility if it runs on an SMP machine.

```
load from ... modified by cpu_parallelism ...
```

DISK_PARALLELISM

This option specifies the number of processes or threads to use for writing data to disk. The default value is calculated based on the number of containers specified for all the table spaces in which objects for the table are stored and other table characteristics.

```
load from ... disk_parallelism 3 ...
```

Other Options

Other LOAD options and file type modifiers that may affect the performance include:

- *Norowwarnings* — If specified, this will usually improve the performance.
- *Savecount* — The larger amount of records loaded before a consistency point, the better for performance.
- *Statistics* — The less statistics generated, the better the performance. However, the combined runtime for the LOAD and the RUNSTATS utilities is very often longer than using the LOAD utility to generate the statistics.

Using the Load Utility from the Control Center

You run the LOAD utility in much the same way as the IMPORT and EXPORT utilities. Use the Control Center and select the target table to be loaded. Click the right mouse button and select the **Load** option (Figure 12–25).

Once invoked, the user can specify all the options available on the command line. The use of the Control Center approach will be demonstrated by an example.

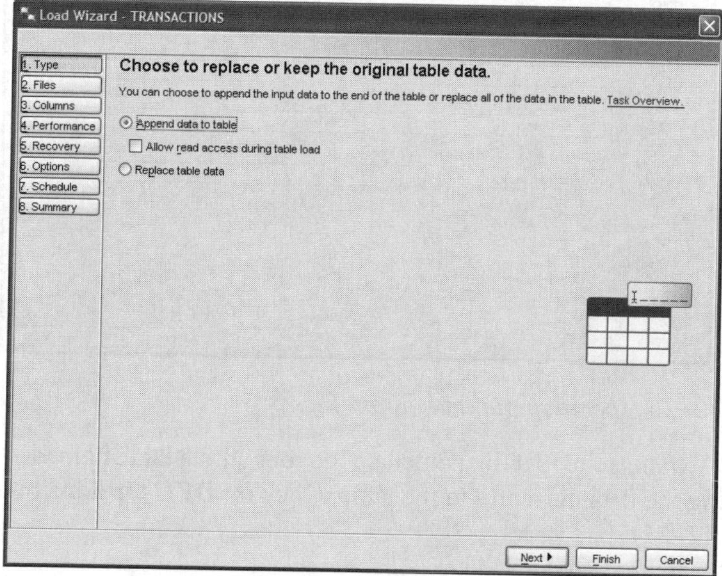

Figure 12–25 *Choose to replace or keep the original table data*

The DBA selects to append to, or replace existing data (Figure 12–26). Click **Next**.

Load Wizard - TRANSACTIONS
1. Type
2. Files
3. Columns
4. Performance
5. Recovery
6. Options
7. Schedule
8. Summary
Specify input and output files.
Most load operations will have at least one input or output file. Other minor file specifications can be found on the 'Options' page.
Input file format
Delimited Text (DEL)
DEL Options
Input file location
Server (BAKLARZ)
Remote host
Full path and file name of user exit program on database server
Full path and file name of input files
C:\sanjose\sales.del
Full path and file name to store progress messages:
C:\sanjose\sanjose.msg
Back
Next
Finish
Cancel

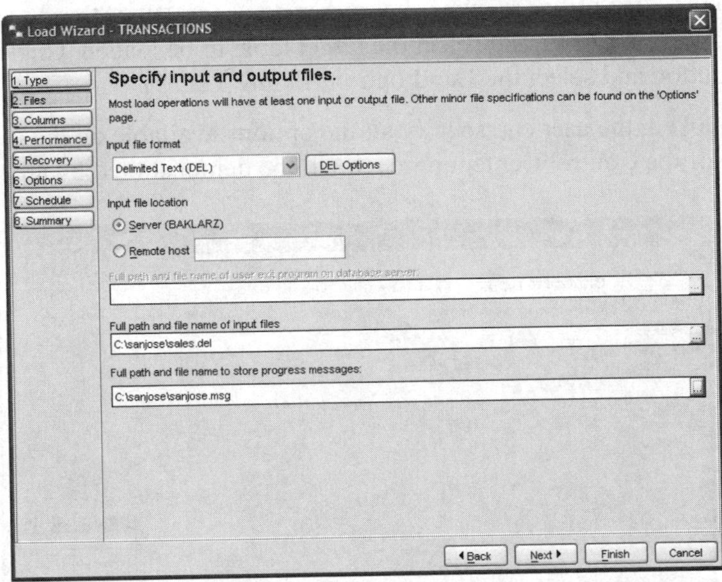

Figure 12–26 *Specify input and output files*

The DBA wants to load a file named `sales.del` into a table named `TRANSACTIONS`, appending the data currently in the table. Click on **DEL Options** button (Figure 12–27).

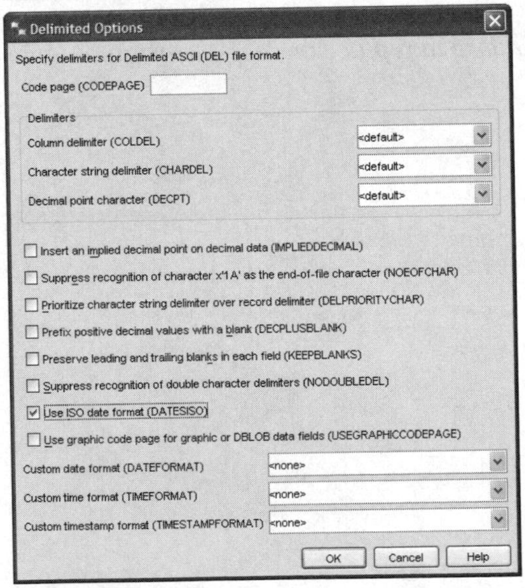

Delimited Options
Specify delimiters for Delimited ASCII (DEL) file format.
Code page (CODEPAGE)
Delimiters
Column delimiter (COLDEL)
<default>
Character string delimiter (CHARDEL)
<default>
Decimal point character (DECPT)
<default>
Insert an implied decimal point on decimal data (IMPLIEDDECIMAL)
Suppress recognition of character x'1A' as the end-of-file character (NOEOFCHAR)
Prioritize character string delimiter over record delimiter (DELPRIORITYCHAR)
Prefix positive decimal values with a blank (DECPLUSBLANK)
Preserve leading and trailing blanks in each field (KEEPBLANKS)
Suppress recognition of double character delimiters (NODOUBLEDEL)
Use ISO date format (DATESISO)
Use graphic code page for graphic or DBLOB data fields (USEGRAPHICCODEPAGE)
Custom date format (DATEFORMAT)
<none>
Custom time format (TIMEFORMAT)
<none>
Custom timestamp format (TIMESTAMPFORMAT)
<none>
OK
Cancel
Help

Figure 12–27 *Delimited Options*

Figure 12–27 shows the options that were selected. Click **OK**.

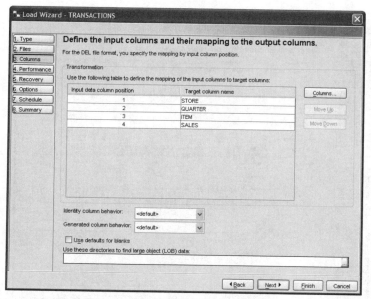

Figure 12–28 *Load from Control Center — Columns tab*

The Columns tab as shown in Figure 12–28 is used to specify whether and how you want the columns from the data files loaded into the table columns.

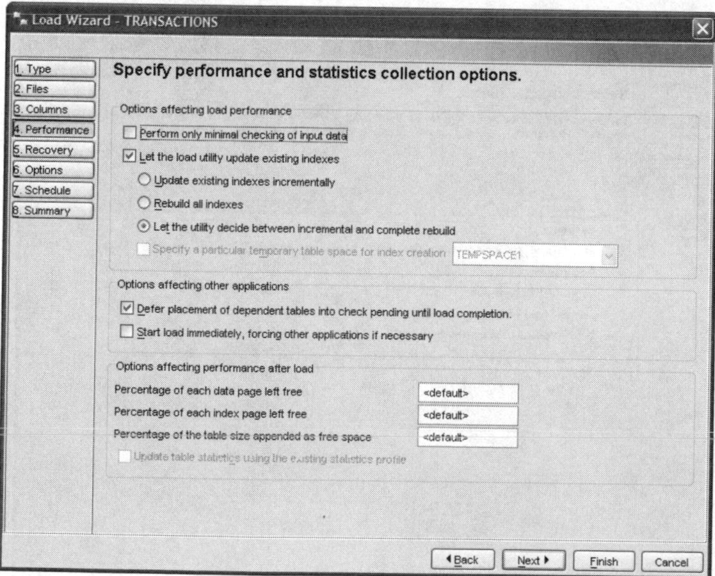

Figure 12–29 *Specify performance and statistics collection options*

The DBA is given a number of parameters that can affect the performance of the LOAD operation (Figure 12–29). Click **Next**.

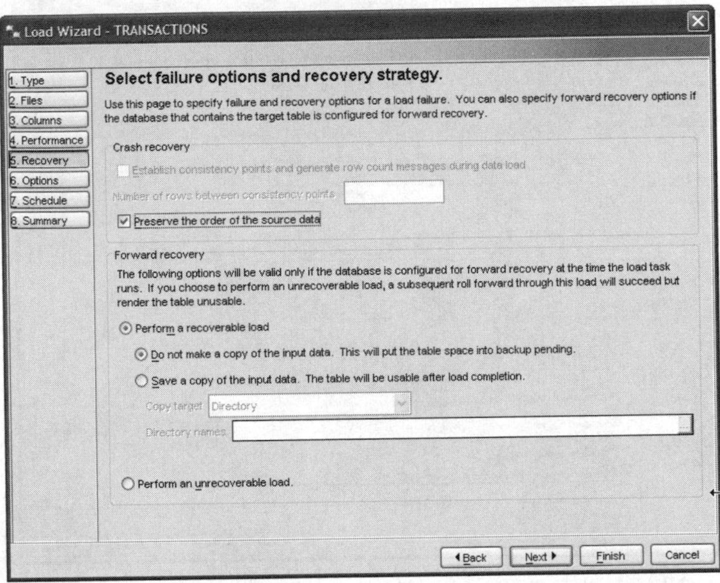

Figure 12–30 *Select failure options and recovery strategy*

The DBA is given a number of options on what actions should take if the load should not complete normally (Figure 12–30). Click **Next**.

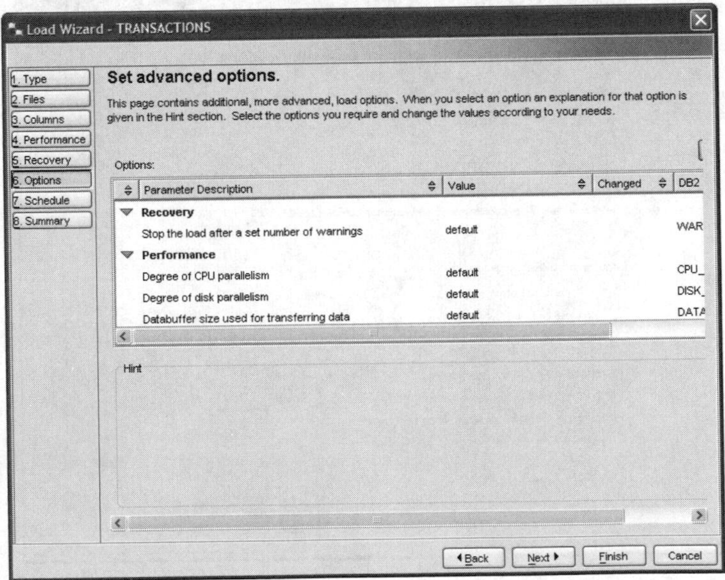

Figure 12–31 *Set advanced options*

Additional options are provided here with respect to recovery, performance, and other miscellaneous parameters. Values can be updated from this panel (Figure 12–31). Click **Next**.

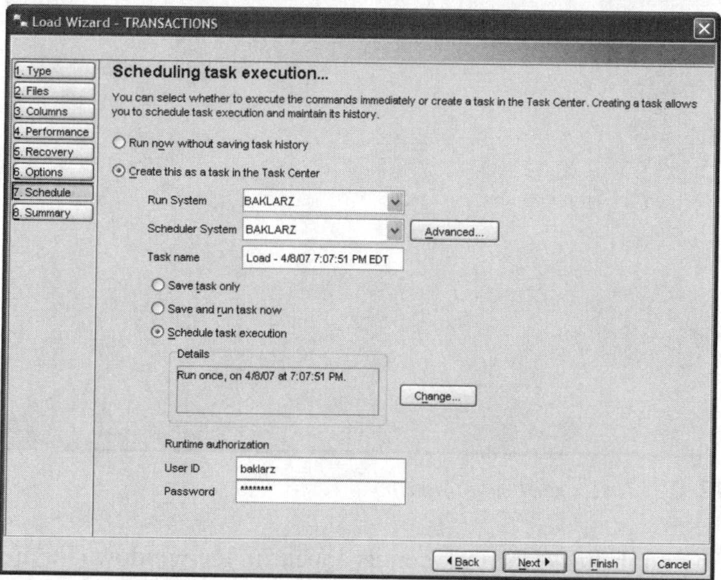

Figure 12–32 *Scheduling task execution*

The DBA is given the option to execute the load now or to schedule it at a later time with the use of the Task Center (Figure 12–32). Enter an authorized id and password, click **Next**.

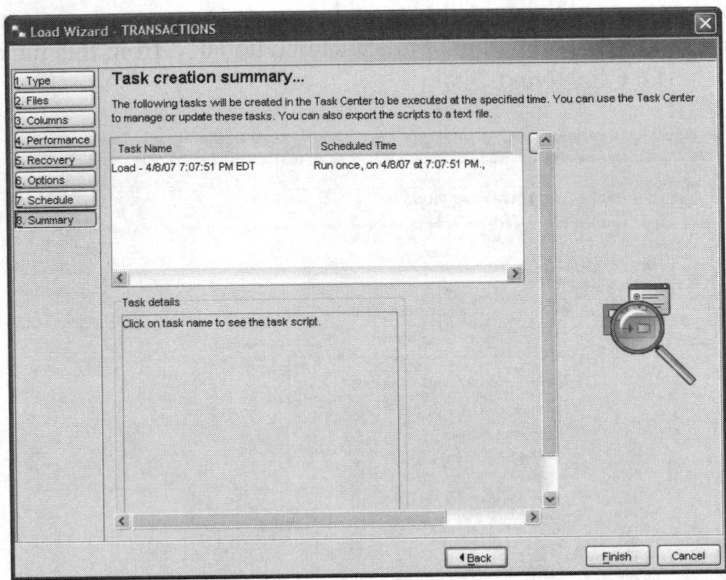

Figure 12–33 *Task creation summary*

By clicking on the task, the task details appear in the window (Figure 12–33). The user can choose to save the command as a script to be invoked at a later time. Click **Finish** to save the task and optionally start the Task Center.

After Load Has Finished

The LOAD utility can put the table space in which the target table resides in one of two pending states or can set the table to a pending state. If this happens, users cannot access the tables in the table space or access the table itself.

To query the state of a table space, use the LIST TABLESPACES command as described in "Data Storage Management" on page 625. The states that the LOAD utility can put the table space into are as follows.

Backup Pending

If a table is loaded with the COPY NO command option and archival logging is switched on, the table spaces involved in the load operation will be put in a BACKUP PENDING state.

This state forces the user to take a backup of the database or table space the target table resides in. This is done to ensure that if needed, the table can be recovered.

If the LOAD utility was invoked with the NONRECOVERABLE or COPY YES command options, the table space will not be put in a backup-pending state. It is recommended that the DBA take a backup of the table space or database as soon as possible if NONRECOVERABLE is used. If not, the DBA will *not* be able to recover it by restoring a older backup and then rolling forward using the log files. If this is attempted, the table will be flagged as invalid. The only operation that can be performed is to drop the table.

Table in Check Pending

The load utility can also put the *table* in check-pending state. This state occurs if constraints other than primary key and unique constraints are defined on the target table. They include the following:

- Foreign key constraints — Used to enforce referential integrity.
- Check constraints — User-defined constraints. Normally used to check for valid data ranges on columns.
- Summary table involved in the scenario — Used to refresh a summary table that has the REFRESH IMMEDIATE option set.

The state of a table is recorded in the SYSCAT.TABLES catalog view. To find the state associated with a table, issue the following select statement:

```
select tabschema,tabname,status, const_checked from
  syscat.tables where
  tabname='MYTAB' and tabschema='MYSCHEMA'
```

The status column is of type CHAR and indicates the state the table is in. Valid values for it are:

- C — Check pending
- N — Normal
- X — Inoperative view

The CONST_CHECKED column is of type CHAR(32). The first character denotes the status of the foreign key constraints, character two denotes the status of the check constraints, and character five denotes the status of the summary table refresh. Valid values for these states are:

- Y — Checked by the system.
- N — Not checked. This is a check-pending state.
- U — Checked by the user.
- W — Was in the state "U" before it was placed in this state. This is also a check-pending state.

The SELECT statement can be rewritten to eliminate all the unnecessary information returned by the previous one (next page).

```
SELECT TABSCHEMA AS SCHEMA,
  TABNAME AS NAME,
  STATUS AS STATE,
  SUBSTR(CONST_CHECKED,1,1) AS FOREIGN_KEYS,
  SUBSTR(CONST_CHECKED,2,1) AS CHECK_CONSTRAINTS,
  SUBSTR(CONST_CHECKED,5,1) AS SUMMARY_TABLES
FROM SYSCAT.TABLES
  WHERE TABNAME='MYTAB' AND TABSCHEMA='MYSCHEMA'
```

To remove the check-pending state on the table, the SET INTEGRITY statement can be used. The usage of this statement is discussed in "The SET INTEGRITY Statement" on page 758.

The DBA can check for records that could not be loaded because of formatting or null value violations by looking in the dump file (as specified with the MODIFIED BY DUMPFILE option). In addition, the exception table (if specified) can be queried to find records that were rejected because of duplicate values. The remote file can be queried by using the LOAD QUERY command. It contains information about the number of rows read, rejected, and loaded, as well as any error or warning messages generated by the LOAD utility. In the event of failure, an SQL error code with a short description will be returned. Also, the DB2DIAG.LOG file can be checked. It can give useful information about the sequence of events that preceded the failure.

Multi-Dimensional Clustering Considerations

The following restrictions apply to multi-dimensional clustering (MDC) tables:

- The SAVECOUNT option of the LOAD utility is not supported.
- The TOTALFREESPACE file type modifier is not supported since these tables manage their own free space.

When using the LOAD utility with MDC, violations of unique constraints will be handled as follows:

- If the table included a unique key prior to the load operation and duplicate records are loaded into the table, the original record will remain and the new records will be deleted during the delete phase.
- If the table did not include a unique key prior to the load operation and both a unique key and duplicate records are loaded into the table, only one of the records with the unique key will be loaded and the others will be deleted during the delete phase.

Note, that there is no explicit technique for determining which record will be loaded and which will be deleted.

The LOAD QUERY Command

The LOAD QUERY command is used to interrogate a LOAD operation and generate a report on its progress. The user may direct it to summarize or to display the difference or delta since the last invocation.

Load Query Syntax

The syntax of the LOAD QUERY command is provided to add to the discussion of the command. Figure 12–34 shows the syntax diagram.

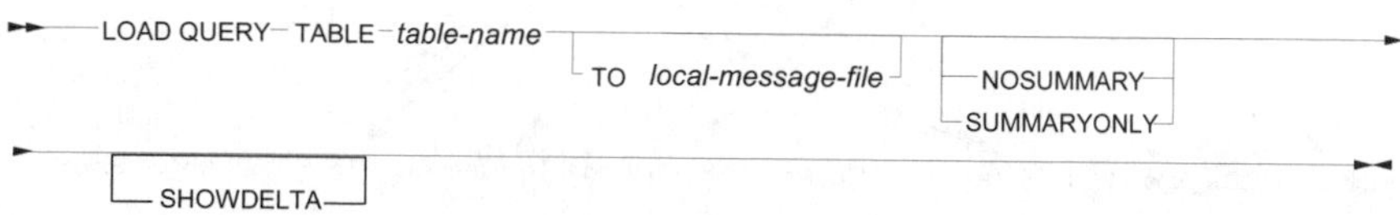

Figure 12–34 *The LOAD QUERY command*

The key parameters are:

- `table-name` — The name of the table that is being loaded.
- `TO local-message-file` — The name of a file on the server (where the LOAD is executed). The load query report will be output to this file. This cannot be the same file as the message file specified in the LOAD command. If the file specified exists, all new output will be appended to it.
- NOSUMMARY — Indicates that no summary information should be generated.
- SUMMARYONLY — Will generate summary information about the number of records read, loaded, rejected, and so on.
- SHOWDELTA — Will cause only the new information since the last invocation of LOAD QUERY to be displayed.

Using LOAD QUERY and LOAD

In this example, a load will be performed on a table named SALES from a file named SALES.DEL with the character delimiter (*) and the column delimiter (|). New data will be added to the table.

There are two summary tables defined on the SALES table. The first is a summary table on the sales per employee, and the second is defined to summarize the sales per product. The first, EMP_SALES, is defined with the option REFRESH DEFERRED, and the second, PROD_SALES, is defined with the option REFRESH IMMEDIATE.

The SALES table also has a foreign key constraint defined that references the PRODUCT table. It also has a check constraint defined on the AMOUNT column. This constraint ensures that any row inserted or updated in the table has an amount that is greater than zero. Figure 12–35 shows the relationships between these tables.

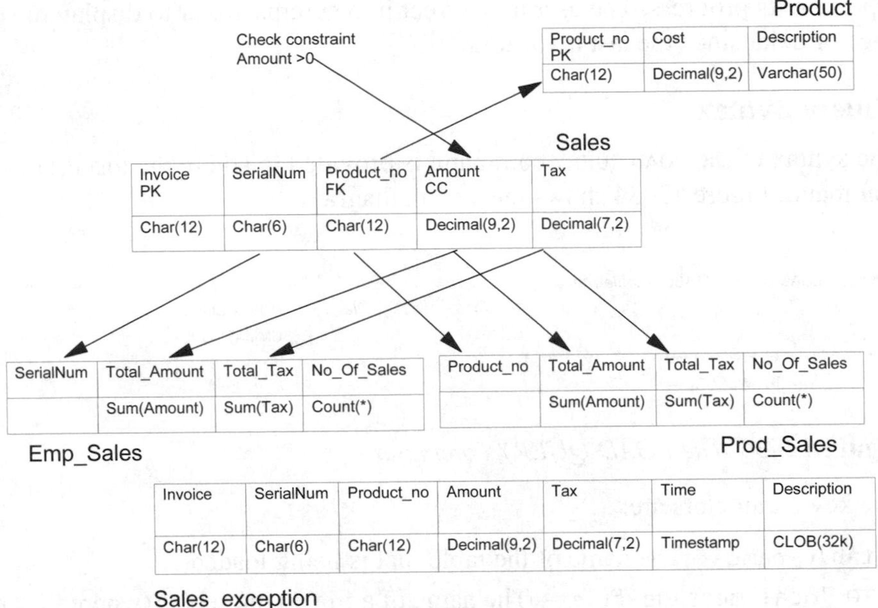

Figure 12–35 *The SALES table dependencies*

After evaluating the information, the DBA decided to load the SALES table with the following options:

```
LOAD FROM SALES.DEL OF DEL
  MODIFIED BY COLDEL| CHARDEL*
  SAVECOUNT 100
  MESSAGES MSGS.TXT
  TEMPFILES PATH D:\TEMP
  INSERT INTO SALES FOR EXCEPTION SALES_EXCEPTION
  STATISTICS YES AND INDEXES ALL
  COPY NO
  CPU_PARALLELISM 4
  DISK_PARALLELISM 3
  INDEXING MODE INCREMENTAL
```

The LOAD utility will move all the duplicate rows to the exception table SALES_EXCEPTION during the delete phase.

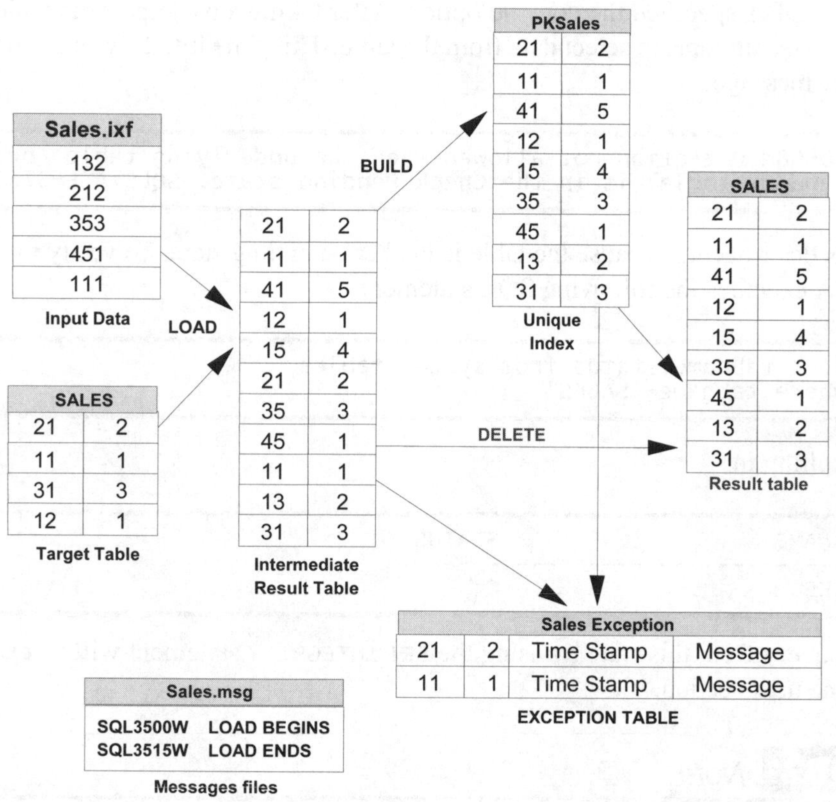

Figure 12–36 *Loading the SALES table*

It will not make a copy of the data loaded during the load, but it will force the user to take a backup of the table space(s) involved.

During the load of the SALES table, the DBA decided to monitor the load progress using the following command. He would be able to query this file to determine the status of the LOAD at that time.

```
load query table sales TO D:\messages\load\Sales.msg
```

After loading the data into the SALES table, the DBA attempts to issue an INSERT statement on the SALES table. It fails with the following error message:

```
SQL0290N Table space access is not allowed. SQLSTATE=55039
```

This indicates that the table space is in a backup-pending state. The reason for this is the DBA specified the COPY NO option. After taking a backup of the table space, the DBA attempts to select data from the table. This time it fails with the following error message:

```
SQL0668N Operation not allowed when the underlying table (or a
dependent table) is in the Check Pending state. SQLSTATE=57016
```

This error occurs because the table is in check-pending state. To verify this, the DBA executes the following SQL statement:

```
select tabname,status from syscat.tables
  where tabname='SALES'
```

Resulting in:

```
TABNAME                    STATUS
-------------------------- ------
SALES                      C
```

Recovery from this state by using the SET INTEGRITY statement will be examined in the next section.

DB2 *Note*

The LOAD QUERY command now returns the table state of the target table into which data is being loaded as well as the status information it previously included on a load operation in progress. The command can be used to query table states whether or not a load operation is in progress on a particular table.

The SET INTEGRITY Statement

The integrity or validity of data in a database is of crucial importance. It is difficult to ensure the validity of data being inserted into a database; many RDBMS products, however, including DB2, provide the ability to define some rule-based constraints or checks that can be incorporated into the database. In DB2, the following checks can be used to minimize the risk of inserting incorrect data into a table:

- The fields in a row are checked to see if they conform to the data type and length of the columns with which they are associated. For example, the value "g553g" does not match a column data type of DECIMAL, and therefore the row will be rejected, thus ensuring the validity of the data in the database.

- If a *primary key* constraint has been defined on a table, then each row in the table must have a unique value in the column or columns that collectively form the primary key. If a row is inserted with the same key as an existing one, the new row will be rejected.
- If a *unique* constraint has been defined on a table, each row in the table must comply with this constraint by having a unique value or combination of values that make up the unique key.
- If a *foreign key* constraint has been defined, each row in the table must have a value in the foreign key column or columns that matches a primary key of a row in the parent table. In some cases, a null value may be acceptable if the column or columns defined as part of the foreign key are also defined as nullable.
- If a *check* constraint has been defined on a column, each row must comply with the constraint. For example, a check constraint on a salary column of an employee table may prevent an application or user from inserting a new employee record or row for which the salary is less than zero. Any row inserted into the table that has a salary value of less than zero will be rejected, thus minimizing the risk of inserting incorrect data into the table.

In most cases, the enforcing of these rules or constraints is done automatically. For instance, whenever a row is inserted, updated, imported, or loaded, the following will always be checked:

- Validity of the data format and length
- Primary key values
- Unique constraints

Whenever a row is inserted, updated, or imported, the following checks will also be done:

- Compliance with foreign key constraints
- Compliance with check constraints
- Updating of summary tables defined with `IMMEDIATE CHECKED` option

The second list above is *not* checked or executed when data is *loaded* into a table. Because it is not checked, the validity of the data remains in doubt until such time as the data is checked and found to be consistent. For this reason, DB2 restricts access to the table by placing it in a check-pending state. This prevents the data in the table from being accessed and indicates that explicit checking of the data is required.

A table might also be placed into this state if a new constraint is defined on the table, and the checking of the constraint is not performed immediately. This is done because there is no guarantee that the existing rows in the table comply with the new constraint.

Here is an abbreviated syntax of the `SET INTEGRITY` statement (Figure 12–37):

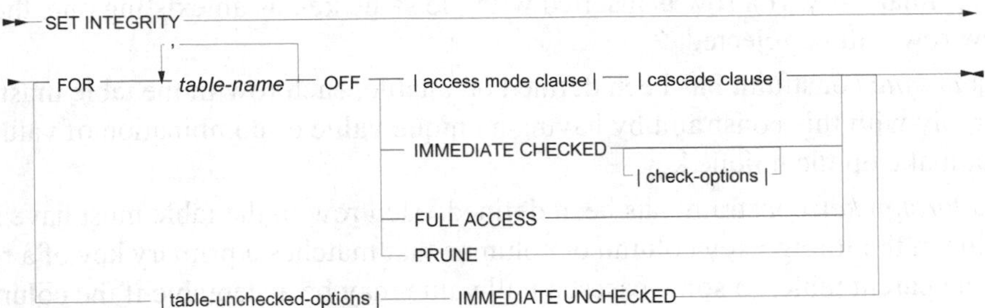

Figure 12–37 *SET INTEGRITY command*

The validity of the existing data in a table can be checked by using one of these statements:

- `SET INTEGRITY` (also known as `SET CONSTRAINTS`)
- `REFRESH TABLE`

The `SET INTEGRITY` statement can be used to do the following:

- *Set* a table to check-pending state and mark one or more of the following as *not* checked: check constraints, foreign key constraints, and the refreshing of refresh immediate summary tables.

  By marking any one of the above as *not* checked, the table is set to check-pending state. Primary key and unique key constraint checking cannot be turned off and will still be enforced. Because the table is set to the check-pending state, access to the table data is restricted.

- *Reset* the check-pending state of a table by *checking* all or some of the following constraints: check constraints, foreign key constraints, and the refreshing of refresh immediate summary tables.
- *Reset* a check-pending state by *marking* any of the following constraints as checked: check constraints, foreign key constraints, and the refreshing of refresh immediate summary tables. The actual checking of the constraints will not be done. This is referred to as deferred checking.

The `REFRESH TABLE` statement can be used on summary tables only. It will update the data in the summary table by making use of the current data in the table that it is derived from.

DB2 Note

Prior to Version 8, following a load operation the target table remained in check pending state if it contained generated columns. The load utility will now generate column values, and you no longer need to issue the SET INTEGRITY statement after a load operation into a table that contains generated columns and has no other table constraints.

If existing data is to be checked, the user can specify that it should be done incrementally. This means that only the data that has been added to the table since checking has turned off has to be checked.

The following example is a continuation of the LOAD example in "Using LOAD QUERY and LOAD" on page 755. In the previous example, after the LOAD completed, the table space was in a backup-pending state. After a backup was made, a SELECT statement failed with the following error message:

```
SQL0668N Operation not allowed when the underlying table (or a
dependent table) is in the Check Pending state. SQLSTATE=57016
```

This message indicates that the table is in a check-pending state. As mentioned before, this pending state can occur on tables that have foreign key constraints or check constraints defined. Use the following statement to find the reason for the check-pending state on the SALES table.

```
SELECT TABSCHEMA AS SCHEMA,
  TABNAME AS NAME,
  STATUS AS State,
  SUBSTR(CONST_CHECKED,1,1) AS FOREIGN_KEYS,
  SUBSTR(CONST_CHECKED,2,1) AS CHECK_CONSTRAINTS,
  SUBSTR(CONST_CHECKED,5,1) AS SUMMARY_TABLES
FROM SYSCAT.TABLES
  WHERE TABNAME='SALES' AND TABSCHEMA='DB2ADMIN'
```

The result is shown below. The value "C" in the STATUS column indicates that the table is in a check-pending state.

```
SCHEMA    NAME      STATE FOREIGN_KEYS CHECK_CONSTRAINTS SUMMARY_TABLES
--------- --------- ----- ------------ ----------------- --------------
DB2ADMIN  SALES     C     N            N                 Y
```

The "N" shown in the output indicates the reason for the check-pending state. In our case it is because one or more constraints have not been checked. To remove the check-pending state on the table, use the SET INTEGRITY statement:

```
SET INTEGRITY FOR SALES IMMEDIATE CHECKED
  FOR EXCEPTION IN SALES USE SALES_EXCEPTION
```

The statement generates the following message:

```
SQL3602W Check data processing found constraint violations and
  moved them into the exception table. SQLSTATE-01603
```

At this point, the table should now be accessible.

Using Set Integrity from the Control Center

The SET INTEGRITY statement can also be executed from the Control Center. To do so, right-click on the table in question and choose the **Set Integrity** option. Figure 12–38 illustrates how you can choose the constraint checking options.

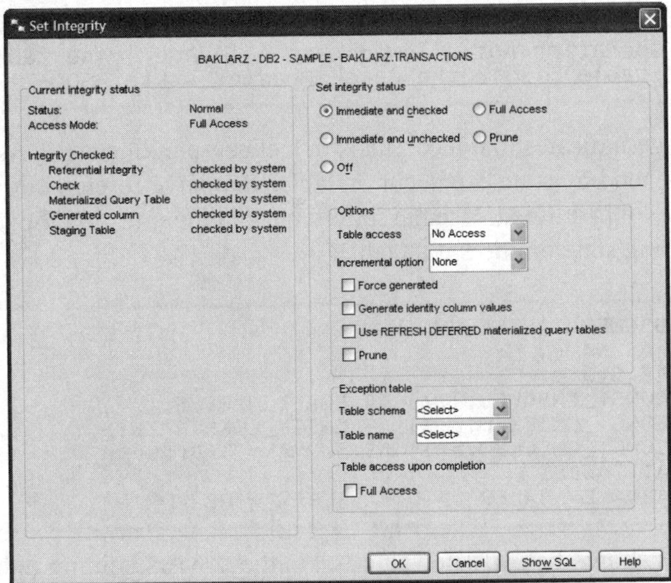

Figure 12–38 *Set Integrity from the Control Center*

During the execution of the SET INTEGRITY statement, all the rows that do not comply with either of the two constraints defined on the SALES table will be copied to the SALES_EXCEPTION exception table. This exception table can also be used during the LOAD operation.

Figure 12–39 shows how a foreign key constraint defined on the SALES table is evaluated. All the rows in the SALES table that refer to a nonexistent value in the

PRODUCT table will be deleted from the SALES table and copied to the exception table. The same process will be used to delete the rows in the SALES table that do not comply with the check constraint defined on the table. Copies of these rows will also be placed in the SALES_EXCEPTION table.

After completion of the SET INTEGRITY operation, the user can query the message column (if defined) in the SALES_EXCEPTION table to determine the reason a given row was rejected. These rows can then be modified and reinserted into the SALES table at a later time.

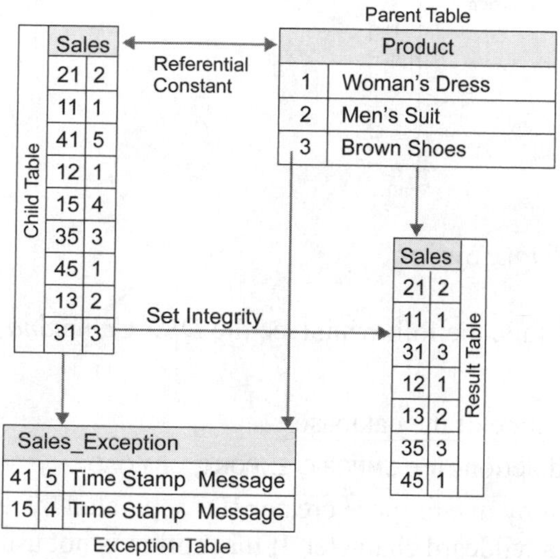

Figure 12–39 *SET INTEGRITY and the use of the exception table*

The DB2MOVE Utility

The db2move utility can be used to move data between different DB2 databases that may reside on different servers. It is very useful when a large number of tables need to be copied from one database to another. The utility can run in one of three modes: EXPORT, IMPORT, or LOAD.

When running in the *export* mode, it will use the EXPORT utility to export data from the table or tables specified into data files of type IXF. It will also produce a file named DB2MOVE.LST that records all the names of the tables exported and the file names produced when they were exported. It will also produce various message files that record any errors or warning messages generated during the execution of the utility.

If the db2move utility is executed in *import* mode, the IMPORT utility will be used to import data files of type IXF into a given database. It will attempt to read the DB2MOVE.LST file to find the link between the file names of the data files and the table names into which the data must be imported.

In the *load* mode, the input files specified in the DB2MOVE.LST file will be loaded into the tables using the LOAD utility.

Here is an abbreviated syntax of the db2move utility (Figure 12–40):

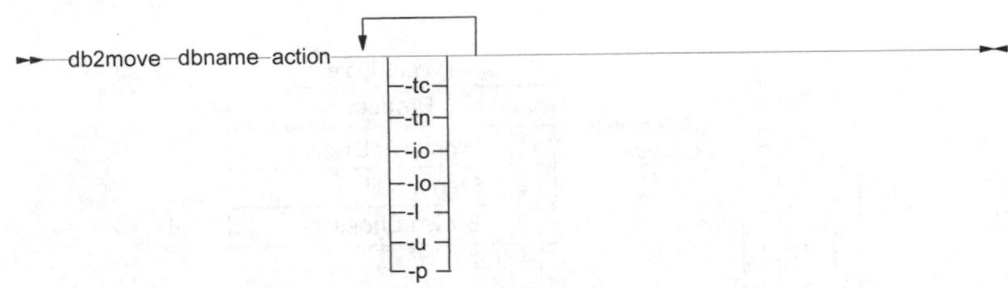

Figure 12–40 *db2move Syntax*

Key parameters include the following (see the *DB2 Command Reference* for more detail):

- dbname — The name of the database.
- action — Valid actions are IMPORT, EXPORT, or LOAD.
- -tc — Followed by one or more creator IDs separated by a comma. The "*" may be used as a wildcard character. If this option is not used, the default behavior of this utility is to work with all the creator IDs.
- -tn — Flag only valid if used with the EXPORT action. If specified, it should be followed by one or more (maximum ten) table names separated by commas.
- -io — Flag used to specify the import action to take. If specified, it should be followed by any one of the following options: INSERT, INSERT_UPDATE, REPLACE, CREATE, or REPLACE_CREATE. If not specified when the IMPORT action is specified, the option REPLACE_CREATE will be used as the default.
- -lo — Flag used to specify the load option to use. Valid options are INSERT and REPLACE. If not specified when the LOAD action is specified, INSERT will be used as the default load option.
- -l — Specify the absolute path names for the directories to be used when importing, exporting, or loading LOB values into or from separate files. If specified with the EXPORT action, the directories will be cleared before the LOBs are exported to files in the directory or directories.
- -u — Followed by a userid that is to be used to run the utility. If not specified,

the userid of the logged-on user will be used to execute the utility.

- `-p` — Followed by the password to be used to authenticate the userid that is used when executing the utility.

Here is an example of using the `db2move` utility.

An existing database, `SAMPLE`, needs to be copied to a new database on another server. The new database name is `NEWSAMPL`. The user has not defined any tables in the new database and plans to do this using the `db2move` utility. To export all the tables in the `SAMPLE` database, the user issues the following command:

```
db2move sample export
```

This produces the following files:

- `EXPORT.OUT` — The results of the `EXPORT` action
- `DB2MOVE.LST` — A file containing a list of file names and the table names they originate from
- `TABNNN.IXF` — The IXF files containing the data from the tables
- `TABNNN.MSG` — The messages file associated with the export operation on each table

The user now wants to recreate the database structure in the `NEWSAMPL` database and populate it with the data in the IXF files. The following command can now be used:

```
db2move newsampl import -io REPLACE_CREATE
```

The use of the `-io` option is not required in our case because the default option is `REPLACE_CREATE`.

The files used as input by the utility are:

- `DB2MOVE.LST` — The list file containing the table names and file names of the data files for the tables
- `TABNNN.IXF` — The actual data files of type IXF

The output files of this operation are:

- `IMPORT.OUT` — This file contains a summary of the results of the individual import operations.
- `TABNNN.MSG` — These files contains error and warning messages generated during the import of the various files.

Data Maintenance

The physical distribution of the data stored in tables has a significant effect on the performance of applications using those tables. The way the data is stored in a table is affected by the update, insert, and delete operations on the table. For example, a delete operation may leave empty pages of data that may not be reused later. Also, updates to variable-length columns may result in the new column value not fitting in the same data page. This can cause the row to be moved to a different page and so produce internal gaps or unused space in the table. As a consequence, DB2 may have to read more physical pages to retrieve the information required by the application.

These scenarios are almost unavoidable. However, as the database administrator, you can use the data maintenance commands provided in DB2 to optimize the physical distribution of the data stored in your tables.

There are three related utilities or commands that can help you organize the data in your tables. These are:

- REORGCHK
- REORG
- RUNSTATS

DB2 Note

Most of the commands used in this section require that the SCHEMA name be prefixed to the table name: SCHEMA.TEST_CANDIDATE, where *schema* should be replaced with the userid or schema that the object was created with.

Analyzing Data's Physical Organization

It has been discussed that certain SQL operations may produce internal gaps in tables. So the question you may ask is, how can I determine the physical organization of my tables or indexes? How can I know how much space is currently being used and how much is free?

Questions like these can be answered by using the REORGCHK utility. This utility is used to analyze the system catalog tables and gather information about the physical organization of my tables and indexes. The user has the option of using the current information in the catalog or to make the REORGCHK utility update the information before using it.

With the information collected from the system catalog tables, the REORGCHK utility displays the space allocation characteristics of the tables and indexes. The utility uses a number of formulas to help you decide if your tables and indexes require physical reorganization.

These formulas are general recommendations that show the relationship between the allocated space and the space that is being used for the data in your tables. Three formulas are used for tables, and three are used for indexes.

It is recommended that you establish a data maintenance policy to ensure that the data in your table is stored as efficiently as possible. If you don't, you may discover that your applications start to experience degradation in performance. This may be caused by the poor physical organization of your data, so before this happens, do preventive maintenance on your tables.

Here is an abbreviated syntax of the REORGCHK utility:

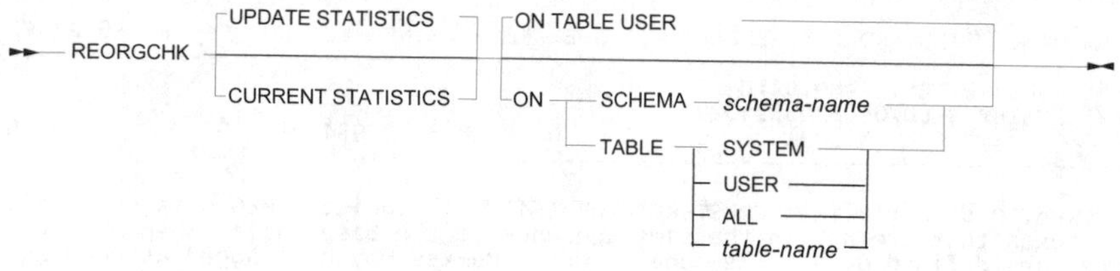

Figure 12–41 *REORGCHK command*

Some of the key parameters to the REORGCHK command include (see the *DB2 Command Reference* for further detail):

- UPDATE STATISTICS — updates table statistics, and uses the updated statistics to determine if a table reorganization is required.
- CURRENT STATISTICS — uses current table statistics to determine if a table reorganization is required.

To use the REORGCHK utility you must have one of the following authorities: SYSADM, DBADM, or CONTROL privilege on the table. The following is an example of using the REORGCHK utility. This utility will be executed against the table TEST_CANDIDATE.

```
reorgchk update statistics on table baklarz.test_candidates
```

The output of the REORGCHK utility is shown in Figure 12–42.

```
Doing RUNSTATS ....

Table statistics:

F1: 100 * OVERFLOW / CARD < 5
F2: 100 * (Effective Space Utilization of Data Pages) > 70
F3: 100 * (Required Pages / Total Pages) > 80

SCHEMA.NAME                 CARD     OV    NP    FP ACTBLK    TSIZE  F1  F2  F3 REORG
--------------------------------------------------------------------------------------
Table: BAKLARZ.TEST_CANDIDATE
                               8      0     1     1      -      920   0   - 100 ---
--------------------------------------------------------------------------------------

Index statistics:

F4: CLUSTERRATIO or normalized CLUSTERFACTOR > 80
F5: 100 * (Space used on leaf pages / Space available on non-empty leaf pages) >
    MIN(50, (100 - PCTFREE))
F6: (100 - PCTFREE) * (Amount of space available in an index with one less level /
    Amount of space required for all keys) < 100
F7: 100 * (Number of pseudo-deleted RIDs / Total number of RIDs) < 20
F8: 100 * (Number of pseudo-empty leaf pages / Total number of leaf pages) < 20

SCHEMA.NAME    INDCARD LEAF ELEAF LVLS NDEL KEYS LR NR  LO  NO  F4  F5 F6 F7 F8 REORG
--------------------------------------------------------------------------------------
Table: BAKLARZ.TEST_CANDIDATE
Index: SYSIBM.SQL070408203315020
                     8    1     0    1    0    8 3  3 984 984 100   -  -  0  0 -----
--------------------------------------------------------------------------------------

CLUSTERRATIO or normalized CLUSTERFACTOR (F4) will indicate REORG is necessary
for indexes that are not in the same sequence as the base table. When multiple
indexes are defined on a table, one or more indexes may be flagged as needing
REORG.  Specify the most important index for REORG sequencing.

Tables defined using the ORGANIZE BY clause and the corresponding dimension
indexes have a '*' suffix to their names. The cardinality of a dimension index
is equal to the Active blocks statistic of the table.
```

Figure 12–42 *REORGCHK results*

Note that four headings have been shorted in order to display the output data properly:

- LR — LEAF_RECSIZE
- NR — NLEAF_RECSIZE
- LO — LEAF_PAGE_OVERHEAD
- NO — NLEAF_PAGE_OVERHEAD

The output of REORGCHK is divided into two sections. The first section shows the table statistics and formulas. The second section displays information about the table's indexes and associated formulas.

Interpreting the Output from REORGCHK

The REORGCHK utility uses formulas that may help you decide whether a table requires reorganization. An explanation of the elements that are used to calculate these formulas are examined in this section:

```
Table statistics:

F1: 100 * OVERFLOW / CARD < 5
F2: 100 * (Effective Space Utilization of Data Pages) > 70
F3: 100 * (Required Pages / Total Pages) > 80

SCHEMA.NAME                     CARD    OV    NP    FP ACTBLK    TSIZE  F1  F2  F3 REORG
-----------------------------------------------------------------------------------------
Table: BAKLARZ.TEST_CANDIDATE
                                   8     0     1     1      -      920   0   - 100 ---
-----------------------------------------------------------------------------------------
```

- SCHEMA.NAME — Column indicates the schema and the name of the table. Remember that the authorization ID of the creator of an object is used as the default schema. REORGCHK can check a set of tables at one time.
- CARD — Indicates the number of data rows in the base table.
- OV (OVERFLOW) — The overflow indicator. It indicates the number of overflow rows. An overflow may occur when a new column is added to a table or when a variable-length value increases its size.
- NP (NPAGES) — Indicates the total number of pages that contain data.
- FP (FPAGES) — Indicates the total number of pages allocated to the table.
- ACTBLK — Total number of active blocks for a multidimensional clustering (MDC) table. This field is only applicable to tables defined using the ORGANIZE BY clause. It indicates the number of blocks of the table that contain data.
- TSIZE — Indicates the table size in bytes. This value is calculated from the result of multiplying the number of rows in the table times the average row length.
- TABLEPAGESIZE — Indicates the page size of the table space in which the table resides.
- REORG — Column has a separate indicator for each one of the first three formulas. A hyphen (-) indicates that reorganization is not recommended. An asterisk (*) indicates that reorganization is recommended.

The formulas F1, F2, and F3 provide guidelines for table reorganization. The formulas are shown in the REORGCHK output.

- *F1* works with the number of overflow rows. It recommends a table reorganization if 5% or more of the total number of rows are overflow rows.
- *F2* works with the free or unused space. It recommends a table reorganization if the table size (TSIZE) is less than or equal to 70% the size of the total space allocated to the table. In other words, it recommends to reorganize a table when

more than 30% of the allocated space is unused.

- *F3* works with free pages. It recommends a table reorganization when more than 20% of the pages in a table are free. A page is considered free when it contains no rows.

Whenever the formulas find that table reorganization is needed, an asterisk will be shown in the REORG column of the output.

For example, if the overflow rows of a table exceed the recommended value, the REORG column will look like this:

```
REORG
-----
*--
```

Remember, these values are only general guidelines. You may use your own thresholds. However, most of the time you will find these values adequate for your environment.

Another part of REORGCHK involves interpreting the output gathered from indexes. To do this, some information about the structure of indexes is needed. Indexes in DB2 are created using a B+ tree structure. These data structures provide an efficient search method to locate the entry values of an index. The logical structure of a DB2 index is shown in Figure 12–43:

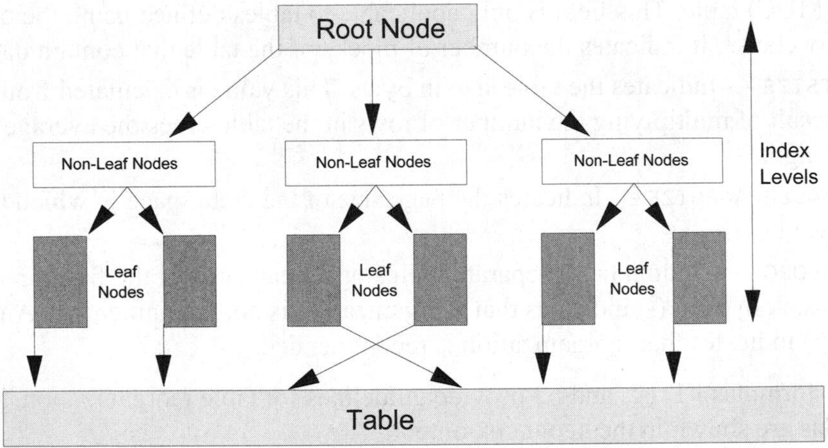

Figure 12–43 *DB2 index structure*

An index can have several levels. The fewer levels an index has, the more quickly DB2 can access the table or data pages. The index shown in Figure 12–43 has two levels. Here is a review of the REORGCHK index information.

```
Index statistics:

F4: CLUSTERRATIO or normalized CLUSTERFACTOR > 80
F5: 100 * (Space used on leaf pages / Space available on non-empty leaf pages) >
    MIN(50, (100 - PCTFREE))
F6: (100 - PCTFREE) * (Amount of space available in an index with one less level /
    Amount of space required for all keys) < 100
F7: 100 * (Number of pseudo-deleted RIDs / Total number of RIDs) < 20
F8: 100 * (Number of pseudo-empty leaf pages / Total number of leaf pages) < 20

SCHEMA.NAME    INDCARD LEAF ELEAF LVLS NDEL KEYS LR NR  LO  NO  F4  F5 F6 F7 F8 REORG
--------------------------------------------------------------------------------------
Table: BAKLARZ.TEST_CANDIDATE
Index: SYSIBM.SQL070408203315020
                     8    1    0    1    0    8 3  3 984 984 100   -  -  0  0 -----
--------------------------------------------------------------------------------------
```

- SCHEMA.NAME — Column indicates the schema and table name to which the index belongs. Remember that the creator of an object is used as the default schema. This will show statistics about all the indexes of a table. The information is also collected for system-defined indexes, such as primary key indexes.
- INDCARD — Indicates the number of index entries in the index.
- LEAF — Indicates the number of leaf nodes of the index.
- ELEAF — Number of pseudo empty index leaf pages.
- LVLS (LEVELS) — Indicates the total number of levels of the index.
- NDEL — Number of pseudo deleted RIDs.
- KEYS — Number of unique index entries that are not marked deleted.
- LR (LEAF_RECSIZE) — Record size of the index entry on a leaf page. This is the average size of the index entry excluding any overhead and is calculated from the average column length of all columns participating in the index.
- NR (NLEAF_RECSIZE) — Record size of the index entry on a non-leaf page. This is the average size of the index entry excluding any overhead and is calculated from the average column length of all columns participating in the index except any INCLUDE columns.
- LO (LEAF_PAGE_OVERHEAD) — Reserved space on the index leaf page for internal use.
- NO (NLEAF_PAGE_OVERHEAD) — Reserved space on the index non-leaf page for internal use.
- REORG — Column has a separate indicator for each one of the index formulas. An asterisk indicates that reorganization is recommended, and a hyphen indicates that the reorganization is not recommended.

The formulas F4, F5, F6, F7, and F8 provides guidelines for index reorganization. The formulas are shown in the REORGCHK output.

- *F4* indicates the CLUSTERRATIO or normalized CLUSTERFACTOR. This ratio shows the percentage of data rows that are stored in same physical sequence as the index. The clustering ratio of an index should be greater than 80%.
- *F5* calculates space reserved for index entries. Less than 50% of the space allocated for the index should be empty.
- *F6* measures the usage of the index pages. The number of index pages should be more than 90% of the total entries that NLEVELS can handle.
- *F7* measures the number of pseudo-deleted RIDs on non-pseudo-empty pages and should be less than 20%.
- *F8* measures the number of pseudo-empty leaf pages and should be less than 20% of the total number of leaf pages.

Whenever the formulas find that an table reorganization is needed, an asterisk will be shown in the REORG column of the output.

For example, if the CLUSTERRATIO of an index is below the recommended level, the REORG column will appear as:

```
REORG
-----
*----
```

DB2 Note

The REORGCHK utility is an analysis tool provided with DB2. To reorganize your tables, you must use the REORG utility.

REORGCHK Options

You can use the CURRENT STATISTICS option of the REORGCHK utility to use the statistics in the system catalog tables at that time. For example, to analyze the current statistics of table TEST_TAKEN:

```
reorgchk current statistics on table baklarz.test_taken
```

To review the current statistics of all the tables in a database, including the system catalog and user tables:

```
reorgchk current statistics on table all
```

You can also verify the organization of the system catalog tables using the SYSTEM option. Alternatively, you can select all the tables under the current user schema name by specifying the USER keyword:

```
reorgchk current statistics on table system
```

If you don't specify the CURRENT STATISTICS parameter, REORGCHK will call the RUNSTATS utility.

DB2 Note

REORGCHK cannot be run from the Control Center. You can use the Command Center to run the REORGCHK command and to capture the output for analysis.

Table Reorganization

After using the REORGCHK utility, you may find the physical reorganization of a table necessary. This reorganization is done using the REORG command. To use the REORG utility you must have one of the following authorities: SYSADM, SYSCTRL, SYSMAINT, DBADM, or CONTROL privilege on the table.

The REORG utility will delete all the unused space and write the table and index data in contiguous pages. With the help of an index, it can also be used to place the data rows in the same physical sequence as the index. These actions can be used to increase the CLUSTERRATIO of the selected index.

Assume that, after running the REORGCHK utility, you find that it is necessary to reorganize the TEST_TAKEN table.

Here is an abbreviated syntax of the REORG utility:

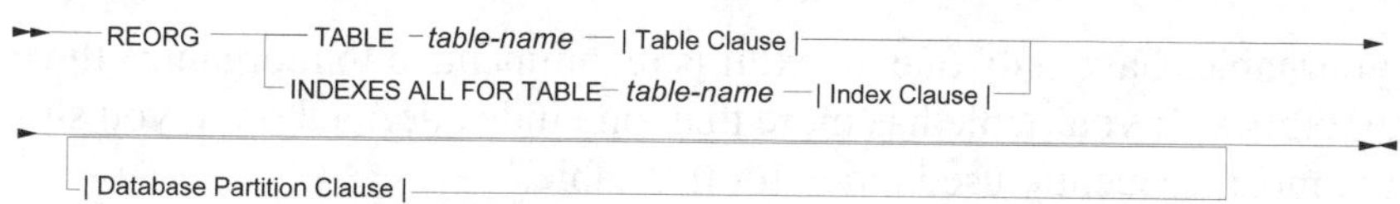

Figure 12–44 *REORG command*

Some of the key parameters to the REORG command include (see the *DB2 Command Reference* for further details):

- ALLOW READ ACCESS — allows read access to the table during reorganization.
- ALLOW WRITE ACCESS — allows write access to the table during reorganization.

- RESUME — resumes a previously paused in-place table reorganization.

This command will reorganize the TEST_TAKEN table and all of its indexes, but will *not* put the data in any specific order.

```
reorg table baklarz.test_taken
```

DB2 *Note*

When using REORG, it is mandatory to use the fully qualified name of the table.

DB2 *Note*

DB2 has the ability to perform an online REORG and supports READ/WRITE operations for the entire table, except for the small portion of the table that is being REORGed. Also, the reorg can be performed "in-place," so there is no requirement to allocate a large amount of temporary space during its operation. Only Type 2 indexes are supported for this operation.

Using an Index to Reorganize a Table

With the help of an index, REORG will put the table data in the same physical order as the selected index is. This operation can help improve the response time in the execution of your applications. This is because the data pages of the table will be placed in sequential order according to an index key. This will help DB2 find the data in contiguous space and in the desired order, reducing the seek time needed to read the data.

If DB2 finds an index with a very high cluster ratio, it may use it to avoid a sort, thus improving the performance of applications that require sort operations.

When your tables have only one index, it is recommended to reorganize the table using that index. If your table has more than one index defined on it, you should select the most frequently used index for that table.

DB2 *Note*

DB2 allows read and update operations on a table and its existing indexes during an index reorganization using the new REORG INDEXES command.

As an example, assume that the table TEST_CENTER has an index called BY_COUNTRY and that most of the queries that use the table are grouped by country.

Therefore, you might want to reorganize the TEST_CENTER table using the BY_COUNTRY index.

The REORG command is as follows:

```
reorg table baklarz.test_center index by_country
```

The INDEX option tells the REORG utility to use the specified index to reorganize the table. After the REORG command has completed, the physical organization of the table should match the order of the selected index. In this way, the key columns will be found sequentially in the table.

In Figure 12–45, the *high* cluster ratio index was used to REORG the table shown. The *low* cluster ratio index is shown to emphasize the difference between using and not using an index to perform the reorganization.

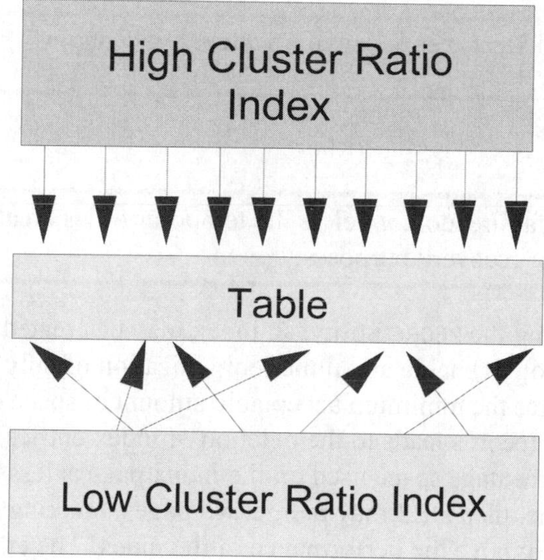

Figure 12–45 *Cluster ratio*

The arrows in Figure 12–45 illustrate the position of the index keys in the table. In high cluster ratio index, the keys will be in sequential order. In a low cluster ratio index, the keys will be distributed throughout the table.

A *clustering index* defined on the table may assist DB2 in keeping future data in a clustered index order by trying to insert new rows physically close to the rows for which the key values of the index are in the same range. You can only have one clustering index for a table.

After reorganizing a table using the index option, DB2 will not force the subsequent inserts or updates to match the physical organization of the table. You may wish to run the REORG utility on a regular basis.

Using a Temporary Table Space for Reorganization

While REORG is executing, it creates temporary files (or tables) in the table space where the table resides. You can specify a different table space for the REORG utility. If you want to have control over the location of these tables, you need to specify the USE option.

If the page size of the table space where the table being reorganized resides is 8 KB, for instance, and you want to use the USE option, the table space specified with this option must have the same page size of 8 KB.

In this example, the temporary tables created during the processing of the REORG utility will be placed in the temporary table space, TEMPSPACE1.

```
reorg table baklarz.test_center index by_country
  use tempspace1
```

DB2 *Note*

In the event of a failure, do *not* delete the temporary files created by REORG. DB2 will need them for recovery purposes.

In addition to using the REORG utility, an index may be created with the MINPCTUSED option to enable an online reorganization of only the index. This parameter indicates the minimum acceptable amount of space used on index pages. If the deletion of records leads to the deletion of index entries on a page in the index and the percentage space used on the index page is less than the MINPCTUSED value, then DB2 may merge two pages, marking one as completely empty. This will impove the performance of the index. The empty page will not be deleted, however; therefore, the size of the index file (SMS) or storage used by the index (DMS) will be unaffected. To delete the empty page and reduce the amount of storage space used, the user must explicitly reorganize the table.

Using the REORG Utility from the Control Center

You can also REORG a table from the Control Center by right-clicking on the table and selecting **Reorganize**. Figure 12–46 gives an example of how a temporary table space and index to use for the REORG is specified.

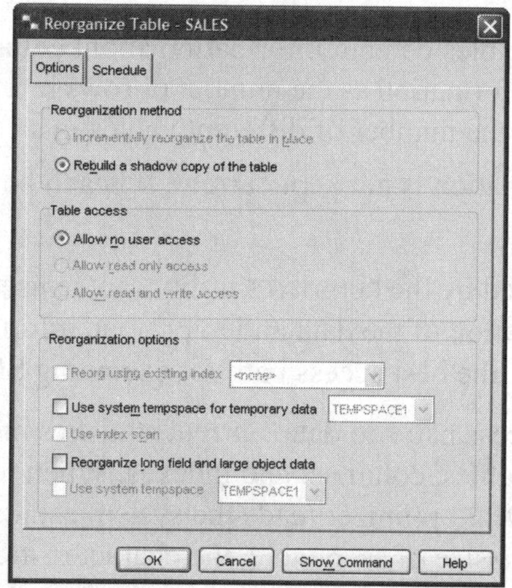

Figure 12–46 *Reorganize Table*

The user has the option to see the command that is generated and to save it or schedule it for later execution (Figure 12–47):

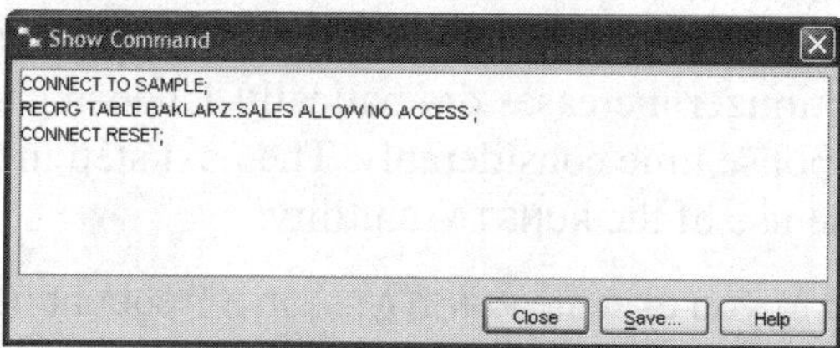

Figure 12–47 *REORG command generated*

Recommended Actions After Reorganizing a Table

Table reorganization may help to improve the performance of your applications. There are some additional steps that you should follow. These actions will allow your existing applications to benefit from the table reorganization:

1. Use the `RUNSTATS` command on the tables and their indexes. This will provide the optimizer with the updated information about the new physical organization of each table and its indexes.
2. Use the `REBIND` utility on the packages that access the reorganized table. This will allow your applications to take advantage of any changes selected by the optimizer to improve the access strategy of your SQL statements.

Generating Statistics

The system catalog tables contain information about columns, tables, and indexes. They contain such information as the number of rows in a table, the use of space by a table or index, and the number of different values in a column.

However, this information is not kept current. It has to be generated by a utility called RUNSTATS.

The statistics collected by the RUNSTATS utility can be used in two ways: to display the physical organization of the data and to provide information that the DB2 optimizer needs to select the best access path for executing SQL statements.

To have efficient access paths to data, current statistics must exist that reflect the actual state of your tables, columns, and indexes. Whenever a dynamic SQL statement is issued, the DB2 optimizer reads the system catalog tables to review the available indexes, the size of each table, the characteristics of a column, and other information to select the best access path for executing the query.

If the statistics do not reflect the current state of the tables, the DB2 optimizer will not have the correct information to make the best choice in selecting an access path to execute your query. This becomes more crucial as the complexity of the SQL statements increases. When only one table is accessed without indexes, there are fewer choices available to the optimizer. However, when the SQL statement involves several tables, each one with one or more indexes, the number of choices available to the optimizer increases dramatically. Choosing the correct access path can reduce the response time considerably. The next step in improving performance involves the use of the RUNSTATS utility.

It is recommended to you execute RUNSTATS on a frequent basis on tables that have a large number of updates, inserts, or deletes. For tables with a great deal of insert or delete activity, you may decide to run statistics after a fixed period of time or after the insert or delete activity.

DB2 *Note*

It is recommended to use the RUNSTATS utility after a REORG of a table.

An important feature of DB2 is that it allows you to reorganize and use the RUNSTATS utility on the system catalog tables. This feature of DB2 can improve the access plans generated when querying the system catalog tables. DB2 may access these tables when you issue an SQL statement, even though you are referencing only user tables. Therefore, it is very important to have current statistics on the system catalog tables.

Using the RUNSTATS Utility

To use the RUNSTATS utility you must have one of the following authorities: SYSADM, SYSCTRL, SYSMAINT, DBADM CONTROL privilege on the table, or LOAD authority.

Figure 12–48 shows an abbreviated syntax of the RUNSTATS utility:

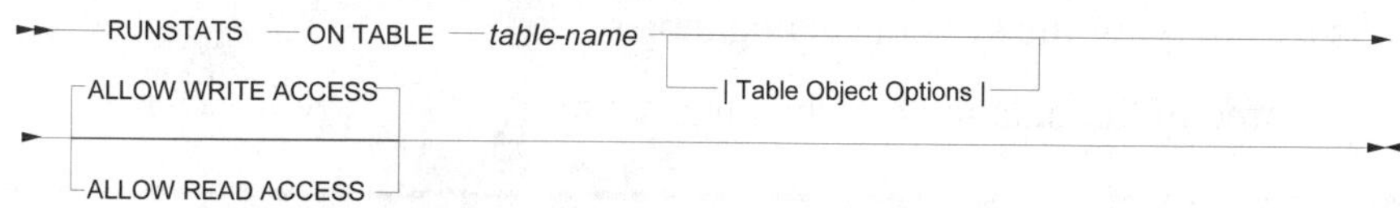

Figure 12–48 *RUNSTATS command*

Some of the key parameters to the RUNSTATS command include (see the *DB2 Command Reference* for further detail):

- FOR INDEXES — collects and updates statistics for indexes only.
- AND INDEXES — collects and updates statistics for both the table and the indexes.
- DETAILED — calculates extended index statistics that are gathered for large indexes.
- SAMPLED — when used with the DETAILED option, a sampling technique is used to estimate the extended index statistics.
- ALLOW WRITE ACCESS — allows users to read and write to the table while statistics are calculated.
- ALLOW READ ACCESS — allows users read access to the table while statistics are calculated.

DB2 Note

The RUNSTATS command has enhanced the statistics it collects, including: statistics on column combinations, prefetching statistics on the table, index statistics, able to accept a list of index names (previously available only with the API), accept a list of columns on which statistics are to be collected, accept distribution statistics limits (NUM_FREQVALUES and NUM_QUANTILES values at the table level), without having to change the configuration parameters, and then disconnect and reconnect all users. The utility also performs faster by taking a sample collection of DETAILED index statistics.

Suppose you are the database administrator and have noticed that every time your decision support system tries to resolve a user request, it takes a considerable amount of time before data is retrieved. You decide to investigate by using the RUNSTATS utility on some of the system catalog tables. This example will use the SYSIBM.SYSCOLUMNS table:

```
runstats on table sysibm.syscolumns
```

The RUNSTATS utility does not produce an explicit result. You can only see its results by querying the system catalog tables.

Here is some of the data updated by RUNSTATS:

```
TABSCHEMA    TABNAME      CARD  NPAGES  FPAGES  OVERFLOW
----------   ----------   ----  ------  ------  --------
SYSIBM       SYSCOLUMNS   5303     286     286        33
SYSIBM       SYSTABLES     368      45      45         1
```

This output was obtained by selecting all the columns of the SYSSTAT.TABLES catalog view. If any of the values were -1 (negative one) this would indicate that there are no statistics available for that object. The columns of the SYSSTAT.TABLES view have the same meaning as those of the REORGCHK utility:

- CARD — Indicates the number of data rows in the table
- NPAGES — Indicates the total number of pages that contain data
- FPAGES — Indicates the total number of pages that have been allocated to the table
- OVERFLOW — Indicates the number of overflow rows

Identifying Updated Statistics

It is not difficult to identify the absence of available statistics for a specific object. The -1 (negative one) value in the statistical information columns indicates this state. However, it is also important to identify the time of the last update of the object's statistics.

When you perform RUNSTATS on an object, the utility records the timestamp of its execution in the system catalog tables. Depending on the type of object, you can find the timestamp information in SYSCAT.TABLES or SYSCAT.INDEXES. In both views, the information is stored in the STATS_TIME column.

Old statistics may also affect the access path selection. They can mislead the optimizer to choose a improper access plan for an SQL statement.

Having current statistics is the best way to help the optimizer choose the best access path for a particular SQL statement.

Collecting Statistics for Tables and Indexes

It is possible to perform RUNSTATS on a table and all of its indexes at the same time. This is shown in the following command:

```
runstats on table baklarz.test_taken and indexes all
```

The REORGCHK utility executes the command shown above when it calls the RUNSTATS utility. The INDEXES ALL option indicates that statistics for all the indexes of a table are required. The AND option specifies that you want statistics for the table and the indexes.

Collecting Statistics for Indexes Only

After creating a new index on a table, you may find it useful to gather statistics only for the indexes of that table. If table statistics have never been generated, then this command will generate both table and index statistics; otherwise, only index statistics will be generated.

```
runstats on table baklarz.test_taken for indexes all
```

Collecting Distribution Statistics on Table Columns

There may be some columns in which the values are not distributed in a uniform manner or in which the values are concentrated in a particular range.

This kind of nonuniform distribution of data may mislead the optimizer when choosing the most appropriate access method. However, the RUNSTATS utility provides the ability to show this non-uniform distribution to the optimizer. This may improve the access plans for such tables.

In this example, suppose that 75% of the DB2 certification program exams are taken in one testing center and the other 25% are distributed in other testing centers. This nonuniform distribution of values is stored in the TEST_TAKEN table.

The following command can be used to collect distribution statistics:

```
runstats on table baklarz.test_taken with distribution
```

The WITH DISTRIBUTION option is used to instruct DB2 to collect data about the distribution of values for the columns in a table. This option is related to three database configuration parameters: NUM_FREQVALUES, NUM_QUANTILES, and

STAT_HEAP_SZ. These parameters will limit the action of the WITH DISTRIBUTION option.

- NUM_FREQVALUES — Indicates the number of most frequent values that DB2 will collect. For example, if it is set to 10, only information for the 10 most frequent values will be obtained.
- NUM_QUANTILES — Indicates the number of quantiles that DB2 will look for. This is the amount of information DB2 retains about the distribution of values for columns in the table.
- STAT_HEAP_SZ — Indicates how much memory DB2 uses for collecting these statistics.

This procedure is demanding, and it is not recommended for all your tables. Only tables presenting a high volume of nonuniform values are candidates for this option.

Collecting Detailed Information About Indexes

It is possible to collect data that will give more information about an index, in this example, information on the indexes of the table TEST_TAKEN:

```
runstats on table baklarz.test_taken for detailed
  indexes all
```

The DETAILED option is used to gather this information. The statistics collected are stored in the CLUSTERFACTOR and PAGE_FETCH_PAIRS columns of the SYSIBM.SYSINDEXES system catalog table.

This option generates statistics similar to the CLUSTERRATIO. However, CLUSTERFACTOR and PAGE_FETCH_PAIRS provide a more accurate measurement of the relationship between the index and the data pages. These two values can give the optimizer a more detailed way to model the I/O operations and select a better access path for an SQL statement. The DETAILED option is also affected by the STAT_HEAP_SZ database parameter.

Access to Tables During RUNSTATS

The RUNSTATS utility allows applications different types of access to the table being analyzed:

- ALLOW WRITE ACCESS — Other applications have read/write access to the table.
- ALLOW READ ACCESS — Other applications have read-only access to the table.

You specify this level of access (also known as the *share level*) using the SHRLEVEL option in the RUNSTATS command. For example, while executing RUNSTATS on the

TEST_CANDIDATE table, you could prevent other applications from writing to the table by using the following command:

```
runstats on table baklarz.test_candidate shrlevel reference
```

The default level of access allowed to other applications during a RUNSTATS is CHANGE.

Recommended Actions After RUNSTATS

Now that the system catalog tables have been updated, you should perform the following procedures. This will give your applications the benefit of the recently collected statistics about your tables.

- Do a REBIND on the packages that access the reorganized table. This will provide your applications with any changes selected by the DB2 optimizer to improve the access strategy for your SQL statements.
- Dynamic SQL statements will experience immediate benefits from the execution of the RUNSTATS utility. Packages in this situation do not need to be rebound.

Collecting Statistics from the Control Center

By right-clicking on a table in the Control Center, you can click on **Runstats** and update the table's statistics through the graphical interface. You can specify what statistics you would like to collect for both the table and the indexes on that table. Figure 12–49 shows a RUNSTATS against the SALES table. The Index tab displays additional options on what statistics should be gathered on the indexes associated with the table.

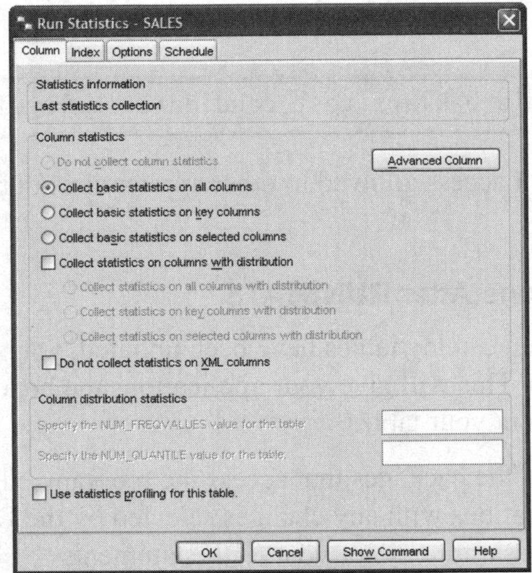

Figure 12–49 *RUNSTATS from the Control Center*

The user has the option to review the command generated and to save or schedule it to be executed at a later time. Figure 12–50 shows the command generated:

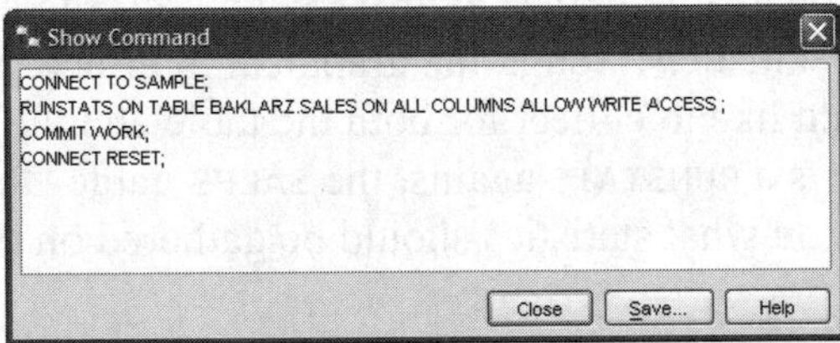

Figure 12–50 *RUNSTATS command generated*

The Rebind Utility

The `REBIND` utility provides the ability to recreate a package with the information available in the system catalog tables. This may allow your embedded SQL applications to use a different access path selected by the optimizer.

The `REBIND` utility is recommended after doing `REORG` or `RUNSTATS`. The DB2 SQL optimizer will use the new organization and recently collected statistics to generate an access path. This access path may be better suited to the new physical organization of your data.

Here is an abbreviated syntax of the `REBIND` utility:

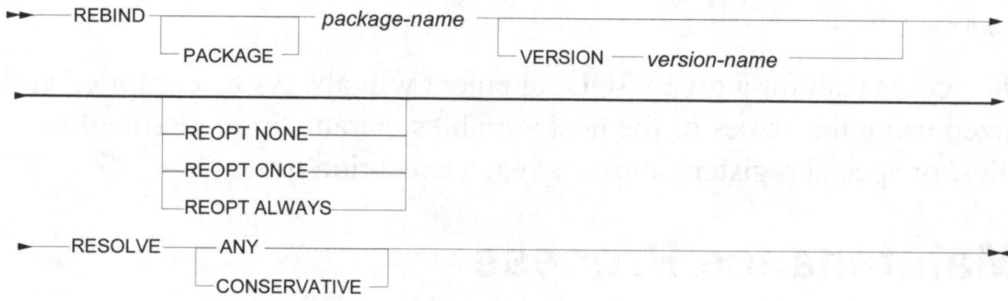

Figure 12–51 *REBIND command*

For example, suppose you have an application called `db2cert` that uses the table `BAKLARZ.TEST_TAKEN`. You have just created a new index for the table, and you need to use `REBIND` so that the `db2cert` application can try to use the new index for data access.

```
rebind db2cert
```

If you made significant changes to your database and updated all the statistics, you might want to recreate the packages for *all* applications that use the database. In this scenario, you might want to use the `db2rbind` tool. The `db2rbind` tool allows you to do an explicit rebind of all packages that are currently in the `SYSCAT.PACKAGES` catalog view. The following command rebinds all packages in the `SAMPLE` database and logs the results to `db2rbind.log`.

```
db2rbind sample /l db2rbind.log
```

The `REOPT` options are useful for updating the behavior of the application based on new indexes, statistics, parameter markers, or other optimizations that may have occurred in the database.

- `NONE`

  The access path for a given SQL statement containing host variables, parameter markers, global variables, or special registers will not be optimized using real values for these variables. The default estimates for these variables will be used instead, and this plan is cached and used subsequently. This is the default behavior.

- `ONCE`

  The access path for a given SQL statement will be optimized using the real values of the host variables, parameter markers, global variables, or special registers when the query is first executed. This plan is cached and used subsequently.

- ALWAYS

  The access path for a given SQL statement will always be compiled and re-optimized using the values of the host variables, parameter markers, global variables, or special registers known at each execution time.

Data Maintenance Process

As shown in Figure 12–52, the data maintenance process starts with the RUNSTATS and REORGCHK utilities. The REORGCHK utility can execute the RUNSTATS utility at the same time. However, it is recommended to call RUNSTATS separately, so you can control the utility's options and customize it for your environment.

After performing RUNSTATS, the REORGCHK utility reviews the statistics collected, applies six formulas, and then gives recommendations about whether a REORG is needed.

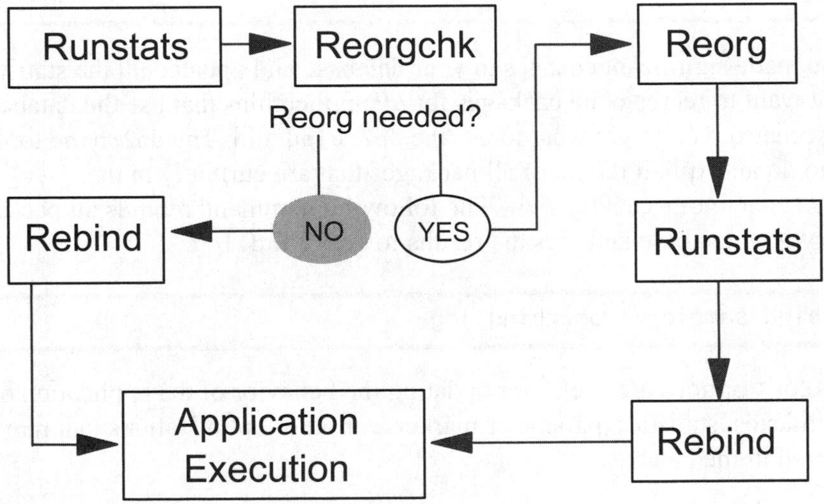

Figure 12–52 *The data maintenance process*

If reorganization is recommended, use the REORG utility on the selected objects and then do RUNSTATS and REBIND. You must perform a REBIND on any packages affected by the above operations, so they can take advantage of the benefits of the new physical organization and updated statistics. After performing subsequent update, insert, and delete operations, as part of the data maintenance process, repeat by first executing the RUNSTATS utility.

Establish a routine for RUNSTATS and the REBIND processes. Updated statistics will give you precise information about your database state.

Modeling a Production Environment

You can use the SYSSTAT schema to update system catalog statistical information. You can enter values for statistics such as table cardinality, column distribution, or index cluster ratio. In doing so, you will be able to model different volumes of data on test databases.

This is useful when you want to be sure that the access paths your applications use in your production environment are the same as those in your development environment. The access paths selected by the optimizer in each environment may differ because of different data volumes.

By updating the SYSSTAT views, you will be able to provide the optimizer with the same environment found in different databases. The update procedure is performed using the SQL UPDATE statement.

There are five updatable views under the SYSSTAT schema. These views are:

- SYSSTAT.TABLES
- SYSSTAT.COLUMNS
- SYSSTAT.INDEXES
- SYSSTAT.COLDIST
- SYSSTAT.FUNCTIONS

These catalog views can be used to provide a "what-if" analysis for your database applications. For example, you can increase the cardinality of a table or the cluster ratio of an index.

You can use the REBIND utility to model the behavior of your static SQL applications in the "what-if" analysis process. You can create or drop an index and then use the REBIND utility to see how the access plan is affected.

As a general recommendation, only update the SYSSTAT schema view in a development environment.

The DB2LOOK Utility

The DB2LOOK utility can be used to do one of three tasks. It can generate a report of database statistics. This report file can be a postscript, LaTeX, or a normal text file. (LaTeX, like HTML, is a markup language used to represent documents.)

DB2LOOK can also be used extract statistics and/or the Data Definition Language (DDL) statements for the creation of tables, indexes, views, and so on that are needed to generate a Command Line Processor (CLP) script file used to recreate database objects and/or to update the statistics.

Why is it useful? If an application developer needs access to a database that is the same as the production database except for the data it contains, the DB2LOOK utility can be used to extract the DDL and statistics into a script. This script can then be used to create a "development" database and update the statistics without actually copying the production data to the development database. An application programer can now use the development database for testing code. In addition, performance evaluation can be undertaken using utilities like Visual Explain, which use the database statistics to report on how an SQL statement will be executed and give an indication of its likely performance.

Here is an abbreviated syntax of the db2look utility:

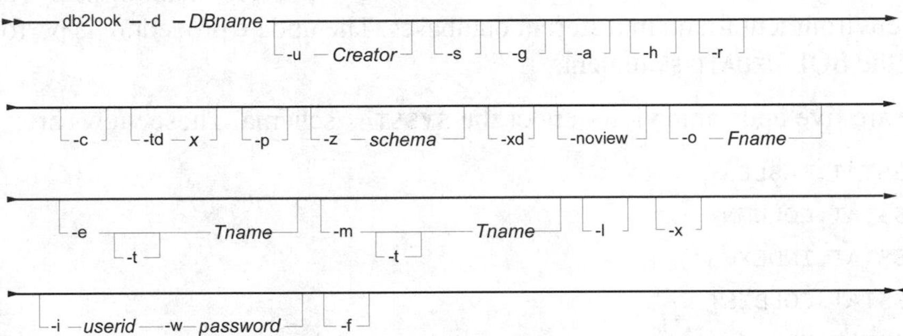

Figure 12–53 *DB2LOOK command*

Some of the key parameters to the db2look command include (see the *DB2 Command Reference* for further detail):

- -d DBname — The name of the database must be specified. This is not optional.
- -u Creator — If specified, only information about objects created by the Creator will be extracted.
- -a — Option will allow information to be extracted for all objects in the database. If neither -u or -a is specified, the USER environment variable is used. When using Windows NT, no default value is specified for this environment variable, in which case a SET USER=XXXX statement can be used prior to the invocation of the utility to set the USER environment variable.
- -s — Flag will cause the utility to format the output to LaTeX file and then convert it to a postscript file. This requires LaTeX software to be installed.
- -g — Flag is similar to the -s option. The difference is a graph that will be created to show fetch page pairs for indices. This requires LaTeX and Gnuplot software to be installed.

- `-p` — If specified, this flag will cause the information extracted to be formatted as a plain text file.
- `-o filename` — Specifies the file name that is to be used for the output files. The extension need not be specified. If the output file is a LaTeX file, the `tex` extension will be used. If the output file is a postscript file, `ps` will be used, and if it is a text file, then `txt` will be used. If the utility is used to generate a CLP script file, no extension will be added to the file name.
- `-e` — Flag will inform the utility to extract the necessary DDL statements to recreate some objects in the database, including tables, indexes, views, and triggers.
- `-l` — Option indicate that DDL statements for the creation of table spaces, buffer pools and database partition groups.
- `-x` — Should be used to extract various `GRANT` statements used to duplicate the authorization aspects of the database and the objects in it.
- `-m` — If this flag is specified, the utility will run in mimic mode. It will generate a text file that contains all the SQL statements required to update the statistics in the updatable catalog views of a target database to reflect that of the source database.
- `-c` — Flag indicates to the utility that no `COMMIT`, `CONNECT`, or `CONNECT RESET` statements should be generated in the output file. This flag is ignored if the `-m` flag is not specified.
- `-r` — Flag will cause the utility to not execute the `RUNSTATS` command prior to the extraction of statistics from the catalog.
- `-i userid` — Specifies the userid to use when running the `DB2LOOK` utility against a remote database.
- `-w password` — Specifies the password to use when running the `DB2LOOK` utility against a remote database.

Here is an example of using the `DB2LOOK` command that could be applied to a production database. The `SAMPLE` database contains many tables that are used to show the capabilities of the DB2 database. Application programmers may want a copy of the `SAMPLE` database to use themselves without destroying the contents of the original copy. The DBA decides to extract the DDL script from the `SAMPLE` database to use it to build a database named `TESTSMPL` on the server that is to be used for development only. The command the DBA uses to extract the DDL is:

```
db2look -d sample -a -o sample.ddl -e -x -l
```

Maintaining Data

The DBA edits the SAMPLE.DDL file, replaces SAMPLE with TESTSMPL in the CONNECT statement and executes the following command:

```
db2 -tvf sample.ddl
```

The Control Center allows a user-friendly method to invoke the DB2LOOK utility. Simply right-click the mouse on the required database object and select the **Generate DDL** option (Figure 12–54).

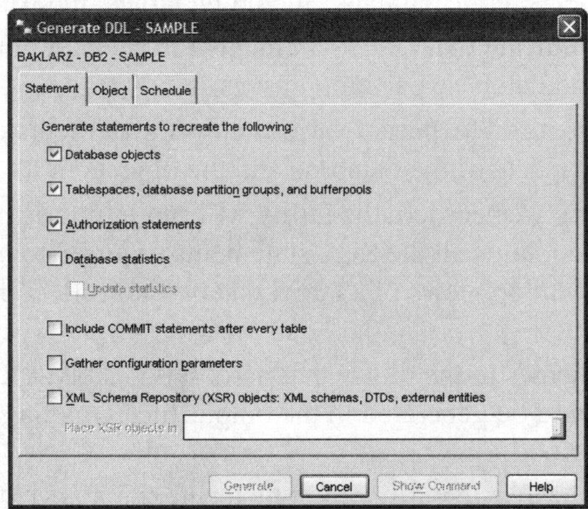

Figure 12–54 *Generate DDL*

Executing DB2LOOK from the Control Center

The DB2LOOK utility can be invoked remotely, so the user does not specify the output file name in which the output will be stored. Instead, the user can look at the script file produced by invoking the Script Center to view and edit the script, as shown in Figure 12–55.

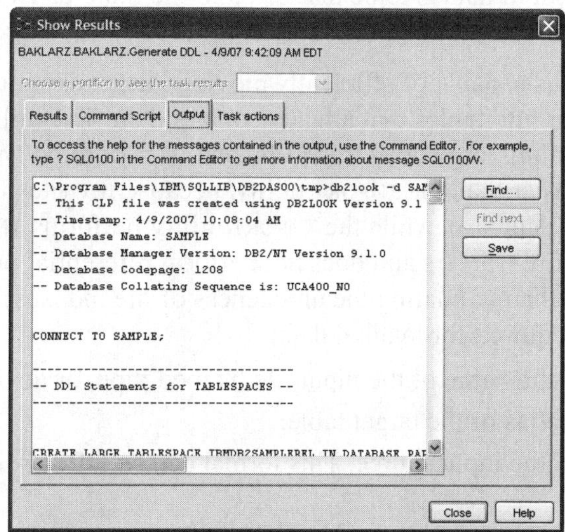

Figure 12–55 *Task Center listing the DB2LOOK output script*

Summary

This chapter has dealt with the issues of data movement, organization, and placement in your database. Various utilities in DB2 that move data into database tables and to extract data from tables have been reviewed. These included the EXPORT, IMPORT, and LOAD utilities. Included in this discussion was a summary of the various file types allowed by DB2. The numerous options provided with these commands give you flexibility in their use. These utilities can be invoked either graphically through the Control Center or by any of the command line tools.

The EXPORT utility exports data from a database to an operating system file, which can be in one of several external file formats. The following information is required when exporting data:

- A SELECT statement specifying the data to be exported.
- The path and name of the operating system file that will store the exported data.
- The format of the data in the input file. This format can be IXF, WSF, or DEL.

The IMPORT utility inserts data from an input file into a table or updatable view. If the table or view receiving the imported data already contains data, you can either replace or append to the existing data. The IMPORT utility requires the following information:

- The path and the name of the input file.
- The name or alias of the target table or view.
- The format of the data in the input file. This format can be IXF, WSF, DEL, or ASC.

- Whether the input data is to be inserted into the table or view, or whether existing data in the table or view is to be updated or replaced by the input data.

The LOAD utility is capable of efficiently moving large quantities of data into newly created tables, or into tables that already contain data. The utility can handle most data types, including large objects (LOBs) and user-defined types (UDTs). The LOAD utility is faster than the IMPORT utility, because it writes formatted pages directly into the database, while the IMPORT utility performs INSERTs. The LOAD utility does not fire triggers and does not perform referential or table constraints checking (other than validating the uniqueness of the indexes). The following information is required for loading data:

- The path and the name of the input file, named pipe, or device.
- The name or alias of the target table.
- The format of the input source. This format can be DEL, ASC, PC/IXF, or CURSOR.
- Whether the input data is to be appended to the table, or is to replace the existing data in the table.

Getting data into relational tables is just the first step. DB2 utilities and commands are provided to maintain the data. This includes the analysis of data in tables and indexes with the REORGCHK utility, physically changing the organization of the table and index data using the REORG command, and how to update the statistics of table and index data using the RUNSTATS command.

When an indexed table has been modified many times, the data in the indexes may become fragmented. If the table is clustered with respect to an index, the table and index can get out of cluster order. Both of these factors can adversely affect the performance of scans using the index, and can impact the effectiveness of index page prefetching. REORG INDEXES can be used to reorganize all of the indexes on a table, to remove any fragmentation and restore physical clustering to the leaf pages. Tables that have been modified so many times that data is fragmented and access performance is noticeably slow are candidates for the REORG TABLE command. After reorganizing a table, use RUNSTATS to update the table statistics. After running RUNSTATS, a REBIND should be issued to ensure that the applications are aware of the updated statistics in your environment.

CHAPTER 13

Database Recovery

- LOG FILES
- LOGGING
- BACKUP
- RESTORE
- ROLLFORWARD RECOVERY
- HIGH AVAILABILITY SCENARIOS

One of the fundamental functions of any database management system is the ability to recover from events that would lead to the integrity of the database being compromised. DB2 is no different in this regard and has a number of features and functions available to help you manage your environment and ensure that you can perform adequate recovery of your data.

In this chapter, the concept of logging in a relational database system as it relates to the recovery of a database will be discussed. In addition, the major utilities involved in the area of database recovery, BACKUP and RESTORE, will be reviewed.

Database Recovery Concepts

While DB2 has mechanisms to provide automatic recovery from situations that threaten the integrity of its databases, it cannot cater to all situations, especially unforeseen external events. While it is impossible to cover every possible scenario, careful planning can ensure that recovery is possible for the majority of situations with minimum loss of data.

Some situations you should consider are:

- System outage — The operating system fails due to a hardware or software problem. An interruption to the power supply also falls under this category.
- Transaction failure — A transaction fails before completion. What happens to changes made to the database before the point of failure?
- Media failure — A disk drive failure causes a partial or complete loss of data on the disk.
- Disaster — A wide range of nontrivial damage to more than just a single component of the system. The facility at which the system is located suffers damage that impacts the system's operation.

Unit of Work

To ensure consistency of the data in a database, it is often necessary for applications to apply a number of changes together as a unit. This is called a *unit of work*. A unit of work is a recoverable sequence of operations within an application process. It is the basic mechanism that an application uses to ensure database integrity. At any time, an application process has a single unit of work, but the life of an application process may involve many units of work.

Transaction

Units of work are also known as *transactions*. A unit of work is started implicitly when the first SQL statement is issued against the database. The application must end the transaction by issuing a `COMMIT` or a `ROLLBACK` statement. The `COMMIT` statement tells the database manager to apply all database changes (inserts, updates, deletes, creates, alters, grants, revokes) to the database at once. The `ROLLBACK` statement tells the database manager not to apply the changes but to return the affected rows back to their state before the beginning of the transaction.

Types of Recovery

Recovery can be one of the following: crash, version, or roll-forward. Each type will now be examined.

Crash Recovery

Crash recovery protects a database from being left in an inconsistent or unusable state. Units of work against the database can be interrupted unexpectedly. For example, should a power failure occur before all of the changes that are part of a unit of work are completed and committed, the database will be left in an inconsistent state.

The database is made consistent again by undoing the uncommitted transactions. The RESTART DATABASE command initiates this function. If the AUTORESTART database configuration parameter is set to ON (which is the default), the first connection to the database after a failure will initiate the RESTART DATABASE.

Version Recovery

Version recovery allows for the restoration of a previous version or image of the database that was made using the BACKUP command.

Restoration of the database will rebuild the entire database using a backup of the database made at some point in time earlier. A backup of the database allows you to restore a database to a state identical to the time when the backup was made. Every unit of work from the time of the backup to the end of the log files is lost. (These can be recovered using roll-forward recovery.)

The version recovery method requires a full database backup for each version you may want to restore in the future. DB2 supports version recovery by default.

Roll-Forward Recovery

This technique extends the version recovery by using full database backups in conjunction with log files to provide the capability of restoring a database or selected table spaces to a particular point in time.

By using a full database backup as a baseline, if all the log files are available covering the time period from the time of the backup to the current time, you can choose to have DB2 apply all the units of work for any or all table spaces in the database, up to any time within the time period covered by the logs.

Roll-forward recovery is specified at a database level in DB2 and has to be explicitly enabled.

DB2 Note

The catalog table space `SYSCATSPACE`, when used in table space roll-forward recovery, *must* be rolled forward to the end of the logs. It can be rolled forward to a point in time as part of database roll-forward recovery.

Recovery Strategies

Some of the factors to consider when formulating a recovery strategy include:

- Will the database be recoverable or nonrecoverable?
- How near to the time of failure will you need to recover the database (the point of recovery)?
- How much time can be spent recovering the database?
- How large a window do you have for all recovery activities?
- What storage resources are available for storing backups and log files?

In general, a database maintenance and recovery strategy should ensure that all information is available when it is required for database recovery. In addition, you should include elements that reduce the likelihood and impact of database failure.

Recoverable and Nonrecoverable Databases

Recoverable databases in DB2 are distinguished by the `LOGRETAIN` and `USEREXIT` or `LOGARCHMETH1` and `LOGARCHMETH2` database configuration parameters being enabled. This means that crash, version, *and* roll-forward recovery techniques are available for use.

Nonrecoverable databases *do not* support roll-forward recovery.

The decision whether a database should be recoverable depends on factors such as:

- If the database is query only, then there will be no units of work in the log, therefore the database may not need to be recoverable.
- If there is little volatility in the database (that is, few changes to the data) and the data can be recreated easily, then you may wish to consider not having your database recoverable.
- Databases that have data that is not easily recreated should be made recoverable.
- If there is a lot of update activity, a recoverable database should be considered.

Online and Offline Access

When performing the various database recovery activities, the database can be considered *offline* or *online*.

Online means that other applications can connect to the database during the operation being performed. Conversely, offline means that no other application can use the database while the operation is in progress. Offline and online are not available for all recovery activities.

Use of Log Files

All DB2 databases have logs associated with them. These logs keep a record of all changes made to database objects and data. All the changes are first written to log buffers in memory before being flushed to the log files on disk at `COMMIT` time.

For example, in case of a mishap such as power failure, the log files would be used to bring the database back to a consistent state. All units of work would be reapplied using the log files, and then all uncommitted units of work would be rolled back.

Log files have a predefined, configurable size. Therefore, when one log file is filled, logging continues in another log file. Figure 13–1 shows how multiple log files are being used to manage concurrent transactions.

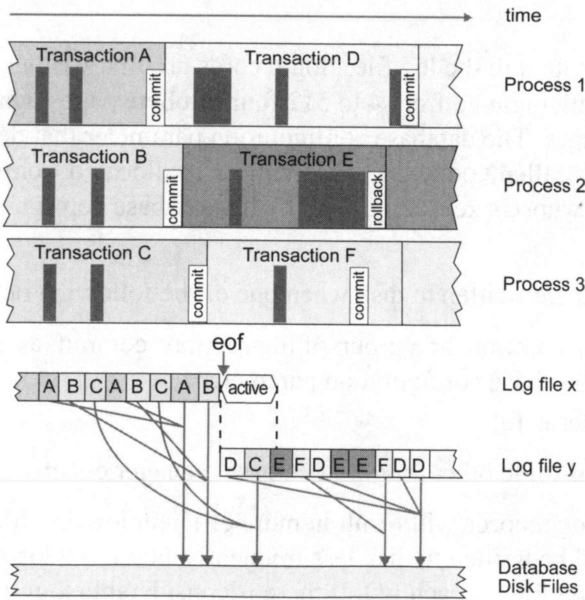

Figure 13–1 *Transaction log file use*

The top part of the diagram represents the evolution of three user processes (1 – 3) accessing the same database. The boxes represent database changes such as inserts or updates. The life of every transaction is also depicted (A – F). The lower-middle section of the diagram shows how the database changes are synchronously recorded in the log files (x,y). The letter in each box indicates the transaction to which the database change belongs.

DB2 Note

DB2 uses a write-ahead-logging scheme to ensure data integrity by having any updates, deletes, or inserts of data written first to the log files. At a later time, these changes are then written to the relational database.

When a `COMMIT` is issued, the log buffer containing the transaction is written to disk. This is represented by the arrows and the small wavy lines. Transaction E is never written to disk because it ends with a `ROLLBACK` statement. When log file x runs out of room to store the first database change of transaction D, the logging process switches to log file y. Log file x remains active until all transaction C changes are written to the database disk files. The period of time during which log file x remains active after logging is switched to log file y is represented by the hexagon.

Log Buffers

Before being written to the log files, log records are first written into buffers. The size of these buffers range from 4 to 512 four-kilobyte pages, with the default setting of eight pages. The database configuration parameter that defines the size of the log buffer is called `LOGBUFSZ`. The memory is allocated from an area called the database heap, whose size is controlled by the database configuration parameter `DBHEAP`.

The log records are written to disk when one of the following occurs:

- A transaction commits or a group of transactions commit, as defined by the `MINCOMMIT` database configuration parameter.
- The log buffer is full.
- As a result of some other *internal* database manager event.

Buffering the log records will result in more efficient logging file I/O because the log records will be written to disk less frequently, and more log records will be written to the log files at each I/O. If there is considerable logging activity in the system, increase the size of the log buffers to improve performance.

Primary and Secondary Log Files

There are two types of log files: primary and secondary.

- *Primary* log files establish a fixed amount of storage allocated to the recovery log files. These files are preallocated during the first connection to the database. The database configuration parameter `LOGPRIMARY` determines the number of primary log files created of a size specified by the `LOGFILSIZ` database configuration parameter.
- *Secondary* log files are allocated one at a time as needed (up to the value of the database configuration parameter `LOGSECOND`) when the primary log files become full. The size of secondary log files is also specified by the `LOGFILSIZ` database configuration parameter.

  One recommendation is to use secondary log files for databases that have periodic needs for large amounts of log space. For example, an application that is run once a month may require log space beyond that provided by the primary log files.

DB2 Note

The default value of `LOGFILSIZ` is 1000 pages for Linux and UNIX-based versions of DB2. For Windows, the value is 250 pages. The page size is always 4 KB.

Types of Logging

There are two types of logging that can occur in DB2: circular and archival.

- *Circular logging* supports nonrecoverable databases. This type of logging uses active log files only (see below for details). Primary and secondary log files are used as described above. When a log file has had all of its transactions committed or rolled back, then it can be reused. Roll-forward recovery is not possible with this logging method, whereas crash recovery and version recovery are available. This is the default logging method when a DB2 database is created.

  The circular logging method is shown in Figure 13–2.

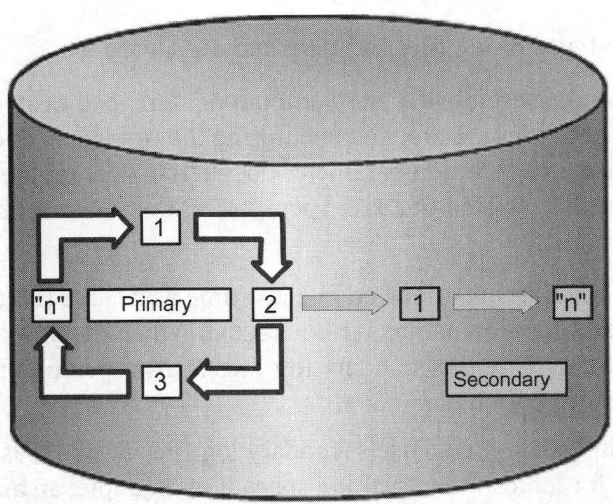

Figure 13–2 *Circular logging*

- *Archival logging* is where log files are archived when they become inactive. Archival logging is not the default logging method. It is the only method that will allow you to support roll-forward recovery and implement recoverable databases. There are three types of log files associated with this method, shown in Figure 13–3.

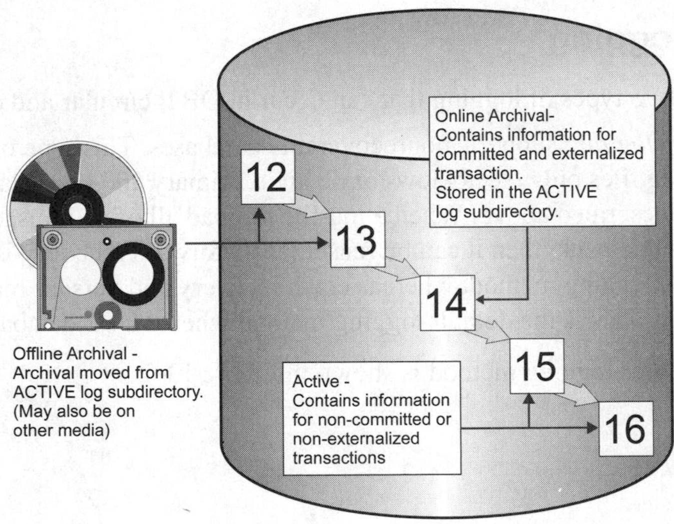

Figure 13–3 *Archival logging*

Log files can be classified as follows:

- *Active* — Indicated by numbers 15 and 16. These files contain information related to units of work that have not yet been committed (or rolled back). They also contain information about transactions that have been committed but whose changes have not yet been written to the database files.

  Active log files are used by crash recovery to prevent a failure from leaving the database in an inconsistent state. The RESTART DATABASE situation (for crash recovery) and ROLLFORWARD command (for point-in-time recovery or recovery to the end of the logs) use the active logs to reapply or roll back units of work if necessary to bring the database to a point of consistency.

DB2 Note

DB2 supports log mirroring at the database level. The DB2 configuration parameter, MIRRORLOGPATH, enables the database to write an identical copy of the log files to a different path.

- *Online Archived* — Indicated by number 14. When all changes in the active log are no longer needed for normal processing, the log is closed and becomes an archived log.

  These files contain information related to completed transactions no longer required for restart recovery. They are called *online* because they reside in the same subdirectory as the active log files.

- *Offline Archived* — Indicated by numbers 12 and 13. These log files have been moved from the active log file directory. The method of moving these files could be a manual or automated process such as that invoked by a user exit. Archived log files can be placed offline simply by moving them to another directory or storing them on tape or other medium. They can also be managed by an external storage manager such as IBM's TSM (Tivoli Storage Manager) products.

There are two sets of database configuration parameters that allow you to configure a database for archival logging:

- LOGRETAIN, USEREXIT
- LOGARCHMETH1, LOGARCHMETH2

LOGRETAIN and USEREXIT can still be used in DB2 9 but they are deprecated which means they will not be supported in a future release. It is recommended that the newer LOGARCHMETH1/2 configuration parameters are used instead.

LOGRETAIN and USEREXIT

When the LOGRETAIN database configuration parameter is enabled, log files are not deleted when they become inactive. When the USEREXIT database configuration parameter is enabled, DB2 will call the user exit program when a log file is ready for archiving. The database name, path of the log file, and several other parameters are passed to the program.

If the user exit option is enabled, you have the option of issuing the ARCHIVE LOG command to force a log archive.

DB2 Note

The default setting for LOGRETAIN and USEREXIT is NO; thus circular logging is the default.

LOGARCHMETH1 and LOGARCHMETH2

The LOGARCHMETH1 parameter specifies the media type of the primary destination for archived logs. LOGARCHMETH1 can contain one of five values:

- OFF (default)

  Specifies that the log archiving method is not to be used. If both LOGARCHMETH1 and LOGARCHMETH2 are set to OFF, the database is considered to be using circular logging and will not be rollforward recoverable.

- LOGRETAIN

  This value can only be used for LOGARCHMETH1 and is equivalent to setting the LOGRETAIN configuration parameter to RECOVERY.

- USEREXIT

  This value is only valid for LOGARCHMETH1 and is equivalent to setting the userexit configuration parameter to ON.

- DISK

  This value must be followed by a colon(:) and then a fully qualified existing path name where the log files will be archived. For example, if you set LOGARCHMETH1 to DISK:/u/db2user/archived_logs the archive log files will be placed in a directory called /u/db2user/archived_logs.

- TSM

  This value indicates that log files should be archived on the local TSM server using the default management class. If followed by a colon(:) and a TSM management class, the log files will be archived using the specified management class.

- VENDOR

  Specifies that a vendor library will be used to archive the log files. This value must be followed by a colon(:) and the name of the library. The APIs provided in the library must use the backup and restore APIs for vendor products.

The LOGARCHMETH2 parameter specifies the media type of the secondary destination for archived logs. The value of this parameter can be either OFF or set to a file path. If a path is specified, log files will be archived to both this destination and the destination specified by the LOGARCHMETH1 database configuration parameter.

ROLL-FORWARD Recovery

Roll-forward recovery can use online archived logs, offline archived logs, and active logs to rebuild a database or table space either at the end of the logs or at a specific point in time. The roll-forward function achieves this by reapplying committed units of work that are found in the archived and active logs to the restored database.

Database Recovery

DB2 *Note*

The current log file path is indicated by the database configuration parameter LOGPATH. When a database is created, the log files are placed under the default database directory. The NEWLOGPATH database configuration parameter is used to change the log file location.

Log File Usage

There are some considerations to bear in mind in relation to the use of log files. These considerations are as follows.

Erasing Logs

If an active log is erased, the database becomes unusable and must be restored before it can be used again.

If an archive log is erased, you will only be able to roll-forward changes up to the first log erased.

It is critical that all log files be protected by the security subsystem of the operating system. Other than the process of moving archive logs out of the log path directory, no other user or application other than DB2 has any need to access the log files.

Using the Not Logged Initially Option

The NOT LOGGED INITIALLY option exists for the CREATE TABLE and ALTER TABLE statements. When this option is used, no loggable activity within the unit of work that creates or alters the table or activates this option at a later time is logged. This is an advantage when inserting or updating a large amount of data into a table for the first time. This option is also suitable for work tables where data can be easily recreated.

The advantage of this option is the improvement in performance due to the absence of logging overhead; the disadvantage is the lack of recoverability of the unit of work.

Logging Using Raw Devices

Normally, log files use the standard operating system file systems to support their implementation (e.g., NTFS for Windows, JFS for AIX).

In addition to the standard file systems, you can use raw devices for logging. By using raw devices, you can avoid the overhead of using the file system, and therefore logging performance should be improved. This support is available on the Windows, AIX, and Solaris operating systems.

This involves using an unformatted hard disk partition (Windows) or a raw logical volume (AIX). The database configuration parameter NEWLOGPATH is set to point to the raw device.

Some considerations for using raw devices for logging are:

- Primary log files (extents) are still used according to the LOGPRIMARY and LOGFILSIZ database configuration parameters. The amount of space in the raw device must be at least (LOGPRIMARY * (LOGFILSIZ + 2)) + 1) pages of 4 KB each.
- Secondary log files are not used. You may have to increase the number and/or size of primary log files to compensate for this.

Refer to the *DB2 Administration Guide* for more details about logging using raw devices. Logging using raw devices is deprecated in DB2 9, which means that it will not be supported in a future release.

Block Transactions When Log Directory is Full

The DBM configuration parameter BLK_LOG_DSK_FUL can be used to prevent “disk full” errors from being generated when DB2 cannot create a new log file in the active log path. DB2 attempts to create the log file every five minutes and writes a message to the db2diag.log file after each attempt. An analysis of the db2diag.log file can confirm if the application is hanging.

DB2 *Note*

The maximum amount of log space has been increased from 32GB to 256GB. Infinite active logging is also new and allows an active unit of work to span the primary logs and archive logs, enabling a transaction to use an infinite number of log files.

Version Recovery Using Backup and Restore

Version recovery is implemented using the BACKUP and RESTORE commands. These two commands will now be examined in greater detail.

Backing Up a Database

The BACKUP command can be invoked from the Command Line Processor, Command Center, application programming interface, or Control Center.

Before taking a backup, consider the following:

- You must have SYSADM, SYSCTRL, or SYSMAINT authority to invoke BACKUP.
- The database may be local or remote. The backup itself remains on the database server.
- The BACKUP command can interface with an external storage manager such as TSM to directly manage the backup image.
- BACKUP can directly send its output to tape via the operating system.
- BACKUP can directly send its output to disk on all platforms.
- Multiple backup files may be created to contain the backed-up data from the database.

When you invoke the BACKUP command, you should be aware of the following:

- DB2 must be started.
- The database must be in a normal or backup-pending state.
- When using the BACKUP utility, refer to the database name by its alias. In most cases this will be the same name as the database.
- You can run the backup in online mode via the ONLINE parameter or in offline mode, which is the default. Online mode allows other applications to remain connected to the database and do active work while the backup is proceeding. Alternately, for an offline backup, only the backup job itself may be connected to the database.

  For online mode, the database must be recoverable; that is, archive logging must be enabled. When running in online mode, DB2 attempts to acquire S (share) locks on tables with LOBs (large objects). This might result in failures running the utility due to applications connected to the database holding incompatible locks.

In addition, consider the following to improve the backup performance:

- The value of the PARALLELISM parameter. Using this parameter can reduce the amount of time required to complete the backup. It defines the number of processes or threads that are started to read data from the database. Each process or thread is assigned to back up a specific table space. When it completes backing up the table space, it requests another. Increasing the value requires additional processor and memory resources. The default value is one.
- The backup buffer size and number of buffers. If you use multiple buffers and I/O channels, you should use at least twice as many buffers as channels to ensure that the channels do not have to wait for data. The size of the buffers should ideally be a multiple of the table space extent size. If you have differing extent sizes, choose a multiple of the largest extent size. If the buffer size if not specified the value is taken from the database manager configuration parameter BACKBUFSZ, which by default is 1024 (4 KB) pages.

Backup Images Created by Backup

Backup images are created at the target specified when the BACKUP utility is invoked:

- In the directory for disk backups
- At the device specified for tape backups
- At an external storage manager server

The *recovery history file* is updated automatically with summary information whenever you carry out a backup of a database. This information is useful when tracking the backup history of a database. Other utilities' activities are also recorded in this file.

The file name(s) created on disk will consist of a concatenation of the following information, separated by periods; on other platforms, a four-level subdirectory tree structure is used:

- *Database alias* — A one- to eight-character database alias name that was supplied when the backup command was invoked.
- *Type* — Type of backup taken, where "0" is for full database, "3" is for table space.
- *Instance name* — A one- to eight-character name of the instance.
- *Node number* — The node number.
- *Catalog node number* — The node number of the database's catalog node.

- *Time stamp* — A 14-character representation of the date and time the backup was performed. The timestamp is in the format yyyymmddhhmmss, where:

  yyyy is the year (1995 to 9999), mm is the month (01 to 12),
  dd is the day of the month (01 to 31), hh is the hour (00 to 23),
  mm is the minutes (00 to 59), ss is the seconds (00 to 59).
- *Sequence number* — A three-digit sequence number used as a file extension.

On all operating systems, the format would appear as:

```
DB_alias.Type.Inst.nodennnn.catnnnn.timestamp.seq_num
```

For example, a database named SAMPLE in the DB2 instance is backed up to disk as a file named:

```
SAMPLE.0.DB2.NODE0000.CATN0000.20070410092203.001
```

In versions of DB2 prior to DB2 9, the format on Windows would appear as:

```
DB_alias.Type\Inst\nodennnn\catnnnn\yyyymmdd\hhmmss.seq_num
```

The previous example would have backed up the SAMPLE database as:

```
V:\SAMPLE.0\DB2\NODE0000\CATN0000\20070410\092203.001
```

For tape-directed output, file names are not created; however, the above information is stored in the backup header for verification purposes.

Examples of Using Backup

Some of the key parameters of the BACKUP command (Figure 13–4) include (see the *DB2 Command Reference* for further details):

- ONLINE — Specifies an online backup, offline is the default.
- INCREMENTAL — Specifies a backup of all data since the last full backup.
- DELTA — Specifies a backup of data since the most recent backup operation of any type.

You can run the BACKUP command from the DB2 Command Line Processor or DB2 Command Center. For example, this command backs up the database SAMPLE to the C:\DBBACKUP directory on a Windows system. The other parameters take their default values:

```
BACKUP DATABASE SAMPLE TO C:\DBBACKUP
```

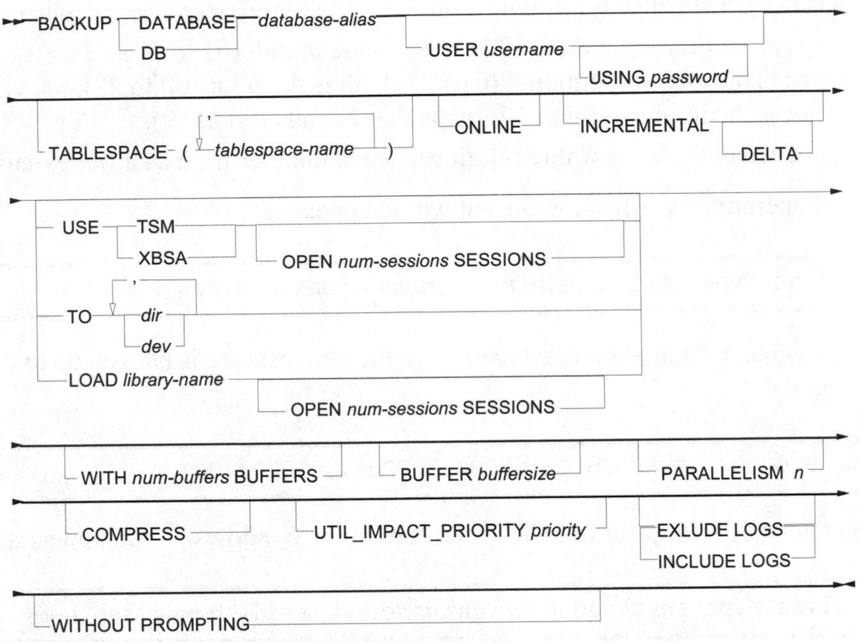

Figure 13–4 *BACKUP command*

This command backs up the database SAMPLE to a tape device on an AIX system. Two buffers of 512 (4 KB) pages each are allocated. Two parallel tasks are used to backup in parallel.

```
BACKUP DATABASE SAMPLE TO /dev/rmt0
       WITH 2 BUFFERS
       BUFFER 512
       PARALLELISM 2
```

You can also use the Control Center to invoke a backup. After right-clicking on the database you wish to back up, select the Backup Database option, as shown in Figure 13–5.

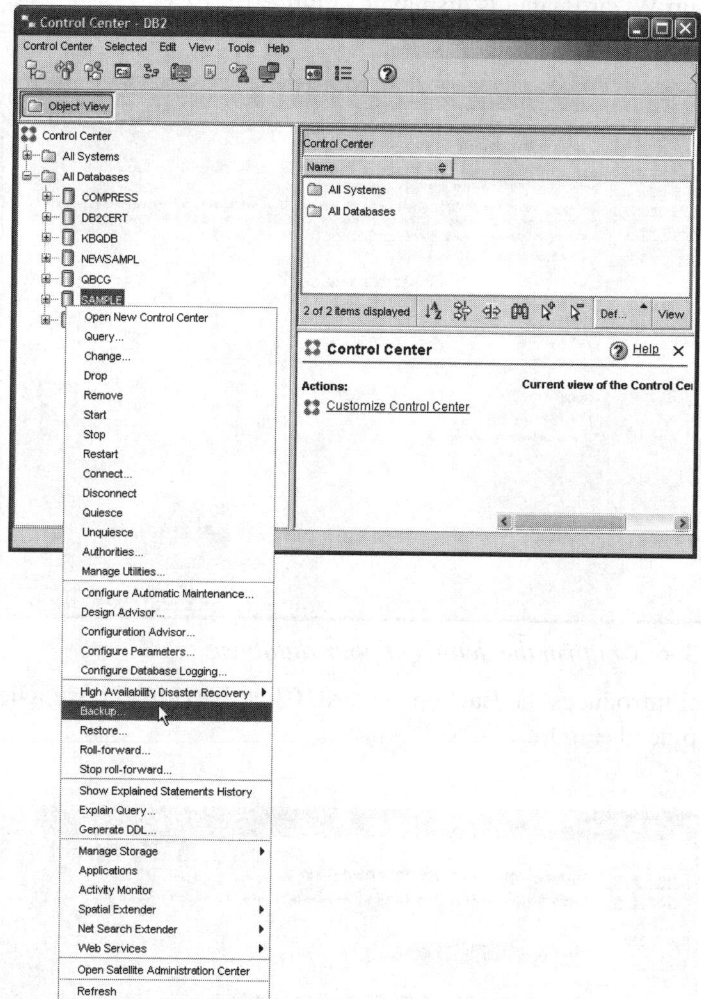

Figure 13–5 *Backing up a database from the Control Center*

The Backup Wizard panel is displayed (Figure 13–6):

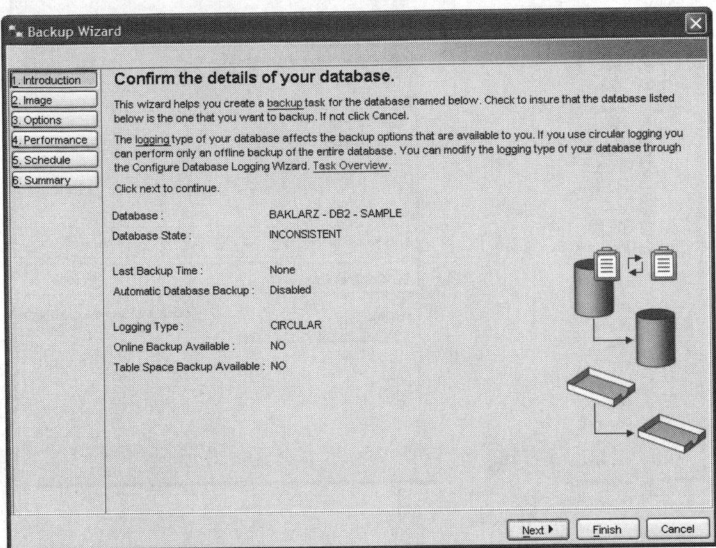

Figure 13–6 *Confirm the details of your database*

This panel introduces the Backup Wizard. Click **Next** to choose where the backup image is placed (Figure 13–7).

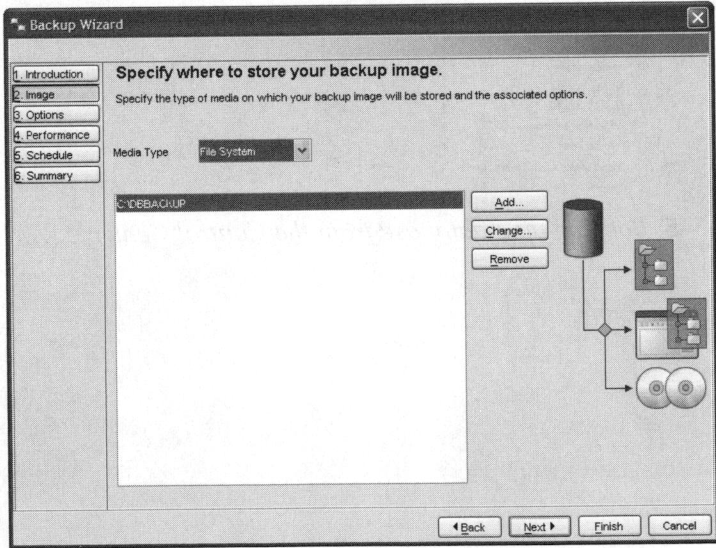

Figure 13–7 *Specify where to store your backup image*

Here you can choose whether to perform the backup to a file system, tape, TSM, XBSA, or third-party. In this example, select File System, click on Add, select the directory DBBACKUP, and click OK to get back to this panel. Click **Next**.

DB2 Note

The DB2 backup can now interface with solutions from storage vendors that have implemented the XBSA (Backup Services APIs) industry standard interface.

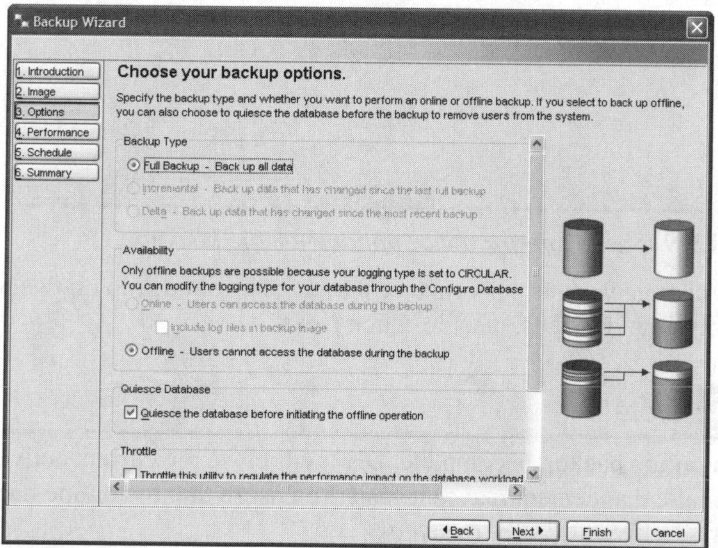

Figure 13–8 *Choose your backup options*

If archive logging was enabled, this panel would offer the DBA the choice of performing the backup procedure online (Figure 13–8). Archive logging also enables the incremental backup to be performed. For this example, click **Next** to display the performance options that are available during backup (Figure 13–9).

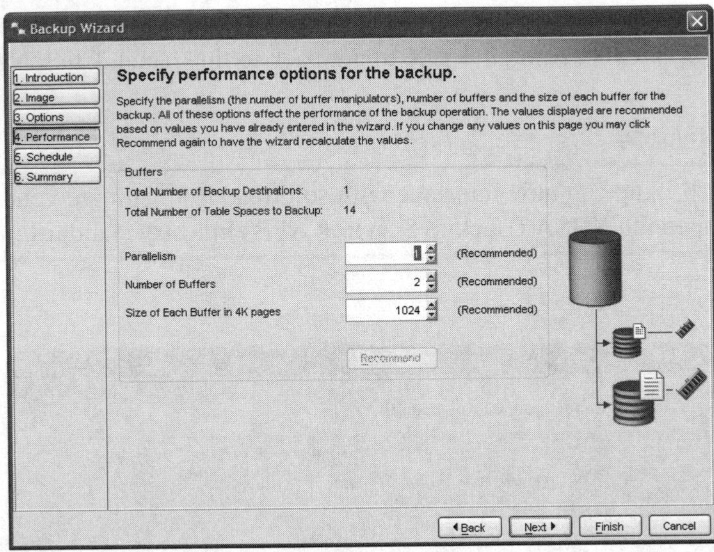

Figure 13–9 *Specify performance options for the backup*

You can change various performance parameters for backup on this panel, but normally you should let DB2 decide. Click **Next**.

DB2 Note

After an online backup is complete, DB2 will close the current active log. This operational enhancement makes it easier to ensure that the online backup has the necessary archived logs for recovery.

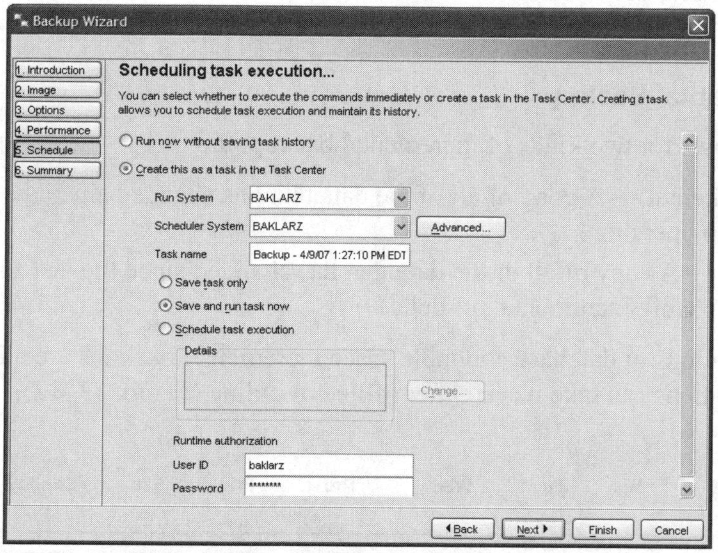

Figure 13–10 *Scheduling task execution*

You can perform the backup procedure to execute immediately or schedule it as a task for the Task Center (Figure 13–10). Select the radio button Save and run task now, enter a valid user ID and password, then click **Next**.

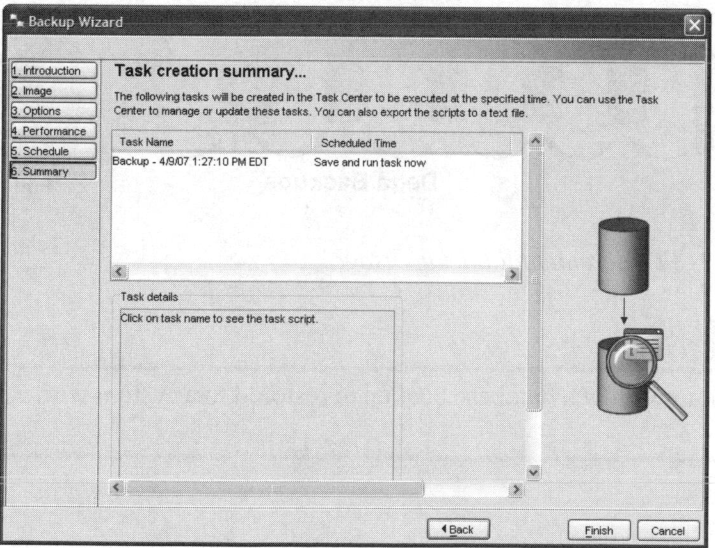

Figure 13–11 *Task creation summary*

Before launching the backup procedure, you have the option to save the script into a file (Figure 13–11). Click **Finish**.

In both cases, you can monitor and view the results of running the BACKUP command through the Journal, which can be invoked from the Control Center.

Incremental Backup

DB2 allows for two kinds of incremental backup, they are:

- Incremental — A copy of all of the data that has changed since the last full backup operation.
- Delta — A copy of all of the data that has changed since the last successful backup (full, incremental, or delta).

Combinations of database and table space incremental backups are allowed, and the operations can take place either offline or online (Figure 13–12).

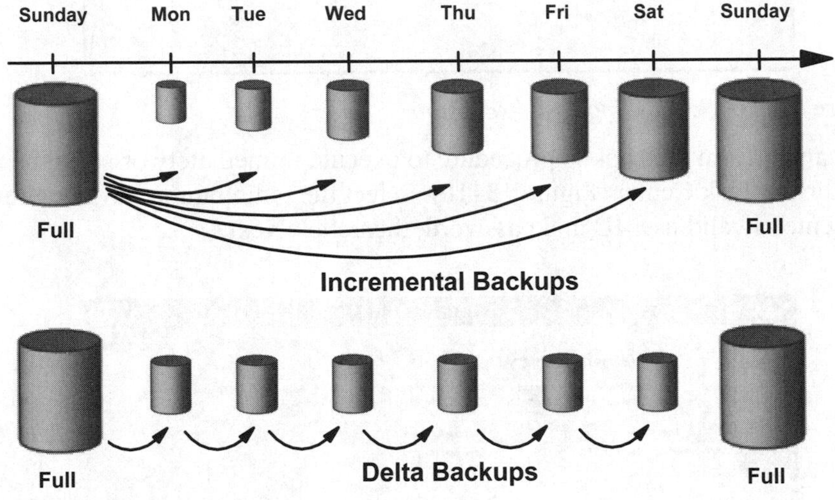

Figure 13–12 *Incremental backup usage*

DB2 *Note*

DB2 will now allow a database backup to restored to a system with a different code page.

Restoring a Database

The RESTORE command can be invoked from the Command Line Processor, Command Center, application programming interface, or Control Center.

Before performing a restore, consider the following:

- You must have SYSADM, SYSCTRL, or SYSMAINT authority to perform a RESTORE to an existing database and SYSADM or SYSCTRL if performing a RESTORE to an new database.
- You can only use this command if the database has been previously backed up with the BACKUP command.
- The RESTORE command can interface with an external storage manager such as TSM to directly use a backup image managed by the external storage manager.
- RESTORE requires an exclusive connection to the database; no applications can be running against the database when the utility is started. Once it starts, it prevents other applications from accessing the database until the restore is completed.
- The database may be local or remote.

When you invoke the RESTORE command, you should be aware of the following:

- DB2 must be started.
- You can restore to a new or an existing database.
- You can run the restore in online mode via the ONLINE parameter for table space restores only.
- The TAKEN AT parameter requires the timestamp for the backup. If there is more than one backup image in the same directory, this parameter is required. The timestamp can be exactly as it was displayed after the completion of a successful backup, that is, the format yyyymmddhhmmss. It can also be a partial timestamp as long as it is not ambiguous in identifying a backup image. If this parameter is not specified when using TSM, the latest the backup image is used for restoration.

In addition, consider the following to improve the performance of RESTORE:

- The value of the PARALLELISM parameter. Using this parameter can reduce the amount of time required to complete the restore. It defines the number of processes or threads that started for restore processing. The default value is one.

DB2 Note

There is no affiliation between a thread/process with a table space during the recovery process.

- Increasing the restore buffer size and number of buffers. You can improve the performance of RESTORE by increasing the restore buffer size (BUFFER parameter) and number of buffers (WITH n BUFFERS parameter).

  The minimum value for the BUFFER parameter is 8 pages; the default value is 1024 pages. The restore buffer pool size must be a positive integer multiple of the backup buffer size specified during the backup operation.

  For example, if a backup buffer size of 1024 pages was specified and an attempt made to restore this backup with a buffer size of 16 pages, the actual restore buffer size would be 1024. If the specified restore buffer size were 2049, the actual restore buffer size would be 2048.

DB2 Note

If a failure occurs during a database restore, the database will not be usable until a successful restore is completed.

Examples of Using Restore

Some of the key parameters to the RESTORE command include (see the *DB2 Command Reference* for further detail):

- ONLINE — Applicable only when performing a table space-level restore.
- HISTORY FILE — Specifies to restore only the history file from the backup image.
- INCREMENTAL — Without any additional parameters, this specifies a manual cumulative restore operation.
- INCREMENTAL AUTO/AUTOMATIC — Specifies an automatic cumulative restore operation.
- REDIRECT — Specifies a redirected restore operation. This command should be followed by one or more SET TABLESPACE CONTAINERS commands, and then by a RESTORE DATABASE command with the CONTINUE option.
- WITHOUT ROLLING FORWARD — Specifies the database is not to be put in rollforward pending state after it has been successfully restored.

You can run the RESTORE command from the Command Line Processor or Command Center. For example:

```
RESTORE DATABASE DB2CERT FROM C:\DBBACKUP
```

An abbreviated syntax of the RESTORE command is found in Figure 13–13.

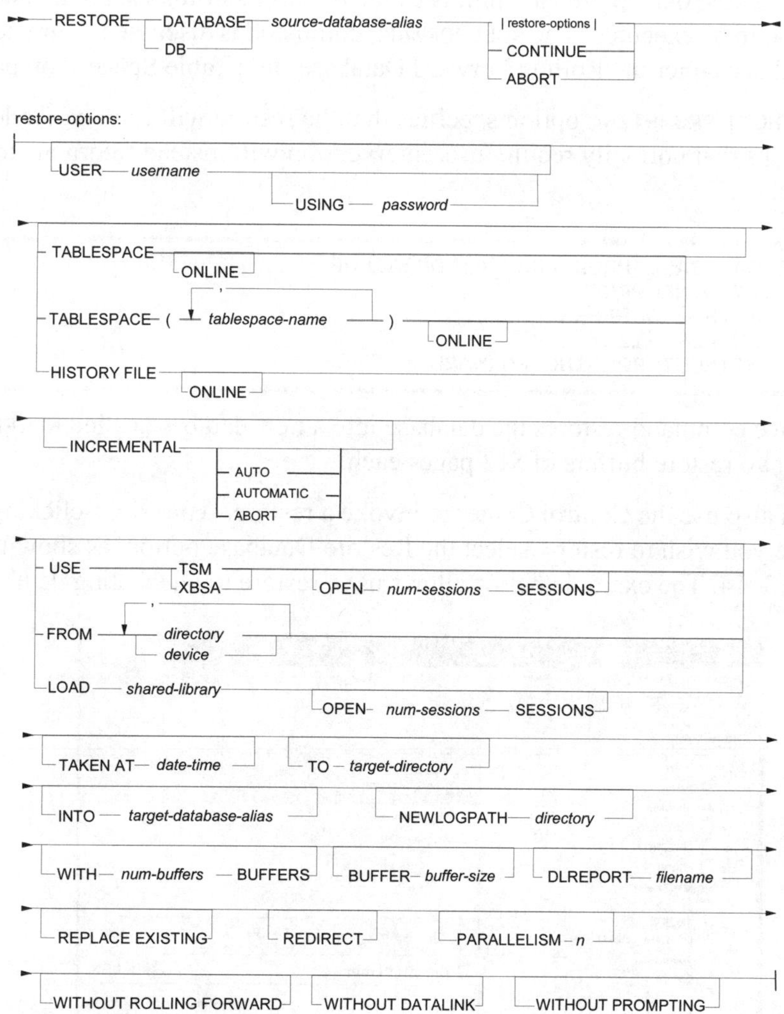

Figure 13–13 *RESTORE command*

This command restores the database `SAMPLE` from the `C:\DBBACKUP` directory on a Windows system. The other parameters use their default values. This may leave the database in a roll-forward pending state that requires the `ROLLFORWARD` command be executed before the database can be accessed.

```
RESTORE DATABASE PROD FROM C:\DBBACKUP
        WITHOUT ROLLING FORWARD
        WITHOUT PROMPTING
```

The above RESTORE command eliminates the requirement for the ROLLFORWARD command to be executed. The ROLLFORWARD command is discussed in greater detail later in this chapter in "Rolling Forward Databases and Table Spaces" on page 829.

The WITHOUT PROMPTING option specifies that the restore will run unattended and any actions that normally require user intervention will instead return an error message.

```
RESTORE DATABASE PROD FROM C:\DBBACKUP
        INTO NEWPROD
        WITH 2 BUFFERS
        BUFFER 512
        WITHOUT ROLLING FORWARD
```

The above command restores the database into a new database called NEWPROD and assigns two restore buffers of 512 pages each.

You can also use the Control Center to invoke a restore. After right-clicking on the database you wish to restore, select the Restore Database option, as shown in Figure 13–14. The example below allows us to restore to an existing database.

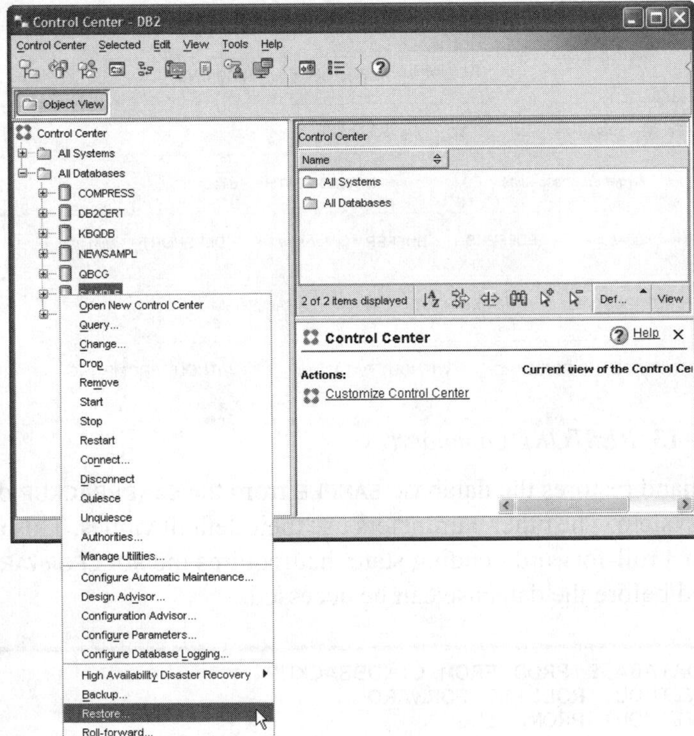

Figure 13–14 *Restoring a database using the Control Center*

The first panel confirms the details of the database that you want to recover (Figure 13–15). The wizard allows you to restore to an existing database, create a new database (redirected restore), or restore the history file of the database. Select the Restore to an existing database option, and click **Next**.

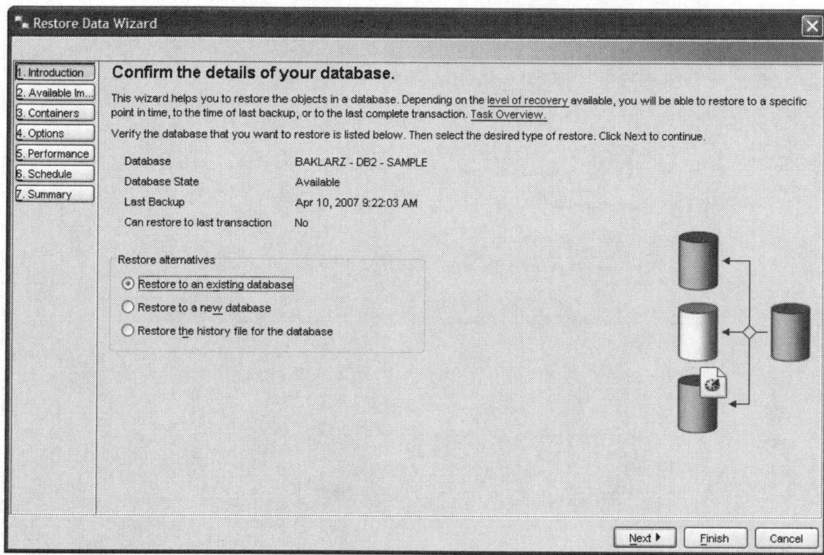

Figure 13–15 *Database details*

The second panel displays the previous backups that were performed. One of the backups needs to be selected before continuing on with backup options (Figure 13–16).

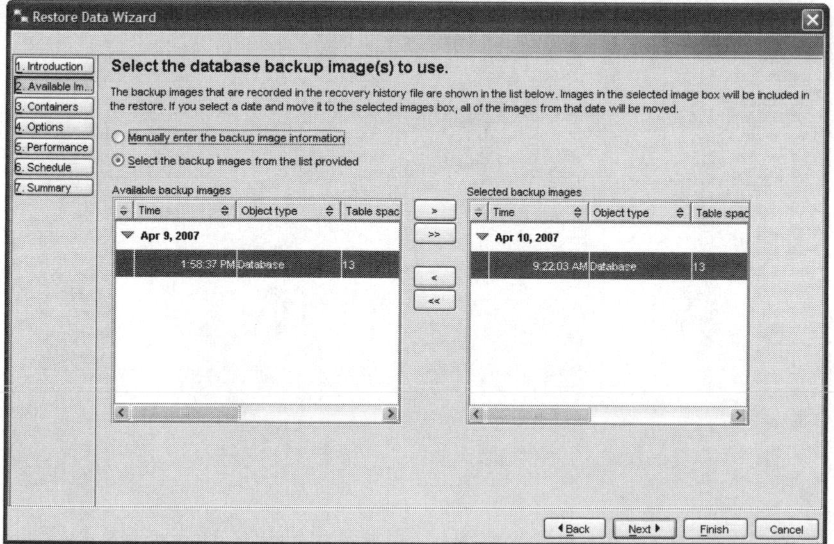

Figure 13–16 *Selecting which backup to restore*

The Containers tab allows you to redefine the containers that a table space uses. You should only do this if you want to change the containers from those defined in the backup image (Figure 13–17). This is known as a *redirected restore*. Click **Next**.

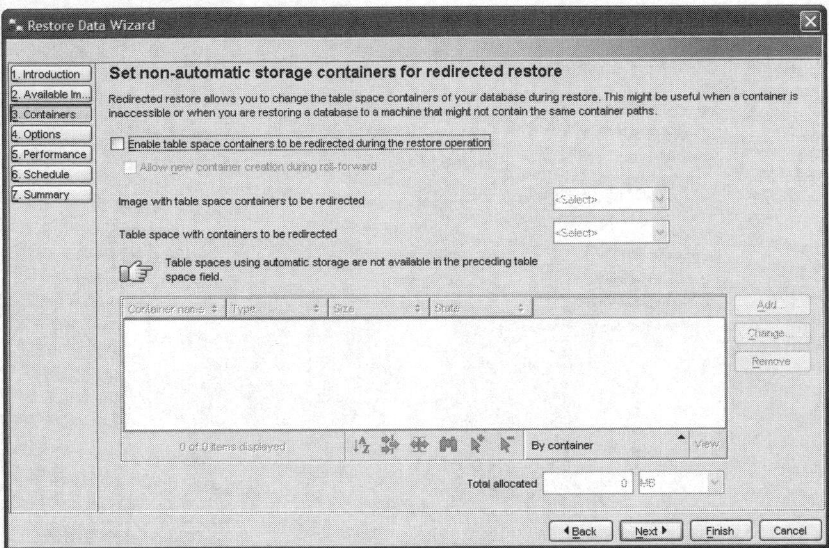

Figure 13–17 *Set your containers for a redirected restore*

The option of quiescing the database is given before initiating an offline restore (Figure 13–18). Click **Next** (you do not need to select an option on this panel).

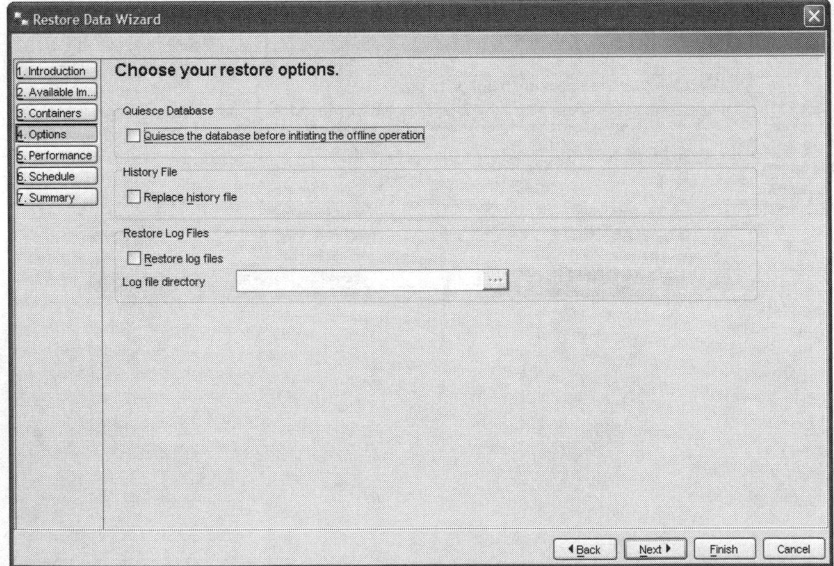

Figure 13–18 *Choose your restore options*

These next panel contains parameters that affect the performance of restore, similar to backup (Figure 13–19). Change the values if desired, click **Next**.

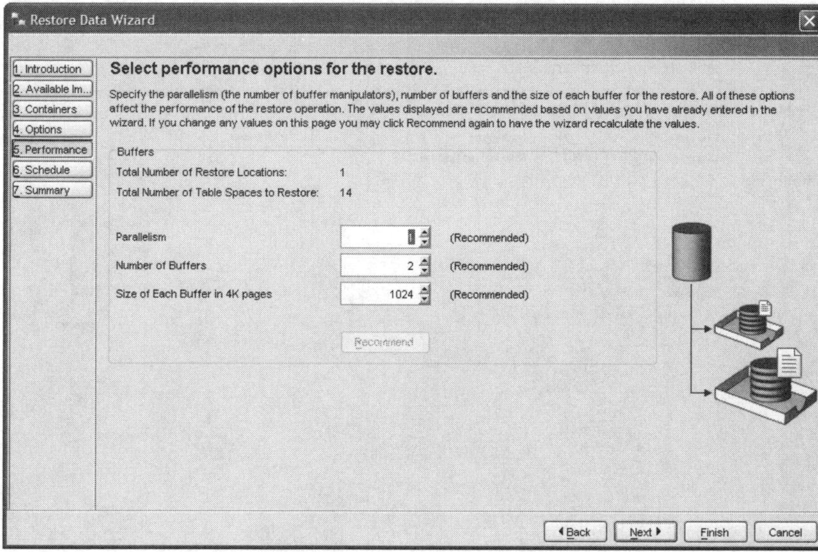

Figure 13–19 *Select performance options for the restore*

The scheduling panel gives you the option of executing the restore operation immediately or scheduling it through the Task Center (Figure 13–20). Click **Next**.

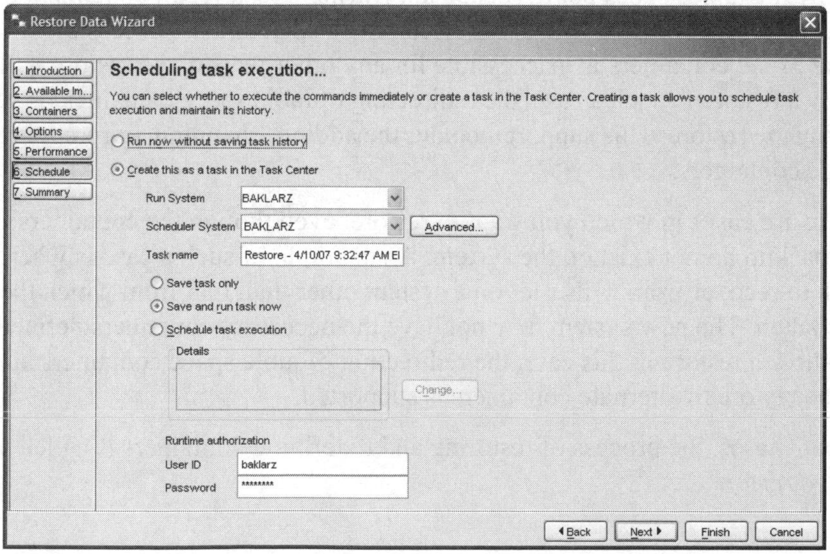

Figure 13–20 *Scheduling task execution*

The final panel summarizes the task that was created to execute the restore (Figure 13–21).

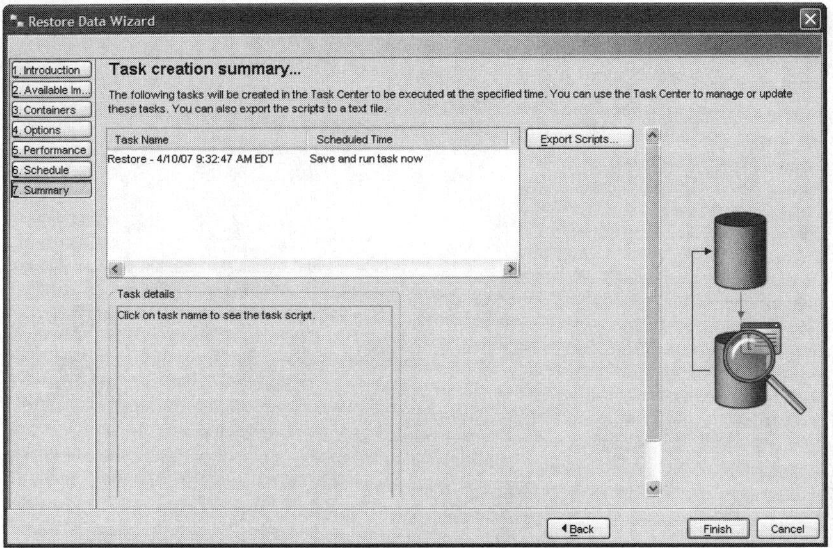

Figure 13–21 *Restore command summary*

Redefining Table Space Containers During Restore

During a backup of a database, a record is kept of all the table space containers in use by the table spaces being backed up. During a restore, all containers listed in the backup are checked to see if they currently exist and are accessible. If one or more of the containers is inaccessible for any other reason, the restore will fail. To allow a restore in such a case, the redirecting of table space containers is supported during the restore. This support includes the adding, changing, or removing of table space containers.

There are cases in which you want to restore, even though the containers listed in the backup do not exist on the system. An example of such a case is where you wish to recover from a disaster on a system other than that from which the backup was taken. The new system may not have the necessary containers defined.
To allow a restore in this case, the redirecting of table space containers at the time of the restore to alternate containers is supported.

In both cases, the process of restoring and redefining containers is called a *redirected restore.*

DB2 *Note*

A redirected restore can also be useful for backing up a production database at the primary site to a database at a designated backup site, which will typically be configured with less resources, such as the amount of disk available for containers.

As shown previously, you can use the restore dialog in the Control Center to perform a redirected restore or use the Command Center or Command Line Processor. For the next example, assume that the PRODUCT database was created using the following command:

```
CREATE DATABASE PRODUCT
  AUTOMATIC STORAGE NO
  ON 'C:\'
  USER TABLESPACE
    MANAGED BY DATABASE
    USING ( FILE 'C:\TS\USERDATA\USERDATA.DAT' 512 ) ;
```

In addition, a full backup was performed on the database:

```
BACKUP DATABASE PRODUCT
  TO "C:\DBBACKUP";
```

The next restore command will create the NEWPROD database from the contents of the PROD backup. This is an example of a redirected restore:

```
RESTORE DATABASE PRODUCT FROM C:\DBBACKUP
        INTO NEWPROD
        REDIRECT
        WITHOUT ROLLING FORWARD
```

The above command requests that the PRODUCT database be restored into a new database called NEWPROD. However, since PRODUCT has table spaces with specific SMS and DMS containers and containers cannot be shared by databases, new containers for the new database must be defined. The RESTORE utility returns the following messages:

```
SQL1277W  A redirected restore operation is being performed.  Table
space configuration can now be viewed and table spaces that do not
use automatic storage can have their containers reconfigured.
DB20000I The RESTORE DATABASE command completed successfully.
```

DB2 *Note*

All commands associated with a single redirected restore operation must be invoked from the same window or CLP session.

To list the containers to be redefined, issue the `LIST TABLESPACES` command, which produces the following output. Note that from the previous `RESTORE` command, you are connected to the `NEWPROD` database, with restricted functionality.

```
           Tablespaces for Current Database

 Tablespace ID                          = 0
 Name                                   = SYSCATSPACE
 Type                                   = System managed space
 Contents                               = All permanent data. Regular table space.

 State                                  = 0x2001100
   Detailed explanation:
     Restore pending
     Storage must be defined
     Storage may be defined

 Tablespace ID                          = 1
 Name                                   = TEMPSPACE1
 Type                                   = System managed space
 Contents                               = System Temporary data
 State                                  = 0x2001100
   Detailed explanation:
     Restore pending
     Storage must be defined
     Storage may be defined

 Tablespace ID                          = 2
 Name                                   = USERSPACE1
 Type                                   = Database managed space
 Contents                               = All permanent data. Large table space.
 State                                  = 0x2001100
   Detailed explanation:
     Restore pending
     Storage must be defined
     Storage may be defined
```

Note that all the table spaces are in the "Storage must be defined" state. To continue, define new containers for all the table spaces using the `SET TABLESPACE CONTAINERS` command as follows:

```
SET TABLESPACE CONTAINERS FOR 0
    USING (PATH "D:\NEWPROD1");

SET TABLESPACE CONTAINERS FOR 1
    USING (PATH "D:\NEWPROD2");

SET TABLESPACE CONTAINERS FOR 2
    USING (FILE "D:\NEWPROD3\USER.DAT" 5120);
```

Now that the containers are defined, continue the redirected restore with the following statement:

```
RESTORE DATABASE PRODUCT CONTINUE
```

This completes the redirected restore. Note that table spaces that were SMS and ones that were DMS must stay with their respective storage types during the redirection.

You should also be aware of the following considerations when using redirected restores:

- Directory and file containers are automatically created if they do not exist. No redirection is necessary unless the containers are inaccessible for some other reason. DB2 does not automatically create device containers.
- The ability to perform container redirection on any restore provides considerable flexibility in managing table space containers. For example, even though DB2 does not directly support adding containers to SMS table spaces, you could accomplish this by simply specifying an additional container on a redirected restore. Similarly, you could move a DMS table space from file containers to device containers.

Restoring to an Existing Database

DB2 uses *database seeds* to determine the database that a given database backup was created from. A database seed is an unique identifier of a database that remains constant for the life of the database. This seed is assigned by DB2 when the database is first created.

When restoring to an existing database, the following functions are performed:

- Delete table, index, long field, and large object contents for the existing database and replace them with the contents from the backup.
- Replace table space entries for each table space being restored.
- Retain the recovery history file unless the existing one is damaged, in which case it will be replaced with the one from the backup image.
- Retain the authentication for the existing database.
- Retain the database directories for the existing database that define where the database resides and how it is cataloged.

Certain functions depend on the database seed. When the database seeds are different:

- Delete the logs associated with the existing database.

- Copy the database configuration file from the backup.
- Change the database configuration file to indicate that the default log file path should be used for logging.

When the database seeds are the same:

- Retain the current database configuration file, unless it is damaged.
- Delete the logs if the image is of a nonrecoverable database.
- The LOGPATH parameter from the database configuration file in the backup is used to set the log file directory path.

Restoring to a New Database

When restoring to a new database, the following functions are performed:

- Create a new database, using the database name and alias that was specified by the target database alias. If not specified, a database with the name and alias of the source database alias will be created.
- Restore the database configuration file from the backup.
- Modify the database configuration file to indicate that the default log file path should be used for logging.
- Restore the authentication type from the backup.
- Restore the recovery history file for the database.

Restoring an Automatic Storage Database

An automatic storage database provides the simplest form of recovery and redirected restore. If the database was created with only automatic storage tables spaces, the RESTORE command only needs to specify the new paths for the restored database. These paths can be the same, or completely different from the original database design. For instance, if the original database was created with the following command:

```
CREATE DATABASE PRODUCT AUTOMATIC STORAGE YES
  ON /db2/path01, /db2/path02
```

The RESTORE command would include the new path specification for the database:

```
RESTORE DATABASE PRODUCT FROM C:\DBBACKUP
    ON /db2/path03, /db2/path04, /db2/path05
```

Roll-Forward Recovery

Roll-forward recovery enables *recoverable* databases. When enabled, in addition to what can be performed for version recovery, the following can be performed:

- Recovery at an individual table space level
- Point in time recovery using the ROLLFORWARD command
- Online processing of BACKUP and RESTORE commands

As previously mentioned, roll-forward recovery is enabled by enabling either or both the LOGRETAIN or USEREXIT database configuration parameters. When roll-forward recovery is enabled, the database goes into backup-pending state, which requires that a full database backup be taken before the database can be used.

Backing Up a Database

The points made here are in addition to the considerations discussed in the version recovery section earlier in this chapter.

Before taking a backup, consider the following:

- By using the TABLESPACE option of the BACKUP command, you can back up individual table spaces. This can reduce the overall time it takes to back up the database by backing up only the more volatile table spaces. The PARALLELISM parameter can also used to back up multiple table spaces in parallel.
- A table space backup and a table space restore cannot be run at the same time, even if the backup and restore are working on different table spaces.
- If you have the index or large object components of a table in different table spaces, the set of table spaces encompassing the entire table should be backed up together to ensure a consistent point of recovery.

When you invoke the BACKUP command, you should be aware of the following point in addition to the points made in the version recovery discussion:

- The database or table spaces must be in a normal or backup-pending state for BACKUP to function.

Example of Backing Up at the Table Space Level

You can run the BACKUP command from the Command Line Processor or Command Center. The same function can also be done graphically from the Control Center. For example, using the Command Line Processor:

```
BACKUP DATABASE PROD
       TABLESPACE (SYSCATSPACE,USERSPACE1) TO C:\DBBACKUP
```

This command backs up the catalog table space SYSCATSPACE and user table space in the PROD database to the C:\DBBACKUP directory on a Windows system. Default values are used for the other parameters.

Restoring a Database

Before performing a restore, consider the following:

- You can restore a backup copy of a full database or table space backup to an existing database. The backup image may differ from the existing database in its alias name, database name, or its database seed.
- Database restores can be in offline mode only.
- Table spaces can be restored in offline or online mode. While in online mode, connections to the database can be made. This is advantageous in the case of table space restoration when other table spaces can still be used concurrently while the restore is executing.
- A database enabled for roll-forward recovery must be rolled forward after it is restored unless the WITHOUT ROLLING FORWARD option is used. However, this option cannot be used if the backup was taken with the ONLINE option or if the backup image is of table spaces only.
- Even though the restore and roll-forward are separate functions, your recovery strategy may have restore as the first phase of a complete roll-forward recovery of a database. After a successful restore, a database that was configured for roll-forward recovery at the time the backup was taken enters a roll-forward-pending state, being unusable until the ROLLFORWARD command has been run successfully.
- When the ROLLFORWARD command is issued, if the database is in roll-forward-pending status, the database is rolled forward. If the database is not in roll-forward-pending status, but the table spaces are, when you issue the ROLLFORWARD command and specify a list of table spaces, only those table spaces are rolled forward. If you do not specify a list, all table spaces that are in roll-forward-pending status are rolled forward.
- Another database RESTORE is not allowed when the roll-forward process is running.
- You can only restore a table space if the table space currently exists and is the *same* table space. This means it must have the same name and has not been dropped and recreated between taking the backup image and restoration.
- You cannot use a table space backup image to restore the table space to a different database.
- If you have the index or large object components of a table in different table spaces, the set of table spaces encompassing the entire table should be restored together to ensure a consistent point of recovery.

- You can restore selected table spaces from a full database backup image. All log files associated with the table space must exist from the time the backup was created.

Example of Restoring at the Table Space Level

You can run the RESTORE command from the Command Line Processor or Command Center. Of course, the same function can also be done from the Control Center. From the Command Line Processor, for example:

```
RESTORE DATABASE PROD
        TABLESPACE (USERSPACE1) ONLINE FROM C:\DBBACKUP
```

This command restores the table space USERSPACE1 in database PROD from the C:\DBBACKUP directory in online mode on a Windows system. Connections can still be made to the database. Default values are used for the other parameters. This command will leave the table space in a roll-forward-pending state, which requires that the ROLLFORWARD command be executed before the table space can be accessed.

Rolling Forward Databases and Table Spaces

The ROLLFORWARD command can be invoked from the Command Line Processor, application programming interface (API), or Control Center.

Before performing a roll-forward, consider the following:

DB2 *Note*

When using point-in-time (PIT) rollforward recovery, the local time can be specified rather than UTC time with the USING LOCAL TIME option of the ROLLFORWARD command.

- You must have SYSADM, SYSCTRL, or SYSMAINT authority to invoke ROLLFORWARD.
- The database may be local or remote.
- The database must be recoverable.
- A database must be restored successfully (using the RESTORE command) before it can be rolled forward.
- A table space, besides being restored, can also be put into roll-forward-pending state from a media error or some other unexpected event.
- A database roll-forward runs in offline mode. The database is not available for use until the roll-forward completes. Online roll-forward for table spaces is

available, except for the catalog table space `SYSCATSPACE`, which requires an offline roll-forward. Other table spaces are available for use during online roll-forward.

- You can use any backup image that you have as long as you have the necessary log files to cover the period you wish to roll-forward.
- Frequent backups reduce the execution time of `ROLLFORWARD`, as less log data has to be read between the time of the backup and the recovery point.

Generally, the sequence of commands when invoking `ROLLFORWARD` is as follows:

- Issue the `ROLLFORWARD` command without the `STOP/COMPLETE` option.
- Issue the `ROLLFORWARD` command with the `QUERY STATUS` option. The `QUERY STATUS` option can indicate that log file(s) may be missing if the point in time returned is earlier than expected for rolling forward to the end of the log.
- Issue the `ROLLFORWARD` command with the `STOP/COMPLETE` option. After this command is invoked, it is not possible to roll forward additional changes.

When you invoke the `ROLLFORWARD` command, you should be aware of the following:

- If you need to cancel a roll-forward operation, you can use `ROLLFORWARD` with the `CANCEL` option. This places the database into restore-pending state, whether or not a roll-forward is in progress against the database.
- If you issue `ROLLFORWARD` with the `CANCEL` option and specify a list of table spaces that are in roll-forward pending state, they are put in restore-pending state.
- You cannot use `ROLLFORWARD` with the `CANCEL` option to cancel a roll-forward operation that is running. You can only use it to cancel a roll-forward operation that completed but did not have a `ROLLFORWARD STOP` issued for it or for a roll-forward operation that failed before completing.
- A log uses a timestamp associated with the completion of a unit of work. The timestamp in the logs uses Coordinated Universal Time (UTC). The format is `yyyy-mm-dd-hh.mm.ss.nnnnnn` (year, month, day, hour, minutes, seconds, microseconds). When you want to roll-forward to a point in time, you have to specify the time using the local time or UTC time.
- If you are rolling forward one or many table spaces to a point in time, you must roll-forward at least to the minimum recovery time, which is the last update to the system catalogs for the table spaces. The minimum recovery time is shown in the output of the `LIST TABLESPACES SHOW DETAIL` command.

Table Space States During Roll-Forward

Different states are associated with a table space to indicate its current status:

- A table space will be placed in *roll-forward-pending* state after restoration or following an I/O error. The table space must be rolled forward to remove the roll-forward-pending state. If the cause was an I/O error, this situation must be corrected before doing a roll-forward.
- A table space will be placed in *roll-forward-in-progress* state when a roll-forward operation is in progress on that table space. The state remains until roll-forward operations are completed successfully. If the `STOP/COMPLETE` option was not used on a point in time recovery, the table space will also stay in this state.
- A table space will be placed in the *restore-pending* state after a `ROLLFORWARD` with `CANCEL` option or an unrecoverable error occurs in the execution of `ROLLFORWARD`. The table space must be restored and rolled forward again.
- A table space will be placed in the *backup-pending* state after a `ROLLFORWARD` to a point in time or after a `LOAD NO COPY` operation. The table space must be backed up before it can be used.

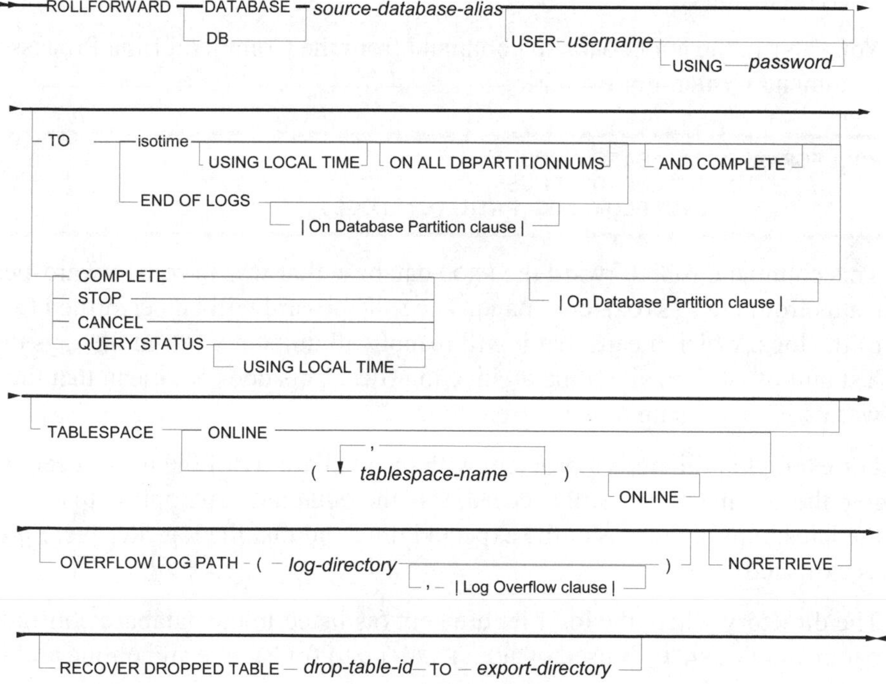

Figure 13–22 *Rollforward command summary*

Examples of Rolling Forward

Some of the key parameters to the ROLLFORWARD command (Figure 13–22) include:

- isotime — the point in time where all committed transactions are to be rolled forward. This value is a timestamp, expressed in Coordinated Universal Time (UTC). The CURRENT TIMEZONE special register specifies the difference between UTC and local time at the database server.
- USING LOCAL TIME — allows the user to rollforward to a point in time that is t the user's local time, rather than the UTC time.
- COMPLETE/STOP — stops the rolling forward of log records, and completes the rollforward recovery process by rolling back any incomplete transactions and turning off the rollforward pending state of the database.
- CANCEL — cancels the rollforward recovery operation and places the database or one or more table spaces in restore pending state.
- ONLINE — specifies a table space-level rollforward recovery operation to be performed online.
- NORETRIEVE — specifies the administrator controls which log files will be rolled forward on the stand-by machine, allowing the ability to disable the retrieval of archived logs.

You can run the ROLLFORWARD command from the Command Line Processor or Command Center. For example:

```
ROLLFORWARD DATABASE PROD
            TO END OF LOGS
            OVERFLOW LOG PATH (C:\LOGS)
```

This command rolls forward the PROD database that was in roll-forward-pending status from the RESTORE command. The roll-forward will be performed to the end of the logs, which means that it will reapply all units of work in the logs up to the last unit of work in all online archive log files. This does not mean that the roll-forward will process up to the current time.

For example, if there is a problem with the availability of the most recent active log, the command will still succeed. Use the QUERY STATUS option to ensure that the latest unit of work is at the expected time and that the log files were processed as expected.

The directory where the log files are kept (as listed in the database configuration parameter LOGPATH) is used by ROLLFORWARD to find active and online archive logs.

The OVERFLOW LOG PATH parameter specifies the directory where offline archive log files are kept so that ROLLFORWARD can use them for reapplying units of work.

This command rolls forward the USERSPACE1 table space that is in roll-forward-pending status from the RESTORE command. The ONLINE parameter allows concurrent access to other table spaces. The AND COMPLETE parameter instructs DB2 to complete the rolling forward, roll back any incomplete units of work, and to enable the database to become available for general use by turning off the roll-forward-pending state.

```
ROLLFORWARD DATABASE PROD
            TO END OF LOGS AND COMPLETE
            TABLESPACE (USERSPACE1) ONLINE
```

This command lists the log files that DB2 has rolled forward, the next archive file required, and the timestamp (in UTC) of the last committed transaction since roll-forward processing began.

```
ROLLFORWARD DATABASE PROD
            QUERY STATUS
```

The information returned contains the following:

- Rollforward status — The status may be database or table space roll-forward pending, database or table space roll-forward in progress, database or table space roll-forward processing stop, or no roll-forward pending.
- Next log file to be read — A string containing the name of the next required log file.
- Log files processed — A string containing the names of the processed log files that are no longer needed for recovery and can be removed from the directory.
- Last committed transaction — A string containing a timestamp in ISO format (yyyy-mm-dd-hh.mm.ss). This timestamp marks the last transaction committed after the completion of roll-forward recovery. The timestamp applies to the database. For table space roll-forward, it is the timestamp of the last transaction committed to the database.

Here is sample output of the QUERY STATUS option (Figure 13–23):

```
                 Rollforward Status

Input database alias                 = PROD
Number of nodes returned status      = 1
Node number                          = 0
Rollforward status                   = DB working
Next log file to be read             = S0000019.LOG
Log files processed                  = S0000014.LOG - S0000018.LOG
Last committed transaction           = 2007-04-10-00.09.51.000000
```

Figure 13–23 *Rollforward status (1)*

Note the status is DB WORKING, meaning that this is a database roll-forward and that it is still in progress, as the STOP/COMPLETE option has not been specified.

Database Recovery

This command stops the rolling forward of log records and completes the roll-forward recovery process by rolling back any incomplete transactions and turning off the roll-forward-pending state of the database. This allows access to the database or table spaces that have been rolled forward. The keywords STOP and COMPLETE are equivalent. When rolling table spaces forward to a point in time, the table spaces are placed in backup-pending state.

```
ROLLFORWARD DATABASE PROD COMPLETE
```

DB2 Note

For the recovery of a table space, only the log files required to recover the database are processed; log files that not required are skipped.

Here is output of the QUERY STATUS option (Figure 13–24):

```
                        Rollforward Status

Input database alias                   = PROD
Number of nodes returned status        = 1
Node number                            = 0
Rollforward status                     = not pending
Next log file to be read               =
Log files processed                    = S0000014.LOG - S0000018.LOG
Last committed transaction             = 2007-04-10-00.09.51.000000
```

Figure 13–24 *Rollforward status (2)*

Note that the status has now changed to not pending.

```
ROLLFORWARD DATABASE PROD
         TO 2007-04-10-00.00.00.000000
         TABLESPACE (USERSPACE1) ONLINE
```

This command rolls forward the USERSPACE1 table space to a particular point in time. Note that the roll-forward time is UTC, regardless of the local time. Here is the output of the QUERY STATUS option (which is produced by default as a function of the above command) (Figure 13–25):

```
                        Rollforward Status

Input database alias                   = PROD
Number of nodes returned status        = 1
Node number                            = 0
Rollforward status                     = TBS working
Next log file to be read               =
Log files processed                    = -
Last committed transaction             = 2007-04-10-00.09.51.000000
```

Figure 13–25 *Rollforward status (3)*

Note that the status has now changed to `TBS working`, as this is a table space roll-forward. You can keep rolling forward past the nominated time, as there are still units of work that could be applied (note the "Last committed transaction" time is later than the requested point in time) or issue the `ROLLFORWARD` command with the `COMPLETE` option to roll back incomplete units of work and make the table space available for general use.

You can also use the Control Center to invoke a roll-forward. After right-clicking on the database you wish to roll-forward and selecting the **Roll-forward** option, the Roll-Forward Wizard panel is displayed (Figure 13–26). You will not be able to enter this panel unless the database is in roll-forward-pending state.

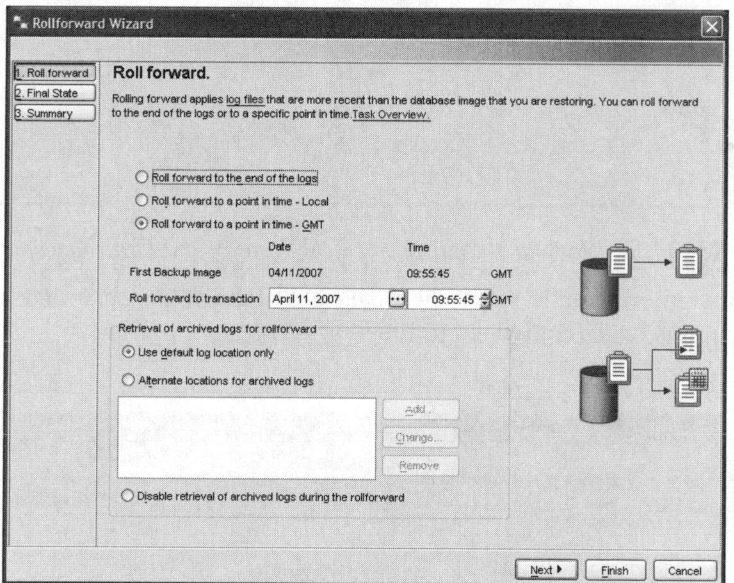

Figure 13–26 *Rollforward Wizard*

In this panel, you can see options for end of log recovery, point in time recovery, and the options for using the archived logs. Click on **Next**.

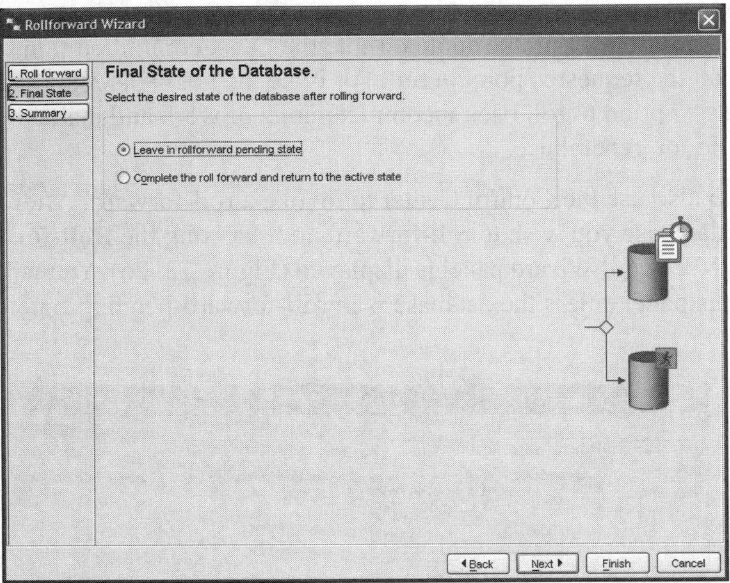

Figure 13–27 *Rollforward Wizard — Final State of the Database*

This panel allows you to select the final state of the database, either in in roll-forward-pending state (equivalent to the `STOP/COMPLETE` option) or in an active state.

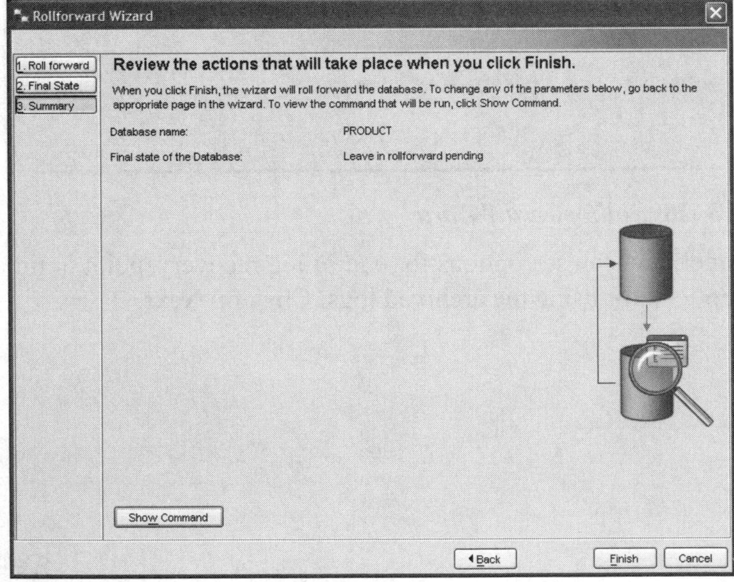

Figure 13–28 *Rollforward Wizard — Review*

In the last panel of the Rollforward Wizard, you can press the **Show Command** button to see the command that will be issued by DB2.

Managing Log Files

In this section, aspects of log file management will be reviewed, such as how log files are named and how to avoid losing them.

Log File Naming Scheme

Log file names are of the format `Snnnnnnn.LOG`, where `nnnnnnn` is a seven-digit number ranging from `0000000` to `9999999`. When a database is first created, logs starting from `S0000000.LOG` are created.

DB2 restarts the log file numbering sequence at `S0000000.LOG` under the following conditions:

- When the database configuration file is changed to enable archival logging
- When the database configuration file is changed to disable archival logging
- When the log file sequence wraps, that is after log `S9999999.LOG` is used

When the `ROLLFORWARD` command has been run and you have issued the `STOP/COMPLETE` option successfully, the last log used is truncated and logging begins with the next sequential log. Any log in the log path directory with a sequence number greater than the last log used by `ROLLFORWARD` is reused. You can make a copy of the old logs and place them in a different directory if you want to be able to reexecute the `ROLLFORWARD` command using the old logs.

DB2 *Note*

DB2 allows the database administrator to force the archive of a log on demand. This allows greater flexibility in managing log files, especially in situations that support offsite recovery.

Log File Placement for Recovery

DB2 ensures that an incorrect log is not applied during roll-forward recovery, but it cannot detect the location of the required logs.

If you moved log files to a location other than specified by the `LOGPATH` database configuration parameter, use the `OVERFLOW LOG PATH` parameter of the `ROLLFORWARD` command to specify the path for DB2 to search.

If you are rolling forward changes in a database or table space and ROLLFORWARD cannot find the next log, then ROLLFORWARD stops and returns the next log name in the SQL Communications Area (SQLCA).

If you change the log path directory via the NEWLOGPATH database configuration parameter, any existing archive logs are unaffected and do not get moved to the new path. You must keep track of the location of these logs.

Losing Logs

Log files can be erased in the following ways:

- Dropping a database erases all logs in the current log path directory. You may need to back these logs up for any future restoration purposes.
- As noted previously, when recovering to a point in time, log files chronologically past the point in time are reused. If you need to restore again past the point in time used earlier, you cannot do so because the logs were reused. You must back up the original set of logs to a different location and copy them back for the restoration.
- If you change the log path directory and then remove the subdirectory or erase any logs in that subdirectory requested by DB2 in the log path, DB2 will look for logs in the default log path (SQLOGDIR) when the database is opened. If the logs are not found, the database will enter a backup-pending state.
- If you lose the log containing the point in time of the end of the online backup and you are rolling forward the corresponding restored image, the database will not be useable. To make the database usable, you must restore the database from a different backup and all its associated logs.

Prune Logfile Command

This command will delete all log files created prior to a specified log file. It will only do so from the active log path, so if any log files have been moved to another path they will not be considered by this command. For example:

```
PRUNE LOGFILE PRIOR TO S0000100.LOG
```

This command will delete all log files in the active log path up to and including S0000099.LOG.

Other Recovery Considerations

Additional considerations related to recovery will be covered here, such as the time taken to recover a database, the recovery history file, and how to recover dropped tables.

Recovery Time Required

The time required to recover a database is composed of:

- The time required to complete the restore of the backup.
- If the database is recoverable, the time it takes to roll-forward through the logs.

When formulating a recovery plan, you should plan a sufficient amount of time for your business operations to be affected while the database is being recovered.

Testing your overall recovery plan will assist you in determining whether the time required to recover the database is reasonable given your business requirements. Following each test, you may want to increase the frequency with which you take a backup. If roll-forward recovery is part of the strategy, this will reduce the number of logs that are archived between backups and reduce the time taken in rolling forward through the units of work.

Storage Considerations for Log Files

To prevent a media failure from destroying a database and your ability to rebuild it, you should keep the database backup, the database logs, and the database itself on other devices. Use the `LOGPATH` database configuration parameter to move the logs to a new device once the database is created.

Because the log files can occupy a large amount of disk space, if you plan on using roll-forward recovery, you have to plan how to manage the archive logs. You can:

- Dedicate enough space in the database log path directory to retain the logs
- Manually copy the archive logs to a storage device or directory other than the database log path directory
- Use a user exit program to copy the logs to another storage device

When using disk mirroring of the log files, you need to account for twice the amount of disk storage.

The Quiesce Command

You can issue the `QUIESCE TABLESPACES FOR TABLE` command to create a point of consistency that can be used for subsequent roll-forward recovery. When you quiesce table spaces for a table, the request will wait (through locking) for all running transactions that are accessing objects in the table spaces to complete, at the same time blocking new requests against the table spaces. When the quiesce request is granted, all outstanding transactions are already completed (committed or rolled back), and the table spaces are in a consistent state.

You can look in the recovery history file to find quiesce points and check whether they are past the minimum recovery time to determine a desirable time to stop the roll-forward.

```
QUIESCE TABLESPACES FOR TABLE PRODUCT.EMPLOYEE SHARE
```

In the example above, when the quiesce share request is received, the transaction requests intent share locks for the table spaces and one for the table.

When the transaction obtains the locks, the state of the table spaces is changed to `QUIESCED SHARE`. The state is granted to the quiescer only if there is no conflicting state held by other users.

DB2 *Note*

`QUIESCE` can now force all users off an instance or database and put it into a quiesced mode for database maintenance activities.

The table cannot be changed while the table spaces for the table are in `QUIESCED SHARE` state. Other share mode requests to the table and table spaces will be allowed. When the unit of work commits or rolls back, the locks are released, but the table spaces for the table remain in `QUIESCED SHARE` state until the state is explicitly reset by issuing the following command:

```
QUIESCE TABLESPACES FOR TABLE PRODUCT.EMPLOYEE RESET
```

The `QUIESCE` command can be invoked from the Command Line Processor, Command Center, or application programming interface.

The Recovery History File

A recovery history file is created with each database and is automatically updated whenever there is a:

- Archive of a log
- `BACKUP` of a database or table space
- `RESTORE` of a database or table space
- `ROLLFORWARD` of a database or table space
- `CREATE` of a table space
- `ALTER` of a table space
- `RENAME` of a table space
- `QUIESCE` of a table space

- DROP of a table
- LOAD of a table
- REORG of a table

You can use the summarized backup information in this file to recover all or part of the database to a point in time. The information in the file includes:

- The part of the database that was copied and the copy procedure
- The time that the copy was made
- The location of the copy
- The last time a restore was done

Every backup operation includes a copy of the recovery history file. The file is linked to the database, so when a database is dropped, the file is deleted.

If the current database is unusable and the file is damaged or deleted, an option in the RESTORE command allows only the recovery history file to be restored.

The file is managed with the PRUNE HISTORY command. Entries in the file earlier than a specified date and time can be deleted with this command.

The LIST HISTORY command reports on information in the recovery history file. For example:

```
LIST HISTORY ALL FOR DB2CERT
```

This command produces the following output (Figure 13–29):

```
                    List History File for product

Number of matching file entries = 5

 Op Obj Timestamp+Sequence Type Dev Earliest Log Current Log  Backup ID
 -- --- ------------------ ---- --- ------------ ------------ --------------
  B  D  20070410175928001   F    D  S0000000.LOG S0000000.LOG
 ----------------------------------------------------------------------------
 Contains 2 tablespace(s):

 00001 SYSCATSPACE
 00002 USERSPACE1
 ----------------------------------------------------------------------------
    Comment: DB2 BACKUP PRODUCT OFFLINE
 Start Time: 20070410175928
   End Time: 20070410175930
     Status: A
 ----------------------------------------------------------------------------
 EID: 1 Location: C:\DBBACKUP

 Op Obj Timestamp+Sequence Type Dev Earliest Log Current Log  Backup ID
 -- --- ------------------ ---- --- ------------ ------------ --------------
  X  D  20070411094344      1    D  S0000000.LOG C0000000
 ----------------------------------------------------------------------------
 ----------------------------------------------------------------------------
    Comment:
 Start Time: 20070411094344
   End Time: 20070411094412
```

Database Recovery

```
   Status: A
----------------------------------------------------------------------------
 EID: 2 Location: C:\LOGS\DB2\PRODUCT\NODE0000\C0000000\S0000000.LOG

Op Obj Timestamp+Sequence Type Dev Earliest Log Current Log  Backup ID
-- --- ------------------ ---- --- ------------ ------------ --------------
 B  D  20070411094412001    F    D  S0000001.LOG S0000001.LOG
----------------------------------------------------------------------------
 Contains 2 tablespace(s):

 00001 SYSCATSPACE
 00002 USERSPACE1
----------------------------------------------------------------------------
   Comment: DB2 BACKUP PRODUCT OFFLINE
Start Time: 20070411094412
  End Time: 20070411094421
    Status: A
----------------------------------------------------------------------------
 EID: 3 Location: C:\DBBACKUP

Op Obj Timestamp+Sequence Type Dev Earliest Log Current Log  Backup ID
-- --- ------------------ ---- --- ------------ ------------ --------------
 X  D  20070411094434       1    D  S0000001.LOG C0000000
----------------------------------------------------------------------------

----------------------------------------------------------------------------
   Comment:
Start Time: 20070411094434
  End Time: 20070411094501
    Status: A
----------------------------------------------------------------------------
 EID: 4 Location: C:\LOGS\DB2\PRODUCT\NODE0000\C0000000\S0000001.LOG

Op Obj Timestamp+Sequence Type Dev Earliest Log Current Log  Backup ID
-- --- ------------------ ---- --- ------------ ------------ --------------
 R  D  20070411094916001    F       S0000001.LOG S0000001.LOG 20070411094412
----------------------------------------------------------------------------
 Contains 2 tablespace(s):

 00001 SYSCATSPACE
 00002 USERSPACE1
----------------------------------------------------------------------------
   Comment: RESTORE PRODUCT NO RF
Start Time: 20070411094916
  End Time: 20070411094930
    Status: A
----------------------------------------------------------------------------
 EID: 5 Location:

----------------------------------------------------------------------------
```

Figure 13–29 *History file information*

Here is a backup and restore event displayed. Note that the full name and path of the backup is shown.

For further details on the contents of the recovery history file, please refer to the *DB2 Command Reference* and the *DB2 Administration Guide*.

Tables Related to Other Tables

If you want to roll-forward a table space to a point in time, and a table in the table space participates in a referential constraint with another table in another table space, you should roll-forward both table spaces to the same point in time; otherwise, both tables will be placed into check-pending state.

Similarly, for an underlying table for a summary table that is in another table space or vice versa, you should roll-forward both table spaces to the same point in time; otherwise, the summary table is placed into check pending state.

When tables affect other tables via triggers, you should consider backing up and recovering the related table spaces together as well keeping the same consistency points and therefore the integrity of the data. The updates to the database as a result of triggers *firing* will still occur during roll-forward processing.

Dropped Table Recovery

Tables that have been accidentally dropped can be recovered using the following technique:

Prior to the table being accidentally dropped:

- Use the `CREATE` or `ALTER TABLESPACE` statement with the `DROPPED TABLE RECOVERY ON` option. DB2 will write additional log and recovery history file entries to support recovery of dropped tables.

When a table has been dropped and needs to be recovered, do the following:

- Extract the DDL from the recovery history file using the `LIST HISTORY DROPPED TABLES` command. This will provide you with not only the list of tables that have been dropped but also the statements needed to recreate them.
- Restore a database or table space from a backup image. Of course, this image must have coexisted before the table was dropped.
- Roll-forward the database or table space using the `RECOVER DROPPED TABLE` option. This option requires you to specify both a `tableid` and an export directory. The `tableid` is taken from the `LIST HISTORY` command, and the export directory is the directory where DB2 will place an export file of the data for the dropped table.
- Recreate the table with the extracted DDL from the history file.
- Import the recovered data.

This technique should only be used on regular table spaces.

Reorganization of Tables

If you reorganize a table, you should back up the affected table spaces after the operation completes. If you later issue the roll forward command and you did not back up, you will have to roll forward through the entire `REORG` operation.

Large Objects

If a table contains long field or large object (LOB) columns, you should consider placing this data into a separate table space. With the amount of time and disk space potentially required to back up LOB data, by putting it in a separate table space, you can decide to back it up at a lower frequency than the regular table spaces.

You can also choose not to log LOB columns when creating or altering tables, which will also save log file space. This is feasible if the LOB data is easily recreatable.

Offline and Online Table Space States

During database start-up/activation, DB2 checks to make sure that all of the table space containers are accessible.

If a container is not accessible, the table space will be placed into an *offline* state in addition to the other recovery states it may have, such as back-up-pending, restore-pending, roll-forward-pending, and so on. So a table space may have a state of, for example, `BACKUP PENDING + OFFLINE`.

To get a table space back into an *online* state after resolving the container problem:

- Disconnect all applications and reconnect to or restart the database.
- If the database still has applications connected to it, use the `ALTER TABLESPACE` statement with the `SWITCH ONLINE` option.

The table space can also be dropped while in an *offline* state.

If the container problem cannot be resolved, to restart the database cleanly so that there are no errors, use the `RESTART DATABASE` command with the `DROP PENDING TABLESPACES` option. This will instruct DB2 to start the database successfully, even though the list of supplied table spaces is in error. Once the database is started, the only operation that can be performed on those table spaces that cannot be recovered is to drop them.

High Availability

DB2 supports high availability functionality, where in the event that one machine running a DB2 instance fails, another machine automatically takes over the processing for the failed machine (Figure 13–30).

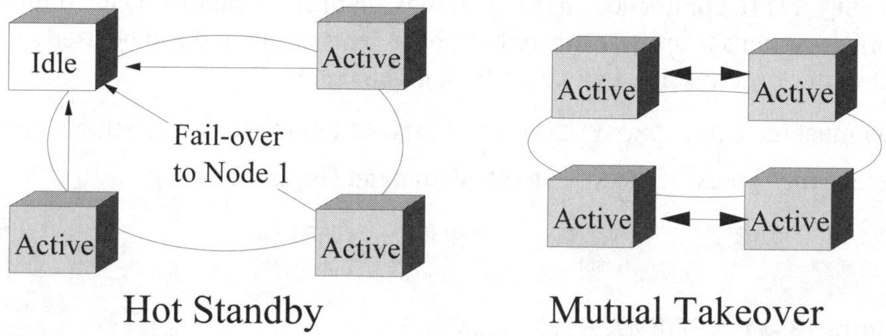

Figure 13–30 *High availability scenarios*

For example, on AIX, this support uses and is enabled by the High Availability Cluster Multi-Processing (HACMP™) product. HACMP provides increased availability through clusters of processors that share resources such as disks or network access. If one processor fails, another in the cluster can substitute for the failed one. Additional high-availability programs are available depending on the operating environment.

A brief description of the hot standby and mutual takeover modes follows.

- *Hot standby* — Active processors are being actively used to run the DB2 instance and a DB2 server is in standby mode ready to take over the instance if there is an operating system or hardware failure involving the first processor.
- *Mutual takeover* — The various processors are either used to run separate DB2 instances or used to run a DB2 instance while another processor is used to run DB2 applications. If there is an operating system or hardware failure on one of the processors, the other processor takes over the tasks of the failing processor. Once the failover is complete, the remaining processor is doing the work of both processors.

DB2 *Note*

Other popular high availability software programs include Microsoft Cluster Server (MSCS), Sun® Cluster (SC), and Steeleye® (for Linux environments), and Veritas™ Cluster Server.

SET WRITE Command

Advances in disk technology have increased database availability by providing the ability to create a duplicate or mirrored copy. By splitting a consistent copy of the data, the primary or production database can continue normal operations while the copy can be used either online or offline operations.

The `SET WRITE` command is used in high-availability scenarios by enabling the disk storage systems to split a mirrored database. This command can be used to supsend I/O writes or to resume I/O writes for a given database.

You must have `SYSADM`, `SYSCTRL`, or `SYSMAINT` authority to issue this command.

Here is the syntax of the `SET WRITE` command (Figure 13–31):

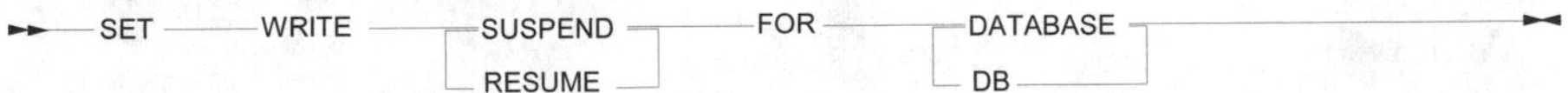

Figure 13–31 *SET WRITE command*

The key parameters to the `SET WRITE` command include (see the *DB2 Command Reference* for further detail):

- `SUSPEND` — This will suspend I/O writes and put all tablespaces into a `SUSPEND_WRITE` state. Writes to the logs are also suspended by this command.
- `RESUME` — This will resume I/O writes and remove the `SUSPEND_WRITE` state from all of the tablespaces and make the tablespaces available for update activities.

DB2 Note

You can use the `DB2 LIST TABLESPACES` command to view the state of the table space in `SUSPEND_WRITE`.

DB2INIDB Command

The `db2inidb` command (Figure 13–32) is used to initialize a mirrored database in a split mirror envirionment. The mirrored database can be initialized as a clone of the primary database, placed in roll-forward-pending state, or used as a backup image to restore the primary database.

You must have `SYSADM`, `SYSCTRL`, or `SYSMAINT` authority to issue this command.

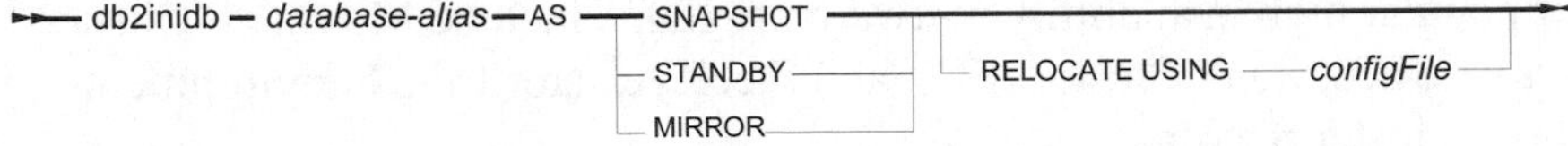

Figure 13–32 *db2inidb command*

The key parameters to the `db2inidb` command include (see the *DB2 Command Reference* for further detail):

- `SNAPSHOT` — specifies that the mirrored database will be initialized as a clone of the primary database.
- `STANDBY` — specifies the database will be placed in roll-forward-pending state. Logs from the primary database can be applied to the standby database. The standby will be able to take place of the primary database if it goes down.
- `MIRROR` — specifies the mirrored database will be a backup image that can be used to restore the primary database.
- `RELOCATE USING configfile` — specifies the database files are to be relocated based on the information listed in the configuration file.

Using Split Mirror to Clone a Database

Creating a snapshot or clone of the primary database can be useful to run queries or reports, thereby offloading the workload off the primary database. The steps to create a clone database are:

1. Suspend I/O on the primary database:

   ```
   db2 set write suspend for database
   ```

2. Split the mirror.
3. Resume I/O on the primary database:

   ```
   db2 set write resume for database
   ```

4. Attach the mirrored database to another instance.
5. Start the database instance:

   ```
   db2start
   ```

6. Initialize the mirrored database as a clone of the primary database:

   ```
   db2inidb database_alias as snapshot
   ```

DB2 *Note*

The write resume command forces a restart for databases in `SUSPEND_WRITE` state. This command can only be applied to the primary database, not the mirrored databases.

Database Recovery

Using Split Mirror as a Standby Database

A stand-by database is created to increase availability by decreasing the potential recovery time to assume operational workload. The stand-by database is constantly rolling forward through the log and continually fetching logs from the primary system. The steps to create a mirrored stand-by database are:

1. Suspend I/O on the primary database:
   ```
   db2 set write suspend for database
   ```
2. Split the mirror.
3. Resume I/O on the primary database:
   ```
   db2 set write resume for database
   ```
4. Attach the mirrored database to another instance.
5. Place the mirrored database in rollforward pending state:
   ```
   db2inidb database_alias as standby
   ```
   Recommend taking a backup of the mirrored database at this time, before any records are written to the standby.
6. Set up a user exit program to retrieve the log files from the primary system.
7. Roll the database forward to the end of the logs or a point-in-time.
8. Continue retrieving log files, and rolling the database forward through the logs until the end of the logs or the point-in-time required has been reached for the standby database.
9. Bring the standby database online by issuing the `ROLLFORWARD` command with the `STOP` option specified. The DB2 clients are now ready to reconnect to the standby database.
   ```
   db2 rollforward database <db> to end of logs and stop
   ```

DB2 Note

The `WRITE RESUME` command must be issued from the same window or CLP session as the `WRITE SUSPEND` command.

Using Split Mirror as a Backup Image

A backup image of the mirrored system can be restored on the primary system when the primary database needs recovery.

The steps to create a backup image of the mirrored database are:

1. Suspend I/O on the primary database:

```
db2 set write suspend for database
```

2. Split the mirror.
3. Resume I/O on the primary database:

```
db2 set write resume for database
```

4. A failure occurs on the primary system, requiring a restore from a backup image.
5. Stop the primary database instance:

```
db2stop
```

6. Use operating system-level commands to copy the split-off data over to the primary system. Do not copy the split-off log files, because the primary logs will be required for rollforward recovery.
7. Start the primary database instance:

```
db2start
```

8. Initialize the primary database:

```
db2inidb database_alias as mirror
```

9. Bring the standby database online by issuing the ROLLFORWARD command with the STOP option specified. The DB2 clients are now ready to reconnect.

```
db2 rollforward db <db> to end of logs and stop
```

High-Availability Disaster Recovery

DB2 database high-availability disaster recovery (HADR) is a database replication feature that provides a high-availability solution for both partial and complete site failures. HADR protects against data loss by replicating data changes from a source database, called the primary, to a target database, called the standby. The changes made on the primary database are captured in the log file and shipped to the secondary system to be applied there.

HADR has been designed with the following goals:

- Ultra-fast failover with the option for zero transaction loss

  The HADR solution provides ultra-fast failover with typically sub-minute recovery times. Other technologies (for example, database clustering) typically require longer recovery times. HADR is applicable to all sorts of workloads and normally requires no modification to applications.

- Easy setup and administration

  The HADR solution is simple to set up and administer. HADR can be set up via the Control Center, or via the setting of five simple database configuration parameters.

- Negligible impact on performance

  The architecture behind HADR insures that the performance impact on the primary database is negligible.

- Software upgrades without interruption

  HADR takes availability to a new level by giving DBAs the ability to upgrade their software without taking an outage. The primary system can be upgraded while the secondary system continues to run the workload. When maintenance is complete, the primary can catch up on the work that was done on the secondary, and then resume accepting transactions.

- Automatic failover for applications

  Availability characteristics have to be extended to the client as well. If an outage occurs, the HADR solution delivers an automatic client reroute capability. The clients will automatically switch to the backup system without intervention from the user or an external recovery monitor.

How High-Availability Disaster Recovery works

The easiest way to think about HADR is to think log shipping — only that individual transactions are shipped from memory as opposed to entire log files.

The problem with log shipping was that you could always be out the number of transactions in the log file. For performance reasons, you typically create larger log files — which means more transactions in the log being shipped and potentially more transactions lost in the event of a failure.

HADR starts with two machines — a primary server and a standby server. The standby server must have an identical copy of the database that is found on the primary server. The primary server processes transactions and ships log entries to the standby server, while the standby server receives log entries from the primary and reapplies the transactions on the standby.

If the primary server fails, the standby can take over the transactional workload in seconds as the standby becomes the new primary server. If the failed machine becomes available again, it can be automatically reintegrated back into the HADR pair and the old primary server becomes the new standby server.

The architecture of HADR is shown in Figure 13–19.

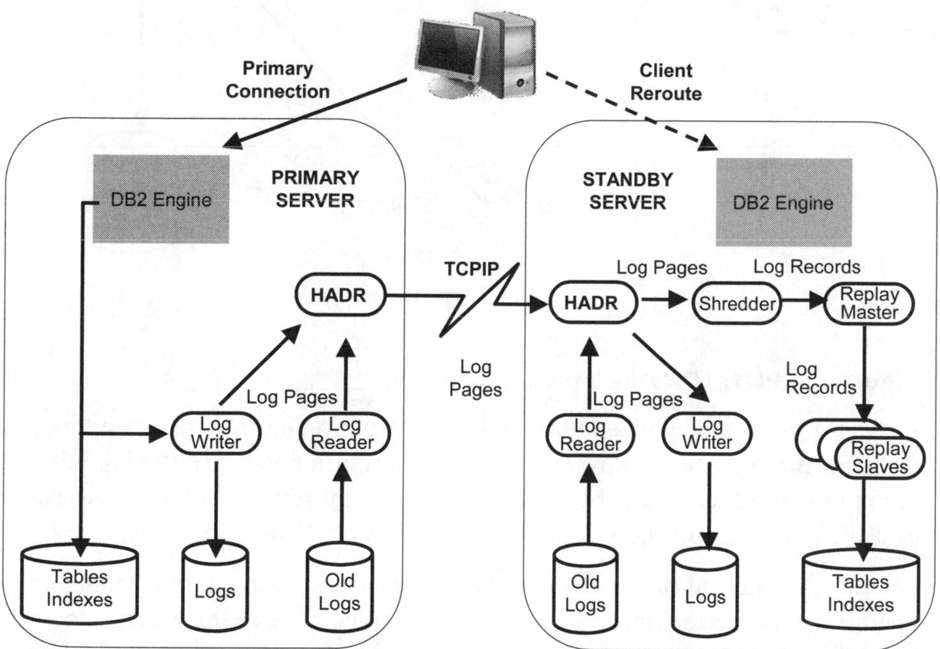

Figure 13–33 *HADR architecture overview*

As transactions run against the database, they are “replayed” on the standby server. The log buffer entries get streamed across the network wire (using any TPC/IP network connection), shredded, and run on the standby.

You define the synchronization mode when setting up an HADR solution. HADR supports three synchronization modes: asynchronous, near-synchronous, and synchronous, as shown in Figure 13–34.

DB2 Note

It's not only a `COMMIT` operation that flushes the log buffer; there are parameters and other operations that affect the timeliness of a log flush too. For simplicity, the following explanations assume that only a `COMMIT` will flush the log buffer.

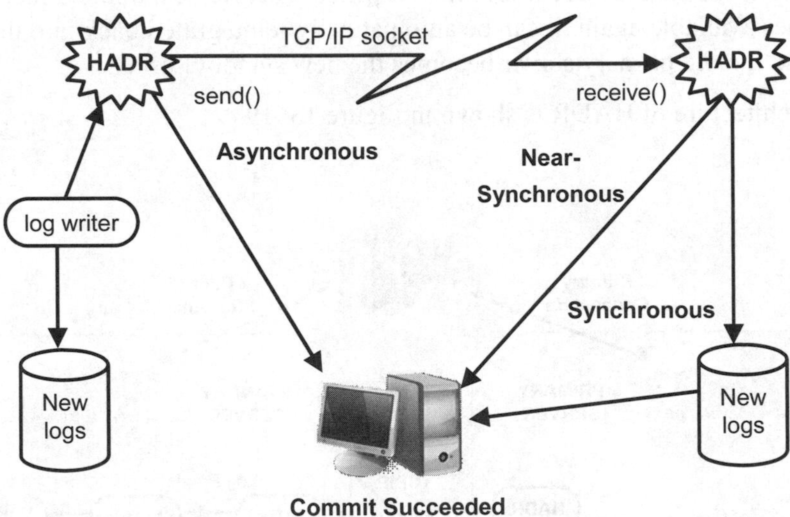

Figure 13–34 *HADR synchronization modes*

In *synchronous* mode, when the client application requests a `COMMIT` operation, the database manager will not return a successful return code until the log buffer containing the transaction has been sent to the standby server, replayed, and hardened to disk. With this setting, you are guaranteed never to lose a transaction.

On the opposite end of the spectrum is *asynchronous* mode. In this mode, a `COMMIT` operation completes when a `send()` socket call is made to the wire protocol. The transaction is put into the wire with little consideration after that point. If data is lost on the wire or something happens to the primary or standby servers while the transaction is being streamed, you could lose transactions.

In between these two settings is *near-synchronous*, which is the mode that is recommend to most customers when deploying an HADR solution. This is the default mode for HADR. In this mode, a successful return code is not given to the client application until the log buffer (which contains the transaction) is flowed across the wire and that buffer is in memory on the standby server. In this case, you could potentially lose the transactions in a log buffer in the rare case that you experienced the simultaneous failure of both the primary and standby servers and you then chose to start up the standby server as your new primary.

Setting Up HADR

The ability to quickly and easily set up an HADR environment was one of the main design goals of this new feature. DB2 provides the Configure HADR Databases wizard to set up the primary and standby servers for HADR. This wizard helps you perform the tasks required to set up an HADR environment.

The HADR wizard is invoked from the Control Center by right-clicking on the database that you want to use. Note that HADR always manages failover at the database level. The first panel (Figure 13–35) introduces the HADR feature and gives the user some background information on what is required to set up the environment.

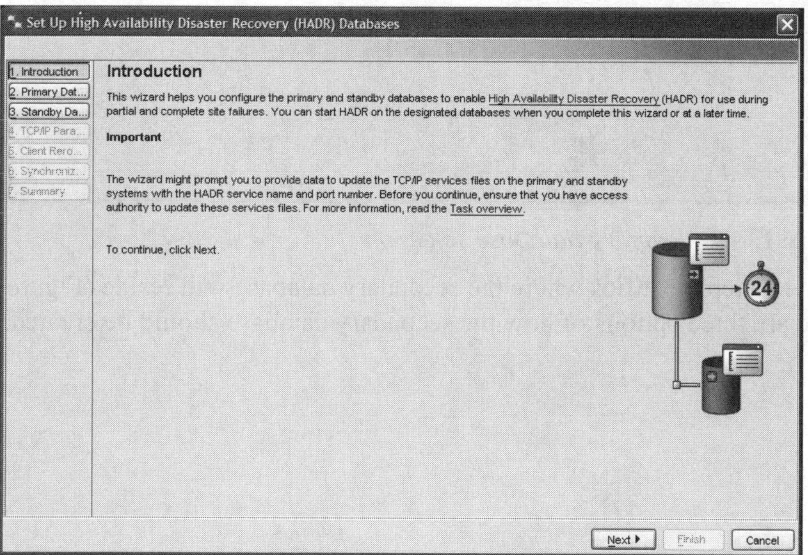

Figure 13–35 *HADR Introduction Screen*

The next step in the process is to check the status of the database and determine whether it is eligible for HADR recovery (Figure 13–36). One of the key requirements is that archive logging must be turned on. If this is not enabled, the wizard will take you through the steps required to turn on archive logging. In addition, the tool gives you options on how to handle index records.

Index creation is always logged in a DB2 database. However, only the `CREATE INDEX` command is captured, not the actual index records that are generated in the database. HADR will replay the `CREATE INDEX` command on the standby server when the server goes into primary mode. This means that before the database can be available for use, it must complete the creation of the index. In order to avoid the index build time, DB2 can log the actual index record creation, thus eliminating the index creation overhead.

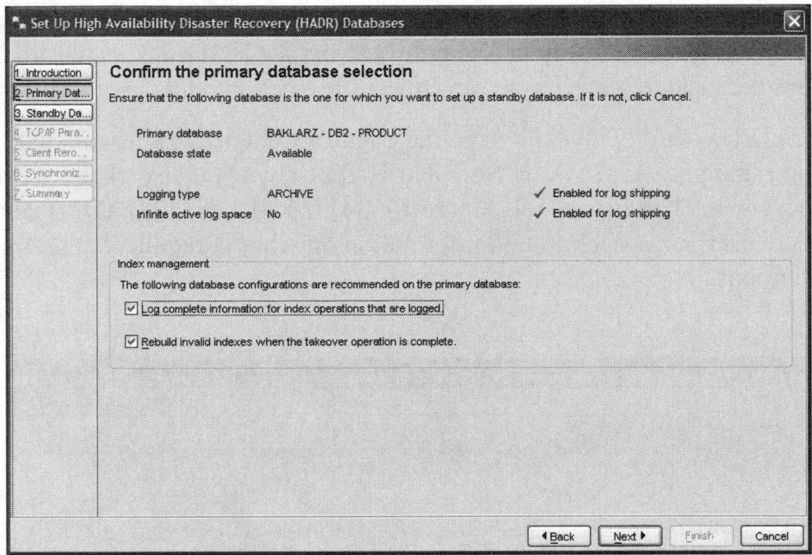

Figure 13–36 *Primary database selection*

The next step identifies where the secondary database will reside (Figure 13–37). There are three options of how the secondary database should be created.

Set Up High Availability Disaster Recovery (HADR) Databases

1. Introduction
2. Primary Dat...
3. Standby Da...
4. Backup Ima...
5. Restore dat...
6. TCP/IP Para...
7. Client Rero...
8. Synchroniz...
9. Summary

Identify a standby database

Select the standby system and instance. If the standby system and instance are not currently cataloged, click Add to catalog them.

System name BAKLARZ Add...
Instance name BACKUP Add...

Standby database initialization options

Use a backup image of the primary database to initialize a standby database

You can select from a list of existing backup images or create a new backup image. The following pages will help you to initialize the standby database using the DB2 backup and restore utilities.

Use another existing database as the standby database

The following values show the cataloged alias name identical to the primary database name.

Database name PRODUCT

Database alias name PRODALT

Use suspended I/O and online split mirror to initialize a standby database

To create a split mirror, consult the storage vendor documentation applicable for your device. Exit from this wizard to perform the split mirror procedure. Once you have created the mirror database, return to this wizard to configure the new database as the standby database. For more information, see Suspended I/O and online split mirror.

Back Next Finish Cancel

Figure 13–37 *Secondary database setup*

The database can be created from an existing primary database backup, created via a split/mirror process, or created through a manual process. If the database is to be created from an existing backup, an additional panel will be displayed that lets you select which backup image to use (Figure 13–38).

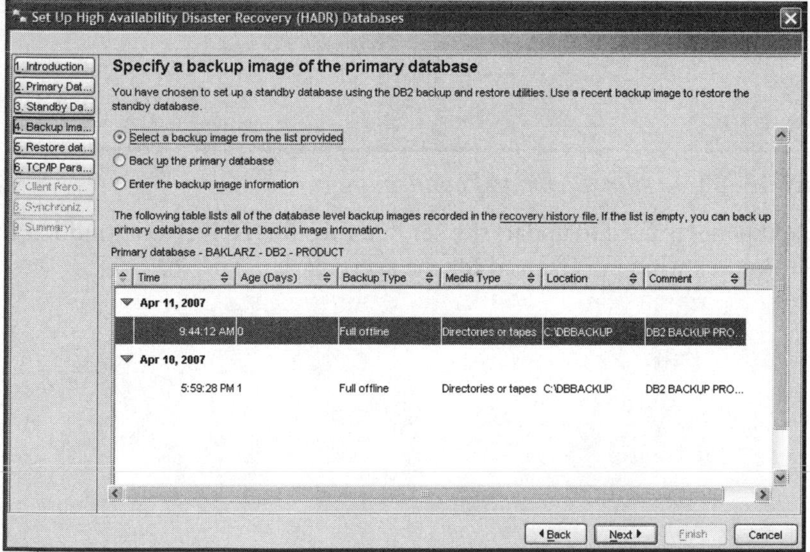

Figure 13–38 *Backup selection*

Figure 13–39 summarizes the commands that will be issued to create the secondary database. If additional RESTORE options are required, there is a button beside the command that will allow for further customization.

If SPLIT/MIRROR was selected, the wizard will not continue since it needs the secondary database to be available before continuing on. Once the split/mirror processing has finished, the user would select "Use another existing database."

In addition to moving the database, any external stored procedures, functions, or objects that are required for application execution must also be moved to the secondary server. These external objects are often the pieces that are forgotten when recovering a database.

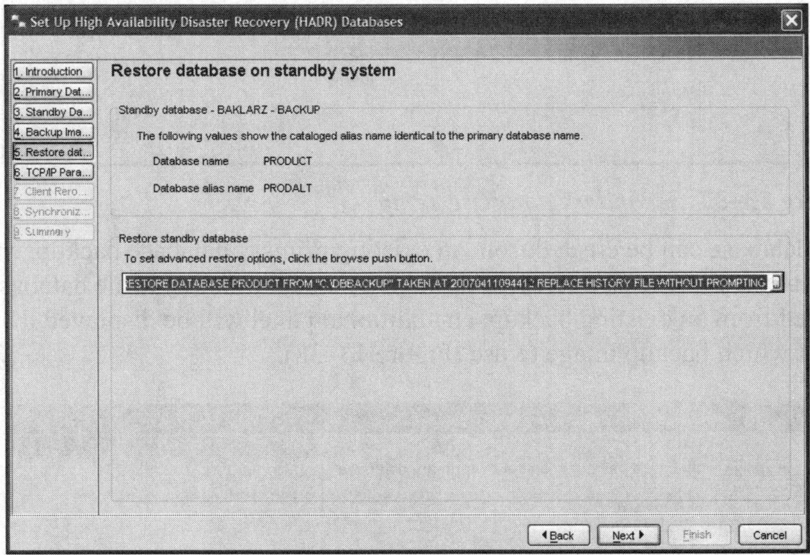

Figure 13–39 *Restore command confirmation*

The next panel is used to update the service files for TCP/IP communication so that HADR knows what port is used for the secondary database.

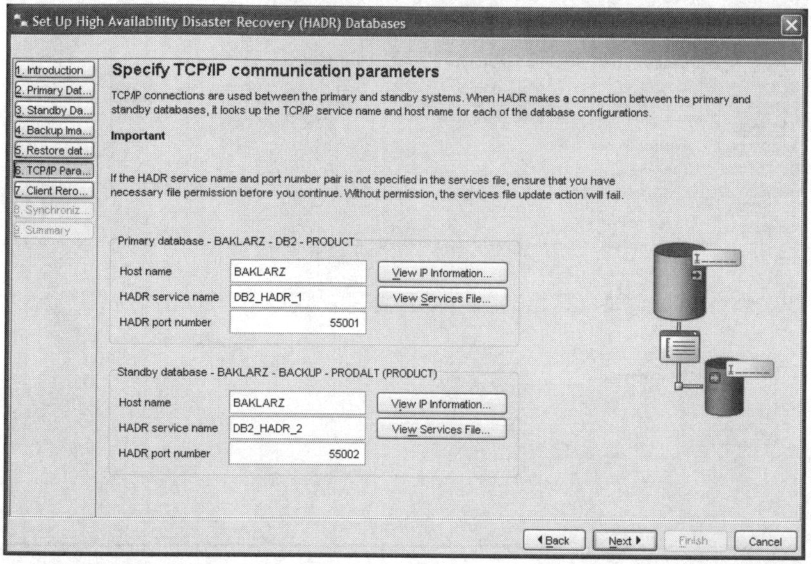

Figure 13–40 *TCP/IP Parameters*

Figure 13–41 displays the client configuration panel that catalogues the secondary database so that the client can automatically switch to it upon a failure.

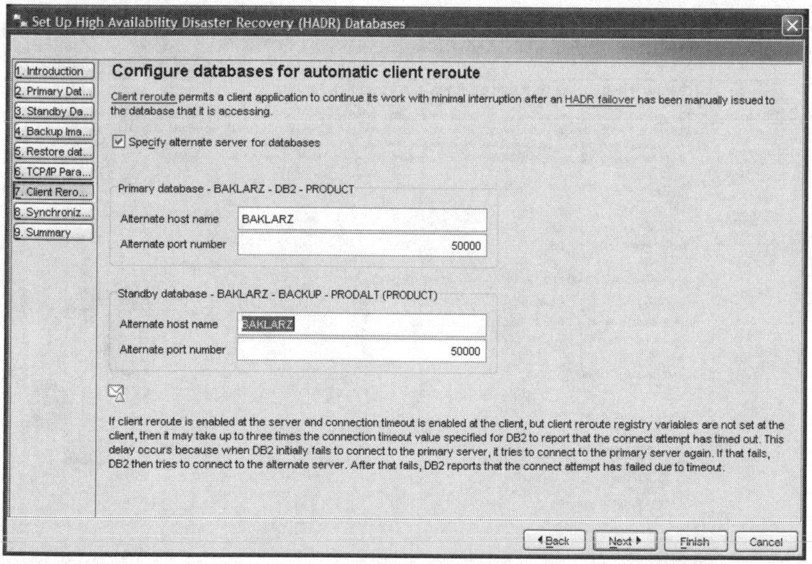

Figure 13–41 *Automatic client reroute configuration*

The next panel (Figure 13–42) lets the user chose type of synchronization is to take placed between the two servers. By default, near-synchronous log page shipping is used.

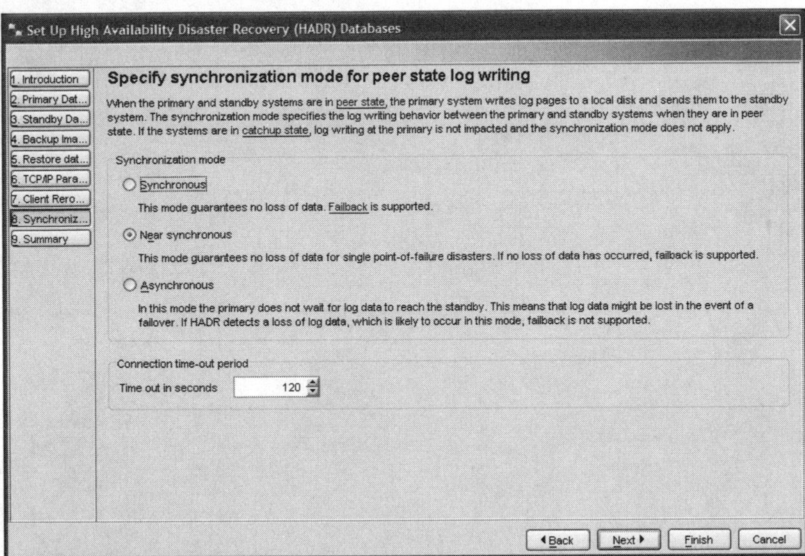

Figure 13–42 *HADR synchronization modes*

The final panel summarizes the actions that will take place when the wizard completes (Figure 13–43).

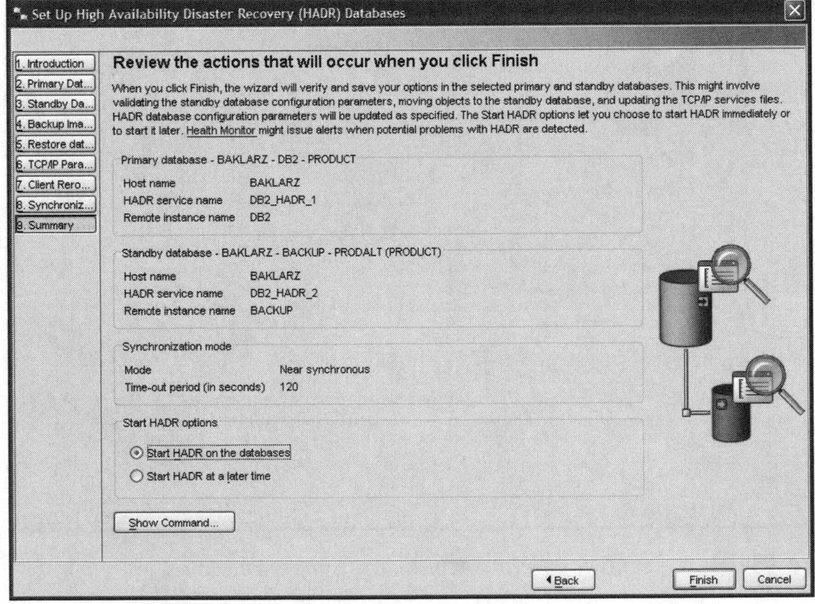

Figure 13–43 *Summarization of HADR setup*

The commands that will be issued by the wizard can be reviewed by clicking on the Show SQL button (Figure 13–44).

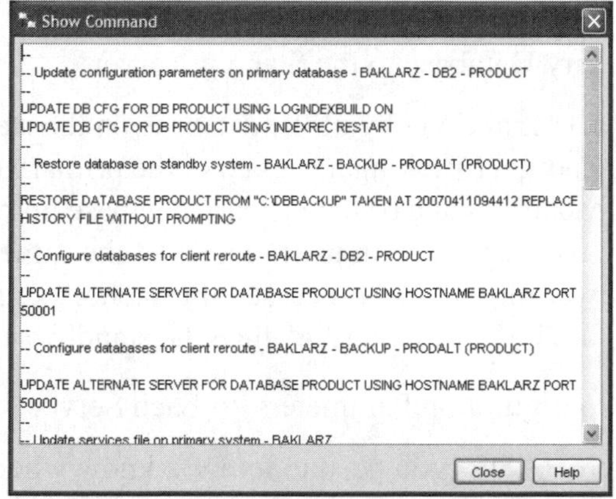

Figure 13–44 *SQL command summary*

Once the finish button is pressed, the wizard will display a progress window that tracks the commands as they execute (Figure 13–45).

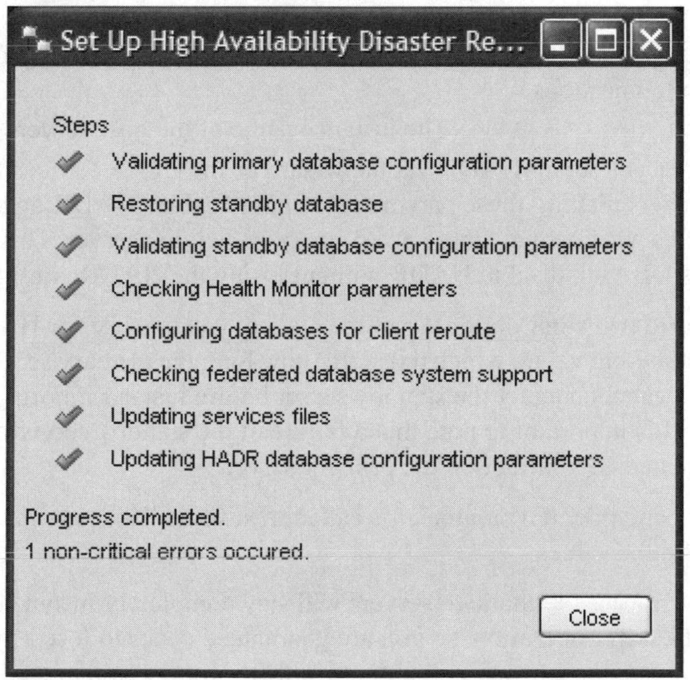

Figure 13–45 *Command progress*

Manual HADR Setup

HADR can be easily set up using commands or scripts. To manually set up HADR, you need to perform three simple steps to have a high-availability cluster:

1. Clone the Primary Database to the Standby Server

   The first step is to make a copy of the database on the standby server. You can do this simply enough by taking a backup of the primary (online if needed) and restoring that backup image of the primary database onto the standby server. Now you have two servers with exact copies of the same database. However, the primary server might have processed transactions during the restore operation and therefore be "further ahead" than the standby server.

2. Update Five Configuration Parameters on Each Server

   Before you start HADR, you need to let DB2 know where the primary and standby servers are on the network. To do this, update the required HADR database configuration parameters as follows:

   - `HADR_LOCAL_HOST` — The host name of the local server
   - `HADR_REMOTE_HOST` — The host name of the peer in the HADR cluster
   - `HADR_LOCAL_SVC` — The port number that the server listens on for HADR communications
   - `HADR_REMOTE_SVE` — The port number that the peer listens on for HADR communications
   - `HADR_REMOTE_INST` — The instance name of the peer server

   Whether you set up HADR via the wizard or the CLP, you need to set these parameters. Setting these parameters neither enables HADR on a database nor indicates whether a database is a primary or standby server. This separation allows DBAs to disable HADR without losing the HADR configuration.

   There are two other optional parameters that you can use for HADR. The first is the time-out value, which tells DB2 how long the primary server should wait for if it cannot contact the standby server before it starts ignoring the standby server. It's important to note that a failure of the standby server or the network does not cause a failure on the primary server.

   The second optional parameter is called `SYNCMODE`. This parameter can take on one of three values:

   - `SYNC` means the that two servers will stay completely in sync down to the last `COMMIT` operation, so you are guaranteed never to lose a transaction.
   - `NEARSYNC` means that you will never lose a transaction unless both the primary and standby servers fail simultaneously, and you then start the standby

up as the primary.

- ASYNC means that log buffers are sent asynchronously to the standby server every time a transaction commits, which has less impact on the production server.

3. Start HADR on the Standby and Primary Servers

At this point, you have two servers that each have a copy of the same database and you have specified how each server can talk to each other (over TCP/IP). All that is left to do is start HADR.

You start HADR on the standby server with the following command:

```
db2 start HADR on database PRODUCT as STANDBY
```

The other option is to use the Control Center and use the HADR panel to manage the databases (Figure 13–46).

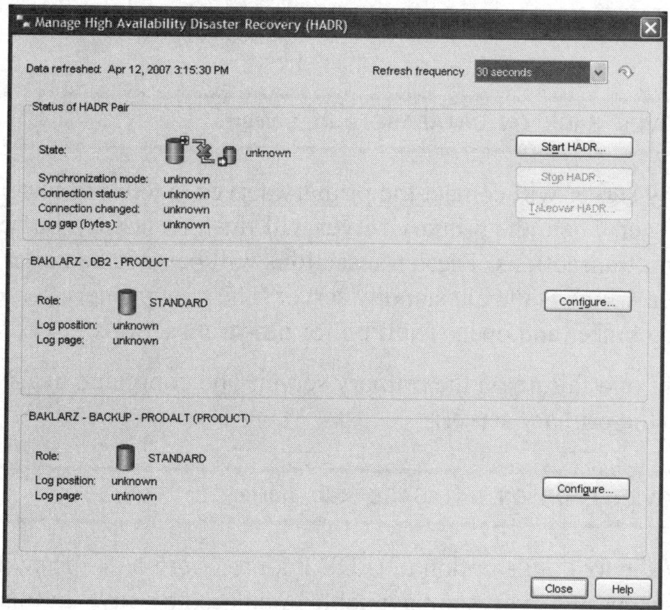

Figure 13–46 *Managing HADR databases*

The START HADR command causes the standby server to contact the primary server and "catch up" with the transactions it missed while it was down. The standby server will tell the primary server what location it is in the log file and will pull over any log files that have been created since the backup was created to catch up to the current active log.

The next step is to start HADR on the primary server with the following command to get the two databases in peer state:

```
db2 start HADR on database PRODUCT as PRIMARY
```

After this command completes, any time the log buffer is flushed to disk on the primary server, the log buffer that contains the transaction is sent to the standby server and applied to keep it synchronized.

Once HADR is set up, you can manage its operations using the CLP or a wizard.

Performing a Takeover

HADR has two forms of takeover. The first is sometimes called a normal takeover or a switch roles takeover. In this form, the primary database becomes the standby and the standby database turns into the primary. This can be extremely useful for performing maintenance such as applying maintenance. To perform the takeover in this manner, you simply log on to the standby server and run the following command:

```
db2 TAKEOVER HADR ON DATABASE <db_name>
```

The standby server will contact the primary server to tell it to turn itself into a standby server. Then, the primary server will flush its last log buffer and force off any in-flight transactions. These transactions will be switched over to the new primary server, which is the old standby server. The new primary server then receives the final log buffer and opens itself up for new transactions.

In the event of a failure on the primary server, one command turns the standby server into the primary server:

```
db2 TAKEOVER HADR ON DATABASE <db_name> BY FORCE
```

The use of the BY FORCE option tells DB2 not to coordinate the switching of roles (since the primary server is not available to talk to anyway). In this mode, the standby server becomes the primary database and begins to accept new transactions from end user applications.

When the old primary database comes back online, you need to start HADR on that server as a standby. This will cause the failed database to contact the new primary server and resynchronize itself into a peer state with it. This reintegration is guaranteed if you are using the synchronous mode and possible (as long as no transactions were lost) using the near-synchronous and asynchronous modes.

Monitoring HADR

DB2 provides many mechanisms by which to monitor HADR. For example, DBAs can use SQL to retrieve information about the status of HADR or use the Control Center. An example of some HADR-specific output from the Control Center is shown in Figure 13–47.

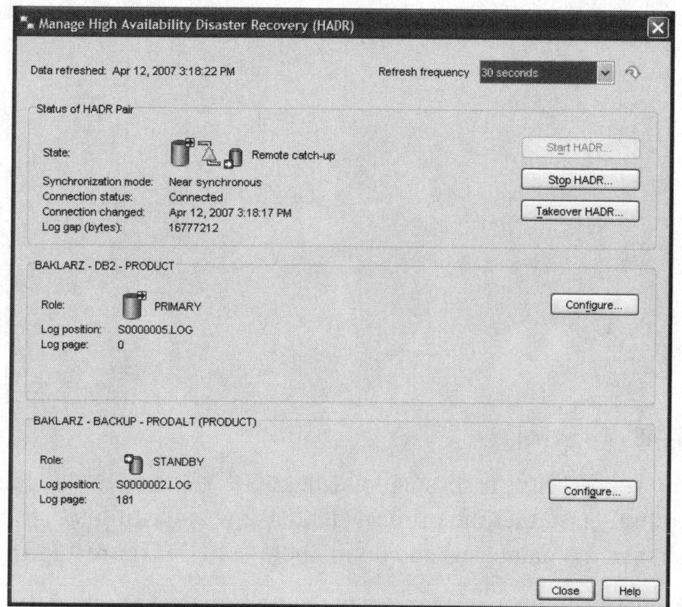

Figure 13–47 *HADR Status*

The state of the two servers is “remote catch-up.” This indicates that the standby server still needs to apply logs from the primary database before it can be in peer state. Below this section is more detailed information on the status of the servers.

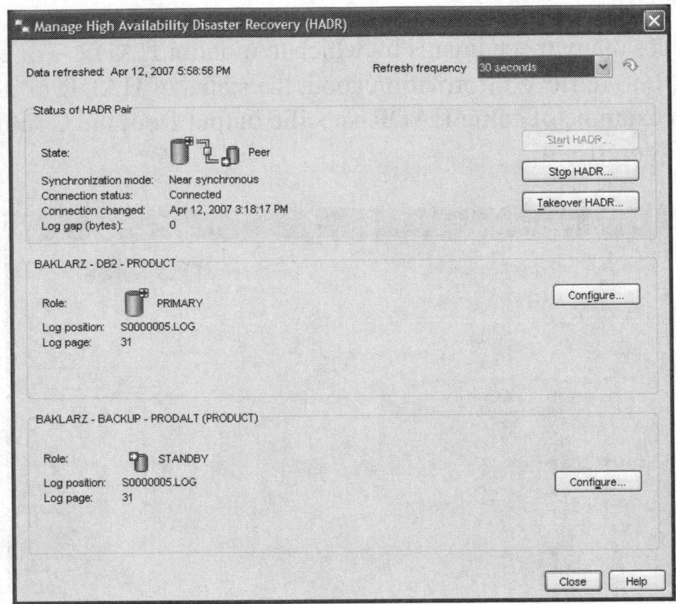

Figure 13–48 *Peer state*

The standby server was processing log file `S0000002.LOG` and it needed to catch up to the `S0000005.LOG` that the primary database was writing to. Once the logs have been caught up, the databases end up in "peer state" (Figure 13–48).

Peer state means that the two servers are synchronized and that the log buffers are shipped directly from the primary to the standby server when flushed.

The connection status of the HADR pair is also returned in the database snapshot output. In this case, you can see if two servers are connected and the time they were connected at. The connection status could also show that the two servers were disconnected or congested. The following SQL statement returns the HADR status by querying the contents of the `SYSIBMADM.SNAPHADR` administrative view (Figure 13–49):

```
SELECT SUBSTR(DB_NAME, 1, 8) AS DBNAME, HADR_ROLE, HADR_STATE,
   HADR_SYNCMODE, HADR_CONNECT_STATUS
   FROM SYSIBMADM.SNAPHADR

DBNAME   HADR_ROLE  HADR_STATE   HADR_SYNCMODE HADR_CONNECT_STATUS
-------- ---------- ------------ ------------- -------------------
PRODUCT  PRIMARY    PEER         NEARSYNC      CONNECTED

  1 record(s) selected.
```

Figure 13–49 *HADR status*

Other information includes Heartbeats missed (a key indicator if something on the network is causing a problem for HADR), Log gap running average (which could identify network latency or if the standby server can't keep up for some reason), and more.

Automatic Failover for Applications with Automatic Client Reroute

Automatic Client Reroute (ACR) is a feature that was first introduced in the DB2 V8.2 release. ACR isn't tied to HADR technology; it can be used with HADR, clustering software, in a partitioned database environment, with replication, and so on. ACR provides a method by which applications can be automatically and transparently reconnected to the standby server without the application or end user being exposed to a communications error.

For the ACR feature, you identify an alternate server to connect to if the primary database becomes unavailable in the server's configuration.

```
UPDATE ALTERNATE SERVER FOR DATABASE PRODUCT
  USING HOSTNAME BACKUP PORT 756
```

Whenever a DB2 client makes a successful connection to the primary database server, the alternate server information is returned to the client and stored there.

In the event of a failure, once the ACR technology has verified that the primary database has indeed experienced an outage, the connection is transferred to the alternate server.

Software Upgrades on the Fly

One aspect of availability involves planned maintenance. This involves database and non-database specific tasks. You can use HADR to apply maintenance to your software or hardware without taking the database down. For example, you might want to apply a Fix Pack to DB2, a service pack to your operating system, or swap out some hardware components.

With HADR, you can take the standby server "down," apply maintenance, and bring it back online. HADR will then automatically resynchronize the standby and catch up to the primary by applying the transactions it missed during the maintenance period. Once peer state is achieved, you simply perform a switch roles takeover and then take the new standby down, apply the patch and have HADR resynchronize itself with the new primary server. An example is shown below.

1. Applications are currently connect to the primary server. A TAKEOVER command is issued from the standby server (Figure 13–50).

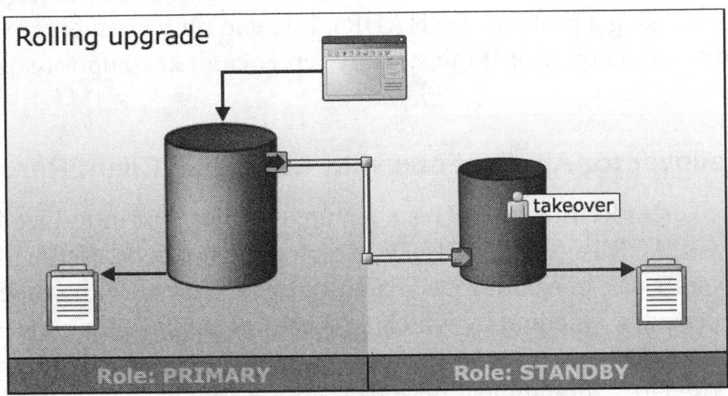

Figure 13–50 *Standby takeover*

2. The primary server reverse roles with the standby. Applications start using the standby server as the new primary. Transaction logs now get applied in the reverse direction (Figure 13–51).

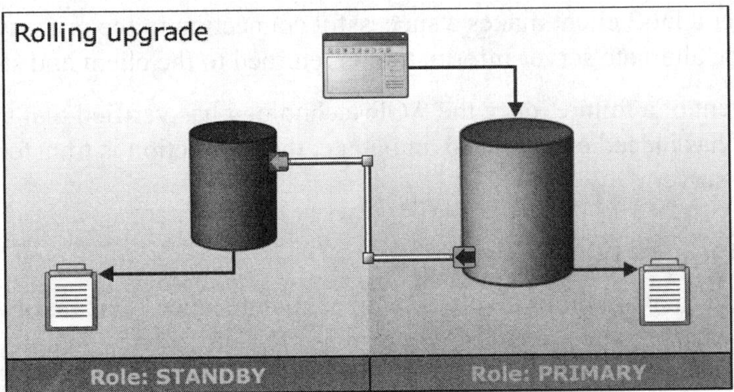

Figure 13–51 *Role reversal*

3. At this point in time, maintenance can be applied on the original primary server (now labelled as standby). Hardware, software, database, and network maintenance can be performed on this server at this time since the clients are currently accessing the standby server.

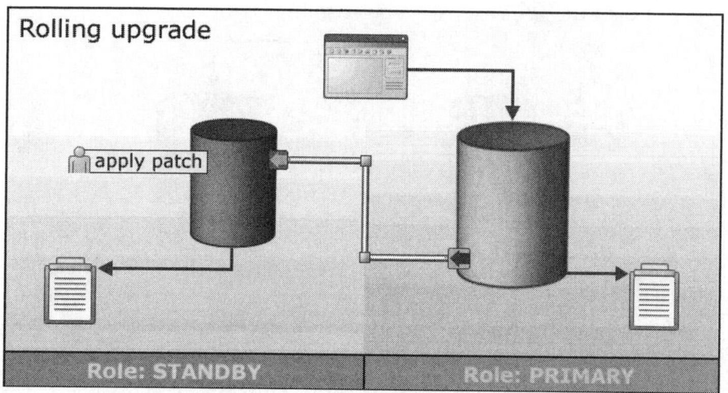

Figure 13–52 *Role reversal*

4. Once the work on the system is complete, the standby server gets rebooted. The primary server does not send any transactions to the standby because it is considered "offline" (Figure 13–53).

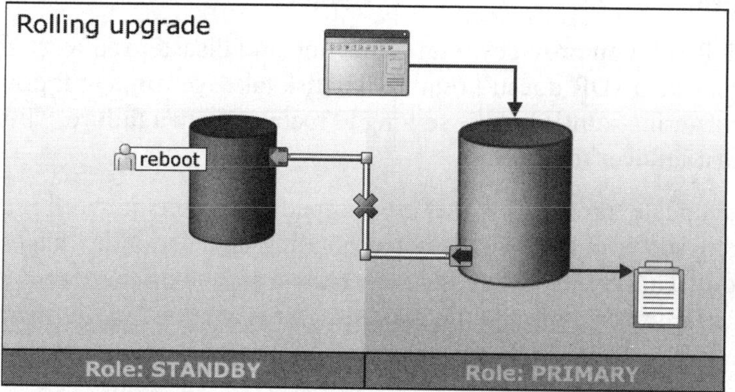

Figure 13–53 *Standby server rebooted*

5. As the standby server starts up, the primary begins to send transactions to it in order for it to "catch up" (Figure 13–54). Once the standby has read all of the primary logs, it will be considered to be in "peer state."

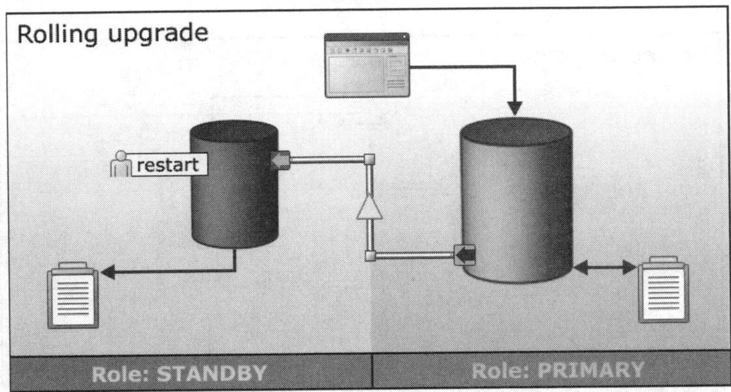

Figure 13–54 *Standby catching up on transactions*

6. The entire process can now be repeated on the secondary server. The current standby can initiate a takeover and shutdown the primary server for maintenance.

HADR Benefits

The HADR solution provides total protection and disaster recovery for an entire solution stack. HADR doesn't require the disk takeover time at failover that makes typical clustering solutions take so long to recover from a failure. This feature leads to very fast failover times.

All of the update transactions that are shipped across the network require DB2 on the standby server to retrieve the corresponding data and index pages into the buffer pool. This greatly reduces restart recovery time on the standby server in the event of a failure because the memory structures are "hot" with the most recent updates.

HADR does limit the activity on the HADR standby database — it can only be used for failover. However, there is nothing to prevent you from using the standby server for other DB2 and non-DB2 activities.

Summary

This chapter discussed concepts and facilities of DB2 recovery. These included:

- *Unit of work* — A recoverable sequence of operations within an application process. This could involve one or many SQL statements depending upon the business logic required. Either all the SQL covering the unit of work gets applied or none of it.

There are three kinds of recovery to consider:

- *Crash recovery* — Protects the database from being left in an inconsistent or unusable state. Unexpected interruptions that leave incomplete units of work are handled by crash recovery, which rolls back the changes made by uncommitted transactions.
- *Version recovery* — Allows the restoration of a database from a backup image taken at an earlier point in time. Table spaces can also be version recovered.
- *Roll-forward recovery* — Extends version recovery by using full database backups in conjunction with log files to provide the capability of recovering to any point in time covered by the log files.

Recoverable databases support crash, version, and roll-forward recovery. DB2 supports recoverable databases by allowing the `LOGRETAIN` and/or `USEREXIT` database configuration parameters. Nonrecoverable databases support crash and version recovery. DB2 implements this type of database by not allowing the use of the above two parameters.

Offline access to the database means that access to the database is in exclusive mode; no one else can connect to the database. Online access means that other applications can concurrently connect to the database when the particular operation is being performed.

Primary log files establish a fixed, preallocated amount of storage to the recovery log files. Enough disk space for the primary log files must be allocated before the database is connected to. Secondary log files are used when the primary log files become full and are allocated one at a time when required.

There are two kinds of logging supported by DB2:

- *Circular logging* — Supports nonrecoverable databases, as primary log files are reused in a circular manner.
- *Archival logging* — Supports recoverable databases by archiving logs once they have been written to; that is, log files are not reused.

Log files can be characterized as one of the following:

- *Active log files* — The log files written to by DB2 that support crash recovery.

Database Recovery

- *Archive log files* — The log files that have been written to by DB2 and are no longer needed to support crash recovery. Online archive log files reside in the active log path directory. Offline archive log files do no reside in the active log path directory. They can be moved manually or by an external storage management product.

The following DB2 commands enable the recoverability of databases:

- The `BACKUP` command creates images of databases or table spaces that are used for restoration purposes, this operation can occur either online or offline. Incremental backup is also supported.
- The `RESTORE` command takes the backup images created by the `BACKUP` command and restores databases or table spaces.
- The `ROLLFORWARD` command supports roll-forward recovery by reapplying units of work captured in the log up to the nominated point in time that roll-forward recovery stops.
- The `QUIESCE` command establishes a point of consistency for related table spaces that can be used in roll-forward operations later on. It does this by taking locks on tables which ensures that no other application can update the tables being quiesced.

To improve the availability of DB2, you can use high-availability products such as HACMP on AIX to implement hot standby and mutual takeover modes. This allows automatic switching of DB2 operations to a backup machine if the primary machine fails without interruption to operations. This can significantly improve the operational availability of DB2.

Several storage vendors have provided advanced disk mirroring capabilities. DB2 has provided commands to use this technology and can initialize a mirrored database as a:

- `SNAPSHOT` — a clone of the primary database.
- `STANDBY` — a database in roll-forward-pending state, ready to take place of the primary system if it goes down.
- `MIRROR` — a backup image that can be used to restore the primary database.

In addition to using HACMP, DB2 also offers the High-Availability Disaster Recovery (HADR) feature to provide improved availability. This feature can help guard from many different failures, but also allow for rolling upgrades of hardware and software on the production system.

CHAPTER 14

Monitoring and Tuning

- PLANNING
- DB2 ARCHITECTURE OVERVIEW
- DATABASE MONITORING
- SQL MONITORING
- TUNING CONFIGURATION PARAMETERS
- PROBLEM DETERMINATION
- SELF-TUNING MEMORY MANAGER

Understanding the performance of the DB2 database management system, its databases, and active applications in a dynamic environment requires monitoring. This means that a database administrator should gather information regarding the usage of the database. An application programmer may also require SQL statement execution information. Gathering database information using DB2's monitoring facilities and information regarding SQL statement processing will be discussed.

In this chapter, the various DB2 facilities for the monitoring and gathering of information that is input into the tuning process will be reviewed. The *Explain Facility*, *Snapshot Monitor*, and *Event Monitor* are the main tools used to monitor DB2 databases and SQL statements.

These tools may be used to perform the following tasks:

- Understand user and application activity within DB2
- Better understand how an SQL statement is processed
- Determine the sources and causes of problems
- Tune configuration parameters
- Improve database and application performance

Elements of Performance

Performance is the way a computer system behaves given a particular work load. Performance is measured through one or more of the system's response time, throughput, and availability. It is affected by:

- The resources available
- How well the resources are utilized

Performance tuning should be undertaken when you want to improve the cost-benefit ratio of your system. Specific situations include:

- You want to process a larger, more demanding work load without increasing processing costs that may include having to acquire additional hardware.
- Obtaining faster system response time, or higher throughput, without increasing processing costs.
- Reducing processing costs without negatively affecting service to the client(s).

Translating performance from technical terms to economic terms is difficult. Performance tuning costs money through labor and machine resources, so the cost of tuning must be weighed against the benefits that tuning may or may not deliver.

Some of these benefits, including less resource usage and the ability to add more users to the system, are tangible, whereas other benefits, such as increased customer satisfaction, are less tangible from a monetary perspective.

Tuning Guidelines

The following guidelines should be considered in developing an overall approach to performance tuning.

Remember the Law of Diminishing Returns

Your greatest performance benefits usually come from your initial efforts. Further changes generally produce smaller and smaller benefits and require greater effort.

Do Not Tune Just for the Sake of Tuning

Tune to relieve identified constraints. If you tune resources that are not the primary cause of performance problems, this can have little or no effect on response time until you have relieved the major constraints, and it can actually make subsequent tuning work more difficult. If there is any significant improvement potential, it lies in improving the performance of the resources that are major factors in the response time.

Consider the Whole System

You can never tune one parameter or system in isolation. Before you make any adjustments, consider how it will affect the system as a whole.

Change One Parameter at a Time

Do not change more than one performance tuning parameter at a time. Even if you are sure that all the changes will be beneficial, you will have no way of evaluating how much each change has contributed. You also cannot effectively judge the trade-off you have made by changing more than one parameter at a time. Every time you adjust a parameter to improve one area, you almost always affect at least one other area that may not have been considered.

Measure and Reconfigure by Levels

For the same reasons that you should change only one parameter at a time, tune one level of your system at a time. You can use the following list of levels within a system as a guide:

- Hardware
- Operating system
- Application server and requester
- Database
- SQL statements
- Application programs

Check for Hardware and Software Problems

Some performance problems may be corrected by applying service to your hardware, your software, or to both. Do not spend excessive time monitoring and tuning your system when simply applying service may be the solution to the problem.

Understand the Problem Before Upgrading Hardware

Even if it seems that an additional storage or processor resource could immediately improve performance, take the time to understand where the bottlenecks are. You may spend money on additional disk storage only to find that you do not have the processor resource to exploit it.

Put Fall Back Procedures in Place Before You Start Tuning

Because changes are being made to an existing system, you must be prepared to back out those changes out if they do not have the desired effect or have a negative effect on the system.

Performance Improvement Process

Monitoring and tuning a database and its applications should be performed using the following basic process:

- Establish performance indicators.
- Define performance objectives.
- Develop a performance monitoring plan.
- Implement the plan.
- Analyze the measurements. Determine if the objectives have been met. If so, consider reducing the number of measurements to keep to a minimum the amount of resource consumed for monitoring.
- Determine the major constraints in the system.
- Decide where you can afford to make trade-offs and which resources can bear an additional load. Most tuning activities involve trade-offs among system resources and various elements of performance.
- Adjust the configuration of the system. If you think that it is feasible to change more than one tuning option, implement one at a time.
- Based on the results, start another iteration of the monitoring cycle.

You may want to follow the above process for periodic monitoring or when significant changes occur to the system and/or work load taken on by the system.

How Much Can a System Be Tuned?

There are limits to how much you can improve the efficiency of a system. Consider how much time and money you should spend on improving system performance and how much the spending of additional time and money will help the users of the system.

Your system may perform adequately without any tuning at all, but it probably will not perform to its potential. Each database is unique. As soon as you develop your own database and applications for it, investigate the tuning parameters available and learn how you can customize their settings to reflect your situation. In some circumstances, there will only be a small benefit from tuning a system. In most circumstances, however, the benefit may be significant.

There are wizards available from the DB2 Control Center that assist in tuning the database parameters. The performance Configuration Advisor can be found by clicking the right mouse button on the database you want to tune.

If your system encounters performance bottlenecks, it is likely that tuning will be effective. If you are close to the performance limits, and you increase the number of users on the system by about 10%, the response time may rise by much more than 10%. In this situation, you will need to determine how to counterbalance this degradation in performance by tuning your system. However, there is a point beyond which tuning cannot help. At that point, you should consider revising your goals and expectations within that environment. Or you should change your system environment by considering more disk storage, faster/additional processors, additional memory, or faster networking solutions.

A Less Formal Approach

If you do not have enough time to set performance objectives and to monitor and tune in a comprehensive manner, you can address performance by listening to your users. Find out if they are having performance-related problems. You can usually locate the problem or determine where to start looking for the problem by asking a few simple questions. For example, you can ask your users:

- What do you mean by slow response? Is it 10% slower than you expect it to be or ten times slower?
- When did you notice the problem? Is it recent or has it always been there?
- Do you know of other users who are complaining of the same problem? Are those complaining one or two individuals or a whole group?
- Are the problems you are experiencing related to a specific transaction or application program?
- Do your problems appear during regular periods, such as at lunch hour, or are they continuous?

DB2 Architecture Overview

To understand performance and what can be monitored, a brief overview of DB2 from an architectural perspective will be presented. The architectural components that will be examined include:

- Process model
- DB2 memory usage
- SQL compiler/optimizer

Process Model

The process model or server architecture for DB2 is known as an *n-n process model*. The main feature of this architecture is its ability to ensure database integrity. It isolates all database applications from critical database resources. These resources include database control blocks and critical database files. A high-level view of the DB2's architecture can be found in Figure 14–1.

During the database connection process, a DB2 coordinating agent is assigned to each database application. Each DB2 agent works on behalf of the database application and handles all of the SQL requests. The application and database agents communicate using Inter-Process Communication (IPC) techniques (such as message queues, shared memory, and semaphores). DB2 coordinating agents work with DB2 subagents if intra-partition parallelism is enabled.

DB2 Note

The DB2 agents are *threads* in Windows and *processes* in Linux and UNIX operating systems.

This architecture provides a firewall to protect the database resources from an errant application.

A many to one process model is made possible by the DB2 connection concentrator. The use of a concentrator can improve performance by allowing many more client connections to be processed and reducing memory use for each connection. The connection concentrator is enabled when the value of `MAX_CONNECTIONS` is greater than the value of `MAX_COORDAGENTS`.

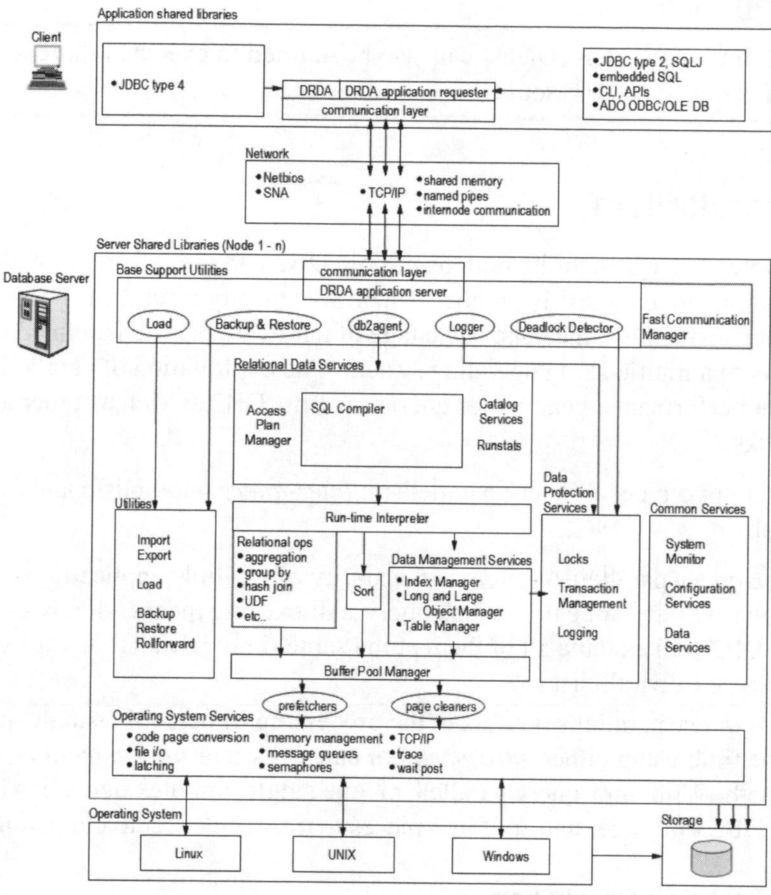

Figure 14–1 *DB2 Architecture Overview*

Fenced/Not Fenced Resources

A database stored procedure is a dynamically loadable library (DLL) that can be invoked from a database application by using the CALL statement. The library is stored on the DB2 database server, and it can execute as a *fenced* resource or a *not fenced* resource. A fenced resource is one that executes in a separate process from the database agent. A not fenced resource will execute in the same process as the database agent.

A not fenced resource will have better performance than a fenced resource since there is less interprocess communication overhead. However, a not fenced resource can overwrite DB2 control blocks if it is not well tested.

DB2 Note

User-defined functions (UDFs) can also be defined to execute as a fenced or unfenced (not fenced) resource.

Query Parallelism

In Chapter 1, the scalability options of how DB2 can grow from a small uniprocessor machine to a massively parallel system was briefly discussed. There are certain elements inside DB2 that take advantage of hardware parallelism in addition to the benefits of a multitasking operating system. The exploitation of parallelism has significant performance benefits for queries against DB2 as well as other administrative tasks.

There are two types of query parallelism: *inter-query* parallelism and *intra-query* parallelism.

- *Inter-query* parallelism refers to the ability of multiple applications to query a database at the same time. Each query will execute independently of the others, but DB2 will execute all of them at the same time. DB2 has always supported this type of parallelism.
- *Intra-query* parallelism refers to the processing of parts of a single query at the same time using either *intra-partition* parallelism or *inter-partition* parallelism or both. With intra-query parallelism, one single complex query can be taken by the DB2 optimizer and split into pieces that can be executed in parallel.

Intra-Partition Parallelism

Intra-partition parallelism refers to the ability to break up a query into multiple parts. This type of parallelism subdivides what is usually considered a single database operation such as index creation, database load, or SQL queries into multiple parts, many or all of which can be executed in parallel within a single database partition. Intra-partition parallelism is best suited to take advantage of the symmetric multiprocessor (SMP) system.

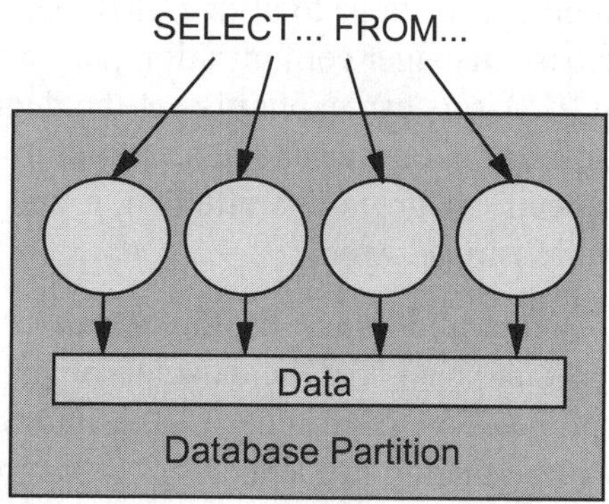

Figure 14–2 *Intra-partition parallelism*

Figure 14–2 shows a query broken into four pieces that can be executed in parallel, with the results returned more quickly than if the query were run in a serial fashion. To utilize intra-partition parallelism, you need to configure the database appropriately. You can choose the degree of parallelism or let the system do it for you. The degree of parallelism is the number of pieces of a query that execute in parallel. It will be discussed later in this section.

In a parallel environment, the DB2 optimizer considers access plans that do not run a complete query but break the query down into different parts (also called *query decomposition*). The DB2 optimizer considers different groupings of operators that can be sent to different processes or threads to be executed. The parts are called Subsection Pieces (SSPs) with one SQL statement consisting of one or many subsection pieces.

DB2 Note

The use of subsection pieces or SSPs will only be considered by the optimizer if intra-partition parallelism is enabled.

A subsection piece is a sequence of one or more database operators belonging to the same SQL query that, when executed, completes the processing part of that query. A subsection piece must be executed in one DB2 process or thread. A subsection piece may receive data from other DB2 subsection pieces or feed data to another subsection piece or return data to the user. Subsection pieces can be cloned or duplicated by the optimizer to speed up the processing.

DB2 provides the capability to change the *degree of parallelism*. The degree of parallelism limits the number of SSPs a query can be broken down into.

The optimizer handles all of this behind the scenes; therefore, users do not need to change anything in their applications to utilize SMP parallelism other than setting the intra-parallel database manager configuration parameter to yes and setting the degree of parallelism >1. Users can explicitly set the degree of parallelism for the DB2 instance, the application, or the statement. In addition, if a section is built by the optimizer with a specific degree of parallelism, it will be reduced if the instance default degree of parallelism is lower.

When breaking a query into multiple SSPs, the optimizer will also determine if the SSPs will work on the same data or if the data can be partitioned among the SSPs. In determining the optimal way to split the section into SSPs and to partition the data, the optimizer will be mainly influenced by the degree of parallelism and the cardinality of the data.

In an SMP environment, the SSPs will be duplicates or clones of each other. DB2 will then execute the SSPs in parallel and return the results faster than if the query were run on one processor. Each SSP copy will work on a subset of the data. As determined by the optimizer, this subset may be based on the data values or on equal divisions of the data based on the number of rows.

DB2 *Note*

If the degree of parallelism is set to a value >1, the number of SSPs created is equal to that value.

Inter-Partition Parallelism

Inter-partition parallelism refers to the ability to break up a query into multiple parts across multiple partitions of a partitioned database on one machine or multiple machines. The query is performed in parallel. Inter-partition parallelism is best suited to take advantage of clusters or massively parallel processing (MPP) systems.

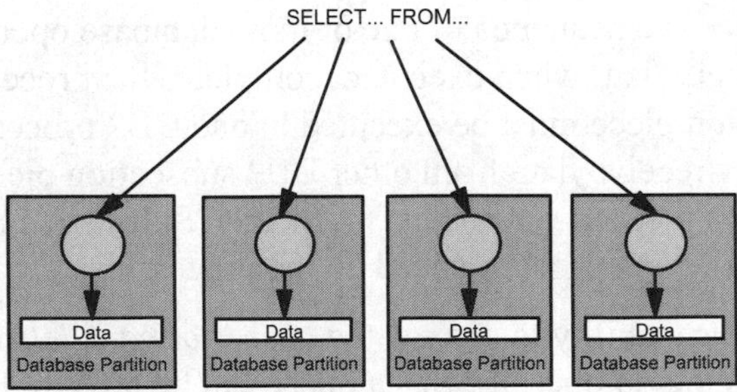

Figure 14–3 *Inter-partition parallelism*

Figure 14–3 shows a query broken into four pieces that can be executed in parallel, with the results returned more quickly than if the query were run in a serial fashion in a single partition. The degree of parallelism is largely determined by the number of partitions you create and how you define your nodegroups. The DB2 Data Partitioning Feature allows for inter-partition parallelism as well as combining intra-partition and inter-partition parallelism. This product is covered in detail in the *DB2 Administration Guide.*

DB2 Memory Usage

Database activity involves disk access (I/O) and memory access (CPU). Each of the DB2 configuration parameters affects either the memory or disk resources. Because disk access is much slower than memory access is, the key database performance tuning objective is to decrease the amount of disk activity. If you are able to eliminate I/O wait time, the database requests are CPU bound, and increasing performance would then require faster CPUs or multiple CPUs.

Figure 14–4 shows the relationship of the various configurable meymory parameters. Memory is allocated on the server or the client. The number of memory segments allocated for the Database Global Memory depends on the number of currently active databases.

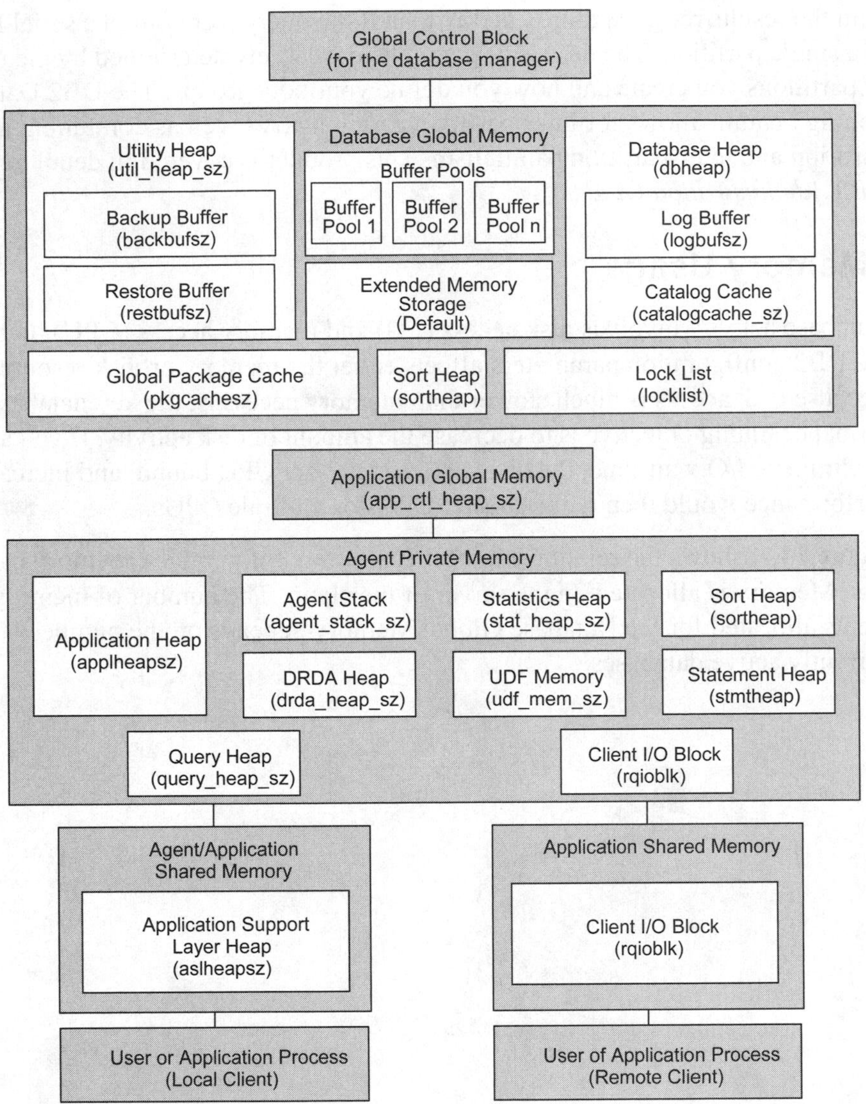

Figure 14–4 *Memory used by DB2*

Each DB2 application has an associated DB2 *coordinating agent*. The database agent accesses the database resources on behalf of the application. Therefore, there are tuning parameters that adjust resource usage of the database agent. The Agent Private Memory exists for each agent, and the size is determined by the values of the following parameters:

- Application heap size (APPLHEAPSZ)
- Sort heap size (SORTHEAP)
- Statement heap size (STMTHEAP)
- Statistics heap size (STAT_HEAP_SZ)
- Query heap size (QUERY_HEAP_SZ)
- DRDA heap size (DRDA_HEAP_SZ)
- UDF shared memory set size (UDF_MEM_SZ)
- Agent stack size (AGENT_STACK_SZ)

If intra-partition parallelism is enabled by setting the intra-parallel database manager configuration parameter to yes, which is the default value in an SMP environment, the coordinating agent distributes database requests to *subagents*, and these agents perform the requests for the application. Once the coordinating agent is created, it handles all database requests on behalf of its application by coordinating the subagents that perform requests on the database.

The application control heap is used as a global work area for all the agents (coordinating and subordinate) working for the application. The database parameter is APP_CTL_HEAP_SZ.

The memory area, known as application shared memory, is used to determine the amount of memory used to communicate between the application and its DB2 coordinating agent. Record blocking occurs within this memory area. The DBM parameter is ASLHEAPSZ.

Prefetching Data into the Buffer Pool

Prefetching pages means that one or more pages are retrieved from disk in the expectation that they will be required by an application. Prefetching index and data pages into the buffer pool can help improve performance by reducing the I/O wait time. In addition, parallel I/O enhances prefetching efficiency. The two types of prefetching are:

- Sequential prefetch — consecutive pages are read into the buffer pool before the pages are required by an application.
- List prefetch — also known as list sequential prefetch, prefetches a set of non-consecutive data pages.

The two methods of reading data are in addition to a normal read. A normal read is used when only one or a few consecutive pages are retrieved.

Prefetching is important to the performance of intra-partition parallelism, which uses multiple subagents when scanning an index or a table. Such parallel scans introduce larger data consumption rates, which require higher prefetch rates.

The cost of inadequate prefetching is higher for parallel scans than serial scans. If prefetching does not occur for a serial scan, the query runs more slowly because the agent always needs to wait for I/O. If prefetching does not occur for a parallel scan, all subagents might need to wait because one subagent is waiting for I/O.

Because of its importance, prefetching is performed more aggressively with intra-partition parallelism. The sequential detection mechanism tolerates larger gaps between adjacent pages so that the pages can be considered sequential. The width of these gaps increases with the number of subagents involved in the scan.

SQL Compiler Overview

The SQL compiler performs a number of tasks during the creation of the compiled form of the SQL statements. These phases are described below and are also shown in Figure 14–5 on page 886. As you can see in this figure, the representation of the query is stored in an internal in-memory structure known as the *Query Graph Model.*

- Parse query — The first task of the SQL compiler is to analyze the SQL query to validate the syntax. If any syntax errors are detected, the SQL compiler stops processing, and the appropriate SQL error is returned to the application attempting to compile the SQL statement. When parsing is complete, an internal representation of the query is created.
- Check Semantics — The second task of the compiler is to further validate the SQL statement by checking to ensure that the parts of the statement make sense given the other parts, for example, ensuring that the data types of the columns input into scalar functions are correct for those functions.

  Also during this stage, the compiler adds the behavioral semantics to the query graph model, such as the effects of referential constraints, table check constraints, triggers, and views.
- Rewrite query — The SQL compiler uses global semantics provided in the query graph model to transform the query into a form that can be optimized more easily. For example, the compiler might move a predicate, altering the level at which it is applied, in an attempt to improve query performance. This particular process is called *general predicate pushdown*.

  Any changes made to the query are rewritten back to the query graph model.
- Optimize access plan — The SQL optimizer portion of the SQL compiler uses the query graph model as input and generates many alternative execution plans for satisfying the user's request. It estimates the execution cost of each alternative plan using the statistics for tables, indexes, columns, and functions, and chooses the plan with the smallest estimated execution cost.

The optimizer uses the query graph model to analyze the query semantics and to obtain information about a wide variety of factors, including indexes, base tables, derived tables, subqueries, correlation, and recursion.

The output from this step of the SQL compiler is an access plan. The access plan provides the basis for the information captured in the *explain tables*. The information used to generate the access plan can be captured with an *explain snapshot*.

- Generate executable code — The final step of the SQL compiler uses the access plan and the query graph model to create an executable access plan, or section, for the query. This code generation step uses information from the query graph model to avoid repetitive execution of expressions that only need to be computed once for a query. Examples for which this optimization is possible include code page conversions and the use of host variables.

  Information about access plans for static SQL is stored in the system catalog tables. When the package is executed, DB2 will use the information stored in the system catalog tables to determine how to access the data and provide results for the query. It is this information that is used by the `db2expln` tool.

  It is recommended that the RUNSTATS command be done periodically on tables used in queries where good performance is desired. The optimizer will then be better equipped with relevant statistical information on the nature of the data. If the RUNSTATS command is not run, or the optimizer determines that RUNSTATS was run on empty or near-empty tables, the optimizer may either use defaults or attempt to derive certain statistics based on the number of pages used to store the table on disk.

  Accurate statistics on tables is of critical importance given the fact that query access plans are based entirely on a cost-based optimizer which relies on accurate statistics in order to make accurate calculations of query access plan costs. In far too many cases the cause of poor performance has been inaccurate statistics, and in many cases tables involved in poor access plans had never had statistics gathered for them.

  In DB2 9, statistics are automatically gathered for new databases. Existing databases that are migrated to DB2 9 will need to have this feature turned on. DB2 monitors the insert/update/delete activity that goes on for each table in the database. When a large amount of activity has occurred, the table will be marked as a candidate for automatic statistics collection. A periodic process will look at those tables marked as candidates and determine (through sampling) if the catalog statistics are out of date. If the statistics require updating, the process will schedule a RUNSTATS operation on that table to update the catalog statistics to more accurate values. The table activity indicator will then be reset.

DB2 Note

DB2 automatically manages statistics for new databases created with DB2 9.

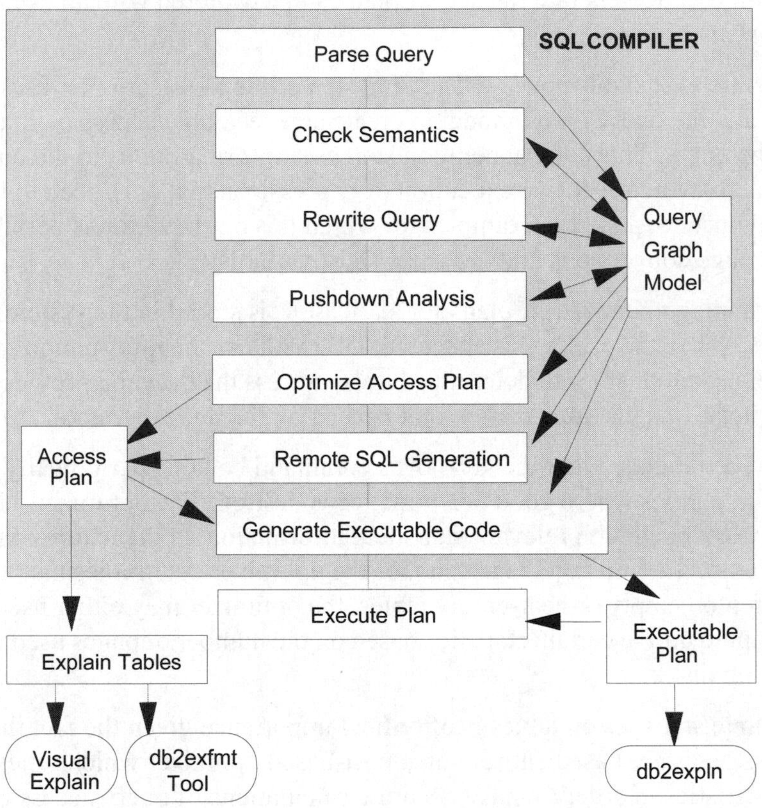

Figure 14–5 *Steps performed by SQL compiler*

Explain information must be captured before you can review it using one of DB2's explain tools. You can decide to capture detailed information regarding the access plan. While the query is being compiled, the information can be captured into a file of special tables known as explain tables.

DB2 Sorting Methods

When an SQL query requires the data to be returned in a defined sequence or order, the result may or may not require sorting. DB2 will attempt to perform the ordering through index usage. If an index cannot be used, the sort will occur. A sort involves two steps:

1. A sort phase
2. Return of the results of the sort phase

How the sort is handled within these two steps results in different categories or types by which the sort can be described. When considering the sort phase, the sort can be categorized as *overflowed* or *nonoverflowed.* When considering the return of the results of the sort phase, the sort can be categorized as *piped* or *non-piped.*

Overflowed and Nonoverflowed

If the information being sorted cannot fit entirely into the sort heap (a block of memory that is allocated each time a sort is performed), it overflows into temporary database tables. Sorts that do not overflow always perform better than those that do.

Piped and Non-Piped

If sorted information can return directly without requiring a temporary table to store a final, sorted list of data, it is referred to as a piped sort. If the sorted information requires a temporary table to be returned, it is referred to as a non-piped sort. A piped sort always performs better than a non-piped sort.

The DB2 optimizer will determine if a nonoverflowed sort can be performed and if a piped sort can be performed by comparing the expected result set with the value of the SORTHEAP database configuration parameter, and so forth.

DB2 *Note*

To obtain an ordered result set, a sort is not always required. If an index scan is the access method used, then the data is already in the order of the index, and sorting is not required.

Monitoring the DB2 System

The first step in the database monitoring process is defining your objectives. Defining the objectives is very important in selecting the best facility to meet your requirements.

An objective can be:

- Understanding how a given query will be optimized in a specific environment. For example, there is a query used in an application that does not perform well.
- Understanding how applications use database manager resources at a specific point of time. For example, database concurrency is reduced if a specific application is started.

Understanding which database manager events have occurred when running applications. For example, you notice a degradation in overall performance when certain applications are run.

Once your monitoring objectives have been determined, decide on the process and tools to implement and maintain the overall health of the DB2 system. This entire process is summarized in Figure 14–6.

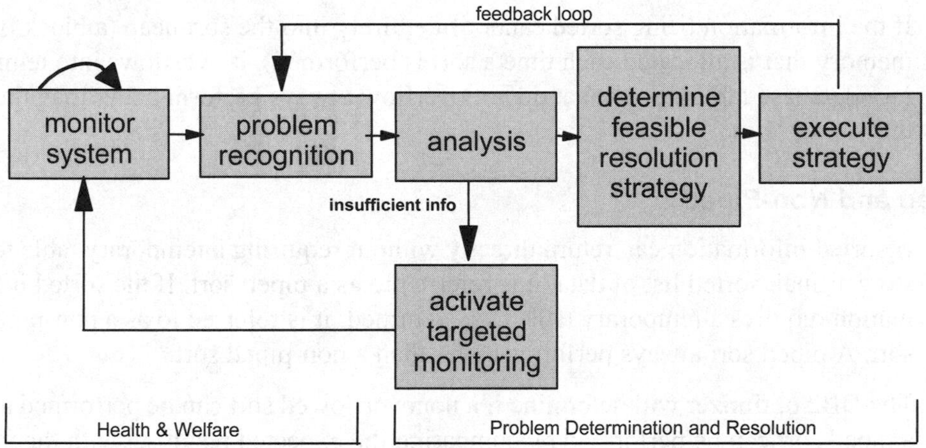

Figure 14–6 *DB2 monitoring process*

DB2 Health Monitor

The Health Monitor is a server-side tool that constantly monitors the health of the instance, even without user interaction. If the Health Monitor finds that a defined threshold has been exceeded (for example, the available log space is not sufficient), or if it detects an abnormal state for an object (for example, an instance is down), the Health Monitor will raise an alert. When an alert is raised two things can occur:

- Alert notifications can be sent by e-mail or to a pager address, allowing you to contact whoever is responsible for a system.

- Preconfigured actions can be taken. For example, a script or a task (implemented from the Task Center) can be run.

A health indicator is a system characteristic that the Health Monitor checks. The Health Monitor comes with a set of predefined thresholds for these health indicators (Figure 14–7). The Health Monitor checks the state of your system against these health-indicator thresholds when determining whether to issue an alert. Using the Health Center, commands, or APIs, you can customize the threshold settings of the health indicators, and define who should be notified and what script or task should be run if an alert is issued. The following are the categories of health indicators:

- Application concurrency
- Database management system
- Database
- Logging
- Memory
- Package and catalog caches
- Sorting
- Table space storage

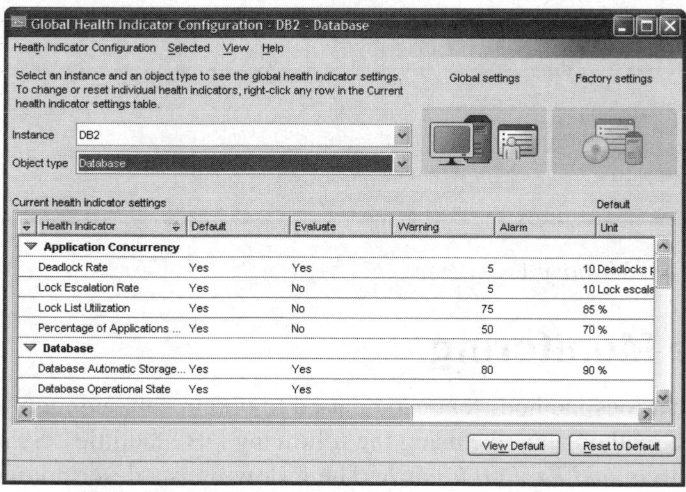

Figure 14–7 *Health Indicator settings*

The Health Center provides the graphical interface to the Health Monitor. You use it to configure the Health Monitor, and to see the rolled-up alert state of your instances and database objects. Using the Health Monitor's drill-down capability, you can access details about current alerts and obtain a list of recommended actions that describe how to resolve the alert. You can follow one of the recommended actions to address the alert. If the recommended action is to make a database or database manager configuration change, a new value will be recommended and you can implement the recommendation by clicking on a button. In other cases, the recommendation will be to investigate the problem further by launching a tool, such as the CLP or the Memory Visualizer (Figure 14–8).

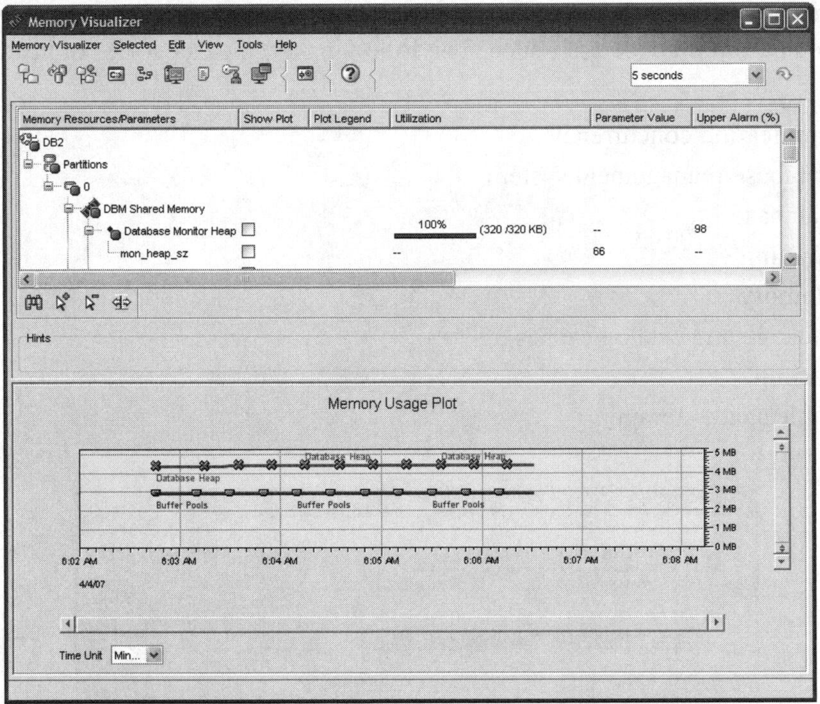

Figure 14–8 *Memory Visualizer*

Database Monitoring

There are various methods that can be used to obtain detailed monitoring information. These methods involve using the following DB2 facilities: *Snapshot Monitor, Event Monitor, and Explain Facility.* The following is a description of the information provided by the Explain Facility and the database monitors:

- Choose the Snapshot or Event Monitor if you want to gather data about DB2's operation, performance, and the applications using it. This data is maintained as DB2 runs and can provide important performance and trouble-shooting information.
- Choose the Explain Facility if you want to analyze the access plan for an SQL

statement or a group of SQL statements.

This section will give you information to decide which of the existing facilities is the best for your needs. It shows how to capture data using the Explain Facility, the Snapshot Monitor, the Event Monitor, and how to interpret the collected information.

This section also gives you information on how to diagnose problems in DB2 and CLI/ODBC/JDBC applications.

Database Monitors

Database monitors are used to collect detailed resource usage information. Monitoring activity may be performed from a DB2 client or a DB2 server. The monitor interface can be invoked using CLP commands, graphical monitors, or monitoring APIs. DB2 provides different kinds of monitoring, which differ in the way monitoring data is gathered. The two ways of monitoring are:

- *Snapshot Monitoring* — Provides information regarding database activity at a specific point in time. It is a picture of the current state of DB2 activity. The amount of data returned to the user when a snapshot is taken is determined using monitor switches. These switches can be set at the instance or application level.
- *Event Monitoring* — Records the occurrence of specific milestones of DB2 events. This can allow you to collect information about transient events, including deadlocks, connections, and SQL statements.

The system monitor provides multiple means of presenting monitor data to the administrator. For snapshot and event monitors, you have the option of storing monitor information in files, SQL tables, viewing it on the screen, or processing it with a client application.

The two monitoring options are discussed in the following pages.

DB2 Note

Snapshots can now be taken using SELECT statements against a set of new user-defined table functions. Event monitors can now write data to SQL tables, as well as to files or pipes.

Snapshot Monitoring

Snapshots are useful for determining the status of a database system. Taken at regular intervals, they can be useful for observing trends and anticipating potential performance bottlenecks. The Snapshot Monitor provides cumulative information in the form of counters. These counters can be reset. The snapshot information is provided in special data structures that can be examined by the application issuing the snapshot.

The amount of data returned by the Snapshot Monitor is set according to switches. The monitor switches, along with the information they provide, are displayed in Table 14–1.

Table 14–1 *Data Returned by the Snapshot Monitor*

Group	Information Provided	Monitor Switch	DBM Parameter
Sorts	Number of heaps used, overflows, sort performance	SORT	DFT_MON_SORT
Locks	Number of locks held, number of deadlocks	LOCK	DFT_MON_LOCK
Tables	Measure activity (rows read, rows written)	TABLE	DFT_MON_TABLE
Bufferpools	Number of reads and writes, time taken	BUFFERPOOL	DFT_MON_BUFPOOL
Unit of work	Start times, end times, completion status	UOW	DFT_MON_UOW
SQL	Start time, stop time, statement identification	STATEMENT	DFT_MON_STMT
Timestamps	Monitors timestamp	TIMESTAMP	DFT_MON_TIMESTAMP

The monitor switches can be turned on and off at the instance (DBM configuration) level or at the application level (using the `UPDATE MONITOR SWITCHES` command). There is also base information provided by the Snapshot Monitor that is gathered regardless of the monitor switches settings.

Setting the instance configuration parameters for monitor switches will affect all databases within the instance. Every application connecting to a database will inherit the default switches set within the DBM configuration.

DB2 Note

DB2 Snapshot Monitors can only be used by users having SYSADM, SYSCTRL, or SYSMAINT authority. Event Monitors require SYSADM or DBADM authority.

For example, to capture detailed information about SQL statements executing in DB2, the appropriate monitor switches must be turned on. The commands are:

```
UPDATE DBM CONFIGURATION USING DFT_MON_STMT ON
```

You can alternatively use this command:

```
UPDATE MONITOR SWITCHES USING STATEMENT ON
```

The UPDATE DBM CONFIGURATION command will modify the database manager configuration. Therefore, SQL statement information will be captured for applications accessing all databases within the instance.

DB2 Note

When you change the value of the database manager configuration parameters, you usually need to stop and start the instance to make those changes effective; however, the changes of the default monitor switches will be effective immediately. Therefore, you don't need to stop and start the instance.

On the other hand, the UPDATE MONITOR SWITCHES command will only capture SQL statements for the application that activated the switch. (In this example, the application is the command line processor.)

DB2 Note

Even if none of the switches are turned on, there will be some basic information captured by the Snapshot Monitor.

Viewing Snapshot Monitor Data

When a monitor switch is turned on, the monitor data starts being collected. To view the monitor data, a *snapshot* must be taken.

DB2 Note

There is a minor performance effect when the data is recorded. Issuing the snapshot incurs additional performance overhead.

A snapshot is requested using the DB2 command `GET SNAPSHOT`. This command can be executed in different ways. It can be executed within the Command Center GUI tool, embedded in an application using the appropriate API, or executed from the Command Center or CLP.

Before the output of the Snapshot Monitor is examined, how the snapshot information is captured will be discussed. Use the Command Center interface to capture database monitor snapshots. While taking a snapshot, it is possible to define a particular area of interest.

There are different levels of monitoring used with the Snapshot Monitor. These levels allow you to focus your analysis in a particular area of interest.

The following Snapshot Monitor levels are available:

- *Database manager* — Captures information for an active instance
- *Database* — Captures database(s) information
- *Application* — Captures application(s) information
- *Bufferpools* — Captures buffer pool activity information
- *Table space* — Captures information for table spaces within a database
- *Table* — Captures information for tables within a database
- *Lock* — Captures information for locks held by applications against a database
- *Dynamic SQL cache* — Captures point-in-time statement information from the SQL statement cache for the database

Snapshot Monitor switches and levels are combined to provide different monitoring information when taking a snapshot. The two are very closely related. If the proper monitor switch is not turned on, the snapshot level used may not return any data.

As said before, the `GET SNAPSHOT` command is used to review the Snapshot Monitor data.

To gather lock information for the Certification database, execute the following DB2 command from the Command Center:

```
GET SNAPSHOT FOR LOCKS ON SAMPLE
```

The output of the snapshot is displayed in the Command Center Results window. It is a good idea to save the output to a file for analysis purposes.

The output of the SNAPSHOT FOR LOCKS command is shown in Figure 14–9. If you want detailed information about locks, as shown in Figure 14–9, you must turn on the Lock Monitor Switch.

Analyzing the snapshot, you can see that the first application (application ID *LOCAL.DB2.070404102103) is in Lock-Wait status. It is attempting to acquire a select lock on a row having an X lock held by the second application (application ID *LOCAL.DB2.070404102055). To release the lock, the application holding it must complete its transaction using a COMMIT or ROLLBACK statement.

DB2 Note

The LOCKTIMEOUT database configuration parameter controls the maximum time that an application should wait in Lock-Wait status. Its default value is to wait until the locked resource is available.

```
                Database Lock Snapshot

Database name                              = SAMPLE
Database path                              = C:\DB2\NODE0000\SQL00002\
Input database alias                       = SAMPLE
Locks held                                 = 6
Applications currently connected           = 2
Agents currently waiting on locks          = 1
Snapshot timestamp                         = 04/04/2007 06:25:36.077524

Application handle                         = 11
Application ID                             = *LOCAL.DB2.070404102103
Sequence number                            = 00002
Application name                           = db2bp.exe
CONNECT Authorization ID                   = BAKLARZ
Application status                         = Lock-wait
Status change time                         = Not Collected
Application code page                      = 1252
Locks held                                 = 3
Total wait time (ms)                       = Not Collected

List Of Locks
 Lock Name                   = 0x01000000010000000100 7B0056
 Lock Attributes             = 0x00000000
 Release Flags               = 0x40000000
 Lock Count                  = 1
 Hold Count                  = 0
 Lock Object Name            = 0
 Object Type                 = Internal Variation Lock
 Mode                        = S

 Lock Name                   = 0x53514C4332463041F12CF8E241
 Lock Attributes             = 0x00000000
 Release Flags               = 0x40000000
 Lock Count                  = 1
 Hold Count                  = 0
 Lock Object Name            = 0
 Object Type                 = Internal Plan Lock
 Mode                        = S

 Lock Name                   = 0x03000701000000000000000054
 Lock Attributes             = 0x00000000
 Release Flags               = 0x00000001
```

Monitoring and Tuning

```
 Lock Count                        = 1
 Hold Count                        = 0
 Lock Object Name                  = 263
 Object Type                       = Table
 Tablespace Name                   = IBMDB2SAMPLEREL
 Table Schema                      = BAKLARZ
 Table Name                        = ONEROW
 Mode                              = IS

Application handle                                 = 7
Application ID                                     = *LOCAL.DB2.070404102055
Sequence number                                    = 00002
Application name                                   = db2bp.exe
CONNECT Authorization ID                           = BAKLARZ
Application status                                 = UOW Waiting
Status change time                                 = Not Collected
Application code page                              = 1252
Locks held                                         = 3
Total wait time (ms)                               = Not Collected

List Of Locks
 Lock Name                         = 0x030007010800600F0000000052
 Lock Attributes                   = 0x00000008
 Release Flags                     = 0x40000000
 Lock Count                        = 1
 Hold Count                        = 0
 Lock Object Name                  = 257949704
 Object Type                       = Row
 Tablespace Name                   = IBMDB2SAMPLEREL
 Table Schema                      = BAKLARZ
 Table Name                        = ONEROW
 Mode                              = X

 Lock Name                         = 0x53514C4332463041F12CF8E241
 Lock Attributes                   = 0x00000000
 Release Flags                     = 0x40000000
 Lock Count                        = 1
 Hold Count                        = 0
 Lock Object Name                  = 0
 Object Type                       = Internal Plan Lock
 Mode                              = S

 Lock Name                         = 0x03000701000000000000000054
 Lock Attributes                   = 0x00000000
 Release Flags                     = 0x40000000
 Lock Count                        = 1
 Hold Count                        = 0
 Lock Object Name                  = 263
 Object Type                       = Table
 Tablespace Name                   = IBMDB2SAMPLEREL
 Table Schema                      = BAKLARZ
 Table Name                        = ONEROW
 Mode                              = IX
```

Figure 14–9 *Output of GET SNAPSHOT for locks on SAMPLE*

The information provided by the Snapshot Monitor is a valuable resource to solve many problems. At the time of the snapshot shown in Figure 14–9, there was a concurrency problem in the database. Therefore, the LOCKS monitoring level was used to analyze the database activity.

The information from APPLICATIONS Snapshot Monitor level as shown in Figure 14–10 was taken using the following command:

```
GET SNAPSHOT FOR APPLICATIONS ON SAMPLE
```

This command can produce large volumes of output depending what is currently running on the system. The report in Figure 14–10 contains only a small portion of the total output produced by this command.

```
                Application Snapshot

Application handle                          = 11
Application status                          = Lock-wait
Status change time                          = Not Collected
Application code page                       = 1252
Application country/region code             = 1
DUOW correlation token                      = *LOCAL.DB2.070404102103
Application name                            = db2bp.exe
Application ID                              = *LOCAL.DB2.070404102103
Sequence number                             = 00002
TP Monitor client user ID                   =
TP Monitor client workstation name          =
TP Monitor client application name          =
TP Monitor client accounting string         =

Connection request start timestamp          = 04/04/2007 06:21:02.994726
Connect request completion timestamp        = 04/04/2007 06:21:02.995921
Application idle time                       = Not Collected
CONNECT Authorization ID                    = BAKLARZ
Client login ID                             = BAKLARZ
Configuration NNAME of client               = BAKLARZ
Client database manager product ID          = SQL09010
Process ID of client application            = 3740
Platform of client application              = NT
Communication protocol of client            = Local Client

Inbound communication address               = *LOCAL.DB2

Database name                               = SAMPLE
Database path                               = C:\DB2\NODE0000\SQL00002\
Client database alias                       = SAMPLE
Input database alias                        = SAMPLE
Last reset timestamp                        =
Snapshot timestamp                          = 04/04/2007 06:34:16.182354
...
```

Figure 14–10 *Partial output of Get Snapshot for applications command*

The snapshot provides detailed data about the activity of applications. Using this snapshot, you can see application activity, such as how may rows have been read, updated, or deleted by an application. To obtain more information regarding database objects shown in an application snapshot, such as tables or locks, the appropriate monitor switches and monitoring levels should be used.

To review a table level snapshot, issue the following command:

```
GET SNAPSHOT FOR TABLES ON SAMPLE
```

The output from the table level snapshot is shown in Figure 14–11. By using a table snapshot, further information can be obtained, such as which table has the most activity in the database.

```
            Table Snapshot

First database connect timestamp       = 04/04/2007 06:20:55.046159
Last reset timestamp                   =
Snapshot timestamp                     = 04/04/2007 06:47:52.738505
Database name                          = SAMPLE
Database path                          = C:\DB2\NODE0000\SQL00002\
Input database alias                   = SAMPLE
Number of accessed tables              = 1

Table List
 Table Schema          = BAKLARZ
 Table Name            = ONEROW
 Table Type            = User
 Data Object Pages     = 1
 Rows Read             = 5
 Rows Written          = 1
 Overflows             = 0
 Page Reorgs           = 0
```

Figure 14–11 *GET SNAPSHOT for tables on the SAMPLE database*

DB2 *Note*

To collect the snapshot information shown in Figure 14–11, the `TABLE` monitor switch (`DFT_MON_TABLE`) must be set to `ON`.

The table snapshot output shows different tables being accessed. In our example, user and catalog tables were accessed. Catalog tables are used by DB2 for different activities, such as checking the authorizations granted to the user requesting an SQL statement, reviewing distinct types used, and so on.

The snapshots that have been presented show data related to DB2 logical objects, such as tables, locks, and applications. Snapshots can be used to provide information related to the physical database environment, such as disk activity and memory usage. This kind of information is gathered using a table space level snapshot using the command below. Partial output follows in Figure 14–12.

```
GET SNAPSHOT FOR TABLESPACES ON SAMPLE
```

```
                 Tablespace Snapshot

First database connect timestamp         = 04/04/2007 06:20:55.046159
Last reset timestamp                     =
Snapshot timestamp                       = 04/04/2007 06:52:53.450568
Database name                            = SAMPLE
Database path                            = C:\DB2\NODE0000\SQL00002\
Input database alias                     = SAMPLE
Number of accessed tablespaces           = 15

Tablespace name                          = SYSCATSPACE
  Tablespace ID                          = 0
  Tablespace Type                        = Database managed space
  Tablespace Content Type                = All permanent data. Regular table space.
  Tablespace Page size (bytes)           = 4096
  Tablespace Extent size (pages)         = 4
  Automatic Prefetch size enabled        = Yes
  Buffer pool ID currently in use        = 1
  Buffer pool ID next startup            = 1
```

```
Using automatic storage                       = Yes
Auto-resize enabled                           = Yes
File system caching                           = Yes
Tablespace State                              = 0x'00000000'
 Detailed explanation:
   Normal
Tablespace Prefetch size (pages)              = 4
Total number of pages                         = 16384
Number of usable pages                        = 16380
Number of used pages                          = 9804
Number of pending free pages                  = 0
Number of free pages                          = 6576
High water mark (pages)                       = 9804
Initial tablespace size (bytes)               = 33554432
Current tablespace size (bytes)               = 67108864
Maximum tablespace size (bytes)               = NONE
Increase size (bytes)                         = AUTOMATIC
Time of last successful resize                =
Last resize attempt failed                    = No
Rebalancer Mode                               = No Rebalancing
Minimum Recovery Time                         =
Number of quiescers                           = 0
Number of containers                          = 1

Container Name                              = C:\DB2\NODE0000\SAMPLE\T0000000\C0000000.CAT
    Container ID                              = 0
    Container Type                            = File (extent sized tag)
    Total Pages in Container                  = 16384
    Usable Pages in Container                 = 16380
    Stripe Set                                = 0
    Container is accessible                   = Yes

Table space map:

 Range  Stripe Stripe  Max          Max  Start  End     Adj.    Containers
 Number Set    Offset  Extent       Page Stripe Stripe
 [   0] [   0]      0    4094     16379      0   4094    0      1 (0)

Buffer pool data logical reads                = Not Collected
Buffer pool data physical reads               = Not Collected
Buffer pool temporary data logical reads = Not Collected
Buffer pool temporary data physical reads= Not Collected
Asynchronous pool data page reads             = Not Collected
Buffer pool data writes                       = Not Collected
Asynchronous pool data page writes            = Not Collected
Buffer pool index logical reads               = Not Collected
Buffer pool index physical reads              = Not Collected
Buffer pool temporary index logical reads= Not Collected
Buffer pool temporary index physical reads = Not Collected
Asynchronous pool index page reads            = Not Collected
Buffer pool index writes                      = Not Collected
Asynchronous pool index page writes           = Not Collected
Total buffer pool read time (millisec)        = Not Collected
Total buffer pool write time (millisec)       = Not Collected
Total elapsed asynchronous read time          = Not Collected
Total elapsed asynchronous write time         = Not Collected
Asynchronous data read requests               = Not Collected
Asynchronous index read requests              = Not Collected
No victim buffers available                   = Not Collected
Direct reads                                  = Not Collected
Direct writes                                 = Not Collected
Direct read requests                          = Not Collected
Direct write requests                         = Not Collected
Direct reads elapsed time (ms)                = Not Collected
Direct write elapsed time (ms)                = Not Collected
Number of files closed                        = Not Collected
```

Figure 14–12 *Partial output of GET SNAPSHOT for table spaces on SAMPLE*

The snapshot in Figure 14–12 is organized according to the I/O and buffer pool activity for each table space. The data captured shows different counters representing time (expressed in milliseconds) or times that a different activity has occurred.

Along with the table space information, this monitor level shows information about the buffer pool usage. Buffer pool information is only gathered if the BUFFERPOOL monitor switch is turned on.

Any I/O prefetching activity is shown as asynchronous reads, and any buffer pool asynchronous page cleaning is shown as asynchronous writes. The term direct read/write corresponds to the number of read operations that do not use the buffer pool.

Reviewing the Snapshot Monitor Switch Status

At any time, you can determine the current settings of database monitor switches by issuing the following command:

```
GET MONITOR SWITCHES
```

The switch states are shown in Figure 14–13. The timestamps correspond to the last time the switches were reset or turned on.

```
            Monitor Recording Switches

Switch list for db partition number 0
Buffer Pool Activity Information  (BUFFERPOOL) = OFF
Lock Information                        (LOCK) = OFF
Sorting Information                     (SORT) = OFF
SQL Statement Information          (STATEMENT) = OFF
Table Activity Information             (TABLE) = ON  04/04/2007 06:46:02.581767
Take Timestamp Information         (TIMESTAMP) = ON  04/04/2007 06:20:30.546036
Unit of Work Information                 (UOW) = OFF
```

Figure 14–13 *Monitor switch settings*

The monitor switch settings for an application are shown in Figure 14–13. If you want to know the instance settings for the monitor switches, use the following command:

```
GET DBM MONITOR SWITCHES
```

Resetting the Snapshot Monitor Switches

As demonstrated, the data returned by a Snapshot Monitor is based primarily on counters. These counters are associated with a monitor switch.

Monitor switches are initialized or reset when one of the following occurs:

- Application-level monitoring is used, and the application connects to the database.

- Database-level monitoring is used, and the first application connects.
- Table-level monitoring is used, and the table is first accessed.
- Table-space level monitoring is used, and the table space is first accessed.
- Issuing the `RESET MONITOR` command.
- Turning on a particular monitor switch.

Monitor switches can be reset at any time by issuing the command:

```
RESET MONITOR FOR DATABASE SAMPLE
```

Resetting the monitor switches effectively starts all of the counters at zero, and further snapshots are based on the new counter values.

To reset the monitor switches for all databases within an instance, the `RESET MONITOR ALL` command should be used.

DB2 Note

Every application has its own copy of the snapshot monitor values. Resetting the monitor switches only affects the counters of the application that issues the reset.

Event Monitoring

While Snapshot Monitoring records the state of database activity when the snapshot is taken, an Event Monitor records the database activity when an *event* or *transition* occurs. Some database activities that need to be monitored cannot be easily captured using the Snapshot Monitor. These activities include deadlock scenarios. When a deadlock occurs, DB2 will resolve the deadlock by issuing a `ROLLBACK` for one of the transactions. Information regarding the deadlock event cannot be easily captured using the Snapshot Monitor because the deadlock was probably resolved before a snapshot could be taken.

Event Monitors are created using SQL Data Definition Language (DDL) like other database objects. Event Monitors can be turned on or off much like the Snapshot Monitor switches.

DB2 Note

`SYSADM` or `DBADM` authority is required to create an Event Monitor.

When an Event Monitor is created, the type of event to be monitored must be stated. The Event Monitor can monitor the following events:

- *Database* — Records an event record when the last application disconnects from the database.
- *Tables* — Records an event record for each active table when the last application disconnects from the database. An active table is a table that has changed since the first connection to the database.
- *Deadlocks* — Records an event record for each deadlock event.
- *Tablespaces* — Records an event record for each active table space when the last application disconnects from the database.
- *Bufferpools* — Records an event record for buffer pools when the last application disconnects from the database.
- *Connections* — Records an event record for each database connection event when an application disconnects from a database.
- *Statements* — Records an event record for every SQL statement issued by an application (dynamic and static).
- *Transactions* — Records an event record for every transaction when it completes (`COMMIT` or `ROLLBACK` statement).

The output of an Event Monitor is stored in an SQL table, directory, or in a named pipe. The existence of the pipe or the file will be verified when the Event Monitor is activated. If the target location for an Event Monitor is a named pipe, then it is the responsibility of the application to promptly read the data from the pipe. If the target for an Event Monitor is a directory, then the stream of data will be written to a series of files.

The following system catalog tables are used to store Event Monitor definitions:

- `SYSCAT.EVENTMONITORS` — Contains a record for each Event Monitor, including the current state of the Event Monitor, and identifies the target output as an SQL table, file, or pipe.
- `SYSCAT.EVENTS` — Contains a record for each event being monitored. A single Event Monitor can be defined to monitor multiple events (e.g., `DEADLOCKS` and `STATEMENTS`).
- `SYSIBM.EVENTTABLES` — Contains a row for every target table of an Event Monitor that writes to an SQL table.

Analyzing Event Monitor Output

These utilities are available to analyze Event Monitor data:

- *db2eva* — A GUI tool that can be invoked from a command line (used to read data written to SQL tables).

- *db2evmon* — A text-based tool that will read the event records and generate a report (used to read files).

A deadlock situation will now be created to demonstrate the Event Monitor. To do this, you need two DB2 Command Center windows with the AUTOCOMMIT feature turned off (db2 -c-). Don't forget to make sure you have created an event monitor for DEADLOCKS and activate it. Here are the steps to create a deadlock situation:

- In the first window, issue: LOCK TABLE TEST_TAKEN IN SHARE MODE
- In the second window, issue: LOCK TABLE TEST IN SHARE MODE
- Back in the first window, issue: LOCK TABLE TEST IN EXCLUSIVE MODE
- Back in the second window, issue: LOCK TABLE TEST_TAKEN IN EXCLUSIVE MODE

These steps will generate a deadlock situation that will be resolved by DB2. The data captured by the Event Monitor will now be analyzed.

Event Analyzer/Monitor

The Event Analyzer displays the Event Monitor records that have been previously collected. To invoke the Event Analyzer, execute the DB2EVA command. If you are working on a Windows machine, you can select the **Event Analyzer** icon in the DB2 folder.

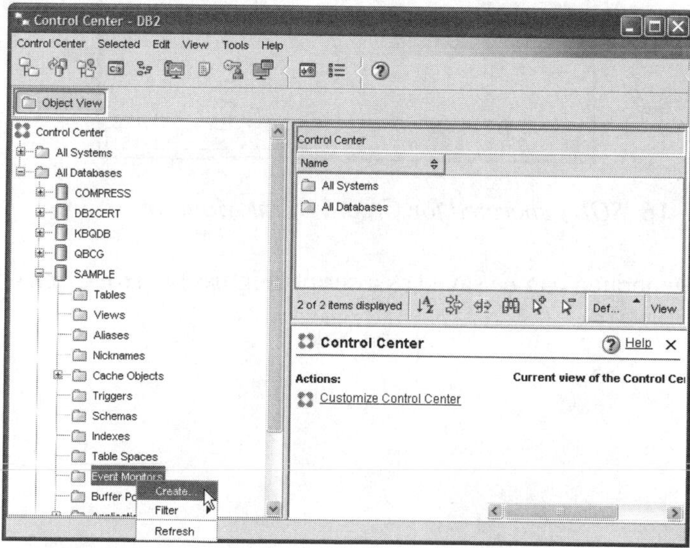

Figure 14–14 *Invoking the Event Monitor from the Control Center*

An alternative to selecting the **Event Analyzer** icon is to right-click on the Event Monitor object in the Control Center as shown in Figure 14–14.

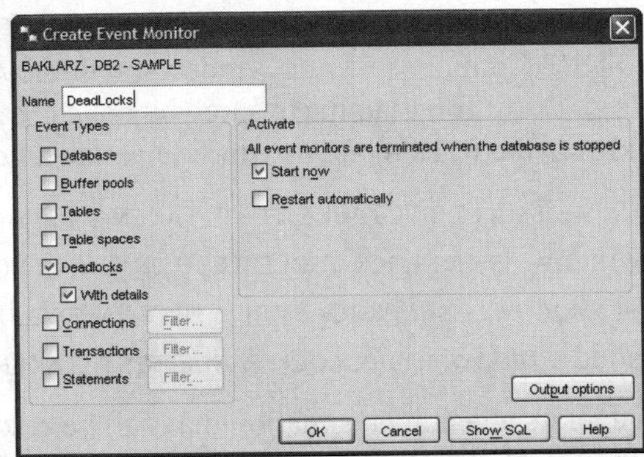

Figure 14–15 *Create Event Monitor*

In this example, the event monitor named **Deadlocks** will be created to monitor deadlocks (Figure 14–15). Note that this monitor could also be used to monitor additional events as besides deadlock events.

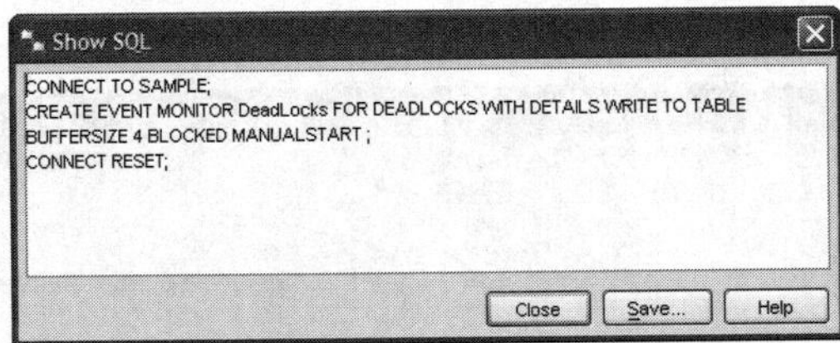

Figure 14–16 *SQL generated for Create Event Monitor*

The SQL generated can be saved as a script (Figure 14–16). Click Close and OK.

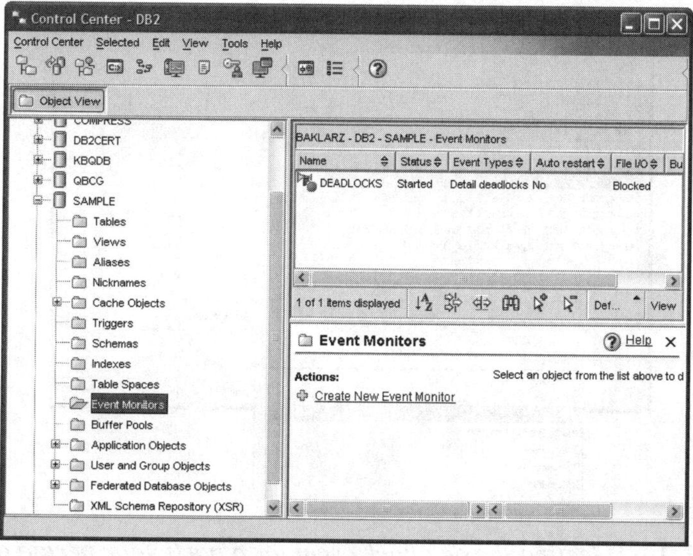

Figure 14–17 *Deadlock Monitor activated*

After creating the monitor, it can be displayed from the Control Center (Figure 14–17).

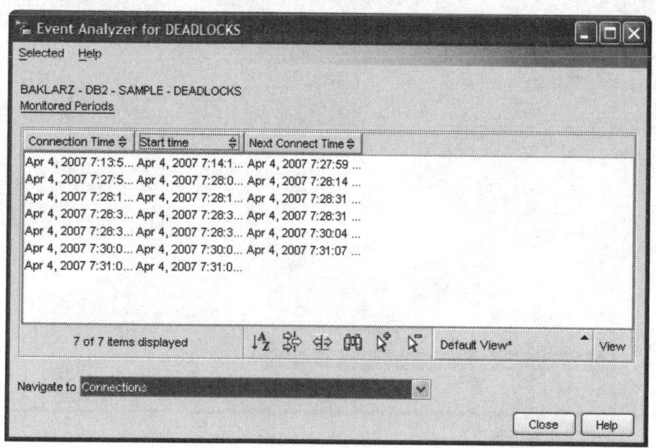

Figure 14–18 *Monitored Periods View of an Event Monitor*

From the Monitored Periods View window, as shown in Figure 14–18, you can analyze the event records for a specific time frame when the Event Monitor was active. Select the time interval you want to analyze, and then select the **DEADLOCKS** event from the pulldown menu. This is shown in Figure 14–19.

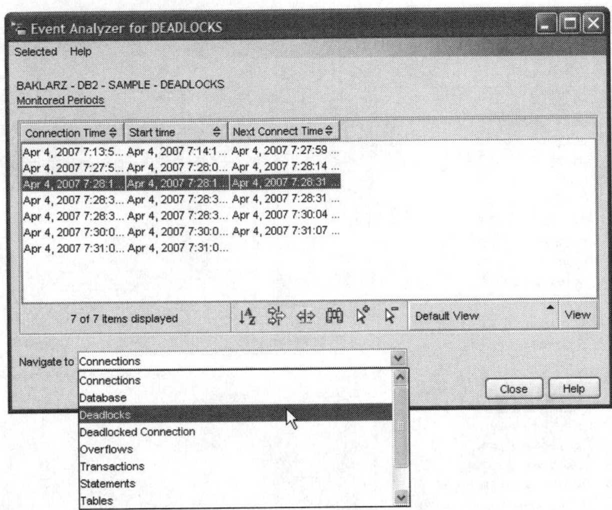

Figure 14–19 *Selecting the deadlock event for a particular period of time*

After selecting the deadlock Event Monitor, notice the information in the Deadlocks View window as shown in Figure 14–20.

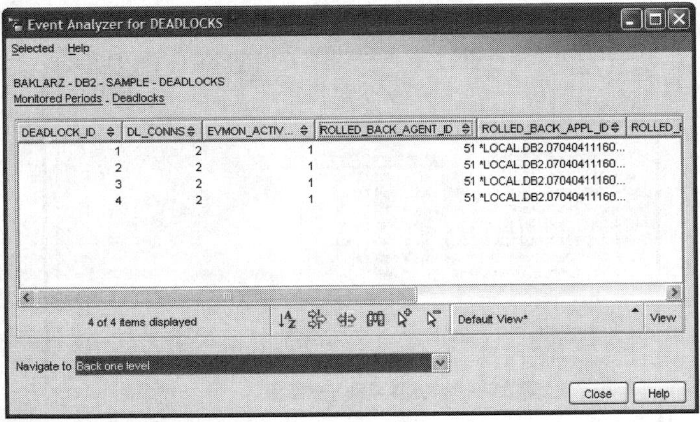

Figure 14–20 *Deadlock event view*

The Deadlocks View window indicates that a number deadlocks were detected.

Figure 14–20 displays a number of connections that caused deadlocks. Drill down to **Deadlocked Connections**, and then Deadlocked Connections window is shown in Figure 14–21.

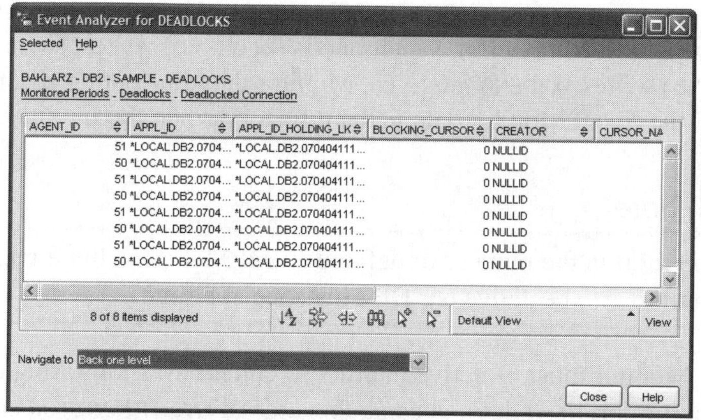

Figure 14–21 *Deadlocked Connections view*

The Event Analyzer will only display previously captured data. Therefore, there is no overhead in using the Event Analyzer as there is with the Snapshot Monitor. The Event Analyzer may not contain the desired information as it can only display the event records that have been previously captured. For example, if you select **Open as Statements** and no statement information was defined for the Event Monitor, the display will not contain SQL statement information.

Event Monitoring Using File Output

As mentioned, Event Monitors are database objects created using SQL DDL statements. In this example, a deadlock Event Monitor will be created to store its event records in the "\EVENTMONITORS\DEADLOCK\EVMON1" directory.

DB2 Note

When using file output, the Event Monitor output directory will not be created by DB2. It must be created by the database administrator, and the instance owner must be able to write to the specified directory.

The following SQL statement creates an Event Monitor using file output. In our example, the Event Monitor is called EVMON1.

```
CREATE EVENT MONITOR evmon1 FOR DEADLOCKS
  WRITE TO FILE 'C:\eventmonitors\deadlock\evmon1'
  MAXFILES 3 MAXFILESIZE 1000;
```

This Event Monitor is defined to allocate up to three files, each 4 MB in size, for a total monitor storage area of 12 MB. Other Event Monitor options include specifying the size of the write buffer, synchronous (BLOCKED) writes, asynchronous (UNBLOCKED) writes, APPEND the Event Monitor data to existing records, or REPLACE the Event Monitor data in the directory when the monitor is activated.

DB2 Note

There is no limit in the number of defined Event Monitors, but a maximum of 32 Event Monitors can be active per DB2 instance at a time.

An Event Monitor must be active in order to collect the monitoring data. Once the Event Monitor has been defined using the CREATE EVENT MONITOR statement, it must be activated. The following statement is used to activate an Event Monitor.

```
SET EVENT MONITOR evmon1 STATE = 1
```

DB2 Note

The directory must exist when the monitor is activated, or else the statement will fail with an SQL1614N error: An I/O error occurred when activating an event monitor. Reason code = "2". SQLSTATE=58030.

When the Event Monitor has been activated, Event Monitor records are written to the files contained in the defined directory or pipe (such as /EVENTMONITORS/DEADLOCKS/EVMON1 in our example).

An Event Monitor can be started automatically each time the database is started using the AUTOSTART option. This option is specified at creation time.To turn off an Event Monitor, the SET EVENT MONITOR STATE statement is once again used:

```
SET EVENT MONITOR evmon1 STATE = 0
```

Turning off an Event Monitor will also flush all of its contents.

Even when an Event Monitor has been turned off, it is still defined in the system catalog tables. However, it is not recording monitor information.

To determine if an Event Monitor is active or inactive, use the SQL function EVENT_MON_STATE or view the status in the Control Center. The EVENT_MON_STATE function returns a value of "1" if the Event Monitor is active and "0" if the monitor is not active.

A sample SQL statement using the `EVENT_MON_STATE` function to query the state of the `EVMON1` Event Monitor is as follows:

```
SELECT EVMONNAME, EVENT_MON_STATE(EVMONNAME)
FROM SYSCAT.EVENTMONITORS WHERE EVMONNAME = 'EVMON1';

EVMONNAME                          2
---------------------------------- -----------
EVMON1                                       1

  1 record(s) selected.
```

Just like other database objects, Event Monitors can be dropped from the database. An example of removing the `EVMON1` Event Monitor is as follows:

```
DROP EVENT MONITOR evmon1
```

Event Monitor files cannot be analyzed directly. An application must be used. There are a few alternatives provided by DB2 for analyzing Event Monitor data that will be discussed. First some of the Event Monitor records will be examined.

To ensure that all of the event records have been written to disk (some may be buffered), simply turn the Event Monitor off. You can also use the `BUFFER` option of `FLUSH EVENT MONITOR` command as follows:

```
FLUSH EVENT MONITOR evmon1 BUFFER
```

It forces the Event Monitor buffers to be written out. The `FLUSH EVENT MONITOR` command with the `BUFFER` option does not generate a partial record. Only the data already present in the Event Monitor buffers are written out.

If an Event Monitor is monitoring database, table space, or table events, it will write complete event records when the last application using the database disconnects. As already explained, you can use the `FLUSH EVENT MONITOR` command to record the partial event records.

To generate the Event Monitor report for the evmon1 monitor, issue the following command indicating where the event monitor files are located:

```
db2evmon -path /eventmonitors/deadlock/evmon1
```

or

```
db2evmon -db sample -evm evmon1
```

The -PATH option of the DB2EVMON command is used to indicate the path where the Event Monitor files reside.

DB2 Note

It is a good idea to name the directories used for Event Monitor files using the type of Event Monitor (deadlock) and its name (evmon1).

The output of the DB2EVMON utility will be displayed on the screen by default. It is best to redirect the output to a file for analysis. A portion of the Event Monitor output for the evmon1 Event Monitor as shown in Figure 14–22 will now be examined.

The files are sequentially numbered and have a file extension of "evt" (e.g., 00000000.EVT and 00000001.EVT). The maximum size and number of Event Monitor files is specified when the monitor is defined.

DB2 Note

An Event Monitor will turn itself off if the defined file space has been exceeded.

```
------------------------------------------------------------------------
                          EVENT LOG HEADER
  Event Monitor name: EVMON1
  Server Product ID: SQL09010
  Version of event monitor data: 8
  Byte order: LITTLE ENDIAN
  Number of nodes in db2 instance: 1
  Codepage of database: 1208
  Territory code of database: 1
  Server instance name: DB2
------------------------------------------------------------------------

------------------------------------------------------------------------
  Database Name: SAMPLE
  Database Path: C:\DB2\NODE0000\SQL00002\
  First connection timestamp: 04/04/2007 07:54:11.647498
  Event Monitor Start time:   04/04/2007 07:58:34.645670
------------------------------------------------------------------------

------------------------------------------------------------------------
  Database Name: SAMPLE
  Database Path: C:\DB2\NODE0000\SQL00002\
  First connection timestamp: 04/04/2007 08:04:46.267796
  Event Monitor Start time:   04/04/2007 08:04:46.495034
------------------------------------------------------------------------

5) Deadlock Event ...
  Deadlock ID:   1
  Number of applications deadlocked: 2
  Deadlock detection time: 04/04/2007 08:06:46.288693
  Rolled back Appl participant no: 2
  Rolled back Appl Id: *LOCAL.DB2.070404120455
  Rolled back Appl seq number: : 0002

6) Connection Header Event ...
  Appl Handle: 186
  Appl Id: *LOCAL.DB2.070404120455
  Appl Seq number: 00002
  DRDA AS Correlation Token: *LOCAL.DB2.070404120455
```

```
   Program Name     : db2bp.exe
   Authorization Id: BAKLARZ
   Execution Id     : BAKLARZ
   Codepage Id: 1252
   Territory code: 1
   Client Process Id: 1476
   Client Database Alias: SAMPLE
   Client Product Id: SQL09010
   Client Platform: Unknown
   Client Communication Protocol: Local
   Client Network Name: BAKLARZ
   Connect timestamp: 04/04/2007 08:04:49.828772
7) Deadlocked Connection ...
```

Figure 14–22 *Deadlock event monitor records*

In Figure 14–22, a deadlock event record and two deadlock connection event records are shown. The information identifies the two applications involved in the deadlock and the reason for the deadlock.

In this example, the deadlock involves two shared locks: one on the BAKLARZ.TEST_TAKEN table and the other on the BAKLARZ.TEST table. The Event Monitor shows the ID of the application that was rolled back and the time when the deadlock occurred.

Additional Utilities

DB2 provides several additional tools that can be used to monitor and manage specific events. The following will be reviewed:

- DB2 Governor
- Inspect Command
- Audit Facility Administrator Tool
- Storage Management Tool
- Indoubt Transaction Manager
- Database Benchmarking Tool
- DB2PD

DB2 Governor

When monitoring DB2, you can detect where bottlenecks are occurring in the system, where certain types of database activity are occurring, and if DB2 is using all the server's resources to their full extent. You can also analyze the behavior of database applications to see if certain applications are more resource intensive than others. However, if an application is resource intensive or is stopping other applications from obtaining resources, the DBA must first detect the application using monitoring techniques and then change the behavior of the application or explicitly force the application off the system.

The *DB2 Governor* is a server application that performs such checking automatically. The governor can also force an application that is deemed to be using too many resources on the server. (Please note that you can also use the `FORCE APPLICATIONS` command of DB2 to force an application or all applications off of the instance. Please refer to the *DB2 Command Reference* for further details on this command.)

The governor collects statistics about applications running against a database. It then checks these statistics against rules that have been specified for that database. Such rules might include:

- Increase the priority of application *X* so that it always completes quickly.
- Slow down a subset of applications, namely *A*, *B*, and *C*.
- Don't let any unit of work run for more than 15 minutes.

The governor then enforces these rules by changing the parameters for the specified applications or by forcing the application off the system. You start and stop the DB2 Governor the same way you might start and stop monitoring DB2. For example, using a governor configuration file (which contains the governor rules) called `MYGOV.CFG`, you can start the governor monitoring the `SAMPLE` database using the `DB2GOV` utility at the operating system command prompt.

```
db2gov START SAMPLE mygov.cfg gov.log
```

The file that was specified, `GOV.LOG`, is where the DB2 Governor will log any actions it takes. You can then stop the governor running against the `SAMPLE` database.

```
db2gov STOP SAMPLE
```

You can have multiple instances of the DB2 Governor running against multiple databases. The DB2 Governor does incur a performance impact when running against a DB2 database because it collects statistics and monitors the activity of database applications at regular intervals. You can examine the logs generated by the DB2 Governor using the `DB2GOVLG` tool.

Inspect Command

This command provides the ability to check the pages of the database for their architectural integrity. The command can select to check the structures of table objects and of table spaces.

Here are some of the key options of the INSPECT command (Figure 14–23):

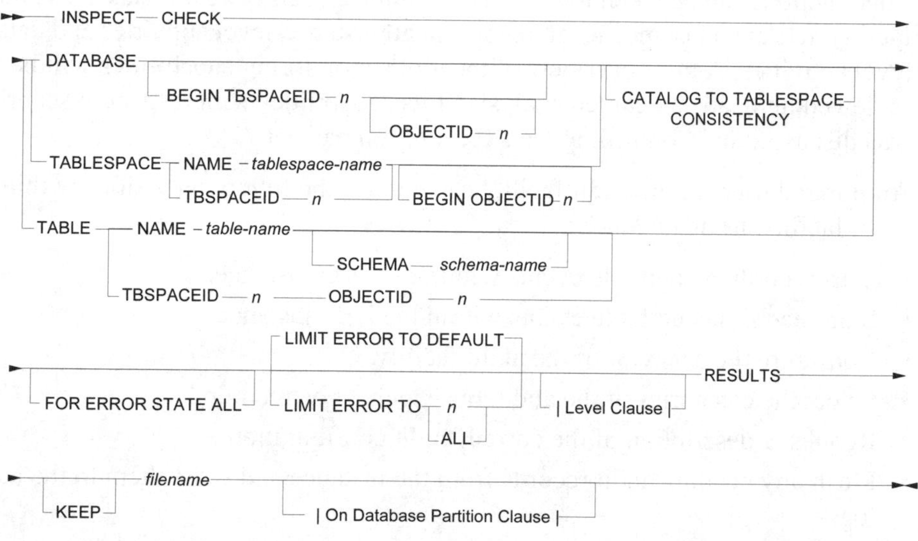

Figure 14–23 *INSPECT Command*

Some of the key parameters to the INSPECT command include (see the *DB2 Command Reference* for further details):

- CHECK — specifies check processing.
- DATABASE — specifies whole database.
- CATALOG TO TABLESPACE CONSISTENCY — specifies to include checking for the consistency of physical tables in the table space to the tables listed in the catalog.
- LIMIT ERROR TO n — specifies number of pages in error for an object to limit reporting.
- LIMIT ERROR TO DEFAULT — specifies the default number of pages (extent size of the object) be used to limit reporting.
- KEEP — specifies to always keep the result output file.

Note that while the DB2DART command (Database Analysis and Reporting Tool) can also be used to check for architectural integrity, this tool runs offline, so no users can using the system while it is in operation.

Audit Facility Administrator Tool

DB2 provides an audit facility to assist in the detection of unknown or unanticipated access to data. The DB2 audit facility generates and permits the maintenance of an audit trail for a series of predefined database events. The records generated from this facility are kept in an audit log file (db2audit.log). The analysis of these records can reveal usage patterns which would identify system misuse. Once identified, actions can be taken to reduce or eliminate such system misuse. The audit facility acts at an instance level, recording all instance-level activities and database level activities. A brief overview of the tool's monitoring capabilities will be reviewed here, and a detailed analysis of its capabilities with respect to security was discussed in "Controlling Data Access" on page 167.

Authorized users of the audit facility can control the following actions within the audit facility, using *db2audit*:

- Start recording auditable events within the DB2 instance.
- Stop recording auditable events within the DB2 instance.
- Configure the behavior of the audit facility.
- Select the categories of the auditable events to be recorded.
- Request a description of the current audit configuration.
- Flush any pending audit records from the instance and write them to the audit log.
- Extract audit records by formatting and copying them from the audit log to a flat file or ASCII delimited files. Extraction is done for one of two reasons: In preparation for analysis of log records, or in preparation for pruning of log records.
- Prune audit records from the current audit log.

The categories of events available for auditing are:

- Audit (AUDIT) — Generates records when audit settings are changed or when the audit log is accessed.
- Authorization Checking (CHECKING) — Generates records during authorization checking of attempts to access or manipulate DB2 objects or functions.
- Object Maintenance (OBJMAINT) — Generates records when creating or dropping data objects.
- Security Maintenance (SECMAINT) — Generates records when granting or revoking object or database privileges, or DBADM authority. Records are also generated when the database manager security configuration parameters SYSADM_GROUP, SYSCTRL_GROUP, or SYSMAINT_GROUP are modified.
- System Administration (SYSADMIN) — Generates records when operations requiring SYSADM, SYSMAINT, or SYSCTRL authority are performed.
- User Validation (VALIDATE) — Generates records when authenticating users or retrieving system security information.
- Operation Context (CONTEXT) — Generates records to show the operation context when a database operation is performed. This category allows for better interpretation of the audit log file. When used with the log's event correlator

field, a group of events can be associated back to a single database operation. For example, an SQL statement for dynamic SQL, a package identifier for static SQL, or an indicator of the type of operation being performed, such as CONNECT, can provide needed context when analyzing audit results.

In most cases, you will configure the audit facility for a more restricted or focused view of the events you wish to audit. For example, you may want to only audit those events that fail. In this case, the audit facility could be configured as follows:

```
db2audit configure scope audit,
         checking,
         objmaint,
         secmaint,
         sysadmin,
         validate status failure
```

Storage Management Tool

A Storage Management tool is available through the Control Center, by right-clicking on a database icon in the Control Center window and select `Manage Storage`. From this tool you can access the Storage Management view that displays a snapshot of the storage for a particular database, database partition group, or table space.

Statistical information can be captured periodically and displayed depending on the object chosen:

- For table spaces, information is displayed from the system catalogs and database monitor for tables, indexes, and containers defined under the scope of the given table space.
- For databases or database partition groups, information is displayed for all the table spaces defined in the given database or database partition group.
- For databases, information is also collected for all the database partition groups within the database.

You can use the information displayed in this view to monitor various aspects of your storage, such as space usage for table spaces, data skew (database distribution) for database partition groups, and capture cluster ratio of indexes for database partition groups and table spaces.

From the Storage Management view (Figure 14–24) you can also set thresholds for data skew, space usage, and index cluster ratio. A warning or alarm flag will let you know if a target object exceeds a specified threshold.

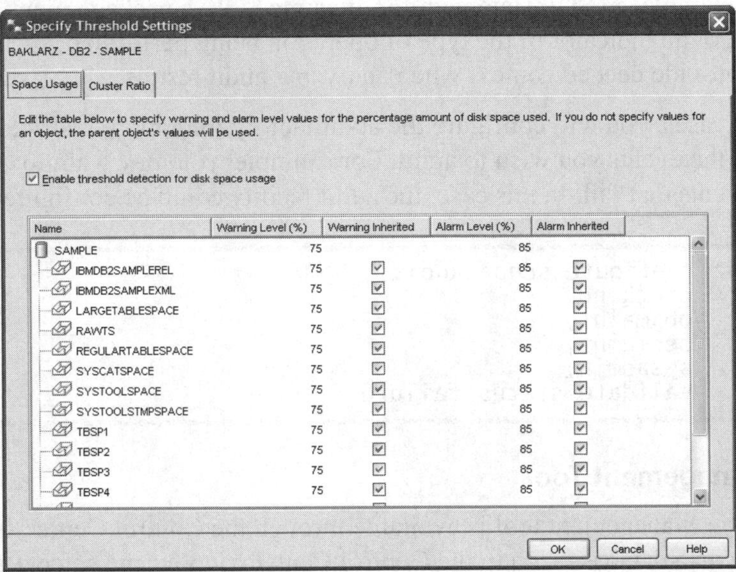

Figure 14–24 *Storage Management Tool*

Indoubt Transaction Manager

Invoking the Indoubt Transaction Manager will check the status of the current indoubt transactions for a given database. Usually, the transaction manager will attempt to resynchronize indoubt transactions. However, it is possible that an indoubt transaction may not be resolved automatically.

For example, an indoubt transaction may involve more than just your DB2 system. If a third-party tool involved in the transaction cannot be reached due to communication failure, or is unavailable, the indoubt transaction may not be resolved automatically. If something like this has happened, or if you cannot wait for the transaction manager to automatically resolve indoubt transactions, there are actions you can take to manually and heuristically resolve indoubt transactions and free up log space.

The Indoubt Transaction Manager is available from the command line by typing:

```
db2indbt
```

Database Benchmarking Tool

The `db2batch` command is a useful tool to benchmark SQL statements. It can read SQL statements from either a flat file or standard input, dynamically preparing and describing the statements, and returning the answer set.

Here are some of the key parameters of the `db2batch` command (Figure 14–25):

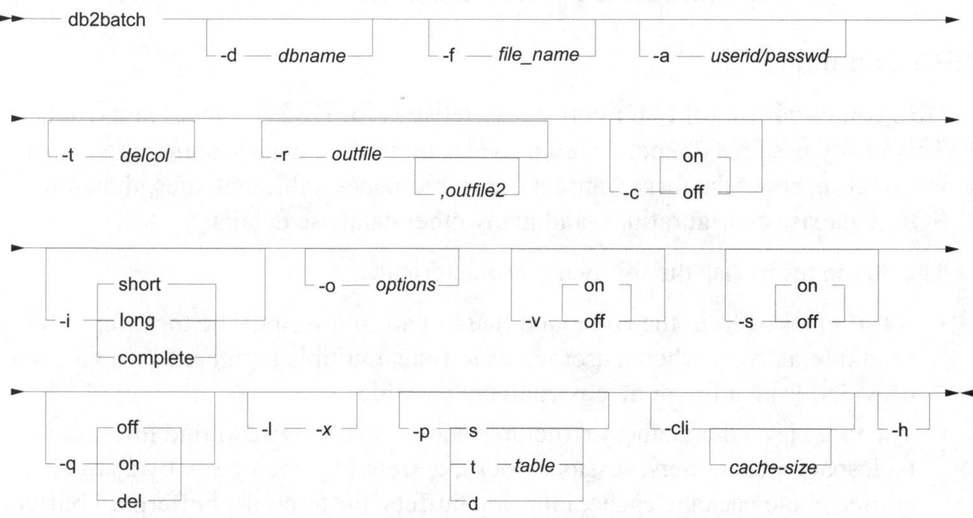

Figure 14–25 *db2batch Command*

The key parameter of the `db2batch` command is `-o` (options). The valid options are (see the *DB2 Command Reference* for the other options):

- f rows_fetch (–1 to n) — Specifies number of rows to be fetched (–1 indicates all rows to be fetched).
- r rows_out (–1 to n) — Specifies the number of fetched rows to be sent to output.
- p perf_detail — Specifies the level of performance information to be returned.
  - 0 — No timing is to be done.
  - 1 — Return elapsed time only.
  - 2 — Return elapsed time and CPU time.
  - 3 — Return a summary of monitoring information.
  - 4 — Return a snapshot for the database manager, database, application, and statement.
  - 5 — Return a snapshot for the database manager, database, application, statement, bufferpools, table spaces and FCM (if in a multi-partitioned

environment).

- o query_optimization_class — Specifies the query optimization class.
- e explain_mode — Specifies the explain mode which `db2batch` runs
  - 0 — Run query only (default).
  - 1 — Populate explain tables only.
  - 2 — Populate explain tables and run query.
  - –1 x — Specifies the termination character.

DB2PD Command

DB2 comes with a utility for collecting statistics for DB2 instances and databases. This utility is called `db2pd`. `db2pd` provides more than twenty options to display information about database transactions, tablespaces, table statistics, dynamic SQL, database configurations, and many other database details.

The `db2pd` utility has the following characteristics:

- It can invoked from the command line or part of a script. The tool can also be used interactively when a user wants to issue multiple commands. Input can be provided from a file or an environment variable.
- The tool views the memory structures being used by DB2 to find information on tablespaces, containers, sessions, locks, current SQL being run by a session, entries in the package cache, logs, log buffers, bufferpools, bufferpool buffers, and more.
- The tool does not acquire any latches or locks that would interfere with the activity on the system.
- The tool does not perform any file I/O to or from any database files as this could interfere with database activity.
- The tool can report on a combination of requests (tablespaces, users, and locks) or on all options.
- The tool can be run for multiple iterations to capture information for situations where there is a need to see a snapshot of certain outputs during a certain time-frame.
- It allows one database, any number of databases, or all databases to be reported.
- It has the ability to pick specific agents, applications, or other specific options for reported information such as locks held by an application or locks mapped to a transaction identifier.

The format of the `db2pd` command is:

```
db2pd -inst instance -db database options
```

An instance or database name may be required for some of the commands. If information from all the databases is required, then the -alldatabases or -everything option should be used. There are an extensive number of options available with the db2pd command. A brief summary of these options is found below — more information can be found in the *DB2 Command Reference*.

- -inst — Returns all instance-scope information.
- -help — Displays the online help information.
- -version — Displays the current version and service level of the installed DB2 product.
- -dbpartitionnum num — Specifies that the command is to run on the specified database partition server.
- -alldbpartitionnums — Specifies that this command is to run on all active database partition servers in the instance. db2pd will only report information from database partition servers on the same physical machine that db2pd is being run on.
- -database database — Specifies that the command attaches to the database memory sets of the specified database.
- -alldatabases — Specifies that the command attaches to all memory sets of all the databases.
- -everything — Runs all options for all databases on all database partition servers that are local to the server.
- -file filename — Specifies to write the output to the specified file.
- -command filename — Specifies to read and execute the db2pd command options that are specified in the file.
- -interactive — Specifies to override the values specified for the DB2PDOPT environment variable when running the db2pd command.
- -full — Specifies that all output is expanded to its maximum length. If not specified, output is truncated to save space on the display.
- -hadr — Reports high availability disaster recovery (HADR) information.
- -utilities — Reports utility information.
- -repeat num sec count — Specifies that the command is to be repeated after the specified number of seconds. If a value is not specified for the number of seconds, the command repeats every five seconds. You can also specify the number of times the output will be repeated. If you do not specify a value for count, the command is repeated until it is interrupted.
- -applications — Returns information about applications.
- -fmp — Returns information about the process in which the fenced routines are executed.
- -agents — Returns information about agents.

- `-transactions` — Returns information about active transactions.
- `-bufferpools` — Returns information about the buffer pools.
- `-logs` — Returns information about the log files.
- `-locks` — Returns information about the locks.
- `-tablespaces` — Returns information about the table spaces.
- `-dynamic` — Returns information about the execution of dynamic SQL.
- `-static` — Returns information about the execution of static SQL and packages.
- `-fcm` — Returns information about the fast communication manager.
- `-memsets` — Returns information about the memory sets.
- `-mempools` — Returns information about the memory pools.
- `-memblocks` — Returns information about the memory pools.
- `-dbmcfg` — Returns the settings of the database manager configuration parameters.
- `-dbcfg` — Returns the settings of the database configuration parameters.
- `-catalogcache` — Returns information about the catalog cache.
- `-sysplex` — Returns information about the list of servers associated with the database alias indicated by the db parameter. If the -database parameter is not specified, information is returned for all databases.
- `-tcbstats` — Returns information about tables and indexes.
- `-reorg` — Returns information about table and data partition reorganization.
- `-recovery` — Returns information about recovery activity.
- `-reopt` — Returns information about cached SQL statements that were reoptimized using the `REOPT ONCE` option.
- `-osinfo` — Returns operating system information. If a disk path is specified, information about the disk will be printed.
- `-storagepaths` — Returns information about the automatic storage paths defined for the database.
- `-pages` — Returns information about the buffer pool pages.
- `-stack` — Produces stack trace files in the DIAGPATH directory.
- `-dump` — Produces stack trace and binary dump files in the `DIAGPATH` directory.

The following command will request information on the status of the log files in the `SAMPLE` database:

```
db2pd -db sample -logs
```

The results from this command can be found in Figure 14–26.

```
Database Partition 0 -- Database SAMPLE -- Active -- Up 0 days 05:44:26

Logs:
Current Log Number            0
Pages Written                 214
Method 1 Archive Status       n/a
Method 1 Next Log to Archive  n/a
Method 1 First Failure        n/a
Method 2 Archive Status       n/a
Method 2 Next Log to Archive  n/a
Method 2 First Failure        n/a

Address    StartLSN         State      Size        Pages     Filename
0x0510D254 0x000011D28000 0x00000000 1000        1000      S0000000.LOG
0x0510D2F4 0x000012110000 0x00000000 1000        1000      S0000001.LOG
0x0510D394 0x0000124F8000 0x00000000 1000        1000      S0000002.LOG
```

Figure 14–26 *db2pd results*

One of the primary benefits of the db2pd command is that is does not require a DB2 command line in the Windows environment to run. In addition, this tool can often get information from DB2 before other utilities because of contention within the database engine.

SQL Monitoring

If you want to know how a query will be executed by DB2, you must analyze its *access plan*, which is the method for retrieving data from a relational table. The explain facilities will provide information about how DB2 accesses the data to resolve the SQL statements.

Before describing the capabilities and features of the explain facilities, you should understand at a high level how SQL statements are processed by the DB2 database engine. Each SQL statement is analyzed by DB2, and then it is determined how to process the statement during a static bind or when executed dynamically. The method used to retrieve data from tables is called the *access plan*.

The component within DB2 that determines the access plan to be used is known as the optimizer. During the static preparation of an SQL statement, the SQL compiler is called on to generate an access plan. The access plan contains the data access strategy including index usage, sort methods, locking semantics, and join methods. The executable form of the SQL statement is stored in the system catalog tables when a BIND command is executed (assuming a deferred binding method). This is called a *package*.

Monitoring and Tuning

DB2 Note

The method for retrieving data from a specific table, such as whether indexes are used, is called the access path. The access plan involves a set of access paths.

Sometimes, the complete statement is not known at application development time. In this case, the compiler is invoked during program execution to generate an access plan for the query that can be used by the database manager to access the data. Such an SQL statement is called a dynamic SQL statement. The access plans for a dynamic SQL statement are not stored in the system catalogs. They are temporarily stored in memory (known as the global package cache). The compiler will not be invoked if the access plans for the dynamic SQL statements already exist in the package cache.

Explain Tables

DB2 uses explain tables to store access plan information so that users can see the decisions the optimizer has made. These tables are called:

- `EXPLAIN_ARGUMENT` — Represents the unique characteristics for each individual operator.
- `EXPLAIN_INSTANCE` — Main control table for all explain information. Each row of data in the explain tables is explicitly linked to one unique row in this table. Basic information about the source of the SQL statements being explained and environment information is kept in this table.
- `EXPLAIN_OBJECT` — Contains data objects required by the access plan generated to satisfy the SQL statement.
- `EXPLAIN_OPERATOR` — Contains all the operators needed to satisfy the SQL statement.
- `EXPLAIN_PREDICATE` — Identifies which predicates are applied by a specific operator.
- `EXPLAIN_STATEMENT` — Contains the text of the SQL statement in two forms. The original version entered by the user is stored in addition to the rewritten version that is the result of the compilation process.
- `EXPLAIN_STREAM` — This table represents the input and output data streams between individual operators and data objects. The data objects themselves are represented in the `EXPLAIN_OBJECT` table. The operators involved in a data stream are represented in the `EXPLAIN_OPERATOR` table.

The explain tables have to be created before any explain information can be gathered. The CLP input file, called `EXPLAIN.DDL`, located in the misc directory of the

SQLLIB directory, contains the definition of the explain tables. To create the explain tables, you can connect to the database and use the following command:

```
db2 -tvf EXPLAIN.DDL
```

Explain tables are created the first time you use Visual Explain.

Gathering Explain Data

There are different kinds of explain data that can be collected. They differ in the explain table columns that will be populated. The explain data options are:

- EXPLAIN — Captures detailed information of the access plan and stores the information in the explain tables. No snapshot information is stored.
- EXPLAIN SNAPSHOT — Captures the current internal representation of an SQL query and related information. The snapshot information is stored in the SNAPSHOT column of the EXPLAIN_STATEMENT table.

Not all explain tools require the same kind of explain data. Some tools use the data captured using the EXPLAIN option and others, such as Visual Explain, require snapshot data.

After creating the explain tables, you can start capturing the explain data that will populate them. Not all SQL statements can be explained. The explainable SQL statements include: SELECT, SELECT INTO, UPDATE, INSERT, DELETE, VALUES, and VALUES INTO statements.

Depending on the number of SQL statements or kind of application you want to explain, you should use different methods. These methods include the following:

- EXPLAIN statement — Gathers explain data for an SQL statement
- CURRENT EXPLAIN MODE special register — Specifies the gathering of explain data for dynamic SQL statements
- CURRENT EXPLAIN SNAPSHOT special register — Specifies the gathering of explain snapshot data for dynamic SQL statements
- BIND options — Specify the gathering of explain data for static and/or dynamic embedded SQL statements in a package

Each of these methods will be examined in turn.

EXPLAIN Statement

The EXPLAIN statement is useful when you want to gather explain information for a single dynamic SQL statement. The EXPLAIN statement can be invoked either from the Command Line Processor, Command Center, or from within an application.

You can control the amount of explain information that the EXPLAIN statement will store in the explain tables. The default is to only capture regular explain table information and not the snapshot information. If you wish to modify this behavior, use the following EXPLAIN statement options:

- WITH SNAPSHOT— Captures explain and explain snapshot data into the explain tables.

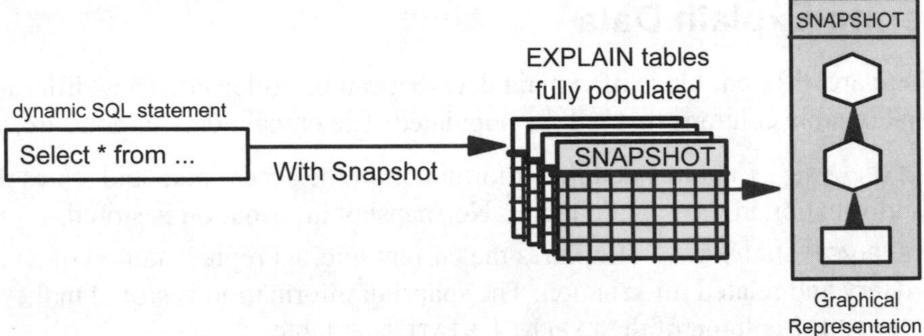

- FOR SNAPSHOT — Only captures the explain snapshot information. No other explain information is captured other than that normally found in the EXPLAIN_INSTANCE and EXPLAIN_STATEMENT tables.

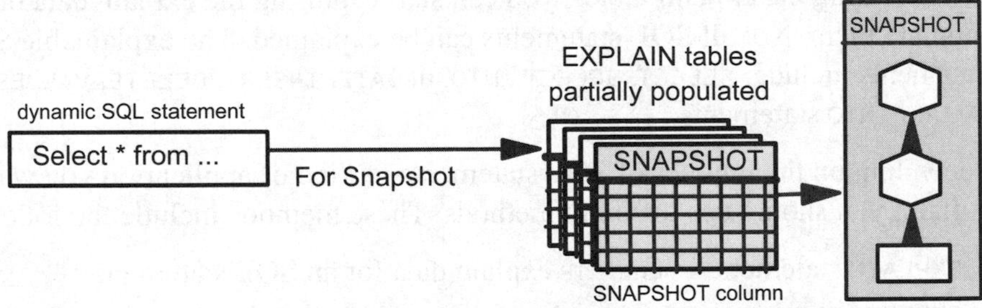

The default case is used when no other explain option is specified. In the default case, the EXPLAIN statement will only gather the explain data. No explain snapshot data is captured.

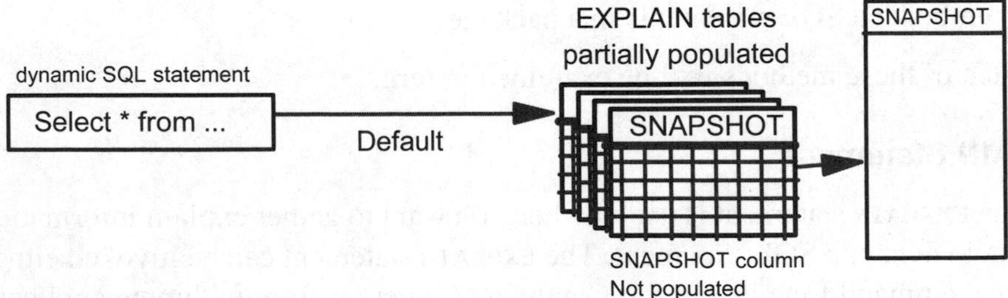

To issue the EXPLAIN statement, the user must have INSERT privilege on the explain tables.

DB2 Note

The SQL statement being explained using the EXPLAIN statement will not be executed; only the explain data is captured.

An example of gathering access plan information using the EXPLAIN statement will now be examined. The explain statement is shown below. This example collects all the available explain information for the explain tables.

```
EXPLAIN ALL WITH SNAPSHOT FOR "SELECT * FROM TEST_CANDIDATE"
```

DB2 Note

Instead of the keyword ALL, used in our example, the keywords PLAN and PLAN SELECTION can be used. Your EXPLAIN statement must include one of them.

The EXPLAIN statement shown in the last example populates a number of explain tables including the SNAPSHOT column of the EXPLAIN_STATEMENT table.

The SNAPSHOT_TAKEN column in the EXPLAIN_INSTANCE table indicates the existence of a Visual Explain snapshot for each explained statement.

The EXPLAIN statement can also be embedded in an application that populates the explain tables. Once the explain tables are populated, they can be queried. Special operators can be examined to determine if the ideal access plan was used for the query.

Explain Special Register

Another way to collect explain information is to use the explain special registers. There are two special registers used by DB2 for gathering explain information for dynamic SQL statements. These registers can be set interactively, or they can be used in a dynamic embedded SQL program. The values of special registers are modified using the SET statement.

The special registers are:

- CURRENT EXPLAIN MODE — Used to populate only the explain data. No snapshot will be taken.

- CURRENT EXPLAIN SNAPSHOT — Used to capture only the explain snapshot data.

The following statements are used to set the value of the explain special registers:

```
SET CURRENT EXPLAIN MODE     option
SET CURRENT EXPLAIN SNAPSHOT option
```

The explain registers options are:

- NO — No explain information is captured for dynamic SQL statements.
- YES — Explain tables or snapshot information will be populated for dynamic SQL statements while executing the SQL statement, and the result is returned.
- EXPLAIN — Explain tables or snapshot information will be populated for dynamic SQL statements without executing the SQL statement. Use this state to obtain explain information without executing the SQL statement.

The following two options are for the CURRENT EXPLAIN MODE register only. They will be illustrated in the section that discusses the Index Advisor.

- RECOMMEND INDEXES
- EVALUATE INDEXES

DB2 *Note*

Once you have set a register to YES or EXPLAIN, any subsequent dynamic SQL statements will be explained until the register is reset to NO.

Explain BIND Options

The BIND command is discussed in "Development Considerations" on page 997. However, in this section, the bind options related to the explain information will be reviewed.

There are two explain BIND options that can be specified: EXPLAIN and EXPLSNAP. The EXPLSNAP option collects explain snapshot information. If you want to view the access plan using Visual Explain, you use the EXPLSNAP option. The EXPLAIN option only populates the explain information without including a snapshot.

DB2 *Note*

Explain snapshots cannot be performed for DRDA application servers.

Figure 14–27 shows options of the BIND command and the explain tables that are populated when the options are used.

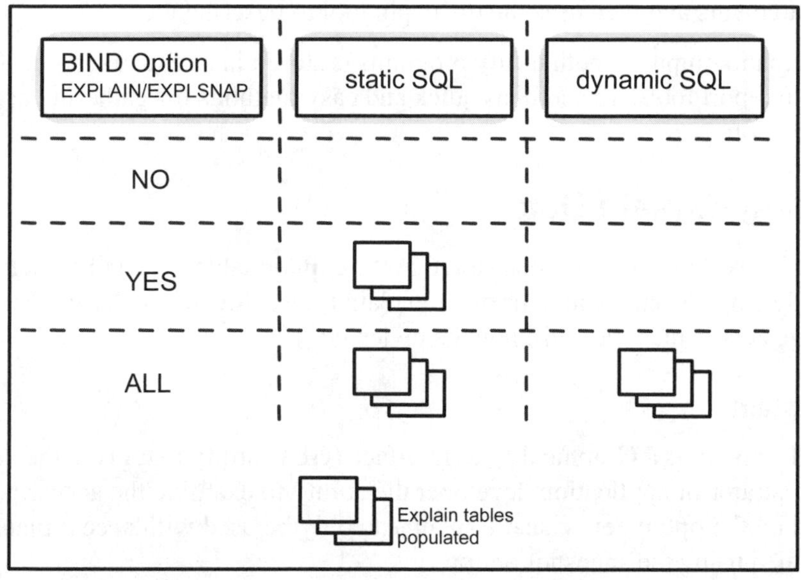

Figure 14–27 *Using the EXPLAIN or EXPLSNAP option for BIND command*

Explain data using a bind option will now be captured.

```
BIND checkid.bnd EXPLSNAP ALL
```

In this example, the explain snapshot information will be populated for all of the static SQL statements defined in the `CHECKID.BND` package. Because the ALL option was specified, the dynamic SQL statements issued during package execution will also have explain snapshot information gathered at run time.

The method of obtaining explain information during binds is useful for an administrator to determine the access plans of static or dynamic statements executed from packages.

To examine the access plan data for individual dynamic SQL statements, the special register technique is an easier method to use.

Using the Explain Report Tools to Gather and Analyze Explain Data

There are alternative methods of gathering explain data that is stored in a report rather than in the explain tables. They are the *dynexpln* tool and the *db2expln* tool.

The `db2expln` tool describes the access plan selected for static SQL statements in the packages stored in the system catalog tables, and the `dynexpln` tool describes the access plan selected for dynamic SQL statements. It creates a static package for the statements and then uses the db2expln tool to describe them.

The explain output of both utility programs is stored in a readable report file. The explain report tools are useful as quick and easy methods for gathering access plan information.

Examining Explain Data

Once the explain data has been stored in the explain tables, it can be queried or displayed using Visual Explain or other explain tools. How to use Visual Explain and analyze access plan data will now be reviewed.

Visual Explain

Visual Explain is a Graphical User Interface (GUI) utility that gives the database administrator or application developer the ability to examine the access plan determined by the optimizer. Visual Explain can only be used with access plans explained using the snapshot option.

Visual Explain can be used to analyze previously generated explain snapshots or to gather explain data and explain dynamic SQL statements. If the explain tables have not been created when you start Visual Explain, it will create them for you. You can invoke Visual Explain from either the Command Center or Control Center.

From the Control Center interface, right-click the database icon, you will notice that there is an option called **Show Explained Statements History,** as shown in Figure 14–28.

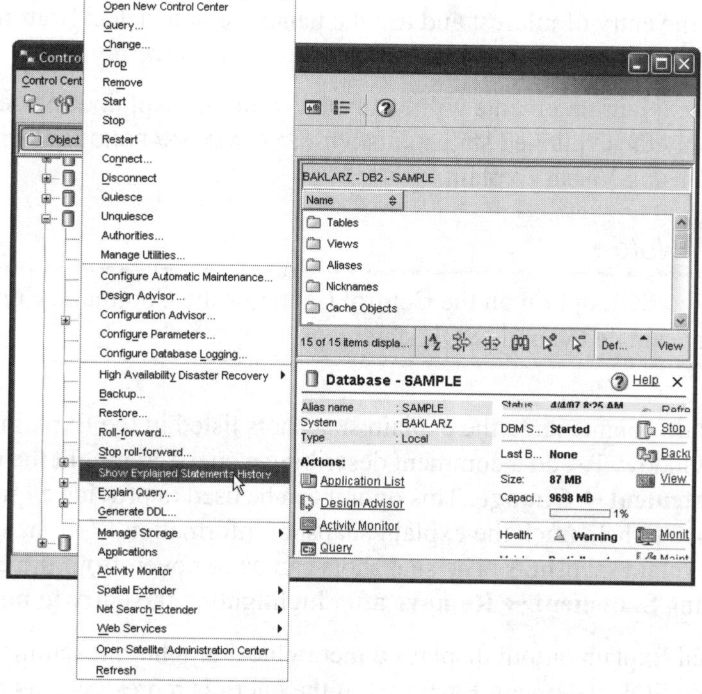

Figure 14–28 *DB2 Control Center — Accessing Visual Explain*

The **Explain SQL...** option, also shown in Figure 14–28, allows you to gather explain data and show the graphical representation of a dynamic SQL statement. This is the easiest way to explain a single SQL statement.

Once the Explained Statement History window has been opened, all of the explained statements will be listed as shown in Figure 14–29. Because it can be customized to your environment, the displayed information may differ. In Figure 14–29, the total costs and the SQL statements are shown.

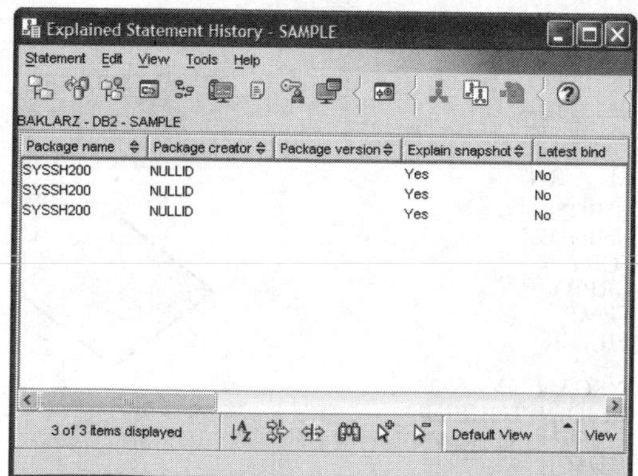

Figure 14–29 *Customized display of Explained Statement History panel*

To examine an access plan in detail, simply double-click the explained statement or highlight the entry of interest and use the panel menu to select **Statement ➔ Show access plan** on the Explained Statement History window.

All of the explain statements will be displayed in the Explained Statement History list, but only the explained statements with EXPLAIN SNAPSHOT information can be examined using Visual Explain.

DB2 *Note*

The Explain SQL option on the Control Center or the Command Center are useful to explain a single dynamic SQL statement.

You can add comments to the explain snapshots listed in the Explained Statement History window. To add a comment describing a query, highlight the entry and then select **Statement ➔ Change**. This option can be used to provide a query tag, which can be used to help track the explain snapshot information. You may also wish to remove explain snapshots. The snapshots can be removed from the explain tables by selecting **Statement ➔ Remove** after highlighting the entry to be removed.

The Visual Explain output displays a hierarchical graph representing the components of an SQL statement. Each part of the query is represented as a graphical object. These objects are known as *nodes*. There are two basic types of nodes:

- *OPERATOR* nodes indicate an action that is performed on a group of data.
- *OPERAND* nodes show the database objects on which an operator action takes place. An operand is an object that the operators act on. These database objects are usually tables and indexes.

There are many operators that can be used by the DB2 optimizer to determine the best access plan. Some of the operators used by Visual Explain are shown in Figure 14–30.

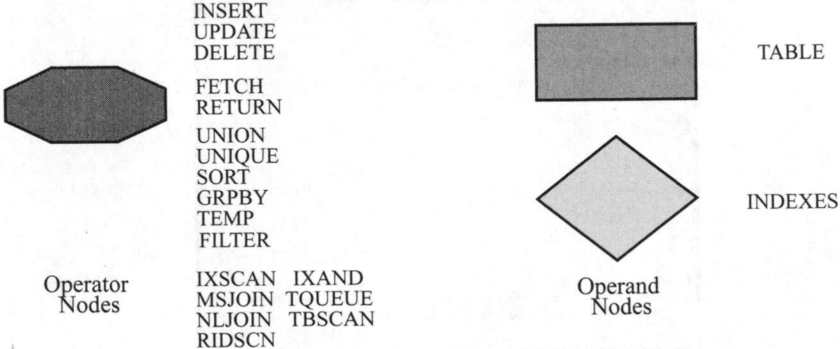

Figure 14–30 *Operators and operands displayed in Visual Explain*

These operators indicate how data is accessed (IXSCAN, TBSCAN, RIDSCN, IXAND), how tables are joined internally (MSJOIN, NLJOIN), and other factors, such as if a sort will be required (SORT). More information about the operators can be found using Visual Explain Online Help.

The objects shown in a Visual Explain graphic output are connected by arrows showing the flow of data from one node to another. The end of an access plan is always a RETURN operator.

For the next set of examples, assume the following table was created within the SAMPLE database:

```
CREATE TABLE ALLEMP LIKE EMPLOYEE;
INSERT INTO ALLEMP SELECT * FROM EMPLOYEE;
```

The access plan shown in Figure 14–31 is a simple SQL statement: SELECT * FROM ALLEMP. In this example, there are two operators and a single operand. The operand is the ALLEMP table, and the operators include a table scan (TBSCAN) and a RETURN operator.

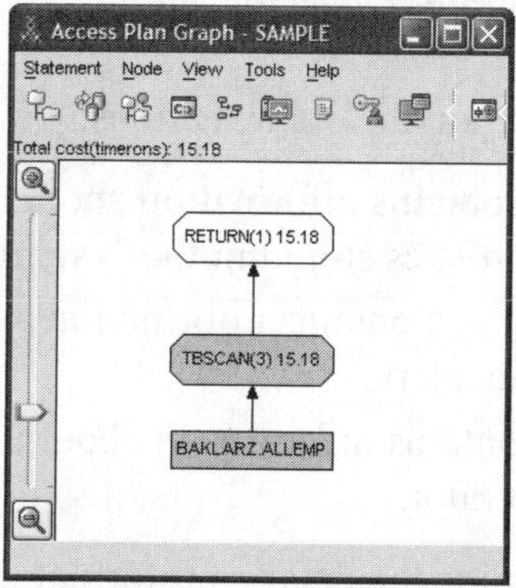

Figure 14–31 *Visual Explain: Graphical access plan for SQL statement*

Generating explain data for an SQL statement is the only way to analyze the access plan determined by the DB2 optimizer.

Each node, shown in an access plan graph, has detailed information that can be accessed by double-clicking the node or by choosing the **Show details** option from the **Node** menu item.

To display the details of the table scan operation, select the **TBSCAN** operator node and then select **Show details** from the **Node** menu item. The information about the TBSCAN operation, shown in the access plan, is displayed in Figure 14–32.

Monitoring and Tuning

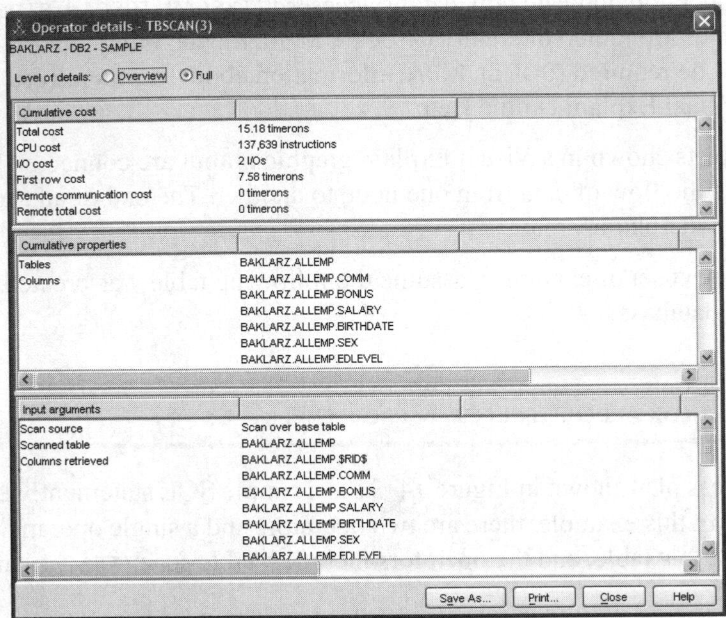

Figure 14–32 *Visual Explain: Operator details*

This window contains several different sections:

- Cumulative costs — Contains information about the estimated cumulative costs calculated using the statistics stored in the system catalog tables.
- Cumulative properties — Contains information about the table, columns, and so forth used to satisfy the query.
- Input arguments — Contains information about the input arguments that affect the behavior of the operator.

It is also possible to examine the detailed information about the operands. Select a operand node and then select **Show statistics** from the **Node** menu item. Figure 14–33 shows operand details for the ALLEMPS table.

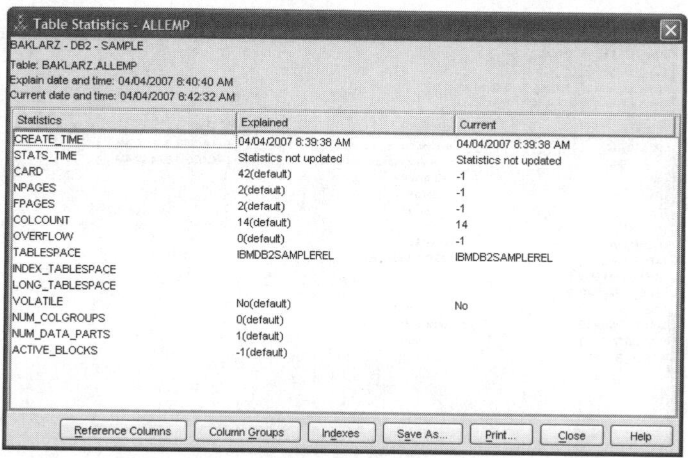

Figure 14–33 *Visual Explain: Detailed statistics information for an operand*

Detailed information for operand nodes shows the table or index statistics, including table space information, the number of columns, and the number of rows in the object. Figure 14–33 shows the explained and current statistics from the system catalog tables. These statistics are used by the DB2 optimizer to determine the access plan. Figure 14–33 shows that there were no statistics gathered for the ALLEMP table.

When the optimizer has no statistics to work with for a table, or if the statistics for a table indicate that the cardinality of the table is relatively small, then the optimizer itself will attempt to calculate the cardinality of the table. The optimizer does this by using certain factors, including the average column length of the table and the number of pages used by the table.

Current statistics are the key to good access plans. If DB2 is not aware of the characteristics of objects involved in a query, it may not be able to generate a good access plan. To ensure the latest statistics are available for the optimizer, a DB2 utility must be used. This utility is called RUNSTATS. Here is an example of gathering statistics for the ALLEMP table.

```
RUNSTATS ON TABLE BAKLARZ.ALLEMP
            WITH DISTRIBUTION AND DETAILED INDEXES ALL
```

Statistics for the ALLEMP table are stored in the system catalog tables. After running the RUNSTATS utility, rebind the packages against the database and re-explain the SQL statement. You will note that the values for the current statistics have changed, and probably the total cost of the access plan generated would change too. Figure 14–34 shows that the updated ALLEMP statistics have changed.

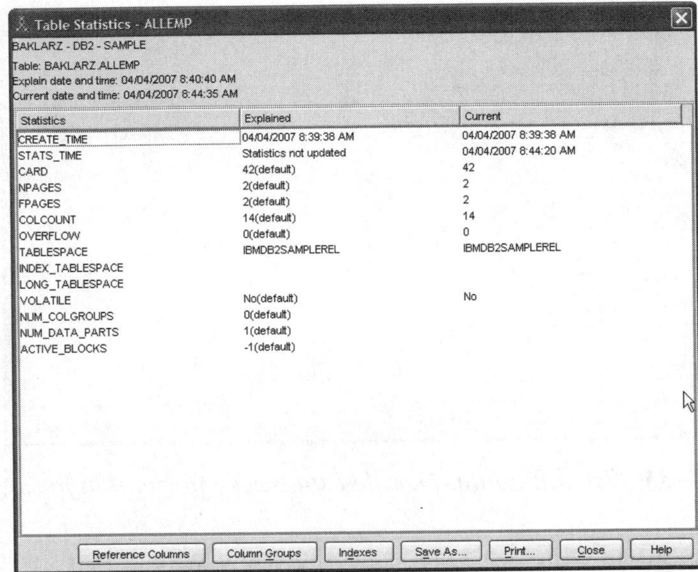

Table Statistics - ALLEMP

BAKLARZ - DB2 - SAMPLE

Table: BAKLARZ.ALLEMP
Explain date and time: 04/04/2007 8:40:40 AM
Current date and time: 04/04/2007 8:44:35 AM

Statistics	Explained	Current
CREATE_TIME	04/04/2007 8:39:38 AM	04/04/2007 8:39:38 AM
STATS_TIME	Statistics not updated	04/04/2007 8:44:20 AM
CARD	42(default)	42
NPAGES	2(default)	2
FPAGES	2(default)	2
COLCOUNT	14(default)	14
OVERFLOW	0(default)	0
TABLESPACE	IBMDB2SAMPLEREL	IBMDB2SAMPLEREL
INDEX_TABLESPACE		
LONG_TABLESPACE		
VOLATILE	No(default)	No
NUM_COLGROUPS	0(default)	
NUM_DATA_PARTS	1(default)	
ACTIVE_BLOCKS	-1(default)	

Reference Columns | Column Groups | Indexes | Save As... | Print... | Close | Help

Figure 14–34 *Visual Explain: Table statistics after RUNSTATS*

When determining the access plan for dynamic SQL statements, the DB2 optimizer always uses the current statistics. For a static SQL statement, DB2 uses the statistics available at `BIND` time (when the package was created). To ensure that current statistics are used with static SQL statements that were compiled before the statistics were updated, the packages must be recreated. This can be accomplished using the `REBIND` command.

In Figure 14–35, the total cost for the SQL statements is not the same in both cases. They differ because different statistics were used by DB2 when the explain snapshot was captured.

Package name	Packag...	Packa...	Explain sn...	Lates...	Dynamic...	Explain date	Explain time	Total cost	Statemer
SYSSH200	NULLID		Yes	No	Yes	Feb 26, 2007	8:49:44 PM	22.819	
SYSSH200	NULLID		Yes	No	Yes	Feb 26, 2007	8:58:28 PM	15.211	
SYSSH200	NULLID		Yes	No	Yes	Feb 28, 2007	1:39:38 PM	15.175	
SYSSH100	NULLID		Yes	No	Yes	Apr 4, 2007	8:29:38 AM	15.175	
SYSSH100	NULLID		Yes	No	Yes	Apr 4, 2007	8:37:50 AM	15.175	
SYSSH100	NULLID		Yes	No	Yes	Apr 4, 2007	8:40:40 AM	15.175	
SYSSH100	NULLID		Yes	No	Yes	Apr 4, 2007	8:47:48 AM	15.175	

Figure 14–35 *Visual Explain: List of explained statements*

In our example, the difference of the total cost of the explained queries is very small. This is because the DB2 optimizer estimates some statistics for tables if the statistics have not been gathered. Therefore, the default statistics were quite close to the actual statistics, hence, the similar total costs. The statistics are estimated based on the number of pages in the tables, row length, and so on. Due to the dynamic nature of databases, the estimated, or catalog, statistics may be very different than what the database really looks like. In these cases, the access plan chosen by DB2 may be inefficient.

Please refer to "Maintaining Data" on page 701 for detailed information about the RUNSTATS and REBIND commands.

DB2 Note

Updated statistics become critical as your SQL statements grow in complexity.

Visual Explain can be used to see the decisions that the optimizer made for sorting. In Figure 14–36, you can see that an index was used to provide the ordered result from the TEST_CANDIDATE table.

```
SELECT * FROM TEST_CANDIDATE
  WHERE CID=CANDIDATE_ID('111')
```

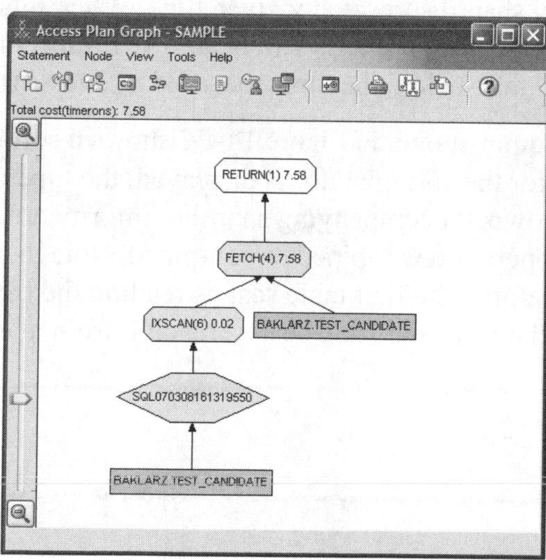

Figure 14–36 *Sort request satisfied by an index*

The sort heap is used for each application sort request. The DB2 optimizer may decide to attempt to perform a nonoverflowed piped sort. However, if there is not enough available memory to allocate another sort heap at run time, then the sort may be performed using a temporary table instead.

There is a database manager parameter that is used to control the total amount of memory allocated for sorting on the DB2 server. The parameter is called SHEAPTHRES. The SHEAPTHRES parameter should be set to the maximum amount of memory for all sort heaps allowed to be allocated at any given time.

As already explained, if intra-partition parallelism is enabled, a sort operations can be processed in parallel, and it can be a private sort or a shared sort, which uses memory from two different memory sources. The size of the shared sort memory area is statically predetermined (and not preallocated) at the time of the first connection to a database based on the value of SHEAPTHRES. The size of the private sort memory area is unrestricted.

The SHEAPTHRES parameter is used differently for private and shared sorts.

For private sorts, this parameter is an instance-wide soft limit on the total amount of memory that can be consumed by private sorts at any given time. When the total private-sort memory consumption for an instance reaches this limit, the memory allocated for additional incoming private-sort requests will be considerably reduced.

For shared sorts, this parameter is a database-wide hard limit on the total amount of memory consumed by shared sorts at any given time. When this limit is reached, no further shared-sort memory requests will be allowed (until the total shared-sort memory consumption falls below the limit specified by SHEAPTHRES).

The Visual Explain output shown in Figure 14–37 shows a sort operator. If the detailed information for the sort operator is displayed, the type of sort and the columns involved are shown. Accompanying snapshot information could be used to determine if the sort operation was piped or non-piped. Note that there are two relational table scan operators. The first table scan is reading the base table TEST_CANDIDATE, and the second table scan is reading from a temporary sort table.

```
SELECT LNAME, INITIAL, FNAME
  FROM TEST_CANDIDATE
ORDER BY LNAME
```

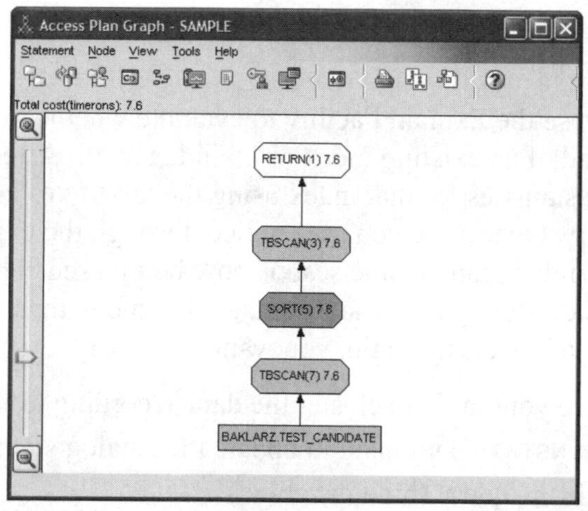

Figure 14–37 *Visual Explain with sort operator*

There are a number of sorting-related performance variables that can be monitored using the DB2 Snapshot Monitor. These parameters include:

- *Percentage of overflowed sorts* — This variable can be monitored to determine if the optimizer is attempting to use a sort heap and fails. If the percentage is high, consider increasing the SORTHEAP and/or SHEAPTHRES values.
- *Percentage of piped sorts accepted* — This variable can be monitored to determine if piped sorts are being chosen but not accepted by the optimizer. If the percentage is low, consider increasing the SORTHEAP and/or SHEAPTHRES.

As with the buffer pool allocation, it is important to allocate as much memory as possible to the sort heap (and set the threshold accordingly) without over-allocating memory and causing memory paging to occur.

Guidelines on Using Explain Output

There are a number of ways in which analyzing the explain data can help you to tune your queries and environment. For example:

- *Are indexes being used?*

  Creating appropriate indexes can have a significant benefit on performance. Using the explain output, you can determine if the indexes you have created to help a specific set of queries are being used. In the explain output, you should look for index usage in the following areas:

  - Join Predicates
  - Local Predicates

- GROUP BY clauses
- ORDER BY clauses
- The select list

You can also use the Explain Facility to evaluate whether a different index can be used instead of an existing index or no index at all. After creating a new index, collect statistics for that index using the RUNSTATS command and recompile your query. Over time, you may notice, through the explain data, that instead of an index scan, a table scan is now being used. This can result from a change in the clustering of the table data. If the index that was previously being used now has a low cluster ratio, you want to:

- Reorganize your table to cluster the data according to that index.
- Use the RUNSTATS command to update the catalog statistics.
- Recompile the query (bind or rebind).
- Reexamine the explain output to determine whether reorganizing the table has affected the access plan.

- *Is the type of access appropriate for the application?*

  You can analyze the explain output and look for types of access to the data that, as a rule, are not optimal for the type of application being executed. For example:

  - Online Transaction Processing (OLTP) Queries

    OLTP applications are prime candidates to use index scans with range-delimiting predicates because they tend to return only a few rows that are qualified using an equality predicate against a key column. If your OLTP queries are using a table scan, you may want to analyze the explain data to determine the reasons why an index scan was not used.

  - Read-Only Queries

    The search criteria for a *read-only* type query may be vague causing a large number of rows to qualify. If the user usually looks only at a few screens of the output data, she may want to try to ensure that the entire answer set need not be computed before some results are returned. In this case, the goals of the user are different from the basic operating principle of the optimizer, which attempts to minimize resource consumption for the entire query, not just the first few screens of data.

    For example, if the explain output shows that both merge scan join and sort operators were used in the access plan, the entire answer set will be materialized in a temporary table before any rows are returned to the application. In this case, you can attempt to change the access plan by using the OPTIMIZE FOR clause on the SELECT statement. In this way, the optimizer can attempt to choose an access plan that does not produce the entire answer set in a temporary table before returning the first rows to the application.

Index Advisor

The *Index Advisor* is an administrative tool that provides assistance in the designing of indexes on tables. It is useful in the following situations:

- Finding the best indexes for a problem query
- Finding the best indexes for a set of queries (work load) subject to resource limits that are optionally applied
- Testing out an index on a workload without having to create the index

There are two concepts associated with this facility: *workload* and *virtual indexes*.

A work load is a set of SQL statements (SELECT, INSERT, UPDATE, DELETE) that DB2 has to process over a given period of time. The information in the workload is concerned with the type and frequency of the SQL statements over a given period of time. The index advisor uses this workload information in conjunction with the database information to recommend indexes. The goal of the advising engine is to minimize the total workload cost.

Virtual indexes are indexes that do not exist in the current database schema. These indexes could be either recommendations that the facility has made or indexes that are being proposed to create but wish to model the effect using the advisor facility.

The advisor facility uses two tables that are extensions to the EXPLAIN tables:

- ADVISE_WORKLOAD —This table is where you describe the workload to be considered. Each row in the table represents an SQL statement and is described by an associated frequency. There is an identifier called WORKLOAD_NAME for each workload that is a field in the table. All SQL statements that are part of the same workload should have the same WORKLOAD_NAME.
- ADVISE_INDEX — This table stores information about recommended indexes. Information is placed into this table by the SQL compiler, the db2advis command (DB2 Index Advisor Command), or manually using SQL statements.

By setting the CURRENT EXPLAIN MODE special register to RECOMMEND INDEXES, the ADVISE_INDEX table will be populated when the EXPLAIN function is invoked.

When the CURRENT EXPLAIN MODE special register is set to EVALUATE INDEXES, the ADVISE_INDEX table will be used as input into the EXPLAIN process, reading the virtual index definitions and using them in the EXPLAIN process as if they were real indexes.

The DB2 Index Advisor can be invoked using the db2advis command or by invoking it from the Control Center. This example connects to the SAMPLE database and recommends indexes for each table referenced by the queries in the input file. The maximum allowable time for finding a solution is 3 minutes.

```
db2advis -d sample -f sql.in -t 3
```

Configuring Database Resources

Monitoring database activity should be performed with a purpose in mind. The purpose of monitoring may be to achieve greater concurrency or to reduce the amount of disk access wait time. Another key purpose of monitoring database activity is to provide input for configuring various DB2 (instance) and database parameters to optimize memory utilization and increase performance.

Some of the key DBM and DB configuration parameters and how they relate to each other will be examined. Some of these parameters are used to determine the size of the memory allocated for each DB2 instance, database, or application.

DB2 *Note*

A `SHOW DETAILS` option has been added to the `GET DATABASE` and `GET DATABASE MANAGER CONFIGURATION` commands that will list both the current value and the value that will be used at the next instance start or database activation.

One of the most important factors affecting database performance is the size of each buffer pool in the database. When you create or alter a buffer pool, you have to set the size of each one. If you set the size to minus 1, then the default size is used, which is specified by the `BUFFPAGE` parameter in the database configuration file. Each buffer pool is the data cache between the applications and the physical disk. You can place your data in separate buffer pools by specifying a buffer pool for a particular table space. Also, it is possible for multiple table spaces to use one buffer pool.

If there were no buffer pools, then all database activity would result in disk access. If the size of each buffer pool is too small, the buffer pool hit ratio will be low, and the applications will wait for disk access activity to satisfy SQL queries. If one or more buffer pools are too large, memory on the server may be wasted. If the total amount of space used by all buffer pools is larger than the physical memory available on the server, then operating system paging (disk activity) will occur. Accessing a buffer pool that has been paged out to disk is inefficient.

If you create your own buffer pools in addition to the default buffer pool `IBMDEFAULTBP`, you must be careful how you allocate space for each one. There is no point in allocating a large buffer pool to a table space containing a large number of small, rarely used tables and a small buffer pool to a table space containing a large, frequently accessed table. The size of buffer pools should reflect the size of tables in the table space and how frequently they are updated or queried.

The DB2 optimizer will utilize the different buffer pools to achieve the best query performance. There is a parameter that provides the optimizer with information regarding the average number of active applications (AVG_APPLS). This parameter is used by the optimizer to determine how much of each buffer pool may be used for each application.

DB2 allows the addition, alteration, and dropping of buffer pools without stopping database activity. With the ability to change buffer pool allocations and update configuration parameters online, memory usage can be customized to specific tasks. For example, if you have a prime shift memory allocation that is optimized for query performance (a large buffer pool), a script can be executed to optimize memory usage for a load operations during the time reserved for batch operations. The script would:

- Reduce the buffer pool size
- Increase the utility and sort heap
- Run loads with the configuration optimized for load
- Return parameters to prime shift values when the loads have completed

DB2 *Note*

Buffer pool allocations and the altering of database manager and database configuration parameters that affect memory can now be changed online while DB2 is running.

Another memory block shared at the database level is called the database heap (DBHEAP). There is one database heap per database, and the database manager uses it on behalf of all applications connected to the database. It contains control block information for tables, indexes, table spaces, buffer pools, and so forth.

DB2 *Note*

DB2 allows certain DBM (INSTANCE_MEMORY) and DB (DATABASE_MEMORY, MAXAPPLS) configuration parameters to be set to AUTOMATIC, thereby allowing the database to select the values of these parameters.

There are many I/O caches that can be configured, including a log file cache (LOGBUFSZ) and a system catalog table cache (CATALOGCACHE_SZ). The log buffer is used as a buffer for writing log records to disk. Every transaction involves writing multiple log records. To optimize disk write performance, the writes are buffered in memory and periodically flushed to disk. The catalog cache is used to store the system catalog tables in memory. As an SQL statement is compiled or referenced, the database object information needs to be verified. If the information is in memory, then there is no need to perform disk activity to access the data. The package cache (PCKCACHESZ) is used to reduce the need to reload access plans (sections) of a package. This caching can improve performance when the same section is used multiple times within a program.

DB2 *Note*

The access plans are cached for static and dynamic SQL statements in the package cache.

Record blocking is a distributed caching technique used to send a group of records across the network to the client instead of a single record at a time. The decrease in network traffic increases application performance and allows for better network throughput. The records are blocked by DB2 according to the cursor type and bind parameter. If the optimizer decides to return the query output in blocks, the amount of data in each block is determined by the ASLHEAPSZ parameter.

The application heap (APPLHEAPSZ) contains a number of memory blocks that are used by DB2 to handle requests for each application.

The sort heap (SORTHEAP) determines the maximum number of memory pages that can be used for each sort. The sort heap area is allocated in the agent private memory if intra-partition parallelism is disabled. However, if intra-partition parallelism is enabled, a sort operation is processed in parallel, and the sort heap area is allocated in the agent private memory or the database global memory depending on which type of sort, a *private sort* or a *shared sort*, is performed. For a private sort, a sort heap area is allocated independently for each parallel agent in the private agent memory. For a shared sort, a sort heap area is allocated in the database global memory, and each parallel agent shares this sort heap. The SORTHEAP parameter is used by the optimizer to determine if the sorting can be performed in memory or on disk. DB2 will always attempt to perform the sort in memory.

The SHEAPTHRES parameter is used to control the amount of memory that can be allocated for sort heaps in a DB2 server.

One of the key performance parameters that affects the amount of memory used on the DB2 server as a data cache (database level) will now be modified. The default buffer pool size can be updated to 200 MB using the following command:

```
UPDATE DB CFG FOR SAMPLE USING BUFFPAGE 50000
```

Allocating at least half of the physical memory on a machine to buffer pool space is usually a good starting point when adjusting the size of buffer pools. This assumes a dedicated DB2 database server and a single database active at any given time. For example, to effectively use a database server with 400 MB of RAM, the total size of all the buffer pools could amount to 200 or 300 MB.

Any modification to the database configuration file will not be effective until all applications using the database are disconnected. The subsequent database connection will use the new database configuration parameters. If you change the DBM (instance) configuration parameters, the new values will not be effective until the instance has been stopped and restarted.

The size of the memory used to perform record blocking will now be modified. The memory area used for record blocking is known as the application support layer heap (`ASLHEAPSZ`). The following command would set the record blocking to be 200 KB in size (the units are 4 KB).

```
UPDATE DATABASE MANAGER CONFIGURATION USING ASLHEAPSZ 50
```

Any changes to the database manager configuration will not take effect until the instance is stopped and restarted except default database monitor switch parameters, such as `DFT_MON_BUFPOOL`, `DFT_MON_LOCK`, `DFT_MON_SORT`, `DFT_MON_TABLE`, `DFT_MON_UOW`, and `DFT_MON_STMT`.

In this example, when the instance is restarted, records will be sent across the network from the DB2 server to the application in 200 KB blocks (likely more than a single row). If the average row length were 1 KB, then 200 records would be returned in a single block of data (assuming more than 200 records are in the final result table).

DB2 *Note*

Record blocking occurs for remote and local DB2 client applications.

DB2 also provides graphical tools that enable you to configure DB2 easily. The Configuration Advisor is a tool that asks you to define what you want to use the database for: to define size requirements and certain country specific information. Then, using your input as a guideline, the Advisor tunes certain parameters to better fit your needs in DB2. Right-click on a database icon in the Control Center window and select Configuration Advisor. This will bring up the Configuration Advisor window as shown in Figure 14–38.

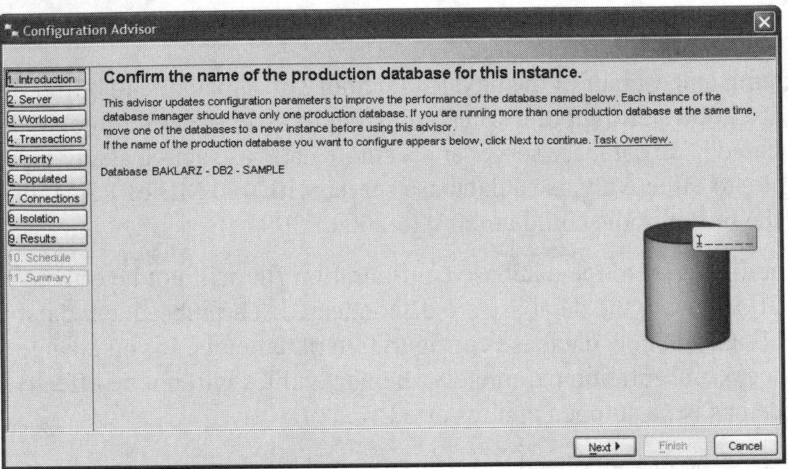

Figure 14–38 *Configuration Advisor*

The various tabs in the Advisor panel indicate the range of questions that the Advisor might ask. Once the Advisor has been filled in, you can go to the Results panel and see the new values of the parameters. In complex environments, the Advisor may not be able to make all the changes that are needed, so you may want to review the different parameters to see what has been changed and left unchanged. Figure 14–39 gives an idea of what the Results panel might look like. You do not need to apply the changes immediately in the Advisor. Instead, you can save a command to make the result come into effect as a script file, which can be run later from the Task Center.

DB2 *Note*

The `AUTOCONFIGURE` command invokes the Performance Configuration Wizard for a given database. There are options available when using `AUTOCONFIGURE` that assist you to define values for several database manager and database configuration parameters that can improve transaction or query performance.

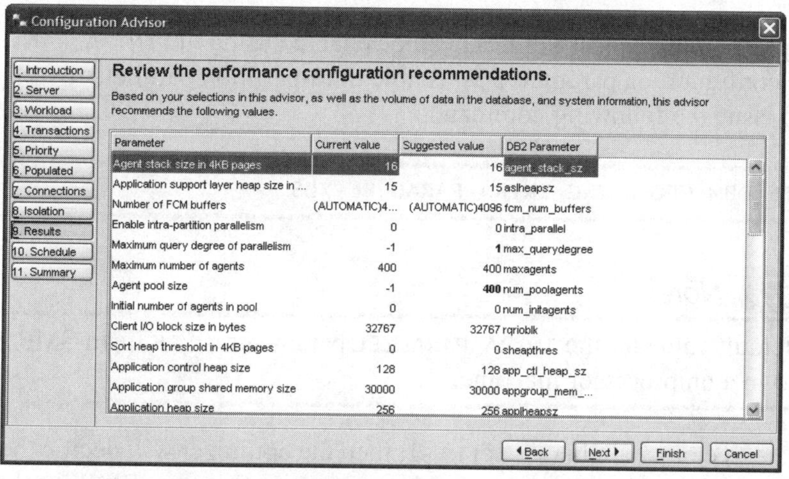

Figure 14–39 *Configuration Advisor — Results panel*

Another tool provided by DB2 is a user interface to the database manager and database configuration files. Using the Control Center, you can configure either the database manager or each database, using online help to guide you along. Figure 14–40 shows how you can configure the `SAMPLE` database from the Control Center. The configuration tool also provides hints for each database configuration parameter.

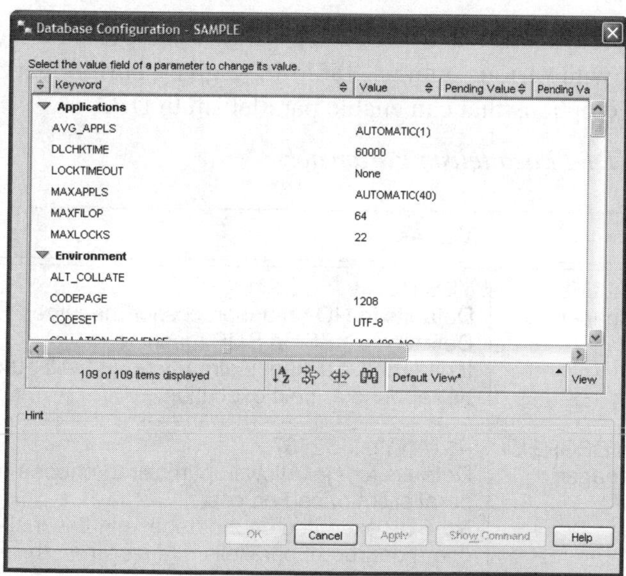

Figure 14–40 *Configure database using Control Center*

Configuring Intra-Partition Parallelism

Intra-partition parallelism in DB2 can be enabled using the INTRA_PARALLEL DBM configuration parameter. To enable intra-partition parallelism in DB2, you would issue the following command:

```
UPDATE DBM CFG USING INTRA_PARALLEL YES
```

DB2 *Note*

The default value for the INTRA_PARALLEL parameter is YES in an SMP machine and NO in a uniprocessor machine.

If the degree of parallelism is set to –1, then the optimizer will decide the degree of parallelism for each SQL query. For instance, on a four-way SMP machine, a simple insert statement will gain no advantage from being run in parallel across the CPUs, so using the –1 setting will result in this type of statement running on only one CPU (a degree of parallelism of 1).

Setting the DBM configuration parameter MAX_QUERYDEGREE to 2 in a uni-processor machine environment could improve I/O performance slightly. This is because the uni-processor may not have to wait for input or output tasks to complete before working on a new query, thus improving the performance of I/O bound applications.

Embedded SQL applications and CLI applications can override the default degree of parallelism with various options. Table 14–2 gives a brief overview of the parameters and options that can enable parallelism in DB2.

Table 14–2 *DB2 Parallelism Parameters*

Parameter	Values
INTRA_PARALLEL Database Manager Configuration	YES/NO. Defaults to NO on uni-processor machine. Defaults to YES on SMP machine. If changed, packages already bound will automatically be rebound at next execution.
MAX_QUERYDEGREE Database Manager Configuration	–1 (ANY), 1-32767. Defaults to –1 - Allows optimizer to choose degree of parallelism based on cost. No SQL executed on a database in this instance can use a degree of parallelism higher than this value.

Parameter	Values
DFT_DEGREE Database Configuration	–1 (ANY), 1-32767. Defaults to 1 (no parallelism). Provides the default value for: CURRENT DEGREE special register. DEGREE bind option. Maximum for any SQL in this database.
CURRENT DEGREE Special Register for dynamic SQL	–1 (ANY), 1-32767. Sets degree of parallelism for dynamic SQL. Defaults to DFT_DEGREE.
DEGREE Precompile or bind option for static SQL	–1 (ANY), 1-32767. Sets degree of parallelism for static SQL. Defaults to DFT_DEGREE. To change: `PREP STATIC.SQL DEGREE 2.`
RUNTIME DEGREE SET RUNTIME DEGREE command	–1 (ANY), 1-32767. Sets degree of parallelism for running applications. To change (setting degree to 4 for the application whose handler number is 100): `SET RUNTIME DEGREE FOR (100) to 4` Only affects queries issued after SET RUNTIME is executed.
DB2DEGREE CLI configuration file	–1 (ANY), 1-32767. Default is 0. Sets degree of parallelism for CLI applications. CLI application issues a SET CURRENT DEGREE statement after database connection.

The maximum query degree of parallelism for an active application is specified using the `SET RUNTIME DEGREE` command. The application can set its own runtime degree of parallelism by using the `SET CURRENT DEGREE` statement. The actual runtime degree used is the lower of:

- `MAX_QUERYDEGREE` DBM configuration parameter
- Application runtime degree
- SQL statement compilation degree

More information on parallelism support in DB2 can be found in the *DB2 Administration Guide*.

Monitoring and Tuning

Diagnostics and Problem Determination

DB2 offers a range of tools that can be used to determine the cause of problems or errors in the DB2 system. Potential problems include:

- Operating-system-specific

- Hardware- or I/O-specific
- Application-specific
- Communications-specific

In a complex environment, such as a distributed DB2 database system or a high-volume OLTP database system, there is a possibility that problems could occur. You need tools to analyze anything that might be characterized as an error. In more serious cases, you may want to determine the cause of a system crash. This kind of trouble-shooting needs to be done as quickly and efficiently as possible.

Error Messages and SQL Codes

DB2 has a large number of error codes that explain the possible problems within the database system. This means DB2 can report on problems within a database but also on problems within any of the tools and functions that are supplied with DB2.

These messages are divided into a few different categories. Each message has an error code associated with it. The prefix of the error code dictates what category the error code falls under:

- ADM — Administration Notification messages
- ASN — DB2 Replication Support messages
- CCA — Configuration Assistant messages
- CLI — CLI/ODBC application messages
- CLP — Command Line Processor messages
- DBA — Control Center or DBA Utility messages
- DBI — DB2 Installation messages
- DWC — Data Warehouse Center messages
- DXX — XML Extender messages
- GSE — Spatial Extender messages
- ICC — Information Catalog Center messages
- SAT — DB2 Satellite Edition messages
- SPM — Syncpoint Manager messages
- SQJ — DB2 embedded SQL in Java (SQLJ) messages
- SQL — SQL messages

Because the DB2 environment can be complex, there are a large number of error messages. During installation and setup of DB2, administrators may encounter some DBI, DBA, and CCA messages as they become accustomed to the new system. Another example might be users running adhoc queries against a DB2 database. They could receive SQL errors because of inaccurate SQL syntax or because they were not granted access to certain tables. If you have the specific code associated with an error, you can view the error message text in two ways: first, by consulting the *DB2 Messages Reference*, which details all the error codes in DB2; Second, by querying the code using the CLP or Command Center:

```
DB2 ? SQL0818
```

If an SQL statement fails, you receive an SQL error code as well as an SQLSTATE code. The SQLSTATE code is a standard code based on the ISO/ANSI SQL92 standard. It is unchanged across all the members of the DB2 Family, including RDBMSs on host systems. The SQL error codes may be unique to DB2 for Linux, UNIX, and Windows.

The SQL codes can be in two formats: a negative code (or in the format SQLxxxxN) or positive code (or in the format SQLxxxxW). The *negative* codes signify SQL *errors*, and the *positive* codes signify SQL *warnings* (a zero SQL code means that the SQL completed successfully).

Sometimes the SQL codes contain reason codes within the error message text. These reason codes usually provide more detailed information to supplement the message text. Some examples of reason codes include operating system return codes and communications protocol return codes. The *DB2 Messages Reference* provides some detail on common return codes. Sometimes, however, it may be necessary to consult other system documentation.

When using the Administration tools that come with DB2, the Journal records any messages that are returned to the user.

For example, if you try to use the Control Center to access the SAMPLE database while an offline backup is in progress, a pop-up dialog box will inform you that the database is in use. This message is then recorded in the Journal. Figure 14–41 gives an example of the messages logged by the Journal.

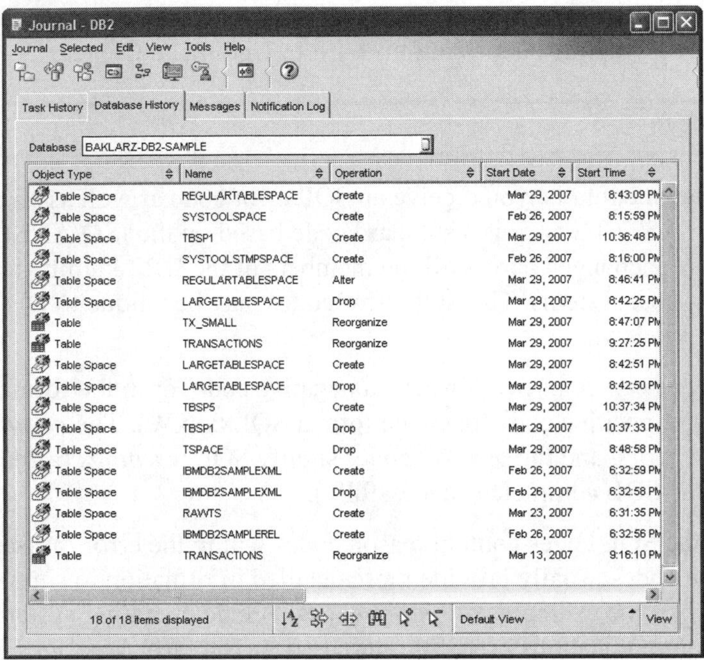

Figure 14–41 *Messages in the journal*

Diagnostic and Service Logs

DB2 will allow you to log most administrative tasks within the system. There are diagnostic log files for each DB2 instance, a diagnostic log for the Administration Tools that come with DB2, a report log for the DB2 Governor, and logs to document DB2 installation. The focus will be on the diagnostic logs for each DB2 instance.

DB2 will not log any Data Definition Language (DDL) statements or Data Manipulation Language (DML) statements. DB2 *will* log different administrative tasks, such as activating databases, backing up databases, starting and stopping DB2, or starting DB2 communications support.

These kinds of messages, when logged by DB2, are known as *informational* messages. However, in a trouble-shooting scenario, the messages that you will be looking for are *error* and *warning* messages. This is also known as *First Failure Data Capture (FFDC)* information. FFDC information is diagnostic information about an error that is captured automatically by the DB2 Administration Server when the error occurs. This information captured by the DB2 Administration Server FFDC includes:

- Administration notification logs — When significant events occur, DB2 writes information to the administration notification log. The information is intended for use by database and system administrators. Many notification messages provide additional information to supplement the SQLCODE that is provided. The type of event and the level of detail of the information gathered are determined by the NOTIFYLEVEL configuration parameter. On Windows, administration notification messages are written to the event log.
- Dump files — Sometimes, when a DB2 process or thread fails and signals an error, it will also log extra information in external binary dump files. These files are more-or-less unreadable and are intended for DB2 Customer Service personnel.
- Trap files — DB2 creates a trap file if an operating system trap/segmentation violation/exception occurs.

DB2 *Note*

The log previously known as the db2alert.log has been removed and the alerts are now written to the administration notification and diagnostic logs.

The FFDC information is logged in the directory specified by the DIAGPATH database manager configuration parameter. FFDC information is logged separately for each DB2 instance and is logged for both DB2 Server instances and DB2 Administration Server. The default DIAGPATH value is null at instance creation time. By default, the diagnostic files are written to the instance directory (in the db2dump subdirectory in UNIX platforms).

The DIAGPATH parameter is a database manager configuration parameter, so you could change it in the Control Center by right-clicking on the appropriate instance and clicking on **Configure**. You could also use the CLP or Command Center:

```
UPDATE DBM CFG USING DIAGPATH 'C:\NEWDIAGPATH'
```

The level of diagnostic information, DIAGLEVEL, is also a database manager configuration parameter. The DIAGLEVEL parameter can be set to the following values:

- 0 — No administration notification messages captured. (This setting is not recommended.)
- 1 — Severe errors only. Only fatal and unrecoverable errors are logged. To recover from some of these conditions, you may need assistance from DB2 service.
- 2 — All errors. Conditions are logged that require immediate attention from the system administrator or the database administrator. If the condition is not

resolved, it could lead to a fatal error. Notification of very significant, non-error activities (for example, recovery) may also be logged at this level. This level will capture Health Monitor alarms.

- 3 — All errors and warnings. Conditions are logged that are non-threatening and do not require immediate action but may indicate a non-optimal system. This level will capture Health Monitor alarms, Health Monitor warnings, and Health Monitor attentions. This is the default.
- 4 — All errors, warnings, and informational messages.

The default `DIAGLEVEL` is usually sufficient for normal DB2 operation. However, during the initial set-up of DB2, or when errors are occurring, the `DIAGLEVEL` could be updated to 4 in order to gather as much information as possible.

```
UPDATE DBM CFG USING DIAGLEVEL 4
```

DB2 *Note*

You must set *notifylevel* to a value of 2 or higher for the Health Monitor to send any notifications to the contacts defined in its configuration.

Tracing Problems in a DB2 Database

Sometimes problems occur in DB2 or applications using DB2, and the FFDC information is not sufficient to determine the source of the problem. At this point, DB2 Customer Service may ask the DBA to run traces against the application, against the CLI/ODBC/JDBC driver, or against the database itself.

An abbreviated syntax of the `DB2TRC` command is found in Figure 14–42.

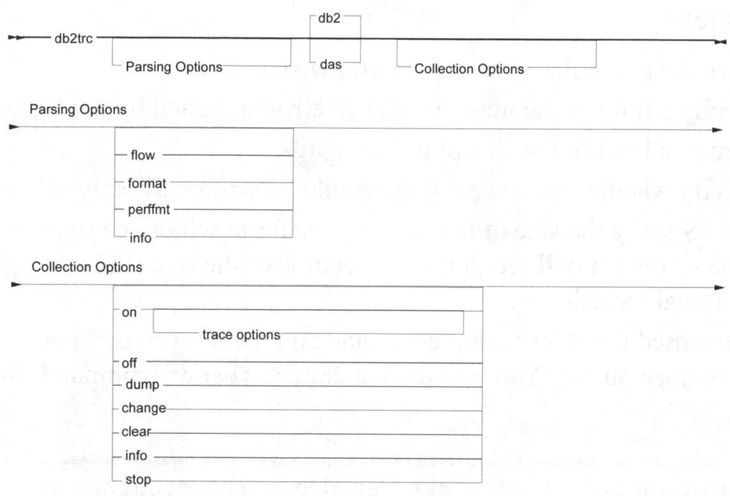

Figure 14–42 *DB2TRC Command*

Tracing or debugging the DB2 application is primarily a task for the application developer who created the program. DB2 embedded SQL programs provide extensive error-reporting functions using the SQLCA structure. This allows application developers to monitor their code executing against DB2.

Tracing against DB2 itself is somewhat similar to CLI/ODBC/JDBC tracing. You specify where you want the trace output to go and then turn on tracing. Tracing also has a significant performance impact on DB2. However, you have some flexibility when tracing inside DB2. You can filter what you want to monitor. You can specify how large a memory buffer you wish to use to hold trace information. You can specify how many DB2 errors the trace retains. Tracing against DB2 can be started with the **db2trc** command. You have to specify certain options to gather the trace information. You take a DB2 trace in four steps:

- Switch on tracing (`db2trc on`).
- Dump the trace output (`db2trc dmp`).
- Switch off tracing (`db2trc off`).
- Format the trace output (`db2trc flow` or `db2trc format`).

Using the `flow` option, you can specify that you would like the trace output formatted in order of DB2 thread/process. Using the `format` option, you can specify that you want the trace output formatted in chronological order.

Monitoring and Tuning

When switching on tracing, you can specify some additional options (only a subset are shown here):

- `-m` — Mask the particular record types you wish to trace.
- `-e` — Specify a limit to the number of DB2 errors retained by the trace.
- `-r` — Specify a limit to the size of trace records.
- `-f` — Specify whether the trace output should be written directly to a file.
- `-l` or `-i` — Specify the size of the memory buffer in which the trace output is stored. The `-l` option will retain the last records of the trace. The `-i` option will retain the initial records.

After you have used the `db2trc dmp` command and the `db2trc off` command, you can format the trace output. You execute the `db2trc format` command, for example:

```
C:\SQLLIB\BIN> db2trc format mytrace.dmp mytrace.out
 Trace wrapped       :YES
 Size of trace       :3996054 bytes
 Records in trace    :39450
 Records formatted :39450
```

A trace file formatted with the `db2trc fmt` command might look something like the following:

```
14719     DB2 fnc_retcode    SW- query graph        sqlnq_ftb::new (1.33.60.55)
          pid 138; tid 117; cpid 139; time 7951153; trace_point 254
          return_code = 000000 = 0

14720     DB2 fnc_entry      SW- query graph        sqlnq_ftb::sqlnq_ftb (1.30.60.56)
          pid 138; tid 117; cpid 139; time 7951153; trace_point 0
          called_from 0081F618

14721     DB2 cei_entry      oper_system_services sqlogmblk (1.20.15.82)
          pid 138; tid 117; cpid 139; time 7951153; trace_point 0
          called_from 10047AE9

14722     DB2 cei_data       oper_system_services sqlogmblk (1.25.15.82)
          pid 138; tid 117; cpid 139; time 7951153; trace_point 1
          4c05 9601 8c00 0000 0000 0000        L..........
```

For more information on tracing in DB2, please refer to the *DB2 Information Center.*

CLI/ODBC/JDBC Trace Facility

DB2 CLI and DB2 JDBC trace file analysis can benefit application developers in a number of ways. First, subtle program logic and parameter initialization errors are often evident in the traces. Second, DB2 CLI and DB2 JDBC traces may suggest ways of better tuning an application or the databases it accesses. For example, if a DB2 CLI trace shows a table being queried many times on a particular set of attributes, an index corresponding to those attributes might be created on the table to improve application performance. Finally, analysis of DB2 CLI and DB2 JDBC trace files can help application developers understand how a third-party application or interface is behaving.

The DB2 CLI and DB2 JDBC drivers offer comprehensive tracing facilities. By default, these facilities are disabled and use no additional computing resources. When enabled, the trace facilities generate one or more text log files whenever an application accesses the appropriate driver (DB2 CLI or DB2 JDBC). These log files provide detailed information about:

- The order in which CLI or JDBC functions were called by the application
- The contents of input and output parameters passed to and received from CLI or JDBC functions the return codes and any error or warning messages generated by CLI or JDBC functions

DB2 CLI and DB2 JDBC Trace Configuration

The configuration parameters for both DB2 CLI and DB2 JDBC traces facilities are read from the DB2 CLI configuration file `db2cli.ini`. By default, this file is located in the \sqllib path on the Windows platform and the /sqllib/cfg path on Linux or UNIX platforms. You can override the default path by setting the `DB2CLIINIPATH` environment variable. On the Windows platform, an additional db2cli.ini file may be found in the user's profile (or home) directory if there are any user-defined data sources defined using the ODBC Driver Manager. This `db2cli.ini` file will override the default file.

To view the current db2cli.ini trace configuration parameters from the command line processor, issue the following command:

```
GET CLI CFG FOR SECTION COMMON
```

For example, the following command issued from the command line processor updates the `db2cli.ini` file and enables the JDBC tracing facility:

```
UPDATE CLI CFG FOR SECTION COMMON USING jdbctrace 1
```

DB2 *Note*

Tracing a CLI/JDBC application will slow down the application's performance considerably. Also, a large amount of data is written to the output trace file and may use up a large amount of disk space.

DB2 CLI Trace Options and the db2cli.ini File

When an application using the DB2 CLI driver begins execution, the driver checks for trace facility options in the `[COMMON]` section of the `db2cli.ini` file. These trace options are specific trace keywords that are set to certain values in the db2cli.ini file under the `[COMMON]` section.

The DB2 CLI trace keywords that can be defined are (see the *DB2 Information Center* for further detail):

- `TRACE=0|1` — enables or disables tracing
- `TRACEFILENAME=0 | <any positive integer>` — specifies how often trace information is written to the DB2 CLI trace log file.
- `TRACEPATHNAME=<fully_qualified_trace_path_name>` — specifies where all DB2 CLI trace information is to be written. There is no default path to which DB2 CLI trace output log files are written, and the path specified must exist at application execution time (the DB2 CLI driver will not create the path).
- `TRACEFLUSH=0 | <any positive integer>` — specifies how often trace information is written to the DB2 CLI trace log file.
- `TRACEREFRESHINTERVAL=0 | <any positive integer>` — any value greater than 0 causes the DB2 CLI trace facility to reread the `TRACE` and `TRACEPIDLIST` keywords from the db2cli.ini file at the specified interval (every n seconds).
- `TRACECOMM=0|1` — enable tracing of communications between the client and server (CLI functions processed completely on the client and server, number of bytes sent and received with the server, and time spent communicating between the client and server).
- `TRACETIMESTAMP=0|1|2|3` — specifies the addition of various timestamp information with trace records.
- `TRACEPIDTID=0|1` — specifies to add process and thread ID information to be included in the trace.
- `TRACEPIDLIST=<no value> | <pid1,pid2, pid3,...>` — restricts which process ID values the CLI traces will generate.
- `TRACETIME=0|1` — specifies to calculate the elapsed time between CLI function calls and returns will be calculated and included in the DB2 CLI trace.
- `TRACESTMTONLY=0|1` — 0 specifies trace information for all DB2 CLI function call swill be written to the DB2 CLI trace log file, 1 specifies only information related to `SQLExecute()` and `SQLExecDirect()`function calls will be written to the log file. This trace option can be useful in determining the number of times a statement is executed in an application.

An example db2cli.ini file trace configuration using these DB2 CLI keywords and values is:

```
[COMMON]
TRACE=1
TRACEFILENAME=\TEMP\CLITRACE.TXT
TRACEFLUSH=1
```

The output form the DB2 CLI trace is a sequence of CLI/ODBC API calls. The following example demonstrates what the ODBC trace output would look like for an unsuccessful connection attempt to a DB2 database.

```
SQLAllocHandle( fHandleType=SQL_HANDLE_ENV, hInput=0:0, phOutput=&12d1d5c )

SQLAllocHandle( phOutput=0:1 )
    <--- SQL_SUCCESS   Time elapsed - +1.000000E-002 seconds

SQLSetEnvAttr( hEnv=0:1, fAttribute=SQL_ATTR_ODBC_VERSION, vParam=2,cbParam=0)
    ---> Time elapsed - +0.000000E+000 seconds

SQLSetEnvAttr( )
    <--- SQL_SUCCESS   Time elapsed - +0.000000E+000 seconds

SQLAllocHandle( fHandleType=SQL_HANDLE_DBC, hInput=0:1, phOutput=&12d1d4c )
    ---> Time elapsed - +0.000000E+000 seconds
SQLAllocHandle( phOutput=0:1 )
    <--- SQL_SUCCESS   Time elapsed - +0.000000E+000 seconds

SQLGetInfo( hDbc=0:1, fInfoType=SQL_DRIVER_ODBC_VER, rgbInfoValue=&12d1e30,
 cbInfoValueMax=12, pcbInfoValue=&128324 )
    ---> Time elapsed - +0.000000E+000 seconds

SQLGetInfo( rgbInfoValue="03.00", pcbInfoValue=5 )
    <--- SQL_SUCCESS   Time elapsed - +0.000000E+000 seconds

SQLDriverConnect( hDbc=0:1, hwnd=11:1402, szConnStrIn="DSN=SAMPLE;", cbConnStrIn=-3,
 szConnStrOut=&12d1e50, cbConnStrOutMax=256, pcbConnStrOut=&129130,
 fDriverCompletion=SQL_DRIVER_COMPLETE_REQUIRED )
    ---> Time elapsed - +0.000000E+000 seconds
( DBMS NAME="DB2/NT", Version="08.01.0000", Fixpack="0x21010104" )
( StmtOut="SET CURRENT DEGREE 'ANY'" )
( COMMIT=0 )

SQLDriverConnect( szConnStrOut="DSN=SAMPLE;UID=baklarz;PWD=******;DB2DEGREE=ANY;
LOBMAXCOLUMNSIZE=1048575;LONGDATACOMPAT=1;DBALIAS=SAMPLE;PATCH1=131072;"
  ,pcbConnStrOut=121 )
    <--- SQL_SUCCESS   Time elapsed - +1.502000E+000 seconds
( DSN="SAMPLE" )
( UID="baklarz" )
( PWD="******" )
( DB2DEGREE="ANY" )
( LOBMAXCOLUMNSIZE="1048575" )
( LONGDATACOMPAT="1" )
( DBALIAS="SAMPLE" )
( PATCH1="131072" )
```

DB2 JDBC Trace Options and the db2cli.ini File

When an application using the DB2 JDBC driver begins execution, the driver also checks for trace facility options in the db2cli.ini file. As with the DB2 CLI trace options, DB2 JDBC trace options are specified as keyword/value pairs located under the [COMMON] section of the db2cli.ini file.

The DB2 JDBC trace keywords that can be defined are:

- `JDBCTRACE=0|1` — enables or disables tracing.
- `JDBCTRACEPATHNAME=<fully_qualified_trace_path_name>` — specifies where all DB2 JDBC trace information is to be written. There is no default path to which DB2 JDBC trace output log files are written, and the path specified must exist at application execution time.
- `JDBCTRACEFLUSH=0 | <any positive integer>` — specifies how often trace information is written to the DB2 JDBC trace log file.

An example `db2cli.ini` file trace configuration using these DB2 JDBC keywords and values is:

```
[COMMON]
JDBCTRACE=1
JDBCTRACEPATHNAME=\TEMP\JDBCTRACE\
JDBCTRACEFLUSH=1
```

Enabling DB2 JDBC tracing does not enable DB2 CLI tracing. Some versions of the DB2 JDBC driver depend on the DB2 CLI driver to access the database. Consequently, Java developers may also want to enable DB2 CLI tracing for additional information on how their applications interact with the database through the various software layers. DB2 JDBC and DB2 CLI trace options are independent of each other and can be specified together in any order under the `[COMMON]` section of the `db2cli.ini` file.

DB2 CLI Driver Trace Versus ODBC Driver Manager Trace

It is important to understand the difference between an ODBC driver manager trace and a DB2 CLI driver trace. An ODBC driver manager trace shows the ODBC function calls made by an ODBC application to the ODBC driver manager. In contrast, a DB2 CLI driver trace shows the function calls made by the ODBC driver manager to the DB2 CLI driver on behalf of the application.

An ODBC driver manager might forward some function calls directly from the application to the DB2 CLI driver. However, the ODBC driver manager might also delay or avoid forwarding some function calls to the driver. The ODBC driver manager may also modify application function arguments or map application functions to other functions before forwarding the call on to the DB2 CLI driver.

Reasons for application function call intervention by the ODBC driver manager include:

- The Microsoft cursor library will map calls such as `SQLExtendedFetch()` to multiple calls to `SQLFetch()` and other supporting functions to achieve the same end result.

- ODBC driver manager connection pooling will usually defer `SQLDisconnect()` requests (or avoid them altogether if the connection gets reused).

For these and other reasons, application developers may find an ODBC driver manager trace to be a useful complement to the DB2 CLI driver trace.

For more information on capturing and interpreting ODBC driver manager traces, refer to the ODBC driver manager documentation. On the Windows platforms, refer to the Microsoft ODBC 3.0 Software Development Kit and Programmer's Reference, also available online at: www.msdn.microsoft.com.

DB2 CLI Driver, DB2 JDBC driver, and DB2 traces

Internally, some versions of the DB2 JDBC driver make use of the DB2 CLI driver for database access. For example, the Java `getConnection()` method may be internally mapped by the DB2 JDBC driver to the DB2 CLI `SQLConnect()` function. As a result, Java developers might find a DB2 CLI trace to be a useful complement to the DB2 JDBC trace.

The DB2 CLI driver makes use of many internal and DB2 specific functions to do its work. These internal and DB2 specific function calls are logged in the DB2 trace. Application developers will not find DB2 traces useful, as they are only meant to assist IBM Service in problem determination and resolution.

DB2 CLI Driver and DB2 JDBC traces and CLI or Java Stored Procedures

On all workstation platforms, the DB2 CLI and DB2 JDBC trace facilities can be used to trace DB2 CLI and DB2 JDBC stored procedures.

Most of the DB2 CLI and DB2 JDBC trace information and instructions mentioned previously is generic and applies to both applications and stored procedures equally. However, unlike applications which are clients of a database server (and typically execute on a machine separate from the database server), stored procedures execute at the database server. Therefore, the following additional steps must be taken when tracing DB2 CLI or DB2 JDBC stored procedures:

DB2 *Note*

Ensure the trace keyword options are specified in the `db2cli.ini` file located at the DB2 server.

If the `TRACEREFRESHINTERVAL` keyword is not set to a positive, non-zero value, ensure all keywords are configured correctly prior to database startup time (that is, when the db2start command is issued). Changing trace settings while the database server is running may have unpredictable results. For example, if the TRACEPATHNAME is changed while the server is running, then the next time a stored procedure is executed, some trace files may be written to the new path, while others are written to the original path. To ensure consistency, restart the server any time a trace keyword other than TRACE or TRACEPIDLIST is modified.

Trouble-shooting Information

Extensive information on problem determination in DB2 can be found in the *DB2 Information Center*. Also, there are a number of readme files, technical hints and tips, as well as online DB2 publications available in the DB2 Technical Library on the World Wide Web. The DB2 Technical Library is located at: www.software.ibm.com/data/db2/library.

Self-Tuning Memory Manager

The previous sections in this chapter discussed different techniques for tuning the database. However, many of these techniques can be time-consuming and require continual revision and analysis by the DBA. Rather than go through many iterations to get the best performance from DB2, it may be more convenient to use the Self-Tuning Memory Manager (STMM) to optimize the database.

STMM was designed to measure and analyze how DB2 database memory was being consumed and dynamically reallocate memory to optimize workload performance. STMM can also manage DB2 memory usage so that it balances its requirements with the operating system, other applications, and other databases (in the same or other instances).

STMM can dynamically and automatically tune the main shared database memory consumers in a DB2 data server. The objects that STMM controls includes:

- Sort heaps (SHEAPTHRES_SHR and SORTHEAP)
- Locking heaps (LOCKLIST and MAXLOCKS)
- Package cache (PCKCACHESZ)
- Buffer pools

The sum of these heaps form the main shared memory working set for the database that is identified by the DATABASE_MEMORY database configuration parameter.

STMM's hands-off online memory tuning requires no database administrator (DBA) intervention. In laboratory settings, STMM arrived at the optimal memory parameters settings for performance in most cases within an hour. This means that a DB2 system can be "expertly tuned" in a very short amount of time.

The STMM feature is turned on by default for any new nonpartitioned database that you create in DB2 9. In a partitioned database environment, STMM is fully supported, but it is not turned on by default.

DB2 *Note*

The SAMPLE database that ships with DB2 9 does not have STMM enabled.

When operational, STMM automatically senses the underlying workload on the data server and tunes the supported memory set based on its need. STMM can adapt quickly to workload shifts by dynamically reallocating memory heaps for optimal performance.

STMM's self-tuning memory algorithms are particularly useful for these situations:

- **When an inexperienced DBA is given a database to tune and does not understand how DB2 uses memory.**

  STMM is well suited for inexperienced DBAs — those who are new to or unfamiliar with the DB2 memory model, or those who are new to a data server's workload characteristics. DBAs can also benefit from STMM in environments in which the server has lots of free memory.

- **When the application workload is unknown so the memory requirements cannot be determined.**

  DBAs often get handed new applications with unknown workload memory requirements. Since STMM is so deeply integrated into the DB2 engine, it is able to sense workload memory requirements and quickly tune the configuration. STMM requires absolutely no DBA interaction once it's turned on.

- **When workloads vary during the day and there isn't the time to react to these changes.**

  DB2 can optimally maintain memory allocations on servers that have dramatically varying memory needs from one hour to the next. STMM constantly reevaluates the memory requirements based on the workload — it can holistically maintain an optimal level of performance for the data server throughout the day's business cycle. STMM can update the memory allocations up to 120 times per hour to ensure that DB2 is optimizing the memory required by the currently running workload.

- **Tuning databases with different size bufferpools.**

  Experienced DBAs often spend a lot of time managing systems with multiple buffer pools and often varying pages sizes. Sometimes it's difficult for a DBA to tune memory when multiple buffer pools are in the database environment, because as the number of buffer pools increases, the number of possible configurations increases exponentially. STMM can transfer memory between buffer pools of varying page sizes, and the DBA can decide which buffer pools STMM should auto-tune and which ones it should ignore. This leaves the DBA free to tune the important buffer pools and leave the less important ones to DB2.

- **Inadequate time for hands-on tuning.**

  A substantial amount of DBA time can be freed up by not getting snapshots of the database's memory allocations and creating and running scripts to capture the performance information. By enabling STMM in a production or test environment, a couple of hours of STMM analysis will result in a good starting configuration that can be further hand-tuned.

STMM is also especially useful for multi-database or multi-instance environments running in Windows or AIX. STMM can share memory among all of the instances and databases to optimize the throughput of the system.

Operating System Memory Management and STMM

On Linux, HP-UX, and Solaris systems, the overall database memory working set (Figure 14–43) is static from DB2's perspective and allocated at startup. Due to the memory management implementation of these operating systems and the way DB2 interacts with them, the total memory working set cannot grow and shrink dynamically without recycling the data server. For this reason, STMM will not be able to interact with the OS to feed its supported heaps or return memory to the OS when it's not needed.

DB2 Note

STMM is still be very useful in these environments because it will auto tune the shared database memory working set.

On Windows and AIX systems, DB2 can allocate and deallocate OS memory at will after startup. This means that in these two environments, STMM can grow and shrink memory segments dynamically as needed after startup.

In Figure 14–43, you can see the subdivision of the database memory is divided into the sort heap, lock list, package cache heap, buffer pools, utility heap, and database heap. As the data server's workload becomes heavier, some of these heaps grow while other heaps are allocated at database startup time and can be changed only using administrative commands. For example, more memory is allocated to the sort heap when running a query that has heavy sorting requirements or that is performing a hash join. The exception to this rule is for the buffer pool and lock list heaps; DB2 allocates all the defined memory to these heaps at startup for performance reasons.

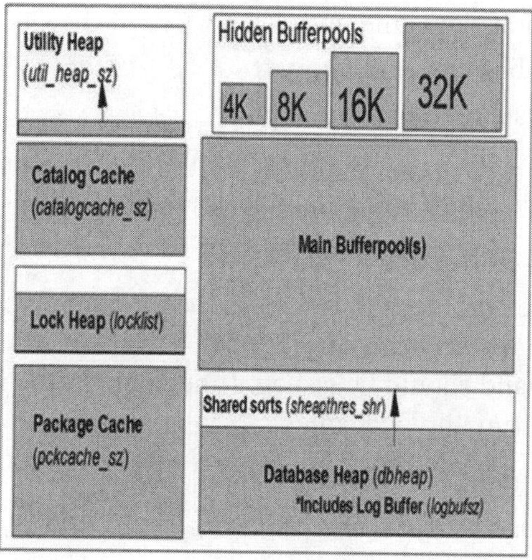

Figure 14–43 *DB2 memory*

Memory to most of the heaps in Figure 14–43 is allocated on an as-needed basis and is delivered to these heaps from the working memory set. The size of the database heaps are controlled by configuration parameters.

To track the memory allocation inside the database shared memory and memory working sets, the `db2mtrk` utility can be used (Figure 14–44):

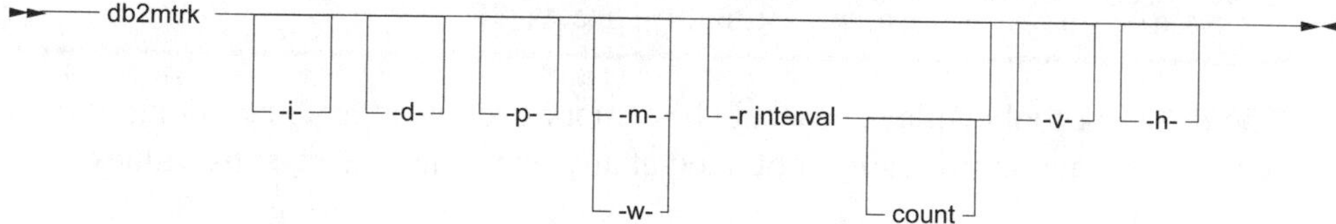

Figure 14–44 *DB2MTRK command*

This command displays the following memory pool allocation information:

- Current size
- Maximum size (hard limit)
- Largest size (high water mark)

- Type (identifier indicating function for which memory will be used)
- Agent who allocated pool (only if the pool is private)

The parameters of the DB2MTRK command are:

- -i — Show instance level memory
- -d — Show database level memory
- -p — Show private memory
- -m — Show maximum values for each pool
- -w — Show high watermark values for each pool
- -r interval *count* — Repeat mode

  The repeat mode continues to report on the memory every "interval" number of seconds. The count parameter is optional, and if specified indicates how many times the command should be issued. If no count value is supplied, the utility will continue to run until cancelled.
- -v — Verbose output.
- -h — Show help screen.

  If you specify -h, only the help screen appears. No other information is displayed.

For instance the db2mtrk -d command will show the current database memory usage. In this example, only the SAMPLE database was active:

```
Tracking Memory on: 2007/04/14 at 15:40:51
Memory for database: SAMPLE
   utilh      pckcacheh catcacheh bph (1)     bph (S32K) bph (S16K) bph (S8K)
   64.0K      128.0K    64.0K     1.2M        704.0K     448.0K     320.0K

   bph (S4K) shsorth    lockh     dbh         other
    256.0K     0         320.0K    4.3M        128.0K
```

The db2mtrk tool displays how much memory each heap is using, along with current values, maximum values obtained at any one time, and starting values.

STMM Example

The following example demonstrates the the dramatic impact that STMM can have on a workload. An application with the following specification was run against an untuned DB2 database:

- 370 client connections
- static OLTP-like workload
- 2TB database

- 128GB of RAM
- 13 buffer pools, each with the DB2 default size of 1,000 pages

The results of STMM tuning are shown in Figure 14–45.

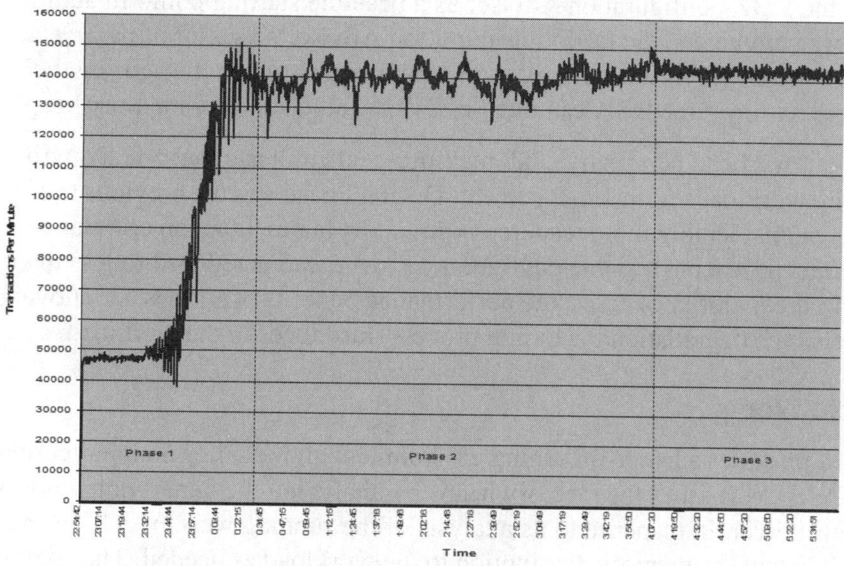

Figure 14–45 *STMM managing buffer pools*

There are three distinct phases of tuning that this application goes through:

1. Initial Tuning

   During Phase 1 the application produced about 47,000 transactions per minute (tpm). STMM delivered a dramatic performance increase as it allocated additional memory to the bufferpools and performance nearly tripled to about 140,000 tpm.

2. Incremental Tuning

   In Phase 2, STMM continues to run, but extends the time between its sleep and wake periods since the performance demands weren't as extreme as those in Phase 1. During Phase 2, STMM is profiling the application as it continues to tune the data server by adjusting the various heap sizes.

3. Stable Performance

   In Phase 3, performance had reached a stable 143,000 tpm. The variance of the performance has stabilized (illustrated by the straight line). STMM took time to learn and observe the workload to determine the optimal configuration after addressing the immediate performance problems.

The test illustrates STMMs capability of taking a default configuration and optimizing it within hours of operation. While most DBAs will have a reasonable configuration for the database to start with, STMM can help optimize the configuration even further in a very short period of time. DBAs should initially tune their servers using the DB2 Configuration Advisor as a baseline starting point. In addition to memory parameters, the DB2 Configuration Advisor sets a lot of parameters that aren't as sensitive as the memory tuning parameters. After configuring the initial memory settings, the DBA can then let STMM auto-tune the memory heaps.

From an overhead perspective, lab measurements indicate that STMM will impact existing workloads from 1 to 5 percent. During Phase 1 in the previous test, STMM is using considerably more resources while it trying to attain an optimal configuration. Once it reaches a stable configuration, overhead is reduced to less than 1 percent. In the majority of cases, the performance benefits of STMM far outweigh any performance degradation the tuning process introduces to the workload.

How STMM Works

STMM provides a hands-off tuning environment and requires no intervention from a DBA. STMM tunes the memory heaps by analyzing the underlying workload on the data server. In response to its analysis of the running workload, STMM can quickly adapt the memory distribution to the workload as needed. The analysis performed by STMM is iterative; STMM will determine its "wake-up" (when it collects statistics and performs analysis) and "sleep" (when it's dormant) cycles depending on results of the analysis.

By default, the STMM tuning interval occurs once every 3 minutes. Depending on the outcome of the most recent analysis and the amount of memory needed, STMM can schedule to wake up and rerun analysis from 30 seconds to 10 minutes. If STMM determines that no changes are needed to optimize the system, it may schedule a longer sleep time. In contrast, if STMM finds that it needs to allocate a large amount of memory to a heap, it may schedule a shorter sleep time.

The total amount of memory that STMM can allocate or deallocate from any heap is limited to 50 percent increases and 20 percent decreases. This form of dampening control pevents huge fluctuations in performance when STMM is running.

STMM can operate in three different modes, depending on the value of the `DATABASE_MEMORY` configuration parameter:

- `DATABASE_MEMORY=AUTOMATIC`

  In this mode, DB2 will decide how much memory to allocate to the DB2 database shared memory region and how much to leave to the operating system. STMM takes memory from and returns it to the OS on an "as needed" basis. DB2 will try to maintain some amount of free physical memory on the server at all times. If more free memory exists and is available on the server, DB2 will consume more memory as long as it finds a good use for it.

Using the `AUTOMATIC` setting addresses issues that DBAs have when they don't know how much memory to allocate to a database.

DB2 *Note*

`DATABASE_MEMORY=AUTOMATIC` mode is supported only for the AIX and Windows operating systems. If you try to set this parameter to `AUTOMATIC` on Linux, HP-UX, or Solaris, you will receive an error message.

- `DATABASE_MEMORY=X` (4KB pages)

  The value assigned to the `DATABASE_MEMORY` parameter gives DB2 the maximum amount of memory that will be allocated to the shared database memory set. In this mode, STMM still dynamically tunes the supported memory heaps used by DB2, but the memory set is constant. DB2 will not be able to balance memory usage with other DB2 data serves on the same machine.

- `DATABASE_MEMORY=COMPUTED`

  In DB2 8, setting `DATABASE_MEMORY=AUTOMATIC` meant that DB2 would aggregate all of the memory allocations for the heaps and set the `DATABASE_MEMORY` to this calculated value. In DB2 9, the `AUTOMATIC` setting in DB2 8 has been renamed to `COMPUTED`. During the migration of a DB2 8 database to DB2 9, the the `AUTOMATIC` keyword will be changed to `COMPUTED`.

Figure 14–46 illustrates the various memory heaps that are supported by STMM, including multiple buffer pools. DB2 can pass memory in either mode of operation from any of these heaps to another heap at any point in time. The arrows in the figure represent the potential movement of memory between the different memory consumers.

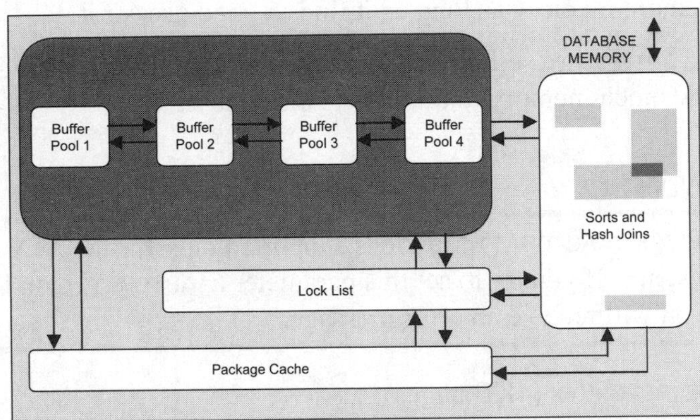

Figure 14–46 *Memory Heaps*

In DB2 9, the default is for all buffer pools to be managed by STMM. Note that buffer pools are the only memory heaps that can have multiple instances in a database. DB2 9 takes advantage of this because it has the unique ability to trade memory between these buffer pools, even if they use different memory page sizes. For example, if DB2 needs to move memory from an 8KB-based buffer pool to a 4KB-based buffer pool, it will do so with a single transfer that is split into two 4KB pages.

DB2 9 provides DBAs with a granular control mechanism over what heaps are tuned by STMM. The `ALTER BUFFERPOOL` can specify with buffer pools that you want STMM to manage for you and those that you want to manage yourself.

Using STMM in DB2 9

All of the memory parameters that STMM is able to manage in DB2 9 now have new optional settings of `AUTOMATIC` and `MANUAL`, in addition to the traditional ability to specify a static value. By default, all of the configuration parameters required to enable STMM are set to `ON` and the corresponding memory heaps are set to `AUTOMATIC` (for nonpartitioned databases).

If a database is being migrated to DB2 9, or an existing database being enabled for STMM, the following steps need to be taken:

- Turn on STMM
- Detemine the amount of memory available for STMM
- Configure non-participating Heaps

Turn On STMM

In order to turn on STMM, the `SELF_TUNING_MEM` parameter must be set to `ON`.

The easiest way to see the setting of this parameter is to use the `GET DATABASE CONFIGURATION FOR <DATABASE_NAME>` command. To update the parameter, use the following command:

```
UPDATE DATABASE CONFIGURATION FOR <database_name>
  USING SELF_TUNING_MEM ON
```

You can also use the Control Center to manage STMM, as shown in Figure 14–47.

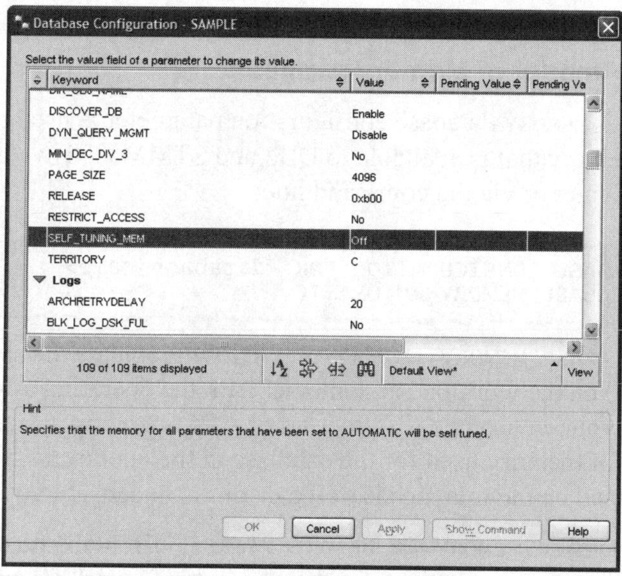

Figure 14–47 *Enabling STMM*

The `SELF_TUNING_MEM` parameter is dynamic, so you can turn STMM on and off at any time.

In DB2 9, all of the STMM parameters are enabled at the database level. However, the configuration of the `SHEAPTHRES` heap in DB2 8 takes place at the instance level. For this reason, depending on the way you set this parameter, STMM will behave differently.

- If `SHEAPTHRES` is greater than 0, DB2 will use the DB2 8.2 sort memory mode in that some sort memory consumers will use private memory and others will use shared memory. If you set `SHEAPTHRES` greater than 0, STMM will not be able to tune the sort heap.

- If SHEAPTHRES=0, the new DB2 9 memory model is used. This is the default for all new instances. Using this memory model, all of the sort memory consumers will use shared memory all the time.

The SHEAPTHRES database manager configuration parameter is not dynamic, so changing its setting will require that you recycle the database instance.

DB2 Note

If you migrate an existing DB2 8 instance, you must manually change this parameter since the underlying policy of a migration between versions of DB2 is not to change the operating environment.

Define the Amount of Memory Available

The DATABASE_MEMORY database configuration parameter is used to define the amount of memory that is available to DB2 and STMM. This value can be set in the Control Center or via the command line:

```
UPDATE DATABASE CONFIGURATION FOR <database_name>
  USING DATABASE_MEMORY AUTOMATIC
```

If you set DATABASE_MEMORY=AUTOMATIC, DB2 will regulate the amount of memory it needs based on the workload and interact with the operating system and within itself to tune your environment (Windows or AIX operating systems only). The total amount of memory used for the database in this mode can grow and shrink over time, based on the total needs of the database in consideration of the server.

If you set DATABASE_MEMORY=<# OF 4KB PAGES>, DB2 will consume this amount of memory. The memory settings for the entire shared working set will be static and DB2 will not be able to grant or take memory from the operating system.

Configure Each Heap Supported by STMM

Each supported memory parameter is set to AUTOMATIC by default. If you do not want STMM to tune certain memory parameters, or if there are specific bufferpools that should not be modified, the value should be set to MANUAL. Setting the value to MANUAL has the effect of disabling STMM for that particular heap and assigning it the last value used by STMM. The other alternative would be to set the value explicitly. The GET DATABASE CONFIGURATION command will display the actual memory settings for the objects rather than the MANUAL keyword.

The enablement of buffer pools for STMM is a little different from that of the memory heaps discussed thus far, since no configuration parameters are associated with these objects. To enable a buffer pool for STMM, you need to use the AUTOMATIC setting for the SIZE parameter.

You can create buffer pools to be managed by STMM or alter existing pools. For example, you can change the IBMDEFAULTBP buffer pool such that STMM manages its memory as follows:

```
ALTER BUFFERPOOL IBMDEFAULTBP SIZE AUTOMATIC
```

If you wanted to create a new buffer pool where STMM would manage its memory, use this:

```
CREATE BUFFERPOOL <bufferpool_name> SIZE AUTOMATIC
```

Buffer pools can be enabled for STMM using the IMMEDIATE or DEFERRED keyword. If you use the IMMEDIATE keyword, the memory request will take place immediately, while DEFERRED will delay the change until the next time the database is recycled.

DBAs should be aware of a few considerations if they intend to run a mix of AUTOMATIC and MANUAL memory heaps:

- If you set DATABASE_MEMORY=<# OF 4KB PAGES>, you need to ensure that there are at least two of the supported heaps set to AUTOMATIC — otherwise STMM will not be able transfer memory from one heap to another.
- In an environment with a mix of memory heaps set to AUTOMATIC and specified values, STMM will try to maintain the 20 percent overflow buffer and use the rest of the free memory for the heaps set to AUTOMATIC.
- DBAs should also note that the LOCKLIST and MAXLOCKS heaps are tuned together; therefore, when LOCKLIST=AUTOMATIC, then MAXLOCKS=AUTOMATIC. Because of this relationship, DB2 will not allow you to set LOCKLIST=<# OF 4KB PAGES> and MAXLOCK=AUTOMATIC.

Disabling STMM

STMM can be turned off in two ways:

- Set SELF_TUNING_MEM=OFF

  This parameter is dynamic, the so effects will be immediate when you initiate this change. When STMM is disabled using this approach, all of the settings for STMM remain in system. Setting SELF_TUNING_MEM=ON will enable STMM with the previous configuration.

- Set heap size to MANUAL

  Any of the STMM supported heap parameters can be set to MANUAL or to a specific numeric value. This will have the effect of STMM no longer tuning that heap. In most cases, this change can performed dynamically. In circumstances for which a heap cannot be dynamically disabled, it will perform a deferred change and the output of the GET DATABASE CONFIGURATION FOR <DATABASE_NAME> will inform you of the pending change.

Monitoring STMM

Once STMM tuning has started, you may want to see what values STMM has determined as optimal for each heap. You can use the GET DATABASE CONFIGURATION FOR <DATABASE_NAME> SHOW DETAIL command to see these values. An example of this output is shown in Figure 14–48.

```
       Database Configuration for Database kbqdb
Description                                     Parameter  Current Value     Delayed Value
--------------------------------------------------------------------------------------------
Database configuration release level                       = 0x0b00
Database release level                                     = 0x0b00

Database territory                                         = US
Database code page                                         = 1252
Database code set                                          = IBM-1252
Database country/region code                               = 1
Database collating sequence                                = UNIQUE          UNIQUE
Alternate collating sequence              (ALT_COLLATE) =
Database page size                                         = 4096            4096

Dynamic SQL Query management           (DYN_QUERY_MGMT) = DISABLE            DISABLE

Discovery support for this database       (DISCOVER_DB) = ENABLE             ENABLE

Restrict access                                            = NO
Default query optimization class         (DFT_QUERYOPT) = 5                  5
Degree of parallelism                      (DFT_DEGREE) = 1                  1
Continue upon arithmetic exceptions   (DFT_SQLMATHWARN) = NO                 NO
Default refresh age                   (DFT_REFRESH_AGE) = 0                  0
Default maintained table types for opt (DFT_MTTB_TYPES) = SYSTEM             SYSTEM
Number of frequent values retained     (NUM_FREQVALUES) = 10                 10
Number of quantiles retained            (NUM_QUANTILES) = 20                 20

Backup pending                                             = NO

Database is consistent                                     = YES
Rollforward pending                                        = NO
Restore pending                                            = NO

Multi-page file allocation enabled                         = YES

Log retain for recovery status                             = NO
User exit for logging status                               = NO

Self tuning memory                    (SELF_TUNING_MEM) = ON (Active)        ON
Size of database shared memory (4KB)  (DATABASE_MEMORY) = AUTO(63312)        AUTO(63312)
Database memory threshold               (DB_MEM_THRESH) = 10                 10
Max storage for lock list (4KB)              (LOCKLIST) = AUTO(14701)        AUTO(14701)
Percent. of lock lists per application       (MAXLOCKS) = AUTO(98)           AUTO(98)
Package cache size (4KB)                   (PCKCACHESZ) = AUTO(767)          AUTO(767)
Sort heap thres for shared sorts (4KB) (SHEAPTHRES_SHR) = AUTO(269)          AUTO(269)
Sort list heap (4KB)                         (SORTHEAP) = AUTO(53)           AUTO(53)
```

Figure 14–48 *STMM Details*

In addition to the information found in the database configuration, STMM also places diagnostic information in the `DB2DIAG.LOG` file and in a special `STMM.#.LOG` file. The STMM log file is updated at each interval and includes diagnostic information, configuration updates, heap allocations, and other information. If the database were to crash, or shutdown, STMM knows to start DB2 with the last used memory configuration settings.

The STMM log is located in the `sqllib\<instance_name>\stmmLog` directory in Windows and in the `sqllib/db2/db2dump/stmmLog` directory in UNIX and Linux. The STMM log file can contain a large amount of information, so DB2 has a self-pruning algorithm that prevents more than five, 10MB STMM log files from existing at a time. When this threshold is reached, DB2 will delete the first log file in the chain and create a new one for additional logging.

Summary

DB2 agents are represented by threads in Windows and processes in Linux and UNIX operating environments. While the DB2 process model usually has one coordinating agent represent a client or application connection to DB2, the connection concentrator improves performance by allowing multiple client connections to be handled by each coordinating agent. Important database manager and database configuration parameters were reviewed and their effect on performance.

The Health Center is part of IBM's autonomic computing strategy to have complex systems able to self-manage and self-tune itself. Health indicators are used by the Health Monitor to evaluate specific aspects of database manager or database performance. Health indicators measure either a finite set of distinct states or a continuous range of values to determine whether the state is healthy or unhealthy. If the change in the state is determined to be unhealthy, an alert can be issued in response. Health Monitor information can be accessed through the Health Center, Web Health Center, the Command Line Processor, or APIs.

There are two types of monitors available to analyze database activity, the Snapshot and Event Monitor. The Snapshot Monitor provides point-in-time information regarding resource usage. Many of the elements returned from a snapshot are counters and high-water marks. An Event Monitor is defined through the Control Center or by using a DDL statement. Once activated, the monitored events can be written to SQL table, a file, or to a named pipe.

The DB2 optimizer is one of the most advanced in the relational database industry. The optimizer will generate an access plan during query compilation. Access plans are stored in the system catalog tables for static SQL applications. Access plans for dynamic SQL statements are generated at query execution time and stored in memory.

To gain an understanding of the access plan (strategy) chosen by the DB2 optimizer, the Explain Facility may be used. The Explain Facility will populate relational tables with detailed information for the SQL statements. These tables can then be queried to determine the plan information regarding index usage and other database resources. There is a snapshot column in the explain tables that is used to store a graphical representation of the access plan. This graphical version of the plan can be examined using Visual Explain.

Diagnostics and problem determination information is provided in DB2. This information comes in the form of SQLCODE, and SQLSTATE codes, CLI/JDBC and DB2 traces, and other First Failure Data Capture (FFDC) information.

Finally, the Self-tuning Memory Manager (STMM) can help save time and effort when tuning a DB2 database. Using this feature as the first step in tuning a database will ensure an optimized configuration in the quickest amount of time.

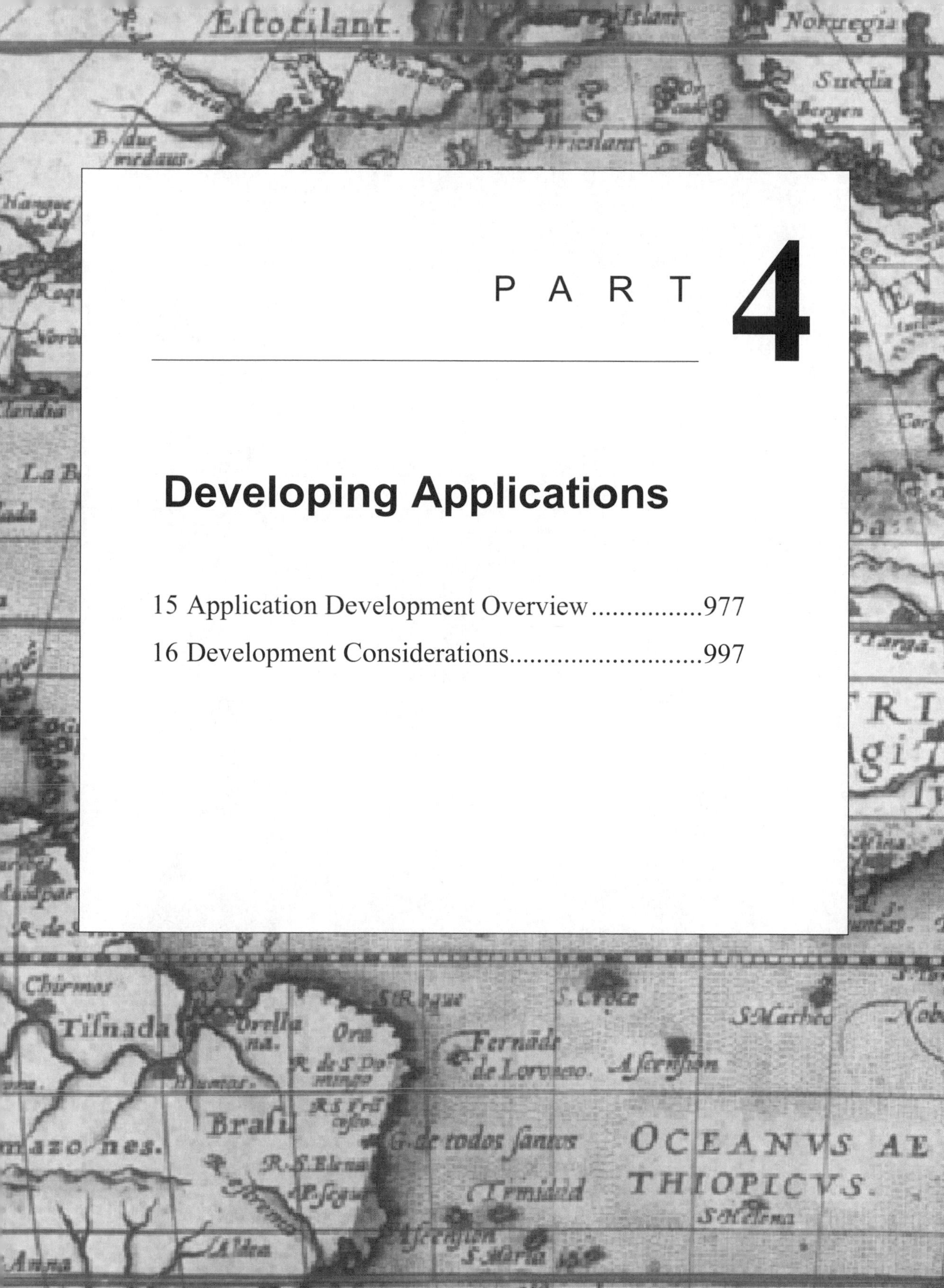

PART 4

Developing Applications

CHAPTER 15

Application Development Overview

- DEVELOPMENT ENVIRONMENT
- PROGRAMMING INTERFACES

Applications represent the interface to the database, and as a DB2 Database administrator, you may have to provide support to developers when they write applications that access the database. DB2 does not have its own programming language. Instead, it allows data to be manipulated using interfaces that pass SQL statements. It also provides an Application Programming Interface for managing and administering the database.

A DB2 application can perform specific queries or process well-defined transactions. An application that performs transaction processing is sometimes referred to as an Online Transaction Processing (OLTP) application. An application that performs ad hoc queries is sometimes referred to as a Decision Support System (DSS) or Online Analytical Processing (OLAP) application. DB2 can be used as the data server for both types of applications.

In this chapter, we will explore the DB2 application development environment, become familiar with many of the options available for developing DB2 applications, and examine some common features of DB2 applications.

DB2 Application Development Environment

You can develop applications at a DB2 server or a client. You can develop and test applications that run on one operating system and access databases on the same or a different operating system. For example, you can create an application that runs on the Windows operating system but accesses a database on a UNIX platform such as AIX. Once you have developed your applications, you can distribute them to other systems, where they can be executed using the DB2 runtime client component that is included in all DB2 products.

To supplement or extend client applications, DB2 programming can also involve development of components that run on the server either as parts of the database manager or as separate modules.

Software Requirements

Before developing applications for DB2, the following products need to be installed and configured:

- Non-DB2 application development utilities, including a compiler or interpreter
- DB2 installed locally or remotely
- DB2 Client
- IBM Database Enterprise Developer Edition (optional)
- Application Development Framework (optional)

The DB2 client is included as part of the DB2 installation. This client contains a set of drivers that support all the programming languages supported in DB2.

Non-DB2 Application Development Utilities

DB2 allows for application development through a variety of programming languages and third-party application development tools. You must ensure that the proper programming tools and products are installed on each of the development machines. For example, if you are planning to develop an application using a programming language like C, C++, COBOL, or FORTRAN, you need to have the appropriate compilers for creating application modules such as executables and libraries. For Java programs, you need the Java Development Kit (JDK). Third-party or ODBC application development environments such as Lotus Notes and Microsoft Visual Basic have their own requirements.

DB2 Note

FORTRAN and REXX support have been stabilized since DB2 Universal Database Version 5.2.

Because each compiler or development tool has different attributes, you may need to configure it for use with DB2. Instructions for setting up development tools and a list of supported compilers is provided in the *DB2 Application Development Guide: Getting Started with Database Application Development.*

DB2 Database

The data server can either be installed on the same system where the application is being developed or on a remote machine. Generally, if the database is to be accessed by a single developer, it may as well reside on the same system where the application is being developed. When many developers need to access a database, a common data server may be more suitable.

Most of the time, the database location for development purposes is chosen based on convenience and may not be its final location. This is because the location and platform of the data server has little influence over the application development process on the client. For example, if the database were moved from a development platform of DB2 on Windows XP to a production platform of DB2 on AIX, it is unlikely that the application would require any changes. However, you may need to bind the application to the new database. We will discuss the bind process in more detail later.

DB2 provides a sample database that you require for running the supplied sample programs. The sample database can be created using the `db2sampl` command or through the First Steps tool found in the DB2 folder. You may use the sample database for development purposes or choose to create a customized database. A database can be created using the Control Center, Command Center, Command Line Processor (CLP) or a script. A database can only be created by a user with `SYSADM` or `SYSCTRL` privileges. Upon creating the database, the user who created the database will be the `DBADM` (by default). This user can then grant privileges to other users who can create database objects and populate them with data to be used for development purposes.

Once you have successfully created a database and all of its objects, you should verify that your environment has been set up properly by establishing a connection to the database. You can test the connection to the database using the DB2 CLP, Command Center, Configuration Assistant, or the Control Center.

DB2 Clients

A DB2 client provides the runtime environment that's required for DB2 applications to access a data server's resources. For example, a DB2 client contains the communications infrastructure to communicate with remote data servers. You can also execute SQL, bind packages, use data manipulation utilities (`IMPORT`, `LOAD`, `EXPORT`, and so on), catalog remote nodes and databases, and more using a DB2 client. In fact, most of the database administration tasks DBAs perform are typically done from a DB2 client workstation.

There are two different types of client:

- **DB2 Runtime Client** — Provides the minimum *client* footprint (about 20–30 MB) to support connectivity to DB2 9 data servers (the exception to this is if you choose to support communication via specific API drivers, covered later in this section). When you install a DB2 Runtime Client, you install a set of drivers that support all the programming languages supported in DB2 9, some of which include: ADO.NET, ADO, OLE DB, ODBC, JDBC, SQLJ, static SQL, and more.
- **DB2 Client** — Includes all the functions found in the DB2 Runtime Client *plus* tools for client-server configuration, and database administration, as well as application development files that accelerate application development such as header files, samples, and more. For example, this client includes the Configuration Assistant which provides graphical tool for client administration and connectivity. A DB2 Client's footprint is directly correlated to the components you select to install and can take between 200 MB — 800 MB depending on the options you select. The process to install a DB2 Client is very similar to that of a DB2 data server.

For independent software vendors (ISVs) and enterprises that want to set up connectivity between client workstations and DB2 data servers with minimal disk footprint, they can alternatively use a standalone *driver.* A driver can be used to set up connectivity using a specific API; for example, there's a driver for JDBC/SQLJ connections and one for ODBC/CLI connections.

Drivers are sometimes preferred over DB2 clients since they have a small footprint (for example, the IBM Driver for JDBC and SQLJ is about 2 MB) and therefore are easily embedded within an application. They also come with royalty-free distribution licenses for this very purpose.

The main difference between a DB2 Runtime Client and a driver is that a DB2 Runtime Client supports all the connectivity APIs supported by DB2 9, whereas a driver only supports the API for which it was created.

For example, as of the time this book was written, there was no specific driver for .NET applications and therefore to connect an application written using the ADO.NET API to a DB2 data server, you need to install one of the DB2 clients.

The drivers available in DB2 9 are:

- **IBM Driver for JDBC and SQLJ** — Used to support Java-based connectivity to a DB2 data server. This driver is about 2 MB in size and can easily be embedded within your application. This driver is common between the version of DB2 that runs on the distributed platforms and DB2 for z/OS; however; in other words, it's the same code. A DB2 Connect license enables this driver to connect to DB2 for i5/OS and DB2 for z/OS data sources
- **IBM Driver for ODBC and CLI** — Used to support open database connectivity (ODBC) or call level interface (CLI) connectivity to a DB2 9 data server (essentially the same concept as the IBM Driver for JDBC and SQLJ for Java, only this driver is for ODBC and CLI connections). This driver is about 2 MB in size and can easily be embedded within your application. If you want to use this driver to connect to a DB2 for z/OS or DB2 i5/OS data server, you need to additionally license the DB2 Connect software.

You can use a DB2 client to connect to a DB2 9 or DB2 8 data server. If you are connecting to a DB2 8 data server you must be aware of some of the functions and SQL you try to execute on this server. If it was introduced in DB2 9, it won't obviously work on a DB2 8 server. For the most part, we strongly recommend running your DB2 data servers and DB2 clients at the same version level, and ideally at the same maintenance level.

IBM Database Enterprise Developer Edition

The client that is included with the DB2 product only supports development of applications on the particular platform the product was purchased for. For instance, a DB2 for Windows server would only contain libraries and utilities that support development of applications on the Windows platform. If you needed support for pre-compiled applications on an AIX server, then the IBM Database Enterprise Developer Edition would be required.

The IBM Database Enterprise Developer Edition product enables an application developer to design, build, and prototype applications for deployment on any of the IBM Information Management client or server platforms. Using the software that comes with this product, you can develop and test applications that run on one operating system and access databases on the same or on a different operating system. For example, you can create an application that runs on a Windows operating system but accesses a database on a UNIX platform such as AIX.

Application Development Framework

The following integrated development environments and other development tools facilitate DB2 database application development:

- IBM integrated database application development environments
  - DB2 Developer Workbench
  - Rational Application Developer
  - Rational Application Architect
- Database application plug-ins for integrated development environments
  - IBM Database Add-ins for Visual Studio 2005
- Tools for developing SQL Statements
  - SQL Assist Wizard
  - SQL Builder
  - SQL Editor
  - Command line processor
- Database application monitoring and performance tuning tools
  - Event monitors
  - Explain tools
  - CLI/ODBC/JDBC Static Profiling
- Tools for developing web applications
  - WebSphere Studio Application Developer
  - Rational Web Developer
  - DB2 Alphablox®

DB2 Programming Interfaces

There are many programming methods available to a DB2 application developer. These include:

- Embedded SQL — Static and dynamic
- Call Level Interface (CLI), Open Database Connectivity (ODBC)
- Java Interfaces — JDBC, SQLJ
- Native DB2 Application Programming Interfaces (APIs)
- Microsoft Data Objects — ADO .NET, OLE DB .NET, ODBC .NET, DB2 .NET
- Perl DBI, PHP, Ruby
- Other interfaces, third-party, and ODBC end-user tools

Why are there so many different programming methods? Each programming method has its unique advantages. We will examine each of the methods and provide examples of their advantages and disadvantages.

Embedded SQL

SQL (Structured Query Language) is the database interface language used to access and manipulate data in DB2 databases. You can embed SQL statements in your applications, enabling them to perform any task supported by SQL, such as retrieving or storing data.

An application in which you embed SQL statements is called a host program. A programming language that you compile, and in which you embed SQL statements, is called a host language. The program and language are defined this way because they host or accommodate SQL statements. Using DB2, you can code your embedded SQL applications in the C/C++, COBOL, FORTRAN, and Java (SQLJ) programming languages.

There are two types of embedded SQL statements: static and dynamic. These are discussed in the following sections.

Static Embedded SQL

Static SQL statements are ones in which the SQL statement type and the database objects accessed by the statement, such as column names, are known prior to running the application. The only unknowns are the data values the statement is searching for or modifying. The database objects being accessed must exist when a static embedded application module is bound to the database.

The development process involves the combination of SQL with a third-generation programming language. When the embedded SQL program is executed, it uses predefined SQL statements that have been bound to the database as application packages. Thus, the access plan to data is retained in the database in a ready-to-execute package.

There are many performance benefits to having ready-to-execute database logic stored within the database. Static embedded SQL programs have the least runtime overhead of all the DB2 programming methods and execute faster. The package is in a form that is understood by the data server. However, as you might have guessed already, this method of developing applications is not the most flexible because every SQL statement that the end user executes needs to be known and understood during the development process.

The transactions are grouped into packages and stored in the database. The SQL statements are embedded within programming modules. The programming modules, which contain embedded SQL statements, must be precompiled. The modified programming modules, created by the precompiler, are then compiled and linked to create the application. During the precompile phase, the SQL statements are analyzed and packages are created. Figure 15–1 illustrates these various steps.

We will examine all of the steps for creating static embedded DB2 applications in the next chapter.

Static applications for DB2 can be coded using C/C++, Java, COBOL, or FORTRAN. DB2 provides support for static SQL statements in Java programs using the SQLJ (Embedded SQL for Java) standard.

Generally, static statements are well suited for high-performance applications with predefined transactions. A reservation system is a good example of such an application.

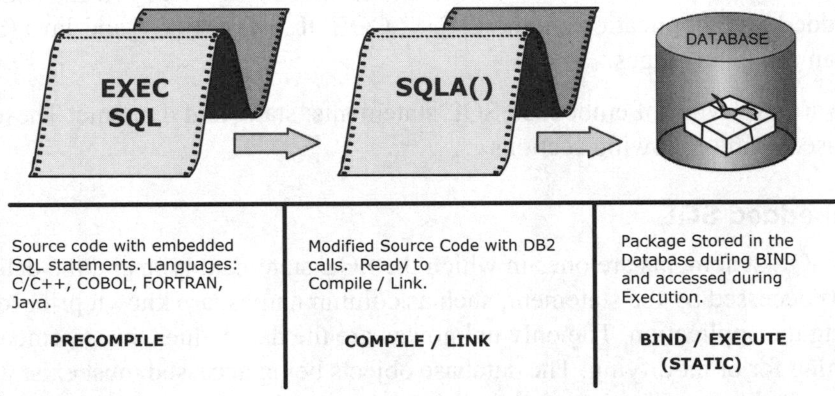
EXEC
SQL
SQLA()
DATABASE
Source code with embedded SQL statements. Languages: C/C++, COBOL, FORTRAN, Java.
PRECOMPILE
Modified Source Code with DB2 calls. Ready to Compile / Link.
COMPILE / LINK
Package Stored in the Database during BIND and accessed during Execution.
BIND / EXECUTE (STATIC)

Figure 15–1 *SQL statements prepared during application development*

Advantages

- Ready-to-use packages may be optimal for faster execution
- Use programming skills in COBOL, C/C++, or FORTRAN

Disadvantages

- Must define SQL statements during development
- Requires precompiling

Dynamic Embedded SQL

Dynamic SQL statements are those statements that your application builds and executes at runtime. An interactive application that prompts the end-user for key parts of an SQL statement, such as the names of the tables and columns to be searched, is a good example of dynamic SQL. The application builds the SQL statement while it is running and then submits the statement for processing.

Dynamic embedded SQL, as shown in Figure 15–2, still requires the precompile, compile, and link phases of application development. The binding or selection of the most effective data access plan is performed at program execution time, as the SQL statements are *dynamically prepared.* Choosing the access path at program execution time has some advantages and some drawbacks.

The database objects being accessed must exist when a static embedded application module is bound to the database. Dynamic embedded SQL modules do not require that these database objects exist when the application is precompiled. However, the database objects must exist at runtime.

An embedded static SQL programming module will have its data access method determined during the static bind phase, using the database statistics available at bind time. An embedded dynamic SQL programming module will have its data access method determined during the statement preparation and will utilize the database statistics available at query execution time.

Therefore, there is no need to rebind dynamic embedded SQL programming modules to the database following a collection of database statistics. The database statistics are collected when the RUNSTATS command is issued. The results are stored in the system catalog tables. There is, of course, a query execution time overhead to choose the access path, since each dynamically prepared SQL statement must be optimized.

In Figure 15–2, the development steps for embedded dynamic SQL program modules are shown. Using embedded dynamic SQL statements does not remove the precompile phase of development, but it does provide the execution of dynamic SQL statements.

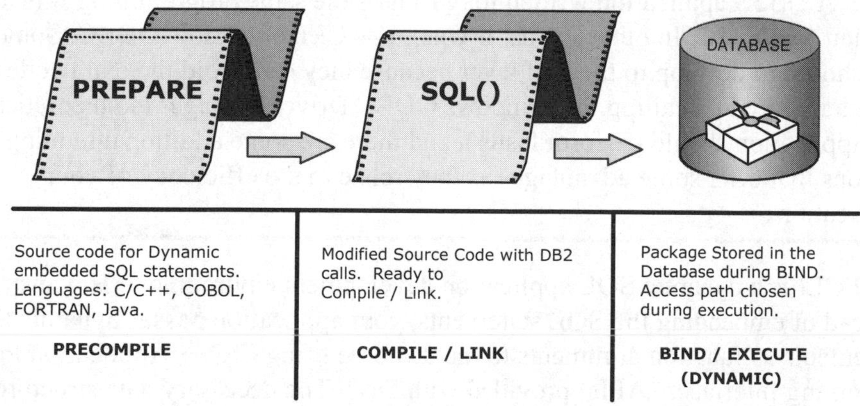
PREPARE
SQL()
DATABASE
Source code for Dynamic embedded SQL statements. Languages: C/C++, COBOL, FORTRAN, Java.
PRECOMPILE
Modified Source Code with DB2 calls. Ready to Compile / Link.
COMPILE / LINK
Package Stored in the Database during BIND. Access path chosen during execution.
BIND / EXECUTE (DYNAMIC)

Figure 15–2 *SQL statements prepared during application execution*

Generally, dynamic SQL statements are well suited for applications that run against a rapidly changing database where transactions need to be specified at runtime. An interactive query interface is a good example of such an application.

Advantages

- Current database statistics are used for each SQL statement.
- Database objects do not have to exist before runtime.
- They are more flexible than static SQL statements.

Disadvantages

- Since SQL statements are optimized at runtime, they may take more time to execute.

Call Level Interface and ODBC

The DB2 Call Level Interface (CLI) is a programming interface that your C and C++ applications can use to access DB2 databases. DB2 CLI is based on the Microsoft Open Database Connectivity Standard (ODBC) specification and the X/Open and ISO Call Level Interface standards. Because DB2 CLI is based on industry standards, application programmers who are already familiar with these database interfaces may benefit from a shorter learning curve. Many ODBC applications can be used with DB2 without any modifications. Likewise, a CLI application is easily ported to other data servers.

DB2 *Note*

Note: A DB2 9 application written for CLI uses the same programming skill as one written for ODBC. In other words, if you know CLI, you know ODBC. Some people choose to develop to the CLI layer because they can avoid the extra code path length required by calling the Windows ODBC Driver Manager (so theoretically the application should perform faster), and there are some additional binding options that offer some advantages as they relate to the efficiency of your application.

DB2 CLI is a dynamic SQL application development environment. However, instead of embedding the SQL statements, your application passes dynamic SQL statements as function arguments to the database using C/C++ Application Programming Interfaces (APIs) provided with DB2. The necessary data structures used to communicate between the database and the application are allocated transparently by DB2.

Because the SQL statements are issued through direct API calls, CLI programs are not precompiled. Also, CLI applications use common access packages provided with DB2; hence, there is no need to bind the program modules separately. You only need to bind the DB2 CLI packages once to each database you want to access using any DB2 CLI or ODBC applications on a client.

Many differences exist between developing an embedded SQL application module and developing a CLI module. Since an application is usually composed of a number of program modules, the modules can use different DB2 programming techniques. It can be beneficial to use different DB2 programming interfaces in a single application.

The CLI application development environment is shown in Figure 15–3.

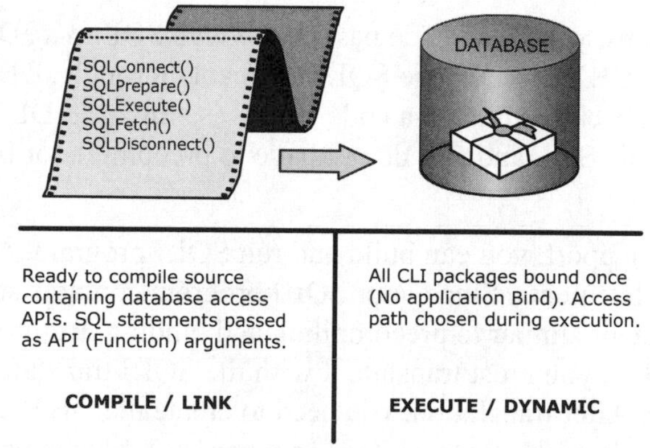

Figure 15–3 *Application development using CLI or ODBC*

Advantages

- Precompiler *not* required
- Binding an application package to the database *not* required
- Current database statistics used
- Can store and retrieve sets of data
- Can use scrollable and updatable cursors
- Easy porting to other database platforms

Disadvantages

- Must have C/C++ programming skills
- Dynamic binding can result in slower query execution

Java Interfaces (JDBC and SQLJ)

DB2 provides support for many different types of Java programs including applets, applications, servlets, and advanced DB2 server-side features. Java programs that access and manipulate DB2 databases can use the Java Database Connectivity (JDBC) API and Embedded SQL for Java (SQLJ) standard. Both of these vendor-neutral SQL interfaces provide data access to your application through standardized Java methods. The greatest benefit of using Java regardless of the database interface is its *write once, run anywhere* capability, allowing the same Java program to be distributed and executed on various operating platforms in a heterogeneous environment without recompiling. And since the two Java database interfaces supported by DB2 are industry open standards, you have the added benefit of using your Java program against a variety of database vendors.

For JDBC programs, your Java code passes *dynamic* SQL to a JDBC driver that comes with DB2. DB2 executes the SQL statements through JDBC APIs and the results are passed back to your Java code. JDBC is similar to DB2 CLI because JDBC uses dynamic SQL and you do not have to precompile or bind a JDBC program.

With DB2 SQLJ support, you can build and run SQLJ programs that contain *static* embedded SQL statements. Since your SQLJ program contains static SQL, you need to perform steps similar to precompiling and binding. Before you can compile an SQLJ source file, you must translate it with the SQLJ translator to create native Java source code. After translation, you need to create the DB2 packages using the DB2 for Java profile customizer (`db2sqljcustomize`). Mechanisms contained within SQLJ rely on JDBC for many tasks like establishing connections.

Choosing between SQLJ and JDBC for your Java program involves many of the same considerations and tradeoffs as for static versus dynamic embedded SQL in other languages (Table 15–1). SQLJ may be beneficial because static SQL can be faster. Java programs containing embedded SQL can also be subjected to static analysis of SQL statements for the purposes of syntax checking, type checking, and schema validation. On the other hand, not all data objects to be accessed may be known before execution, requiring JDBC for dynamic SQL. A Java programmer can create a powerful application by including both static and dynamic constructs with ease since SQLJ shares environment and state information with JDBC.

Table 15–1 *Differences Between JDBC and SQLJ*

JDBC	SQLJ
SQL via API calls	SQL is embedded

Table 15–1 *Differences Between JDBC and SQLJ*

JDBC	SQLJ
Dynamic SQL	Static SQL
Precompiling not required	Translate SQLJ and create packages

Advantages

Java programs written for DB2 offer:

- Increased portability to other database systems and operating platforms
- Easy access to databases across the Internet from multiple client platforms
- Representation of the NULL state built into Java types
- Object-oriented application development and data access model

Disadvantages

- Must have Java programming skills
- Can be slower since Java is interpreted

Native DB2 APIs

DB2 supplies native Application Programming Interfaces (APIs), which can be used to directly manipulate DB2 instances and databases. They are also called administrative or database manager APIs. Some tasks must be coded using these APIs since there is no equivalent SQL statement to perform the operation.

The DB2 APIs are provided in many programming languages, including C/C++, COBOL, and FORTRAN. Information is exchanged between the application and database using special data structures. If the source program module contains only DB2 APIs, there is no need to precompile, and a database package is not created.

The native DB2 APIs are not directly used for coding SQL statements on their own. For example, the function `sqlaintp()` is commonly used to retrieve the complete text for a DB2 error message, so an embedded SQL application can then display the error message to the end-user. The DB2 APIs are grouped by functional category (see Table 15–2). For details on using these APIs, see the *DB2 API Reference*.

Table 15–2 *Types of Native (Administrative) DB2 APIs*

Backup/Recovery	Database Monitoring
Database Control	Operational Utilities

Table 15–2 *Types of Native (Administrative) DB2 APIs*

Database Manager Control	Data Utilities
Database Directory Management	General Application Programming
Client/Server Directory Management	Application Preparation
Network Support	Remote Server Utilities
Database Configuration	Table Space Management
Node and Nodegroup management	

Advantages

- Enables advanced features of DB2 (e.g., table space administration)
- No precompiling or binding required

Disadvantages

- Requires host language compiler/linker
- Can be more difficult to implement
- Cannot issue SQL statements
- Not easily ported to other data servers

DB2 *Note*

A new ADMIN_CMD stored procedure has been introduced into DB2 that supports the execution of many of the DB2 utilities through the use of the SQL CALL statement. This will reduce the need to use many of these low-level API calls. Using an SQL CALL statement is particularly useful for the Java developer who does not have to use JNI (Java Native Interface) to call these API functions.

Microsoft Data Objects (DAO, RDO, ADO, OLE-DB)

These access methods are included here for historical purposes. There may still be some applications that you support that were written in Microsoft Visual Basic or Microsoft Visual C++ that conform to the Data Access Object (DAO) and Remote Data Object (RDO) specifications. These applications interface with DB2 using DB2's ODBC (CLI) driver (Figure 15–4). DB2 also supports ActiveX Data Object (ADO) applications via the OLE:ODBC bridge, or a native OLE DB driver for DB2.

ActiveX Data Objects (ADO) allow you to write an application to access and manipulate data through an OLE DB provider. The OLE DB API was designed by Microsoft to allow data access to a much broader set of data providers than are available through ODBC. The primary benefits of ADO are high speed, ease of use, low memory overhead, and a small disk footprint.

Remote Data Objects (RDO) provide an information model for accessing remote data sources through ODBC. RDO offers a set of objects that make it easy to connect to a database, execute queries and stored procedures, manipulate results, and commit changes to the server. It is specifically designed to access remote ODBC relational data sources and makes it easier to use ODBC without complex application code. It is a primary means of accessing a relational database that is exposed with an ODBC driver.

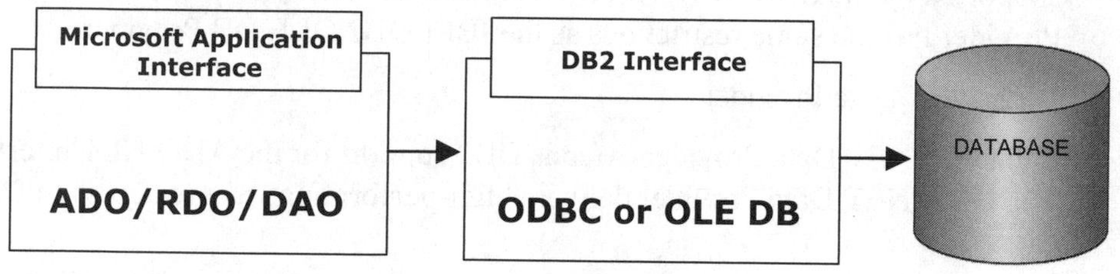

Figure 15–4 *Applications using Microsoft data objects*

Microsoft Visual Basic is a widely used tool that permits development of rich featured applications using a variety of data access models including ADO, DAO, and RDO.

Advantage

- Provide standardized programming model independent of data source

Disadvantage

- Data objects available on Microsoft Windows platforms only

DB2 .NET Provider Support

DB2 ships with a .NET managed provider, `IBM.DATA.DB2`, which is specifically designed to work with DB2 servers. This native managed provider can give you significant performance improvement over the OLE DB and ODBC bridges, and it also provides the ability to exploit the specific features of DB2 servers.

Users who need to use .NET features to access DB2 have three options:

- ODBC .NET Data Provider

  The ODBC .NET Data Provider makes ODBC calls to a DB2 data source using the DB2 CLI Driver. Therefore, the connection string keywords supported by the ODBC .NET Data Provider are the same as those supported by the DB2 CLI driver. Also, the ODBC .NET Data Provider has the same restrictions as the DB2 CLI driver.

- OLE DB .NET Data Provider

  The OLE DB .NET Data Provider uses the IBM DB2 OLE DB Driver, which is referred to in a ConnectionString object as IBMDADB2. The connection string keywords supported by the OLE DB .NET Data Provider are the same as those supported by the IBM OLE DB Provider for DB2. Also, the OLE DB .NET Data Provider has the same restrictions as the IBM DB2 OLE DB Provider.

- DB2 .NET Data Provider

  The DB2 .NET Data Provider extends DB2 support for the ADO.NET interface. The DB2 .NET Data Provider delivers high-performing, secure access to DB2 data.

  The DB2 .NET Data Provider allows your .NET applications to access the following database management systems:

  - DB2 Database for Linux, UNIX, and Windows, Version 9 and Version 8
  - DB2 Universal Database Version 6 (or later) for OS/390® and z/OS®, through DB2 Connect
  - DB2 Universal Database Version 5, Release 1 (or later) for AS/400® and iSeries®, through DB2 Connect
  - DB2 Universal Database Version 7.3 (or later) for VSE & VM, through DB2 Connect

  To develop and run applications that use DB2 .NET Data Provider you need the .NET Framework, Version 2.0 or 1.1. In addition to the DB2 .NET Data Provider, the IBM Database Development Add-In enables you to quickly and easily develop .NET applications for DB2 databases in Visual Studio 2005. You can also use the Add-In to create database objects such as indexes and tables, and develop server-side objects, such as stored procedures and user-defined functions.

Other Interfaces and Tools

There are numerous third-party application building tools and end-user applications that interface with DB2 using one or more programming methods described previously (Figure 15–5). However, many of these tools and applications provide their own front-end data access methods, making the underlying interface to the database transparent to application developers and end users. This can provide a simpler alternative to developing applications than using a high-level programming language.

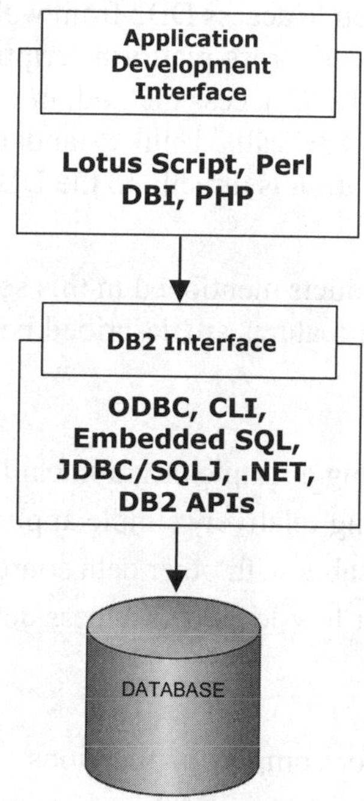

Figure 15–5 *Application development using other interfaces*

ODBC Tools

There might be cases where you need to perform a basic task, such as querying the database, developing reports, and analyzing data. ODBC end-user tools such as Lotus Notes and Microsoft Access can assist in creating applications to perform these tasks. With Lotus products, you can develop applications using LotusScript, a full-featured, object-oriented programming language that comes with a wide array of objects, events, methods, and properties, along with a built-in program editor.

Perl DBI

Perl DBI is an application programming interface that provides database access for the Perl language. Like ODBC, Perl DBI provides a standardized database interface independent of the actual database being used. DB2 supports the Perl Database Interface (DBI) specification for data access through the DBD::DB2 driver.

This driver works in conjunction with the DBI to access DB2 via CLI. The ability to access DB2 from a Perl environment is particularly useful for database testing and maintenance scripts on UNIX platforms and Windows. Perl applications are also commonly used for writing CGI scripts for Web access.

PHP

PHP can be used as a method to access DB2 from web-based applications. PHP is a server-side, HTML-embedded, cross-platform scripting language. It supports DB2 access using the Unified-ODBC access method, in which the user-level PHP communicates to DB2 using ODBC calls. Unlike standard ODBC, with the Unified-ODBC method, communication is directly to the DB2 CLI layer, not through the ODBC layer.

Each of the third-party products mentioned in this section has its own benefits and drawbacks. Some common features are described below.

Advantages

- Quick access to data using a simple or graphical interface
- Faster way for developing relatively simple applications
- Development skills reusable with other data sources
- Provide abstraction over low-level data access details

Disadvantages

- Sometimes unsuitable for complex applications
- May not be able to access certain DB2 features and functions

Ruby and Ruby on Rails

Ruby is a fully-integrated object-oriented programming language used to develop web applications. The main features of this programming language include:

- Simplicity — simple programming language syntax
- Flexibility — no compiler required
- Portability — works on many types of UNIX, Linux, and Windows
- Ease of use — object-oriented programming language

Ruby on Rails (also known as Rails) is a framework for developing web applications that access databases according to the Model-View-Control architectural framework. The main features of the Rails framework include:

- Provides access to supporting code that facilitates efficient web application development

- Provides a full stack framework including database management, object-relational-mapping, modeling business logic, and more

Ruby applications can be developed to access DB2 databases through the use of a Ruby driver.

Summary

DB2 supports applications on a wide variety of operating platforms and numerous methods of coding the applications.

Applications can contain embedded SQL or be coded using standard APIs like CLI, ODBC, and JDBC. Applications can also be developed using other interfaces such as Perl DBI and ActiveX Data Objects. There are many IBM and non-IBM products like Visual Basic, and end-user tools such as Lotus Notes and Microsoft Access, which make the process of application development faster and easier.

Depending on the type of application, one or more programming techniques can be used. DB2 allows applications to be developed that use many popular programming languages including C/C++, COBOL, FORTRAN, and Java. The IBM Database Enterprise Developer Edition product enables an application developer to design, build, and prototype applications using these programming languages across all supported DB2 platforms.

Finally, DB2 also supports newer application development languages and web tools, including Perl, PHP, Python, and Ruby.

CHAPTER 16

Development Considerations

- PACKAGES
- BINDING
- CLI AND ODBC SETTINGS
- JDBC AND SQLJ SETTINGS
- DB2 DEVELOPER WORKBENCH

Embedded SQL programming was introduced in the previous chapter. Even though many of the alternatives to embedded SQL programming offer faster and easier ways to develop applications, it is nevertheless useful to understand and know how to program using embedded SQL. Static statements offer great performance benefits and are only possible through embedded SQL. If you are migrating applications from mainframes such as zSeries or using COBOL, you may prefer embedded SQL.

A precompiler for a variety of programming languages is provided with the IBM Database Enterprise Developer Edition. The precompiler is used to convert embedded SQL statements into a series of Application Programming Interface (API) requests (as was discussed in the previous chapter).

Embedded SQL Overview

Figure 16–1 illustrates the steps involved in building an embedded SQL application. These steps are as follows:

1. Create source files that contain programs with embedded SQL statements.
2. Connect to a database, then precompile each source file.

   The precompiler converts the SQL statements in each source file into DB2 run-time API calls to the database manager. The precompiler also produces an access package in the database and, optionally, a bind file, if you specify that you want one created. We will discuss packages and bind files in the following sections.
3. Compile the modified source files (and other files without SQL statements) using the host language compiler.
4. Link the object files with the DB2 and host language libraries to produce an executable program.
5. Bind the bind file to create the access package if this was not already done at precompile time or if a different database is to be accessed.
6. Run the application. The application accesses the database using the access plan in the package.

Creating Packages

A *package* is a database object that contains optimized SQL statements. A *package* corresponds to a single source programming module, and *sections* corresponds to the SQL statements contained in the source program module.

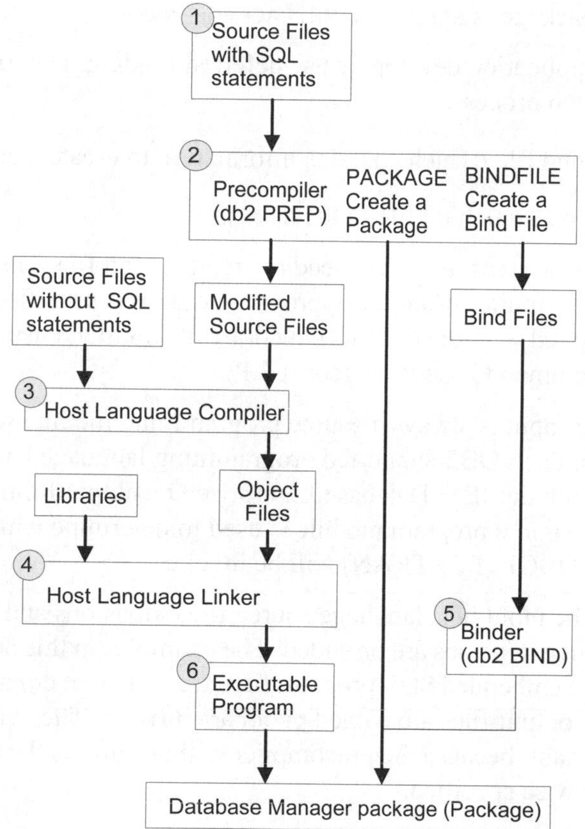

Figure 16–1 *Process for creating embedded SQL applications*

A programming module that contains embedded *static* SQL statements requires precompiling, during which time the precompiler generates a package (by default). This package contains a number of sections that correspond to embedded SQL statements. A section is the compiled form of an SQL statement. While every section corresponds to one statement, every statement does not necessarily have a section. An optimized *access plan* will be stored in the section. The package can be stored directly in the database, or the data needed to create a package can be stored in a bind file. Creating a bind file and binding it in a separate step is known as *deferred binding*.

A program module that contains embedded *dynamic* SQL statements has an associated package and sections, but in this case, the sections are used as placeholders for the SQL statement that will be dynamically prepared. There are no access plans stored in the sections because they are in embedded static SQL modules.

Like views and tables, packages have an associated schema name. The fully qualified name of a package is `SCHEMA-NAME.PACKAGE-NAME`.

In most cases, application developers use deferred binding. Deferred binding requires a two-step process:

1. Creating a bind file (which contains information to create a package)
2. Binding the package bind file to the database

Let's examine these steps. First, we need to create a bind file. The bind file is generated by the precompiler when the appropriate option is specified. The precompiler can be invoked with the `PREP` or `PRECOMPILE` command using the Command Center or the Command Line Processor (CLP).

The precompiler input is always a source programming module with embedded SQL statements. Each DB2-supported programming language has its own precompiler provided with the IBM Database Enterprise Developer Edition. The file extension of the source program module is used to determine which precompiler (e.g., C, C++, COBOL, FORTRAN) will be invoked.

In Table 16–1, the input host language source file extensions and the modified source file output extensions are provided. The examples in this book are written in C. Therefore, the embedded SQL program files are named `program-name.sqc`, and the precompiler output files are named `program-name.c`. The name of the source module is important, because the precompiler will use this as the name of the package unless otherwise specified.

Table 16–1 *Precompile File Extensions*

Host Language	File Extension (Input - Source)	File Extension (Output - Modified Source)
C	.sqc	.c
C++ (case sensitive - AIX)	.sqC	.C
C++ (case insensitive - Windows)	.sqx	.cxx
COBOL - Use TARGET and/or OUTPUT options to use other extensions	.sqb	.cbl
FORTRAN (UNIX)	.sqf	.f
FORTRAN (Windows)	.sqf	.for

If you issue these DB2 commands/statements then you would create an application package called DB2CERT.PROG1 in the DB2CERT database (Example 16–1).

```
CONNECT TO SAMPLE USER DB2CERT;
PRECOMPILE PROG1.SQC;
CONNECT RESET;
```

Example 16–1 *Precompiling an application*

This package would contain a lot of information about the embedded SQL statements, apart from the host variable values required to execute the embedded SQL statements that are contained in the file PROG1.SQC. There are additional steps required before you have an executable application. All database objects specifically referenced (tables, views, etc.) must exist during the precompile phase because in this example deferred binding is not being used. The other inconvenient aspect of not creating a separate bind file is that the entire database would need to be provided, along with the application to the end user, since the package only exists in the database. The data needed to create the package is not contained in a separate bind file in this example.

Let's look at an example of deferred binding with the DB2 commands/statements (Example 16–2):

```
CONNECT TO SAMPLE USER DB2CERT;
PRECOMPILE PROG1.SQC BINDFILE;
CONNECT RESET;
```

Example 16–2 *Precompiling an application*

This example demonstrates the use of the precompiler option BINDFILE. This option is used to generate an output file that contains all of the data needed to create the package for the source module. By using this option, this data is stored in a file called PROG1.BND. You can change the name of the output bind file, but in this example, we did not rename the bind file. To avoid confusion between source program modules, bind files, and package names, try to avoid renaming any of these objects. If you want to create the package using a different name, use the option PACKAGE USING <PACKAGE-NAME>. If you want to create the package using a different schema name, use the option COLLECTION <SCHEMA-NAME>.

The name of the package is determined when the PROG1.BND file is bound to the database. If the same user were to bind this package, the name of the package would be DB2CERT.PROG1. If the database objects do not exist during precompile, only warnings will be generated, and the bind file is created (Object existence and authentication SQL codes are treated as warnings instead of as errors.) The BIND command verifies the existence and access privileges of database objects and will only be successful once the required objects are present.

DB2 Note

Database objects referenced in embedded static SQL programs must exist in the database during package creation (`PRECOMPILE` without `BINDFILE` option or `BIND`) unless the `DEFERRED_PREPARE` option is set to `YES`.

For each source program module containing embedded static SQL statements, a corresponding package must exist in the database. Assume that we are creating an application that accesses two different DB2 databases. The objects referenced in the application must exist in the database for the package to be created successfully. Therefore, we will develop the application using two different program modules. Each program module or source file represents a database package. If we keep the SQL statements for each database in separate packages, the bind will be successful. We can then compile and link the program modules together into a single executable.

Any `PRECOMPILE` error messages will be reported to the display or to a message file. The error message file can be specified using the `MESSAGES` option when issuing the `PRECOMPILE` command. It is recommended to send the messages to an output file so you can examine the file to determine the cause of the errors. Errors during precompile could include invalid host variable definitions and incorrect SQL statements.

When precompiling, you can also determine whether the SQL embedded in the program conforms to different syntaxes and standards. For example, you can check to see if the application works against DB2 for z/OS or is ISO/ANS SQL92 compliant. This is done using the `LANGLEVEL`, `SQLFLAG`, and `SQLRULES` options when precompiling the program.

It is important to remember that an embedded dynamic SQL programming module does have associated packages but does *not* contain access plans or executable sections. For example, suppose an SQL program contains four static SQL statements and two dynamic SQL statements in a single source module. There would be four SQL sections (each with an access plan) created and stored in the database within a single package.

Binding Applications

The most common method of binding in application development is *deferred binding*. When deferred binding is used, the information about the SQL statements is stored in the bind file created by the precompile process. This bind file must be bound against the database to create a package. Once the package exists in the database, there is no longer any need to bind the application.

The SQL statements from the bind file are examined during the bind process, and the current database statistics are used to determine the best method of data access. At this point, an access plan is chosen by the DB2 optimizer. This access plan is then stored in the database system catalog tables. An access plan is *only* created for static embedded SQL statements. Embedded dynamic SQL statements have a package and a section number assigned, but there is *no* access plan created until the statement is executed.

The bind process needs to be performed following each successful precompile of the application source modules. When the bind file is created, a timestamp is stored in the package. The timestamp is sometimes referred to as a *consistency token*. This same timestamp is also stored in the database when the bind is completed and is used to ensure that the resulting application executes the proper SQL statement.

The modified source module (output from the precompile) will attempt to execute the SQL statements by package name and section number. If the required package and section are not found, the following message will be returned:

```
SQL0805N Package 'pkgschema.pkgname' was not found.
SQLSTATE=51002
```

If the required package and section exist in the database system catalogs, the timestamp is then checked. If the timestamp in the application executable does not match the timestamp stored in the system catalog tables in the database, the following message is returned:

```
SQL0818N A timestamp conflict occurred.
SQLSTATE=51003
```

To avoid this problem, you can use the `VERSION` option during the precompilation step. The `VERSION` option allows multiple packages that share both the schema and package-id to coexist in the system catalogs. This option will allow you to introduce and test a new version of a package on the system without affecting users of the existing version of the package. The support of the version option will allow ongoing package maintenance to occur without interruption of end-user access to the system. The `PREP`, `BIND`, `REBIND` and `DROP PACKAGE` facilities have been enhanced to support package versioning.

Authorization Considerations for Static SQL

If the package does not yet exist in the database, the user who issues the BIND must have BINDADD authority for the database or be a member of a group that has this authority. The user must also have one of these privileges: IMPLICIT_SCHEMA on the database (if the schema name of the package does not exist) or CREATEIN on the schema (if the schema name does already exist). The person who binds the package by default becomes the package owner, unless the OWNER keyword is specified during the BIND. In addition, since static statements execute with privileges of the package owner authorization ID, that userid must also have the proper privileges for all of the referenced objects in the SQL statements referenced in the bind file information. These privileges must be explicitly granted to the user binding the packages or to PUBLIC. If the privileges are granted to a group of which the user is a member but are not granted explicitly to the user, the bind will fail.

Unqualified database objects in embedded static SQL programs are by default qualified with the userid of the package owner. Alternatively, you may specify the QUALIFER keyword during the BIND to indicate the qualifier name for unqualified objects in static SQL statements.

Table 16–2 summarizes the behavioral characteristics of static SQL with respect to authorization ID used for statements and the qualifier for unqualified database objects depending on whether the OWNER and QUALIFIER options are used during the BIND:

Table 16–2 *Static SQL — Authorization and Qualifier Summary*

BIND Keyword	Authorization ID	Qualification Value for Unqualified Objects
OWNER and QUALIFIER NOT specified	ID of the user binding the package	ID of the user binding the package
OWNER specified	ID of the user specified in OWNER bind option	ID of the user specified in OWNER bind option
QUALIFIER specified	ID of the user binding the package	ID of the user specified in the QUALIFIER bind option
OWNER and QUALIFIER specified	ID of the user specified in OWNER bind option	ID of the user specified in the QUALIFIER bind option

Once the package exists in the database, any person with EXECUTE privilege on the package can issue any of the SQL statements contained in the package, even if the individual does not have explicit privilege on the database object. This is a feature of embedded static SQL program modules. It allows end users access to a portion of data contained in a table without defining a view or column-level privileges.

Authorization Considerations for Dynamic SQL

Unlike static SQL, dynamically prepared statements can be made to execute under the authorization ID of either the user that binds the package (the package owner) or the user who executes the application, depending on which option is used for the DYNAMICRULES keyword during the bind.

Under DYNAMICRULES RUN (the default), the person who runs a dynamic SQL application must have the privileges necessary to issue each SQL statement (it specifies that the authorization ID of the user executing the package is to be used) as well as the EXECUTE privilege on the package. The privileges may be granted to the user's authorization ID, to any group of which the user is a member or to PUBLIC. With DYNAMICRULES RUN, the person binding the application only needs the BINDADD authority on the database, if the program contains no static SQL.

When using the DYNAMICRULES BIND option, authorizations and privileges required are similar to static SQL. That is, the user that binds a dynamic SQL application (the authorization ID of the package owner) must have BINDADD authority as well as the privileges necessary to perform all the dynamic and static SQL statements in the application. The user that runs the application inherits the privileges associated with the package owner authorization ID and therefore only needs the EXECUTE privilege on the package.

DB2 *Note*

If you bind packages with DYNAMICRULES BIND, and have SYSADM or DBADM authority or any authorities that the user of the package should not receive, consider explicitly specifying OWNER to designate a different authorization ID. This prevents the package from automatically inheriting SYSADM, DBADM, or other unnecessary privileges on dynamic SQL statements from the userid that binds the application.

The authorization ID privileges and qualifier values used for DYNAMICRULES RUN and BIND options are summarized in Table 16–3:

Table 16–3 *Dynamic SQL — Authorization and Qualifier Summary*

DYNAMICRULES Option	Authorization ID	Qualification Value for Unqualified Objects
RUN (default)	ID of user executing package	Owner's authorization ID whether or not the owner is explicitly specified. It can be superseded by the CURRENT SCHEMA special register.

Table 16–3 *Dynamic SQL — Authorization and Qualifier Summary (Continued)*

DYNAMICRULES Option	Authorization ID	Qualification Value for Unqualified Objects
BIND	The implicit or explicit value of OWNER bind option	The implicit or explicit value of the QUALIFIER bind option.

Examining Packages and Timestamps

We have briefly discussed packages and timestamps. Let's examine how we can verify that the bind file and the packages in the database match. When the BIND command is successful, a single entry in the system catalog view SYSCAT.PACKAGES is created. There are a number of columns defined for this table. We will not go into a complete explanation here, but let's look at the timestamp column. The timestamp associated with a package is actually stored in the column named UNIQUE_ID. If you were to successfully issue the command in Example 16–3, the SYSCAT.PACKAGES view would have a new entry for this bind file with the package name DB2LOOK and the authorization user ID as the package schema. Any error or warning messages would be written to the file called MSG1.OUT.

```
BIND DB2LOOK.BND MESSAGES MSG1.OUT
```

Example 16–3 *Binding an application*

To examine the timestamp contained in the DB2LOOK.BND file, there is a utility provided with DB2 called db2bfd (Example 16–4).

```
db2bfd -b db2look.bnd
```

Example 16–4 *Examining the bind file information*

Here is an example of the output of the db2bfd tool (Example 16–5):

```
db2look.bnd:  Header Contents

Header Fields:

Field                Value
-----                -----
releaseNum           0x800
Endian               0x4c
numHvars             460
maxSect              59
numStmt              271
optInternalCnt       4
optCount             10

Name                 Value
------------------   -----
Isolation Level      Uncommitted Read
```

```
Creator             "NULLID  "
App Name            "DB2LOOK "
Timestamp           "060629:User defined timestamp"
Cnulreqd            Yes
Sql Error           No package
Block               Block All
Validate            Bind
Date                Default/local
Time                Default/local

*** All other options are using default settings as specified by the server ***
```

Example 16–5 *Sample bind output*

Note that the timestamp is encoded as 060629. This timestamp is the exact time when the PRECOMPILE command was used to generate the bind file.

To confirm that this bind file (db2look.bnd) has been bound to the database, issue this SQL statement once connected to the database (Example 16–6):

```
SELECT PKGSCHEMA, PKGNAME, UNIQUE_ID
  FROM SYSCAT.PACKAGES
  WHERE PKGNAME = 'DB2LOOK';

  PKGSCHEMA PKGNAME UNIQUE_ID
  --------  ------- -------------------
  NULLID    DB2LOOK X'3036303632390000'
```

Example 16–6 *Bind information for DB2LOOK*

The output of this SQL statement should contain a single row result with a UNIQUE_ID matching the bind file, as shown in Example 16–5. The UNIQUE_ID is returned as a hexadecimal value.

Binding Utilities

The CLP is a dynamic SQL application that is provided with DB2. The packages associated with the utilities, like the DB2 CLP, are included in the sqllib directory, in the bnd subdirectory.

The bind files associated with the DB2 CLP and other utilities are found in a list file called db2ubind.lst.

Specifically, the bind files associated with the DB2 CLP are: db2clpcs.bnd, db2clprr.bnd, db2clpur.bnd, db2clprs.bnd, and db2clpnc.bnd.

DB2 Note

Each of the CLP bind files is created with different isolation levels. This allows a user the ability to change the isolation level when using the CLP utility, using the `CHANGE ISOLATION LEVEL` command.

These bind files must have been bound to the database you wish to access using the DB2 Command Center, the DB2 CLP or the Configuration Assistant (CA).

DB2 Note

To bind the DB2 utilities (e.g., `CLP`, `IMPORT`, `EXPORT`) issue this command: `bind @db2ubind.lst blocking all`.

To bind a number of packages using a single `BIND` command, add the "@" character in front of the source filename. When this character is encountered, DB2 will assume that the file contains a list of bind files and is not a bind file itself.

Blocking

Record blocking is a feature of DB2 that reduces data access time across networks when an application is retrieving a large amount of data. The record blocking is based on cursor type and the amount of storage allocated on the DB2 server to perform record blocking. Cursors are used in applications to manipulate multirow result sets from a DB2 server.

The DBM configuration parameter known as `ASLHEAPSZ` specifies the amount of memory used to buffer data on the server for applications requesting multiple data records. For applications executing on remote clients, the buffer is specified by the DBM configuration parameter known as `RQRIOBLK`.

You can think of record blocking as data retrieval caching. The record blocking options are described in Table 16–4. Usually, you would specify `BLOCKING ALL` for applications that perform many queries. An *ambiguous cursor* is a cursor that has been defined without any reference to its intended usage in an SQL statement. As we will see, all cursors are defined using a `SELECT` statement. They are used in a `SELECT`, `DELETE`, or `UPDATE` statement.

The default blocking option for static embedded applications is `BLOCKING UNAMBIG`. The default blocking option for CLI applications and the CLP is `BLOCKING ALL`.

Table 16–4 *Record Blocking Options*

BLOCKING <option>	Record Blocking Behavior
UNAMBIG	All cursors except those specified as FOR UPDATE are blocked.
ALL	Ambiguous cursor are blocked.
NO	No cursors are blocked.

Record blocking affects the way you, as an application developer, declare your cursors within your application. The more specific you are with your cursor declaration, the more likely DB2 will use record blocking appropriately. If record blocking is enabled, the cache is allocated when the cursor is opened. It is deallocated when the cursor is closed. Therefore, to avoid wasting memory resources on the server, avoid keeping cursors open if they are no longer required.

DB2 *Note*

All cursors used for dynamic SQL statements are assumed to be ambiguous.

Support for CLI and ODBC Programming

We have been discussing static and dynamic SQL statement processing by embedding the SQL statements in an application module. A precompile or preparation stage is required to map these SQL statements to DB2 API calls. We are required to manipulate SQLDA data structures to handle dynamic SQL. These can become quite complex and, more importantly, are not easily ported to various database vendors. An alternative method of developing database applications using callable SQL interfaces has become a popular technique of creating powerful yet highly portable applications.

A callable SQL interface involves invoking APIs (also referred to as functions or function calls in this chapter) that allow the developer to access database information directly; therefore, there is no need for precompiling the application and there is no database-specific language to learn. One such callable SQL interface is Microsoft's Open Database Connectivity (ODBC). There are slightly different callable SQL interface standards known as Call Level Interface (CLI) as defined by groups such as X/Open and ISO.

DB2 has its own CLI which is based on the X/Open, ISO, and ODBC standards. The focus of the discussion here will be application development using DB2 CLI. We will also cover ODBC briefly but will not go into too much detail because the two standards are very similar.

All of the SQL statements are dynamically prepared and executed using CLI or ODBC. The programming techniques and runtime environment for CLI are quite different than those for embedded SQL. We will discuss many of these differences.

Embedded Dynamic Versus Call Level Interface

Developing an application using CLI is different than using embedded SQL techniques. So before we examine how to code CLI applications, let's examine some of the key differences.

The DB2 CLI environment is different from embedded SQL in the following ways:

- No explicit cursors are required.
- There is no precompile stage.
- No application-level packages created. There is a set of CLI packages that is bound once for all CLI applications.
- No `COMMIT`/`ROLLBACK` statement is used to control transaction processing. An API called `SQLEndTran()` is used to commit or rollback a transaction.
- No SQLDA data structure is required.
- No SQLCA data structure is used because the errors are analyzed using SQLSTATES and return codes through special error-handling APIs.
- No host variables are used in SQL statements; parameter markers are used instead.

The differences listed above are important to understand before attempting to develop CLI applications. There are some unique features provided with CLI that are not available in an embedded SQL environment including:

- Manipulation of multiple rows of data at a time (array fetch/insert)
- The ability to have bidirectional (scrollable) cursors
- Easier to query the system catalog tables because there are predefined APIs to query system catalog table resources

ODBC Versus CLI

The ODBC and CLI standards overlap in many areas. They are both based on a set of APIs that access data sources using programs written in the C/C++ programming language. The initial ODBC standard was based on an early version of the X/Open CLI standard, and they have evolved over the years.

The ODBC standard is based on levels of conformance. The DB2 ODBC driver currently conforms to ODBC level 3.51. This includes all core, level 1, and level 2 functions. As the ODBC standard continues to evolve, so may DB2's ODBC conformance.

The DB2 product provides both a CLI driver and an ODBC driver. In the CLI environment, the application communicates directly with the CLI driver. In an ODBC environment, the ODBC Driver Manager provides the interface to the application. It also dynamically loads the ODBC driver for the necessary database server that the application connects to. It is the driver that implements the ODBC function set, with the exception of some extended functions implemented by the Driver Manager. Figure 16–2 illustrates the relationship between the application and DB2 in both the ODBC and CLI environments.

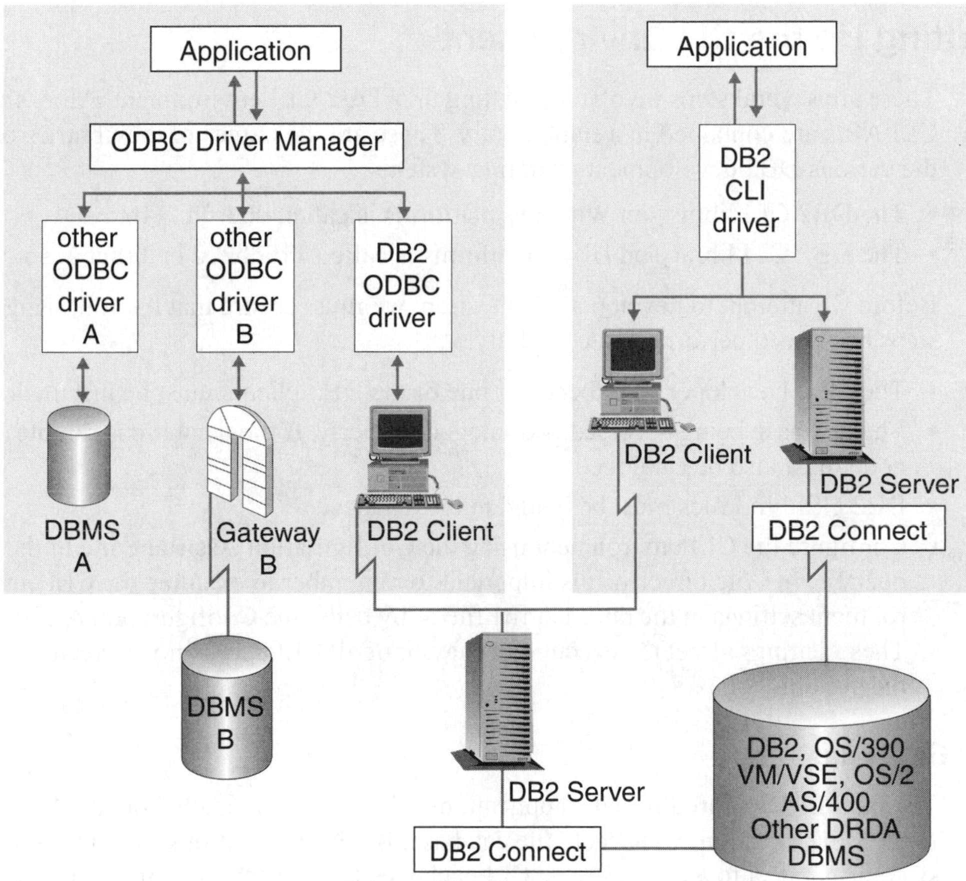

Figure 16–2 *DB2 CLI versus ODBC*

A DB2 CLI application does not require the ODBC driver or the ODBC driver manager to operate. The advantage of coding an ODBC application is the ease of portability. Also, the application can access more than one database vendor product. Therefore, you could develop an application that accesses data from multiple database vendor products quite simply with the ODBC interface. The DB2 CLI driver can only access DB2 Family data sources.

DB2 *Note*

The installation of the ODBC driver is *only* required if ODBC applications are being executed. To run CLI applications, only the DB2 runtime client needs to be installed. It includes the DB2 CLI driver.

Setting Up the CLI Environment

There are several steps involved in setting up a DB2 CLI environment. All of the CLI APIs are contained in a static library. These are the names of the libraries on the various DB2 development operating systems:

- The DB2 CLI library on Windows platforms is called `db2cli.lib`.
- The DB2 CLI library on UNIX platforms is called `libdb2.a` or `libdb2.so`.

Before we attempt to develop an application, we must ensure that the following steps have been performed successfully:

- The DB2 Developer Workbench or one of the DB2 clients must be installed.
- The database being accessed is cataloged properly. If the database is remote, a node must also be cataloged.
- DB2 CLI bind files must be bound to the database.
- Configure the CLI environment using the Configuration Assistant or edit the `db2cli.ini` file directly. It is important to remember to examine the CLI environment settings in the `db2cli.ini` file or by using the Configuration Assistant. These settings affect the execution behavior of all CLI applications executing on the system.

CLI Bind Files

The bind files required for CLI applications will be automatically bound when the first CLI application connects to the database. If CLI applications from multiple systems connect to a database, the CLI packages from each client platform and unique build level (fixpak level) need to be bound to the database. The bind may not be successful if the user does not have BINDADD authority on the database. Therefore, the database administrator may be required to bind the necessary bind files manually using the DB2 `BIND` command or the Configuration Assistant (CA). Each of the supported DB2 servers use different bind files (Table 16–5).

Table 16–5 *CLI Bind List Files*

Bind File	DB2 Server
db2cli.lst	DB2 for Linux, UNIX, Windows
ddcsvm.lst	DB2 for VM (SQL/DS)
ddcsvse.lst	DB2 for VSE (SQL/DS)
ddcsmvs.lst	DB2 for z/OS
ddcs400.lst	DB2 for iSeries (OS/400)

For example, to manually bind the CLI packages from a DB2 Command Window on Windows against a DB2 for AIX database, you would issue the following command after connecting to the database (Example 16–7):

```
DB2 BIND @db2cli.lst BLOCKING ALL
    MESSAGES DB2CLI.MSG GRANT PUBLIC
```

Example 16–7 *Binding CLI packages*

Likewise, if the DB2 database resides on zSeries, you could use this command (Example 16–8):

```
DB2 BIND @ddcsmvs.lst BLOCKING ALL SQLERROR CONTINUE
    MESSAGES MVSBIND.MSG GRANT PUBLIC
```

Example 16–8 *Binding packages on DB2 z/OS*

Configuring CLI

Usually it is not necessary to modify the DB2 CLI configuration file (`db2cli.ini`). It is important to understand that the file exists and may require small modifications. Some of the reasons for modifying the CLI configuration file include:

- Increase CLI application performance
- Change default CLI behavior
- Enable workarounds for specific applications

The db2cli.ini file is located in the sqllib/cfg directory of the instance owner in UNIX environments and in the sqllib directory for Windows 32-bit operating systems.

A sample db2cli.ini file is found in Figure 16–3.

```
; Comment Goes Here
[SAMPLE]
CURSORHOLD=0
TNXISOLATION=4
DEFERREDPREPARE=1
DB2DEGREE=4
PATCH1=4
```

Figure 16–3 *Example db2cli.ini configuration*

There are many more options that can be specified in the CLI configuration file, but these options were selected because they can dramatically affect an application's execution environment. The keywords and values shown here may not be applicable to your environment.

The first line is a comment about this section of the file. Multiple databases may be configured in this file. The second line contains the database alias name in brackets, [SAMPLE]. The SAMPLE database can still be accessed from a DB2 CLI application without an entry in the db2cli.ini file, but if there is no section for the SAMPLE database, all of the default values for the parameters will be used. This may not be desirable.

The five lines below the database name contain keywords and corresponding values. The supported keywords are defined in the *DB2 Call Level Interface Guide and Reference, Volume 1*, but let's examine the keywords defined in Figure 16–3 and explain them in Table 16–6.

Table 16–6 *Configuring a DB2 CLI Environment*

Keyword	Meaning
CURSORHOLD	0 = cursor no hold (the cursors are destroyed when the transaction is committed). 1 = cursor hold (default). The default value of this keyword is 1. This means that the cursors are maintained across units of work. This is quite different from embedded SQL since all cursors exhibit the cursor without hold behavior unless the DECLARE CURSOR statement includes the phrase WITH HOLD.

Table 16–6 *Configuring a DB2 CLI Environment (Continued)*

Keyword	Meaning
TXNISOLATION	1 - Uncommitted Read 2 - Cursor Stability (default) 4 - Read Stability 8 - Repeatable Read 32 - No Commit (DB2 for iSeries only) This keyword identifies the isolation level used for concurrency.
DEFERREDPREPARE	0 = Deferred Prepare is not used. 1 = Deferred Prepare is used (default). Defers sending the PREPARE request until the corresponding execute request is issued. The two requests are then combined into one command/reply flow (instead of two) to minimize network flow and to improve performance.
DB2DEGREE	0-32767/ANY (Default is 0) Sets the degree of parallelism for the execution of SQL statements.
PATCH1 PATCH2	The keywords Patch1 and Patch2 are used for work-arounds to known problems when using certain applications or environments. In our example, we used PATCH1=4 to map timestamp values to date values. To use multiple PATCH1 values, simply add the values together to form the keyword value. For example, if you want the patches 1, 4, and 8, then specify PATCH1=13. Unlike PATCH1, to specify multiple patches for PATCH2, the values are specified in a comma delimited string, for example PATCH2="7,15".

The DB2 CA or ODBC Administrator Tool on the Windows platform allows you to configure the CLI environment without editing the db2cli.ini file directly. The interface is easy to use and explains each parameter that can be modified (Figure 16–4).

Development Considerations

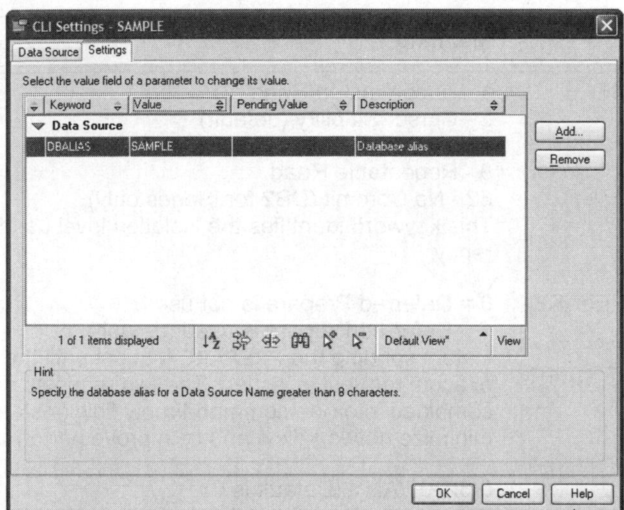

Figure 16–4 *CLI/ODBC settings panel in the Configuration Assistant*

Accessing a DB2 Database via ODBC

To access a DB2 database from ODBC, the following are required on the DB2 client where the ODBC application executes:

- DB2 runtime client or server must be installed. If the database is on a remote DB2 system, it should be cataloged correctly and be accessible for connecting to.
- The ODBC Driver Manager must be installed.
- An ODBC driver for DB2 must be installed and registered with the ODBC driver manager.
- The DB2 database must be registered as an ODBC data source with the driver manager.

There must be an ODBC driver manager installed on the computer where the ODBC application has been installed. For all Microsoft operating systems, the ODBC driver manager is provided by Microsoft.

The IBM DB2 ODBC driver or another ODBC driver for DB2 must be installed and registered. The Microsoft ODBC driver manager and the DB2 ODBC driver are automatically installed on Windows 32-bit platforms during DB2 installation as long as the ODBC component, highlighted by default, is not unchecked. The DB2 ODBC driver is also registered with the driver manager during installation of DB2 on Windows platforms. On Windows platforms, you can run the Microsoft ODBC Administrator from the Control Panel to verify that “IBM DB2 ODBC Driver” is shown in the list. On UNIX platforms, the DB2 ODBC driver and databases available through it are specified using '.odbc.ini' and '.odbcinst.ini' files in the home directory of the user running the ODBC application. Note that the files start with a '.'.

The database must be identified to the ODBC driver manager as an available data source. The data source can be made available to all users of the system (a system data source) or only to the current user (a user data source). On Windows, you can register the data source with the driver manager using the CA, as shown in Figure 16–5. Databases configured though the CA are selected as system ODBC data sources by default, unless you explicitly uncheck the selection. For non-Windows platforms, this is accomplished by using the appropriate ODBC Administration tool or by configuring the driver manager manually.

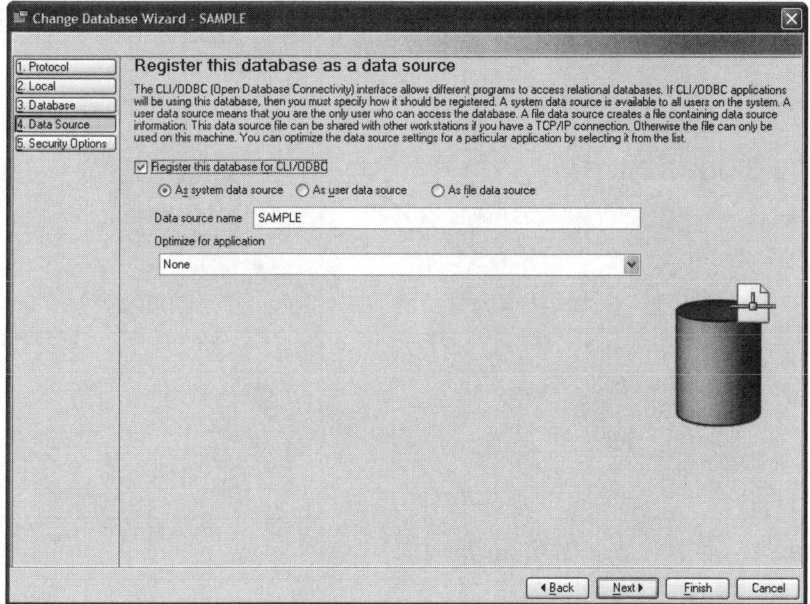

Figure 16–5 *Database properties*

ODBC Development Considerations

For ODBC application development, you must obtain an ODBC Software Development Kit.

The steps of binding of CLI packages and customizing CLI using db2cli.ini or CA are also applicable to ODBC applications that will access DB2 data sources. These steps are performed in the same way as for CLI applications.

Support for Java Programming

DB2 supports many types of Java programs. Applets and applications are two main types of Java programs. Before explaining how to code applets and applications for DB2, let's first examine these two types.

Java applications rely on the DB2 client code to connect to the DB2 database. You start your application from the desktop or command line, like any other application. The DB2 JDBC driver handles the JDBC API calls from your application. These calls to the DB2 JDBC driver are translated to DB2 CLI calls via Java native methods.The JDBC driver uses the CLI driver on the client to communicate the requests to the server, receives the results, and passes them to the Java application. Thus an application requires at least the DB2 runtime client code to be installed where the application executes.

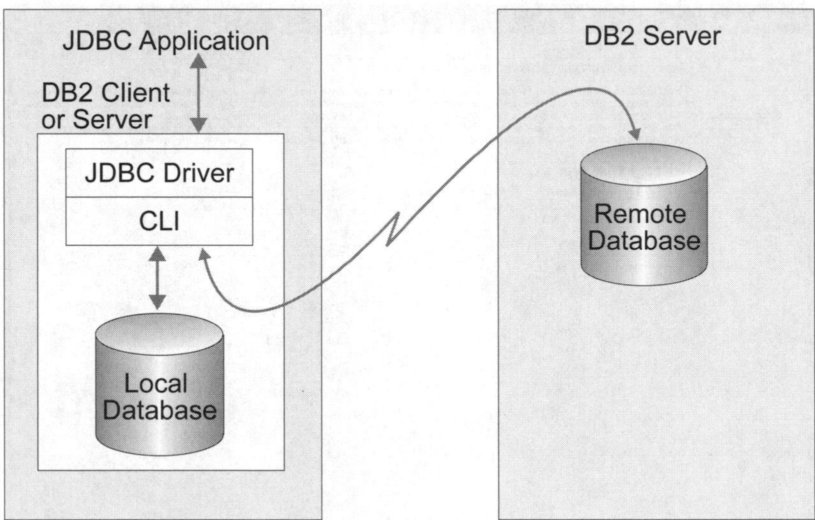

Figure 16–6 *Java applications for DB2*

Java applets do not require any DB2 client code to be installed on the system where they execute. You need only a Java-enabled Web browser on the client machine to run your applet. Typically, you would embed the applet in a HyperText Markup Language (HTML) page. When you load your HTML page, the browser downloads the Java applet to your machine, which then downloads the Java class files and DB2's JDBC driver. When your applet calls the JDBC API to connect to DB2, the JDBC driver establishes a separate network connection with a DB2 JDBC applet server residing on the Web server. The JDBC server communicates with the database via the DB2 CLI driver and sends the results back to the client through the separate connection. Figure 16–7 illustrates the flow of communications wih a Java applet that uses JDBC.

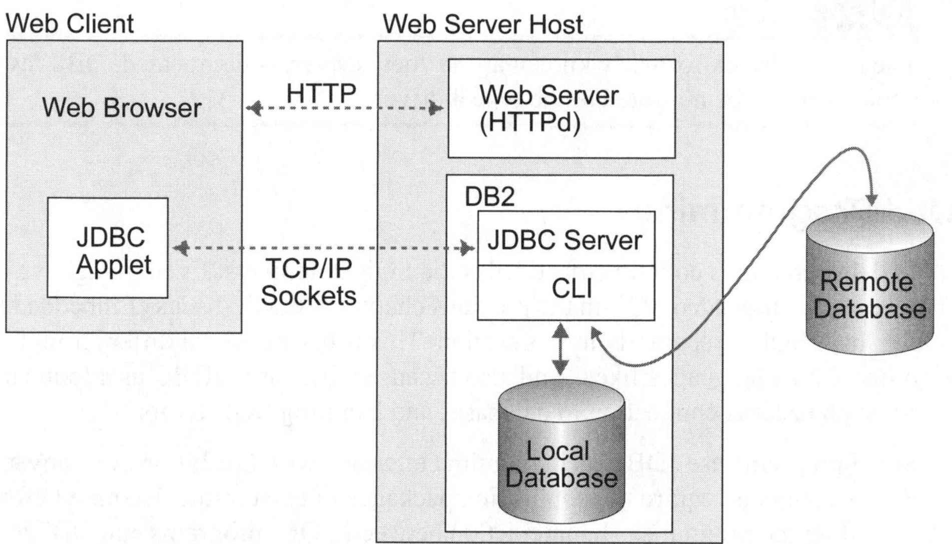

Figure 16–7 *Java applets for DB2*

DB2 also supports user-defined functions and stored procedures written in Java.

Java programs that access DB2 databases can do so using JDBC or SQLJ interfaces. The JDBC API allows you to write Java programs that make dynamic SQL calls to databases. SQLJ extends JDBC to support embedded static SQL. The next few sections deal with coding Java programs for DB2 using JDBC and SQLJ.

JDBC Programming

If your DB2 application or applet uses JDBC, you need to familiarize yourself with the JDBC specification and understand how to call JDBC APIs to access a database and manipulate data in that database. Here we introduce some commonly used terms and constructs to help you better understand JDBC programs for DB2.

DB2's JDBC Drivers

DB2 JDBC drivers are installed during the installation of DB2 client or server code. DB2 provides an *app* driver: `COM.ibm.db2.jdbc.app.DB2Driver`. You would use this driver for *applications* that run on machines where DB2 is installed. DB2 also comes with a *net* driver: `COM.ibm.db2.jdbc.net.DB2Driver`. You would use this driver when your Java program executes on a machine that does not have DB2 installed, that is, for running applets. The class files for the drivers are packaged in `db2java.zip`.

The JDBC classes are found in the `java.sql` package.

DB2 Note

The type 3 driver, formerly known as the “net” driver, is deprecated. DB2 Java applets should be migrated to the type 4 driver.

SQLJ Programming

SQLJ source files contain embedded static SQL statements. Even though we covered static embedded SQL in the previous chapter, we will discuss Embedded SQL for Java (SQLJ) separately in this section. This is because Java differs from the traditional host languages like C and also because SQLJ uses JDBC as a foundation for such tasks as connecting to databases and handling SQL errors.

SQLJ programs use JDBC as the runtime interface with DB2; however, any static SQL statements require the application packages to exist in the database before executing the programs. The interaction between SQLJ programs and DB2 is shown in Figure 16–8.

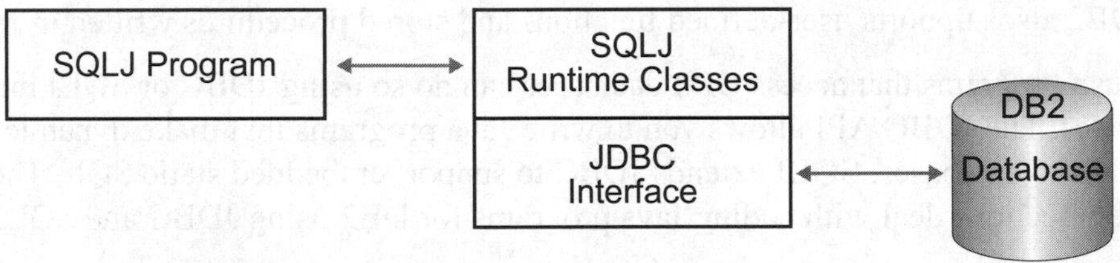

Figure 16–8 *SQLJ's interface with DB2*

Because SQLJ applications and applets access the database through DB2's JDBC support, they require the JDBC classes (`java.sql.*`) and DB2's JDBC driver classes contained in `db2java.zip`. The SQLJ translator that replaces embedded SQL statements in the SQLJ program uses classes in `sqlj.zip` (in the `sqllib/java` directory). However, the interfaces and classes in `sqlj.zip` are not required for executing the program. To execute SQLJ programs, the SQLJ runtime classes (`sqllib/java/runtime.zip`) are needed to authenticate and execute any SQL packages that were bound to the database at the precompiling and binding stage.

DB2 Developer Workbench

The DB2 9 Developer Workbench (DB2 DWB) replaces the DB2 8 Development Center. This newly designed tool is based on the Eclipse framework and replaces the DB2 Development Center.

Developer Workbench makes it easy to:

- Create, view, and edit database objects (such as tables and schemas)
- Explore and edit data in tables and rows
- Visually build SQL and XQuery statements
- Develop and deploy stored procedures, user defined functions (UDFs), routines, and scripts
- Debug SQL and Java stored procedures
- Develop SQLJ applications
- Develop queries and routines for XML data
- Perform data movement (such as load and extract)
- Collaborate and share projects with team members
- Migrate projects from DB2 Development Center

However, there's so much more to this list. For example, the DB2 DWB includes an SQL editor that's enriched with syntax colorization and code assistants, as well as teaming support, compare utilities, and more.

The DB2 DWB is a separate tool and is maintained separate from a DB2 data server. You can download it from www-304.ibm.com/jct03001c/software/data/db2/ad/dwb.html.

The DB2 DWB is really meant for power-DBAs that aren't coding experts but require rapid development assistance for the building of business logic for their data servers. Depending on your environment, you may elect to use another tool like Toad for DB2. Pure developers will likely choose to use the plug-ins provided with DB2 9 into their respective IDEs, though they are free to (and in many cases will) use the DB2 DWB. For the most part, you can perform the same tasks in any of the tools that IBM ships or the integration points into specific IDEs.

Figure 16–9 shows the main screen of the workbench.

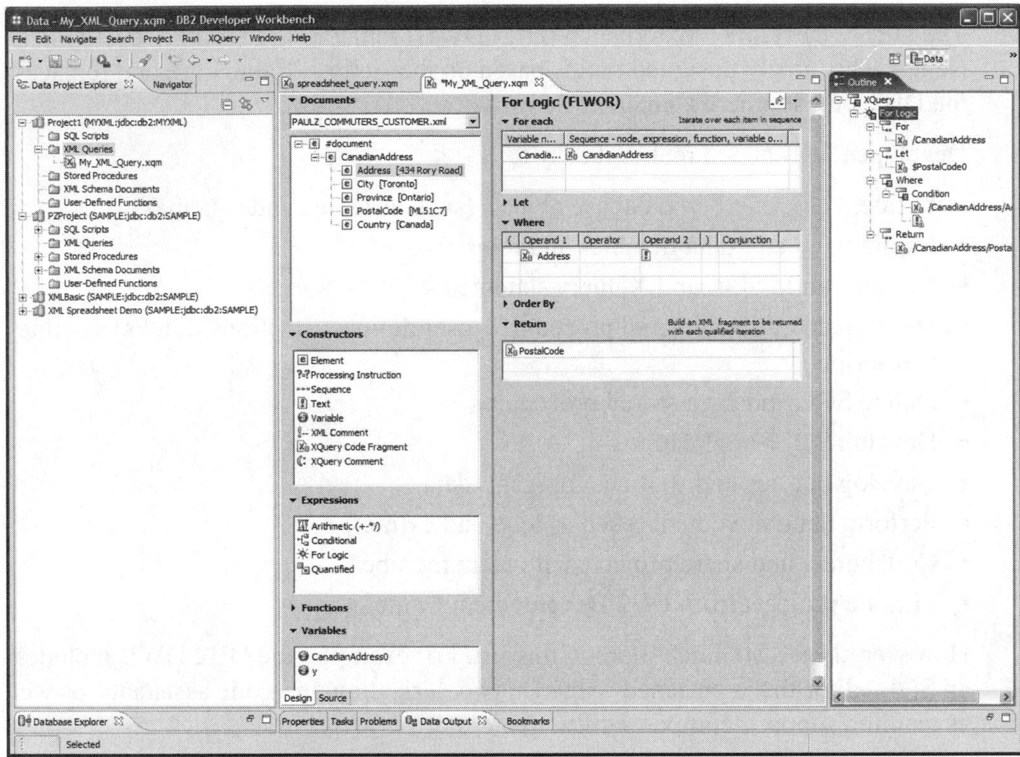

Figure 16–9 *The DB2 Developer Workbench*

Summary

The process of creating static embedded SQL program modules was discussed in this chapter. By embedding SQL statements into a programming language, we can manipulate the data contained in a DB2 database. The programming modules containing the SQL statements must be converted from SQL statements to DB2 library APIs. This step is known as the precompilation step, since it is always performed before the programming module is compiled and linked.

This chapter also discussed CLI, ODBC, and JDBC development and what steps are required to develop and execute programs using these interfaces.

Finally, we introduced the DB2 Developer Workbench Center. This tool can be used to develop, test, and debug user-defined functions and stored procedures.

PART 5

Appendices

APPENDIX A

DB2 9 Certification Test Objectives

This appendix provides the test objectives for the following exams:

- DB2 9 Fundamentals (730)
- DB2 9 DBA for Linux, UNIX and Windows (731)
- DB2 9 for Linux, UNIX, and Windows Advanced DBA (734)
- DB2 9 DBA for Linux, Unix, and Windows Upgrade (736)

How does one certify? There are three basic steps:

1. Understand certification test objectives.
2. Review study guides, online tutorials, or take an education course. Then test your knowledge by taking an assessment exam at www.ibm.com/software/data/education/cert/assessment.html. These assessments are offered through Prime/Prometric at a low nominal fee of $10 USD.
3. Register and take the certification exam.

For more information on IBM Data Management skills programs please visit:
`www.ibm.com/software/data/education.html`.
Detailed information on the IBM Professional Certification program, including the DB2 Database certification exams, can be found at:
`www.ibm.com/certify`.
Experience with DB2 9 is the best route to preparing for the DB2 certification exams. This certification guide is intended to be used alongside your day-to-day use of DB2 while preparing for the exams.

DB2 Certification Levels

There are five job roles and three levels of certified solution expert associated with the DB2 product in the distributed environment. The following diagram lists the exam numbers and the corresponding certification level associated with it.

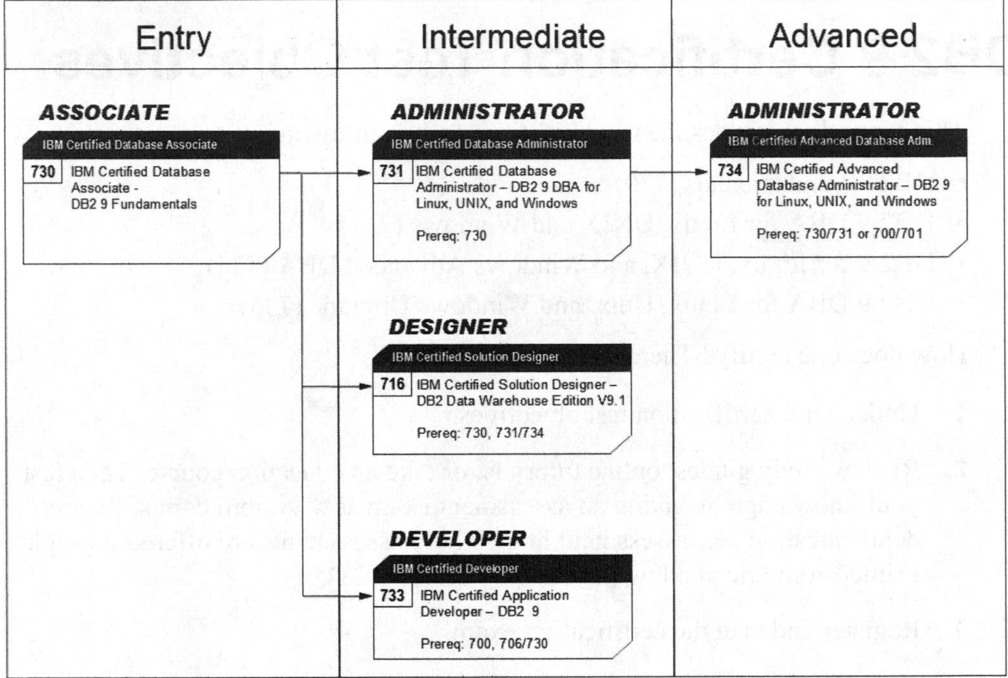

Exam 736 (DB2 9 DBA for Linux, Unix, and Windows Upgrade) has only 38 questions and can be taken instead of Exam 731 — if you earned the DBA certification for V8.

These certification levels are accurate at time of publication, but additional exams may be added to these levels over time. For more information on the certification levels, please refer to the IBM certification site: www.ibm.com/certify.

DB2 9 Fundamentals (730)

The Database Associate is an entry-level DBA or a user of any of the DB2 family of products. This individual is knowledgeable about the fundamental concepts of DB2 9 through either hands-on experience or formal and informal education. The database associate should have an in-depth knowledge of the basic to intermediate tasks required in day-to-day administration, basic SQL (Structured Query Language), understand how DB2 9 is packaged and installed, understand how to create databases and database objects, and have a basic knowledge of database security and transaction isolation.

To attain the IBM Certified Database Associate – DB2 9 Fundamentals certification, candidates must pass one test.

Section 1 — Planning (14%)

- Knowledge of restricting data access
- Knowledge of the features or functions available in DB2 tools (just tools that come with product — distributed space — i.e., control center, configuration advisor, configuration assistant, command line processor)
- Knowledge database workloads (OLTP vs. warehousing)
- Knowledge of non-relational data concepts (extenders)
- Knowledge of XML data implications (non-shredding)

Section 2 — Security (11%)

- Knowledge of DB2 products (client, server, etc.)
- Knowledge of different privileges and authorities
- Knowledge of encryption options (data and network)
- Given a DDL SQL statement, knowledge to identify results (grant/revoke/connect statements)

Section 3 — Working with Databases and Database Objects (17%)

- Ability to identify and connect to DB2 servers and databases
- Ability to identify DB2 objects
- Knowledge of basic characteristics and properties of DB2 objects
- Given a DDL SQL statement, knowledge to identify results (ability to create objects)

Section 4 — Working with DB2 Data using SQL (23.5%)

- Given a DML SQL statement, knowledge to identify results
- Ability to use SQL to SELECT data from tables

- Ability to use SQL to SORT or GROUP data
- Ability to use SQL to UPDATE, DELETE, or INSERT data
- Knowledge of transactions (i.e., commit/rollback and transaction boundaries)
- Ability to call a procedure or invoke a user defined function
- Given an XQuery statement, knowledge to identify results

Section 5 — Working with DB2 Tables, Views and Indexes (23.5%)

- Ability to demonstrate usage of DB2 data types
- Given a situation, ability to create table
- Knowledge to identify when referential integrity should be used
- Knowledge to identify methods of data constraint
- Knowledge to identify characteristics of a table, view or index
- Knowledge to identify when triggers should be used
- Knowledge of schemas
- Knowledge of data type options for storing XML data

Section 6 — Data Concurrency (11%)

- Knowledge to identify factors that influence locking
- Ability to list objects on which locks can be obtained
- Knowledge to identify characteristics of DB2 locks
- Given a situation, knowledge to identify the isolation levels that should be used

DB2 for LUW Database Administration (731)

If you are knowledgeable with DB2 9 and are capable of performing the intermediate to advanced skills required in the day-to-day administration of DB2 instances and databases, you may benefit from this certification role.

To attain the IBM Certified Database Administrator – DB2 9 DBA for Linux, UNIX and Windows certification, candidates must pass 2 tests: Test 730 (DB2 9 Fundamentals) and Test 731.

Candidates who have passed exam 700 – DB2 UDB V8.1 Family Fundamentals, or who have acquired the IBM Certified Database Administrator – DB2 UDB V8.1 for Linux, UNIX and Windows certification (by passing both exams 700 and 701), only need to pass exam 731 – DB2 9 DBA for Linux, UNIX and Windows to obtain the Certified Database Administrator certification.

Section 1 — DB2 Server Management (20.5%)

- Ability to configure/manage DB2 instances (e.g. scope)
- Ability to obtain/modify database manager configuration information
- Ability to obtain/modify database configuration information
- Knowledge of the DB2 force command
- Ability to configure client/server connectivity
- Ability to schedule jobs
- Ability to use Automatic Maintenance (i.e., RUNSTAT, Backup, REORG)
- Ability to configure client server connectivity using DISCOVERY
- Skill in interpreting the notify log
- Ability to obtain and modify DB2 registry variables
- Ability to use self-tuning memory management and autoconfig
- Ability to use throttling utilities

Section 2 — Data Placement (17.5%)

- Ability to create a database
- Skill in discussing the use of schemas
- Skill in discussing the various table space states
- Ability to create and manipulate the various DB2 objects
- Ability to create and discuss the characteristics of an SMS table space
- Ability to create and discuss the characteristics of an automated managed table space

- Knowledge of partitioning capabilities (e.g., table partitioning, hash partitioning, MDC, Hybrid)
- Knowledge of XML structure (indexing for performance)
- Knowledge of compression data

Section 3 — Database Access (11.5%)

- Knowledge of the creation and management of indexes
- Ability to create constraints on tables (e.g., RI, informational, unique)
- Ability to create views on tables
- Skill in examining the contents of the System Catalog tables
- Ability to use the GUI Tools for administration
- Knowledge of how to enforce data uniqueness

Section 4 — Analyzing DB2 Activity (13%)

- Ability to capture and analyze EXPLAIN/VISUAL EXPLAIN information
- Ability to capture snapshots using Get Snapshots or SQL functions
- Ability to create and activate event monitors
- Ability to configure Health Monitor using the Health Center
- Ability to identify the functions of Problem Determination Tools (e.g., db2pd, db2mtrk)

Section 5 — DB2 Utilities (14.5%)

- Ability to use `EXPORT` utility to extract data from a table
- Ability to use `IMPORT` utility to insert data into a table
- Ability to use the `LOAD` utility to insert data into a table
- Knowledge to identify when to use `IMPORT` vs. `LOAD`
- Ability to use the `REORG`, `REORGCHK`, `REBIND` and `RUNSTATS` utilities
- Ability to use DB2Move, DB2Look, and DB2Batch
- Knowledge of the functionality of the DB2 Advisors (db2advis utility)
- Ability to use the DB2 Control Center

Section 6 — High Availability (14.5%)

- Ability to perform database-level and table space level `BACKUP` & `RESTORE`
- Knowledge to identify and explain issues on index recreation
- Knowledge of database logging
- Knowledge of crash recovery
- Knowledge of version recovery

- Knowledge of Roll Forward recovery
- Knowledge of and ability to perform HADR
- Knowledge of and ability to perform Log Mirroring
- Knowledge of Configurable Online Parameters

Section 7 — Security (8.5%)

- Knowledge of DB2 authentication
- Knowledge of DB2 authorizations
- Ability to set user and/or group privileges
- Knowledge of the DB2 Security Infrastructure (e.g., LBAC and security plug-ins)

DB2 for LUW Advanced DBA (734)

An IBM Certified Advanced Database Administrator is the lead DBA for the DB2 products on one or more of the following platforms: Linux, UNIX (including AIX, HP-UX, and Sun Solaris), and Windows. This individual has extensive experience as a DBA and extensive knowledge of DB2 9. This person is capable of performing the advanced tasks such as performance, high availability, security and networking that are required.

To earn an IBM Certified Advanced Database Administrator Certification for DB2 9, you must pass the following exams:

1. Exam 734 – DB2 9 for Linux, UNIX, and Windows Advanced Database Administrator
2. Either Exam 736 – Upgrade Exam for DB2 9 for Linux, UNIX, and Windows Database Administrator OR Exam 731 – Full Exam for DB2 9 for Linux, UNIX, and Windows Database Administrator
3. Either Exam 700 – DB2 V8 Family Fundamentals OR Exam 730 – DB2 9 Fundamentals

The test contains six sections with 51 multiple-choice questions. You must score 64% or greater to pass the exam. The percentages after each section title reflect the approximate distribution of the total question set across the sections.

Section 1 — Database Design (14%)

- Ability to design, create and manage table spaces
- Ability to design, create and manage buffer pools
- Ability to design and configure federated database access

Section 2 — Data Partitioning and Clustering (15%)

- Ability to design, create, and manage database partitioning
- Ability to design, create and manage multi-dimensional clustered tables
- Ability to design, create, and manage table partitioning
- Knowledge of Balance Configuration Unit (BCU)

Section 3 — High Availability and Diagnostics (20%)

- Ability to manage database logs for recovery
- Ability to use advanced backup features
- Ability to use advanced recovery features
- Ability to enhance database availability

- Ability to use diagnostic tools (db2pd, db2mtrk, inspect, db2dart, db2diag)

Section 4 — Performance and Scalability (33%)

- Identify and use DB2 registry variables that affect database system performance
- Identify and use configuration parameters that affect database system performance
- Knowledge of query optimizer concepts
- Ability to manage and tune database, instance and application memory and I/O
- Ability to use data compression
- Ability to analyze performance problems
- Ability to manage a large number of users and connections
- Ability to determine the more appropriate index
- Ability to exploit parallelism

Section 5 — Security (8%)

- Knowledge of external authentication mechanisms
- Ability to implement data encryption
- Ability to implement Label Based Access Control (LBAC)
- Ability to use DB2 Audit

Section 6 — Connectivity and Networking (10%)

- Ability to configure client server connectivity (e.g., db2discovery)
- Ability to manage connections to host systems
- Ability to identify and resolve connection problems

IBM Certified DBA for DB2 9 for LUW, Upgrade (736)

If you are one of the many people who has earned an IBM Certified Database Administrator – DB2 UDB V8.1 for Linux, UNIX and Windows Certification, the is an upgrade exam available.

As with Version 8, there are two different exams that you can take to upgrade to the V9 DBA Certification:

1. Exam 736 – IBM Certified Database Administrator for DB2 9 for Linux, UNIX, and Windows, Upgrade Exam
2. Exam 731 – IBM Certified Database Administrator for DB2 9 for Linux, Unix and Windows, Full Exam

The Upgrade Exam 736 is only an option for candidates who are already certified as an IBM Certified Database Administrator – DB2 UDB V8.1 for Linux, UNIX and Windows. If you pass the exam you will earn you the same certificate that you'd earn from passing Exam 731.

Section 1 — Server Management (29%)

- Understand the functionality of AUTOCONFIGURE
- Ability to manually configure communications (protocol image (IPV6))
- Ability to enable automatic maintenance
- Ability to enable Self-Tuning Memory Manager
- Ability to enable Utility Throttling

Section 2 — Data Placement (21%)

- Ability to CREATE DATABASE (new default behavior)
- Ability to create and manage Automatic Storage table spaces
- Knowledge of Table Partitioning
- Knowledge of Data Row Compression

Section 3 — XML Concepts (13%)

- Ability to use XML data types
- Ability to create and manage XML indexes
- Ability to use basic XML functions (XMLPARSE, XMLSERIALIZE, XMLVALIDATE, XMLQUERY)
- Understanding XQuery fundamentals
- Using DB2 Utilities with XML data

Section 4 — Analyzing DB2 Activity (16%)

- Ability to use DB2 utilities (db2bfd, db2mtrk, db2pd)
- Ability to monitor deadlocks
- Ability to use administrative routines and SNAPSHOT functions

Section 5 — High Availability (10.5%)

- Ability to use RECOVER DATABASE command
- Knowledge of High Availability Disaster Recovery (HADR)

Section 6 — Security (10.5%)

- Understanding of Label Based Access Control (LBAC)
- Knowledge of new authentication types

APPENDIX B

DB2DEMO Installation

Introduction

Now that you've read this book, you probably want to try out some of the examples against DB2. The DB2DEMO program lets you explore the various features of DB2, including:

- SQL Features
  - Referential Integrity
  - Domains and Constraints
  - Triggers
  - Recursive SQL
  - Outer Joins
- Advanced Object-Relational Features
  - Large Object Support (BLOBs)
  - User-defined Types
  - User-defined Functions
  - Table functions
  - Row-types and Typed Tables
  - Reference Types
  - SQL PL Stored Procedure Language
- XML Support
  - SQL/XML Functions
  - XML Data type
  - XQuery Language Extensions
- Business Intelligence Features
  - Star Schema support
  - Multi-dimensional Analysis
  - Dynamic Bitmap indexes

    - Automatic Summary Tables
    - Compression
    - Table partitioning
- Manageability
- Performance

This demo lets you try out many of these features of DB2, including showing you some of the administrative and performance features. The only thing you need to do is check that you have requirements and then install the code!

Installation Requirements

This program is meant to be used for demonstrating the functionality of the DB2 9 product. In order to use this program, you need the following configuration:

- Windows Operating System (Windows 2000/XP/2003/Vista)
- Browser (Internet Explorer, Firefox, or any suitable browser)
- Access to a DB2 system with the SAMPLE database

Your workstation or laptop should have a minimum of 384M of memory to run Windows and DB2, although more than 512M is ideal. The DB2DEMO program itself needs approximately 3MB of disk space for the program and help files, but this can grow to 20MB to hold the sample tables that are created during the demonstration.

The program will work with DB2 Version 7+, but not all features will work if you use a down-level server. In addition to having a DB2 server available, the SAMPLE database must be created beforehand, otherwise the program will not be able to run any of the examples. The SAMPLE database is normally created as part of the First Steps program after the DB2 installation is complete. If you need to create the sample database, use the db2sampl command.

While the SAMPLE database is the default database used by the DB2DEMO program, any database can be accessed by the program on all of the DB2 supported platforms, including:

- AIX
- HP
- SUN
- Linux (all platforms)
- Windows 2000, Windows XP, Windows 2003
- iSeries (DB2 Connect Required)
- z/OS (DB2 Connect Required)

Although the database can reside on one of these machines, the actual client (demo) must run on Windows 2000/XP/2003/Vista. For details on how to do this, please see the installation procedure section.

The DB2DEMO program can also be used against other DB2 databases in your environment, but many of the examples are strictly for the DB2 on the Linux, UNIX, and Windows platforms.

DB2 Database Server

The DB2 database server can be installed from the DB2 web site:

`www-306.ibm.com/software/data/db2/express/download.html`

DB2 Express-C is a version of DB2 Express Edition (DB2 Express) for the community. DB2 Express-C is a no-charge data server for use in development and deployment of applications, including XML, C/C++, Java, .NET, PHP, and more. DB2 Express-C can be run on up to 2 dual-core CPU servers, with up to 4 GB of memory, any storage system setup and with no restrictions on database size or any other artificial restrictions.

Installing the DB2DEMO Program

Installation File

The DB2DEMO installation program consists of only one file that contains the executable along with all of the supporting files required to run the program. The file name when downloaded from the internet is DB2DEMOSETUP.EXE.

Before beginning the installation, make sure that you have about 10M of disk space available (half of this is temporary space that will be released when the installation is complete).

DB2DEMO can be downloaded from the IBM developerWorks website:

`www-128.ibm.com/developerworks/db2/library/demos/db2demo/index.html`

Setup and Installation of the Program

From within the directory that you placed the DB2DEMOSETUP program, you double-click your left mouse button on this file name, or execute it from a command line:

```
C:\DOWNLOADS>DB2DEMOSETUP.EXE
```

After clicking on the DB2DEMOSETUP program, there will be some temporary messages displayed while the program unpacks some files, and then you will be presented with the first installation screen (next page).

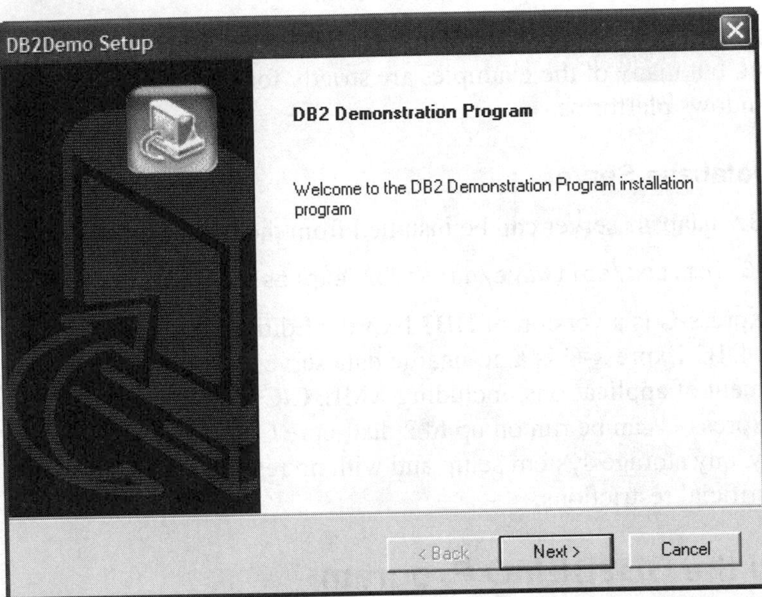

Make sure that you have exited any programs that may be currently running (just to be on the safe side) and the hit OK to continue on to the next step. The next screen gives you the copyright and legal information for the program. Please read it and say "YES" to continue:

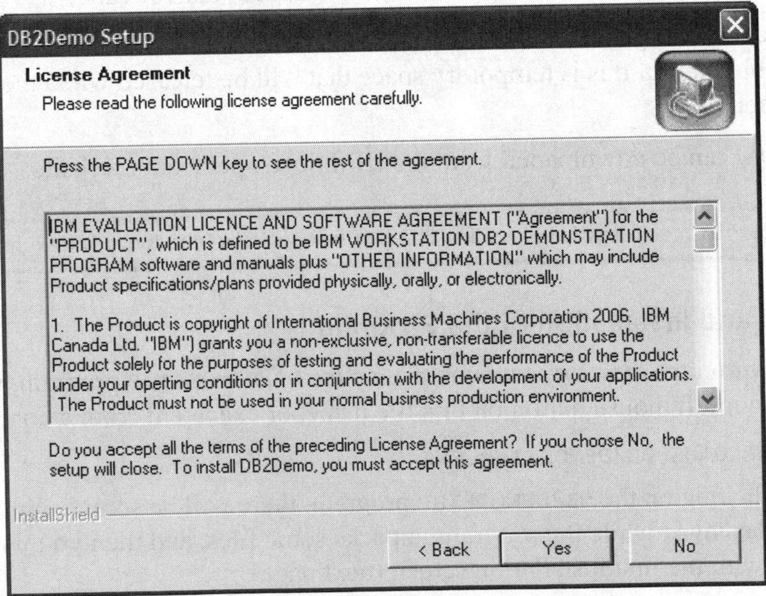

The next screen that appears is the directory screen:

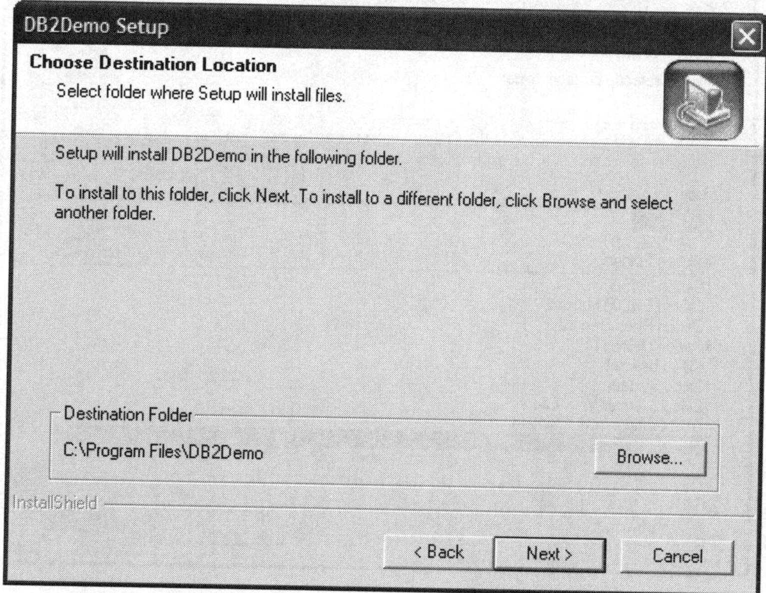

Select a drive and directory to place the `DB2DEMO` program into. By default, the name of the directory is called `C:\Program Files\DB2DEMO` and it is placed on the C: drive. The above example shows how the installation directory can be changed.

Use the Drives and Directories list boxes to change the value of the field to point to the installation directory you want. When you are ready to go, hit the **Next** button. At this point in time, the installation program will ask you for the Program Group that the `DB2DEMO` program will be placed into.

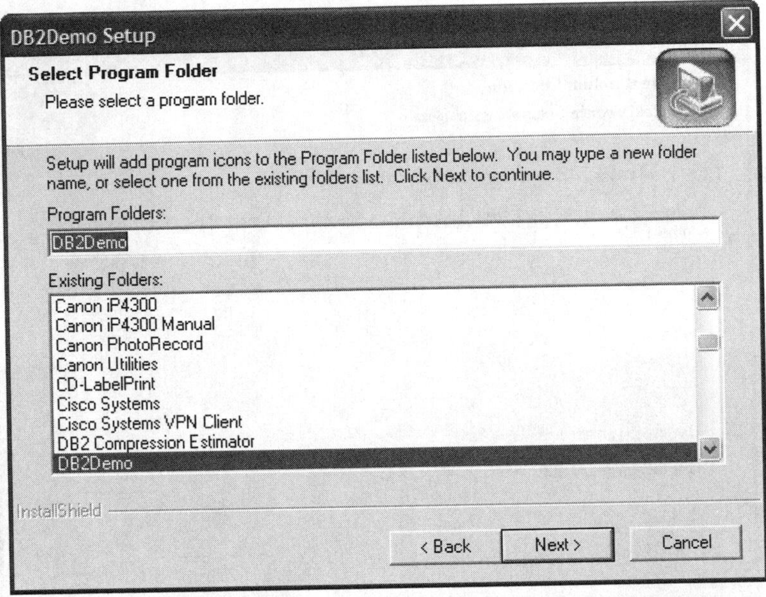

Once you have selected the group name, the program will confirm the installation information:

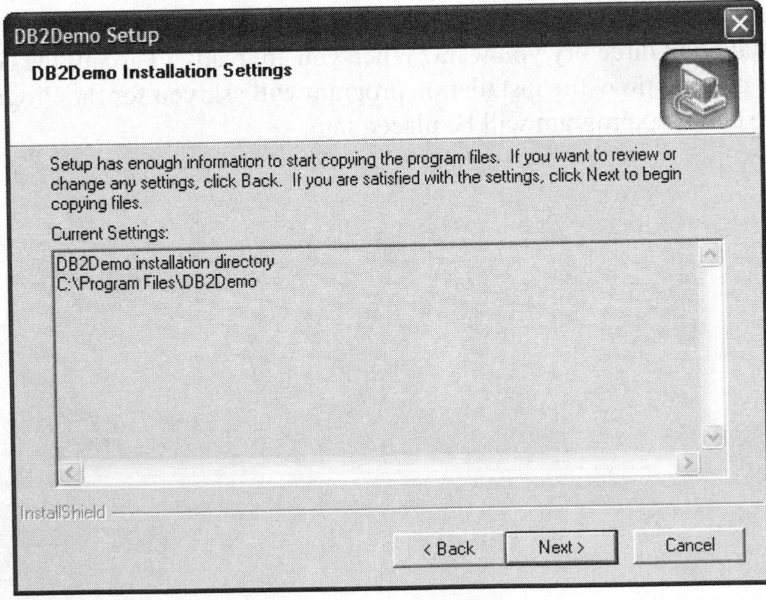

Once you hit the continue button, the program will begin copying files:

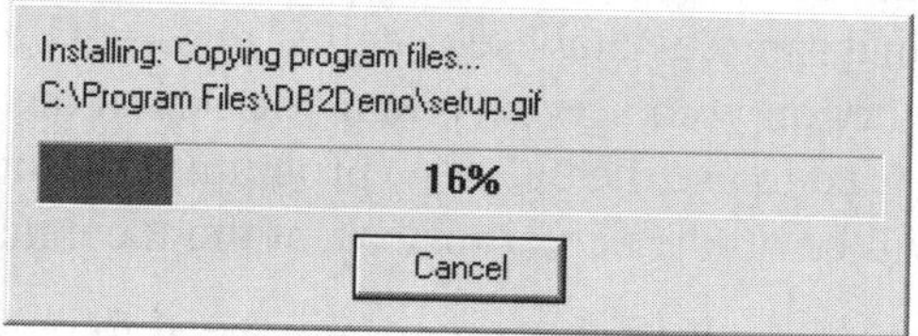

When copying is complete, the final completion box will be displayed.

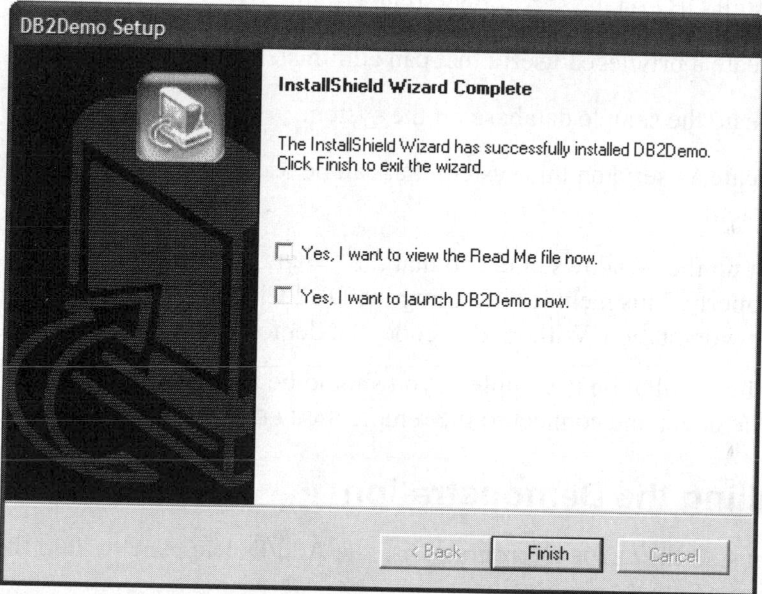

Depending on which operating system you were installing on, you may be asked to reboot the machine, or be given an option to try out the demo program, or look at the additional README information that is supplied with the program. You can also start up DB2DEMO by going into the DB2DEMO group and selecting the DB2DEMO icon from the DB2DEMO group (or whatever you called it) and clicking on it:

To see how the program works, check out the section on running the program. If you want to run the DB2DEMO program against another server, please read the instructions on customization.

Advanced Installation

The SAMPLE database can be installed on any server supported by DB2. The program that creates that sample database is called db2sampl and can be found in the sqllib\bin directory on your server. When you install the database on a different machine, you still need to use the DB2DEMO program on Windows 2000 or Windows XP, but the data will be on the server instead of the local machine.

In order to install this on a different server, you need to be very familiar with DB2 commands and the security of the machine you are working on. The steps required to run this demo against a different server are:

1. Install DB2 on the server operating system.
2. Create a privileged userid that can administer the DB2 system.
3. Create the sample database on the system.
4. Create a userid on this system that can be used to connect from the remote system.
5. Set up the Windows client so that the SAMPLE database has been catalogued properly. This includes installing the DB2 Client Application Enabler code on the workstation. Without this code, the demonstration program cannot run.

Once the installation is complete, you should be able to run the DB2DEMO program from the client and connect to the remote SAMPLE database.

Uninstalling the Demonstration

To uninstall the DB2DEMO program, use the Add/Delete panel within the Services group to delete the application:

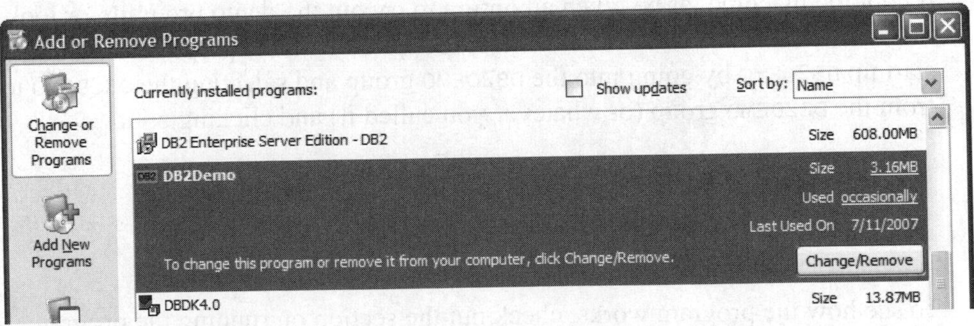

Select the DB2 Demonstration program and the various files will be deleted. The directory may not be deleted if you have personalized any of the files.

Using the DB2DEMO Program

To start the demonstration program, go either to a command or use Windows explorer to start the `DB2DEMO` program in the `DB2DEMO` directory (or wherever you choose to place it).

DB2Demo ▸ DB2 DB2Demo

Or you can run it from a command line:

```
DB2DEMO [filename.sql] {option1=value option2=value ...}
```

Once you have started the program, you will see the introduction screen:

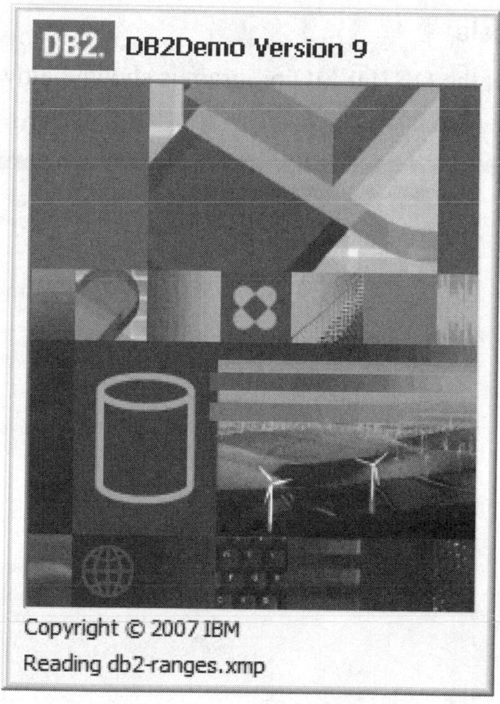

A number of brief messages will display, and finally the demonstration screen will be displayed.

Note: The program will use a number of defaults to start up:

- password=
- userid=
- database="SAMPLE"
- file="DB2DEMO.SQL"
- font="Tahoma"
- fontsize="10"
- schema=(userid if blank)
- autostart="on"
- sqllib="c:\program files\ibm\sqllib" or DB2INSTPROF value if set
- instance="DB2" or DB2INSTANCE value if set

If the `DB2DEMO.SQL` file cannot be found, an error message will be displayed and the command section of the screen will be blank. Errors can also occur when connecting to the `SAMPLE` database. If there is a failure of any type, the program will display the error and bring up the demonstration screen. At this point you need to check your connectivity to the `SAMPLE` database.

Overview of the Panels

The main screen of the DB2DEMO program is shown below.

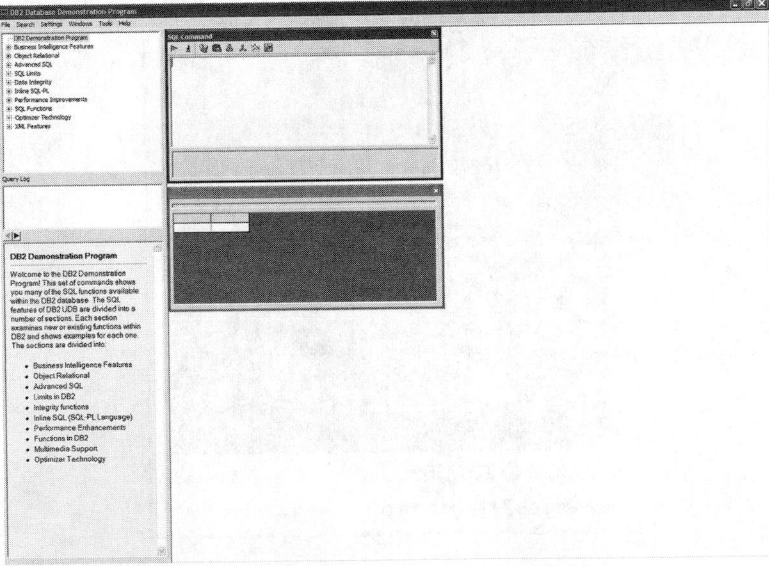

The demonstration screen is divided into a number of sections. On the far left-hand side of the screen are:

- SQL Commands
- Query Log
- Help

This section is not moveable. The middle section of the screen contains:

- SQL Input
- Error Messages
- Output

These windows can be resized and moved around in the remaining space on the screen. Finally, there is a toolbar on the far right-hand side of the screen that allows you to launch any of the DB2 administrative tools.

In addition to these screens, there are a number of windows which will be displayed depending on what you are doing:

- Performance Monitor
- Graphing/Plotting Menu
- XML/Long string display

The following section describes the function of each of the windows found in the main demonstration screen.

Main Panel Window

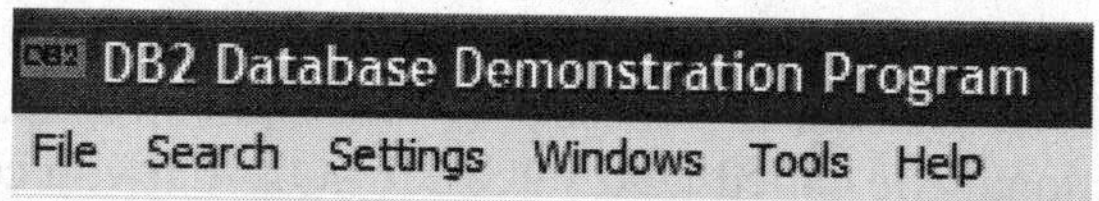

The main panel has six menu items. Each one of these sections is described below.

File

The file menu has two options:

When you have finished using the DB2DEMO program, click on the exit button to close the application and disconnect from the database. Note that the program keeps a connection open to the database at all times. This means that any utilities that need an exclusive lock on the system will not run until you exit the DB2DEMO application.

The Open option will load a new SQL file into the DB2DEMO program. When you want to load a new set of SQL commands, click on the File button and then select the file you want to load from the menu:

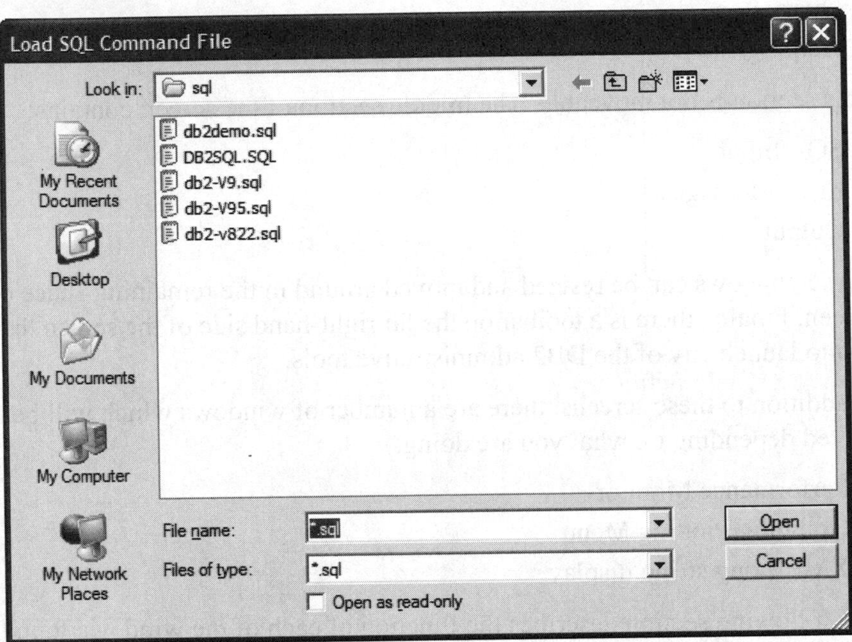

When you hit the LOAD button, the file will be loaded into the demonstration program. If you don't want to change the current set of SQL, just click on the cancel button.

DB2 Note

There is an additional file called DB2V9CERT.SQL that you can use to explore many of the examples that are described in this book.

Search

The Search option allows you find all of the scripts (examples) in the current set of SQL statements that have the characters that you are looking for:

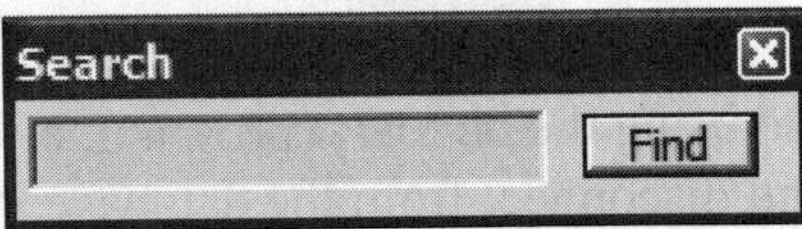

When a search term is entered, the set of commands in the command window is expanded to show the individual examples that have the keyword in the description line.

For instance, the normal command window looks similar to the following screen:

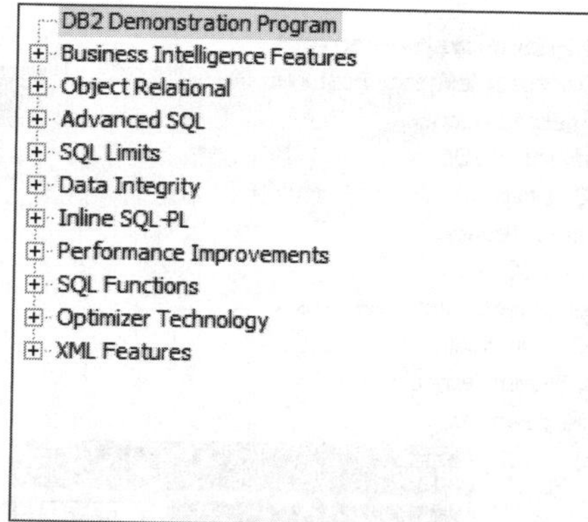

The search field is filled in with "union" and the Find button pressed.

This will result in the command window being modified to show the examples with "union" in the description highlighted:

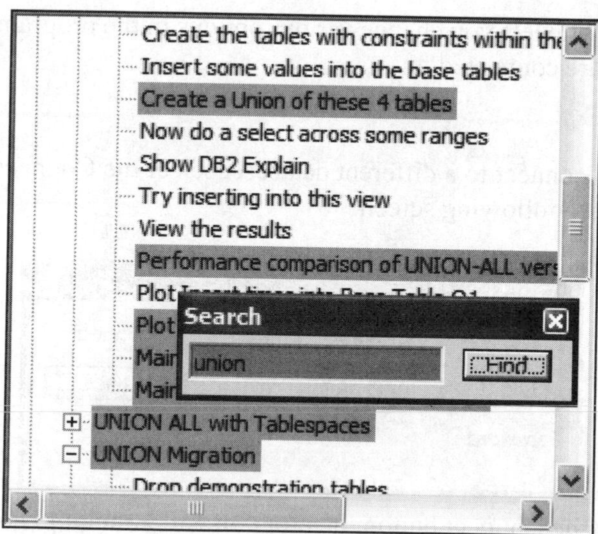

Note also that the search field turns green to indicate that a value was found. In the event that the value was not found, the field will turn red:

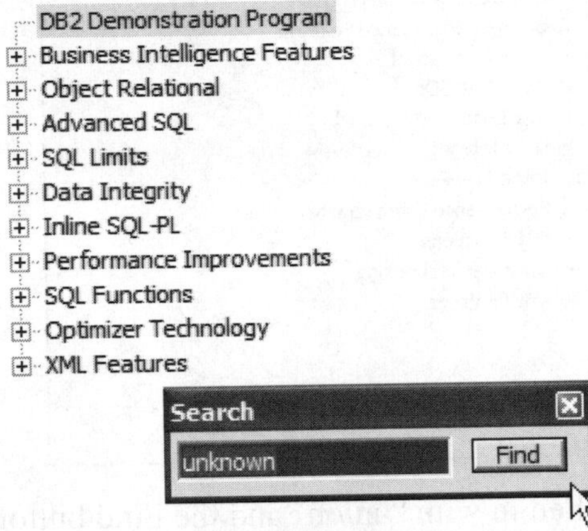

Settings

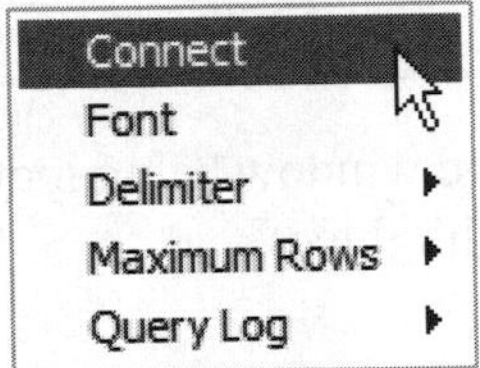

The settings menu lets you change various options in the program, including which database you are connected to.

Connect

If you want to connect to a different database, select the Connection option. This will bring up the following screen:

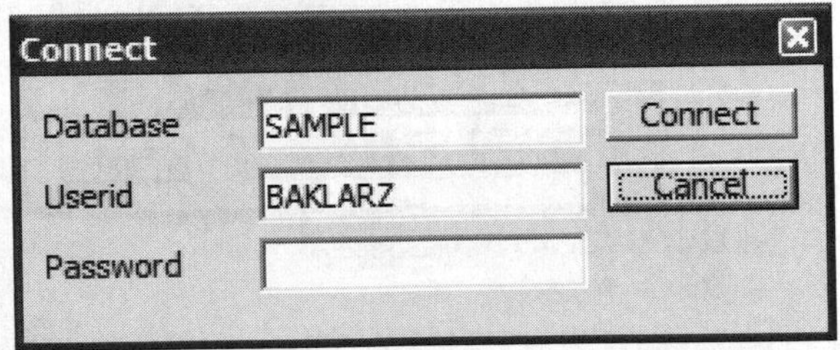

When you hit the Connect button the program will attempt to connect to the database using the userid and password that you have supplied. If you do not supply a userid or password, your default userid will be used as part of the connection.

Font

The fonts used by the program are controlled by this menu. When pressed, a panel will appear that gives the user the opportunity to change the size of the font and the type of font used in the SQL input window:

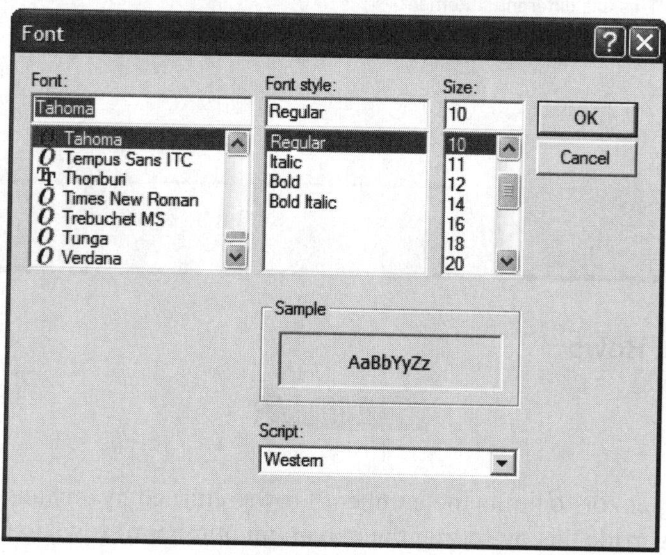

Delimiter

The delimiter option lets you change which delimiter is used to separate SQL and XQuery statements in the program. By default this value is a semicolon (;), but it can also be the at sign (@), a dollar sign ($), and the hash sign (#). When creating triggers, stored procedures, and functions you will need to use a different delimiter since the semicolon is a statement delimiter within the SQL PL language. The same is true with XQuery where the semicolon is also used. In this case, it may be easier to use the hash symbol (#) to separate each statement.

This option will set the delimiter to always be the character selected. However, you can change the delimiter for a block of SQL by having the first character of the string be one of these special characters. In this case, every statement will need to be delimited by this character in the SQL.

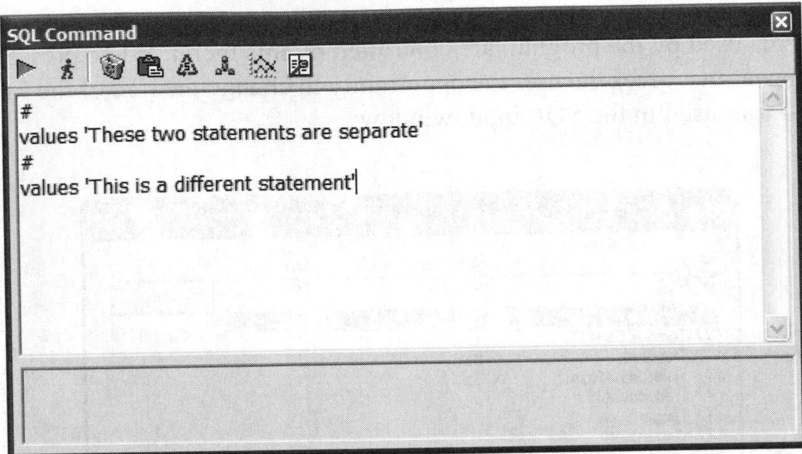

Maximum Rows

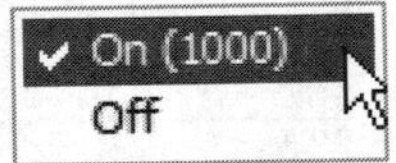

By default, DB2DEMO limits the number of rows returned by any answer set to 1000. You can override this by setting the maximum number of rows to Off.

Query Log

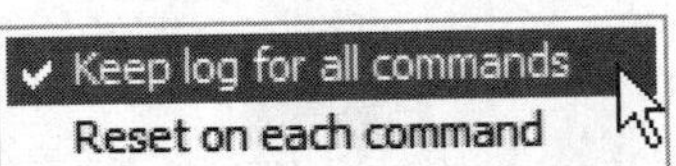

The query log keeps track of the commands that have been executed in the program. By default, all commands are tracked in the query log window. This setting can be changed so that the log is cleared whenever a new command stream is executed. This is sometimes useful when you want to debug an SQL script.

Windows

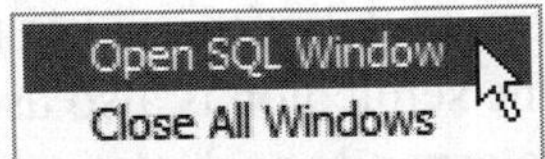

There are two options in the Windows menu. The first option will open up another SQL window (next page).

Normally the DB2DEMO program will open up an SQL window when the program starts. However, you may want to have an additional window open to compare two different sets of SQL. There is no limit to the number of SQL windows that can be opened, but it may become difficult to track which window is active when too many are displayed!

If you want to clear all of the SQL windows, select the Close All Windows option. Note that this will get rid of all of the SQL windows, so if you want to continue running SQL commands you will need to open at least one SQL window.

Tools

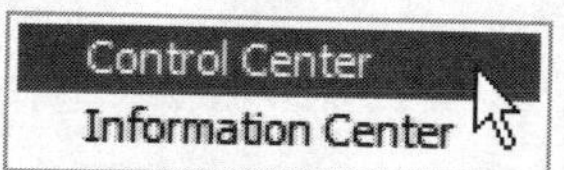

The DB2 Control Center and the Information Center are both available from the Tools menu. Note that these DB2 programs must be installed in order for the DB2DEMO program to access them.

Help

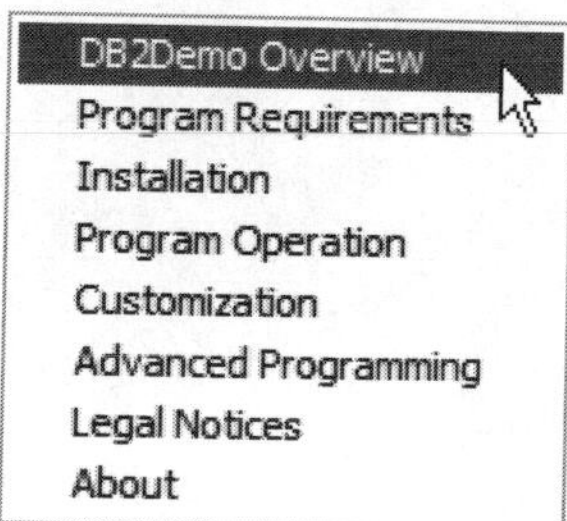

The Help menu contains links to all of the help topics associated with the DB2DEMO program.

SQL Input Window

The DB2 Input window is used to display and execute commands. You can enter any SQL or XQuery in this input window and then hit the RUN key to execute it. Note that XQuery commands must always start with XQUERY in order for DB2 to properly execute it. Near the bottom of this screen is the message panel which gets updated with status information:

If you want additional error information, click anywhere in the status box and a larger error description will be displayed.

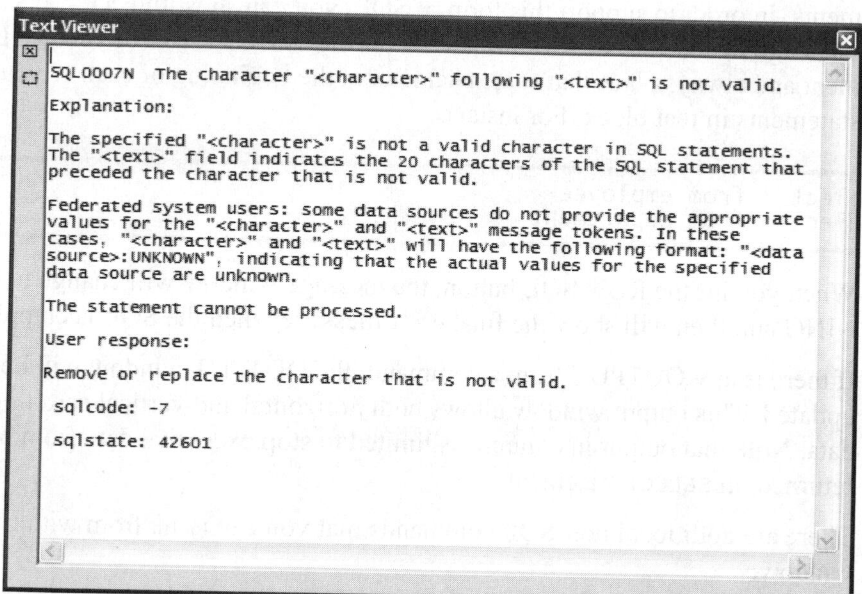

Note that the larger error message is only available when running with DB2 V9. At the top of the SQL Input window are a number of buttons. The buttons (from LEFT to RIGHT) are:

- Run SQL

  When you hit the Run SQL button it will submit the SQL to DB2 to execute. The types of SQL that you can execute from this program are:

```
UPDATE, INSERT, DELETE, CREATE, DROP, VALUES, GRANT, REVOKE,
WITH, XQUERY
```

  You cannot run a LOAD, CONNECT, or any utility from this screen. Generally, most SQL will run. The worst that can happen is you get an error message back from DB2!

  To enter an SQL statement in this window, place the cursor in the input area and click with the LEFT mouse button, and then start typing. You can separate multiple SQL commands by placing a " ; " at the end of each statement:

```
select * from employee;
select * from department;
```

  Occasionally you need to use a different delimiter. Triggers and SQL PL stored procedures make use of the semi-colon (;) as a delimiter between multiple statements. In order to support this form of SQL, you can substitute a "#", "$", or "@" sign instead. To do this, use the "#" as the first character of your SQL statement and always place that same character at the beginning of each of your SQL statements in that block. For instance:

```
#select * from employee
#select * from department
```

When you hit the RUN SQL button, the message window will change to RUNNING and then will show the final error message when the SQL is complete.

If there is any OUTPUT from a command, the OUTPUT window will be updated. This output window allows both horizontal and vertical scrolling of data. Note that output in columns is limited to stop excessive data from being returned on `SELECT` statements.

There are additional non-SQL commands that you can issue from within this window:

- %VIEW SELECT ...

  This command will let you view a field in the database that is larger than 255 characters. Normally this is used to look at the results of an EXPLAIN statement against the database. The field is extracted from the `SELECT` statement and then placed into a separate window.

- Other commands

  More advanced commands can be found in the Advanced Programming section. These additional commands let you load new scripts into the program, run operating system commands, create menus, and do a variety of other tasks.

- Autorun On/Off

  When you click on an SQL command, it will have the SQL statements in the example placed into the SQL Input window and executed immediately if the Autorun button is set. You can change this behavior if you want to view the SQL before it gets executed. Pressing the key will change it to the Stop icon.

- Clear SQL

  The Clear button clears all SQL from the input area.

- Clear and Paste

  The Clear and Paste button will clear the contents of the current SQL window and place the contents of the clipboard into it. If you don't want to clear the contents of the existing window, you should use the standard Window shortcuts — Cntl-Insert and Shift-Insert, to cut and paste.

- Show last command (5)

  The re-cycle button with a 5 in the middle tells the program to retrieve the last SQL command issued. It keeps a list of the last five commands that were typed in.

- Explain SQL

  DB2 has the Visual Explain facility which gives you a graphical snapshot of the way a transaction will run in the database engine. Unfortunately, this utility can only be invoked directly through the Control Center! Instead of using the graphical explain, this button will invoke a textual explain facility which will display a character (text) representation of how a statement will execute. While not as detailed as a Visual Explain, it can give you some valuable insight into how the statement will execute. Consider the following SQL statement in an SQL windows:

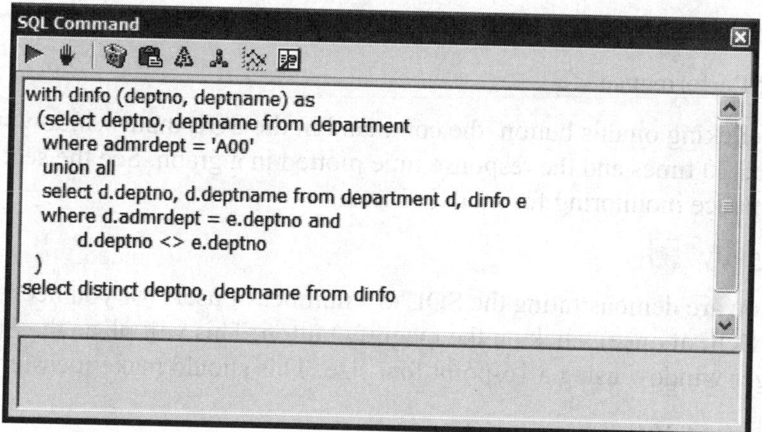

SQL Command
with dinfo (deptno, deptname) as
(select deptno, deptname from department
where admrdept = 'A00'
union all
select d.deptno, d.deptname from department d, dinfo e
where d.admrdept = e.deptno and
d.deptno <> e.deptno
)
select distinct deptno, deptname from dinfo

Here is the corresponding explain output:

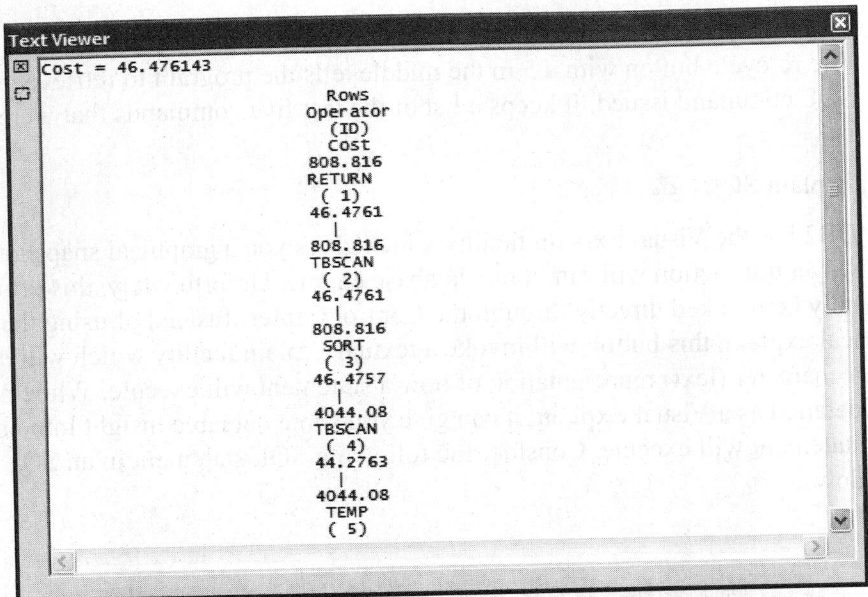

- Plot Performance

  By clicking on this button, the command in the SQL input window will be executed 20 times and the response time plotted in a graph. See the section on performance monitoring for more information.

- Magnify

  If you are demonstrating the SQL to a number of users (or you need to see all of the SQL at once), click on the magnify button. This will place the SQL into a larger window using a 16-point font size. This should make it easier to read.

SQL Output Window

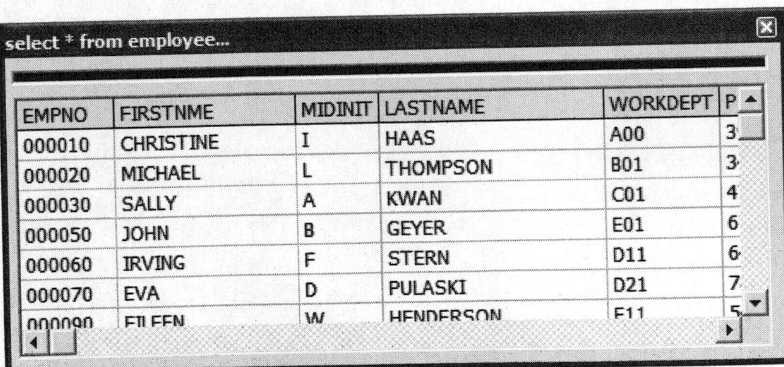

EMPNO	FIRSTNME	MIDINIT	LASTNAME	WORKDEPT	P
000010	CHRISTINE	I	HAAS	A00	3
000020	MICHAEL	L	THOMPSON	B01	3
000030	SALLY	A	KWAN	C01	4
000050	JOHN	B	GEYER	E01	6
000060	IRVING	F	STERN	D11	6
000070	EVA	D	PULASKI	D21	7
000090	EILEEN	W	HENDERSON	E11	5

The SQL Output panel shows the results of the query done in the SQL Input window. To resize a column, click on the column separator on the title line (column descriptions) and move it to the right or left. This will re-size the individual column.

If one of the columns is too large to display on the screen, you can left-click on the column to have the value placed into a separate window. For instance, many of the XML examples produce strings that are too long to display in a normal window. The DB2DEMO program has the ability to format the XML to make it easier to read. For instance, the following panel contains an SQL statement that creates a large XML string:

SQL Command

```
select
 XML2CLOB
  (
  XMLELEMENT(NAME "DoctorRecord",
     XMLELEMENT(NAME "DoctorID", d.doc_id),
     XMLELEMENT(NAME "Firstname", d.doc_firstname),
     XMLELEMENT(NAME "Lastname",  d.doc_lastname),
     XMLELEMENT(NAME "Extension", d.doc_extension)
     )
```

This SQL results in the output displaying as follows:

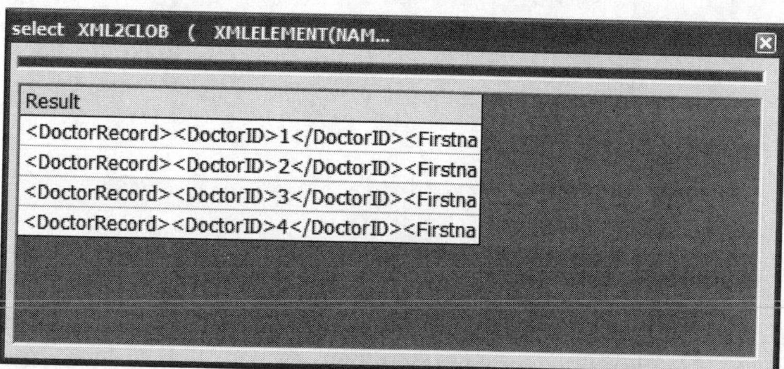

This does not lend itself well to understanding the structure of the resulting XML! By clicking on the large character column, DB2DEMO will format it into a separate window that is easier to view:

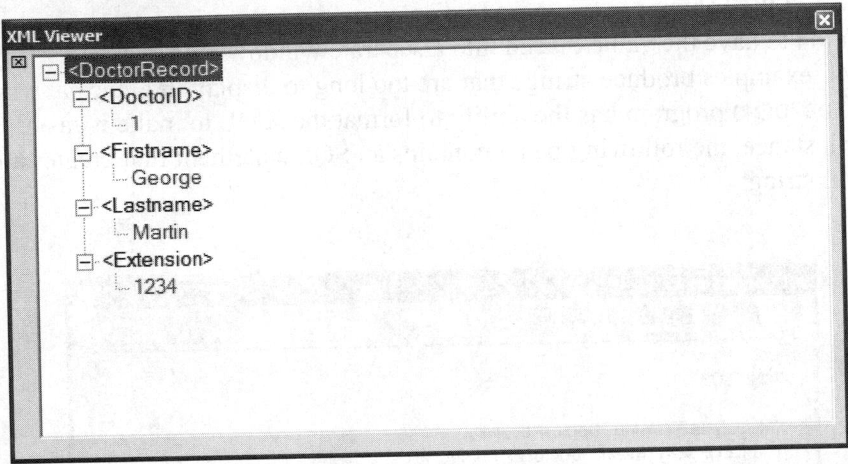

Command Window

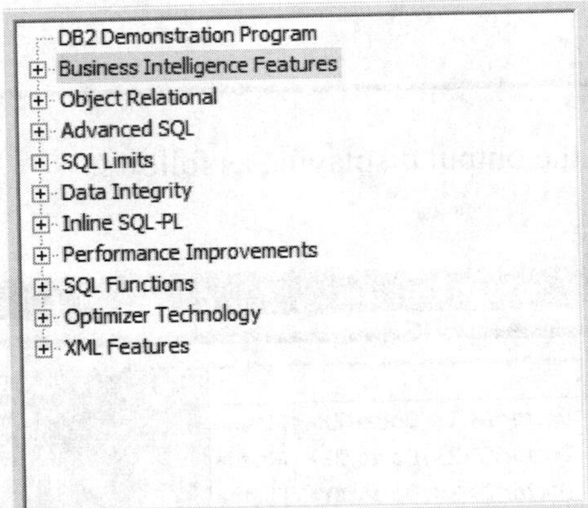

The command window contains all of the examples of SQL that are demonstrated in the DB2DEMO program. By default, the DB2DEMO program will automatically execute the SQL found in the command window when you click on an item. If you want to stop automatic execution, click on the Run On/Off button and it will toggle between on (green) and off (red).

In order to execute one of the sample SQL commands, you need to click on one of the sections shown in the SQL Example. If you click on a [+] sign, it will expand to show the various SQL commands:

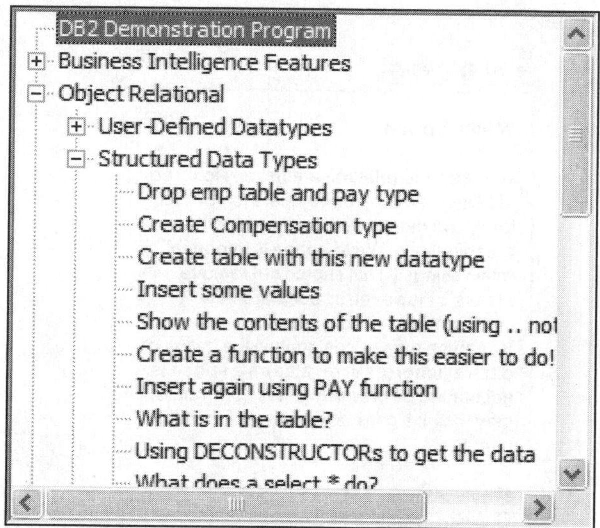

There are two types of commands that can be issued from this screen:

- SQL Commands

  When you click on an SQL command, it will have the SQL statements in the example placed into the SQL Input window and executed immediately if the Autorun button is set. You can change this behavior if you want to talk about the SQL before it gets executed (see the Autorun button). If you click on the [-] when the list is already opened, it will close up again into a single item.

  You will also notice that when clicking on any of the items that the SQL information box also gets updated. Usually this box will contain information on the command that is being executed. You can use the scroll bars to go up and down to see what the SQL is trying to accomplish.

  When the SQL executes, the DB2 Input message window will change to "Running" and then be updated with any error codes. Always take a look at this window to determine what the status of the SQL is.

- Tutorial

  A tutorial will place information in the help panel that also includes buttons to try the different examples in the text. For instance, the XML tutorial will create a screen similar to:

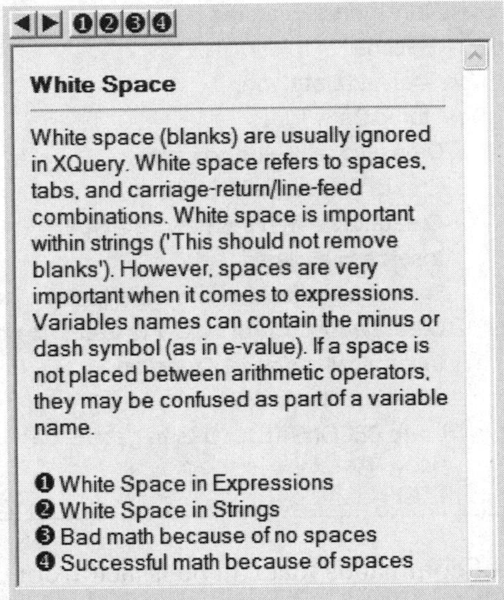

  If the tutorial contains multiple panels, a user can page through the entire presentation by clicking with the LEFT arrow (at the top) or use the RIGHT arrow to page backwards. The numbers represent different XQuery (or SQL) examples that will get executed when pressed.

Query Log

Underneath the command window is the Query Log. This window tracks all of the SQL commands that were issued in any of the SQL Input windows. When an SQL command completes, this window is updated to include the command that was executed, the records returned, the return code, and the total run time.

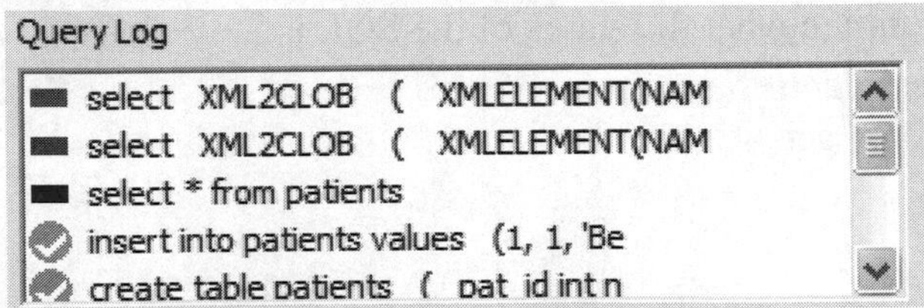

Depending on the type of SQL executed, you will see either a success or failure code, or a color bar that indicates which output window corresponds to the result set. The icons that are found on this panel are:

- Execution Error

  If an SQL statement fails, the query log will contain the error icon along with a short description of the SQL statement. If the user clicks on the error icon, two additional lines are displayed:

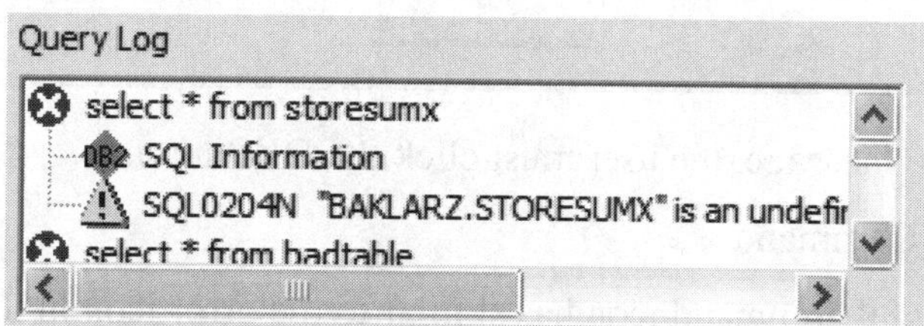

  The SQL information line gives the user the exact SQL statement that was executed. By clicking on this line, a new SQL window will be displayed with the statement in the input box:

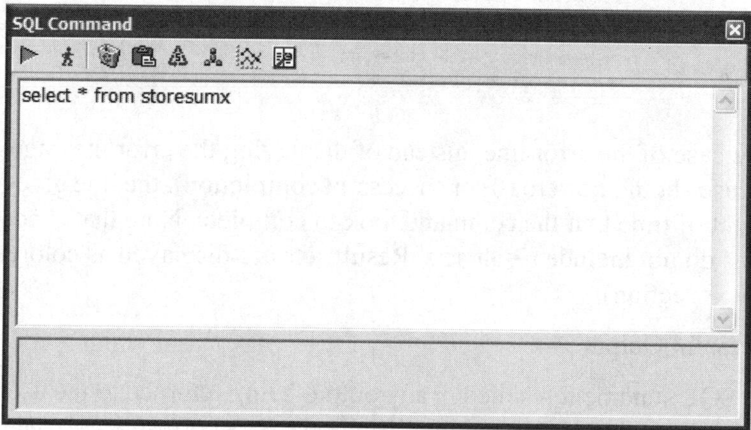

  You can correct the SQL in this new window and execute it, independent of any other SQL windows that you may have open. This SQL window is available for all SQL statements that were executed, whether they succeeded, failed, or generated an answer set.

The second line contains the error message that was generated by the SQL statement. If the user clicks on this line, a separate message window will appear with the entire error message displayed:

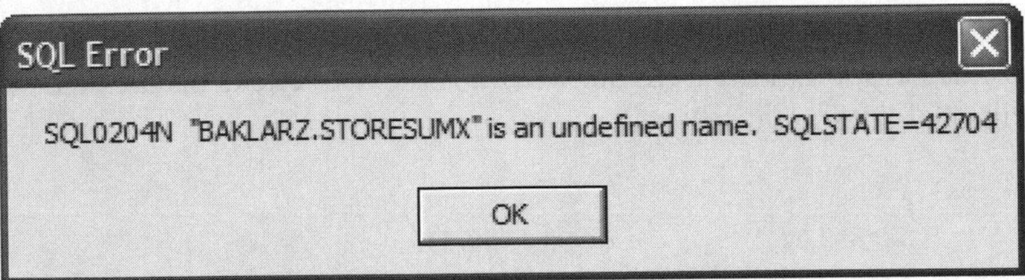

To close the message, the user must click the OK button.

- Successful Command

  The successful command icon has similar to the error icon in that it has both an SQL information line and an error return line:

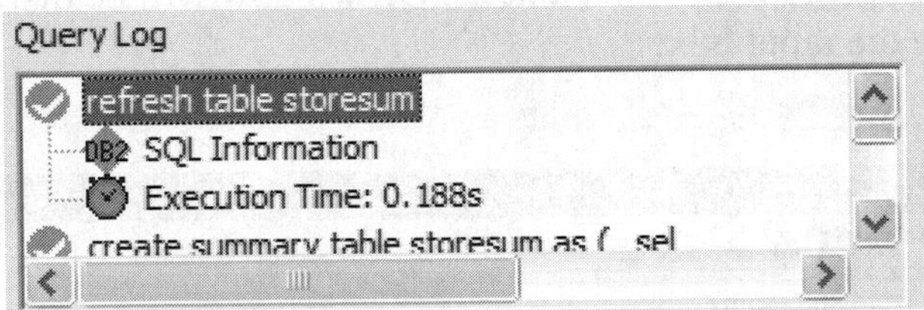

  In the case of the error line, instead of displaying the error message (which in this case should be zero (0) or successful completion), the line gives the user the amount of time that the command took to complete. Note that successful commands do not include result sets. Result sets are displayed as colored bars (see the next section).

- Successful Output

  If an SQL statement resulted in any output being returned to the user, the icon in the query log would be a colored bar. These bars correspond to the output window that was produced by the SQL statement:

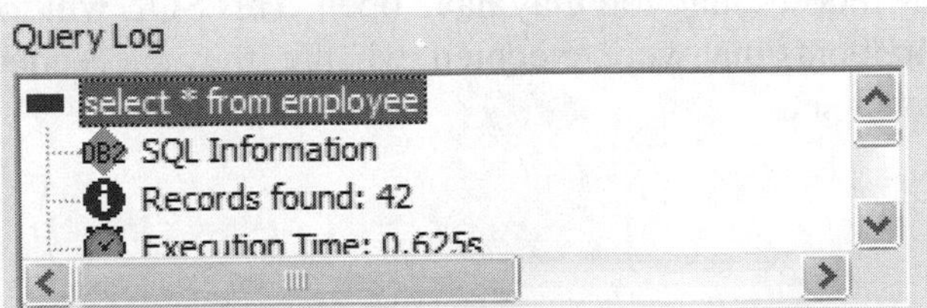

Note the color of the bar on the output window:

select * from employee...

EMPNO	FIRSTNME	MIDINIT	LASTNAME	WORKDEPT	P
000010	CHRISTINE	I	HAAS	A00	3
000020	MICHAEL	L	THOMPSON	B01	3
000030	SALLY	A	KWAN	C01	4
000050	JOHN	B	GEYER	E01	6
000060	IRVING	F	STERN	D11	6
000070	EVA	D	PULASKI	D21	7
000090	EILEEN	W	HENDERSON	E11	5

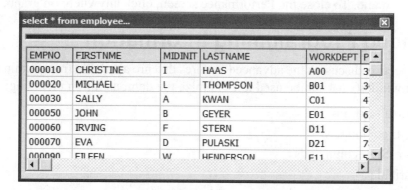

Opening up the log record will display three separate lines of information. The first line includes the SQL statement, which a user can edit and resubmit. The second line contains the number of records found in the answer set, and the final line gives the total execution time of the query.

Performance Monitoring

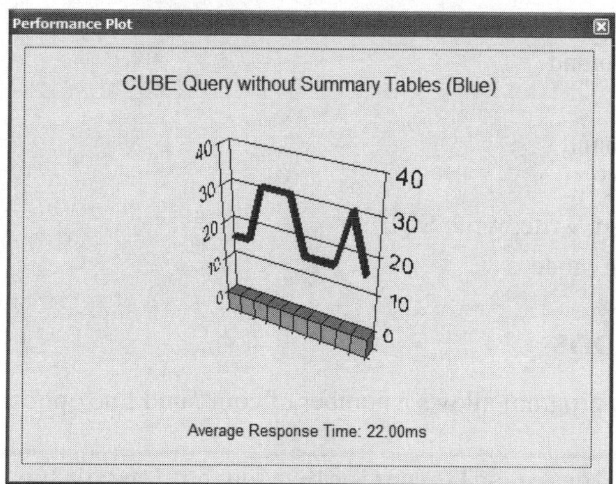

The performance screen is used to see how fast SQL transactions run. To use this performance chart, first execute an SQL command in the SQL Input window. Then click on the performance button to start the performance graph.

When you click on this button, the SQL found in the SQL Input window will run 20 times (no output is displayed during multiple executions) and the performance will be charted.

Note that the plot shows the number of milliseconds taken to execute the command, and the number at the top right-hand corner is the average execution time of the command. To close the Performance screen, click anywhere on graph.

Advanced Programming Information

This section discusses the advanced features that are available from within the SQL Input window that can be used to customize the demonstration including:

- Startup options
- SQL commands
- Non-SQL commands
- Variables
- Performance monitoring and graphing
- Comparing performance of 2 SQL statements
- Plotting data
- Message support
- Loading commands
- Loading large objects
- Operating system commands
- DB2 commands
- Clear command
- If section
- Exit command
- Explain SQL
- Open, close, write, write SQL
- Debugging mode

Startup Options

The DB2DEMO program allows a number of command line options:

```
DB2DEMO [filename.sql] {option1=value option2=value ...}
```

Each option consists of the option name followed by an equal sign and a value in quotes (either single or double quotes). Options are separated by spaces.

- password=

  By default the DB2DEMO program will not supply a userid or password to DB2. The program assumes that you have been authenticated by the operating system and that DB2 will use the default userid and password to connect to the database. If this is not the case, then you need to supply a userid and password before the program can connect you to the database.

- userid=

  As with the password parameter, DB2DEMO does not supply the userid to the DB2 system and assumes that the system defaults will be used. If this is not the case, then you need to supply the userid and password to DB2.

- database="SAMPLE"

  The DB2DEMO program uses portions of the SAMPLE database to demonstrate various features of DB2. If you do not have the SAMPLE database available, either create it using the "First Steps" facility of DB2 or run the DB2SAMPL program found within the \SQLLIB\BIN directory.

  If you want to use the program to run queries against other databases, then this is possible by either selecting a different database by using this option or using the Connect panel from within the DB2DEMO program.

- file="DB2DEMO.SQL"

  By default the DB2DEMO program will load the DB2DEMO.SQL file to demonstrate various DB2 features. However, you can create custom scripts and load them into the program via the command line or using the "Load File" feature from within the program itself.

- font="Tahoma"

  The default font used by DB2DEMO is Tahoma. The program will allow different fonts to be set, including

  - Arial
  - Lucida Console
  - Courier New
  - MS Sans Serif
  - Tahoma

  To change the font as part of the command line, use the font="font name" syntax, making sure you enclose the entire font name in quotes.

- fontsize="10"

  The default font size of the program is 10, but you can override this to any size up to 24 point. Anything larger than that would be too difficult to read!

- autostart="on"

  If the DB2DEMO cannot connect to the database, it attempts to start the DB2 instance. If you do not want the database to be started (especially if you are connecting to a remote database), set autostart="off".

- schema=(userid)

  The schema for all of the examples used by DB2DEMO is set to the current user that is connected. The assumption is that you are the owner of the SAMPLE database, so any administrative commands will include your userid as the high-level schema name. If the SAMPLE tables are owned by someone else, you will need to override the schema value that is generated by DB2DEMO. The first time you connect, the schema will be set to your current userid (even when doing a default connection with no userid or password). If you don't want this behavior, set schema to a value that DB2DEMO can use instead.

- sqllib=(DB2INSTPROF) instance=(DB2INSTANCE)

  The current location of the SQLLIB library (usually c:\program files\ibm\sqllib) is contained in the sqllib variable. This along with the DB2INSTANCE value (usually DB2) is used by the program when running a number of the DB2 commands. You can override these values if you have multiple versions of DB2 running on the same machine.

If you want to override these options permanently, you can place them all into a file called DB2DEMO.INI. This file is read before the command line options. The format of the file is:

```
* Comments have an asterisk at the beginning
option=value
```

Options in this file do no require quotes around them. This file can also contain the name of variables that you want to set for your script to use. The format is identical to assigning a value to an option. For instance, the following script will set the database to DEMO and the variable TITLE to a value. Then within the SQL scripts (or help panels), you can refer to the variable TITLE using the DB2DEMO variable format: %[title]. Make sure you do not use quotes around the values, otherwise the quotes will be included as part of the variable definition.

```
* DB2DEMO Options
database=DEMO
title=Test of New DB2DEMO Scripts
complexGIF=<img scr='c:\some directory\file.gif' alt="I can't find the GIF">
```

Querying the settings of the variables in the program (using the %DUMPVARS command) will display the settings for these variables:

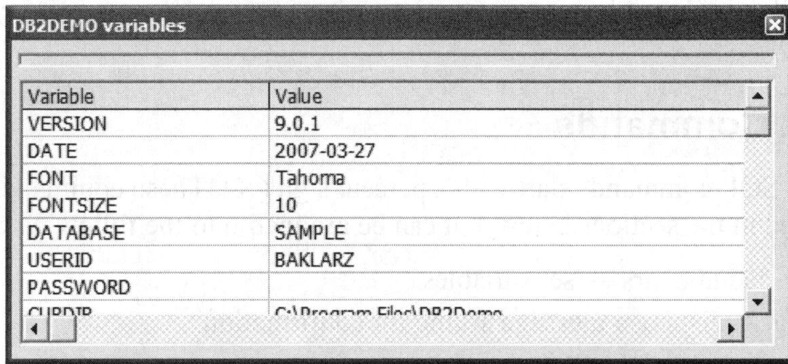
DB2DEMO variables

Variable	Value
VERSION	9.0.1
DATE	2007-03-27
FONT	Tahoma
FONTSIZE	10
DATABASE	SAMPLE
USERID	BAKLARZ
PASSWORD	

In summary, the order in which options are set by DB2DEMO are:

- Startup (default) values
- Options from the DB2DEMO.INI file
- Command line options

SQL Commands

The SQL Input window can be used to issue SQL and other types of commands. In most examples, the SQL input window will contain one SQL command:

```
select * from employee
```

However, there are occasions where you need to issue more than one SQL command. In order to do this, follow each SQL command with a semicolon (;):

```
select * from employee;
select count(*) from department;
```

If the SQL that you are using requires the use of a semicolon (like a trigger definition), use the dollar sign ($), hash symbol (#), or at sign (@) at the beginning of each SQL statement instead of the semicolon:

```
#select * from employee
#select count(*) from department
```

If the parser does not see a "$", "#" or "@" in the first position, it assumes that you will be using a semicolon. If one of the special symbols is found, then it will parse statements using these delimiters instead.

Hopefully you won't have may situations where semicolons are required as part of your SQL.

Non-SQL Commands

All non-SQL commands start with a percent sign (%). These commands are described in the sections below, but can be grouped into the following categories:

- %var, %dumpvars — set variables
- %msg — display a message asking for confirmation
- %graph — graph an SQL statements performance
- %cmd — issue an operating system command
- %load, %loadsql — load data and sql commands
- %view — examine text objects
- %plot — plot data based on the output window
- %db2 — issue commands to DB2 via the db2 command line interface
- %clear — clear the SQL Input area
- %connect — connect to another database
- %tables — list tables in the database
- %describe — describe table column layout
- %open, %write, %writesql, %close — I/O commands

If a command starts with a % and then is followed by one or more spaces, or is followed by an asterisk(*), the command will be considered to be a comment, up to and including the semicolon. For instance, the following is a comment line:

```
%* This is a comment;
%  And so is this;
```

The remainder of the commands are described below.

Variables

There are situations where you may want to create variables that get substituted into your SQL, rather than having to rewrite the SQL every time. The format to set a variable is:

```
%var var1=val1
     var2="value 2 with double quotes"
```

```
    var3='value 3 with single quotes'
    var4=
    var5;
```

Note that multiple variables can be set within a %var command block. There is no need to have separate var statements for each set of values, but the following is perfectly legal:

```
%var var1=val1;
%var var2="value 2 with double quotes";
```

The important thing to remember is that the semi-colon delimits the end of the %var command.

Some key information about variables and to the values that can be assigned to them:

- Variable Names

  Variable names are not case sensitive, so upper and lowercase letters in a name make no difference. The length of a variable name is also unlimited, but you probably don't want anything too long and the name can only consist of letters, numbers, and the "_-" characters. A blank always signifies the end of a variable name. The following are examples of good variable names:

```
val1 this_is_a_long_name a123
```

  However, these would not be treated too kindly in the program:

```
!avd asd%%qwe
```

- Variable Contents

  Anything can be placed into a variable, including spaces and special characters. If the value you are assigning to a variable does not contain blanks, then you can place it right after the equal sign. Note: You must always use the format variable=value with no spaces in between, otherwise the program will assume that these are two separate variables.

```
%var city=Toronto;
```

  If you do not place a value after the equal sign, (city=) or use the variable name without an equal sign (city), then the program will assign a null value to this object.

Strings that contain blanks or special characters can be enclosed within single (') or double (") quotes. Just make sure you end your strings and use the same delimiters!

```
%var city="New York";
```

- Variable Usage

  Once you have defined a variable, you can use it in a SELECT statement, or any other command, by placing the name of the variable in between the following characters %[]:

```
%var deptno=A00;
select * from employee where workdept = '%[deptno]';
```

Although it would be nice to make variables consistent with CLI and static SQL design (colon followed by variable name like :deptno), this was a simpler design to build. The variables can also be used in any expressions, not just SQL statements. An SQL statement has all of the variables substituted before it actually goes to DB2. This select statement would be changed to read:

```
select * from employee where workdept = 'A00';
```

As many variables as you like can be used in an SQL statement (or in any of the executable statements in this section). You could also use variables within VAR statements:

```
%var dept=A00;
%var
   dept-A=%[dept]A
   dept-B=%[dept]B;
```

The final result of all of these substitutions is that the variable %[dept-A] would have a value of A00A and %[dept-B] would contain A00B.

This example shows a subtle trick with variable substitution. Substitution of the line is done before it is executed. The following statement will not work as intended:

```
%var
   dept=A00
   dept-A=%[dept]A
   dept-B=%[dept]B;
```

The reason for this odd behavior is that the entire `%var` command gets substitution applied to it before each of the assignment statements takes place. This means that `%[dept]` does not exist yet when this is first executed, so the value of dept-A would be `%[dept]A`. The example shown earlier works since the first statement is executed and dept is set to `A00`. Then the next `%var` statement executes and the substitution works since dept now has a value.

Remember that if a variable is not defined prior to use, the brackets and variable name are kept within the statement.

- Displaying Variables Contents

  From the SQL window you can issue the `%DUMPVARS` command. This will display the names of all defined variables and their contents in the SQL output window. You can use this for debugging purposes.

Text Support

In order to show text columns in a window rather than a column in a table, the `%view` command can be used. The syntax of the view function is:

```
%view SELECT text_column from table where ....
```

The object_column refers to the text (char) column that you want to view. If you do not specify a column, an SQL error message will be displayed. The logic can be any SQL that results in the answer set you want to view. However, only the first record of the answer set will be displayed, even if multiple records are returned.

Performance Monitoring and Graphing

The `DB2DEMO` program has the ability to plot the performance of an SQL statement on a small graph. You can automatically start the graph from the SQL window by issuing the graph commands.

The format of the graph command is:

```
%graph
   title="Some title"
   color=red
   repeat=10
   sql="select * from employee";
```

Each one of these statements is optional, but you really should supply some SQL to plot! The parameters within the graph command are:

- "title="text" — Set the title of the graph

  The title of the graph window will contain the text found in the quotes. You must place the title within quotes unless your title has no blanks in it.

- color=red/blue/green — Set color of the next plot

  This command lets you select the color of the next plot that will be produced.

- repeat=count — How many times to execute the SQL

  This option tells the program to repeat the SQL a fixed number of times. The default is 10, but you can set this value to anything between 1 and 50.

- sql="select..." — Plot the performance of the sql

  When the graph is plotted, the SQL found in the quoted string will be executed multiple times in the graph window, resulting in a display similar to the following:

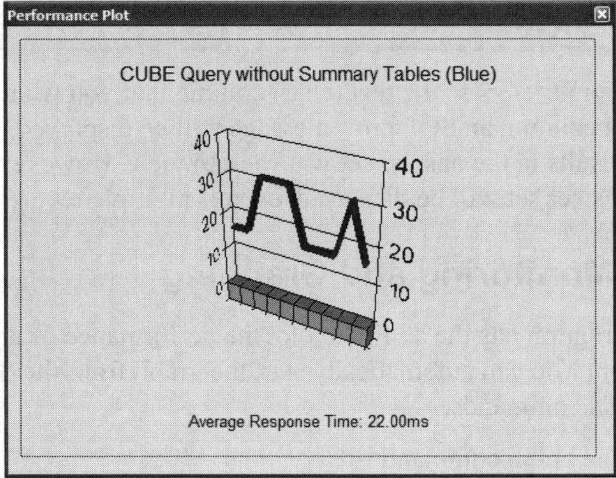

Note that the sql can span multiple lines between quotes:

```
%graph
   title="Some title"
   color=red
   sql="
       select *
       from employee
       ";
```

Make sure you do not imbed a semi-colon from within the SQL being plotted! This will confuse the program.

The actual commands that were used to create this previous plot are:

```
[1] %graph
[2]     color=blue
[3]     title="CUBE Query without Summary Tables (Blue)"
[4]     repeat=20
[5]     sql="
          select store, quarter, item, sum(quantity)
                        from transactions
            group by cube(store, quarter, item)"
```

- [1] Graph command
- [2] Set the graph color to blue
- [3] Title of the plot
- [4] Repeat the SQL 20 times in the performance plot
- [5] SQL to run for the plot

The plot will finish when 20 iterations of the statement have completed. You can stop the plot by closing the window, or issuing another SQL command out of the SQL input window.

Comparing the Performance of 2 SQL Statements

If you only want to show the performance of a single (or two) SQL statement, you can use the `%COMPARE` command to plot the results. This is similar to the plot command, but only works on SQL statements. The syntax of the command is:

```
%compare
   title="Some title"
   repeat=[1..50]
   sql1="
        select *
        from employee
        "
   label1="What is this"
   sql2="select * from department"
   label2="Another SQL";
```

The title refers to the reason of the plot, while the label1 and label2 keywords describe what the individual SQL plots are. The SQL within the SQL1 and SQL2 strings are executed “x” number of times and the average value is then plotted. You may want to consider setting the repeat value to at least 10 or 20 so that variations in performance can be smoothed out. By default this value is 1.

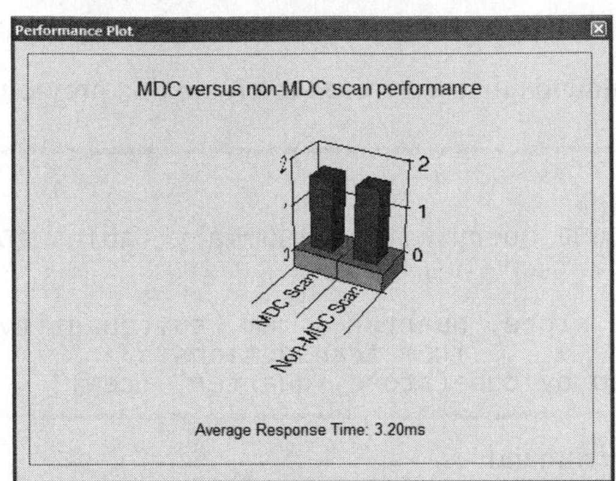

Plotting Data from the Output Window

The DB2DEMO program can also plot values that are found in the SQL output window. Before you can plot data, you must have created some results in the output window. If there are no results in this window, the plot button will not work and an error message will be displayed.

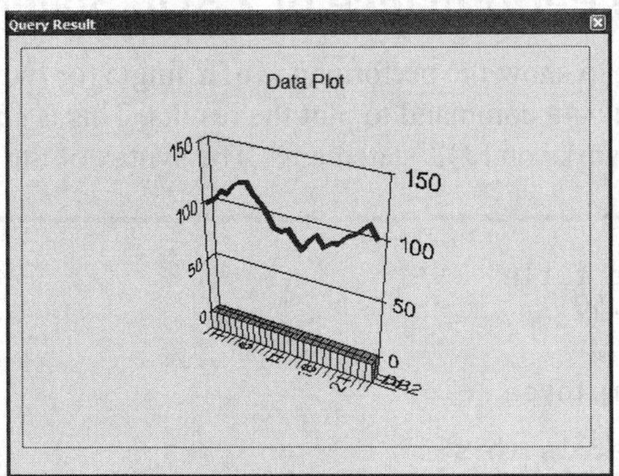

Before you show a plot, you must execute an SQL statement!

```
select lastname, salary from employee
```

There are four options that you can change on this screen:

- Plot Type

  There are five different types of plots that can be generated by the program. These are:

  - 3D Line Chart
  - 3D Bar Chart
  - 2D Line Chart
  - 2D Bar Chart
  - Pie Chart

  Depending on which type of plot you selected, you will need to specify which Grouping Columns, Labels, and Data Columns you want to use.

- Grouping Column

  For either 3D or 2D line charts, you must specify a Grouping Column. This is the column that is used to determine when a lines value ends. For instance, the following select statement (using data from the SAMPLE database) will generate a sequence of values:

```
select lastname, salary from employee
```

- Labels

  Labels refers to the column that is used to tag the line being drawn.

- Data Columns

  This is the actual data you want plotted on the screen. Once you have selected the columns and plot type you want, create the following command to generate your plot.

```
%PLOT
{ LINE | 2DLINE | BAR | 2DBAR | PIE | MENU }
  DATA=Column with data to plot
[ GROUP=Grouping Column ]
[ LABEL=Column with labels ]
```

Message Support

The DB2DEMO demonstration program has the ability to generate a message that can be used to execute only portions of some SQL. This facility is used as part of the table creation process so that the demonstration can be customized without having to edit the actual SQL. The message command has a number of subcommands that relate to the message being displayed. Here is a sample message:

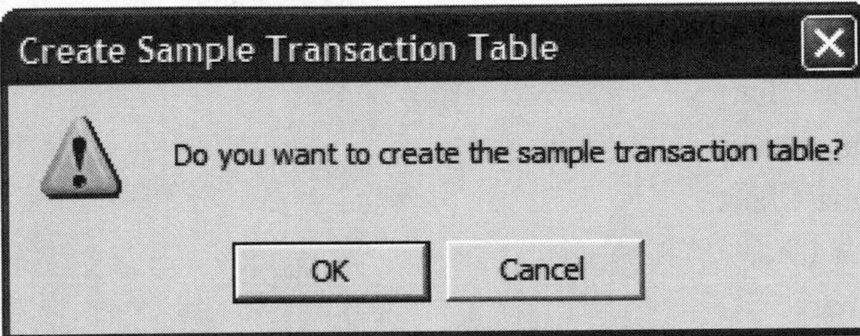

The top of the message contains the title, while the center section contains the prompt for the user. Below the message are two buttons that allow the user to continue with the script or cancel execution.

The message command has the following syntax:

```
%msg
   title="Some title"
   text="Some information about this menu"
   ;
```

Loading Commands

Occasionally you may want to create your own .SQL file and use that from within the demonstration program without having to reload the program. You can load your own commands by issuing the following command:

```
%loadsql filename;
```

When you issue this command, the contents of the filename will be loaded into the program and the existing commands removed. Sometimes it is useful to place the following section of code into your `.SQL` file to allow for quick testing of your `.SQL` file without having to key in this command every time:

```
%loadsql myops.sql;
```

If you do not know the name of the file, click on the file button, and then select Load SQL File from the menu. A list of files will be displayed (.SQL). Locate the file you are looking for, then press the load button.

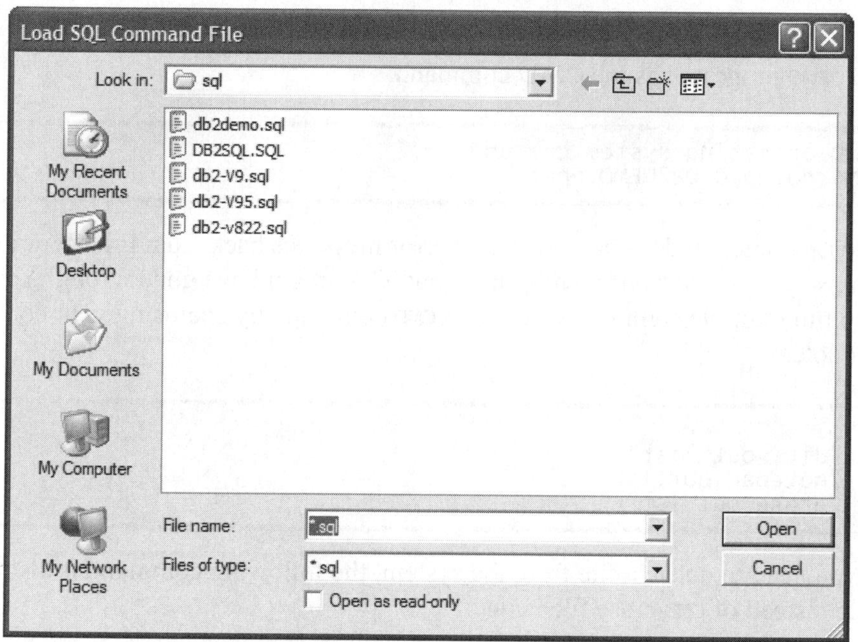

Loading BLOBs or XML Files

The DB2DEMO program has a facility for loading large objects into the database. The format of the LOAD command is:

```
%load into table_name
   values (a,b,?,....,?)
   [filename1] [filename2] ... [filename10];
```

The table_name refers to the table that you want to insert into, and the values clause includes the data that you want inserted. For every column that needs data from a file, a question mark (?) is placed in that position. Following the values portion is a set of file names, each enclosed in brackets []. For each question mark there needs to be an associated file name, otherwise the program will issue an error message. The program will take the contents of that file and place it into the associated column. The following example is taken from the Large Objects section of the demonstration. This section of code loads the advertisements into the ADS table:

```
%load into ads values (1,'Sales Call',?,?) [salescall.gif] [salescall.txt];
%load into ads values (2,'Car Sales ',?,?) [car.gif] [car.txt];
%load into ads values (3,'Furniture ',?,?) [furniture.gif] [furniture.txt];
%load into ads values (4,'China     ',?,?) [china.gif] [china.txt];
```

Operating System Commands

You may want to issue operating system commands from the SQL window, so the DB2DEMO program has the CMD command:

```
%CMD operating system command;
%CMD notepad DB2DEMO.ops;
```

The CMD function does not return any error messages back from the operating system, so you are on your own figuring out what might have gone wrong! You can also run multiple commands from one CMD command by enclosing your commands in quotes:

```
%CMD
   "dir >out.list"
   "notepad out.lst"
   "erase out.lst"
```

If you need to delete a file from the system, the following command is also available instead of CMD erase filename:

```
%erase filename;
```

DB2 Command

Occasionally you have to issue a command against the DB2 database that you cannot accomplish through the SQL interface provided by the DB2DEMO program. This command lets you send one or more commands to the DB2 database for execution through the DB2 interface. The results of the commands that are issued are automatically placed into an output file and displayed to the user when the command completes.

The syntax of this command is:

```
%DB2
   [ "db2 command string" ]*
```

You do not need to enclose the command in quotes if you are only issuing one command to DB2. However, if you want to issue multiple commands, enclose each one in a set of quotes.

For instance, the following command will issue a select command (note that this will not work for you since you need to connect before running any commands in the DB2 command line!):

```
%DB2  SELECT * FROM EMPLOYEE
```

If you want this to work, you need a couple of commands (including the CONNECT):

```
%DB2 "connect to sample"
     "select * from employee"
```

Note how the two commands are enclosed in quotes so that the system knows that they need to be issued separately. Also, you do not need to supply a semi-colon as a terminator for the commands since this is added by the program automatically.

Clear Command

Use the %CLEAR command to clear the contents of the SQL input window. This is usually used as part of a script to hide the commands that were used to load data.

IF/END Block

The IF/END block is used as a simple structure to control script execution. The IF statement can contain only one argument, which tests for the existence of a table within the database.

```
%IF [exists=table_name | notexists=table_name] ;
... statements ...
%ENDIF;
```

If the table exists (or not exists), the statements following the %IF statement will be executed until the corresponding %ENDIF statement is found. If the statement is NOT true, all of the statements up to the %ENDIF statement will be ignored. Any type of statements are allowed within the IF/ENDIF block, except for IF/ENDIF statements themselves. For example:

```
%IF NOTEXISTS=SAMPLE ;
   %MSG TEXT="Do you want me to create the SAMPLE table?";
   create table sample (name char(5));
%ENDIF;
```

Note the use of the %MSG command to stop execution of the program. If you click OK in the message box, execution will continue with the creation of the SAMPLE table. If you click CANCEL, all execution in this script will stop. If you want the script to stop without input from the user, use the %EXIT command to stop execution:

```
%IF EXISTS=SAMPLE ;
   %exit;
%ENDIF;
```

One final note. Both the IF and ENDIF statements must end with a semicolon, similar to all other commands.

Connect

The %CONNECT command lets you connect to another database. The syntax of the connect command is:

```
%CONNECT
   DATABASE=database name
     [ USERID=userid ]
     [ PASSWORD=password ]
```

These options tell the program how to attach to the database. You normally specify the name of the database and then optionally the userid and password that you want to connect as. These parameters are described in more detail below:

- DATABASE=value

  This the name of the database that you want to connect to. The database itself must be defined in the local client catalog or in a LDAP directory for this to work. You should supply this value as part of the connect command, or else the connect command will just re-connect to the existing database.

- USERID=value

  The userid field is optional, and can be used with or without the password field. If you do not supply a userid, the system will use your current userid and password.

- PASSWORD=value

  The password is optional and is usually associated with a userid.

The connect command resets the current connection, so if your connect command fails, you will not be able to issue any SQL commands at that point.

If you enter the %CONNECT command with no arguments, or use the CONNECT command from the pulldown menu (options), the following menu will be displayed:

Enter the appropriate information on this panel and then press CONNECT or CANCEL. Note that the password does not display when using the menu.

Exit Command

The EXIT command will result in any SQL following it to be ignored when the script is executed. The following SQL illustrates this point:

```
select * from employee;
%exit;
select * from workdept;
```

In this example, the select * from workdept code will never get executed. The exit command is used primarily as a convenience when testing large SQL command scripts. You can stop execution after a particular SQL statement and check results without having to erase all of the SQL in the command sequence. Once you are satisfied that the SQL up to that point is working, you can erase the EXIT command and see how the entire SQL string works.

List Tables Command

The TABLES command is used to list the tables that are found in the current database. The syntax of this command is:

```
%TABLES
  [ pattern ]
```

If you do not supply any values to the TABLES command, the program will display the names of all tables found within the database. However, you can optionally supply a pattern which will be used by the program to find all the names of the tables that contain these letters.

For instance, the command:

```
%TABLES emp
```

This will result in a display of all tables that have the letters "EMP" found as part of the name (in any position, not just the beginning).

Describe Table Command

The DESCRIBE command is used to show the columns that make up the contents of a table. The syntax of this command is:

```
%DESCRIBE
  [ table name ]
```

If you do not supply any values to the DESCRIBE command, the program will display the column names of all tables found within the database. However, you can optionally supply a pattern which will be used by the program to describe all the tables that contain these letters. For instance, the command:

```
%DESCRIBE emp
```

This will result in a display of all columns that belong to tables that have the letters "EMP" found as part of the name (in any position, not just the beginning).

Explain SQL Statement

The EXPLAIN command is used to show the optimization that DB2 will use when executing a particular SQL command. The EXPLAIN command produces a textual representation of what the statement will do within the DB2 engine. A visual representation of this is also available through the DB2 Control Center, but it cannot be viewed directly from within this program.

The syntax of this command is:

```
%EXPLAIN
    "sql statements"
```

Note that you can have multiple SQL statements defined, but only the last one will have an explain statement produced. Each statement requires quotes around it. In the event you want to change the optimization level, or some other parameter as part of the explain, you need to place each SQL statement in a separate quoted string.

For example:

```
%EXPLAIN
   "set current refresh age 0"
   "select sum(sales) from transactions"
```

Do not enclose semicolons within the quoted strings. These are not required as part of the command.

I/O Commands

DB2DEMO has four commands that allow you to interact with the file system. These commands are:

- %OPEN filename — Open a file for output.

  The OPEN command will open a file for output. If the file exists, it will be deleted and written over. The filename is placed after the OPEN command.

- %WRITE 'string' — Write a string to a file.

  Anything following the WRITE command will be placed into the file. The line will be appended with a newline character automatically.

- %WRITESQL select ... — Write contents of an SQL statement out to a file.

  The WRITESQL statement will execute the SELECT statement and will write out the results to the file. If more than one column is specified in the select list, each value will be separated with a comma.

- %CLOSE — Close a file.

  Once the file is closed it can be read by other programs.

The following SQL will take the contents of the EMPLOYEE table and place it into the EMPLOYEE.TXT file:

```
%open c:\employee.txt;
%writesql select * from employee;
%close;
%cmd notepad c:\employee.txt
```

Debugging Mode

If you want to test your scripts, you can turn on a debug mode in DB2DEMO that will run all of the SQL found in your script. This mode is useful for checking the correctness of all of your SQL. There are two options on the DEBUG command. By default, the DEBUG command will run all of the commands without waiting. If you add the optional "wait" parameter after the command, the program will stop when it encounters any error, other than an object not being found as a result of a DROP statement. If you hit "OK" at the error message, it will continue to run the scripts. If you hit "CANCEL", the script will stop running.

```
%debug wait
```

An error will stop the program:

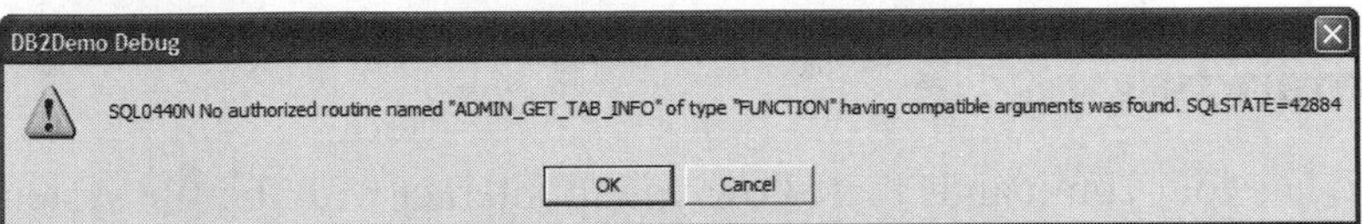

Hitting CANCEL will stop the execution of any more SQL.

Customizing the DB2DEMO Program

Script Overview

The DB2DEMO.SQL (or presentation script) is what drives the demonstration program. Within this file, the demo will find the sections, sql commands, and help files that will be presented as part of the demo. You can modify this file to add new examples or create your own customized presentation script.

By default, when the DB2DEMO program is started, it looks for a script file called DB2DEMO.SQL. However, you can override this by adding the commands option after the program name:

```
DB2DEMO MYDEMO.SQL
```

Instead of using the standard input file, the demo program will read this file instead. This gives you the option of creating custom scripts for demonstrations or to try new exotic SQL without losing the original demonstration file.

The DB2DEMO.SQL file has the following format:

```
<include filename="filename.xmp"/>
<section title="Major Section on Object Relational">
  <info>
  This section contains all sorts of information on Object
  Relational extensions in DB2.
  </info>
  <example title="User-Defined Functions">
    <info>
    Along with all of the new built-in functions, the user now has
    the ability to create their own functions.  These functions
    can do a variety of things, but this section will show how
    one can create functions that manipulate multimedia objects
    in the database.
    </info>
```

```
    <sql>
    SELECT * FROM EMPLOYEE
    </sql>
  </example>
</section>
```

The DB2DEMO.SQL file is freeform, but generally it follows the type of outlining shown above. The file uses XML tags to describe the objects within the script and the elements must be properly nested. Each tag (<section>, <example>, <info>, <sql>) and their corresponding closing tags must be on their own line. For instance, the following code is correct:

```
<section title="This is a title">
  <sql>
  ...
  </sql>
</section>
```

However, the following will not work:

```
<section title="This is a title"><sql>...</sql></section>
```

The script file can contain a number of elements, including:

- Comments <-- Comment --> — Used for commenting out portions of the code.
- Include File <include file="filename"\> — Used for including other files into the script.
- Section <section title="Information about this section"> — Used to start a major new section in the script.
- Example <example title="Information about this example"> — Defines an individual example within the script.
- Info tag <info> — Describes the section or example that is being viewed on the screen.
- SQL tag <sql> — Includes the SQL that will be executed as part of an example

Comments

You can imbed comments within a file by using the standard XML comment "<!--" characters at the beginning of a line. Anything after the line is ignored until a corresponding "-->" is found. This is useful for documenting what you are doing or for commenting out code that you do not want to use in the file.

For instance, the following script is used to describe what the script does:

```
<!--
   This section is used to demonstrate XQuery commands.
-->
<section ...>
```

Including Files

You can place some of your SQL into separate files and bring them together by using the <include> command. The "file=" attribute is used to specify the name of the file. The file name must be placed in quotes and the command must be closed with the /> symbol. The file name can be any valid Windows file name and the convention used by DB2DEMO has the major example files called x.SQL and subsections called x.XMP (for example). You can nest the include files up to 10 levels, at which point the program will raise an error message for too deep a nesting of files.

For example, the following script loads in all of the examples associated with the DB2DEMO program:

```
<section title="DB2 Demonstration Program">
  <info>
  Welcome to the DB2 Demonstration Program!  This set of
  commands shows you many of the SQL functions available within
  the DB2 database.
  </info>
</section>
<include file="db2-viper.sql"/>
<include file="db2-bi.xmp"/>
<include file="db2-objrel.xmp"/>
<include file="db2-advsql.xmp"/>
<include file="db2-limits.xmp"/>
<include file="db2-integrity.xmp"/>
<include file="db2-inlinesqlpl.xmp"/>
<include file="db2-performance.xmp"/>
<include file="db2-functions.xmp"/>
<include file="db2-optimizer.xmp"/>
```

Sections

Sections are used to group a number of examples or tutorials together. Sections can also be used to group other sections. A section is displayed in the command window as an entry that has a [+] beside the name when it is not expanded. Here is an example of a command window with all of the sections closed:

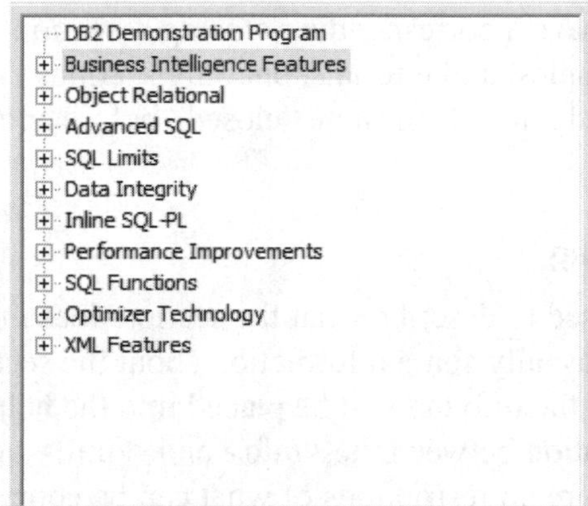

In order to execute one of the sample SQL commands, a user needs to click on one of the sections shown above. If you click on a [+] sign, it will expand to show the various SQL commands and screens:

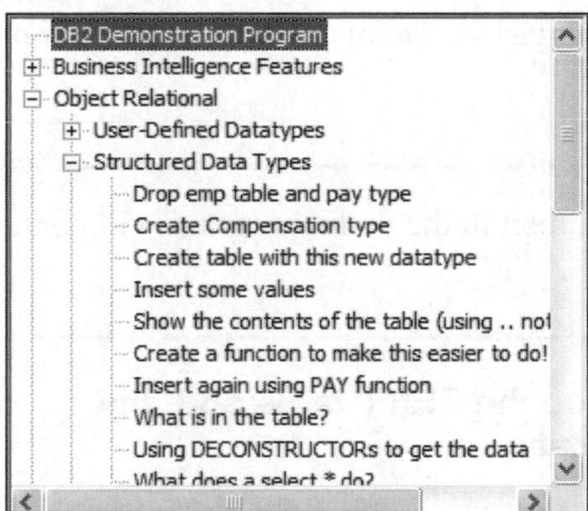

Note how the Structured Data Types section is nested below Object Relational.

The syntax of the section command is:

```
<section title="Description of section">
  <info>
  ... information about the section ...
  </info>
  ... other <section>, <example>, or <tutorial> commands
</section>
```

The title="..." tag is optional, but it should be used to describe what the section is doing. For instance, in the previous example, the Objection Relational section was started with:

```
<section title="Object Relational">
```

Each section must have a corresponding closing </section>. Sections can contain other sections, examples, and tutorials, but only sections can be nested. In other words, examples and tutorials must be "closed" before another section can be started.

Section: <info> tag

The <info> tag is used to describe what the section does in detail. The use of the tag is optional, but usually some information about the section would be useful! The material within the info tag will be placed into the help panel on the main screen. The information between the <info> and </info> tags can contain any HTML tags. There are no restrictions of what can be contained within these two tags, aside from the info tags themselves. For instance, the following HTML can be placed between the info tags:

```
<section title="Drop the TEST table and any datatypes">
  <info>
  This section contains information about dropping the
  <u>TEST</u> table.
  </info>
</section>
```

The resulting help screen in the demo program will contain:

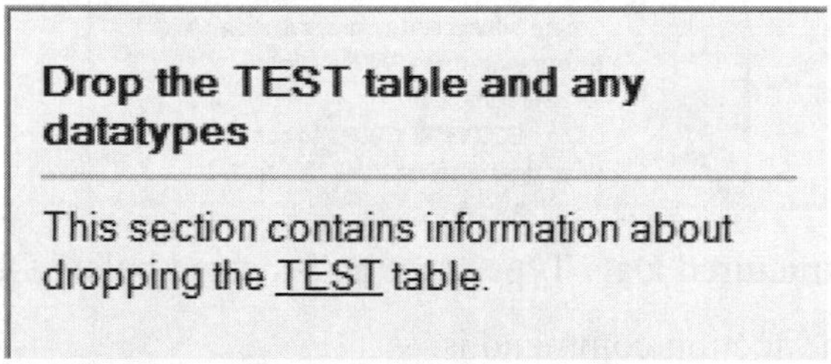

Drop the TEST table and any datatypes

This section contains information about dropping the TEST table.

The title of the example gets placed at the top of the help window, followed by any text or HTML that was found within the <info> and </info> tags.

If you do not want to use the default title from the <section> command, you can place a title attribute within the info tag:

```
<section title="Drop the TEST table and any datatypes">
  <info title="Dropping Tables">
  This section contains information about dropping the
  <u>TEST</u> table.
  </info>
</section>
```


The resulting help screen will have a different title at the top:

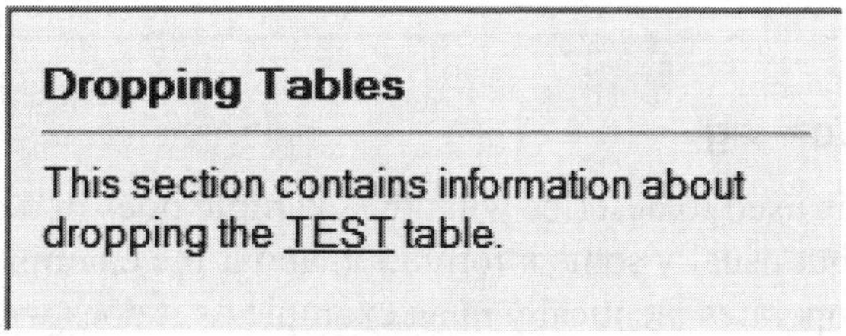

Dropping Tables

This section contains information about dropping the TEST table.

Examples

An example tag is used to demonstrate some SQL feature in DB2. The example tag typically includes an information tag to describe the SQL that will run (<info>) but it is not necessary. It should, however, contain an sql tag <sql> to run the example being described.

The syntax of the example command is:

```
<example title="Description of example">
  <info>
  ... information about the example ...
  </info>
  <sql>
  ... sql commands
  </sql>
</example>
```

Example tags cannot be nested. Each example should only describe one concept although the SQL can contain more than one SQL statement. The example tag usually has a title associated with it. If you do not supply a title, the entry will be blank in the command window. The example tag must also be closed with the </example> tag.

The following shows an example command that runs some SQL to drop some tables in the database:

```
<example title="Drop RI tables">
  <info>
  This command drops the existing RI tables and constraints.
  This needs to be done so that the following examples will work.
  If you fail to execute this command, the following examples
  will fail.
  </info>
  <sql>
drop table ridept;
drop table riempl;
  </sql>
</example>
```

Example: <info> tag

The <info> tag is used to describe what the example does in detail. The use of the tag is optional, but usually some information about the example would be useful! The <info> tag operates identically in an example as it does with a section. See the section tag for more information on its usage.

Example: <sql> tag

When you click on an example, any SQL associated with the command will be placed into the SQL input window and executed. The SQL can contain SQL statements, XQuery commands, or any of the special commands found within the DB2DEMO program.

The types of SQL that can execute from within the program are:

```
UPDATE, INSERT, DELETE, CREATE, DROP, VALUES
GRANT, REVOKE, WITH, BEGIN ATOMIC, CALL
```

You cannot run a LOAD, CONNECT or any utility from this screen. Generally, most SQL will run. The worst that can happen is that your SQL will fail. For more information on the SQL syntax, check your DB2 Information Center for the SQL Getting Started manual.

SQL statements can be placed freeform after a <sql> definition statement. The only restriction is that strings cannot be placed across multiple lines. For instance, the following is not valid:

```
SELECT * FROM EMPLOYEE WHERE LASTNAME='
BAKER'
```

You can separate multiple SQL commands by placing a ; at the end of each line:

```
select * from employee;
select * from workdept;
```

If your SQL requires the use of the semicolon, then you can use a hash (#), at (@) or dollar ($) sign instead at the beginning of every statement:

```
#select * from employee
#select * from workdept
```

There are additional SQL and non-SQL statements that can be run from within an SQL window. These are discussed in detail in the Advanced Programming section.

Example: <sql button="x"> tag

An example can have up to nine buttons associated with it. These buttons can contain any SQL that would normally found in the sql block. Rather than executing as part of the example, the sql is associated with a button that is found above the help panel rather than executing automatically as part of an example.

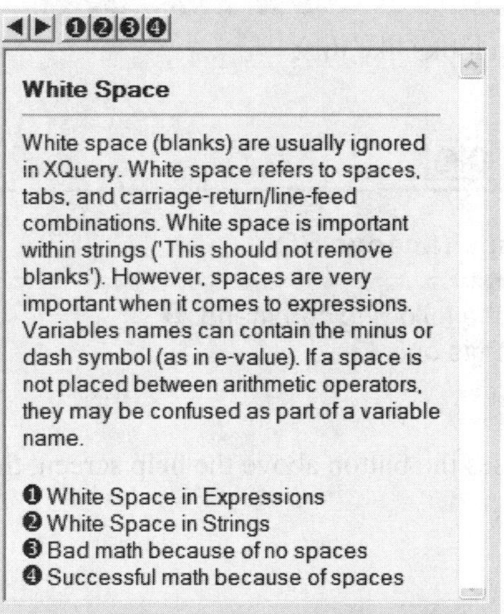

The buttons are numbered from 1 to 9 (...). The text describes what the buttons are supposed to do, and clicking on the button above the help section will actually "show" the sql or XQuery command execute. The button icons found in the info section are created by using the special `DB2DEMO` variables `%[B1]` through `%[B9]`. When these special variables are used in text, they are replaced with the icons 1 through 9.

When an sql block is defined with a button, an icon is created above the help panel that corresponds to its button number. Button number 0 exists as well, but it corresponds to an sql block with no button number. This is also the SQL that gets executed automatically when the example is loaded.

When a button is pressed, the SQL that has been defined for it is automatically placed into the SQL section and executed. In order to describe what the buttons does, the text section should include a reference to this button. In order to display the button icon, use the special DB2DEMO variable %[b1]..%[b9] within the script. The DB2DEMO program will translate this variable into the proper icon to display. These icons (or GIF files) are generated automatically by DB2DEMO in the event you create your script in a directory which does not have these files. The following example illustrates the use of the button attributes:

```
<example title="Simple SELECT example">
  <info title="Miscellaneous SQL">
  Try the following command: %[b1]
  <br>
  And this one: %[b2]
  </info>
  <sql button="1">select * from employee</sql>
  <sql button="2">select * from department</sql>
</example>
```

The resulting screen looks like this:

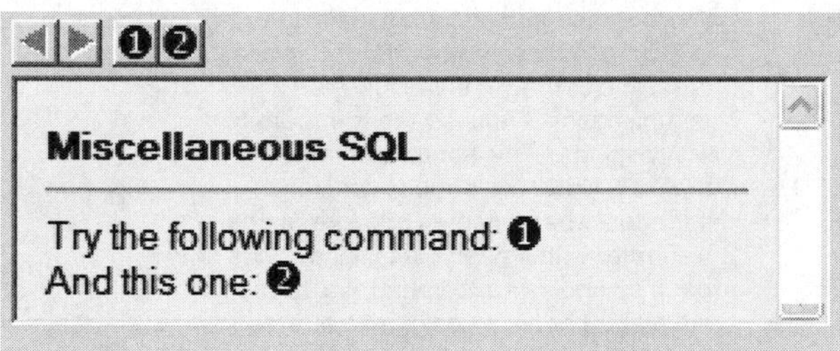

When the user presses the button above the help screen, the corresponding SQL will get executed.

If the second button is pressed, the sql screen will now have the following in it:

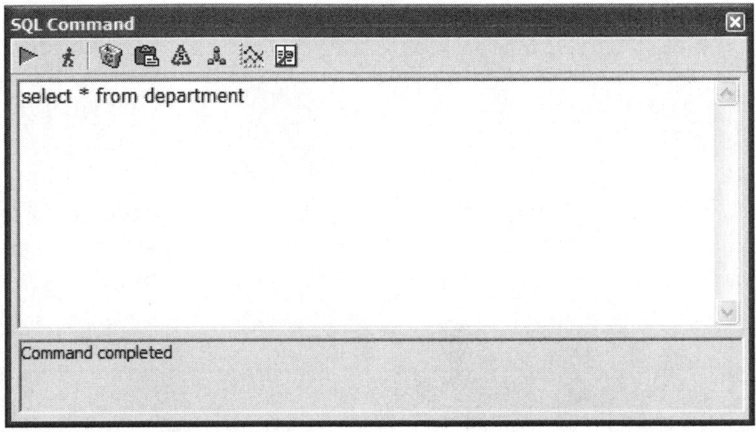

Support

We've tried to think of everything, but occasionally things go wrong. If you have a problem with the demonstration code, please send us a note with your e-mail address, name, and a description of the problem. We can be reached at baklarz@ca.ibm.com.

Index

Symbols

A

B

C

D

G

H

I

J

L

M

N

O

P

Q

R

S

T

U

V

W

X

THIS BOOK IS SAFARI ENABLED

INCLUDES FREE 45-DAY ACCESS TO THE ONLINE EDITION

The Safari® Enabled icon on the cover of your favorite technology book means the book is available through Safari Bookshelf. When you buy this book, you get free access to the online edition for 45 days.

Safari Bookshelf is an electronic reference library that lets you easily search thousands of technical books, find code samples, download chapters, and access technical information whenever and wherever you need it.

TO GAIN 45-DAY SAFARI ENABLED ACCESS TO THIS BOOK:

- Go to **http://www.awprofessional.com/safarienabled**
- Complete the brief registration form
- Enter the coupon code found in the front of this book on the "Copyright" page

If you have difficulty registering on Safari Bookshelf or accessing the online edition, please e-mail customer-service@safaribooksonline.com.